These books have been down many roads,

From Wall Street to the Information Highway,

And everywhere in between.

(Even those off the beaten path.)

They've welcomed the occasional passenger,

Keynes, Marx, Smith,

And treasured every word.

It's an exciting roadtrip now in its Third Edition

And riding shotgun is David Colander,

The author that brought passion to economics

And watched it spread to students.

What's his secret?

Keep reading,

Soon you'll discover why

Students drive it.

MIDDLEBURY COLLEGE
MIDDLEBURY, VERMONT 05753

Dear Colleague,

I'm pleased to say that earlier editions of this book were very well-received. There were lots of economists out there who share my view (1) that a knowledge of history and institutions is necessary to put economic theory in context and (2) that learning economics can be enjoyable–an economics textbook need not be an impersonal conveyance of a dismal science. Economics is fun, challenging, and exciting, and should be taught as such.

This book does not present economics as a pretentious science, nor does it present economics as a touchy-feely subject. Economics is presented for what it is–an enormously powerful, but simultaneously, potentially confusing, engine of analysis that provides an interesting approach to understanding the economic problems of society. It is a straightforward presentation of economic ideas–warts and all.

It is a principles book primarily written for students who will not necessarily continue studying economics; it attempts to integrate the broader dimensions of economic reasoning with the models that form the core of what we teach in principles.

Despite its differences, my book is not a radical departure from the standard principles book. Institutions are important; they don't get changed overnight, and the standard principles book has become an institution. Because of my belief in the importance of institutions, I follow my 15% rule–a textbook can differ from the existing books by, at most, 15%. So in writing this book I attempted to stay true to my underlying beliefs, while simultaneously providing the core material that is known as principles of economics.

The end result is a book that differs from the standard book in the following ways. It is a book that has:

1) a writing style that is much more conversational. I talk to the student, not at the student. I find this style gets them to read the chapters.

2) a stronger focus on policy issues and applying economic reasoning. The models are there, but so too are the institutional stepping stones.

3) a stronger focus on the broader context of the models rather than a presentation of models for models' sake. Thus, there's more discussion of limitations of models than in other books.

4) a focus on economic reasoning as a useful way of approaching policy issues, not on models as a way of answering policy issues. The answer is only to be found in context–in applying economic reasoning with an understanding of the institutional, political and historical context within which a problem developed.

I hope that you will take a look at the book, and consider teaching from it. If you are used to all economics texts differing only in packaging, this one will surprise you. All the same stuff is there and covered from a mainstream perspective, but the flavor is different. The flavor is not soybean mush–economics reduced to a common non-controversial denominator. Instead, the flavor is spicy beef, with a sweet-and-sour tang that invites students to read. I'm pleased to say that there's something in it to provoke just about everyone. It's an approach that the students have responded to so positively in the earlier editions, and I think you'll find that they will respond even more positively to the Third Edition.

Sincerely,

David Colander

"I agree with my students: Colander's Economics is a real find."

Ed Raupp
Waldorf College

"My students tell me, 'I actually read this book!'"

Roger Conover
Azusa Pacific University

"My students are quite pleased with the book."

Reza Hoshmand
University of Hawaii-West Oahu

"The text works with the students and doesn't talk at or above them."

Antoinette James Criss
Randolph-Macon Woman's College

"It is the best principles book I've used in 24 years."

Charles L. Fisk, Jr.
St. Leo College

What remains the same. . .

Supporting economic sensibility

This text encourages students to look at the world as a latticework of ascending cost/benefit frameworks in which one is deciding on the optimal degree of rationality. It is not a "taught technique" but a "learned reasonableness" that provides insights into complicated issues. It is a critical thought approach.

Beyond the facts

David Colander's writing is thoughtful and thought-provoking. He insists on illustrating how economic ideas are relevant and challenging. He goes beyond the facts to explain why the facts are exciting.

Passion without bias

To keep students interested, rather than focusing on the technique, David Colander presents some ideas in a debate format with two passionate believers on both sides arguing the points. Students are exposed to differing views; they get caught up in the debate, and think about ideas much more deeply than they otherwise would.

A flavorful style

Colander's conversational tone ebbs and flows depending on the nature of the material. It eliminates the sense some students have that textbooks provide the truth; he encourages them to think. Even those professors who don't like Colander's writing style agree that their students respond to it. It keeps students reading. Before they know it, they've finished the chapter and have used economic reasoning to analyze the new material.

This style presents models within context

Models without context are meaningless, and thus you'll find more historical and institutional issues in this book's appendixes than in other principles books. The discussion conveys the sense that geography, history, and psychology are important.

"Colander ranks with the best!"

Dr. Mike Williams
Bethune-Cookman College

"In over 20 years of teaching this is the first introductory text I would be delighted to use again!"

Professor Gordon Weil
Wheaton College

What has changed. . .

Core material is much more manageable

Instructors voiced their request for more "guidance" as to which parts should be considered core and which parts were supplemental. Colander reworked the text to make the core about 100 pages smaller, placing supplemental, mathematical, institutional, and historical material in the appendixes.

Greater flexibility

Now the instructor can more easily custom design a course. As one reviewer noted, the book sets the standard for flexibility in textbooks.

Coverage of the latest policy issues

Colander has paid particular attention to providing the latest information and the most up-to-date discussion of policy possible. To allow students to keep the statistics up to date, he has placed much more reliance on economic data obtainable over the Internet. Thus, throughout the book, students will find Internet addresses where the data can be updated.

Changes in Macro

A new chapter (18) has been added on structural macro policy. And the monetary policy discussions have been reworked to focus more on policy regimes than on specific policy actions. The Third Edition includes a reworked, cleaner presentation of the AS/AD framework. This framework is fully integrated with the AE/AP framework without compromising analytic integrity. Colander has also rewritten the discussion of the governmental component of GDP statistics.

Changes in Micro

An extra chapter (4) on applications of supply and demand has been added to the introductory material. This allows early discussion of policy. The elasticity chapter (21) has been significantly rewritten. Supply elasticity and demand elasticity are covered in one chapter and arc elasticity is fully developed.

Improved Ancillary Package

The Ancillary Package was revised, reworked, and expanded to make it the best on the market–a complete learning system. Among these innovative ancillaries are a reworked Test Bank, new PowerPoint Presentation, a new Instructor's Assistant with problem sets and syllabi, several new and innovative multimedia products, and a host of revised print supplements. Please turn to pages 14-15 for a detailed description of this revamped and complete learning package.

The Third Edition has undergone numerous changes in structure and organization.

Brief Contents

Introduction

Chapter 1: Economics and Economic Reasoning: Old Chapter 1 shortened. The discussion of the production possibility curve was taken out and integrated with the chapter on evolution of economic systems, which was moved up to Chapter 2 to accommodate it.

Chapter 2: Economic Organization: Old Chapter 3 combined with the Chapter 1 discussion of production possibility curve. Discussion of comparative advantage expanded. Core chapter shortened considerably with historical material moved to an appendix.

Chapters 3 and 4: Supply and Demand, Applications of Supply and Demand: Old Chapter 2, the central supply and demand chapter, divided into two chapters–one on the analytics of supply and demand and one on applications. This division allows a much earlier discussion of applications of the supply-demand model. Appendixes on algebraic solutions to supply and demand added.

Chapters 5 and 6: U.S. and Worm Economic Institutions: The cores of old Chapters 4 and 5 shortened considerably, with much of the specific institutional discussion moved to appendixes.

Macro

Chapter 7: Growth, Business Cycles, Unemployment, and Inflation: old Chapter 8; Improved discussion of calculation of real income; slightly expanded discussion of growth. More emphasis on the difficulty of determining potential income and "target rate of unemployment."

Chapter 8: National Income Accounting: Old Chapter 9 with a condensed discussion of national economic accounting; technical issues put in appendix. Revised to include new conventions about government investment spending.

Chapter 9: Money, Banking, and the Financial Sector: Combination of Old Chapters 12 and 13 with much of the institutional specifics of financial institutions and T-accounts analysis moved to appendixes. It was moved up earlier to emphasize importance of monetary and financial issues in modern macroeconomics.

Chapter 10: Development of Modern Macro: Combination and simplification of Old Chapters 8 and 9. This chapter went through a major revision. It is now a similar, but more carefully presented, discussion of the basic macro model that is used by a majority of other texts. The distinction between partial and aggregate equilibriums is still emphasized, but focus is not on theory, but on developing a working policy model. Appendixes are reduced considerably, and policy focus supersedes the oratorical focus.

Chapter 11: The AP/AE Model: Modification of Old Chapter 10 with the multiplier simplified to focus on expenditures-income relationship. Algebraic appendix of components model.

Chapter 12: Activist Demand Management Policy: Modification of Old Chapter 11 with focus shifting away from fiscal policy toward a broader concept of demand management, centered around macro policy model.

Chapter 13: Monetary Policy: Modification of Old Chapter 14; updated to reflect new focus on federal funds rate. T-accounts discussion moved to appendix.

Chapter 14: Inflation and Its Relationship to Unemployment and Growth: Modification of Old Chapter 15. Additional discussion of growth trade-offs added to bring in Classical viewpoint better, with streamlined discussion of the debate about the Phillips curve.

Chapter 15: International Dimensions: Old Chapter 16; updated examples and statistics.

Chapter 16: Open Economy Macro: Old Chapter 17 combined with discussion of trade policy to allow a broader policy discussion.

Chapter 17: Art of Traditional Macro Policy: Old Chapter 19 updated. Added discussion about the importance of regimes as opposed to policy.

Chapter 18: Structural Supply-Side Macro Policies: A totally new chapter that brings the structural policies of the '90s into clear focus.

Chapter 19: Deficits and Debt: Old Chapter 18. Updated and revised with discussion of recent decrease in measured deficit.

Chapter 20: Growth and Development. Old Chapter 20 updated and revised.

Micro

Chapter 21: Elasticities: Combination of parts of Old Chapters 20 and 21 to consolidate discussion of elasticity. Reworked derivations to focus on arc elasticity in order to provide clarity and to follow up on the application of supply and demand material in Chapter 4.

Chapter 22: The Logic of Individual Choice: Old Chapter 20 minus discussion of elasticity.

Chapter 23: Production Cost: Old Chapter 23 revised and updated.

Chapter 24: Production Cost: Old Chapter 24 revised and updated. Addition of an appendix on isoquants and isocosts.

Chapter 25: Perfect Competition: Old Chapter 25 revised and updated.

Chapter 26: Monopoly: Old Chapter 26 revised and updated. Addition of an appendix of algebraic derivation of monopoly equilibrium.

Chapter 27: Monopolistic Competition, Oligopoly and Strategic Pricing: Old Chapter 27 revised.

Chapter 28: Competition in the Real World: Old Chapter 28 revised and updated.

Chapter 29: Politics and Economics: Old Chapter 34 revised and updated to account for new farm laws. It is moved up to allow earlier discussion of policy issues.

Chapter 30: Microeconomic Policy and Economic Reasoning: Old Chapter 35 shortened with case studies moved to appendixes.

Chapter 31: The Role of Government: Old Chapter 33 revised and updated.

Chapter 32: Economics and the Environment: Old Chapter 36 revised and updated.

Chapter 33: Antitrust and Industrial Policies. Old Chapter 29 revised and updated. It was moved down and included in policy sections to give professors more flexibility in choosing which applications chapter to focus on.

Chapter 34: Who Gets What?: Old Chapter 30 revised and updated.

Chapter 35: Work and Labor Market. Old Chapter 35 revised and updated with technical discussion of marginal products moved to appendix.

Chapter 36: Nonwage and Asset Income: Old Chapter 31 revised and updated.

Chapter 37: International Trade Restrictions: Old Chapter 37 revised and updated with technical discussion of absolute and comparative advantage moved to appendix.

Chapter 38: Growth and Microeconomics of Developing Countries: Old Chapter 38 revised and updated.

Chapter 39: Socialist Economies in Transition: Old Chapter 39 revised and updated.

A test drive.

Key Points
Each chapter opens with a numbered list of key points or learning objectives. The bulleted points reinforce an integrated learning strategy, help organize the chapter material, and make review more efficient.

Summary
The summaries provide a review of the key points and their related discussions within the chapter.

Key Terms List
The page-referenced key terms list at each chapter's end provides quick review of the terms that have been boldfaced in the text and that all students should know.

Colloquial Glossary
A glossary of colloquial words enables ESL students to become more familiar with conversational English.

Glossary
Key terms are listed at the back of the text for easy reference.

CHAPTER

Four
Using Supply and Demand

It is by invisible hands that we are bent and tortured worst.
~ Nietzsche

After reading this chapter, you should be able to:

1. Demonstrate the effect of a price ceiling and a price floor on a market.
2. Explain real-world events using supply and demand.
3. Discuss exchange rates using supply and demand.
4. Explain the effect of taxes and tariffs on equilibrium prices and quantity.
5. State the relevance to macroeconomics of the fallacy of composition.
6. Explain why interrelated supply and demand curves may undermine partial equilibrium demand/supply analysis.

In the last chapter I introduced you to the concepts of supply and demand. In this chapter I will: (1) show you the power of supply and demand; (2) show you how the invisible forces interact to change the outcome of supply and demand analysis; and (3) discuss when it is appropriate to apply supply and demand analysis directly, and when one must adjust supply and demand analysis with other issues kept at the back of one's mind.

SUPPLY AND DEMAND IN ACTION

I ended the last chapter with a generic example of supply and demand. Let's start this chapter with another example, this one from the real world.

OPEC and Oil Price Fluctuations

Exhibit 1(a) shows the changes in the price of oil from 1973 to 1996. Exhibit 1(b) demonstrates the supply/demand forces that caused the substantial rise in the price of oil adjusted for inflation from 1973 to 1981, when the supply of oil was severely restricted. Prior to the 1970s, the price of oil had been relatively stable. In the early 1970s, at a series of meetings of countries who were members of the Organization of Petroleum Exporting Countries (OPEC), some delegates who had studied economics pointed out that OPEC could get more revenue by selling less oil.

Their argument went as follows: If the countries could get together and restrict supply, the price of oil would rise dramatically. Each country would sell fewer barrels, but a lot more dollars per barrel sold, thereby increasing revenues.

Exhibit 1(b) shows just how this worked. Initially the quantity supplied was

Video Series, Economics USA: Supply and Demand, Segment 15

CHAPTER SUMMARY

- Price ceilings cause shortages; price floors cause surpluses.
- By minding one's Ps and Qs—the shifts of and movements along curves—one can describe almost all events in terms of supply and demand.
- The determination of prices of currencies—the determination of exchange rates—can be determined by supply and demand analysis, in the same way supply and demand analysis applies to any other good.
- Taxes and tariffs shift the supply and demand curves depending on who pays the tax. They raise the equilibrium price (inclusive of tax) and decrease the quantity.
- In macro, small side effects that can be assumed away in micro are multiplied enormously. Thus they can significantly change the results and cannot be ignored. To ignore them is to fall into the fallacy of composition.
- When supply and demand curves are interdependent, a movement along one curve can cause the other to shift—moving the equilibrium. Such interdependence violates the "other things constant" assumption.

KEY TERMS

appreciation *(91)*
depreciation *(90)*
exchange rates *(90)*
excise tax *(95)*
fallacy of composition *(97)*
fixed exchange rates *(92)*
nonconvertible currency *(91)*
partial equilibrium analysis *(97)*
price ceiling *(86)*
price floor *(91)*
quota *(95)*
rent control *(93)*
tariff *(95)*

Colloquial Glossary

A

Ad infinitum. (adjective). Latin for "forever" (literally, it means "unto infinity.")

Ads. (noun). Short for "advertisements."

Ain't. (verb). An ungrammatical form of "isn't," sometimes used to emphasize a point even when the speaker knows that "isn't" is the correct form.

Airtight. (adjective). Completely secure; impregnable.

All the rage. (descriptive phrase). Extremely popular, but the popularity is likely to be transitory.

Allied forces. (descriptive phrase). In World War II the Allied forces were made up of military from more than 20 countries, some of whom were the United States, Canada, Great Britain, France, Poland, the Netherlands, the USSR, and China. They were allied against a group of opponents

group of people whose large number is attributed to the "boom" in babies that occurred when military personnel, many of whom had been away from home for four or five years, were discharged from service after the end of World War II.

Back off. (verb). To retreat from.

Back to the drawing board. (descriptive phrase). To start all over again after having your plan or project turn out to be useless.

Backfire. (verb). To injure the person or entity who intended to inflict injury.

Bads. (noun). Bad things; the opposite of good things.

Bailed out. (descriptive phrase). To be rescued. It has other colloquial meanings as well, but they do not appear in this book.

Bale. (noun). A bundle, usually of an agricultural produce,

Key Terms

The vocabulary essential to understanding economics is boldfaced within the running text at the point where the term is first introduced. The definition that follows is highlighted in italics for easy reviewing.

Margin Questions

Ten questions are presented in the margins of each chapter so students can have a conceptual check as they go along. They encourage students to reflect on what they read and to use economic reasoning.

Margin Key Points

Each key point is repeated in the margin next to the appropriate text discussion, to reinforce the importance of the material.

The invisible hand, however, was only temporarily beaten. The quantity demanded responded to the change in the price of oil—as the price rose, the quantity demanded fell as people switched to fuel-efficient cars and set their thermostats lower. The high price of oil also inspired a large number of non-OPEC suppliers (and OPEC members who could hide their oil sales from other members) to increase significantly the quantity of oil they supplied (an upward movement along the original supply curve). The high price of oil also encouraged oil companies to explore for more oil. These new discoveries of oil shifted oil's total supply curve outward, even as OPEC countries held their oil back. By 1981, the cartel's high price policy was undermined by these outward shifts, and oil prices began to decline.

Exhibit 1(c) shows the effect of the shift out of the supply curve for oil. By the late 1980s, the invisible hand had effectively broken OPEC's limitation on supply, and price adjusted for inflation fell to between $12 and $14 a barrel as shown in Exhibit 1(c). By the 1990s the price of oil had fallen to where it would have been (after adjustment for inflation) had OPEC never organized to limit supply.

Before these supply and demand adjustments occurred, U.S. political forces instituted measures to counteract the sudden jump in oil prices. The invisible foot put downward pressure on the price of oil in the United States. The United States imposed a **price ceiling**—*a government-imposed limit on how high a price can be charged*—on oil. This political pressure prevented the price of oil from rising enough to make the quantity supplied equal the quantity demanded. The result was an oil shortage. The quantity of oil demanded was greater than the quantity of oil supplied. There were dire predictions that people would freeze to death or wouldn't be allowed to use energy-intensive products.

Exhibit 1(d) shows how a price ceiling would cause such shortages. Suppose the price ceiling, the limit the government set on prices, is $10 per barrel, below the supply/demand equilibrium price of $16 per barrel. Quantity supplied is 1 billion barrels, while quantity demanded is 1.8 billion barrels. The difference between quantity supplied and quantity demanded reflects the number of people who want oil but cannot buy it. When the invisible foot or invisible handshake prevents price from rising to the equilibrium price, the invisible hand doesn't disappear. It places upward pressure on price while the invisible foot places downward pressure on price. In this case the invisible hand won out, and the price ceilings were eliminated, allowing the price of oil to rise substantially. The rise in price eliminated the shortages.

The above example of a price ceiling provides an important lesson about the way markets work. Price ceilings below the equilibrium price create excess demand which must be rationed in some other way—in this case by long lines at the pump. People don't like price increases, but at least price increases prevent shortages, which they often like even less.

Examples of Shifts in Supply and Demand

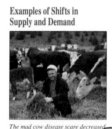

The mad cow disease scare decreased

Supply and demand can shift in many ways and one of the calisthenics of introductory economics involves describing various events with the supply/demand graph. So in the next two sections I give you two exercises that give you practice in using supply and demand curves. In the first I list six events, labeling them 1 through 6. I also provide six graphs of supply and demand shifts in Exhibit 2, labeling them *a* through *f*.

Here are the six events:

1. In 1996 European Union consumption of beef and derivative products dropped between 20 percent and 30 percent in response to reports that "mad cow disease" from beef had killed some Britons. The EU banned imported British beef and supermarkets there began to look for alternative sources of beef. Other countries followed suit. The price of beef and derivative products dropped in the EU. To restore confidence in its beef industry, the British government banned the sale of older cattle by British farmers. Beef prices rose slightly, but not to their previous level. Market:

Margin notes

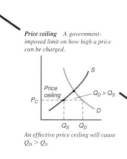

Price ceiling *A government-imposed limit on how high a price can be charged.*

An effective price ceiling will cause $Q_D > Q_S$.

Q-1: If the price ceiling had been set at $8 rather than $10, what would have happened to the size of the shortage?

1 Price ceilings cause shortages; price floors cause surpluses.

Margin Highlights

Highlighted comments provide both a running summary of the argument and a reiteration of central points.

Supply of produced goods involves a much more complicated process than demand and is divided into analysis of factors of production and the transformation of those factors into goods.

taco company combines your labor with other inputs like meat, cheese, beans, and tables, and produces many tacos (production) which it supplies to customers in the goods market. For produced goods, supply depends not only on individuals' decisions to supply factors of production; it also depends on firms' ability to produce—to transform those factors of production into usable goods.

The supply process of produced goods can be much more complicated. Often there are many layers of firms—production firms, wholesale firms, distribution firms, and retailing firms—each of which passes on in-process goods to the next layer of firms. Real-world production and supply of produced goods is a multistage process.

The supply of nonproduced goods is more direct. Individuals supply their labor in the form of services directly to the goods market. For example, an independent contractor may repair your washing machine. That contractor supplies his labor directly to you.

Thus, the analysis of the supply of produced goods has two parts: an analysis of

End-of-Chapter Questions

At least 25 questions (includes margin questions) vary in complexity, and require a short answer. *Wall Street Journal* questions are marked with an icon. Citations for these are listed in the Instuctor's Manual.

NEW!

Wall Street Journal Icons

These icons alert students to questions ripped from the *Wall Street Journal*.

End-of-Chapter Problems and Exercises

To get students to actually *think* about the chapter material, Colander offers involved problems, numerical in nature, that sometime call for graphical solutions. Many come from current events.

QUESTIONS FOR THOUGHT AND REVIEW

1. Demonstrate graphically the effect of a price ceiling.
2. Say that the price and quantity both fell. What would you say was the most likely cause?
3. Say that price fell and quantity remained constant. What would you say was the most likely cause?
4. In 1996 the exchange rate for the South African rand fell precipitously from 29 cents per rand to 22 cents per rand when there was political trouble in the country. Explain why the political turmoil had that effect in reference to a graphical supply and demand analysis.
5. Demonstrate graphically the effect of a price floor.
6. Demonstrate graphically why rent controls might increase the total payment that new renters pay for an apartment.
7. Oftentimes, to be considered for a job, you have to know someone in the firm. What does this observation tell you about the wage paid for that job?
8. Graphically show the effects of a minimum wage on the number of unemployed.
9. Demonstrate graphically the effect of a tax of $4 per unit on equilibrium price and quantity.
10. Using a graph like the one you drew for question 8 above, show graphically what the quota would be that led to the same price and quantity.
11. In most developing countries, there are long lines of taxis at airports, and these taxis often wait two or three hours. What does this tell you about the price in that market? Demonstrate with supply and demand analysis.
12. In the text, the supply and demand situation between Mexican pesos and U.S. dollars was shown in reference to the supply and demand for pesos. Go through the same analysis in terms of the supply and demand for dollars.

PROBLEMS AND EXERCISES

1. "Scalping" is the name given to the buying of tickets at a low price and reselling them at a high price. The following information about a Florida State–Notre Dame game in 1993 comes from a newspaper. At the beginning of the season:
   a. Tickets sell for $27 and are sold out in preseason.
   b. Halfway through the season, both teams have maintained unbeaten records. Resale price of tickets rises to $200.
   c. One week before the game, both teams have remained unbeaten and are ranked 1-2. Ticket price rises to $600.
   d. Three days before the game, price falls to $400.
   Demonstrate, using supply/demand analysis and words, what might have happened to cause these fluctuations in price.
2. In some states and localities "scalping" is against the law, although enforcement of these laws is spotty (difficult).
   a. Using supply/demand analysis and words, demonstrate what a weakly enforced antiscalping law would likely do to the price of tickets.
   b. Using supply/demand analysis and words, demonstrate what a strongly enforced antiscalping law would likely do to the price of tickets.
3. Apartments in New York City are often hard to find. One of the major reasons is that there is rent control.
   a. Demonstrate graphically how rent controls could make apartments hard to find.
   b. Often one can get an apartment if one makes a side payment to the current tenant. Can you explain why?
   c. What would be the likely effect of eliminating rent controls?
   d. What is the political appeal of rent controls?
4. Until recently, angora goat wool (mohair) has been designated as a strategic commodity (it used to be utilized in some military clothing). Because of that, in 1992 for every dollar's worth of mohair sold to manufacturers, ranchers received $3.60.
   a. Demonstrate graphically the effect of the elimination of this designation and subsidy.
   b. Explain why the program was likely kept in existence for so long.
   c. Say that a politician has suggested that the government should pass a law that requires all consumers to pay a price for angora goat wool high enough so that the sellers of that wool would receive $3.60 more than the market price. Demonstrate the effect of the law graphically. Would consumers support it? How about suppliers?
5. In one of the boxes, a gray market in Russian rubles is discussed.
   a. Draw the supply and demand curves for rubles in terms of dollars and show the Russian government's then-official price of .64 rubles per dollar.
   b. Show the gray market price of dollars mentioned in that box.
   c. Show what the black market price of rubles would have likely been if the Russian government had strictly enforced the exchange laws.

ANSWERS TO MARGIN QUESTIONS

1. The shortage would have increased; the lower the price ceiling relative to equilibrium price, the larger the shortage. *(86)*
2. The demand curve would have shifted out, increasing both price and quantity, as in the diagram below. *(88)*

3. I remind Jean that a shift factor changes demand, not quantity demanded. *(89)*
4. Quantity decreases but it is unclear what happens to price. *(89)*
5. To conduct the analysis in terms of the supply and demand for dollars, one must put the peso price of dollars on the vertical axis and the quantity of dollars on the horizontal axis, as in the diagram below: *(91)*

6. In a fixed exchange rate system the government works with the market, buying and selling currency to see that quantity supplied equals quantity demanded. In a nonconvertible exchange rate system, the government enacts a statutory provision setting the exchange rate by law. *(92)*
7. I state that the tax will most likely raise the price by less than $2 since the tax will cause the quantity demanded to decrease. This will decrease quantity supplied, and hence decrease the price the suppliers receive. In the diagram below, Q falls from Q_1 to Q_2 and the price the supplier receives falls from $4 to $3, making the final price $5, not $6. *(95)*

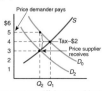

8. Firms prefer quotas to tariffs because with quotas, they receive rents; with tariffs, the government receives tax revenues. *(96)*
9. The fallacy of composition is relevant for macroeconomic issues because it reminds us that, in the aggregate, small effects that are immaterial for micro issues can add up and be material. *(98)*
10. When supply and demand are interdependent, a movement along one curve will cause a shift in the other curve, violating the "other things constant" assumption that is necessary for partial equilibrium analysis to apply. *(99)*

Answers to Margin Questions

Answers to the margin questions appear at the end of each chapter so students can get quick feedback. Answers to remaining questions and problems are in the Instructor's Manual.

Graphs

Analytical graphs are simple and straightforward so that students can easily follow what's happening. Consistent use of color allows differentiation between movements along curves and shifts of curves.

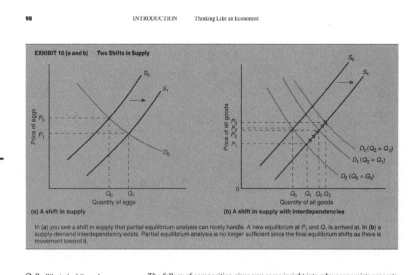

EXHIBIT 10 (a and b)   Two Shifts in Supply

(a) A shift in supply

(b) A shift in supply with interdependencies

In (a) you see a shift in supply that partial equilibrium analysis can nicely handle. A new equilibrium at P_1 and Q_1 is arrived at. In (b) a supply-demand interdependency exists. Partial equilibrium analysis is no longer sufficient since the final equilibrium shifts as there is movement toward it.

Q–9 Why is the fallacy of composition relevant for macroeconomic

The fallacy of composition gives you some insight into why economists separate micro from macro. One of the important side effects of decisions that must be consid-

Internet Addresses

Internet addresses have been added based on data for immediate student updates.

The text discussion is further enlivened, both visually and conceptually, by a series of boxed-off text. These boxes serve one of two purposes:

A REMINDER

1. Those entitled "A Reminder" serve as a review for students; they summarize and consolidate key material.

THE DYNAMIC LAWS OF SUPPLY AND DEMAND	A REMINDER ☑
1. When quantity demanded is greater than quantity supplied, prices tend to rise; when quantity supplied is greater than quantity demanded, prices tend to fall. 2. The larger the difference between quantity supplied and	quantity demanded, the faster prices will rise (if there is excess demand) or fall (if there is excess supply). 3. When quantity supplied equals quantity demanded, prices have no tendency to change.

demanded is a phenomenon economists call the **first dynamic law of supply and demand:**

> *When quantity demanded is greater than quantity supplied, prices tend to rise; when quantity supplied is greater than quantity demanded, prices tend to fall.*

It's called a *dynamic law* because *dynamic* refers to change and this law refers to how prices change, not to what prices will be.

How much pressure will there be for prices to rise or fall? That too will likely depend on differences between quantity supplied and quantity demanded. The greater

---

ADDED DIMENSION

2. "Added Dimension" boxes either extend the text material or provide another perspective on it, relating the material to the real world and deepening students' understanding.

BLACK AND GRAY MARKETS IN CURRENCY — ADDED DIMENSION

Foreign exchange markets are a good example of supply and demand forces at work. Whenever there's excess supply or demand for something, there's incentive for suppliers and demanders to get together to eliminate the excess.

Let's consider the issue in relation to the former Soviet Union. In 1989, at the official price of 0.64 rubles per dollar, the quantity of dollars demanded far exceeded the quantity of dollars supplied. In the former Soviet Union, adventurous individuals (who weren't worried about the wrath of the invisible foot—that is, about being prosecuted for violating foreign exchange laws) traded in a black market at a higher price.

A black market, which involves trades of a good that can't legally be traded, is a natural result of government price restrictions. Often the government knows that such trading goes on and chooses, for political reasons, not to enforce its own laws strictly. (There are situations like this in the United States. Here the speed limit is 55 miles per hour on many secondary roads but almost everyone drives at 65 miles per hour, which police tend to accept as a fact of life.)

When a black market is unofficially condoned, trading on it becomes more open and it's often called a gray market. Since risk of prosecution is less, upward pressure on price from the invisible foot is less; so gray market prices are usually closer to the supply/demand equilibrium than are black market prices.

The Soviet foreign exchange market became a gray market in late 1989. (The gray market price of a dollar was between 5 and 15 rubles rather than the 0.64 rubles you'd get at the official rate.) If you went to the former Soviet Union at that time, individuals would come up to you on the street and offer to trade rubles for dollars at something near the gray market price. In 1991 the Soviet Union broke apart and Russia began to let the ruble be freely tradable. Because of political and economic problems, however, the ruble's value fell enormously and it cost thousands of rubles to buy one dollar.

In my next example, let's consider rent control in Paris in 1948 (this case is discussed in the *Classic Readings* supplement). **Rent control** is *a price ceiling on rents, set by government.* During World War I, to stabilize housing prices and help out those fighting for France, rents were frozen. Upon the return of veterans, the freeze was held in the interest of society. In 1926, rent control was reviewed but by that time, lifting the controls would have resulted in huge increases in rents. Rents were allowed to rise only slightly. Again, during World War II, rents were frozen and rents in Paris

Rent Controls

Rent control   A price ceiling on rents, set by government and applying to what a landlord can charge for apartments.

The Appendix Solution

The appendix solution makes the core of the book much more manageable by placing over 100 pages of the supplemental, mathematical, institutional, and historical material in the appendixes. Tailoring the course is now easier than ever. As one reviewer noted, the book sets the standard for flexibility in textbooks.

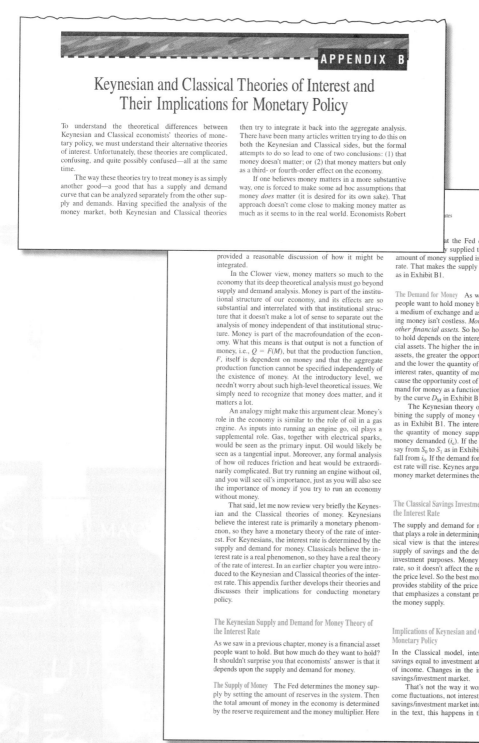

APPENDIX B.

Keynesian and Classical Theories of Interest and Their Implications for Monetary Policy

To understand the theoretical differences between Keynesian and Classical economists' theories of monetary policy, we must understand their alternative theories of interest. Unfortunately, these theories are complicated, confusing, and quite possibly confused—all at the same time.

The way these theories try to treat money is as simply another good—a good that has a supply and demand curve that can be analyzed separately from the other supply and demands. Having specified the analysis of the money market, both Keynesian and Classical theories

then try to integrate it back into the aggregate analysis. There have been many articles written trying to do this on both the Keynesian and Classical sides, but the formal attempts to do so lead to one of two conclusions: (1) that money doesn't matter; or (2) that money matters but only as a third- or fourth-order effect on the economy.

If one believes money matters in a more substantive way, one is forced to make some ad hoc assumptions that money *does* matter (it is desired for its own sake). That approach doesn't come close to making money matter as much as it seems to in the real world. Economists Robert

provided a reasonable discussion of how it might be integrated.

In the Clower view, money matters so much to the economy that its deep theoretical analysis must go beyond supply and demand analysis. Money is part of the institutional structure of our economy, and its effects are so substantial and interrelated with that institutional structure that it doesn't make a lot of sense to separate out the analysis of money independent of that institutional structure. Money is part of the macrofoundation of the economy. What this means is that output is not a function of money, i.e., $Q = F(M)$, but that the production function, F, itself is dependent on money and that the aggregate production function cannot be specified independently of the existence of money. At the introductory level, we needn't worry about such high-level theoretical issues. We simply need to recognize that money does matter, and it matters a lot.

An analogy might make this argument clear. Money's role in the economy is similar to the role of oil in a gas engine. As inputs into running an engine go, oil plays a supplemental role. Gas, together with electrical sparks, would be seen as the primary input. Oil would likely be seen as a tangential input. Moreover, any formal analysis of how oil reduces friction and heat would be extraordinarily complicated. But try running an engine without oil, and you will see oil's importance, just as you will also see the importance of money if you try to run an economy without money.

That said, let me now review very briefly the Keynesian and the Classical theories of money. Keynesians believe the interest rate is primarily a monetary phenomenon, so they have a monetary theory of the rate of interest. For Keynesians, the interest rate is determined by the supply and demand for money. Classicals believe the interest rate is a real phenomenon, so they have a real theory of the rate of interest. In an earlier chapter you were introduced to the Keynesian and Classical theories of the interest rate. This appendix further develops their theories and discusses their implications for conducting monetary policy.

The Keynesian Supply and Demand for Money Theory of the Interest Rate

As we saw in a previous chapter, money is a financial asset people want to hold. But how much do they want to hold? It shouldn't surprise you that economists' answer is that it depends upon the supply and demand for money.

The Supply of Money The Fed determines the money supply by setting the amount of reserves in the system. Then the total amount of money in the economy is determined by the reserve requirement and the money multiplier. Here

at the Fed can perfectly determine the money supplied to the economy and that that amount of money supplied isn't influenced by the interest rate. That makes the supply of money perfectly vertical, as in Exhibit B1.

The Demand for Money As we saw in a previous chapter, people want to hold money because it's useful to them as a medium of exchange and as a store of wealth. But holding money isn't costless. *Money pays lower interest than other financial assets.* So how much money people want to hold depends on the interest rate on those other financial assets. The higher the interest rate on other financial assets, the greater the opportunity cost of holding money and the lower the quantity of money demanded. At lower interest rates, quantity of money demanded is larger because the opportunity cost of holding money is lower. Demand for money as a function of the interest rate is shown by the curve D_M in Exhibit B1.

The Keynesian theory of interest comes from combining the supply of money with the demand for money as in Exhibit B1. The interest rate is determined where the quantity of money supplied equals the quantity of money demanded (i_e). If the supply of money increases, say from S_0 to S_1 as in Exhibit B1(b), the interest rate will fall from i_0. If the demand for money increases, the interest rate will rise. Keynes argued that, in the short run, the money market determines the interest rate.

The Classical Savings Investment Theory of the Interest Rate

The supply and demand for money isn't the only market that plays a role in determining the interest rate. The Classical view is that the interest rate is determined by the supply of savings and the demand for those savings for investment purposes. Money doesn't affect the interest rate, so it doesn't affect the real economy. It only affects the price level. So the best monetary policy is a policy that provides stability of the price level. It's a long-run policy that emphasizes a constant predetermined growth rate of the money supply.

Implications of Keynesian and Classical Theories for Monetary Policy

In the Classical model, interest rate fluctuations keep savings equal to investment at the full-employment level of income. Changes in the interest rate equilibrate the savings/investment market.

That's not the way it works in Keynes's model. Income fluctuations, not interest rate fluctuations, bring the savings/investment market into equilibrium. As discussed in the text, this happens in the following way: Income

Student Supplements

Drill and Review Study Guide (also available as splits)

This comprehensive guide reinforces textbook principles and helps students practice the tools of economics. The preface shows students how to better use the text, their own lecture notes, and the guide itself. This new guide is particularly helpful to effectively prepare for multiple-choice and short-answer exams. The guide has two main components:

1. A chapter-by-chapter drill and review.

2. Various kinds of Pretests (with answers):

   - *Chapter at a Glance* lists the important points of each chapter.

   - *Short-Answer Questions* are based upon a specific learning objective from the chapter.

   - *Word Scrambles* are designed to be a diversion for the student.

   - Matching Terms and Concepts to their definitions allow for review of key terms.

   - *Problems and Exercises* focus on numerical and graphical aspects of the chapter.

   - *Multiple-Choice Questions* test the breadth of the student's knowledge of the text material.

   - Answers to all questions provide detailed rationale to all questions including specific references to text pages.

   - *Pretests* give students practice taking timed, cumulative exams.

Student Workbook (also available as splits)

This workbook complements the textbook through review and examination preparation. Each chapter contains the following components:

- *Chapter at a Glance* lists the important points in each chapter.

- *Jeopardy and Double Jeopardy* prepares students for recall-type exam questions.

- *Problems and Applications* use 10 short questions to prepare students for all three types of test questions: recall, analytical, and graphical.

- *Brain Teasers* (1 to 3 per chapter) are a more rigorous version of *Problems and Applications*.

- *Multiple-Choice Questions.*

- *Potential Essay Questions* prepare students for short-answer, essay-type exam questions.

- *Food for Thought* provides the opportunity to combine subjective judgment and economic tools to answer questions with no "right" answer.

Note: Answers to all questions, except *Food for Thought*, are provided at the end of each chapter.

Classic Readings in Economics

This collection of original texts–written by such authors as Karl Marx, Adam Smith, and John Maynard Keynes–shows the ever-changing direction of economic thinking while raising the kind of questions students should consider during their study of economics.

Economics: An Honors Companion

Students with a mathematics background can use the Honors Companion to study the underlying mathematical techniques of basic economic concepts. Each chapter presents these concepts through exposition and graphs and then defines the attendant mathematics using the student's knowledge of economic relationships. Numerical examples are also included as are end-of-chapter problems.

Case Studies in Microeconomics/Case Studies in Macroeconomics: Selections from The Wall Street Journal

Written specifically for the Colander text, this book serves three purposes:

1. Familiarize the student with applications of economic ideas–as they are applied to the real-world cases.

2. Show students how to effectively read *The Wall Street Journal.*

3. Give students some practice in reading critically and expressing themselves.

Macro/Micro-interactive

This companion software is organized into three segments–introduction, core principles, and applications–with each module having three levels of interactivity. The first, **INTRO,** introduces users to an economic concept and provides a tie-in to the invisible forces relevant to the module. The second, **EXPLORE,** allows the user to experiment with an economic concept by various on-screen manipulations. The third, **APPLY,** allows users to test what they have learned in the previous two sections.

Link-Miller: Microeconomics CD-ROM/ Macroeconomics CD-ROM

These interactive tutorials cover core topics in introductory microeconomics and macroeconomics: supply and demand, pure competition, tax incidence, elasticities, monopoly, and costs and production (microeconomics); national accounts, aggregate expenditures I, aggregate expenditures II, aggregate supply and demand, money and banking and monetary policy (macroeconomics). The CD-ROMs review through illustrations and automated discussions of basic concepts. Interactive exercises focusing on the construction of key economic graphs and charts allow students to see "real" outcomes of economic exercises and learn where common errors occur.

WinEcon CD-ROM

This Windows software provides over 75 hours of interactive learning that cover the *entire* syllabus for a principles of economics course–the first computer-based learning package to do so! It offers self-assessment questions and exams, economic databases, an economic glossary, and references to leading economics textbooks. WinEcon will be available both for student purchase and as a site license.

Instructor Supplements

Instructor's Manual

The IM is designed to let the professor see, at a glance, the learning aids from within the text and from those supplements available for each chapter of the text. Each chapter includes:

- The Laugher Curve. Updated by a Helsinki economist, this joke-filled Web site *http://www.etla.fi/pkm/joke.html* proves that–if you try hard enough–"economic"can spell "comic."
- A list of the chapter's objectives.
- A detailed lecture outline–key terms are boldfaced and definitions are given.
- Additional Resources–references to Macroeconomic and Microeconomic Case Studies, Classic Readings, Macro and Micro Interactive Software, the Honors Companion, the Irwin/McGraw-Hill Economics Video Series, Experiments in Teaching Economics, and the Economics U\$A video series.
- Classroom aids: a précis of current articles that illustrate key points in the text.

Wall Street Journal Package

- **10-week Student Subscription and Applications Booklet**
  This special *Wall Street Journal* Edition of Colander's **Economics** includes a bound-in booklet describing *The Wall Street Journal* and its use. Students will receive an exclusive 10-week *WSJ* subscription by simply completing and mailing the Business Reply Card found in the text.
- **Complimentary 1-Year Subscription for Instructors**
  Upon receiving 20 *WSJ* orders from your students, *WSJ* will send you a complimentary 1-year subscription. Talk to your Irwin/McGraw-Hill representative for details on how to subscribe.
- **Complimentary Fax Service–***Irwin/McGraw-Hill Economics Fax Newsletter*
  Adopters of this special *Wall Street Journal* Edition can take advantage of a free weekly fax service during each semester. Each fax includes *Week at a Glance:* 10 questions and answers on articles from the previous week of *The Wall Street Journal*; *Article Analysis:* a reprint of one or two articles from *The Wall Street Journal* followed by five analytical questions and their answers with references to text chapters; and *Economic Highlights:* a summary of economic data reported in *The Wall Street Journal* that relate to the principles course. In-depth coverage is provided for select data when available and appropriate.

Instructor's Assistant

This valuable aid allows instructors to incorporate any number of supplements into a classroom. It presents core material for the entire Colander textbook and ancillaries in a format that can be tailored to specific needs. Included are (1) syllabi for a microeconomics course, a macroeconomics course, and a one-term principles course; (2) problem sets with answers for each chapter; and (3) sample mid-terms and final exams. It is available in printed and word processing formats.

Test Banks A and B

The test banks now boast a more interesting and diverse collection of over 10,000 true/false and multiple-choice questions that cover all 39 chapters. Questions are categorized by *difficulty* (easy, medium, hard); *skill* (recall, comprehension, application); and *type* (word problem, graph, calculation). Rationale and text page references for ALL questions are provided. User friendly questions are easily translated into standard word processing systems. Brownstone software offers these test banks in computerized form.

Test Bank C

The nearly 500 questions found in this revised test bank are short-answer, essay, and graphical in nature.

PowerPoint® Presentations

These Windows® programs–for microeconomics and for macroeconomics–offer more than 800 slides that can be used to create classroom presentations designed specifically to illustrate the key issues, graphs, and tables in the Third Edition. Slides contain the key points and illustrations in each chapter.

CD-ROM

This multimedia software offers secured access to the following programs: Instructor's Manual; Instructor's Assistant; PowerPoint; Computerized Test Bank; and Interactive Visualization software. This CD-ROM has the capacity to construct presentations from these programs or from any other software the instructor may have.

Annotated Instructor's Edition

This version of the text is fully annotated with teaching tips and information on incorporating the ancillaries.

Experiments in Teaching Economics

This is an introduction to experimental economics for the principles instructor and a "how to" guide for integrating experimental demonstrations into the classroom. Eight simple yet powerful teaching devices and educationally motivating tools bring students into the study of economics.

Color Transparency Acetates

Nearly 200 text graphs and illustrations are available in transparency acetates.

Economics U\$A Videos

Each of the 30-minute segments from this series of 28 will enhance the principles and concepts covered in the text.

Irwin/McGraw-Hill Economics Issues Video Series

These videos can supplement classroom discussions or can be used as a basis for small group discussions.

Gross Domestic Product, 1959–96—Continued
(Billions of dollars, except as noted; quarterly data at seasonally adjusted annual rates)

Net Exports of Goods and Services			Government Consumption Expenditures and Gross Investment					Final Sales of Domestic Product	Gross Domestic Purchases[1]	Addendum: Gross National Product[2]	Percent Change from Preceding Period	
			Total	Federal			State and Local				Gross Domestic Product	Gross Domestic Purchases[1]
Net Exports	Exports	Imports	Total	Total	National Defense	Non-defense						
−1.7	20.6	22.3	112.0	67.2	55.7	11.5	44.8	503.0	508.9	510.1	—	—
2.4	25.3	22.8	113.2	65.6	54.9	10.8	47.6	523.3	524.1	529.8	3.8	3.0
3.4	26.0	22.7	120.9	69.1	57.7	11.4	51.8	541.9	541.5	548.4	3.5	3.3
2.4	27.4	25.0	131.4	76.5	62.3	14.2	55.0	579.1	582.8	589.4	7.4	7.6
3.3	29.4	26.1	137.7	78.1	62.2	15.9	59.6	611.7	614.1	621.9	5.5	5.4
5.5	33.6	28.1	144.4	79.4	61.3	18.1	65.0	658.0	657.6	668.0	7.4	7.1
3.9	35.4	31.5	153.0	81.8	62.0	19.7	71.2	709.4	715.3	724.5	8.5	8.8
1.9	38.9	37.1	173.6	94.1	73.4	20.7	79.5	774.0	785.9	793.0	9.5	9.9
1.4	41.4	39.9	194.6	106.6	85.5	21.0	88.1	823.1	832.2	839.1	5.8	5.9
−1.3	45.3	46.6	212.1	113.8	92.0	21.8	98.3	901.4	911.8	916.7	9.2	9.6
−1.2	49.3	50.5	223.8	115.8	92.4	23.4	108.0	972.7	983.4	988.4	7.9	7.8
1.2	57.0	55.8	236.1	115.9	90.6	25.3	120.2	1,033.4	1,034.4	1,042.0	5.4	5.2
−3.0	59.3	62.3	249.9	117.1	88.7	28.3	132.8	1,116.9	1,128.4	1,133.1	8.7	9.1
−8.0	66.2	74.2	268.9	125.1	93.2	31.9	143.8	1,227.4	1,245.3	1,246.0	9.9	10.4
.6	91.8	91.2	287.6	128.2	94.7	33.5	159.4	1,365.2	1,382.0	1,395.4	11.7	11.0
−3.1	124.3	127.5	323.2	139.9	101.9	38.0	183.3	1,482.8	1,500.0	1,512.6	8.3	8.5
13.6	136.3	122.7	362.6	154.5	110.9	43.6	208.1	1,636.9	1,617.1	1,643.9	8.9	7.8
−2.3	148.9	151.1	385.9	162.7	116.1	46.6	223.1	1,802.0	1,821.2	1,836.1	11.5	12.6
−23.7	158.8	182.4	416.9	178.4	125.8	52.6	238.5	2,003.8	2,050.5	2,047.5	11.4	12.6
−26.1	186.1	212.3	457.9	194.4	135.6	58.9	263.4	2,264.2	2,317.5	2,313.5	13.0	13.0
−24.0	228.7	252.7	507.1	215.0	151.2	63.8	292.0	2,540.6	2,581.5	2,590.4	11.6	11.4
−14.9	278.9	293.8	572.8	248.4	174.2	74.2	324.4	2,791.9	2,799.1	2,819.5	8.9	8.4
−15.0	302.8	317.8	633.4	284.1	202.0	82.2	349.2	3,087.8	3,130.9	3,150.6	11.9	11.9
−20.5	282.6	303.2	684.8	313.2	230.9	82.3	371.6	3,256.6	3,262.6	3,273.2	4.1	4.2
−51.7	277.0	328.6	735.7	344.5	255.0	89.4	391.2	3,519.4	3,566.2	3,546.5	8.4	9.3
−102.0	303.1	405.1	796.6	372.6	282.7	89.9	424.0	3,835.0	4,004.5	3,933.5	11.0	12.3
−114.2	303.0	417.2	875.0	410.1	312.4	97.7	464.9	4,154.5	4,294.9	4,201.0	7.1	7.3
−131.5	320.7	452.2	938.5	435.2	332.4	102.9	503.3	4,412.6	4,553.7	4,435.1	5.8	6.0
−142.1	365.7	507.9	992.8	455.7	350.4	105.3	537.2	4,668.1	4,834.5	4,701.3	6.1	6.2
−106.1	447.2	553.2	1,032.0	457.3	354.0	103.3	574.7	5,038.7	5,155.6	5,062.6	7.6	6.6
−80.4	509.3	589.7	1,095.1	477.2	360.6	116.7	617.9	5,407.0	5,519.1	5,452.8	7.7	7.0
−71.3	557.3	628.6	1,176.1	503.6	373.1	130.4	672.6	5,735.8	5,815.1	5,764.9	5.6	5.4
−20.5	601.8	622.3	1,225.9	522.6	383.5	139.1	703.4	5,919.0	5,937.2	5,932.4	3.0	2.1
−29.5	639.4	669.0	1,263.8	528.0	375.8	152.2	735.8	6,237.4	6,274.0	6,255.5	5.5	5.7
−62.7	657.8	720.5	1,290.4	522.6	362.7	159.9	767.8	6,532.4	6,615.7	6,563.5	4.9	5.4
−94.4	719.1	813.5	1,314.7	516.4	352.0	164.3	798.4	6,876.2	7,030.1	6,931.9	5.8	6.3
−94.7	807.4	902.0	1,358.3	516.6	345.5	171.0	841.7	7,216.7	7,348.4	7,246.7	4.6	4.5
−120.2	844.3	964.5	1,414.8	525.5	348.8	176.7	889.3	7,579.6	7,736.5	7,598.9	3.8	4.9

[1] Gross domestic product (GDP) less exports of goods and services plus imports of goods and services

[2] GDP plus net receipts of factor income from rest of the world.

[3] 3rd quarter estimates

Source: Department of Commerce, Bureau of Economic Analysis

ANNOTATED INSTRUCTOR'S EDITION

MACROECONOMICS
Third Edition

DAVID C. COLANDER
Middlebury College

Boston, Massachusetts   Burr Ridge, Illinois   Dubuque, Iowa
Madison, Wisconsin   New York, New York   San Francisco, California   St. Louis, Missouri

Dedicated to the memory of Frank Knight and Thorstein Veblen, both of whose economics have significantly influenced the contents of this book.

1 2 3 4 5 7 8 9 0 VH/VH 9 0 9 8 7

ISBN 0-256-17266-8

Editorial director: *Michael W. Junior*
Publisher: *Gary Burke*
Senior developmental editor: *Tom Tompson*
Developmental editor: *Catherine Schwent*
Senior project manager: *Denise Santor-Mitzit*
Senior production supervisor: *Bob Lange*
Art director: *Keith McPherson*
Photo research coordinator: *Keri Johnson*
Compositor: *Shepard Poorman Communications Corp.*
Typeface: *10/12 Times Roman*

Printer: *Von Hoffmann Press, Inc*

Library of Congress Cataloging-in-Publication Data

Colander, David C.
   Macroeconomics / David C. Colander. / 3rd ed.
     p. cm.
    0-256-17217-X   0-07-115226-1 (International)
    Includes index
    ISBN 0-256-17217-X.—ISBN 0-256-17266-8 (student's ed.).—ISBN
   0-07-115226-1 (International ed.)
    1. Macroeconomics.   I. Title
HB172.5.C638   1997
339—dc21   97-25681

http://www.mhcollege.com

Preface

One of the first lessons of writing is: Know for whom you are writing. This book is written for students; this preface, however, is written for professors. Why? The answer is simple—the students for whom this book is written don't read prefaces; they don't read anything in a textbook unless it is assigned (and sometimes they don't read that). Their interests lie in the real world, not in texts. The style and structure of the body of this text is made to turn on such students, as much as they can be turned on, to economic ideas. Alas, I recognize that I will fail with many, but I sincerely believe that my success rate of actually getting students to read this textbook will likely be higher than will be the success rate for other economics textbooks written in standard professorial style.

I also recognize that students will never get a chance to read this text unless the professor chooses the book, which is why I write this preface for professors—they read prefaces. (If you're one of those rare students who read textbook prefaces, read on; it will give you a sense of what will be coming in the course.)

Excerpts from Preface to the First Edition

Before I started writing this book I had done quite a bit of research on economics education. As part of that research, Arjo Klamer and I had surveyed and interviewed graduate students in a number of top graduate programs. Two of the most disturbing things we discovered were that economic institutions and economic literature were being given short shrift in graduate economics education. For example, in response to the question, "How important is a knowledge of economic literature to being successful as an economist?" only 10 percent of the students responded that it was very important, while 43 percent said it was unimportant. In response to the question, "How important to achieving success as an economist is having a thorough knowledge of the economy?" only 3 percent said it was very important, while 68 percent said it was unimportant.

I believe that the majority of the profession is concerned with these results. Certainly the students we interviewed were concerned. They said they believe that institutions and literature were very important. Their survey responses simply indicated their perception of how people succeed in the profession, not that the current situation was the way it should be. Almost all economists I know believe that students need to know economic literature and have a thorough knowledge of the institutions. Without the appropriate background knowledge of institutions and literature, all the technical skills in the world aren't going to provide one with the economic sensibility necessary to understand what's going on in the economy or to decide whether or not a model is relevant.

As I thought about these results and considered my own teaching, I realized that the problem was not only in graduate schools; it had filtered down to undergraduate texts. As I looked through the texts, I saw excellent discussions of technical issues and of models, but little discussion of economic sensibility. These books didn't even try to provide the intellectual context within which those models developed or the institutional context to which these models were to be applied. The standard texts had settled into teaching technique for the sake of technique and had shifted away from teaching economic sensibility.

I decided that if I were serious about playing a role in reinstituting economic sensibility and a knowledge of institutions and literature in economics education, I would have to write an introductory textbook that did that. I took it as a challenge. Meeting that challenge was what drove me to write this book; it is what kept me going when all my rational instincts told me it was too much time and too much work.

Teaching Economic Sensibility

The question I faced was: How do you incorporate economic sensibility into a textbook? Economic sensibility is more than a knowledge of modeling techniques; it is a mindset in which one's lens of the world is a latticework of ascending cost/benefit frameworks in which one is deciding on the optimal degree of rationality. Economic sensibility is an enforced reasonableness that provides insight into complicated issues; it is a perspective, not a technique. The argument I heard in favor of teaching technique was that economic sensibility could not be taught. I reject that argument. Economic sensibility may be hard to teach because it does not come naturally for most people, but it can and must be taught. The question is: How do you teach it? The answer I came to: Enthusiastically.

Economics with Passion

I am first and foremost an economics teacher; I am excited by economics. I find economic ideas relevant, challenging, and exciting. In my lectures, I try to convey that excitement, and if the lecture is going right, I can feel the excitement in my students. Then off they go to read the text. All too often when they return to class, the fire in their eyes is gone; the textbook has lulled them into complacency. Those who know me know that I can put up with many things (not quietly, but nonetheless put up with), but one of those things isn't complacency. I want students to think, to argue, to challenge, to get passionate about the ideas. I encourage this reaction from students not just because economists' ideas deserved to be treated passionately, but also because, through a combination of passion and reason, eventually students achieve economic sensibility. I decided what was missing from most textbooks was the passion. I promised myself my book would retain the passion.

Now there's no way I'm going to get passionate about Slutsky equations, phase diagrams, indifference curves, or an AS/AD model. Mathematicians may get passionate about such things, I don't. I do get passionate about the insight economics gives one into the problems we, as individuals and as society, must face: the budget deficit, TANSTAAFL, the environment, and agricultural subsidies. If the techniques help in understanding the ideas, fine, but if they don't, goodbye to the techniques.

Passion without Bias

While not all textbooks are written by passionless people, the conventional wisdom is that authors should hide their passion to make their books more marketable. In some ways this makes sense—often passion and ideological bias go together. Many economists' passions are ideologically linked, and if you remove the ideology, you remove the passion. Good economic sensibility cannot be—and cannot even appear to be—biased; if passion is purged in maintaining neutrality, it is purged for a good cause.

But passion and ideological bias need not go together. I believe it is possible for a passionate textbook to be reasonably objective and unbiased. And I set out to write a book that would be as unbiased as possible (but not more so) and to do so without masking my passion for economic ideas. Various techniques allow me to do this. For example, to keep the students interested in the ideas rather than focusing on technique, I present some ideas in a debate format with two passionate believers on both sides arguing the points. The debate format makes the arguments come alive; they are no longer technical issues that must be memorized; they are passionate ideas, and as the students get caught up in the debate, they think about the ideas much more deeply than they otherwise would.

A Conversational Tone

To transmit that sense of passion to the students, I needed a writing style that allowed it to come through. Quite honestly, textbookese douses passion faster than a cold shower. So this book is not written in textbookese. It's written in conversational English—I'm talking to the students. When they read the book, they will know me; they may not like me the way my mother likes me, but they will know me.

The conversational tone is not a monotone; it ebbs and flows depending on the nature of the material. Sometimes, in the analytic parts, the style approaches textbookese; the important technical aspects of economics require technical writing. When we hit those parts, I tell the students, and encourage them to stick with me. But, even here I try to provide intuitive explanations that students can relate to.

The use of conversational style has two effects. First, it eliminates the sense some students have that textbooks provide the "truth." When the textbook author is a real person with peccadilloes and warts, the students won't accept what he or she says unless it makes sense to them. Approaching a textbook with a Missouri "show me" attitude stimulates true learning. Second, the conversational style keeps the students awake. If students' heads are nodding as they read a chapter, they're not learning. Now I know this book is not *Catcher in the Rye;* it's a textbook conveying sometimes complex ideas. But the excitement about economic ideas and the real world comes through.

The approach I take allows me to deal simply with complicated ideas. For example, in the book I discuss modern interpretations of Keynesian and Classical economics, real business cycles, strategic pricing, the theory of the second best, rent-seeking, Pareto optimality, and challenges to Pareto optimality. The conversational style conveys the essence of these complex topics to students in a nontechnical fashion without tying the students' brains up in technical tourniquets. The style allows me to relate the ideas to concrete examples rather than mathematical formulas, providing intuitive discussions of the ideas that capture the economic sensibility.

Models in Historical and Institutional Context

Discussing only the minimum of techniques necessary for the students to understand the ideas allows me more leeway to get into, and discuss, institutional and historical issues as they relate to current policy. Models without context are meaningless, and thus you'll find more historical and institutional issues in this book than in other principles books. The book has numerous maps; the discussion conveys the sense that geography, history, and psychology are important, even though it touches on them only tangentially.

One of the ways in which this historical and institutional approach shows up is in the complete coverage of the changing nature of economic systems. Socialism is undergoing enormous changes, and students are interested in what is happening and why it is happening. Their questions cannot be answered with technical models, but they can be discussed informally in a historical context. And that's what this book does.

The Invisible Forces

I've incorporated in the book a pedagogical device I've found useful where I want to include the social and political forces that affect reality. That device is to convey to students a picture of reality being controlled not only by the invisible hand, but also by the invisible foot (politics) and the invisible handshake (social and cultural forces). This *invisible forces* imagery lets me relate economists' abstract models to the real world; it allows me to discuss the real-world interface between economics, politics, and social forces. What makes this device effective is that students can picture these three invisible forces fighting each other to direct real-world events; that image allows them to put economic models into perspective.

Some Prefatory Comments on the Third Edition

This third edition marks a substantial revision of the second. The changes include the usual revisions and updates, together with some reorganization and some reworking of previous material. The need to update statistics, discussion of institutions, and discussion of policy is obvious. Keeping up with the ongoing policy issues requires a rewrite here, a change in discussion there, a new statistic here, and a deletion there. Such changes occur in every chapter; they reflect my attempt to provide a book that has the latest information and the most up-do-date discussion of policy possible. To allow students to keep the statistics up to date, I have placed much more reliance on data obtainable over the Internet. Thus, throughout the book, I have placed Internet addresses where the data can be updated by the student.

Let me give one example of these changes from microeconomics and one example from macroeconomics. In micro, antitrust rules were changed since the last edition—in 1997, the Justice Department announced that it was going to take the likelihood of a merger lowering price into account when it rules on mergers. That information needed to be added. Also, the AT&T situation, which I had used as a case study, turned into an even more interesting case as the Baby Bells started to merge and compete with AT&T in both local and long distance telephone markets. These discussions, and many like them, were updated.

In macro, the nature of GDP statistics changed in 1996 when the government started separating out its capital expenditures from current expenditures. That change meant rewriting the entire discussion of the governmental component of GDP statistics. In macro policy, the big story was the continued slow, steady expansion of the economy through the middle of 1997. That expansion lowered unemployment below what almost every economist had predicted back in 1995, and in doing so, drove U.S. unemployment lower than economists had previously believed achievable without accelerating inflation (even as European unemployment remained high). This experience provoked a needed discussion within the profession about the stability of the natural rate of unemployment. To keep the text up-to-date, the macro policy discussion had to be modified to take this recent experience into account.

In macro policy, the pendulum swung even further away from debates about discretionary fiscal policy and toward debates about the appropriate monetary régime and issues of structural policy. To take these changes into account I added a new chapter on structural macro policy and reworked the monetary policy discussion to focus more on policy régimes than on specific policy actions.

A second set of changes occurred at the suggestions of the many helpful reviewers and users of the second edition. Before I began working on the third edition, the publisher collected a large number of reviews and suggestions about what was good and not so good in the second edition, and about how the book could be modified to better fit the diverse needs of the teachers who use it. These suggestions resulted in a number of changes.

Ancillaries

Many reviewers' suggestions concerned ancillaries. Most agreed that the book had the broadest, most interesting set of ancillaries of any principles book, but that the quality of some of them could be improved. I took this advice seriously and, in this edition, I took direct oversight of the print ancillaries. I asked Jenifer Gamber, who is also the managing editor of the *Eastern Economic Journal,* to become our drill sergeant, seeing to it that we all kept up and delivered high-quality material.

Together with Jenifer, I wrote the *Drill and Review Study Guide,* making it into what we believe is the most useful tool for students it can be. Doug Copeland continued his excellent work on the *Student Workbook,* and Tom Adams carefully reworked the *Instructor's Manual* to make it more useful and to provide answers to the in-text questions. Jenifer and I developed the Annotated Instructor's Edition that shows how the ancillaries fit into teaching the book. And Patrick O'Neill added an *Instructor's Assistant* that provides problem sets, syllabi, and suggested tests—on disk and in print—to make professors' lives a little easier.

Reviewers also told us that, while the test bank was solid, it needed more diverse and more interesting questions. In revising the test bank we worked hard to incorporate such questions. In doing so we added over 3,000 new questions so that not only is the test bank the largest in the field, it is also the highest in quality. I'm also happy to say that the publisher has adopted a new test-generating program that is much easier to use and that allows users to download tests into standard word processing programs.

These revised print ancillaries, together with the innovative ancillaries of the last edition—the *Honors Companion,* the *Classic Readings,* the *Wall Street Journal Case Studies* in Micro and Macro, and the *Experiments in Economics,* make the third edition's printed ancillaries a complete learning package.

In addition to the print supplements, there have been improvements and additions to the electronic components of our package. For the student, we have revised the Interactive Visualization software created by Paul Estensen to accompany the second edition and we have added Excel problem sets written by Byron Brown at Michigan State University. For the instructor, we have added PowerPoint slide presentations and we will make available an Instructor's CD-ROM that contains the *Instructor's Manual,* the *Instructor's Assistant,* the computerized test banks, the PowerPoints, the Interactive Visualization software, and the Excel problem sets. This remarkable multimedia program will also allow instructors to create presentations from any of the materials on the CD-ROM or from additional material on disks.

I'm very proud of the ancillary package. I think you will find that its quality is high, its diversity enormous, and its usefulness exceptional. It makes the book a complete learning system.

Changes to the Textbook

Reviewers offered numerous suggestions about how to improve the text—how to make the book more teachable by a wider range of instructors. Many of these suggestions have been incorporated into this third edition. One central issue concerned length. Most reviewers were in agreement that the book was too long, and that all principles books are becoming too encyclopedic. But it quickly became evident that there was little agreement as to what constituted the core of the course. The reality

is that there are many ways to teach the introductory course, and that what are extra pages for one instructor is highly desired content for another.

Faced with this conclusion—cut, but cut what I want cut—I had to make some difficult decisions. In making those decisions I tried to find out what reviewers objected to about a full-coverage principles book. Was it length per se, or was it the difficulty such large books created about what should be covered? Some teachers felt required to cover everything in the book. In a 10-, 12-, or even 15-week semester, that is virtually impossible. In discussing this issue with reviewers what I found was that most felt that the biggest problem was not size, as long as that size did not increase the cost, but a lack of "guidance" as to which parts should be considered core and which parts were supplemental. They wanted a smaller core to teach.

Faced with this dual objective function—shorten, but include diverse topics, I decided upon what might be called the "appendix solution." I cut the core chapters significantly—by about 100 pages. But rather than totally eliminating the remaining material, I reworked it so that it would fit into appendixes. This somewhat large number of appendixes allows you to tailor your course to what you want it to be.

Let me give a specific example of how the appendix solution works. Many teachers liked the historical discussion of the evolution of economies in the second edition. Others felt they didn't have time to cover that much history, and that that history was not part of the core course. So I reworked the chapter for the third edition, put much of the history in an appendix, and integrated the core discussion with the discussion of production possibility curves in Chapter 1. Thus, a brief discussion of the evolution of systems is in the chapter, and a much longer discussion of economic systems is in the appendix for those who want it.

This appendix solution also allowed me to move a significant amount of mathematical, institutional, and historical material to appendixes, and even to add some analytic material. For example, appendixes covering the algebraic presentation of supply and demand, the algebraic presentation of monopoly, and isoquants and isocost analysis are newly included in this edition. As one reviewer noted, the book sets the standard for flexibility in textbooks.

There were also numerous changes made in the structure and organization of the text, so let me give you a list of those changes.

Introduction

Chapter 1: Economics and Economic Reasoning: Old Chapter 1 was shortened. Discussion of the production possibility curve was taken out and integrated with the chapter on evolution of economic systems, which was moved up to Chapter 2 to accommodate it.

Chapter 2: Economic Organization: Old Chapter 3 was combined with the Chapter 1 discussion of production possibility curve. Discussion of comparative advantage expanded. Core chapter shortened considerably with historical material moved to an appendix.

Chapters 3 and 4: Supply and Demand: Using Supply and Demand: Old Chapter 2, the central supply and demand chapter, divided into two chapters—one on the analytics of supply and demand and one on applications. This division allows a much earlier discussion of applications of the supply-demand model. Appendixes on algebraic solutions to supply and demand added.

Chapters 5 and 6: U.S. and World Economic Institutions: The cores of old Chapters 4 and 5 shortened considerably, with much of the specific institutional discussion moved to appendixes.

Macro

Chapter 7: Growth, Business Cycles, Unemployment, and Inflation: Old Chapter 8; Improved discussion of calculation of real income; slightly expanded discussion of growth. More emphasis on the difficulty of determining potential income and "target rate of unemployment."

Chapter 8: National Income Accounting: Old Chapter 9 with a condensed discussion of national income accounting; technical issues put in appendix. Revised to include new conventions about government investment spending.

Chapter 9: Money, Banking and the Financial Sector: Combination of old Chapters 12 and 13 with much of the institutional specifics of financial institutions and T–accounts analysis moved to appendixes. It was moved up earlier to emphasize importance of monetary and financial issues in modern macroeconomics.

Chapter 10: Development of Modern Macro: Combination and simplification of old Chapters 8 and 9. This chapter went through a major revision. It is now a similar, but more carefully presented, discussion of the basic macro model that is used by a majority of other texts. The distinction between partial and aggregate equilibrium is still emphasized, but the focus is not on theory, but on developing a working policy model. Appendices are reduced considerably, and policy focus supersedes theoretical focus.

Chapter 11: The AP/AE Model: Modification of old Chapter 10 with the multiplier simplified to focus on expenditures-income relationship. Algebraic appendix of components model.

Chapter 12: Activist Demand Management Policy: Modification of old Chapter 11 with focus shifting away from fiscal policy toward a broader concept of demand management, centered around macro policy model.

Chapter 13: Monetary Policy: Modification of old Chapter 14; updated to reflect new focus on federal funds rate. T-accounts discussion moved to appendix.

Chapter 14: Inflation and Its Relationship to Unemployment and Growth: Modification of old Chapter 15. Additional discussion of growth trade-offs added to bring in Classical viewpoint better, with streamlined discussion of the debate about the Phillips curve.

Chapter 15: International Dimensions: Old Chapter 16. Updated examples and statistics.

Chapter 16: Open Economy Macro: Old Chapter 17 combined with discussion of trade policy to allow a broader policy discussion.

Chapter 17: Art of Traditional Macro Policy: Old Chapter 19 updated. Added discussion about the importance of regimes as opposed to policy.

Chapter 18: Structural Supply-Side Macro Policies: A totally new chapter that brings the structural policies of the '90s into clear focus.

Chapter 19: Deficits and Debt: Old Chapter 18. Updated and revised with discussion of recent decrease in measured deficit.

Chapter 20: Growth and Development. Old Chapter 20 updated and revised.

A Change Not Made: My Colloquial Writing Style

One change not made in this edition, even though it put off some professors, is my colloquial writing style. It's pretty clear that my writing style (and my style in general) isn't professorial. I agree; it isn't. But in my view, students would learn a lot more if professors were a lot less professorial. If students see us as people, they will be encouraged to think through what we have to say, and to challenge us when they think we're wrong. That's the purpose of education—to get students to think. True, it would be nice if students had a love of learning and were thirsting for knowledge. Unfortunately, the reality is that 99 percent of them don't. It's our job as teachers to make learning fun and exciting for students who don't want to learn, and either get them to learn, or to flunk them out. Being less professorial makes us more real to students and makes learning more fun.

I see the course and the book as an entry point to an enormous store of information, not as the ultimate source. I want to motivate students to learn on their own, to read on their own, to think on their own. These desires have to be taught, and they can only be taught in a language that students can relate to. I believe in going in steps with students, not in leaps. The traditional textbookese is too much a leap for most students to make. It's not a step from the stuff they normally read; it's a leap that most of them aren't willing to make—the same type of leap it is for most of us teachers of economics to read the *Journal of Economic Theory*. There may be some relevant information in those articles, but most of us teachers aren't going to find out because the language the ideas are presented in is incomprehensible to us. So too with a text; it has to talk to students, otherwise they don't read it. I'm pleased to say that students have uniformly related to my style, even if they think my jokes are sometimes corny.

People to Thank

A book this size is not the work of a single person, despite the fact that only one is listed as author. So many people have contributed so much to this book that it is hard to know where to begin thanking them. But I must begin somewhere, so let me begin by thanking the innumerable referees of three editions who went through the various versions of the text and kept me on track:

First Edition

Jack Adams
University of Arkansas

Stan Antoniotti
Bridgewater State College

Mahmoud P. Arya
Edison Community College

James Q. Aylsworth
Lakeland Community College

George Bohler
University of North Florida

Bijit K. Bora
Carleton College

Gerald E. Breger
Grand Rapids Junior College

Mario Cantu
Northern Virginia Community College

Tom Carroll
Central Oregon Community College

Carol A. M. Clark
Guilford College

Roy Cohn
Illinois State University

Eleanor Craig
University of Delaware

Jerry L. Crawford
Arkansas State University

Ed Dennis
Franklin Pierce College

Phillip Droke
Highline Community College

Fred Englander
Fairleigh Dickinson University

Valerie Englander
St. John's University

Sharon Erenberg
Eastern Michigan University

Rhona C. Free
Eastern Connecticut State University

Joseph Garwood
Valencia Community College

Bernard Gauci
Hollins College

Robert Gentennar
Hope College

Jack B. Goddard
Northeastern State University

Deniek Gondwee
Gettysburg College

Richard Hansen
Southeast Missouri State University

Raymond N. Harvey
Niagara County Community College

Robert Jantzen
Iona College

Walter Johnson
University of Missouri

Diane E. Kraas
Augustana College

Leonard Lardaro
University of Rhode Island

Randall Lutter
State University of New York at Buffalo

Raymond Mack
Community College of Allegheny County Boyce Campus

Drew Mattson
Anoka-Ramsey Community College

Bruce McCrea
Lansing Community College

H. Neal McKenzie
Dalton College

Debbie A. Meyer
Brookdale Community College

Craig Milnor
Clarke College

William Morgan
University of Wyoming

Mark Morlock
California State University–Chico

H. Richard Moss
Ricks College

Theodore Muzio
St. Vincent College

Hillar Neumann, Jr.
Northern State University

Maureen O'Brien
University of Minnesota–Duluth

Amar Pari
State University of New York College at Fredonia

E. Dale Peterson
Late of Mankato State University

Richard Rosenberg
University of Wisconsin

Linda Schaeffer
California State University–Fresno

Ted Scheinman
Mt. Hood Community College

Timothy Schibik
University of Southern Indiana

Dorothy Siden
Salem State College

R. J. Sidwell
Eastern Illinois University

G. Anthony Spira
University of Tennessee

Mitch Stengel
University of Michigan–Dearborn

Robert Stonebreaker
Indiana University of Pennsylvania

Frank Taylor
McLennan Community College

Wade Thomas
State University of New York College at Oneonta

Joe Turek
Illinois Benedictine College

Alejandro Velez
St. Mary's University

David Weinberg
Xavier University

Kenneth Woodward
Saddleback College

Second Edition

Fatma Antar
Manchester Community College

John Atkins
Pensacola Junior College

Bruce Barnett
Grossmont College

Peter S. Barth
University of Connecticut

William W. Boorman
Palm Beach Community College

Ginny Brannon
Arapahoe Community College

H. L. Brockman
Central Piedmont Community College

Chris Clark
BCIT

Eleanor D. Craig
University of Delaware

Douglas Copeland
Johnson County Community College

Norman V. Cure
Macomb Community College

James W. Eden
Portland Community College

John P. Farrell
Oregon State University

Peter Fortura
Algonquin College

Ann J. Fraedrich
Marquette University

Louis Green
San Diego State University

John B. Hall
Portland State University

Paul A. Heise
Lebanon Valley College

Joseph A. Ilacqua
Bryant College

Susan Kamp
University of Alberta

R. E. Kingery
Hawkeye Community College

Robert Kirk
Indiana University/Purdue University Indianapolis

Evanthis Mavrokordatos
Tarrant County Junior College, N.E.

Diana L. McCoy
Truckee Meadows Community College

Shah M. Mehrabi
Montgomery College

Dennis D. Miller
Baldwin Wallace College

James E. Needham
Cuyahoga Community College

Tim Payne
Shoreline Community College

Harmanna Poen
Houston Community College

Edward R. Raupp
Augsburg College

Donald Reddick
Kwantlen College

Mitchell Redlo
Monroe Community College

Balbir S. Sahni
Concordia University

Dennis Shannon
Belleville Area College

Amrick Singh Dua
Mt. San Antonio College

John D. Snead
Bluefield State College

John Somers
Portland Community College

Annie Spears
University of Prince Edward Island

Delores W. Steinhauser
Brookdale Community College

John Stoudenmire
Methodist College

Deborah L. Thorsen
Palm Beach Community College

Marion Walsh
Lansing Community College

James Watson
Jefferson College

Edgar W. Wood
University of Mississippi

Third Edition

Thomas J. Adams
Sacramento City College

Diann Benesh
University of Wisconsin–Eau Claire

David Berrian
Shoreline Community College

David Black
University of Toledo

Geoffrey Black
Marist College

Michael D. Brasselero
Front Range Community College (Colorado)

Kathleen K. Bromley
Monroe Community College (Rochester)

Sidney L. Carroll
University of Tennessee–Knoxville

Marc C. Chopin
Louisiana Tech University

Curtis Clarke
Mountain View College (Texas)

John Costley
Iowa Wesleyan College

James Craven
Clark College (Washington)

Lisa C. DeFelice
University of New Hampshire–Durham

James Eden
Portland Community College

James P. Egan
University of Wisconsin–Eau Claire

David N. Feglio
University of Oregon

David W. Findlay
Colby College

Mary Gade
Oklahoma State University

John W. Graham
Rutgers University

Mark E. Haggerty
Clarion University of Pennsylvania

David R. Hakes
University of Northern Iowa

George E. Hoffer
Virginia Commonwealth University

Alexander Holmes
University of Oklahoma

Scott Hunt
Columbus State Community College (Ohio)

Philip A. Klein
The Pennsylvania State University

Morris Knapp
Miami-Dade Community College

Penny Kugler
Central Missouri State University

Randy LaHote
Washtenaw Community College (Michigan)

Jodey Lingg
City University of Renton (Washington)

Robert T. McLean
Harrisburg Area Community College

Jon R. Miller
University of Idaho

Reynold Nesiba
Augustana College (North Dakota)

Norman P. Obst
Michigan State University

Albert Okunade
University of Memphis

Patrick O'Neill
University of North Dakota

Dan Powroznik
Chesapeake College

Leila J. Pratt
University of Tennessee–Chattanooga

Renee Prim
Gonzaga University

James J. Rakowski
University of Notre Dame

George D. Santopietro
Radford University (Virginia)

Jacob Sonny
Dowling College (New York)

Susan Snyder
Virginia Polytechnic Institute

Ken Woodward
Saddleback College (California)

I cannot thank these reviewers enough. They corrected many of my stupid mistakes, they explained to me how a text can contribute to good teaching, and they kept me focused on combining teaching economic sensibility with economic models. They provided me with page upon page of detailed comments and suggestions for improvement. The book strongly reflects their input and is much more usable because of that input.

The formal reviewers are only a small portion of the total reviewers. There were many faculty and students who have informally pointed out aspects of the book that they liked, or did not like. There are so many that I can't remember, and don't have room to list, them all, but I hope by listing a few of them I can give you a sense of the importance of these informal reviewers. Some of these individuals (who happen to come to mind at the moment) are:

Roger Adkins, Zahiruddin Alim, John Atkins, Anis Bahreinian, Jim Barbour, Robin Bartlett, Roger Beck, John Bethune, Paula Bracy, Allen Bradley, Jim Bryan, Scott Callan, Tom Cate, Kristine Chase, John Conant, John Cornwall, Richard Cornwall, James Craven, Robert Crofts, Mahmoud Davoudi, Roger Dimick, Rohini Divecha, Jim Esen, Susan Feiner, Ann Fender, Windsor Fields, Richard Fryman, Art Gibb, Derrick Gondwe, Leland Gustafson, John H. Hoag, Janet Harris, Ric Holt, Dave Horlacher, Jim Hubert, Jim Kelsey, Rose Kilburn, Alfred Konuwa, Roger Koppl, Chris Kuehl, Harry Landreth, June Lapidus, Robert Liebman, Peyton Lingle, Lew Marler, Peter Matthews, Tom Mayer, Susan McGowan, Pat McMahon, Wendy Morrison, Frank Mossadeghi, Joy Newcomb, Michael Paganelli, Tom Porebski, Abdul Qayum, Mary Jean Rivers, James R. Scheib, Sunder Rameswamy, John Ranlett, Nancy Roberts, Sam Rosenberg, Barkley Rosser, Ted Scheinman, Peter Sephton, Scott Sewell, Ben Slay, James Smith, Noel Smith, Paul Sommers, Howard Stein, Terry Stokes, Kit Taylor, James Thomas, Roger Traver, Lisa Tuttle, S. V. Char, David Wagenblast, Kristi Weir,

Geraldine Welch, Bruce Welz, Paul Wonnacott, Phani Wunnava, Peter Wyman. There are many more.

Often their helpful comments were in the form of questions, and in trying to answer them it became clear that the problem was a reflection of my failure of exposition, not in their understanding. I thank all these individuals (and apologize to the many, many unlisted ones).

I am happy to say that my group of friends throughout the profession is expanding. One of the pleasant aspects of the book is that it led to a large number of invitations to speak throughout the country. At those talks, I met some wonderful economics educators. These talks played a role in the development of an informal group of economics educators who are concerned about the way economics is taught. Together, we've been putting some pressure on the economics establishment to pay more time to teaching and to concern itself more with content teaching issues. The petition we organized (published with all our signatures in the *AER*) of almost 500 undergraduate professors of economics committed to changing the way economics is taught in graduate school made an impact, as did the positive reception given to earlier editions of this text. The graduate schools know economists committed to quality undergraduate teaching—which includes conveying a sense of history and institutions—are out there. Eventually, I think we will begin to see some change in the profession—not large change, mind you—institutions don't allow large, sudden change, but positive, glacial changes in the right direction. My sincere thanks to all who have helped in this effort.

Massaging the Manuscript into a Book

Once the manuscript takes its final form there are still an almost infinite number of jobs to be done on it. Figures must be checked, arguments checked, drafts read, re-read, and reread once again. In this third edition, I had immense help in these undertakings from Jenifer Gamber, who is a superbly trained economist and a great organizer. She found last minute data and saw to it that the answers to all the questions were reasonable.

Another person who helped is Umar Serajuddin. Umar worked for me in the year following his graduation from Middlebury; he played an important role in seeing to it that the arguments in the book didn't get confused. He has now gone on to graduate school and I am sure that he will do well. Other students who helped in various tasks include Aaron Coburn, Senake Gajameragedara, and Munir Qazi Alam. Then, of course, there are all the students in my classes who gave many helpful suggestions. I thank them all.

In developing this book many people at Irwin/McGraw-Hill were extremely important and helpful. One is Wendy Hagel, a sales rep who convinced me that Irwin/McGraw-Hill was the right publisher for me.

Other individuals who were instrumental in various editions include Scot Stratford, Gary Nelson, and Catherine Schwent. I thank them and wish them well.

The preparation of this edition was punctuated by a merger of Irwin with McGraw-Hill. Such mergers are always traumatic, and would have been more so were it not for the professionalism and knowledge of Gary Burke, my publisher, and Tom Thompson, my developmental editor. Gary is an old friend from way back—he published my first book—and Tom is superb in all that he does. Tom is organized; he has a sense of humor, and maintains a level head when confusion reigns. I'm delighted to be working with both of them and hope that it will be a long and fruitful relationship. I thank them both.

I would also like to thank upper-level management at Irwin/McGraw-Hill—specifically Mike Junior, John Black, and Jeff Sund. I had less contact with them, but I fully recognize their guiding hands. Their belief in the project made it possible for an antibureaucratic author to fit in with a formal publishing institution.

The actual production process of a four-color introductory book is complicated. It requires enormous efforts. Luckily, I had Denise Santor-Mitzit, senior project manager, directing the manuscript through the process. She did a superb job, as did all the players in the production process: Tom Serb, the copy editor; Laurie Entriger, the designer who made the book look good; Jon Christopher, the production supervisor, who worked with Shepard Poorman, the typesetter, and Von Hoffmann Press, the printer.

Of course, as they did their superb job, they created more work for me, reading the galley proofs, the page proofs, and doing all the final checking that must be done in an effort to eliminate those pesky errors that occur out of nowhere. Jenifer Gamber, James Craven, and Helen Reiff went over the manuscript with their fine-tooth combs and discerning eyes, and I went over it with my rake and 20-400 vision, and together we caught things overlooked until then. Finally, Paul Sommers went over the manuscript with his 20-10 vision, catching numerous mistakes the rest of us had missed. I thank them enormously for doing what I cannot do, and apologize to them for complaining that they are so picky.

After you have what you believe is a good book, the process still isn't done. You still have to get people to look at it. David Littlehale quickly got a sense of what I was trying to do with the book and captured the essence of it when he explained that I was being "aggressively neutral." I thank him. Nelson Black oversaw the marketing effort on this third edition.

Then, there are the sales reps who are the core of a textbook publishing company. As I traveled around the country giving lectures, I met with many of the Irwin/McGraw-Hill sales reps, discussing the book and learning to see it through their eyes. There are a number I remember very well; they sent me books and comments, and talked with me for hours about publishing and Irwin/McGraw-Hill. Since our talks were often honest, blunt, and off the record, I won't mention them, but I will thank them sincerely. Irwin/McGraw-Hill has a great set of sales representatives out there, and I thank them for getting behind the book.

Creating the Package

These days an introductory economics book is much more than a single book; it is an entire package, and numerous people have worked on the package. Jenifer Gamber took charge of developing these ancillaries and has done a stupendous job. She is totally organized, driven, caring, and a superb economist. I've enjoyed working with her immensely, and suspect we'll be working together for a long time.

The supplements authors were as follows:

Jenifer Gamber, supplements coordinator for all the print ancillaries, coauthor of the *Study Guide,* the *Case Studies,* and the *Test Banks* (with David Colander), and author of the *Economics Fax Newsletter.*

Tom Adams, *Instructor's Manual*

Patrick O'Neill, *Instructor's Assistant*

Douglas Copeland, *Student Workbook*

Gerald Nelson, *Discover Econ Software*

Anthony Zambelli, *PowerPoint Presentations*

Paul Estenson, *Micro/Macroeconomics Visualization Software*

Andreas Ortmann and Dave Colander, *Experiments in Teaching and Understanding Economics*

Harry Landreth and Dave Colander, *Classic Readings in Economics*

Sunder Ramaswamy, Kailash Khandke, Jenifer Gamber, and Dave Colander, *Honors Companion*

There are stories to go with each of these authors—and enormous thanks to be given to them all, but the publisher has told me this preface must be short, so I will simply say thank you to all the supplements authors for making a high-quality and innovative supplements package to the text.

Finally, there's the group of people who helped me at every stage of the process. My colleagues at Middlebury and the Middlebury administration were supportive throughout the project. Helen Reiff and Jenifer Gamber helped in a variety of ways that went beyond their other duties.

Then, there's my wife, Pat. She made it possible for me to put enormous effort into economics while still feeling that our family remained a family. My love and admiration for her remain as unbounded as ever.

As you can see, although my name is on the book, many people besides me deserve the credit. I thank them all.

About the Author

David Colander is the Christian A. Johnson Distinguished Professor of Economics at Middlebury College. He has authored, coauthored, or edited 23 books and over 70 articles on a wide range of economic topics.

He earned his B.A. at Columbia College and his M.Phil and Ph.D. at Columbia University. He also studied at the University of Birmingham in England and at Wilhelmsburg Gymnasium in Germany. Professor Colander has taught at Columbia College, Vassar College, and the University of Miami, as well as having been a consultant to Time-Life Films, a consultant to Congress, a Brookings Policy Fellow, and Visiting Scholar at Nuffield College, Oxford. Recently, he spent two months in Bulgaria, where he worked with former professors of political economy on how to teach Western economics.

He belongs to a variety of professional associations and has served on the Board of Directors and as vice president and president of both the History of Economic Thought Society and the Eastern Economics Association. He has also served on the Editorial Boards of the *Journal of Economic Perspectives, The Journal of Economic Methodology, The Journal of the History of Economic Thought,* and *The Eastern Economics Journal.*

He is married to a pediatrician, Patrice, which is fortunate, since they have a family of five boys. In their spare time, the Colanders have designed and built their oak post-and-beam house on a ridge overlooking the Green Mountains to the east and the Adirondacks to the west. The house is located on the site of a former drive-in movie theater. (They replaced the speaker poles with fruit trees and used the I-beams from the screen as support for the second story of the carriage house and the garage. Dave's office and library are in the former projection room.)

Brief Contents

Contents

PART

2

Macroeconomics

I

Macroeconomic Problems, Concepts, and Institutions

IV
Structural Macro Policy Debates

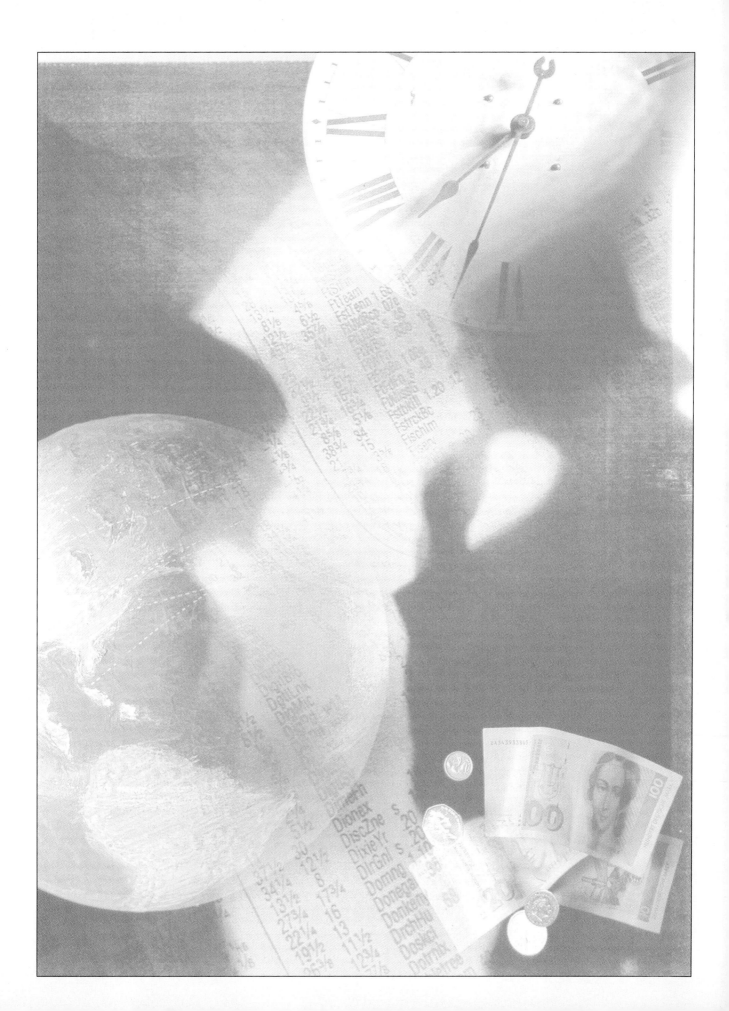

PART

One INTRODUCTION

Part I is an introduction, and an introduction to an introduction seems a little funny. But other sections have introductions, so it seemed a little funny not to have an introduction to Part I; and besides, as you will see, I'm a little funny myself (which, in turn, has two interpretations; you will, I'm sure, decide which of the two is appropriate). It will, however, be a very brief introduction, consisting of questions you probably have and some answers to those questions.

SOME QUESTIONS AND ANSWERS

Why study economics?

Because it's neat and interesting and helps provide insight into events that are constantly going on around you.

Why is this book so big?

Because there's lot of important information in it and because the book is designed so

your teacher can pick and choose. You'll likely not be required to read all of it, especially if you're on the quarter system. But once you start it, you'll probably read it all anyhow. (Would you believe?)

Why does this book cost so much?

To answer this question you'll have to read the book.

Will this book make me rich?

No.

Will this book make me happy?

It depends.

This book doesn't seem to be written in a normal textbook style. Is this book really written by a professor?

Yes, but he is different. He misspent his youth working on cars; he married his high school sweetheart after they met again at their 20th high school reunion. Twenty-five years after graduating from high school, his wife went back to medical school and got her MD because she was tired of being treated poorly by doctors. Their five kids make sure he doesn't get carried away in the professorial cloud.

Will the entire book be like this?

No, the introduction is just trying to rope you in. Much of the book will be hard going. Learning happens to be a difficult process: no pain, no gain. But the author isn't a sadist; he tries to make learning as pleasantly painful as possible.

What do the author's students think of him?

Weird, definitely weird—and hard. But fair, interesting, and sincerely interested in getting us to learn. (Answer written by his students.)

So there you have it. Answers to the questions that you might never have thought of if they hadn't been put in front of you. I hope they give you a sense of me and the approach I'll use in the book. There are some neat ideas in it. Let's now briefly consider what's in the first six chapters.

A SURVEY OF THE FIRST SIX CHAPTERS

This first section is really an introduction to the rest of the book. It gives you the background necessary to have the later chapters make sense. Section I, "Thinking Like an Economist," consists of four chapters. Chapter 1 gives you an overview of the entire field of economics as well as an introduction to my style. Chapter 2 gives you some history of economic systems and shows you how important institutions are. It gives you a sense of how economic forces interact with political and social forces. Chapters 3 and 4 introduce you to supply and demand, and show you not only the power of those two concepts, but also the limitations.

Section II, "Economic Institutions," consists of two chapters that introduce you to some important economic institutions. Chapter 5 concentrates on domestic institutions; Chapter 6 concentrates on international institutions. Now let's get on with the show.

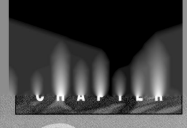

One
Economics and
Economic Reasoning

In my vacations, I visited the poorest quarters of several cities and walked through one street after another, looking at the faces of the poorest people. Next I resolved to make as thorough a study as I could of Political Economy.

~ Alfred Marshall

After reading this chapter, you should be able to:

1 List three coordination problems that any economic system must solve and explain how they relate to scarcity.

2 State five important things to learn in economics.

3 Explain how to make decisions by comparing marginal costs and marginal benefits.

4 Define opportunity cost and explain its relationship to economic reasoning.

5 Explain real-world events in terms of three "invisible forces."

6 Differentiate between microeconomics and macroeconomics.

7 Distinguish among positive economics, normative economics, and the art of economics.

When an artist looks at the world, he sees color. When a musician looks at the world, she hears music. When an economist looks at the world, she sees a symphony of costs and benefits. The economist's world might not be as colorful or as melodic as the others' worlds, but it's more practical. If you want to understand what's going on in the world that's really out there, you need to know economics.

I hardly have to convince you of this fact if you keep up with the news. Unemployment is up; inflation is down; interest rates are up; businesses are going bankrupt. . . . The list is endless. So let's say you grant me that economics is important. That still doesn't mean that it's worth studying. The real question then is: How much will you learn? Most of what you learn depends on you, but part depends on the teacher and another part depends on the textbook. On both these counts, you're in luck; since your teacher chose this book for your course, you must have a super teacher.[1]

I have always found that my students do better when they are *involved*, especially at the beginning of the course. Ask simple questions to get things started and to make your students feel comfortable. You might find that better responses to your tougher questions later in the course will be the result.

---

[1]This book is written by a person, not a machine. That means that I have my quirks, my odd sense of humor, and my biases. All textbook writers do. Most textbooks have the quirks and eccentricities edited out so that all the books read and sound alike—professional but dull. I choose to sound like me—sometimes professional, sometimes playful, and sometimes stubborn. In my view, that makes the book more human and less dull. So forgive me my quirks—don't always take me too seriously—and I'll try to keep you awake when you're reading this book at 3 A.M. the morning of the exam. If you think it's a killer to read a book this long, you ought to try writing one.

THE ECONOMY AND ECONOMICS

Economics *The study of how human beings coordinate their wants.*

1 Three central coordination problems any economic system must solve are what to produce, how to produce it, and for whom to produce it.

Video Series, Economics U$A: Resources and Scarcity, Segment 1.2

Wants are changeable and partially society-determined.

The quantity of goods, services, and usable resources depends upon technology and human action.

Let's begin with some definitions. An **economy** is the *institutional structure through which individuals in a society coordinate their diverse wants and desires.* An **economic system** is *the system by which the economy is organized.* For example, if an economy is organized through markets, it is a market economic system. **Economics** is *the study of economies.* That is, economics is the study of how human beings coordinate their wants and desires, given the institutional structures of the society. By "institutional structures" I mean decision-making mechanisms, social customs, and political realities of that society.

One of the key words in the above explanation of the term "economics" is *coordination.* Coordination can mean many things. In the study of economics, coordination refers to how the three central problems facing any economy are solved. These central problems are:

1. What, and how much, to produce.
2. How to produce it.
3. For whom to produce it.

In answering these questions, economies generally find that individuals want more than is available, given how much they're willing to work. That means that in our economy there is a perceived problem of **scarcity**—*the goods available are too few to satisfy individuals' desires.* This is a *perceived* problem because if individuals could be encouraged to work more and want less, that scarcity problem could be reduced and perhaps even eliminated. No known society, however, has ever managed to eliminate perceived scarcity.

Scarcity is so prevalent in economies that many economists begin with scarcity when defining economics. They define *economics* as the study of the allocation of scarce resources to satisfy individuals' wants or desires. There are two reasons I don't use that definition. The first reason is that wants are changeable and partially society-determined. The scarcity definition of economics makes it sound to some as if wants are unchangeable. But they change all the time, and the way we fulfill wants can affect those wants. For example, if you work on Wall Street you will probably want upscale and trendy clothes. Up here in Vermont, I wear Levis and flannel, but if I worked on Wall Street I'm sure I'd want those ritzy clothes too (although for the life of me I cannot understand anyone wanting to wear anything but Levis and flannel).

The second reason I avoid the allocation of scarce resources definition is that I want to emphasize that the quantity of goods, services, and usable resources depends on technology and human action which underlie production; production is an important element of economics. Individuals' imagination, innovativeness, and willingness to do what needs to be done can greatly increase available goods and resources. Who knows what technologies are in our future—Nannites or micro machines that change atoms into whatever we want could conceivably eliminate scarcity of goods as we know it. But would that eliminate economics? No; the economy would still face a coordination problem—society would have to allocate the jobs and activities to individuals. Thus, in my view, the definition of economics centering on coordination includes the scarcity definition since it does not deny the existence of perceived scarcity. It does not, however, make a judgment about whether that perception is correct or not, and hence the coordination definition is more general.

In all known economies, coordination has involved coercion—limiting people's wants and increasing the amount of work individuals are willing to do to fulfill those wants. The reality of our society is that many people would rather play than help solve society's problems. So the basic economic problem involves inspiring people to do things that other people want them to do, and not to do things that other people don't want them to do. Thus, an alternative definition of economics is that it is the study of how to get people to do things they're not wild about doing (such as studying)

RESOURCES, INPUTS, TECHNOLOGY, AND OUTPUT

ADDED DIMENSION

One of the important jobs of an economy is production. Production involves transforming *inputs* into *outputs*. For example, seeds, soil, and labor (inputs) combine to produce wheat (output). Many introductory economics texts call inputs *resources* and divide those inputs into three resources: land, labor, and capital. Economists in the 1800s, often called *Classical economists,* discussed production as a means of transforming land, labor, and capital into outputs. Classical economists divided all inputs into those three categories because they were interested in answering the question: How is income divided among landowners, workers, and capitalists? The three divisions helped them focus on that question: landowners' income was rent, workers' income was wages, and capitalists' income was profit.

Modern advanced analysis of production doesn't follow this threefold division. Instead, the modern analysis is more abstract and tells how inputs in general are transformed into outputs in general. Modern economic theory has moved away from the traditional division because the

In the 1990s oil has remained an important natural resource.
Bettman Newsphotos

division of income among these three groups isn't central to the questions economists are now asking.

But that leaves open the problem: What division of resources makes the most sense? The answer depends on what question you're asking. In the most abstract categorization, the ultimate resources are space (represented by land), time (represented by labor), and matter (represented by capital). Thus, in one way of looking at it, the traditional distinction is still relevant. But in another way, it isn't. It directs our focus of analysis away from some important inputs. For example, one of the inputs that economists now focus on is *entrepreneurship,* the ability to organize and get something done. Entrepreneurship is an important input that's distinct from labor. Most listings of general resources today include entrepreneurship.

Here's another important point about resources. The term *resource* is often used with the qualifier *natural,* as in the phrases *natural resources.* Coal, oil, and iron are all called *natural resources.* Be careful about that qualifier *natural.* Whether something is or isn't a natural resource depends on the available technology. And technology is unnatural. For example, at one time a certain black gooey stuff was not a resource—it was something that made land unusable. When people learned that the black gooey stuff could be burned as a fuel, oil became a resource. What's considered a resource depends on technology. If solar technology is ever perfected, oil will go back to being black gooey stuff.

and not to do things they are wild about doing (such as eating all the lobster they like), so that the things some people want to do are consistent with the things other people want to do.

Five important dimensions of economic learning are:

1. *Economic reasoning.*
2. *Economic terminology.*
3. *Economic insights* economists have about issues, and theories that lead to those insights.
4. Information about *economic institutions.*
5. Information about the *economic policy options* facing society today.

By no coincidence this book discusses economic reasoning, economic terminology, economic insights, economic institutions, and economic policy options. Let's consider each in turn.

WHAT ECONOMICS IS ABOUT

2 Five important dimensions of economic learning are:
1. Economic reasoning.
2. Economic terminology.
3. Economic insights.
4. Economic institutions.
5. Economic policy options.

Economic Reasoning

Economic reasoning *Making decisions on the basis of costs and benefits.*

I ask my students to think of examples in their own lives in which they use economic reasoning. You will likely get a roomful of blank stares at the beginning of class, but ask again at the end of your treatment of the chapter. You should see a big difference.

If one is trying out an experimental approach to teaching economics, this is a good place to introduce the bonus allocation experiment presented in *Experiments in Teaching and in Understanding Economics* supplement.

Video Series, Economics U$A: Resources and Scarcity, Segment 1.1

The most important dimension of economics that you'll learn is **economic reasoning**—*how to think like an economist, making decisions on the basis of costs and benefits*. People trained in economics think in a certain way. They analyze everything critically; they compare the costs and the benefits of every issue and make decisions based on those costs and benefits. For example, say you're trying to decide whether protecting baby seals is a good policy or not. Economists are trained to put their emotions aside and ask: What are the costs of protecting baby seals, and what are the benefits? Thus, they are open to the argument that the benefits of allowing baby seals to be killed might exceed the costs. To think like an economist is to address almost all issues using a cost/benefit approach.

Economic reasoning, once learned, is infectious. If you're susceptible, being exposed to it will change your life. It will influence your analysis of everything, including issues normally considered outside the scope of economics. For example, you will likely use economic reasoning to decide the possibility of getting a date for Saturday night, and who will pay for dinner. You will likely use it to decide whether to read this book, whether to attend class, whom to marry, and what kind of work to go into after you graduate. This is not to say that economic reasoning will provide all the answers. As you will see throughout this book, real-world questions are inevitably complicated, and economic reasoning simply provides a framework within which to approach a question.

Economic Terminology

Second, there's economic terminology, which is tossed around by the general public with increasing frequency. *GDP, corporations,* and *money supply* are just a few of the terms whose meaning any educated person in modern society needs to know. If you go to a party and don't know these terms and want to seem intelligent, you'll have to nod knowingly. It's much better to actually *know* when you nod knowingly.

Economic Insights

Economic theory *Generalizations about the workings of an abstract economy.*

"Economics" by Alfred Marshall in *Classic Readings in Economics* (a supplement available with this text).

Third, you'll learn about some general insights economists have gained into how the economy functions—how an economy seems to proceed or progress without any overall plan or coordinating agency. It's almost as if an invisible hand were directing economic traffic. These insights are often based on **economic theory**—*generalizations about the workings of an abstract economy*. Theory ties together economists' terminology and knowledge about economic institutions and leads to economic insights.

We're so used to an economy that's functioning smoothly that we may not realize how amazing it is that the economy coordinates the diverse wants of 266 million people so well. Imagine for a moment that you're a visitor from Mars. You see the U.S. economy functioning relatively well. Stores are filled with goods. Most people have jobs. So you ask, "Who's in charge of organizing and coordinating the economic activities of the 266 million people in the United States?" The answer you get is mind boggling: "No one. The invisible hand of the market does it all." Economic theory helps explain such mind-boggling phenomena.

Economic Institutions

Economic institutions *Physical or mental structures that significantly influence economic decisions.*

Differences in economic institutions can help explain differences in economies among countries.

Fourth, you'll learn about economic institutions: how they work, and why they sometimes don't work. An **economic institution** is *a physical or mental structure that significantly influences economic decisions*. Corporations, governments, and cultural norms are all economic institutions. Many economic institutions have social, political, and religious dimensions. For example, your job often influences your social standing. In addition, many social institutions, such as the family, have economic functions. If any institution significantly affects economic decisions, I include it as an economic institution because you must understand that institution if you are to understand how the economy functions.

Economic institutions differ significantly among countries. For example, in Germany banks are allowed to own companies; in the United States they cannot. This contributes to a difference in the flow of resources into investment in Germany as compared to the flow in the United States. Or alternatively, in Japan, antitrust laws

---

FIVE IMPORTANT DIMENSIONS OF ECONOMICS

A REMINDER ✓

To understand the economy, you need to learn:

1. *Economic reasoning.*
2. *Economic terminology.*
3. *Economic insights* economists have gained in thinking about economics.
4. Information about *economic institutions.*
5. Information about *economic policy options* facing society today.

(laws under which companies can combine or coordinate their activities) are loose; in the United States they are more restrictive. This causes differences in the nature of competition in the two countries.

Besides helping you understand the economy, knowledge of economic institutions also directly benefits you. How do firms decide whom to hire? How do banks operate? How does unemployment insurance work? What determines how much a Japanese car will cost you? How much does the government require your boss to deduct from your paycheck? Knowing the answers to these real-world questions will make your life easier.

Fifth, you'll learn about economic policy options facing our country. An **economic policy** is *an action (or inaction) taken, usually by government, to influence economic events.* Examples of economic policy questions are: How should the government deal with the next recession? (Alas, we can be sure that there will be a next recession.) What should the government do about the budget deficit? Will lowering interest rates stimulate the economy? Should government allow two large companies to merge? You won't get specific answers to these questions; instead, you'll simply learn what some of the policy options are, and what advantages and disadvantages each option offers.

Economic Policy Options

Economic policy   Action to influence the course of economic events.

Let's now look at each of these five dimensions more carefully. We'll start with economic reasoning. In the economic way of thinking, every choice has costs and benefits, and decisions are made by comparing the two. The **economic decision rule** is simple:

> *If the relevant benefits of doing something exceed the relevant costs, do it.*
> *If the relevant costs of doing something exceed the relevant benefits, don't do it.*

A GUIDE TO ECONOMIC REASONING

3 If the relevant benefits of doing something exceed the relevant costs, do it. If the relevant costs of doing something exceed the relevant benefits, don't do it.

Marginal Costs and Marginal Benefits

While the economic decision rule is simple, applying it is not. What are the relevant costs and relevant benefits? It is the expected *incremental* or additional costs incurred and the expected *incremental* benefits of a decision that matter. Economists use the term *marginal* when referring to additional or incremental. Marginal costs and marginal benefits are key concepts.

A **marginal cost** is *the additional cost to you over and above the costs you have already incurred.* That means eliminating **sunk costs**—*costs that have already been incurred and cannot be recovered*—from the relevant costs when making a decision. Consider, for example, attending class. You've already paid your tuition; it is a sunk cost. So the marginal (or additional) cost of going to class does not include tuition.

Marginal costs   Additional costs above what you've already incurred.

Similarly with marginal benefit. A **marginal benefit** is *the additional benefit above what you've already derived.* The marginal benefit of reading this chapter is the *additional* knowledge you get from reading it. If you already knew everything in this chapter before you picked up the book, the marginal benefit of reading it now is zero. The marginal benefit is not zero if by reading the chapter you learn that you are prepared for class; before, you might only have suspected you were prepared.

Marginal benefits   Additional benefits above what you've already derived.

ADDED DIMENSION ECONOMIC KNOWLEDGE IN ONE SENTENCE: TANSTAAFL

Once upon a time, Tanstaafl was made king of all the lands. His first act was to call his economic advisers and tell them to write up all the economic knowledge the society possessed. After years of work, they presented their monumental effort: 25 volumes, each about 400 pages long. But in the interim, King Tanstaafl had become a very busy man, what with running a kingdom of all the lands and everything. Looking at the lengthy volumes, he told his advisers to summarize their findings in one volume.

Despondently, the economists returned to their desks, wondering how they could summarize what they'd been so careful to spell out. After many more years of rewriting, they were finally satisfied with their one-volume effort, and tried to make an appointment to see the king. Unfortunately, affairs of state had become even more pressing than before, and the king couldn't take the time to see them. Instead he sent word to them that he couldn't be bothered with a whole volume, and ordered them, under threat of death (for he had become a tyrant), to reduce the work to one sentence.

The economists returned to their desks, shivering in their sandals and pondering their impossible task. Thinking about their fate if they were not successful, they decided to send out for one last meal. Unfortunately, when they were collecting money to pay for the meal, they discovered they were broke. The disgusted delivery man took the last meal back to the cook, and the economists started down the path to the beheading station. On the way, the delivery man's parting words echoed in their ears. They looked at each other and suddenly they realized the truth. "We're saved!" they screamed. "That's it! That's economic knowledge in one sentence!" They wrote the sentence down and presented it to the king, who thereafter fully understood all economic problems. (He also gave them a good meal.) The sentence?

There Ain't No Such Thing As A Free Lunch—
TANSTAAFL

Q–1: Say you bought stock A for $10 and stock B for $20. The price of each is currently $15. Assuming taxes are not an issue, which would you sell if you need $15?

Comparing marginal (additional) costs with marginal (additional) benefits will often tell you how you should adjust your activities to be as well off as possible. If the marginal benefit of engaging in an activity exceeds the marginal cost of doing so, you should do it. But if the marginal benefit is less than the marginal cost, you should do something else.

As an example, let's consider a discussion I might have with a student who tells me that she is too busy to attend my classes. I respond, "Think about the tuition you've spent for this class—it works out to about $30 a lecture." She answers that the book she reads for class is a book that I wrote, and that I wrote it so clearly she fully understands everything. She goes on:

> I've already paid the tuition and whether I go to class or not, I can't get any of the tuition back, so the tuition is a sunk cost and doesn't enter into my decision. The marginal cost to me is what I could be doing with the hour instead of spending it in class. I value my time at $75 an hour [people who understand everything value their time highly], and even though I've heard that your lectures are super, I estimate that the marginal benefit of your class is only $50. The marginal cost, $75, exceeds the marginal benefit, $50, so I don't attend class.

Ask your students if they have ever made a decision they have later regretted. Does this mean that they are irrational? Not necessarily. Oftentimes, the full costs and benefits are not known before a decision is made. The decision is based upon expected costs and benefits.

I would congratulate her on her diplomacy and her economic reasoning, but tell her that I give a quiz every week, that students who miss a quiz fail the quiz, that those who fail all the quizzes fail the course, and that those who fail the course do not graduate. In short, she is underestimating the marginal benefits of attending my course. Correctly estimated, the marginal benefits of attending my class exceed the marginal costs. So she should attend my class.

There's much more to be said about economic reasoning, but that will come later. For now, all you need remember is that, in economic thinking, *all actions have a cost—and a benefit,* and decisions are made on the basis of the economic decision rule: *If relevant benefits exceed relevant costs, do it. If relevant costs exceed relevant benefits, don't do it.*

Remember the economic decision rule: If relevant benefits exceed relevant costs, do it. If relevant costs exceed relevant benefits, don't do it.

Economics and Passion

Recognizing that everything has a cost is reasonable, but it's a reasonableness that many people don't like. It takes some of the passion out of life. It leads you to consider possibilities like these:

· Saving some people's lives with liver transplants might not be worth the additional cost. The money might be better spent on nutritional programs that would save 20 lives for every 2 lives you might save with transplants.
· Maybe we shouldn't try to eliminate all pollution, because the additional cost of doing so may be too high. To eliminate all pollution might be to forgo too much of some other good activity.
· Buying a stock that went up 20 percent wasn't necessarily the greatest investment if in doing so you had to forgo some other investment that would have paid you a 30 percent return.
· It might make sense for the automobile industry to save $12 per car by not installing a safety device, even though without the safety device some people will be killed.

You get the idea. This kind of reasonableness is often criticized for being cold-blooded. But, not surprisingly, economists first reason *economically*; the social and moral implications of their conclusions are integrated later.

Economists' reasonableness isn't universally appreciated. Businesses love the result; others aren't so sure, as I discovered some years back when my then-girlfriend told me she was leaving me. "Why?" I asked. "Because," she responded, "you're so, so . . . reasonable." It took me many years after she left to learn what she already knew: There are many types of reasonableness, and not everyone thinks an economist's reasonableness is a virtue. I'll discuss such issues later; for now, let me simply warn you that, for better or worse, studying economics will lead you to view questions in a cost/benefit framework.

Putting economists' cost/benefit rules into practice isn't easy. To do so, you have to be able to choose and measure the costs and benefits correctly. Economists have devised the concept of opportunity cost to help you do that. The **opportunity cost** of undertaking an activity is *the benefit forgone by undertaking that activity.* The benefit forgone is the benefit that you might have gained from choosing the next-best alternative. To obtain the benefit of something, you must give up (forgo) something else—namely, the next-best alternative. All activities that have a next-best alternative have an opportunity cost.

Let's consider some examples. The opportunity cost of going out once with Natalia (or Nathaniel), the most beautiful woman (attractive man) in the world, might well be losing your solid steady, Margo (Mike). The opportunity cost of cleaning up the environment might be a reduction in the money available to assist low-income individuals. The opportunity cost of having a child might be two boats, three cars, and a two-week vacation each year for five years.

Examples are endless, but let's consider two that are particularly relevant to you: your choice of courses and your decision about how much to study. Let's say you're a full-time student and at the beginning of the term you had to choose four or five courses to take. Taking one precluded taking some other, and the opportunity cost of taking an economics course may well have been not taking a course on theater. Similarly with studying: you have a limited amount of time to spend studying economics, studying some other subject, sleeping, or partying. The more time you spend on one activity, the less time you have for another. That's opportunity cost.

Notice how neatly the opportunity cost concept takes into account costs and benefits of all other options, and converts these alternative benefits into costs of the decision you're now making. This conversion helps you to compare marginal costs and marginal benefits and to select the activity with the largest difference between marginal benefits and marginal costs.

I like to point out to my students that economists don't have all the answers to difficult moral and societal questions. But economists usually have answers on efficiency criteria that must be weighed against other normative criteria.

Economic reasoning is based on the premise that everything has a cost.

Q–2: Can you think of a reason why a cost/benefit approach to a problem might be inappropriate? Can you give an example?

Opportunity Cost

4 Opportunity cost is the basis of cost/benefit economic reasoning; it is the benefit forgone, or the cost, of the next-best alternative to the activity you've chosen. In economic reasoning, that cost is less than the benefit of what you've chosen.

Opportunity costs have always made choice difficult, as we see in the early 19th-century engraving, "One or the Other." *Bleichroeder Print Collection, Baker Library, Harvard Business School.*

The relevance of opportunity cost isn't limited to your individual decisions. Opportunity costs are also relevant to government's decisions, which affect everyone in society. A common example is the guns-versus-butter debate. The resources that a society has are limited; therefore, its decision to use those resources to have more guns (more weapons) means that it must have less butter (fewer consumer goods). Thus, when society decides to spend $50 billion more on an improved health care system, the opportunity cost of that decision is $50 billion not spent on helping the homeless, paying off some of the national debt, or providing for national defense.

The opportunity cost concept has endless implications. It can even be turned upon itself. For instance, it takes time to think about alternatives; that means that there's a cost to being reasonable, so it's only reasonable to be somewhat unreasonable. If you followed that argument, you've caught the economic bug. If you didn't, don't worry. Just remember the opportunity cost concept for now; I'll infect you with economic thinking in the rest of the book.

Economics and the Invisible Forces

Economic forces are the necessary reactions to scarcity.

When an economic force operates through the market, it becomes a market force.

5 Economic reality is controlled by three invisible forces:
1. The invisible hand (economic forces);
2. The invisible handshake (social and historical forces); and
3. The invisible foot (political and legal forces).

Social and cultural forces—the invisible handshake—can play a significant role in the economy.

The opportunity cost concept applies to all aspects of life and is fundamental to understanding economic forces. **Economic forces** are *the necessary reactions to scarcity.* When goods are scarce, those goods must be rationed. **Rationing** is *a structural mechanism for determining who gets what.* The society must determine what that rationing mechanism will be; society must deal with the scarcity, thinking about and deciding how to allocate the scarce good. For example, economic forces might be embodied in a variety of rationing methods: by lottery, by putting prices on goods, or by some other mechanism.

Let's consider some specific real-world rationing mechanisms. Dormitory rooms are often rationed by lottery, and permission to register in popular classes is often rationed by a first-come, first-registered rule. Food in the United States, on the other hand, is generally rationed by price. If price did not ration food, there wouldn't be enough food to go around. All scarce goods or rights must be rationed in some fashion. These rationing mechanisms are examples of economic forces in action.

One of the important choices that a society must make is whether to allow these economic forces to operate freely and openly or to try to rein them in. A **market force** is *an economic force that is given relatively free rein by society to work through the market.*

Market forces ration by changing prices. When there's a shortage, the price goes up. When there's a surplus, the price goes down. Much of this book will be devoted to analyzing how the market works like an invisible hand, guiding economic forces to coordinate individual actions and allocate scarce resources. The **invisible hand** is *the price mechanism, the rise and fall of prices that guides our actions in a market.*

Societies can't choose whether or not to allow economic forces to operate—economic forces are always operating. However, societies may choose whether to allow market forces to predominate. Other forces play a major role in deciding whether to let market forces operate. I'll call these other forces the **invisible handshake**—*social and historical forces*—and the **invisible foot**—*political and legal forces.* Economic reality is determined by a contest among these three invisible forces.

Let's consider an example in which the invisible handshake prevents an economic force from becoming a market force: the problem of getting a date for Saturday night. If a school (or a society) has significantly more people of one gender than the other (let's say more men than women), some men may well find themselves without a date—that is, men will be in excess supply—and will have to find something else to do, say study or go to a movie by themselves. An "excess supply" person could solve the problem by paying someone to go out with him or her, but that would probably change the nature of the date in unacceptable ways. It would be revolting to the person who offered payment and to the person who was offered payment. That unacceptability is an example of the invisible handshake in action—the complex of social and

Ideas are encapsulated in metaphors, and Adam Smith's "invisible hand" metaphor has been a central one in economics since 1776. It's a neat metaphor, but it sometimes makes economic forces seem to be the only forces guiding the direction of society. And that just ain't so.

In the 1970s and 1980s, a number of modern-day economists attempted to broaden the dimensions of economic analysis. To explain what they were doing, they introduced metaphors for two other invisible forces. The term *invisible handshake* was coined by Arthur Okun, former chairman of the president's Council of Economic Advisers and an economist at the Brookings Institution, an economic think tank. Okun argued that social and historical forces—the

invisible handshake—often prevented the invisible hand from working.

The term *invisible foot* was coined by Stephen Magee, chairman of the Department of Finance at the University of Texas. Magee summarized the argument of a large number of economists that individuals often use politics and laws to get what they want, expressing this phenomenon with the invisible foot metaphor. Government action to benefit particular pressure groups is the invisible foot. By the late 1980s, these two additional terms were commonly used by the group of economists who were struggling to integrate economic insights with social and political insights.

cultural norms that guides and limits our activities. People don't try to buy dates because the invisible handshake prevents them from doing so. The invisible handshake makes the market solution for dating inappropriate.

Now let's consider another example in which it's the invisible foot—political and legal influences—that stops economic forces from becoming market forces. Say you decide that you can make some money delivering mail in your neighborhood. You try to establish a small business, but suddenly you experience the invisible foot in action. The U.S. Postal Service has a legal exclusive right to deliver regular mail, so you'll be prohibited from delivering regular mail in competition with the post office. Economic forces—the desire to make money—led you to want to enter the business, but in this case the invisible foot squashes the invisible hand.

Often the invisible foot and invisible handshake work together against the invisible hand. For example, in the United States there aren't enough babies to satisfy all the couples who desire them. Babies born to particular sets of parents are rationed—by luck. Consider a group of parents, all of whom want babies. Those who can, have a baby; those who can't have one, but want one, try to adopt. Adoption agencies ration the available babies. Who gets a baby depends on whom people know at the adoption agency and on the desires of the birth mother, who can often specify the socioeconomic background (and many other characteristics) of the family in which she wants her baby to grow up. That's the economic force in action; it gives more power to the supplier of something that's in short supply.

If our society allowed individuals to buy and sell babies, that economic force would be translated into a market force. The invisible hand would see to it that the quantity of babies supplied would equal the quantity of babies demanded at some price. The market, not the adoption agencies, would do the rationing.[2]

Most people, including me, find the idea of selling babies repugnant. But why? It's the strength of the invisible handshake backed up and strengthened by the invisible foot.

What is and isn't allowable differs from one society to another. For example, in Russia, until recently, private businesses were against the law, so not many people started their own businesses. In the United States, until the 1970s, it was against the law to hold gold except in jewelry and for certain limited uses such as dental supplies,

Video Series, Economics USA: Resources and Scarcity, Segment 1.3

Q-5: Your study partner, Joan, states that market forces are always operative. Is she right? Why or why not?

Economic forces are always operative; society can allow market forces to operate.

Ask your students to suggest some method to ration scarce goods. Rationing high grades is often a good example.

Questions concerning the selling of organs or babies get students excited. I often throw out a suggestion that our society should allow babies to be bought and sold, arguing that doing so would increase happiness all around. The suggestions usually wake the class up and set the tone for a class where the students should expect the unexpected.

---

[2]Even though it's against the law, some babies are nonetheless "sold" on a semilegal, or what is called a gray, market. In the early 1990s, the "market price" for a healthy baby was about $30,000. If it were legal to sell babies (and if people didn't find it morally repugnant to have babies in order to sell them), the price would be much lower, because there would be a larger supply of babies.

The invisible hand, invisible foot, and invisible handshake at work.

What happens in society can be seen as a reaction to, and interaction of, the invisible hand (economic forces), the invisible foot (political forces), and the invisible handshake (social and historical forces).

ECONOMIC TERMINOLOGY

I like to point out that although there is a lot of terminology in economics, it should not be the focus of students' study. Terms, like graphs and math, are only tools that we use to arrive at economic insights.

I like to help my students learn terminology within the context of solving a problem.

ECONOMIC INSIGHTS

For a light-hearted look at some economists' language and some examples of economic reasoning, see Chapter 1 in *Case Studies in Economics* (a supplement offered with this text).

so most people refrained from holding gold. Ultimately a country's laws and social norms determine whether the invisible hand will be allowed to work.

The invisible foot and invisible handshake are active in all parts of your life. The invisible foot influences many of your everyday actions. You don't practice medicine without a license; you don't sell body parts or certain addictive drugs. These actions are all against the law. But many people do sell alcohol; that's not against the law if you have a permit. The invisible handshake also influences us. You don't make profitable loans to your friends (you don't charge your friends interest); you don't charge your children for their food (parents are supposed to feed their children); many sports and media stars don't sell their autographs (some do, but many consider the practice tacky); you don't lower the wage you'll accept in order to get a job away from someone else (you're no scab). The list is long. You cannot understand economics without understanding the limitations that political and social forces—the invisible foot and the invisible handshake—place on economic actions.

In summary, what happens in a society can be seen as the reaction to, and interaction of, these three forces: the invisible hand (economic forces), the invisible foot (political and legal forces), and the invisible handshake (social and historical forces). Economics has a role to play in sociology, history, and politics, just as sociology, history, and politics have roles to play in economics.

Economics is about the real world. Throughout this book I'll use the invisible forces analogy to talk about real-world events and the interrelationships of economics, history, sociology, and politics.

Economic terminology needs little discussion. It simply needs learning. As terms come up, you'll begin to recognize them. Soon you'll begin to understand them, and finally you'll begin to feel comfortable using them. In this book I'm trying to describe how economics works in the real world, so I introduce you to many of the terms that occur in business and in discussions of the economy. Learning economic vocabulary, like learning German or French vocabulary, isn't fun. It's not something that's easily taught in classes. It's something that's learned by study and repetition outside the class. Learning vocabulary takes repetition and memorization, but no one ever said all learning is fun.

Whenever possible I'll integrate the introduction of new terminology into the discussion so that learning it will seem painless. In fact I've already introduced you to a number of economic terms: *opportunity cost, the invisible hand, market forces, economic forces,* just to name a few. By the end of the book I'll have introduced you to hundreds more.

Economists have thought about the economy for a long time, so it's not surprising that they've developed some insights into the way it works.

General insights are often embodied in an *economic theory*—a formulation of highly abstract, deductive relationships that capture inherent empirically observed tendencies of economies. Theories are inevitably too abstract to apply in specific cases and, thus, a theory is often embodied in an **economic model**—*a framework that places the generalized insights of the theory in a more specific contextual setting*—or in an **economic principle**—*a commonly held economic insight stated as a law or general assumption.* Then these theories, models, and principles are empirically tested (as best one can) to ensure that they correspond to reality. While these models and principles are less general than theories, they are still usually too general to apply in specific cases. Theories, models, and principles must be combined with a knowledge of real-world economic institutions to arrive at specific policy recommendations.

To see the importance of principles, think back to grade school when you learned to add. You didn't memorize the sum of 147 and 138; instead you learned a principle of addition. The principle says that when adding 147 and 138, you first add 7 + 8, which you memorized was 15. You write down the 5 and carry the 1, which you add

---

WINSTON CHURCHILL AND LADY ASTOR

There are many stories about Nancy Astor, the first woman elected to Britain's Parliament. A vivacious, fearless American woman, she married into the English aristocracy and, during the 1930s and 1940s, became a bright light on the English social and political scenes, which were already quite bright.

One story told about Lady Astor is that she and Winston Churchill, the unorthodox genius who had a long and distinguished political career and who was Britain's prime minister during World War II, were sitting in a pub having a theoretical discussion about morality. Churchill suggested that as a thought experiment Lady Astor ponder the question: If a man were to promise her a huge amount of money—say a million pounds—for the privilege, would she sleep with him? Lady Astor did ponder the question for a while and finally answered, yes, she would, if the money were guaranteed. Churchill then asked her if she would sleep with him for five pounds. Her response was sharp: "Of course not. What do you think I am—a prostitute?" This time Churchill won the battle of wits by answering, "We have already established that fact; we are now simply negotiating about price."

One moral that economists might draw from this story is that economic incentives, if high enough, can have a powerful influence on behavior. An equally important moral of the story is that noneconomic incentives can also be very strong. Why do most people feel it's wrong to sell sex for money, even if they would be willing to do so if the price were high enough? Keeping this second moral in mind will significantly increase your economic understanding of real-world events.

---

to 4 + 3 to get 8. Then add 1 + 1 = 2. So the answer is 285. When you know that one principle, you know how to add millions of combinations of numbers.

In the same way, knowing a theory gives you insight into a wide variety of economic phenomena, even though you don't know the particulars of each phenomenon. For example, much of economic theory deals with the *pricing mechanism* and how the market operates to coordinate *individuals' decisions*. Economists have come to the following insights:

> *When the quantity supplied is greater than the quantity demanded, price has a tendency to fall.*
> *When the quantity demanded is greater than the quantity supplied, price has a tendency to rise.*

Using these generalized insights, economists have developed a theory of markets that leads to the further insight that, under certain conditions, the market will coordinate individuals' decisions, allocating scarce resources efficiently—that is, providing goods as cheaply as possible. An efficient economy is one that achieves a goal as cheaply as possible. Economists call this insight the **invisible hand theory**—*a market economy, through the price mechanism, will allocate resources efficiently.*

Theories, and the models used to represent them, are enormously efficient methods of conveying information, but they're also necessarily abstract. They rely upon simplifying assumptions, and *if you don't know the assumptions, you don't know the theory.* The result of forgetting assumptions could be similar to what happens if you forget that you're supposed to add numbers in columns. Forgetting that, yet remembering all the steps, can lead to a wildly incorrect answer. For example,

$$471$$
$$+ \ 327$$
$$\overline{5037 \text{ is wrong.}}$$

Knowing the assumptions of theories and models allows you to progress beyond gut reaction and better understand the strengths and weaknesses of various economic systems. Let's consider a central economic assumption: the assumption that individuals behave rationally—that what they choose reflects what makes them happiest, given the constraints. If that assumption doesn't hold, the invisible hand theory doesn't hold.

The Invisible Hand Theory

When the quantity supplied is greater than the quantity demanded, price has a tendency to fall.

When the quantity demanded is greater than the quantity supplied, price has a tendency to rise.

Q-6: There has been a superb growing season and the quantity of tomatoes supplied exceeds the quantity demanded. What is likely to happen to the price of tomatoes?

You've got to know the assumption if you are to know the theory.

Often I go to the board and add up some numbers incorrectly. The students usually catch me. It forces them to pay attention and brings them into the flow of the class. I, of course, tell them afterwards that I made the mistake on purpose. They, of course, don't believe me.

Q-7: John, your study partner, is a free market advocate. He argues that the invisible hand theory tells us that the government should not interfere with the economy. Do you agree? Why or why not?

ADDED DIMENSION   DEALING WITH MATH ANXIETY

Knowing my students, I can see the red flags rising, the legs tensing up, the fear flooding over many of you. Here it comes—the math and the graphs.

I wish I could change things by saying to you, "Don't worry—mathematics and graphical analysis are easy." But I can't. That doesn't mean math and graphical analysis aren't easy. They are. They're wonderful tools that convey ideas neatly and efficiently. But I've had enough teaching experience to know that somewhere back in elementary school some teacher blew it and put about 40 percent of you off mathematics for life. A tool that scares you to death is not useful; it can be a hindrance, not a help, to learning. I also know that nothing your current teacher or I now can say, write, or do is going to change that for most of those 40 percent. On the other hand, I've had a little bit of luck with about 10 percent of the 40 percent (which makes 4 percent—4 out of 100 students) with the following "conspiracy explanation." So I'll try it on you. Here's what I tell them.

Economics is really simple. Economists know that it is, and they also know that if word got around about how simple economics is, few students would take economics. But economists are smart. They make economics seem more difficult than it is by couching simple economic ideas in graphs. The graphs convince many students that economics is really hard, allowing economics professors to teach simple ideas that the students think are hard.

About 4 percent of my students become so mad at the thought of being duped that they overcome their math anxiety. The rest just wonder whether this teacher is for real.

If avoiding being duped means something to you, believe the preceding story; if it doesn't, don't. But whatever you do, try to follow the numerical and graphical examples carefully, because they not only cement the knowledge into your minds; they also present in a rigorous manner the ideas I'm discussing.

The ideas conveyed in the numerical and graphical examples will be explained in words—and the graphical analysis (the type of mathematical explanation most used in introductory economics) generally will simply be a more precise presentation of the accompanying discussion in words. In some economics courses, understanding the words may be enough, but in most, the exams pose the questions in graphical terms, so there's no getting around the need to understand the ideas graphically. And it is simple. (Appendix B discusses the basics of graphical analysis.)

Presenting the invisible hand theory in its full beauty is an important part of any economics course. Presenting the assumptions upon which it is based and the limitations of the invisible hand is likewise an important part of the course. I'll do both throughout the book.

Economic Theory and Stories

Economic theory, and the models in which that theory is presented, often developed as a shorthand way of telling a story. These stories are important; they make the theory come alive and convey the insights that give economic theory its power. In this book I present plenty of theories and models, but they're accompanied by stories that provide the context that makes them relevant.

At times, because there's much new terminology, discussing models and theories takes up much of the presentation time and becomes a bit oppressive. That's the nature of the beast. As Albert Einstein said, "Theories should be as simple as possible, but not more so." When a theory or a model becomes oppressive, pause and think about the underlying story that the theory is meant to convey. That story should make sense and be concrete. If you can't translate the theory into a story, you don't understand the theory.

For additional discussion of mathematical tools in technically oriented courses see *Economics: An Honors Companion* (a supplement offered with this text). Assign chapters 1–3 as background reading.

Often economic theories are presented in mathematical—graphical or algebraic—models. In this book I keep models to a minimum, but I cannot avoid them completely. Graphical models are used so much by economists that they must be included. So part of the course will consist of translating the verbal discussions of the economy into graphical models. To prepare you for those graphical models I have written a brief introduction to the basics of graphical presentation in Appendix B.

Microeconomics and Macroeconomics

Microeconomics is the study of how individual choice is influenced by economic forces.

Economic theory is divided into two parts: microeconomic theory and macroeconomic theory. Microeconomic theory considers economic reasoning from the viewpoint of individuals and firms and builds up from there to an analysis of the whole economy. I define **microeconomics** as *the study of individual choice, and how that choice is influenced by economic forces*. Microeconomics studies such things as the pricing policies of firms, households' decisions on what to buy, and how markets allocate resources among alternative ends. Our discussion of opportunity cost was based on microeconomic theory. The invisible hand theory comes from microeconomics.

As one builds up from microeconomic analysis to an analysis of the entire society, everything gets rather complicated. Many economists try to uncomplicate matters by taking a different approach—a macroeconomic approach—first looking at the aggregate, or whole, and then breaking it down into components. A micro approach would analyze a person by looking first at each individual cell and then building up. A macro approach would start with the person and then go on to his or her components— arms, legs, fingernails, feelings, and so on. Put simply, microeconomics analyzes from the parts to the whole; macroeconomics analyzes from the whole to the parts.

In recent years the analysis of macroeconomic issues—inflation, unemployment, business cycles, and growth—has been supplemented by more and more microeconomic analysis. I define **macroeconomics** as *the study of inflation, unemployment, business cycles, and growth primarily from the whole to the parts*. It focuses on aggregate relationships and supplements that analysis with microeconomic insights.

Neither macro nor micro is prior to the other. Clearly, macro results follow from micro decisions, but micro decisions are made within a macro context, and can only be understood within that context. For example, say everyone expects total output to be low. Given those expectations, each person or firm produces a low level of output. Those expectations are determined by the macroeconomic conditions. To analyze the economy appropriately, one must simultaneously develop a microfoundation of macro and a macrofoundation of micro. The macrofoundation of micro provides the institutional and expectational context within which micro decisions are made, and the microfoundation of macro provides the contextual relation between individual decisions and aggregate outcomes.

To know whether you can apply economic theory to reality, you must know about economic institutions. Economic institutions are complicated combinations of historical circumstance and economic, cultural, social, and political pressures. Economic institutions are all around you and affect your everyday life. For example, let's consider three economic institutions: schools, corporations, and cultural norms. Where you go to school plays an important role in the kind of job you'll get. Corporations determine what products are available to buy. Cultural norms determine what you identify as legitimate business activities. Understanding economic institutions requires the wisdom of experience, tempered with common sense—all combined with a desire to understand rather than to accept without question.

Since cultural norms may be an unfamiliar concept to you, let's consider how such norms affect economies. A **cultural norm** is *a standard people use when they determine whether a particular activity or behavior is acceptable*. For example, religious rules once held that Catholics shouldn't eat meat on Friday, so Friday became a day to eat fish. The prohibition ended in the 1960s, but the tendency to eat fish on Friday has endured. In the United States today, more fish is consumed on Fridays than on any other day of the week. This fact can be understood only if you understand the cultural norm that lies behind it. Similarly, in the United States more hams are bought in April and more turkeys are bought in November and December than in other months; more pork is consumed per capita in Sweden than in Israel. Can you explain why?

Economic institutions sometimes seem to operate in ways quite different than economic theory predicts. For example, economic theory says that prices are determined by supply and demand. However, businesses say that prices are set by rules of thumb—often by what are called cost-plus-markup rules. (That is, you determine what your costs are, multiply by 1.4 or 1.5, and the result is the price you set.) Economic theory says that supply and demand determine who's hired; experience suggests that hiring is often done on the basis of whom you know, not by economic forces.

6 Microeconomics considers economic reasoning from the viewpoint of individuals and builds up; macroeconomics considers economic reasoning from the aggregate and builds down.

Macroeconomics is the study of inflation, unemployment, business cycles, and growth; it focuses on aggregate relationships.

Some exciting new work being done in macroeconomics focuses on the limitations of the representative individual assumption. Three readable articles are: Axel Leijonhufvud's Southern Economic Association's presidential address, "Towards a Not Too Rational Economics," published in the *Southern Economic Journal*, April, 1993; my "The Macro Foundations of Micro," published in the *Eastern Economic Journal*, Fall 1993; and Alan Kirman's "Whom or What Does the Representative Individual Represent?" published in the *Journal of Economic Perspective*, Spring 1992.

ECONOMIC INSTITUTIONS

Ask your students to discuss some general cultural norms that they are familiar with. What norms exist in their community or even in their family?

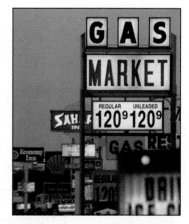

In retail markets most prices are posted and are determined by a cost-plus-markup rule.

These apparent contradictions have two complementary explanations. First, economic theory abstracts from many issues. These issues may account for the differences. Second, there's no contradiction; economic principles often affect decisions from behind the scenes. For instance, supply and demand pressures determine what the price markup over cost will be. In this case, the invisible handshake is guided by the invisible hand. In all cases, however, to apply economic theory to reality—to gain the full value of economic insights—you've got to have a sense of economic institutions.

ECONOMIC POLICY OPTIONS

The final goal of the course is to present the economic policy options facing our society today. For example, should the government restrict mergers between firms? Should it run a budget deficit? Should it do something about the international trade deficit? Should it decrease taxes?

I saved my discussion of this goal for last because there's no sense talking about policy options unless you know some economic terminology, some economic theory, and something about economic institutions. Once you know something about those, you're in a position to consider the policy options available for dealing with the economic problems our society faces.

Q–8: Canada spends 8 percent of its gross domestic product (GDP) on health care. The United States spends 14 percent. Yet both countries have essentially the same level of healthiness. Based on this information, would you advise the United States to adopt a system like Canada's?

Policies operate within institutions, but policies can also influence the institutions within which they operate. Some policies are even designed to change institutions directly. Policies that affect institutions are much more difficult to analyze (because their effects on institutions are generally indirect and nebulous) and to implement (since existing institutions often create benefits for specific individuals who don't want them changed) than are policies that don't affect institutions. For example, consider establishing a government program to promote research. Seems like a good thing— right? But such a policy might undermine the role of existing institutions already promoting research, and the net result of the program might be less, not more, research. When analyzing such policies, we need to take this effect on institutions into account.

To carry out economic policy effectively one must understand how institutions might change as a result of the economic policy.

Let's consider another example: welfare policy and the institution of the two-parent family. In the 1960s, the United States developed a variety of policy initiatives designed to eliminate poverty. These initiatives directed income to single parents with children, and assumed that family structure would be unchanged by these policies. But family structure did not remain unchanged; it changed substantially, and, very likely, these policies to eliminate poverty played a role in increasing the number of single-parent families. The result was a failure of the programs to eliminate poverty. Now this is not to say that we should not have programs to eliminate poverty, or that two-parent families are preferable to one-parent families; it is only to say that we must build into our policies their effect on institutions.

Q–9: True or False? Economists should focus their policy analysis on institutional changes because such policies offer the largest gains.

On the other hand, policies that directly change institutions, while much more difficult to implement than policies that don't, also offer the largest potential for gain. Let's consider an example. In the 1990s, a number of countries decided to replace socialist institutions with market economies. The result: output in those countries fell enormously as the old institutions fell apart. Eventually, these countries hope, once the new market institutions are predominant, output will bounce back and further gains will be made. The temporary hardships these countries are experiencing show the enormous difficulty of implementing policies involving major institutional changes.

Objective Policy Analysis

Good policy analysis is as objective as possible.

You may wish to share with your students the reasons behind your choice of a dissertation or thesis topic. Were there normative issues that influenced your decision?

Good economic policy analysis is **objective analysis**—*analysis that keeps the analyst's value judgments separate from the analysis.* Objective analysis does not say, "This is the way things should be," reflecting a goal established by the analyst. That would be **subjective analysis**—*analysis that reflects the analyst's view of how things should be.* Instead, objective analysis says, "This is the way the economy works, and if society (or the individual or firm for whom you're doing the analysis) wants to achieve a particular goal, this is how it might go about doing so." Objective analysis keeps, or at least tries to keep, subjective views—value judgments—separate.

To make clear the distinction between objective and subjective analysis, economists have divided economics into three categories: *positive economics, normative economics,* and the *art of economics.* **Positive economics** is *the study of what is, and how the economy works.* It asks such questions as: How does the market for hog bellies work? How do price restrictions affect market forces? These questions fall under the heading of economic theory. **Normative economics** is *the study of what the goals of the economy should be.* In discussing such questions, economists must carefully delineate whose goals they are discussing. One cannot simply assume that one's own goals for society are society's goals. Normative economics asks such questions as: What should the distribution of income be? What should tax policy be designed to achieve?

The **art of economics** *relates positive economics to normative economics*; it is the application of the knowledge learned in positive economics to the achievement of the goals one has determined in normative economics. It looks at such questions as: To achieve a certain distribution of income, how would you go about it, given the way the economy works?[3] Most policy discussions fall under the art of economics.

In each of these three branches of economics, economists separate their own value judgments from their objective analysis as much as possible. The qualifier "as much as possible" is important, since some value judgments inevitably sneak in. We are products of our environment, and the questions we ask, the framework we use, and the way we interpret empirical evidence all embody value judgments and reflect our backgrounds.

Maintaining objectivity is easiest in positive economics, where one is working with abstract models to understand how the economy works. Maintaining objectivity is harder in normative economics. You must always be objective about whose normative values you are using. It's easy to assume that all of society shares your values, but that assumption is often wrong.

It's hardest to maintain objectivity in the art of economics because it embodies the problems of both positive and normative economics. Because noneconomic forces affect policy, to practice the art of economics one must make judgments about how these noneconomic forces work. These judgments are likely to embody one's own value judgments. So one must be exceedingly careful to be as objective as possible in practicing the art of economics.

One of the best ways to find out about feasible economic policy options is to compare our economic policies with those of other countries. For example, health care is supplied quite differently in various countries. To decide how to improve health care policy in the United States, policy makers study how Canada and Britain do it, and make judgments about whether the approach those countries take will fit our existing institutions. Comparative institutional analysis is an important part of the art of economics.

When you think about the policy options facing society, you'll quickly discover that the choice of policy options depends on much more than economic theory. One must take into account historical precedent plus social, cultural, and political forces. In an economics course, I don't have time to analyze these forces in as much depth as I'd like. That's one reason there are separate history, political science, sociology, and anthropology courses.

I don't pretend that these forces play an insignificant role in policy decisions. That's why I use the invisible force terminology when I cover these other issues. It allows me to integrate the other forces without explaining in depth how they work. I'll use this terminology when discussing policy and applying economic insights to

7a *Positive economics* is the study of what is, and how the economy works.

7b *Normative economics* is the study of what the goals of the economy should be.

7c The *art of economics* is the application of the knowledge learned in positive economics to the achievement of the goals determined in normative economics.

In the art of economics, it is difficult to be objective but it is important to try.

Q–10: State whether the following five statements belong in positive economics, normative economics, or the art of economics.
1. We should support the market because it is efficient.
2. Given certain conditions, the market achieves efficient results.
3. Based on past experience and our understanding of markets, if one wants a reasonably efficient result, markets should probably be relied upon.
4. The distribution of income should be left to markets.
5. Markets allocate income according to contributions of factors.

Policy and the Invisible Forces

This book consistently takes the position that policy decisions are extremely complicated and that the models the students learn have too many simplifying assumptions for those models to be applied directly to policy analysis.

---

[3]This three-part distinction was made back in 1896 by a famous economist, John Neville Keynes, father of John Maynard Keynes, the economist who developed macroeconomics. This distinction was instilled into modern economics by Milton Friedman and Robert Lipsey in the 1950s. They, however, downplayed the art of economics, which J. N. Keynes had seen as central to understanding the economists' role in policy.

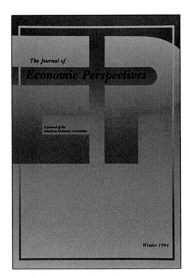

Students find the *Journal of Economic Perspectives* the most relevant of the journals published by the American Economic Association.

policy questions. In economics, we focus the analysis on the invisible hand, and much of economic theory is devoted to how the economy would operate if the invisible hand were the only force operating. But as soon as we apply theory to reality and policy, we must take into account the other invisible forces.

An example will make my point more concrete. Most economists agree that holding down or eliminating tariffs (taxes on imports) and quotas (numerical limitations on imports) makes good economic sense. They strongly advise governments to follow a policy of free trade. Do governments follow free trade policies? Almost invariably they do not. The invisible foot—politics—leads society in a different direction. If you're advising a policy maker, you need to point out that these other forces must be taken into account, and how other forces should (if they should) and can (if they can) be integrated with your recommendations.

Here's another example. Economic analysis devoid of institutional content would say that the world would be more efficient if we allowed U.S. citizenship to be bought and sold. But to advise policies that would legally allow a market for buying and selling U.S. citizenship would be to recommend a kind of efficiency that goes against historical, cultural, and social norms. The invisible handshake and the invisible foot would prevent the policies from being introduced, and any economist who proposed them would probably be banished to an ivory or other type of tower.

CONCLUSION

"Economics" by Alfred Marshall and "Of the Principle Which Gives Occasion to the Division of Labour" by Adam Smith in *Classic Readings in Economics.*

There's tons more that could be said by way of introducing you to economics, but an introduction must remain an introduction. As it is, this chapter should have:

1. Introduced you to economic reasoning.
2. Surveyed what we're going to cover in this book.
3. Given you an idea of my writing style and approach.

We'll be spending long hours together over the coming term, and before entering into such a commitment it's best to know your partner. While I won't know you, by the end of this book you'll know me. Maybe you won't love me as my mother does, but you'll know me.

This introduction was my opening line. I hope it also conveyed the importance and relevance that belong to economics. If it did, it has served its intended purpose. Economics is tough, but tough can be fun.

CHAPTER SUMMARY

- The three coordination problems any economy must solve are what to produce, how to produce it, and for whom to produce it.
- Learning economics consists of learning economic reasoning, economic terminology, economic insights, economic institutions, and economic policy options.
- Economic reasoning structures all questions in a cost/benefit frame: If the relevant benefits of doing something exceed the relevant costs, do it. If the relevant costs exceed the relevant benefits, don't.
- Often economic decisions can be made by comparing marginal costs and marginal benefits.

- "There ain't no such thing as a free lunch" (**TANSTAAFL**) embodies the opportunity cost concept.
- Economic forces, the forces of scarcity, are always working.
- Economic reality is controlled and directed by three invisible forces: the invisible hand, the invisible foot, and the invisible handshake.
- Economics can be divided into microeconomics and macroeconomics.
- Economics also can be subdivided into positive economics, normative economics, and the art of economics.

KEY TERMS

art of economics *(19)*
cultural norm *(17)*
economic decision rule *(9)*
economic forces *(12)*
economic institution *(8)*
economic model *(14)*
economic policy *(9)*
economic principle *(14)*
economic reasoning *(8)*
economic system *(6)*

economic theory *(8)*
economics *(6)*
economy *(6)*
invisible foot *(12)*
invisible hand *(12)*
invisible hand theory *(15)*
invisible handshake *(12)*
macroeconomics *(17)*
marginal benefit *(9)*
marginal cost *(9)*

market force *(12)*
microeconomics *(16)*
normative economics *(19)*
objective analysis *(18)*
opportunity cost *(11)*
positive economics *(19)*
rationing *(12)*
scarcity *(6)*
subjective analysis *(18)*
sunk costs *(9)*

QUESTIONS FOR THOUGHT AND REVIEW

The number after each question represents the estimated degree of critical thinking required. (1 = almost none; 10 = deep thought.)

1. What is the textbook author's reasoning for focusing the definition of economics on coordination rather than on scarcity? *(4)*
2. You rent a car for $29.95. The first 150 miles are free, but each mile thereafter costs 15 cents. You drive it 200 miles. What is the marginal cost of driving the car? *(4)*
3. For some years, China has had a one-child-per-family policy. For cultural reasons, there are now many more male than female children born in China. How is this likely to affect who pays the cost of dates in China in 15 or 20 years? Explain your response. *(5)*
4. List two microeconomic and two macroeconomic problems. *(2)*
5. Does economic theory prove that the free market system is best? Why? *(4)*
6. Calculate, using the best estimates you can make:
   a. Your opportunity cost of attending college.
   b. Your opportunity cost of taking this course.
   c. Your opportunity cost of attending yesterday's lecture in this course. *(6)*

7. List two recent choices you made and explain why you made those choices in terms of marginal benefits and marginal costs. *(5)*
8. Individuals have two kidneys but most of us need only one. People who have lost both kidneys through accident or disease must be hooked up to a dialysis machine, which cleanses waste from their bodies. Say a person who has two good kidneys offers to sell one of them to someone whose kidney function has been totally destroyed. The seller asks $30,000 for the kidney, and the person who has lost both kidneys accepts the offer. Who benefits from the deal? Who is hurt? Should a society allow such market transactions? Why? *(9)*
9. Is a good economist always objective? Why? *(4)*
10. Recently many states have adopted new EPA (Environmental Protection Agency) gasoline standards designed to reduce air pollution. What would you advise politicians if they reevaluate these air pollution policies? *(8)*
11. In 1996, the German comedian Harald Schmidt attempted to mimic the successful David Letterman show in Germany. The format didn't entertain its German audience. What economic policy lesson can be learned from Harald Schmidt's failure? *(8)*

PROBLEMS AND EXERCISES

1. State whether the following are microeconomic or macroeconomic policy issues:
   a. Should the U.S. government use a policy of free trade with China to encourage China to advance human rights?
   b. Will the fact that more and more doctors are selling their practices to managed care networks increase the efficiency of medical providers?
   c. Should the current federal income tax structure be eliminated in favor of a flat tax?
   d. Should the federal minimum wage be raised?
   e. Should AT&T and MCI be allowed to jointly build local phone networks?
   f. Should commercial banks be required to provide loans

in all areas of the territory from which they accept deposits?

2. State whether the following statements belong in positive economics, normative economics, or the art of economics.
   a. In a market, when supply exceeds demand, price tends to fall.
   b. When determining tax rates, the government should take into account the income needs of individuals.
   c. What society feels is fair is determined largely by cultural norms.
   d. When deciding which rationing mechanism is best (lottery, price, first-come/first-served), one must take into account the goals of society.
   e. California currently rations water to farmers at

subsidized prices. Once California allows the trading of water rights, it will allow economic forces to be a market force.

3. Give two examples of the invisible handshake and explain how they keep economic forces from becoming market forces.

4. Give two examples of the invisible foot and explain how they might interact with the invisible hand.

5. Name three ways a limited number of dormitory rooms could be rationed. How would economic forces determine individual behavior in each? How would the three invisible forces determine whether those economic forces become market forces?

6. State the opportunity cost of each of the following decisions that confront a student completing an economics major at Opportunity State University. (To attend O.S.U., you must be a full-time student.)
   a. Before enrolling as a freshman at O.S.U.
   b. After enrolling at O.S.U., but before the first class.
   c. Only one class is needed to complete the major.
   d. The student has completed the major and graduated from O.S.U.

7. Go to two stores: a supermarket and a convenience store.
   a. Write down the cost of a gallon of milk in each.
   b. The prices are most likely different. Using the terminology used in this chapter, explain why that is the case and why anyone would buy milk in the store with the higher price.
   c. Do the same exercise with shirts or dresses in Wal-Mart (or its equivalent) and Saks (or its equivalent).

8. Adam Smith, who wrote *The Wealth of Nations* and is seen as the father of modern economics, also wrote *The Theory of Moral Sentiments* in which he argued that society would be better off if people weren't so selfish and were more considerate of others. How does this view fit with the discussion of economic reasoning presented in the chapter?

ANSWERS TO MARGIN QUESTIONS

The numbers in parentheses refer to the page number of each margin question.

1. Since the price of both stocks is now $15, it doesn't matter which one you sell (assuming no differential capital gains taxation). The price you bought them for doesn't matter; it's a sunk cost. Marginal analysis refers to the future gain, so what you expect to happen to future prices of the stocks—not past prices—should determine which stock you decide to sell. *(10)*

2. A cost/benefit analysis requires that you put a value on a good, and placing a value on a good can be seen as demeaning it. Consider love. Try telling an acquaintance that you'd like to buy his or her spiritual love, and see what response you get. *(11)*

3. John is wrong. The opportunity cost of reading the chapter is primarily the time you spend reading it. Reading the book prevents you from doing other things. Assuming that you already paid for the book, the original price is no longer part of the opportunity cost; it is a sunk cost. Bygones are bygones. *(12)*

4. Whenever there is scarcity, the scarce good must be rationed by some means. Free health care has an opportunity cost in other resources. So if it is not rationed, to get the resources to supply that care, other goods would have to be more tightly rationed than they currently are. It is likely that unless health care were rationed in some way, perhaps not by the market, the opportunity cost of supplying free health care would be larger than most societies would be willing to pay. *(12)*

5. Joan is wrong. Economic forces are always operative; market forces are not. *(13)*

6. According to the invisible hand theory, the price of tomatoes will likely fall. *(15)*

7. He is wrong. The invisible hand theory is a positive theory and does not tell us anything about policy. To do so would be to violate Hume's dictum that a "should" cannot be derived from an "is." This is not to say that government should or should not interfere; whether government should interfere is a very difficult question. *(15)*

8. The answer is not so simple. The adviser must take a careful look at many more issues, such as who has health coverage, who pays for the coverage, how much personal choice is allowed, and how readily available is the most advanced technology. It is a question in the art of economics and such questions never have simple answers. *(18)*

9. False. While such changes have the largest gain, they may also have the largest cost. The policies economists should focus on are those that offer the largest net gain—benefits minus costs—to society. *(18)*

10. (1) Normative; (2) Positive; (3) Art; (4) Normative; (5) Positive. *(19)*

Economics in Perspective

All too often, students study economics out of context. They're presented with sterile analysis and boring facts to memorize, and are never shown how economics fits into the larger scheme of things. That's bad; it makes economics seem boring—but economics is not boring. Every so often throughout this book, sometimes in the appendixes and sometimes in boxes, I'll step back and put the analysis in perspective, giving you an idea from whence the analysis sprang and its historical context. In educational jargon, this is called *enrichment*.

I begin here with economics itself.

First, its history: In the 1500s there were few universities. Those that existed taught religion, Latin, Greek, philosophy, history, and mathematics. No economics. Then came the *Enlightenment* (about 1700) in which reasoning replaced God as the explanation of why things were the way they were. Pre-Enlightenment thinkers would answer the question, "Why am I poor?" with, "Because God wills it." Enlightenment scholars looked for a different explanation. "Because of the nature of land ownership" is one answer they found.

Such reasoned explanations required more knowledge of the way things were, and the amount of information expanded so rapidly that it had to be divided or categorized for an individual to have hope of knowing a subject. Soon philosophy was subdivided into science and philosophy. In the 1700s, the sciences were split into natural sciences and social sciences. The amount of knowledge kept increasing, and in the late 1800s and early 1900s social science itself split into subdivisions: economics, political science, history, geography, sociology, anthropology, and psychology. Many of the insights about how the economic system worked were codified in Adam Smith's *The Wealth of Nations,* written in 1776. Notice that this is before economics as a subdiscipline developed, and Adam Smith could also be classified as an anthropologist, a sociologist, a political scientist, and a social philosopher.

Throughout the 18th and 19th centuries, economists such as Adam Smith, Thomas Malthus, John Stuart Mill, David Ricardo, and Karl Marx were more than economists; they were social philosophers who covered all aspects of social science. These writers were subsequently called *Classical economists*. Alfred Marshall continued in that classical tradition, and his book, *Principles of Economics,* published in the late 1800s, was written with the other social sciences much in evidence. But Marshall also changed the questions economists ask; he focused on those questions that could be asked in a graphical supply/demand framework. In doing so he began what is called *neoclassical economics.* Marshall's analysis forms the basis of much of what's currently taught in undergraduate microeconomics courses.

In the 1930s, as economists formalized Marshall's insights, many other social science insights were removed. By the 1950s, these social sciences were cemented into college curricula and organized into college departments. Economists learned economics; sociologists learned sociology.

For a while economics got lost in itself, and economists learned little else. Marshall's analysis was downplayed, and the work of more formal economists of the 1800s (such as Léon Walras, Francis Edgeworth, and Antoine Cournot) was seen as the basis of the science of economics. Economic analysis that focuses only on formal interrelationships is called *Walrasian economics.*

Thus, in the 1990s, there are two branches of neoclassical economics: Marshallian and Walrasian. **Marshallian economics** is *economic analysis that sees economics as a way of thinking and integrates insights from other disciplines.* **Walrasian economics** is *economic analysis that sees economics as a logical science; it analyzes economic issues separately from social and cultural issues.* This book falls solidly in the Marshallian tradition. It sees economics as a way of thinking—as an engine of analysis used to understand real-world phenomena, not as a logical exercise in deductive reasoning. My strong belief is that in undergraduate school one should learn Marshallian economics; in graduate school one can learn Walrasian economics.

Marshallian economics is an art, not a science. It is primarily about policy, not theory. It sees institutions as well as political and social dimensions of reality as important, and it shows you how economics ties into those dimensions.

KEY TERMS

Marshallian economics   *(23)*   Walrasian economics   *(23)*

QUESTIONS FOR THOUGHT AND REVIEW

1. What event occurred in the 1700s that might have led philosophers to question the "Because God wills it" answer to the "Why am I poor" question? This question requires library research.
2. Explain how Adam Smith could be called:
   a. An anthropologist

   b. A sociologist
   c. A political scientist
3. How do Marshallian and Walrasian economics differ from each other? How would you categorize:
   a. Your professor?
   b. The author of this book?

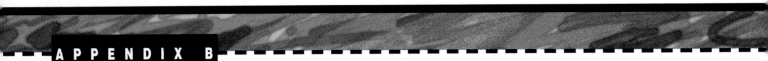

A P P E N D I X   B

Graphish
The Language of Graphs

A picture is worth 1,000 words. Economists, being efficient, like to present ideas in **graphs,** *pictures of points in a coordinate system in which points denote relationships between numbers.* But a graph is worth 1,000 words only if the person looking at the graph knows the graphical language; *Graphish,* we'll call it. (It's a bit like English.) Graphish is usually written on graph paper. If the person doesn't know Graphish, the picture isn't worth any words and Graphish can be babble.

I have enormous sympathy for students who don't understand Graphish. A number of my students get thrown for a loop by graphs. They understand the idea, but Graphish confuses them. This appendix is for them, and for those of you like them. It's a primer in Graphish.

Two Ways to Use Graphs

In this book I use graphs in two ways:

1. To present an economic model or theory visually; to show how two variables interrelate.

2. To present real-world data visually. To do this, I use primarily bar charts, line charts, and pie charts.

Actually, these two ways of using graphs are related. They are both ways of presenting visually the *relationship* between two things.

Graphs are built around a number line, or axis, like the one in Exhibit B1(a). The numbers are generally placed in order, equal distances from one another. That number line allows us to represent a number at an appropriate point on the line. For example, point *A* represents the number 4.

The number line in Exhibit B1(a) is drawn horizontally, but it doesn't have to be; it can also be drawn vertically, as in Exhibit B1(b).

How we divide our axes, or number lines, into intervals, is up to us. In Exhibit B1(a), I called each interval 1; in Exhibit B1(b), I called each interval 10. Point *A* appears after 4 intervals of 1 (starting at 0 and reading from left to right), so it represents 4. In Exhibit B1(b), where each

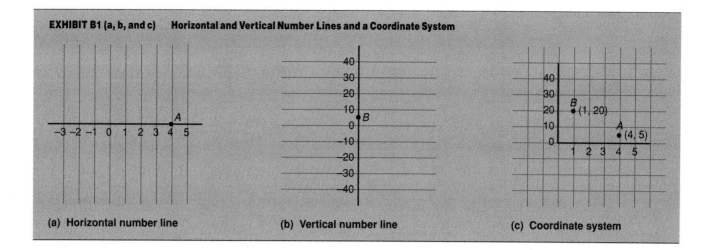

EXHIBIT B1 (a, b, and c)   Horizontal and Vertical Number Lines and a Coordinate System

(a) Horizontal number line

(b) Vertical number line

(c) Coordinate system

interval represents 10, to represent 5, I place point *B* halfway in the interval between 0 and 10.

So far, so good. Graphish developed when a vertical and a horizontal number line were combined, as in Exhibit B1(c). When the horizontal and vertical number lines are put together they're called *axes*. (Each line is an axis. *Axes* is the plural of *axis*.) I now have a **coordinate system**—*a two-dimensional space in which one point represents two numbers*. For example, point *A* in Exhibit B1(c) represents the numbers (4, 5)—4 on the horizontal number line and 5 on the vertical number line. Point *B* represents the numbers (1, 20). (By convention, the horizontal numbers are written first.)

Being able to represent two numbers with one point is neat because it allows the relationships between two numbers to be presented visually instead of having to be expressed verbally, which is often cumbersome. For example, say the cost of producing 6 units of something is $4 per unit and the cost of producing 10 units is $3 per unit. By putting both these points on a graph, we can visually see that producing 10 costs less per unit than does producing 6.

Another way to use graphs to present real-world data visually is to use the horizontal line to represent time. Say that we let each horizontal interval equal a year, and each vertical interval equal $100 in income. By graphing your income each year, you can obtain a visual representation of how your income has changed over time.

Graphs can be used to show any relationship between two variables. (*Variables* are what economists call the units that are measured on the horizontal and vertical axes.) As long as you remember that graphs are simply a way of presenting a relationship visually, you can keep graphs in perspective.

Using Graphs in Economic Modeling   I use graphs throughout the book as I present economic models, or simplifica-

tions of reality. A few terms are often used in describing these graphs, and we'll now go over them. Consider Exhibit B2(a), which lists the number of pens bought per day (column 2) at various prices (column 1).

We can present the table's information in a graph by combining the pairs of numbers in the two columns of the table and representing, or plotting, them on two axes. I do that in Exhibit B2(b).

By convention, when graphing a relationship between price and quantity, economists place price on the vertical axis and quantity on the horizontal axis.

I can now connect the points, producing a line like the one in Exhibit B2(c). With this line, I interpolate the numbers between the points (which makes for a nice visual presentation). That is, I make the **interpolation assumption**—*the assumption that the relationship between variables is the same between points as it is at the points*. The interpolation assumption allows us to think of a line as a collection of points and therefore to connect the points into a line.

Even though the line in Exhibit B2(c) is straight, economists call any such line drawn on a graph a *curve*. Because it's straight the curve in B2(c) is called a **linear curve**—*a curve that is drawn as a straight line*. Notice that this curve starts high on the left-hand side and goes down to the right. Economists say any curve that looks like that is *downward-sloping*. They also say that a downward-sloping curve represents an **inverse relationship**—*a relationship between two variables in which when one goes up, the other goes down*. In this example, the line demonstrates an inverse relationship between price and quantity—that is, when the price of pens goes up, the quantity bought goes down.

Exhibit B2(d) presents a **nonlinear curve**—*a curve that is drawn as a curved line*. This curve, which really is curved, starts low on the left-hand side and goes up to the right. Economists say any curve that goes up to the right is *upward-sloping*. An upward-sloping curve represents a **direct relationship**—*relationship in which when one variable goes up, the other goes up too.* The direct relationship I'm talking about here is the one between the two variables (what's measured on the horizontal and vertical lines). *Downward-sloping* and *upward-sloping* are terms you need to memorize if you want to read, write, and speak Graphish, keeping graphically in your mind the image of the relationships they represent.

Slope   One can, of course, be far more explicit about how much the curve is sloping upward or downward by defining it in terms of **slope**—*the change in the value on the vertical axis divided by the change in the value on the horizontal axis.* Sometimes slope is presented as "rise over run":

$$\text{Slope} = \frac{\text{Rise}}{\text{Run}} = \frac{\text{Change in value on vertical axis}}{\text{Change in value on horizontal axis}}$$

Slopes of Linear Curves   In Exhibit B3, I present five linear curves and measure their slope. Let's go through an example to show how we can measure slope. To do so, we must pick two points. Let's use points *A* (6, 8) and *B* (7, 4) on curve *a*. Looking at these points, we see that as we move from 6 to 7 on the horizontal axis, we move from 8 to 4 on the vertical axis. So when the number on the vertical axis falls by 4, the number on the horizontal axis increases by 1. That means the slope is −4 divided by 1, or −4.

Notice that the inverse relationships represented by the two downward-sloping curves, *a* and *b,* have negative

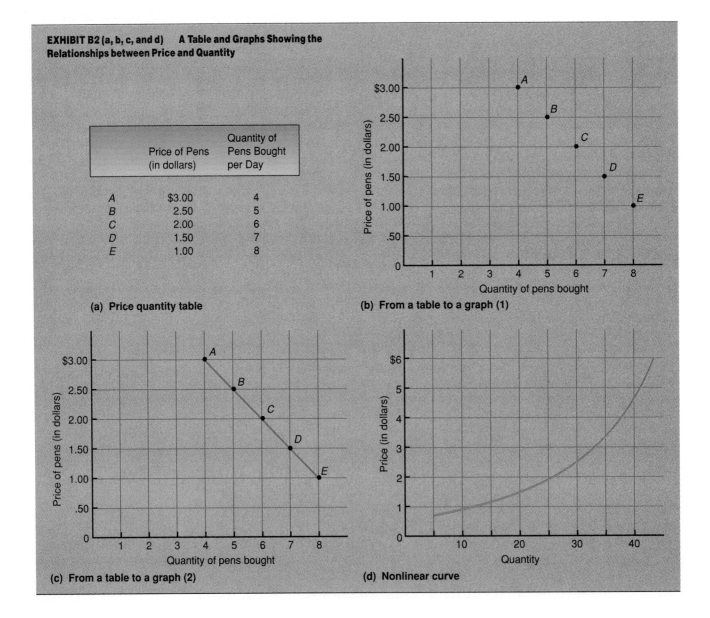

EXHIBIT B2 (a, b, c, and d)   A Table and Graphs Showing the Relationships between Price and Quantity

	Price of Pens (in dollars)	Quantity of Pens Bought per Day
A	$3.00	4
B	2.50	5
C	2.00	6
D	1.50	7
E	1.00	8

(a) Price quantity table

(b) From a table to a graph (1)

(c) From a table to a graph (2)

(d) Nonlinear curve

slopes, and that the direct relationships represented by the two upward-sloping curves, *c* and *d*, have positive slopes. Notice also that the flatter the curve, the smaller the numerical value of the slope; and the more vertical, or steeper, the curve, the larger the numerical value of the slope. There are two extreme cases:

1. When the curve is horizontal (flat), the slope is zero.
2. When the curve is vertical (straight up and down), the slope is infinite (larger than large).

Knowing the term *slope* and how it's measured lets us describe verbally the pictures we see visually. For example, if I say a curve has a slope of zero, you should picture in your mind a flat line; if I say "a curve with a slope of minus one," you should picture a falling line that makes a 45° angle with the horizontal and vertical axes. (It's the hypotenuse of an isosceles right triangle with the axes as the other two sides.)

Slopes of Nonlinear Curves   The preceding examples were of *linear (straight) curves*. With *nonlinear curves*—the ones that really do curve—the slope of the curve is constantly changing. As a result, we must talk about the slope of the curve at a particular point, rather than the slope of the whole curve. How can a point have a slope? Well, it can't really, but it can almost, and if that's good enough for mathematicians, it's good enough for us.

Defining the slope of a nonlinear curve is a bit more difficult. The slope at a given point on a nonlinear curve is determined by the slope of a linear (or straight) line that's tangent to that curve. (A line that's tangent to a

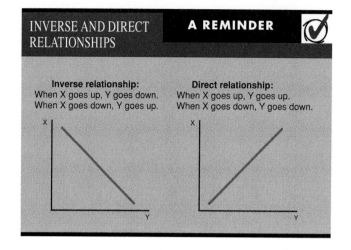

INVERSE AND DIRECT RELATIONSHIPS   **A REMINDER**

Inverse relationship:
When X goes up, Y goes down.
When X goes down, Y goes up.

Direct relationship:
When X goes up, Y goes up.
When X goes down, Y goes down.

curve is a line that just touches the curve, and touches it only at one point in the immediate vicinity of the given point.) In Exhibit B3, the line *LL* is tangent to the curve *ee* at point *E*. The slope of that line, and hence the slope of the curve at the one point where the line touches the curve, is +1.

Maximum and Minimum Points   Two points on a nonlinear curve deserve special mention. These points are the ones for which the slope of the curve is zero. I demonstrate those in Exhibit B4(a) and (b). (At point *A*, we're at the top of the curve so it's at a maximum point; at point *B*, we're at the bottom of the curve so it's at a minimum point.) These maximum and minimum points are often referred to by economists, and it's important to realize

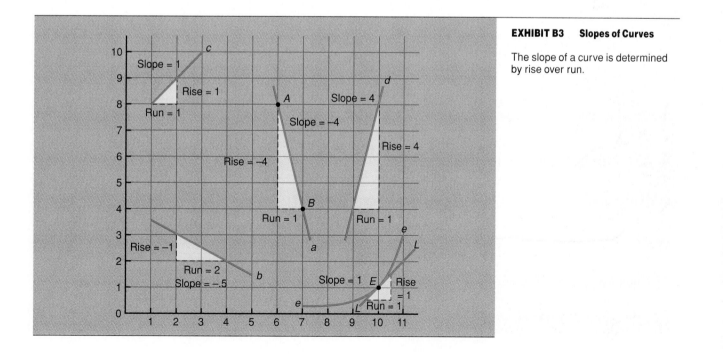

EXHIBIT B3   Slopes of Curves

The slope of a curve is determined by rise over run.

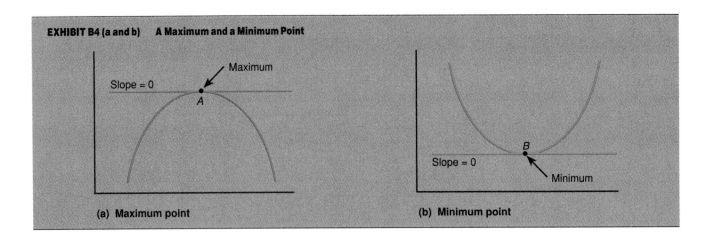

EXHIBIT B4 (a and b)   A Maximum and a Minimum Point

(a) Maximum point

(b) Minimum point

that the value of the slope of the curve at each of these points is zero.

There are, of course, many other types of curves, and much more can be said about the curves I've talked about. I won't do so because, for purposes of this course, we won't need to get into those refinements. I've presented as much Graphish as you need to know for this book.

Presenting Real-World Data in Graphs

The previous discussion treated the Graphish terms that economists use in presenting models which focus on hypothetical relationships. Economists also use graphs in presenting actual economic data. Say, for example, that you want to show how exports have changed over time. Then you would place years on the horizontal axis (by convention) and exports on the vertical axis, as in Exhibit B5(a) and (b). Having done so, you have a couple of choices: you can draw a **line graph**—*a graph where the data are connected by a continuous line*; or you can make a **bar graph**—*a graph where the area under each point*

is filled in to look like a bar. Exhibit B5(a) shows a line graph and Exhibit B5(b) shows a bar graph.

Another type of graph is a **pie chart**—*a circle divided into "pie pieces," where the undivided pie represents the total amount and the pie pieces reflect the percentage of the whole pie that the various components make up.* This type of graph is useful in visually presenting how a total amount is divided. Exhibit B5(c) shows a pie chart, which happens to represent the division of grades on a test I gave. Notice that 5 percent of the students got As.

There are other types of graphs, but they're all variations on line and bar graphs and pie charts. Once you understand these three basic types of graphs, you shouldn't have any trouble understanding the other types.

Interpreting Graphs about the Real World

Understanding Graphish is important, because if you don't, you can easily misinterpret the meaning of graphs.

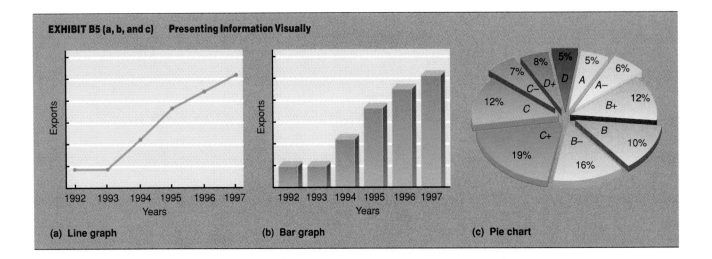

EXHIBIT B5 (a, b, and c)   Presenting Information Visually

(a) Line graph

(b) Bar graph

(c) Pie chart

For example, consider the two graphs in Exhibit B6(a) and (b). Which graph demonstrates the larger rise in income? If you said (a), you're wrong. The intervals in the vertical axes differ, and if you look carefully you'll see that the curves in both graphs represent the same combination of points. So when considering graphs, always make sure you understand the markings on the axes. Only then can you interpret the graph.

Let's now review what we've covered.

- A graph is a picture of points on a coordinate system in which the points denote relationships between numbers.
- A downward-sloping line represents an inverse relationship or a negative slope.
- An upward-sloping line represents a direct relationship or a positive slope.
- Slope is measured by rise over run, or a change of y (the number measured on the vertical axis) over a change in x (the number measured on the horizontal axis).
- The slope of a point on a nonlinear curve is measured by the rise over run of a line tangent to that point.
- At the maximum and minimum points of a nonlinear curve, the value of the slope is zero.
- In reading graphs, one must be careful to understand what's being measured on the vertical and horizontal axes.

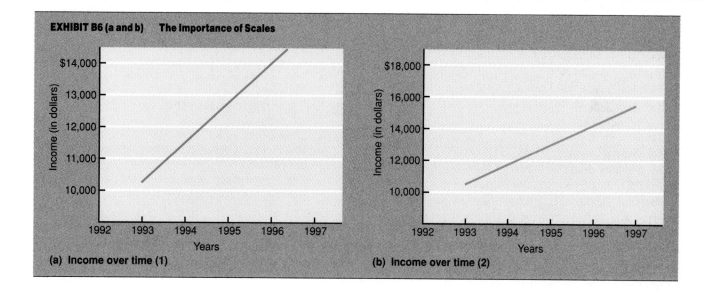

EXHIBIT B6 (a and b)   The Importance of Scales

(a) Income over time (1)

(b) Income over time (2)

KEY TERMS

bar graph *(28)*
coordinate system *(25)*
direct relationship *(26)*
graph *(24)*

interpolation assumption *(25)*
inverse relationship *(25)*
line graph *(28)*
linear curve *(25)*

nonlinear curve *(25)*
pie chart *(28)*
slope *(26)*

QUESTIONS FOR THOUGHT AND REVIEW

1. Create a coordinate space on graph paper and label the following points:
   a. (0, 5)
   b. (−5, −5)
   c. (2, −3)
   d. (−1, 1)

2. Graph the following costs per unit, and answer the questions that follow.

Horizontal Axis: Output	Vertical Axis: Cost per Unit
1	$30
2	20
3	12
4	6
5	2
6	6
7	12
8	20
9	30

a. Is the relationship between cost per unit and output linear or nonlinear? Why?
b. In what range in output is the relationship inverse? In what range in output is the relationship direct?
c. In what range in output is the slope negative? In what range in output is the slope positive?
d. What is the slope between 1 and 2 units?
3. Within a coordinate space, draw a line with:
   a. Zero slope.
   b. Infinite slope.
   c. Positive slope.
   d. Negative slope.
4. Calculate the slope of lines *a* to *e* in the following coordinate system.

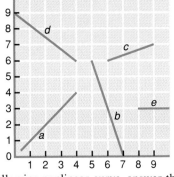

5. Given the following nonlinear curve, answer the following questions:

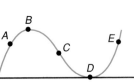

a. At what point(s) is the slope negative?
b. At what point(s) is the slope positive?
c. At what point(s) is the slope zero?
d. What point is the maximum? What point is the minimum?
6. State what type of graph or chart you would use to show the following real-world data:
   a. Interest rates from 1929 to 1997.
   b. Median income levels of various ethnic groups in the United States.
   c. Total federal expenditures by selected categories.
   d. Total costs of producing 100–800 shoes.

Two
The Economic Organization
of Society

*In capitalism man exploits man; in socialism it's the other way
'round.*

~ Abba Lerner

After reading this chapter, you should be able to:

1 Define capitalism and socialism.

2 Explain how capitalist and Soviet-style socialist economies solve the three central economic problems.

3 Explain how markets coordinate economic activities.

4 Demonstrate opportunity cost with a production possibility curve.

5 State the principle of increasing marginal opportunity cost.

6 Relate the concept of comparative advantage to the production possibility curve.

7 Explain why economic reasoning involves contextual reasoning that requires a knowledge of history and institutions.

The political and economic turmoil in the formerly socialist countries has been much in the news in the 1990s. And with good reason. The Soviet Union no longer exists; most republics of the former Soviet Union have forsaken socialism and are struggling to introduce market economies. Similarly, China is undergoing enormous change; it is introducing markets throughout its economy, even while the Communist party is maintaining political control.

These events involve some of the most far-reaching changes in the nature of economic systems that the world has seen since the 1930s—changes so major that some social scientists have called these developments "the end of history." Although such a sweeping statement is more than a tad too strong, the developments are certainly important. In this chapter I relate these recent developments to some broader issues involving economic systems and the workings of markets, and to a graphical tool—the production possibility curve.

In Chapter 1, I discussed how an **economic system**—*the set of economic institutions that coordinate individual wants in a society*—works via the interaction of three invisible forces: the invisible hand (economic forces), invisible foot (political and legal forces), and invisible handshake (social and historical forces). In this chapter I discuss those forces in reference to two economic systems, capitalism and socialism.

ECONOMIC SYSTEMS: CAPITALISM AND SOCIALISM

An economic system must coordinate individuals' wants and desires. It must solve the problems: What, How, and For whom.

Let's first, however, review the three main coordination problems an economic system must solve. Those three problems are:

1. What, and how much, to produce.
2. How to produce it.
3. For whom to produce it.

These three decisions that an economic system must make are necessarily vague, because people's wants are vague. But when people feel that an economic system isn't giving them what they want, the result isn't always so vague. Failure to solve the problems appropriately can result in a revolutionary change in the system, as recently happened in the former Soviet Union.

To illustrate the many ways scarce resources can be distributed, see "The Bonus Allocation Experiment," in Experiments in Teaching and in Understanding Economics.

Societies face a universal problem when trying to solve the three problems: Usually what individuals want to do isn't consistent with what "society" wants them to do. Society would often like people to consider what's good for society when making their individual decisions, and to agree that what society wants for them is what they want, too. For example, say society has garbage, and society determines that your neighborhood is the best place to set up a garbage dump. Even if you agree a garbage dump is needed, you probably won't want it in your neighborhood. This **NIMBY**—*Not In My Back Yard*—attitude—*a mindset of approving a project but not wanting it to be nearby*—has become familiar in the 1990s.

NIMBY   Not In My Back Yard. Phrase used by people who may approve of a project, but don't want to be near it.

Individual goals and social goals also conflict when decisions are being made about how much to produce and consume. Individuals generally like to consume much more than they like to produce. So society must provide incentives for the people who comprise it to produce more and consume less to alleviate that scarcity. A sure sign that an economic system isn't working is when people perceive that there are important things that need to be done, but are sitting around doing nothing because the system doesn't provide them with the incentive to do them.

The coordination problems faced by society are immense.

How hard is it to make the three decisions I've listed? Imagine for a moment the problem of living in a family: the fights, arguments, and questions that come up. "Do I have to do the dishes?" "Why can't I have piano lessons?" "Bobby got a new sweater. How come I didn't?" "Mom likes you best." Now multiply the size of the family by millions. The same fights, the same arguments, the same questions—only for society the problems are millions of times more complicated than for one family.

How are these complicated coordination problems solved? The two main economic systems the world has used in the past 50 years—capitalism and socialism—answer this question differently.

Capitalism

1a Capitalism is an economic system based on private property and the market. It gives private property rights to individuals, and relies on market forces to coordinate economic activity.

Capitalism is *an economic system based upon private property and the market in which, in principle, individuals decide how, what, and for whom to produce.* Under capitalism, individuals are encouraged to follow their own self-interest, while market forces of supply and demand are relied upon to coordinate those individual pursuits. Distribution of goods is to each individual according to his or her ability, effort, and inherited property.

Reliance upon market forces doesn't mean that political, social, and historical forces play no role in coordinating economic decisions. These other forces do influence how the market works. For example, for a market to exist, government must allocate and defend **private property rights**—*the control a private individual or firm has over an asset or a right.* The concept of private ownership must exist and must be accepted by individuals in society. When you say, "This car is mine," it means that it is unlawful for someone else to take it without your permission. If someone takes it without your permission, he or she is subject to punishment through the legal system.

Q–1: John, your study partner, is telling you that the best way to allocate property rights is through the market. How do you respond?

Markets work through a system of rewards and payments. If you do something, you get paid for doing that something; if you take something, you pay for that something. How much you get is determined by how much you give. This relationship seems fair to most people. But there are instances when it doesn't seem fair. Say someone is unable to work. Should that person get nothing? How about Joe down the street who was given $10 million by his parents? Is it fair that he gets lots of toys, like Corvettes and skiing trips to Aspen, and doesn't have to work, while the rest of us have to work 40 hours a week and maybe go to school at night?

I'll put those questions about fairness off at this point—they are very difficult questions. For now, all I want to present is the underlying concept of fairness that capitalism embodies: "Them that works, gets; them that don't, starve."[1] In capitalism, individuals are encouraged to follow their own self-interest.

In capitalist economies, individuals are free to do whatever they want as long as it's legal. The market is relied upon to see that what people want to get, and want to do, is consistent with what's available. Price is the mechanism through which people's desires are coordinated and goods are rationed. If there's not enough of something to go around, its price goes up; if more of something needs to get done, the price given to individuals willing to do it goes up. If something isn't wanted or doesn't need to be done, its price goes down. Under capitalism, fluctuations in prices play a central role in coordinating individuals' wants.

> When I discuss the role of self-interest in coordinating production, I take on the role of Gordon Gecko in the movie, *Wall Street,* and have students defend the "greed is good" speech.

Is the market a good way to coordinate individuals' activities? Much of the book will be devoted to answering that question. The answer that I, and most U.S. economists, come to is: Yes, it is a reasonable way. True, it has problems: The market can be unfair, mean, and arbitrary, and sometimes it is downright awful. Why then do economists support it? For the same reason that Oliver Wendell Holmes supported democracy—it is an awful system, but, based on experience with alternatives, it is better than all others we've thought of.

> *Under capitalism, fluctuations in prices coordinate individuals' wants.*

The primary debate among economists is not about using markets; it is about how markets should be structured, and whether they should be modified and adjusted by government regulation. Those are much harder questions, and on these questions, opinions differ enormously.

By almost all accounts, capitalism has been an extraordinarily successful economic system. Since much of this book will be devoted to explaining capitalist economies' success, and since capitalism is probably somewhat familiar to you already, I focus on socialism in this section.

Socialism

The view that markets are a reasonable way to organize society has not always been shared by all economists. Throughout history strong arguments have been made against markets. These arguments are both philosophical and practical. The philosophical argument against the market is that it brings out the worst in people—it glorifies greed. It encourages people to beat out others rather than to be cooperative. As an alternative some economists have supported **socialism**—which is, in theory, *an economic system based on individuals' good will toward others, not on their own self-interest;* in principle, society decides what, how, and for whom to produce.

Socialism in Theory   You can best understand the idea behind theoretical socialism by thinking about how decisions are made in a family. In most families, benevolent parents decide who gets what, based on the needs of each member of the family. When Sabin gets a new coat and his sister Sally doesn't, it's because Sabin needs a coat while Sally already has two coats that fit her and are in good condition. Victor may be slow as molasses, but from his family he still gets as much as his superefficient brother Jerry gets. In fact, Victor may get more than Jerry because he needs extra help.

> Q–2:   Are there any activities in a family that you believe should be allocated by a market? What characteristics do those activities have?

Markets have little role in most families. In my family, when food is placed on the table we don't bid on what we want, with the highest bidder getting the food. In my family, every person can eat all he or she wants, although if one child eats more

---

[1]How come the professor gets to use rotten grammar but screams when he sees rotten grammar in your papers? Well, that's fairness for you. Actually, I should say a bit more about writing style. All writers are expected to know correct grammar; if they don't, they don't deserve to be called writers. Once one knows grammar, one can individualize his or her writing style, breaking the rules of grammar where the meter and flow of the writing require it. In college you're still proving that you know grammar, so in papers handed in to your teacher, you shouldn't break the rules of grammar until you've proved to the teacher that you know them. Me, I've done lots of books, so my editors give me a bit more leeway than your teachers will give you.

than a fair share, that child gets a lecture from me on the importance of sharing. "Be thoughtful; be considerate. Think of others first," are lessons that many families try to teach.

In theory, socialism is an economic system that tries to organize society in the same way as these families are organized, trying to see that individuals get what they need. Socialism tries to take other people's needs into account and adjust people's own wants in accordance with what's available. In socialist economies, individuals are urged to look out for the other person; if individuals' inherent goodness won't make them consider the general good, government will make them. In contrast, a capitalist economy expects people to be selfish; it relies on markets and competition to direct that selfishness to the general good.[2]

Difficulty in Defining Socialism   Socialism means different things to different people. Thus, it is difficult to provide an unambiguous definition of socialism. For example, a number of Western European countries, such as Sweden, consider themselves democratic socialist countries. They, however, use markets and allow investment decisions to be determined by capitalist firms. Since they do so they are often considered as modified capitalist countries. In my view, they could be considered either, and if you keep in mind that economic systems are best viewed on a continuum, leaving ambiguity about what to call countries in the middle of the continuum, you will be able to see why both could be right.

In this chapter, to keep the contrasts sharp, I shall concentrate on definitions at the end of each continuum. Thus, when I talk about socialism I will be focusing on a particular type of socialism that is on the end of the continuum.

Socialism in Practice   Few economists argue directly in favor of greed. Most accept that it would be great if everyone wanted to be good to others. However, they point out that in practice, economic systems based upon people's goodwill have tended to break down. This is certainly true of the major countries that tried socialism starting in the 1900s. In practice socialist governments had to take a strong role in guiding the economy. Socialism became an economic system based on government ownership of the means of production, with economic activity governed by central planning. What I am describing as "socialism in practice" is often called **Soviet-style socialism**—*an economic system that uses administrative control or central planning to solve the coordination problems: what, how, and for whom.*

Defining Soviet-style socialism precisely is difficult because it embodied both political and economic features. I will concentrate on the economic features. Specifically, in a Soviet-style socialist economic system, government planning boards set society's goals and then directed individuals and firms as to how to achieve those goals.

In the 1980s, a number of countries had Soviet-style socialist economies. By the late 1990s most of these countries had rejected Soviet-style socialism, were experimenting with capitalism, and were searching for a third way of organizing society.

Why did these countries reject the economic system they had followed for almost 50 years? Some economists argue that Soviet-style socialism self-destructed because socialism did not offer acceptable solutions to the three central coordination problems. They claim socialism didn't provide individuals with incentives to produce enough. Soon, they claim, the world will have only one economic system: capitalism. Other economists argue that Soviet-style socialism deviated from the socialistic path. They argue that the failure of Soviet-style socialism is no reflection of the failure of true socialism because true socialism was never tried.

1b Socialism is, in theory, an economic system that tries to organize society in the same way as most families are organized—all people contribute what they can, and get what they need.

"Selections from 'Manifesto of the Communist Party,' " by Karl Marx and Friedrich Engels, in *Classic Readings in Economics.*

Q-3: Which would be more likely to attempt to foster individualism: socialism or capitalism?

Soviet-style socialism   *An economic system that uses administrative control or central planning to solve the coordination problems: what, how, and for whom.*

Q-4: What is the difference between socialism in theory and socialism in practice?

---

[2]As you probably surmised, the above distinction is too sharp. Even capitalist societies want people to be selfless, but not too selfless. Children in capitalist societies are generally taught to be selfless at least in dealing with friends and family. The difficulties parents and societies face is finding a midpoint between the two positions: selfless but not too selfless; selfish but not too selfish.

Central economic problem	Capitalism's solution	Soviet-style socialism's solution
What to produce?	What firms believe people want and will make the firm a profit.	What central planners believe socially beneficial.
How to produce?	Businesspeople decide how to produce efficiently, guided by their desire to make a profit.	Central planners decide, guided by what they believe is good for the country (ideally).
For whom to produce?	Distribution according to ability and inherited wealth.	Distribution according to individual's need (as determined by central planners).

EXHIBIT 1   Capitalism's and Soviet-style Socialism's Solutions to the Three Economic Problems

Let's briefly discuss how a Soviet-style socialist country, if one existed today, and a capitalist country might solve the what, how, and for whom problems. Consider two goods: designer jeans and whole wheat bread. Compared to their cost in the formerly socialist countries, in most capitalist societies designer jeans are relatively inexpensive while whole wheat bread is relatively expensive. Why? One reason is that central planners decide that designer jeans are frivolous luxury items, so they direct firms to produce few or no designer jeans, and to charge a high price for those they do produce. Similarly, they decide that whole wheat bread is good for people, so they direct firms to produce large quantities and to price it exceptionally low. Planners, not market forces, determine what, how, and for whom to produce.

The difference between Soviet-style socialist and capitalist economies is not that Soviet-style socialist economies are planned economies and capitalist economies are unplanned. Both economies involve planning. Planning simply involves deciding—before the production takes place—what will be produced, how to produce it, and for whom it will be produced. The differences between capitalism and Soviet-style socialism are in who does the planning, what the planners are trying to do, and how the plans are coordinated.

In capitalist countries, businesspeople do the planning. Businesspeople decide that they can sell designer jeans, Jazz Jackrabbit CDs, or economics textbooks. They target their likely customers and decide how much to produce and what price to charge. In Soviet-style socialist countries, government planners decide what people need and should have.

In an idealized capitalist society, businesses design their plans to maximize their profit; the market is relied upon to see that individual self-interest is consistent with society's interest. In an idealized socialist society, the government designs its plans to make society better. In a capitalist economy, coordination of plans is left to the workings of the market. In a Soviet-style socialist economy, coordination is done by government planners.

Exhibit 1 summarizes how capitalism and Soviet-style socialism solve the three central economic problems: what, how, and for whom.

Capitalism and socialism have not existed forever. Capitalism came into wide-spread existence in the mid-1700s; socialism came into existence in the early 1900s. Before capitalism and socialism other forms of economic systems existed, including **feudalism**—*an economic system in which traditions (the invisible handshake) rule*. In feudalism if your parents were serfs (small farmers who lived on a manor) you would be a serf. Feudalism dominated the Western world from about the 8th century to the 15th century.

Differences between Soviet-Style Socialism and Capitalism

"Individualism and Collectivism," by F.A. Hayek, in *Classic Readings in Economics*.

Q–5: The difference between capitalism and Soviet-style socialism is that Soviet-style socialism involves planning and capitalism does not. True or false? Why?

"The Chief Features of the Industrial Revolution," by Arnold Toynbee, in *Classic Readings in Economics*.

2 Exhibit 1 shows capitalism's and Soviet-style socialism's solutions to planning problems.

Evolving Economic Systems[3]

Feudalism *An economic system in which traditions rule.*

For a consideration of the similarities between evolution of economic and biological systems, see Chapter 3 in *Case Studies in Economics*.

---

[3]The appendix to this chapter traces the development of economic systems from feudalism to mercantilism to capitalism to socialism to modern–day forms of welfare capitalism in a bit more detail.

ADDED DIMENSION   TRADITION AND TODAY'S ECONOMY

In a tradition-based society, the invisible handshake (the social and cultural forces embodied in history) gives a society inertia (a tendency to resist change) that predominates over economic and political forces.

"Why did you do it that way?"

"Because that's the way we've always done it."

Tradition-based societies had markets, but those were peripheral, not central, to economic life. In feudal times what was produced, how it was produced, and for whom it was produced were primarily decided by tradition.

In today's U.S. economy, the market plays the central role in economic decisions. But that doesn't mean that tradition is dead. As I said in Chapter 1, tradition still plays a significant role in today's society, and, in many aspects of society, tradition still overwhelms the invisible hand. Consider the following:

1. The persistent view that women should be homemakers rather than factory workers, consumers rather than producers.

2. The raised eyebrows when a man is introduced as a nurse, secretary, homemaker, or member of any other profession conventionally identified as women's work.

3. Society's unwillingness to permit the sale of individuals or body organs.

4. Parents' willingness to care for their children without financial compensation.

Each of these tendencies reflects tradition's influence in Western society. Some are so deep-rooted that we see them as self-evident. Some of tradition's effects we like; others we don't—but we often take them for granted. Economic forces may work against these traditions, but the fact that they're still around indicates the continued strength of tradition in our market economy.

Mercantilism   An economic system in which government doles out the rights to undertake economic activities.

Douglass North, an economic historian who has emphasized the central role that institutions play in the economy.   *Reuters/ Bettmann.*

Ask your students to suggest alternative coordination mechanisms to self-interest. This usually starts great discussions.

Throughout the feudalistic period merchants and artisans (small hand manufacturers) grew in importance and wealth and, eventually, their increased importance led to a change in the economic system from feudalism to **mercantilism**—*an economic system in which government (the invisible foot) determines the what, how, and for whom decisions by doling out the rights to undertake certain economic decisions.* Mercantilism remained the dominant economic system until the 1700s when the **Industrial Revolution**—*a time when technology and machines rapidly modernized industrial production and mass produced goods replaced handmade goods*—led to a decrease in power of small producers, an increase in power of capitalists, and eventually to a revolution instituting capitalism as the dominant economic system.

Some economists prefer to call the system that evolved from mercantilism a *market economic system* rather than capitalism. Their justification for doing so is that the key element of the new system is not the power of the capitalists but the central reliance on markets to coordinate economic activities. They argue that the market system is not fundamentally changed if the power shifts from a small group of capitalists to corporations, or even to nonprofit organizations, as long as the market remains central. I agree with their argument, but I use the term capitalism because of its widespread usage, not because I believe that capitalist control is the central element of our modern market economy.

I mention feudalism and mercantilism because aspects of both continue in economies today. For example, governments in Japan and Germany play significant roles in directing their economies. Their economic systems are sometimes referred to as *neomercantilist economies.*

The Need for Coordination in an Economic System   As economic systems evolved from mercantilism to a market economy, many people asked: Who will coordinate economic activities if the government does not? It was in answering this question that modern economics developed. To answer that question, a British moral philosopher named Adam Smith developed, in his famous book *The Wealth of Nations* (1776), the concept of the invisible hand, and used it to explain how markets could coordinate the economy without the active involvement of government. Smith wrote:

THE RISE OF MARKETS IN PERSPECTIVE

Back in the Middle Ages, markets developed spontaneously. "You have something I want; I have something you want. Let's trade" is a basic human attitude we see in all aspects of life. Even children quickly get into trading: chocolate ice cream for vanilla, two Zebots for a ride on a motor scooter. Markets institutionalize such trading by providing a place where people know they can go to trade. New markets are continually being formed. Today there are markets for baseball cards, pork bellies (which become bacon and pork chops), rare coins, and so on.

Throughout history, societies have tried to prevent some markets from operating because they feel those markets are ethically wrong or have undesirable side effects. Societies have the power to prevent markets, to make some kinds of markets illegal. In parts of the United States, the addictive drug market, the baby market, and the sex market, to name a few, are illegal. In socialist countries, markets in a much wider range of goods (such as clothes, cars, and soft drinks) and activities (such as private business for individual profit) have been illegal.

But, even if a society prevents the market from operating, society cannot escape the invisible hand. If there's excess supply, there will be downward pressure on prices; if there's excess demand, there will be upward pressure on prices. To maintain an equilibrium in which the quantity supplied does not equal the quantity demanded, a society needs a strong force to prevent the invisible hand from working. In the Middle Ages, that strong force was religion. The Church told people that if they got too far into the market mentality—if they followed their self-interest—they'd go to Hell.

Until recently, in socialist society the state provided the preventive force. The educational system in socialist countries emphasized a more communal set of values. They taught students that a member of socialist society does not try to take advantage of other human beings but, rather, lives by the philosophy "From each according to his ability; to each according to his need."

For whatever reason—whether it be that true socialism wasn't really tried, or that people's self-interest is too strong—the "from each according to his ability; to each according to his need" approach didn't work in socialist countries. They have switched (some say succumbed) to greater reliance on the market.

Man has almost constant occasion for the help of his brethren, and it is in vain for him to expect it from their benevolence only. He will be more likely to prevail, if he can interest their self-love in his favour, and show them that it is for their own advantage to do for him what he requires of them. Whoever offers to another a bargain of any kind proposes to do this. Give me that which I want, and you shall have that which you want, is the meaning of every such offer; and it is in this manner that we obtain from one another the far greater part of those good offices which we stand in need of. It is not from the benevolence of the butcher, the brewer, or the baker, that we expect our dinner, but from their regard to their own interest. We address ourselves, not to their humanity but to their self-love, and never talk to them of our own necessities but of their advantages.

Smith argued that the market's invisible hand would guide suppliers' actions toward the general good. No government coordination was necessary.

Evolutionary Changes within Systems   Revolutionary shifts that give rise to new economic systems are not the only way economic systems change. Systems also evolve. For example, both capitalism and socialism have changed over the years, evolving with changes in the three invisible forces. A brief look at their evolution will give us a good sense of the struggle among the invisible forces that dominate our lives. In the 1930s, during the Great Depression, capitalist countries integrated a number of what might be called socialist institutions into their existing institutions. Distribution of goods was no longer, even in theory, only according to ability; need also played a role. Governments began to play a larger role in the economy, taking control over some of the who, what, and for whom decisions. For example, most capitalist nations established welfare and social security systems, providing an economic safety net for people whose incomes could not fill their needs. Capitalism became what is sometimes called **welfare capitalism**—*an economic system in which the market is allowed to operate but in which government plays dual roles in determining distribution and making the what, how, and for whom decisions.* In some countries the governments

3 Markets coordinate economic activity by using the price mechanism to direct individuals' self-interest into society's interest.

"Of the Principle Which Gives Occasion to the Division of Labour," by Adam Smith, in *Classic Readings in Economics.*

Economic systems are always evolving with changes in the three invisible forces.

It is interesting to ask students to think about socialist institutions that are integrated into our capitalist economy.

Welfare capitalism   *Economic system in which the market operates but government regulates markets significantly.*

"Can Capitalism Survive?" by
Joseph Schumpeter, in *Classic Readings in Economics.*

played such an important role that they could reasonably be called market-modified socialist economies. Some countries today, such as Sweden, call their economic system a socialist, rather than a capitalist, system.

In the 1980s, in socialist countries the reverse process took place: socialism integrated capitalist institutions into its existing institutions. By the 1990s, most of the formerly socialist countries had given up Soviet-style socialism and began to let the market determine the what, how, and for whom decisions. Some government activities in former Socialist economies were privatized—sold to the private sector. Similarly in the 1990s, in capitalist countries governments became even more market oriented and tried to pull back their involvement in the market in favor of private enterprise. For example, governments in Western Europe and the United States tried to eliminate aspects of their welfare systems. In the 1980s and 1990s economic systems have moved more toward the capitalist end of the spectrum.

I sometimes assign students countries and have them bring the class up to date on developments in their assigned country.

A Blurring of the Distinction between Capitalism and Socialism   The result of these recent changes has been a blending of economic systems and a blurring of the distinctions between capitalism and socialism. China still ostensibly has a socialist system, but a recent trip to China convinced me that it is a very capitalist type of socialism. If the trend toward use of market mechanisms in socialist countries continues, in the 21st century only one general type of economic structure may exist. It won't be pure socialism and it won't be pure capitalism. It will be a blend of the two.

THE PRODUCTION POSSIBILITY CURVE: ECONOMIC REASONING, TRADE, AND ECONOMIC SYSTEMS

The choices that a society must make are often presented in terms of a production possibility curve. The production possibility curve is related to the concept of opportunity cost that you were introduced to in Chapter 1. It is a tool that can nicely be used to discuss choices societies must make about economic systems. Applying economic reasoning outside of historical and institutional context, however, has difficulties and I'll discuss these difficulties too. To illustrate the power of these tools I conclude the chapter with a discussion of the ongoing debate in the United States between Republicans and Democrats about economic policy. I show how Republican and Democratic positions are both supportable by economic reasoning, but that the presentations of both positions often miss the central economic insight that there ain't no such thing as a free lunch.

The Production Possibility Table

A production possibility table lists a choice's opportunity costs.

As I discussed in the last chapter the concept of opportunity costs—every decision has a cost in forgone opportunities—lies at the center of economic reasoning. Opportunity cost can be seen numerically with a **production possibility table**—*a table that lists a choice's opportunity costs by summarizing what alternative outputs you can achieve with your inputs.* An **output** is simply *a result of an activity,* and an **input** is *what you put into a production process to achieve an output.* For example, your grade in a course is an output and your study time is an input.

Let's present the study time/grades example numerically. Say you have exactly 20 hours a week to devote to two courses: economics and history. (So, maybe I'm a bit optimistic.) Grades are given numerically and you know that the following relationships exist: if you study 20 hours in economics, you'll get a grade of 100, 18 hours—94, and so forth.[4]

Let's say that the best you can do in history is a 98 with 20 hours of study a week; 19 hours of study guarantees you a 96, and so on. The production possibility table in Exhibit 2(a) shows the highest combination of grades you can get with various allocations of the 20 hours available for studying the two subjects. One possibility is

Much of what managers of firms do is make decisions that involve trade-offs like those described by the production possibility table.

---

[4]Throughout the book I'll be presenting numerical examples to help you understand the concepts. The numbers I choose are often arbitrary. After all, you have to choose something. As an exercise, you might choose different numbers than mine, numbers that apply to your own life, and work out the argument using those numbers. For students who don't want to make up their own numbers, the study guide has examples with different numbers.

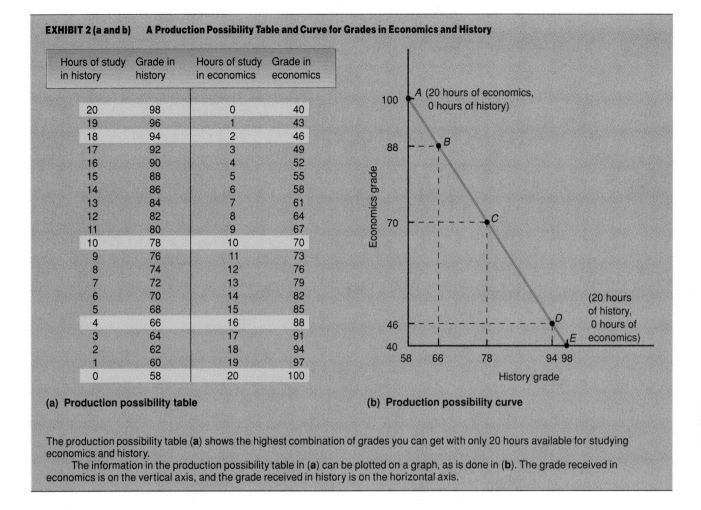

EXHIBIT 2 (a and b)   A Production Possibility Table and Curve for Grades in Economics and History

Hours of study in history	Grade in history	Hours of study in economics	Grade in economics
20	98	0	40
19	96	1	43
18	94	2	46
17	92	3	49
16	90	4	52
15	88	5	55
14	86	6	58
13	84	7	61
12	82	8	64
11	80	9	67
10	78	10	70
9	76	11	73
8	74	12	76
7	72	13	79
6	70	14	82
5	68	15	85
4	66	16	88
3	64	17	91
2	62	18	94
1	60	19	97
0	58	20	100

(a) Production possibility table

(b) Production possibility curve

The production possibility table (**a**) shows the highest combination of grades you can get with only 20 hours available for studying economics and history.

The information in the production possibility table in (**a**) can be plotted on a graph, as is done in (**b**). The grade received in economics is on the vertical axis, and the grade received in history is on the horizontal axis.

getting 100 in economics and 58 in history. Another is getting 70 in economics and 78 in history.

Notice that the opportunity cost of studying one subject rather than the other is embodied in the production possibility table. The information in the table comes from experience: we are assuming that you've discovered that if you transfer an hour of study from economics to history, you'll lose 3 points on your grade in economics and gain 2 points in history. Thus, the opportunity cost of a 2-point rise in your history grade is a 3-point decrease in your economics grade.

Since this is the first graph you will present in class, work through it deliberately. Pay special attention to questions about the law of diminishing marginal opportunity costs. In my experience, this is an area of difficulty for students.

The information in the production possibility table can also be presented graphically in a diagram called a production possibility curve. A **production possibility curve** is *a curve measuring the maximum combination of outputs that can be obtained from a given number of inputs*. It is a graphical presentation of the opportunity cost concept.

A production possibility curve is created from a production possibility table by mapping the table in a two-dimensional graph. I've taken the information from the table in Exhibit 2(a) and mapped it into Exhibit 2(b). The history grade is mapped, or plotted, on the horizontal axis; the economics grade is on the vertical axis.

As you can see from the bottom row of Exhibit 2(a), if you study economics for all 20 hours and study history for 0 hours, you'll get grades of 100 in economics and 58 in history. Point *A* in Exhibit 2(b) represents that choice. If you study history for all 20 hours and study economics for 0 hours, you'll get a 98 in history and a 40 in

The Production Possibility Curve

Production possibility curve *A curve measuring the maximum combination of outputs that can be obtained from a given number of inputs.*

Video Series, Economics U$A: Markets: Do They Meet Our Needs? Segments 2.1-2.3

For computer exercises involving opportunity cost and trade, use module "Comparative Advantage and Trade" in *Micro/Macro Interactive.*

4 Remember this graph:

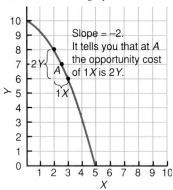

The slope tells you the opportunity cost of good *X* in terms of good *Y.* You have to give up 2*Y* to get 1*X* when you're around point *A.*

You may want to ask your students to write a paragraph explaining the principle of increasing marginal opportunity costs after you have discussed it.

economics. Point *E* represents that choice. Points *B, C,* and *D* represent three possible choices between these two extremes.

Notice that the production possibility curve slopes downward from left to right. That means that there is an inverse relationship (a trade-off) between grades in economics and grades in history. The better the grade in economics, the worse the grade in history, and vice versa. That downward slope represents the opportunity cost concept—you get more of one benefit only if you get less of another benefit.

The production possibility curve not only represents the opportunity cost concept, it also measures the opportunity cost. For example, in Exhibit 2(b), say you want to raise your grade in history from a 94 to a 98 (move from point *D* to point *E*). The opportunity cost of that 4-point increase would be a 6-point decrease in your economics grade, from 46 to 40.

To summarize, the production possibility curve demonstrates that:

1. There is a limit to what you can achieve, given the existing institutions, resources, and technology.
2. Every choice you make has an opportunity cost. You can get more of something only by giving up something else.

Increasing Marginal Opportunity Cost I chose an unchanging trade-off in the study time/grade example because it made the initial presentation of the production possibility curve easier. Since, by assumption, you could always trade two points on your history grade for three points on your economics grade, the production possibility curve was a straight line. But is that the way we'd expect reality to be? Probably not. The production possibility curve is generally bowed outward, as in Exhibit 3(b).

Why? Because some resources are better suited for the production of some kinds of goods than they are for the production of some other kinds of goods. To make the answer more concrete, let's talk specifically about society's choice between defense spending (guns) and spending on domestic needs (butter). The graph in Exhibit 3(b) is derived from the table in Exhibit 3(a).

EXHIBIT 3 (a and b) A Production Possibility Table and Curve

The table in (a) contains information on the trade-off between the production of guns and butter. This information has been plotted on the graph in (b). Notice in (b) that as we move along the production possibility curve from *A* to *F,* trading butter for guns, we get fewer and fewer guns for each pound of butter given up. That is, the opportunity cost of choosing guns over butter increases as we increase the production of guns. This concept is called the principle of increasing marginal opportunity cost. The phenomenon occurs because some resources are better suited for the production of butter than for the production of guns, and we use the better ones first.

% of resources devoted to production of guns	Number of guns	% of resources devoted to production of butter	Pounds of butter	Row
0	0	100	15	A
20	4	80	14	B
40	7	60	12	C
60	9	40	9	D
80	11	20	5	E
100	12	0	0	F

(a) Production possibility table

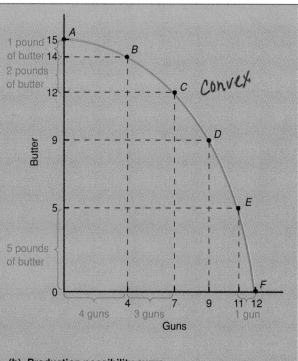

(b) Production possibility curve

Let's see what the shape of the curve means in terms of numbers. Let's start with society producing only butter (point *A*). Giving up a little butter (one pound) initially gains us a lot of guns (4), moving us to point *B*. The next two pounds of butter we give up gains us slightly fewer guns (point *C*). If we continue to trade butter for guns, we find that at point *D* we gain almost no guns from giving up a pound of butter. The opportunity cost of choosing guns over butter increases as we increase the production of guns.

The reason the opportunity cost of guns increases as we consume more guns is that some resources are relatively better suited to producing guns, while others are relatively better suited to producing butter. Put in economists' terminology, some resources have a **comparative advantage** over other resources—*the ability to be better suited to the production of one good than to the production of another good*. In this example, some resources have a comparative advantage over other resources in the production of butter, while other resources have a comparative advantage in the production of guns.

When making small amounts of guns and large amounts of butter, in the production of those guns we use the resources whose comparative advantage is in the production of guns. All other resources are devoted to producing butter. Because the resources used in producing guns aren't good at producing butter, we're not giving up much butter to get those guns. As we produce more and more of a good, we must use resources whose comparative advantage is in the production of the other good—in this case, more suitable for producing butter than for producing guns. As we remove resources from the production of butter to get the same additional amount of guns, we must give up increasing amounts of butter. An alternative way of saying this is that the opportunity cost of producing guns becomes greater as the production of guns increases. As we continue to increase the production of guns, the opportunity cost of more guns becomes very high because we're using resources to produce guns that have a strong comparative advantage for producing butter.

Let's consider two more specific examples. Say the United States suddenly decides it needs more wheat. To get additional wheat, we must devote additional land to growing it. This land is less fertile than the land we're already using, so our additional output of wheat per acre of land devoted to wheat will be less. Alternatively, consider the use of relief pitchers in a baseball game. If only one relief pitcher is needed, the manager sends in the best; if he must send in a second one, then a third, and even a fourth, the likelihood of winning the game decreases.

For many of the choices society must make, opportunity costs tend to increase as we choose more and more of an item. The reason is that resources are not easily adaptable from the production of one good to the production of another. Such a phenomenon about choice is so common, in fact, that it has acquired a name: the **principle of increasing marginal opportunity cost**. That principle states:

In order to get more of something, one must give up ever-increasing quantities of something else.

In other words, initially the opportunity costs of an activity are low, but they increase the more we concentrate on that activity. Sometimes this law is called the flowerpot law because, if it didn't hold, all the world's food could be grown in a flowerpot. But it can't be. As we add more seeds to a fixed amount of soil, there won't be enough nutrients or room for the roots, so output per seed decreases.

Comparative Advantage, Trade, and the Production Possibility Curve

The same comparative advantage argument I just used to explain the shape of the production possibility curve can be used to show how trade (and hence how the markets that facilitate that trade) make society better off. To keep the analysis simple, let's consider two individuals. Sunder is a whiz at creative writing; he can turn out four creative writing papers a day or one economics paper a day, or any proportional combination thereof. Ti is an economics whiz; she can turn out four economics papers

---

Q–6: If no resource had a comparative advantage in the production of any good, what would the shape of the production possibility curve be? Why?

Comparative advantage   *To be better suited to the production of one good than to the production of another good.*

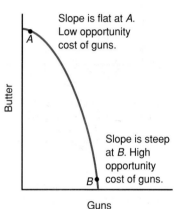

Slope is flat at *A*. Low opportunity cost of guns.

Slope is steep at *B*. High opportunity cost of guns.

Guns

Remember: when the slope is flat, there's a low opportunity cost of guns (a high opportunity cost of butter). When the slope is steep, there's a high opportunity cost of guns (a low opportunity cost of butter).

5 The principle of increasing marginal opportunity cost states that opportunity costs increase the more you concentrate on the activity. In order to get more of something, one must give up ever-increasing quantities of something else.

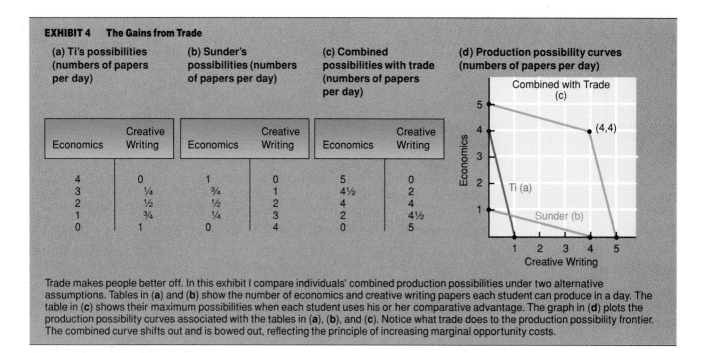

EXHIBIT 4   The Gains from Trade

(a) Ti's possibilities (numbers of papers per day)

Economics	Creative Writing
4	0
3	¼
2	½
1	¾
0	1

(b) Sunder's possibilities (numbers of papers per day)

Economics	Creative Writing
1	0
¾	1
½	2
¼	3
0	4

(c) Combined possibilities with trade (numbers of papers per day)

Economics	Creative Writing
5	0
4½	2
4	4
2	4½
0	5

(d) Production possibility curves (numbers of papers per day)

Trade makes people better off. In this exhibit I compare individuals' combined production possibilities under two alternative assumptions. Tables in (a) and (b) show the number of economics and creative writing papers each student can produce in a day. The table in (c) shows their maximum possibilities when each student uses his or her comparative advantage. The graph in (d) plots the production possibility curves associated with the tables in (a), (b), and (c). Notice what trade does to the production possibility frontier. The combined curve shifts out and is bowed out, reflecting the principle of increasing marginal opportunity costs.

For a classroom experiment, see "A Demonstration of Gains from Trade," in *Experiments in Teaching and in Understanding Economics.*

Q–7: Show, using production possibility curves, that Steve and Sarah would be better off specializing in their baking activities, and then trading, rather than baking only for themselves, given the following production possibility tables.

(a) Steve's Production per Day		(b) Sarah's Production per Day	
Loaves of Bread	Dozens of Cookies	Loaves of Bread	Dozens of Cookies
4	0	4	0
3	2	3	1
2	4	2	2
1	6	1	3
0	8	0	4

a day or one creative writing paper a day, or any proportional combination thereof. Their respective paper-writing production possibility tables and curves per day are shown in Exhibit 4. The blue line represents Sunder's production possibility curve; the red line represents Ti's production possibility curve.

Sunder and Ti's teacher has given each of them a weekly assignment to do four economics and four creative writing papers. Ti spends four days writing four creative writing papers and one day writing four economics papers. Sunder does the reverse. This will leave no time for partying.

The following week their teacher allows Ti and Sunder to collaborate on their assignment. The team must turn in eight creative writing papers and eight economics papers. Ti and Sunder will receive a collective grade. The question facing Ti and Sunder is how to divide up the work. If they work as they did the week before, it will take each of them all week.

Fortunately Ti is taking an economics course and has just learned about comparative advantage. She points out to Sunder that they can do much better if they avail themselves of their comparative advantages. Since Ti has a comparative advantage in economics and Sunder has a comparative advantage in creative writing, it pays for them to specialize in their respective strengths. Let's say they do that. Their new production possibility table per day is shown in the Exhibit 4(c). They both specialize, and in one day the team can turn out four economics papers and four creative writing papers. Now it takes them only two days to do their assignment, leaving them three days to party (or to study for other courses, or to work at a part-time job to pay for their education).

Note two things about the combined production possibility curve shown in Exhibit 4(d). First, it is considerably further out than what the combination of the individual production possibility curves would be. When individuals trade, using their comparative advantages, their combined production possibility curve shifts out. The combined possibility curve more than doubles each of their individual production possibility curves, so when the gains from trade are divided up, individuals can reach points beyond their individual production possibility curve. The shifting out of the production possibility curve is a geometric representation of the gains to trade. Second, the curve is bowed outward, like the production possibility curve we drew above in Exhibit 3(b). That outward bow comes from using comparative advantage.

The above examples give a visual sense of the power of markets to make people better off. Markets allow people to trade—to utilize their comparative advantages—and thereby to improve society's combined production possibility curve. Adam Smith, the founder of modern economics, saw this aspect of markets and trade as what differentiated human beings from animals. He wrote:

> This division of labour, from which so many advantages are derived, is not originally the effect of any human wisdom, which foresees and intends that general opulence to which it gives occasion. It is the necessary, though very slow and gradual consequence of a certain propensity in human nature which has in view no such extensive utility; the propensity to truck, barter, and exchange one thing for another. . . . [This propensity] is common to all men, and to be found in no other race of animals, which seem to know neither this nor any other species of contracts. . . . Nobody ever saw a dog make a fair and deliberate exchange of one bone for another with another dog. Nobody ever saw one animal by its gestures and natural cries signify to another, this is mine, that yours; I am willing to give this for that.

The argument that the division of labor and trade makes individuals better off also holds for countries. Trade shifts out countries' production possibility curves, making them better off. There are, of course, exceptions to this proposition. (Remember all models are dependent on the assumptions of the model.) These exceptions are considered later in microeconomics courses when trade is looked at in more depth. But the general argument that trade and markets make people better off because they allow individuals and economies to assert their comparative advantages carries through and is a primary reason why economists generally support markets.

Efficiency We would like, if possible, to get as much output as possible from a given amount of inputs or resources. That's **productive efficiency**—*achieving as much output as possible from a given amount of inputs or resources.* We would like to be efficient. The production possibility curve helps us see what is meant by productive efficiency. Consider point *A* in Exhibit 5(a), which is inside the production possibility curve. If we are producing at point *A,* we are using all our resources to produce 4 guns and 6 pounds of butter. Point *A* represents **inefficiency**—*getting less output from inputs which, if devoted to some other activity, would produce more output.* That's because with the same inputs we could be getting either 4 guns and 8 pounds of butter (point *B*) or 6 pounds of butter and 6 guns (point *C*). As long as we prefer more to less, both points *B* and *C* represent **efficiency**—*achieving a goal using as few inputs as possible.* We always want to move our production out to a point on the production possibility curve.

Why not move out farther, to point *D*? If we could, we would, but by definition the production possibility curve represents the most output we can get from a certain combination of inputs. So point *D* is unattainable, given our resources and technology.

When technology improves, when more resources are discovered, or when the economic institutions get better at fulfilling our wants, we can get more output with the same inputs. What this means is that when technology or an economic institution improves, the entire production possibility curve shifts outward from *AB* to *CD* in Exhibit 5(b). How the production possibility curve shifts outward depends on how the technology improves. For example, say we become more efficient in producing guns, but not more efficient in producing butter. Then the production possibility curve shifts outward to *AC* in Exhibit 5(c).

Policies that costlessly shift the production possibility curve outward are the most desirable policies because they don't require us to decrease our consumption of one good to get more of another. Alas, such policies are the most infrequent. Improving

6 When individuals trade using their comparative advantages, their combined production possibility curve shifts out.

Markets allow specialization and the division of labor. They allow individuals to develop their comparative advantages, thereby increasing the production possibilities of society.

Efficiency involves achieving a goal as cheaply as possible. Efficiency has meaning only in relation to a specified goal.

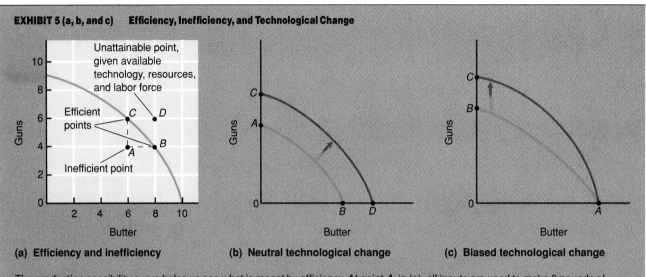

EXHIBIT 5 (a, b, and c)   Efficiency, Inefficiency, and Technological Change

(a) Efficiency and inefficiency

(b) Neutral technological change

(c) Biased technological change

The production possibility curve helps us see what is meant by efficiency. At point *A*, in (**a**), all inputs are used to make 6 pounds of butter and 4 guns. This is inefficient since there is a way to obtain more of one without giving up any of the other, that is, to obtain 6 pounds of butter and 6 guns (point *C*) or 4 guns and 8 pounds of butter (point *B*). All points inside the production possibility curve are inefficient. With fixed inputs and given technology, we cannot go beyond the production possibility curve. For example, point *D* is unattainable.

A technological change that improves production techniques will shift the production possibility curve outward, as shown in both (**b**) and (**c**). How the curve shifts outward depends on how technology improves. For example, if we become more efficient in the production of both guns and butter, the curve will shift out as in (**b**). If we become more efficient in producing guns, but not in producing butter, then the curve will shift as in (**c**).

---

technology and institutions and discovering more resources are not costless; generally there's an opportunity cost of doing so that must be taken into account.

Q–8: Your firm is establishing a trucking business in Saudi Arabia. The firm has noticed that women are paid much less than men in Saudi Arabia, and the firm suggests that hiring women would be more efficient than hiring men. What should you respond?

An increase in output that goes to only one person and not to anyone else would not necessarily be efficient.

Video Series, Economics U\$A: Resources and Scarcity Segment 1.1, 1.2

Distribution and Production Efficiency   In discussing the production possibility curve, I avoided questions of distribution: Who gets what? But such questions cannot be ignored in real-world situations. Specifically, if the method of production is tied to a particular income distribution and choosing one method will help some people but hurt others, we can't say that one method of production is efficient and the other inefficient, even if one method produces more total output than the other. As I stated above, the term efficiency involves achieving a goal as cheaply as possible. The term has meaning only in regard to a specified goal. Say, for example, that we have a society of ascetics who believe that consumption above some minimum is immoral. For such a society, producing more for less (productive efficiency) would not be efficient since consumption is not its goal. Or say that we have a society that cares that what is produced is fairly distributed. An increase in output that goes to only one person and not to anyone else would not necessarily be efficient.

In our society, however, most people prefer more to less, and many policies have relatively small distributional consequences. On the basis of the assumption that more is better than less, economists use their own kind of shorthand for such policies and talk about efficiency as identical to productive efficiency—increasing total output. But it's important to remember the assumption under which that shorthand is used: that the distributional effects that accompany the policy aren't undesirable and that we, as a society, prefer more output.

Some Examples of Shifts in the Production Possibility Curve

All decisions must be made in context.

To see whether you understand the production possibility curve, let us now consider some situations that can be shown with the production possibility curve. In Exhibit 6 I demonstrate four situations with production possibility curves. Below Exhibit 6, I list five situations. To test your understanding of the curve, match the situation to the curve (a graph can match more than one situation).

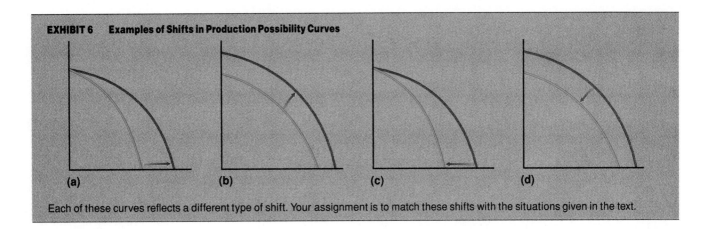

EXHIBIT 6   Examples of Shifts in Production Possibility Curves

(a)   (b)   (c)   (d)

Each of these curves reflects a different type of shift. Your assignment is to match these shifts with the situations given in the text.

1. A new genetic material is found that doubles the speed at which agricultural goods grow.
2. Nanites (micro machines) are perfected that lower the cost of manufactured goods.
3. A meteoroid hits the world and destroys half the natural resources.
4. A world trade war erupts and trade restrictions grow enormously.
5. Soviet-style socialist countries give up on the socialist system and switch to a market system.

The correct answers are:
1–a; 2–a; 3–d; 4–d; 5–d.
If you got them all right, you are well on your way to understanding the production possibility curve.

Q–9: When a natural disaster hits the midwestern United States, where most of the U.S. butter is produced, what happens to the U.S. production possibility curve for guns and butter?

If I have time, I discuss recent developments in biotechnology and communications (the information superhighway), and speculate on the effect these developments will have on our economy. This usually generates a good discussion. For example, what implications does cloning have for Social Security?

Some of you may have rightly wondered about one of the answers in the above examples, specifically the last one. (If you wondered about others, a review is in order for you.) The appropriate wondering is the following: According to what I have said previously, the shift by socialist countries toward markets should shift the production possibility curve out, not in; so wouldn't the correct answer be that it shifts the production possibility curve out because it introduces markets that allow trade?

The answer to that question is: Yes, it should *eventually* shift the production possibility curve out. But in the short and medium run (i.e., within 5 to 10 years) the change will shift it in. The explanation of why this is so brings us back to our discussion of economic systems and allows me to tie together that discussion with the discussion of opportunity costs as represented by the production possibility curve.

The production possibility curve presents choices in a timeless fashion and therefore makes opportunity costs clear-cut; there are two choices, one with a higher cost and one with a lower cost. The reality is that most choices are dependent on other choices; they are made sequentially with a time dimension. With sequential choices you cannot simply reverse your decision. Once you have started on a path, to take another path you have to return to the beginning. Thus following one path often lowers the costs of options along that path, but it raises the costs of options along another path.

Such sequential decisions can best be seen within the framework of a **decision tree**—*a visual description of sequential choices*. A decision tree is shown in Exhibit 7.

The Production Possibility Curve and Economic Systems

This institutional interpretation of the production possibility curve is slightly different than that presented in some other texts. This institutional approach is more consistent with Marshall's partial equilibrium approach than is the noninstitutional approach, and hence is consistent with this text's focus on the importance of institutions.

The production possibility curve presents choices in a timeless fashion, but most choices are dependent upon previous choices.

Decision tree *A visual description of sequential choices.*

EXHIBIT 7   A Decision Tree

Decisions are often made sequentially. The systemic and institutional decisions (at low levels of the decision tree) place one on one branch of the decision tree and preclude, or at least significantly increase the costs of, other decisions.

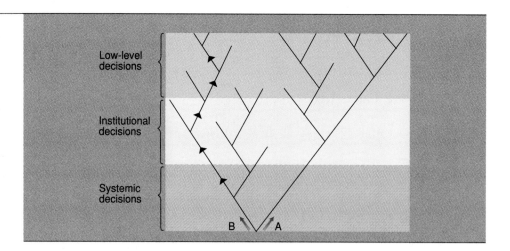

Q–10: Using the pursuit of an undergraduate college degree as a framework, give an example of each of the following: systemic choice, institutional choice, low-level choice. Which of the choices will most likely be the most costly?

In my class, I use this section to introduce some of the ideas about complexity and the work at the Sante Fe Institution on complex systems.

7 Because decisions are contextual, what the production possibility curve for a particular decision looks like depends on the existing institutions, and the analysis can be applied only in that institutional and historical context.

Once you make the initial decision to go on path A, the costs of path B options become higher; they include the costs of reversing your path and starting over. The decision trees of life have thousands of branches; each decision you make rules out other paths, or at least increases your costs highly. (Remember that day you decided to blow off your homework? That decision may have changed your future life.)

I find it helpful sometimes to divide decisions into three levels—low level, institutional, and systemic choices, as I have done in Exhibit 7. Low-level choices are choices that involve general acceptance of the path one has taken. (Do I spend an extra hour on economics rather than on creative writing?) Institutional choices involve choices that make major institutional changes. (Do I bag this college and transfer to a different college?) Systemic choices are fundamental choices that determine the set of institutional and low-level choices available. (Do I drop college entirely, run off with Kasey, and live on a desert island?) Low-level decisions are made sequentially and are based upon the institutional and systemic choices already made. That means that each time you make an institutional or systemic choice, it changes your production possibility curve—shifting it out in some dimensions and shifting it in in others—but initially the overall production possibility curve shifts in as you learn to operate within the new institution or new system.

Another way of putting this same point is that all *decisions are made in context*: What makes sense in one context may not make sense in another. For example, say you're answering the question: Would society be better off if students were taught literature, or if they were taught agriculture? The answer depends on the institutional context. In a developing country whose goal is large increases in material output, teaching agriculture may make sense. In a developed country, where growth in material output is less important, teaching literature may make sense.

Recognizing the contextual nature of decisions is important when interpreting the production possibility curve. Because decisions are contextual, what the production possibility curve for a particular decision looks like depends on the existing institutions, and the analysis can be applied only in institutional and historical context. The production possibility curve is not a purely technical phenomenon. The curve is an engine of analysis to make contextual choices, not a definitive tool to decide what one should do in all cases.

From the above discussion, it should be clear where economic systems fit into this discussion. The choice of economic systems is not the type of decision that the production possibility curve is designed to address. Usually, the curve takes the system as given. The production possibility curve is most useful when analyzing questions that involve policy decisions given existing systems and institutions—slight movements in the production of one good or another.

I sometimes compare the decision the formerly socialist countries made to my recent decision to give up my beloved Macintosh and to become more Windows-oriented. Mac has a different operating system than Windows, and my wonderful efficiency in Mac does not prevent me from being a total klutz in Windows. Why did I change? Because I believe that eventually, as Windows affords me a wider choice of software, the change will make me more efficient. But sometimes I wonder, and in fact this paragraph is being typed on my Mac. Thus, I have no trouble understanding the difficulties and the switches back and forth that the formerly socialist countries are making.

Actually, this analogy to a computer operating system is only partially appropriate. With economic systems the problem of changing operating systems or even high-level institutions is even more complex than the analogy is meant to illustrate. Imagine if every software program you used had a mind of its own, and when that program saw that it was going to be made obsolete, it started spewing out viruses and sabotaging the new system. Now, that's the correct analogy. And now you should understand why the formerly socialist countries may indeed have problems for many years to come.

A Mac user on a Windows computer can be a total klutz.

The Production Possibility Curve and Tough Choices

The production possibility curve represents the tough choices society must make. Look at questions such as: Should we save the spotted owl or should we allow logging in the Western forests? Should we expand the government health care system or should we strengthen our national defense system? Should we emphasize policies that allow more consumption now or should we emphasize policies that allow more consumption in the future? Such choices involve difficult trade-offs which can be pictured by the production possibility curve.

Not everyone recognizes these choices. For example, politicians often talk as if the production possibility curve were nonexistent. They promise voters the world, telling them, "If you elect me, you can have more of everything." When they say that, they obscure the hard choices and increase their probability of getting elected.

Economists do the opposite. They promise little except that life is tough, and they continually point out that seemingly free lunches often involve significant hidden costs. Alas, political candidates who exhibit such reasonableness seldom get elected. Economists' reasonableness has earned economics the nickname, *the dismal science.*

The difference between economists' and politicians' approaches can be seen by considering the debate between Democrats and Republicans. Both Democrats and Republicans state that they want to eliminate the government budget deficit. But neither side is totally forthcoming on how they will accomplish this goal in conjunction with their other goals. For the Democrats these other goals include the continuation of popular government programs; for the Republicans these other goals include the desire to cut taxes significantly. The problem arises when the actual numbers are looked at closely; it is clear that each party has its own goals that are incompatible with the deficit-cutting goal that the two parties share. So if each party intends to achieve its deficit-cutting goal and its other goals, there must be another side to each party's program, explaining how the incompatibility can be resolved.

Neither side emphasizes this other side of its program—the side that would make the programs compatible with eliminating the deficit. For the Democrats that other side would be raising taxes; for Republicans that other side would be much more significant cuts in existing programs than they are calling for. In effect, they are telling the public that their program will put society at a position like *A* in Exhibit 8.

Economists differ as to where on the production possibility curve the economy should be, but all economists agree that the outcome promised by either the Republicans or the Democrats is a point like *A*, beyond the production possibility curve, and hence impossible to achieve. Republicans and Democrats alike respond to economists that their policies will make the economy grow—that they will shift the production possibility curve out to a curve consistent with *A*.

Economists continually point out that seemingly free lunches often involve significant hidden costs.

"The American Political-Economic System," by Adolph Berle, in *Classic Readings in Economics.*

The newspaper is a wonderful place to find examples of politial rhetoric. The last page of Section A of *The Wall Street Journal* is dedicated to political news.

EXHIBIT 8   Impossible Promises

Politicians have a tendency to argue as if the economy can operate outside of the economy's production possibility curve. Doing so allows them to avoid the "no free lunch" proposition. Economists emphasize that there is no such thing as a free lunch.

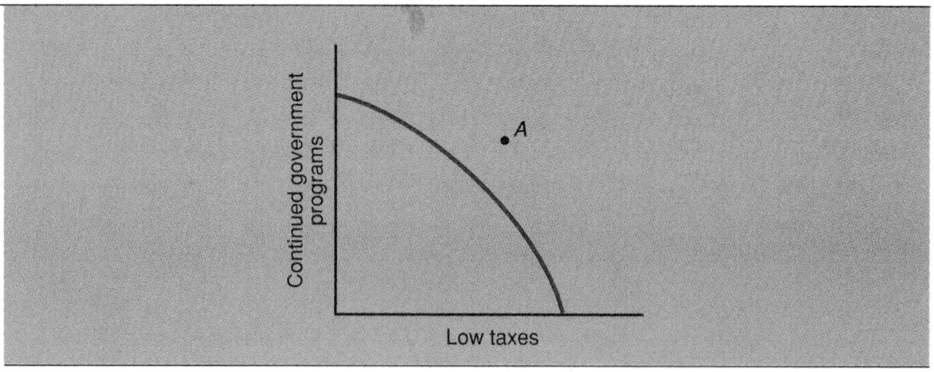

In my class, I use this section to start a discussion about some issue which is currently hot politically.

In justifying their belief that growth will alleviate the inconsistency, the Democrats and Republicans face different problems. The problem for Democrats is to explain how the United States, following similar programs to those that it has followed in the recent past, will experience different results than in the past. Continued slow growth is the more likely alternative.

The problem for Republicans is that they are offering a new set of programs that the United States has not tried in the recent past. This set of programs involves a major change in institutions—one that cuts down the size of government programs and expands the size of the private sector. While this change may eventually lead to more growth, in the short run it is unlikely to do so. Why? As I discussed above, while such major institutional changes can have significant long-run positive effects, in the short run, usually such changes cause significant transition problems. The Republicans, like the Democrats, emphasize the benefits and hide the costs of their programs.

Economists and the production possibility curve analysis emphasize opportunity costs.

Economists and the production possibility curve analysis do not answer the question: Which of these two programs is better? What economists and the production possibility curve analysis do is to focus the analysis of those programs on the opportunity costs, always asking the question: What are the costs of achieving the positive goals being claimed? In doing so TANSTAAFL is emphasized again and again. It is with that TANSTAAFL theme that economic systems must live every day; the production possibility curve analysis brings home that theme graphically.

CONCLUSION

I will often bring the latest Dilbert cartoon in and discuss why it is so popular.

I will end the discussion here; the issues involved in formally analyzing sequential choices quickly become enormously complicated. That's why I avoid such an analysis and formally present only the simple timeless production possibility curve. That's hard enough. But as I will emphasize throughout this course, the tools you will be learning here are powerful but simple, and that simplicity means that much care must be used in their application—to see that the tools fit the situation for which they are used. Businesses tell me that they have much more of a problem with new employees who think they understand things, but actually don't, than they do with new employees who recognize how little they know—who are willing to learn the institutional ropes—and recognize that the time for changing institutions is only when they understand the structural role that the institutions play.

What this means is that economic reasoning is extraordinarily strong, and it really helps you if you apply it in the appropriate time and context. It remains strong when inappropriately applied; but it leads you to the wrong conclusion. The reality is that history and institutions are fundamentally important for making good economic decisions. Economic reasoning alone does not tell anyone, "This is right and this is wrong policy." What economic reasoning does is to provide a framework of analysis that focuses the decision on precisely what are the opportunity costs, and what are the alternative ways of measuring those costs. Fitting that reasoning together with your gut intuitive sense of what is right and wrong is what makes a good economist.

CHAPTER SUMMARY

- Any economic system must solve three central problems:
  - What, and how much, to produce.
  - How to produce it.
  - For whom to produce it.
- In capitalism, the what, how, and for whom problems are solved by the market.
- In Soviet-style socialism, the what, how, and for whom problems were solved by government planning boards.
- Political, social, and economic forces are active in both capitalism and socialism.
- Economic systems are in a constant state of evolution.
- Markets use the price mechanism to coordinate economic activity.

- In feudalism, tradition rules; in mercantilism, the government rules; in capitalism, the market rules.
- In welfare capitalism, the market, the government, and tradition each rule components of the economy.
- The production possibility curve embodies the opportunity cost concept.
- In general, in order to get more and more of something, we must give up ever-increasing quantities of something else.
- Trade allows people to assert their comparative advantage and improve society's production possibility curve.
- Production possibility curves must be interpreted within the contextual nature of decisions.

KEY TERMS

capitalism *(32)*
comparative advantage *(41)*
decision tree *(45)*
economic system *(31)*
efficiency *(43)*
feudalism *(35)*
Industrial Revolution *(36)*

inefficiency *(43)*
input *(38)*
mercantilism *(36)*
NIMBY *(32)*
output *(38)*
principle of increasing marginal
  opportunity cost *(41)*

private property rights *(32)*
production possibility curve *(39)*
production possibility table *(38)*
productive efficiency *(43)*
socialism *(33)*
Soviet-style socialism *(34)*
welfare capitalism *(37)*

QUESTIONS FOR THOUGHT AND REVIEW

The number after each question represents the estimated degree of critical thinking required. (1 = almost none; 10 = deep thought.)

1. Is capitalism or socialism the better economic system? Why? *(9)*
2. What three problems must any economic system solve? *(2)*
3. How does Soviet-style socialism solve these three problems? *(3)*
4. How does capitalism solve these three problems? *(3)*
5. What arguments can you give for supporting a socialist organization of a family and a capitalist organization of the economy? *(6)*
6. Design a grade production possibility table and curve that embody the principle of increasing marginal opportunity cost. *(4)*

7. What would the production possibility curve look like if there were decreasing marginal opportunity costs? Explain. What is an example of decreasing marginal opportunity costs? *(8)*
8. Show how a production possibility curve would shift if a society became more productive in its output of widgets but less productive in its output of wadgets. *(5)*
9. How does the theory of comparative advantage relate to production possibility curves? *(6)*
10. When all people use economic reasoning, inefficiency is impossible, because if the benefit of reducing that inefficiency were greater than the cost, the efficiency would be eliminated. Thus, if people use economic reasoning, it's impossible to be on the interior of a production possibility curve. Is this statement true or false? Why? *(8)*

11. An overhaul of the Social Security system (a system that began in 1935) has been much in the news in the 1990s. Some plans include privatizing much of the program. What does this suggest about how the three invisible forces and consequently the U.S. economic system are evolving? *(8)*

12. Why, in the near term, would socialist countries' switch to a market system cause those countries' production possibility curves to shift in? What institutional and societal characteristics are necessary to carry through that switch successfully? *(8)*

13. If trade shifts the production possibility curve out, why would some politicians oppose actions to promote trade?   *(8)*

PROBLEMS AND EXERCISES

1. Poland, Bulgaria, and Hungary (all former socialist countries) were in the process of changing to a market economy in the early 1990s.
   a. Go to the library and find the latest information about their transitions.
   b. Explain what has happened in those countries, using the invisible hand, invisible handshake, and invisible foot metaphors.

2. Economists Edward Lazear and Robert Michael have calculated that the average family spends two-and-one-half times as much on each adult as they do on each child.
   a. Does this mean that children are deprived and that the distribution is unfair?
   b. Do you think these percentages change with family income? If so, how?
   c. Do you think that the allocation would be different in a family in a Soviet-style socialist country than in a capitalist country? Why?

3. One of the specific problems Soviet-style socialist economies had was keeping up with capitalist countries technologically.
   a. Can you think of any reason inherent in a centrally planned economy that would make innovation difficult?
   b. Can you think of any reason inherent in a capitalist country that would foster innovation?
   c. Joseph Schumpeter, a famous Harvard economist of the 1930s, predicted that as firms in capitalist societies grew in size they would innovate less. Can you suggest what his argument might have been?
   d. Schumpeter's prediction did not come true. Modern capitalist economies have had enormous innovations. Can you provide explanations why?

4. In 1993 President Clinton introduced a health care plan that would increase government involvement in the economy.
   a. Why might he have done so at precisely the time when government-controlled economies were floundering?
   b. Many economists predicted that a government-controlled health care program would have serious problems. What do you think their argument was?
   c. What other major areas of the U.S. economy are run by government? Can you give reasons why they are government-run, rather than being privately run?

5. A country has the following production possibility table:

Resources Devoted to Clothing	Output of Clothing	Resources Devoted to Food	Output of Food
100%	20	0%	0
80	16	20	5
60	12	40	9
40	8	60	12
20	4	80	14
0	0	100	15

   a. Draw the country's production possibility curve.
   b. What's happening to marginal opportunity costs as output of food increases?
   c. Say the country gets better at the production of food. What will happen to the production possibility curve?
   d. Say the country gets equally better at producing food and producing clothing. What will happen to the production possibility curve?

6. Suppose a country has the following production possibility table:

Resources Devoted to Clothing	Output of Clothing	Resources Devoted to Food	Output of Food
100%	15	0%	0
80	14	20	4
60	12	40	8
40	9	60	12
20	5	80	16
0	0	100	20

   a. Draw the country's production possibility curve.
   b. What is the combined production possibility curve for this country and the country in question 5 if the countries do not trade and they produce devoting equal proportionate resources on each good?
   c. What would be the combined production possibility curve of the two countries if they took advantage of their comparative advantages?

7. Assume the United States can produce Toyotas at the cost of $8,000 per car and Chevrolets at $6,000 per car. In Japan, Toyotas can be produced at 1,000,000 yen and Chevrolets at 500,000 yen.
   a. In terms of Chevrolets, what is the opportunity cost of producing Toyotas in each country?

b. Who has the comparative advantage in producing Chevrolets?

c. Assume Americans purchase 500,000 Chevrolets and 300,000 Toyotas each year. The Japanese purchase far fewer of each. Using productive efficiency as the guide, who should most likely produce Chevrolets and who should produce Toyotas, assuming Chevrolets are going to be produced in one country and Toyotas in the other?

8. Lawns produce no crops but occupy more land (25 million acres) in the United States than any single crop, such as corn. This means that the United States is operating inefficiently and hence is at a point inside the production possibility curve. Right? If not, what does it mean?

9. Groucho Marx is reported to have said that "The secret of success is honest and fair dealing. If you can fake those, you've got it made." What would likely happen to society's production possibility curve if everyone could fake honesty? Why? (Hint: Remember that society's production possibility curve reflects more than just technical relationships.)

ANSWERS TO MARGIN QUESTIONS

1. He is wrong. Property rights are required for a market to operate. Once property rights are allocated, the market will allocate goods, but the market cannot distribute the property rights that are required for the market to operate. *(32)*

2. Most families allocate basic needs through control and command. The parents do (or try to do) the controlling and commanding. Generally they are well-intentioned, trying to meet their perception of their children's needs. However, some family activities which are not basic needs might be allocated through the market. For example, if one child wants a go-cart and is willing to do extra work at home in order to get it, go-carts might be allocated through the market, with the child earning chits that can be used for such nonessentials. *(33)*

3. Capitalism places much more emphasis on fostering individualism. Socialism tries to develop a system in which the individual's needs are placed second to society's needs. *(34)*

4. In theory, socialism is an economic system based upon individuals' good will. In practice, socialism follows the Soviet model and involves central planning and government ownership of the primary means of production. *(34)*

5. False. Both socialism and capitalism involve planning. The difference is in who does the planning. In Soviet-style socialism, central planners did the planning. In capitalism, the managers of firms do the planning, with consumers deciding whether those plans are correct. *(35)*

6. If no resource had a comparative advantage, the production possibility curve would be a straight line connecting the points of maximum production of each product as in the graph below.

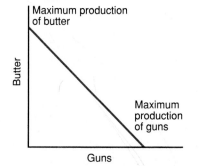

At all points along this curve, the opportunity cost of producing guns and butter is equal. *(41)*

7. If Steve and Sarah do not trade, and divide their time identically, their combined production possibility table is shown in **(a)**. If they do collaborate, their production possibility table is shown in **(b)**. The corresponding production possibility curves are drawn beneath the tables. The production possibility curve with trade is further to the right than the one without trade. Steve and Sarah can each end up with more bread and cookies if they trade than if they worked on their own. *(42)*

(a) Combined, No Trade		(b) Combined, Trade	
Loaves of Bread	Dozens of Cookies	Loaves of Bread	Dozens of Cookies
8	0	8	0
6	3	6	4
4	6	4	8
2	9	2	10
0	12	0	12

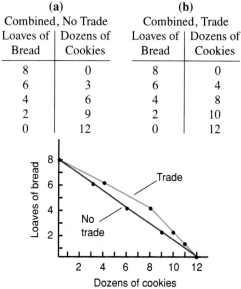

8. I remind them of the importance of cultural forces. In Saudi Arabia women are not allowed to drive. *(44)*

9. The production possibility curve shifts in along the butter axis as in the graph below. *(45)*

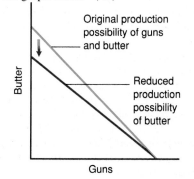

10. Choosing which college to attend is a systemic choice. Choosing a major is an institutional choice. Choosing electives within that major is a low-level choice.

Changing colleges would likely be extremely costly once you are choosing electives within a major at a college. Many of your credits would likely not transfer. *(46)*

APPENDIX A

The History of Economic Systems

Remember the distinction between market and economic forces: Economic forces have always existed—they operate in all aspects of our lives; but market forces have not always existed. Markets are social creations societies use to coordinate individuals' actions. Markets developed, sometimes spontaneously, sometimes by design, because they offered a better life for at least some—and usually a large majority of—individuals in a society.

To understand why markets developed, it is helpful to look briefly at the history of the economic systems from which our own system descended.

Feudal Society: Rule of the Invisible Handshake

Let's go back in time to the year 1000 when Europe had no nation-states as we now know them. (Ideally, we would have gone back farther and explained other economic systems, but, given the limited space, I had to draw the line somewhere—an example of trade-off.) There was no coordinated central government, no unified system of law, no national patriotism, no national defense, although a strong religious institution simply called the Church fulfilled some of these roles. There were few towns; most individuals lived in walled manors or "estates." These manors "belonged to" the "lord of the manor." (Occasionally the "lord" was a lady, but not often.) I say "belonged to" rather than "were owned by" because most of the empires or federations at that time were not formal nation-states that could organize, administer, and regulate ownership. No documents or deeds gave ownership of the land to an individual. Instead tradition ruled, and in normal times nobody questioned the lord's right to the land.

The land "belonged to" the lord because the land "belonged to" him—that's the way it was.

Without a central nation-state, the manor served many functions a nation-state would have served had it existed. The lord provided protection, often within a walled area surrounding the manor house or, if the manor was large enough, a castle. He provided administration and decided disputes. He also decided *what* would be done, *how* it would be done, and *who* would get what, but these decisions were limited. In the same way that the land belonged to the lord because that's the way it always had been, what people did and how they did it were determined by what they always had done. Tradition ruled the manor more than the lord did.

The Life of a Serf Individuals living on the land were called *serfs*. What serfs did was determined by what their fathers had done. If the father was a farmer, the son was a farmer. A woman followed her husband and helped him do what he did. That was the way it always had been and that's the way it was—tradition again.

Most serfs were farmers, and surrounding the manor were fields of about a half acre each. Serfs were tied by tradition to their assigned plots of land; according to tradition, they could not leave those plots and had to turn over a portion of their harvest to the lord every year. How much they had to turn over varied from manor to manor, but payments of half the total harvest were not unheard of. In return, the lord provided defense and organized the life of the manor—boring as it was. Thus, there was a type of trade between the serf and the lord, but it was nonnegotiable and did not take place through a market.

Problems of a Tradition-Based Society   This system is known as **feudalism**—*an economic system divided into small communities in which a few powerful people protect those who are loyal to them*. It developed about the 8th and 9th centuries and lasted until about the 15th century, though in isolated countries such as Russia it continued well into the 19th century, and in all European countries its influence lingered for hundreds of years (as late as about 140 years ago in some parts of Germany). Such a long-lived system must have done some things right, and feudalism did: it solved the what, how, and for whom problems in an acceptable way.

But a tradition-based society has problems. In a traditional society, because someone's father was a baker, the son must also be a baker, and because a woman was a homemaker, she wouldn't be allowed to be anything but a homemaker. But what if Joe Blacksmith, Jr., the son of Joe Blacksmith, Sr., is a lousy blacksmith and longs to knead dough, while Joe Baker, Jr., would be a superb blacksmith but hates making pastry? Tough. Tradition dictated who did what. In fact, tradition probably arranged things so that we will never know whether Joe Blacksmith, Jr., would have made a superb baker.

As long as a society doesn't change too much, tradition operates reasonably well, although not especially efficiently, in holding the society together. However, when a society must undergo change, tradition does not work. Change means that the things that were done before no longer need to be done, while new things do need to get done. But if no one has traditionally done these new things, then they don't get done. If the change is important but a society can't figure out some way for the new things to get done, the society falls apart. That's what happened to feudal society. It didn't change when change was required.

The life of a serf was difficult, and feudalism was designed to benefit the lord. Some individuals in feudal society just couldn't take life on the manor, and they set off on their own. Because there was no organized police force, they were unlikely to be caught and forced to return to the manor. Going hungry, being killed, or both, however, were frequent fates of an escaped serf. One place to which serfs could safely escape, though, was a town or city—the remains of what in Roman times had been thriving and active cities. These cities, which had been decimated by plagues, plundering bands, and starvation in the preceding centuries, nevertheless remained an escape hatch for runaway serfs because they relied far less on tradition than did manors. City dwellers had to live by their wits; many became merchants who lived predominantly by trading. They were middlemen; they would buy from one group and sell to another.

Trading in towns was an alternative to the traditional feudal order because trading allowed people to have an income independent of the traditional social structure.

Markets broke down tradition. Initially merchants traded using barter (exchange of one kind of good for another): silk and spices from the Orient for wheat, flour, and artisan products in Europe. But soon a generalized purchasing power (money) developed as a medium of exchange. Money greatly expanded the possibilities of trading because its use meant that goods no longer needed to be bartered. They could be sold for money, which could then be spent to buy other goods.

In the beginning, land was not traded, but soon the feudal lord who just had to have a silk robe but had no money was saying, "Why not? I'll sell you a small piece of land so I can buy a shipment of silk." Once land became tradable, the traditional base of the feudal society was undermined. Tradition that can be bought and sold is no longer tradition—it's just another commodity.

From Feudalism to Mercantilism

Toward the end of the Middle Ages (mid-15th century), markets went from being a sideshow, a fair that spiced up peoples' lives, to being the main event. Over time, some traders and merchants started to amass fortunes that dwarfed those of the feudal lords. Rich traders settled down; existing towns and cities expanded and new towns were formed. As towns grew and as fortunes shifted from feudal lords to merchants, power in society shifted to the towns. And with that shift came a change in society's political and economic structure.

As these traders became stronger politically and economically, they threw their support behind a king (the strongest lord) in the hope that the king would expand their ability to trade. In doing so, they made the king even stronger. Eventually, the king became so powerful that his will prevailed over the will of the other lords and even over the will of the Church. As the king consolidated his power, nation-states as we know them today evolved. *The invisible foot—government—became an active influence on economic decision making.*

As markets grew, feudalism evolved into **mercantilism**—*an economic system in which the government determines the what, how, and for whom decisions by doling out the rights to undertake certain economic activities.* Political rather than social forces came to control the central economic decisions.

The evolution of feudal systems into mercantilism occurred in somewhat this way: As cities and their markets grew in size and power relative to the feudal manors and the traditional economy, a whole new variety of possible economic activities developed. It was only natural that individuals began to look to a king to establish a new tradition that would determine who would do what. Individuals in particular occupations organized into groups called *guilds,* which were similar to strong labor unions today. These guilds, many of which had financed and supported the king, now expected the king and his government to protect their interests.

As new economic activities, such as trading companies, developed, individuals involved in these activities similarly depended on the king for the right to trade and for help in financing and organizing their activities. For example, in 1492, when Christopher Columbus had the wild idea that by sailing west he could get to the East Indies and trade for their riches, he went to Spain's Queen Isabella and King Ferdinand for financial support.

Since many traders had played and continued to play important roles in financing, establishing, and supporting the king, the king was usually happy to protect their interests. The government doled out the rights to undertake a variety of economic activities. By the late 1400s, Western Europe had evolved from a feudal to a mercantilist economy.

The mercantilist period was marked by the increased role of government, which could be classified in two ways: by the way it encouraged growth, and by the way it limited growth. Government legitimized and financed a variety of activities, thus encouraging growth. But government also limited economic activity in order to protect the monopolies of those it favored, thus limiting growth. So mercantilism allowed the market to operate, but it kept the market under its control. The market was not allowed to respond freely to the laws of supply and demand.

From Mercantilism to Capitalism

Mercantilism provided the source for major growth in Western Europe, but mercantilism also unleashed new tensions within society. Like feudalism, mercantilism limited entry into economic activities. It used a different form of limitation—the invisible foot (politics) rather than the invisible handshake (social and cultural tradition)—but individuals who were excluded still felt unfairly treated.

The most significant source of tension was the different roles played by craft guilds and owners of new businesses, who were called industrialists or **capitalists**—*businesspeople who have acquired large amounts of money and use it to invest in businesses.* Craft guild members were artists in their own crafts: pottery, shoemaking, and the like. New business owners destroyed the art of production by devising machines to replace hand production. Machines produced goods cheaper and faster than craftsmen.[2] The result was an increase in supply and a downward pressure on the price, which was set by govern-

ment. Craftsmen didn't want to be replaced by machines. They argued that machine-manufactured goods didn't have the same quality as hand-crafted goods, and that the new machines would disrupt the economic and social life of the community.

Industrialists were the outsiders with a vested interest in changing the existing system. They wanted the freedom to conduct business as they saw fit. Because of the enormous cost advantage of manufactured goods over crafted goods, a few industrialists overcame government opposition and succeeded within the mercantilist system. They earned their fortunes and became an independent political power.

Once again the economic power base shifted, and two groups competed with each other for power—this time, the guilds and the industrialists. The government had to decide whether to support the industrialists (who wanted government to loosen its power over the country's economic affairs) or the craftsmen and guilds (who argued for strong government limitations and for maintaining traditional values of workmanship). This struggle raged in the 1700s and 1800s. But during this time, governments themselves were changing. This was the Age of Revolutions, and the kings' powers were being limited by democratic reform movements—revolutions supported and financed in large part by the industrialists.

The Need for Coordination in an Economy One argument craftsmen put forward was that coordination of the economy was necessary, and the government had to be involved. If government wasn't going to coordinate economic activity, who would? To answer that question, a British moral philosopher named Adam Smith developed the concept of the invisible hand, in his famous book *The Wealth of Nations* (1776), and used it to explain how markets could coordinate the economy without the active involvement of government.

As stated in the chapter, Smith argued that the market's invisible hand would guide suppliers' actions toward the general good. No government coordination was necessary.

With the help of economists such as Adam Smith, the industrialists' view won out. Government pulled back from its role in guiding the economy and adopted a **laissez-faire** policy—the *economic policy of leaving coordination of individuals' wants to be controlled by the market.* (*Laissez faire,* a French term, means "Let events take their course; leave things alone.")

The Industrial Revolution The invisible hand worked; **capitalism**—*an economic system in which individuals decide how, what, and for whom to produce*—thrived. Beginning about 1750 and continuing through the late 1800s, machine production increased enormously, almost totally replacing hand production. This phenomenon has

---

[2]Throughout this section I use *men* to emphasize that these societies were strongly male-dominated. There were almost no businesswomen. In fact, a woman had to turn over her property to a man upon her marriage, and the marriage contract was written as if she were owned by her husband!

been given a name, the **Industrial Revolution**—the *period of about 1750–1900 during which technology and machines rapidly modernized industrial production*. The economy grew faster than ever before. Society was forever transformed. New inventions changed all aspects of life. James Watt's steam engine (1769) made manufacturing and travel easier. Eli Whitney's cotton gin (1793) changed the way cotton was processed. James Kay's flying shuttle (1733),[3] James Hargreaves's spinning jenny (1765), and Richard Arkwright's power loom (1769), combined with the steam engine, changed the way cloth was processed and the clothes people wore.

The need to mine vast amounts of coal to provide power to run the machines changed the economic and physical landscapes. The repeating rifle changed the nature of warfare. Modern economic institutions replaced guilds. Stock markets, insurance companies, and corporations all became important. Trading was no longer financed by government; it was privately financed (although government policies, such as colonial policies giving certain companies monopoly trading rights with a country's colonies, helped in that trading). The Industrial Revolution, democracy, and capitalism all arose in the middle and late 1700s. By the 1800s, they were part of the institutional landscape of Western society. Capitalism had arrived.

Welfare Capitalism
From Capitalism to ~~Socialism~~

Capitalism was marked by significant economic growth in the Western world. But it was also marked by human abuses—18-hour workdays, low wages, children as young as five years old slaving long hours in dirty, dangerous factories and mines—to produce enormous wealth for an elite few. Such conditions and inequalities led to criticism of the capitalist or market economic system.

Marx's Analysis
The best-known critic of this system was Karl Marx, a German philosopher, economist, and sociologist who wrote in the 1800s and who developed an analysis of the dynamics of change in economic systems. Marx argued that economic systems are in a constant state of change, and that capitalism would not last. Workers would revolt, and capitalism would be replaced by a socialist economic system.

Marx saw an economy marked by tensions among economic classes. He saw capitalism as an economic system controlled by the capitalist class (businessmen). His class analysis was that capitalist society is divided into capitalist and worker classes. He said constant tension between these economic classes causes changes in the system. The capitalist class made large profits by exploiting the **proletariat** class—*the working class*—and extracting what he called *surplus value* from workers who, according to Marx's labor theory of value, produced all the value inherent in goods. Surplus value was the additional profit, rent, or interest that, according to Marx's normative views, capitalists added to the price of goods. What economic analysis sees as recognizing a need that society has and fulfilling it, Marx saw as exploitation.

Marx argued that this exploitation would increase as production facilities became larger and larger and as competition among capitalists decreased. At some point, he believed, exploitation would lead to a revolt by the proletariat, who would overthrow their capitalist exploiters.

By the late 1800s, some of what Marx predicted had occurred, although not in the way that he thought it would. Production moved from small to large factories. Corporations developed, and classes became more distinct from one another. Workers were significantly differentiated from owners. Small firms merged and were organized into monopolies and trusts (large combinations of firms). The trusts developed ways to prevent competition among themselves and ways to limit entry of new competitors into the market. Marx was right in his predictions about these developments, but he was wrong in his prediction about society's response to them.

The Revolution that Did Not Occur
Western society's response to the problems of capitalism was not a revolt by the workers. Whereas Marx said capitalism would fall because of the exploitation of workers by the owners of businesses or capitalists, what actually happened was that the market economy was modified by political forces. Governments stepped in to stop the worst abuses of capitalism. The hard edges of capitalism were softened.

Evolution, not revolution, was capitalism's destiny. The democratic state did not act, as Marx argued it would, as a mere representative of the capitalist class. Competing pressure groups developed; workers gained political power that offset the economic power of businesses.

In the late 1930s and the 1940s, workers dominated the political agenda. During this time, capitalist economies developed an economic safety net which included government-funded programs, such as public welfare and unemployment insurance, and established an extensive set of regulations affecting all aspects of the economy. Today, depressions are met with direct government policy. Antitrust laws, regulatory agencies, and social programs of government softened the hard edges of capitalism. Laws were passed prohibiting child labor, mandating a certain minimum wage, and limiting the hours of work.

---

[3]The invention of the flying shuttle frustrated the textile industry because it enabled workers to weave so much cloth that the spinners of thread from which the cloth was woven couldn't keep up. This challenge to the textile industry was met by offering a prize to anyone who could invent something to increase the thread spinners' productivity. The prize was won when the spinning jenny was invented.

ADDED DIMENSION SHAREHOLDERS AND STAKEHOLDERS

Corporations (businesses) are technically owned by the owners of capital (shareholders). In theory, at least, they control corporations by electing the officers (the people who make the *what, how,* and *for whom* production decisions). In practice, however, effective control of corporations is generally in the hands of a small group of managing officers.

In the debate about the possible future evolution of capitalism, the question of who controls business decisions is likely to take center stage. Some reformers in the United States argue that the current U.S. system is wrong in both theory and practice. They argue that corporations should reflect the need of stakeholders (all the individuals who have a stake in a corporation's activities). Stakeholders include the corporation's stockholders and officers as well as workers, customers, and the community where the corporation operates. An economy in which all stakeholders, not just shareholders, elect the officers who make the *what, how,* and *for whom* decisions would still use the market. It would still be a market economy, but it would no longer be a capitalist economy.

Capitalism became what is sometimes called **welfare capitalism**, an *economic system in which the market is allowed to operate, but in which government plays key roles in determining distribution and making the what, how, and for whom decisions.*

Due to these developments, government spending now accounts for about a fifth of all spending in the United States, and for more than half in some European countries. Were an economist from the late 1800s to return from the grave, he'd probably say socialism, not capitalism, exists in Western societies. Most modern-day economists wouldn't go that far, but they would agree that our economy today is better described as a welfare capitalist economy than as a capitalist, or even a market, economy. Because of these changes, the U.S. and Western European economies are a far cry from the competitive "capitalist" economy that Karl Marx criticized. Markets operate, but they are constrained by the government.

The concept *capitalism* developed to denote a market system controlled by one group in society, the capitalists. Looking at Western societies today, we see that domination by one group no longer characterizes Western economies. Although in theory capitalists control corporations through their ownership of shares of stock, in practice corporations are controlled in large part by managers. There remains an elite group who control business, but "capitalist" is not a good term to describe them. Managers, not capitalists, exercise primary control over business, and even their control is limited by laws or the fear of laws being passed by governments.

Governments in turn are controlled by a variety of pressure groups. Sometimes one group is in control; at other times, another. Government policies similarly fluctuate. Sometimes they are proworker, sometimes proindustrialist, sometimes progovernment, and sometimes prosociety.

From Feudalism to Socialism

You probably noticed that I crossed out "Socialism" in the previous section's heading and replaced it with "Welfare Capitalism." That's because capitalism did not evolve to socialism as Karl Marx predicted it would. Instead, Marx's socialist ideas took root in feudalist Russia, a society that the Industrial Revolution had in large part bypassed. Arriving at a different place and a different time than Marx predicted it would, you shouldn't be surprised to read that socialism arrived in a different way than Marx predicted. The proletariat did not revolt to establish socialism. Instead, World War I, which the Russians were losing, crippled Russia's feudal economy and government. A small group of socialists overthrew the czar (Russia's king) and took over the government in 1917. They quickly pulled Russia out of the war, and then set out to organize a socialist society and economy.

Russian socialists tried to adhere to Marx's ideas, but they found that Marx had concentrated on how capitalist economies operate, not on how a socialist economy should be run. Thus, Russian socialists faced a huge task with little guidance. Their most immediate problem was how to increase production so that the economy could emerge from feudalism into the modern industrial world. In Marx's analysis, capitalism was a necessary stage in the evolution toward the ideal state for a very practical reason. The capitalists exploit the workers, but in doing so capitalists extract the necessary surplus—an amount of production in excess of what is consumed. That surplus had to be extracted in order to provide the factories and machinery upon which a socialist economic system would be built. But since capitalism did not exist in Russia, a true socialist state could not be established immediately. Instead, the socialists created **state socialism**—*an economic system in which government sees to it that people* *work for the common good until they can be relied upon to do that on their own.*

Socialists saw state socialism as a transition stage to pure socialism. This transition stage still exploited the workers; when Joseph Stalin took power in Russia in the late 1920s, he took the peasants' and small farmers' land and turned it into collective farms. The government then paid farmers low prices for their produce. When farmers balked at the low prices, millions of them were killed.

Simultaneously, Stalin created central planning agencies that directed individuals what to produce and how to produce it, and determined for whom things would be produced. During this period, *socialism* became synonymous with *central economic planning,* and Soviet-style socialism became the model of socialism in practice.

Also during this time, Russia took control of a number of neighboring states and established the Union of Soviet Socialist Republics (USSR), the formal name of the Soviet Union. The Soviet Union also installed Soviet-dominated governments in a number of Eastern European countries. In 1949 most of China, under the rule of Mao Zedong, adopted Soviet-style socialist principles.

Since the late 1980s, the Soviet socialist economic and political structure has fallen apart. The Soviet Union as a political state broke up, and its former republics became autonomous. Eastern European countries were released from Soviet control. Now they faced a new problem: transition from socialism to a market economy. Why did the Soviet socialist economy fall apart? Because workers lacked incentives to work; production was inefficient; consumer goods were either unavailable or of poor quality; and high Soviet officials were exploiting their positions, keeping the best jobs for themselves and moving themselves up in the waiting lists for consumer goods. In short, the parents of the socialist family (the Communist party) were no longer acting benevolently; they were taking many of the benefits for themselves.

Recent political and economic upheavals in Eastern Europe and the Soviet Union suggest the kind of socialism these societies tried did not work. However, that failure does not mean that socialist goals are bad; nor does it mean that no type of socialism can ever work. To overthrow socialist-dominated governments it is not necessary to accept capitalism, and many citizens of these countries are looking for an alternative to both systems. Most, however, want to establish market economies.

From Socialism to ?

The upheavals in the former Soviet Union and Eastern Europe have left only China as a major power using a socialist economic system. But even in China there have been changes, and the Chinese economy is socialist in name only. Almost uncontrolled markets exist in numerous sectors of the economy. These changes have led some socialists to modify their view that state socialism is the path from capitalism to true socialism, and instead to joke: "Socialism is the longest path from capitalism to capitalism."

Economic Systems of the Future

Our economic system will probably be different 30 years from now. If the debate between socialism and capitalism disappears, another debate will rise up to take its place. A new topic for debate may be: Who should be the decision makers in a market economy? In the U.S. economy in the late 1980s, a handful of financiers became celebrities by reaping billions of dollars in profits for themselves. Many people came to wonder whether an economic system that so glorified greed was really desirable, and in the 1990s some of those same financiers found themselves in jail, with the financial institutions they had controlled in ruins. Such widespread reactions may well lead to further evolution of the capitalist system.

Also in the 1990s, the Asian tigers—a collection of Asian countries such as Singapore, South Korea, and Thailand—are the economic stars. As I will discuss in a later chapter, these economies are similar to Japan's economy, which, in turn, has many similarities to mercantilism. In Japan, government and industrialists work closely together, and government plays a key role in the economy. Given the success of the Asian tigers, many in the United States are pushing for a type of mercantilism similar to theirs. And so it's safe to predict that the rest of the 1990s and the 2000s will see further evolution of economic systems. The lesson of history seems to be that change remains the one constant in economic systems.

KEY TERMS

capitalism   *(54)*
capitalists   *(54)*
feudalism   *(53)*

Industrial Revolution   *(55)*
laissez-faire   *(54)*
mercantilism   *(53)*

proletariat   *(55)*
state socialism   *(56)*
welfare capitalism   *(56)*

QUESTIONS FOR THOUGHT AND REVIEW

1. Why did feudalism evolve into mercantilism? Could feudalism stage a return? Why?

2. Why did mercantilism evolve into capitalism? Could mercantilism stage a return? Why?

3. In feudalism, how should the *what, how,* and *for whom* questions be answered?

4. How did the Knights of the Round Table get their food? For example, did they go to the market and buy it?

5. Why did traders in the Middle Ages support the king? What relevance do such actions have to modern-day lobbying?

6. In what way did mercantilism foster economic growth, and in what way did it limit economic growth?

7. Your study partner, Joan, is arguing that mercantilism went down with the king; it was overthrown by the Age of Revolution. How do you respond?

8. Some intellectuals have argued "history has ended" because of recent developments in socialist economies. Respond, basing your answer on Marx's analysis.

9. A common joke in socialist countries in the early 1990s was that a person went into a free market store and asked how much a loaf of bread cost. "One dollar," said the clerk. "But that's outrageous. Down the street at the state-run store, it only costs a nickel." "So why don't you buy it there?" said the clerk. "Well," said the customer, "they don't have any." Using supply/demand analysis, show why this situation makes economic sense.

10. The Heisenberg principle has been interpreted as meaning that it's impossible to know the true nature of reality because in analyzing that reality, you change it. How might the Heisenberg principle apply to Marx's economic analysis?

Three

Supply and Demand

Teach a parrot the terms supply *and* demand *and you've got an economist.*

~ Thomas Carlyle

After reading this chapter, you should be able to:

1 State the law of demand.

2 Explain the importance of opportunity cost and substitution to the laws of supply and demand.

3 Distinguish a shift in demand from a movement along the demand curve.

4 Draw a demand curve from a demand table.

5 State the law of supply.

6 Distinguish a shift in supply from a movement along the supply curve.

7 Draw a supply curve from a supply table.

8 State the three dynamic laws of supply and demand.

Supply and demand. Supply and demand. Roll the phrase around your mouth, savor it like a good wine. *Supply* and *demand* are the most-used words in economics. And for good reason. They provide a good off-the-cuff answer for any economic question. Try it.

Why are bacon and oranges so expensive this winter? *Supply and demand.*

Why are interest rates falling? *Supply and demand.*

Why can't I find decent wool socks any more? *Supply and demand.*

The importance of the interplay of supply and demand makes it only natural that, early in any economics course, you must learn about supply and demand. Let's start with demand.

DEMAND

Poets and songwriters use literary license. Take the classic song by the Rolling Stones entitled "You Can't Always Get What You Want." Whether the statement is or isn't true depends on how you define *want*. If you define *want* as "being sufficiently desirous of something so that you do what's necessary to buy the good," then in a market in which prices are flexible, you *can* always get what you want. The reason: What you want depends on what the price is. If, however, you define *want* as simply "being desirous of something," then there are many unfulfilled "wants," such as my wanting an expensive sports car.

I want to own a Maserati. But, I must admit, I'm not willing to do what's necessary to own one. If I really wanted one, I'd mortgage everything I own, increase my income by doubling the number of hours I work, not buy anything else, and get that car. But I don't do any of those things, so there's a question of whether I really want the car. Sure, I'd want one if it cost $10,000, but from my actions it's clear that, at $240,000, I don't really want it. If *want* is defined as "being sufficiently desirous of something that you will do what's necessary to buy the good," you can always get what you want, because your willingness to pay the going price for something is the only way to tell whether you really want it. What you want at a low price differs from what you want at a high price. The quantity you demand varies inversely—in the opposite direction—with the price.

Prices are the tool by which the invisible hand—the market—coordinates individuals' desires and limits how much people are willing to buy—how much they really want. When goods become scarce, the market reduces people's desires for those scarce goods; as their prices go up, people buy fewer goods. As goods become abundant, their prices go down, and people want more of them. The invisible hand sees to it that what people want (do what's necessary to get) matches what's available. In doing so, the invisible hand coordinates individuals' wants. While you can't always get what you want at a low price, you can get it at some price—maybe a super-high price.

It isn't surprising that the Stones chose the other definition of *want;* it's unlikely that their song would have become a hit had they put in the appropriate qualifier. You can't dance to "You Can't Always Get What You Want at the Price You Want."

The Law of Demand

1 The law of demand states that the quantity of a good demanded is inversely related to the good's price. When price goes up, quantity demanded goes down. When price goes down, quantity demanded goes up.

You may also wish to explain the law of demand in terms of the law of diminishing marginal utility.

Video Series, Economics U$A: Markets: Do They Meet Our Needs? Segment 2.1

What makes the qualifier appropriate is the **law of demand**:

More of a good will be demanded the lower its price, other things constant.

Or alternatively:

Less of a good will be demanded the higher its price, other things constant.

This law is fundamental to the invisible hand's ability to coordinate individuals' desires: as prices change, people change how much of a particular good they're willing to buy.

To see that the law of demand makes intuitive sense, just think of something you'd really like but can't afford. If the price is cut in half, you—and other consumers—become more likely to buy it. Quantity demanded goes up as price goes down.

Just to be sure you've got it, let's consider a real-world example: demand for vanity—specifically, vanity license plates. In 1989, the North Carolina state legislature increased the vanity plates' price from $30 to $40. In response, the quantity demanded fell from 60,334 at $30 a year to 31,122 at $40 a year. Assuming other things remained constant, that is the law of demand in action.

The Demand Curve

Demand curve   *The graphic representation of the law of demand.*

A **demand curve** is *the graphic representation of the law of demand.* Exhibit 1 shows a demand curve.

As you can see, in graphical terms, the law of demand states that the quantity demanded of a good is inversely related to that good's price, other things constant. As the price goes up, the quantity demanded goes down. An alternative way of saying the same thing is that price and quantity demanded are inversely related, so the demand curve slopes downward to the right.

Important Qualifications of the Law of Demand

Relative price   *The price of a good compared to the price of another good or combination of goods.*

To understand the law of demand, you must understand the terminology used to discuss that law and the assumptions upon which that law is based.

Relative Price   One important qualification to remember is that *the law of demand refers to a good's relative price.* The **relative price** of a good is *the price of that good compared to the price of another good or combination of goods.* For example, if the price of a compact disc is $11 and the price of an apple is 50 cents, the relative price of CDs compared to the price of apples is $11/50¢ = 22. In other words, you can buy 22 apples with one CD or one CD with 22 apples.

The actual price you pay for the goods you buy is called the **money price.** You don't say that a CD has a price of 22 apples; you say that a CD has a price of $11.

But don't let that fool you. While the $11 may not look like a relative price, it is. It is the price of the CD compared to a composite price for all other goods. That composite price for all other goods is the price of money. What's the price of money? It's simply how much you'll pay for money. Most people will pay $1 for $1, so the price of $1 is $1. The money price of $11 means that you can trade one CD for 11 one-dollar bills.

Money is not desired for its own sake. You want dollar bills only because you can trade them for something else. You have in the back of your mind a good sense of what else you could do with that $11—what the opportunity cost of spending it on a CD is. You could buy, say, three Big Macs, a super-size order of fries, and a large vanilla shake for $11. The opportunity cost of buying the CD is that big tray of fast food. Thus the money price of an item represents the price of that item relative to the prices of all other goods.

As long as your sense of what that opportunity cost is doesn't change, money price is a good representation of relative price. Over short periods the opportunity cost of $1 doesn't change. Over longer periods, though, because of inflation, money prices are not a good representation of relative prices. Say, for instance, that money prices (including your wage) on average go up 10 percent. (When this happens, economists say the price level has gone up by 10 percent.) Also say the money price of a CD goes up by 2 percent. Has the relative price of CDs gone up or down? Since the average money price has gone up 10 percent and the money price of a CD has risen by 2 percent, the relative price of a CD has fallen by 8 percent. The law of demand would say that the quantity of CDs demanded would increase because the relative price has gone down, even though the money price has gone up.

The use of money prices makes life easier for members of society, but it makes life harder for economics students, who must remember that even though they see the money price of an item as an absolute number, it is actually a relative price.

I emphasize that the law of demand refers to relative price because the explanation for it involves demanders' ability to substitute some other good for that good. If a good's relative price goes up, some people will substitute some other good for it because that substitute's relative price goes down. For example, if the money price of compact discs rises and the money price of tapes doesn't rise, individuals will substitute tapes for CDs.

Other Things Constant   Notice that in stating the law of demand, I put in the qualification: other things constant. That's three extra words, and unless they were important I wouldn't have put them in. But what does "other things constant" mean? Say that over a period of two years, the price of cars rises as the number of cars sold likewise rises. That seems to violate the law of demand, since the number of cars sold should have fallen in response to the rise in price. Looking at the data more closely, however, we see that a third factor has also changed: individuals' income has increased. As income increases, people buy more cars, increasing the demand for cars.

The increase in price works as the law of demand states—it decreases the number of cars bought. But in this case, income doesn't remain constant; it increases. That rise in income increases the demand for cars. That increase in demand outweighs the decrease in quantity demanded that results from a rise in price, so ultimately more cars are sold. If you want to study the effect of price alone—which is what the law of demand refers to—you must make adjustments to hold income constant when you make your study. That's why the qualifying phrase "other things constant" is an important part of the law of demand.

This qualifying phrase, "other things constant," places a limitation on the implications that can be drawn from any analysis based on the law of demand. **Other things constant** means that *all other factors that could affect the analysis are assumed to remain constant (whether they actually remain constant or not).* Alfred Marshall, one of the originators of this law, emphasized these limitations, arguing that it is as much of a mistake to apply supply-demand analysis to areas where these

The distinction between relative and absolute price changes should be emphasized. It is an idea that will be used repeatedly in the study of economics.

Mentioning some significant relative price changes over time helps students grasp the concept. Washing machines, for example, have risen in price over many time periods, but when adjusted for inflation, have significantly fallen in price. I sometimes assign students a year—such as 1977—and ask them to find an advertisement from the newspaper from that year and compare it with today's advertised prices.

Q-1: If the price of houses falls 2% but the price of all other goods has fallen 6%, what does the law of demand predict would happen to the quantity of houses demanded?

2a The law of demand is based upon opportunity cost and individuals' ability to substitute. If the relative price of a good rises, the opportunity cost of purchasing that good will also rise and demanders will substitute for it a good with a lower opportunity cost.

"Other things constant" places a limitation on the application of the law of demand.

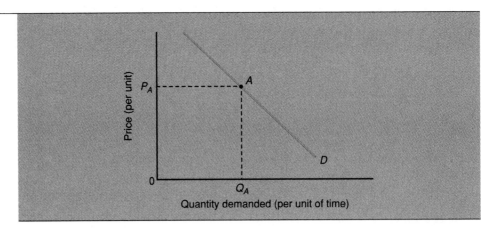

EXHIBIT 1   A Sample Demand Curve

The law of demand states that the quantity demanded of a good is inversely related to the price of that good, other things constant. As the price of a good goes up, the quantity demanded goes down, so the demand curve is downward sloping.

Partial equilibrium analysis *Analysis in which other things can reasonably be assumed to remain constant.*

The emphasis on **partial** equilibrium here is important because it will establish the distinction between micro supply and demand analysis presented both here and in the micro section of the book, and the macro aggregate supply and demand analysis, which will be used in setting out the macro model.

assumptions do not hold as it is not to apply it to those areas where it does apply. To emphasize this point he argued that the law of demand is directly applicable to partial equilibrium issues—issues in which other things can reasonably be assumed to remain constant—and that supply-demand analysis should be called **partial equilibrium analysis** — *analysis in which other things can reasonably be assumed to remain constant.*

He admonished his students to remember that partial equilibrium analysis is incomplete because it assumes other things equal. That it is incomplete does not mean that it cannot be used for other issues, but when applied to issues where other things do not remain constant, it must be used with an educated common sense and one must keep in the back of one's mind what does not remain constant.

How much of a good somebody wants to buy depends on many other things besides its price. These include individuals' tastes, prices of other goods, and even the weather. Those other factors must remain constant if you're to make a valid study of the effect of an increase in the price of a good on the quantity demanded. In practice, it's impossible to keep all other things constant, so you have to be careful when you say that when price goes up, quantity demanded goes down. It's likely to go down, but it's always possible that something besides price has changed.

Shifts in Demand versus Movements along a Demand Curve

To distinguish between the effects of price and the effects of other factors on how much of a good is demanded, economists have developed the following precise terminology—terminology that inevitably shows up on exams. The first distinction to make is between demand and quantity demanded.

- **Demand** refers to *a schedule of quantities of a good that will be bought per unit of time at various prices, other things constant.*
- **Quantity demanded** refers to *a specific amount that will be demanded per unit of time at a specific price, other things constant.*

Q–2: In the 1980s and 1990s, as animal rights activists made wearing fur coats déclassé, the _____ decreased. Should the missing words be "demand for furs" or "quantity of furs demanded"?

I make sure to point out that the shift factors of demand determine the position of the demand curve and that when one of the factors changes, the whole curve shifts.

In graphical terms, the term "demand" refers to the entire demand curve. Demand tells how much of a good will be bought *at various prices.* "Quantity demanded" refers to a point on a demand curve, such as point *A* in Exhibit 1. This terminology allows us to distinguish between *changes in quantity demanded* and *shifts in demand.* A change in the quantity demanded refers to the effect of a price change on the quantity demanded. It refers to a **movement along a demand curve**— *the graphic representation of the effect of a change in price on the quantity demanded.* A **shift in demand** refers to *the effect of anything other than price on demand.* **Shift factors of demand** are *factors that cause shifts in the demand curve.* A change in anything besides price causes a shift of the entire demand curve.

Exhibit 2 distinguishes between a shift in demand—a shift of the entire demand curve as shown by arrow A—and a change in quantity demanded—a movement along a demand curve as shown by arrow B. Summarizing:

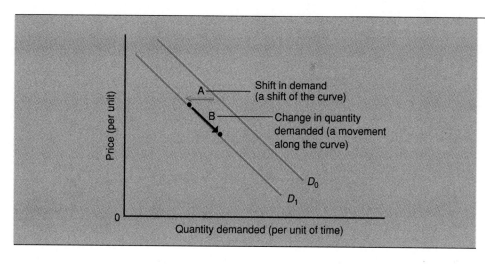

EXHIBIT 2   Shift in Demand versus Change in Quantity Demanded

A shift in demand—a shift in the entire demand curve—brought about by a shift in a nonprice factor is shown by arrow A. A change in quantity demanded—a movement along a demand curve—brought about by a change in price of that good is shown by arrow B.

If how much is demanded is affected by price, we call that effect a change in the quantity demanded. Since a demand curve tells us how much is demanded at different prices, a change in the quantity demanded is represented graphically by a movement along the demand curve.

If how much is demanded is affected by a factor other than the price of the good (by a shift factor of demand), there is said to be a shift in demand.

3 Changes in quantity demanded are shown by movements along a demand curve. Shifts in demand are shown by a shift of the entire demand curve.

Important shift factors of demand include:

1. Society's income.
2. The prices of other goods.
3. Tastes.
4. Expectations.

These aren't the only shift factors. In fact anything—except price changes of that good—that affects demand (and many things do) is a shift factor. While economists agree these shift factors are important, they believe that no shift factor influences how much is demanded as consistently as does price of the specific item. That's what makes economists focus first on price as they try to understand the world. That's why economists make the law of demand central to their analysis.

Shift Factors of Demand

Important shift factors of demand include:

1. Society's income.
2. The prices of other goods.
3. Tastes.
4. Expectations.

A Review

Let's test your understanding by having you specify what happens to your demand curve for cassettes in the following examples: First, let's say you buy a CD player. Next, let's say that the price of cassettes falls; and finally, say that you won $1 million dollars in a lottery. What happens to the demand for cassettes in each case? If you answered: It shifts in; it remains unchanged; and it shifts out—you've got it.

The Demand Table

As I emphasized in Chapter 1, introductory economics depends heavily on graphs and graphical analysis—translating ideas into graphs and back again into words. So let's graph the demand curve.

Exhibit 3(a), a demand table, describes Alice's demand for renting videocassettes. For example, at a price of $2, Alice will rent (buy the use of) six cassettes per week and at a price of 50 cents she will rent nine.

There are five points about the relationship between the number of videos Alice rents and the price of renting them that are worth mentioning. First, the relationship follows the law of demand: as the rental price rises, quantity demanded decreases. Second, quantity demanded has a specific *time dimension* to it. In this example demand refers to the number of cassette rentals per week, not the number of cassettes rented per day, hour, or year. Without the time dimension, the table wouldn't provide us with any useful information. Nine cassette rentals per year is quite a different

EXHIBIT 3 (a and b)   From a Demand Table to a Demand Curve

The demand table in (a) is translated into a demand curve in (b). Each combination of price and quantity in the table corresponds to a point on the curve. For example, point A on the graph represents row A in the table: Alice demands 9 videocassette rentals at a price of 50 cents. A demand curve is constructed by plotting all points from the demand table and connecting the points by a line.

	Price per cassette (in dollars)	Cassette rentals demanded per week
A	$0.50	9
B	1.00	8
C	2.00	6
D	3.00	4
E	4.00	2

(a) A demand table

(b) A demand curve   (per week)

concept from nine cassette rentals per week. Third, the cassette rentals that Alice buys are interchangeable—the ninth cassette rental doesn't significantly differ from the first, third, or any other cassette rental.

The concept of interchangeable goods causes economists significant problems in discussing real-world demand schedules because the quality of goods often differs in the real world. A pink Volkswagen is quite different from a gray Aston Martin, yet they're both cars. Luckily, in textbooks interchangeable goods cause few problems because we can pick and choose among examples. Textbook authors simply avoid examples that raise significant quality problems. However, it's only fair to point out that in the real world economists spend a great deal of time adjusting their analyses for differences in quality among goods.

The fourth and fifth points are already familiar to you. Fourth, the price the table refers to is a relative price even though it is expressed as a money price, and fifth, the schedule assumes that everything else is held constant.

From a Demand Table to a Demand Curve

Exhibit 3(b) translates the demand table in Exhibit 3(a) into a graph. Point A (quantity = 9, price = $.50) is graphed first at the (9, $.50) coordinates. Next we plot points B, C, D, and E in the same manner and connect the resulting dots with a solid line. The result is the demand curve, which graphically conveys the same information that's in the demand table. Notice that the demand curve is downward sloping (from left to right), indicating that the law of demand holds in the example. When a curve slopes downward to the right, we say that there is an *inverse* relationship between the price and the quantity demanded.

4 To derive a demand curve from a demand table, you plot each point in the demand table on a graph and connect the points.

The demand curve represents the *maximum price* that an individual will pay for various quantities of a good; the individual will happily pay less. For example, say someone offers Alice six cassette rentals at a price of $1 each (point F of Exhibit 3(b)). Will she accept? Sure; she'll pay any price within the shaded area to the left of the demand curve. But if someone offers her six rentals at $3.50 each (point G), she won't accept. At a rental price of $3.50 apiece, she's willing to buy only three cassette rentals.

Individual and Market Demand Curves

Normally, economists talk about market demand curves rather than individual demand curves. A **market demand curve** is *the horizontal sum of all individual demand curves*. Market demand curves are what most firms are interested in. Firms don't care whether individual A or individual B buys their good; they care that *someone* buys their good.

EXHIBIT 4 (a and b)   From Individual Demands to a Market Demand Curve

The table (a) shows the demand schedules for Alice, Bruce, and Cathy. Together they make up the market for videocassette rentals. Their total quantity demanded (market demand) for videocassette rentals at each price is given in column 5. As you can see in (b), Alice's, Bruce's, and Cathy's demand curves can be added together to get the total market demand curve. For example, at a price of $2, Cathy demands 0, Bruce demands 3, and Alice demands 6, for a market demand of 9 (point D).

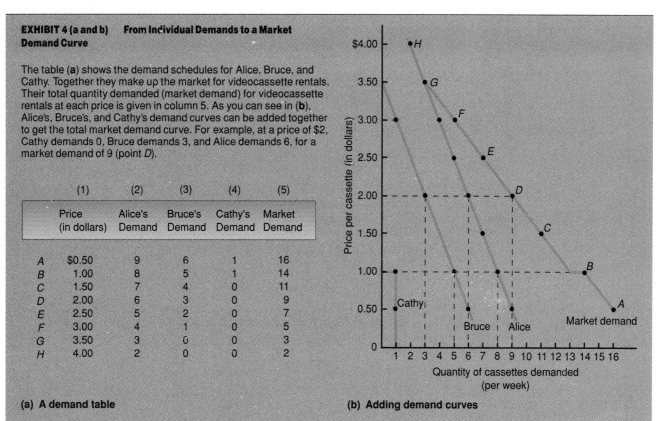

	(1)	(2)	(3)	(4)	(5)
	Price (in dollars)	Alice's Demand	Bruce's Demand	Cathy's Demand	Market Demand
A	$0.50	9	6	1	16
B	1.00	8	5	1	14
C	1.50	7	4	0	11
D	2.00	6	3	0	9
E	2.50	5	2	0	7
F	3.00	4	1	0	5
G	3.50	3	0	0	3
H	4.00	2	0	0	2

(a) A demand table

(b) Adding demand curves

It's a good graphical exercise to add individual demand curves together to create a market demand curve. I do that in Exhibit 4. In it I assume that the market consists of three buyers, Alice, Bruce, and Cathy, whose demand tables are given in Exhibit 4(a). Alice and Bruce have demand tables similar to the demand tables discussed previously. At a price of $3 each, Alice rents four cassettes; at a price of $2, she rents six. Cathy is an all-or-nothing individual. She rents one cassette as long as the price is equal to or below $1; otherwise she rents nothing. If you plot Cathy's demand curve, it's a vertical line. However, the law of demand still holds: as price increases, quantity demanded decreases.

The quantity demanded by each demander is listed in columns 2, 3, and 4 of Exhibit 4(a). Column 5 gives total market demand; each entry is the sum of the entries in columns 2, 3, and 4. For example, at a price of $3 apiece (row F), Alice demands four cassette rentals, Bruce demands one, and Cathy demands zero, for a total market demand of five cassette rentals.

Exhibit 4(b) shows three demand curves: one each for Alice, Bruce, and Cathy. The market, or total, demand curve is the horizontal sum of the individual demand curves. To see that this is the case, notice that if we take the quantity demanded at $1 by Alice (8), Bruce (5), and Cathy (1), they sum to 14, which is point B (14, $1) on the market demand curve. We can do that for each price. Alternatively, we can simply add the individual quantities demanded, given in the demand tables, prior to graphing (which we do in column 5 of Exhibit 4(a)), and graph that total in relation to price. Not surprisingly, we get the same total market demand curve.

In practice, of course, firms don't measure individual demand curves, so they don't sum them up in this fashion. Instead, they estimate total demand. Still, summing up individual demand curves is a useful exercise because it shows you how the market demand curve is made up of the sum (the horizontal sum, graphically speaking) of the individual demand curves, and it gives you a good sense of where market demand curves come from. It also shows you that, even if individuals don't respond to small

Q–3: Derive a market demand curve from the following two individual demand curves:

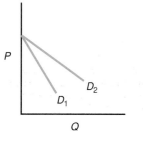

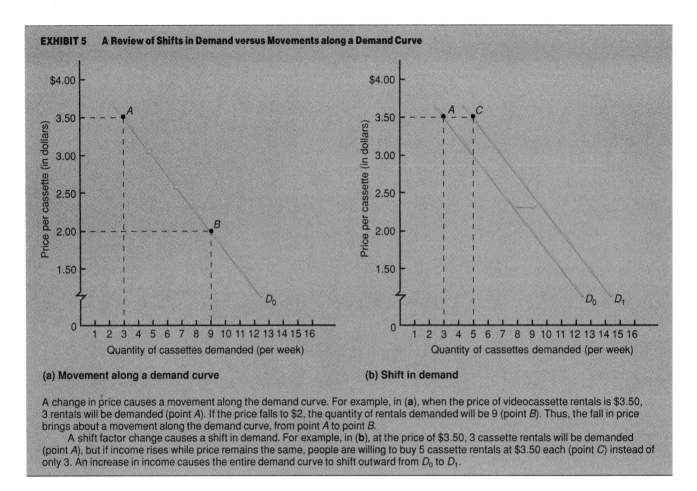

EXHIBIT 5   A Review of Shifts in Demand versus Movements along a Demand Curve

(a) Movement along a demand curve   **(b) Shift in demand**

A change in price causes a movement along the demand curve. For example, in (**a**), when the price of videocassette rentals is $3.50, 3 rentals will be demanded (point *A*). If the price falls to $2, the quantity of rentals demanded will be 9 (point *B*). Thus, the fall in price brings about a movement along the demand curve, from point *A* to point *B*.

A shift factor change causes a shift in demand. For example, in (**b**), at the price of $3.50, 3 cassette rentals will be demanded (point *A*), but if income rises while price remains the same, people are willing to buy 5 cassette rentals at $3.50 each (point *C*) instead of only 3. An increase in income causes the entire demand curve to shift outward from D_0 to D_1.

For the market, the law of demand is based on two phenomena:

1. At lower prices, existing demanders buy more.

2. At lower prices, new demanders enter the market.

A Review

The difference between shift in demand and movement along a demand curve is that a change in a shift factor causes a shift in the entire demand curve, while a change in the price of a good causes a movement along a demand curve.

changes in price, the market demand curve can still be smooth and downward sloping. That's because for the market, the law of demand is based on two phenomena:

1. At lower prices, existing demanders buy more.

2. At lower prices, new demanders (some all-or-nothing demanders like Cathy) enter the market.

Now let's make sure you understand the distinction between a change in quantity demanded and a shift in demand.

Exhibit 5(a) shows the effect of a change in the price of cassette rentals from $3.50 each to $2 each. Point *A* (quantity demanded 3, price $3.50) represents the starting point. Now the price falls to $2 and the quantity demanded rises from 3 to 9, so we move along the demand curve to point *B*. Notice the demand curve (D_0) has already been drawn to demonstrate the effect that price has on quantity.

Now let's say that price of $3.50 doesn't change but income rises and, as it does, quantity demanded rises to 5. Thus, at a price of $3.50 apiece, 5 cassette rentals are demanded rather than only 3. That point is represented by point *C* in Exhibit 5(b). But if a rise in income causes a rise in quantity demanded at a price of $3.50 per cassette, it will also likely cause an increase in the quantity demanded at all other prices. The demand curve will not remain where it was, but will shift to D_1 to the right of D_0. Because of the change in income, the entire demand curve has shifted. Thus, we say a change in this shift factor has caused a shift in demand.

Let's try another example. Say the local theater decides to let everyone in for free. What will happen to demand for videocassettes? If your answer is there will be a shift in demand—the entire demand curve will shift inward—you've got it. Just to be sure, let's try one last example. Say tastes change: couch potatoes are out, outdoor exercise is in. What will happen to the demand for cassettes? The entire demand curve shifts in some more.

The difference between shifts in demand and movements along the demand curve deserves emphasis:

A change in any factor besides price causes a shift in demand (a shift of the entire demand curve).
A change in price of a good causes a change in the quantity demanded (a movement along an existing demand curve).

In one sense, supply is the mirror image of demand. Individuals control the **factors of production**—*inputs, or resources, necessary to produce goods.* Individuals' supply of these factors to the market mirrors other individuals' demand for those factors. For example, say you decide you want to rest rather than weed your garden. You hire someone to do the weeding; you demand labor. Someone else decides she would prefer more income instead of more rest; she supplies labor to you. You trade money for labor; she trades labor for money. Her supply is the mirror image of your demand.

For a large number of goods and services, however, the supply process is more complicated than demand. As Exhibit 6 shows, for many goods there's an intermediate step in supply. Individuals supply factors of production to **firms**—*organizations of individuals that transform factors of production into usable goods.*

Let's consider a simple example. Say you're a taco technician. You supply your labor to the factor market. The taco company demands your labor (hires you). The

SUPPLY

Factors of production   Resources, or inputs, necessary to produce goods.

Video Series, Economics U$A: Markets: Do They Meet Our Needs? Segment 2.2

Firms   Organizations of individuals that transform factors of production into usable goods.

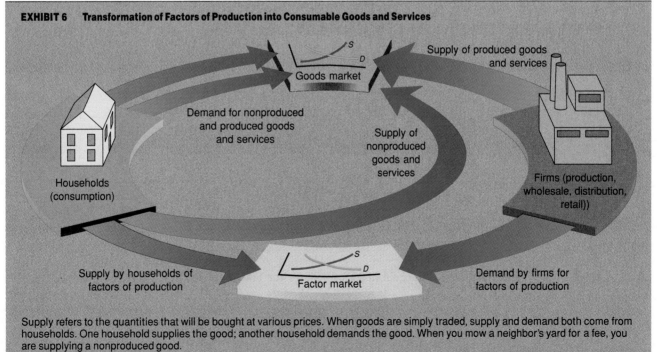

EXHIBIT 6   Transformation of Factors of Production into Consumable Goods and Services

Goods market

Supply of produced goods and services

Demand for nonproduced and produced goods and services

Supply of nonproduced goods and services

Households (consumption)

Firms (production, wholesale, distribution, retail))

Supply by households of factors of production

Factor market

Demand by firms for factors of production

Supply refers to the quantities that will be bought at various prices. When goods are simply traded, supply and demand both come from households. One household supplies the good; another household demands the good. When you mow a neighbor's yard for a fee, you are supplying a nonproduced good.

With produced goods and services, such as a television and insurance, the supply process is more complicated. Households supply factors; firms demand factors and use those factors to produce goods and services. These produced goods are then supplied to households.

Most students can relate to factory outlet stores, which are an attempt to bypass the retail stage. I often mention how important distribution (and other service areas) is to today's economy.

Supply of produced goods involves a much more complicated process than demand and is divided into analysis of factors of production and the transformation of those factors into goods.

taco company combines your labor with other inputs like meat, cheese, beans, and tables, and produces many tacos (production) which it supplies to customers in the goods market. For produced goods, supply depends not only on individuals' decisions to supply factors of production; it also depends on firms' ability to produce—to transform those factors of production into usable goods.

The supply process of produced goods can be much more complicated. Often there are many layers of firms—production firms, wholesale firms, distribution firms, and retailing firms—each of which passes on in-process goods to the next layer of firms. Real-world production and supply of produced goods is a multistage process.

The supply of nonproduced goods is more direct. Individuals supply their labor in the form of services directly to the goods market. For example, an independent contractor may repair your washing machine. That contractor supplies his labor directly to you.

Thus, the analysis of the supply of produced goods has two parts: an analysis of the supply of factors of production to households and to firms, and an analysis of why firms transform those factors of production into usable goods and services.

The Law of Supply

In talking about supply, the same convention exists that we used for demand. Supply refers to the various quantities offered for sale at various prices. Quantity supplied refers to a specific quantity offered for sale at a specific price.

There's also a law of supply that corresponds to the law of demand. The law of supply states that the quantity supplied of a good is positively related to that good's price, other things constant. Specifically the **law of supply** states:

More of a good will be supplied the higher its price, other things constant.

5 The law of supply states that the quantity supplied of a good is directly related to the good's price. When price goes up, quantity supplied goes up. When price goes down, quantity supplied goes down.

Or alternatively:

Less of a good will be supplied the lower its price, other things constant.

Price regulates quantity supplied just as it regulates quantity demanded. Like the law of demand, the law of supply is fundamental to the invisible hand's (the market's) ability to coordinate individuals' actions.

What accounts for the law of supply? When the price of a good rises, individuals and firms can rearrange their activities in order to supply more of that good to the market, substituting production of that good for production of other goods. Thus, the same psychological tendency of individuals that underlies the law of demand—their determination to want more for less—underlies the law of supply. Individuals and firms want the highest price they can get for the smallest possible quantity they can supply.

Q-4: In the 1980s and 1990s, as animal activists caused a decrease in the demand for fur coats, the prices of furs fell. This made _____ decline. Should the missing words be "the supply" or "the quantity supplied"?

With firms, there's a second explanation of the law of supply. Assuming firms' costs are constant, a higher price means higher profits (the difference between a firm's revenues and its costs). The expectation of those higher profits leads it to increase output as price rises, which is what the law of supply states.

The Supply Curve

A **supply curve** is *the graphic representation of the law of supply.* The law of supply is shown graphically in Exhibit 7.

Notice how the supply curve slopes upward to the right. That upward slope captures the law of supply. It tells us that the quantity supplied varies *directly*—in the same direction—with the price.

Important Qualifications to the Law of Supply

The same qualifications hold for the law of supply that held for the law of demand.

2b The law of supply, like the law of demand, is based on opportunity cost and the individual firm's ability to substitute. Suppliers will substitute toward goods for which they receive higher relative prices.

Relative Price   The first qualification is that the law of supply refers to relative price. The reason is that, like the law of demand, the law of supply is based on individuals' and firms' ability to substitute production of one good for another, or vice versa. If the price of corn rises relative to the price of wheat, farmers will grow less wheat and more corn. If both prices rise by equal percentages, the relative price won't change and it won't be worthwhile to substitute one good for another.

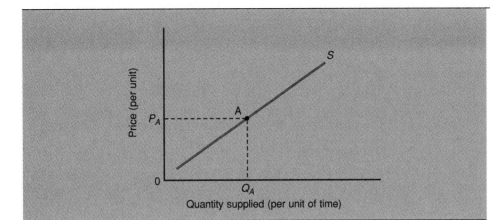

EXHIBIT 7   A Sample Supply Curve

The supply curve demonstrates graphically the law of supply, which states that the quantity supplied of a good is directly related to that good's price, other things constant. As the price of a good goes up, the quantity supplied also goes up, so the supply curve is upward sloping.

Other Things Constant   As with the law of demand, the other important qualification of the law of supply is that it assumes other things are held constant. Thus, if the price of wheat rises and quantity supplied falls, you'll look for something else that changed—for example, a drought might have caused a drop in supply. Your expectations would go as follows: Had there been no drought, the quantity supplied would have increased in response to the rise in price, but because there was a drought, the supply decreased, which caused prices to rise.

As with the law of demand, the law of supply represents economists' off-the-cuff response to the question: What happens to quantity supplied if price rises? If the law seems to be violated, economists search for some other variable that has changed. As was the case with demand, these other variables that might change are called shift factors. The same distinctions in terms made for demand apply to supply.

> **Supply** refers to *a schedule of quantities a seller is willing to sell per unit of time at various prices, other things constant.*
>
> **Quantity supplied** refers to *a specific amount that will be supplied at a specific price.*

In graphical terms, supply refers to the entire supply curve because a supply curve tells us how much will be offered for sale at various prices. "Quantity supplied" refers to a point on a supply curve, such as point *A* in Exhibit 7.

The second distinction that is important to make is between the effects of a change in price and the effects of shift factors on how much of a good is supplied. Changes in price cause changes in quantity supplied; such changes are represented by **a movement along a supply curve**—*the graphic representation of the effect of a change in price on the quantity supplied.* If the amount supplied is affected by anything other than price, that is by a shift factor of supply, there will be a **shift in supply**—*the graphic representation of the effect of a change in a factor other than price on supply.*

The distinction between a shift in supply and a change in quantity supplied is shown in Exhibit 8.

Again, here I am setting up the macro/micro distinction which will be carried through to the macro section. Macro analysis refers to the price level; micro supply demand analysis refers to **relative** prices.

Shifts in Supply versus Movements along a Supply Curve

6 Just as with demand, it is important to distinguish between a shift in supply (a shift of the entire supply curve) and a movement along a supply curve (a change in the quantity supplied due to a change in price).

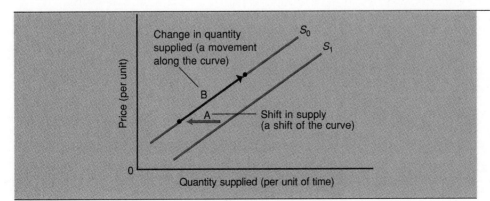

EXHIBIT 8   Shift in Supply versus Change in Quantity Supplied

A shift in supply—a shift in the entire supply curve—brought about by a shift in a nonprice factor is shown by arrow A. A change in quantity supplied—a movement along a supply curve—brought about by a change in price is shown by arrow B.

A shift in supply—a shift of the entire supply curve—is shown by arrow A. A change in the quantity supplied—a movement along the supply curve—is shown by arrow B.

Shift Factors of Supply

Important shift factors of supply include:

1. The prices of inputs used in the production of a good.

2. Technology.

3. Suppliers' expectations.

4. Taxes and subsidies.

Some important shift factors of supply include:

1. Changes in the prices of inputs used in the production of a good.
2. Changes in technology.
3. Changes in suppliers' expectations.
4. Changes in taxes and subsidies.

These aren't all the shift factors; as was the case with demand, anything that affects supply, other than price, is a shift factor. Each of these shift factors will cause a shift in supply, whereas a change in the price causes a movement along the supply curve.

A Review

A shift of the supply curve is often due to a change in the costs of production.

To cement the difference into your mind, ask yourself what might cause you to shift your supply curve of labor out, and what might cause you to shift your supply curve of labor in. Say for example, that you suddenly decide that you absolutely need a new car. What is likely to happen to your labor supply curve? How about if you suddenly won a million dollars in the lottery? And finally, how about if the wage you could earn doubled? If you came up with the answers: shift out, shift in, and no change—you've got it down. If not, it's time for a review.

Do we see such shifts in the supply curve often? Yes. A good example is computers. For the past 30 years, technological changes have continually shifted computers' supply curve out.

The Supply Table

7 To derive a supply curve from a supply table, you plot each point in the supply table on a graph and connect the points.

Remember Exhibit 4(a)'s demand table for cassette rentals. In Exhibit 9(a), columns 2 (Ann), 3 (Barry), and 4 (Charlie), we follow the same reasoning to construct a supply table for three hypothetical cassette suppliers. Each supplier follows the law of supply: When price rises, each supplies more, or at least as much as each did at a lower price.

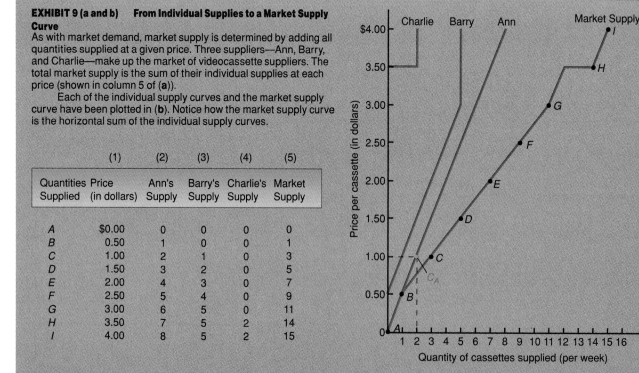

EXHIBIT 9 (a and b)   From Individual Supplies to a Market Supply Curve

As with market demand, market supply is determined by adding all quantities supplied at a given price. Three suppliers—Ann, Barry, and Charlie—make up the market of videocassette suppliers. The total market supply is the sum of their individual supplies at each price (shown in column 5 of (**a**)).

Each of the individual supply curves and the market supply curve have been plotted in (**b**). Notice how the market supply curve is the horizontal sum of the individual supply curves.

	(1)	(2)	(3)	(4)	(5)
Quantities Supplied	Price (in dollars)	Ann's Supply	Barry's Supply	Charlie's Supply	Market Supply
A	$0.00	0	0	0	0
B	0.50	1	0	0	1
C	1.00	2	1	0	3
D	1.50	3	2	0	5
E	2.00	4	3	0	7
F	2.50	5	4	0	9
G	3.00	6	5	0	11
H	3.50	7	5	2	14
I	4.00	8	5	2	15

(a) A supply table

(b) Adding supply curves

SUPPLY, PRODUCTION, AND PROFIT

Many goods must be produced—that is, inputs must be physically transformed before they become desirable goods. Production is complicated and requires a separate analysis before it can be integrated into our analysis.

In what's called *Walrasian economics* (named after famous Swiss economist Leon Walras), the problem of production is assumed away; his is an analysis of a trading economy. This is important to recognize since it's Walrasian economics that provides the logical underpinnings for supply/demand analysis. In Walrasian economics individuals have certain goods they trade; at some prices they sell, at some (lower) prices they buy. It is in this sense that supply is simply the mirror image of demand.

An easy way to see that supply is a mirror image of demand is to think about your supply of hours of work. When we talk of work, we say you're supplying hours of work at $6 per hour. But that same supply of work can be thought of as demand for leisure time. If, at $6 an hour, you choose to work 8 hours a day, you're simultaneously choosing to keep 16 hours for yourself (24 hours a day minus the 8 hours spent working). If we talk in terms of leisure, we speak of demand for leisure; if we talk of work, we speak of supply of labor. One is simply the mirror image of the other.

Another approach to economics is *Marshallian economics* (named after Alfred Marshall, a famous English economist). Marshallian economics does include an analysis of production. It relates costs of production with what firms are willing to sell. The reason production is difficult to integrate with an analysis of supply is that, with many production processes, per-unit costs fall as production increases. For example, in the 1920s Henry Ford produced a lot more Model T cars than either he or any of his competitors had produced before. As he produced more, costs per unit fell and the price of cars fell. Even today many businesses will tell you that if they can increase demand for their good, their per-unit costs and their price will go down. Such examples don't violate the law of supply. Costs per unit fall because of the nature of production. As the nature of production changes, the upward-sloping supply curve shifts outward.

There's another point we should mention about supply. Sometimes students get the impression from textbooks that supply and demand simply exist—that firms can go out, find demand curves, and start supplying. That's not a realistic picture of how the economy works. Demand curves aren't there for students or firms to see. Producing goods and supplying them inevitably involves risk and uncertainty. A company like General Motors may spend $1 billion designing a certain type of car, only to find that consumers don't like its style, or that another company has produced a car consumers like better. In that case, GM suffers a large loss.

To compensate for the potential for losses, suppliers also have the potential to make a profit on goods they sell. When the price of a good is high compared to costs of the resources used in production, expected profits are high, so more producers are encouraged to take the risk. When the price of a good is low compared to the costs, fewer firms take the risk because expected profits are low. Thus, profit is a motivating force of supply in a market economy.

Exhibit 9(b) takes the information in Exhibit 9(a)'s supply table and translates it into a graph of each supplier's supply curve. For instance, point C_A on Ann's supply curve corresponds to the information in columns 1 and 2, row C. Point C_A is at a price of $1 per cassette and a quantity of 2 cassettes per week. Notice that Ann's supply curve is upward sloping, meaning that price is positively related to quantity. Charlie's and Barry's supply curves are similarly derived.

The supply curve represents the set of *minimum* prices an individual seller will accept for various quantities of a good. The market's invisible hand stops suppliers from charging more than the market price. If suppliers could escape the market's invisible hand and charge a higher price, they would gladly do so. Unfortunately for them, and fortunately for consumers, a higher price encourages other suppliers to begin selling cassettes. Competing suppliers' entry into the market places a limit on the price any supplier can charge.

The market supply curve is derived from individual supply curves in precisely the same way that the market demand curve was. To emphasize the symmetry, I've made the three suppliers quite similar to the three demanders. Ann (column 2) will supply 2 at $1; if price goes up to $2 she increases her supply to 4. Barry (column 3) begins supplying at $1, and at $3 supplies 5, the most he'll supply regardless of how high price rises. Charlie (column 4) has only two units to supply. At a price of $3.50 he'll supply that quantity, but higher prices won't get him to supply any more.

We sum horizontally the individual supply curves to get the market supply curve. In Exhibit 9(a) (column 5), we add together Ann's, Barry's, and Charlie's supply to

From a Supply Table to a Supply Curve

Q–5: Derive the market supply curve from the following two individual supply curves.

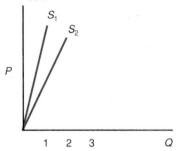

Individual and Market Supply Curves

arrive at the market supply curve, which is graphed in Exhibit 9(b). Notice each point on it corresponds to the information in columns 1 and 5 for each row. For example, point *H* corresponds to a price of $3.50 and a quantity of 14.

The market supply curve's upward slope is determined by two different sources: by existing suppliers supplying more and by new suppliers entering the market. Sometimes existing suppliers may not be willing to increase their quantity supplied in response to an increase in prices, but a rise in price often brings brand new suppliers into the market. For example, a rise in teachers' salaries will have little effect on the amount of teaching current teachers do, but it will increase the number of people choosing to be teachers.

The law of supply is based on two phenomena:
1. *At higher prices, existing suppliers supply more.*
2. *At higher prices, new suppliers enter the market.*

THE MARRIAGE OF SUPPLY AND DEMAND

When there is positive news about a company, there is a temporary excess demand for its stock.

I like to check for a current example of this in *The Wall Street Journal*, and use it as an illustration.

Thomas Carlyle, the English historian who dubbed economics "the dismal science," also wrote this chapter's introductory tidbit, "Teach a parrot the words *supply* and *demand* and you've got an economist." In Chapters 1 and 2, I hope I convinced you that economics is *not* dismal. In the rest of this chapter I hope to convince you that, while supply and demand are important to economics, parrots don't make good economists. If students think that when they've learned the terms *supply* and *demand* they've learned economics, they're mistaken. Those terms are just labels for the ideas behind supply and demand, and it's the ideas that are important. What's relevant about supply and demand isn't the labels but how the concepts interact. For instance, what happens if a freeze kills the blossoms on the orange trees? The quantity of oranges supplied isn't expected to equal the quantity demanded. It's in understanding the interaction of supply and demand that economics becomes interesting and relevant.

The Dynamic Laws of Supply and Demand

Q–6: Explain what a sudden popularity of "Economics Professor" brand casual wear would likely do to prices of that brand.

When you have a market in which neither suppliers nor demanders can organize and in which prices are free to adjust, economists have a good answer for the question: What happens if quantity supplied doesn't equal quantity demanded? If there is **excess supply** (a surplus), *quantity supplied is greater than quantity demanded,* and some suppliers won't be able to sell all their goods. Each supplier will think: "Gee, if I offer to sell it for a bit less, I'll be the lucky one who sells my good; someone else will be stuck with not selling their good." But because all suppliers with excess goods will be thinking the same thing, the price in the market will fall. As that happens, demanders will increase their quantity demanded. So the movement toward equilibrium caused by excess supply is on both the supply and demand sides.

8 The three dynamic laws of supply and demand are:
1. If quantity demanded is greater than quantity supplied, prices tend to rise; when quantity supplied is greater than quantity demanded, prices tend to fall.
2. The larger the difference between quantity demanded and quantity supplied, the greater the pressure for prices to rise (if there is excess demand) or fall (if there is excess supply).
3. When quantity demanded equals quantity supplied, prices have no tendency to change.

The reverse is also true. Say that instead of excess supply, there's **excess demand** (a shortage)—*quantity demanded is greater than quantity supplied*. There are more demanders who want the good than there are suppliers selling the good. Let's consider what's likely to go through demanders' minds. They'll likely call long-lost friends who just happen to be sellers of that good and tell them it's good to talk to them and, by the way, don't they want to sell that . . . ? Suppliers will be rather pleased that so many of their old friends have remembered them, but they'll also likely see the connection between excess demand and their friends' thoughtfulness. To stop their phones from ringing all the time, they'll likely raise their price. The reverse is true for excess supply. It's amazing how friendly suppliers become to potential demanders when there's excess supply.

This tendency for prices to rise when the quantity demanded exceeds the quantity supplied and for prices to fall when the quantity supplied exceeds the quantity demanded is a phenomenon economists call the **first dynamic law of supply and demand:**

> *When quantity demanded is greater than quantity supplied, prices tend to rise; when quantity supplied is greater than quantity demanded, prices tend to fall.*

It's called a *dynamic law* because *dynamic* refers to change and this law refers to how prices change, not to what prices will be.

How much pressure will there be for prices to rise or fall? That too will likely depend on differences between quantity supplied and quantity demanded. The greater the difference, the more pressure there is on individuals to raise or lower prices. If you're a seller (supplier) and all your old friends are calling you (there's major excess demand), you'll simply put a message on your answering machine saying, "The price has gone up 200 percent or 300 percent. If you're still interested in talking about old times, stay on the line. Otherwise, it was nice knowing you." If, however, only a couple of old friends call you (there's only minor excess demand), you'll probably raise your price only slightly. Or if you're a buyer (demander) and there's major excess supply, you'll leave the following message: "If you're trying to sell me anything, I'm broke and can only pay less than what you ask."

Thus, the **second dynamic law of supply and demand** is:

> *In a market, the larger the difference between quantity supplied and quantity demanded, the greater the pressure on prices to rise (if there is excess demand) or fall (if there is excess supply).*

People's tendencies to change prices exist as long as there's some difference between quantity supplied and quantity demanded. But the change in price brings the laws of supply and demand into play. As price falls, quantity supplied decreases as some suppliers leave the business (the law of supply); and as some people who originally weren't really interested in buying the good think, "Well, at this low price, maybe I do want to buy," quantity demanded increases (the law of demand). Similarly, when price rises, quantity supplied will increase (the law of supply) and quantity demanded will decrease (the law of demand).

Whenever quantity supplied and quantity demanded are unequal, price tends to change. If, however, quantity supplied and quantity demanded are equal, price will stay the same because no one will have an incentive to change it. This observation leads to the **third dynamic law of supply and demand:**

> *When quantity supplied equals quantity demanded, prices have no tendency to change.*

The Graphical Marriage of Supply and Demand

Exhibit 10 shows supply and demand curves for cassette rentals and demonstrates the operation of the dynamic laws of supply and demand. Let's consider what will happen to the price of cassettes in four cases:

1. When the price is $3.50 each;
2. When the price is $3 each;
3. When the price is $1.50 each; and
4. When the price is $2.50 each.

1. When price is $3.50, quantity supplied is 7 and quantity demanded is only 3. Excess supply is 4. At a price of $3, individual demanders can get all they want, but most suppliers can't sell all they wish; they'll be stuck with

For those classes with access to computers, *Micro/Macro Interactive* software includes a module, "Using the Market Model." Students can predict the effects of shifts in supply and demand on price.

Video Series, Economics U$A: Supply and Demand, Segment 15

Communication is centrally important for the working of markets.

To illustrate the second dynamic law of supply, ask your students to compare the upward pressure on the price for tickets to the Super Bowl with that of a Slim Whitman concert.

EXHIBIT 10   The Marriage of Supply and Demand

Combining Ann's supply from Exhibit 9 and Alice's demand from Exhibit 4, let's see the dynamic laws of supply and demand. These laws tell us the pressures on price when there is excess demand (there is upward pressure on price) or excess supply (there is downward pressure on price). Understanding these pressures is essential to understanding how to apply economics to reality.

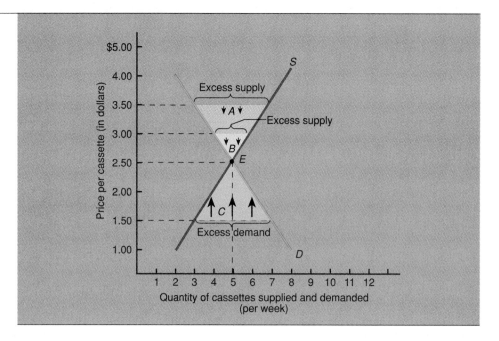

Q–7: In a flood, it is ironic that usable water supplies tend to decline because the pumps and water lines are damaged. What will a flood likely do to the prices of bottled water?

For classes with students with the background in mathematical tools, *Economics: An Honors Companion* provides a student-friendly presentation of basic economic concepts. See pages 135–139 for the basics of supply and demand.

cassettes that they'd like to rent. Suppliers will tend to offer their goods at a lower price and demanders, who see plenty of suppliers out there, will bargain harder for an even lower price. Both these forces will push the price as indicated by the *A* arrows in Exhibit 10. (Dynamic Law 1.)

2. When price falls from $3.50 to $3.00, the pressures are the same kind as in (1), only they're weaker, because excess supply is now only 2. There aren't as many dissatisfied suppliers searching for ways to sell their cassettes. Generally, the rate at which prices fall depends on the size of the gap between quantity supplied and quantity demanded. This smaller pressure is shown by the *B* arrows in Exhibit 10. (Dynamic Law 2.)

Now let's start from the other side.

3. Say price is $1.50. The situation is now reversed. Quantity supplied is 3 and quantity demanded is 7. Excess demand is 4. Now it's demanders who can't get what they want and suppliers who are in the strong bargaining position. The pressures will be on price to rise in the direction of the *C* arrows in Exhibit 10. (Dynamic Law 1.)

4. At $2.50, price is at its equilibrium: quantity supplied equals quantity demanded. Suppliers offer to sell 5 and demanders want to buy 5, so there's no pressure on price to rise or fall. Price will tend to remain where it is (point *E* in Exhibit 10). (Dynamic Law 3.)

EQUILIBRIUM

"The Price System in Microcosm: A P.O.W. Camp," by R. A. Radford, in *Classic Readings in Economics.*

The concept of equilibrium appears often throughout this text. You need to understand what equilibrium is and what it isn't. The concept itself comes from physics—classical mechanics. **Equilibrium** is *a concept in which opposing dynamic forces cancel each other out.* For example, a hot air balloon is in equilibrium when the upward force exerted by the hot air in the balloon equals the downward pressure exerted on the balloon by gravity. In supply and demand analysis, equilibrium means that the upward pressure on price is exactly offset by the downward pressure on price. **Equilibrium price** is *the price toward which the invisible hand drives the market.*

So much for what equilibrium is. Now let's consider what it isn't.

First, equilibrium isn't inherently good or bad. It's simply a state in which dynamic pressures offset each other. Some equilibria are awful. Say two countries are engaged in a nuclear war against each other and both sides are blown away. An equilibrium will have been reached, but there's nothing good about it.

PUBLIC CHOICE AND RENT-SEEKING ECONOMIC MODELS

Economics is a developing discipline, so the models used in one time period aren't necessarily the models used in another. In their research, economists debate which models are best and how to integrate more insights into their existing models.

Two groups of economists who've recently pushed back the frontiers of economics are the *public choice economists* and the *neoclassical political economists*. Public choice economists, led by Gordon Tullock and James Buchanan, argue that the political dimension must be part of economists' models. To integrate the political dimension, they apply economic analysis to politics and consider how economic forces affect the laws that are enacted and how, in turn, those laws affect economics. Their work was instrumental in leading to the invisible foot metaphor discussed in Chapter 1, and won James Buchanan a Nobel prize in 1986.

Neoclassical political economists share with public choice economists the view that the political dimension must be part of economists' models, and have developed a variety of formal models that significantly modify earlier models' predictions. Many of their models focus on rent seeking (how suppliers can restrict supply and thereby create rents for themselves). *Rent* is defined as an income earned when supply is restricted. For example, say a carpenter's union limits the number of people who can do carpentry. The supply of carpenters will decrease and existing carpenters will earn a higher wage that includes a rent component. Rents can be created either by using politics (the invisible foot) or by special agreements (the invisible handshake). Hence, neoclassical political economists are at the forefront of the movement to broaden economic analysis.

Although the formal analyses of both these groups haven't been adopted by the majority of economists, other economists often use their informal results and insights. Throughout this book I'll discuss these and other groups' views, but I'll focus on the mainstream model that the majority of economists use.

Second, equilibrium isn't a state of the world. It's a characteristic of the model—the framework you use to look at the world. The same situation could be seen as an equilibrium in one framework and as a disequilibrium in another. Say you're describing a car that's speeding along at 100 miles an hour. That car is changing position relative to objects on the ground. Its movement could be, and generally is, described as if it were in disequilibrium. However, if you consider this car relative to another car going 100 miles an hour, the cars could be modeled as being in equilibrium because their positions relative to each other aren't changing.

Understanding that equilibrium is a characteristic of the framework of analysis, not of the real world, is important in applying economic models to reality. For example, in the preceding description I said equilibrium occurs where quantity supplied equals quantity demanded. In a model where the invisible hand is the only force operating, that's true. In the real world, however, other forces—political and social forces—are operating. These will likely push price away from that supply/demand equilibrium. Were we to consider a model that included all these forces—political, social, and economic—equilibrium would be likely to exist where quantity supplied isn't equal to quantity demanded. In the real world, the invisible hand, foot, and handshake often work in different directions and vary in strength. For example:

In the real world, there exist other forces besides pure supply and demand. Political pressure (the invisible foot) and social pressures (the invisible handshake) can be powerful actors in the determination of equilibrium.

- In agricultural markets, farmers use political pressure (the invisible foot) to obtain higher than supply/demand equilibrium prices. Generally they succeed, so agricultural prices rise above the supply/demand equilibrium price. The laws of supply and demand assume no political pressures on prices.
- In labor markets, social pressures often offset economic pressures and prevent unemployed individuals from accepting work at lower wages than currently employed workers (the invisible handshake). Similarly, when there's a strike, social pressures prevent people who don't have jobs from taking jobs strikers have left. People who do take those jobs are called names like *scab* or *strikebreaker,* and they don't like those names. A pure supply and demand model, though, assumes everyone who wants a job will try to become a scab.
- In product markets, suppliers conspire to limit entry by other suppliers. They work hard to get Congress to establish tariffs and make restrictive regulations (the invisible foot). They also devise pricing strategies that scare off other suppliers and allow them to hold their prices higher than a supply/demand equilibrium. A pure supply and demand model assumes no conspiring at all.

Agricultural markets have significant government intervention.

If one is familiar with experiments and wants to conduct a double auction experiment, this is a good place to do it. But it is not a minor undertaking; it requires significant commitment and knowledge of experiments to run successfully. If *Experiments in Teaching and in Understanding Economies* by Ortman and Colander is your first introduction to experiments, it's probably best not to do it. You might, however, sit in on a colleague's experiment to get a feel for it. Otherwise, assuming all goes as planned, Ortman has made a video of some of his experiments. This video can be obtained through your McGraw-Hill/Irwin representative, and will give you a sense of the experiment. Experiments are a great way to teach and bring the class into economics, but to run them well requires quite a bit of background.

CHANGES IN SUPPLY AND DEMAND

• In the housing rental markets, consumers often organize politically and get local government to enact rent controls (ceilings on rents that can be charged for apartments). Here's an example of government (the invisible foot) putting downward pressure on price.

If social and political forces were included in the analysis, they'd provide a counterpressure to the dynamic forces of supply and demand. The result would be an equilibrium with continual excess supply or excess demand if the market were considered only in reference to economic forces. The invisible hand pushing toward a supply/demand equilibrium would be thwarted by other invisible forces pushing in the other direction.

A formal political/social/economic model that included all these forces simultaneously would be complicated, and economists are still working on perfecting one. Meanwhile economists, in their formal analysis, focus on a pure supply and demand model in which only the invisible hand is operating. That model lets you see clearly the economic forces at work. When economists apply the pure supply/demand model to reality, however, they discuss the effects of these other forces.

In this book I'll introduce you to both the formal model (in which only market forces are operating) and the informal model (in which all forces are operating).

To ensure that you understand the supply and demand graphs throughout the book and can apply them, let's go through three examples. Exhibit 11(a) deals with an increase in demand; Exhibit 11(b) deals with a decrease in supply.

Let's consider again the supply and demand for cassette rentals. In Exhibit 11(a), the supply is S_0 and initial demand is D_0. They meet at an equilibrium price of $2.25 per cassette and a quantity demanded of 8 cassettes per week (point A). Now say

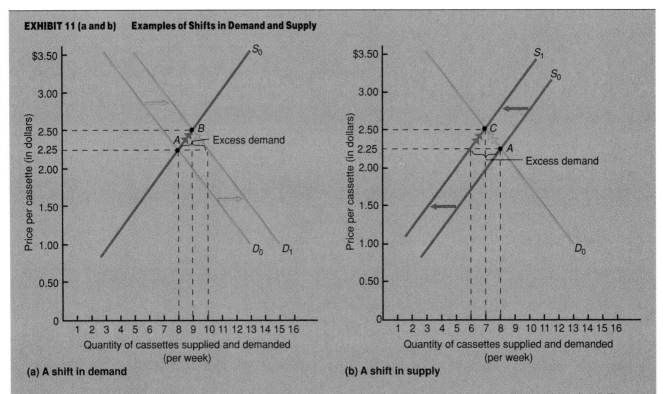

EXHIBIT 11 (a and b)   Examples of Shifts in Demand and Supply

(a) A shift in demand

(b) A shift in supply

When there is an increase in demand (the demand curve shifts outward), there is upward pressure on the price, as shown in (**a**). If demand increases from D_0 to D_1, the quantity of cassette rentals that was demanded at a price of $2.25, 8, increases to 10, but the quantity supplied remains at 8. This excess demand tends to cause prices to rise. Eventually, a new equilibrium is reached at the price of $2.50, where the quantity supplied and the quantity demanded is 9 (Point *B*).

If supply of cassette rentals decreases, then the entire supply curve shifts inward to the left, as shown in (**b**), from S_0 to S_1. At the price of $2.25, the quantity supplied has now decreased to 6 cassettes, but the quantity demanded has remained at 8 cassettes. The excess demand tends to force the price upward. Eventually, an equilibrium is reached at the price of $2.50 and quantity 7 (point *C*).

■n Chapter 1, I distinguished between an economic force and a market force. Economic forces are operative in all aspects of our lives; market forces are economic forces that are allowed to be expressed through a market. My examples in this chapter are of market forces—of goods sold in a market—but supply and demand can also be used to analyze situations in which economic, but not market, forces operate. An economist who is adept at this is Gary Becker of the University of Chicago. He has applied supply and demand analysis to a wide range of issues, even the supply of and demand for children.

Becker doesn't argue that children should be bought and sold. But he does argue that economic considerations play a large role in people's decisions on how many children to have.

In farming communities, children can be productive early in life; by age six or seven, they can work on a farm. In an advanced industrial community, children provide pleasure, but generally don't contribute productively to family income. Even getting them to help around the house can be difficult.

Becker argues that since the price of having children is lower for a farming society than for an industrial society, farming societies will have more children per family. Quantity of children demanded will be larger. And that's what we find. Developing countries that rely primarily on farming often have three, four, or more children per family. Industrial societies average fewer than two children per family.

demand for cassette rentals increases from D_0 to D_1. At a price of $2.25, the quantity of cassette rentals supplied will be 8 and the quantity demanded will be 10; excess demand of 2 exists.

As the first dynamic law of supply and demand dictates, the excess demand pushes prices upward in the direction of the small arrows, decreasing the quantity demanded and increasing the quantity supplied. As it does so, movement takes place along both the supply curve and the demand curve. The first dynamic law of supply and demand tells us that price will be pushed up.

The upward push on price decreases the gap between the quantity supplied and the quantity demanded. As the gap decreases, the upward pressure decreases, as the second dynamic law requires. But as long as that gap exists at all, price will be pushed upward until the new equilibrium price ($2.50) and new quantity (9) are reached (point B). At point B the third dynamic law of supply and demand takes hold: quantity supplied equals quantity demanded. So the market is in equilibrium. Notice that the adjustment is twofold: The higher price brings about equilibrium by both increasing the quantity supplied (from 8 to 9) and decreasing the quantity demanded (from 10 to 9).

Exhibit 11(b) begins with the same situation that we started with in Exhibit 11(a); the initial equilibrium quantity and price are 8 cassettes per week and $2.25 per cassette (point A). In this example, however, instead of demand increasing, let's assume supply decreases—say because some suppliers change what they like to do, and decide they will no longer supply cassettes. That means that the entire supply curve shifts inward to the left (from S_0 to S_1). At the initial equilibrium price of $2.25, the quantity demanded is greater than the quantity supplied. Two more cassettes are demanded than are supplied. (Excess demand = 2.)

As the dynamic laws of supply and demand require, this excess demand exerts upward pressure on price. Price is pushed in the direction of the small arrows. As the price rises, the upward pressure on price is reduced (in accord with the second dynamic law of supply and demand) but will still exist until the new equilibrium price, $2.50, and new quantity, 7, are reached. At $2.50, the quantity supplied equals the quantity demanded. The adjustment has involved a movement along the demand curve and the new supply curve. As price rises, quantity supplied is adjusted upward and quantity demanded is adjusted downward until quantity supplied equals quantity demanded where the new supply curve intersects the demand curve at point C, an equilibrium of 7 and $2.50.

I leave a final example as an exercise for you. Demonstrate graphically how the price of computers could have fallen dramatically in the past 10 years, even as demand increased. (Hint: Supply has shifted even more, so even at lower prices, far more computers have been supplied than were being supplied 10 years ago.)

Q–8: Demonstrate graphically the effect of a heavy frost in Florida on the equilibrium quantity and price of oranges.

I like to ask my students to search their hometown paper for examples of the laws of supply and demand in action.

Q–9: Say a hormone has been discovered that increases cows' milk production by 20 percent. Demonstrate graphically what effect this discovery would have on the price and quantity of milk sold in a market.

Q–10: Demonstrate graphically the likely effect of an increase in the price of gas on the equilibrium quantity and price of compact cars.

CONCLUSION

Throughout the book I'll be presenting examples of supply and demand. So I'll end this chapter here because its intended purposes have been served. What were those intended purposes? First, the discussion and examples should have exposed you to enough economic terminology and economic thinking to allow you to proceed to my more complicated examples. Second, the discussion should also have set your mind to work putting the events around you into a supply/demand framework. Doing that will give you new insights into the events that shape all our lives. Finally, this chapter should have made you wary of applying supply/demand analysis to the real world without considering the other invisible forces out there battling the invisible hand.

CHAPTER SUMMARY

- The law of demand (supply): More (less) of a good will be demanded (supplied) the lower its price, other things constant.
- A market demand (supply) curve is the sum of all individual demand (supply) curves.
- A change in quantity demanded (supplied) is a movement along the demand (supply) curve. A change in demand (supply) is a shift of the entire demand (supply) curve.

- The laws of supply and demand refer to relative prices; they hold true because individuals can substitute.
- When quantity demanded is greater than quantity supplied, prices tend to rise. When quantity supplied is greater than quantity demanded, prices tend to fall.
- When quantity supplied equals quantity demanded, prices have no tendency to change.
- When demand shifts out, the equilibrium price rises. When supply shifts out, the equilibrium price falls.

KEY TERMS

demand *(62)*
demand curve *(60)*
equilibrium *(74)*
equilibrium price *(74)*
excess demand *(72)*
excess supply *(72)*
factors of production *(67)*
firms *(67)*
first dynamic law of supply and demand *(73)*
law of demand *(60)*

law of supply *(68)*
market demand curve *(64)*
money price *(60)*
movement along a demand curve *(62)*
movement along a supply curve *(69)*
other things constant *(61)*
partial equilibrium analysis *(62)*
quantity demanded *(62)*
quantity supplied *(69)*
relative price *(60)*

second dynamic law of supply and demand *(73)*
shift factors of demand *(62)*
shift in demand *(62)*
shift in supply *(69)*
supply *(69)*
supply curve *(68)*
third dynamic law of supply and demand *(73)*

QUESTIONS FOR THOUGHT AND REVIEW

The number after each question represents the estimated degree of critical thinking required. (1 = almost none; 10 = deep thought.)

1. Draw a demand curve from the following demand table. *(1)*

P	Q
37	20
47	15
57	10
67	5

2. Draw a market demand curve from the following demand table. *(1)*

P	D_1	D_2	D_3	Market Demand
37	20	4	8	32
47	15	2	7	24
57	10	0	6	16
67	5	0	5	10

3. It has just been reported that eating meat is bad for your health. Using supply and demand curves, demonstrate the

report's likely effect on the price and quantity of steak sold in the market. *(3)*

4. New York City has had residential rent control for many years. Using supply/demand analysis, explain what effect eliminating those controls would probably have. *(4)*

5. Draw a market supply curve from the following supply table. *(2)*

P	S_1	S_2	S_3
37	0	4	14
47	0	8	16
57	10	12	18
67	10	16	20

6. Show, using supply and demand curves, the likely effect of a minimum wage law. If you were a worker, would you support or oppose minimum wage laws? Why? *(6)*

7. Distinguish the effect of a shift factor of demand on the demand curve from the effect of a change in price on the demand curve. *(3)*

8. Say the United States were to legalize the sale of certain currently illegal drugs. Using supply/demand analysis, show what effect legalization would have on the price of those drugs and on the quantity bought. *(7)*

9. Mary has just stated that normally, as price rises, supply will increase. Her teacher grimaces. Why? *(5)*

10. Supply/demand analysis states that equilibrium occurs where quantity supplied equals quantity demanded, but in U.S. agricultural markets quantity supplied almost always exceeds quantity demanded. How can this be? *(5)*

PROBLEMS AND EXERCISES

1. You're given the following individual demand tables for comic books.

Price	John	Liz	Alex
$ 2	4	36	24
4	4	32	20
6	0	28	16
8	0	24	12
10	0	20	8
12	0	16	4
14	0	12	0
16	0	8	0

   a. Determine the market demand table.
   b. Graph the individual and market demand curves.
   c. If the current market price is $4, what's total market demand? What happens to total market demand if price rises to $8?
   d. Say that an advertising campaign increases demand by 50 percent. Illustrate graphically what will happen to the individual and market demand curves.

2. Draw hypothetical supply and demand curves for tea. Show how the equilibrium price and quantity will be affected by each of the following occurrences:
   a. Bad weather wreaks havoc with the tea crop.
   b. A medical report implying tea is bad for your health is published.
   c. A technological innovation lowers the cost of producing tea.
   d. Consumers' income falls.

3. This is a question concerning what economists call "the identification problem." Say you go out and find figures on the quantity bought of various products. You will find something like the following:

Product	Year	Quantity	Average Price
VCRs	1990	100,000	$210
	1991	110,000	220
	1992	125,000	225
	1993	140,000	215
	1994	135,000	215
	1995	160,000	220

   Plot these figures on a graph.
   a. Have you plotted a supply curve, a demand curve, or what?
   b. If we assume that the market for VCRs is competitive, what information must you know to determine whether these are points on a supply curve or on a demand curve?
   c. Say you know that the market is one in which suppliers set the price and allow the quantity to vary. Could you then say anything more about the curves you have plotted?
   d. What information about shift factors would you expect to find to make these points reflect the law of demand?

4. You're a commodity trader and you've just heard a report that the winter wheat harvest will be 2.09 billion bushels, a 44 percent jump, rather than an expected 35 percent jump to 1.96 billion bushels.
   a. What would you expect would happen to wheat prices?
   b. Demonstrate graphically the effect you suggested in *a*.

5. In the United States, gasoline costs consumers about $1.20 per gallon. In Italy it costs consumers about $4 per gallon. What effect does this price differential likely have on:
   a. The size of cars in the United States and in Italy?
   b. The use of public transportation in the United States and in Italy?
   c. The fuel efficiency of cars in the United States and in Italy? What would be the effect of raising the price of gasoline in the United States to $4 per gallon?

ANSWERS TO MARGIN QUESTIONS

1. Since all other prices fell 6%, the relative price of houses has actually risen 4%. The law of demand would predict that the quantity of houses demanded would fall.   *(61)*

2. *Demand for furs.* The other possibility, *quantity demanded*, is used to refer to movements along (not shifts of) the demand curve.   *(62)*

3. When adding two demand curves, you sum them horizontally, as in the accompanying diagram.   *(65)*

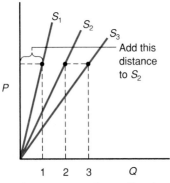

4. "The quantity supplied" declined because there was a movement along the supply curve. The supply curve itself remained unchanged.   *(68)*

5. When adding two supply curves, sum horizontally the two individual supply curves, as in the diagram below.   *(71)*

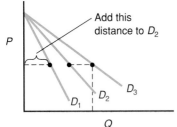

6. Customers will flock to stores demanding that funky "Economics Professor" look, creating excess demand. This excess demand will soon catch the attention of suppliers, and prices will be pushed upward.   *(72)*

7. As substitutes—tap water—decrease, demand for bottled water increases enormously, and there will be upward pressure on prices. The other invisible forces will, however, likely work in the opposite direction—against "profiteering" in people's misery.   *(74)*

8. A heavy frost in Florida will decrease the supply of oranges, increasing the price and decreasing the quantity demanded, as in the accompanying graph.   *(77)*

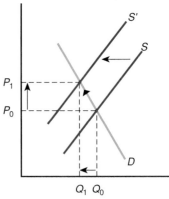

9. A discovery of a hormone that will increase cows' milk production by 20 percent will increase the supply of milk, pushing the price down and increasing the quantity demanded, as in the accompanying graph.   *(77)*

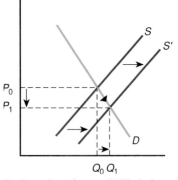

10. An increase in the price of gas will likely increase the demand for compact cars, increasing their price and increasing the quantity supplied, as in the accompanying graph.   *(77)*

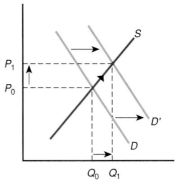

Algebraic Representation of Demand, Supply, and Equilibrium

In the chapter I discussed demand, supply, and the determination of equilibrium price and quantity in words and graphs. These concepts can also be presented in equations. In this appendix I do so, using straight-line supply and demand curves.

The Laws of Supply and Demand in Equations

Since the law of supply states that quantity supplied is positively related to price, the slope of an equation specifying a supply curve is positive. (The quantity intercept term is generally less than zero since suppliers are generally unwilling to supply a good at a price less than zero.) An example of a supply equation is:

$$Q_S = -5 + 2P,$$

where Q_S is units supplied and P is the price of each unit in dollars per unit. The law of demand states that as price rises, quantity demanded declines. Price and quantity are negatively related, so a demand curve has a negative slope. An example of a demand equation is:

$$Q_D = 10 - P,$$

where Q_D is units demanded and P is the price of each unit in dollars per unit.

Determination of Equilibrium   The equilibrium price and quantity can be determined in three steps using these two equations. To find the equilibrium price and quantity for these particular demand and supply curves, you must find the quantity and price that solve both equations simultaneously.

Step 1: Set the quantity demanded equal to quantity supplied:

$$Q_S = Q_D \rightarrow -5 + 2P = 10 - P.$$

Step 2: Solve for the price by rearranging terms. Doing so gives:

$$3P = 15$$
$$P = \$5.$$

Thus, equilibrium price is $5.

Step 3: To find equilibrium quantity, you can substitute $5 for P in either the demand or supply equation. Let's do it for supply: $Q_S = -5 + (2 \times 5) = 5$ units. I'll leave it to you to confirm that the quantity you obtain by substituting $P = \$5$ in the demand equation is also 5 units.

The answer could also be found graphically. The supply and demand curves specified by these equations are depicted in Exhibit A1. As you can see, demand and supply intersect; quantity demanded equals quantity supplied at a quantity of 5 units and a price of $5.

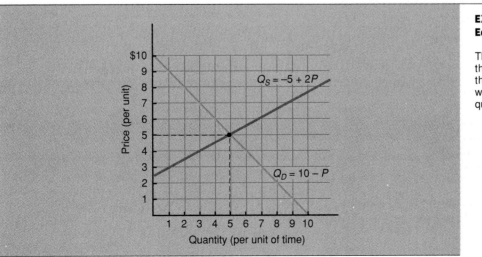

EXHIBIT A1   Supply and Demand Equilibrium

The algebra in this appendix leads to the same results as the geometry in the chapter. Equilibrium occurs where quantity supplied equals quantity demanded.

Movements along a Demand and Supply Curve The demand and supply curves above represent schedules of quantities demanded and supplied at various prices. Movements along each can be represented by selecting various prices and solving for quantity demanded and supplied. Let's create a supply and demand table using the above equations—supply: $Q_S = -5 + 2P$; demand: $Q_D = 10 - P$.

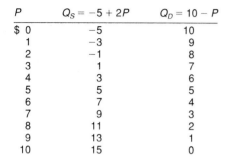

P	$Q_S = -5 + 2P$	$Q_D = 10 - P$
$0	−5	10
1	−3	9
2	−1	8
3	1	7
4	3	6
5	5	5
6	7	4
7	9	3
8	11	2
9	13	1
10	15	0

As you move down the rows, you are moving up along the supply schedule, as shown by increasing quantity supplied, and moving down along the demand schedule, as shown by decreasing quantity demanded. Just to confirm your equilibrium quantity and price calculations, notice that at a price of $5, quantity demanded equals quantity supplied.

Shifts of a Demand and Supply Schedule What would happen if suppliers' expectations changed so that they would be willing to sell more goods at every price? This shift factor of supply would shift the entire supply curve out to the right. Let's say that at every price, quantity supplied increases by three. Mathematically the new equation would be $Q_S = -2 + 2P$. The quantity intercept increases by 3. What would you expect to happen to equilibrium price and quantity? Let's solve the equations mathematically first.

Step 1: To determine equilibrium price, set the new quantity supplied equal to quantity demanded:

$$10 - P = -2 + 2P.$$

Step 2: Solve for the equilibrium price:

$$12 = 3P$$
$$P = \$4.$$

Step 3: To determine equilibrium quantity, substitute P in either the demand or supply equation:

$$Q_D = 10 - (1 \times 4) = 6 \text{ units}$$
$$Q_S = -2 + (2 \times 4) = 6 \text{ units}.$$

Equilibrium price declined to $4 and equilibrium quantity rose to 6, just as you would expect with a rightward shift in a supply curve.

Now let's suppose that demand shifts out to the right. Here we would expect both equilibrium price and equilibrium quantity to rise. We begin with our original supply and demand curves—supply: $Q_S = -5 + 2P$; demand: $Q_D = 10 - P$. Let's say at every price, the quantity demanded rises by 3. The new equation for demand would be $Q_D = 13 - P$. You may want to solve this equation for various prices to confirm that at every price, quantity demanded rises by 3. Let's solve the equations for equilibrium price and quantity

Step 1: Set the quantities equal to one another:

$$13 - P = -5 + 2P.$$

Step 2: Solve for equilibrium price:

$$18 = 3P$$
$$P = \$6.$$

Step 3: Substitute P in either the demand or supply equation:

$$Q_D = 13 - (1 \times 6) = 7 \text{ units}$$
$$Q_S = -5 + (2 \times 6) = 7 \text{ units}.$$

Equilibrium price rose to $6 and equilibrium quantity rose to 7 units, just as you would expect with a rightward shift in a demand curve.

Just to make sure you've got it, I will do two more examples. First, suppose the demand and supply equations for wheat per year in the United States can be specified as follows (notice that the slope is negative for the demand curve and positive for the supply curve):

$$Q_D = 500 - 2P$$
$$Q_S = -100 + 4P.$$

P is the price in dollars per thousand bushels and Q is the quantity of wheat in thousands of bushels. Remember that the units must always be stated. What is the equilibrium price and quantity?

Step 1: Set the quantities equal to one another:

$$500 - 2P = -100 + 4P.$$

Step 2: Solve for equilibrium price:

$$600 = 6P$$
$$P = \$100.$$

Step 3: Substitute P in either the demand or supply equation:

$$Q_D = 500 - (2 \times 100) = 300$$
$$Q_S = -100 + (4 \times 100) = 300.$$

Equilibrium quantity is 300 thousand bushels.

As my final example, take a look at Alice's demand curve depicted in Exhibit 4(b) in the chapter. Can you write an equation that represents the demand curve in that figure? It is $Q_D = 10 - 2P$. At price of zero, the quantity of cassette rentals Alice demands is 10, and for every increase in price of $1, the quantity she demands falls by 2. Now look at Ann's supply curve shown in Exhibit 9(b) in the chapter. Ann's supply curve mathematically is $Q_S = 2P$. At a zero price, the quantity Ann supplies is zero, and for every $1 increase in price, the quantity she supplies rises by 2. What is the equilibrium price and quantity?

Step 1: Set the quantities equal to one another:

$$10 - 2P = 2P$$

Step 2: Solve for equilibrium price:

$$4P = 10.$$
$$P = \$2.5.$$

Step 3: Substitute *P* in either the demand or supply equation:

$$Q_D = 10 - (2 \times 2.5) = 5, \text{ or}$$
$$Q_S = 2 \times 2.5 = 5 \text{ cassettes per week.}$$

Ann is willing to supply 5 cassettes per week at $2.50 per rental and Alice demands 5 cassettes at $2.50 per cassette rental. Remember that in Exhibit 10 in the chapter, I showed you graphically the equilibrium quantity and price of Alice's demand curve and Ann's supply curve. I'll leave it up to you to check that the graphic solution in Exhibit 10 is the same as the mathematical solution we came up with here.

Conclusion

We'll stop there. There's much more that can be done, but this is an economics book, not a math text. The purpose of this appendix was simply to introduce you to the algebraic presentation and show you that it is an alternative way of presenting the same concepts the graphs present.

QUESTIONS FOR THOUGHT AND REVIEW

1. Suppose the demand and supply for milk is described by the following equations: $Q_D = 600 - 100P$; $Q_S = -150 + 150P$, where *P* is price in dollars, Q_D is quantity demanded in millions of gallons per year, and Q_S is quantity supplied in millions of gallons per year.
   a. Create demand and supply tables corresponding to these equations.
   b. Graph supply and demand and determine equilibrium price and quantity.
   c. Confirm your answer to (*b*) by solving the equations mathematically.
2. Suppose a growth hormone is introduced that allows dairy farmers to offer 125 million more gallons of milk per year at each price.
   a. Construct new demand and supply curves reflecting this change. Describe with words what happened to the supply curve and to the demand curve.
   b. Graph the new curves and determine equilibrium price and quantity.
   c. Determine equilibrium price and quantity by solving the equations mathematically.
   d. Suppose the government set the price of milk at $3 a gallon. Demonstrate the effect of this regulation on the market for milk. What is quantity demanded? What is quantity supplied?

3. Write demand and supply equations that represent demand, D_0, and supply, S_0, in Exhibit 11(a) in the chapter.
   a. Solve for equilibrium price and quantity mathematically.
   b. Rewrite the demand equation to reflect the shift in demand to D_1. What happens to equilibrium price and quantity as shown in Exhibit 11 in the chapter? Confirm by solving the equations for equilibrium price and quantity.
4. Write demand and supply equations that represent demand D_0, and supply, S_0, in Exhibit 11(b) in the chapter.
   a. Solve for equilibrium price and quantity mathematically.
   b. Rewrite the supply equation to reflect the shift in supply to S_1. What happens to equilibrium price and quantity as shown in Exhibit 11 in the chapter? Confirm by solving the equations for equilibrium price and quantity.
5. a. How is a shift in demand reflected in a demand equation?
   b. How is a shift in supply reflected in a supply equation?
   c. How is a movement along a demand (supply) curve reflected in a demand (supply) equation?

Four
Using Supply and Demand

It is by invisible hands that we are bent and tortured worst.

~ Nietzsche

After reading this chapter, you should be able to:

1 Demonstrate the effect of a price ceiling and a price floor on a market.

2 Explain real-world events using supply and demand.

3 Discuss exchange rates using supply and demand.

4 Explain the effect of taxes and tariffs on equilibrium prices and quantity.

5 State the relevance to macroeconomics of the fallacy of composition.

6 Explain why interrelated supply and demand curves may undermine partial equilibrium demand/supply analysis.

In the last chapter I introduced you to the concepts of supply and demand. In this chapter I will: (1) show you the power of supply and demand; (2) show you how the invisible forces interact to change the outcome of supply and demand analysis; and (3) discuss when it is appropriate to apply supply and demand analysis directly, and when one must adjust supply and demand analysis with other issues kept at the back of one's mind.

SUPPLY AND DEMAND IN ACTION

I ended the last chapter with a generic example of supply and demand. Let's start this chapter with another example, this one from the real world.

OPEC and Oil Price Fluctuations

Exhibit 1(a) shows the changes in the price of oil from 1973 to 1996. Exhibit 1(b) demonstrates the supply/demand forces that caused the substantial rise in the price of oil adjusted for inflation from 1973 to 1981, when the supply of oil was severely restricted. Prior to the 1970s, the price of oil had been relatively stable. In the early 1970s, at a series of meetings of countries who were members of the Organization of Petroleum Exporting Countries (OPEC), some delegates who had studied economics pointed out that OPEC could get more revenue by selling less oil.

*Video Series, Economics USA:
Supply and Demand, Segment 15*

Their argument went as follows: If the countries could get together and restrict supply, the price of oil would rise dramatically. Each country would sell fewer barrels, but get a lot more dollars per barrel sold, thereby increasing revenues.

Exhibit 1(b) shows just how this worked. Initially the quantity supplied was 2 billion barrels per year and the price per barrel was $6. Total OPEC revenue was $12 billion ($6 × 2 billion). The agreement to reduce supply through OPEC shifted

EXHIBIT 1 (a, b, c, and d)   Supply, Demand, and Changing Oil Prices

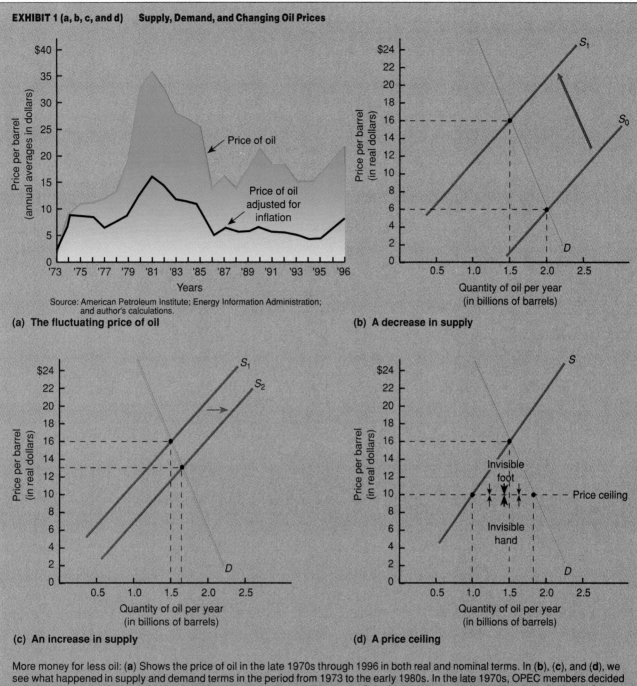

(a) **The fluctuating price of oil**

Source: American Petroleum Institute; Energy Information Administration; and author's calculations.

(b) **A decrease in supply**

(c) **An increase in supply**

(d) **A price ceiling**

More money for less oil: (**a**) Shows the price of oil in the late 1970s through 1996 in both real and nominal terms. In (**b**), (**c**), and (**d**), we see what happened in supply and demand terms in the period from 1973 to the early 1980s. In the late 1970s, OPEC members decided to limit their supply of oil to 1.5 billion barrels, represented by a shift to curve S_1 in (**b**). Initially, supplying 2 billion barrels of oil at $6 per barrel gave them a revenue of $12 billion, but with restricted supply, the real price of oil per barrel rose to $16, giving OPEC members a revenue of $24 billion (1.5 billion × $16). New exploration shifted the supply curve out in the early 1980s, lowering the inflation-adjusted price to between $12 and $14, as in (**c**).

Graph (**d**) shows the response of a market to a price ceiling such as the one imposed in the 1970s in the United States. In (**d**) the invisible hand is not allowed to operate; quantity demanded exceeds quantity supplied; and the result is shortage. In the 1970s, people lined up to buy limited supplies of gas for their cars.

supply back from S_0 to S_1. The quantity of oil supplied fell to 1.5 billion barrels and the price of oil adjusted for inflation rose to $16 per barrel. The members' revenue rose to $24 billion ($16 × 1.5 billion). By cutting production by 25 percent they doubled their revenues! The invisible handshake (which in this case operated through a very visible agreement to limit supply) had beaten the invisible hand, at least temporarily.

The invisible hand, however, was only temporarily beaten. The quantity demanded responded to the change in the price of oil—as the price rose, the quantity demanded fell as people switched to fuel-efficient cars and set their thermostats lower. The high price of oil also inspired a large number of non-OPEC suppliers (and OPEC members who could hide their oil sales from other members) to increase significantly the quantity of oil they supplied (an upward movement along the original supply curve). The high price of oil also encouraged oil companies to explore for more oil. These new discoveries of oil shifted oil's total supply curve outward, even as OPEC countries held their oil back. By 1981, the cartel's high price policy was undermined by these outward shifts, and oil prices began to decline.

Exhibit 1(c) shows the effect of the shift out of the supply curve for oil. By the late 1980s, the invisible hand had effectively broken OPEC's limitation on supply, and price adjusted for inflation fell to between $12 and $14 a barrel as shown in Exhibit 1(c). By the 1990s the price of oil had fallen to where it would have been (after adjustment for inflation) had OPEC never organized to limit supply.

Before these supply and demand adjustments occurred, U.S. political forces instituted measures to counteract the sudden jump in oil prices. The invisible foot put downward pressure on the price of oil in the United States. The United States imposed a **price ceiling**—*a government-imposed limit on how high a price can be charged*—on oil. This political pressure prevented the price of oil from rising enough to make the quantity supplied equal the quantity demanded. The result was an oil shortage. The quantity of oil demanded was greater than the quantity of oil supplied. There were dire predictions that people would freeze to death or wouldn't be allowed to use energy-intensive products.

Exhibit 1(d) shows how a price ceiling would cause such shortages. Suppose the price ceiling, the limit the government set on prices, is $10 per barrel, below the supply/demand equilibrium price of $16 per barrel. Quantity supplied is 1 billion barrels, while quantity demanded is 1.8 billion barrels. The difference between quantity supplied and quantity demanded reflects the number of people who want oil but cannot buy it. When the invisible foot or invisible handshake prevents price from rising to the equilibrium price, the invisible hand doesn't disappear. It places upward pressure on price while the invisible foot places downward pressure on price. In this case the invisible hand won out, and the price ceilings were eliminated, allowing the price of oil to rise substantially. The rise in price eliminated the shortages.

The above example of a price ceiling provides an important lesson about the way markets work. Price ceilings below the equilibrium price create excess demand which must be rationed in some other way—in this case by long lines at the pump. People don't like price increases, but at least price increases prevent shortages, which they often like even less.

Price ceiling *A government-imposed limit on how high a price can be charged.*

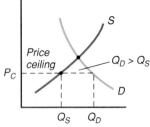

An effective price ceiling will cause $Q_D > Q_S$.

Q–1: If the price ceiling had been set at $8 rather than $10, what would have happened to the size of the shortage?

■ Price ceilings cause shortages; price floors cause surpluses.

Examples of Shifts in Supply and Demand

The mad cow disease scare decreased the demand for British beef.

Supply and demand can shift in many ways and one of the calisthenics of introductory economics involves describing various events with the supply/demand graph. So in the next two sections I give you two exercises that give you practice in using supply and demand curves. In the first I list six events, labeling them 1 through 6. I also provide six graphs of supply and demand shifts in Exhibit 2, labeling them *a* through *f*.

Here are the six events:

1. In 1996 European Union consumption of beef and derivative products dropped between 20 percent and 30 percent in response to reports that "mad cow disease" from beef had killed some Britons. The EU banned imported British beef and supermarkets there began to look for alternative sources of beef. Other countries followed suit. The price of beef and derivative products dropped in the EU. To restore confidence in its beef industry, the British government banned the sale of older cattle by British farmers. Beef prices rose slightly, but not to their previous level. Market: British beef.

EXHIBIT 2   Shifts in Supply and Demand

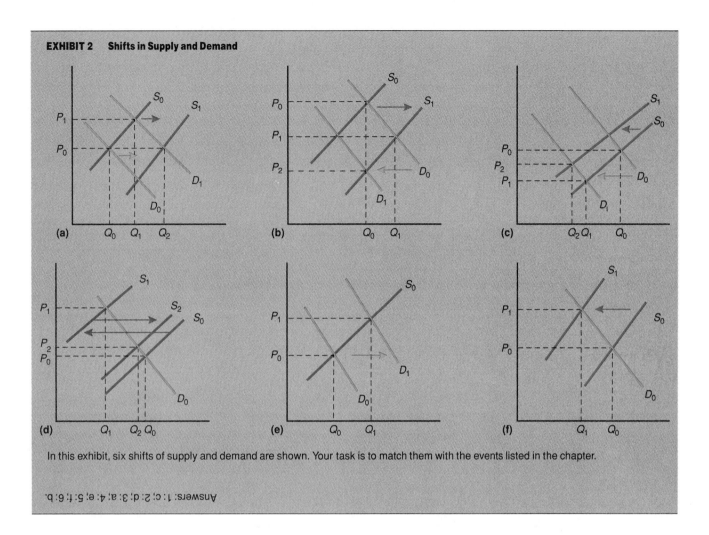

In this exhibit, six shifts of supply and demand are shown. Your task is to match them with the events listed in the chapter.

Answers: 1: c; 2: d; 3: a; 4: e; 5: f; 6: b.

2. In 1990 the UN placed trade sanctions on oil from Iraq after the Iraqi invasion of Kuwait in August of that year. In addition, during the 1991 Iraqi conflict, oil production throughout the Middle East was disrupted. Oil prices rose 12.1 percent during the conflict, but declined thereafter as production in some Middle-Eastern countries resumed. The trade sanctions on oil from Iraq remained in place. Market: World oil.

3. As China opened its markets to the world, per capita income has risen in China and more and more Chinese have wanted to purchase computers. The more than 13,000 traditional Chinese characters, however, have presented an enormous problem for a Chinese-character keyboard. Few exist; they are complicated and difficult to use. With improved voice and handwriting recognition technology, firms have developed keyboardless computers for the Chinese market. Market: Computers in China.

4. In the mid-1990s the 76 million U.S. baby boomers started to put away more and more savings for retirement. This saving was directed toward the purchase of financial assets, driving up the price of stocks. Market: Financial assets.

5. In 1991 Congress imposed a 10 percent tax on the sale of luxury boats. In response, some boat owners held onto their old boats longer. Others bought boats in the Bahamas to escape the tax. Market: Luxury boats. (Because of the uproar from the producers of luxury boats, Congress eliminated the tax in 1993.)

6. Throughout the 1990s, technological advances in personal computers have resulted in the dramatic decline in the price of high-end PCs. In the late 1990s, new programming languages have enabled the Internet to provide services similar to the

"The Price System in Microcosm: A P.O.W. Camp," by R.A. Radford, in *Classic Readings in Economics.*

Designing a keyboardless computer to access the Chinese computer market has proved difficult.

PCs, from word processing to data management. Users need what is called a Dumb box, which costs less than one-third of the price of a high-end PC. Market: High-end PCs.

Each of the events may involve a shift in demand, a shift in supply, or a shift in both supply and demand. Your job is to match the events with the graph that best describes it. A word of warning: the shifts of supply and demand could be in either direction, so be careful as you go through the matches.

Now that you have done those exercises (you have, haven't you?), let's go through the explanations to see that you got them right.

Q–2: If instead of the cattle's "mad cow disease" having been thought to be potentially transmissible to people, there had been a discovery that beef increases the IQ of most people who eat it, what would have been the effect on price and quantity?

Mad Cow Disease Fears of mad cow disease reduced the demand for beef. This change in tastes is a shift factor of demand that shifted the demand curve for British beef to the left. We would expect the price of beef to decline and the quantity of beef supplied to decline also. That was not the end of the story, however. Legislative action by the British government then mandated that older beef could not be sold. Farmers, then, at every price, were willing to supply less beef—a shift to the left in the supply curve. Exhibit 2(c) depicts these shifts. Originally, the drop in demand led to a fall in prices to P_1. At that price, suppliers were willing to sell Q_1, less than the original quantity, Q_0. Government action then shifted supply to S_1. The price of beef rose to P_2 but the shift in supply was not enough for price to rise to its original level. The quantity demanded fell even more, to Q_2.

Iraqi Oil Here is a case of shifting supply. Since Iraq was banned from exporting oil and production from other Middle Eastern countries was disrupted, the world supply of oil fell. This is depicted by a leftward shift in the supply of oil. Oil prices rose and quantity demanded fell. As oil production resumed after the conflict, supply shifted out, but not to its original position. Exhibit 2(d) shows these shifts.

PCs in China In this case, the rise in income resulted in a shift out in the demand for PCs. Quantity supplied rose, as did price. Lured by the increasing market for PCs in China, firms began to research ways to supply more user-friendly computers and overcome the character barrier. The technological improvements led to a shift to the right in the supply curve of PCs to China. Their prices declined and quantity demanded rose. Exhibit 2(a) shows this scenario. First demand shifted from D_0 to D_1. The price of PCs rose to P_1 and the quantity of computers supplied rose to Q_1. The supply curve then shifted out to S_1 with technological innovation. Price returned to P_0 and the quantity demanded increased further to Q_2.

2 Supply and demand can shed light on a variety of real-world events.

Chinese and Japanese characters each convey a complete idea. A simple novel will contain about 3,500 different characters. This posed a serious technical problem for computer manufacturers.

Financial Assets and the Baby Boomers The swell in the population called the baby boomers has resulted in shifting demand for all sorts of products as the boomers entered college, then bought houses, and now are demanding more health care and financial assets. In this case, demographic changes have resulted in a shift out in the demand curve for financial assets, resulting in a rise in stock market prices and an increase in the quantity of stocks and mutual funds supplied. This is depicted in Exhibit 2(e). This figure could also be used to describe the huge rise in housing prices in the 1980s as baby boomers began to purchase houses.

Excise Taxes In Chapter 3's discussion of shift factors, I explained that taxes levied on the supplier will shift the supply curve to the left. The 10 percent excise tax will shift the supply curve to the left. That some boat owners hold onto their older boats and others look elsewhere to buy boats is substitution at work, and a movement up along the demand curve. Exhibit 2(f) shows this scenario. After the tax, price is P_1 and quantity of boats demanded declines to Q_1.

Computers and the Internet   The rapid developments in chip design in the 1990s have resulted in a lower cost of producing high-end PCs. This shifts the supply curve to the right. Innovation on the Internet, however, has provided a substitute for the PC, namely the Dumb box. As would-be PC users instead buy Dumb boxes, the demand for high-end PCs shifts to the left. Exhibit 2(b) shows the initial shift in the supply curve from S_0 to S_1, resulting in a lower price, P_1, and an increase in number of computers demanded to Q_1. Innovations on the Internet then shifted the demand curve for high-end PCs from D_0 to D_1, further depressing PC prices but lowering the quantity of PCs supplied.

A Review   As you can see, supply and demand analysis can get quite complicated. That is why you must separate shifts in demand and supply from movements along the supply and demand curves. Remember: Anything that affects demand and supply other than price of the good will shift the curves. Changes in the price of the good result in movements along the curves. Another thing to recognize is that when both curves are shifting you can get a change in price but little change in quantity, or a change in quantity but little change in price.

To test your understanding, I'll now give you six generic results. Your job is to decide what shifts produced those results. This exercise is a variation of the first. It goes over the same issues, but this time without the graphs. On the left–hand side of the table below I list combinations of movements of observed prices and quantities, labeling them 1–6. On the right I give six shifts in supply and demand, labeling them *a–f*.

Price and Quantity Changes		*Shifts in Supply and Demand*
1.	P↑ Q↑	*a.* Supply shifts in. No change in demand.
2.	P↑ Q↓	*b.* Demand shifts out. Supply shifts in.
3.	P↑ Q?	*c.* Demand shifts in. No change in supply.
4.	P↓ Q?	*d.* Demand shifts out. Supply shifts out.
5.	P? Q↑	*e.* Demand shifts out. No change in supply.
6.	P↓ Q↓	*f.* Demand shifts in. Supply shifts out.

You are to match the shifts with the price and quantity movements that best fit each described shift, using each shift and movement only once. My recommendation to you is to draw the graphs that are described in *a–f*, decide what happens to price and quantity, and then find the match in 1–6.

Now that you've worked them, let me give you the answers I came up with. They are: 1: *e*; 2: *a*; 3: *b*; 4: *f*; 5: *d*; 6: *c*. How did I come up with the answers? I did what I suggested you do—took each of the scenarios on the right and predicted what happens to price and quantity. For case *a*, supply shifts in and there is a movement up along the demand curve. Since the demand curve is downward sloping, the price rises and quantity declines. This matches number 2 on the left. For case *b*, demand shifts out. Along the original supply curve, price and quantity would rise. But supply shifts in, leading to even higher prices, but lower quantity. What happens to quantity is unclear, so the match must be number 3. For case *c*, demand shifts in. There is movement down along the supply curve with lower price and lower quantity. This matches number 6. For case *d*, demand shifts out and supply shifts out. As demand shifts out, we move along the supply curve to the right and price and quantity rise. But supply shifts out too, and we move out along the new demand curve. Price declines, erasing the previous rise, and the quantity rises even more. This matches number 5.

I'll leave it up to you to confirm my answers to *e* and *f*. Notice that when supply and demand both shift, the change in either price or quantity is uncertain—it depends

Q–3: Jean, your study partner, has just stated that the increase in Dumb boxes will shift the quantity demanded of high-end PCs to the right. How do you respond?

Anything other than price that affects demand or supply will shift the curves.

For more practice with shifting demand and supply curves, see Micro/Macro Interactive, module "Using the Market Model."

If you don't confuse your "shifts of" with your "movements along," supply and demand provide good off-the-cuff answers for any economic questions.

Q–4: If both demand and supply shift in, what happens to price and quantity?

EXHIBIT 3   Diagrammatic of Effects of Shifts of Demand and Supply on Price and Quantity

This exhibit provides a summary of the effects of shifts in supply and demand on price and quantity. Notice that when both curves shift, the effect on either price or quantity depends on the relative size of the shifts.

	No change in supply.	Supply shifts out.	Supply shifts in.
No change in demand.	No change.	P↓ Q↑ Price declines and quantity rises.	P↑ Q↓ Price rises. Quality declines.
Demand shifts out.	P↑ Q↑ Price rises. Quantity rises.	P? Q↑ Quantity rises. Price could be higher or lower depending upon relative size of shifts.	P↑ Q? Price rises. Quantity could rise or fall depending upon relative size of shifts.
Demand shifts in.	P↓ Q↓ Price declines. Quantity declines.	P↓ Q? Price declines. Quantity could rise or fall depending upon relative size of shifts.	P? Q↓ Quantity declines. Price rises or falls depending upon relative size of shifts.

upon the relative size of the shifts. As a summary, in Exhibit 3 I present a diagrammatic of the combinations.

Exchange Rate Determination

There is a difference of opinion whether it is helpful to present the supply-demand analysis of exchange rates at this early point in the semester. I generally skip doing so because it requires students to think of prices of currencies, which can confuse them. However, many professors find it a perfect example and focus on it.

3 As long as one remembers what prices and quantities go on each axis, exchange rate determination can be described by supply and demand graphs.

Various currencies are exchanged for one another in foreign exchange markets.

Enough exercises. Let's now turn to another example of supply and demand in action—the determination of **exchange rates**—*the rate at which one currency exchanges for another.* I recently went on an around-the-world trip, and I discovered what any of you will discover if you travel outside the United States: To buy goods in another country, generally you must trade your country's currency for the other country's currency. That is, you must buy foreign currency with your currency. What this means is that that foreign currency has a price in reference to your currency, just as any other good does.

For what price will currencies exchange? Supply and demand analysis tells us. To see how, let's look at the Mexican peso and the U.S. dollar over the mid-1990s and see what supply and demand forces are associated with the changes that occurred. Exhibit 4(a) shows the price of the Mexican peso in terms of the U.S. dollar. The peso's price, called the exchange rate, is in terms of dollars per peso. So a peso costs 13 cents or, alternatively, 1 dollar bought about 7½ pesos in 1996.

Notice that in 1994 the peso experienced a **depreciation**—*a decrease in the value of a currency.* That is, the exchange rate of the peso fell enormously. What happened? Up until 1994, investors had high hopes for the Mexican economy and bought more and more Mexican assets. In 1994, however, there were political upheavals and rumors that the Mexican economy was in trouble. Many foreign investors stopped investing and many Mexicans tried to get their money out of Mexico. As they did, the value of the peso fell. Now let us translate these real-world events in Mexico into supply and demand curves.

The first thing we must do is specify our axes. Price and quantity are no longer enough since there are two monies—dollars and pesos—and consequently two prices—a peso price of dollars and a dollar price of pesos. Exhibit 4(b) shows the

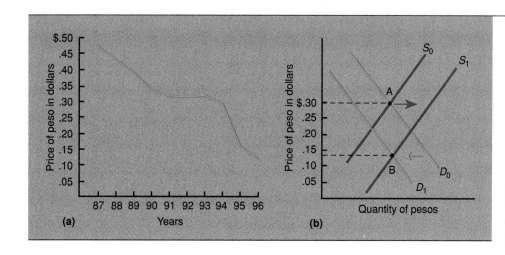

(a) Years

(b) Quantity of pesos

EXHIBIT 4 (a and b)   Exchange Rate Value of the Peso and Supply and Demand

The movements in the exchange rate value of the peso shown in (**a**) can be explained by the supply and demand for pesos as shown in (**b**). Political and economic problems led Americans to want to sell their holdings of pesos, shifting the demand for pesos to the left (from D_0 to D_1). At the same time Mexicans wanted to sell their pesos, shifting the supply of pesos to the right (from S_0 to S_1). The value of the peso in this example fell to about 13 cents per peso.

supply and demand for pesos in terms of U.S. dollars. The quantity of pesos is on the horizontal axis and the price of pesos in terms of dollars is on the vertical axis.

In this example, the demand for pesos is the demand of U.S. citizens for Mexican pesos; this demand reflects their demand for Mexican goods and assets. The supply of pesos is the demand of Mexican citizens for U.S. dollars; this demand reflects their demand for U.S. goods and assets. In 1993 when prospects for Mexico looked good, the demand for Mexican goods and assets, and thus the demand for pesos, was high. The price of one peso in terms of dollars was 30 cents (labeled A in Exhibit 4(b)). One dollar bought three and one-third pesos.

When the rumors started spreading that Mexico was in trouble, many people wanted to sell their pesos since they thought the peso's price would fall and because they did not see Mexico as such a good place to invest. Remember, one needs pesos to invest in Mexico. Mexicans who wanted to sell pesos shifted the supply curve for pesos out from S_0 to S_1. Simultaneously, the demand for pesos fell from D_0 to D_1 as few people wanted to invest in Mexico. The new equilibrium price of pesos fell substantially so that now a peso cost only 13 cents. One dollar bought about seven and a half pesos. That new equilibrium is labeled B in Exhibit 4(b).

What did this fall in the value of the peso mean for Mexican and U.S. citizens? The value of the U.S. dollar experienced an **appreciation**—*an increase in value*—and rose relative to the peso. This made U.S. goods much more expensive for Mexicans and threw the Mexican economy into a recession. For foreign tourists, it also made trips to Mexico cheaper—meaning I took my wife and kids to Isla Mujeres for a couple of weeks, and the cost was less than 50 percent of what it would have been just one year earlier.

Price floors and price ceilings also play a role in currency markets. For example, a government may pass a law stating that the exchange rate will be set at a specified rate, regardless of supply and demand. Governments that set a specified rate of exchange regardless of supply and demand have made their currencies *nonconvertible*. A **nonconvertible currency** is *a currency that cannot be freely exchanged except at the government set rate*. If the specified rate is lower than the equilibrium exchange rate, the law will be the equivalent to a price ceiling. Since we considered the example of a price ceiling in the price-of-oil example earlier in this chapter, this time let's consider the case of a **price floor**—*a government-imposed limit on how low a price can be charged*. In Exhibit 5, I demonstrate this case.

There the price of pesos is set at 30 cents, even though the equilibrium price is 25 cents. As you can see, at a price floor of 30 the quantity of pesos supplied (Q_S) is greater than the quantity of pesos demanded (Q_D). People want to sell more pesos than others want to buy.

Passing a law is one thing; enforcing it is quite another. And the nature of the enforcement depends on how strong the government's not-so-invisible foot is—what the penalties are for violating the law, and how strictly the law is enforced.

There are many different currencies in the world.

Q–5: The exchange rate could also be analyzed in terms of the supply and demand for dollars with the peso price of dollars on the vertical axis. Draw the relevant graph and explain what happened in reference to that graph.

Price floor   *A government-imposed limit on how low a price can be charged.*

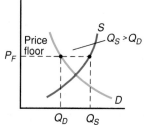

An effective price floor will cause $Q_S > Q_D$.

EXHIBIT 5   Nonconvertible Currency: Price Floor

A nonconvertible currency is an example of a price floor. In this example, the equilibrium price in pesos is 25 cents, but the price floor is 30 cents. In this case, the quantity supplied exceeds the quantity demanded.

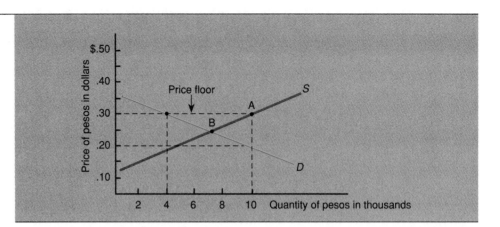

It is very hard to catch two people who meet and agree to exchange dollars for pesos. Countries who do try to enforce their nonconvertible currency laws usually have some undercover agents out there offering to exchange currencies. Government agents offer tourists a better exchange rate than they would get at the official exchange rate—and if tourists take the offer they are arrested. The fear of arrest in a foreign country keeps many people from accepting the swell exchange rate deals they're offered by their taxi driver or a fellow who walks up to them while they're waiting to cross the street.

What would the black market exchange rate be? Consider Exhibit 5 again. The quantity supplied at 30 cents is 10,000. Extending a line down to the demand curve, we see that at 10,000 the price demanders are willing to pay is 20 cents. So the black market price will be somewhere between 30 cents and 20 cents per peso. The box on black and gray markets gives some more insight into what happens with nonconvertible currencies.

With fixed exchange rates, government sets the exchange rate and makes a commitment to buy and sell sufficient currency at that exchange rate so that quantity supplied always equals quantity demanded.

Fixed Exchange Rates   In Western industrial countries nonconvertible currencies are not the rule, but a number of countries have **fixed exchange rates**—*rates, set by government, at which a currency can be freely exchanged among individuals.* At first glance, a fixed exchange rate looks very much like a nonconvertible currency, but there is a major difference. With a nonconvertible currency, the government passes a law. Quantity supplied and quantity demanded are brought into equilibrium by enforcing the law—the price is set by the invisible foot. With fixed exchange rates, the government passes no law. It doesn't try to work against market forces; it simply tries to guide the invisible hand. It works with, rather than against, market forces. It does so by setting an exchange rate and making a commitment to buy and sell sufficient currency at that exchange rate so that quantity supplied always equals quantity demanded. For example, if quantity supplied is less than quantity demanded, the government must sell (supply) its currency. If quantity supplied is greater than quantity demanded, the government must buy (demand) its currency.

Q–6: How does a fixed exchange rate system differ from a nonconvertible exchange rate system?

The way in which a fixed exchange rate works is shown in Exhibit 6. The demand and supply for the currency is initially at D_0 and S_0. Equilibrium price begins at the fixed exchange rate of P_0. If, however, conditions change so that either supply or demand shifts, the exchange rate will fluctuate. Suppose demand shifts in to D_1. At the official exchange rate, there will be excess supply, labeled A. To keep the exchange rate from declining, the government must eliminate that excess supply by buying (reducing the supply of) its own currency. This is shown by a shift in the supply curve to S_1. The exchange rate remains at P_0, but equilibrium quantity is now Q_1. Where countries get into trouble is if they run out of foreign currency to eliminate excess supply of their own currency. In this case, they can either borrow funds from other countries or let their currencies fluctuate and risk a disruption in their economy. Either option is hazardous. In the mid-1990s, Mexico did both. It borrowed from other countries to stabilize the peso, allowing it to remain somewhat fixed.

BLACK AND GRAY MARKETS IN CURRENCY

ADDED DIMENSION

Foreign exchange markets are a good example of supply and demand forces at work. Whenever there's excess supply or demand for something, there's incentive for suppliers and demanders to get together to eliminate the excess.

Let's consider the issue in relation to the former Soviet Union. In 1989, at the official price of 0.64 rubles per dollar, the quantity of dollars demanded far exceeded the quantity of dollars supplied. In the former Soviet Union, adventurous individuals (who weren't worried about the wrath of the invisible foot—that is, about being prosecuted for violating foreign exchange laws) traded in a black market at a higher price.

A black market, which involves trades of a good that can't legally be traded, is a natural result of government price restrictions. Often the government knows that such trading goes on and chooses, for political reasons, not to enforce its own laws strictly. (There are situations like this in the United States. Here the speed limit is 55 miles per hour on many secondary roads but almost everyone drives at 65 miles per hour, which police tend to accept as a fact of life.)

When a black market is unofficially condoned, trading on it becomes more open and it's often called a gray market. Since risk of prosecution is less, upward pressure on price from the invisible foot is less; so gray market prices are usually closer to the supply/demand equilibrium than are black market prices.

The Soviet foreign exchange market became a gray market in late 1989. (The gray market price of a dollar was between 5 and 15 rubles rather than the 0.64 rubles you'd get at the official rate.) If you went to the former Soviet Union at that time, individuals would come up to you on the street and offer to trade rubles for dollars at something near the gray market price. In 1991 the Soviet Union broke apart and Russia began to let the ruble be freely tradable. Because of political and economic problems, however, the ruble's value fell enormously and it cost thousands of rubles to buy one dollar.

In my next example, let's consider rent control in Paris in 1948 (this case is discussed in the *Classic Readings* supplement). **Rent control** is *a price ceiling on rents, set by government*. During World War I, to stabilize housing prices and help out those fighting for France, rents were frozen. Upon the return of veterans, the freeze was held in the interest of society. In 1926, rent control was reviewed but by that time, lifting the controls would have resulted in huge increases in rents. Rents were allowed to rise only slightly. Again, during World War II, rents were frozen and rents in Paris right after the end of World War II stood at about $10 a month. This was a good situation for those occupying apartments, but it had drawbacks. For instance, there was an enormous shortage of apartments. The situation is shown in Exhibit 7.

Before World War I, demand for rental housing was D_{1918} and equilibrium price was about $2 a month. No shortage existed. However, rent was then frozen at $2 a month. More and more French moved to Paris to help in the war effort and the population continued to grow. The demand for apartments shifted close to D_{1926}. Given this demand, at $2 a month there was a shortage of apartments, shown by A. To eliminate the shortage, rents would have had to rise to $10 a month.

What was the result of the rent control? Because of the low rents, repairs were not made to existing buildings and no new buildings were being constructed. There

Rent Controls

Rent control   *A price ceiling on rents, set by government and applying to what a landlord can charge for apartments.*

"Rent Control: An Example of Price Fixing," by Bertrand de Jouvenel in *Classic Readings in Economics.*

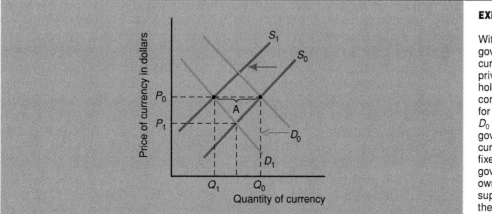

EXHIBIT 6   Fixed Exchange Rate

With a fixed exchange rate, the government adjusts its supply of the currency to offset any fluctuation in private demand or supply, thereby holding the price of the currency at a constant level. In this case demand for the currency has shifted in from D_0 to D_1. In the absence of any government action the price of the currency would fall to P_1. But in a fixed exchange rate system the government steps in and buys its own currency, thereby shifting the supply from S_0 to S_1 and holding the price of its currency constant.

EXHIBIT 7   Rent Control in Paris

A price ceiling imposed on housing rent in Paris during World War I created a shortage of housing when World War I ended and veterans returned home. The shortage is shown by A. The shortage would have been eliminated if rents had been allowed to rise to $10 per month.

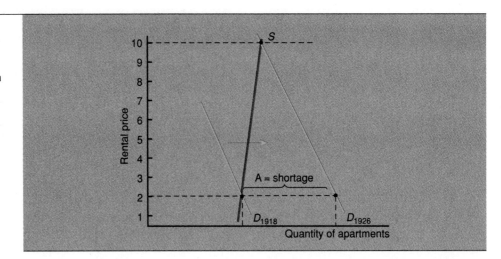

When price ceilings exist, demanders will sometimes pay bribes to suppliers.

For more detail regarding this example of rent control along with additional discussion questions, see Chapter 2 in *Case Studies in Economics*.

With price ceilings, existing goods are no longer rationed entirely by price. Other methods of rationing existing goods arise called nonprice rationing.

Video Series, Economics U$A: Economic Efficiency, Segment 18.3

were many people who could not find housing. To get into a rent-controlled apartment individuals had to pay large bribes, running into the hundreds of dollars. Or they had to live doubled up with relatives because they couldn't find apartments of their own. Eventually, the situation got so bad that the rent controls were lifted.

The system of rent controls is not only of historical interest. Below I list some phenomena that exist in New York City in the 1990s. (These phenomena come from the *Case Studies* supplement.)

- A couple pays $350 a month for a two-bedroom Park Avenue apartment with a solarium and two terraces, while another individual pays $1,200 a month for a studio apartment shared with two roommates.
- The vacancy rate for apartments in New York City is currently 3.5 percent. Anything under 5 percent is considered a housing emergency.
- The actress Mia Farrow pays $2,900 a month (a fraction of the market-clearing rent) for 10 rooms on Central Park West. It is an apartment her mother first leased 40 years ago.
- Would-be tenants make payments, called key money, to current tenants or landlords to get apartments.

Your assignment is to explain how these phenomena might have come about, and to demonstrate, with supply and demand, the situation that likely caused them. (Hint: New York City does have rent control.)

Now that you have done your assignment (you have, haven't you?) let me give you my answers so that you can check them with your answers.

The situation is identical with that presented above in Exhibit 7. Take the first item. The couple lives in a rent-controlled apartment while the individual with roommates does not. If rent control were eliminated, rent on the Park Avenue apartment would rise and rent on the studio would most likely decline. Item 2: The housing emergency is a result of rent control. Below-market rent results in excess demand and little vacancy. Item 3: That Mia Farrow rents a rent-controlled apartment is the result of nonprice rationing. Instead of being rationed by price, other methods of rationing arise. These other methods of rationing scarce resources are called nonprice rationing. In New York City, strict rules determine the handing down of rent-controlled apartments from family member to family member. Item 4: New residents must search for a long time to find apartments to rent and many discover that illegal payments to landlords are the only way to obtain a rent-controlled apartment. Key money is a black-market payment for a rent-controlled apartment. Because of the limited supply of apartments, individuals are willing to pay far more than the controlled price. Landlords can use other methods of rationing the limited supply of apartments—instituting first-come, first-serve policies, and, in practice, selecting tenants based upon gender, race, or other personal characteristics, even though such discriminatory selection is illegal.

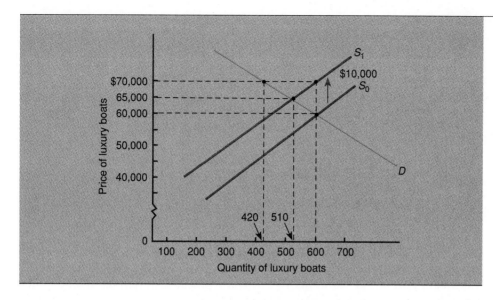

EXHIBIT 8   The Effect of an Excise Tax

An excise tax on suppliers shifts the entire supply curve up by the amount of the tax. Since at a price equal to the original price plus the tax there is excess supply, the price for the good rises by less than the tax, while quantity supplied and demanded falls.

Let's consider an example of the invisible foot entering into a market and modifying the results of supply/demand analysis in the form of a tax or a subsidy. An **excise tax** *is a tax that is levied on a specific good.* The luxury tax on expensive cars that the United States imposed in 1991 is an example. A **tariff** *is an excise tax on an imported good.* What effect will excise taxes and tariffs have on the price and quantity in a market?

The Effect of an Excise Tax on Price and Quantity   To lend some sense of reality, let's take the example from the early 1990s when the United States put a tax on some luxury goods, such as expensive boats. This tax was paid by the supplier. Say the price of a boat before the luxury tax was $60,000, and 600 boats were sold at that price. Now the government places a tax of $10,000 on such boats. What will the new price of the boat be, and how many will be sold?

If you were about to answer: The new price will be $70,000, be careful. Ask yourself whether I would have given you that question if the answer were that easy. By looking at supply and demand curves in Exhibit 8 you can see why $70,000 is the wrong answer.

To sell 600 boats, suppliers must be fully compensated for the tax. So the tax of $10,000 on the supplier shifts the supply curve up from S_0 to S_1. However, at $70,000, demanders are not willing to purchase 600 boats. They are willing to purchase only 420 boats. Quantity supplied exceeds quantity demanded at $70,000. Suppliers lower their prices until quantity supplied equals quantity demanded at $65,000, the new equilibrium price. Demanders increase the quantity of boats they are willing to purchase to 510, still less than the original 600 at $60,000. Why? At the higher price of $65,000 some people choose not to buy boats and others find substitute vehicles or purchase their boats outside the United States.

Notice that at the new equilibrium the new price is $65,000, not $70,000. The reason is that at the higher price, the quantity of boats people demand is less. This is a movement up along a demand curve to the left. Excise taxes reduce the quantity of goods demanded. That's why boat manufacturers were up in arms after the tax was imposed and why the revenue generated from the tax was less than expected. Instead of collecting $10,000 × 600 ($6 million), revenue collected was only $10,000 × 510 ($5.1 million). The tax was repealed in 1993.

Quantity Restrictions: Quotas   The next example I want to consider is the imposition of a quantity control—a legal restriction on the quantity that can be bought or sold. The most common type of quantity control is the international **quota**—*a quantitative restriction on the amount that one country can export to another.* A recent instance of a quota occurred when the United States wanted to restrict U.S. imports of Japanese cars. I show the effect in Exhibit 9(a).

The Effects of Taxes, Tariffs, and Quotas

4 Taxes and tariffs raise price and reduce quantity.

A tax on suppliers shifts the supply curve up by the amount of the tax.

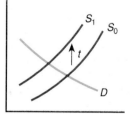

Q–7:   Your study partner, Umar, has just stated that a tax on demanders of $2 per unit will raise the equilibrium price from $4 to $6. How do you respond?

For a review of tariffs and quotas and computer simulations of their effects on the market, see *Micro/Macro Interactive,* module "International Trade."

Quota   *A quantitative restriction on the amount that one country can export to another.*

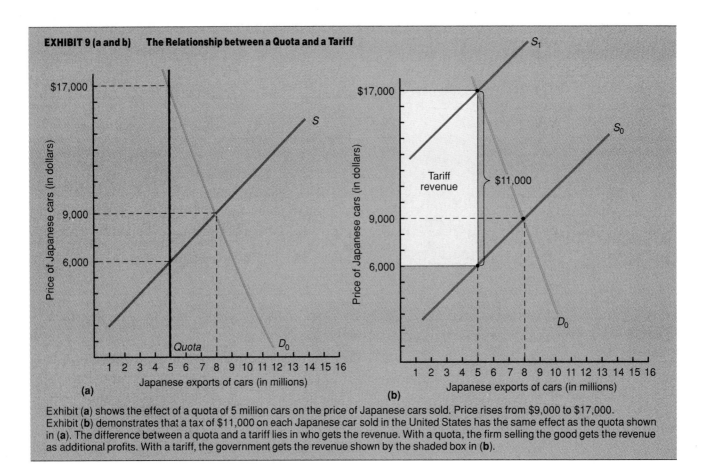

EXHIBIT 9 (a and b)   The Relationship between a Quota and a Tariff

Exhibit (a) shows the effect of a quota of 5 million cars on the price of Japanese cars sold. Price rises from $9,000 to $17,000.
Exhibit (b) demonstrates that a tax of $11,000 on each Japanese car sold in the United States has the same effect as the quota shown in (a). The difference between a quota and a tariff lies in who gets the revenue. With a quota, the firm selling the good gets the revenue as additional profits. With a tariff, the government gets the revenue shown by the shaded box in (b).

The market price of a Japanese car is $9,000. At that price, U.S. consumers demand, and Japanese car makers are willing to supply, 8 million cars. But, when the United States places an import quota of, say, 5 million cars into the United States, U.S. consumers are willing to pay $17,000 a car even though Japanese firms are willing to sell them for $6,000 apiece. Of course, sellers will accept what consumers are willing to pay, and the price of Japanese cars rises to $17,000. Notice what the effect of the quota is. It raises the price of Japanese cars in the United States.

The Relationship of a Quota and a Tariff   Above we considered the effect of both quotas and taxes, and I noted that a tax is the equivalent of a tariff. Both devices increase price and reduce quantity. Let's now compare the effects of the quota above with the results of a tariff that would have achieved the same amount of restriction in output.

I show the effects of such a tariff in Exhibit 9(b). There you can see that a tariff of $11,000 shifts the supply curve back sufficiently to end up with the same sale of 5 million Japanese cars obtained with the quota. Consumers still pay $17,000 for Japanese cars.

Is there a difference between the two cases? The answer is yes. In the quota case, the higher price brings in more revenue to the company. In the tariff case, the revenue goes to the government. So which of the two do you think companies favor? The quota, of course—it means more profits as long as your company is one of those who receives the rights to fill those quotas. In fact, once quotas are instituted Japanese firms compete intensely to get them.

There is such a U.S. tariff on light trucks from Japan, which is why here in the United States you see few light trucks that were built in Japan. You will see Japanese trucks. But these, however, most likely were not produced in Japan. As Japan has internationalized its production facilities, many of the cars and trucks built by Japanese companies are no longer produced in Japan. They are produced in countries such

A quota of Q_1 has the same effect as a tax t.

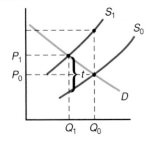

Q–8: Why do firms prefer quotas to tariffs?

as Canada and France and, especially, in the United States. In fact, Japanese auto companies are the largest exporters of cars from the United States.

I hope the above section has convinced you of the power of supply and demand analysis. Now let's discuss some of its limitations. I emphasized in Chapter 3 that understanding supply and demand involves much more than simply being able to say what happens when the curves shift (although you had better be able to do that if you want to understand economic reasoning). It also involves *understanding the assumptions upon which the analysis is based*. One of the most important of these assumptions is the other-things-constant assumption.

To emphasize this other-things-constant assumption, supply/demand analysis is called **partial equilibrium analysis**—*analysis that is partial or incomplete because it holds other things constant*. It limits its direct analysis to relative price effects. It holds all other effects constant, but keeps them at the back of one's mind, to be added later as required. Understanding the partial equilibrium nature of supply/demand analysis is fundamental to using the analysis appropriately. Supply and demand is an engine of analysis—a first step, not the complete analysis. Supply/demand analysis is appropriately used only in combination with reason and educated common sense, and its results are adjusted whenever other material things do not remain constant.

What do I mean by "material things"? I mean factors that can affect the results in a substantive way. Let's take an example. Say you're considering the effect of a fall in the wage rate. In partial equilibrium supply/demand analysis, you would look at the effect that fall would have on workers' decisions to supply labor, and on business's decision to hire workers. But might there be other material effects? For instance, might the fall in the wage lower people's income, and thereby shift back demand for firms' goods? And might that effect materially affect firms' demand for workers? If these effects do occur, and are material—that is, important enough to affect the result—those additional feedback effects have to be added back to the analysis in order for you to have a complete analysis.

Deciding on the materiality of effects requires a knowledge of the structure of the economy. All actions have a multitude of ripple or feedback effects—they create waves, like those that spread out from a stone thrown into a pool. These waves bounce back, and then hit other waves, which create new waves which . . . . The art of applying supply/demand analysis is determining which of these multitude of ripple effects affect the analysis in a material way, and hence must be added back to the analysis.

There is no single answer to the question of which ripples must be included, and much debate among economists involves which ripple effects to include. But there are some general rules. Partial equilibrium analysis, used without adjustment, is most appropriate for questions where the relative prices refer to the prices of goods that are a small percentage of the entire economy. That is when the other-things-constant assumption will most likely hold. As soon as one starts analyzing goods that are a large percentage of the entire economy, the other-things-constant assumption is likely not to hold true. The reason is found in the **fallacy of composition**—*the false assumption that what is true for a part will also be true for the whole.*

Let's consider the fallacy of composition more carefully. When you are analyzing one individual's actions, small effects of an individual's actions can reasonably be assumed to be immaterial—they are too small to change the results of partial equilibrium analysis. However, when you are analyzing the whole, or a significant portion of the whole, these small effects add up to a big effect. To see this, think of one supplier lowering the price of his or her good. People will substitute that good for other goods, and the quantity demanded of the good will increase. But what if all suppliers lower their prices? Since all prices have gone down, why should demanders switch? The substitution story can't be used in the aggregate. There are many such examples.

THE LIMITATIONS OF SUPPLY AND DEMAND ANALYSIS

Using supply and demand analysis involves understanding the assumptions upon which the analysis is based.

Supply/demand analysis is appropriately used only in combination with reason and educated common sense.

The emphasis on the feedback effects here sets up the discussion of the dynamic micro-foundations of macro in the macro chapters. I have found that it gives students a good sense of the difference between micro and macro.

Partial equilibrium analysis, used without adjustment, is most appropriate for questions where the relative prices refer to the prices of goods that are a small percentage of the entire economy.

The Fallacy of Composition

5 When analyzing the aggregate, small effects that can be put aside in micro, can add up, and hence cannot be forgotten.

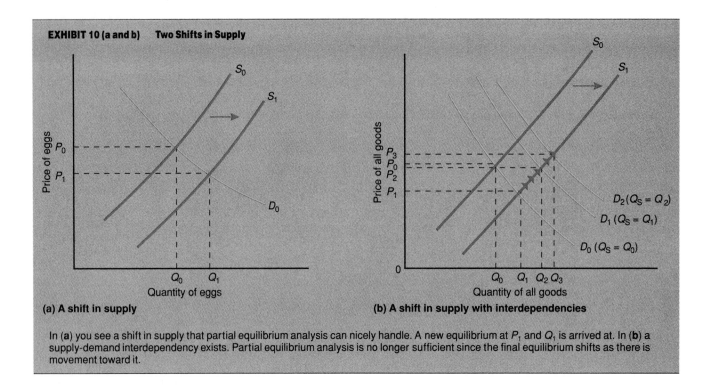

EXHIBIT 10 (a and b)   Two Shifts in Supply

(a) A shift in supply

(b) A shift in supply with interdependencies

In (a) you see a shift in supply that partial equilibrium analysis can nicely handle. A new equilibrium at P_1 and Q_1 is arrived at. In (b) a supply-demand interdependency exists. Partial equilibrium analysis is no longer sufficient since the final equilibrium shifts as there is movement toward it.

Q–9 Why is the fallacy of composition relevant for macroeconomic issues?

I like to use the example of the people in the stands at a football game. It may be rational for one person to stand up to get a better view. But if everyone stood up to get a better view, everyone would be worse off—no one would have the better view and everyone's legs would get tired from standing.

Examples: Chickens, Eggs, and Composite Goods

New growth theory focuses on such interdependencies.

The fallacy of composition gives you some insight into why economists separate micro from macro. One of the important side effects of decisions that must be considered in macro, but not in micro, is the side effect of spending decisions. Your spending decision is someone else's income, and someone else's spending decision creates your income. The circular flow diagram presented in Chapter 3 demonstrated that interconnection.

In our economy people can spend what they want; there is no direct mechanism in the economy that coordinates our spending decisions. Thus the composite of all spending decisions may be lots of spending, or little spending. As that spending changes, output changes, and the economy experiences a business cycle.

Let's now consider some examples of when partial equilibrium results can be used and when they cannot. First, in Exhibit 10(a), let's look at the effect of an increase in the supply of eggs due to a bio-technological change. Say that, through hormone injections, the technological change significantly increases the egg production of chickens. The supply curve shifts out, causing the relative price of eggs to fall from P_0 to P_1, and the quantity of eggs produced will increase from Q_0 to Q_1, as in Exhibit 10(a). If we were to be precise, we would have also pointed out that the demand for eggs would have also been affected by the indirect ripple effects of the technological change—it made the economy richer and increased its income. But common sense suggests that the ripple or repercussion effect on income does not meet the materiality condition—it is too small to include in the analysis. So for this question, it is reasonable to apply the results of supply/demand analysis directly, if other assumptions are also met.

Now let's consider a technological change that affects the production of all goods in the economy. So, instead of being an analysis of eggs, the analysis is of a composite good representing all goods. I consider this case in Exhibit 10(b). The technological change shifts the supply curve out as before—from S_0 to S_1, which would suggest that price will fall and quantity will increase. But can we stop the analysis there? The answer is: Not necessarily. While in the example of eggs we could leave out the income ripple effects, in this composite good example we cannot. Since we are talking about the supply of a composite of all goods, when the technological change signifi-

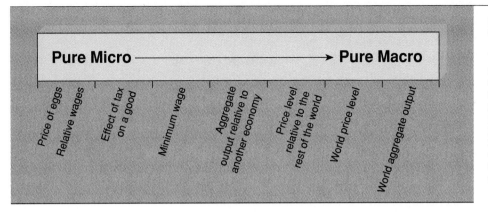

cantly increases people's output, it significantly increases their income. Therefore the technological change will also likely affect the demand for their goods—people will have higher income, and will demand more. So as the supply curve shifts out we can expect that the demand curve will shift out too. To determine what the effect will be on price and output we will need to have an additional analysis of these interdependent shifts.

Let's say that we have determined that, because of the shift in supply, the demand curve will shift out to D_1. Can we then say that the new equilibrium will be at price P_2 and quantity Q_2? No, we can't. It isn't only shifts of supply of a composite good that can affect income, and hence demand; it is also movements along a supply curve. But if such movements affect demand, as we move along the supply curve the demand curve will shift! There is no simple geometric way of showing what the solution will be. In fact, there is no simple mathematical way of determining the equilibrium. A number of possibilities exist. For example, there could be no equilibrium: the situation could be like a dog chasing its tail—whenever it tries to catch its tail, the tail moves, and the faster the dog chases, the faster the tail moves. There would simply be an unending chase between the two. But the situation could also be like an explosion, or like a dampening wave system where the chase will end. (Technically we have relationships that can only be analyzed in a differential equation format.)

The painful reality is that there are many possible interrelationships between a shift factor and a movement along a curve. When such interrelationships exist in the real world, they must be added back to the analysis before partial equilibrium supply/demand analysis can be applied to policy analysis.

The lesson is abstract, but it has direct policy relevance. Say you're predicting the effect of a 10 percent increase in price by your firm on the quantity demanded. If other firms in the industry don't follow suit, there will probably be a large drop-off in your quantity demanded. But if other firms do follow suit and raise their price, other things will not remain constant and there will likely be little effect on demand. So in your analysis you must take into account the interdependent effect of your decisions on your competitors' decisions.

The degree of interdependencies differs among various sets of issues. That is why we distinguish between micro and macro. In introductory macro we focus on problems and issues where the existence of an interconnection between supply and demand is obvious. In introductory micro (partial equilibrium analysis) we focus on policy issues where the interconnection is not so obvious. This allows us to abstract from the interconnections.

Of course, the lines between micro and macro are not hard and fixed. Thus, we must make choices and some issues could go into either. Exhibit 11 demonstrates the choices that must be made.

Issues to the far right are definitely pure macroeconomic issues. To the far left are pure microeconomic issues. The areas in the middle are ambiguous.

6 When there is an interdependence between supply and demand, a movement along one curve can cause a shift of the other curve. Thus, supply and demand used alone is not enough to determine where the equilibrium will be.

Q–10: Why does any interdependence between supply and demand cause a problem for partial equilibrium analysis?

Why a Separate Macroeconomics Exists

We distinguish between micro and macro because the degree of interdependence differs among various sets of issues.

An understanding of this possible interdependence is of central relevance to macroeconomics. In the aggregate, whenever firms produce (whenever they supply), they create income (demand for their goods). So in macro, when aggregate supply changes, or when there is movement along an aggregate supply curve, aggregate demand changes. *Aggregate supply decisions and aggregate demand decisions are interdependent.* This interdependence is one of the primary reasons we have a separate macroeconomics. In macroeconomics, the "other things constant" assumption central to microeconomic supply/demand analysis cannot hold. In macroeconomics, output creates income and income is spent on output. When the output side increases, so does the income side.

It is to account for interdependency between aggregate supply decisions and aggregate demand decisions that we have a separate micro analysis and a separate macro analysis.

It is to account for these interdependencies that we have a separate macro analysis and micro analysis. In macro we use curves whose underlying foundations are much more complicated than the partial equilibrium supply and demand curves we use in micro.

One final comment: The fact that there may be an interdependence between supply and demand does not mean that you can't use supply and demand analysis; it simply means that you must modify its results with the interdependency that, if you've done the analysis correctly, you've kept in the back of your head. Thus using supply and demand analysis is generally a step in any good economic analysis, but you must remember that it may be only a step.

CONCLUSION

I'll stop the analysis here. If you've made it through the chapter, you should have a good sense of the power of supply and demand and also of the limitations. Combined, these should give you a good theoretical foundation for doing economics. The next two chapters give you an institutional foundation for your study of economics.

CHAPTER SUMMARY

- Price ceilings cause shortages; price floors cause surpluses.
- By minding one's Ps and Qs—the shifts of and movements along curves—one can describe almost all events in terms of supply and demand.
- The determination of prices of currencies—the determination of exchange rates—can be determined by supply and demand analysis, in the same way supply and demand analysis applies to any other good.
- Taxes and tariffs shift the supply and demand curves depending on who pays the tax. They raise the equilibrium price (inclusive of tax) and decrease the quantity.
- In macro, small side effects that can be assumed away in micro are multiplied enormously. Thus they can significantly change the results and cannot be ignored. To ignore them is to fall into the fallacy of composition.
- When supply and demand curves are interdependent, a movement along one curve can cause the other to shift—moving the equilibrium. Such interdependence violates the "other things constant" assumption.

KEY TERMS

appreciation *(91)*
depreciation *(90)*
exchange rates *(90)*
excise tax *(95)*
fallacy of composition *(97)*

fixed exchange rates *(92)*
nonconvertible currency *(91)*
partial equilibrium analysis *(97)*
price ceiling *(86)*
price floor *(91)*

quota *(95)*
rent control *(93)*
tariff *(95)*

QUESTIONS FOR THOUGHT AND REVIEW

1. Demonstrate graphically the effect of a price ceiling.
2. Say that the price and quantity both fell. What would you say was the most likely cause?
3. Say that price fell and quantity remained constant. What would you say was the most likely cause?
4. In 1996 the exchange rate for the South African rand fell precipitously from 29 cents per rand to 22 cents per rand when there was political trouble in the country. Explain why the political turmoil had that effect in reference to a graphical supply and demand analysis.
5. Demonstrate graphically the effect of a price floor.
6. Demonstrate graphically why rent controls might increase the total payment that new renters pay for an apartment.
7. Oftentimes, to be considered for a job, you have to know someone in the firm. What does this observation tell you about the wage paid for that job?
8. Graphically show the effects of a minimum wage on the number of unemployed.
9. Demonstrate graphically the effect of a tax of $4 per unit on equilibrium price and quantity.
10. Using a graph like the one you drew for question 8 above, show graphically what the quota would be that led to the same price and quantity.
11. In most developing countries, there are long lines of taxis at airports, and these taxis often wait two or three hours. What does this tell you about the price in that market? Demonstrate with supply and demand analysis.
12. In the text, the supply and demand situation between Mexican pesos and U.S. dollars was shown in reference to the supply and demand for pesos. Go through the same analysis in terms of the supply and demand for dollars.

PROBLEMS AND EXERCISES

1. "Scalping" is the name given to the buying of tickets at a low price and reselling them at a high price. The following information about a Florida State–Notre Dame game in 1993 comes from a newspaper. At the beginning of the season:
   a. Tickets sell for $27 and are sold out in preseason.
   b. Halfway through the season, both teams have maintained unbeaten records. Resale price of tickets rises to $200.
   c. One week before the game, both teams have remained unbeaten and are ranked 1-2. Ticket price rises to $600.
   d. Three days before the game, price falls to $400.
   Demonstrate, using supply/demand analysis and words, what might have happened to cause these fluctuations in price.
2. In some states and localities "scalping" is against the law, although enforcement of these laws is spotty (difficult).
   a. Using supply/demand analysis and words, demonstrate what a weakly enforced antiscalping law would likely do to the price of tickets.
   b. Using supply/demand analysis and words, demonstrate what a strongly enforced antiscalping law would likely do to the price of tickets.
3. Apartments in New York City are often hard to find. One of the major reasons is that there is rent control.
   a. Demonstrate graphically how rent controls could make apartments hard to find.
   b. Often one can get an apartment if one makes a side payment to the current tenant. Can you explain why?
   c. What would be the likely effect of eliminating rent controls?
   d. What is the political appeal of rent controls?
4. Until recently, angora goat wool (mohair) has been designated as a strategic commodity (it used to be utilized in some military clothing). Because of that, in 1992 for every dollar's worth of mohair sold to manufacturers, ranchers received $3.60.
   a. Demonstrate graphically the effect of the elimination of this designation and subsidy.
   b. Explain why the program was likely kept in existence for so long.
   c. Say that a politician has suggested that the government should pass a law that requires all consumers to pay a price for angora goat wool high enough so that the sellers of that wool would receive $3.60 more than the market price. Demonstrate the effect of the law graphically. Would consumers support it? How about suppliers?
5. In one of the boxes, a gray market in Russian rubles is discussed.
   a. Draw the supply and demand curves for rubles in terms of dollars and show the Russian government's then-official price of .64 rubles per dollar.
   b. Show the gray market price of dollars mentioned in that box.
   c. Show what the black market price of rubles would have likely been if the Russian government had strictly enforced the exchange laws.

ANSWERS TO MARGIN QUESTIONS

1. The shortage would have increased; the lower the price ceiling relative to equilibrium price, the larger the shortage. *(86)*

2. The demand curve would have shifted out, increasing both price and quantity, as in the diagram below. *(88)*

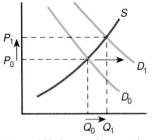

3. I remind Jean that a shift factor changes demand, not quantity demanded. *(89)*

4. Quantity decreases but it is unclear what happens to price. *(89)*

5. To conduct the analysis in terms of the supply and demand for dollars, one must put the peso price of dollars on the vertical axis and the quantity of dollars on the horizontal axis, as in the diagram below: *(91)*

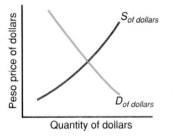

6. In a fixed exchange rate system the government works with the market, buying and selling currency to see that quantity supplied equals quantity demanded. In a nonconvertible exchange rate system, the government enacts a statutory provision setting the exchange rate by law. *(92)*

7. I state that the tax will most likely raise the price by less than $2 since the tax will cause the quantity demanded to decrease. This will decrease quantity supplied, and hence decrease the price the suppliers receive. In the diagram below, Q falls from Q_1 to Q_2 and the price the supplier receives falls from $4 to $3, making the final price $5, not $6. *(95)*

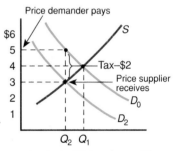

8. Firms prefer quotas to tariffs because with quotas, they receive rents; with tariffs, the government receives tax revenues. *(96)*

9. The fallacy of composition is relevant for macroeconomic issues because it reminds us that, in the aggregate, small effects that are immaterial for micro issues can add up and be material. *(98)*

10. When supply and demand are interdependent, a movement along one curve will cause a shift in the other curve, violating the "other things constant" assumption that is necessary for partial equilibrium analysis to apply. *(99)*

Algebraic Representation of Interferences with Supply and Demand

In Appendix A of Chapter 3, I showed how equilibrium could be determined algebraically. In this appendix I show how that equilibrium can be changed by various interferences in the market.

Price Ceilings and Price Floors

Let's start out by considering a price ceiling and price floor using the same example we used in the Chapter 3 appendix.

$$Q_S = -5 + 2P$$
$$Q_D = 10 - P.$$

This gave us the solution:

$$P = 5$$
$$Q = 5.$$

Now, say that a price ceiling of $4 is imposed. Would you expect a shortage or a surplus? If you said "shortage" you're doing well. If not, review the chapter before continuing with this appendix. To find out how much the shortage is we must find out how much will be supplied and how much will be demanded at the price ceiling. Substituting $4 in for price in both lets us see that $Q_S = 3$ units and $Q_D = 6$ units. There will be a shortage of 3 units. Next, let's consider a price floor of $6. To determine the surplus we follow the same exercise. Substituting $6 into the two equations gives a quantity supplied of 7 units and a quantity demanded of 4 units, so there is a surplus of 3 units.

Taxes and Subsidies

Next, let's consider the effect of a tax of $1 placed on the supplier. That tax would decrease the price received by suppliers by $1. In other words:

$$Q_S = -5 + 2(P - 1).$$

Multiplying the terms in parentheses by 2 and collecting terms results in

$$Q_S = -7 + 2P.$$

This supply equation has the same slope as in the previous case, but a new intercept term—just what you'd expect. To determine the new equilibrium price and quantity, follow steps 1 to 3 from Appendix B of Chapter 3. Setting this new equation equal to demand and solving for price gives

$$P = 5\frac{2}{3}.$$

Substituting this price into the demand and supply equations tells us equilibrium quantity:

$$Q_S = Q_D = 4\frac{1}{3} \text{ units.}$$

Of that price, the supplier must pay $1 in tax, so the price the supplier receives net of tax is $4⅔.

Next, let's say that the tax were put on the demander rather than on the supplier. In that case, the tax increases the price for demanders by $1 and the demand equation becomes

$$Q_D = 10 - (P + 1), \text{ or}$$
$$Q_D = 9 - P.$$

Again solving for equilibrium price and quantity requires setting the demand and supply equations equal to one another and solving for price. I leave the steps to you. The result is:

$$P = 4\frac{2}{3}.$$

This is the price the supplier receives. The price demanders pay is $5⅔. The equilibrium quantity will be 4⅓ units.

These are the same results we got in the previous cases showing that, given the assumptions, it doesn't matter who actually pays the tax: The effect on equilibrium price and quantity is identical no matter who pays it.

QUESTIONS FOR THOUGHT AND REVIEW

1. Suppose the demand and supply for milk is described by the following equations: $Q_D = 600 - 100P$; $Q_S = -150 + 150P$, where P is the price in dollars; Q_D is quantity demanded in millions of gallons per year; and Q_S is quantity supplied in millions of gallons per year.
   a. Solve for equilibrium price and quantity of milk.

b. Would a government-set price of $4 create a surplus or a shortage of milk? How much? Is $4 a price ceiling or a price floor?

2. Suppose the U.S. government imposes a $1 per gallon of milk tax on dairy farmers. Using the demand and supply equations from question 1:

   a. What is the effect of the tax on the supply equation? The demand equation?

   b. What is the new equilibrium price and quantity?

   c. How much do dairy farmers receive per gallon of milk after the tax? How much do demanders pay?

3. Repeat question 2a to 2c assuming the tax is placed on the buyers of milk. Does it matter who pays the tax?

4. Repeat question 2a to 2c assuming the government pays a $1-per-gallon-of-milk subsidy to farmers.

5. Suppose the demand for cassettes is represented by $Q_D = 16 - 4P$, and the supply of cassettes is represented by $Q_S = 4P - 1$. Determine if each of the following is a price floor, price ceiling, or neither. In each case, determine the shortage or surplus.

   a. $P = \$3$.

   b. $P = \$1.50$.

   c. $P = \$2.25$.

   d. $P = \$2.50$.

Five

U.S. Economic Institutions

The business of government is to keep the government out of business—that is, unless business needs government aid.

~ Will Rogers

After reading this chapter, you should be able to:

1 Provide a bird's-eye view of the U.S. economy.

2 Explain the role of consumer sovereignty in the U.S. economy.

3 Summarize briefly the advantages and disadvantages of various types of business.

4 Explain why, even though households have the ultimate power, much of the economic decision making is done by business and government.

5 List two general roles of government and seven specific roles of government.

You saw in Chapters 3 and 4 that supply and demand are the driving forces behind the invisible hand. But the invisible hand doesn't operate in an invisible world; it operates in a very real world—a world of institutions that sometimes fight against, sometimes accept, and sometimes strengthen the invisible hand. Thus, to know how the invisible hand works in practice, we need to have some sense of economic institutions and data about the U.S. economy.

The powerful U.S. economic machine generates enormous economic activity and provides a high standard of living (compared to most other countries) for almost all its inhabitants. It also provides economic security for its citizens. Starvation is far from most people's minds. Ultimately, what underlies the U.S. economy's strength is its people and its other resources. The United States has vast central plains that are extraordinarily fertile, as are areas in its West and South. It is the world's second-largest producer, and largest exporter, of grains. It has excellent ports and almost eight million kilometers (five million miles) of roads.

The positive attributes of the U.S. economy don't mean that the United States has no problems. Critics point out that crime is rampant, drugs are omnipresent, economic resources such as oil and minerals are declining, the environment is deteriorating, the distribution of income is skewed toward the rich, and enormous economic effort goes into economic gamesmanship (real estate deals, stock market deals, deals about deals) that seems simply to reshuffle existing wealth, not to create new wealth. Internationally, the U.S. relative economic position has deteriorated substantially since the 1950s and 1960s. In some people's eyes, Japan has replaced the United States as the world's economic leader. Rather than lending money to other countries as it had done in the 1950s and 1960s, beginning in the 1980s the United States borrowed enormous

Ask your students to research the economic geography of their local community. They may need to conduct some interviews with public officials and businesspeople to find their data, especially if they are from a small town or rural area.

A BIRD'S-EYE VIEW OF THE U.S. ECONOMY

1 Ultimately the U.S. economy's strength is its people and its other resources.

There are more chapters in this book than can be lectured on in most classes. I generally lecture on only half the chapters. But that doesn't mean I don't assign more chapters. I believe it is quite legitimate to assign and test students on chapters I have not lectured on. I explain to students that active learning—is one of the skills I am giving them practice in, and that they should be thankful that I am not spoon-feeding them. This approach works reasonably well for the bright-but-lazy student (there's a lot of them); these students quickly figure out whether the professor will cover all the relevant material, and if so, won't read the chapters.

⊞ ADDED DIMENSION THE IMPORTANCE OF INSTITUTIONS

◼t should be clear from the first four chapters that I believe institutions are enormously important to the working markets. The two chapters in this section are designed to give you an introduction to the institutions of the United States and the world. You will need to be familiar with them to be able to apply economic thinking to any real-world issue. Remember, economics is the study of how individuals in a society coordinate their diverse wants and desires within the institutional structure.

To say that this material is important is not to say that these chapters require long lectures. It does mean that you must familiarize yourself with the information. Often professors will simply assign the chapters and test you on your reading of them. That's the way I do it. And I emphasize to students that this information, while important, can be learned quite easily.

amounts from other countries and is now the biggest debtor nation in the world. In short, the U.S. economy of the 1990s is great, but it's far from perfect.

Diagram of the U.S. Economy

Q–1: Into what three groups are market economies generally broken up?

I like to use the diagram as the centerpiece of this lecture on economic institutions. I discuss it briefly at the beginning, and then return to it as the components are discussed in depth.

Exhibit 1 diagrams a market economy such as that of the United States. Notice it's divided up into three groups: business, households, and government. Households supply factors of production to business and are paid by business for doing so. The market where this interaction takes place is called a *factor market*. Business produces goods and services and sells them to households and government. The market where this interaction takes place is called the *goods market*.

Notice also the arrows going out to and coming in from both business and households. Those arrows represent the international connection, which I'll discuss in Chapter 6. Finally, consider the arrows connecting government with households and business. Government taxes business and households. It buys goods and services from business and buys labor services from households. Then, with some of its tax revenue, it provides services (roads, education) to both business and households and gives some

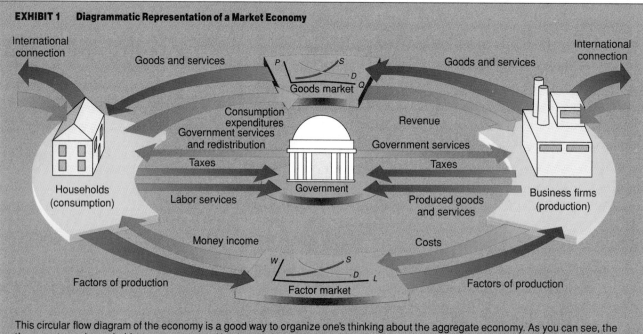

EXHIBIT 1   Diagrammatic Representation of a Market Economy

International connection

Goods and services

P *S* *D* Q
Goods market

Consumption expenditures
Government services and redistribution
Taxes
Households (consumption)
Labor services
Money income
Factors of production

Government

Revenue
Government services
Taxes
Produced goods and services
Costs

W *S* *D* *L*
Factor market

Goods and services

International connection

Business firms (production)

Factors of production

This circular flow diagram of the economy is a good way to organize one's thinking about the aggregate economy. As you can see, the three sectors—households, government, and business—interact in a variety of ways.

of its tax revenue directly back to individuals. In doing so, it redistributes income. But government also serves a second function. It oversees the interaction of business and households in the goods and factor markets. Government, of course, is not independent. The United States, for instance, is a democracy, so households vote to determine who shall govern.

Now let's look briefly at the individual components.

BUSINESS

President Calvin Coolidge once said, "The business of America is business." That's a bit of an overstatement, but business is responsible for over 80 percent of U.S. production. (Government is responsible for the other 20 percent.) In fact, any time a household decides to produce something, it becomes a business. **Business** is simply the name given to *private producing units in our society.*

Businesses in the United States decide *what* to produce, *how* much to produce, and *for whom* to produce it. They make these central economic decisions on the basis of their own feelings, which are influenced by market incentives. Anyone who wants to can start a business, provided he or she can come up with the required cash and meet the necessary regulatory requirements. Each year, about 770,000 businesses are started.

Businesses in the United States decide what *to produce,* how *much to produce, and* for whom *to produce it.*

For a story of the tribulations of an employee turned entrepreneur, see Chapter 3, *"Case Studies in Economics."*

Entrepreneurship and Business

Don't think of business as something other than people. Businesses are ultimately made up of a group of people organized together to accomplish some end. In terms of numbers, most businesses are one- or two-person operations. Home-based businesses, at least if they're part-time activities, are easy to start. All you have to do is say you're in business, and you are. If that business becomes complex enough and big enough to have employees (especially if it needs its own building), the difficulties begin. Before the business may expand its operations, a large number of licenses, permits, approvals, and forms must be obtained from various government agencies. That's one reason why **entrepreneurship** (*the ability to organize and get something done*) is an important part of business.

Entrepreneurship is the ability to organize and get something done; it is an important part of business.

Ask your students think of products or services that are the product of entrepreneurial vision—something that was invented before there was any clear demand for it. Post-it notes and in-line skates are good examples.

Consumer Sovereignty and Business

To say that businesses decide what to produce isn't to say that **consumer sovereignty** (*the consumer's wishes rule what's produced*) doesn't reign in the United States. Businesses decide what to produce based on what they believe will sell. A key question a person in the United States should ask about starting a business is: Can I make a profit from it? **Profit** is *what's left over from total revenues after all the appropriate costs have been subtracted.* Businesses that guess correctly what the consumer wants generally make a profit. Businesses that guess wrong generally operate at a loss.

People are free to start businesses for whatever purposes they want. No one asks them: "What's the social value of your term paper assistance business, your Twinkies business, your fur coat business, or your textbook publishing business?" Yet the U.S. economic system is designed to channel individuals' desire to make a profit into the general good of society. That's the invisible hand at work. As long as the business doesn't violate a law and does conform to regulations, people in the United States are free to start whatever business they want, if they can get the money to finance it. That's a key difference between the U.S. market economy and a traditional Soviet-style socialist economy where people weren't free to start a business even if they could get the financing.

2 Although businesses decide what to produce, they are guided by consumer sovereignty.

There's an important if *in people's freedom to start a business:* If *they can get the money to finance it.*

Q–2: In the United States the invisible hand ensures that only socially valuable businesses are started. True or false? Why?

✓ A REMINDER   ECONOMIC GEOGRAPHY OF THE UNITED STATES

Geographic economic information is vitally important. To understand an economy you should know: Where are goods produced? Where are natural resources found? What natural resources does it lack? What are normal transportation routes? To simplify their analyses, economists often discuss economic problems without discussing geographic dimensions. But no discussion of an economy should forget that geographic dimensions of economic problems are significant. To determine whether to send my students off to the library to learn this information, I give them a quiz. I present them with two lists like those below. The list on the right gives 20 places in the United States. The list on the left gives a particular economic characteristic, such as an industry, product, activity, or natural condition that has been turned to economic advantage. Students are required to match the numbers with important characteristics of each area.

If you answer fewer than 15 correctly, I strongly suggest learning more geographic facts. The study guide has a number of other projects, information, and examples. An encyclopedia has even more, and your library has a wealth of information. You could spend the entire semester acquiring facts. I'm not suggesting that, but I *am* suggesting that you follow the economic news carefully and pay attention to *where* various *whats* are produced.

THE QUIZ

In the first column, I list 20 economic characteristics. In the second and third columns, I list 20 states, cities, or areas of the country. Associate the locale with the proper characteristic by printing the letter on the line. Can you locate each of the locales in the map?

_____ 1. excellent climate for spacecraft launching
_____ 2. major concentration of investment and banking services
_____ 3. film and TV industry
_____ 4. significant fishing and lobstering industries
_____ 5. the maple sugar state
_____ 6. concentration of textile industries
_____ 7. gold is a major product
_____ 8. major oil reserves
_____ 9. iron ore and iron extraction
_____ 10. major automobile production
_____ 11. major port for oil
_____ 12. tourism is a major industry, especially at Mardi Gras
_____ 13. significant irrigation farming
_____ 14. island's seasonal economy driven by summer residents and tourists
_____ 15. nearly all energy needs supplied by hydroelectric power
_____ 16. significant natural gas reserves
_____ 17. staging area for shipment of prime beef
_____ 18. concentration of lead mining
_____ 19. extensive silver mines
_____ 20. major timber production and port for shipping wood products to Japan and the Far East.

a. Colorado
b. Detroit and surrounding area
c. Florida
d. Georgia, South Carolina, and North Carolina
e. Houston
f. Idaho
g. Kansas City
h. Maine
i. Martha's Vineyard (Mass.)
j. New Orleans

k. New York City
l. Northern Minnesota
m. Oklahoma
n. Oregon
o. Pennsylvania and West Virginia
p. Seattle and surrounding area
q. South Dakota
r. Southern California
s. Nevada
t. Vermont

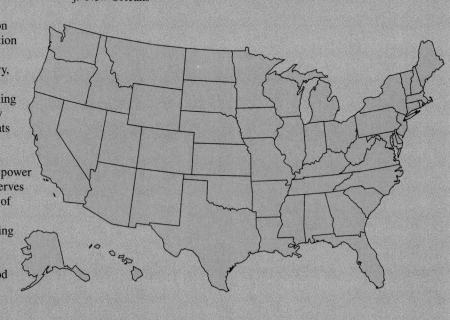

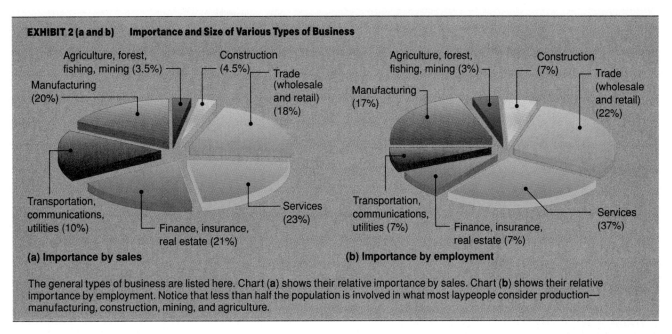

EXHIBIT 2 (a and b)   Importance and Size of Various Types of Business

Agriculture, forest, fishing, mining (3.5%)
Construction (4.5%)
Manufacturing (20%)
Trade (wholesale and retail) (18%)
Transportation, communications, utilities (10%)
Finance, insurance, real estate (21%)
Services (23%)

(a) Importance by sales

Agriculture, forest, fishing, mining (3%)
Construction (7%)
Manufacturing (17%)
Trade (wholesale and retail) (22%)
Transportation, communications, utilities (7%)
Finance, insurance, real estate (7%)
Services (37%)

(b) Importance by employment

The general types of business are listed here. Chart (**a**) shows their relative importance by sales. Chart (**b**) shows their relative importance by employment. Notice that less than half the population is involved in what most laypeople consider production—manufacturing, construction, mining, and agriculture.

Source: *Survey of Current Business* (1996), http://www.bea.gov, and *Employment and Earnings* (1997), Bureau of Labor Statistics, http://stats.bis.gov.

Exhibit 2(a) shows a selection of various categories of U.S. businesses with their relative amounts of receipts (the total income firms take in) for each category. Total receipts aren't necessarily the best indicator of the importance of various types of business to the economy. Exhibit 2(b) ranks businesses by their relative employment. Notice that services are much more important when businesses are ranked by employment than when they are ranked by sales.

The three primary forms of business are sole proprietorships, partnerships, and corporations. Of the 18 million businesses in the United States, approximately 69 percent are sole proprietorships, 8 percent are partnerships, and 23 percent are corporations, as we see in Exhibit 3(a). In terms of total receipts, however, we get a quite different picture, with corporations far surpassing all other business forms, as Exhibit 3(b) shows. In fact, the largest 500 corporations account for almost 90 percent of the total receipts of all U.S. businesses.

Categories of Business

Q–3: Is the category "finance, insurance, and real estate" more important when measured by sales or when measured by employment?

Forms of Business

Q–4: Are most businesses in the United States corporations? If not, what are most businesses?

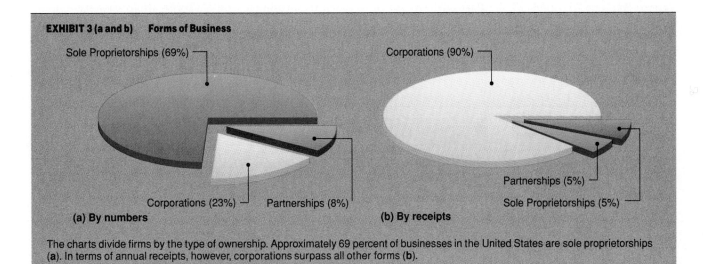

EXHIBIT 3 (a and b)   Forms of Business

Sole Proprietorships (69%)
Corporations (23%)
Partnerships (8%)

(a) By numbers

Corporations (90%)
Partnerships (5%)
Sole Proprietorships (5%)

(b) By receipts

The charts divide firms by the type of ownership. Approximately 69 percent of businesses in the United States are sole proprietorships (**a**). In terms of annual receipts, however, corporations surpass all other forms (**b**).

Source: IRS, *Statistics of Income,* Fall 1996. http://www.irs.ustreas.gov.

Producing physical goods is only one of a society's economic tasks. Another task is to provide services (activities done for others). Services do not involve producing a physical good. When you get your hair cut, you buy a service, not a good. Much of the cost of the physical goods we buy actually is not a cost of producing the good, but is a cost of one of the most important services: distribution (getting the good to where the consumer is). After a good is produced, it has to get to the individuals who are going to consume it at the time they need it. If the distribution system gets botched up, it's as if the good had never been produced.

Let's consider a couple of examples. Take Christmas trees. Say you're sitting on 60,000 cut spruce trees in the Vermont mountains, but an ice storm prevents you from shipping them until December 26. Guess what? You're now stuck with 60,000 spruce trees and the problem of somehow getting rid of them. Or take hot dogs. How many of us have been irked that a hot dog that cost 25¢ to fix at home costs $3 at a football game? But a hot dog at home isn't the same as a hot dog at a game. Distribution of the good is as important as production; you're paying the extra $2.75 for distribution.

Take a chance and ask your students if any of them have started a business of his or her own. You might be surprised. What form of business was it? Why did they choose that form?

Sole proprietorships—*businesses that have only one owner*—are the easiest to start and have the fewest bureaucractic hassles. **Partnerships**—*businesses with two or more owners*—create possibilities for sharing the burden, but they also create unlimited liability for each of the partners. **Corporations**—*businesses that are treated as a person, and are legally owned by their stockholders who are not liable for the actions of the corporate "person"*—are the largest form of business when measured in terms of receipts.

The advantages and disadvantages of each are summarized in Exhibit 4.

Since corporations are the most complex, let's consider them more carefully. When a corporation is formed, it issues **stock** (*certificates of ownership in a company*) which is sold or given to individuals. Proceeds of the sale of that stock make up what is called the *equity capital* of a company. Ownership of stock entitles you to vote in the election of a corporation's directors.

Limited liability   Owner of business is liable only to the extent of his or her own investment.

Corporations were developed as institutions to make it easier for company owners to be separated from company management. A corporation provides the owners with **limited liability**—*the stockholder's liability is limited to the amount that stockholder has invested in the company.* With the other two forms of business, owners can lose everything they possess even if they have only a small amount invested in the company, but in a corporation the owners can lose only what they have invested in that corporation. If you've invested $100, you can lose only $100. In the other kinds of business, even if you've invested only $100, you could lose everything; the business's losses must be covered by the individual owners. Corporations' limited liability makes it easier for them to attract investment capital. Corporations pay taxes but they also offer their individual owners ways of legally avoiding taxes.

3 The advantages and disadvantages of the three forms of business are shown in the table.

A corporation's stocks can be distributed among as few as three persons or among millions of stockholders. Stocks can be bought and sold either in an independent transaction between two people (an *over-the-counter* trade) or through a broker

---

EXHIBIT 4   Advantages and Disadvantages of Various Forms of For-Profit Businesses

	Sole Proprietor	Partnership	Corporation
Advantages	1. Minimum bureaucratic hassle 2. Direct control by owner	1. Ability to share work and risks 2. Relatively easy to form	1. No personal liability 2. Increasing ability to get funds 3. Ability to shed personal income and gain added expenses
Disadvantages	1. Limited ability to get funds 2. Unlimited personal liability	1. Unlimited personal liability (even for partner's blunder) 2. Limited ability to get funds	1. Legal hassle to organize 2. Possible double taxation of income 3. Monitoring problems

Small corporations' stock is usually traded *over-the-counter,* which doesn't mean you go in a store and walk up to the counter. *Over-the-counter* means that the stock is traded in informal markets in which brokers contact other brokers directly. An over-the-counter share has a *bid* price and a higher *ask* price. The bid price is the price someone has offered to pay for shares; the ask price is the price a shareholder has told her brokers she wants to get for her shares. Trades are usually made at some price between the bid and ask figures, with the broker collecting a commission for arranging a trade.

Large corporations' stock is usually traded on a *stock exchange*—a formal market in which stocks are bought and sold. The table shows a typical stock exchange listing. Each stock sold on the New York Stock Exchange has only one price listed. That's because the exchange has a "specialist" market-maker system, in which a particular broker markets a particular group of stocks. This specialist always stands ready to buy or sell shares of a stock at some price. The specialist sets a price and then varies it according to whether he or she is receiving more buy orders or more sell orders.

In order to buy or sell a New York Stock Exchange stock, you contact a stockbroker and say you want to buy or sell whatever stock you've decided on—say Ford Motor Company. The commission you're charged for having the broker sell you the stock (or sell it for you) varies. Any purchase of fewer than 100 shares of one corporation is called an *odd lot* and you'll be charged a higher commission than if you buy a 100-share lot or more.

There are a number of stock exchanges. The largest and most familiar is the New York Stock Exchange. Somewhere around 50 million individuals own stock they bought on the New York Stock Exchange.

To judge how stocks as a whole are doing, a number of indexes have been developed. These include Standard and Poor's (S&P 500), the Wilshire Index, and the Dow Jones Industrial Average. The Dow Jones is the one you're most likely to hear about in the news.

When a share of a corporation's existing stock is sold on the stock exchange, corporations get no money from that sale. The sale is simply a transfer of ownership from one individual (or organization) to another. The only time a corporation gets money from the sale of stock is when it first issues the shares.

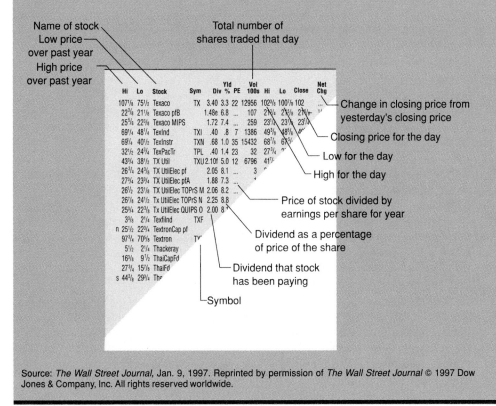

and a *stock exchange.* The Added Dimension box "Trading in Stocks" provides a brief introduction to the stock market.

In corporations, ownership is separated from control of the firm. Most stockholders have little input into the decisions a corporation makes. Instead, corporations are often controlled by their managers, who often run them for their own benefit as well as for the owners'. The reason is that owners' control of management is limited.

Eighty percent of the largest 200 corporations are controlled by managers, with little effective stockholder control.

A large percentage of most corporations' stock is not even controlled by the owners; instead, it is controlled by financial institutions such as mutual funds (financial institutions that invest individuals' money for them) and by pension funds (financial institutions that hold people's money for them until it is to be paid out to them upon their retirement). Thus, ownership of corporations is another step removed from individuals. Studies have shown that 80 percent of the largest 200 corporations in the United States are essentially controlled by managers and have little effective stockholder control.

Q–5: It is obvious that all for-profit businesses in the United States will maximize profit. True or false? Why?

Why is the question of who controls a firm important? Because economic theory assumes business owners' goal is to maximize profits, which would be true of corporations if stockholders made the decisions. Managers don't have the same incentives to maximize profits that owners do. There's pressure on managers to maximize profits, but that pressure can often be weak or ineffective.

HOUSEHOLDS

In the economy, householders vote with their dollars.

The second classification we'll consider in this overview of U.S. economic institutions is households. **Households** (*groups of individuals living together and making joint decisions*) are the most powerful economic institution. They ultimately control government and business, the other two economic institutions. Households' votes in the political arena determine government policy; their decisions about supplying labor and capital determine what businesses will have available to work with; and their spending decisions or expenditures (the "votes" they cast with their dollars) determine what business will be able to sell.

4 Although, in principle, ultimate power resides with the people and households (consumer sovereignty), in practice the representatives of the people—firms and government—are sometimes removed from the people and, in the short run, are only indirectly monitored by the people.

While the ultimate power does in principle lie with the people and households, we, the people, have assigned much of that power to representatives. As I discussed above, corporations are only partially responsive to owners of their stocks, and much of that ownership is once-removed from individuals. Ownership of 1,000 shares in a company with a total of 2 million shares isn't going to get you any influence over the corporation's activities. As a stockholder, you simply accept what the corporation does.

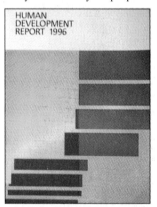

People are a country's most important resource.

A major decision that corporations make independently of their stockholders concerns what to produce. True, ultimately we, the people, decide whether we will buy what business produces, but business spends a lot of money telling us what services we want, what products make us "with it," what books we want to read, and the like. Most economists believe that consumer sovereignty reigns—that we are not fooled or controlled by advertising. Still, it is an open question in some economists' minds whether we, the people, control business or the business representatives control people.

Because of this assignment of power to other institutions, in many spheres of the economy households are not active producers of output but merely passive recipients of income. That's why much of the discussion of the household sector focuses on the distribution of household income. Thus, my consideration of households will be short and will focus on their income and their role as suppliers of labor.

Household Types and Income

The U.S. population of about 266 million is composed of about 100 million households. Exhibit 5 looks at three ways income is divided up among households. Notice the relatively low incomes of families where the husband is absent and of black families. Because income determines how many goods and services a person will get, these two groups have fared especially poorly in the *for whom* department.

Q–6: What was the median income of a black family in 1995?

One political concern about income is whether it is fairly (equitably, as opposed to equally) distributed, and whether all households have sufficient income. That's a tough question to answer. For now, let me simply note that the poverty level for a

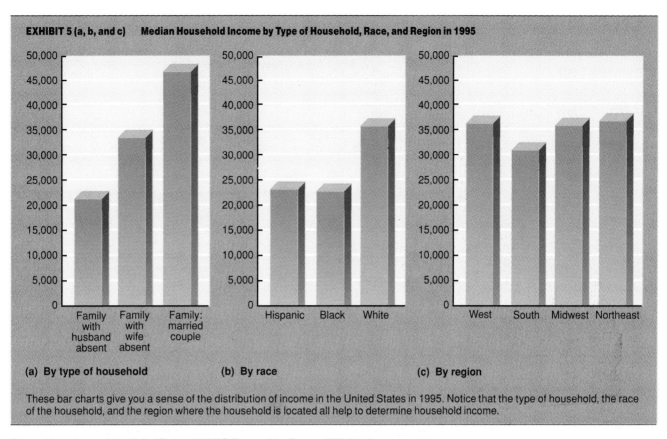

EXHIBIT 5 (a, b, and c)   Median Household Income by Type of Household, Race, and Region in 1995

(a) **By type of household**

(b) **By race**

(c) **By region**

These bar charts give you a sense of the distribution of income in the United States in 1995. Notice that the type of household, the race of the household, and the region where the household is located all help to determine household income.

Source: *Money Income in the United States: 1995.* U.S. Bureau of the Census, 1996, http://www.census.gov.

family of four in the United States is defined by the U.S. Department of Commerce as an income below $15,569 per year (1995 figure). By this definition, about 13.8 percent of all households in the United States were below the poverty level in the mid-1990s. This percentage is divided unequally between whites and blacks, with 29.3 percent of all black households below the poverty level and 8.5 percent of all white households below it.

The largest source of household income is wages and salaries (the income households get from labor). Households supply the labor with which businesses produce and government governs. The total U.S. labor force is about 134 million, about 5.4 percent (7.2 million) of whom were unemployed in 1996. The average U.S. workweek is 42.3 hours for males and 35.7 hours for females.

Households as Suppliers of Labor

Exhibits 6(a) and (b) divide U.S. employment by types of jobs and predicted growth rates of certain jobs. Notice that many of the jobs are service jobs, since the United States has become largely a service economy. Exhibit 6(b) shows that this greater emphasis on services rather than goods is continuing. Many of the fastest-growing jobs are in service industries; many of the fastest-declining are in manufacturing and agriculture.

Other divisions of jobs show even more differences. For example, physicians earn about $150,000 per year; lawyers often earn $100,000 per year, and CEOs of large corporations often make $2,000,000 per year or more. A beginning McDonald's employee generally makes about $12,000 per year.

One of the biggest changes in the labor markets in recent times has been unions' decline in importance. Labor unions are an economic institution closely associated with households. They were initially created to balance businesses' power. By organizing into unions, workers became an economic institution and gained a larger say in the production process. Unions pushed U.S. wages up relative to wages in other countries, and established in the United States some of the best working conditions in

In recent times, the power of the unions declined.

(a)			Median Earnings per Week	
Job category	Millions of Females	Millions of Males	Female	Male
Managerial and professional	17,754	18,744	$616	$852
Technical, sales	24,194	13,489	394	567
Service	10,210	6,967	273	357
Precision products	1,219	12,368	373	560
Machine operators	4,447	13,750	307	422
Farming, fishing, and forestry	677	2,889	255	300

(b) Fastest-growing jobs*	Fastest-declining jobs*
Personal and home care aides	Farmers
Systems analysts and computer scientists	Typists and word processors
Physical and corrective therapy assistants	Bookkeeping, accounting, and auditing clerks
Medical assistants	Bank tellers

*Projection for 1994–2005, based on moderate growth assumptions.

Source: *Employment and Earnings,* Bureau of Labor Statistics, and *Occupational Outlook Handbook,* 1996–1997. http://stats.bls.gov.

In going through this list, I talk about a computer voice recognition system, and how that will change word processing.

the world. But unions also had a negative effect; part of businesses' response to the high U.S. wages has been to move production facilities to countries where workers receive lower wages. That's one reason the U.S. manufacturing sector has declined relative to the service sector, and union membership and influence have fallen substantially. Service workers have far fewer unions, and their jobs are much more difficult to move to other countries.

GOVERNMENT

5a Two general roles of government are (1) as a referee and (2) as an actor.

The third major U.S. economic institution I'll consider is government. Government plays two general roles in the economy. It's both a referee (setting the rules that determine relations between businesses and households) and an actor (collecting money in taxes and spending that money on its own projects, such as defense and education). Let's first consider government's role as an actor.

Government as an Actor

The United States has a federal government system, which means we have various levels of government (federal, state, and local), each with its own powers. All levels of government combined consume about 20 percent of the country's total output and employ about 19 million individuals. The various levels of government also have a number of programs that redistribute income through taxation or through an array of social welfare and assistance programs designed to help specific groups.

State and Local Government State and local governments employ over 16 million people and spend almost $1 trillion a year. As you can see in Exhibit 7(a), state and local governments get much of their income from taxes: property taxes, sales taxes, and state and local income taxes. They spend their tax revenues on public welfare, administration, education (education through high school is available free in U.S. public schools), and roads, as Exhibit 7(b) shows. These activities fall within microeconomics, which we'll discuss in the microeconomics sections of this book.

Q–7: The largest percentage of federal expenditure is in what general category?

Federal Government Probably the best way to get an initial feel for the federal government and its size is to look at the various categories of its tax revenues and expenditures in Exhibit 8. Notice income taxes make up about 41 percent of the federal government's revenue, while social security taxes make up about 40 percent. That's more than 80 percent of the federal government's revenues, most of which shows up

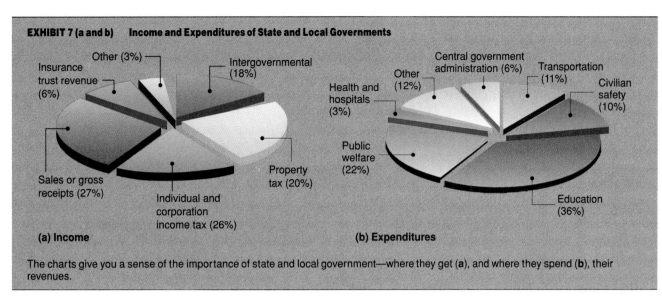

EXHIBIT 7 (a and b)   Income and Expenditures of State and Local Governments

(a) Income

Other (3%)
Insurance trust revenue (6%)
Intergovernmental (18%)
Sales or gross receipts (27%)
Individual and corporation income tax (26%)
Property tax (20%)

(b) Expenditures

Central government administration (6%)
Transportation (11%)
Other (12%)
Health and hospitals (3%)
Civilian safety (10%)
Public welfare (22%)
Education (36%)

The charts give you a sense of the importance of state and local government—where they get (**a**), and where they spend (**b**), their revenues.

Source: *Survey of Current Business,* 1996, Bureau of Economic Analysis, http://www.bea.gov.

as a deduction from your paycheck. In Exhibit 8(b), notice that the federal government's two largest categories of spending are income maintenance and defense, with expenditures on interest payments close behind.

Even if government spending made up only a small proportion of total expenditures, government would still be central to the study of economics. The reason is that, in a market economy, government controls the interaction of business and households. Government sets the rules of interaction and acts as a referee, changing the rules when it sees fit. Government decides whether the invisible hand will be allowed to operate freely.

Government is involved in every interaction between households and business in the form of laws regulating that interaction. For example, in the United States today:

1. Businesses are not free to hire and fire whomever they want. They must comply with equal opportunity and labor laws. Even closing a plant requires 60 days' notice for many kinds of firms.

Government as a Referee

"The American Political-Economic System," by Adolph A. Berle, in *Classic Readings in Economics.*

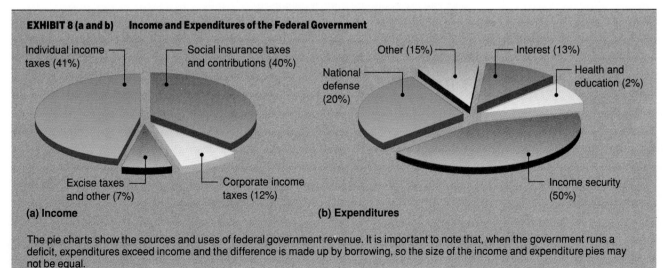

EXHIBIT 8 (a and b)   Income and Expenditures of the Federal Government

(a) Income

Individual income taxes (41%)
Social insurance taxes and contributions (40%)
Excise taxes and other (7%)
Corporate income taxes (12%)

(b) Expenditures

Other (15%)
Interest (13%)
National defense (20%)
Health and education (2%)
Income security (50%)

The pie charts show the sources and uses of federal government revenue. It is important to note that, when the government runs a deficit, expenditures exceed income and the difference is made up by borrowing, so the size of the income and expenditure pies may not be equal.

Source: *Survey of Current Business,* 1996, Bureau of Economic Analysis, http://www.bea.gov.

2. Many working conditions are subject to government regulation: safety rules, wage rules, overtime rules, hours-of-work rules, and the like.

3. Businesses cannot meet with other businesses to agree on prices they will charge.

4. Workers in a union cannot require all workers in a firm to join the union before they are hired. In many states, they cannot require workers to join the union at all.

A recent price-fixing case that I sometimes discuss is the Archer Daniels Midlands case.

Most of these laws evolved over time. Up until the 1930s, household members, in their roles as workers and consumers, had few rights. Businesses were free to hire and fire at will and, if they chose, to deceive and take advantage of consumers.

Over time, laws have changed. New laws to curb business abuses have been passed, and government agencies have been formed to enforce these laws. Now many people think the pendulum has swung too far the other way. They believe businesses are saddled with too many regulatory burdens.

One big question that I'll address throughout this book is: What referee role should the government play in an economy? For example, should government redistribute income from the rich to the poor through taxation? Should it allow a merger between two companies? Should it regulate air traffic? Should it regulate prices?

Because considering government's role will be a central element of the entire book, I'll present a few terms and roles now to establish a framework for the later chapters.

Economic Roles of Government   I first consider the economic roles of government. These roles tend to be somewhat less controversial than its political roles.

5b Seven specific roles of government are:

1. Providing a stable structure within which markets can operate.
2. Promoting workable, effective competition.
3. Correcting for external effects of individuals' decisions.
4. Providing public goods that the market doesn't adequately supply.
5. Ensuring economic stability and growth.
6. Providing acceptably fair distribution of society's production among its individuals.
7. Encouraging merit and discouraging demerit goods or activities.

Providing a Stable Institutional Framework   A basic economic role of government is to provide a stable institutional framework (the set of rules determining what we can and can't do). Before people conduct business, they need to know the rules of the game and have a reasonable belief about what those rules will be in the future. The modern economy requires contractual arrangements to be made among individuals. These arrangements must be enforced if the economy is to operate effectively. Ultimately only the government can create a stable environment and enforce contracts through its legal system. Where governments don't provide a stable environment, as often happens in developing countries, economic growth is difficult; usually such economies are stagnant. Liberia in the 1990s is an example. As two groups there fought for political control, the Liberian economy stagnated. Eventually the fight broke into civil war and the economy almost collapsed.

Almost all economists believe that providing an institutional framework within which the market can operate is an important function of government. However, they differ significantly as to what the rules for such a system should be. Even if the rules are currently perceived as unfair, an argument can be made for keeping them. Individuals have already made decisions based on the existing rules, so it's unfair to them to change the rules in midstream. Stability of rules is a benefit to society.

Recent economic reforms in the former Soviet Union provide a good example of this point. First, the Soviets modified their rules to encourage profits and entrepreneurship. Within a year they changed the rules again, attacking entrepreneurs as profiteers and confiscating their earnings. Then they began to encourage entrepreneurship again, but the second time few entrepreneurs came forward because of fear that the rules would change once again. Then there was a conservative coup; then a reestablishment of the market. Finally the entire political structure fell apart, and the Soviet Union was no more.

Governments have a hard time balancing degrees of unfairness.

When rules are perceived as unfair and changing them is also perceived as unfair, which often happens, the government finds itself in the difficult position of any referee, trying to strike a balance between the two degrees of unfairness.

Promoting Effective and Workable Competition   One of the most difficult economic functions of government is its role in protecting and promoting competition. As I discussed above, U.S. ideology sees monopoly power as bad. **Monopoly power** is *the ability of individuals or firms currently in business to prevent other individuals or firms from entering the same kind of business;* thereby monopoly power can raise existing firms' prices. Similarly, U.S. ideology sees **competition** (*individuals' or firms' ability to enter freely into business activities*) as good. Government's job is to promote competition and prevent monopoly power from limiting competition.

Government's job is to promote competition and prevent monopoly power from limiting competition.

What makes this a difficult function for government is that most individuals and firms believe that competition is far better for the other guy than it is for themselves, that their monopolies are necessary monopolies, and that competition facing them is unfair competition. For example, farmers support competition, but they also support government farm subsidies and import restrictions, which make it harder for foreign individuals to compete in the United States. Likewise, firms support competition, but they also support tariffs, which protect them from foreign competition. Professionals, such as architects and engineers, support competition, but they also support professional licensing, which limits the number of competitors who can enter their field.

Correcting for Externalities   When two people freely enter into a trade or agreement, they both believe that they will benefit from that trade. But unless they're required to do so, traders are unlikely to take into account any **externality**—*the effect that an action may have on a third party that the person who undertook that action did not take into account.* An externality can be positive (in which case society as a whole benefits even more than the two parties) or negative (in which case society as a whole benefits less than the two parties). In either case, externalities provide a potential role for government. If one's goal is to benefit society as much as possible, actions with positive externalities should be encouraged, and actions with negative externalities should be restricted.

Externality   *Effect of an action on third parties that the person who undertook that action did not take into account.*

An example of a positive externality is education. When someone educates herself or himself, it is not only the person who is helped. All society benefits since better-educated people make better citizens and can often figure out new approaches to solving problems—solutions that benefit everyone.

Q–8: If there were no externalities, there would be no role for government. True or False? Why?

An example of a negative externality is pollution. For example, when people use air conditioners, they'll probably let loose a small amount of chlorofluorocarbons, which go up into the earth's atmosphere and contribute to the destruction of the ozone layer. The ozone layer protects all living things by filtering some of the sun's ultraviolet light rays, which can contribute to cancer and other harmful or fatal conditions. Neither the firms that produce the air conditioners nor the consumers who buy them pay for the negative effects those chlorofluorocarbons have on society. This means that the destruction of the ozone layer is an externality—the result of an action that is not taken into account by market participants.

When externalities exist, government has a potential role: to step in and change the rules so that the actors must take into account the effect of their actions on society as a whole. I emphasize that the role is a *potential* one, because government often has difficulty dealing with externalities in such a way that society gains. For example, even if the U.S. government totally banned chlorofluorocarbons, the problem wouldn't be solved because ozone layer destruction is an international, rather than a national, problem. I also emphasize *potential* because government isn't simply an institution trying to do good. It's an institution that reflects, and is often guided by, politics and vested interests. It's not clear that, given the political realities, government intervention to correct externalities would improve the situation. In later chapters I'll have a lot more to say about government's role in correcting for externalities.

When externalities exist governments have a potential role.

Providing for Public Goods   **Public goods** are *goods whose consumption by one individual does not prevent their consumption by other individuals.* This means that when a supplier supplies a public good to one person, he or she supplies the good to all. In

Video Series, Economics USA: Public Goods and Responsibility, Segments 26.1–26.3.

contrast, a **private good** is *one that, when consumed by one individual, cannot be consumed by other individuals*. An example of a private good is an apple; once I eat that apple, no one else can consume it.

An example of a public good is national defense. National defense must protect all individuals in the country; it cannot protect some people but leave others unprotected. Everyone agrees that national defense is needed. But will everyone, as individuals, supply it, or will everyone rely on someone else doing it? Self-interested people would like to enjoy the benefits of defense while letting someone else pay for it. Because national defense is a public good, if someone else defends the country you're defended for free; you can be a **free rider**—*a person who participates in something for free because others have paid for it*. Everyone has an incentive to be a free rider, but if everyone is a free rider, there won't be any defense. In such cases government can step in to require that everyone pay part of the cost of national defense to make sure that no one is a free rider.

Government can provide public goods such as defense and require that everyone pay part of the cost to make sure no one is a free rider.

Ensuring Economic Stability and Growth   In addition to providing general stability, government has the potential role of providing economic stability. If it's possible, most people would agree that government should prevent large fluctuations in the level of economic activity; maintain a relatively constant price level; and provide an economic environment conducive to economic growth. These aims, which became U.S. government goals in 1946 when the Employment Act was passed, are generally considered macroeconomic goals. They're justified as appropriate aims for government to pursue because they involve **macroeconomic externalities** (*externalities that affect the levels of unemployment, inflation, or growth in the economy as a whole*).

Macroeconomic externality   *Effect of an individual decision that affects the levels of unemployment, inflation, or growth in an economy as a whole, but is not taken into account by the individual decision maker.*

Here's how a macroexternality could occur. When individuals decide how much to spend, they don't take into account the effects of their decision on others; thus, there may be too much or too little spending. Too little spending often leads to unemployment. But in making their spending decision, people don't take into account the fact that spending less might create unemployment. So their spending decisions can involve a macroexternality. Similarly, when people raise their price and don't consider the effect on inflation, they too might be creating a macroexternality.

Political Roles of Government   The other group of possible roles for government, *political roles*, involves more controversial issues.

Providing for a Fair Distribution of Society's Income   The first, and probably most controversial, of these roles concerns income distribution. Many believe the government should see that the economic system is fair, or at least is perceived as fair, by the majority of the people in the society.

But determining what's fair is a difficult philosophical question. Let's simply consider two of the many manifestations of the fairness problem. Should the government use a **progressive tax** (*a tax whose rates increase as a person's income increases*) to redistribute money from the rich to the poor? (A progressive income tax schedule might tax individuals at a rate of 15 percent for income up to $20,000; at 25 percent for income between $20,000 and $40,000; and at 35 percent for every dollar earned over $40,000.) Or should government impose a **regressive tax** (*a tax whose rates decrease as income rises*) to redistribute money from the poor to the rich? Or should government impose a flat or **proportional tax** (*a tax whose rates are constant at all income levels, no matter what your total annual income is*)? Such a tax might be, say, 25 percent of every dollar of income. The United States has chosen a somewhat progressive income tax, while the social security tax is a proportional tax up to a specified earned income.

Q–9: Is a progressive tax fairer than a proportional tax?

Another tax question government faces is: Should there be *exemptions* (items of income that aren't taxed at all)? An exemption might be granted for $2,500 of income multiplied by the number of people, including children, supported by the taxpayer. A single mother with five children wouldn't be taxed at all on $15,000 ($2,500 × 6) of

No introductory book is able to provide you with all the information you should have about the economy. You should know about:

- Financial institutions, such as banks, insurance companies, and stock markets.
- The state of the economy: unemployment rates, inflation rates, and growth rates.
- The operations of business, such as advertising and assembly line production.

I'll provide general information on such topics, but you should get up-to-date specifics by following the economic news. Such current information is integral to any economics course. Where should you look? The following sources provide a good beginning:

- Cursory: Business section of your local paper and network news on TV. A slim treatment of the economic issues, but at least it introduces you to the terms.

- One step up from cursory: *Time, Newsweek, U.S. News & World Report;* a national newspaper's business sections (*New York Times, Los Angeles Times, Washington Post*); CNN on TV.
- Reasonably thorough: *Business Week, Forbes, Fortune* magazines; "Wall Street Week," "The Lehrer News Hour" or "Nightly Business Report" on PBS, and "Market Place" on NPR.
- Excellent: *The Wall Street Journal, The Economist, The Financial Times.*
- Web sites of various government agencies and Federal Reserve Banks. For a list of these see the Colander web site http://www.mhhe.com/economics/Colander.

her annual income. Or is that a *tax loophole* (a legal but unfair exemption)? Economists can tell government the effects of various types of taxes and forms of taxation, but we can't tell government what's fair. That is for the people, through the government, to decide.

Determining Demerit and Merit Goods or Activities   Another controversial role for government involves deciding what's best for people independently of their desires. The externality justification of government intervention assumes that individuals know what is best for themselves.

But what if people don't know what's best for themselves? What if they do know but don't act on that knowledge? For example, people might know that addictive drugs are bad for them, but because of peer pressure, or because they just don't care, they may take addictive drugs anyway. Government action prohibiting such activities through law or high taxes may then be warranted. Goods or activities like this are **demerit goods or activities** that are *deemed bad for people even though they choose to use the goods or engage in the activities.* Addictive drugs are a demerit good; using addictive drugs is a demerit activity.

Alternatively, there are some activities that government believes are good for people, even if people may not choose to engage in them. For example, government may believe that going to the opera or contributing to charity is a good activity. But in the United States only a small percentage of the population goes to the opera, and not everyone in the United States contributes to charity. Similarly, government may believe that whole-wheat bread is more nutritious than white bread. But many consumers prefer white bread. Things like whole-wheat bread and activities like contributing to charity are known as **merit goods or activities**—*activities and goods that government believes are good for you even though you may not choose to engage in the activities or consume the goods*—and government support for them through subsidies or tax benefits may be warranted.

The reasons for government intervention are often summed up under the phrase "market failure." **Market failures** are *situations where the market does not lead to a desired result.* Market failures are pervasive in the economy—the market is always failing in one way or another. But the fact that there are market failures does not mean that government intervention will improve the situation. There are also **government**

I often assign students to groups and make each group responsible for presenting a 5-minute summary of what's available from various information sources in the box above.

Demerit goods or activities   Things government believes are bad for you, although you may like them.

Merit goods or activities   Things government believes are good for you, although you may not think so.

Q-10:   If there is a market failure, government intervention will eliminate the problem. True or false? Why?

failures—*situations where the government intervenes and makes things worse.* Government failures are pervasive in the government—the government is always failing in one way or another. So real-world policy usually ends up choosing which failure will be least problematic.

The Limits of Government Action

Economists on all sides of the political spectrum speak in the voice of reason: "Look at all the costs; look at all the benefits. Then decide whether government should or should not intervene."

Pick out a local issue that involves potential economic intervention by the government, and ask your students to research and discuss the costs and benefits of the government intervention.

Economic theory doesn't say government should or shouldn't play any particular role in the economy. Those decisions depend on costs and benefits of government action. The public often perceives economic theory and economists as suggesting the best policy is a policy of laissez-faire, or government noninvolvement in the economy. Many economists do suggest a laissez-faire policy, but that suggestion is based on empirical observations of government's role in the past, not on economic theory.

Still, economists as a group generally favor less government involvement than does the general public. I suspect that the reason is that economists are taught to look below the surface at the long-run effect of government actions. They've discovered that the effects often aren't the intended effects, and that programs frequently have long-run consequences that make the problems worse, not better. Economists, both liberal and conservative, speak in the voice of reason: "Look at all the costs; look at all the benefits. Then decide whether government should or should not intervene."

Political pressures often force government to act, regardless of what rational examination suggests. A good example is new air safety regulations after a plane crash. The public generally favors these overwhelmingly. Most economists I know say: "Wait. Don't act in haste. Consider the benefits and costs that would result." After careful consideration, advantages and disadvantages aren't always clear; some economists favor more regulation, some economists favor less regulation—but they all make their assessments on the basis of rational examination, not emotion.

CHAPTER SUMMARY

- The invisible hand doesn't operate in an invisible world. Knowing economics requires knowing real-world information.
- Views about government's appropriate role in the economy have changed over time.
- In the United States, businesses make the *what, how much,* and *for whom* decisions.
- Businesses, households, and government can be categorized in a variety of ways.
- Although businesses decide what to produce, they succeed or fail depending on their ability to meet consumers' desires. That's consumer sovereignty.
- The three main forms of business are corporations, sole proprietorships, and partnerships.
- Income is unequally divided among households. Whether that's bad, and whether anything should be done about it, are debatable.
- Government plays two general roles in the economy: (1) as a referee, and (2) as an actor.

- Government has seven possible specific roles in a capitalist society:

  1. Providing a stable institutional and legal structure within which markets can operate.
  2. Promoting workable and effective competition.
  3. Correcting for external effects of individuals' decisions.
  4. Providing public goods that the market doesn't adequately supply.
  5. Ensuring economic stability and growth.
  6. Providing an acceptably fair distribution of society's products among its individuals.
  7. Encouraging merit and discouraging demerit goods or activities.

- In deciding whether government has a role to play, economists look at the costs and benefits of a given role.

KEY TERMS

business *(107)*
competition *(117)*
consumer sovereignty *(107)*
corporation *(110)*
demerit goods or activities *(119)*
entrepreneurship *(107)*
externality *(117)*
free rider *(118)*

government failure *(119)*
households *(112)*
limited liability *(110)*
macroeconomic externality *(118)*
market failure *(119)*
merit goods or activities *(119)*
monopoly power *(117)*
partnership *(110)*

private good *(118)*
profit *(107)*
progressive tax *(118)*
proportional tax *(118)*
public good *(117)*
regressive tax *(118)*
sole proprietorship *(110)*
stock *(110)*

QUESTIONS FOR THOUGHT AND REVIEW

The number after each question represents the estimated degree of critical thinking required. (1 = almost none; 10 = deep thought.)

1. Why does an economy's strength ultimately reside in its people? *(7)*
2. A market system is often said to be based on consumer sovereignty—the consumer determines what's to be produced. Yet business decides what's to be produced. Can these two views be reconciled? How? If not, why? *(5)*
3. The United States is sometimes classified as a postindustrial society. What's meant by this? And, if it's an accurate classification, is it good or bad to be a postindustrial society? *(7)*
4. Why is entrepreneurship a central part of any business? *(3)*
5. You're starting a software company in which you plan to sell software to your fellow students. What form of business organization would you choose? Why? *(5)*
6. What are the two largest categories of federal government expenditures? *(2)*
7. You've set up the rules for a game and started the game, but now realize that the rules are unfair. Should you change the rules? *(6)*
8. Say the government establishes rights to pollute so that without a pollution permit you aren't allowed to emit pollutants into the air, water, or soil. Firms are allowed to buy and sell these rights. In what way will this correct for an externality? *(9)*
9. What are two general roles of government and seven specific roles? *(3)*
10. According to polls, most U.S. economists classify themselves as liberal, but they generally favor less government involvement in the economy than does the general public. Why? *(6)*

PROBLEMS AND EXERCISES

1. Go to a store in your community.
   a. Ask what limitations the owners faced in starting their business.
   b. Were these limitations necessary?
   c. Should there have been more or fewer limitations?
   d. Under what heading of reasons for government intervention would you put each of the limitations?
   e. Ask what kinds of taxes the business pays and what benefits it believes it gets for those taxes.
   f. Is it satisfied with the existing situation? Why? What would it change?
2. You've been appointed to a county counterterrorist squad. Your assignment is to work up a set of plans to stop a group of 10 terrorists the government believes are going to disrupt the economy as much as possible with explosives.
   a. List their five most likely targets in your county, city, or town.
   b. What counterterrorist action would you take?
   c. How would you advise the economy to adjust to a successful attack on each of the targets?
3. The technology is now developing so that road use can be priced by computer. A computer in the surface of the road picks up a signal from your car and automatically charges you for the use of the road.
   a. How could this technological change contribute to ending bottlenecks and rush hour congestion?
   b. What are some of the problems that might develop with such a system?
   c. How would your transportation habits likely change if you had to pay to use roads?

4. Tom Rollins heads a new venture called Teaching Co. He has taped lectures at the top universities, packaged the lectures on audio- and videocassettes, and sells them for $90 and $150 per eight-hour series.
   a. Discuss whether such an idea could be expanded to include college courses that one could take at home.
   b. What are the technical, social, and economic issues involved?
   c. If it is technically possible and cost-effective, will the new venture be a success?

5. In 1938 Congress created a Board of Cosmetology in Washington, D.C., to license beauticians. In 1992 this law was used by the Board to close down a hair-braiding salon specializing in cornrows and braids operated by Mr. Uqdah, even though little is taught in cosmetology schools about braiding and cornrows.
   a. What possible reason can you give for why this Board exists?
   b. What options might you propose to change the system?
   c. What will be the political difficulties of implementing those options?

ANSWERS TO MARGIN QUESTIONS

1. Market economies are generally broken up into business, households, and government. *(106)*

2. False. In the United States individuals are free to start any type of business they want, provided it doesn't violate the law. The invisible hand sees to it that only those businesses that customers want earn a profit. The others make losses and eventually go out of business, so in that sense only businesses that customers want stay in business. *(107)*

3. As can be seen in Exhibit 2, the "finance, insurance, and real estate" sector is more important when measured by sales. *(109)*

4. As can be seen in Exhibit 3, most businesses in the United States are sole proprietorships, not corporations. Corporations, however, generate the most revenue. *(109)*

5. While profits are important to business, because of internal monitoring problems it is not clear that managers maximize profit. They may waste profit potential in high-priced benefits for themselves and in inefficiency

generally. The market, however, provides a limit on inefficiency, and firms that exceed that limit and make losses go out of business. *(112)*

6. As can be seen in Exhibit 5, the median income of a black family in 1995 was approximately $22,500. *(112)*

7. The largest percentage of federal expenditure is for income security. *(114)*

8. False. While externalities provide a role for government in many activities, there are other potential roles such as setting up the rules of economic interaction and providing merit goods. *(117)*

9. It depends. Most people would say that a progressive tax is fairer because they implicitly equate fairness with a tax rate that is higher when the income is higher. That, however, is a value judgment upon which opinions can differ. *(118)*

10. False. While government intervention may eliminate the problem, it may also make the situation worse. There's government failure as well as market failures. *(119)*

APPENDIX A

A Deeper Look at Business

In the chapter, I briefly discussed the role of business in the economy. In this appendix, I expand that discussion to include more institutional data.

To begin, recall my comments about the importance of entrepreneurship. Let me give you a sense of what entrepreneurship means by considering what it is like to start a small business.

Trials and Tribulations of Starting a Business

In 1986, Susan and Ralph decided that it would be fun to open a kitchen shop in a prosperous Vermont town. They

planned to sell kitchen utensils and light food and drink, including coffee, muffins, cheese, and wine.

They found a building, bought it, and, after getting a building permit, began remodeling. Because it was to be the home of a business, the building had to meet strict fire, electrical, and plumbing codes. Because Susan and Ralph planned to sell wine, they had to apply for a liquor license.

Their plans initially called for an upstairs store area, but state inspectors told Susan and Ralph that, in a building and zone like theirs, an upstairs store was against the law. So much for upstairs.

They had to establish contacts with suppliers, get

The Vermont Country Kitchen, a small business like many found across the United States. It went out of business in 1997.

insurance, and obtain permits from the town to comply with zoning, health, and sanitation codes and regulations surrounding the sale of prepared food.

Then, of course, there are taxes. Any business with employees must withhold taxes from their wages and send those taxes periodically to the various taxing authorities. This includes social security taxes, federal income taxes, and state income taxes. There are also unemployment compensation taxes, property taxes, and sales taxes that the business, not the employees, must pay.

All this costs a lot of money. Susan and Ralph had to open a business checking account with their bank. (They couldn't run all that expense through their personal checking account because sound accounting practice requires people to keep their business checks separate from their personal checks.) They had to have some money to put in the business account. They used some of their savings, but they needed more funds. That meant they had to apply for a loan from the bank. The bank required them to present a formal business plan.

It took two years and well over $200,000 to start the business. And this was a small business. Somebody without training and background in handling forms, taxes, and bureaucratic regulations usually doesn't do well in business. To such a person, entry into business isn't free; it isn't even possible. Still, many people enter business, and many succeed. Eight years after start-up, 54 percent of new businesses are still in business; 18 percent have failed; and 28 percent will have terminated operations voluntarily.

Levels of Business

Businesses in the United States are organized on a variety of **stages of production**—*the various levels, such as man-*ufacturing, wholesaling, or retailing, that U.S. businesses adopt.* For most products, the manufacturer doesn't sell the product to you. Often products are sold five or six times before they reach the consumer. Each of these levels is called a stage of production. Thus, most firms *provide a service*—getting you the good when you want it—rather than producing the good. Firms are continually deciding whether to combine these stages of production under one firm, or whether to divide the stages up and allow many firms. Recently, for example, retailing firms such as Wal-Mart have been vertically integrating and combining various stages into their firms. Factory outlets are examples of manufacturing firms undertaking retailing functions.

The Relative Importance of Manufacturing   The percentage of manufacturing output relative to total output has remained constant over the last 50 or so years; in 1950, it was about 22 percent, and in the late 1990s, it was still about 21 percent. But in terms of jobs, manufacturing has declined significantly, falling from about 34 percent in 1950 to about 19 percent in the late 1990s. The reason is twofold: first, manufacturing has become more productive, so we get more output per worker; and second, we now import many more components of the products we produce. In the 1990s, parts of manufactured goods are produced throughout the world, and in the United States service jobs such as retailing have replaced manufacturing jobs.

The growing importance of the service sector to the economy has led some observers to say that we're in a postindustrial society. In their view, the U.S. economy today is primarily a service economy, not a production economy. So classifying the economy may or may not be helpful, but you should note how important the provision of services and the distribution of goods are to our economy.

From Manufacturer to You   To give you a sense of the path of a good from manufacturer to ultimate buyer, let's consider a hypothetical example of a window. Clearview Window Corporation bought the glass, wood, and machines needed to make the window from other companies, perhaps spending a total of $20 per window. Those purchases all fell within what is classified as wholesale trade. Clearview Window then assembled the components (cost of assembly: $60), making Clearview's total cost of the window $80.

I needed a window for my house, so I went down to Buildright, a local building supply store, which sells both wholesale to general contractors and retail to plain people who walk in off the street. Wholesale customers get a 20 percent discount from the retail price, which is deducted at the end of the month from the total bill they've run up. These wholesale customers charge their own customers the full retail price. I'm a plain person, so when I ordered

EXHIBIT A1   The Largest Businesses

Ten Largest U.S. Corporations*	Sales	Assets
	(in millions)	
General Motors	$168,829	$217,123
Ford Motor	137,137	243,283
Exxon	110,009	91,296
Wal-Mart Stores	93,627	37,871
American Telephone and Telegraph	79,609	88,884
International Business Machines	71,940	80,290
General Electric	70,028	228,035
Mobil	66,724	42,138
Chrysler	53,195	53,756
Phillip Morris	53,139	53,811
*Ranking by sales.		

Ten Largest Retailing Companies	Sales	Assets
Wal-Mart Stores	$93,627	$37,841
Sears Roebuck	35,181	36,020
Kmart	34,654	12,925
Dayton Hudson	23,516	15,550
JC Penney	21,419	16,760
Federated Department Stores	15,049	7,500
May Department Stores	12,187	10,743
Dillard Department Stores	6,097	5,567
Nordstrom	4,114	2,750
Fred Meyer	3,429	1,500

Source: *Fortune* Magazine, April 29, 1996.

my window, Buildright told me the cost would be $200. However, it didn't have the right size in stock.

Buildright stacked my order with orders from other customers and called up its Clearview distributor (who has a franchise from Clearview Window in the territory where I live) to place one big order for a number of windows, including mine. The Clearview distributor charged Buildright $140 for my window. The Clearview distributor keeps a pile of windows in stock which he replenishes from a shipment of newly made windows that come in once a month from the Clearview plant. For my window, he pays about $100 plus freight.

So it costs Clearview $80 to make my window; Clearview sells it to the distributor for $100 plus freight. The distributor needs to cover his costs for storage, handling, inventory, and billing, and of course he has to make a profit, so he sells the window to Buildright for $140. The owner of Buildright has to cover expenses and make a profit, so he sells me the window for $200 ($160—a 20 percent discount—if he thought I was a wholesale customer).

Producing the good is only a small component of the cost. Distribution—getting the good where it is wanted when it is wanted—makes up 60 percent of the total cost of the window in this example. That large percentage is not unusual. The same story holds true for most goods you buy.

Given the importance of distribution, firms are always looking for new ways to make the distribution process more efficient. Recent approaches include *just-in-time* inventory systems in which computers track a firm's needs; the needed inputs are shipped to the firm just in time, and its outputs are similarly shipped to customers just in time. Another new practice is for retail firms to keep instantaneous tabs on what is selling. That is why, when you buy something, the clerk has to type a whole load of numbers into the computerized cash register (or have the scanner read the bar code with a whole

load of numbers). This practice lets the store know what's selling and what isn't so it knows what to order. This makes the distribution process more efficient, and thereby reduces the firm's costs, although it sometimes makes checkouts a pain.

Sizes of Business

Another way to classify businesses is by size. Contrary to popular belief, many sectors of United States business contain small (fewer than 500 employees), not large, firms. This is especially true in retail trade and construction industries. The notable exception is manufacturing, which has a group of large producers such as auto manufacturers.

Exhibit A1 looks at the largest businesses in various types of activities. Notice the enormous size of some of the businesses, especially in the industrial category. General Motors has sales of well over $150 billion; Wal-Mart has sales of almost $100 billion. GE has assets (the physical and financial property that it controls) of over $200 billion. Compare these figures to the total output of a country like Nepal ($3.5 billion) and you have a sense of the size of some U.S. businesses.

The fact that a business is in the top 10 one year doesn't necessarily mean it will be in the top 10 the next year. Take IBM ("Big Blue")—until the 1990s, it was close to the top of the top 10 of all categories. Then, like many large companies, IBM went through major restructuring (downsizing) due to its inability to satisfy its customers, and it decreased in relative importance.

A sector's relative size does not necessarily capture its importance to the economy. Take agriculture, for example. It's small in terms of both payroll and revenue, but if it stopped doing its job of providing our food, its importance would quickly become apparent. Similarly, the financial sector is relatively small, but modern industry

BALANCE SHEET AND INCOME STATEMENT

Accounting for revenues and expenditures is an important part of business. Elaborate methods of keeping track of those revenues and expenses have developed over the years. A firm's balance sheet (a statement of the firm's net worth at a point in time) is shown in (a) below.

COMPANY NAME
Balance Sheet
December 31, 1996

Assets*		Liabilities and stockholders' equity*	
Current assets........	$13,859	Current liabilities......	$12,675
Property, plant, and		Long-term liabilities....	5,843
equipment..........	20,362	Stockholders' equity....	15,703
		Total liabilities and stockholders'	
Total assets.........	$34,221	equity.............	$34,221

*Dollars in millions.

(a) Balance sheet

COMPANY NAME
Income Statement*
For the Year Ended December 31, 1996

Sales	$8,710
Cost of goods sold	5,980
Gross profit	2,730
Operating expenses	1,509
Fixed interest payment	165
Income before federal income taxes	1,056
Federal income taxes	509
Net income	$ 547

* Dollars in millions.

(b) Income statement

As you can see, the balance sheet is divided into assets on the left side and liabilities and stockholders' equity (also called *net worth*) on the right side. An *asset* is anything of value. An asset need not be a physical item. It might be a right to do something or use something. For example, landing rights are important assets of airline companies. A *liability* is an obligation. When a firm borrows money, it takes on a liability because it has an obligation to pay the money back to the lender. The totals of the two sides must be equal, since *stockholders' equity (net worth)* is defined as the difference between assets and liabilities. That is:

$$\text{Assets} = \text{Liabilities} + \text{Stockholders' equity}$$
$$\text{or}$$
$$\text{Assets} = \text{Liabilities} + (\text{Assets} - \text{Liabilities})$$
$$\text{Assets} = \text{Assets}.$$

The two sides of the equation are equal by definition. Both assets and liabilities are divided into various subcategories on a balance sheet, but at this stage, all you need to remember is the sheet's general structure.

A firm's income statement is shown in (b). Whereas a balance sheet measures a stock concept (a firm's position at a point in time), an income statement measures a flow concept (the amount of income and expenses passing through a company during a particular period of time). A firm's sales, or total revenue, is given at the top. Then the cost of goods sold is subtracted from total revenue. The resulting number is called *gross profit*, although many income statements don't list gross profits. Next, operating costs and fixed interest payments are subtracted, giving earnings before taxes. Finally, income taxes are subtracted, giving the firm's net income.

The annual report of any company generally is glossy and upbeat about the future.

couldn't function without a highly developed financial sector. Just as a missing bolt can bring a car to a sudden halt, so too can problems in one sector of the economy bring a sudden halt to a much larger part of the economy.

Goals of Business

Another way to classify businesses is by their goals. They can be either for-profit businesses or nonprofit businesses.

For-profit businesses keep their earnings after they pay expenses (if there are any to keep); **nonprofit businesses** are *businesses that try only to make enough money to cover their expenses with their revenues*. If a nonprofit business winds up with a profit, that money goes into "reserves" where it's saved to use in case of later losses.

The goal of a nonprofit business is to serve the community or some segment of the community. Nonprofit businesses include all government-run businesses, some hospitals, some pension funds, foundations, many fund-raising organizations such as the American Cancer Society, most universities and colleges, and many museums. Working for a nonprofit organization doesn't mean working for free. Salaries are an expense of a business, and are paid by both for-profit and nonprofit firms. In fact, salaries paid to individuals managing nonprofit organizations can be higher than they are in for-profit organizations, and perks of the job can be substantial.[1] But perks are classified as "expenses" and aren't included in "profits."

Why discuss the goals of business? Because the goals of business are central to economic theory and economists' insight into how economies function. In a pure capitalist country, all businesses are for-profit businesses. In a pure socialist country, all businesses are nonprofit. As I discussed in Chapter 2, the United States is far from a pure capitalist country, and nonprofit businesses play significant roles in the U.S. economy.

---

[1]*Perks* is short for *perquisites*. An example of a "substantial" perk might be the business supplying you with a limousine and driver in New York City or Washington, D.C., an unlimited expense account, trips to Europe and the Far East, and a condo in Honolulu.

KEY TERMS

nonprofit businesses   *(125)*   stages of production   *(123)*

QUESTIONS FOR THOUGHT AND REVIEW

1. Jill has been advised by Jack to start her own business since she is a superb mechanic and can fix a car's engine easily. Unfortunately, she hates forms and bureaucracy. What would you advise?
2. A nonprofit company will generally charge lower prices than a for-profit company in the same business because the nonprofit company doesn't factor a profit into its prices. True or false? Why?
3. The social security system is inconsistent with pure capitalism, but is almost an untouchable right of Americans. How can this be?
4. How do goals of profit and non-profit firms differ?

APPENDIX B

Households, Culture, and Ideology

People Power

An important way households influence government and business is in their cultural and ideological beliefs. Those beliefs determine what is allowable and what isn't. When those beliefs differ from the existing situation, "people power" has the potential to change the existing institutions significantly. For example, in Eastern Europe by the late 1980s, people's beliefs had become so inconsistent with the existing institutions that people demanded and brought about major economic and political reforms even though there was no formal mechanism, such as free elections, for them to exert their power. People power goes beyond the power people exert in elections. People in an economy have a cultural sensibility, or outlook, which limits actions of both government and business.

Households can exert people power to keep government and business in line. Do people accept the existing situation, or do they feel business or government is wrong? To keep people power on their side, U.S. businesses spend a lot of money on public service and advertisements stating that they, the businesses, are good citizens.

Because of the importance of these cultural and social limitations to business (the invisible handshake), you need some sense of which way the invisible handshake will push. While summarizing the sensibility of a country's people is impossible, it is necessary to make the attempt because it is through those sensibilities—through informal, invisible channels—that households exert much of their power on the economy. Thus, in the next section, I will present my view of the sensibility of the American people.

The Social, Cultural, and Ideological Sensibilities of the American People

As I've pointed out, the actual U.S. economy is best described as welfare capitalism or a mixed economy due to a number of government programs designed to blunt the sharp edge of the market's forces. However, the American **ideology** (*set of values held so deeply that they are not questioned by the majority of the population*) is, in word if not in deed, "Let the market do it." Like apple pie and motherhood, competition and freedom to undertake economic activities are seen as sacred. Small enterprises and entrepreneurships are especially prized, and many people aspire to starting their own business.

Apple pie and motherhood have changed over the years, and so has competition. In the Great Depression of the 1930s, the U.S. population's unbridled faith in the market was tested. Under President Franklin D. Roosevelt's New Deal in the 1930s, numerous government programs were developed to ease the market's harshness. Laws were passed establishing minimum prices at which goods could be sold. Labor was given the right to organize to achieve its ends; a new farm program limited price fluctuations of agricultural goods; a welfare system, including social security programs and unemployment insurance, was established. These laws and programs are generally viewed as good, although that view started to be questioned in the mid-1990s. For example, the welfare system was modified to include a work component. Some people even started advocating privatizing the social security system.

With the advent of World War II (1941–45), defense spending zoomed and government spending as a percentage of total U.S. spending increased from less than 10 percent of total U.S. income in the early 1930s to more than 50 percent of total U.S. income in 1944. After the war, that percentage declined, but the march of government programs to regulate the market continued. In the decade following the war, the government sector's role increased further and the economy grew rapidly. In 1946, the government took responsibility for maintaining high employment. In the 1960s and 1970s, the *safety net* (a set of programs that guaranteed individuals a minimum standard of living) was expanded.

During the postwar period there developed what's called a **military-industrial complex** (*a combination of defense industry firms and the U.S. armed forces, which have vested interests in keeping defense spending flowing, regardless of whether that spending is good for society*). As outside threats to the United States decreased, the military-industrial complex has been squeezed, and defense spending's percentage of the federal budget has been falling in the 1990s. In the mid- and late 1990s, defense spending has fluctuated around $270 billion (approximately 17 percent of the federal government budget).

The military-industrial complex is the best known of the vested interests trying to protect themselves, but it's not unique. Other groups' vested interests might also be described as complexes. For example, we could say there's a social-educational complex that protects education interests, while a health industry-welfare complex protects medical benefits. These complexes compete for government expenditures.

These developments may seem to go against the cultural and ideological support the American public gives the market. Support for the market and tolerance of vested interests seem contradictory, but people's ideological views need not be consistent, and they often aren't. A large role for government in the market has been accepted by most people, although in the late 1990s there has been a backlash reaction against government and government programs. Still, programs that restrict the market (for example, the social security system) are considered as fundamentally American as the market.

Another important aspect of a people's sensibility is their view of morality. Compared to other countries, the United States has a relatively strict standard of economic morals—activities such as direct bribery and payoffs are illegal. (In some countries, these activities aren't illegal. In numerous others, they're illegal but openly tolerated.) The U.S. government bureaucracy, while considered by many to be inefficient, is generally thought to be honest and not corrupt; moreover, by international standards it's actually efficient. Around the fringes of standard morality there's still room for influence peddling, discreet payoffs, and trading favors, but by international standards of corruption they're small potatoes.

There's much more to be said about the cultural sensibilities of the American people, but I'll stop here. Those of you unfamiliar with U.S. cultural and social norms can best find out about them by following the newspapers and by having discussions with friends. My goal here isn't to cover the American people's social and cultural sensibilities completely—that would take a whole book by itself—but simply to remind you how important they are: How an economy functions, what types of policies can be instituted, and what people's perceptions of the economic problems are, are all shaped by its people's social, cultural, and ideological sensibilities. The invisible handshake is an important determinant of economic events.

KEY TERMS

ideology   *(127)*   military-industrial complex   *(127)*

QUESTIONS FOR THOUGHT AND REVIEW

1. Do you agree with the author's summary of American ideology? If you don't, how would you modify the discussion?
2. As the military-industrial complex has decreased in importance, do you think any other "complexes" have grown in importance? Which?
3. How can Americans support the government-run social security system if they favor markets?

Six

An Introduction
to the World Economy

*As for foreign exchange, it is almost as romantic as young love, and
quite as resistant to formulae.*

~ H. L. Mencken

After reading this chapter, you should be able to:

1 Explain what is meant by *the industrial countries of the world* and *the developing countries of the world*.

2 State where in the world various resources are found and where goods are produced.

3 State two ways international trade differs from domestic trade.

4 Make sense of an exchange rate table in the newspaper.

5 Explain two important causes of a trade deficit.

6 List five important international economic institutions.

There was a time when you could proceed from a discussion of the U.S. economy to a discussion of macroeconomics and microeconomics, the two divisions of economics. No longer. International issues must now also be taken into account in just about every economic decision the United States or a firm in the United States faces. The U.S. economy is now integrated with the world economy, and we cannot reasonably discuss U.S. economic issues without discussing the role that international considerations play in these issues.

Consider the clothes on your back. Most likely they were made abroad. Similarly with the cars you drive. It's likely that half of you drive a car that was made abroad. Of course, it's often difficult to tell. Just because a car has a Japanese or German name doesn't mean that it was produced abroad. Some Japanese and German companies now have manufacturing plants in the United States, and some U.S. firms have manufacturing plants abroad. When goods are produced by **global corporations** (*corporations with substantial operations on both the production and sales sides in more than one country*), corporate names don't always tell much about where a good is

International issues must now be taken into account in just about any economic decision a country or a firm faces.

Ask your students to name some global corporations that they are familiar with. What special problems might a global or multinational firm encounter?

Global corporation *Corporation with substantial operations on both the production and sales sides in more than one country.*

129

Ten largest banks in the world:
1. *Deutsche*
2. *Sanwana*
3. *Sumitomo*
4. *Dai-Ichi Kangyo*
5. *Fuji*
6. *Sakura*
7. *Mitsubishi*
8. *Norinchukin*
9. *Credit Agricole Matuel*
10. *Industry Bank of Japan*
Source: American Banker,
August 5, 1996.

produced. As global corporations' importance has grown, most manufacturing decisions are made in reference to the international market, not the domestic U.S. market.

The economic focus has shifted to the world economy in finance as well as manufacturing. In 1970, the world's 10 largest banks were all headquartered in the United States. Today not even one is in the United States.

The international connection means international economic problems and the policies of other countries—European trade policy, developing countries' debt problems, questions about the United States's competitiveness, transfer of U.S. technology to China, Japanese microeconomic policy, Organization of Petroleum Exporting Countries (OPEC) pricing policies—all have moved to the center of the economic stage. This chapter introduces you to such issues.

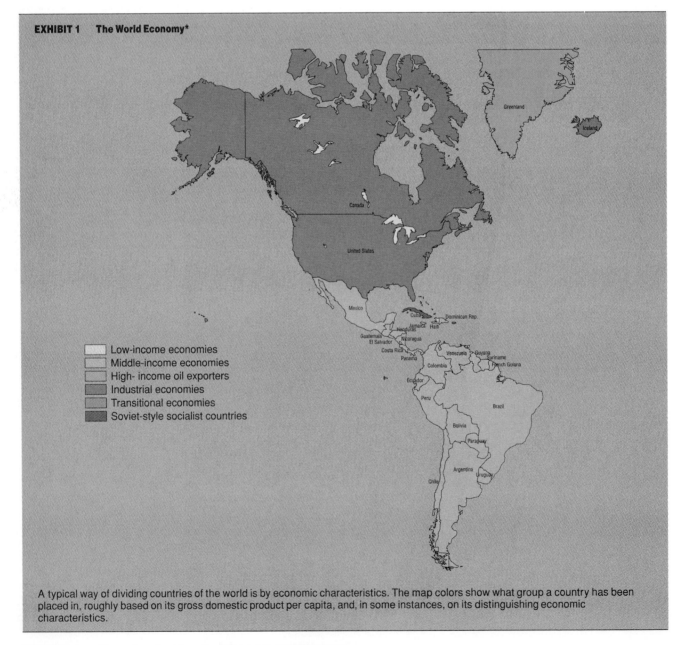

EXHIBIT 1   The World Economy*

Low-income economies
Middle-income economies
High-income oil exporters
Industrial economies
Transitional economies
Soviet-style socialist countries

A typical way of dividing countries of the world is by economic characteristics. The map colors show what group a country has been placed in, roughly based on its gross domestic product per capita, and, in some instances, on its distinguishing economic characteristics.

*Groupings of countries are based on International Monetary Fund (IMF) groupings.

Exhibit 1's map of the world is divided into categories based on per capita output (output per person) and other relevant economic characteristics. *Industrial economies* (such as the United States, Germany, and Britain) have a large industrial production base. A second group of countries, such as Kuwait and Saudi Arabia, have high incomes, but don't have the industrial base. Since their high income is primarily based on oil exports, those countries are known as *high-income oil exporters*. The next two classifications, *middle-income economies* and *low-income economies* (or as they are sometimes called, *developing countries*), make up the majority of countries in the world. The *transitional economies* consist of the formerly socialist economies. These economies are in a period of flux and will probably be much in the news in the late 1990s. It is unclear what form of economic organization these transitional economies

INTERNATIONAL ECONOMIC STATISTICS: AN OVERVIEW

1 The industrial countries of the world have a large industrial base and a per capita income of about $20,000 a year; the developing countries of the world include low- and medium-income economies that have a per capita income of between $300 and $2,000 a year.

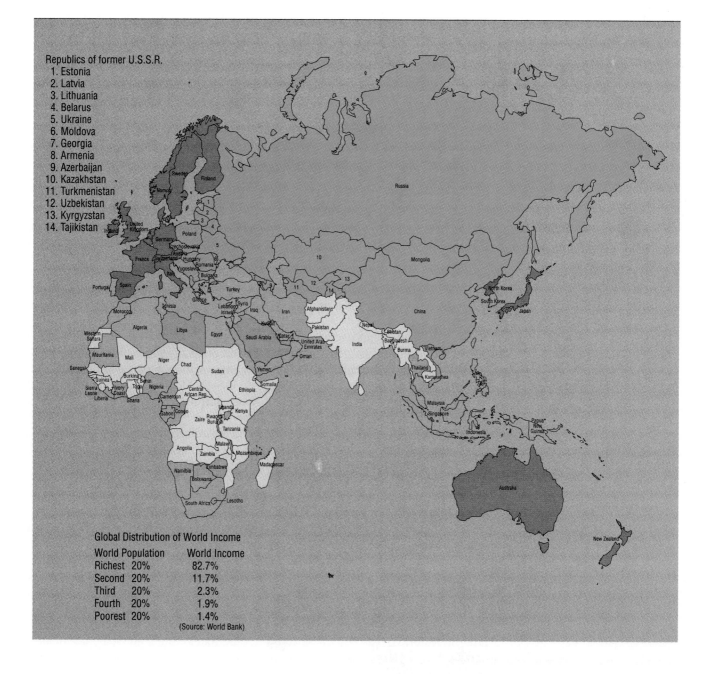

Republics of former U.S.S.R.
1. Estonia
2. Latvia
3. Lithuania
4. Belarus
5. Ukraine
6. Moldova
7. Georgia
8. Armenia
9. Azerbaijan
10. Kazakhstan
11. Turkmenistan
12. Uzbekistan
13. Kyrgyzstan
14. Tajikistan

Global Distribution of World Income

World Population		World Income
Richest	20%	82.7%
Second	20%	11.7%
Third	20%	2.3%
Fourth	20%	1.9%
Poorest	20%	1.4%

(Source: World Bank)

will take. The final category is *Soviet-style socialist economies;* in the mid-1990s, only North Korea and Cuba still fit in this category. (Note, however, that some market economies, such as Sweden, have structures which could be considered socialist.)

Alternative Methods of Classification

I like to give students the opportunity to study a country of their choice and present a short report. The *Instructor's Manual* has such an exercise that lists questions for the students to answer about their country.

This isn't the only method of classification. An alternative method is by region: Latin American, African, Middle Eastern, Asian, Western European, North American, and Eastern European countries. Since geographically grouped countries often share a cultural heritage, they also often face similar problems.

None of these classifications is airtight. Each country is different from every other, so no grouping works perfectly. Exhibit 1's classification system based largely on output per person is the most commonly used, and should give you a sense of what's meant by such classifications. The next time you hear "the industrial nations of the world" or "the developing countries of the world," you should be able to close your eyes and picture the relevant group of economies on a map or, at least, have a general idea of which countries are meant.

Economic Geography

Q–1: On the map in Exhibit 1, Russia looks much larger than Africa. In reality, it isn't. Why does it look larger?

Most classifications are based on a country's total output or production. Production statistics, however, don't necessarily capture a nation's importance or the strategic role it plays in the world economy. Consider Saudi Arabia. Its total output isn't particularly large, but since it's a major supplier of oil to the world, its strategic importance goes far beyond the relative size of its economy. Without its oil, many of the industrial countries of the world would come to a grinding halt. Similarly, Panama's production is minuscule, but its location on a narrow isthmus between the Atlantic and Pacific Oceans and the fact that the Panama Canal runs through its territory make Panama vital to the world economy.

These examples demonstrate why we need, besides a knowledge of countries' productive capacities, a knowledge of economic geography: Where do the world's natural resources lie? Which countries control them? What are the major trade routes? How are goods shipped from one place to another?

Exhibit 2 locates some of the world's major energy resources and trade routes. Note the major flow of energy resources from the Middle East: You can see why it is so important to the world economy (oil and the Suez Canal). Other such resource maps would show why many countries treat South Africa with care (gold, many other alloying metals, and diamonds) and why Chile (with about 27 percent of all copper) is important to the world economy.

2 Some major producing areas for some important raw minerals are:
Aluminum—Guinea, Australia
Cobalt—Zaire, Zambia, Russia
Copper—Chile, U.S., Poland
Iron—Russia, Brazil, Australia
Zinc—Canada, Australia, Russia

Differing Economic Problems

For a discussion of global joblessness and differences in institutions and growth among various nations see Chapter 5 in *Case Studies in Economics.*

The economic problems countries face are determined by a variety of factors such as per capita income levels. High-income countries generally face quite different problems than low-income countries. Even two countries within the same group often face different problems. For example, a significant U.S. problem is its trade deficit. As I'll discuss later in the chapter, the United States **imports** (*buys goods produced in foreign countries*) much more than it **exports** (*sells domestic goods to foreign countries*). A significant Japanese problem is its trade surplus; Japan exports much more than it imports.

Q–2: If you were tracing the flow of copper trade in a map like the one in Exhibit 2, where would you find the information?

Although the identical economic insights apply to all countries, institutions differ substantially among countries. For example, many developing countries have few financial institutions, so when people there want to save, there's no way for them to do so. Similarly with transportation systems. If a firm wants to ship a good from Kansas City to Seattle, it can use trucks, trains, or planes. However, if an African firm wants to ship a good from one city to another in Zaire—say from Kinshasa to Lubumbashi—it must import trucks that can travel on unpaved or even nonexistent roads.

The European Union (EU) is a group of European countries.

Some groups of countries have formal **free trade associations**—*groups of countries that have reduced or eliminated trade barriers among themselves.* For example, most of the countries in Europe are organized in a free trade association that is called the *European Union.* Other groups have loose trading relationships because of cultural or historical reasons. These loose trading relationships are sometimes called trading

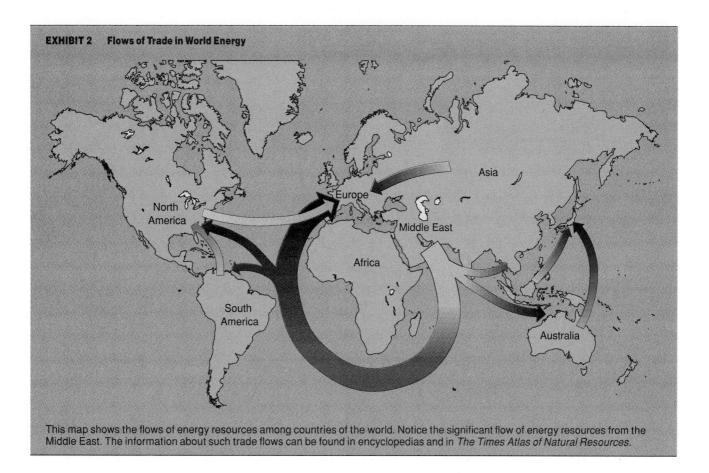

EXHIBIT 2 Flows of Trade in World Energy

This map shows the flows of energy resources among countries of the world. Notice the significant flow of energy resources from the Middle East. The information about such trade flows can be found in encyclopedias and in *The Times Atlas of Natural Resources.*

zones. For example, many European countries maintain close trading ties with many of their former colonies in Africa where they fit into a number of overlapping trading zones. European companies tend to see that central area as their turf. Similarly, the United States, Canada, and Mexico have created the **North American Free Trade Agreement (NAFTA)** (*a U.S.–Canada–Mexico free trade zone that is phasing in reductions in tariffs*). The United States also has close ties in Latin America, making the Western hemisphere another trading zone. Another example of a trading zone is that of Japan and its economic ties with other Far East countries; Japanese companies often see that area as their commercial domain.

These trading zones overlap, sometimes on many levels. For instance, Australia and England, Portugal and Brazil, and the United States and Saudi Arabia are tied together for historical or political reasons, and those ties lead to increased trade between them that seems to deviate from the above trading zones. Similarly, as companies become more and more global, it is harder and harder to associate companies with particular countries. Let me give an example: Do you know who the largest exporters of cars from the United States are? The answer is: Japanese automobile companies!

Thus, there is no hard and fast specification of trading zones, and one can only understand many of the relationships if one has a knowledge of history and politics.

History and politics strongly influence trading patterns, but, ultimately, economic issues underlie trade. Countries trade because they gain from trade and, as we saw in Chapter 2, gains from trade are determined by comparative advantage. A country has a **comparative advantage** in producing a good *if it can produce that good at a lower opportunity cost (forgone production of another good) than another country can.* Put in more simple terminology: Companies produce goods where the cost of producing goods is lowest.

I like to keep a file of *Wall Street Journal* clippings on NAFTA, and distribute a selection of them to my class as discussion starters. This is also a useful way to clear up some common misunderstandings about the likely economic effects of the agreement.

Several additional free trade associations are developing and expanding, in part in response to the EU and NAFTA. Examples are ASEAN, Andean Group, Mercosur, and ANZCERTA.

Comparative Advantage and Trade

For computer exercises comparative advantage, use module "Comparative Advantage and Trade" in *Micro/Macro Interactive.*

ADDED DIMENSION   KEY PROVISIONS OF THE NORTH AMERICAN FREE TRADE AGREEMENT

NAFTA (North American Free Trade Agreement) is a comprehensive plan to eliminate existing barriers to trade between Canada, the United States, and Mexico. NAFTA is open to the inclusion of further participants, but each member country reserves the right to veto the admission of any new applicant.

Some trade restrictions remain in place and some tariffs will only be phased out over a prolonged period of time. Overall, the agreement will remove tariffs on about 10,000 consumer goods within 15 years. Some of NAFTA's key provisions are:

Agriculture   Existing tariffs on agricultural produce will gradually be phased out. NAFTA foresees a complete elimination of all barriers by the end of a 15-year interim period. The domestic farming sectors may still be subject to government intervention as long as trade in agricultural products will not be distorted by that intervention.

Automobiles   Existing tariffs on automobiles will be phased out over a period of 10 years. Restrictions apply to auto parts imported from outside of the free trade zone. After a transition period of eight years, 62.5 percent of the value added to each automobile must have originated within North America if the automobile is to be allowed to avoid tariffs.

Banking   NAFTA allowed U.S. and Canadian banks to purchase up to 8 percent of Mexican banks immediately. All restrictions on acquiring Mexican banks will be removed by the year 2000.

Disputes   Trade disputes are subject to arbitration by special appointed judges.

Energy   Access to Mexican oil resources will continue to remain closed to foreign investors. Canadian and U.S. companies will, however, gain access to contracts offered by Mexican oil and electricity monopolies within 10 years.

Immigration   NAFTA aims to remove restrictions on the free movement of certain special labor groups, chiefly business executives and professionals. Barriers to northward immigration of Mexican wage laborers will remain intact.

Patents and Copyright Protection   Mexico pledges to protect the rights to intellectual property. Under the agreement, foreign patents on pharmaceuticals will be honored for a period of 20 years.

Textiles   NAFTA establishes strict guidelines on the free trade of textiles. It foresees the creation of strict rules of origin and manufacture of garments. Tariffs will be phased out over a 5-year interim period.

A country has a comparative advantage in a good if it can produce that good at a lower opportunity cost than another country can. (Remember it is a lower opportunity cost, not necessarily a lower absolute cost.)

I like to emphasize the principle of comparative advantage early in the principles course. Even at this stage you may wish to work through some numerical samples. Then you can show the gains from trade and the motivation for international trade.

For a classroom experiment that demonstrates comparative advantage, see "A Demonstration of Gains from Trade," in *Experiments in Teaching and in Understanding Economics.*

In thinking about trade and comparative advantage, a common belief is that because wages are lower in developing countries as compared to wage levels in developed countries, the cost of producing all goods is lower in developing countries. While that is certainly true for some manufactured goods (which is why the production of these manufactured goods has moved to developing countries), it is not true for all manufactured goods, and it is certainly not true for many services and other economic activities. Costs of production have many elements, of which labor is only one, and many of these other costs are much lower in developed countries. For instance, the infrastructure and expertise necessary to produce highly technical manufactured goods often does not exist in developing countries, making the cost of producing them prohibitively expensive. Hence the developing country must import these goods and services from developed countries. To do that they must produce goods that the developed country wants.

The point of the above argument is that both developed and developing countries have comparative advantages in different goods. How do I know? Because trade is a two-way street. If one country could produce all goods at a lower cost, all production would flow to that country, and its **exchange rate**—*the rate at which one country's currency exchanges for another country's currency*—would rise. Then the comparative cost structure would change. To understand this, it is necessary to consider specifically the nature of international trade.

*Inter*national trade differs from *intra*national (domestic) trade in two ways. First, international trade involves potential barriers to the flow of inputs and outputs. Before they can be sold in the United States, international goods must be sent through U.S. Customs; that is, when they enter the United States they are inspected by U.S. officials and usually charged fees, known as *customs*. A company in Texas can produce output to sell in any U.S. state without worrying that its right to sell will be limited; a producer outside the U.S. boundary cannot. At any time, a foreign producer's right to sell in the United States can be limited by government-imposed **quotas** (*limitations on how much of a good can be shipped into a country*), **tariffs** (*taxes on imports*), and **nontariff barriers** (*indirect regulatory restrictions on imports and exports*).

The last category, indirect regulatory restrictions on imports and exports, may be unfamiliar to you, so let's consider an example. U.S. building codes require that plywood have fewer than, say, three flaws per sheet. Canadian building codes require that plywood have fewer than, say, five flaws per sheet. The different building codes are a nontariff barrier, making trade in building materials between the United States and Canada difficult.

The second way international trade differs from domestic or intranational trade is countries' use of different currencies. When people in one country sell something to people in another, they must find a way to exchange currencies as well as goods. **Foreign exchange markets** (*markets where one currency can be exchanged for another*) have developed to provide this service.

How many dollars will an American have to pay to get a given amount of the currency of another country? That depends on the supply of and demand for that currency. To find what you'd have to pay, you look in the newspaper for the exchange rate set out in a foreign exchange table. Exhibit 3 shows such a table.

If you want shekels, you'll have to pay about 31¢ apiece. If you want punt, one punt will cost you $1.67. (If you're wondering what shekels and punt are, look at Exhibit 3.)

Unless you collect currencies, the reason you want the currency of another country is that you want to buy something that country produces or an existing asset of that country. Say you want to buy a Hyundai car that costs 10,140,000 South Korean won. Looking at the table you see that the exchange rate is $1 for 845 won. Dividing 845 into 10,140,000 won tells you that you need $12,000 to buy the car. So before you can buy the Hyundai, somebody must go to a foreign exchange market with $12,000 and exchange those dollars for 10.14 million won. Only then can the car be bought in the United States. Most final buyers don't do this; the importer does it for them. But whenever a foreign good is bought, someone must trade currencies.

One reason a U.S. economics course must consider international issues early on is the U.S. **balance of trade** (*the difference between the value of goods and services a country imports and the value of the goods and services it exports*). A country is running a **trade deficit** when its *imports exceed exports;* and a country is running a **trade surplus** when its *exports exceed imports.*

Exhibit 4 shows that since the mid-1970s the United States has been running a trade deficit, which increased substantially in the late 1980s. Although it declined a bit in the mid-1990s, most economists consider the trade deficit a figure to watch. In 1987, when the trade deficit was at its highest, U.S. imports were about 13 percent of its total output; exports were about 10 percent. The 3 percent difference meant the United States imported about $140 billion worth of goods and services more than it exported.

Running a trade deficit isn't necessarily bad. In fact, while you're doing it, it's rather nice. If you were a country, you probably would be running a trade deficit now since, most likely, you're consuming (importing) more than you're producing (exporting).

EXHIBIT 3   A Foreign Exchange Rate Table

From the exchange rate table, you learn how much a dollar is worth in other countries. For example, on this day, Jan. 7, 1997, one dollar would buy 5.322 French francs or 115.75 yen. The table also tells you how many dollars other currencies can buy. For example, one British pound could buy 1.688 dollars.

Wednesday, January 8, 1997

EXCHANGE RATES

The New York foreign exchange selling rates below apply to trading among banks in amounts of $1 million and more, as quoted at 4 p.m. Eastern time by Dow Jones Telerate Inc. and other sources. Retail transactions provide fewer units of foreign currency per dollar.

Country	U.S. $ equiv. Wed.	U.S. $ equiv. Tues.	Currency per U.S. $ Wed.	Currency per U.S. $ Tues.
Argentina (Peso)	1.0012	1.0012	.9988	.9988
Australia (Dollar)	.7805	.7902	1.2812	1.2655
Austria (Schilling)	.09043	.09101	11.058	10.988
Bahrain (Dinar)	2.6525	2.6525	.3770	.3770
Belgium (Franc)	.03080	.03105	32.470	32.205
Brazil (Real)	.9607	.9615	1.0409	1.0401
Britain (Pound)	1.6880	1.6946	.5924	.5901
30-Day Forward	1.6869	1.6935	.5928	.5905
90-Day Forward	1.6843	1.6910	.5937	.5914
180-Day Forward	1.6802	1.6867	.5952	.5929
Canada (Dollar)	.7399	.7370	1.3516	1.3568
30-Day Forward	.7414	.7386	1.3488	1.3539
90-Day Forward	.7442	.7413	1.3437	1.3489
180-Day Forward	.7479	.7450	1.3370	1.3422
Chile (Peso)	.002352	.002356	425.25	424.40
China (Renminbi)	.1201	.1201	8.3272	8.3276
Colombia (Peso)	.0009985	.0009985	1001.50	1001.50
Czech. Rep (Krouna)				
Commercial rate	.03662	.03677	27.307	27.194
Denmark (Krone)	.1663	.1677	6.0118	5.9633
Ecuador (Sucre)				
Floating rate	.0002766	.0002787	3615.00	3587.50
Finland (Markka)	.2121	.2135	4.7150	4.6841
France (Franc)	.1879	.1893	5.3220	5.2838
30-Day Forward	.1882	.1896	5.3126	5.2741
90-Day Forward	.1889	.1903	5.2935	5.2558
180-Day Forward	.1901	.1914	5.2617	5.2243
Germany (Mark)	.6352	.6394	1.5744	1.5639
30-Day Forward	.6364	.6407	1.5714	1.5607
90-Day Forward	.6389	.6432	1.5652	1.5547
180-Day Forward	.6430	.6472	1.5552	1.5450
Greece (Drachma)	.004049	.004068	246.98	245.80
Hong Kong (Dollar)	.1292	.1292	7.7390	7.7390
Hungary (Forint)	.006139	.006164	162.89	162.23
India (Rupee)	.02787	.02786	35.875	35.890
Indonesia (Rupiah)	.0004233	.0004233	2362.15	2362.63
Ireland (Punt)	1.6664	1.6714	.6001	.5983
Israel (Shekel)	.3079	.3085	3.2474	3.2412
Italy (Lira)	.0006483	.0006510	1542.50	1536.00

Country	U.S. $ equiv. Wed.	U.S. $ equiv. Tues.	Currency per U.S. $ Wed.	Currency per U.S. $ Tues.
Japan (Yen)	.008639	.008681	115.75	115.20
30-Day Forward	.008676	.008718	115.26	114.71
90-Day Forward	.008750	.008791	114.28	113.76
180-Day Forward	.008865	.008907	112.80	112.28
Jordan (Dinar)	1.4075	1.4075	.7105	.7105
Kuwait (Dinar)	3.3367	3.3389	.2997	.2995
Lebanon (Pound)	.0006445	.0006445	1551.50	1551.50
Malaysia (Ringgit)	.4018	.4002	2.4885	2.4990
Malta (Lira)	2.7624	2.7701	.3620	.3610
Mexico (Peso)				
Floating rate	.1278	.1277	7.8220	7.8330
Netherland (Guilder)	.5655	.5699	1.7685	1.7547
New Zealand (Dollar)	.7072	.7106	1.4140	1.4073
Norway (Krone)	.1540	.1548	6.4926	6.4599
Pakistan (Rupee)	.02529	.02529	39.540	39.540
Peru (new Sol)	.3814	.3840	2.6218	2.6039
Philippines (Peso)	.03800	.03802	26.318	26.300
Poland (Zloty)	.3460	.3475	2.8900	2.8780
Portugal (Escudo)	.006307	.006369	158.55	157.02
Russia (Ruble) (a)	.0001787	.0001788	5595.00	5594.00
Saudi Arabia (Riyal)	.2666	.2667	3.7503	3.7502
Singapore (Dollar)	.7116	.7124	1.4053	1.4037
Slovak Rep. (Koruna)	.03259	.03259	30.688	30.688
South Africa (Rand)	.2141	.2142	4.6705	4.6690
South Korea (Won)	.001184	.001184	844.75	844.65
Spain (Peseta)	.007546	.007603	132.52	131.53
Sweden (Krona)	.1431	.1435	6.9865	6.9697
Switzerland (Franc)	.7334	.7387	1.3635	1.3537
30-Day Forward	.7357	.7411	1.3593	1.3494
90-Day Forward	.7401	.7454	1.3511	1.3416
180-Day Forward	.7470	.7523	1.3386	1.3293
Taiwan (Dollar)	.03638	.03637	27.489	27.493
Thailand (Baht)	.03902	.03906	25.625	25.605
Turkey (Lira)	.00000911	.00000915	109755.00	109235.00
United Arab (Dirham)	.2723	.2723	3.6720	3.6720
Uruguay (New Peso)				
Financial	.1145	.1145	8.7300	8.7300
Venezuela (Bolivar)	.002098	.002096	476.70	477.12
SDR	1.4315	1.4326	.6986	.6980
ECU	1.2308	1.2404		

Special Drawing Rights (SDR) are based on exchange rates for the U.S., German, British, French, and Japanese currencies. Source: International Monetary Fund.

European Currency Unit (ECU) is based on a basket of community currencies.

a-fixing, Moscow Interbank Currency Exchange.

Video Series, Economics U$A: Exchange Rates, Segments 28.1–28.3

Q–5: Will a debtor nation necessarily be running a trade deficit?

How can you do that? By living off past savings, getting support from your parents or a spouse, or borrowing.

Countries have the same options. They can live off foreign aid, past savings, or loans. For example, the U.S. economy is currently financing its trade deficit by selling off assets—financial assets such as stocks and bonds, or real assets such as real estate and corporations. Since the assets of the United States total many trillions of dollars, it can continue to run trade deficits of similar size for decades to come.

The United States has not always run a trade deficit. Following World War II it ran trade surpluses with other countries, so it was an international lender. Thus, it acquired large amounts of foreign assets. Because of the large trade deficits the United States ran in the 1980s, now the United States is a large debtor nation. The United States has borrowed more from abroad than it has lent abroad.

As the United States has gone from being a large creditor nation to being the world's biggest debtor, international considerations have been forced upon the nation. The cushion of being a creditor—of having a flow of interest income—has been replaced by the trials of being a debtor and having to pay out interest every year without getting anything for it.

A WORLD ECONOMIC GEOGRAPHY QUIZ

Economic geography isn't much covered in most economics courses because it requires learning enormous numbers of facts, and college courses aren't a good place to learn facts. College is designed to teach you how to interpret and relate facts. Unfortunately, if you don't know facts, much of what you learn in college isn't going to do you much good. You'll be relating and interpreting air. The following quiz presents some facts about the world economy. Below I list characteristics of 20 countries or regions in random order. Beneath the characteristics, in alphabetical order, I list 20 countries or regions. Associate the characteristics with the country or region.

If you answer 15 or more correctly, you have a reasonably good sense of economic geography. If you don't, I strongly suggest learning more facts. The study guide has other projects, information, and examples. An encyclopedia has even more, and your library has a wealth of information. You could spend the entire semester acquiring facts. I'm not suggesting that; I am suggesting following the economic news carefully, paying attention to where various commodities are produced, and picturing in your mind a map whenever you hear about an economic event.

_____ 1. Former British colony, now small independent island country famous for producing rum.

_____ 2. Large sandy country contains world's largest known oil reserves.

_____ 3. Very large country with few people produces 25 percent of the world's wool.

_____ 4. Temperate country ideal for producing wheat, soybeans, fruits, vegetables, wine, and meat.

_____ 5. Small tropical country produces abundant coffee and bananas.

_____ 6. Has world's largest population and world's largest hydropower potential.

_____ 7. Second-largest country in Europe; famous for wine and romance.

_____ 8. Former Belgian colony has vast copper mines.

_____ 9. European country; exports luxury clothing, footwear, and automobiles.

_____ 10. Country that has depleted many of its own resources but which has the highest level of GDP of any country in the world.

_____ 11. Long, narrow country of four main islands; most thickly populated country in the world; exports majority of the world's electronics products.

_____ 12. Recently politically reunified country; one important product is steel.

_____ 13. Second-largest country in the world; a good neighbor to the United States; leading paper exporter.

_____ 14. European country for centuries politically repressed; now becoming industrialized; chemicals are one of its leading exports.

_____ 15. 96 percent of its people live on 4 percent of the land; much of the world's finest cotton comes from here.

_____ 16. Politically and racially troubled African nation has world's largest concentration of gold.

_____ 17. Huge, heavily populated country eats most of what it raises but is a major tea exporter.

_____ 18. Country that is a top producer of oil and gold; has recently undergone major political and economic changes.

_____ 19. Has only about 50 people per square mile but lots of trees; timber and fish exporter.

_____ 20. Sliver of a country on Europe's Atlantic coast; by far the world's largest exporter of cork.

A. Argentina
B. Australia
C. Barbados
D. Canada
E. China
F. Costa Rica
G. Egypt
H. France
I. Germany
J. India
K. Italy
L. Japan
M. Portugal
N. Russia
O. Saudi Arabia
P. South Africa
Q. Spain
R. Sweden
S. United States
T. Zaire

Answers: 1-C, 2-O, 3-B, 4-A, 5-F, 6-E, 7-H, 8-T, 9-K, 10-S, 11-L, 12-I, 13-D, 14-Q, 15-G, 16-P, 17-J, 18-N, 19-R, 20-M.

Exchange rates, imports, and exports are all tied together in what are called **balance of payments accounts.** *These accounts record all transactions between the residents of a country and residents of all foreign nations.* In Exhibit 5(a), I present a highly simplified balance of payments account for Brazil in 1995.

Balance of Payments Accounts

EXHIBIT 4   U.S. Trade Balance

The balance of trade is the difference between the value of goods and services a country imports and the value of goods and services it sells abroad, or exports. As you can see from the graph, since the early 1980s the United States has imported many more goods and services than it has exported. Thus, economists say the United States is running a trade deficit. The trade deficit declined somewhat in the early 1990s, but returned to high levels in the late 1990s.   Source: U.S. Dept. of Commerce, http://www.census.gov.

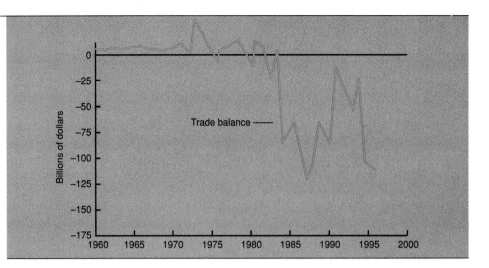

A balance of payments account is comprised of a current account, a capital account, and an official transaction account.

There are a couple things to notice about these balance of payments accounts. First, a balance of payments account is comprised of a current account, a capital account, and an official transactions account. The current account is made up primarily of foreign demand for domestic (in this case Brazil's) goods and services (exports) and domestic demand for other countries' goods and services (imports). In 1995 Brazil imported more than it exported, so its current account was in deficit. The capital account is comprised of foreign demand for domestic assets (inflows) and domestic demand for other countries' assets (outflows). The official transactions account is the amount of domestic currency that the government buys or sells.

The second thing to notice is that the capital and current accounts represent the private demand and supply for the country's domestic currency—in this case Brazilian reals. Since Brazil must purchase foreign goods, services, and assets by using foreign currencies, current account imports and capital account outflows represent the private supply of Brazilian reals. The foreign demand for Brazilian goods, services, and assets represents the private demand for Brazilian reals. Exhibit 5(b) shows the corresponding supply and demand curves for Brazilian reals.

When the balance of payments account is in equilibrium, the quantity of a currency supplied equals the quantity of currency demanded.

With fixed exchange rates, where the government specifies an exchange rate and maintains that rate by buying or selling currencies, these private supplies and demands need not be equal. When the balance of payments is in deficit, the quantity of a currency supplied exceeds the quantity of a currency demanded and the government must purchase the excess supply. When the balance of payments is in surplus, the quantity of a currency demanded exceeds the quantity of a currency supplied and the government must sell currency to eliminate the excess demand.

With flexible exchange rates these private supplies and demands must be equal and the balance on the current and capital accounts must be zero, which is why I stated above that ultimately a country cannot have a lower cost in everything. If it did, the demand for its exports would be enormous and would push up the value of the country's currency. (A country can, however, temporarily have a lower cost in all produced goods if it has large capital inflows.)

Q–6: In a fixed-rate exchange régime, the market is not allowed to operate. True or false? Why?

The official transactions account measures the net amount of its currency that a country buys. In this example of Brazil, the Brazilian government has sold currency, so the actual exchange rate is lower than it would be if the country had a totally flexible exchange rate and the official transactions account were zero. This is shown

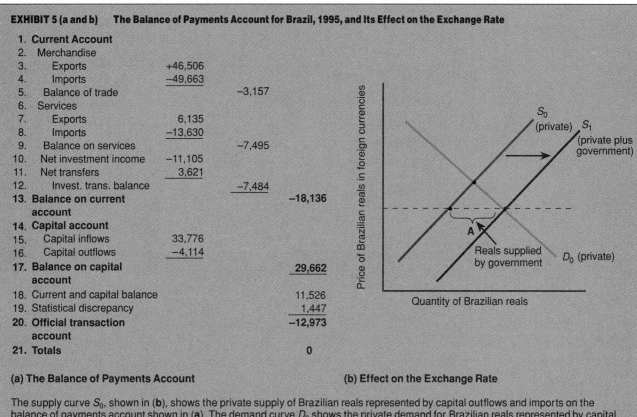

EXHIBIT 5 (a and b)   The Balance of Payments Account for Brazil, 1995, and Its Effect on the Exchange Rate

1. **Current Account**			
2. Merchandise			
3. Exports	+46,506		
4. Imports	−49,663		
5. Balance of trade		−3,157	
6. Services			
7. Exports	6,135		
8. Imports	−13,630		
9. Balance on services		−7,495	
10. Net investment income	−11,105		
11. Net transfers	3,621		
12. Invest. trans. balance		−7,484	
13. **Balance on current account**			−18,136
14. **Capital account**			
15. Capital inflows	33,776		
16. Capital outflows	−4,114		
17. **Balance on capital account**			29,662
18. Current and capital balance			11,526
19. Statistical discrepancy			1,447
20. **Official transaction account**			−12,973
21. **Totals**			0

(a) The Balance of Payments Account

(b) Effect on the Exchange Rate

The supply curve S_0, shown in (**b**), shows the private supply of Brazilian reals represented by capital outflows and imports on the balance of payments account shown in (**a**). The demand curve D_0 shows the private demand for Brazilian reals represented by capital inflows and exports on the balance of payments accounts. If the balance of payments is in surplus, the quantity of Brazilian reals demanded exceeds the quantity supplied and there is upward pressure on the exchange rate value of the real. A balance of payments surplus and corresponding shortage of Brazilian reals is shown by **A**. Because there is a balance of payments surplus in the private flows, the Brazilian government must be selling reals, shifting the supply curve for the real to the right. This holds the price of the real lower than it otherwise would be. This sale shows up on the official transactions account so that the balance of payments, including the official transaction account, is in equilibrium at the government-set exchange rate.

Source: International Financial Statistics (http://www.imf.org)

in Exhibit 5(b) as a shift in the supply of Brazilian reals to the right and a lower exchange rate than there would have been without government intervention.

With the above background on the balance of payments accounts, let us reconsider the U.S. trade deficit shown in Exhibit 4. Since the dollar is primarily market-determined (the official transaction account transactions are small), the U.S. trade deficit could also be seen as a capital account surplus—there was a large foreign demand for U.S. assets relative to the U.S. demand for foreign assets. If that demand for U.S. assets is to be met, the United States must run a trade deficit. So, as is often the case in economics, there is another side of the picture.

Asset demand, in turn, depends on the return to owning those assets. Say you earn 8 percent interest on assets in the United States and a 4 percent return in Japan. Where would you rather invest your money? I hope you said "In the United States, because you earn twice as much there." The importance of interest rates in determining the return on assets means that interest rates play a key role in exchange rate determination.

I'll stop consideration of the balance of payments accounts here; the issues quickly get complicated. We will discuss them fully in a later chapter. The above discussion, however, should give you an initial introduction to exchange rate

The U.S. trade deficit can also be seen as a capital account surplus.

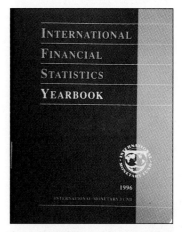

Asset demand plays an important role in the determination of exchange rates.

determination and a sense of why I began this chapter with the quotation, "As for foreign exchange, it is almost as romantic as young love, and quite as resistant to formulae."

In determining the size of the trade deficit, two factors are important:

1. U.S. competitiveness and the value of the dollar.
2. The state of the U.S. economy compared to that of other countries.

Let's look at each factor.

U.S. Competitiveness   Probably the single most important issue in determining whether a country runs a trade deficit or a trade surplus is its **competitiveness** (*the ability to produce goods and services more cheaply than other countries*). Competitiveness depends upon productivity—a country's output per worker and its technological innovativeness (its ability to develop new and different products).

In the 1960s and early 1970s, the United States was highly competitive. Even though U.S. workers were paid substantially more than foreign workers, U.S. goods were cheaper, better, and more desired than foreign goods. In the 1950s, the label MADE IN JAPAN was a sign of low-quality, cheap goods. That has changed since the late 1970s. While the United States lost its competitive edge, Japan gained one. Today MADE IN JAPAN is a sign of quality.

Japan's rise from a defeated country after World War II, with few natural resources, little land, and a devastated economy, into an international economic power that outcompetes the United States in many aspects of economics was an important economic story of the 1980s. One reason for Japan's rise was cultural. Japanese culture emphasizes hard work and savings. Another reason was the relative values of the Japanese yen and U.S. dollar. Throughout much of the 1960s, 1970s, and 1980s, the yen's relative value was low. A major determinant of a country's competitiveness is the value of its currency. A currency that is low in value relative to other currencies encourages the country's exports by lowering their prices and discourages its imports by raising their prices. (In 1965, $1 bought about 300 yen; in the late 1990s, $1 bought as little as 100 yen.) Similarly, the dollar's relatively high value during the 1960s undermined U.S. competitiveness.

In the late 1980s the dollar's value relative to the yen fell substantially, making U.S. goods more competitive. That fall didn't immediately reduce the U.S. trade deficit, and it became apparent that the problems of the United States in international competitiveness have additional causes. But it did eventually help improve U.S. competitiveness. By 1993, the fall of the yen had pushed Japanese car prices up sufficiently so that U.S. cars seemed like bargains, causing a recovery of the U.S. automobile industry in the mid-1990s. However, the fall in the dollar's value had a downside: It meant that U.S. assets were cheaper for foreigners. They could buy not only the products we made, but also the firms that make those products, the buildings within which those products were made, and the land upon which those buildings stood. When the relative value of the dollar is low we inevitably hear complaints that foreigners are "buying up America." These complaints ended in 1996 when the value of the dollar rose.

The State of the U.S. Economy   A second factor in determining the trade balance is the state of the economy. The level of U.S. income affects the trade balance, and the trade balance affects the level of U.S. income. The reason for the first effect is simple. Say the United States is running a trade deficit. When U.S. income rises, the U.S. imports more, so the trade deficit increases.

The second effect—the trade balance's effect on U.S. income—isn't so simple. Say the United States has a trade deficit. When the United States imports more (or exports less), the trade deficit worsens and the rise in imports means U.S. production falls, which means U.S. citizens have less income; they spend less and U.S. income falls even more. So an increase in the trade deficit lowers income. It also works the opposite way: When the United States exports more (imports less), U.S. production rises; as U.S. production rises, U.S. citizens have more income; they spend more and

Determinants of the Trade Deficit

5 Two important causes of a trade deficit are:
1. A country's competitiveness; and
2. The relative state of a country's economy.

Competitiveness   *A country's ability to produce goods and services more cheaply than other countries.*

Q-7:   If the dollar/yen exchange rate changed from $1/¥100 to $1/¥200, what would be the effect on U.S. competitiveness?

In discussions of our trade deficit with Japan, students will often repeat the popular notion that the Japanese don't buy goods that are produced in the United States. When this idea comes up, I like to show a graph of our largest export markets. It comes as a surprise to many students (and some instructors, too) that Japan is one of our largest export markets.

The trade balance is dependent on the state of the economy.

U.S. income rises even more. This effect of the growth of exports on domestic income is what economists mean when they say a country has "export-led growth." A country with export-led growth has a trade surplus that stimulates growth in income.

Large trade deficits often inspire politicians to call for trade restrictions prohibiting imports. Most economists, liberal and conservative alike, generally oppose such restrictions. The reason is that even though trade restrictions directly decrease the trade deficit, they also have negative effects on the economy that work in the opposite direction.

One negative effect is that trade restrictions reduce domestic competition. When a group of U.S. producers can't compete with foreign producers—either in price or in quality—that group often pushes for trade restrictions to prevent what they call "unfair" foreign competition. U.S. producers benefit from the trade restrictions, but consumers are hurt. Prices to consumers rise and the quality of the goods they buy falls.

A second negative effect is that trade restrictions bring retaliation. If one country limits imports, the other country responds; the first country responds to that . . . The result is called a *trade war,* and a trade war hurts everyone.

Such a trade war occurred in the 1930s and significantly contributed to the Great Depression of that period. To prevent trade wars, countries have entered into a variety of international agreements and organizations. The most important is the **World Trade Organization (WTO)**, which is *an organization committed to getting countries to agree not to impose new tariffs or other trade restrictions except under certain limited conditions.* The WTO is the successor to the **General Agreement on Tariffs and Trade (GATT)**, *an agreement among many subscribing countries on certain conditions of international trade,* to which you will still occasionally see references, even though the WTO has taken its place. One of the differences between the WTO and GATT is that the WTO includes some enforcement mechanisms.

True to form, the U.S. trade deficit of the 1980s and 1990s has brought about significant political pressure for import restrictions on foreign goods—especially Japanese goods. In the United States, Patrick Buchanan's support in the 1996 Republican primaries derived partly from his advocacy of trade restrictions. Supporters of trade restrictions against Japan argue that the current arrangement isn't fair, that Japan has many more barriers to U.S. goods than the United States has barriers to Japanese goods. Japan bashing in the United States, and United States bashing in Japan, have become common, and a trade war between the two countries is a definite possibility.

Just as international trade differs from domestic trade, so does international economic policy differ from domestic economic policy. When economists talk about U.S. economic policy, they generally refer to what the U.S. federal government can do to achieve certain goals. In theory, at least, the U.S. federal government has both the power and the legal right of compulsion to make U.S. citizens do what it says. It can tax, it can redistribute income, it can regulate, and it can enforce property rights.

There is no international counterpart to a nation's federal government. Any meeting of a group of countries to discuss trade policies is voluntary. No international body has powers of compulsion. Hence, dealing with international problems must be done through negotiation, consensus, bullying, and concessions.

To discourage bullying and to encourage negotiation and consensus, governments have developed a variety of international institutions to promote negotiations and coordinate economic relations among countries. These include the United Nations (UN), World Trade Organization (WTO), World Bank, World Court, International Monetary Fund (IMF), and regional organizations such as the Organization of Petroleum Exporting Countries (OPEC), European Union (EU), and North American Free Trade Agreement (NAFTA).

These organizations have a variety of goals. For example, the **World Bank** is *a multinational, international financial institution that works with developing countries to secure low-interest loans,* channeling such loans to them to foster economic

Economists' View of Trade Restrictions

Q–8: What are two reasons economists generally oppose trade restrictions?

After presenting the economist's view of trade restrictions, ask for your students' reaction.

World Trade Organization (WTO)
An organization committed to reducing trade barriers.

Video Series, Economics U$A: International trade, Segments 27.1–27.3

INTERNATIONAL ECONOMIC POLICY AND INSTITUTIONS

Governmental International Institutions

6 Five important international economic institutions are:
1. The UN.
2. The WTO.
3. The World Bank.
4. The IMF.
5. The EU.

Since governmental membership in international organizations is voluntary, their power is limited.

Q–9: If the United States chooses not to follow a World Court decision, what are the consequences?

growth. The **IMF** is *a multinational, international financial institution concerned primarily with monetary issues.* It deals with international financial arrangements. When developing countries encountered financial problems in the 1980s and had large international debts that they could not pay, the IMF helped work on repayment plans.

In addition to these formal institutions, there are informal meetings of various countries. These include the **Group of Five** that *meets to promote negotiations and coordinate economic relations among countries.* The Five are Japan, Germany, Britain, France, and the United States. The **Group of Seven** also *meets to promote negotiations and coordinate economic relations among countries.* The Seven are the five countries just named plus Canada and Italy.

Since governmental membership in international organizations is voluntary, their power is limited. When the United States doesn't like a World Court ruling, it simply states that it isn't going to follow the ruling. When the United States is unhappy with what the United Nations is doing, it withholds some of its dues. Other countries do the same from time to time. Other member countries complain, but can do little to force compliance. It doesn't work that way domestically. If you decide you don't like U.S. policy and refuse to pay your taxes, you'll wind up in jail.

What keeps nations somewhat in line when it comes to international rules is a moral tradition: Countries want to (or at least want to look as if they want to) do what's "right." Countries will sometimes follow international rules to keep international opinion favorable to them. But perceived national self-interest often overrides international scruples.

Global Corporations

Q–10: What is a global corporation?

Chapter 5 introduced you to U.S. corporations. More and more of these and other corporations are transcending national boundaries. They have branches on both the production and sales sides throughout the world. As they do, they become global, or multinational, corporations rather than national corporations.

Global corporations offer enormous benefits for countries. They create jobs; they bring new ideas and new technologies to a country, and they provide competition for domestic companies, keeping them on their toes. But global corporations also pose a number of problems for governments. One is their implications for domestic and international policy. A domestic corporation exists within a country and can be dealt with using policy measures within that country. A global corporation exists within many countries and there is no global government to regulate or control it. If it doesn't like the policies in one country—say taxes are too high or regulations too tight—it can shift its operations to other countries.

EXHIBIT 6   Global Corporations

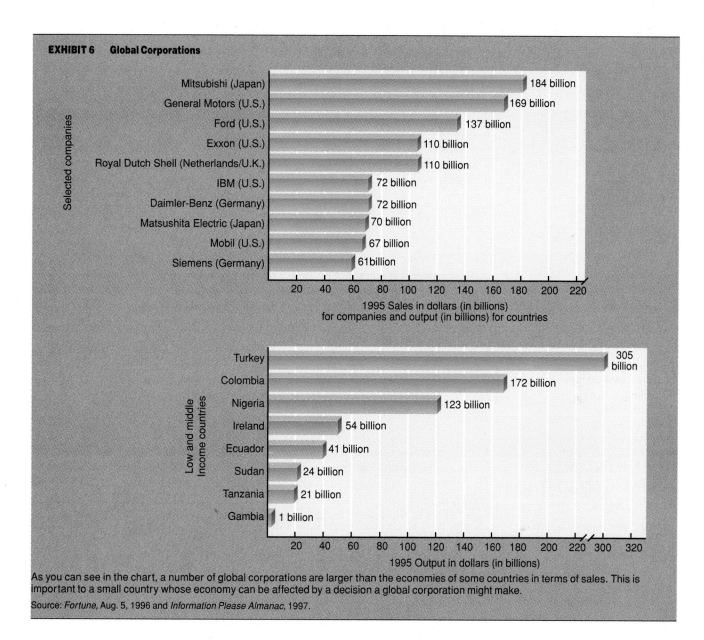

Selected companies (1995 Sales in dollars, in billions):

Company	Sales
Mitsubishi (Japan)	184 billion
General Motors (U.S.)	169 billion
Ford (U.S.)	137 billion
Exxon (U.S.)	110 billion
Royal Dutch Shell (Netherlands/U.K.)	110 billion
IBM (U.S.)	72 billion
Daimler-Benz (Germany)	72 billion
Matsushita Electric (Japan)	70 billion
Mobil (U.S.)	67 billion
Siemens (Germany)	61 billion

1995 Sales in dollars (in billions) for companies and output (in billions) for countries

Low and middle Income countries (1995 Output in dollars, in billions):

Turkey	305 billion
Colombia	172 billion
Nigeria	123 billion
Ireland	54 billion
Ecuador	41 billion
Sudan	24 billion
Tanzania	21 billion
Gambia	1 billion

1995 Output in dollars (in billions)

As you can see in the chart, a number of global corporations are larger than the economies of some countries in terms of sales. This is important to a small country whose economy can be affected by a decision a global corporation might make.

Source: *Fortune*, Aug. 5, 1996 and *Information Please Almanac*, 1997.

Countries often compete for these global corporations by changing their regulations to encourage companies to use them as their home base. For instance, firms might register their oil tankers in Liberia to avoid paying U.S. wages, and put their funds in Bahamian banks to avoid U.S. financial disclosure laws.

At times it seems that global corporations are governments unto themselves, especially in relation to poorer countries. Consider Exhibit 6's lists of some large global corporations and their sales and of some small and middle-size economies and their output. In terms of sales, a number of global corporations are larger than the economies of middle-size countries. This comparison is not quite accurate, since sales do not necessarily reflect power; but when a company's decisions can significantly affect what happens in a country's economy, that company has significant economic power.

When global corporations have such power, it is not surprising that they can sometimes dominate a country. The corporation can use its expertise and experience to direct a small country to do its bidding rather than the other way around.

Another problem global corporations present for governments involves multiple jurisdiction. Global corporations can distance themselves from questionable economic activities by setting up *dummy corporations*. A dummy corporation exists only

At times it seems that global corporations are governments unto themselves.

on paper, and is actually controlled by another corporation. Sometimes when a corporation really wants to separate itself from the consequences of certain actions, it creates dummy dummy and dummy dummy dummy corporations, in which one paper corporation controls another paper corporation, which in turn controls another paper corporation. Each corporation is incorporated in a different nation, which makes it difficult, if not impossible, to trace who is actually doing what and who can be held accountable.

Before you condemn globals, remember: Globals don't have it so easy.

Before you condemn globals, remember: Globals don't have it so easy either. Customs and laws differ among countries. Trying to meet the differing laws and ambiguous limits of acceptable action in various countries is often impossible. For example, in many countries bribery is an acceptable part of doing business. If you want to get permission to sell a good, you must pay the appropriate officials *baksheesh* (as it's called in Egypt) or *la mordita* (as it's called in Mexico). In the United States, such payments are called bribes and are illegal. Given these differing laws, the only way a U.S. company can do business in some foreign countries is to break U.S. laws.

Moreover, global corporations often work to maintain close ties among countries and to reduce international tension. If part of your company is in an Eastern European country and part in the United States, you want the two countries to be friends. So beware of making judgments about whether global corporations are good or bad. They're both simultaneously.

THE IMPORTANCE OF KNOWING ABOUT OTHER COUNTRIES

I've covered a lot of ground in the chapter, and I've only touched on some of the many international issues. For example, I haven't given you a sense of very many countries. (In Appendix A, I briefly discuss the European Union and Japan.) Still, I hope I have conveyed to you the importance of international issues, and given you a foundation upon which to build in the remainder of the book.

CHAPTER SUMMARY

- To understand the U.S. economy, one must understand its role in the world economy.
- Knowledge of the facts about the world economy is necessary to understand the world economy.
- Countries can be classified in many ways. One way is to characterize them as industrial, middle-income, or low-income economies.
- International trade differs from domestic trade because (1) there are potential barriers to trade and (2) countries use different currencies.
- The relative value of a currency can be found in an exchange rate table.

- The U.S. trade deficit is large. It is financed by selling U.S. assets to foreign owners.
- U.S. competitiveness and the state of the U.S. economy compared to other countries are important in determining the trade deficit's size.
- Exchange rates, imports, and exports are all tied together in the balance of payments accounts.
- International policy coordination must be achieved through consensus among nations.
- Global corporations are corporations with significant operations in more than one country.

KEY TERMS

balance of payments accounts   *(137)*
balance of trade   *(135)*
comparative advantage   *(133)*
competitiveness   *(140)*
exchange rate   *(134)*
exports   *(132)*
foreign exchange market   *(135)*
free trade associations   *(132)*
General Agreement on Tariffs and Trade
  (GATT)   *(141)*

global corporations   *(129)*
Group of Five   *(142)*
Group of Seven   *(142)*
IMF   *(142)*
imports   *(132)*
nontariff barriers   *(135)*
North American Free Trade Agreement
  (NAFTA)   *(133)*
quotas   *(135)*
tariffs   *(135)*

trade deficit   *(135)*
trade surplus   *(135)*
World Bank   *(141)*
World Trade Organization (WTO)
  (141)

QUESTIONS FOR THOUGHT AND REVIEW

The number after each question represents the estimated degree of critical thinking required. (1 = almost none; 10 = deep thought.)

1. A good measure of a country's importance to the world economy is its area and population. True or false? Why?   *(5)*
2. How does a trading zone differ from a free trade association?   *(3)*
3. The United States exports large amounts of wheat while Japan exports large amounts of cars. What is a likely underlying economic explanation?   *(5)*
4. If one country has a lower cost of producing all goods what will likely happen?   *(7)*
5. What are the two ways in which international trade differs from domestic trade?   *(3)*
6. Find the exchange rate for Swedish krona in Exhibit 3 and also the krona's most current rate from your newspaper.   *(3)*
7. If the current account is in deficit and a country has a flexible exchange rate, what can you say about its capital account?   *(6)*
8. What is the difference between a fixed and a flexible exchange rate?   *(4)*

9. If one U.S. dollar will buy .67 Swiss francs, how many U.S. dollars will one Swiss franc buy?   *(5)*
10. The U.S. economy is falling apart because the United States is the biggest debtor nation in the world. Discuss.   *(7)*
11. What is likely to happen to the U.S. trade deficit if the U.S. economy grows rapidly? Why?   *(5)*
12. Why do most economists oppose trade restrictions?   *(5)*
13. What is the relationship between GATT and the WTO?   *(3)*
14. How would the author of the text counter Pat Buchanan's argument that "imports, particularly from Japan and from low-wage nations such as China, have undermined American jobs and wages"?   *(9)*
15. Look up a recent foreign exchange rate table from *The Wall Street Journal* (section C).   *(5)*
    a. How many Portuguese escudos will you receive for $100?
    b. Say you want to buy a Volvo directly from Sweden. The foreign car dealer quotes a price of 235,794 Swedish krona. How many dollars will you have to exchange to purchase the Volvo?

PROBLEMS AND EXERCISES

1. This is a library research question.
    a. What are the primary exports of Brazil, Honduras, Italy, Pakistan, and Nigeria?
    b. Which countries produce most of the world's tin, rubber, potatoes, wheat, marble, and refrigerators?
2. This is an entrepreneurial research question. You'd be amazed about the information that's out there if you use a bit of initiative.
    a. Does the largest company in your relevant geographic area (town, city, whatever) have an export division? Why or why not?
    b. If you were an adviser to the company, would you suggest expanding or contracting its export division? Why or why not?
    c. Go to a store and look at 10 products at random. How many were made in the United States? Give a probable explanation why they were produced where they were.
3. From 1990 to 1993, the share of U.S. exports to Western Europe and Japan fell from 41 percent to 35 percent, while the share going to Latin America and Asia rose from 32 percent to 38 percent.
    a. What are likely reasons why this change occurred?
    b. What would you predict would happen to these percentages if the Japanese economy boomed?
    c. Why would President Clinton have urged the Japanese to stimulate their economy during this period?

4. Exchange rates can be found in a variety of sources.

    a. Using Exhibit 3, determine the U.S. dollar equivalent of the:

        (1) Lira

        (2) Zloty

        (3) Rand

        (4) Forint

    b. Determine the most recent dollar equivalent of those same currencies. (Use the Web or a recent newspaper.)

    c. Using the information in *a* or *b*, calculate the number of dollars you could get from one unit of each of the above currencies.

5. Demonstrate graphically the private supply and demand for a currency when:

    a. The government has a deficit in its official transactions account.

    b. The government sets the value of its currency above the level that the private market would set it at.

6. When you include the government in the graph in Problem 5, what do the total supply and demand curves (private plus government) look like?

ANSWERS TO MARGIN QUESTIONS

1. While Russia is very large, in terms of square miles of land the continent of Africa is larger. It does not look so on the map because of the nature of the projections used to make the round earth flat. These projections expand the relative size of countries the closer they are to the North or South Pole, and reduce the relative size of countries close to the equator. *(132)*

2. I would find this information in an encyclopedia under "copper" or in *The Times Atlas of Natural Resources.* (The primary producers of copper are Chile, the United States, Poland, and Russia.) *(132)*

3. A quota is a quantitative limitation on trade. A tariff is a type of tax on imports. *(135)*

4. You will receive 42,525 pesos. *(135)*

5. A debtor nation will not necessarily be running a trade deficit. "Debt" refers to accumulated past deficits. If a country had accumulated large deficits in the past, it could run a surplus now but still be a debtor nation. *(136)*

6. False. The market is allowed to operate, while the government plays an active role in the market, buying and selling currency to hold the exchange rate constant. *(138)*

7. The rise in the value of the dollar would significantly raise the price of U.S. goods to the Japanese and lower the price of Japanese goods to U.S. citizens, thereby lowering U.S. competitiveness. *(140)*

8. Most economists oppose trade restrictions because of their negative effects, such as the reduction of domestic competition and the likelihood that countries upon whom trade restrictions are imposed, in retaliation, will impose trade restrictions of their own, thus beginning a trade war. *(141)*

9. The World Court has no enforcement mechanism. Thus, when a country refuses to follow the Court's decisions, the country cannot be directly punished except through indirect international pressures. *(142)*

10. A global corporation is a corporation with both production and sales facilities in a variety of different countries. *(142)*

Our International Competitors

In the chapter I gave you a brief introduction to the international economic problems the United States faces and to some of the international institutions that exist to coordinate international economic activity. In this appendix I introduce two of our most important rivals, the European Union and Japan, giving you a brief background of their histories and economic institutions. I also briefly discuss a third competitor—the developing world—and explain why, with the relatively new North American Free Trade Agreement (NAFTA), questions of our economic and political relations with Mexico have been much in the news in the 1990s and are likely to continue to be.

The European Union

In 1957, several governments of Europe formed the European Economic Community. This organization has undergone many changes since its founding, changes that have strengthened the economic and political ties among the countries. The Community is now called the **European Union (EU)**, which is *both an economic free trade area and a loose political organization*. In the EU, as in any economic union, members allow free trade among themselves to help their economies by providing a larger marketplace and more competition for their own companies. Over time, the EU has expanded from 6 countries to the 15 shown in the map in Exhibit A1. Some other European countries, primarily those in eastern Europe, are hoping to join in the next few years.

The EU's initial goals were:

1. To remove barriers to trade among member nations;
2. To establish a single commercial policy toward nonmember countries;
3. To better coordinate member countries' economic policies; and
4. To promote competitiveness with other countries.

Meeting those goals hasn't been easy, but the EU has made significant progress.

Why did the countries of the EU combine? Two primary reasons were to establish better markets for European companies and to compete better against U.S. goods. In the 1950s and 1960s, when the United States was highly competitive with other countries and had a trade surplus, it could look beneficently at, and even encourage, such developments. In the 1990s, however, U.S. goods are far less competitive and there's a large trade deficit, so the United States finds it much harder to encourage a potential competitor. The EU's gains likely will come at the expense of the United States.

These U.S. fears have increased as cooperation among EU countries has grown. In 1992, most trade barriers among member nations were removed, and the EU adopted a single commercial policy toward outside nations. The movement toward economic integration has not gone easily, however, and attempts at further unification have been fraught with political difficulties and confusion. Specifically, the movement toward a common currency called the Euro and a single monetary policy broke down in the 1990s and now might not take place until the 21st century, if at all.

In the second half of the 1990s the EU's economy slowed and unemployment was a serious concern for almost all EU countries. Despite this slowdown, the EU makes a formidable competitor for the United States. Exhibit A2 gives you a statistical comparison of the United States, Japan, and the European Union.

Developments in the EU have been made even more important by recent events in Eastern Europe. Eastern European countries have changed from socialist to more market-oriented economic systems and are attempting to establish closer economic and political ties with the West. East and West Germany are reunified. These developments will open up new markets for which both the United States and the EU will compete. In that competition, the EU has both cultural and geographic advantages over the United States.

In response to the EU's increasing strength, the United States has entered into a free trade agreement with Canada and Mexico called the North American Free Trade Agreement (NAFTA). Once the agreement is in place (it is being phased in over 15 years), U.S. firms will be able to produce in Mexico—or vice versa—subject to Mexican regulations and at Mexican wage rates, and ship directly to the United States without international legal hurdles. NAFTA raises significant questions about the short-run effects of free trade, such as: Should goods sold in the United States all be subject to the same regulations regardless of where they are produced? Will free trade with Mexico and Canada increase jobs or decrease jobs in the United States? The agreement should be much in the news in the 1990s.

Besides entering into NAFTA, the United States also argued strongly against high EU protective barriers on imports from foreign countries. Since there are no international organizations specifically designed to coordinate

EXHIBIT A1   Map of EU Countries

Members of the European Union in 1996 include Austria, Belgium, Denmark, Finland, France, Germany, Great Britain, Greece, Ireland, Italy, Luxembourg, The Netherlands, Portugal, Spain, and Sweden.

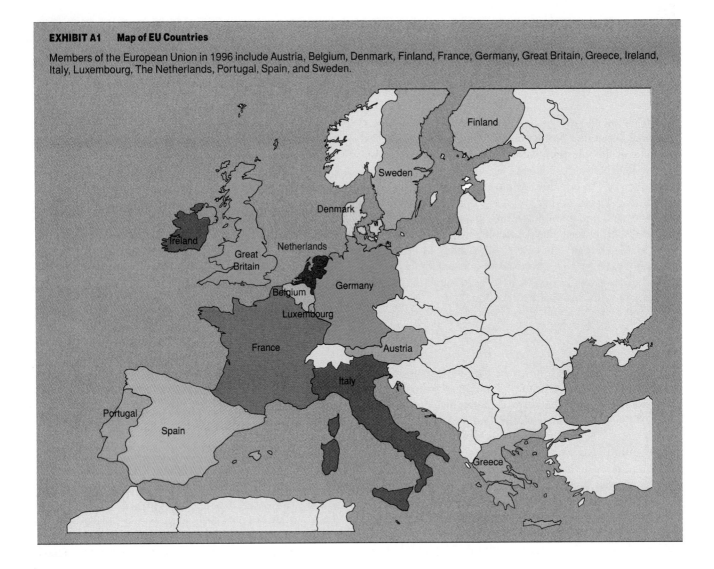

EXHIBIT A2   Summary Statistical Comparison of the United States, the European Union, and Japan

	United States	Japan	European Union
Area (square miles)	3,566,278	145,850	1,060,161
Population (millions)	266	126	373
GDP per capita (U.S. dollars)	$28,000	$26,000	$21,500
Unemployment rate	5.1%	2.9%	10.7%
Inflation	2.9%	0.1%	2.3%

Source: U.S. Census Bureau (http://www.census.gov), Japanese Ministry of Finance (http://stat.go.jp), Europa (http://europa.eu.int).

and facilitate international trade among trading areas, a new policy problem of the 1990s may be trade wars among "free trading" areas.

"Japan, Inc."

Japan is a little country with a lot of people—about 126 million, half as many people as the United States—but it fits them into 146,000 square miles, about 4 percent of the area of the United States. Almost two-thirds of Japan

is covered with forest, and much of the rest of the land has poor soil. It has almost no oil; its coal is very low grade; it must import nearly 100 percent of its petroleum and all of its iron ore (used to make steel) and bauxite (used to make aluminum). It has some copper and other minerals such as zinc, but not enough. Even with heavy forestation, it doesn't have enough lumber for domestic use and must make substantial expenditures for imported lumber.

Besides being small, crowded, and poorly endowed, Japan is a chain of islands and has a language that is ex-

GERMANY: THE LEADING EU COUNTRY

The largest European Union economy is Germany. Germany has been on the losing end of two world wars and, nonetheless, has emerged as one of the leading economies of the world. One reason is cultural: German culture reinforces hard work and makes saving a virtue. Also, the country's coal and iron resources helped it establish a strong industrial base as long ago as the early 1900s.

After losing World War II in 1945, Germany was divided into East and West Germany. East Germany, which had a large part of the manufacturing base of prewar Germany, was controlled by a Communist government. West Germany was controlled by the victorious Allied forces, who encouraged it to set up a democratic market economy. The Allies limited West German military spending, while the United States, through the Marshall Plan (an assistance plan for Europe which the United States ran after World War II), pumped in large amounts of money to help the West German economy recover from the war. And recover it did. In the 1960s and 1970s, the West German economy grew so fast that it was called an *economic miracle*.

West Germany's economic story contrasted significantly with East Germany's. East Germany grew more than any of the other Eastern bloc Communist economies, but its growth didn't match West Germany's. To prevent East Germans from emigrating to West Germany, East Germany closed its borders with West Germany in 1961 and built a wall between the two countries. Economic and political changes in East Germany at the end of the 1980s led to the introduction of a market economy in East Germany, an opening of the border, and physical destruction of the wall. In 1990, East and West Germany were reunified.

The problems of economic and political reunification were immense. They placed enormous strains on the German political and economic system. To fund the reunification, the German government borrowed (it ran deficits) and raised taxes. Interest rates rose in Germany, placing significant strains on the European Union. In the 1990s, the German economy remained relatively strong, but it was no longer the economic miracle. It found itself with many of the same difficulties as the United States. In fact, in the mid-1990s, Germany had significantly higher unemployment than did the United States, and more serious government budget problems.

The German economy is much more centralized than is the U.S. economy. Banks play a much more important role than do banks in the United States, and often control a variety of German companies. In the United States such control would be illegal. Thus, while Germany, like the United States, is a market economy, it is a different kind of market economy.

---

tremely difficult to learn. These facts have tended, until the middle of the 20th century, to isolate it from the rest of the world. Japan broke its isolation by entering World War II, which it lost, leaving its economy in ruins.

By almost all objective analyses, then, one would expect Japan to be a poor, underdeveloped country. It isn't. Instead, it is one of the most successful and developed countries in the world. In the 1980s its economic strength earned it the nickname *Japan, Inc*. In the 1990s, while still successful, Japan has had its problems. Its stock market crashed in the early 1990s, and the government has spent considerable resources propping up its financial sector. Moreover, with the rise in the value of the yen in the early 1990s and the subsequent rise in price of its exports, Japanese exports declined and the Japanese economy fell into a recession; unemployment rose because exports fell due to limited demand. With these events, Japan has lost its "supereconomy" status, and has joined the ranks of the other industrialized economies. It is successful, but it is less successful than it was in the 1980s.

Some Reasons for the Japanese Economy's Success   There are many reasons for Japan's success. Some reasons are cultural: The Japanese have a strong commitment to hard work and saving; and Japanese have a highly cooperative spirit that reduces fractions within organizations. Some reasons are institutional: Their educational system is much more demanding than the United States's, and the government and business work in a partnership that encourages and shelters business.

The Japanese savings tradition is also encouraged by government policies that keep prices of consumer goods high, make borrowing for consumer goods comparatively expensive, and maintain only skimpy government pension and welfare systems. One of the reasons the Japanese save a much higher percentage of their incomes than most other people do is that they worry about supporting themselves in adversity and in their old age.

Japan as a Neomercantilist Country   Another reason that some economists cite for Japanese development is its government's strong role in stimulating export-led growth. These economists argue that Japan's economic growth is not an example of the power of the invisible hand, but of the three invisible forces working together to direct an economy toward growth. In many economists' view, the Japanese economic system is as closely related to mercantilism as it is to capitalism. Some have called the Japanese economic system **neomercantilism**—*a market economy guided by government*.

The power of Japan's neomercantilist approach is striking. In the 1940s, with few resources and raw

For every economy that works well, there are many more economies that aren't achieving their goals. Considering one of them helps us keep our perspective. Take Pakistan, a country of about 130,000,000 people. Pakistan is poor; the average per capita income is about $400. In the United States the equivalent figure is about $28,000. Pakistan's political structure is, in theory, democratic, but the army plays a major role in determining who will rule. Coups d'états (overthrows of the government) and unexplained deaths of high leaders are common. The resulting political instability keeps out most foreign investments.

Pakistan is an Islamic republic which has had significant fights with India ever since the two nations were created out of the former single British commonwealth country. The British commonwealth "India" was divided into "India" and "Pakistan" in 1947 after World War II. In 1971, Pakistan's internal strife led to half the country declaring its independence and forming a separate country, Bangladesh.

Pakistan's economy is primarily agricultural, although it also manufactures textiles and chemicals. One out of every 66 people has a TV; one out of every 176 has a car. In the United States the equivalent figures are one TV for every 1.2 people, and one car for every 1.8 people. Housing is poor for the majority of the people, and many barely get enough to eat. Income distribution is highly unequal, with a small group being very rich and a great majority being extremely poor.

Most industry has heavy government involvement and is highly inefficient. Without large tariff barriers, it could not compete. Such dependency on the government's prevention of competition breeds corruption. Most Pakistanis have little faith that their government bureaucracy will work for the benefit of society.

---

materials and devastated by World War II, Japanese firms, under government direction, borrowed in order to finance the purchase of raw materials from abroad. The Japanese government directed firms to allocate a large portion of output for export. They started with small products, paid workers low wages, saved their profits, and learned about international markets. Then they plowed back those savings into more raw materials, more manufacturing, and more exports. They continued this process, each time manufacturing more sophisticated products than before.

Japan put off making improvements in housing, transportation, highways, parks, cultural institutions, and public health while it directed its efforts to rebuilding and developing technology. Government policy encouraged and sheltered business.

The Japanese government developed an aggressive trading policy under the control of its **Ministry of International Trade and Industry (MITI)**—*the Japanese government agency that guides the Japanese economy*. The agency encourages businesses to cooperate, not to compete, with one another in order to be more efficient. Thus, in Japan, firms are organized into alliances called *keiretsus*. The largest six of these keiretsus account for 25 percent of Japanese output.

The government instituted strong tariffs that are still in force. They prohibit altogether the import of some articles that might compete with Japanese manufacturers. In short, Japan does not follow a laissez-faire policy in either the domestic or the international economy, and it is successful.

Not all economists agree that the government's role in Japanese economic development has been positive. Some economists argue that hard work and high savings led to growth that was partially offset by the government's involvement. They point out that MITI often backed the losing, not the winning, industries. The companies and technologies *it didn't back*, not the ones it did back, were the growth sectors of the Japanese economy. They argue that Japanese growth occurred in spite of, not because of, government involvement.

The Japanese Cooperative Spirit Japan's labor market is remarkably different from that in the United States. Large companies have what are called *permanent employees*. By tradition, a man, once hired, stays with the same company for his entire working life. Women are unlikely to be permanent employees and are expected to resign their jobs when they get married. The relationship between the company and the worker is close—a worker is a member of the corporate family and his social life revolves around the company. The nature of the Japanese labor market is now changing significantly. Some women can be permanent employees and more and more employees are being laid off and are moving to other companies.

Labor unions exist in Japan, but are organized according to industry. In the United States, unions are more likely to be organized by type of skill. Organization by industry allows Japanese workers to do many different jobs within a firm. Until recently, U.S. organized workers would not work outside their specialty.

Japan's pay structure is also different from that in the United States. Japanese workers know that their bonuses, gifts, and special allowances depend on how well their company is doing. Until recently, most U.S. workers received only a wage or salary and no bonus. Another Japanese characteristic contributing to its economic success is the tradition of cooperation between unions and business; in the United States, labor and management are frequently in conflict.

Japan, Inc., versus the United States   The Japanese and U.S. economies are both successful, but they differ significantly from each other. There is less competition among firms in Japan than in the United States. Japanese firms work closely with government in planning their industrial strategy. U.S. firms often see government as an opponent, not a partner. Similarly with labor and business: In Japan they generally cooperate; in the United States they generally are somewhat confrontational.

The Japanese Ministry of International Trade and Industry (MITI) plays a key role in determining what will be produced and who will produce it. MITI's goal has been to establish strong export-led growth, and that goal has been accomplished, although, as I have said, whether it was because of MITI, or in spite of MITI, is debatable. MITI also has an economic planning board that oversees many parts of the Japanese economy. Japan is no laissez-faire economy.

Don't Overestimate the Differences   The differences between the U.S. and Japanese economies are large, but shouldn't be overestimated. Both economies rely on markets. In both, profit incentives motivate production.

As global corporations bridge the gap between these two economies, the differences (once very large) are shrinking. U.S. labor unions and firms are cooperating more, while Japanese firms and labor unions are cooperating less.

With both systems successful, it is difficult to say that one set of institutions is better than the other. They are merely distinct from each other. The differences reflect social, cultural, and geographical conditions in the two countries. Some people have suggested that the United States should adopt a neomercantilist system like Japan's. Maybe it should, but it is not at all clear that Japanese institutions could be transferred to the United States. What works in one country can bomb in another.

The argument that policies that work in one country cannot necessarily be translated into policies that work in another country doesn't mean Japan's experience is of no relevance to the United States. In itself, the fact that a policy works in one country means that that policy deserves consideration by other countries. That's tough for an economist with a strong distrust of government to say, but it must be said. An open mind is a necessary attribute of a good economist.

Developing Countries as Competitors

Japan and the EU have developed industrial economies similar to the United States's economy. There is, however, a much larger group of countries out there that are at various lower levels of industrial development. Many of them are anxious for industrial development and will likely provide significant competition for the U.S. economy. If Japan and the EU can't out-compete the United States, these other countries often can with low wage rates and governments eager to give global corporations whatever they want. If U.S. firms don't take advantage of this low-cost labor, Japanese and European firms will, and will export the output to the United States.

Of these developing countries, Mexico is of special interest to the United States. The reason is NAFTA, which will allow easy access into the U.S. market for firms producing in Mexico. As NAFTA brings in freer trade, U.S. companies are likely to experience significant Mexican competition. In return, of course, U.S. companies will have a new open market to sell to—Mexico. As inevitably happens with competition, some people will be helped, and some will be hurt.

Conclusion

Knowing about other countries' economies helps us keep our own economy in perspective. I don't have the space here (an example of scarcity) to look at other countries' tax structures, public finances, support of education, labor markets . . . the list is endless. But as you wonder about any of the economic policies that are discussed throughout this book, take a few minutes to ask somebody from a foreign country about his or her country's economy, and go to the library and look up another country's way of handling its economy (even if you look no further than an encyclopedia). See how that country compares to the United States. Then try to explain what does or doesn't work in that country and whether it would or would not work in the United States. Doing so will make the course more meaningful and your understanding of economics stronger.

KEY TERMS

European Union (EU)   *(147)*   Ministry of International Trade and   neomercantilism   *(149)*
                                        Industry (MITI)   *(150)*

QUESTIONS FOR THOUGHT AND REVIEW

1. What is the difference between EU and Euro?
2. If your ancestors emigrated to the United States, state what the annual per capita income in your ancestors' country is today. If your ancestors did not immigrate, what is the annual per capita income of native Americans?
3. What effect has the establishment of the EU had on the U.S. economy? Why?
4. Japan's successful economy is an example of the power of the invisible hand. True or false? Why?

PART

Two

MACROECONOMICS

In the early 1990s, unemployment in Europe hit 11 percent, and Europe's growth rate fell to zero. In the United States, the situation was somewhat better, but still there was serious concern about the level of unemployment and growth. People turned to macroeconomists for suggestions about what to do. This section of the book explains the ideas of competing groups of macroeconomists about such issues. It tells you how the ideas developed, and what relevance they have for policy in the 1990s.

The specific focus of macroeconomics is the study of unemployment, business cycles (fluctuations in the economy), growth, and inflation. While the macroeconomic theories studied have changed considerably over the past 60 years, macroeconomics' focus on those problems has remained. Thus, we'll define macroeconomics as the study of the economy in the aggregate with specific focus on unemployment, inflation, business cycles, and growth.

In the following chapters, I provide you with the background necessary to discuss the modern debate about these issues. Let's begin with a little history.

Macroeconomics emerged as a separate subject within economics in the 1930s when the U.S. economy fell into a Great Depression. Businesses collapsed and unemployment rose until 25 percent of the workforce—millions of people—were out of work.

The Depression changed the way economics was taught and the way in which economic problems were conceived. Before the 1930s, economics was microeconomics (the study of partial-equilibrium supply and demand). After the 1930s, the study of the core of economic thinking was broken into two discrete areas: microeconomics, as before, and macroeconomics (the study of the economy in the aggregate).

Macroeconomic policy debates have centered on a struggle between two groups: Keynesian (pronounced KAIN-sian) economists and Classical economists. Should the government run a budget deficit or a surplus? Should the government increase the money supply when a recession threatens? Should it decrease the money supply when inflation threatens? Can government prevent recessions? Keynesians generally answer one way; Classicals, another.

Each group has many variants. On the Classical side are neo-Classicals, New Classicals, and monetarists. On the Keynesian side are neo-Keynesians, New Keynesians, and post-Keynesians, just to name a few. At the introductory level we needn't concern ourselves with these various subdivisions. We'll focus on Keynesians and Classicals.

While there are many differences between Keynesians and Classicals, the fundamental policy difference is the following: Classical economists generally oppose government intervention in the economy; they favor a laissez-faire policy.[1] Keynesians are more likely to favor government intervention in the economy. They feel a laissez-faire policy can sometimes lead to disaster. Both views represent reasonable economic positions. The differences between them are often subtle and result from their taking slightly different views of what government can do and slightly different perspectives on the economy.

Section I, Macroeconomic Problems (Chapters 7–9), introduces you to the macroeconomic problems, terminology, and statistics used in tracking the economy's macroeconomic performance. Section II, Macroeconomic Models (Chapters 10–11), provides the background you need to understand macroeconomic theory sufficiently so that you can understand the policy debates that have been going on for the last 60 years and continue unabated. In these chapters the terms of the debate between Keynesians and Classicals will become clear.

Section III, Traditional Macro Policy Debates (Chapters 12–17), introduces you to the traditional macroeconomic policy. It leads you through the advantages of fiscal policy, monetary policy, exchange rate policy, and trade policy. Section IV, Structural Macro Policy Debates (Chapters 18–20), introduces you to important policy debates that are ongoing today. It gives you insight into what structural macro policies are and why they are so hard to implement.

---

[1]"Laissez-faire" (introduced to you in Chapter 2) is a French expression meaning "Leave things alone; let them go on without interference."

Seven

Economic Growth, Business Cycles, Unemployment, and Inflation

*Remember that there is nothing stable in human affairs; therefore
avoid undue elation in prosperity, or undue depression in adversity.*

~ Socrates

After reading this chapter, you should be able to:

1 Summarize some relevant statistics about growth, business cycles, unemployment, and inflation.

2 Name five sources of growth.

3 List four phases of the business cycle.

4 Explain how unemployment is measured and state some microeconomic categories of unemployment.

5 Relate the target rate of unemployment to potential income.

6 Define inflation and distinguish a real concept from a nominal concept.

7 Differentiate between cost-push and demand-pull inflation and expected and unexpected inflation.

8 State two important costs of inflation.

Like people, the economy has moods. Sometimes it's in wonderful shape—it's expansive; at other times, it's depressed. Like people whose moods are often associated with specific problems (headaches, sore back, an itch), the economy's moods are associated with various problems.

Macroeconomics is the study of the aggregate moods of the economy, with specific focus on problems associated with those moods—the problems of growth, business cycles, unemployment, and inflation. These four problems are the central concern of macroeconomics. The macroeconomic theory we'll consider is designed to explain how supply and demand forces in the aggregate interact to create these problems. The macroeconomic policy controversies we'll consider concern these four problems. So it's only appropriate that in this first chapter we consider an overview of these problems, their causes, their consequences, and the debate about what to do about them. It introduces you to some of the terms we'll be using and gives you a sense of the interrelationship of these problems. Just how are business cycles and growth related to inflation and unemployment? The chapter won't answer all your questions (if it did, we wouldn't need the other chapters), but it will provide you with a framework for the remaining chapters.

We'll start with the problems of growth.

The four central problems of macro are growth, business cycles, unemployment, and inflation.

GROWTH

1a U.S. economic output has grown at an annual 2.5 to 3.5 percent rate.

Generally the U.S. economy is growing or expanding. Economists use changes in **real gross domestic product (real GDP)**—*the market value of goods and services produced in an economy stated in the prices of a given year*—as the primary measurement of growth. When people produce and sell their goods, they earn income, so when an economy is growing, both total output and total income are increasing. Such growth gives most people more this year than they had last year. Since most of us prefer more to less, growth is easy to take.

The U.S. Department of Commerce traced U.S. economic growth in output since about 1890 and discovered that, on average, output of goods and services grew about 3.5 percent per year, although in recent years this rate has decreased to slightly under 3 percent. This 2.5 to 3.5 percent growth rate is sometimes called the *secular trend growth rate*. The rate at which the actual output grows in any one year fluctuates, but on average, the U.S. economy has been growing at that long-term trend. Since population has also been growing, per capita economic growth (growth per person) has been less than 2.5 to 3.5 percent. This growth trend can be divided into two components, one reflecting growth of population, and one consisting of increased productivity (output per input). When economists talk about economic growth, they generally mean this long-term growth trend of real GDP of 2.5 to 3.5 percent per year.

The Benefits and Costs of Growth

Politically, growth, or predictions of growth, allows governments to avoid hard questions.

Economic growth (per capita) allows everyone in society, on average, to have more. Thus, it isn't surprising that most governments are generally searching for policies that will allow them to grow. Indeed, one reason market economies have been so successful is that they have consistently channeled individual efforts toward production and growth. Individuals feel a sense of accomplishment in making things grow and, if sufficient economic incentives and resources exist, individuals' actions can lead to a continually growing economy.

Politically, growth, or predictions of growth, allows governments to avoid hard distributional questions of who should get what part of our existing output: With growth there is more to go around for everyone. A growing economy generates jobs, so politicians who want to claim that their policies will create jobs generally predict those policies will create growth. For example, in the presidential election of 1996, opposing candidates Bill Clinton and Robert Dole both claimed their policies would bring about high growth and thereby create jobs.

Of course, there are also costs to material growth—pollution, resource exhaustion, and destruction of natural habitat. These costs lead some people to believe that we would be better off in a non-material-growth society that de-emphasized material growth. (That doesn't mean we shouldn't grow emotionally, spiritually, and intellectually; it simply means we should grow out of our material good fetish.) Many people believe these environmental costs are important, and the result is often an environmental–economic growth stalemate.

To reconcile the two goals, some have argued that spending on the environment can create growth and jobs, so the two need not be incompatible. Unfortunately, there's a problem with this argument. It confuses growth and jobs with increased material consumption—what most people are worried about. As more material goods made available by growth are used for pollution control equipment, less is available for the growth of an average individual's personal consumption, since the added material goods created by growth have already been used. What society gets, at best, from these expenditures is a better physical environment, not more of everything. Getting more of everything would violate the TANSTAAFL law.

The Sources of Growth

Economists have thought a lot about growth, and have many ideas about it. But they have no magic recipe of policies that can be directly related to growth. They, however, have specified some of the ingredients of that recipe. Five of the most important causes of growth are the following:

1. Institutions with incentives compatible with growth;
2. Technological development;
3. Available resources;
4. Capital accumulation—investment in productive capacity; and
5. Entrepreneurship.

Let's consider each in turn.

Institutions with Incentives Compatible with Growth

Throughout this book I have emphasized the importance of economic institutions. Those institutions are vitally necessary for growth. **Growth-compatible institutions**—*institutions that foster growth*—must have *incentives* built into them that lead people to put out effort—to work hard—and must discourage people from activities that inhibit growth such as spending a lot of their time in leisure pursuits or in gaining income for themselves by creating impediments for others. Let's consider some examples of each.

When individuals get much of the gains of growth themselves, they have incentives to work harder. That's why private ownership of property plays an important role in growth. Many economists focus on private property ownership and markets when considering pro-growth policies. In the former Soviet Union, individuals didn't get much of the gain of their own initiative, and hence often spent their time in pursuits other than activities fostering economic growth. Another example of a growth-compatible institution is the corporation, a legal fiction that gives owners limited liability, thereby encouraging large enterprises because people are more willing to invest their savings when they have limited liability than they would be if they did not.

Many developing countries follow a type of mercantilist policy in which government approval is necessary before any economic activity is allowed. Government officials' income often comes from bribes offered to them by individuals who want to be able to undertake economic activity. Such policies inhibit economic growth. Many regulations, even reasonable ones, also tend to inhibit economic growth because they inhibit entrepreneurial activities. But I should mention that to ensure that the growth is of a socially desirable type, some regulation is necessary. The policy problem is in deciding between necessary and unnecessary regulation.

Technological Development

Growth is sometimes thought of as the same things getting bigger, or as getting more of the same things. That's an incorrect view of growth. While growth in some ways involves more of the same, a much larger aspect of growth involves changes in technology—*changes* in the goods we buy, and *changes* in the way we make goods. Think of what this generation spends its income on—CDs, cars, computers, fast food—and compare that to what the preceding generation spent money on—LP records, cars that would now be considered obsolete, and tube and transistor radios. (When I was eleven, I saved $30—the equivalent of over $100 now—so I could afford a 6-transistor Motorola radio; personal computers didn't exist.)

Contrast this with the goods the next generation might spend its income on: video brain implants (little gadgets in your head to receive sound and full-vision broadcasts—you simply close your eyes and tune in whatever you want, if you've paid your cellular fee for that month), electric cars (gas cars will be considered so quaint, but so polluting), and instant food (little pills that fulfill all your nutritional needs, letting your brain implant gadget supply all the ambiance)—Just imagine! You probably can get the picture even without a video brain implant.

How does society get people to work on these new developments to change the very nature of what we do and how we think? One way is through economic incentives; another is with institutions that foster creativity and bold thinking—like this

2 Five important ingredients of growth are:
1. Institutions with incentives compatible with growth;
2. Technological development;
3. Available resources;
4. Capital accumulation—investment in productive capacity; and
5. Entrepreneurship.

You may wish to ask your students what factors, other than those discussed in the text, they believe will foster growth in the future.

The hot issue in growth theory in the early 1990s is endogenous growth theory, in which technological change is endogenized. For some relatively readable articles on these developments see the Winter, 1994 issue of *The Journal of Economic Perspectives.*

Q–1: In what way do regulations inhibit growth and in what way are they necessary?

The nature of products in a society is continually changing.

Technological change does more than cause economic growth; it changes the entire social and political dimensions of society.

The discussion of growth naturally leads to a discussion of the trade-offs that are necessary to sustain economic growth. I like to expand this discussion by asking students about their valuation of each of the alternatives involved.

A per capita growth rate of 1 percent per year means on average people will be able to consume 1 percent more per year. Most of you, I suspect, are hoping to do better than that, and most of you will do better, both because you're in college studying economics (so you'll do better than average) and because most individuals in their working years can expect to consume slightly more each year than they did the previous year. Since income also tends to increase with age up to retire-

ment, and ends completely at death, a specific individual's income, and hence his or her consumption, will generally increase by more than the per capita growth in income.

So, if the future is like the past, the average (living) person can look forward to a rate of increase in consumption significantly above average. The average dead person will have a rather significant decrease.

U.S. educational institutions do a good job of fostering creativity.

What is a resource depends on the technology used. A resource in one time period may not be a resource in another.

Q–2: The Soviet Union invested a lot but did not grow. What explanation for this can you give?

Q–3: Does your going to school increase the capital of the economy?

book; a third is through institutions that foster hard work. There are, of course, trade-offs. Institutions that foster hard work and require discipline—such as the Japanese educational system—don't do as good a job at fostering creativity as the U.S. educational system, and vice versa: the U.S. educational system isn't great at fostering hard work. Thus, many of the new technologies of the 1980s have been thought up in the United States, but have been translated into workable products in Japan.

Still, the United States has done well on the technology front. Important developments in biotechnology, computers, and communications have developed in the United States, and those developments have helped fuel growth in the 1990s. Those new industries are absent from European Union countries, which is one important reason why those countries have grown far more slowly than has the United States.

Available Resources   If an economy is to grow it will need resources. England grew in the late 1700s because it had iron and coal; and the United States grew in the 20th century because it had a major supply of many resources, and it imported people, a resource it needed.

Of course, you have to be careful in thinking about what is a resource. A resource in one time period may not be a resource in another, or it may depend on the technology being used. So creativity can replace resources, and if you develop new technology fast enough, you can overcome any lack of existing resources. Even if a country doesn't have the physical resources it needs, if it can import them, it can grow—as did Japan following World War II.

Investment and Accumulated Capital   At one point, capital accumulation (where capital was thought of as buildings and machines) and investment were seen as forming *the* key element in growth. While buildings and machines are still considered *a* key element in growth, it is now generally recognized that the growth recipe is far more complicated. One of the reasons for this recognition is the empirical evidence; for instance, the former Soviet Union invested a lot and accumulated lots of capital goods, but their economy didn't grow much because that capital was often internationally obsolete. Another reason for this de-emphasis on capital accumulation is a recognition that products change, and useful buildings and machines in one time period may be useless in another. The value of the capital stock depends on the future, and there is no real way of measuring the value of capital independently of its future expectation of earnings. Capital's role in growth is extraordinarily difficult to accurately measure empirically.

A third reason for this de-emphasis on capital accumulation is that it became clear that capital was far more than machines. Capital also includes **human capital**—that is, *people's knowledge*. **Social capital**—*the habitual way of doing things that guides people in how they approach production*—is another type of capital. For example, the existence of money and a well-developed financial market makes many investment projects possible that otherwise wouldn't be possible, and hence such

---

ADDED DIMENSION

INTERPRETING EMPIRICAL EVIDENCE

When I first went to college, I thought that there were facts and there were theories, and that theories were tested by comparing them to the facts. Alas, my college professors delighted in twisting any neat divisions I made, and my neat distinction between fact and theory is one of the things that bit the dust.

The difficulty is that facts are simply empirical observations. What is a fact depends on who is doing the observing. Economic facts (data) must often be collected through more complicated methods than simple observation. Numbers must be collected (presenting first the collector and then the viewer with possible errors). Numbers must be combined, and often subsets of numbers must be chosen (opening up the possibility of more errors). Finally numbers must be interpreted.

Much of the debate in economics is conducted in the statistical trenches—looking at the data and attempting to pull out "facts" from that data. The "fact" that business cycles' peaks and troughs were reduced after World War II was pretty much accepted as a fact until Christina Romer, an economist at Princeton, reanalyzed the data and came up with a different conclusion. She found that no postwar change in business cycles had occurred. Many economists disagreed with her findings, but whether she was right or wrong is not the important point. The important point is that after she presented her new interpretation, the "fact" was in dispute, and no longer a fact. The moral: Beware of "facts."

---

institutions are a type of social capital. In a way, anything that contributes to growth can be called a type of capital, and anything that slows growth can be called a destruction of capital. With the concept of capital including such a wide range of things, it is difficult to say what is *not* capital, which makes the concept of capital less useful.

> The concept of social capital as a description of the value of institutions as an ongoing concern is not used much in economics, but I find it is a useful concept to complement human capital.

Entrepreneurship   In an earlier chapter I defined entrepreneurship as the ability to get things done. That ability involves creativity, vision, and a talent for translating that vision into reality. When a country's population demonstrates entrepreneurship, it can overcome deficiencies in other ingredients that contribute to growth.

Turning the Sources of Growth into Growth   The five sources of growth cannot be taken as givens. Even if each of these five ingredients exist, they may not exist in the right proportions. For example, economic growth depends upon people saving and investing rather than consuming their income. Investing now helps create machines that in the future can be used to produce more output with less effort. Growth also depends upon technological change—finding new, better ways to do things. For instance, when Nicolas Appert discovered canning (the ability to cook and store food in a sealed container so it wouldn't spoil), the economic possibilities of society expanded enormously. But if, when technological changes occur, the savings aren't there to finance the investment, the result will not be growth. It is the *combination* of investing in machines and technological change that plays a central role in the growth of any economy.

There are, of course, many other sources of growth. Nonetheless, this brief introduction should identify some growth issues to keep in the back of your mind as we consider other goals, because policies that sometimes seem to help alleviate other problems, like unemployment or inflation, can have negative effects on growth.

While the secular, or long-term, trend is a 2.5 to 3.5 percent increase in GDP, there are numerous fluctuations around that trend. Sometimes real GDP is above the trend; at other times GDP is below the trend. This phenomenon has given rise to the term business cycle. A **business cycle** is *the upward or downward movement of economic activity, or real GDP, that occurs around the growth trend*. Exhibit 1 graphs the fluctuations in GDP for the U.S. economy since 1860.

Until the late 1930s, economists took such cycles as facts of life. They had no convincing theory to explain why business cycles occurred, nor did they have policy suggestions to smooth them out. In fact, they felt that any attempt to smooth them through government intervention would make the situation worse.

BUSINESS CYCLES

Business cycle   *The upward or downward movement of economic activity that occurs around the growth trend.*

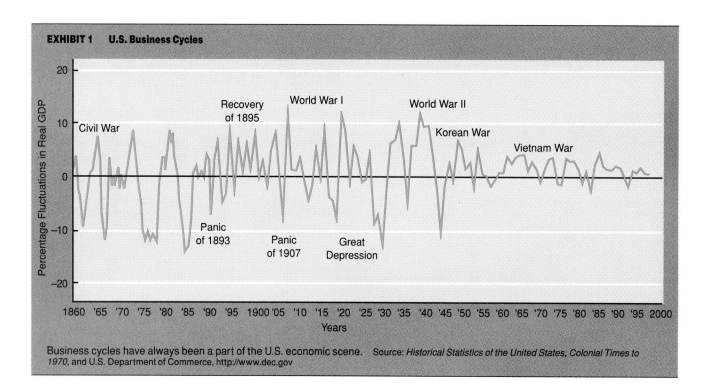

EXHIBIT 1   U.S. Business Cycles

Business cycles have always been a part of the U.S. economic scene.   Source: *Historical Statistics of the United States, Colonial Times to 1970,* and U.S. Department of Commerce, http://www.dec.gov

Keynesian *A macroeconomist who generally favors activist policies.*

Classical *A macroeconomist who generally favors laissez-faire or non-activist policies.*

If prolonged contractions are a type of cold the economy catches, the Great Depression of the 1930s was double pneumonia.

Since the 1940s, however, many economists have not taken business cycles as facts of life. They have hotly debated the nature and causes of business cycles and of the underlying growth. In this book I distinguish two groups of macroeconomists: **Keynesians** (who *generally favor activist government policies*) and **Classicals** (who *generally favor laissez-faire or non-activist policies*). Classical economists argue that fluctuations in economic activity are to be expected in a market economy. Indeed, it would be strange if fluctuations did not occur when individuals are free to decide what they want to do. We should simply accept these fluctuations as we do the seasons of the year. If you have no policy to deal with some occurrence, you might as well accept that occurrence. Keynesian economists argue that fluctuations can and should be controlled. They argue that *expansions* (the part of the business cycle above the long-term trend) and *contractions* (the part of the cycle below the long-term trend) are symptoms of underlying problems of the economy, which should be dealt with by government actions. Classical economists respond that individuals have **rational expectations**—*expectations about the future based on the best current information*—and will anticipate government's reaction, thereby undermining government's attempts to control cycles. Which of these two views is correct is still a matter of debate.

If prolonged contractions (recessions) are a type of cold the economy catches, the Great Depression of the 1930s was double pneumonia. Production of goods and services fell by 30 percent from 1929 to 1933, leading to changes in the U.S. economy's structure. The new structure included a more active role for government in reducing the severity of cyclical fluctuations. Look at Exhibit 1 and compare the periods before and after World War II. (World War II began in 1941 and ended in 1945.) Notice that the downturns and panics since 1945 have generally been less severe than before.

This change in the nature of business cycles can be better seen in Exhibit 2. Notice that since the late 1940s business cycles' duration has increased, but, more important, the average length of expansions has increased while the average length of contractions has decreased.

How to interpret these statistics is the subject of much controversy. As is the case with much economic evidence, the data are subject to different interpretations. Some economists argue the reduction in fluctuations' severity is an illusion.

Cycles	Duration (in months)	
	Pre-World War II (1845–1945)	Post-World War II (1945–1996)
Number	22	9
Average duration (trough to trough)	50	60
Length of longest cycle	99 (1870–79)	117 (1961–70)
Length of shortest cycle	28 (1919–21)	28 (1980–82)
Average length of expansions	29	51
Length of shortest expansion	10 (1919–20)	12 (1980–81)
Length of longest expansion	80 (1938–45)	106 (1961–69)
Average length of recessions	21	11
Length of shortest recession	7 (1918–19)	6 (1980)
Length of longest recession	65 (1873–79)	16 (1981–82)

EXHIBIT 2   Duration of Business Cycles, Pre-World War II and Post-World War II

Source: National Bureau of Economic Research (http://nber.harvard.edu) and *Survey of Current Business* (http://www.bea.doc.gov).

If the severity of the fluctuations has been reduced (which most economists believe has happened), one reason is that changes in institutional structure were made as a result of the Great Depression. Both the financial structure and the government taxing and spending structure were changed, giving the government a more important role in stabilizing the economy. Consideration of that stronger government role is a key element of macroeconomics.

Much research has gone into measuring business cycles and setting official reference dates for the beginnings and ends of contractions and expansions. As a result of this research, business cycles have been divided into phases, and an explicit terminology has been developed. The National Bureau of Economic Research announces the government's official dates of contractions and expansions. In the postwar era (since mid-1945), the average business expansion has lasted about 51 months. A major expansion occurred from 1982 until mid-1990, when the U.S. economy fell into a recession. In mid-1991 it slowly came out of the recession, but slow growth remained.

Business cycles have varying durations and intensities, but economists have developed a terminology to describe all business cycles and just about any position we might find ourself in on the business cycle. Since this terminology is often used by the press it is helpful to go over it. I do so in reference to Exhibit 3 which gives you a visual picture of a business cycle.

The Phases of the Business Cycle

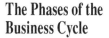 Since 1945 the average expansion has lasted about 51 months.

It is important to make certain that students do not come under the impression that business cycles have a uniform shape, with each stage playing itself out in a uniform manner.

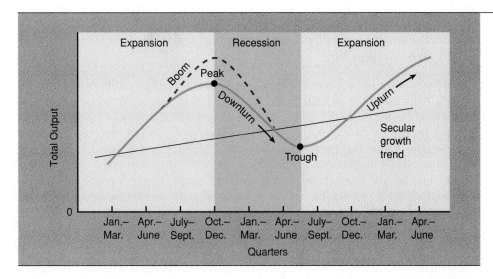

EXHIBIT 3   Business Cycle Phases
Economists have many terms that describe the position of the economy on the business cycle. Some of them are given in this graph.

3 The four phases of the business cycle are:
1. The peak
2. The downturn
3. The trough
4. The upturn.

Let's start at the top. The top of a cycle is called the *peak*. A **boom** is *a very high peak, representing a big jump in output*. (That's when the economy is doing great. Most everyone who wants a job has one and everyone is happy.) Eventually an expansion peaks. (At least, in the past, they always have.) A **downturn** describes *the phenomenon of economic activity starting to fall from a peak*. In a recession the economy isn't doing so great, many people are unemployed, and a number of people are depressed. Formally, a **recession** is *a decline in real output that persists for more than two consecutive quarters of a year*.

A **depression** is *a large recession*. There is no formal line indicating when a recession becomes a depression. In general, a depression is much longer and more severe than a recession. This ambiguity allows some economists to joke, "When your neighbor is unemployed, it's a recession; when you're unemployed, it's a depression." If pushed for something more specific, I'd say that if unemployment exceeds 12 percent for more than a year, the economy is in a depression.

The bottom of a recession or depression is called the *trough*. As total output begins to expand, the economy comes out of the trough; economists say it's in an *upturn*, which may turn into an **expansion**—*an upturn that lasts at least two consecutive quarters of a year*. An expansion leads us back up to the peak. And so it goes.

This terminology is important because if you're going to talk about the state of the economy, you need the terminology to do it. Why are businesses so interested in the state of the economy? They want to be able to predict whether it's going into a contraction or an expansion. Making the right prediction can determine whether the business will be profitable or not. That's why a large amount of economists' activity goes into trying to predict the future course of the economy.

Leading Indicators

Economists have developed a set of indicators to give a good idea of when a recession is about to occur and when the economy is in one. These signs are called **leading indicators**—*indicators that tell us what's likely to happen 12 to 15 months from now*, much as a barometer gives us a clue about tomorrow's weather. They include:

Q-4: List three leading indicators.

I have found that this material doesn't come alive for students unless they have to use it. Consequently, I ask them to go to the library and find, for the last 10 years or so, the data series discussed in this section. Then we discuss the current state of the economy in comparison to recent years, and even make our own forecasts based on the leading indicators. If you're really daring, you might post these forecasts in a conspicuous place so that they can be checked later.

For an example of economists a leading indicator to forecast the economy, see Chapter 6 in *Case Studies in Economics.*

1. Average workweek for production workers in manufacturing.
2. Average weekly claims for unemployment insurance.
3. New orders for consumer goods and materials.
4. Vendor performance, measured as a percentage of companies reporting slower deliveries from suppliers.
5. Index of consumer expectations.
6. New orders for nondefense capital goods.
7. Number of new building permits issued for private housing units.
8. Stock prices—50 common stocks.
9. Interest rate spread—10-year government bond less federal funds rate.
10. Money supply, M2.

These indicators are combined into an index of leading indicators that is frequently reported in the popular press. Economists use leading indicators in making forecasts about the economy. Leading indicators are called *indicators*, not *predictors*, because they're only rough approximations of what's likely to happen in the future. For example, before building a house, you must apply for a building permit. Usually this occurs six to nine months before the actual start of construction. By looking at the number of building permits that have been issued, you can predict how much building is likely to begin in six months or so. But the prediction might be wrong, since getting a building permit does not require someone to actually build. Business economists spend much of their time and effort delving deeper into these indicators, trying to see what they are really telling us, as opposed to what they seem to be telling us. Business economists joke that the leading indicators have predicted six of the past two recessions.

Sifting through the data to find clues in new statistical series is drudgery detective work, but it's the backbone of business economists' work. Just as TV detectives' antics don't reflect what most detectives do, economists' brief appearances on the TV news don't reflect what economists do.

UNEMPLOYMENT

Business cycles and growth are directly related to unemployment in the U.S. economy. **Unemployment** occurs *when people are looking for a job and cannot find one*. The **unemployment rate** is *the number of people who cannot find a job as a percent of those people in the economy who are willing and able to work*. When an economy is growing and is in an expansion, unemployment is usually falling; when an economy is in a downturn, unemployment is usually rising, although often with a lag.

The relationship between the business cycle and unemployment is obvious to most people, but often the seemingly obvious hides important insights. Just why are the business cycle and growth related to unemployment? True, aggregate income must fall in a recession, but, logically, unemployment need not result. A different result could be that everyone's income falls. Looking at the problem historically, we see that unemployment has not always been a problem associated with business cycles.

Unemployment became a problem about the time of the Industrial Revolution. In pre-industrial farming societies, unemployment wasn't a problem; there was always work to be done and all had their assigned tasks. The reason is that pre-industrial farmers didn't receive wages—they received net revenue (the income left after all costs had been paid). That means the average amount they netted per hour (the equivalent of a wage) was flexible. In good years they had a high income per hour; in bad years they had a low income per hour.

The flexibility in people's net income per hour meant that when there were fluctuations in economic activity, people's income rose or fell, but they kept on working. Low income was a problem, but, since people didn't become unemployed, **cyclical unemployment** (*unemployment resulting from fluctuations in economic activity*) was not a problem.

While cyclical unemployment did not exist in pre-industrial society, **structural unemployment** (*unemployment caused by economic restructuring making some skills obsolete*) did. For example, say demand for a product falls because of technological change. Some unemployment would likely result; that unemployment would be called *structural unemployment*. But structural unemployment wasn't much of a problem for government, or at least people did not consider it government's problem. The reason is that unemployment of family members was dealt with internally, by the family. If someone in the family had income, that person would share it with unemployed family members.

The Industrial Revolution changed the nature of work and introduced unemployment as a problem for society. This is because the Industrial Revolution was accompanied by a shift to wage labor and to a division of responsibilities. Some individuals (capitalists) took on ownership of the means of production and *hired* others to work for them, paying them a wage per hour. This change in the nature of production marked a significant change in the nature of the unemployment problem.

First, it created the possibility of cyclical unemployment. With wages set at a certain level, when economic activity fell, workers' income per hour did not fall. Instead, when slack periods occurred, factories would lay off or fire some workers. That isn't what happened on the farm; when a slack period occurred on the farm, the income per hour of all workers fell and few were laid off.

Second, the Industrial Revolution was accompanied by a change in how families dealt with unemployment. Whereas in preindustrial farm economies individuals or families took responsibility for their own slack periods, in a capitalist industrial society factory owners didn't take responsibility for their workers in slack periods. The pink slip (a common name for the notice workers get telling them they are laid off) and the problem of unemployment were born in the Industrial Revolution.

Without wage income, unemployed workers were in a pickle. They couldn't pay their rent, they couldn't eat, they couldn't put clothes on their backs. So what was

Cyclical unemployment *Unemployment resulting from fluctuations in economic activity.*

Structural unemployment *Unemployment resulting from changes in the economy itself.*

Once individuals became dependent on firms for employment, workers found themselves unemployed when firms laid them off and other firms were not hiring.

ADDED DIMENSION   CAPITALISM, THE FEAR OF HUNGER, AND THE DUTCH DISEASE

Using "the fear of hunger" to see that people work may sound rather mean, but looked at from a societal view it can be "kind." For example, consider the socialist countries that wiped out the fear of unemployment. All people were guaranteed a job. (In fact, all people were required by law to have one.) By law, unemployment was eliminated. But this created other problems. People would show up at work but not really work. After all, they couldn't be fired. The results were shoddy products, shortages, and general dissatisfaction. As one cynical citizen said, "We pretend to work and they pretend to pay us." These negative consequences of eliminating unemployment were a significant reason why people pushed for the elimination or modification of socialism. They said, "If this is the result of eliminating unemployment, bring back unemployment." And the formerly socialist countries have done that with a vengeance in the early 1990s.

I use the term *fear of hunger* rather than *fear of unemployment* to emphasize that if people can expect a good income even if they lose their jobs, the fear of unemployment loses some of its bite. For example, in European countries like the Netherlands people were guaranteed almost as much income if they had no job as they would have earned if they did have a job. The result: the unemployment rate rose and the Dutch economy stagnated. The effect of such high support payments to people who didn't work acquired a name: *the Dutch disease.*

No one argues that unemployment or the fear of hunger is good. But many do argue that going too far in eliminating it has such negative effects on growth that unemployment is the better of two bads.

See in *Classic Readings in Economics* "Full Employment in a Free Society," by Lord William Beveridge; "The Specter of Full Employment," by Robert Lekachman; "Full Employment as the Goal," by Henry Hazlitt; and "Unemployment Policy," by Robert E. Lucas for discussion of full employment.

As capitalism evolved, capitalist societies no longer saw the fear of hunger as an acceptable answer to unemployment.

Full employment   *Nearly everyone who wants a job has one.*

Frictional unemployment   *New entrants to the job market and people who have left their jobs to look for and find other jobs.*

After we discuss frictional and structural unemployment, I ask my students to consider an economy in which neither of these unemployment categories exist. We soon come to the conclusion that some degree of unemployment is necessary in a dynamic economy.

1c In the 1980s and 1990s, the target rate of unemployment has been between 5 and 7 percent.

previously a family problem became a social problem. Not surprisingly, it was at that time—the late 1700s—that economists began paying more attention to the problem of unemployment.

Initially, economists and society still did not view unemployment as a societal problem. It was the individual's problem. If people were unemployed, it was their own fault; hunger, or at least the fear of hunger, and people's desire to maintain their lifestyle would drive them to find other jobs relatively quickly. Thus, early capitalism didn't have an unemployment problem; it had an unemployment solution: the fear of hunger.

As capitalism evolved, the hunger solution decreased in importance. Capitalist societies no longer saw the fear of hunger as an acceptable answer to unemployment. Social welfare programs such as unemployment insurance and assistance to the poor were developed to help deal with unemployment.

In the Employment Act of 1946, the U.S. government specifically took responsibility for unemployment. The act assigned government the responsibility of creating **full employment,** *an economic climate in which just about everyone who wants a job could have one.* It was government's responsibility to offset cyclical fluctuations and thereby prevent cyclical unemployment, and to somehow deal with structural unemployment.

Initially government regarded 2 percent unemployment as a condition of full employment. The 2 percent was made up of **frictional unemployment** (*unemployment caused by new entrants into the job market and people quitting a job just long enough to look for and find another one*) and of a few "unemployables," such as alcoholics and drug addicts, along with a certain amount of necessary structural and seasonal unemployment resulting when the structure of the economy changed. Thus, any unemployment higher than 2 percent was considered either unnecessary structural or cyclical unemployment and was now government's responsibility; frictional and necessary structural unemployment were still the individual's problem.

Macroeconomics developed as a separate field and focused on how to combat cyclical unemployment. As you will see in coming chapters, government believed it could offset cyclical unemployment and achieve full employment by seeing to it that there was sufficient aggregate demand.

By the 1950s, government had given up its view that 2 percent unemployment was consistent with full employment. It raised its definition of full unemployment to 3 percent, then to 4 percent, then to 5 percent. By the 1970s and early 1980s, government raised it further, to 6.5 percent unemployment. At that point the term "full employment" fell out of favor (it's hard to call 6.5 percent unemployment "full employment"), and the terminology changed. The term I will use in this book is *target* rate of unemployment. The **target rate of unemployment** is *the lowest sustainable rate of unemployment that policy makers believe is achievable under existing conditions*. In the late 1980s and early 1990s the appropriate target rate of unemployment is a matter of debate, but in the late 1990s most economists place it at somewhere between 5 and 6 percent unemployment.

Why has the target rate of unemployment changed over time? One reason is that, in the 1970s and early 1980s, a low inflation rate, which also was a government goal, seemed to be incompatible with a low unemployment rate. I'll talk about this incompatibility later when I discuss the problem of simultaneous inflation and unemployment. A second reason is demographics: Different age groups have different unemployment rates, and as the population's age structure changes, so does the target rate of unemployment.

A third reason is our economy's changing social and institutional structure. These social and institutional changes affected the nature of the unemployment problem. For example, in the post–World War II period, family wealth increased substantially and borrowing became easier than before, giving many unemployed individuals a bit more leeway before they were forced to find a job. For instance, more family wealth meant that, upon graduation from high school or college, children who couldn't find the job they wanted could live at home and be supported by their parents for a year or two.

Another example of how changing institutions changed the unemployment problem is women's expanding role in the economy. In the 1950s, the traditional view that "woman's place is in the home" remained strong. Usually only one family member—the man—had a job. If he lost his job, no money came in. In the 1970s to 1990s, more and more women entered the workforce so that today over 60 percent of all families are two-earner families. In a two-earner family, if one person loses a job, the family doesn't face immediate starvation. The other person's income carries the family over.

Yet another example involves the changing structure of the economy. In the 1990s the U.S. economy, and much of the European economy, went through major **structural readjustments**—*modifications in the types of goods produced and the methods of production*. Firms laid off high-wage workers even as they were increasing output. The result was that structural unemployment increased as cyclical unemployment decreased. At times this led to the unemployment rate and the level of output moving in the same direction.

Government institutions also changed. Programs like unemployment insurance and public welfare were created to reduce suffering associated with unemployment. But in doing so, these programs changed the way people responded to unemployment. People in the 1990s are more picky about what jobs they take than they were in the 1920s and 1930s. People don't just want any job, they want a *fulfilling* job with a decent wage. As people have become choosier about jobs, a debate has raged over the extent of government's responsibility for unemployment.

Differing views of individuals' responsibility and society's responsibility affect people's views on whether somebody is actually unemployed. Classical economists take the position that, generally, individuals should be responsible for finding jobs. They emphasize that an individual can always find *some* job at *some* wage rate, even if it's only selling apples on the street for 40¢ apiece. Given this view of individual responsibility, unemployment is impossible. If a person isn't working, that's his or her choice; the person simply isn't looking hard enough for a job. For an economist with this view, almost all unemployment is actually frictional unemployment.

Keynesian economists tend to say society owes a person a job commensurate with the individual's training or past job experience. They further argue that the job should be close enough to home so a person doesn't have to move. Given this view, frictional unemployment is only a small part of total unemployment. Structural and cyclical unemployment are far more common.

Target rate of unemployment   The lowest sustainable rate of unemployment that policy makers believe is achievable under existing conditions.

Q–5: Why has the target rate of unemployment changed over time?

Since the 1970s the percentage of women in the workforce has increased enormously.

The unemployment rate in the EU countries is over 10 percent. Discussing this unemployment problem in relation to the welfare state generates useful discussion. It is also helpful to contrast the British and U.S. approach of creating lower-paying, part-time jobs with that of continental Europe of focusing on creating good, high-paying jobs.

Whose Responsibility Is Unemployment?

ADDED DIMENSION   CATEGORIES OF UNEMPLOYMENT

A good sense of the differing types of unemployment and the differing social views that unemployment embodies can be conveyed through three examples of unemployed individuals. As you read the following stories, ask yourself which category of unemployment each individual falls into.

Example 1: Joe is listed as unemployed and collects unemployment insurance. He's had various jobs in the past and was laid off from his last one. He spent a few weeks on household projects, believing he would be called back by his most recent employer—but he wasn't. He's grown to like being on his own schedule. He's living on his unemployment insurance (while it lasts, which usually isn't more than six months), his savings, and money he picks up by being paid cash under the table working a few hours now and then at construction sites.

The Unemployment Compensation office requires him to make at least an attempt to find work, and he's turned up a few prospects. However, some were back-breaking laboring jobs and one would have required him to move to a distant city, so he's avoided accepting regular work. Joe knows the unemployment payments won't last forever. When they're used up, he plans to increase his under-the-table activity. Then, when he gets good and ready, he'll really look for a job.

Example 2: Flo is a middle-aged, small-town housewife. She worked before her marriage, but when she and her husband started their family she quit her job to be a full-time housewife and mother. She never questioned her family values of hard work, independence, belief in free enterprise, and scorn of government handouts. When her youngest child left the nest, she decided to finish the college education she'd only just started when she married.

After getting her degree, she looked for a job, but found the market for middle-aged women with no recent experience was depressed—and depressing. The state employment office where she sought listings recognized her abilities and gave her a temporary job in that very office. Because she was a

"temp," however, she was the first to be laid off when the state legislature cut the local office budget—but she'd worked long enough to be eligible for unemployment insurance.

She hesitated about applying, since handouts were against her principles. On the other hand, while working there she'd seen plenty of people, including her friends, applying for benefits after work histories even slimmer than hers. She decided to take the benefits. While they lasted, she found family finances on almost as sound a footing as when she was working. Although she was bringing in less money, net family income didn't suffer much since she didn't have social security withheld nor did she have the commuting and clothing expenses of going to a daily job.

Example 3: Tom had a good job at a manufacturing plant where he'd worked up to a wage of $450 a week. Occasionally he was laid off, but only for a few weeks, and then he'd be called back. In 1989 the plant was bought by an out-of-state corporation which laid off half the workforce and put in automated equipment. Tom, an older worker with comparatively high wages, was one of the first to go, and he wasn't called back.

Tom had a wife, three children, a car payment, and a mortgage. He looked for other work but couldn't find anything paying close to what he'd been getting. Tom used up his unemployment insurance and his savings. He sold the house and moved his family into a trailer. Finally he heard that there were a lot of jobs in Massachusetts, 800 miles away. He moved there, found a job, and began sending money home every week. Then the Massachusetts economy faltered. Tom was laid off again, and his unemployment insurance ran out again. Relying on his $100,000 life insurance policy, he figured he was worth more to his family dead than alive, so he killed himself.

As these three examples suggest, unemployment encompasses a wide range of cases. Unemployment is anything but a one-dimensional problem, so it's not surprising that people's views of how to deal with it differ.

In the 1960s the average rate of unemployment in Europe was considerably below the average rate of unemployment in the United States. In the 1990s that has reversed and the average unemployment rate in Europe has significantly exceeded that in the United States. One of the reasons for this reversal is that Europe tried to create high-paying jobs, while it left a variety of taxes and social programs in place that discouraged the creation of low-paying jobs.

The United States, on the other hand, actively promoted the creation of jobs of any type. The result has been a large growth of jobs in the United States, many of which are low-paying jobs. An unemployed engineer, had he been in the United States, might well have given up engineering, and become a restaurant manager.

One result of U. S. policy has been continued job anxiety in the United States in the 1990s, despite a fall in the average unemployment rate. People know they can get a job, but they are anxious: Will it be the job they want at the pay they want?

How Is Unemployment Measured?

When there's debate about what the unemployment problem is, it isn't surprising that there's also a debate about how to measure it. When talking about unemployment, economists usually refer to the "unemployment rate" published by the U.S. Depart-

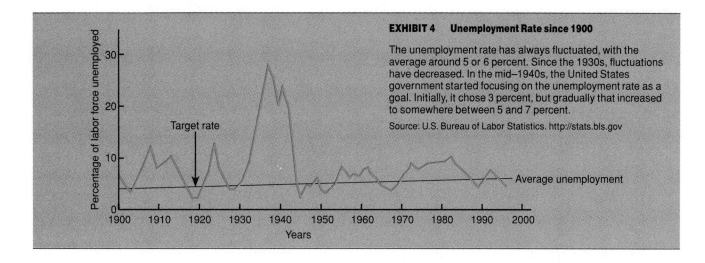

EXHIBIT 4   Unemployment Rate since 1900

The unemployment rate has always fluctuated, with the average around 5 or 6 percent. Since the 1930s, fluctuations have decreased. In the mid–1940s, the United States government started focusing on the unemployment rate as a goal. Initially, it chose 3 percent, but gradually that increased to somewhere between 5 and 7 percent.

Source: U.S. Bureau of Labor Statistics. http://stats.bls.gov

ment of Labor's Bureau of Labor Statistics (BLS). Fluctuations in the official unemployment rate since 1900 appear in Exhibit 4. In it you can see that, during World War II (1941–45), unemployment fell from the high rates of the 1930s depression to an extremely low rate, only 1.2 percent. You can also see that while the rate started back up in the 1950s, reaching 4 or 5 percent, it remained that low up until the 1970s, when the rate began gradually to rise again. After peaking in the early 1980s it began to descend again. In 1990 it was about 5 percent; then in 1991 the economy fell into recession and unemployment rates rose to over 7 percent in 1992. During the expansion that followed the unemployment rate returned to slightly over 5% by 1996.

Calculating the Unemployment Rate   The U.S. unemployment rate is determined by dividing the number of unemployed individuals by the number of people in the **labor force**—*those people in an economy who are willing and able to work*—and multiplying by 100. For example, if the total unemployed stands at 7 million and the labor force stands at 134 million, the unemployment rate is:

$$\frac{7 \text{ million}}{134 \text{ million}} = .052 \times 100 = 5.2\%$$

4a The unemployment rate is measured by dividing the number of unemployed individuals by the number of people in the civilian labor force and multiplying by 100.

To determine the labor force, start with the total civilian population and subtract from that all persons incapable of working, such as inmates of institutions and people under 16 years of age. (The civilian population excludes about 2 million individuals who are in the armed forces.) From that figure another subtraction is made—the number of people not in the labor force, including homemakers, students, retirees, the voluntarily idle, and the disabled. The result is the potential workforce, which is about 134 million people, or about 50 percent of the civilian population (see Exhibit 5).

The civilian labor force can be divided into employed and unemployed. The Bureau of Labor Statistics (BLS) defines people as *employed* if they work at a paid job (including part-time jobs) or if they are unpaid workers in an enterprise operated by a family member. The BLS's definition of *employed* includes all those who were temporarily absent from their jobs that week because of illness, bad weather, vacation, labor–management dispute, or personal reasons, whether or not they were paid by their employers for the time off.

In 1996 the number of unemployed individuals was about 7,200,000. Dividing this number by the labor force (133,900,000) gives us an unemployment rate of 5.4 percent.

How Accurate Is the Official Unemployment Rate?   BLS measures unemployment using a number of assumptions that have been the source of debate. For example, should **discouraged workers**—*people who do not look for a job because they feel they don't have a chance of finding one*—be counted as unemployed? Some Keynesian economists believe these individuals should be considered unemployed. Moreover

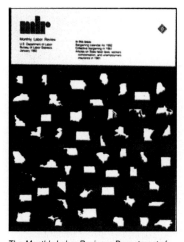

The *Monthly Labor Review*, a Department of Labor publication, is one of the best sources of labor statistics.

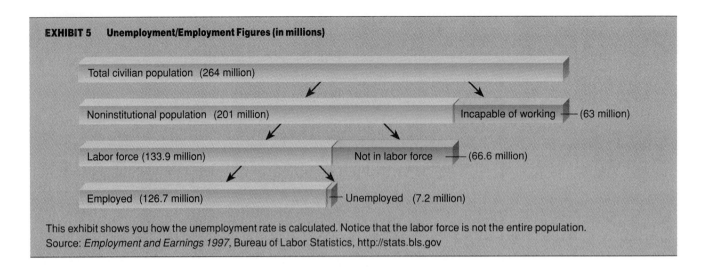

EXHIBIT 5   Unemployment/Employment Figures (in millions)

Total civilian population (264 million)

Noninstitutional population (201 million)   Incapable of working —— (63 million)

Labor force (133.9 million)   Not in labor force ——(66.6 million)

Employed (126.7 million)   — Unemployed (7.2 million)

This exhibit shows you how the unemployment rate is calculated. Notice that the labor force is not the entire population.
Source: *Employment and Earnings 1997*, Bureau of Labor Statistics, http://stats.bls.gov

they question whether *part-time workers who would prefer full-time work,* the **underemployed,** should be classified as employed.

Q–6: Would Keynesians or Classicals be more likely to view the unemployment rate as underestimating the unemployment problems?

The Keynesian argument is that there is such a lack of decent jobs and of affordable transportation to get to the jobs that do exist that many people become very discouraged and have simply stopped trying. Because BLS statisticians define these people as voluntarily idle and do not count them as unemployed, Keynesians argue that the BLS undercounts unemployment significantly.

The Classical argument about unemployment is that being without a job often is voluntary. People say they are looking for a job, but they're not really looking. Many are working "off the books"; others are simply vacationing. Some Classicals contend that the way the BLS measures unemployment exaggerates the number of those who are truly unemployed. A person is defined as unemployed if he or she is not employed and is actively seeking work.

Q–7: In what way is the very concept of unemployment dependent upon the value judgments made by the individual?

So is the official unemployment rate too high or too low? The definition of *unemployment* involves value judgments. Both the Keynesian and the Classical arguments are defensible. But both sides agree the unemployment measure is imperfect, missing many people who should be included and including many people who should not be counted. This means that official unemployment figures must be carefully interpreted and modified in the light of other information, such as the number of people employed, part-time employment, and your own perspective on the problem. In short, measuring and interpreting the unemployment rate (like measuring and interpreting most economic statistics) is an art, not a science.

Despite problems, the unemployment rate statistic still gives us useful information about changes in the economy.

Despite problems, the unemployment rate statistic still gives us useful information about changes in the economy. Except for those times when the BLS changes its procedures, as it did in 1994, the measurement problems themselves are little changed from year to year, so in comparing one year to another, those problems are not an issue. Keynesian and Classical economists agree that a changing unemployment rate generally tells us something about the economy, especially if interpreted in the light of other statistics. That's why the unemployment rate is used as a measure of the state of the economy.

Unemployment and Potential Income

Capacity utilization rate   Rate at which factories and machines are operating compared to the maximum sustainable rate at which they could be used.

The unemployment rate gives a good indication of how much labor is available to increase production and thus provides a good idea of how fast the economy could grow. Capital is the second major input to production. Thus, the **capacity utilization rate,** *the rate at which factories and machines are operating compared to the maximum sustainable rate at which they could be used,* indicates how much capital is available for economic growth.

Exhibit 6 shows the unemployment rates and the capacity utilization rates for selected countries over the last 20 years. Generally U.S. economists in the late 1990s

	Capacity Utilization			Unemployment			Annual Growth in Real Output
	1975	1985	1995	1975	1985	1995	1975–1995
United States	74.6	79.8	82.5	8.5	7.2	5.6	2.5
Japan	81.4	82.5	77.7	1.9	2.6	3.2	3.1
Germany	76.9	79.6	81.7	3.4	8.2	9.4	3.5
United Kingdom	81.9	81.1	81.8	4.6	11.2	8.2	2.4
Canada	83.1	82.5	79.5	6.9	10.5	9.5	2.5
Mexico	85.0	92.0	85.7	*	*	6.3	1.3
Republic of Korea	86.4	74.6	83.3	*	10.9	8.2	8.6

EXHIBIT 6   Unemployment and Capacity Utilization Rates for Selected Countries

Source: Organization for Economic Cooperation and Development (http://www.oecd.org) and author estimates.
(* = unavailable)

feel that 5–6 percent unemployment and 80–85 percent capacity utilization are about as much as we should expect from the economy. To push the economy beyond that would be like driving your car 90 miles an hour. True, the marks on your speedometer might go up to 130, but 90 is a more realistic top speed. Beyond 120 (assuming that's where your car is red-lined), the engine is likely to blow up (unless you have a Maserati).

Economists translate the target unemployment rate and target capacity utilization rate into the level of output with which those rates will be associated. That level of output is called the target level of potential output, or simply potential output (or *potential income*, because output creates income). **Potential output** is *the output that would materialize at the target rate of unemployment and the target rate of capacity utilization.* It is the rate of output beyond which the economy would experience accelerating inflation. Potential output grows at the secular (long-term) trend rate of 2.5 to 3.5 percent per year. When the economy is in a downturn or recession, actual output is below potential output.

Potential output   Output that would materialize at the target rate of unemployment and the target rate of capacity utilization.

As you will see throughout the rest of the book, there is much debate about what the appropriate target rates of unemployment, capacity utilization, and potential income actually are. To capture that debate in the terminology some economists distinguish between high-level potential income and low-level potential income.

5 Potential income is defined as the output that will be achieved at the target rate of unemployment and at the target level of capacity utilization.

Low-level potential income is that level of income that almost all economists agree is sustainable over the long run without that level generating accelerating inflation. High-level potential income is that level of income that may be sustainable, but which may also lead to accelerating inflation. The distinction between the two can be seen by thinking back to the automobile speed example.

Most sports cars have a tachometer that tells how fast the engine is revolving. On the tach there is a yellow caution line—if you're near this line you will probably be OK; and a red double-caution line—you'd better hit the red line for only a short period. Given current institutions, the low-level potential income is the yellow line and the high-level potential income is the red line. Actual potential income—the target rate of potential income that is arrived at through political consensus—is usually between the two; it is usually closer to the yellow than to the red line.

There is debate about where the actual level of potential income is.

To determine what effect changes in the unemployment rate will have on income, we use **Okun's rule of thumb,** which states that *a 1 percentage point change in the unemployment rate will cause income to change in the opposite direction by 2.5 percent.* For example, if unemployment rises from 5 percent to 6 percent, total output of $8 trillion will fall by 2.5 percent, or $200 billion, to $7.8 trillion. In terms of number of workers, a 1 percent increase in the unemployment rate means about 1,300,000 additional people are out of work.

Okun's rule of thumb
A 1-percentage–point change in the unemployment rate will cause income in the economy to change in the opposite direction by 2.5 percent.

These figures are rough, but they give you a sense of the implications of a change. For example, say unemployment falls .2 percentage points, from 5.5 to 5.3 percent. That means about 260,000 more people have jobs and that income will be $40 billion higher than otherwise would have occurred if the increase holds for the entire year.

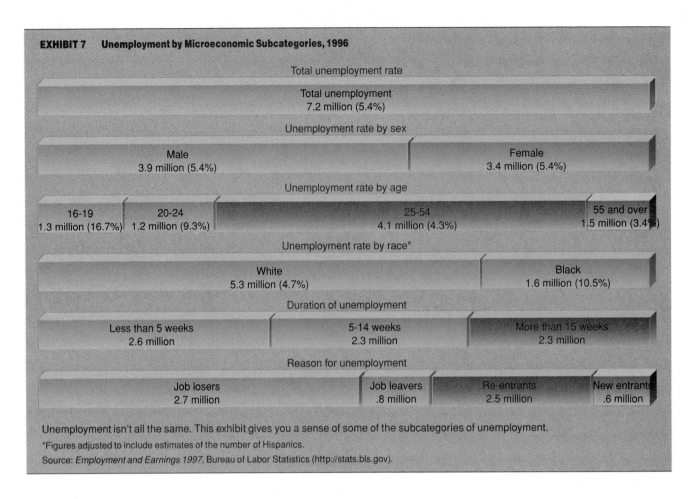

EXHIBIT 7   Unemployment by Microeconomic Subcategories, 1996

Total unemployment rate

| Total unemployment |
| 7.2 million (5.4%) |

Unemployment rate by sex

| Male | Female |
| 3.9 million (5.4%) | 3.4 million (5.4%) |

Unemployment rate by age

| 16-19 | 20-24 | 25-54 | 55 and over |
| 1.3 million (16.7%) | 1.2 million (9.3%) | 4.1 million (4.3%) | 1.5 million (3.4%) |

Unemployment rate by race*

| White | Black |
| 5.3 million (4.7%) | 1.6 million (10.5%) |

Duration of unemployment

| Less than 5 weeks | 5-14 weeks | More than 15 weeks |
| 2.6 million | 2.3 million | 2.3 million |

Reason for unemployment

| Job losers | Job leavers | Re-entrants | New entrants |
| 2.7 million | .8 million | 2.5 million | .6 million |

Unemployment isn't all the same. This exhibit gives you a sense of some of the subcategories of unemployment.

*Figures adjusted to include estimates of the number of Hispanics.

Source: *Employment and Earnings 1997*, Bureau of Labor Statistics (http://stats.bls.gov).

At the end of our discussion of unemployment, my students are usually ready to discuss some policies to deal with the problem. Since we haven't developed monetary and fiscal policy yet, we focus on institutional responses to structural and frictional unemployment, such as job training and employment-related education.

Notice I said "will be $40 billion higher than otherwise would have occurred" rather than simply saying "will increase by $40 billion." As we discussed in the growth section, generally the economy is growing as a result of increases in productivity or increases in the number of people choosing to work. Changes in either of these can cause income and employment to grow, even if there's no change in the unemployment rate. We must point this out because in the 1980s the number of people choosing to work increased substantially, significantly increasing the labor participation rate. Then, in the mid-1990s, as many large firms structurally adjusted their production methods to increase their productivity, unemployment sometimes rose, and employment fell, even as output rose. Thus, when the labor participation rate and productivity change, an increase in unemployment doesn't necessarily mean a decrease in employment or a decrease in income.

Microeconomic Categories of Unemployment

4b Some microeconomic categories of unemployment are reason for unemployment, demographic unemployment, duration of unemployment, and unemployment by industry.

In the post-World War II period, unemployment was seen primarily as cyclical unemployment, and the focus of macroeconomic policy was on how to eliminate that unemployment through a specific set of macroeconomic policies.

Understanding macroeconomic policies is important, but in the 1990s it's not enough. Unemployment has many dimensions, so different types of unemployment are susceptible to different types of policies. Today's view is that you don't use a sledge hammer to pound in finishing nails, and you don't use macro policies to deal with certain types of unemployment; instead you use micro policies. To determine where microeconomic policies are appropriate as a supplement to macroeconomic policies, economists break unemployment down into a number of categories and analyze each category separately. These categories include how people become unemployed, demographic characteristics, duration of unemployment, and industry. (See Exhibit 7.)

FROM FULL EMPLOYMENT TO THE TARGET RATE OF UNEMPLOYMENT

FROM FULL EMPLOYMENT TO THE TARGET RATE OF UNEMPLOYMENT   **ADDED DIMENSION**

As I emphasized in Chapter 1, good economists attempt to remain neutral and objective. It isn't always easy, especially since the language we use is often biased.

This problem has proved to be a difficult one for economists in their attempt to find an alternative to the concept of full employment. An early contender was the natural rate of unemployment. Economists have often used the term natural to describe economic concepts. For example, they've talked about "natural" rights and a "natural" rate of interest. The problem with this usage is that what's natural to one person isn't necessarily natural to another. The term natural often conveys a sense of "that's the way it should be." However, in describing as "natural" the rate of unemployment that an economy can achieve, economists weren't making any value judgments about whether 5.5 percent unemployment is what should, or should not, be. They simply were saying that,

given the institutions in the economy, that is what is achievable. So a number of economists objected to the use of the term *natural*.

As an alternative, a number of economists started to use the term *nonaccelerating inflation rate of unemployment (NAIRU)*, but even users of this term agreed it was a horrendous term. And so most avoided its use and shifted to the relatively neutral term, *target rate of unemployment*.

The target rate of unemployment is the rate that one believes is attainable without causing accelerating inflation. It is not determined theoretically; it is determined empirically. Economists look at what seems to be achievable and is historically normal, adjust that for structural and demographic changes they believe are occurring, and come up with the target rate of unemployment.

Inflation is *a continual rise in the price level*. The price level is an index of all prices in the economy. Even when inflation isn't roaring and inflation itself isn't a problem, the fear of inflation guides macroeconomic policy. Fear of inflation prevents governments from expanding the economy and reducing unemployment. It prevents governments from using macroeconomic policies to lower interest rates. It gets some political parties booted out of office. (Democrat Jimmy Carter lost his bid for a second U.S. presidential term in part because of high inflation at the time.) It gets others elected. (Republican George Bush won the U.S. presidency in 1988 in part because of low inflation in the late 1980s.)

A one-time rise in the price level is not inflation. Unfortunately, it's often hard to tell if a one-time rise in the price level is going to stop, so the distinction blurs in practice, but we must understand the distinction. If the price level goes up 10 percent in a month, but then remains constant, the economy doesn't have an inflation problem. Inflation is an *ongoing rise* in the price level.

From 1800 until World War II the U.S. inflation rate and price level fluctuated; sometimes the price level would rise, and sometimes the price level would fall—there would be deflation. Since World War II the price level has continually risen, which means the inflation rate (the measure of the change in prices over time) has been positive, as can be seen in Exhibit 8. The rate at which the price level rises fluctuates, but the movement has been consistently upward.

INFLATION

6a Inflation is a continual rise in the price level.

Be sure to distinguish between inflation, a persistent increase in price level, and short-run price shocks.

1d Since World War II, the U.S. inflation rate has remained positive and relatively stable.

Since inflation is a sustained rise in the general price level, one must first determine what the general price level was at a given time by creating a **price index,** *a composite of prices—a series of numbers that summarizes what happens to prices of a selection of goods (often called a market basket of goods) over time.* An index converts prices in all other years relative to that base period. There are a number of different measures of the price level. The most often used are the Producer Price Index, the GDP deflator, and the Consumer Price Index. Each has certain advantages and disadvantages.

Before introducing these official price indexes, let's work through the creation of a fictitious price index—the Colander Price Index—and calculate the associated inflation. I'll do so for 1997 and 1998 using 1997 as the base year. A price index is

Measurement of Inflation

EXHIBIT 8   Inflation since 1900

Until 1940, rises in the price level were followed by falls in the price level, keeping the price level relatively constant. Since the 1940s, inflation has almost always been positive, which means that the price level has been continually rising.   Source: U.S. Dept. of Commerce (http://www.doc.gov)

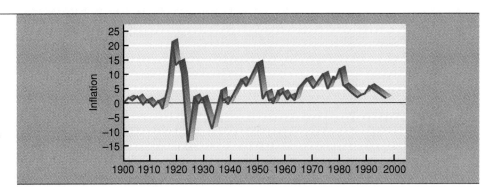

Q–8: Health care costs make up 15 percent of total expenditures. Say they rise by 10 percent, while the other components of the price index remain constant. By how much does the price index rise?

Producer Price Index (PPI)
Composite of prices of certain raw materials.

calculated by dividing the current price of a basket of goods by the base price of a basket of goods. Exhibit 9 lists a market basket of goods I consume in a base year and their associated prices in 1997 and 1998. The market basket of goods is listed in column 1 and represents the quantity of each item purchased in the base year.

The price of the market basket in each year is the sum of the expenditures on each item—the quantity of each good purchased times its market price. The market basket remains the same in each year; only the prices change. The price of the market basket in 1997 is $540 and in 1998 is $675. To calculate the Colander Price Index, divide the price of the market basket by the price of the market basket in the base year and multiply by 100. In this case 1997 is the base year, so the price index in 1998 is

$$\$675/\$540 \times 100 = 125.$$

To make sure you are following this example, calculate the Colander Price Index in 1997.

Pause for answer.

The answer is 100. The base year index is always 100 since you are dividing base years by the base year prices and multiplying by 100.

Inflation in 1998 then is the percent change in the price index. This is calculated in 1998 as

$$(125/100 - 1) \cdot 100 = 25\%.$$

But enough on price indexes in general. Let's now discuss the price indexes most commonly used when talking about inflation.

The **Producer Price Index (PPI)** is *an index or ratio of a composite of prices of a number of important raw materials, such as steel, relative to a composite of the prices of those raw materials in a base year.* It does not correctly measure inflation that most consumers are interested in (people are more interested in final goods). But it does give an early indication of which way inflation will likely head since many of the prices that make it up are the prices of raw materials used as inputs in the production of consumer goods.

EXHIBIT 9   A Simple Year-to-Year Market Basket Comparison

(1)	(2)	(3)	(4)	(5)
		Prices		Expenditures
Basket of Goods	1997	1998	1997	1998
10 pairs jeans	$20.00/pr.	$25.00/pr.	$200	$250
12 flannel shirts	15.00/shirt	20.00/shirt	180	240
100 lbs. apples	0.80/lb.	1.05/lb.	80	105
80 lbs. oranges	1.00/lb.	1.00/lb.	80	80
Total expenditures			$540	$675

MEASUREMENT PROBLEMS WITH THE CONSUMER PRICE INDEX

ADDED DIMENSION

You may have wondered about the fixed basket of goods used to calculate our fictitious price index and the CPI. The basket of goods was fixed in the base year. But buying habits change. The further in time that fixed basket is from the current basket, the worse any fixed-basket price index is at measuring inflation. Four biases that stem from this problem are called the substitution bias, the quality improvement bias, the new product bias, and the discounting bias.

Substitution bias. First of all, changes in prices will change consumption patterns. In our fictitious price index example, the price of apples rose, but the price of oranges did not. It is likely that the basket of goods in 1998 included more oranges and fewer apples than in the base year basket, in which case total expenditures in 1998 would have been less and measured inflation would have been less. Any fixed-basket price index has a substitution bias because it does not take into account the fact that when the price of one good rises, consumers substitute a cheaper item.

Quality improvement bias. The fixed basket of goods is assumed to accurately represent similar products in later years. For example, a car in 1982 is assumed to be the same as a car in 1992. But, in 1992, many cars had airbags as a standard feature. Some of the price increase for cars reflected this quality improvement, but the CPI treated it as if it were a price increase for a

comparable product sold in 1982. The CPI does not reflect quality improvements.

New product bias. A fixed basket of goods leaves no room for the introduction of new products. This would not be a problem if the prices of new products changed at about the same rate as prices of other goods in the basket, but in the 1970s this was not true. For years, the CPI did not include the price of computers whose prices were declining at a 17 percent annual rate! This resulted in the CPI overstating inflation during this period.

Discounting bias. Ever since World War II, consumers have shifted consumption toward discount purchases. The Bureau of Labor Statistics, however, treats a product sold at a discount store as different from products sold at retail stores. Products sold at discount stores are assumed to be of lower quality. To the extent, however, that they are not different, changes in the CPI overstate true inflation.

These and other problems arise because of the choices one must make when constructing a price index. The choices are what to name as the base year, what products to include in the basket, the relative importance to assign each product, and how to account for changes in the quality and for the introduction of new products. In 1996 a commission of economists suggested that, because of these biases, the CPI overstates inflation by about 1 percentage point per year.

The total output deflator, or **GDP deflator** (gross domestic product deflator), *is an index of the price level of aggregate output, or the average price of the components in total output (or GDP), relative to a base year.* GDP is a measure of the total market value of aggregate production of goods and services produced in an economy in a year. (We'll discuss the calculation of GDP in more detail in the next chapter.) A deflator is an adjustment for "too much air." In this context, it is an adjustment for inflation—so that we know how much total output would have risen if there were no inflation.

The GDP deflator is the inflation index economists generally favor because it includes the widest number of goods. As of 1995, the base period used to calculate the GDP deflator changes yearly. (Before 1995 it changed every 5 years.) Unfortunately, since it's difficult to compute, it's published only quarterly and with a fairly substantial lag. (That is, by the time the figures come out, the period the figures measure has been over for quite a while.)

Published monthly, the **Consumer Price Index (CPI)** *measures the prices of a fixed "basket" of consumer goods, weighted according to each component's share of an average consumer's expenditure.* It measures the price of a fixed "basket" of goods rather than measuring the prices of all goods. It is the index of inflation most often used in news reports about the economy and is the index most relevent to consumers. Exhibit 10 shows the relative percentages of the basket's components. As you see, housing, transportation, and food make up the largest percentages of the CPI. To give you an idea of what effect the rise in price of a component of the CPI will have on the CPI as a whole, let's say food prices rise 10 percent in a year and all other prices remain constant. Since food is about 20 percent of the total, the CPI will rise 20% ×

GDP deflator Index of the price level of aggregate output or the average price of the components in GDP relative to a base year.

Consumer Price Index (CPI) Index of inflation measuring prices of a fixed "basket" of consumer goods, weighted according to each component's share of an average consumer's expenditures.

EXHIBIT 10 Composition of CPI

The Consumer Price Index is determined by looking at the prices of goods in the categories listed in this exhibit. These categories represent the rough percentages of people's expenditures. In reality, there are Consumer Price Indexes for two population groups: (1) for all urban consumers (the urban CPI)—about 80 percent of the U.S. population—and (2) for urban wage earners and clerical workers (the wage-earner CPI)—about 32 percent of the U.S. population. The numbers that compose the CPI are collected at 85 separate locations and include prices from over 57,000 housing units and 19,000 business establishments. Source: *CPI Detailed Reports,* 1996, Bureau of Labor Statistics (http://stats.bls.gov).

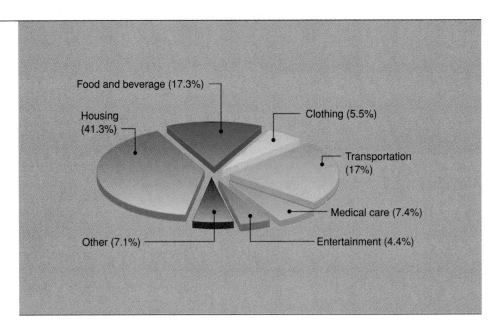

10% = 2%. The CPI and GDP deflator indexes roughly equal each other when averaged over an entire year.

Indexes are not perfect measures of inflation (see the Added Dimension box). Many economists believe that the current CPI index overstates inflation by about 1 percentage point per year and there will likely be slight modifications to the CPI index in the late 1990s.

Real and Nominal Concepts

Real output *Aggregate output adjusted for price level changes.*

One important way in which inflation indices are used is to separate changes in real output from changes in nominal output. **Real output** is *the total amount of goods and services produced, adjusted for price level changes.* It is the measure of output that would exist if the price level had remained constant. **Nominal output** is *output as measured at current prices.* For example, say total output rises from $6.4 trillion to $8 trillion. Nominal output has risen by

$$\frac{\$8 \text{ trillion} - \$6.4 \text{ trillion}}{\$6.4 \text{ trillion}} = \frac{\$1.6 \text{ trillion}}{\$6.4 \text{ trillion}} = 25\%.$$

Q–9: Nominal output has increased from $5 trillion to $6 trillion. The GDP deflator has risen by 15 percent. By how much has real output risen?

Let's say, however, the price level has risen 20 percent, from 100 percent to 120 percent. The inflation index is 120. Because the inflation index has increased, real output (nominal output adjusted for inflation) hasn't risen by 25 percent; it has risen by less than the increase in nominal output. To determine how much less, we use a formula to adjust the nominal figures to account for inflation. This is called *deflating* the nominal figures. To deflate we divide the most recent nominal figure, $8 trillion, by the price index of 120 percent (or 1.2):

$$\text{Real Output} = \frac{\text{Nominal Output}}{120} \times 100 = \frac{\$8 \text{ trillion}}{1.2} = \$6.667 \text{ trillion}.$$

That $6.667 trillion is the measure of output that would have existed if the price level had not changed, that is, the measure of real output. Real output has increased from $6.4 trillion to $6.667 trillion, or by $267 billion.

When you consider price indexes, you mustn't lose sight of the forest for the trees. Keep in mind the general distinction between real and nominal output. The concepts *real* and *nominal* and the process of adjusting from nominal to real by dividing the nominal amount by a price index will come up again and again. So whenever you see the word *real,* remember:

The "real" amount is the nominal amount divided by the price index. It is the nominal amount adjusted for inflation.

6b The "real" amount is the nominal amount divided by the price index. It is the nominal amount adjusted for inflation.

Why Does Inflation Occur?

Inflation results when more people on average raise their nominal prices than lower their nominal prices. Thus, to explain why inflation occurs we must explain why people raise their nominal prices. The logical answer is that they believe that in doing so they can get a larger slice of the total output pie for themselves. But shares of the pie are determined by relative, not nominal, prices. To see the difference, say you raise your nominal price by 10 percent, but everyone else does, too. So the prices of the goods you sell go up by 10 percent, and the prices of the goods you buy go up by 10 percent. Your nominal price has gone up, but your relative price has not, and you're no better off.

Our economy has nominal wage- and price-setting institutions in which people set their relative prices by setting a nominal price. This means that if we are careful, we can gain insight into inflation by considering a representative market and distinguishing two reasons for individuals wanting to raise their relative price (which, given our price-setting institutions, they do by raising their nominal price).

Think back to Chapter 3's discussion of the dynamic laws of supply and demand. There we saw that when the quantity demanded exceeds the quantity supplied, prices tend to rise. Exhibit 11(a) demonstrates this for an individual market. If price is initially P_0 and demand rises from D_0 to D_1, there will be upward pressure on the good's price. When the majority of industries are at close to capacity and they experience increases in demand, we say there's demand-pull pressure. The inflation that results is called **demand-pull inflation**—*inflation that occurs when the economy is at or above full employment*. Where does this increase in demand come from? It can come from numerous sources, but many economists focus on government's demands and increases in the money supply as important causes of increases in demand in markets on average.

Demand-pull inflations are generally characterized by shortages of goods and shortages of workers. Because there's excess demand, firms know that if they raise their prices, they'll still be able to sell their goods, and workers know if they raise their wages, they will still get hired.

Exhibit 11(b) shows a second possible explanation why people might raise their price in an individual market. Say one group of individuals (0-A) figured out a way to limit the quantity supplied to Q_a. To do so, they must keep suppliers A-B out of the market through some type of legal or social pressure. If they succeed, price rises from P_0 to P_1 as supply shifts to the left. When significant proportions of markets (or one very important market, such as the labor market or the oil market) experience restrictions on supply, we say that there is cost-push pressure. The resulting inflation is called **cost-push inflation**—*inflation that occurs when the economy is below full employment, with prices rising even though there are no shortages of goods or workers*.

Although demand-pull and cost-push pressures can be catalysts for starting inflation, they are not causes of continued inflation. For continued price increases, demand-pull and cost-push pressures must continue unabated. Remember, the graphs in Exhibit 11 represent individual markets; they refer to a relative price. If all people raise their relative prices, the overall price level will rise and relative price will be little affected. People will find that they will have to continually raise their relative price to maintain the initial increase. As people come to expect increases in the overall price level, they will raise their relative prices even before the overall price level has risen. Such continued demand-pull and cost-push pressures can quickly generate an accelerating expectational inflation.

In cost-push inflation, because there is no excess demand (there may actually be excess supply), firms are not sure there will be sufficient demand to sell off their goods and workers are not sure that, after raising their wage, they will all be hired, but the ones who actually do the pushing are fairly sure they won't be the ones who can't sell off their goods or the ones fired. A classic cost-push example occurred in the 1970s when OPEC raised its price on oil, triggering cost-push inflation.

The demand-pull/cost-push distinction is helpful as long as one remembers that it must be used with care. The price level is always determined by both demand

It is important to point out that, in the real world, inflation is usually the result of a combination of demand-pull and cost-push forces.

Demand-pull inflation *Inflation that occurs when the economy is at or above full employment.*

7a Cost-push inflation involves a rise in the price level resulting from restrictions on supply due to some sort of legal or social pressure. When excess demand causes the price level to rise, it is referred to as demand-pull inflation.

Cost-push inflation *Inflation that occurs when the economy is below full employment, with prices rising even though there are no shortages of goods or workers.*

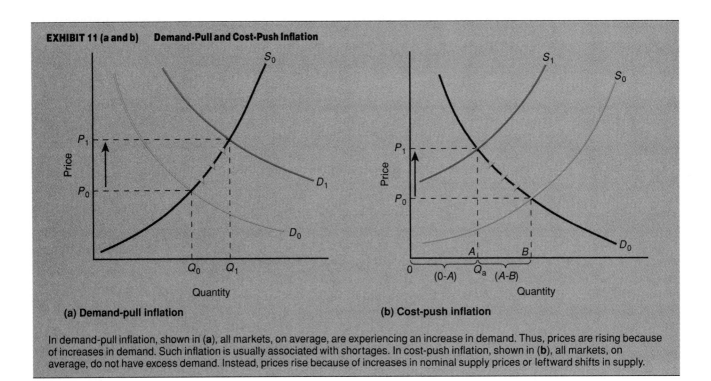

EXHIBIT 11 (a and b)   Demand-Pull and Cost-Push Inflation

(a) Demand-pull inflation

(b) Cost-push inflation

In demand-pull inflation, shown in (a), all markets, on average, are experiencing an increase in demand. Thus, prices are rising because of increases in demand. Such inflation is usually associated with shortages. In cost-push inflation, shown in (b), all markets, on average, do not have excess demand. Instead, prices rise because of increases in nominal supply prices or leftward shifts in supply.

Q-10: Why did some economists see the OPEC oil price rise as a demand-pull, rather than a cost-push, inflation?

pressures and cost pressures. In all inflations, both demand-pull and cost-push pressures play a role. As Alfred Marshall (the 19th-century English economist who originated supply and demand analysis) said, it is impossible to separate the roles of supply and demand in influencing price, just as it is impossible to separate which blade of the scissors is cutting a sheet of paper. Both sides always play a role.

To see the difficulty, let's consider the OPEC oil price rise. What would have happened if all prices rose but total quantity demanded did not rise? The result would have been unemployment, a fall in production, and a decrease in the demand for oil. Prices, on average, wouldn't have continued to rise as demand fell. But prices on average *did* continue to rise because total demand did not stay constant—it rose significantly for reasons that we'll discuss in later chapters. So some economists called it demand-pull inflation rather than cost-push inflation because, in their view, it was the expectation of demand rising that "caused" the inflation. Since inflation is an ongoing rise in prices and, in any ongoing rise, both demand and supply play a role, the cost-push/demand-pull distinction must be used carefully.

Expected and Unexpected Inflation

7b Expected inflation is the amount of inflation that people expect. Unexpected inflation is a surprise to them.

A second helpful distinction is between expected and unexpected inflation. **Expected inflation** is *inflation people expect to occur*. **Unexpected inflation** is *inflation that surprises people*.

To see why this expected/unexpected distinction is important, remember when an individual sets a price (for goods or labor) he or she is actually setting a relative price—relative to some price level that they expect to exist out there. The dynamic laws of supply and demand affect relative prices, not nominal prices.

Now let's say everyone suddenly expects the price level to rise 10 percent. Let's also say that all individual sellers want a ½ percent raise in their relative price. They're not greedy; they just want a little bit more than what they're currently getting. The relative price increase people want must be tacked onto the inflation they expect. In this case, they have to raise their money price by 10½ percent—10 percent to keep up and ½ percent to get ahead. Ten percent of the inflation is caused by expectations of inflation; ½ percent of the inflation is caused by cost-push pressures. Thus, whether or not inflation is expected makes a big difference in individuals' behavior.

Since prices and wages are often set for periods of two months to three years ahead, whether inflation is expected can play an important role in the inflation process. In the early 1970s people didn't expect the high inflation rates that did occur. When inflation hit, people just tried to keep up with it. By the end of the 1970s, people expected more inflation than actually occurred and raised their prices—and, in doing so, caused the inflation rate to increase.

Expectations of inflation play an important role in any ongoing inflation. They can snowball a small inflationary pressure into an accelerating large inflation. Individuals keep raising their prices because they expect inflation, and inflation keeps on growing because individuals keep raising their prices. That's why expectations of inflation are of central concern to economic policy makers.

Costs of Inflation

8 While inflation may not make the nation poorer, it does cause income to be redistributed, and it can reduce the amount of information that prices are supposed to convey.

Inflation has costs, but not the costs that noneconomists often associate with it. Specifically, inflation doesn't make the nation poorer. True, whenever prices go up somebody (the person paying the higher price) is worse off, but the person to whom the higher price is paid is better off. The two offset each other. So inflation does not make society on average any poorer. Inflation does, however, redistribute income from people who cannot or do not raise their prices to people who can and do raise their prices. This often creates feelings of injustice about the economic system. Thus, inflation can have significant distributional or equity effects.

A second cost of inflation is its effect on the information prices convey to people. Consider an individual who laments the high cost of housing, pointing out that it has doubled in 10 years! But if inflation averaged 7 percent a year over the past 10 years, a doubling of housing prices should be expected. In fact, with 7 percent inflation, on average *all* prices double every 10 years. That means the individual's wages have probably also doubled, so he or she is no better off and no worse off than 10 years ago. The price of housing relative to other goods, which is the relevant price for making decisions, hasn't changed. When there's inflation it's hard for people to know what is and what isn't a relative price. People's minds aren't computers, so inflation reduces the amount of information that prices can convey and causes people to make choices that do not reflect relative prices.

Be sure to relate the costs of inflation to distributional effects, and note the importance of unexpected inflation in generating these distributional effects.

Despite these costs, inflation is usually accepted by governments as long as it stays at a low rate. What scares economists is inflationary pressures above and beyond expectations of inflation. In that case, expectations of higher inflation can cause inflation to build up and compound itself. A 3 percent inflation becomes a 6 percent inflation, which in turn becomes a 12 percent inflation. Once inflation hits 5 percent or 6 percent, it's definitely no longer a little thing. Inflation of 10 percent or more is significant. While there is no precise definition, we may reasonably say that inflation has become **hyperinflation** *when inflation hits triple digits—100 percent or more per year.*

Hyperinflation *Exceptionally high inflation of, say, 100 percent or more per year.*

The United States has been either relatively lucky or wise because it has not experienced hyperinflation since the Civil War (1861–65). Other countries, such as Brazil, Israel, and Argentina, have not been so lucky (or have not followed policies as wise as the United States has). These countries have frequently had hyperinflations. But even with inflations at these levels, economies have continued to operate and, in many cases, continued to do well.

In a hyperinflation people try to spend their money quickly, but they still use the money. Let's say the U.S. price level is increasing 1 percent a day, which is a yearly inflation rate of about 4,000 percent.[1] Is an expected decrease in value of 1 percent per day going to cause you to stop using dollars? Probably not, unless you have a good alternative. You will, however, avoid putting your money into a savings account unless that savings account somehow compensates you for the expected inflation (the

---

[1] Why about 4,000 percent and not 365 percent? Because of compounding. In the second day the increase is on the initial price level *and* the 1 percent rise in price level that occurred the first day. When you carry out this compounding for all 365 days, you get almost 4,000 percent.

expected fall in the value of the dollar), and you will try to ensure your wage is adjusted for inflation. In a hyperinflation, wages, the prices firms receive, and individual savings are all in some way adjusted for inflation. Hyperinflations lead to economic institutions with built-in expectations of inflation. For example, usually in a hyperinflation the government issues indexed bonds whose value keeps pace with inflation.

Once these adjustments have been made, substantial inflations will not destroy an economy, but they certainly are not good for it. Such inflations tend to break down confidence in the monetary system, the economy, and the government.

THE INTERRELATIONSHIP OF GROWTH, INFLATION, AND UNEMPLOYMENT

In this chapter, we've talked about growth, inflation, and unemployment. Before we move on, let's briefly address their interrelationship. That interrelationship centers on trade-off between inflation on the one hand and growth and unemployment on the other. If the government could attack inflation without worrying about unemployment or growth, it probably would have solved the problem of inflation by now. Unfortunately, when the government tries to stop inflation, it often causes a recession—increasing unemployment and slowing growth. Similarly, reducing unemployment by stimulating growth tends to increase inflation. To the degree that inflation and unemployment are opposite sides of the coin, the opportunity cost of reducing unemployment is inflation. The government must make a trade-off between low unemployment and slow growth on the one hand and inflation on the other. Opportunity costs must be faced in macro as well as in micro.

CHAPTER SUMMARY

- The secular trend growth rate of the economy is 2.5 to 3.5 percent. Fluctuations around the secular trend growth rate are called *business cycles*.
- Two important causes of growth are appropriate economic incentives and people.
- Phases of the business cycle include peak, trough, upturn, and downturn.
- The target rate of unemployment is the lowest sustainable rate of unemployment possible under existing institutions. It's associated with an economy's potential income. The lower the target rate of unemployment, the higher an economy's potential income.
- The microeconomic approach to unemployment

subdivides unemployment into categories and looks at those individual components.
- A real concept is a nominal concept adjusted for inflation.
- Inflation is a continual rise in the price level. Both cost-push and demand-pull pressures play a role in any inflation.
- Expectations of inflation can provide pressure for an inflation to continue even when other causes don't exist.
- For inflation to continue, cost push and demand pull pressures must continue unabated.
- Two important costs of inflation are an equity cost and an information cost.

KEY TERMS

QUESTIONS FOR THOUGHT AND REVIEW

The number after each question represents the estimated degree of critical thinking required. (1 = almost none; 10 = deep thought.)

1. An economist has just made an argument that rules should be followed because they're rules. Which kind of economist is this person: Keynesian or Classical? Why? *(This question uses material from the section introduction.)*   *(7)*

2. If unemployment fell to 1.2 percent in World War II, why can't it be reduced to 1.2 percent in the 1990s?   *(8)*

3. The index of leading indicators has predicted all past recessions. Nonetheless it's not especially useful for predicting recessions. Explain.   *(7)*

4. Distinguish between structural unemployment and cyclical unemployment.   *(3)*

5. Does the unemployment rate underestimate or overestimate the unemployment problem? Explain.   *(5)*

6. If unemployment rises 2 percent, what will likely happen to income in the United States?   *(7)*

7. Why are expectations central to understanding inflation?   *(5)*

8. The price level of a basket of goods in 1996 was $64. The price level of that same basket of goods in 1997 was $68. If 1996 is the base year, what was the price index in 1997?   *(5)*

9. Inflation, on average, makes people neither richer nor poorer. Therefore it has no cost. True or false? Explain.   *(7)*

10. Who would be more likely to see a psychiatrist: a Keynesian economist or a Classical economist? Why? *(This question uses material from the section introduction.)*   *(8)*

11. Would you expect that inflation would generally be associated with low unemployment? Why?   *(7)*

12. How would a Classical economist likely categorize the unemployment that resulted from Sweden's welfare reform in 1996, which led part-timers to quit their jobs to collect unemployment? How would a Keynesian likely categorize the unemployment?   *(7)*

PROBLEMS AND EXERCISES

1. The following questions require library research.
   a. What are the current unemployment rate, capacity utilization rate, and rate of inflation? What do you predict they will be next year?
   b. Find some predictions for each of these figures for next year.
   c. Are these predictions consistent with your predictions? Why?
   d. In what position on the business cycle does the economy currently find itself?

2. The following questions concern statistics and economic institutions.
   a. Go to the local unemployment office and ask to see the form people fill out to collect unemployment insurance. What are the eligibility criteria?
   b. A friend shows you a newspaper article saying unemployment increased but output also increased. He says that this doesn't make sense, it must be a mistake. What do you tell your friend?
   c. Inflation is 5 percent; real output rises 2 percent. What would you expect to happen to nominal output?
   d. Real output rose 3 percent and nominal output rose 7 percent. What happened to inflation?

3. In H. G. Wells's *Time Machine*, a late Victorian time traveler arrives in England in AD 802700 to find a new race of people, the Eloi, in their idleness. Their idleness is, however, supported by another race, the Morlocks, who are underground slaves and who produce the output. If technology were such that the Elois's lifestyle could be sustained by machines, not slaves, is it a lifestyle that would be desirable? What implications does the above discussion have for unemployment?

4. In 1991, Japanese workers' average tenure with a firm was 10.9 years; in 1991 in the United States the average tenure of workers was 6.7 years.
   a. What are two possible explanations for these differences?
   b. Which system is better?
   c. In the mid-1990s Japan has experienced a recession while the United States economy has been growing. What effect will this likely have on these ratios?

5. One quarter prior to the peak in a business cycle, what is most likely happening to the following indicators (up or down)?
   a. Average workweek
   b. Employees on nonagricultural payrolls
   c. Industrial production
   d. Net change in inventories on hand and on order
   e. New business formation
   f. Personal income minus transfer payments

6. Assume that nominal output rises from $8.5 billion in 2000 to $9.0 billion in 2001. Assume also that the GDP deflator rises from 100 to 105.
   a. What is the percentage increase in nominal output?
   b. What is the percentage increase in the price index?
   c. How much has real output increased?
   d. What is the percentage increase in real output?
   e. By how much would the price index have had to rise for real income to remain constant?

ANSWERS TO MARGIN QUESTIONS

1. Regulations inhibit growth because they discourage and prevent individuals from undertaking entrepreneurial activity. Some regulation is necessary to ensure that growth is of a socially desirable type. *(159)*

2. More capital alone will not lead to growth. Technological change makes older types of capital obsolete, and investment in that older type of capital can be almost a complete waste, as was the case in the former Soviet Union. Its capital didn't embody technological changes. *(160)*

3. To the extent that your going to school increases your knowledge, it increases the social and human capital of the economy. It does not change the physical capital. *(160)*

4. Three leading indicators are the average workweek, the layoff rate, and changes in the money supply. There are others. *(164)*

5. The target rate of unemployment changed over time because (1) low inflation was incompatible with what people thought was the target rate of unemployment, and (2) demographics—the age structure of the population—changed, and people of different ages have different rates of unemployment. *(167)*

6. Keynesians emphasize that since to be counted as unemployed by the BLS one must be looking for a job, the unemployment rate does not include discouraged workers. Classicals emphasize that in order to collect unemployment benefits, some people pretend to be unemployed when they are not really unemployed. Thus, Keynesians would be more likely to view the unemployment rate as underestimating the unemployment problem. *(170)*

7. Unemployment is a hypothetical concept, and what "full employment" means is dependent on a value judgment as to what types of possibilities society owes individuals. *(170)*

8. The price index will rise by $.15 \times .1 = .015 = 1.5\%$. *(174)*

9. Real output equals the nominal amount divided by the price index. Since the price index has risen by 15%, real output equals $5.22 trillion ($6 trillion divided by 1.15). *(176)*

10. The oil price rise involved a change in relative prices. If the world money supply and aggregate demand hadn't expanded, that relative price change would have involved a temporary rise in the price level and unemployment. But aggregate demand did rise significantly, which leads some economists to call the type of inflation during that time a demand-pull inflation. *(178)*

Eight
National Income Accounting

The government is very keen on amassing statistics. . . . They collect them, add them, raise them to the nth power, take the cube root and prepare wonderful diagrams. But you must never forget that every one of these figures comes in the first instance from the village watchman, who just puts down what he damn pleases.

~ Sir Josiah Stamp (head of Britain's revenue department in the late 19th century)

After reading this chapter, you should be able to:

1 State why national income accounting is important.

2 Define GDP, GNP, and NI.

3 Calculate GDP in a simple example, avoiding double counting.

4 Explain why GDP $= C + I + G + (X - M)$.

5 Distinguish between real and nominal values.

6 State some limitations of national income accounting.

Before you can talk about macroeconomics in depth, you need to be introduced to some terminology used in macroeconomics. That terminology can be divided into two parts. The first part deals with the macroeconomic statistics you are likely to see in the newspaper—GDP and its components. The second part discusses problems of using GDP figures. Among other things it distinguishes between real and nominal (or money) concepts. **Real concepts** are *concepts adjusted for inflation;* **nominal concepts** are *concepts specified in monetary terms* with no adjustment for inflation. Real and nominal concepts are used to differentiate and compare goods and services over time and these play a central role in interpreting the movement in components of the national income accounts.

Video Series, Economics USA: Booms and Busts, Segment 3.1

In the 1930s, it was impossible for macroeconomics to exist in the form we know it today because many aggregate concepts we now take for granted either had not yet been formulated or were so poorly formulated that it was useless to talk rigorously about them. This lack of aggregate terminology was consistent with the Classical economists' lack of interest in the aggregate approach in the 1930s; they preferred to focus on microeconomics.

With the advent of Keynesian macroeconomics in the mid-1930s, development of a terminology to describe macroeconomic aggregates became crucial. Measurement is a necessary step towards rigor. A group of Keynesian economists set out to develop an aggregate terminology and to measure the aggregate concepts they defined so that people would have concrete terms to use when talking about

NATIONAL INCOME ACCOUNTING

I often mention the old adage here—there are "lies, damned lies, and statistics."

1 National income accounting enables us to measure and analyze how much a nation is producing and consuming.

National income accounting A set of rules and definitions for measuring economic activity in the aggregate economy.

Measuring Total Economic Output of Goods and Services

2a Gross domestic product (GDP): Aggregate final output of residents and businesses in an economy in a one-year period.

Throughout the material on national income accounting, I like to refer to the circular flow diagram to show where the income and output measures fit in and how they are related.

2b Gross national product (GNP): Aggregate final ouputut of citizens and businesses of an economy in a one-year period.

Take some extra time out of your lecture to concentrate on the difference between GDP and GNP. This distinction is often unclear to students.

GDP is output produced within a country's borders; GNP is output produced by a country's citizens.

Q–1: Which is higher: Kuwait's GDP or its GNP? Why?

Calculating GDP

macroeconomic problems. Their work (for which two of them, Simon Kuznets and Richard Stone, received the Nobel prize) is called **national income accounting**—*a set of rules and definitions for measuring economic activity in the aggregate economy—that is, in the economy as a whole.*

National income accounting provides a way of measuring total, or aggregate, production. In national income accounting, aggregate economic production is broken down into subaggregates (such as consumption, investment, and personal income); national income accounting defines the relationship among these subaggregates. In short, national income accounting enables us to measure and analyze how much the nation is producing and consuming.

In the last chapter I introduced you to economists' primary measure of domestic output: real gross domestic product (real GDP). **Gross domestic product (GDP)** is *the total market value of all final goods and services produced in an economy in a one-year period.* GDP is probably the single most-used economic measure. When economists, journalists, and other analysts talk about the economy, they continually discuss GDP, how much it has increased or decreased, and what it's likely to do.

Up until 1992, the United States (unlike the rest of the world) used gross national product as its primary measure of aggregate output. Economic issues are becoming internationalized, and national income accounting has been affected by that internationalization. In 1992, the United States followed the rest of the world and switched to gross domestic product as its primary measure of aggregate output.

Whereas gross domestic product measures the economic activity that occurs *within* a *country,* the economic activity of the citizens and businesses *of a country* is measured by **gross national product (GNP)**—*the aggregate final output of citizens and businesses of an economy in a one-year period.* So the economic activity of U.S. citizens working abroad is counted in U.S. GNP but isn't counted in U.S. GDP. Similarly for the foreign economic activity of U.S. companies. However, the income of a Mexican or German person or business working in the United States isn't counted in U.S. GNP but is counted in U.S. GDP. Thus, GDP describes the economic output within the physical borders of a country while GNP describes the economic output produced by the citizens of a country. To move from GDP to GNP one must add *net foreign factor income* to GDP. **Net foreign factor income** is defined as *the income from foreign domestic factor sources minus foreign factor incomes earned domestically.* Put another way, one must add the foreign income of one's citizens and subtract the income of residents who are not citizens.

For many countries there's a significant difference between GNP and GDP. For example, consider Kuwait. Its citizens have significant foreign income—income that far exceeds the income of the foreigners in Kuwait. This means that Kuwait's GNP (the income of its citizens) far exceeds its GDP (the income of its residents). For the United States, however, foreign output of U.S. businesses and people for the most part offsets the output of foreign businesses and people within the United States. Kuwait's net foreign factor income has been large and positive, while that of the U.S. has been minimal. In this chapter I focus on GDP, since it is the primary measure presented in government statistics.

Aggregate final output (GDP) consists of millions of different services and products: apples, oranges, computers, haircuts, financial advice. . . . To arrive at total output, somehow we've got to add them all together into a composite measure. Say we produced 7 oranges plus 6 apples plus 12 computers. We have not produced 25 com-applorgs. You can't add apples and oranges and computers. You can only add like things (things that are measured in the same units). For example, 2 apples + 4 apples = 6 apples. If we want to add unlike things, we must convert them into like things. We do that by multiplying each good by its *price*. Economists call this *weighting* the importance of each good by its price. For example, if you have 4 pigs and 4 horses and you price pigs at $200 each and horses at $400 each, the horses are weighted as being twice as important as pigs.

Multiplying the quantity of each good by its market price changes the terms in which we discuss each good from a quantity of a specific product to a *value* measure of that good. For example, when we multiply 6 apples by their price, 25¢ each, we get $1.50; $1.50 is a value measure. Once all goods are expressed in that value measure, they can be added together.

Take the example of seven oranges and six apples. (For simplicity let's forget the computers, haircuts, and financial advice.) If the oranges cost 50¢ each, their total value is $3.50; if the apples cost 25¢ each, their total value is $1.50. Their values are expressed in identical measures, so we can add them together. When we do so, we don't get 13 orples; we get $5 worth of apples and oranges.

If we follow that same procedure with all the final goods and services produced in the economy in the entire year, multiplying the quantity produced by the price per unit, we have all the economy's outputs expressed in units of value. If we then add up all these units of value, we have that year's gross domestic product.

There are two important aspects to remember about GDP. First, GDP represents a flow (an amount per year), not a stock (an amount at a particular moment of time). Second, GDP refers to the market value of *final* output. Let's consider these statements separately.

GDP Is a Flow Concept   In economics it's important to distinguish between flows and stock. Say a student just out of college tells you she earns $8,000. You'd probably think, "Wow! She's got a low-paying job!" That's because you implicitly assume she means $8,000 per year. If you later learned that she earns $8,000 per week, you'd quickly change your mind. The confusion occurred because how much you earn is a *flow* concept; it has meaning only when a time period is associated with it: so much per week, per month, per year. A *stock* concept is the amount of something at a given point in time. No time interval is associated with it. Your weight is a stock concept. You weigh 150 pounds; you don't weigh 150 pounds per week.

GDP is a flow concept, the amount of total final output a country produces per year. The *per year* is often left unstated, but it is important to keep in your mind that it's essential. GDP is usually reported quarterly or every three months, but it is reported on an *annualized basis,* meaning the U.S. Department of Commerce, which compiles GDP figures, uses quarterly figures to estimate total output for the whole year.

The store of wealth, on the other hand, is a stock concept. The stock equivalent to National Income Accounts is the **Wealth Accounts**—*a balance sheet of an economy's stock of assets and liabilities.* These accounts have recently been developed for the United States, making the U.S. National Income Accounts consistent with the United Nations System of National Accounts, which uses an integrated system of

GDP measures economic activity; it adds together all goods and services weighted by their importance.

Two important aspects to remember about GDP are:

1. GDP represents a flow; and

2. GDP represents the market value of final output.

Q-2: How do Wealth Accounts differ from National Income Accounts?

	Dollars (in trillions)		Percent of Component
Private net worth	$24		100%
Tangible wealth		$10.5	
Owner-occupied real estate			$7.5 ... 31
Consumer durables			2.5 ... 10
Other			0.5 ... 2
Financial wealth		13.5	
Corporate equities			4.2 ... 18
Noncorporate equities			2.6 ... 11
Other (Pension reserves, life insurance, etc.)			6.7 ... 28
Government net financial assets	−3.9		100
Federal		−3.6	92
State and local		−0.3	8
Total net worth	**20.1**		

EXHIBIT 1   U.S. National Wealth Accounts in 1994 (net worth)

Source: Bureau of Economic Analysis (http://www.bea.doc.gov) and Board of Governors, Federal Reserve (http://www.bog.frb.fed.us)

Sir Richard Stone—Nobel prize, 1984, for work on national accounting. © *The Nobel Foundation.*

income and wealth accounts. Exhibit 1 shows a summary account of U.S. net worth from the Wealth Accounts for the United States in 1996. These are stock measures; they exist at a moment of time. For example, on December 31, 1994, the accounting date for these accounts, U.S. private net worth was $24 trillion.

GDP Measures Final Output   As a student in my first economics class, I was asked to tell how to calculate GDP. I said, "Add up the value of the goods and services produced by all the companies in the United States to arrive at GDP." I was wrong (which is why I remember it). Many goods produced by one firm are sold to other firms, which use those goods to make something else. GDP doesn't measure total transactions in an economy; it measures *final output.* When one firm sells products to another firm for use in production of yet another good, the first firm's products aren't considered final output. They're **intermediate products**—*products used as input in the production of some other product.* To count intermediate goods as well as final goods as part of GDP would be to double count them. An example of an intermediate good would be wheat sold to a cereal company. If we counted both the wheat (the intermediate good) and the cereal (the final good) made from that wheat, the wheat would be double counted. Double counting would significantly overestimate final output.

If we did not eliminate intermediate goods, a change in organization would look like a change in output. Say one firm that produced steel merged with a firm that produced cars. Both together then produce exactly what each did separately before the merger. Final output hasn't changed, nor has intermediate output. The only difference is that the intermediate output of steel is now internal to the firm. Using only each firm's sales of goods to final consumers (and not sales to other firms) as one's measure of GDP prevents mere changes in organization from affecting the measure of output.

Ask your students to give a few examples of intermediate products and final products. I also like to work through an example of the value added approach to calculating GDP.

Two Ways of Eliminating Intermediate Goods   There are two ways to eliminate intermediate goods from the measure of GDP. One is to calculate only final output. To do so, firms would have to separate goods they sold to consumers from intermediate goods used to produce other goods. For example, each firm would report how much of its product it sold to consumers and how much it sold to other producers for use that year in production of other goods; one would eliminate the latter to exclude double counting.

A second way to eliminate double counting is to follow the value added approach. **Value added** is *the increase in value that a firm contributes to a product or service.* It is calculated by subtracting intermediate goods (the cost of materials that a firm uses to produce a good or service) from the value of its sales. For instance, if a firm buys $100 worth of thread and $10,000 worth of cloth and uses them in making a thousand pairs of jeans which are sold for $20,000, the firm's value added is not $20,000; it is $9,900 ($20,000 in sales minus the $10,100 in intermediate goods that the firm bought).

Value added   *The increase in value that a firm contributes to a product or service. It is calculated by subtracting the cost of materials a firm uses to produce a good or service from the value of its sales.*

3 To avoid double counting, you must eliminate intermediate goods, either by calculating only final output (expenditures approach), or by calculating only final income (income approach) by using the value added approach.

Exhibit 2 provides another example. It gives the cost of materials (intermediate goods) and the value of sales of various businesses who sell to one another. Say we want to measure the contribution to GDP made by a vendor who sells 200 ice cream cones at $2.50 each (they're good cones) for total sales of $500. The vendor bought his cones and ice cream from a middleperson at a cost of $400, who in turn paid the cone factory and ice cream maker a total of $250. The farmer who sold the cream to the factory got $100. Adding up all these transactions, we get $1,250, but that includes intermediate goods. Either by counting only the final value of the vendor's sales, $500, or by adding the value added at each stage of production (column III), we eliminate intermediate sales and arrive at the street vendor's contribution to GDP of $500.

Value added is calculated by subtracting the cost of materials from the value of sales at each stage of production. The aggregate value added at each stage of production is, by definition, precisely equal to the value of final sales, since it excludes all intermediate products. In Exhibit 2, the equality of the value added approach and the final sales approach can be seen by comparing the vendor's final sales of $500 (row 4, column II) with the $500 value added (row 5, column III).

EXHIBIT 2   Value Added Approach Eliminates Double Counting

Participants	I Cost of Materials	II Value of Sales	III Value Added	Row
Farmer	$ 0	$ 100	$100	1
Cone factory and ice cream maker	100	250	150	2
Middleperson (final sales)	250	400	150	3
Vendor	400	500	100	4
Totals	$750	$1,250	$500	5

Calculating GDP: Some Examples   To make sure you understand what value added is and what makes up GDP, let's consider some sample transactions and determine what value they add and whether they should be included in GDP. Let's first consider second-hand sales: When you sell your two-year-old car, how much value has been added? The answer is none. The sale involves no current output, so there's no value added. If, however, you sold the car to a used car dealer for $2,000 and he resold it for $2,500, $500 of value has been added—the used-car dealer's efforts transferred the car from someone who didn't want it to someone who did. I point this out to remind you that GDP is not only a measure of the production of goods; it is a measure of the production of goods *and services.*

Now let's consider a financial transaction. Say you sell a bond (with a face value of $1,000) that you bought last year. You sell it for $1,200 and pay $100 commission to the dealer through whom you sell it. What value is added to final output? You might be tempted to say that $200 of value has been added, since the value of the bond has increased by $200. GDP, however, refers only to value that is added as the result of production or services, not to changes in the values of financial assets. Therefore the price at which you buy or sell the bond is irrelevant to the question at hand. The only value that is added by the sale is the transfer of that bond from someone who doesn't want it to someone who does. Thus, the only value added as a result of economic activity is the dealer's commission, $100. The remaining $1,100 (the $1,200 you got from the bond minus the $100 commission you paid) is a transfer of an asset from one individual to another, but such transfers do not enter into GDP calculations. Only production of goods and services enters into GDP.

Let's consider a different type of financial transaction: The government pays an individual social security benefits. What value is added? Clearly no production has taken place, but money has been transferred. As in the case of the bond, only the cost of transferring it—not the amount that gets transferred—is included in GDP. This is accomplished by including in GDP government expenditures on goods and services, but not the value of government transfers. Thus, social security payments, welfare payments, and veterans' benefits do not enter into calculations of GDP. That's why the government can have a $1.6 trillion budget but only $520 billion ($1.6 trillion minus $1080 billion of transfer payments) is included in GDP.

Finally let's consider the work of a housespouse. (See the Added Dimension Box for further discussion of this issue.) How much value does it add to economic activity in a year? Clearly if the housespouse is any good at what he or she does, a lot of value is added. Taking care of the house and children is hard work. Estimates of the yearly value of a housespouse's services are often in the $35,000 to $45,000 range. Even though much value is added and hence, in principle, housespouse services should be part of GDP, by convention a housespouse contributes nothing to GDP. GDP measures only *market activities;* since housespouses are not paid, their value added is not included in GDP. This leads to some problems in measurement. For example, suppose a woman divorces her housespouse and then hires him to continue cleaning her house for $20,000 per year. Then he will be contributing $20,000 value added. That, since it is a market transaction, is included in GDP.

The housespouse example shows that the GDP measure has some problems. There are other areas in which it also has problems, but these are best left for

Q–3: If a used car dealer buys a car for $2,000 and resells it for $2,500, how much has been added to GDP?

To reinforce the national income identity, I draw a picture of a dollar bill on the blackboard, representing the value of the output for a hypothetical economy. Then I divide the dollar among the factors of production, leaving the profit residual for last, representing the return to entreprenurial skill. The students can see clearly through this demonstration that the total value of output is exhausted as payments are made to factors of production, and thus they see the identity between income and output.

Q–4: How can the government have a $1.6 trillion budget but only have $520 billion of that included in GDP?

A provocative discussion topic is whether the failure of the National Accounts to include spousal housework is or is not discriminating against women.

Although in the example in the book the housespouse is a man, the reality is that most housespouses are women. The fact that GDP doesn't include women is seen, by some, as a type of discrimination against women who work at home since their work is not counted as part of the domestic product. One answer for why it is not counted is that housework does not involve a market transaction and hence could not be measured. That makes some sense, but it does not explain why the services houses provide to homeowners are estimated and included in GDP. Why can't housework also be estimated?

The answer is that it can be estimated, and my suspicion is that not including housespouses' services in GDP does represent the latent discrimination against women that was built into the culture in the 1930s. That latent discrimination against women was so deep that it wasn't even noticed. Anyone who has seen the movie *Rosie the Riveter*, which shows

government programs to get women out from wartime employment and back into their role in the home, will have a good sense of the cultural views of people in the mid-1900s and earlier.

In thinking about whether GDP is biased against women it is important to remember that the concepts we use are culturally determined and, over time, as cultural views change, the concepts can no longer match our changed views. There is no escaping the fact that language is value-loaded. But so, too, is our attempt to point out the values in language. There are many other ways in which GDP makes arbitrary choices and discriminates against groups. The major discussion of the fact that latent discrimination against women was embodied in GDP accounting itself reflects our current values, just as not including housespouses' work reflected earlier values.

intermediate courses. What's important for an introductory economics student to remember is that numerous decisions about how to handle various types of transactions had to be made to get a workable measure. Overall, the terminology of national income accounting is a model of consistency. It focuses on measuring final market output for the entire economy.

The National Income Accounting Identity

National income accounting identity
The relationship defined between output and income whereby one equals the other.

For the implications of accounting identities for political rhetoric, see Chapter 7 in *Case Studies in Economics.*

National income accounting is a form of accounting to which you were introduced in Chapter 5. Accounting is a way of keeping track of things. It is based on certain identities; for a firm, its cost plus profit equals revenues because they are identical to revenues. National income accounting is no different. It too is based on an identity. By definition, whenever a good or service (output) is produced, somebody receives an income for producing it. Thus the **national income accounting identity** is *the accounting equality of output and income.* This identity is subject to a variety of adjustments for taxes paid by households and businesses, but those adjustments are not the main concern here. (Appendix A discusses the adjustments.) Our main concern is with the overall identity, and its implications for our thinking about the aggregate economy can be seen in Exhibit 3, which illustrates the circular flow of income in an economy.[1]

By looking at Exhibit 3 you can see the overall flows of income and expenditures in the economy. The top half of the flows (Flow 1) shows the income households receive for supplying their factor services. The bottom half shows the outflow of expenditures individuals make to firms for the goods and services they buy. The two sides of the flow suggest that there might be two approaches to calculating GDP, and there are; there is the *income approach* and the *expenditures approach*.

In the income approach, we look at the top flow. In the expenditures approach we look at the bottom flow. Let's briefly consider both of these approaches. (In Appendix A we look at the two approaches in detail.)

The Income Approach   The income approach to measuring GDP adds up payments by firms to households called factor payments, to arrive at **national income** (NI), *total income earned by citizens and businesses in a country.* Firms make payments to households for supplying their services as factors of production (Flow 1). These

2c National income is the total income earned by citizens and businesses in a country.

---

[1]An *identity* is a statement of equality that's "true by definition." In algebra, an identity is sometimes written as a triple equal sign ($\equiv$). It is more equal than simply equal. How something can be more equal than equal is beyond me, too, but I'm no mathematician.

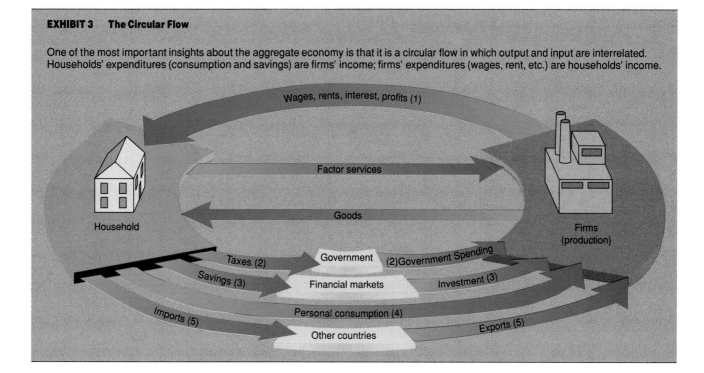

EXHIBIT 3   The Circular Flow

One of the most important insights about the aggregate economy is that it is a circular flow in which output and input are interrelated. Households' expenditures (consumption and savings) are firms' income; firms' expenditures (wages, rent, etc.) are households' income.

payments are broken up into employee compensation, rent, interest, and profits. *Employee compensation* is payments for labor such as wages and salaries. *Rents* are payments for the use of land and buildings. *Interest* includes payments for loans by households to firms. *Profits* are the payments to the owners of the firms; it is what's left over after employee compensation, rents, and interest have been paid out.

Exhibit 4 shows these components for the United States and selected countries. It lists the national income of countries and the components in absolute amounts and in percentages for the US, and in percentages for the remaining countries. As you can see, in all countries compensation to employees is the largest component of national income. When businesses are trying to predict what will likely happen to demand for their goods, they often focus on **disposable personal income**—which is *roughly equal to national income less taxes paid by individuals plus transfer payments made to individuals.* The far right column shows disposable personal income. The importance of employee compensation in income makes it a key statistic that economists focus on. A second key statistic is profits. When profits are high, firms are doing well. One final word of caution: In each country statistics are collected using slightly different methods. This makes international comparison difficult.

Use the circular flow diagram once again to illustrate the flows of income from production.

Q–5: What is the largest factor payments component of national income for the United States?

EXHIBIT 4   National or Domestic Income Breakdown for Selected Countries

(1)	(2)		(3)		(4)		(5)		(6)		(7)
Country	National Income (Billions of $)	=	Employee Compensation (% of NI)	+	Rents (% of NI)	+	Interest (% of NI)	+	Profits (% of NI)	=	Disposable Personal Income (% of NI)
U.S.	$6151		$4449		$127		$403		$1177		$5589
	100%		72%		2%		7%		19%		91%
Japan	4330		66		8		6		19		79
Germany	1829		72		2		7		19		85
United Kingdom	910		62		2		7		29		86
Canada	566		72		7		10		11		92

Source: National Accounts, OECD, (http://www.oecd.org), and embassies of countries.

EXHIBIT 5   Breakdown of GDP for Selected Countries

Country	Nominal GDP (U.S. $ in billions)	Personal Consumption (% of GDP)	Gross Private Investment (% of GDP)	Government Expenditures (% of GDP)	Exports (% of GDP)	Imports (−% of GDP)
United States	$7576	68%	15%	18%	11%	−12%
Brazil	554	63	21	15	9	−7
Germany	2045	57	22	20	23	−22
Japan	4590	60	28	10	9	−8
Pakistan	52	74	17	11	17	−20
Tunisia	16	56	23	25	40	−44
Tanzania	34	93	28	8	27	−56

Source: *World Development Report,* 1996, The World Bank (http://www.world.bank.org) and *Survey of Current Business,* Bureau of Economic Analysis. (Data for U.S. is for 1996; data for other countries is for 1994).

4 GDP=C+I+G+(X−M) is an accounting identity because it is defined as true.

The Expenditures Approach   Now let's turn to the bottom half of Exhibit 3, which gives us a picture (Flows 2–5) of the components of expenditures. Specifically, gross domestic product is equal to the sum of these four categories of expenditures: GDP = C + I + G + (X − M), where C = Consumption, I = Investment, G = Government Consumption and Investment, and (X − M) = Net exports. Let's consider each of these categories in relation to the flows in Exhibit 3.

Personal Consumption   When individuals receive income, they can either spend it on domestic goods, save it, pay taxes, or spend it on foreign goods. These four alternatives are the channels through which income is brought back into the spending stream. The largest and most important of the flows is consumption expenditure (Flow 4). It is also the most obvious way in which income received is returned to firms. The other three flows are slightly more complicated.

Investment   Let's next consider the savings/investment flow through the financial sector (Flow 3). The portion of their income that individuals save leaves the spending stream and goes into financial markets. If these financial markets are working properly they translate that savings back into the spending flow by lending it to individuals who want to spend. Business spending on equipment, structures, and inventories is counted as investment.

Government Consumption and Investment   Let's next consider the taxes/transfer flow (Flow 2) through government. When individuals pay taxes, those taxes are either spent by government on goods and services or are returned to individuals in the form of transfer payments. The transfer payments are spent and included in consumption or saved and channeled to investment. Notice also that there is a connection drawn between the government and the financial market. That's there because if the amount government takes in does not match the amount government spends (i.e., if it runs a deficit), it must borrow from financial markets to make up the difference.

Q–6: What are the four components of expenditures in national income?

Net Exports   Finally, let's consider individuals' spending on foreign goods; that spending escapes the system, and does not add to domestic production. Spending on foreign goods, imports, is subtracted from total expenditures. That flow out is offset by a flow in—foreign demand for U.S goods; that is, U.S. exports (Flow 5). Exports are added to total expenditures. Usually these flows are combined and we talk about net exports.

All expenditures fall into one or another of these four divisions—consumption, investment, government spending, or net exports—so by adding up these four categories, we get total expenditures on U.S. goods and services minus U.S. residents' expenditures on foreign goods. By definition, in national income accounting, those total expenditures on U.S. goods and services equal (with some adjustments for taxes and such) the total amount of production of goods and services (GDP). Exhibit 5 gives the breakdown for GDP of selected countries.

NATIONAL INCOME ACCOUNTING AND DOUBLE-ENTRY BOOKKEEPING

The key to all accounting, including national income accounting, is double-entry bookkeeping, a system of financial record keeping invented in Italy and attributed to Luigi Pacioli (1494). Double-entry bookkeeping is based on redundancy. It requires that accounting terms be defined in such a way that the cost side of the ledger is kept exactly equal to the income side. Since they're exactly equal, in theory one need calculate only one of the two sides, but in practice both sides are calculated, so the accountant can check his or her work. If both sides independently add up to the same figure, it's likely that no mistake was made.

In the national income accounts kept by the U.S. Department of Commerce, the two sides of the ledger are the expenditure accounts and the income accounts. Every entry on one side of the accounts has an offsetting entry on the other side. Whenever production (an increase in output) takes place on the expenditure side, there is a simultaneous increase in income entered on the income side.

As discussed in Chapter 5, in balance sheet accounting (accounting measuring the assets and liabilities of an individual, firm, or country) assets equal liabilities plus net worth. Net worth plays the swing role in balance sheet accounting that profits play in income accounting. *Net worth* is defined as the amount that remains when liabilities are subtracted from assets:

$$\text{Net worth} = \text{Assets} - \text{Liabilities.}$$

Net worth is recorded on the liabilities side of the ledger. Adding liabilities and net worth, we have

$$\text{Assets} = \text{Liabilities} + \text{Net worth.}$$

Substituting in for net worth, we have

$$\text{Assets} = \text{Liabilities} + (\text{Assets} - \text{Liabilities})$$

or

$$\text{Assets} \equiv \text{Assets.}$$

Since by substituting we can get the same term on both sides of the equation, the statement "Assets = Liabilities + Net worth" is true by definition.

In national income accounting, profit plays the swing role. Profits are what is left after all other forms of income are accounted for. Profits are defined as the difference between total output and other income and are counted as income. So we have

$$\text{Output} = \text{Other income} + \text{Profits}$$

$$\text{Profits} = \text{Output} - \text{Other income.}$$

Substituting in for profits gives

$$\text{Output} = \text{Other income} + \text{Output} - \text{Other income.}$$

Therefore,

$$\text{Output} = \text{Output.}$$

This 17th-century engraving "The Money Lender," shows that careful bookkeeping and accounting have been around for a long time. *Bleichroeder Print Collection, Baker Library, Harvard Business School.*

Notice that personal consumption expenditures is the largest component of expenditures in all countries and that there is a rough similarity of the other components in percentage terms.

Equality of Income and Expenditure   The value of the employee compensation, rents, interest, and profits (the flow along the top in Exhibit 3) equals the value of goods bought (the flow along the bottom). How are these values kept exactly equal? That's the secret of double-entry bookkeeping: output must always equal income.

The definition of profit is the key to the equality. Recall that *profit* is defined as what remains after all the firm's other income (employee compensation, rent, and interest) is paid out. For example, say a firm has a total output of $800 and that it paid $400 in wages, $200 in rent, and $100 in interest. The firm's profit is total output less these payments. Profit equals $800 − $700 = $100.

The accounting identity even works if a firm incurs a loss. Say that instead of paying $400 in wages, the firm paid $700, along with its other payments of $200 in rent and $100 in interest. Total output is still $800, but total payments are $1,000. *Profits,* still defined as total output minus payments, are negative: $800 − $1,000 = (−$200). There's a loss of $200. Adding that loss to other income ($1,000 + (−$200))

The *Survey of Current Business,* a Department of Commerce publication, is one of the best sources of GDP figures.

gives total income of $800—which is identical to the firm's total output of $800. It is no surprise that total output and total income, defined in this way, are equal.

The national income accounting identity (Total output = Total income) allows us to calculate GDP either by adding up all values of final outputs (the *expenditures approach*) or by adding up the values of all earnings or income (the *income approach*).

USING GDP FIGURES

The most important way GDP figures are used is to make comparisons of one country's production with another country's and of one year's production with another year's.

Comparing GDP among Countries

Video Series, Economics U$A: Booms and Busts, Segment 3.2

Most countries use somewhat similar measures to calculate GDP. Thus, we can compare various countries' GDP levels and get a sense of their economic size and power.

Per capita GDP is another measure often used to compare various nations' income. To arrive at per capita GDP, we divide GDP by the country's total population. Doing so gives you a sense of the relative standards of living of the people in various countries.

If you look up some of these measures, some of the comparisons should give you cause to wonder. For example, Bangladesh has per capita GDP of only about $210, compared to U.S. per capita GDP of about $28,000. How do people in Bangladesh live? In answering that question, remember GDP measures market transactions. In poor countries, individuals often grow their own food (subsistence farming), build their own shelter, and make their own clothes. None of those activities are market activities, and while they're sometimes estimated and included in GDP, they often aren't estimated accurately. They certainly aren't estimated at the value of what these activities would cost in the United States. Also, remember GDP is an aggregate measure that values activities at the market price in that society. The relative prices of the products and services a consumer buys often differ substantially among countries. In New York City, $1200 a month gets you only a small studio apartment. In Haiti, $1200 a month might get you a mansion with four servants. Thus, GDP can be a poor measure of the relative living standards in various countries.

Q–7: Why are national income statistics not especially good for discussing the income of developing countries?

To avoid this problem in comparing per capita GDP, economists often calculate a different concept, *purchasing power parity,* which adjusts for the different relative prices among countries before making comparisons.

I like to ask my students to discuss whether they think that GDP per capita is a useful measure of economic welfare.

Just how much of a difference the two approaches can make can be seen in the case of China. In May 1992, the International Monetary Fund (IMF) changed from calculating China's GDP using the exchange rate approach to calculating it using the purchasing power parity approach. Upon doing so, the IMF calculated that China's GDP grew over 400 percent in one year. Per capita income rose from about $300 to well over $1,000. When methods of calculation can make that much difference, one must use statistics very carefully.

Economic Welfare over Time

Using GDP figures to compare the economy's performance over time is much better than relying merely on our perceptions.

A second way in which the GDP concept is used is to compare one year with another. Using GDP figures to compare the economy's performance over time is much better than relying merely on our perceptions. Most of us have heard the phrase, *the good old days.* Generally we hear it from our parents or grandparents, who are lamenting the state of the nation or economy. In comparing today to yesterday, they always seem to picture the past with greener grass, an easier life, and happier times. Compared to the good old days, today always comes out a poor second.

Our parents and grandparents may be right when they look back at particular events in their own lives, but if society were to follow such reasoning, it would conclude that all of history has been just one long downhill slide, worsening every year. In actuality, perceptions of the good old days are likely to be biased. It's easy to remember the nice things of yesterday while forgetting its harsh realities. Relying on past perception is not an especially helpful way of making accurate comparisons.

A preferable way is to rely on data that are not changed by emotion or anything else. Looking at GDP over time provides a way of using data to make comparisons over time. For example, say we compare U.S. GDP in 1932 ($58 billion) to GDP in 1996 ($7.6 trillion). Would it be correct to conclude the economy had grown 130 times larger? No. As we discussed in the last chapter, GDP figures aren't affected by emotions, but they are affected by inflation. To make comparisons over time, we can't confine ourselves to a simple look at what has happened to GDP.

In our earlier discussion of supply and demand, I spent quite a bit of space distinguishing between a rise in the price level and a change in relative prices. That's because the distinction is important. A similar important distinction economists make is in comparing output levels over time. Suppose prices of all goods and hence the price level go up 25 percent in one year, but outputs of all goods remain constant. GDP will have risen 25 percent, but will society be any better off? No. To compare GDP over time, you must distinguish between increases in GDP due to inflation and increases in GDP that represent real increases in production and income.

5 A real concept is a nominal concept adjusted for inflation.

Real and Nominal GDP

As I stated in the last chapter, to separate increases in GDP caused by inflation from increases in GDP that represent real increases in production and income, economists distinguish between **nominal GDP** (*GDP calculated at existing prices*) and **real GDP** (*nominal GDP adjusted for inflation*). This distinction is sufficiently important to warrant repetition in this chapter. To adjust nominal output for inflation we create a price index (a measure of how much the price level has risen from one year to the next) and divide nominal GDP by that price index. That price index is the GDP deflator I introduced in the last chapter.[2]

For example, say the price level rises 10 percent (from a GDP deflator of 1 to a GDP deflator of 1.1) and nominal GDP rises from $7 trillion to $8 trillion. Part of that rise in nominal GDP represents the 10 percent rise in the price level. If you divide nominal GDP, $8 trillion, by the new GDP deflator, 1.1, you get $7.27 trillion (the amount GDP would have been if the price level had not risen). That $7.27 trillion is called real GDP. To decide whether production has increased or decreased over time, we simply compare the real income. In this example, real income has risen from $7 trillion to $7.27 trillion, so we can conclude that the real economy has grown by 27/700, or 3.9 percent.

Real GDP is what is important to a society because it measures what is *really* produced. Considering nominal GDP instead of real GDP can distort what's really happening. Let's say the U.S. price level doubled tomorrow. Nominal GDP would also double, but would the United States be better off? No.

We'll use the distinction between real and nominal continually in this course, so to firm up the concepts in your mind, let's go through another example. Consider Somalia in 1987 and 1988, when nominal GDP rose from 159 billion to 268 billion (measured in their local currency units) while the GDP deflator rose from 100 percent to 173.5 percent. Dividing nominal GDP in 1988 by the GDP deflator, we see *real GDP* fell by over 2 percent. So not only did Somalia's economy not grow; it actually shrank.

Nominal GDP *GDP calculated at existing prices.*

Real GDP *Nominal GDP adjusted for inflation.*

Q–8: If real income has risen from $4 trillion to $4.2 trillion and the price level went up by 10 percent, by how much has nominal income risen?

The quotation at this chapter's start pointed out that statistics can be misleading. I want to reiterate that here. Before you can work with statistics, you need to know how they are collected and the problems they have. If you don't, the results can be disastrous. Here's a possible scenario:

A student who isn't careful looks at the data and discovers an almost perfect relationship between imports and investment occurring in a Latin American country. Whenever capital goods imports go up, investment of capital goods goes up by an equal proportion. The student develops a thesis based on that insight, only to learn

SOME LIMITATIONS OF NATIONAL INCOME ACCOUNTING

6 Limitations of national income accounting include:
1. measurement problems;
2. GDP measures national activity, not welfare; and
3. subcategories are often interdependent.

---

[2]Now you know why the total output deflator is called the *GDP deflator*. It is an index of the rise in prices of the goods and services that make up GDP.

Video Series, Economics U$A:
Booms and Busts, Segment 3.2

When I discuss the limitations of national income accounting, I like to make certain to point out that, even though the measures are flawed, the system provides valuable information that is useful for understanding the changes in aggregate economic activity over time.

after submitting the thesis that no data on investments are available for that country. Instead of gathering actual data, the foreign country's statisticians estimate investment by assuming it to be a constant percentage of imports. Since many investment goods are imported, this is reasonable, but the estimate is not a reasonable basis for an economic policy. It would be back to the drawing board for the student, whose thesis would be useless because the student didn't know how the country's statistics had been collected.

If you ever work in business as an economist, statistics will be your life's blood. Much of what economists do is based on knowing, interpreting, and drawing inferences from statistics. Statistics must be treated carefully. They don't always measure what they seem to measure. Though U.S. national income accounting statistics are among the most accurate in the world, they still have serious limitations.

GDP Measures Market Activity, Not Welfare

Welfare is a complicated concept.

The first, and most important, limitation to remember is that GDP does not measure happiness nor does it measure economic welfare. GDP measures economic (market) activity. Real GDP could rise and economic welfare could fall. For example, say some Martians came down and let loose a million Martian burglars in the United States just to see what would happen. GDP would be likely to rise as individuals bought guns and locks and spent millions of dollars on protecting their property and replacing stolen items. At the same time, however, welfare would fall.

Welfare is a complicated concept. The economy's goal should not be to increase output for the sake of increasing output, but to make people better off or at least happier. But a pure happiness measure is impossible. Economists have struggled with the concept of welfare and have decided that the best they can do is to concentrate their analysis on economic activity, leaving others to consider how economic activity relates to happiness. I should warn you, however, that there is no neat correlation between increases in GDP and increases in happiness. You can see that in the accompanying Added Dimension box.

Measurement Errors

Q-9: How can measurement errors occur in adjusting GDP figures for inflation?

GDP figures are supposed to measure all market economic activity, but they do not. Illegal drug sales, under-the-counter sales of goods to avoid income and sales taxes, work performed and paid for in cash to avoid income tax, nonreported sales, and prostitution are all market activities, yet none of them is included in GDP figures. Estimates of the underground, nonmeasured economy's importance range from 1.5 to 20 percent of GDP in the United States and as high as 30 percent in Greece. That is, if measured U.S. GDP is $7.6 trillion, inclusion of the underground, nonmeasured activity would raise it to between $7.71 trillion and $9.12 trillion. If we were able to halt underground activity and direct those efforts to the above-ground economy, GDP would rise significantly. For instance, if we legalized prostitution and marijuana sales and quadrupled tax-collection mechanisms, GDP would rise. But that rise in GDP wouldn't necessarily make us better off.

Measurements of inflation can involve significant measurement errors.

A second type of measurement error occurs in adjusting GDP figures for inflation. In the last chapter I discussed problems using indexes. Measurement of inflation involves numerous arbitrary decisions including what base year to use, how to weight various prices, and how to adjust for changes in the quality of products. Let's take, for example, changes in the quality of products. If the price of a Toyota went up 5 percent from 1995 ($20,000) to 1996 ($21,000), that's certainly a 5 percent rise in price. But what if the 1996 Toyota had a "new improved" 16-valve engine? Can you say that the price of cars rose 5 percent, or should you adjust for the improvement in quality? And if you adjust, how do you adjust? The people who keep track of the price indexes used to measure inflation will be the first to tell you there's no one right answer to any one of these choices. How that question, and a million other similar questions involved in measuring inflation, is answered can lead to significant differences in estimates of inflation and hence in estimates of real GDP growth.

Hundred dollar bills are the favorite bills for illegal transactions.

The only way economists can determine how happy people are is to ask them if they're happy and then develop a happiness index. I've done so in some of my classes by giving students a numerical measure for degrees of happiness:

Ecstatic	5
Very happy	4
Happy	3
Somewhat unhappy	2
Depressed	1

Each student writes down the number that most closely represents his or her average state of happiness for the past year. The average of those calculations forms the "Colander happiness index" for the class—usually between 3 and 3.2. My students are essentially reasonably happy.

In fact, when other economists have taken a type of happiness poll elsewhere, results have been fairly consistent—even in poor countries. Except in times of crisis, people on average are reasonably happy, regardless of their income level, their wealth, or the state of the economy where they live.* I interpret this as meaning there's some level of income

below which we'll be unhappy because we're starving, but above that level more output for a society doesn't mean more happiness for a society.

Now this stability of happiness could mean that economics, economic progress, and growth don't matter, that they're irrelevant to happiness. But we economists are naturally loath to give it such an interpretation. Instead, economists slide over such problems and poll people as to how many prefer a higher income to a lower income. I've also conducted these polls and have yet to find an individual who says he or she prefers less income to more income. (If I found one, of course, I'd volunteer to relieve that person of some income, which would make us both happier.)

The fact that everyone, or almost everyone, prefers more output, but that more output or an increase in income doesn't make everyone happier, is not really a contradiction. I know from watching *Star Trek* (and from reading Lord Tennyson) that it's in striving that human beings acquire happiness. Without striving, the human being is but an empty shell. But enough; if this discussion continues, it will, heaven forbid, turn from economics to philosophy.

*I've given the test to students in Vermont, New York, and Great Britain, and each time the results have been similar. However, when I gave the test to students in Florida at the University of Miami and to students in Bulgaria, the results were different. In Miami they came up consistently higher for each

category. Four students actually checked "ecstatic." I'm not precisely sure what this Florida factor signifies. In Bulgaria, the results were lower (a 2.8 average). Bulgaria was undergoing a wrenching economic change and many incomes had been cut by two-thirds, so this low result was explainable.

One recent study for Canada argued inflation could be either 5.4 or 15 percent, depending on how the inflation index was calculated! Which inflation figure one chose would make a big difference in one's estimate of how the economy was doing. The United States used to switch base years and update its price weights every five years, resulting in the recalculation of history every five years. In 1996, however, it began to use a new measure that updates price weights and the base year every year.

A third limitation of national income accounting concerns possible misinterpretation of the components. In setting up the accounts, a large number of arbitrary decisions had to be made: What to include in "investment"? What to include in "consumption"? How to treat government expenditures? The decisions that were made were, for the most part, reasonable, but they weren't the only ones that could have been made. Once made, however, they influence our interpretations of events. For example, when we see that investment rises, we normally think that our future productive capacity is rising, but remember that investment includes housing investment, which does not increase our future productive capacity. In fact, some types of consumption (say, purchases of personal computers by people who will become computer-literate and use their knowledge and skills to be more productive than they were before they owned computers) increase our productive capacity more than some types of "investment."

The problems of national income accounting have led to a variety of measures of economic activity. One of the most interesting of these is the *Gross Progress Indicator* (GPI) which makes a variety of adjustments to GDP so that it better measures the

Misinterpretation of Subcategories

Q–10: How can some types of consumption increase our productive capacity by more than some types of investment?

ADDED DIMENSION   THE UNDERGROUND ECONOMY

The U.S. government has issued over $400 billion worth of cash. That's about $1,500 for every man, woman, and child. Now ask yourself how much cash you're carrying on you. Add to that the amounts banks and businesses keep, and divide that by the number of people in the United States. The number economists get when they do that calculation is way below the total amount of cash the United States has issued. So what happens to the extra cash?

Let's switch for a minute to a Miami safehouse being raided by drug enforcement officers. They find $50 million in cash. That's what most economists believe happens to much of the extra cash: It goes underground. An underground economy lurks below the real economy.

The underground economy consists of two components: (1) the production and distribution of illegal goods and services; and (2) the nonreporting of legal economic activity.

Illegal activity, such as selling illegal drugs and prostitution, generates huge amounts of cash. (Most people who buy an illegal good or service would prefer not to have the transaction appear on their monthly credit card statements.) This presents a problem for a big-time illegal business. It must explain to the Internal Revenue Service (IRS) where all that money came from. That's where money laundering comes in. Money laundering is simply making illegally gained income look as if it came from a legal business. Any business through which lots of cash moves is a good front for money laundering. Laundromats move lots of cash, which is where the term *money laundering* came from. The mob bought laundromats and claimed a much higher income from the laundromats than it actually received. The mob thus "laundered" the excess money. Today money laundering is much more sophisticated. It involves billions of dollars and international transactions in three or four different countries, but the purpose is the same: making illegally earned money look legal.

The second part of the illegal economy involves deliberately failing to report income in order to escape paying taxes on it. When people work "off the books," when restaurants don't ring up cash sales, when waiters forget to declare tips on their tax returns, they reduce their tax payments and make it look as if they have less income and as if the economy has less production than it actually does.

How important is the underground economy? That's tough to say; it is, after all, underground. A U.S. Department of Commerce economist estimated it at 1.5 percent of the total U.S. economy. The IRS estimates the underground economy at about 10 percent of the total U.S. economy. Some economists estimate it as high as 15 or 20 percent. In other countries, such as Sweden, where the tax rate is higher than in the United States, estimates of the underground economy's size range as high as 30 percent of the above-ground economy.

progress of society rather than simply economic activity. The GPI makes adjustments to GDP for changes in other social goals. For example, if pollution worsens, the GPI falls even though the GDP remains constant. Each of these adjustments requires someone to value these other social goals, and there is significant debate about how social goals should be valued. Advocates of the GPI agree that such valuations are difficult, but they argue that avoiding any such valuation, as is done with the GDP, implicitly values other social goals, such as having no pollution, at zero. Since some index will be used as an indicator of the progress of the economy, it is better to have an index that includes all social goals rather than an index of only economic activity.

GDP Is Worth Using Despite Its Limitations

Measurement is necessary, and the GDP measurements and categories have made it possible to think and talk about the aggregate economy.

By pointing out these problems, economists are not suggesting that national income accounting statistics should be thrown out. Far from it; measurement is necessary, and the GDP measurements and categories have made it possible to think and talk about the aggregate economy. I wouldn't have devoted an entire chapter of this book to national income accounting if I didn't believe it was important. I am simply arguing that national income accounting concepts should be used with sophistication, with an awareness of their weaknesses as well as their strengths.

Used with that awareness, national income accounting is a powerful tool; one wouldn't want to be an economist without it. For those of you who aren't planning to be economists, it's still a good idea for you to understand the concepts of national income accounting. If you do, the business section of the newspaper will no longer seem like Greek to you. You'll be a more informed citizen and will be better able to make up your own mind about macroeconomic debates.

CHAPTER SUMMARY

- National income accounting is the terminology used to talk about the aggregate economy.
- GDP measures aggregate final output of an economy. It's a flow, not a stock, measure of market activity.
- Intermediate goods can be eliminated from GDP in two ways:
    1. By measuring only final sales.
    2. By measuring only value added.
- National income is directly related to national output. Whenever there's output, there's income.
- GDP is divided up into four types of expenditures:

$$GDP = C + I + G + (X - M).$$

- NI = Compensation to employees + Rent + Interest + Profit.
- To compare income over time, we must adjust for price-level changes. After adjusting for inflation, nominal measures are changed to "real" measures.
- Real GDP is the nominal GDP divided by the GDP deflator.
- National income accounting concepts are powerful tools for understanding macroeconomics, but we must recognize their limitations.

KEY TERMS

disposable personal income *(189)*
gross domestic product (GDP) *(184)*
gross national product (GNP) *(184)*
intermediate products *(186)*
national income (NI) *(188)*

national income accounting *(184)*
national income accounting identity *(188)*
net foreign factor income *(184)*
nominal concepts *(183)*

nominal GDP *(193)*
real concepts *(183)*
real GDP *(193)*
value added *(186)*
Wealth Accounts *(185)*

QUESTIONS FOR THOUGHT AND REVIEW

The number after each question represents the estimated degree of critical thinking required. (1 = almost none; 10 = deep thought.)

1. Which will be larger, gross domestic product or gross national product? *(6)*
2. If you add up all the transactions in an economy, do you arrive at GDP, GNP, or something else? *(6)*
3. What's the relationship between a stock concept and a flow concept? Give an example that hasn't already been given in this chapter. *(5)*
4. A company sells 1,000 desks for $400 each. Of these, it sells 750 to other companies and 250 to individuals. What is that company's contribution to GDP? *(4)*
5. The United States is considering introducing a value added tax. What tax rate on value added is needed to get the same increase in revenue as is gotten from an income tax with a rate of 15 percent? Why? *(8)*

6. If the United States introduces universal child care, what will likely happen to GDP? What are the welfare implications of that rise? *(5)*
7. National income accounting equates income and output. Can you think of how accounting rules can be used to show how government can be bad for the people only if the people themselves are bad? *(8)*
8. What is the largest component of national income for most countries? *(2)*
9. If the government increases transfer payments, what will happen to national income? *(6)*
10. If nominal GDP rises from $48 billion to $52 billion and the GDP deflator rises from 100 to 110, what happens to real GDP? *(5)*
11. If society's goal is to make society happier, and higher GDP isn't closely associated with society being happier, why do economists even talk about GDP? *(9)*

PROBLEMS AND EXERCISES

1. There are three firms in an economy: A, B, and C. Firm A buys $250 worth of goods from firm B and $200 worth of goods from firm C, and produces 200 units of output which it sells at $5 per unit. Firm B buys $100 worth of goods from firm A and $150 worth of goods from firm C, and produces 300 units of output which it sells at $7 per

unit. Firm C buys $50 worth of goods from firm A and nothing from firm B. It produces output worth $1,000. All other products are sold to consumers.

   a. Calculate GDP.

   b. If a value added tax (a tax on the total value added of each firm) of 10 percent is introduced, how much revenue will the government get?

   c. How much would government get if it introduced a 10 percent income tax?

   d. How much would government get if it introduced a 10 percent sales tax on final output?

2. State whether the following actions will increase or decrease GDP.

   a. The U.S. legalizes gay marriages.

   b. An individual sells her house on her own.

   c. An individual sells his house through a broker.

   d. Government increases social security payments.

   e. Stock prices rise by 20 percent.

   f. An unemployed worker gets a job.

3. Find personal consumption expenditures (as a percent of GDP) for the following countries. (Requires research.)

   a. Mexico

   b. Thailand

   c. Poland

   d. Nigeria

   e. Kuwait

4. Below are nominal GDP and GDP deflators for four years.

	Nominal GDP	GDP Deflator	Real GDP
1989	$5,251	108.5	
1990	5,546	113.3	
1991	5,723	117.7	
1992	6,039	121.1	

   a. Calculate real GDP in each year.

   b. Did the percent change in nominal GDP exceed the percent change in real GDP in any of the last three years listed?

   c. In which year did society's welfare increase the most?

5. Some economists have proposed that we use a Gross Progress Indicator rather than the GDP as an indication of economic well-being.

   a. List some of the measures that would likely go into the Gross Progress Indicator.

   b. State whether you believe that indicator has gone up or down in the most recent calendar year.

6. Find GDP for the most recent quarter as reported in *The Wall Street Journal*.

   a. What was consumption, investment, government consumption and investment, and net exports?

   b. What was nominal GDP? Real GDP?

   c. By how much did GDP increase? How much of the increase was due to an increase in the aggregate price level?

   d. Which of the components listed in *a* contributed the most to the change in GDP? Did any of the components move in opposite directions?

ANSWERS TO MARGIN QUESTIONS

1. GDP measures the output of the residents of a country— the output within its geographical borders. GNP measures the output of the citizens and businesses of a country. Kuwait is a very rich country whose residents have a high income, much of it from investments overseas. Thus their GNP will be high. However, Kuwait also has large numbers of foreign workers who are not citizens and whose incomes would be included in GDP but not in GNP. In reality, Kuwait citizens' and businesses' foreign income exceeds foreign workers' and foreign companies' income within Kuwait, so Kuwait's GNP is greater than its GDP. *(184)*

2. Wealth Accounts measure stocks—a country's assets and liabilities at a point in time. Income Accounts measure flows—a country's income and expenditures over a period of time. *(183)*

3. Only the value added by the sale would be added to GDP. In this case the value added is the difference between the purchase price and the sale price, or $500. *(187)*

4. The government budget includes transfer payments, which are not included in GDP. Only those government expenditures that are for goods and services are included in GDP. *(187)*

5. The largest factor payments component of national income for the United States is compensation to employees. *(189)*

6. The four components of expenditures in national income are personal consumption, gross private investment, net exports, and government purchases. *(190)*

7. In developing countries, individuals often grow their own food and take part in many activities that are not measured by the GDP statistics. The income figures that one gets from the GDP statistics of developing countries do not include such activities and, thus, can be quite misleading. *(192)*

8. Nominal income must have risen to slightly over $4.6 trillion so that, when it is adjusted for inflation, the real income will have risen to $4.2 trillion. *(193)*

9. Measurement errors occur in adjusting GDP figures for inflation because measuring inflation involves numerous arbitrary decisions such as choosing a base year, adjustment for quality changes in products, and weighting prices. *(194)*

10. Dividing goods into consumption and investment does not always capture the effect of the spending on productive capacity. For example, housing "investment" does little to expand the productive capacity. However, "consumption" of computers or books could expand the productive capacity significantly. *(195)*

National Income Accounting in Detail

As discussed in the chapter, the national income accounts divide up the flow of income in the economy into two sides—the expenditures side and the income side—and equate the two sides. In the chapter I briefly considered the components of the two sides; in this appendix I look at them more closely. First, I go through the components of expenditures. Second, I go through the components of income. And finally, I relate the components of expenditures and the components of income.

The Expenditures Approach

Exhibit A1 gives you a more detailed look at the major expenditure categories used in the expenditures approach to calculating U.S. GDP. It breaks personal consumption expenditures, gross private investment, government consumption expenditures and gross investment, and net exports into their standard subcomponents.

Exhibit A2 demonstrates movements in U.S. GDP and its component parts since 1959. As you can see, the individual parts fluctuate in relative importance. Of the components, investment fluctuates most; personal consumption expenditures fluctuate least. Let's consider each component in turn.

Consumption Expenditure (C)   All goods and services bought by households are lumped together under "personal consumption." This huge category includes such purchases as your visit to the dentist, college tuition, and the new car you buy, as well as all actual and estimated "rents" for existing homes. Consumption is the largest category in GDP, accounting for about 68 percent of the total.

Being so large, consumption is normally broken down into subcategories shown in Exhibit A3: durable consumer goods, nondurable consumer goods, and services. **Durable goods** are defined as *goods expected to last more than one year.* (Why one year? Because one year, although arbitrary, is a reasonable cutoff point.) Durables include cars and household appliances. **Nondurable goods** are *goods that last less than one year.* The food you eat and the movie tickets you buy fall under this heading. Services are activities done for another person (cutting hair, teaching, and mowing a lawn). They are a form of economic activity, but they do not involve production or sale of goods. Exhibit A3 breaks down these subcategories of consumer expenditures into subsubcategories.

Gross and Net Private Investment (*I*)   **Gross private domestic investment** is *expenditures by firms or households on goods, often called capital goods, that are used over and over to make products or provide services.* Housing, tractors, steel mills, and wine barrels are examples. Thus, when economists speak of investment they don't mean the kind of activity taking place when individuals buy stocks or bonds—economists consider that saving, not investing. Gross private investment, the third largest category, makes up about 15 percent of GDP. Exhibit A4 breaks down gross private investment into two subcategories: fixed

GDP, 1996	Dollars (in billions)		% of GDP
Personal consumption expenditures (*C*)	$5151		68%
Durable goods		$ 632	
Nondurable goods		1545	
Services		2974	
Gross private investment (*I*)	1117		15
Fixed investment		1102	
Change in business inventories		15	
Net exports of goods and services (*X* − *M*)	−99		−1
Exports		855	
Imports		954	
Government consumption expenditures and gross investment (*G*)	1406		18
Federal		523	
State and local		883	
	$7576		100%

EXHIBIT A1   GDP via the Expenditures Approach, 1996

Source: *Survey of Current Business,* 1997 (http://www.bea.gov). (Note: Components have been rounded off and do not add up perfectly.)

EXHIBIT A2   Movements of U.S. GDP since 1959

This exhibit demonstrates the approximate movement of GDP and its components since 1959. As you can see, gross private investment and net exports fluctuate significantly over the years, and GDP tends to rise overall each year.

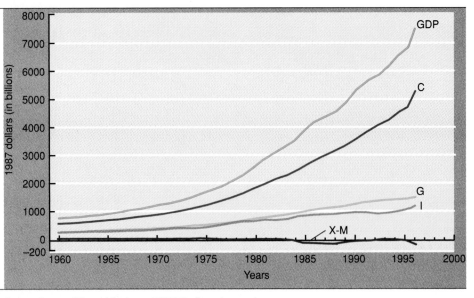

Source: *Survey of Current Business,* 1997 (http://www.bea.gov).

EXHIBIT A3   Breakdown of Consumer Expenditures, 1996

	Dollars (in billions)		% of Expenditures
Durable goods	$ 632		12%
Motor vehicles and parts		$253	
Furniture and household equipment		254	
Other		125	
Nondurable goods	1,545		30
Food		772	
Clothing		264	
Gasoline and oil		122	
Fuel oil and coal		11	
Other nondurable goods		375	
Services	2,974		58
Housing		779	
Household operation		310	
Transportation		205	
Medical care		816	
Other		865	
	$5,151		100%

Source: *Survey of Current Business,* 1997 (http://www.bea.gov).

EXHIBIT A4   Gross Private Investment, 1996

	Dollars (in billions)			% of Investment
Fixed investment	$1102			
Nonresidential		$791		71%
Structures			$214	
Producers' durable equipment			577	
Residential		311		28
Single-family structures			155	
Multifamily structures			21	
Producers' durable equipment			8	
Other			127	
Change in business inventory	15			1
Subtotal gross investment	$1117			100%
Depreciation	858			
Net investment	$ 259			

Source: *Survey of Current Business,* 1997 (http://www.bea.gov).

investment and change in business inventory. Fixed investment is, by far, the larger component. It includes investments in residential and nonresidential buildings and in equipment.

Change in business inventory ("inventory investment" for short) is a different form of investment. It's the increase or decrease in the value of the stocks of inventory that businesses have on hand. Notice I said "increases in the *value* of inventory." Say a car dealership normally keeps 50 cars in stock. Its inventory is 50 cars. In 1996 it increased its stock of cars to 55. Its inventory investment for 1996 was 5 cars times their value. If inventory remains constant from one year to the next, there's no inventory investment. If inventories fall, inventory investment is negative.

Inventory investment is highly volatile. Drawing implications from an increase in inventory investment is difficult, because a change in inventory investment can mean two different things. When firms expect to sell a lot, they usually produce significant amounts for inventory, so an increase in inventory investment may signal expected high sales. But inventory can also increase because goods the firm produces aren't selling. In that case, an increase in inventory investment signals unexpected low sales. Those five extra cars are just sitting on the dealer's lot. Thus, economists keep a close eye on inventory investment as well as on why inventory investment has changed.

Sooner or later, assets such as plants and equipment wear out or become technologically obsolete. Economists call this wearing out process **depreciation**—*the decrease in an asset's value.* Depreciation is part of the cost of producing a good; it is the amount by which plants and equipment decrease in value as they grow older. Much of each year's private investment involves expenditures to replace assets that have worn out. For example, as you drive your car, it wears out. A car with 80,000 miles on it is worth less than the same type of car with only 1,000 miles on it. The difference in value is attributed to depreciation.

To differentiate between total or gross private domestic investment and the new investment that's above and beyond replacement investment, economists use the term **net private investment**—*gross private domestic investment minus depreciation.* In 1996, gross investment was $1117 billion and depreciation was $858 billion, so net investment was $259 billion. Economists pay close attention to net private investment because it gives an estimate of the increase in the country's productive capacity.

Government Purchases (G)   **Government purchases,** *government payments for goods and services and investment in equipment and structures,* are divided into federal expenditures and state and local expenditures. In macroeconomics the main focus is on the federal government because only the federal government is directly concerned with the aggregate economy. This doesn't mean state and local government expenditures don't affect the economy; they do, as do any expenditures. It simply means that state

and local governments generally don't take that effect into account since each is relatively small compared to the total economy.

Government purchases are further divided between consumption expenditures and investment. Consumption expenditures are expenditures on current needs such as salaries of government employees. Government investments are expenditures for structures and equipment such as highways, buildings, computers, and schools. Investments are the purchase of items that provide a service for more than one year. This investment is the public counterpart to private domestic investment.

Government uses its tax revenue to build bridges, buy copying machines, print application forms, pay the president, and meet innumerable other expenses. Many of these government goods and services are paid for from general tax revenue and are provided free to consumers of the goods or services. As a result, they have no price at which to value them. By convention, economists value these goods and services at cost. Thus, if the federal government pays the president a salary of $175,000, the president's contribution to GDP will be valued at $175,000.

Total government purchases (the second-largest component) account for about 18 percent of GDP. Exhibit A5 breaks down purchases by various levels of government.

Notice that state and local governments make more purchases than does the federal government, and federal government expenditures total $523 billion. Each year the federal government budget (about $1.5 trillion) is much larger than these federal government purchases of $523 billion that enter into GDP. The reason is that the remaining part of the federal government budget involves **transfer payments**—*payments made to individuals that aren't payment for a good or service.* Since they're simply a transfer, not a purchase of a good or service, they don't contribute to GDP. The largest of these transfers is social security payments.

Net Exports (X − M)   Some goods and services produced in the United States (such as wheat, computers, and U.S. vacations) are bought by people in foreign countries. Other goods and services (such as French champagne and taxi rides in London) are bought from foreign countries by U.S. residents. If these exports and imports are equal, they net out and make no contribution to GDP. If the value of what the United States sells to foreign countries is greater than what it buys from foreign countries, the United States is producing more than it is spending. In this case **net exports** (*exports minus imports*) are positive, and the difference between exports and imports must be added to GDP, since the increase represents net foreign expenditure on U.S.-produced goods. It's U.S. production bought by foreigners, but U.S. production nonetheless.

If the United States buys more from foreign countries than it sells to them, imports exceed exports, so net exports are negative. In this case, U.S. spending is more than U.S. production. Since GDP measures production, not

EXHIBIT A5   Breakdown of Government Consumption and Investment, 1996

	Dollars (in billions)			% of Total
Federal	$ 523			37%
National defense		$347		
Consumption expenditures			$304	
Gross investment			43	
Nondefense		176		
Consumption expenditures			155	
Gross investment			21	
State and local	883			63
Consumption expenditures		714		
Gross investment		169		
Total	$1406			100%

Source: *Survey of Current Business,* 1997 (http://www.bea.doc.gov).

EXHIBIT A6   Net U.S. Exports, 1996

	Dollars (in billions)		% of Total Exports or Imports
Exports	$855		
Merchandise		$615	72%
Services		240	28
Imports	954		
Merchandise		802	84
Services		152	16
Net exports	$-99		

Source: *Survey of Current Business,* 1997 (http://www.bea.doc.gov).

spending, the excess of imports over exports must be subtracted from U.S. GDP. If it weren't subtracted, we couldn't measure domestic production by measuring expenditures. To some degree, imports and exports offset each other. However, as I said in Chapter 6, in the United States in the early 1990s imports have significantly exceeded exports.

Exhibit A6 presents U.S. exports and imports. In 1996 exports were $855 billion; imports were $954 billion; so net exports were −$99 billion.

GDP and NDP In the discussion of investment, I differentiated gross investment from net investment. Gross investment minus depreciation equals net investment. Economists have created another aggregate term, net domestic product, to reflect the adjustment to investment because of depreciation. **Net domestic product (NDP)** is the sum of consumption expenditures, government expenditures, net foreign expenditures, and investment less depreciation. Thus,

$$GDP = C + I + G + (X - M)$$

$$NDP = C + I + G + (X - M) - \text{depreciation}.$$

NDP takes depreciation into account, and depreciation is a cost of producing goods; so NDP is actually preferable to GDP as the expression of a country's domestic output. However, measuring true depreciation (the actual decrease in an asset's value) is difficult because asset values fluctuate. In fact, it's so difficult that in the real world

accountants don't try to measure true depreciation, but instead use a number of conventional rules of thumb that yield an accepted figure. In recognition of this reality, economists call the adjustment made to GDP to arrive at NDP the *capital consumption allowance* rather than *depreciation*. Since estimating depreciation is difficult, GDP rather than NDP is generally used in discussions.

The Income Approach The alternative way of calculating GDP is the income approach. **Domestic income (DI)** is *the total income earned by residents and businesses in a country.* It has four components: employees' compensation, rents, interest, and profits. Total domestic income equals NDP, not GDP. Why? Because of depreciation, which is a cost, not an income to anyone. An economy's domestic income must be separated from an economy's **national income (NI)**—*the total income earned by citizens and businesses of a country.* Domestic income corresponds to domestic product; national income corresponds to national product. When the United States shifted from GNP to GDP as its primary measure of economic output, it would have been reasonable also to shift to domestic as opposed to national income concepts. Alas, it did not; the primary income statistics reported in the United States are still national income statistics.

To move from domestic income to national income one must add net foreign factor income to domestic income. For the United States in the 1990s, net foreign fac-

	Dollars (in billions)	% of National Income
Compensation to employees	$4449	72%
Rents	127	2
Net interest	403	7
Profits	1172	19
Proprietors' income	$518	
Corporate profits	654	
National income	$6151	100%

EXHIBIT A7   Components of National Income, 1996

Source: *Survey of Current Business,* 1997 (http://www.bea.doc.gov).

tor income has been minimal so there's not a lot of difference between the two concepts, but since the primary income figures reported by the U.S. government are national income figures, I discuss the breakdown of national income rather than domestic income, leaving you to make the adjustments to domestic income concepts by subtracting net foreign factor income from national income concepts.

Compensation to Employees   **Employee compensation** (the largest component of national income) consists of *wages and salaries paid to individuals, along with fringe benefits and government taxes for social security and unemployment insurance.* As you can see in Exhibit A7, compensation to employees made up about 72 percent of national income.

Rents   **Rents** are the *income from property received by households.* Rents received by firms are not included because a firm's rents are simply another source of income to the firm and hence are classified as profits. In most years the rent component of GDP is small, since the depreciation owners take on buildings is close to the income they earn from those buildings.

Interest   **Interest** is *the income private businesses pay to households that have lent the businesses money,* generally by purchasing bonds issued by the businesses. (Interest received by firms doesn't show up in this category for the same reason that rents received by firms don't show up in the *rent* category.) Interest payments by government and households aren't included in national income since by convention they're assumed not to flow from the production of goods and services. In 1996, net interest was 7 percent of national income.

Profits   **Profits** are *the amount that is left after compensation to employees, rents, and interest have been paid out.* (As we discussed earlier, the national income accounts use accounting profits which must be distinguished from economic profits, which are calculated on the basis of opportunity costs.) Profits are normally divided into two categories: (1) profits of unincorporated businesses and proprietors' income, and (2) profits of incorporated businesses. Both require some discussion.

In Chapter 5, I pointed out that in most unincorporated businesses, the owner works for the business. The amount that is left over after paying interest, rent, and compensation to employees is both a compensation for the owner's work (valued at his or her opportunity cost of working elsewhere) and the owner's profit. Thus, if a gift shop owner earns $30,000 a year after paying wages, interest, and rent, and she could have earned $20,000 working elsewhere, her compensation is $20,000 and her profits are $10,000. Tabulation of the national income data doesn't show this separation and, by convention, the entire amount ($30,000 in the example) is included as "profit."

As I also discussed in Chapter 5, corporations are fictitious legal entities. For purposes of calculating national income, they can have no income; all income in national income accounting must be attributed to households.

Corporate profits are, in reality, either paid out to stockholders in *dividends* (payments to the holders of a company's stock), in which case they are considered household income; or are not distributed to stockholders but are instead held within the firm as corporate retained earnings. For national income accounting purposes, these *retained earnings* are undistributed profits, which must be attributed to households. That's what is done. In the national income accounts, all undistributed profit is attributed to households. To do so, the U.S. Department of Commerce simply adds all undistributed profits to household income. In 1996 corporate profits were about 1172 billion (19% of national income).

National Income and Net National Product: Adjustments for Indirect Business Taxes   The sum of compensation to employees, rents, interest, and profits is supposed to equal national income. However, if you added the four components together, you would find national income does not quite equal net national product (NNP). To make the two equal, one must add indirect business taxes to national income. National income plus indirect business taxes equals NNP.

Indirect business taxes include sales taxes (a general tax on sales), excise taxes (a sales tax on a particular item or group of items), business property taxes, customs duties, and license fees. These taxes are ultimately paid by

A REMINDER — GDP, GNP, NDP, AND NNP: A REVIEW

We've covered a lot of definitions quickly, so a review is in order. GDP (the total output of the residents of a society) can be measured in two ways: the expenditures approach and the income approach.

Using the expenditures approach,

$$GDP = C + I + G + (X - M).$$

Much investment is replacement investment—it is made to cover depreciation, and is a cost of production. When one subtracts depreciation from GDP, one arrives at NDP:

$$NDP = GDP - Depreciation.$$

To move from net domestic product to net national product one must add net foreign factor income (foreign earnings of citizens minus domestic earnings of foreigners) to net domestic product:

$$NNP = NDP + Net foreign factor income.$$

To move to national income, one subtracts indirect business taxes from NNP.

$$NI = NNP - Indirect business taxes.$$

National income can be broken up into four components: compensation to employees, rent, interest, and profits:

$$NI = Employee compensation + Rent + Interest + Profits.$$

To move from national income to personal income, one subtracts corporate income taxes, undistributed corporate profits, and social security contributions, and adds transfer payments from the government:

$$PI = NI - Corp. income taxes - undistrib. corp. profits - soc. sec. contrib. + trans. pmts.$$

$$Disposable personal income = Personal income - Personal taxes.$$

---

households, since according to national income accounting, households ultimately receive all the income. How are they paid for by households? Either the firm raises its prices to include the tax or its earnings fall by the amount of the tax. In either case, households pay. When firms add the cost of taxes to their price, households pay the higher prices. When firms subtract the cost of taxes from their earnings, households pay by receiving lower wages or lower dividends (or both) from those firms. But it is firms, not households, that make the actual payment of these taxes, so to go from national income to **net national product**—*GNP adjusted for depreciation*—indirect business taxes must be added back to national (or household) income. That means

$$NNP = NI + Indirect business taxes.$$

Other National Income Terms Two other often-used concepts deserving mention are personal income and disposable personal income. (These can be either national or domestic concepts. Since the United States still reports them as national concepts, I follow that convention here.)

Personal Income National income measures the income individuals receive for doing productive work whereas personal income measures all income actually received by individuals. Individuals receive other income that they do not directly earn (for example, social security payments, welfare payments, food stamps, and veterans' benefits). These payments from government to individuals are not part of national income, but they are available to spend.

Similarly in national income accounting, individuals are attributed income that they do not actually receive. This income includes undistributed corporate profits (retained earnings), employers' contributions to the social security system, and corporate income taxes.

If we add to national income the amounts of such payments that households receive, and subtract from national income the amounts attributed to households but not actually received by them, we arrive at **personal income (PI)**—*national income plus net transfer payments from government minus amounts attributed but not received*. Personal income can be set forth as:

PI = NI + Transfer payments from government
     − Corporate retained earnings
     − Corporate income taxes
     − Social security taxes.

Disposable Personal Income We've accounted for most taxes, but not all. There's still personal income taxes and payroll taxes, which are subtracted from individuals' paychecks or paid directly by self-employed individuals. Personal income taxes and payroll taxes show up on employees' paycheck stubs, but employees don't actually get the money; the government does. Subtracting these personal income taxes from personal income, we arrive at **disposable personal income**—*personal income minus personal income taxes and payroll taxes*:

$$PI - Personal taxes = Disposable personal income.$$

Disposable personal income is what people have readily available to spend. Thus, economists follow disposable personal income carefully.

From GDP to Disposable Personal Income Exhibit A8 reviews the steps involved in moving from GDP to disposable personal income for the United States. Going through these steps should give you a good sense of the relationships among the concepts we've discussed.

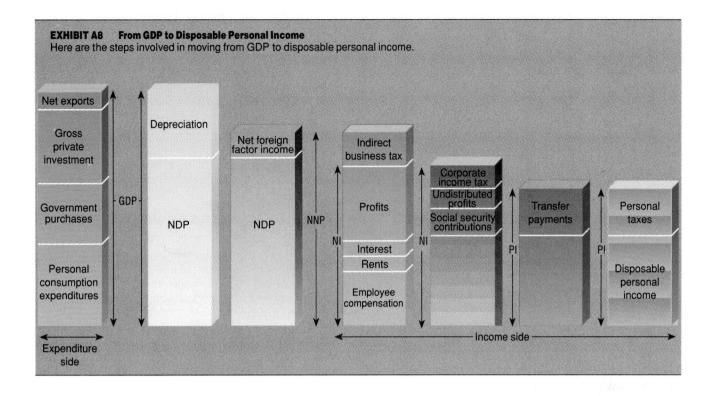

EXHIBIT A8   From GDP to Disposable Personal Income
Here are the steps involved in moving from GDP to disposable personal income.

Conclusion

It is possible to go into the National Income Accounts in much more detail, but, for most students, and most businesspeople, this appendix should provide a sufficient understanding of the accounts so that when you read about them in the paper they make sense. What's important to remember long term is not the specifics—what's important to remember is the general structure of the ac-

counts—how the two sides are made equal by accounting identities, and also that some of the decisions about what is to be included in the accounts are arbitrary. Thus, like all statistics, national income statistics should be used not as definitive statements of what is happening in the economy, but as a guide to understanding. Used in that fashion national income accounting can further your understanding of the aggregate economy.

KEY TERMS

depreciation *(201)*
disposable personal income *(204)*
domestic income (DI) *(202)*
durable goods *(199)*
employee compensation *(203)*
government purchases *(201)*

gross private domestic
  investment *(199)*
interest *(203)*
national income (NI) *(202)*
net domestic product (NDP) *(202)*
net exports *(201)*
net national product *(204)*

net private investment *(201)*
nondurable goods *(199)*
personal income (PI) *(204)*
profits *(203)*
rents *(203)*
transfer payments *(201)*

QUESTIONS FOR THOUGHT AND REVIEW

1. You've been given the following data:

Transfer payments	$ 72	Contribution for social insurance	35
Interest paid by consumers	4	Personal tax and nontax payments	91
Net exports	4	Undistributed corporate profits	51
Indirect business taxes	47	Gross private investment	185
Net foreign factor income	2	Government purchases	195
Corporate income tax	64	Personal consumption	500
		Depreciation	59

On the basis of these data calculate GDP, GNP, NNP, NDP, NI, personal income, and disposable personal income.

2. Rent is $400, investment is $100, interest is $200, savings are $75, profits are −$200, wages are $4,000, and consumption is $3,000. Assuming net foreign factor income and indirect business taxes are zero, what is the level of NDP?

3. Economists normally talk about GDP even though they know NDP is a better measure of economic activity. Why?

4. How does personal income differ from national income?

5. What is the difference between national personal income and domestic personal income?

6. Given the following data about the economy:

Personal consumption	$700
Investment	500
Corporate income tax	215
Proprietors' income	250
Government purchases	300
Profits	250
Wages	700
Net exports	275
Rents	25
Depreciation	25
Indirect business taxes	100
Undistributed corporate profits	60
Net foreign factor income	−3
Interest	150
Social security contribution	0
Transfer payments	0
Personal taxes	165

a. Calculate GDP and GNP with both the expenditures approach and the income approach.

b. Calculate NDP, NNP, NI, and domestic income.

c. Calculate PI.

d. Calculate disposable personal income.

7. You have been hired as a research assistant and are given the following data.

Compensation	$329
Consumption	370
Exports	55
Net foreign factor income	3
Government purchases	43
Gross investment	80
Imports	63
Indirect business taxes	27
Net interest	49
Profits	69
Rental income	1

a. Calculate GNP, GDP, NDP, NNP and NI.

b. What is depreciation in this year?

c. Right after you finish, your boss comes running in to you and tells you that she made a mistake. Imports were really $68 and compensation was $340. She tells you to get her the corrected answers to a and b immediately.

8. You've been called in by your boss with some questions.

a. First, she tells you that she has been told that net private investment was negative and gross private investment was positive this year. She says that that is impossible. What do you tell her?

b. Next, she wants you to tell her what national income in the United States was in 1990. She gives you the following data: 1990 GDP was $5,546.1 billion, net foreign factor income was $21.7 billion, capital depreciated by $607.7 billion, and indirect business taxes stood at $444.0 billion.

c. Finally, she tells you that GDP fell 32 percent in her country last year, and that she must make a state of the economy speech next week. She wants to know how she can portray this fall in the best possible light. What do you tell her?

Nine

Money, Banking, and the Financial Sector

The process by which banks create money is so simple that the mind is repelled.

~ John Kenneth Galbraith

After reading this chapter, you should be able to:

1 Explain why the financial sector is central to almost all macroeconomic debates.

2 Explain what money is.

3 Enumerate the three functions of money.

4 State the alternative definitions of money and their primary components.

5 Explain how banks create money.

6 Calculate both the simple and the approximate real-world money multiplier.

7 Explain how a financial panic can occur and the potential problem with government guarantees to prevent such panics.

In the last two chapters we surveyed the four central problems of macro—growth, business cycles, unemployment, and inflation—and the terminology used to describe those problems. In this chapter we consider the roles of money and financial institutions in the macro economy.

Financial institutions are central to almost all macro-economic debates. The central role that financial institutions play is often not immediately obvious to students. In thinking about the economy, they often focus on the *real sector*—the market for the production and exchange of goods and services. In the real sector, real goods or services such as shoes, operas, automobiles, and textbooks are exchanged. That's an incomplete view of the economy. The *financial sector*—the market for the creation and exchange of financial assets such as money, stocks, and bonds—plays a central role in organizing and coordinating our economy; it makes modern economic society possible. A car won't run without oil; a modern economy won't operate without a financial sector.

For every real transaction there is a financial transaction that mirrors it.

Markets make specialization and trade possible and thereby make the economy far more efficient than it otherwise would be. But the efficient use of markets requires a financial sector that facilitates and lubricates those trades. Let's consider an example of how the financial sector facilitates trade. Say you walk into a store and buy a CD. You shell out a 10-dollar bill and the salesperson hands you the CD. Easy, right? Right—but why did the salesperson give you a CD for a little piece of paper? The answer to that question is: Because the economy has a financial system that has convinced him that that piece of paper has value. To convince him (and you) of that

I like to point out that in capitalism, the financial side of the economy mirrors the real side where the production of goods and services takes place, and that one side of the economy cannot work without the other.

requires an enormous structural system, called the financial sector, underlying the CD transaction and all other transactions. That financial system makes the transaction possible; without it the economy as we know it would not exist.

As long as the financial system is operating smoothly, you hardly know it's there; but should that system break down, the entire economy would be disrupted, and would either stagnate or go into a recession. That's why it is necessary to give you an overview of the financial sector as part of your foundation of macroeconomics.

In thinking about the financial sector's role, remember the following insight. *For every real transaction there is a financial transaction that mirrors it.* For example, when you buy an apple, the person selling the apple is buying 35¢ from you by spending his apple. The financial transaction is the transfer of 35¢; the real transaction is the transfer of the apple.

For larger items, the financial transaction behind the real transaction can be somewhat complicated. When you buy a house, you'll probably pay for part of that house with a mortgage, which requires that you borrow money from a bank. The bank, in turn, borrows from individuals the money it lends to you. There's a similar financial transaction when you buy a car, or even a book, on credit.

Because there's a financial transaction reflecting every real transaction, the financial sector is important for the real sector. If the financial sector doesn't work, the real sector doesn't work. All trade involves both the real sector and the financial sector. Thus in this book I don't have a separate section on the steel sector or even the computer sector of the economy, but I do have a separate section on money, banking, and the financial sector of the economy.

Why Is the Financial Sector Important to Macro?

The financial sector is important in macroeconomics because of its role in channeling flows out of the circular flow—such as savings—back into the circular flow, either in the form of consumer loans (such as you get when you buy something with your credit card), business loans (loans that finance business investment), or loans to government. Think of the financial sector as a gigantic channeling device, something like that shown in Exhibit 1.

The financial sector—financial markets and institutions—channels or transfers savings—outflows from the spending stream in hundreds of different forms—back into spending. This channeling device is extraordinarily complicated and requires years of study to understand fully. However, you don't need that extensive study to understand that what's interesting for macro involves the aggregates—the total amount of flows coming out of, and the total amount of flows returning to, the spending stream—and how well the financial sector does at keeping these aggregate flows

1 The financial sector is central to almost all macroeconomic debates because behind every real transaction, there is a financial transaction that mirrors it.

Q-1: Joe, your study partner, says that since goods and services are produced only in the real sector, the financial sector is not important to the macroeconomy. How do you respond?

The financial sector channels savings back into spending.

If you are covering Appendix B, you can add separate channels for direct finance and for finance that takes place through intermediaries and then list the institutions of direct finance and financial intermediaries along their appropriate channels.

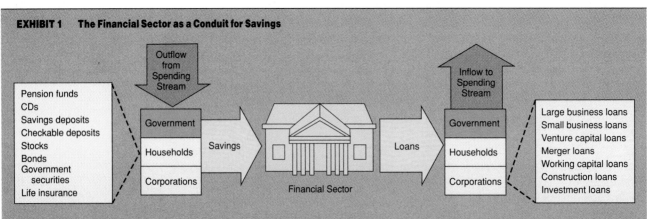

EXHIBIT 1   The Financial Sector as a Conduit for Savings

Financial institutions channel savings—outflows from the spending stream from various entities (government, households, and corporations)—back into the spending stream as loans to various entities (government, households, and corporations). To emphasize the fact that savings take many forms, a breakdown of the type of savings for one entity, households, is shown on the left. The same is done for loans on the right, but for corporations. Each of these loans can itself be broken down again and again until each particular loan is identified individually. The lending process is an individualistic process, and each loan is different in some way from each other loan.

matched, or expanding sufficiently to allow for real growth. If the financial sector expands the flow too much, you get inflationary pressures. If it contracts the flow too much, you get a recession. And if it transfers just the right amount, you get a smoothly running economy.

Flow from the spending stream is channeled into the financial sector as savings when individuals buy **financial assets**—*assets such as stocks or bonds, whose benefit to the owner depends on the issuer of the asset meeting certain obligations.* These obligations by the issuer of the financial asset are called financial liabilities. For every financial asset there is a corresponding financial liability. (Financial assets and liabilities are discussed in detail in Appendix B.)

Price is the mechanism that equilibrates supply and demand in the real sector. Interest rates are the mechanism that equilibrates supply and demand in the financial sector. The channeling of savings into financial assets and the willingness of individuals to incur financial liabilities is strongly influenced by the interest rate on those financial assets and liabilities. In simple terms, the **interest rate** is the *price paid for the use of a financial asset.* When you deposit cash into a deposit account, the bank pays you interest for the use of your financial asset. When the interest rate rises, people are less likely to borrow—sell a financial asset—and more likely to save—buy a financial asset. Thus, when interest rates fall, you often see more borrowing. The funds acquired from the sale of a financial asset reenter the spending stream as consumption and investment.

When financial assets make fixed interest payments, as do most **bonds**—*promises to pay a certain amount plus interest in the future*—the price of the financial asset is determined by the market interest rate. As the market interest rate goes up, the price of the bond goes down. When the market interest rate goes down, the price of the bond goes up. (This inverse relationship between the market interest rate and the price of fixed-payment financial assets is considered in Appendix A.)

Some economists argue that the interest rate does not perfectly translate savings (flows out of the expenditure stream) back into the spending stream. They don't believe that the interest rate equilibrates demand and supply for savings. When it does not, macroeconomic problems can arise.

To get at the problems that can develop, macroeconomics simplifies the flows into two types of financial assets. One type works its way back into the system: bonds, loans, and stocks. These are IOUs issued by savers or their financial intermediaries. The other type of financial asset, when held by individuals, is not necessarily assumed to work its way back into the flow—we'll call this financial asset "money."

What's important about money from a macroeconomic perspective is that, when a person holds money as opposed to holding some other financial asset, the savings that money represents is assumed to escape the circular expenditure flow. If savings is held in some other financial asset, it is assumed that that savings does work its way back into the circular flow. Compared to that complicated maze of interconnected flows that exists in reality, this is an enormous simplification, but it is one that captures a potentially serious problem and possible cause of fluctuations in the economy.

So let's now turn our attention to money.

At this point you're probably saying, "I know what money is; it's currency—the dollar bills I carry around." In one sense you're right: currency is money. But in another sense you're wrong. In fact, a number of short-term financial assets are included as money. To see why, let's consider the definition of money: **Money** is *a highly liquid financial asset that's generally accepted in exchange for other goods, and is used as a reference in valuing other goods, and can be stored as wealth.*

To be *liquid* means to be easily changeable into another asset or good. When you buy something with money you are exchanging money for another asset. So any of your assets that are easily spendable are money. Social customs and standard practices

Stock exchanges, such as the London Stock Exchange shown here, are an important type of financial institution.

The Role of Interest Rates in the Financial Sector

For a mathematical presentation of the relationship between bond prices and interest rates, see Chapter 9 of *Economics: An Honors Companion.*

Savings That Escape the Circular Flow

THE DEFINITION AND FUNCTIONS OF MONEY
2 Money is a financial asset that makes the real economy function smoothly by serving as a medium of exchange, a unit of account, and a store of wealth.

are central to the liquidity of money. The reason you are willing to hold money is that you know someone else will accept it in trade for something else. Its value is determined by its general acceptability to others. If you don't believe that, try spending yuan (Chinese money) in the United States. If you try to buy dinner with 100 yuan, you will be told, no way—give me money.

The U.S. Central Bank: The Fed

The new U.S. $100 bill design incorporates features that are difficult to counterfeit.

The Federal Reserve Bank's home page details the structure of the Fed and is a source of information on interest rates, monetary aggregates, and many other statistics. The address is http://www.frb.fed.us.

So is there any characteristic other than general acceptability that gives value to money? Consider the dollar bill that you know is money. Look at it. It states right on the bill that it is a Federal Reserve Note, which means that it is an IOU (a liability) of the **Federal Reserve Bank (the Fed)**—*the U.S. central bank whose liabilities (Federal Reserve Notes) serve as cash in the United States.* Individuals are willing to accept the Fed's IOUs in return for real goods and services, which means that Fed notes are money.

What, you ask, is a central bank? To answer that question we had better first consider what a bank is. A **bank** is *a financial institution whose primary function is holding money for, and lending money to, individuals and firms.* (There are more complicated definitions and many types of banks, but that will do for now; the issues are discussed more fully in Appendix B.) You got extra currency? Take it to the bank and it will "hold" the extra for you, giving you a piece of paper (or a computer entry) that says you have that much currency held there ("hold" is in quotation marks because the bank does not actually hold the currency). What the bank used to give you was a bank note, and what you used to bring in to the bank was gold, but those days are gone forever. These days what you bring is that Federal Reserve note described above, and what you get is a paper receipt and a computer entry in your checking or savings account. Individuals' deposits in these accounts serve the same purpose as does currency and are also considered money.

Which brings us back to the Federal Reserve Bank, the U.S. central bank. It is a bank that has the right to issue notes (IOUs). By law these Federal Reserve Bank notes are acceptable payment of one's taxes, and by convention these notes are acceptable payment to all people in the United States, and to many people outside the United States. IOUs of the Fed are what most of you think of as cash.

To understand why money is more than just cash, it is helpful to consider the functions of money in more detail. Having done so, we will consider which financial assets are included in various definitions of money.

Functions of Money

3 The three functions of money are:
1. Medium of exchange;
2. Unit of account; and
3. Store of wealth.

As I stated above, money is an asset that can be quickly exchanged for any other asset or good. This definition says money serves three functions:

1. It serves as a medium of exchange.
2. It serves as a unit of account.
3. It serves as a store of wealth.

To get a better understanding of what money is, let's consider each of its functions in turn.

Money as a Medium of Exchange The easiest way to understand money's medium-of-exchange use is to imagine what an economy would be like without money. Say you want something to eat at a restaurant. Without money you'd have to barter with the restaurant owner for your meal. *Barter* is a direct exchange of goods and/or services. You might suggest bartering one of your papers or the shirt in the sack that you'd be forced to carry with you to trade for things you want. Not liking to carry big sacks around, you'd probably decide to fix your own meal and forgo eating out. Bartering is simply too difficult. Money makes many more trades possible because it does not require a double coincidence of wants by two individuals, as simple barter does.

Currency being processed.   *Federal Reserve Bank of Boston.*

The use of money as a medium of exchange makes it possible to trade real goods and services without bartering. It facilitates exchange by reducing the cost of trading. Instead of carrying around a sack full of diverse goods, all you need to carry around is a billfold full of money. You go into the restaurant and pay for your meal with money; the restaurant owner can spend (trade) that money for anything she wants.

Money doesn't have to have any inherent value to function as a medium of exchange. All that's necessary is that everyone believes that other people will accept it in exchange for their goods. This neat social convention makes the economy more efficient.

That social convention depends on there not being too much or too little money. If there's too much money compared to the goods and services offered at existing prices, the goods and services will sell out, and money won't buy you anything. The social convention will break down, or prices will rise. If there's too little money compared to the goods and services offered at the existing prices, there will be a shortage of money and people will have to resort to barter, or prices will fall. Since the Fed controls the supply of money, it also controls the value of money as a medium of exchange.

In order to maintain money's societal usefulness, and to prevent large fluctuations in the price level, the Federal Reserve Bank, or Fed, must issue neither too much nor too little money. (As I stated previously, the Fed is the central bank of the United States; its note liabilities serve as one form of money for the U.S. economy.) People accept money in payment and agree to hold money because they believe the Fed, and the banks the Fed regulates, will issue neither too little nor too much money. This explains why the Fed doesn't freely issue large amounts of money and why it controls (or at least tries to control) the amount of money banks issue. To issue money without restraint would destroy the social convention that gives money its value.

Money as a Unit of Account   A second use of money is as a unit of account. Throughout the book we've emphasized that money prices are actually relative prices. A nominal price, say 25¢, for a pencil conveys the information of a relative price: 1 pencil = $\frac{1}{4}$ of 1 dollar or $\frac{1}{6}$ of a hamburger because money is both our unit of account and our medium of exchange. When you think of 25¢, you think of $\frac{1}{4}$ of a dollar and of what a dollar will buy. The 25¢ a pencil costs only has meaning relative to the information you've stored in your mind about what it can buy. If a hamburger costs $1.50, you can compare hamburgers and pencils (1 pencil = $\frac{1}{6}$ of a hamburger) without making the relative price calculations explicitly.

Having a unit of account makes life much easier. For example, say we had no unit of account and you had to remember the relative prices of all goods. For instance, with three goods you'd have to memorize that an airplane ticket to Miami costs 6 lobster dinners in Boston or 4 pairs of running shoes, which makes a pair of shoes worth $1\frac{1}{2}$ lobster dinners.

Memorizing even a few relationships is hard enough, so it isn't surprising that societies began using a single unit of account. If you don't have a single unit of account, all combinations of 100 goods will require that you remember almost 5,000 relative prices. If you have a single unit of account, you need know only 100 prices. A single unit of account saves our limited memories and helps us make reasonable decisions based on relative costs.

Money is a useful unit of account only as long as its value relative to the average of all other prices doesn't change too quickly. That's because it's not only used as a unit of account at a point in time, it's also a unit of account *over time*. Money is a standard of deferred payment. The value of payments that will be made in the future (such as the college loan payments many of you will be making in the future) is determined by the future value of money. Again, the Fed plays a central role in money's usefulness as a unit of account. If the Fed printed excessive currency to pay all the government's expenses, money's relative price would fall quickly (an increase in supply lowers price), which is another way of saying that the price level would explode and the unit-of-account function of money would be seriously undermined.

Money doesn't have to have any inherent value to function as a medium of exchange.

To begin the discussion of money, I ask students to describe the characteristics of money. They usually describe something that is like a dollar bill. Then I take out a dollar bill and a green rectangular piece of paper and ask them to write a paragraph discussing which one they want and why.

Q–2: Since the cost of printing money is low compared to its value, why doesn't the Fed print up lots of money?

When I discuss money as a unit of account, I start with two goods and ask my students to count the number of prices that are necessary in a two good barter economy. Then I add a good and ask them to do the same calculation for a three-good barter economy. I continue this process, and the number of goods escalates until the point is clear that money serves a valuable function as a unit of account.

See "The Importance of Money," by John Law in *Classic Readings in Economics.*

Money is a useful unit of account only as long as its value relative to other prices doesn't change too quickly.

See "The Price System in Micro-cosm: A P.O.W. Camp," by R.A. Radford in *Classic Readings* for a fuller discussion of the use of cigarettes as a unit of account.

In a hyperinflation, all prices rise so much that our frame of reference is lost.

This three-components-of-money discussion sometimes leaves students with the impression that other things can easily fulfill the functions of money. For the medium of exchange and store of value functions, this is true. However, it is not true for the unit of account function. Because all other financial instruments are valued in money, that unit-of-account function is fundamentally important and tied into the workings of the monetary economy, even if money loses its other two functions.

The use of a unit of account imposes constraints on the economy: specifically, the constraint that the unit of account must be held relatively constant. If it isn't held relatively constant, the role of money as a unit of account will be eroded. Explaining this helps make students understand the need to prevent inflation even though the specific costs of inflation are relatively minor when measured in macroeconomic terms.

As long as money is serving as a medium of exchange, it automatically also serves as a store of wealth.

Q-3: Why do people hold money rather than bonds when bonds pay higher interest than money?

Alternative Definitions of Money

Maintaining the unit-of-account usefulness of money is a second reason the Fed doesn't pay all the government's bills by printing money. Consider a college loan. A hyperinflation would significantly reduce the value of what you have to pay back. So a hyperinflation would help you, right? Actually, probably not—because a hyperinflation would also rapidly destroy money's usefulness as a store of value and unit of account, thereby destroying the U.S. economy.

In a hyperinflation, all prices rise so much that our frame of reference for making relative price comparisons is lost. Is 25¢ for a pencil high or low? If the price level changed 33,000 percent (as it did in 1988 in Nicaragua) or over 100,000 percent (as it did in 1993 in Serbia), 25¢ for a pencil would definitely be low, but would $100 be low? Without a lot of calculations we can't answer that question. A relatively stable unit of account makes it easy to answer.

Given the advantages to society of having a unit of account, it's not surprising that a monetary unit of account develops even in societies with no central bank or government. For example, in a prisoner of war camp during World War II, prisoners had no money, so they used cigarettes as their unit of account. Everything traded was given a price in cigarettes. The exchange rates on December 1, 1944, were:

1 bar of soap: 2 cigarettes
1 candy bar: 4 cigarettes
1 razor blade: 6 cigarettes
1 can of fruit: 8 cigarettes
1 can of cookies: 20 cigarettes

As you can see, all prices were in cigarettes. If candy bars rose to 6 cigarettes and the normal price was 4 cigarettes, you'd know the price of candy bars was high.

Money as a Store of Wealth Whenever you save, you forgo consumption now so that you can consume in the future. To bridge the gap between now and the future, you must acquire a financial asset. This is true even if you squirrel away currency under the mattress. In that case, the financial asset you've acquired is simply the currency itself. Money is a financial asset. (It's simply a bond that pays no interest.) So a third use of money is as a store of wealth. As long as money is serving as a medium of exchange, it automatically also serves as a store of wealth. The restaurant owner can accept your money and hold it for as long as she wants before she spends it. (But had you paid her in fish, she'd be wise not to hold it more than a few hours.)

Money's usefulness as a store of wealth also depends upon how well it maintains its value. If prices are going up 100,000 percent per year, the value of a stated amount of money is shrinking fast. People want to spend their money as quickly as possible before prices rise any more. Thus, once again, money's usefulness as a social convention depends upon the Fed not issuing too much money.

Even if prices aren't rising, you might wonder why people would hold money which pays no interest. Put another way: Why do people hold a government bond which pays no interest? The reason is that money, by definition, is highly liquid—it is more easily translated into other goods than are other financial assets. Since money is also the medium of exchange, it can be spent instantaneously (as long as there's a shop open nearby). Our ability to spend money for goods makes money worthwhile to hold even if it doesn't pay interest.

According to the definition of *money*, what people believe is money and what people will accept as money are determining factors in deciding whether a financial asset is money. Consequently it's difficult to define *money* unambiguously. A number of different financial assets serve some of the functions of money and thus have claims to being called *money*. To handle this ambiguity, economists have defined different concepts of money and have called them M_1, M_2, and L. Each is a reasonable concept of money. Let's consider their components.

M_1 M_1 consists of *currency in the hands of the public, checking account balances, and travelers' checks.* Clearly, currency in the hands of the public (the dollar bills and coins you carry around with you) are money, but how about your checking account deposits? The reason they're included in this definition of money is that just about anything you can do with currency, you can do with a check. You can store your wealth in your checking account; you can use a check as a medium of exchange (indeed, for some transactions you have no choice but to use a check), and your checking account balance is denominated in the same unit of account (dollars) as is currency. If it looks like money, acts like money, and functions as money, it's a good bet it's money. Indeed, checking account deposits are included in all definitions of money.

The same arguments can be made about travelers' checks. (Some advertisements even claim that travelers' checks are better than money because you can get them replaced.) Currency, checking account deposits, and travelers' checks make up the components of M_1, the narrowest definition of money. Exhibit 2 presents the relative sizes of M_1's components.

> **4a** M_1 is the component of the money supply that consists of currency in the hands of the public plus checking accounts and travelers' checks.

> The important point to be made is that the definitions of money expand to include assets that are less and less liquid.

M_2 M_2 is made up of *M_1 plus savings deposits, small-denomination time deposits, and money market mutual fund shares, along with some esoteric financial instruments* that won't concern us here. The relative sizes of the components of M_2 are given in Exhibit 2. (The esoteric instruments are classified as "Other.")

The money in savings accounts (savings deposits) is counted as money because it is readily spendable—all you need do is go to the bank and draw it out. Small-denomination time deposits are also called *certificates of deposit (CDs).*

M_2's components include more financial assets than M_1, some of which don't quite meet all the requirements of being called money. But all the components are highly liquid and play an important role in providing reserves and lending capacity for commercial banks. What makes the M_2 definition important is that economic research has shown that M_2 is the definition of money most closely correlated with the price level and economic activity.

> **4b** M_2 is the component of the money supply that consists of M_1 plus other relatively liquid assets.

> **Q-4:** Which would be a larger number, M_1 or M_2? Why?

Beyond M_2: L   An even wider variety of short-term financial assets (assets whose maturity is less than one year) also have some of the attributes of money. They're liquid and can be "spent" relatively easily. For that reason they're included in some definitions of money. There are definitions for M_3, M_4, and beyond. Most economists concern themselves only with the first two definitions (M_1 and M_2) and the broadest definition, which is called **L** (for *liquidity—the ability to change an asset into an immediately spendable asset*). L is the broadest definition of money and includes almost all short-term assets. In the 1980s and 1990s financial innovation has made it difficult to come up with an unchanging definition of money. Because of that difficulty,

> **4c** The broadest definition of the money supply is L (which stands for liquidity). It consists of almost all short-term financial assets.

No longer reported

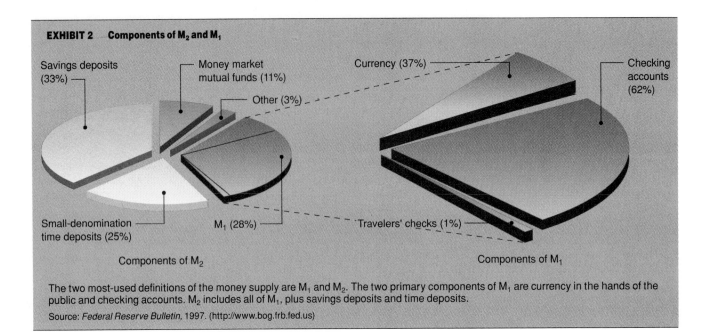

EXHIBIT 2   Components of M₂ and M₁

Savings deposits (33%)

Money market mutual funds (11%)

Other (3%)

Currency (37%)

Checking accounts (62%)

Small-denomination time deposits (25%)

M₁ (28%)

Travelers' checks (1%)

Components of M₂

Components of M₁

The two most-used definitions of the money supply are M₁ and M₂. The two primary components of M₁ are currency in the hands of the public and checking accounts. M₂ includes all of M₁, plus savings deposits and time deposits.

Source: *Federal Reserve Bulletin*, 1997. (http://www.bog.frb.fed.us)

however, measures of money have lost some of their appeal, and broader concepts of asset liquidity have gained greater appeal.

Credit card balances cannot be money since they are assets of a bank. In a sense, they are the opposite of money.

Distinguishing between Money and Credit   You might have thought that credit cards would be included in one of the definitions of *money*. But I didn't include them. In fact, credit cards are nowhere to be seen in a list of financial assets. Credit cards aren't a financial liability of the bank that issues them. Instead credit cards create a liability for their users (money owed to the company or bank that issued the card) and the banks have a financial asset as a result.

Let's consider how a credit card works. You go into a store and buy something with your credit card. You have a real asset— the item you bought. The store has a financial asset—an account receivable. The store sells that financial asset to the bank (for a fee, of course) and gets cash in return. Either the bank collects cash when you pay off your financial liability or, if you don't pay it off, the bank earns interest on its financial asset (usually at a high rate, about 18 percent per year). Credit cards are essentially prearranged loans.

This distinction between credit and money should be kept in mind. Money is a financial asset of individuals and a financial liability of banks. Credit is savings made available to be borrowed. Credit is not an asset of the borrowing public.

Credit cards and credit impact the amount of money people hold. When pre-approved loan credit is instantly available (as it is with a credit card) there's less need to hold money. (If you didn't have a credit card, you'd carry a lot more currency.) With credit immediately available, liquidity is less valuable to people. So credit and credit cards do make a difference in how much money people hold, but because they are not financial assets, they are not money.

Now that we've considered what money is, both in theory and in practice, let's consider the banking system's role in creating money, and what happens if individuals start holding their assets as some form of money rather than as bonds or some other financial asset.

BANKS AND THE CREATION OF MONEY

Banks are financial institutions that borrow from people (take in deposits) and use the money they borrow to make loans to other individuals. Banks make a profit by charging a higher interest on the money they lend out than they pay for the money they borrow. Individuals keep their money in banks, accepting lower interest rates, because doing so is safer and more convenient than the alternatives.

At one time the only checking accounts were those of commercial banks. You put your money in a commercial bank and wrote a check. Then savings banks (banks allowed only to have savings accounts) started allowing individuals to write *negotiable orders of withdrawals* on their savings accounts (NOW accounts). So if you held $10,000 in a savings account you could write an IOU to someone and the savings bank promised to pay it. That IOU looked like a check, and for all practical purposes it was a check. But unlike a checking account, NOW accounts paid interest on depositors' balances. Many people started shifting from checking accounts to NOW accounts, and soon commercial banks complained of unfair competition by savings banks. These complaints led to commercial banks being allowed to pay interest on their checking accounts.

Mutual funds saw how nicely NOW accounts worked and decided to imitate them. Individuals who deposited their money into a mutual fund were allowed to write IOUs based on their deposits (up to three IOUs per month, each for a minimum of, say, $500). The mutual fund invested depositors' money in the money market (short-term bills, commercial paper, and CDs). Hence, accounts with mutual funds are called *money market accounts*. These accounts pay slightly higher interest than savings banks' accounts, and, like the NOW account, are close to a checking account.

So today people have a choice of depository institutions, which is nice for people, but tough for textbook writers and students who have to learn more divisions.

Banking is generally analyzed from the perspective of **asset management** (*how a bank handles its loans and other assets*) and **liability management** (*how a bank attracts deposits and what it pays for them*). When banks offer people "free checking" and special money market accounts paying 4 percent, they do so after carefully considering the costs of those liabilities to them.

To think of banks as borrowers as well as lenders may seem a bit unusual, but borrowing is what they do. When you own a savings account or a checking account, the bank is borrowing from you, paying you a zero (or low) interest rate. It then lends your money to other people at a high interest rate. Much of banks' borrowing is short-term borrowing, meaning banks must pay the money back to the lender either on demand (as in the case of checking accounts or savings accounts) or within a specific period of time (as in the case of certificates of deposit).

In the United States, banks operate in a regulated environment. Regulations limit what kinds of loans banks can make and what types of borrowing banks are allowed to do. The primary regulator of banks and the money supply in the United States is the Federal Reserve Bank (the Fed), which we'll consider in detail in a later chapter.

Banks are centrally important to macroeconomics because they create money. How do banks create money? As John Kenneth Galbraith's epigram at the start of this chapter suggested, the process is simple—so simple it seems almost mystical to many.

The key to understanding how banks create money is to remember the nature of financial assets: Financial assets can be created from nothing as long as an offsetting financial liability is simultaneously created. Since money is any financial asset that can be used as a medium of exchange, unit of account, and store of value, money can be created rather easily. The asset just needs to serve the functions of money. Seeing how dollar bills are created is the easiest way to begin examining the process. Whenever the Fed issues an IOU, it creates money.[1] Similarly, other banks create money by creating financial assets that serve the functions of money. As we saw when we considered the definition of *money,* bank checking accounts serve those functions, so they are money, just as currency is money. When a bank places the proceeds of a loan it makes to you in your checking account, it is creating money. You have a financial asset that did not previously exist.

The First Step in the Creation of Money   To see how banks create money, let's consider what would happen if you were given a freshly printed $100 bill. Remember, the Fed

Video Series, Economics U$A: The Banking System, Segment 8.1
The notion that money is created in the banking system and not by the government seems odd to many people. Make sure that you make it clear that money is created as banks carry out their normal functions of taking deposits and making loans.

It is important to think of banks as both borrowers and lenders.

How Banks Create Money

5 Banks "create" money because a bank's liabilities are defined as money. So when a bank incurs liabilities it creates money.

Video Series, Economics U$A: The Banking System, Segment 8.1
I find it useful to point out the similarities between the money creation process and the multiplier process that students have already become familiar with. It is also fundamentally important to point out the distinction: One deals with the income flow, the other with the money stock.

_____
[1] As we'll see when we discuss the Fed in more detail, dollar bills aren't the Fed's only IOUs.

The Wall Street Journal is must reading material for people who want to follow financial affairs; only the editorial page is highly conservative.

created that $100 bill simply by printing it. The $100 bill is a $100 financial asset of yours and a financial liability of the Fed, which issued it.

If the process of creating money stopped there, it wouldn't be particularly mysterious. But it doesn't stop there. Let's consider what happens next as you use that money.

The Second Step in the Creation of Money

The second step in the creation of money involves the transfer of money from one form—currency—to another—a bank deposit. Say you decide to put the $100 bill in your checking account. To make the analysis easier, let's assume that your bank is a branch of the country's only bank, Big Bank. All money deposited in branch banks goes into Big Bank. After you make your deposit, Big Bank is holding $100 currency for you, and you have $100 more in your checking account. You can spend it whenever you want simply by writing a check. So Big Bank is performing a service for you (holding your money and keeping track of your expenditures) for free. Neat, huh? Big Bank must be run by a bunch of nice people.

But wait. You and I know that bankers, while they may be nice, aren't as nice as all that. There's no such thing as a free lunch. Let's see why the bank is being so nice.

Banking and Goldsmiths

To see why banks are so nice, let's go way back in history to when banks first developed.[2] At that time, gold was used for money and people carried around gold to make their payments. But gold is rather heavy, so if they had to make a big purchase, it was difficult to pay for the purchase. Moreover, carrying around a lot of gold left them vulnerable to being robbed by the likes of Robin Hood. So they looked for a place to store their gold until they needed some of it.

From Gold to Gold Receipts

The natural place to store gold was the goldsmith shop, which already had a vault. For a small fee, the goldsmith shop would hold your gold, giving you a receipt for it. Whenever you needed your gold, you'd go to the goldsmith and exchange the receipt for gold.

Pretty soon most people kept their gold at the goldsmith's, and they began to wonder: Why go through the bother of getting my gold out to buy something when all that happens is that the seller takes the gold I pay and puts it right back into the goldsmith's vault? That's two extra trips.

Consequently, people began using the receipts the goldsmith gave them to certify that they had deposited $100 worth (or whatever) of gold in his vault. At that point gold was no longer the only money—gold receipts were also money since they were accepted in exchange for goods. However, as long as the total amount in the gold receipts directly represented the total amount of gold, it was still reasonable to say, since the receipts were 100 percent backed by gold, that gold was the money supply.

Q–5: Most banks prefer to have many depositors rather than one big depositor. Why?

As technological developments decrease the importance of the medium of exchange role of money in the economy, it is important to point out to students that the process of multiple creation has parallels in debits and credits. The creation of financial assets that are not considered money can increase or decrease velocity and in doing so, can affect the real economy in somewhat the same way as money.

Gold Receipts Become Money

Once this process of using the receipts rather than the gold became generally accepted, the goldsmith found that he had substantial amounts of gold in his vault. All that gold, just sitting there! On a normal day only 1 percent of the gold was claimed by "depositors" and had to be given out. Usually on the same day an amount at least equal to that 1 percent came in from other depositors. What a waste! Gold sitting around doing nothing! So when a good friend came in, needing a loan, the goldsmith said, "Sure, I'll lend you some gold receipts as long as you pay me some interest." When the goldsmith made this loan, he created more gold receipts than he had covered in gold in his vault. He created money.

Pretty soon the goldsmith realized he could earn more from the interest he received on loans than he could earn from goldsmithing. So he stopped goldsmithing and went full-time into making loans of gold receipts. At that point the number of gold receipts outstanding significantly exceeded the amount of gold in the goldsmith's

---

[2]The banking history reported here is, according to historians, apocryphal (more myth than reality). But it so nicely makes the point that I repeat it anyhow.

vaults. But not to worry; since everyone was willing to accept gold receipts rather than gold, the goldsmith had plenty of gold for those few who wanted actual gold.

It was, however, no longer accurate to say that gold was the country's money or currency. Gold receipts were the money. They met the definition of *money*. These gold receipts were backed partially by gold and partially by people's trust that the goldsmiths would pay off their deposits on demand. The goldsmith shops had become banks.

Money is whatever meets the definition of money.

Banking Is Profitable   The banking business was very profitable for goldsmiths. Soon other people started competing with them, offering to hold gold for free. After all, if they could store gold, they could make a profit on the loans to other people (with the first people's money). Some even offered to pay people to store their gold.

The goldsmith story is directly relevant to banks. People store their currency in banks and the banks issue receipts—checking accounts—which become a second form of money. When people place their currency in banks and use their receipts from the bank as money, those receipts also become money because they meet the definition of *money:* They serve as a medium of exchange, a unit of account, and a store of wealth. So money includes both currency that people hold and their deposits in the bank.

Which brings us back to why banks hold your currency for free. They do it, not because they're nice, but because when you deposit currency in the bank, your deposit allows banks to make profitable loans they otherwise couldn't make.

With that background, let's go back to your $100, which the bank is now holding for you. You have a checking account balance of $100 and the bank has $100 currency. As long as other people are willing to accept your check in payment for $100 worth of goods, your check is as good as money. In fact it *is* money in the same way gold receipts were money. But when you deposit $100, no additional money has been created yet. The form of the money has simply been changed from currency to a checking account or demand deposit.

Now let's say Big Bank lends out 90 percent of the currency you deposit, keeping only 10 percent as **reserves**—*currency and deposits a bank keeps on hand or at the Fed or central bank, enough to manage the normal cash inflows and outflows.* This 10 percent is the **reserve ratio** (*the ratio of reserves to total deposits*). Banks are required by the Fed to hold a percentage of deposits; that percentage is called the required reserve ratio. Banks may also choose to hold an additional percentage in excess of that required reserve ratio. This additional percentage of deposits that banks choose to hold is called the excess reserve ratio. The reserve ratio is the sum of the required reserve ratio and the excess reserve ratio. Thus it is at least as large as the required reserve ratio, but it can be larger.

So, like the goldsmith, Big Bank lends out $90 to someone who qualifies for a loan. That person the bank loaned the money to now has $90 currency and you have $100 in a demand deposit, so now there's $190 of money, rather than just $100 of money. The $10 in currency the bank holds in reserve isn't counted as money since the bank must keep it as reserves and may not use it as long as it's backing loans. Only currency held by the public, not currency held by banks, is counted as money. By making the loan, the bank has created $90 in money.

Of course, no one borrows money just to hold it. The borrower spends the money, say on a new sweater, and the sweater store owner now has the $90 in currency. The store owner doesn't want to hold it either. She'll deposit it back into the bank. Since there's only one bank, Big Bank discovers that the $90 it has loaned out is once again in its coffers. The money operates like a boomerang: Big Bank loans $90 out and gets the $90 back again.

The same process occurs again. The bank doesn't earn interest income by holding $90, so if the bank can find additional credible borrowers, it lends out $81, keeping $9 (10 percent of $90) in reserve. The story repeats and repeats itself, with a slightly

The Money Multiplier

It is important to work through the multiplier process carefully and with diligence. The process is often mysterious for students and you want to eliminate that mystery.

Reserve ratio   The ratio of currency (or deposits at the central bank) to deposits a bank keeps as a reserve against currency withdrawals. The reserve ratio consists of required and excess reserves.

Once the simple multiplier is developed, experiment with it by asking about the effects of different values for the reserve requirement. Always explain why the changes occur.

Banks "hold" currency for people and in return allow individuals to write checks for the amount they have on deposit at the bank.

Individuals can withdraw their currency at almost any time from automated tellers.

It is important to point out that the reserve ratio is determined by banks subject to limitations imposed by government. The reserve ratio can include desired excess reserves above and beyond required reserves. For example, in Britain, required reserves are zero, but banks still keep a certain amount of reserves on hand.

6a The money multiplier is the measure of the amount of money ultimately created per dollar deposited by the banking system. When people hold no currency it equals $1/r$.

Appendix C provides an example of the money creation process using T-accounts.

smaller amount coming back to the bank each time. At each step in the process, money (in the form of checking account deposits) is being created.

Determining How Many Demand Deposits Will Be Created   What's the total amount of demand deposits that will ultimately be created from your $100 when individuals hold no currency? To answer that question, we continue the process over and over: 100 + 90 + 81 + 72.9 + 65.6 + 59 + 53.1 + 47.8 + 43.0 + 38.7 + 34.9. Adding up these numbers gives us $686. Adding up $686 plus the numbers from the next 20 rounds gives us $961.08.

As you can see, that's a lot of adding. Luckily there's an easier way. Economists have shown that you can determine the amount of money that will eventually be created by such a process by multiplying the initial $100 in money that was found and deposited by $1/r$, where r is the reserve ratio (the percentage banks keep out of each round). In this case the reserve ratio is 10 percent.

Dividing,

$$1/r = 1/.10 = 10$$

so the amount of demand deposits that will ultimately exist at the end of the process is

$$(10 \times \$100) = \$1,000.$$

The $1,000 is in the form of checking account deposits (demand deposits). The entire $100 in currency that you were given, and which started the whole process, is in the bank as reserves, which means that $900 ($1,000 − $100) of money has been created by the process.

Calculating the Money Multiplier   The ratio $1/r$ is called the **simple money multiplier**—*the measure of the amount of money ultimately created per dollar deposited in the banking system, when people hold no currency.* It tells us how much money will ultimately be created by the banking system from an initial inflow of money. In our example, $1/.10 = 10$. Had the bank kept out 20 percent each time, the money multiplier would have been $1/.20 = 5$. If the reserve ratio were 5 percent, the money multiplier would have been $1/.05 = 20$. The higher the reserve ratio, the smaller the money multiplier, and the less money will be created.

An Example of the Creation of Money[3]   To make sure you understand the process, let's consider an example. Say that the reserve ratio is 20 percent and that John Finder finds $10,000 in currency, which he deposits in the bank. Thus, he has $10,000 in his checking account and the bank has $8,000 ($10,000 − $2,000 in reserves) to lend out. Once it lends that money to Fred Baker, there is $8,000 of additional money in the economy. Fred Baker uses the money to buy a new oven from Mary Builder, who, in turn, deposits the money back into the banking system. Big Bank lends out $6,400 ($8,000 − $1,600 in reserves).

Now the process occurs again. Exhibit 3 shows the effects of the process for 10 rounds, starting with the initial $10,000. Each time it lends the money out, the money returns like a boomerang and serves as reserves for more loans. After 10 rounds we reach a point where total demand deposits are $44,631, and the bank has $8,926 in reserves. This is approaching the $50,000 we'd arrive at using the money multiplier:

$$1/r(\$10,000) = [1/.2](\$10,000) = 5(\$10,000) = \$50,000.$$

If we carried it out for more rounds, we'd actually reach what the formula predicted.

Note that the process ends only when the bank holds all the currency in the economy, and the only money held by the public is in the form of demand deposits. Notice also that the total amount of money created depends on the amount banks hold in reserve.

To see that you understand the process, say that banks suddenly get concerned about the safety of their loans, and they decide to keep **excess reserves**—*reserves*

---

[3]The first three rounds of this example are shown in Appendix C, using T-accounts.

Bank Gets	Bank Keeps (Reserve Ratio: 20%)	Bank Loans (80%) = Person Borrows
$10,000	$ 2,000	$ 8,000
8,000	1,600	6,400
6,400	1,280	5,120
5,120	1,024	4,096
4,096	819	3,277
3,277	656	2,621
2,621	524	2,097
2,097	419	1,678
1,678	336	1,342
1,342	268	1,074
$44,631 (total deposits)	$ 8,926 +	$35,705

Total money existing (after 10 rounds) = $44,631
Eventual Total Money Creation (after infinite rounds)

| $50,000 (total deposits) | $10,000   + | $40,000 |

EXHIBIT 3   The Money-Creating Process

In the money-creating process, the currency keeps coming back to the banking system like a boomerang. With a 20 percent reserve requirement ultimately $(\frac{1}{2}) \times \$10,000 = \$50,000$ will be created. In this example you can see that after ten rounds, most of the creation of deposits will have taken place. As you carry out the analysis further, the money creation will approach the $50,000 shown in the last line.

held by banks in excess of what banks are required to hold. What will happen to the money multiplier? If you answered that it will decrease, you've got it. Excess reserves decrease the money multiplier as much as do required reserves. I mention this example because this is precisely what happened to the banking system in the early 1990s. Banks became concerned about the safety of their loans; they held large excess reserves, and the money multiplier decreased.

In summary, the process of money creation isn't difficult to understand as long as you remember that money is simply a bank's financial liability held by the public. Whenever banks create financial liabilities for themselves, they create financial assets for individuals, and those financial assets are money.

Calculating the Approximate Real-World Money Multiplier   In the example I assumed only banks hold currency. The simple money multiplier reflects that assumption. In reality banks are not the only holders of currency. Firms and individuals hold currency too, so in each round we must also make an adjustment in the multiplier for what people and firms hold. The math you need to calculate the money multiplier formally gets a bit complicated when firms and people hold currency. Since for our purposes a rough calculation is all we need, we will use an approximate money multiplier in which individuals' currency holdings are treated the same as reserves of banks. Thus the

See "100 Percent Reserves," by Irving Fisher in *Classic Readings in Economics.*

In Appendix D, I develop the full multiplier when individuals hold cash. I would only suggest going through this in technically oriented classes. The central idea is sufficiently fulfilled by the approximate real-world multiplier.

6b When people hold currency the approximate money multiplier is $1/(r + c)$.

ADDED DIMENSION   THE REAL-WORLD MONEY MULTIPLIER AND RECENT REFORMS IN BANKING

Life keeps getting tougher. In the old days economics students only had to learn the simple money multiplier. Recent reforms in the U.S. banking system have made that impossible. The Depository Institutions Deregulation Act of 1980 extended the reserve requirement to a wide variety of financial institutions besides banks, but it also lowered the reserve requirement for most deposits. In the 1990s, the average reserve requirement for all types of bank deposits is about 2 percent and banks hold very few excess reserves. (The U.S. reserve requirement on checking accounts is between 3 and 10 percent. In Great Britain, there are no reserve requirements.)

If you insert that low average ratio into the simple money multiplier, you get a multiplier of 50! The real-world money multiplier is much lower than that because of people's holding of currency; the ratio of money people hold as currency, c, is over 40 percent. (For each person in the United States there's about $1,000 in currency. Don't ask me where that currency is, but according to the data it's out there.) Thus, despite the fact that it makes calculating the approximate real-world money multiplier a bit more difficult, these holdings must be included in the story. Otherwise you won't have a sense of how the real-world system works.

Q–6: If banks hold 20 percent of their deposits as reserves, and the ratio of money people hold as currency to deposits is 20 percent, what is the approximate money multiplier?

Q–7: If people suddenly decide to hold more currency, what happens to the size of the approximate money multiplier?

Faith as the Backing of Our Money Supply

All that backs the modern money supply are bank loan customers' promises to pay and government guarantees of banks' liabilities to individuals.

REGULATION OF BANKS AND THE FINANCIAL SECTOR

approximate real-world money multiplier in the economy is:

$$1/(r + c)$$

where r = *the percentage of deposits banks hold in reserve* and c is the *ratio of money people hold in currency to the money they hold as deposits.*[4] Let's consider an example. Say the banks keep 10 percent in reserve and the ratio of individuals' currency holdings to their deposits is 25 percent. This means the approximate real-world money multiplier will be

$$1/(.1 + .25) = 1/.35 = 2.9.$$

The creation of money and the money multiplier are easy to understand if you remember that money held in the form of a checking account (the financial asset created) is offset by an equal amount of financial liabilities of the bank. The bank owes its depositors the amount in their checking accounts. Its financial liabilities to depositors, in turn, are secured by the loans (the bank's financial assets) and by the financial liabilities of people to whom the loans were made. Promises to pay underlie any modern financial system.

The initial money in the story about the goldsmiths was gold, but it quickly became apparent that it was far more reasonable to use gold certificates as money. Therefore gold certificates backed by gold soon replaced gold itself as the money supply. Then, as goldsmiths made more loans than they had gold, the gold certificates were no longer backed by gold. They were backed by promises to get gold if the person wanted gold in exchange for the gold certificate. Eventually the percentage of gold supposedly backing the money became so small that it was clear to everyone that the promises, not the gold, underlay the money supply.

The same holds true with banks. Initially currency (Federal Reserve IOUs) was backed by gold, and banks' demand deposits were in turn backed by Federal Reserve IOUs. But by the 1930s the percentage of gold backing money grew so small that even the illusion of the money being backed by anything but promises was removed. All that backs the modern money supply are bank loan customers' promises to pay and the guarantee of the government to see that the banks' liabilities to individuals will be met.

You just saw how easy it is to create money. The banking system and money make the economy operate more efficiently, but they also present potential problems. For example, say that for some reason suddenly there's an increase in money (that is, in promises to pay) without any corresponding increase in real goods and services. As the money supply increases without an increase in real goods and services to buy with

---

[4]In Appendix D, I discuss the precise calculation of the money multiplier when individuals hold currency.

that money, more money is chasing the same number of goods. The result will be a fall in the value of money (inflation), meaning real trade will be more complicated. Alternatively, if there's an increase in real goods and services but not a corresponding increase in money, there will be a shortage of money, which will hamper the economy. Either the price level will fall (deflation) or there will be a recession.

Video Series, Economics U$A: The Banking System, Segment 8.3, 26.1–26.3

Financial Panics

Societies have continually experienced these problems, and the financial history of the world is filled with stories of financial upheavals and monetary problems. For example, there are numerous instances of private financial firms that have promised the world, but whose promises have been nothing but hot air. One instance occurred in the 1800s in the United States, when banks were allowed to issue their own notes (their own promises to pay). These notes served as part of the U.S. money supply. Sharp financial operators soon got into the process and created banks out in the boonies called wildcat banks because they were situated in places where only a wildcat would go. These wildcat banks issued notes even though they had no deposits, hoping that no one would cash the notes in. Many such banks defaulted on their promises, leaving holders of the notes with only worthless pieces of paper. Merchants quickly caught on, and soon they began checking in a "book of notes" which listed whether the notes the buyer was offering were probably good or not.

See "Why Lombard Street Is Often Very Dull, and Sometimes Extremely Excited," by Walter Bagehot in *Classic Readings in Economics,* which focuses on the role of confidence as a necessary foundation of a banking system.

Anatomy of a Financial Panic

Banking and financial systems are based on promises and trust. People exchange their currency for other financial assets (such as demand deposits) and believe that these demand deposits are as good as currency. In normal times, demand deposits really are as good as currency. When times get bad, people become concerned about the financial firms' ability to keep those promises and they call upon the firms to redeem the checking account promises. But banks have only their reserves (a small percentage of their total deposits) to give depositors. Most of the depositors' assets are loaned out and cannot be collectively gotten back quickly, even though the banks have promised depositors that their deposits will be given back "on demand." Put another way, banks' borrowing is short-term while its lending is long-term; banks borrow short and lend long.

7 Financial systems are based on trust that expectations will be fulfilled. Banks borrow short and lend long, which means that if people lose faith in banks, the banks cannot keep their promises.

Video Series, Economics U$A: Stabilization Policy, Segment 13.3

When a lot of depositors lose faith in a bank and, all at one time, call on the bank to keep its promise to provide currency in exchange for their checking account balances, the bank cannot do so. The result is that the bank fails when depositors lose faith, even though the bank might be financially sound for the long run. Fear underlies financial panics and can undermine financial institutions unless the banks can convert their earning assets into currency quickly.

Q–8: Why does borrowing short and lending long present a potential problem for banks?

Government Policy to Prevent Panic

To prevent such panics, the U.S. government has guaranteed the obligations of various financial institutions. The most important guaranteeing program is the Federal Deposit Insurance Corporation (FDIC), but there are also a variety of government-guaranteed bonds. These guarantees work as follows: The financial institutions pay a small premium for each dollar of deposit to the government-organized insurance company. That company puts the premium into a fund used to bail out banks experiencing a run on deposits. These guarantees have two effects:

Q–9: What are two effects that a government guarantee of financial institutions can have?

1. They prevent the unwarranted fear that causes financial crises. Depositors know that the government will see that they can get their currency back even if the bank fails. This knowledge stops them from responding to a rumor and trying to get their money out of a suspect financial institution before anyone else does.

2. They prevent warranted fears. Why should people worry about whether or not a financial institution is making reasonable loans on the basis of their deposits if the government guarantees the financial institutions' promises to pay regardless of what kind of loans the institutions make?

The Benefits and Problems of Guarantees

The fact that deposits are guaranteed doesn't serve to inspire banks to make certain deposits are covered by loans in the long run.

Many students have never dealt with a bank and, if there's time, it is sometimes helpful to have a loan officer from a local bank come and discuss how he or she decides on making a loan and the problems involved therein. Students really enjoy such real-world presentations.

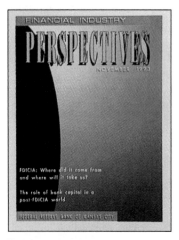

Each reserve bank has its own journal, and these are excellent sources of information and readable articles about financial issues.

Spread   *The difference between a bank's costs of funds and the interest it receives on lending out those funds.*

Government guarantees prevent unwarranted fears. The illusion upon which banks depend (that people can get their money in the short run, even though it's only in the long run that they can *all* get it) can be met by temporary loans from the government. Guarantees can prevent unwarranted fears from becoming financial panics. The guarantee makes the illusion a reality. If people can indeed get their money in the long run, seeing to it that this illusion is reality isn't expensive to the government. As long as the bank has sufficient long-term assets to cover its deposits, the government will be repaid its temporary loan.

Unfortunately, covering the unwarranted fear can also mean preventing the warranted fear from putting an effective restraint or discipline on banks' lending policies. If deposit liabilities are guaranteed, why should depositors worry whether banks have adequate earning assets to cover their deposits in the long run? Thus, when the short-run illusion is also a long-run illusion, and depositors can't get their money even in the long run because of excess loan defaults (that is, their fears were warranted), guaranteeing deposits can be expensive indeed for the taxpayers who must bear the cost of the guaranteed payouts to bank depositors. The U.S. government found this out in the late 1980s in connection with its guarantees of federal savings and loan institutions' deposits.

The Savings and Loan Fiasco of the Late 1980s and Early 1990s   As we said, the United States has guaranteed the deposits of a variety of financial institutions, including savings and loan institutions (S&Ls). S&Ls had developed as institutions to hold savings and invest those savings back into the community. Up until 1980, S&Ls were heavily regulated by the government and weren't allowed to invest in anything except private residential mortgages, which generally are relatively safe investments. The only place S&Ls were allowed to get their funds from was their depositors' savings accounts. During the period when S&Ls were heavily regulated, the U.S. government began to guarantee S&L deposits.

In 1982 financial institutions were deregulated, and S&Ls were allowed to invest in anything they wished and to compete for funds with commercial banks by issuing interest-bearing checking accounts (called *NOW accounts*) and negotiable CDs. They did so. They paid high interest on their deposits and, to justify that high interest, they invested in high-interest financial assets such as high-risk junk (low-grade) bonds and commercial real estate. Unfortunately S&Ls didn't have the management capability to assess the risks, and they made billions of dollars worth of bad loans which would never be paid back. During the 1980s the U.S. economy also changed. Banking policies that had made sense in the late 1970s and early 1980s no longer made sense in the mid-1980s. The result was the savings and loan fiasco of the late 1980s and early 1990s. Many S&Ls failed and didn't have enough money to pay back depositors. The U.S. government, which had guaranteed those deposits, had to bail out the S&Ls by paying the depositors.

Because of the complexity and vast number of deals so many S&Ls made, it will probably be years before the government actually knows the final cost, but it will be somewhere around two hundred billion dollars.

How Could the Savings and Loan Fiasco Happen?   How, you ask, can banks make so many bad loans that they don't have enough money to pay back depositors? A small part of the answer is fraud—banks made loans to friends that they knew were more like gifts than loans. Part of the answer is that it doesn't take many bad loans to pull a bank under. Remember, banks take deposits in and lend those deposits out, hoping to make a profit from the **spread** (*the difference between their costs and the interest they pay out, and the interest they take in minus bad loans*). If, on average, more loans go bad than expected and the banks' costs are higher than expected, banks' profit can evaporate, leaving a loss. When that happens, deposits must be covered by the banks' net worth, which can be small, so there isn't much room for many bad loans. As was just pointed out, the S&Ls paid high interest rates and made many risky loans.

Another part of the answer is that it isn't hard to make a bad loan. Making loans is inherently risky. A person walks in with a grand idea for a mall—all she needs is a $10,000,000 loan. The mall is needed by the community and will be worth $30,000,000 once it's built. She has investors willing to put up $2,000,000 of their own money and she's willing to pay 12 percent interest and give the mall as collateral. She's built successful malls before. So the bank makes the loan.

The building starts, only to have the builder discover there's a stone ledge beneath the site. Blasting is required—costs go up 12 percent. A builders' strike delays construction—costs go up 4 percent. When things are ready to proceed once the strike is settled, it rains daily, slowing construction—costs go up another 8 percent. The economy goes into a recession and one store that had promised to rent space in the mall pulls out. Let's say the store that pulled out was an "anchor" store (that is, the mall relied on that store's presence to attract large numbers of shoppers, who would then wander around and shop in the mall's smaller stores). Now the major industry in town shuts down. The mall's finished value falls 40 percent. You get the picture.

Making loans requires taking chances and, when you take chances, once in a while you lose. S&Ls bet that there would be no recession. When a recession started, they lost their bet, and a number of their loans went bad.

This 18th-century etching by Robert Goez, "The Speculator," captures a popular view of financial activities. It shows a man reduced to rags by bad speculation. *Bleichroeder Print Collection, Baker Library, Harvard Business School.*

The last part of the answer is the government guarantee. Had the government not guaranteed the S&Ls' deposits, depositors (not the government) would have incurred the loss. They likely would have become alarmed as they saw troubles coming to their S&Ls and would have withdrawn their money before the situation became a disaster. But they didn't watch carefully and had no reason to be alarmed, because they knew the government had guaranteed their deposits (at least, up to $100,000).

Should the government have guaranteed S&L deposits? That's an open question. The guarantees did serve their purpose; they prevented unwarranted runs on S&Ls. (That is, depositors didn't all run to the bank at the same time and ask to withdraw their money in currency.) But the guarantee program had serious flaws. If the government was going to guarantee deposits, it should have charged banks much higher fees. Government then would have had enough money to cover the losses resulting from bad loans. Or government should have maintained a strong regulatory presence, limiting the risks the S&Ls undertook.

The S&L crisis didn't answer the debate between the two goals: avoiding unwarranted fears while not limiting warranted fears. Some economists blame the crisis on the bank deregulation that let S&Ls make risky loans and investments. They claim the S&Ls' crisis showed the need for regulation. Others blame government guarantees that stopped the market forces from operating. As usual, both have reasonable arguments.

Q–10: What is a benefit and what is the cost of government guarantees of deposits?

We'll stop our consideration of money and the financial sector there. As you can see, money is central to the operation of the macro economy. If money functions smoothly, it keeps the outflow from the expenditure stream (savings) and the flow back into the expenditure stream at a level that reflects people's desires. Money can be treated simply as a mirror of people's real desires.

When money doesn't function smoothly, it can influence the flows, sometimes creating too large a flow back into the expenditures stream, causing inflationary pressures, and other times creating too small a flow back in, causing a recession.

CONCLUSION

CHAPTER SUMMARY

- The financial sector is the market where financial assets are created and exchanged.
- Every financial asset has a corresponding financial liability.
- Money is a useful financial instrument.
- Money serves as a unit of account, a medium of exchange, and a store of wealth.
- There are various definitions of money: M_1, M_2, and L.

- Since money is what people believe money to be, creating money out of thin air is easy. How banks create money out of thin air is easily understood if you remember that money is simply a financial liability of a bank.
- The simple money multiplier is $1/r$.
- The approximate real-world multiplier is $1/(r + c)$.
- Financial panics are based on fear. They can be prevented by government, but only at a cost.

KEY TERMS

approximate real-world money multiplier *(220)*
asset management *(215)*
bank *(210)*
bond *(209)*
excess reserves *(218)*

Federal Reserve Bank (the Fed) *(210)*
Financial assets *(209)*
interset rate *(209)*
L *(213)*
liability management *(215)*
M_1 *(213)*

M_2 *(213)*
money *(209)*
reserve ratio *(217)*
reserves *(217)*
simple money multiplier *(218)*
spread *(222)*

QUESTIONS FOR THOUGHT AND REVIEW

The number after each question represents the estimated degree of critical thinking required. (1 = almost none; 10 = deep thought.)

1. If financial institutions don't produce any tangible real assets, why are they considered a vital part of the U.S. economy? *(4)*
2. Money is to the economy as oil is to an engine. Explain. *(4)*
3. List the three functions of money. *(1)*
4. Why doesn't the government pay for all its goods simply by printing money? *(4)*
5. What are two components of M_2 that are not components of M_1? *(1)*
6. Assuming individuals hold no currency, calculate the simple money multiplier for each of the following reserve requirements: 5%, 10%, 20%, 25%, 50%, 75%, 100%. *(3)*
7. Assuming individuals hold 20% of their money in the form of currency, recalculate the approximate real-world money multipliers from Question 6. *(5)*

8. If dollar bills (Federal Reserve notes) are backed by nothing but promises and are in real terms worthless, why do people accept them? *(4)*
9. If the U.S. government were to raise the reserve requirement to 100 percent, what would likely happen to the interest rate banks pay on deposits? Why? *(6)*
10. What was the cause of the S&L crisis? What role did government guarantees play in that crisis? *(6)*
11. Is the current U.S. banking system susceptible to panic? If so, how might a panic occur? *(5)*
12. About 30 U.S. localities circulate their own currency with names like "Ithaca Hours" and "Dillo Hours." Doing so is perfectly legal (although by law they are subject to a 10 percent federal tax, which currently the government is not collecting). These currencies are used as payment for rent, wages, goods, etc. Would these currencies be considered money? Explain. *(4)*

PROBLEMS AND EXERCISES

1. While Jon is walking to school one morning, a helicopter flying overhead drops a $100 bill. Not knowing how to return it, Jon keeps the money and deposits it in his bank. (No one in this economy holds currency.) If the bank keeps 5 percent of its money in reserves:
   a. How much money can the bank now lend out?
   b. After this initial transaction, by how much is the money in the economy changed?
   c. What's the money multiplier?
   d. How much money will eventually be created by the banking system from Jon's $100?

2. Go to a local bank.
   a. Ask for a loan application. Inquire if you will be eligible for a loan.
   b. Ask why or why not.
   c. Find out how many different types of accounts they have and how these accounts differ.
   d. Ask if they will cash a $1,000 out-of-state check. If so, how long will it take for them to do so?

3. Categorize the following as components of M_1, M_2, both, or neither.
   a. State and local government bonds.
   b. Checking accounts.
   c. Money market mutual funds.
   d. Currency.
   e. Stocks.
   f. Corporate bonds.
   g. Travelers' checks.

4. For each of the following, state whether it is considered money in the United States. Explain why or why not.
   a. A check you write against deposits you have at Bank USA.
   b. Brazilian reals.
   c. The available credit you have on your MasterCard.
   d. Reserves held by banks at the Federal Reserve Bank.
   e. Federal Reserve notes in your wallet.
   f. Gold bullion.
   g. Grocery store coupons.

5. For each of the following state whether it is included in M_1, M_2, or both:
   a. Checking accounts.
   b. Savings deposits.
   c. Money market mutual funds.
   d. Currency.
   e. Travelers' checks.

ANSWERS TO MARGIN QUESTIONS

1. I would respond by saying that the financial sector is central to the macroeconomy. It facilitates the trades that occur in the real sector. *(208)*

2. For money to have value, it must be in limited supply. People will use paper money as a medium of exchange, unit of account, and store of value only as long as it is limited in supply, which means that the Fed cannot print up lots of money and maintain its use as money. *(211)*

3. Money provides liquidity and ease of payment. People hold money rather than bonds to get this liquidity and hold down transactions costs. *(212)*

4. M_2 would be the larger number, since it includes all of the components of M_1 plus additional components. *(213)*

5. Banks operate on the law of large numbers—the law that, on average, many fluctuations will affect each other, and hence their effect will be much smaller than the sum of all fluctuations—so that they will have some money flowing in and some money flowing out at all times. This allows them to make loans on the "float," the average amount that they are holding. If there is one big depositor at a bank, the law of large numbers does not necessarily hold, and the bank must hold larger reserves in case that big depositor withdraws that money. *(216)*

6. The approximate money multiplier is $1/(r + c)$, which is equal to $1/.4 = 2.5$. *(220)*

7. The approximate real-world money multiplier would decrease since it makes the denominator of the money multiplier larger. *(220)*

8. When banks borrow short and lend long, they are susceptible to a financial panic. Unless they have a place where they can borrow, they may not have the liquidity to pay off depositors immediately. *(221)*

9. Government guarantees of financial institutions can prevent unwarranted fears that cause financial crises, but they can also prevent warranted fears and thereby undermine financial institutions. *(221)*

10. Government guarantees of deposits tend to eliminate unwarranted fears, but they also eliminate warranted fears and hence eliminate a market control of bank loans. *(223)*

The Value of a
Financial Asset

To understand financial assets, you must understand how financial asset prices are determined. Why does an average share of stock sell for about 15 times earnings? How come bond prices rise as market interest rates fall, and fall as market interest rates rise? In answering such questions, the first point to recognize is that $1 today is not equal to $1 next year. Why? Because if I have $1 today I can invest it and earn interest (say 10 percent per year), and next year I will have $1.10, not $1. So if the annual interest rate is 10 percent, $1.10 next year is worth $1 today or, alternatively, $1 next year is worth roughly 91 cents today. A dollar two years in the future is worth even less today, and dollars 30 years in the future are worth very little today.

Present Value and Interest Rate

How much less $1 in the future is worth today depends on the interest rate. If the interest rate is close to zero, $1 is worth only a little bit less; if the interest rate is 5 percent, $1 is worth quite a bit less. The higher the interest rate, the less a dollar is worth in the future. How do I know? Because I pulled out my handy business calculator and pressed in the numbers to calculate the **present value** (*the value now of income payments in the future*).

Exhibit A1 graphically displays, for three different annual interest rates, how much a given amount of money

at various lengths of time in the future is worth now. Notice that: (1) the higher the interest rate, the less a given amount of money in the future is worth now; and (2) how quickly the present value falls at higher annual interest rates. At 15 percent interest, $100 to be received 30 years from now is currently worth $1.50, as shown in Exhibit A1(c).

The present value reasoning also works in reverse. You can determine the future value of a given amount of money today. Say you have $100 now. If you earn 8 percent annual interest on it, it will be $215.89 in 10 years and $466.10 in 20 years. The higher the interest rate and the longer the time frame, the greater the future value will be.

Most of you, I suspect, don't have business calculators. For people who don't, there are bond tables to tell you present values of future dollars. A table or a calculator is extremely helpful in determining the price a bond should sell for. That's because a bond consists of a stream of income payments over a number of years *and* the repayment of the face value of the bond. Each year's interest payment and the eventual repayment of the face value must be calculated separately and then the results added together.

All financial assets can be broken down into promises to pay certain amounts at certain times in the future, or, if the financial asset is a share of stock, not a promise but an

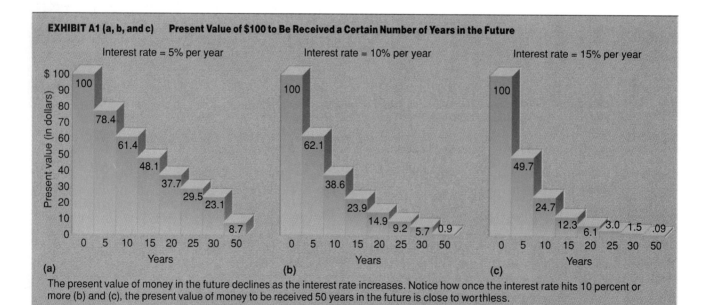

EXHIBIT A1 (a, b, and c)   Present Value of $100 to Be Received a Certain Number of Years in the Future

The present value of money in the future declines as the interest rate increases. Notice how once the interest rate hits 10 percent or more (b) and (c), the present value of money to be received 50 years in the future is close to worthless.

WHAT WILL A BOND SELL FOR?

To determine what a bond will sell for, first remember a bond is a flow of payments over time. Its selling price depends on how much those payments are worth. If it's unlikely those payments will continue (for example, if the company issuing the bond is close to bankruptcy), the bond isn't worth much. This *risk* plays an important role in determining the bond's price.

A second factor in determining a bond's price is the current interest rate in the economy. If the interest rate today (for bonds of similar riskiness) is higher than the bond's coupon rate (which generally represents the interest rate that existed when the bond was originally issued), a bond will sell for less than its face value on the secondary market. Why? Because if it sold at its face value, it would make more sense for people to buy newly issued bonds paying higher interest rates. When a bond sells for less than its face value, its yield (the rate of return you receive per dollar of purchase price per year from a bond) increases. For example, say there's a one-

year 5 percent coupon bond with $100 face value, and this bond is selling for $90. For $90 you'll get a $5 payment (5 percent of $100 from the coupon plus the $100 face value, or a gain of $15 over its initial price of $90. That's a 16.7% yield).

If the interest rate is lower than the coupon rate, bonds will sell for more than their face value. Why? Because at its face value, the bond is much more desirable than newly issued bonds. The market value of the bond will rise until the yield on the bond equals the interest rate on similar newly issued bonds. Only then will the buyer be indifferent between the old and new bonds.

Because of this relationship between interest rates and bond prices, generally whenever market interest rates rise, bond prices fall; whenever market interest rates fall, bond prices rise. Thus, the interest rate in the economy plays an important role in determining a bond's price on the secondary market.

expectation of such payment. So all financial assets (stocks or bonds) can be valued. You simply calculate the present value of all expected future payments. For example, say a share of stock is earning $1 per share and is expected to do so long into the future. If the interest rate is 6½ percent, the present value of that future stream of expected earnings is about $15.

There is, however, a proviso to the preceding reasoning. If promises to pay aren't trustworthy, you don't put the amount that's promised into your calculation; you put in the amount you expect. That's why when a company or a country looks as if it's going to default on loans or stop paying dividends, the value of its bonds and stock will fall considerably. For example, in the late 1980s many people thought Brazil would default on its bonds. That expectation caused the price of Brazilian bonds to fall to about 30¢ on the dollar. Then in the 1990s, when people believed total default was less likely, the value rose.

Asset Prices, Interest Rates, and the Economy

This appendix isn't meant to cover the intricacies of valuation over time. That's done in a finance course. The point of this chapter is to help you understand the relationship between interest rates and asset prices. Increases in interest rates (because they make future flows of income coming from an asset worth less now) make financial asset prices fall. Decreases in interest rates (because they make the future flow of income coming from an asset worth more now) make financial asset prices rise.

Since a slight change in interest rates can lead to a large change in asset prices, many individuals speculate on what's going to happen to interest rates and switch their investments from one type of financial asset to another, causing potential problems for the macroeconomy. So understanding how assets are valued is fundamental to understanding the macroeconomic debate.

KEY TERMS

present value   *(226)*

QUESTIONS FOR THOUGHT AND REVIEW

1. How much is $50 to be received 50 years from now worth if the interest rate is 5 percent? (Use Exhibit A1.)
2. How much is $50 to be received 50 years from now worth if the interest rate is 10 percent? (Use Exhibit A1.)
3. Your employer offers you a choice of two bonus packages: $1,400 today or $2,000 five years from now. Assuming a 5 percent rate of interest, which is the better value? Assuming an interest rate of 10 percent, which is the better value?

4. Suppose the price of a one-year 10 percent coupon bond with a $100 face value is $98.
   a. Are market interest rates likely to be above or below 10 percent? Explain.
   b. What is the bond's yield?
   c. If market interest rates fell, what would happen to the price of the bond?
5. Explain in words why the present value of $100 to be received in 10 years would decline as the interest rate rises.

A Closer Look at Financial Institutions and Financial Markets

Financial Assets and Financial Liabilities

To understand the financial sector and its relation to the real sector, you must understand how financial assets and liabilities work and how they affect the real economy.

An *asset* is something that provides its owner with expected future benefits. There are two types of assets: real assets and financial assets. Real assets are assets such as houses or machinery whose services provide direct benefits to their owners, either now or in the future. A house is a real asset—you can live in it. A machine is a real asset—you can produce goods with it.

Financial assets are *assets, such as stocks or bonds, whose benefit to the owner depends on the issuer of the asset meeting certain obligations.* **Financial liabilities** are *liabilities incurred by the issuer of a financial asset to stand behind the issued asset.* It's important to remember that *every financial asset has a corresponding financial liability;* it's that financial liability that gives the financial asset its value. In the case of bonds, for example, a company's agreement to pay interest and repay the principal gives bonds their value. If the company goes bankrupt and reneges on its liability to pay interest and repay the principal, the asset becomes worthless. The corresponding liability gives the financial asset its value.

For example, a **stock** is *a financial asset that conveys ownership rights in a corporation.* It is a liability of the firm; it gives the holder ownership rights which are spelled out in the financial asset. An equity liability, such as a stock, usually conveys a general right to dividends, but only if the company's board of directors decides to pay them.

A debt liability conveys no ownership right. It's a type of loan. An example of a debt liability is a bond that a firm issues. A **bond** is *a promise to pay a certain amount of money plus interest in the future.* A bond is a liability of the firm but an asset of the individual who holds the bond. A debt liability, such as a bond, usually conveys legal rights to interest payments and repayment of principal.

Real assets are created by real economic activity. For example, a house or a machine must be built. Financial assets are created whenever somebody takes on a financial liability or establishes an ownership claim. For example, say I promise to pay you $1,000,000,000 in the future. You now have a financial asset and I have a financial liability. Understanding that financial assets can be created by a simple agreement of two people is fundamentally important to understanding how the financial sector works.

Financial Institutions A **financial institution** is *a business whose primary activity is buying, selling, or holding financial assets.* For example, some financial institutions (depository institutions and investment intermediaries) sell promises to pay in the future. These promises can be their own promises or someone else's promises. When you open a savings account at a bank, the bank is selling you its own promise that you can withdraw your money, plus interest, at some unspecified time in the future. Such a bank is a **depository institution**—*a financial institution whose primary financial liability is deposits in checking or savings accounts.* When you buy a newly issued government bond or security from a securities firm, it's also selling you a promise to pay in the future. But in this case, it's a third party's promise. So a securities firm is a financial broker that sells third parties' promises to pay. It's a type of marketing firm for financial IOUs.

As financial institutions sell financial assets, they channel savings from savers (individuals who give other people money now in return for promises to pay it back with interest later) to borrowers (investors or consumers who get the money now in return for their promise to pay it and the interest later).

As economists use the term, *to save* is to buy a financial asset. *To invest* (in economic terminology) is to buy real, not financial, assets that you hope will yield a return in the future.[1] How do you get funds to invest if you don't already have them? You borrow them. That means you create a financial asset that you sell to someone else who saves.

Some financial institutions serve several purposes and their various functions may have various names. For example, a depository institution, such as a commercial bank, may also serve as a **contractual intermediary**—*a financial institution that holds and stores individuals' financial assets.* Contractual intermediaries intermediate (serve as a go-between) between savers and investors. For example, a pension fund is a financial institution that takes in individuals' savings, relends those savings, and ultimately, pays back those savings plus interest after the

---

[1]This terminology isn't the terminology most lay people use. When a person buys a stock, in economic terms that person is *saving*, though most lay people call that *investing*.

EXHIBIT B1   1996 Holdings of Selected Financial Institutions

Financial Institutions	Percent of Total Financial Assets	Primary Assets (Uses of Funds)	Primary Liabilities (Sources of Funds)
Depository institutions:			
Commercial banks	36%	Business and consumer loans, mortgages, U.S. government securities, and municipal bonds	Checkable deposits and savings deposits
Savings and loan associations and mutual savings banks	4	Mortgages	Savings deposits (and checkable deposits)
Credit unions	1	Consumer loans	Savings deposits (and checkable deposits)
Contractual intermediaries:			
Pension funds	24	Corporate bonds and stock	Employer and employee contributions
Life insurance companies	10	Corporate bonds and mortgages	Policy obligations
Fire and casualty insurance companies	4	Municipal bonds, corporate bonds and stock, and U.S. government securities	Policy obligations
Investment intermediaries:			
Money market mutual funds	4	Money market instruments	Shares
Mutual funds	11	Stocks and bonds	Shares
Finance companies	4	Consumer and business loans	Commercial paper, stocks, and bonds
Financial brokers:			
Investment banks	0	None	None
Brokerage houses	3	Credit Market Instruments	Security RPS

Source: Federal Reserve System. *Flow of Funds Accounts of the United States,* 1997.

individuals retire. It uses individuals' savings to buy financial assets from people and firms who want to borrow. Similarly, a commercial bank is a financial institution that relends an individual's checking account deposits. A checking deposit is a financial asset of an individual and a financial liability of the bank.

Types of Financial Institutions   Exhibit B1 lists four types of financial institutions and shows the percentage of total U.S. financial assets each holds, along with the sources and uses of funds for each. These percentages give you an idea of the institution's importance, but institutions' importance can come in other ways. For example, although investment banks hold no financial assets, they're important because they facilitate buying and selling such assets. Let's consider each grouping separately.

Depository Institutions   Depository institutions, the first category listed, are financial institutions whose primary financial liability is deposits in checking accounts. They hold approximately 35 percent of all the financial assets in the United States. This category includes commercial banks, savings banks, savings and loan associations (S&Ls), and credit unions. The primary financial liability of each is deposits. For example, the amount in your checking account or savings account is a financial asset for you and a financial liability for the bank holding your deposit.

Banks make money by lending your deposits (primarily in the form of business and commercial loans), charging the borrower a higher interest rate than they pay

the depositor. Those loans from banks to borrowers are financial assets of the bank and financial liabilities of the borrower.

Laws governing financial institutions changed significantly in the 1980s and early 1990s. In the 1970s, each financial institution was restricted to specific types of financial transactions. Savings banks and S&Ls handled savings accounts and mortgages; they were not allowed to issue checking accounts. Commercial banks were not allowed to hold or sell stock; they did, however, issue checking accounts. These restrictions allowed us to make sharp, clear distinctions among financial institutions. Changes in the laws have eliminated many of these restrictions, blurring the distinctions among the various types of financial institutions. Now all depository institutions can issue checking accounts. In the late 1990s, many more changes are likely.

Some differences remain that reflect their history. Commercial banks' primary assets are loans, and their loans include business loans, mortgages, and consumer loans. Savings banks' and S&Ls' primary assets are the same kind as those of commercial banks, but their loans are primarily mortgage loans.

Contractual Intermediaries   The most important contractual intermediaries are insurance companies and pension funds. These institutions promise, for a fee, to pay an individual a certain amount of money in the future, either when some event happens (a fire or death) or, in the case of pension funds and some kinds of life insurance, when the individual reaches a certain age or dies. Insurance

Financial assets are neat. You can call them into existence simply by getting someone to accept your IOU. *Remember, every financial asset has a corresponding financial liability equal to it.* So when you say a country has $1 trillion of financial assets, you're also saying that the country has $1 trillion of financial liabilities. An optimist would say a country is rich. A pessimist would say it's poor. An economist would say that financial assets and financial liabilities are simply opposite sides of the ledger and don't indicate whether a country is rich or poor.

To find out whether a country is rich or poor, you must look at its *real assets.* If financial assets increase the economy's efficiency and thereby increase the amount of real assets, they make society better off. This is most economists' view of financial assets. If, however, they decrease the efficiency of the economy (as some economists have suggested some financial assets do because they focus productive effort on financial gamesmanship), financial assets make society worse off.

The same correspondence between a financial asset and its liability exists when a financial asset's value changes. Say stock prices fall significantly. Is society poorer? The answer

is: It depends on the reason for the change. Let's say there is no known reason. Then, while the people who own the stock are poorer, the people who might want to buy stock in the future are richer since the price of assets has fallen. So in a pure accounting sense, society is neither richer nor poorer when the prices of stocks rise or fall for no reason.

But there are ways in which changes in the value of financial assets might signify that society is richer or poorer. For example, the changes in the values of financial assets might *reflect* (rather than cause) real changes. If suddenly a company finds a cure for cancer, its stock price will rise and society will be richer. But the rise in the price of the stock doesn't cause society to be richer. It reflects the discovery that made society richer. Society would be richer because of the discovery even if the stock's price didn't rise.

There's significant debate about how well the stock market reflects real changes in the economy. Classical economists believe it closely reflects real changes; Keynesian economists believe it doesn't. But both sides agree that the changes in the real economy, not the changes in the price of financial assets, underlie what makes an economy richer or poorer.

policies and pensions are a form of individual savings. Contractual intermediaries lend those savings. As the average age of the U.S. population increases, as it will throughout the 1990s, the share of assets held by these contractual intermediaries will increase.

Investment Intermediaries   Investment intermediaries provide a mechanism through which small savers pool funds to purchase a variety of financial assets rather than just one or two. An example of how pooling works can be seen by considering a mutual fund company, which is one type of investment intermediary.

A mutual fund enables a small saver to diversify (spread out) his or her savings (for a fee, of course). Savers buy shares in the mutual fund which, in turn, holds stocks or bonds of many different companies. When a fund holds many different companies' shares or bonds, it spreads the risk so a saver won't lose everything if one company goes broke. This is called **diversification**— *spreading the risks by holding many different types of financial assets.*

A finance company is another type of investment intermediary. Finance companies make loans to individuals and businesses, as do banks, but instead of holding deposits, as banks do, finance companies borrow the money they lend. They borrow from individuals by selling them bonds and commercial paper. **Commercial paper** is *a short-term promissory note that a certain amount of money plus interest will be paid back on demand.*

Finance companies charge borrowers higher interest than banks do, in part because their cost of funds (the

interest rate they pay to depositors) is higher than banks' cost of funds. (The interest rate banks pay on savings and checking accounts is the cost of their funds.) As was the case with depository institutions, a finance company's profit reflects the difference between the interest rate it charges on its loans and the interest rate it pays for the funds it borrows.

Why do people go to finance companies if finance companies charge higher interest than banks? Because of convenience and because finance companies' loan qualifications are easier to meet than banks'.

Financial Brokers   Financial brokers are of two main types: investment banks and brokerage houses. Investment banks assist companies in selling financial assets such as stocks and bonds. They provide advice, expertise, and the sales force to sell the stocks or bonds. They handle such things as *mergers* and *takeovers* of companies. A merger occurs when two or more companies join to form one new company. A takeover occurs when one company buys out another company. Investment banks do not hold individuals' deposits and do not make loans to consumers. That's why in Exhibit B1 they have zero assets and hence zero liabilities. They are nonetheless financial institutions because they assist others in buying and selling financial assets.

Brokerage houses assist individuals in selling previously issued financial assets. Brokerage houses create a secondary market in financial assets, as we'll see shortly. A **secondary financial market** is a *market in which previously issued financial assets can be bought and sold.*

The market for financial instruments is sometimes rather hectic, as suggested by this famous painting, "The Bulls and The Bears on Wall Street."   © *New York Historical Society.*

Financial Markets

A financial market is a market where financial assets and financial liabilities are bought and sold. The stock market, the bond market, and bank activities are all examples of financial markets.

Financial institutions buy and sell financial assets in financial markets. Sometimes these markets are actual places, like the New York Stock Exchange, but generally a market simply exists in the form of a broker's Rolodex files, computer networks, telephone lines, and lists of people who sometimes want to buy and sell. When individuals want to sell, they call their broker and their broker calls potential buyers; when individuals want to buy, the broker calls potential sellers. A market is an institution that brings buyers and sellers together; a **financial market** is *an institution—such as the Rolodex cards and the telephone—that brings buyers and sellers of financial assets together.*

Primary and Secondary Financial Markets   There are various types of financial markets. A **primary financial market** is *a market in which newly issued financial assets are sold.* These markets transfer savings to borrowers who want to invest (buy real assets). Sellers in this market include *venture capital firms* (which sell part ownerships in new companies) and *investment banks* (which sell new stock and new bonds for existing companies). Whereas investment banks only assist firms in selling their stock, venture capital firms often are partnerships that invest their own money in return for part ownership of a new firm.

Many new businesses will turn to venture capital firms for financing because only established firms can sell stock through an investment bank. Risks are enormous for venture capital firms since most new businesses fail. But potential gains are huge. A company that's already established will most likely use an investment bank to get additional funds. Investment banks know people and institutions who buy stocks; with a new stock offering they

use those contacts. They telephone those leads to try to *place* (sell) the new issue.

Generally new offerings are too large for one investment bank to sell. So it contracts with other investment banks and brokerage houses to sell portions of the new stock or bond issue. Exhibit B2(a) shows an advertisement announcing a stock offering. In this advertisement, a group of investment banks announces it's selling 3,000,000 shares of stock for Petco at $15.50 per share. The lead bankers listed in the first line have subcontracted with all the other investment banks and brokerage houses listed to assist in the sale. Exhibit B2(b) shows a tombstone ad announcing the successful completion of a sale.

There are many different types of buyers for newly issued financial assets. They include rich individuals and financial institutions, such as life insurance companies, pension funds, and mutual funds.

A secondary financial market transfers existing financial assets from one saver to another. (Remember, in economics, when an individual buys a financial asset such as a stock or bond, he or she is a saver. In economics, investment occurs only when savings are used to buy items such as machines or a factory.) A transfer on a secondary market does not represent any new savings; it is savings for one person and dissavings for another. One cancels out the other. The New York Stock Exchange is probably the best-known secondary financial market. It transfer stocks from one stockholder to another.

The secondary market does, however, have an important role to play in new savings. The existence of a secondary market lets the individual buyer of a financial asset know that she can resell it, transferring the asset back into cash at whatever price the secondary market sets. **Liquidity** is this *ability to turn an asset into cash quickly.* Secondary markets provide liquidity for financial assets holders and thereby encourage them to hold financial assets. If no secondary market existed, most people would hesitate to buy a stock or a 30-year bond. What if they needed their money in, say, 10 years? Or 10 weeks?

EXHIBIT B2 (a and b)   Stock Offering Announcements

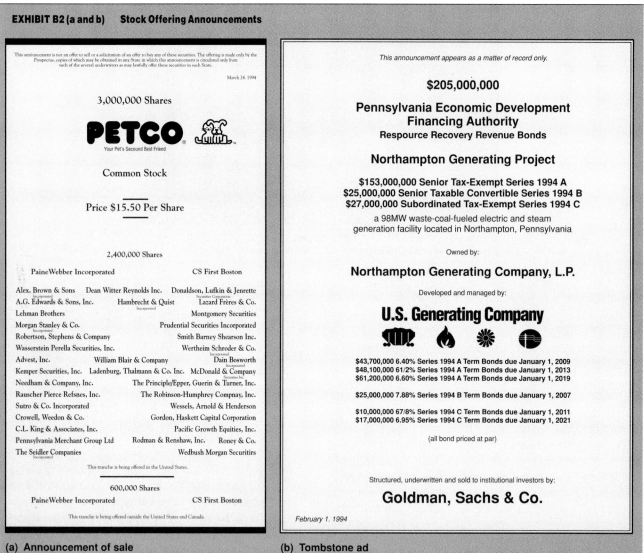

(a) Announcement of sale   **(b) Tombstone ad**

An advertisement (**a**) announcing the availability of a new stock issue notes that it is *not* a "solicitation of an offer to buy," but that a formal prospectus containing all the details is available from the listed investment banks. When the shares have been sold, a second advertisement (**b**) announces completion of the stock or bond offering. The second, self-congratulatory ad is called a *tombstone advertisement*.

Besides the organized secondary financial markets we often hear about—the New York Stock Exchange, AMEX (American Stock Exchange), and Chicago Mercantile Exchange—there are informal *over-the-counter* markets. Over-the-counter markets work like the primary financial markets: Brokers know of other individuals interested in buying what's for sale. Buying and selling takes place over the phone, with the broker acting as an intermediary.

Money Markets and Capital Markets   Financial markets can also be divided into two other categories: **money markets**

(*in which financial assets having a maturity of less than one year are bought and sold*) and **capital markets** (*in which financial assets having a maturity of more than one year are bought and sold*). (*Maturity* refers to the date the issuer must pay back the money that was borrowed plus any remaining interest, as agreed when the asset was issued.) For example, say the U.S. government issues an IOU (sometimes called a *Treasury bill*) that comes due in three months. This will be sold in the money market because its maturity is less than a year. Or say the government or a corporation issues an IOU that comes due in 20 years. This IOU, which is called a *bond*, will be sold in a capital market.

The floor of the New York Stock Exchange often is chaotic.   *UNI/ Bettmann.*

Types of Financial Assets

Now that you've been introduced to financial institutions and markets, we can consider some specific financial assets. Financial assets are generally divided into money market assets and capital market assets.

Money Market Assets   Money market assets are financial assets that mature in less than one year. They usually pay lower interest rates than do longer-term capital assets because they offer the buyer more liquidity. A general rule of thumb is: The more liquid the asset, the lower the return. As in the over-the-counter market, money market and capital market transactions are made over the phone lines using computers. Newly issued money market assets are sold through an investment bank or a securities dealer. Exhibit B3 gives you a visual sense of some of the most important money market assets and their growth over time. Notice how the relative importance of various assets changes over time.

Some of the most important money market assets are negotiable CDs, commercial paper, and U.S. Treasury bills.

Negotiable CDs   A **CD** is *a piece of paper certifying that you have a sum of money in a savings account in the bank for a specified period of time*. It is short for *certificate of deposit*. Think of it as a large amount of savings you agree to hold in an account at the bank for a specified period of time. But what if you need cash before the time is up? That's where the "negotiable" comes in. (Not all CDs are negotiable.) You can sell a negotiable CD in a secondary market and get cash for it if you need cash. The new owner can either sell it again on the secondary market or simply withdraw the money from the bank that issued it, including interest, when the required time is up (when the CD matures).

Commercial Paper   Why borrow from a bank if you can borrow directly from the public? Why not cut out the middleman? Large corporations often do precisely that. The borrowings are called *commercial paper. Commercial paper* is a short-term IOU of a large corporation. Commercial paper pays a higher interest rate than U.S. Treasury bills, but a lower interest rate than banks would charge the corporation. The same reasoning holds for a person who buys commercial paper. Commercial paper

EXHIBIT B3   Principal Money Market Instruments

These pie charts show the growth and relative importance of money market instruments over time. The increasing size of the pies reflects the increasing value over time.   Source: Federal Reserve Bank and author extrapolations.

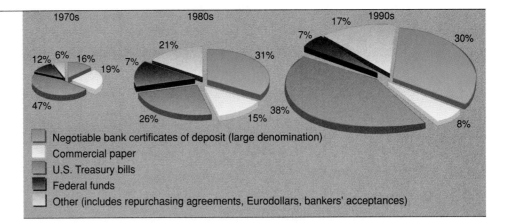

- Negotiable bank certificates of deposit (large denomination)
- Commercial paper
- U.S. Treasury bills
- Federal funds
- Other (includes repurchasing agreements, Eurodollars, bankers' acceptances)

EXHIBIT B4   Principal Capital Market Instruments

These pie charts show the relative importance of capital market instruments since the 1970s. The increasing size of the pies reflects the increasing value over time.   Source: Federal Reserve Bank and author extrapolations.

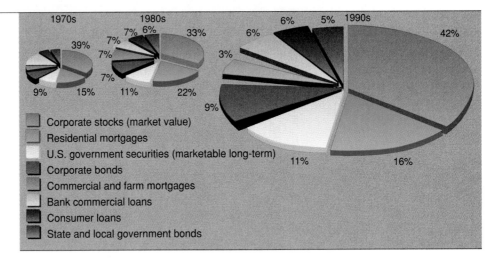

- Corporate stocks (market value)
- Residential mortgages
- U.S. government securities (marketable long-term)
- Corporate bonds
- Commercial and farm mortgages
- Bank commercial loans
- Consumer loans
- State and local government bonds

generally pays a higher interest rate than a CD, which is why people are willing to lend directly to the firm. Since the bank is an intermediary between the lender of funds and the borrower, the firm's action in this case is called **disintermediation**—*the process of lending directly and not going through a financial intermediary.*

U.S. Treasury Bills   These are U.S. government IOUs that mature in less than a year. Since it's unlikely the U.S. government will go broke, IOUs of the U.S. government are very secure, so U.S. Treasury bills need pay a relatively low rate of interest.

Where do these government IOUs come from? Think of what happens when the government spends more than it takes in in revenues; it runs a deficit. That deficit must be financed by borrowing. Selling U.S. Treasury bills is one way the U.S. government borrows money.

Differences among Money Market Assets   Money market assets differ slightly from each other. For example, Treasury bills are safer than commercial paper and pay slightly lower interest. For the most part, however, they are interchangeable, and the interest rates paid on them tend to increase or decrease together.

Capital Market Assets   Capital market assets have a maturity of over one year. Exhibit B4 gives you a visual sense of the principal capital market instruments and their relative importance over time. As you can see, the most important are stocks, bonds, and mortgages. Since mortgages are discussed later in this chapter, we'll focus here on stocks and bonds.

Stocks   A stock is a partial ownership right to a company. The stock owner has the right to vote on company policy, although generally, for smaller shareholders, this right doesn't convey much power. A stockholder can, however, attend the firm's stockholder meeting and ask questions of the firm's officers. Exhibit B5 shows a stock certificate certifying that the holder (who's named on the certificate's face) owns a specified number of shares in the firm—in this case, 120 shares of Cyprus Minerals. This is a valuable certificate, printed on special paper, which will last indefinitely without turning yellow or crumbling away. If the stock certificate is lost or stolen, the owner's investment will still be safe because no one can sell a stock certificate unless the owner has endorsed it on the back (somewhat like a check), which she should not do until the moment she's ready to sell it or confer it as a gift. If a

EXHIBIT B5   A Stock Certificate

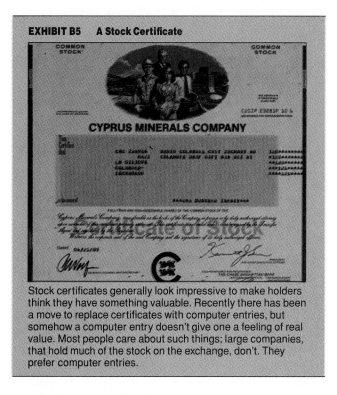

Stock certificates generally look impressive to make holders think they have something valuable. Recently there has been a move to replace certificates with computer entries, but somehow a computer entry doesn't give one a feeling of real value. Most people care about such things; large companies, that hold much of the stock on the exchange, don't. They prefer computer entries.

keep it, hoping that its price will go up and it will be worth more. If the company is paying dividends (periodic payments to owners of its stock), every three months she gets a check for those dividends. She doesn't have to do anything to get these checks—the company mails them automatically to "the shareholder of record."

Stocks have no maturity date. The money you paid for them never has to be paid back to you. Stocks require no periodic payments to you every year. So it's possible to buy a stock and get nothing for it. So why would anyone buy a stock? Because with it comes ownership rights—all the company's income that isn't paid out to factors of production belongs to the stockholders. For example, say you own one share of the million shares Cyprus Minerals has issued, and after paying all costs and debts due, Cyprus Minerals has $6 million in after-tax profits. Your percentage of that $6 million is $6. This $6 can be paid out to stockholders in dividends. Or the company can retain the $6 (which would then be called *retained earnings*), in which case the stock's value will likely increase because the firm can invest the retained earnings and earn more profit. (An increase in the value of a stock is called a *capital gain*.) The company's board of directors decides which option the company will follow.

Notice that a share of stock gives you the right to a percentage of the company's profits this year and all future years. Because it does, the price of a stock depends upon investors' opinions of a company's prospects. A company with excellent prospects sells for a high price; a company whose prospects are dim sells for a low price. What's high? What's low? That depends. A rough rule of thumb is to take a multiple of the company's earnings (its *earnings per share*) to determine the price a person would

stock certificate is lost or destroyed, the owner can get another one from the company because the company keeps a list of its owners (the people who own stock) and their addresses, but the owner must pay a fee.

The owner of a stock can sell it at any time she pleases, provided someone wants to buy it. She will get whatever the going price is at the moment her sale is closed, minus a commission to the broker. Or she can

The divergent interests of debtors and creditors are nicely captured in this late-19th-century drawing by W. W. Chenery.   *Source: Bleichroeder Print Collection, Baker Library, Harvard Business School.*

ADDED DIMENSION   THE DOW

Of all the current economic institutions, perhaps the one you hear most about is Wall Street. Wall Street is a real street in New York City, but the term *Wall Street* is often used to refer to the entire financial sector. Probably the most important institution on Wall Street is the New York Stock Exchange, where ownership rights in corporations are traded. These ownership rights are called *stocks*. Stocks are also called *shares*, because they represent the share of a business the stockholder owns. While individuals who own stocks are chiefly interested in the price of shares they own, they also want to know the general movement of prices in the market as a whole.

A measure indicating this is the *Dow Jones Industrial Average*, commonly called *the Dow*. The Dow Jones average was created in 1884 when newsman Charles Dow (founder of *The Wall Street Journal*) chose a group of what he felt were representative stocks and began reporting their prices as typical of general movements in the market. Initially he chose 12 stocks, added up their prices, divided the total by 12, and arrived at an average price per share.

Unfortunately for the statistician, the financial people who manage the firms represented by the stocks do funny things with stocks, such as splitting stocks or issuing stock dividends. A *stock split* occurs when the company decides to give each owner extra shares—say two shares for each one the owner already has. A stock dividend means that instead of using money to pay you the earnings on your shares, the company gives you one or more additional shares of stock. Stock splits and stock dividends, both of which increase the number of shares in the market, lower the price of all the company's shares but do not make the owners worse off, because the people own more shares. Often, in fact, owners are made better off, because the price of the shares soon starts to rise again.

But after stock splits and stock dividends of any of the stocks comprising the Dow average, dividing by 12 no longer gives us a representative measure of what happened to the average price. Statisticians did some fancy adjusting, and now, even though the number of stocks included in the Dow has risen from 12 to 30, the divisor used is less than .5. So to compute the Dow Jones Industrial Average, you simply add the prices of the following 30 big, well-known companies, and divide by a number slightly less than .5.

Dow Jones Industrial Stocks

Alcoa	Hewlett-Packard
Allied Signal	IBM
American Express	International Paper
AT&T	Johnson & Johnson
Boeing Co.	McDonald's
Caterpillar, Inc.	Merck
Chevron	Minnesota M&M
Coca-Cola	J. P. Morgan
Disney	Philip Morris
Du Pont	Proctor & Gamble
Eastman Kodak	Sears and Roebuck
Exxon	Travelers Group
General Electric	Union Carbide
General Motors	United Technologies
Goodyear Tire and Rubber	Wal-Mart

There are many other measures of the market, such as the Standard & Poor's (S&P) 500 and the Wilshire 5000. But the Dow Jones Average is most used. Most TV news programs include a few spoken words or a message flashed on the screen: "The Dow Jones Average is down 5.63 for the day," or "Dow—+26.9."

ADDED DIMENSION   CAPITAL GAINS AND LOSSES

Capital gains and losses aren't limited to stock. They can occur with any asset—financial or real. A capital gain or loss is simply the change in the value of an asset.

Noneconomists often call capital gains and losses *paper gains and losses* because no money transfers hands as the gain or loss occurs. Often you'll hear, "Oh, it's only a paper loss," as if somehow a capital loss wasn't quite as bad as a loss that has to be paid for in money. It's the same for a "paper gain," which they feel isn't as good as a gain that puts money in your pocket.

Economists don't use the "paper" terminology. They emphasize the opportunity cost concept. When you have a capital gain, you have the option of realizing that gain by selling the asset for the increased price. The opportunity cost of not selling that asset is the price of that asset including the capital gain. Say the price of a share of Cyprus Minerals goes from $21 to $30. If you sell the share, you get the $9 gain (minus transaction costs) in your pocket. If you don't sell the share, the cost of not selling the share is $30. If you didn't sell the share at $21, the cost of not selling it was only $21. Thus, using the opportunity cost framework, a capital gain or loss is as real as any other gain or loss.

be willing to pay for a share. For instance, "15 times earnings" means a share is selling for 15 times the company's annual earnings divided by the number of shares outstanding. If Cyprus Minerals in our previous example was expected to continue earning $6 a share, and stock buyers applied the 15-times-earnings rule of thumb, the stock would sell for $90 a share.

An average company stock sells for somewhere around 15 times earnings. (This average price/earnings ratio fluctuates somewhat over time.) A company with excellent future prospects might sell for 30 or 40 times earnings. A company with poor prospects might sell for merely 2 or 3 times earnings. The price/earnings ratio for a company is reported in the newspaper stock tables.

Bonds   A bond is a promise of the bond-issuer to pay interest of a certain amount at specified intervals (usually semiannually) to the bondholder and to pay the bond's face value when the bond matures. Bonds are different from stocks. They generally have a maturity date when borrowers pay back the money. Exhibit B6(a) shows an unregistered bond.

A bond's value depends on a bond's face value and its coupon rate (the interest rate stated on the bond). Exhibit B6(a)'s bond has a face value of $5,000 and a coupon

rate of 12.75 percent per year. That means that the bondholder receives $637.50 each year in interest payments. When the bond matures, the bond holder receives $5,000.

Printed on the bond is the *maturity date,* October 1, 2002. There's no sense hanging onto that bond after October 1, 2002, because after that it pays no more interest.

If you need the money from the bond before the maturity date, you'll enter into the secondary bond market. Call your bond broker and ask what your bond is selling for. What price you will get depends in large part on the interest rate.

Generally when bonds are issued, their coupon rate is close to the market interest rate prevailing in the economy for bonds of similar risk. These bonds sell *at par* (at their face value). If market interest rates rise, the future stream of income becomes worth less and the bond sells at a discount (at less than its face value). If the market interest rate falls, the future stream of income becomes worth more and the bond sells at a premium (at more than its face value).

Exhibit B6(b) shows a bond table. Let's see what it tells us. FruitL bonds, the first bond issue on the list, pay a coupon rate of 7 percent annual interest and come due in 2011. They sell for $91 for every $100 of their par value (the value stated on the bond), which means that

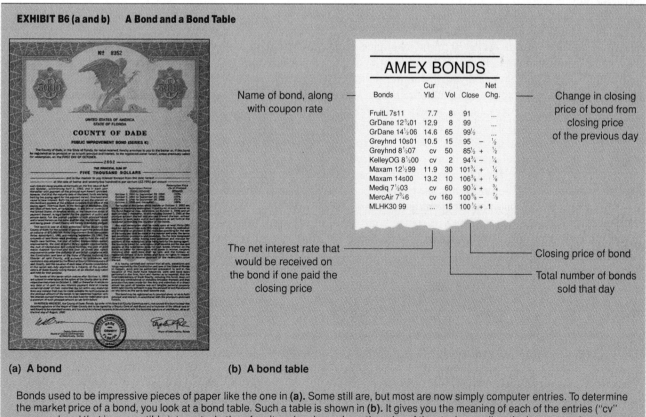

EXHIBIT B6 (a and b)   A Bond and a Bond Table

Name of bond, along with coupon rate

Change in closing price of bond from closing price of the previous day

AMEX BONDS

Bonds	Cur Yld	Vol	Close	Net Chg.
FruitL 7s11	7.7	8	91	...
GrDane 12¾01	12.9	8	99	...
GrDane 14½06	14.6	65	99½	...
Greyhnd 10s01	10.5	15	95	− ½
Greyhnd 8½07	cv	50	85½	+ ½
KelleyOG 8½00	cv	2	94¾	− ¼
Maxam 12½99	11.9	30	101¾	+ ¼
Maxam 14s00	13.2	10	106⅜	+ ⅛
Mediq 7½03	cv	60	90¼	+ ¾
MercAir 7¾6	cv	160	100⅝	− ⅞
MLHK30 99	...	15	100½	+ 1

The net interest rate that would be received on the bond if one paid the closing price

Closing price of bond

Total number of bonds sold that day

(a) A bond   (b) A bond table

Bonds used to be impressive pieces of paper like the one in **(a).** Some still are, but most are now simply computer entries. To determine the market price of a bond, you look at a bond table. Such a table is shown in **(b).** It gives you the meaning of each of the entries ("cv" means a bond that is convertible into a stock; therefore its value depends on the price of the stock as well as the interest rate).

their yield (the net interest rate you get if you buy the bond at the closing price) is 7.7 percent. Each year you get $7.00 from the bond that cost you $91. Dividing $7.00 by $91 gives 7.7 percent.

Notice some other bonds in the table are selling at premiums. They were issued with a face value of $100, but their current prices are over $100. If you sell a Maxam bond for $106 but paid only $100 for it, you make a gain of $6 on the sale price, but the new owner's yield or net annual interest per dollar is lower than the 14 percent stated for these bonds. That's because 14 percent of $100 is $14, but $14 as a percentage of $106 is only 13.2 percent. This 13.2 percent is the bond's yield.

Leading You through Two Financial Transactions

We've covered a lot of material quickly, so the institutions discussed may be a bit of a blur in your mind. To get a better idea of how these financial markets work, let's follow two transactions you'll likely make in your lifetime and see how they work their way through the financial system.

Insuring Your Car   You want to drive. The law requires you to have insurance, so you go to two or three insurance companies, get quotes of their rates, and choose the one offering the lowest rate. Say it costs you $800 for the year. You write a check for $800 and hand the check to the insurance agent who keeps a commission (let's say $80) and then sends her check for $720 to the insurance company. The insurance company has $720 more sitting in the bank than it had before you paid your insurance premium.

The insurance company earns income in two ways: (1) in the difference between the money it receives in payments and the claims it pays out, and (2) in the interest it makes on its financial assets. What does the company use to buy these financial assets? It has payments from its customers (your $720, for example) available because payments come in long before claims are paid out.

Because earnings on financial assets are an important source of an insurance company's income, your $720 doesn't stay in the insurance company's bank for long. The insurance company has a financial assets division which chooses financial assets it believes have the highest returns for the risk involved. Bond salesmen telephone the financial assets division offering to sell bonds. Similarly, developers who want to build shopping malls or ski resorts go to the financial assets division, offering an opportunity to participate (really asking to borrow money).

The financial assets division might decide to lend your $720 (along with $10 million more) to a mall developer who builds in suburban locations. The division transfers the $720 to the mall developer and receives a four-year, 12 percent promissory note (a promise to pay the $720 back in four years along with $86.40 per year in interest payments). The promissory note is a financial as-

set of the insurance company and a financial liability of the developer. When the developer spends the money, the $720 leaves the financial sector and reenters the spending stream in the real economy. At that point it becomes investment in the economic sense.

Buying a House   Most people, when they buy a house, don't go out and pay the thousands of dollars it costs in cash. Instead they go to a bank or similar financial institution and borrow a large portion of the sales price, taking out a mortgage on the house. A **mortgage** is simply *a special name for a secured loan on real estate.* By mortgaging her house, a person is creating a financial liability for herself and a financial asset for someone else. This financial asset is secured by the house. If the person defaults on the loan, the mortgage holder (who, as you will see, may or may not be the bank) can foreclose on the mortgage and take title to the house.

The funds available in banks come primarily from depositors who keep their savings in the bank in the form of savings accounts or checking accounts. Balances in these accounts are often small, but with lots of depositors they add up and provide banks with money to lend out. If you're planning to buy a house, you'll most likely go to a bank.

The bank's loan officer will have you fill in a lengthy form, and the bank will send an appraiser out to the house to assess its value. The appraiser asks questions about the house: Does it meet the electrical code? What kind of pipes does it have? What kind of windows does it have? All this information about you and the house is transferred onto a master form that the loan officer uses to decide whether to make the loan. (Contrary to what many lay people believe, in normal times a loan officer wants to make the loan. Remember, a bank's profits are the difference between what it pays in interest and what it receives in interest; it needs to make loans to make profits. So he or she often looks at hazy answers on the form and puts an interpretation on them that's favorable to making the loan.)

In a month or so, depending on how busy the bank is, you hear back that the loan is approved for, say, $80,000 at 9 percent interest and two points. A point is 1 percent of the loan; it is a charge the bank makes for the loan. So two points means the bank is charging you $1,600 for making you a loan of $80,000 at 9 percent interest. (And you wondered why the bank was anxious to make you a loan!) The bank credits your account with $78,400, which allows you to write a check to the seller of the house at a meeting called the *closing.*

The bank gets a lot of money in deposits, but generally it doesn't have anywhere near enough deposits to cover all the mortgages it would like to make. So the process doesn't stop there. Instead the bank generally sells your mortgage on the secondary market to Fannie Mae (the Federal National Mortgage Association) or Ginnie

Mae (the Government National Mortgage Assocation), which pay, say, $80,400 for the $80,000 mortgage. They're buying your mortgage (which you paid $1,600 in points to be allowed to get) for $400 more than its amount. The bank makes money both ways; when it makes the loan and when it sells the loan.

Fannie Mae and Ginnie Mae are nonprofit companies organized by the government to encourage home ownership. They do this by easing the flow of savings into mortgages. They take your mortgage and a number of similar ones from different areas and make them into a bond package: a $100,000,000 bond fund secured by a group of mortgages. (Remember the long forms and the questions the appraiser asked? Those forms and answers allow Fannie Mae and Ginnie Mae to classify the mortgage and put it in a group with similar mortgages.) They then sell shares in that bond fund to some other institution that gives Fannie Mae and Ginnie Mae money in return. The Maes use that money to buy more mortgages, thereby channeling more savings into financing home ownership.

Who buys Fannie Mae and Ginnie Mae bonds? Let's go back and consider our insurance company. If the insurance company hadn't made the loan to the developer, the company might have decided that Ginnie Mae bonds were the best investment it could make. So who knows? Your insurance company may hold the mortgage to your house.

You, of course, don't know any of this. You simply keep making your mortgage payments to the bank which, for a fee, forwards it to Ginnie Mae, which uses it to pay the interest on the bond it sold to the insurance company.

Summary   We could go through other transactions, but these two should give you a sense of how real-world financial transactions work their way through financial institutions. Financial institutions make money by the fees and commissions they charge for buying and selling loans, and on the difference between the interest they pay to get the money and the interest they receive when they lend the money out.

KEY TERMS

bond *(228)*
capital markets *(232)*
certificate of deposit (CD) *(233)*
commercial paper *(230)*
contractual intermediary *(228)*
depository institution *(228)*

disintermediation *(234)*
diversification *(230)*
financial assets *(228)*
financial institution *(228)*
financial liabilities *(228)*
financial market *(231)*

liquidity *(231)*
money markets *(232)*
mortgage *(238)*
primary financial market *(231)*
secondary financial market *(230)*
stock *(228)*

QUESTIONS FOR THOUGHT AND REVIEW

1. If the government prints new $1,000 bills and gives them to all introductory students who are using the Colander text, who incurs a financial liability and who gains a financial asset?
2. Is the currency in your pocketbook or wallet a real or a financial asset? Why?
3. Joe, your study partner, has just said that, in economic terminology, when he buys a bond he is investing. Is he correct? Why?
4. Joan, your study partner, has just made the following statement: "A loan is a loan and therefore cannot be an asset." Is she correct? Why or why not?
5. What is the difference between an investment bank and a commercial bank?
6. The difference between primary and secondary financial markets is that primary markets are more important. True or false? Why or why not?
7. A company's stock is selling for three times earnings. How is the market valuing the prospects of that company?
8. If the interest rate in the economy goes down, what will likely happen to the price of a previously issued bond?
9. Which market, the primary or secondary, contributes more to the production of tangible real assets? Explain why.
10. Why do money market assets generally yield lower interest payments than capital assets?
11. Suppose that in 1995 you bought a newly issued bond with a $10,000 face value, a coupon rate of 9 percent, and a maturity date of 2020. How much interest would it pay each year? If the interest rate in the economy is 8 percent, would the bond be likely to sell for more or less than $10,000?
12. Consider a company whose stock sells for $24 a share, has about $2 million in annual earnings, and has a million shares outstanding. What's that firm's price/earnings ratio?
13. If a bond with a $5,000 face value and a 7.5 percent coupon rate is selling on the secondary bond market for $4,000, what can you say about the interest rate in the economy?
14. A bond has a face value of $10,000 and a coupon rate of 10 percent. It is issued in 1998 and matures in 2008.
    a. How much does the bond pay annually?
    b. If the bond is currently selling for $9,000, what is its yield?

c. If the interest rate in the economy rises, what will happen to the bond's price? Why?

15. For the following financial instruments, state for whom it is a liability and for whom it is an asset. Also state, if appropriate, whether the transaction occurred on the capital or money markets.

a. Lamar purchases a $100 CD at his credit union.

b. First Bank grants a mortgage to Sandra. The bank then sells the mortgage to FNMA, who packages the mortgage in a fund and sells shares of that fund to Pension USA.

c. Sean purchases a $100 jacket using his credit card with First Bank.

d. City of Providence issues $1 billion in municipal bonds, most of which were purchased by Providence residents, to build a community center.

e. Investment broker sells 100 shares of existing stock to Lanier.

f. Investment broker sells 1,000 shares of new-issue stock to Lanier.

16. State whether you agree or disagree with the following statements:

a. If stock market prices go up, the economy is richer.

b. A real asset worth $1,000,000 is more valuable to an individual than a financial asset worth $1,000,000.

c. Financial assets have no value to society since each has a corresponding liability.

d. The United States has much more land than does Japan. Therefore, the value of all U.S. land should significantly exceed the value of land in Japan.

e. U.S. GDP exceeds Japan's GDP; therefore, the stock market valuation of United States-based companies should exceed that of Japan-based companies.

APPENDIX C

Creation of Money Using T–Accounts

In this appendix I use T-accounts to demonstrate the example of the creation of money given in the text of the chapter.

The basis of financial accounting is the T-account presentation of balance sheets. The balance sheet is made up of assets on one side and liabilities and net worth on the other. By definition the two sides are equal; they balance (just as the T-account must).

To cement the money creation process in your mind, let's discuss how banks create money using transactions that affect the balance sheet. To keep the analysis simple, we limit the example to the case where only banks create money. (In Appendix D we do the more complicated example in which people also hold currency.)

Exhibit C1 shows the initial balance sheet of an imaginary Textland Bank, which we assume is the only

bank in the country. As you can see, Textland has $500,000 in assets: $30,000 in cash, $300,000 in loans, and $170,000 in property. On the liabilities side, it has $150,000 in checking deposits and $350,000 in net worth. The two sides of the balance sheet are equal.

The first thing to notice about this balance sheet is that if all holders of checking accounts (demand deposits) wanted their currency, the bank couldn't give it to them. The currency it holds is only a portion—20 percent—of the total deposits:

$$\$30,000/\$150,000 = .20.$$

Banks rely upon statistical averages and assume that not all people will want their money at the same time. Let's assume Textland Bank has decided 20 percent is an appropriate reserve ratio.

EXHIBIT C1   Textland Bank Balance Sheet   Beginning Balance

Assets		Liabilities and Net Worth	
Currency	$ 30,000	Checking deposits	$ 150,000
Loans	300,000	Net worth	350,000
Property	170,000		
Total assets	$500,000	Total liabilities and net worth	$500,000

EXHIBIT C1   (continued)

Assets		Transaction 1	Liabilities and Net Worth	

Currency (beginning balance).............	$ 30,000		Checking deposits (beginning balance)	$150,000
Currency from John	10,000		John's deposit	10,000
Total currency		$ 40,000	Total demand deposits	$160,000
Loans........................		300,000	Net worth	350,000
Property......................		170,000		
Total assets		$510,000	Total liabilities and net worth	$510,000

Now let's say that John Finder finds $10,000 in currency. He deposits that $10,000 into Textland Bank. After he does so, what will happen to the money supply? The first step is seen in Transaction 1, which shows the effect of John Finder's deposit on the bank's account. The bank gains $10,000 in currency, but its liabilities also increase by $10,000, so, as you can see, the two sides of the balance sheet are still equal. At this point no additional money has been created; $10,000 currency has simply been changed to a $10,000 checking deposit.

Now let's assume the bank uses a reserve ratio of 20 percent, meaning it lends out 80 percent of the currency it receives in new deposits. Say it lends out 80% × $10,000 = $8,000 to Fred Baker, keeping 20 percent × $10,000 =

EXHIBIT C1   (continued)

Assets		Transaction 2	Liabilities and Net Worth	

Currency (after Trans. 1)	$ 40,000		Checking deposits (after Trans. 1)	$160,000
Currency loaned to Fred	− 8,000		Net worth	350,000
Total currency		$ 32,000		
Loans (beginning balance).............	300,000			
Loans to Fred.....................	8,000			
Total loans		308,000		
Property......................		170,000		
Total assets		$510,000	Total liabilities and net worth..................	$510,000

$2,000 in reserve. The change in the bank's balance sheet is seen in Transaction 2. This step creates $8,000 in money. Why? Because John Finder still has $10,000 in his checking account, while Fred Baker has $8,000 currency, so, combining John's checking account balance with Fred's currency, the public has $8,000 in money. As you can see, loans have increased by $8,000 and currency in Textland Bank has decreased by $8,000.

Fred Baker didn't borrow the money to hold onto it. He spends it buying a new oven from Mary Builder, who,

EXHIBIT C1   (continued)

Assets		Transaction 3	Liabilities and Net Worth	

Currency (after Trans. 2)	$32,000		Checking deposits	$160,000
Currency from Mary	8,000		Mary's deposit	8,000
Total currency		$ 40,000	Total demand deposits	$168,000
Loans........................		308,000	Net worth	350,000
Property......................		170,000		
Total assets		$518,000	Total liabilities and net worth	$518,000

in turn, deposits the $8,000 into Textland Bank (the only bank according to our assumptions). Textland's balance sheet now looks like Transaction 3.

Mary Builder has a demand deposit of $8,000, and John Finder has a demand deposit of $10,000. But Text-land Bank has excess reserves of $6,400, since it must keep only $1,600 of Mary's $8,000 deposit as reserves:

$$80\% \times \$8,000 = \$6,400$$

So the bank is looking to make a loan.

At this point the process continues in the fashion described in the chapter text. A good exercise to see that you understand T-accounts is to use T-accounts to demonstrate the next two rounds of the process.

QUESTIONS FOR THOUGHT AND REVIEW

1. Assume that there's only one bank in the country, that the reserve requirement is 10 percent, and that the ratio of individuals' currency holdings to their bank deposits is 20 percent. The bank begins with $20,000 currency, $225,000 in loans, $105,000 in physical assets, $200,000 in demand deposits, and $150,000 in net worth.
   a. An immigrant comes into the country and deposits $10,000 in the bank. Show this deposit's effect on the bank's balance sheet.
   b. The bank keeps enough of this money to satisfy its reserve requirement, and loans out the rest to Ms. Entrepreneur. Show the effect on the bank's balance sheet.
   c. Ms. Entrepreneur uses the money to pay Mr. Carpenter, who deposits 80 percent of what he gets in the bank. Show the effect on the bank's balance sheet.
   d. Show the bank's balance sheet after the money multiplier is all through multiplying (based on the Appendix).

2. Assume there is one bank in the country whose reserve requirement is 20 percent. It has $10,000 in currency; $100,000 in loans; $50,000 in physical assets; $50,000 in demand deposits; and $110,000 in net worth. Mr. Aged withdraws $1,000 from the bank and dies on the way home without spending a penny. He is buried with the currency still in his pocket.
   a. Show this withdrawal's effect on the bank's balance sheet.
   b. What happened to the bank's reserve ratio and what must the bank do to meet reserve requirements?
   c. What is the money multiplier? (Assume no currency holdings.)
   d. What will happen to total money supply because of this event after the money multiplier is through multiplying?

3. Assume reserve requirements are 15 percent. Textland Bank's balance sheet looks like this:

Assets		Liabilities	
Currency	$ 30,000	Deposits	$150,000
Loans	320,000	Net Worth	550,000
Property	350,000		
Total	$700,000	Total	$700,000

   a. How much is the bank holding in excess reserves?
   b. If the bank eliminates excess reserves by making new loans, how much new money would be created (assuming no currency holdings)? Show using T-accounts.

APPENDIX D

Precise Calculation of the Money Multiplier When People Hold Currency

In the text we used the approximate money multiplier to determine what the effect of people holding currency will be. In this appendix we go through a similar example using a precise formula.

Economists have found a simple formula to determine the actual money multiplier when people hold currency. It's $(1 + c)/(r + c)$.

Before we substitute in, it's important to call your attention to the definition of c. It's not the ratio of the money people keep to the total money they receive. It's the ratio of money people hold as currency to the money people hold as demand deposits. The two ratios are, however, related. If people deposit in the bank 80 percent of the money they receive, they're keeping 25 percent of the money they deposit. For example, if they receive $100 and keep $20, they're depositing $80. The ratio of currency to money they receive is

$$20/100 = 20\%.$$

Measuring c (the ratio of currency to the money they deposit), we get

$$c = 20/80 = 25\%.$$

So in our example, $c = .25$.

With this formula we can calculate precisely how much the money multiplier would be when people hold currency. Say banks hold 10 percent of their deposits in reserve ($r = .10$) and individuals hold currency equal to

Bank Gets	Bank Keeps (Reserve Ratio: 20%)	Bank Loans (80%) = Person Borrows	Demand Deposits (77% of What Person Gets)	Person Keeps (23% of What Person Gets)
			$ 7,700	$2,300
$7,700	$1,540	$6,160	4,743	1,417
4,743	949	3,794	2,921	873
2,921	584	2,337	1,799	538
1,799	360	1,439	1,108	331
1,108	222	886	682	204
682	136	546	420	126
420	84	336	259	77
259	52	207	159	48
159	32	127	98	29
98	20	78	60	18
	$3,979		$19,949 +	$5,961
End of money creation process:	$4,000		$20,000 +	$6,000

EXHIBIT D1   The Money-Creating Process

Starting from $10,000 after the first round, $7,700 gets into the bank. By the 10th round, that $10,000 has increased to $25,910.

25 percent of the amount they deposit ($c = .25$). Substituting the numbers into the formula gives

$$(1 + .25)/(.1 + .25) = 3.57.$$

This tells us that when people hold 20 percent of their money as cash and 80 percent as checking account deposits, and banks hold 10 percent of their deposits as reserves, the actual money multiplier is 3.57. So in our example in the text, from that initial $100, $357 in money would be created. Thus our approximate multiplier calculated in the text, 2.9, was too small. Why was it too small? Because it didn't take into account the fact that when people hold money as cash, the money they hold must also be included in the money supply; when banks hold money, it need not be included.

To cement the money creation process in your mind, let's go through the same example we did in the chapter, only this time allowing for individuals to hold cash.

Exhibit D1 shows the effects of the money multiplier process for 10 rounds, starting with the initial $10,000, with a reserve requirement of .2 and a ratio of money

people hold in cash to the money they hold as deposits of .3. (This means that they keep 23 percent ($\frac{c}{1 + c}$) of the cash they receive and deposit 77 percent ($\frac{1}{1 + c}$) in the bank.) Each time it lends the money out, 77 percent of what it lends comes back to the bank like a boomerang and serves as the basis for more loans. After 10 rounds we reach a point where the public holds $5,961 in cash and total demand deposits are up to $19,949. Adding these two gives us a total money supply of $25,910. This is approaching the $26,000 we'd arrived at using the precise calculations of the money multiplier:

$$[(1 + c)/(r + c)](\$10,000) = [(1 + .3)/(.2 + .3)](\$10,000)$$
$$= 2.6(\$10,000) = \$26,000.$$

If we carried it out for a few more rounds, we'd actually reach what the formula predicted.

Note the $10,000 in currency notes is held jointly by the bank and the public. After 10 rounds the bank holds $3,979 in cash and the public holds $5,961 in cash. Thus, a total of $9,940 (approaching $10,000) is held in cash.

However, the money supply, which includes both cash and checking account deposits, has been increased to almost $26,000. The additional money is in the form of checking account deposits.

QUESTIONS FOR THOUGHT AND REVIEW

1. Calculate the effects using both the actual and approximate money multipliers in the following cases:
   a. $r = .1$; $c = .3$; $1,000 enters the banking system.
   b. $r = .2$; $c = .4$; $1,000 enters the banking system.
   c. $r = 0$; $c = .5$; $1,000 enters the banking system.
2. How would your answer to (1) change if banks held .05 of their deposits in excess reserves as well as the values of r in (1)?

3. For what values of c and r is the approximate money multiplier a closer approximation of the precise money multiplier?

Ten
The Modern Macroeconomic Debate

*The Theory of Economics . . . is a method rather than a doctrine,
an apparatus of the mind, a technique of thinking which helps its
possessor to draw correct conclusions.*

~ J. M. Keynes

After reading this chapter, you should be able to:

1 Discuss the historical development of modern macroeconomics.

2 Outline the reasoning behind Say's law.

3 Explain the shape of the *AED* curve and what factors shift the *AED* curve.

4 Explain the shape of the aggregate supply path and what factors shift the aggregate supply path.

5 State which ranges of the macro policy model are relevant for the activist Keynesian and laissez-faire Classical views.

6 Work with the macro policy model, showing the effects of shifts in aggregate equilibrium demand and the aggregate supply path on price level and output.

7 Discuss two reasons why macro policy is more complicated than the model makes it look.

In the late 1990s unemployment was about 10 percent in Europe. In the United States the unemployment rate was much lower, about 5 percent, but there were still significant complaints about *downsizing*—the laying off of workers by large firms—and about the insecurity that many workers felt about the economy. Despite the concerns and the high unemployment rate in Europe, few significant policy actions were taken by any government to deal with that unemployment. Indeed, most of the policy debate among politicians concerned the federal deficit and how to eliminate it, or structural policies which might make the economy more competitive. That policy debate specifically did not focus on fiscal policy (changing the budget deficit to affect the economy), and focused less than in the past on monetary policy (changing the money supply to affect the economy), which had been the traditional macro policies of the 1960s and 1970s. Thus the 1990s marked a significant change in macro policy thinking.

Some governments, it should be noted, took relatively small policy actions that reflected earlier policy responses. Most European countries increased their money supply somewhat whenever unemployment rose (monetary policy). The German government reduced taxes slightly when the German economy fell into a recession (fiscal policy). However, these traditional policy responses were much smaller than they would have been in the 1960s, when governments would have taken—and the

The focus of the macro policy debate keeps changing. At this point in the course I usually discuss the current debate and how the debate has evolved.

majority of the economics profession would have supported—much stronger traditional policy responses. By the 1990s the majority position of the economics profession has changed and is far more hesitant about the use of traditional macroeconomic policies. In this chapter I begin considering why.

In doing so I will present the **macro policy model**—*a model that demonstrates the effects of macro policy on output and prices.* This macro policy model will be the foundation of the policy discussion for much of the remainder of the book. This basic policy model is broad enough to incorporate all views about the macro economy and thus, in its broad outlines presented here, it is accepted by almost all economists.

Still, specific interpretations and empirical estimates of the model are currently being debated, and a sizable minority of economists favor much stronger traditional policy action than governments are currently undertaking. Since debates bring out the points of the model nicely and make learning the model more fun, I will present the model in reference to a debate. For simplicity, I will distinguish only two sides in the debate—Keynesian activists and Classical laissez-faire economists. (Actually, there are almost as many sides as there are economists, and sometimes even more, since many economists change their positions.)

Activist economists are *economists who believe that the government can create and implement policy proposals that can positively impact the economy.* Activist economists are often called Keynesian economists because they follow in the activist tradition of John Maynard Keynes, an economist who played a major role in convincing some economists that activist policy made sense. I will sometimes use the term Keynesian to mean activist because the term is so common. However, I use it with the caveat that many Keynesian economists today would not suggest using the traditional macro policies that, in the past, would have been considered Keynesian policies. It is the activist "do something" thrust in the Keynesian term upon which I am focusing, not the specific policies.

I call economists on the other side of the debate **laissez-faire economists**—*economists who believe that most government policies would probably make things worse, so the best policy is (relatively) little government involvement with the economy*—who advocate minimizing taxes and keeping the government out of the market economy as much as possible. Laissez-faire economists are sometimes called Classical economists because they follow in a Classical economic tradition and because they were called that by Keynes when he was contrasting his activist policies with the then predominant laissez-faire policies. I will use the terms Classical economist and laissez-faire economist interchangeably, although again it is important to recognize that "Classical" is not associated with any specific policy, but instead with a general approach to policy.

In the first part of the chapter I present a brief historical discussion of Classical and Keynesian ideas. Somehow, knowing where the ideas come from makes them a bit more real and a bit more fun to learn. (And that's needed since this is one of those "not so fun" chapters.) Then, in the second part of the chapter I present a simple policy model that provides a framework within which you can think about macro policy issues.

One final introductory comment: Presenting the model in reference to the debate between activist and laissez-faire economists should not mask the enormous amount of agreement about policy issues that exists. Economists are, after all, economists, and there is much more agreement than disagreement in reference to policy and to the model. Moreover, as I stated above, few economists will fall solidly into one camp or the other. So don't overemphasize the differences. Just use the two positions as two boundaries, and recognize that most economists fall somewhere between those boundaries. If you keep in mind that the distinctions drawn are boundaries, not fixed positions of one group or another, presenting the model in reference to the debate will give you a deeper understanding of the assumptions of the model and of the policy debates that make macroeconomics so interesting.

Activist economists   Economists who believe that the government can create and implement policy proposals that will positively impact the economy.

Laissez-faire economists   Economists who believe that most government policies would probably make things worse. They favor less government involvement in the economy.

In the 1960s, it was standard practice to present the Keynesian and Classical models and their historical development and perspective. It no longer is, and, in my view, that is sad. I have found that students really enjoy having things put into historical perspective. I sometimes assign students to look at particular periods of history during earlier recessions, or I summarize an earlier recession myself, as a way of making the policy debates that were going on at the time more real to the students.

Q–1:   Every economist will be either a Keynesian or a Classical. True or false? Why?

Our story of modern macroeconomics begins with the Great Depression of the 1930s. The Depression marked a significant change in U.S. economic institutions and ideology. It was a defining event for a whole generation. In the Depression, not only the deadbeat up the street was unemployed, so were your brother, your mother, your uncle—the hardworking backbone of the country. These people wanted to work, and if the market wasn't creating jobs for them, the market system was at fault.

During the Depression, the popular view of government's proper role in the economy changed considerably. Before, the predominant ideology was laissez-faire: keep the government out of the economy. After the Depression, most people believed that government must have a role in regulating the economy.

The Great Depression also led economists to develop theoretical models that explained unemployment and left room for government intervention in the market. It was during the Depression that it became usual to classify laissez-faire economists—those who generally oppose government intervention—as *Classical economists,* and activist economists—those who generally favor government intervention in the aggregate economy—as *Keynesian economists.*

1 Laissez-faire economists generally oppose government intervention. Activist economists generally favor government intervention.

Classical economists generally oppose government intervention.

Keynesian economists generally favor government intervention in the aggregate economy.

The Emergence of Classical Economics

Classical economics actually began in the late 1700s and early 1800s as economists developed the ideas in Adam Smith's seminal work, *An Inquiry into the Nature and Causes of the Wealth of Nations.* The essence of Classical economics' approach to problems was to use a **laissez-faire** (*leave the market alone*) approach. This policy was based on the view that the market, left to its own devices, was self-adjusting. Wages and prices would adjust to eliminate unemployment. Classicals recognized that in the short run there might be temporary problems, but their analysis focused on the long run.

When the Great Depression hit and unemployment became a problem, most Classical economists avoided the issue (as economists, and most people, tend to do when they don't have a good answer). When pushed by curious students to explain how, if the market's invisible hand was so wonderful, the invisible hand could have allowed the Depression and its 25 percent unemployment, Classical economists referred to supply and demand. Their argument can be seen in supply-and-demand-for-labor curves like those in Exhibit 1.

They explained, "Unemployment results when the **real wage**—*the wage level relative to the price level*—is too high. Workers hold their wage above the equilibrium level—that is, they won't take the lower wages offered. Other forces (government policies and economic institutions such as labor unions) can operate to prevent the invisible hand from working its magic." For example, in Exhibit 1, the equilibrium wage is W_e. If the wage is held at W_1 for some reason, quantity of labor supplied is Q_S and quantity of labor demanded is Q_D. The difference between the two ($Q_S - Q_D$) is unemployment.

Their laissez-faire policy prescription followed from their analysis: The solution to unemployment was to eliminate labor unions and government policies that held wages too high. If these things happened, the wage rate would fall and unemployment would be eliminated.

Laypeople weren't pleased with this argument. (Remember, economists don't try to present pleasing arguments—only arguments they believe are correct.) But laypeople couldn't point to anything wrong with it. It made sense, but it wasn't satisfying. People thought, "Gee, Uncle Joe, who's unemployed, would take a job at half the going wage. But he can't find one—there just aren't enough jobs to go around at any wage."

Most laypeople had a different explanation. The popular lay explanation of the Depression was that an oversupply of goods had glutted the market. All that was

Laissez-faire   Economic policy of leaving coordination of individuals' wants to the control of the market.

Unemployment occurs in the Classical model because of individual decisions about how much labor to supply to the market and how much leisure to take at various real wage rates.

Classical economists' explanation of the Depression focused on the real wage.

Adam Smith, a moral philosopher whose book, *The Wealth of Nations,* is seen as the beginning of modern economics.

**EXHIBIT 1   Unemployment in
the Classical Model**

If social or political forces hold
the wage above the equilibrium
wage (at W_1 rather than W_e), the
result will be unemployment of
$Q_S - Q_D$. To eliminate that
unemployment, the wage
must fall.

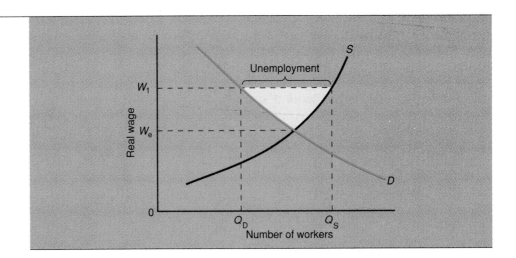

needed to eliminate unemployment was for government to hire the unemployed, even if it were only to dig ditches and fill them back up. The people who got the new jobs would spend their money, creating even more jobs. Pretty soon, the United States would be out of the Depression.

Classical economists argued against this lay view. They argued that money to hire people would have to come from somewhere. It would have to be borrowed. Such borrowing would use money that would have financed private economic activity and jobs; hence, such borrowing would reduce private economic activity. The net effect would mean no increase in the total number of jobs. In short, the Classicals were saying an oversupply of goods was impossible.

This Classical argument that an oversupply of goods was impossible was first made in the 1800s by a French businessman, Jean Baptiste Say. However, it was a British stockbroker, David Ricardo, who made it famous. Say's argument went as follows: People work and supply goods to the market because they want other goods. Thus, the very fact that they supply goods means they have income to demand goods of equal value. This idea can be stated as follows:

Say's law: *Supply creates its own demand.*

Say's Law

2 Say's law—supply creates its own demand.

Say's Law has many different interpretations; the one presented here is the one Keynes attributed to the Classicals.

Say's law implies that savings come back into the circular flow by way of investment.

"Magneto Trouble," by John Maynard Keynes, in *Classic Readings in Economics.*

Say's law is central to the Classical vision of the economy. It says that there can never be a general glut of goods on the market; demand for goods and services as a whole will always be sufficient to buy what is supplied. (See the circular flow diagram in Exhibit 2. In this diagram of the economy, production equals expenditures.)

Not all Classical economists initially accepted Say's law. The most spirited argument against it was put forward by Thomas Malthus, a preacher.[1] Malthus argued that when people saved, part of their income would be lost to the economy and demand for total goods and services would not be as much as total supply. According to Malthus, Say's law was not necessarily true.

Say and Ricardo rejected Malthus's argument. They argued that people's savings were not lost to the economy. When people saved, they did it by lending their savings to other individuals. The people who borrowed the savings would spend what they borrowed on investments: The interest rate would fluctuate to equate savings and investment. So any savings seemingly lost to the economy would be actually translated into investment, making total demand (total buying power in the economy) equal to total supply (total production) through either a direct route (consumption) or an indirect route (investment by way of savings).

[1]Thomas Malthus is most famous for the Malthusian doctrine, which stated that population grows much faster than food production so the future of mankind is starvation. It was the Malthusian doctrine that earned economics the name "the dismal science."

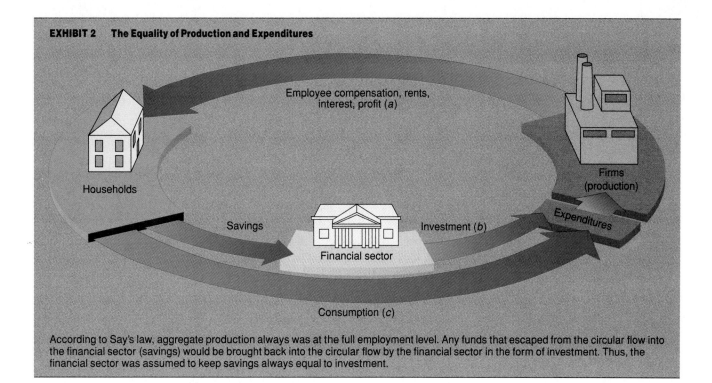

EXHIBIT 2   The Equality of Production and Expenditures

Employee compensation, rents, interest, profit (*a*)

Households

Firms (production)

Expenditures

Savings

Financial sector

Investment (*b*)

Consumption (*c*)

According to Say's law, aggregate production always was at the full employment level. Any funds that escaped from the circular flow into the financial sector (savings) would be brought back into the circular flow by the financial sector in the form of investment. Thus, the financial sector was assumed to keep savings always equal to investment.

The direct route and indirect route appear in Exhibit 2, the familiar circular flow diagram. Say's law states that total expenditures (consumption plus investment, depicted by flows *b* and *c*), would just equal production or income (depicted by flow *a*). The financial sector would translate all savings into investment to maintain a continual equilibrium between supply and demand.

Say's law became a tenet of Classical economics. It didn't say that unemployment could never exist—there could be lots of little pockets of unemployment in various industries if wages didn't adjust. It did say that whatever unemployment existed was a microeconomic, relative wage-price problem and, if wages and prices were allowed to adjust, unemployment would go away on its own. In terms of the discussion of unemployment in an earlier chapter, Classical economists agreed that *frictional* and *structural unemployment* could exist, but they did not agree that *cyclical unemployment* could be caused by a shortage of aggregate demand.

Classical economists buttressed their Say's law analysis of the aggregate economy with the quantity theory of money. The quantity theory determines the price level and Say's law analysis determines real output. (We will discuss the Classical quantity theory in much more detail in later chapters.) In its simplest terms, the **quantity theory of money** says that *the price level varies in response to changes in the quantity of money.* In other words, changes in the price level are caused by changes in the money supply. If the money supply goes up 20 percent, prices go up 20 percent. If the money supply goes down 5 percent, prices go down 5 percent. Thus, money is only a veil, and the analysis of the real economy (of real output) should concentrate on real economic forces.

The quantity theory of money can be nicely seen in the equation of exchange:

$$MV = PQ$$

where: M = money supply
V = velocity of money
P = price level
Q = real output

Q–2: If individuals save part of their income, Say's law will be invalidated. True or false? Why?

Once again it is useful to use the circular flow model to give the students a visual sense of the relationship between income (production) and expenditures.

The Quantity Theory of Money

According to the quantity theory of money, a rise in the money supply will cause an equivalent rise in the price level.

The quantity theory is discussed in more detail in a later chapter.

The quantity theory of money holds that velocity is relatively constant (it is determined by institutional factors). It also holds that real output is determined by real, not monetary, forces. So real output, too, can be treated as relatively constant. This leaves the money supply, M, and price level, P, directly related to each other, and Classicals argued that changes in money supply caused changes in the price level—that the arrow of causation went from left to right: $M\overline{V} \Rightarrow P\overline{Q}$.

Classicals' View of the Great Depression

"The Keynesian Episode," by William H. Hutt, in *Classic Readings in Economics.*

Classical economists recognized that, in the real world, the price and wage levels weren't going to fall to anywhere near the level necessary to bring about equilibrium in the short run. Their interest was primarily in the long run. But in the 1930s the long run kept getting longer and longer, and politicians were becoming more and more dissatisfied with the Classicals' policy prescriptions. As that happened, Classical economists, despite their laissez-faire leanings, started to come up with alternative policy proposals and to develop a theory that explained short-run temporary fluctuations, which, they believed, characterized the Depression.

But they came to these alternative policy prescriptions reluctantly, as a last resort, because they did not see them as getting at the heart of the problem that their model focused on: wage-level rigidities. It was these wage-level rigidities that were causing unemployment, and Classical economists would have favored any policy to rid the economy of these rigidities—i.e., create legislation that would undermine unions.

In the Classical view, the Depression of the 1930s was lasting so long because social and political forces prevented market forces from operating. Thus, their favored solution to the Depression was the laissez-faire solution: stop the measures governments were passing to hold up wages and prices; break up labor unions; and let market forces operate—let wages and prices adjust to their equilibrium levels.

The Emergence of Keynesian Economics

I like to treat this material as a dialogue with my students. The ideas behind the Classical economists' view of the Great Depression and the ensuing policy debate flow easily from the lecture material and engaging the students in a discussion is usually very easy.

"How Keynes Came to America," by John Kenneth Galbraith, in *Classic Readings in Economics.*

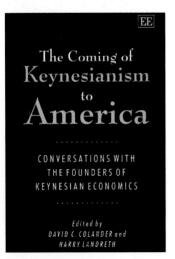

By the late 1930s, many Classical economists were giving up their laissez-faire policy prescriptions. Politicians weren't listening to them; Classical economists sensed it was not the time to push their ideas. For example, in Britain by the 1930s all three of the country's political parties (the Liberal Party, the Labour Party, and the Conservative Party) had abandoned support of a laissez-faire policy. Each party was offering a competing government-organized program to fight unemployment.

Many students weren't listening to them, either: Students wanted to discuss policies to end the Depression. They didn't want to hear about the long run. For example, when Canadian exchange student Robert Bryce came back to Harvard after studying at Britain's Cambridge University where Keynes was a professor, his fellow students asked him to organize seminars to discuss the ideas he'd heard Keynes propound. (It was through Bryce's Harvard seminars that Keynes's ideas were transmitted to the United States.) When students organize their own seminars, you know they're interested.[2]

One more reason why Classical economists were giving up their policy prescriptions is that economists are people too. Despite their training, economists are often compassionate people. Their gut feelings were the same as the general population's: There must be a better way. Thus, during the Depression, some Classical economists advocated a variety of policies that didn't follow from their theory.

While there were many dimensions to Keynes's ideas, the essence was that as wages and the price level adjusted to shocks (such as an unexpected decrease in investment demand), the economy could get stuck in a rut. The reason why it could have problems was that the financial sector didn't translate savings into investment fast enough to prevent a general glut in output. According to Keynes, the level of savings did not determine the level of investment. Instead, the level of investment would change the level of income and thereby change the level of savings.

---

[2]The basis for much of this discussion about Keynesian economics is a set of interviews with early Keynesians. See David Colander and Harry Landreth, *The Coming of Keynesianism to America* (Aldershot, England, and Brookfield, VT: Edward Elgar, 1996).

THE TREASURY VIEW, LLOYD GEORGE, AND KEYNES

ADDED DIMENSION

The Great Depression descended on Britain in the 1920s, before it hit North America. Therefore many debates about what to do about it occurred first in Britain. British Chancellor of the Exchequer Winston Churchill (a Conservative Party member who later became prime minister) followed the advice of his Treasury Department, which was composed of Classical economists. They advised him that Britain should go back on the gold standard (a monetary system that fixes a currency's price relative to gold and other currencies). All countries that use gold to value their currency have *fixed currency exchange rates*. For example, if 1 British pound = 1 ounce of gold, and 1 dollar = 1/2 ounce of gold, then 1 British pound = 2 dollars = 1 ounce of gold.

Churchill followed the Classical economists' advice and returned the pound to the gold standard from which Britain, and all other countries, had departed during World War I. He set a high value on the pound relative to other currencies. As a result, British wages and prices were high relative to those in other countries. Foreign imports were cheap, which was good. British exports were expensive and uncompetitive abroad, which was not good. Unemployment in Britain was high, which was bad. The British Treasury Department's advice on how to eliminate unemployment boiled down to "Keep a stiff upper lip. British wages and prices will eventually fall, or foreign wages and prices will rise."

Regardless of the argument's economic merits, its political merits were dubious. Lloyd George (leader of the opposition Liberal Party) advocated a massive government hiring program to eliminate unemployment. Keynes (a prominent adviser to the Liberal Party, who had, before Lloyd George's proposals, been seen as a Classical economist) modified his economic analysis in part to justify that shift. That was the beginning of the Keynesian approach to macroeconomics.

Needless to say, many of the Classicals were not very pleased with Keynes's shift, and they saw his economic analysis as opportunism. His shifting position led to a well-known joke about economists: If you ask five economists a question, you will get five different answers; if you ask Keynes a question you will get six different answers.

However, stiff upper lips can carry politicians only so far, and soon thereafter the British Conservative Party was also advocating public works programs to help end the Depression. Politics often plays a key role in directing economic thinking.

Source: This account is based on Peter Clarke's book, *The Keynesian Revolution in the Making 1924–1936* (Oxford, England: Oxford University Press, 1988).

Video Series, Economics U$A: Booms and Busts, Segments 4.1–4.3

Given the institutional realities of a relatively fixed price level (which Keynes argued existed in the short run) if, for some reason, people stopped buying—decreased their demand in the aggregate—firms would decrease production, causing people to be laid off; these people would, in turn, buy less—causing other firms to further decrease production, which would cause more workers to be laid off, which would . . . . The cumulative circle of declining production would end with the economy stuck at a low level of income.

The key idea is that, in the short run, equilibrium income is not fixed at the economy's long-run potential income; it fluctuates. Thus, for Keynes, there was a difference between **equilibrium income**—*the level of income toward which the economy gravitates in the short run because of these cumulative circles of declining or increasing production*—and **potential income**—*the level of income that the economy technically is capable of producing without generating accelerating inflation.* Keynes believed that the economy needed some help, at certain times, in reaching its potential income. He focused on short-run equilibrium income because he felt that the forces pushing the economy from its short-run equilibrium income to its long-run potential income would be weak. Long before the long-run equilibrium would be reached, another cumulative circle of production changes would push the economy to another short-run equilibrium income. In Keynes's view, macro analysis should focus on the forces pushing the economy to its short-run equilibrium income.

Market forces that are supposed to bring the economy back to long-run potential income don't work fast, and, at times, will not be strong enough to get the economy out of a recession; the economy would be stuck in a low-income, high-unemployment rut. Thus, Keynes argued, the Classicals' discussion of output in the long run as a reference point from which to discuss temporary deviations of output was flawed. As the economy adjusted to deviations of supply and demand in the aggregate, output would shift and the equilibrium income toward which the economy would gravitate

Equilibrium income *The level of income toward which the economy gravitates in the short run because of cumulative circles of declining production.*

Potential income *The level of income which the economy is capable of producing without generating accelerating inflation.*

Q–3: How might President Frank-lin D. Roosevelt's famous statement, "All we have to fear is fear itself," relate to Keynes's analysis of the aggregate economy?

Keynesian economics provided an explanation as to why the economy could find itself caught in a rut with a glut—and it offered a way to get the economy moving again through the use of government spending policies.

would change. An alternative way of putting the argument is that *short-run aggregate production decisions and expenditure decisions are interdependent*—if producers ex-pected low aggregate expenditures, they would decrease their output (supply). And as they decreased their output, people's incomes would fall, which would further lower aggregate expenditures. In response, producers' expectations of demand would fall still further. As that happened they would decrease their output even more, causing yet another round of adjustment.

Let's consider an example. Say that a large portion of the people in the economy suddenly decide to save more and consume less. Expenditures would decrease and savings would increase. If those savings were not immediately transferred into invest-ment and hence back into expenditures (as the Classicals assumed they would be), investment demand would not increase by enough to offset the fall in consumption demand, and total demand would fall. There would be excess supply. Faced with this excess supply, firms would likely cut back production, which would decrease income. People would be laid off. As people's incomes fell, their desire to consume and their desire to save would decrease. (When you're laid off you don't save.) Eventually income would fall far enough so that once again savings and investment would be in equilibrium, but that equilibrium could be at a lower income level at a point below full employment.

In short, what Keynes argued was that the aggregate economy could get stuck in a rut. Once the economy got stuck in a rut with a glut, it had no way out. The government had to do something to pull the economy out of the rut. This placed Keynesian activists in direct policy opposition to the Classical laissez-faire policy.

THE MACRO POLICY MODEL

Supply/demand models *The micro-economic models in which the shapes of supply and demand curves are based on the principle of substitution and opportunity costs.*

This distinction between partial equi-librium supply and demand models and the macro model is important and needs to be emphasized to students.

Economics: An Honors Companion presents the IS-LM model developed by John Hicks in 1937 representing equilibrium in both the goods and the money markets. The *Honors Companion* follows the text by focus-ing on an alternative dynamic adjust-ment process in the real sector instead of the functioning of the money market as the distinction between Classicals and Keynesians.

The debate between activist and laissez-faire economists can be presented in formal models of the aggregate economy. It would be easy for students if these models were the same as the partial equilibrium **supply/demand models**—*the microeconomic models in which the shapes of supply and demand curves are based on the principle of substitution and opportunity costs.* (Supply/demand models are the models you learned in Chapters 3 and 4.)

The partial equilibrium supply/demand models cannot be used to model the aggregate economy for two reasons. First, macroeconomic models of the economy depend upon macroeconomic relationships between aggregate output and the price level, not upon relationships between output of a single good and its relative price. Second, in the aggregate, *other things do not remain constant,* except under highly restrictive assumptions that do not match our economy. Still, a model with curves that look like their partial equilibrium (micro) counterparts (that is, a demand-side curve that slopes downward, and a supply-side curve that slopes upward) captures the way the economy generally responds to demand-side or supply-side shocks and is the model generally used in introductory economics books. I call this model the macro policy model. In the next section I will introduce you to that model.

The macro policy model provides a working policy model that traces the cumu-lative effect of sudden shifts in the price level, aggregate expenditures, and productive capacity on the aggregate output and the price level. This macro policy model provides a simplified presentation of macro policy issues, which is our primary interest. This model can incorporate both Keynesian and Classical views of the economy, and thus can highlight the difference between activist policy views and laissez-faire policy views.

The Graphical Framework of the Macro Policy Model

The macro policy model consists of two curves. The curve describing the supply side of the aggregate economy is the *aggregate supply path,* and the curve describing the aggregate demand side of the economy is the *aggregate equilibrium demand curve.*

The first thing to note about the macro policy model is that it has the **price level** *(the price of a composite good)* on the vertical axis and the aggregate level of output on the horizontal axis. Those are our axes because when we're talking about the aggre-

When Keynes said, "In the long run, we're all dead," he didn't mean that we can forget the long run. What he meant was that if the long run is sufficiently long so that short-run forces do not let it come about, then for all practical purposes there is no long run. In that case, the short-run problem must be focused on.

Keynes's view of the political and social forces of the time was that voters would not be satisfied waiting for market forces to bring about full employment. Keynes felt that if something were not done in the short run to alleviate unemployment, voters would opt for fascism (as had the Germans) or communism (as had the Russians). He saw both alternatives as undesirable. For him, what would happen in the long run was academic.

Classicals, on the other hand, argued that the short-run problems were not as bad as Keynes made them out to be, so short-run problems should not be focused on to the exclusion of long-run problems. Modern-day Classicals argue that today we are living in Keynes's long run, so that his long-run problems are our short-run problems.

J. M. Keynes.   *Bettmann Newsphotos.*

gate domestic economy, we are not talking about a particular good—we're talking about a composite of all goods, GDP. The axes for the macro policy model are shown in the margin exhibit.

It is important to recognize that this is a fundamentally different framework than the partial equilibrium framework which has the **relative price** *(nominal price of the good relative to the price level)* on the vertical axis and the quantity of a single good on the horizontal axis. This central difference (relative price versus price level) is why macro models do not depend upon concepts of substitution and opportunity cost.

The second thing to note about the macro policy model is that it is an *historical model* (what is also called a first-order-difference model). An **historical model** is *a model that starts at a point in time, and tells one what will likely happen when shocks hit the economy.* It does not try to explain how the economy got to its starting point; the macro economy is too complicated for that. Instead, the model starts from an historically given price and output level and, given the institutional structure, considers how shocks are likely to affect that price and output level. What this means is that we will be basing much of the discussion on the economy's institutional realities and observed empirical regularities.

Let's now consider the two central components of the macro policy model—the *AED* curve and the aggregate supply path.

The **aggregate equilibrium demand (*AED*) curve** is *a curve that shows how a change in the price level will change aggregate equilibrium demand after all the dynamic interactive effects between production and expenditures are taken into account.* A normal-looking *AED* curve is shown in Exhibit 3. Although the curve is called an aggregate equilibrium demand curve, it is important to note that it is not a demand curve in any normal sense. The *AED* curve is more an equilibrium curve. That's why it's called an *aggregate equilibrium demand* curve rather than simply an *aggregate demand* curve. (See the Added Dimension box on "Truth in Labeling" for an explanation.)

Slope of the *AED* Curve   As you can see, the *AED* curve is a downward-sloping curve. A number of explanations have been put forward for why this is so. In this chapter

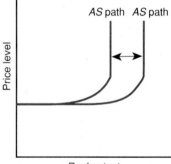

Real output

Aggregate supply and demand axis The axes for the macro policy model are price level (not relative price) and real output (GDP).

The Aggregate Equilibrium Demand Curve Components

Q–4:   Why would calling the *AED* curve an *AD* curve be misleading?

EXHIBIT 3   Determinants of the Slope of the *AED* Curve

The *AED* curve is a downward-sloping curve that looks like a typical demand curve, but it is important to remember that it is not; it is a quite different curve. The reason it slopes downward is not the substitution effect, but is, instead, a set of complicated reasons about how changes in the price level affect the aggregate quantity demanded, and the repercussions these initial shifts set in motion.

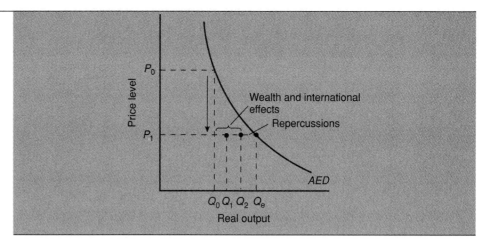

In the appendix, I go though the foundations of the macro policy model—aggregate demand and aggregate supply. There I separate out the effects on aggregate demand due to changes in the price level and those due to interactions between aggregate demand and aggregate supply. When discussing the aggregate demand curve, I go through the wealth effect (Pigou effect), the price level interest rate effect (Keynes effect), the intertemporal price level effect and the international effect as reasons for the downward slope of the *AD* curve. The *AED* curve presented here incorporates the slope of the *AD* curve as well as the interactions between production levels and *AD*.

3a The slope of the *AED* curve is determined by the international effect and the wealth effect (among others) and the repercussions these effects cause.

Q–5: Use the international and wealth effects to explain how a rise in the price level affects aggregate quantity demanded.

I discuss two of them—the *wealth effect* and the *international effect*. (In the Appendix I discuss the reasons why in more detail.) To see how these effects work, let's start at price P_0 and output Q_0 in Exhibit 3. (Remember, as I said above, the model is an historical model so we start at an historically given price and output and determine what would happen if the price level rises and falls from that level.) Now, say that the price level falls to P_1. How will this affect the aggregate amount that people demand? Let's first consider what is called the *wealth effect*. That fall in the price level will make the holders of money and of other financial assets richer. That's because, if the price level falls, the dollar bill in your pocket will buy more than before. As people get richer, they will buy more, which means that the quantity of aggregate demand will increase. So the **wealth effect** tells us that *as the price level falls, people are richer, so they buy more.* In Exhibit 3 the wealth effect increases the aggregate quantity demanded from Q_0 to Q_1

Another reason why aggregate quantity demanded increases with a fall in the price level is the international effect. The **international effect** tells us that *as the price level in the United States falls (assuming the exchange rate does not change), the quantity of U.S. goods demanded will increase.* As the price of U.S. goods relative to foreign goods goes down, U.S. goods become more competitive with foreign goods; U.S. exports increase and U.S. imports decrease. So, in Exhibit 3 when we include the international effect and the wealth effect, a fall in the price level from P_0 to P_1 causes the quantity of aggregate demand to increase to Q_2; the shift from Q_0 to Q_1 is the wealth effect; the shift from Q_1 to Q_2 is the international effect.

There are other effects that have been put forward to explain why the *AED* curve slopes downward, but these two should be sufficient to give you an initial understanding. (The wealth and international effects, as well as the other effects, are considered in more detail in the Appendix.)

Going through the same exercise that I did above for the wealth and international effects for a rise (rather than a fall) in the price level is a useful exercise. Thus, I strongly encourage you to answer the margin question. (If you're having trouble, check your answer with the answer given at the back of the chapter.)

Repercussions and the Multiplier Effect   The wealth effect and the international effect tell us that the quantity of aggregate demand will increase with a fall in the price level, and will decrease with an increase in the price level. The macro policy model, however, does not focus on the quantity of aggregate demand; it is an *equilibrium curve* that relates aggregate equilibrium demand in the goods market to the price level. To determine that equilibrium, one must take into account any repercussions that the

MULTIPLE DIMENSIONS OF CLASSICAL THOUGHT: A CHEER FOR ROBERTSON AND KNIGHT   **ADDED DIMENSION**

Textbooks, by necessity, simplify, and in doing so they often make ideas seem simpler, and positions in debates more clear-cut, than they actually are. Since I am a fan of Dennis Robertson and Frank Knight, two economists whom Keynes labeled as Classical, in this box I will develop their views and position more carefully. As you will see, this more careful presentation places Classical thought in a much more positive light than does the simple presentation in the main body of this chapter's text.

It wasn't only Keynes who was making arguments that the economy could get stuck in a rut. It was also top Classical economists, especially Dennis Robertson and Frederick Hayek in England, and Allyn Young and Lauchlin Currie in the United States. These Classical economists were working on explanations of how an economy could end up at an undesirable equilibrium because of expectational and informational problems of prices transmitting appropriate information to decision makers.

Let's consider the work of Dennis Robertson a bit more carefully. Robertson, a close friend of Keynes, was developing an analysis of a sequence economy which could progress to an undesirable equilibrium if certain conditions held. Robertson's analysis led to many of the same results as those of the Keynesian model, but it was far more sophisticated in its treatment of the dynamic problems an economy can experience. But therein lay the problem: not only was it sophisticated, it was also complicated—so complicated that Robertson's books and work were almost indecipherable to all but a few top economists. Thus, most students were taught the simpler Classical model that we outlined above.

Ironically, one of the reasons Keynes's analysis was so contagious for students was that it could be reduced to a very simple model that, on the surface, seemed to make sense. Students are especially susceptible to simple intuitive models, and thus Keynesian ideas spread like wildfire among the younger economists. Older economists, such as Robertson or Frank Knight, kept saying, no, no, it's more complicated than that; but in the marketplace for ideas, complications don't sell well. The result was that Keynesian economics became macroeconomics.

By the 1950s, Keynesian economics became accepted by most of the profession. It was taught everywhere in the United States. A terminology developed: national income accounting, which was closely tied to Keynesian concepts. As the terminology became generally used, Keynesian economics became as deeply embedded—and as little thought about—as Say's law had been earlier.

That thoughtless acceptance is one of the main reasons why Keynesian economics is not the end of the story and why in this book I emphasize a modern interpretation of the Keynesian model. I should point out, however, that the modern interpretation of the Keynesian model could also be described as Robertsonian Classical rather than Keynesian. As you will see, Keynesian and Classical analyses have been merging in the 1990s and that merging reflects many of the insights of early sophisticated Classical economists. Thus, in the 1990s it is much more difficult to distinguish between Keynesian and Classical thought than it was in the recent past.

TRUTH IN LABELING   **ADDED DIMENSION**

It is very tempting to call the curve representing the demand side of the economy an aggregate demand curve, and many economists have succumbed to the temptation. But there is a problem with doing so. The problem is one of terminology: the curve generally referred to as the aggregate demand curve is not, in any meaningful sense, an aggregate demand curve—a demand curve would hold the quantity of aggregate supply constant. (Remember the other-things-equal assumption necessary to talk meaningfully about a supply or demand curve.) The curve describing the demand side of the aggregate economy does not hold other things constant. All economists agree on this. However, some economists nonetheless refer to the curve as an aggregate demand curve, arguing that, while incorrect, it makes remembering the name of the curve easier for students.

Others, like me, recoil at such misleading terminology. We argue that calling a curve that we know is not an aggregate demand curve an aggregate demand curve violates the truth in labeling precept—it is what in law is called an *attractive nuisance*. An attractive nuisance is an enticing danger—like a polluted swimming hole. It looks enticing, but it is dangerous. In law, owners of attractive nuisances are held strictly liable for the results if they do not strongly prevent people from obtaining access to an attractive nuisance. I feel the same moral law holds for economists. To avoid enticing students into misinterpreting the curve, I call the curve representing the demand side of the economy an aggregate equilibrium demand curve. The *equilibrium* is there to warn students that the AED curve is not a curve that holds the quantity of aggregate supply constant.

change in the quantity demanded has on production (supply decisions) and subsequently on income and expenditures (demand decisions). These repercussions are called **multiplier effects** because they *multiply the initial effect of the price level change on aggregate expenditures as the economy adjusts to equilibrium.*

Q–6: If the U.S. price level rises and the international and wealth effects cause the aggregate quantity demanded to increase by 10, what would likely happen to the quantity of aggregate equilibrium demand?

Specifically, the increase in the aggregate quantity demanded might induce firms to increase the output they supply. This increase, in turn, will increase income and thereby further increase the aggregate quantity demanded. In partial equilibrium analysis (micro) one can forget about such repercussions since, by assumption, the markets being considered are small, and thus the multiplier effects do not meet the materiality criterion—the criterion that they affect the equilibrium in a material, or significant, way. In the aggregate, however, these multiplier effects must be taken into account; the *AED* curve does so. These repercussions amplify the initial wealth and international effects, thereby making the slope of the *AED* curve flatter than it would have been without repercussions. You can see this in Exhibit 3. The wealth effect and the international effect increase output from Q_0 to Q_2. The repercussions multiply that effect so that output increases to Q_e.

Let's consider how these repercussions will likely work in the real world. Say the price level in the United States rises. U.S. citizens will decrease their purchases of U.S. goods, and increase their purchases of foreign goods. (That's the international effect.) U.S. firms will experience declines in demand and will decrease their output. Profits will fall and people will be laid off. Both these effects will cause income to fall, and as income falls, people will demand still less. (If you're unemployed, you cut back your purchases.) This secondary cutback is an example of a multiplier effect.

Shifts in the *AED* Curve   Next, let's consider what causes the *AED* curve to shift. Five important shift factors of aggregate equilibrium demand are foreign income, expectations, exchange rate fluctuations, the distribution of income, and government policies. Let's consider each in turn.

3b Five important initial shift factors of the *AED* curve are:
1. Changes in foreign income.
2. Changes in expectations.
3. Changes in exchange rates.
4. Changes in the distribution of income.
5. Changes in government aggregate demand policy.

Foreign Income   A country is not an island unto itself. How well the U.S. economy does is closely tied to how well its major world trading partners do. When our trading partners go into a recession, the demand for U.S. goods, and hence U.S. exports, will fall, causing the U.S. *AED* curve to shift in. Similarly, a rise in foreign income leads to an increase in U.S. exports and an outward shift of the U.S. *AED* curve.

Expectations   Another important shift factor of aggregate equilibrium demand is expectations. Many different types of expectations can affect the *AED* curve. To give you an idea of the role of expectations, let's consider two expectational shift factors.

Ask your students to list some factors that might shift aggregate equilibrium demand.

Expectations about Future Income: When businesspeople expect demand to be high in the future, they will want to increase their output capacity; their investment demand, a component of aggregate equilibrium demand, will increase. Thus positive expectations about future demand will shift the *AED* curve to the right.

Similarly, when consumers expect the economy to do well, they will be less worried about saving for the future, and they will spend more now—the *AED* curve will shift to the right. Alternatively, if consumers expect the future to be gloomy, they will likely try to save for the future, and will decrease the consumption demand. The *AED* curve will shift to the left.

Anything that affects autonomous components of aggregate expenditures is a shift factor of aggregate equilibrium demand. These components are autonomous consumption, investment, government spending, and net exports.

Expectations of Future Prices: Another type of expectation that shifts the *AED* curve concerns expectations of future prices. If one expects the prices of goods to rise in the future while the current price level remains constant, it pays to buy goods now that you might want in the future—before their prices rise. The current price level hasn't changed, but aggregate quantity demanded at that price level has increased, indicating an outward shift in the *AED* curve. If the current price level falls relative to the future expected price level, people adjust their current quantity demanded (movement along the *AED* curve). An increase in expectations of inflation—an expected rise in the price level—will have a tendency to shift the *AED* curve out.

The effect of expectations of future price levels is seen more clearly in a hyperinflation. In most hyperinflations, people rush out to spend their money quickly—to buy whatever they can to beat the price push. So in hyperinflation, even though prices are rising, aggregate equilibrium demand stays high because the rise in price creates an expectation of even higher prices, and thus the current high price is seen as a low price relative to the future. I said that an increase in expectations of inflation will "have a tendency to" rather than "definitely" shift the *AED* curve out because those expectations of inflation are interrelated with a variety of other expectations. For example, an expectation of a rise in the price of goods you buy could be accompanied by an expectation of a fall in income, and that fall in income would work in the opposite direction, decreasing aggregate equilibrium demand.

This interrelatedness of various types of expectations makes it very difficult to specify precisely what effect certain types of expectation have on the *AED* curve. But it does not negate the importance of expectations as shift factors. It simply means that we often aren't sure what the net effect on aggregate equilibrium demand of a change in expectations will be.

Exchange Rates   Another shift factor of aggregate equilibrium demand is the exchange rate. When a country's currency loses value relative to other currencies, the foreign demand for its goods increases and its demand for foreign goods decreases as individuals do their spending at home. Both these effects mean that the *AED* curve shifts right. By the same reasoning, when a country's currency gains value, the *AED* curve shifts in the opposite direction. You can see these effects on the U.S.–Canadian border. When in the early 1990s the Canadian dollar had a high value relative to the U.S. dollar, many Canadians near the border were making buying trips to the United States. Then in the mid-1990s, when the Canadian dollar fell in value, those buying trips decreased and the Canadian *AED* curve shifted right.

Distribution of Income   Some people save more than others and everyone's spending habits differ. Thus, as income distribution changes, so too will aggregate equilibrium demand. One of the most important of these distributional effects concerns the distribution of income between wages and profits. Workers receive wage income and are more likely to spend the income they receive; firms' profits are distributed to richer people or are retained, and a higher portion of income received as profits will likely be saved. Assuming all savings is not translated into investment, as the real wage decreases but total income remains constant, it is likely that aggregate equilibrium demand will shift in. Similarly, as the real wage increases, it is likely that aggregate equilibrium demand will shift out.

Government Aggregate Demand Policies   One of the most important reasons why the aggregate equilibrium demand curve has been so important in macro policy analysis is that activist macro policy makers think that they can control it, at least to some degree. For example, if the government goes out and spends lots of money without increases in taxes, it shifts the *AED* curve out; if the government raises taxes significantly holding spending constant, the *AED* curve shifts in. Similarly when the Federal Reserve Bank expands the money supply it can often lower interest rates and thereby shift the *AED* curve out. This deliberate shifting of the *AED* curve to influence the level of income in the economy is what most policy makers mean by the term *macro policy*. Expansionary macro policy shifts out the *AED* curve; contractionary macro policy shifts it in.

Multiplier Effects of Shift Factors   As I have emphasized by its name, you cannot treat the *AED* curve like a demand curve. This comes out most clearly when considering shifts in the curve caused by shift factors. The aggregate equilibrium demand curve may shift by more than the amount of the initial shift factor because of the multiplier

Q–7: If expectations of inflation fall, what will likely happen to the *AED* curve?

For computer exercises using the macro policy model, use module "Aggregate Supply and Aggregate Demand" in *Macro Interactive.*

For a discussion of the guesswork that goes into making predictions of future demand and why economists are shy about being too definite about their forecasts, see Chapter 8 in *Case Studies in Macroeconomics.*

The deliberate shifting of the AED *curve to influence the level of income in the economy is what most policy makers mean by the term* macro policy.

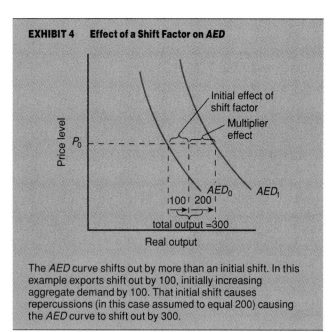

EXHIBIT 4   Effect of a Shift Factor on AED

The *AED* curve shifts out by more than an initial shift. In this example exports shift out by 100, initially increasing aggregate demand by 100. That initial shift causes repercussions (in this case assumed to equal 200) causing the *AED* curve to shift out by 300.

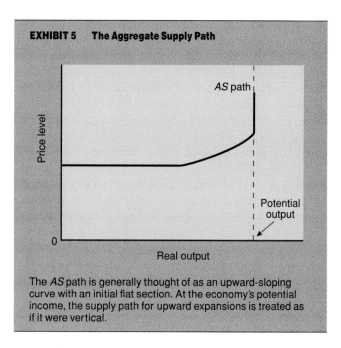

EXHIBIT 5   The Aggregate Supply Path

The *AS* path is generally thought of as an upward-sloping curve with an initial flat section. At the economy's potential income, the supply path for upward expansions is treated as if it were vertical.

effect. The reasoning is the same as I presented above when I was discussing repercussions of the wealth and international effects.

Thus, in Exhibit 4 when an initial shift factor equals 100, the *AED* curve will likely shift out by a multiple of that amount, in this example by 300. The extra 200 shift is the multiplier effect.

To see that you are following the argument consider the following two shifts: (1) a fall in the U.S. exchange rate, increasing net exports by 50; and (2) an increase in government spending of 100. Explain how the *AED* curve will shift in each of these cases, and why that shift will be larger than the initial shift. If you are not sure about these explanations, a review of the multiplier effect discussion above is in order.

This completes my consideration of shift factors of the *AED* curve. The *AED* curve holds all these shift factors constant, so that the slope of the *AED* curve only reflects the initial effects of a change in the price level and the repercussions resulting from that change.

The Aggregate Supply Path

The second component of the macro policy model is the aggregate supply path (*AS* path). The *AS* path specifies the supply path of the economy when there is a shift in aggregate equilibrium demand. Specifically, the **aggregate supply path** is *a curve that tells us how changes in aggregate equilibrium demand will be split between real output changes and price level changes.* Alternatively expressed, it is a curve that traces the price levels that result in the real world when aggregate equilibrium demand shifts, when firms are following their desired competitive pricing strategies given real-world institutions. A standard-looking *AS* path for upward expansions is shown in Exhibit 5.

Be certain to point out that the aggregate supply path presented here represents the empirical observation of aggregate equilibria. Many students will initially make the mistake of thinking of it as representing aggregate supply curve which is essentially the same as its partial equilibrium counterpart. It is not.

Real-World Pricing: The *AS* Path Pricing Strategies and Quantity Adjusting Markets   As you can see, the aggregate supply path is an upward-sloping curve that has a shape similar to that of a supply curve. So why call it an aggregate supply *path*, rather than an aggregate supply *curve?* The reason is to warn students that it is not a true supply curve. Formally, a supply curve can only exist under a market structure which is called perfect competition. In perfect competition firms offer their goods for sale and accept whatever price the market sets to sell all of them.

In introductory economics, the curve describing the aggregate supply-side decisions is often called a supply curve, but its shape is justified on institutional grounds discussed below—grounds that would technically preclude the existence of a supply curve. As I stated above, technically, a supply curve can be used only if one is assuming the goods market is perfectly competitive, and is not in disequilibrium. That is not the assumption that is made in the macro policy model. I call it an aggregate supply path to avoid the definitional inconsistency.

Why emphasize these institutional realities? Because they affect the way the aggregate economy adjusts to aggregate expenditure shocks. A large percentage of the goods markets in our economy have seller-set prices. These markets with seller-set prices are sometimes called **quantity-adjusting markets**—*markets in which firms bring about equilibrium primarily by modifying their supply instead of changing prices.* Empirical estimates suggest that in the short run 90–95 percent of retail markets in the United States are such quantity-adjusting markets. Stores post their prices and agree to sell the goods at that posted price.

In seller-set price markets, central pricing decisions are long-run, not short-run. Firms set pricing strategy for a good early on, and, in the short run, firms tend to hold that price even as demand varies. They meet fluctuations in demand with inventory and by changing the rates of production. Thus, when "Tickle Me Elmo" toys became hot at Christmas 1996, the price remained constant, but a second production shift was added. To say that the price is set in the long run does not mean that price is unresponsive to demand. If demand remains high, material and factor costs will be pulled up, which will affect the firm's long-run pricing strategy. Similarly, when demand for cars fell in the early 1990s, auto firms kept their long-run sticker prices, decreased production, allowed inventory to increase, and offered temporary rebates. When demand increases shortages are allowed to exist when inventory and production can not keep up.

Generally, firms' long-run pricing strategies involve some type of cost plus markup pricing procedure. Firms determine their direct costs and then set price in relation to those costs. If the price is set too high to sell all the firm was planning to sell, firms will hold that price and, initially, build up inventory, and change the quantity of the good they are producing. If inventory gets too high, firms may run sales, temporarily lowering price to eliminate excess inventory, but they will also tie production to sales. So when demand falls, output falls to match demand at the price determined in their long-run pricing strategy. They adjust both quantity (the amount they sell) and price according to competitive conditions.

In seller-set price markets, cutting the stated long-run prices is the exception, not the rule. Since the aggregate supply path is trying to capture the aggregate, it must reflect that general rule.

In quantity-adjusting markets, firms pick a price and quantity strategy, which means that in the short run when they aren't selling as much as expected, they tend to reduce production rather than cut their price sufficiently to sell all they have been producing. That's an important reason why we haven't seen the price level fall in the United States in 50 years. What this means is that the aggregate supply path—the degree to which prices and quantity adjust in response to a shift in demand—can differ from the supply curve.

To say that the U.S. economy is not perfectly competitive is not to say that it is not highly competitive. Ask any businessperson and he or she will tell you that it is competitive. But the competition that takes place among firms is not often price competition. For example, firms may increase their advertising when sales fall, or they may provide higher bonuses for salespeople.

Firms are hesitant to cut price when demand falls, for a variety of reasons. They know that a price-cutting strategy can lead to their direct competitors matching their price cut, eliminating much of the benefit they would get from cutting prices. This

The curve describing the supply-side dimension in the macro policy model is called a supply path rather than a supply curve because it incorporates the institutional realities of seller-set prices.

The approach being followed here involves Marshallian rather than Walrasian dynamics. In the short run, the price level is fixed and dynamic adjustment is brought about by quantity adjustments. Students have no problem feeling comfortable with this assumption, but some professors brought up on Walrasian auctioneer models that have not incorporated dynamic interdependencies may find the presentation unusual. I encourage such professors to discuss the presentation with their colleagues, and to contact me if you have specific questions. I have some more technical papers to which I can refer you.

Generally, firms' long run pricing strategies involve some type of cost plus markup pricing procedure.

To say that the U.S. economy is not perfectly competitive is not to say that it is not highly competitive.

isn't to say that long-run price cuts don't happen; they do. For example, the computer industry is constantly cutting price. Many other examples are possible; in 1995, for instance, brand name cereal manufacturers cut their prices in response to market conditions. But these long-run price cuts are definitely the exception, not the rule.

Slope of the AS Path   From empirical observation, economists have come to the conclusion that the slope of the *AS* path depends on how close the economy is to its potential income. Usually, three ranges are distinguished.

1. A fixed price-level range (a flat *AS* path): When the economy is significantly below its potential output, the price level seems to have a floor—downward shifts in aggregate equilibrium demand do not result in significant falls in the price level, and outward shifts of the *AED* curve do not seem to cause significant rises in the price level. This is Range A in Exhibit 6.

2. A partially flexible price-level range (an upward-sloping *AS* path): At some point, as the economy starts approaching its potential income, the price level starts rising as aggregate equilibrium demand increases. An increase in aggregate equilibrium demand tends to be split into an increase in price level and an increase in aggregate real output. The closer the economy is to its potential income, the larger percentage of that aggregate equilibrium demand increase goes into price increases, and a smaller percentage goes into real output increases. Within this range, however, that rise in price level does not start an accelerating inflation. This is Range B in Exhibit 6.

3. An unsustainable flexible price-level range (a vertical *AS* path): Once the economy reaches its potential income, an excess in aggregate equilibrium demand will result in unsustainable price-level changes. Thus, while real output can exceed potential output temporarily, once this range is entered, a change in the psychology of the economy occurs. It switches away from a stable price-level psychology into an inflationary psychology. In this range, natural resources and labor are in short supply. Significant overall shortages begin occurring, pushing the price level up further. *This point of no return delineated by the economy's potential income provides the supply-side limit of the economy.* All economists agree that once this level of income is reached, expansion of the economy will cause accelerating inflation. Thus, while technically the aggregate supply path extends beyond potential income, for most policy purposes policy makers consider the supply path vertical at that point. This vertical portion emphasizes that, given technology, this is the supply-side limit of any permanent increase in output. This is Range C in Exhibit 6.

Range A   In Range *A*, the price level is fixed; as output changes, the price level doesn't seem to change much. Thus, in the mid-1990s as the U.S. economy expanded and the price level didn't change, we were in that range. This range is also relevant for downward adjustments when there is no underlying inflation since the price level seems to cause a ratchet; it seldom falls. This means that the historically determined price level places a floor on the price level, and any adjustment takes place in real output changes, not in price-level changes.

Range *A*, like the other two ranges, is a policy-operating rule of thumb, not a definitive range. For example, few economists would argue that the price level would never fall when the economy is significantly below its potential income. If the economy remained in that range long enough, the price level would fall. But the political realities are that governments would be forced to respond to the economy's falling significantly below potential income by either introducing policies to get the economy out of this range and closer to its potential income (as the United States has done since the 1950s), or by prohibiting firms from lowering prices (as the U.S. government did in the Great Depression of the 1930s).

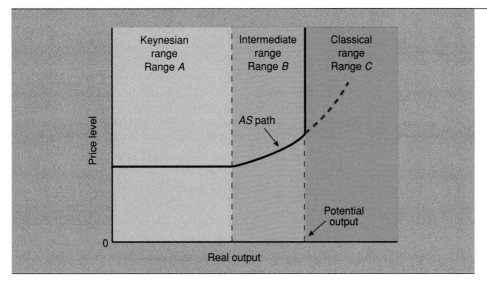

EXHIBIT 6   The Ranges of the Aggregate Supply Path

Most economists believe the economy has three ranges of price-level flexibility. Range *A*, the fixed-price range, is often called the Keynesian range, since in the range, only the income adjustment mechanism is operative. Range *C* (the range above potential output) is often called the Classical range, since in the long run any expansion beyond this point will only lead to accelerating inflation.

Why this asymmetry between upward and downward movements in the price level exists is subject to debate. One explanation involves the implications of seller-set nominal prices, and the difficulty people have in bringing themselves to lower their nominal prices. In such times, competition from new entrants is weaker, and there is an implicit agreement among existing sellers not to "ruin the market" for everyone by lowering price. Another explanation involves society's obvious preference for a boom over a recession. Given this preference, whenever the economy gets to a point where the price level would fall, government policy is undertaken to prevent that fall. Firms build the expectation of government's policy into their pricing strategy, and don't lower prices when demand falls. For whatever reason, empirical evidence indicates that declines in the price level have been very rare.

Empirical evidence indicates that declines in the price level have been very rare.

Range B   In intermediate levels of output (Range *B*), the economy's expansion leaves a trail of a rising price level and a rising real output. The economy begins to approach some supply bottlenecks. Raw materials prices—which are set in flexible price markets—start rising, and selected labor shortages develop. Firms' costs start rising, and they start reevaluating their pricing strategy—increasing prices to pass on the cost increases. At the beginning of Range *B* this occurs in only a few industries—the bottlenecks are scattered, and the price rises are often offset by decreases in prices in other industries that have experienced large technical advances, such as computers.

As the economy moves closer to its potential income, the bottlenecks become more pervasive, and a subtle change occurs in the economy. Firms begin to expect the price level to rise; they build such expectations into their pricing strategy. As that change occurs, the price level changes quickly in response to changes in aggregate equilibrium demand, and the economy leaves Range *B* and moves to Range *C*.

Range C   Range *C* begins at the economy's potential income—it is not a fixed point beyond which the economy cannot expand. Because firms use long-run pricing strategies that tend to hold prices constant in the short run, and hold inventory that can be run down, the economy can temporarily exceed its potential income. But it can only do so temporarily. If the economy has truly exceeded its potential income, there will be significant shortages of labor and raw materials. These shortages will cause prices of raw materials and labor to rise. The rising costs of raw materials and labor will cause firms to change their long-run pricing strategy, increasing prices generally. As

The economy can only exceed its potential income temporarily.

firms begin to expect the price level to rise, they will build that expectation into their pricing strategy, causing accelerating inflation. In this range, it is often said that the economy is in the perfectly flexible price-level range. What that means is that any rise in the price level will generate accelerating inflation.

5 Activist Keynesians see the economy in the fixed price-level range of the *AS* path. Laissez-faire Classicals see the economy in the unsustainable flexible price-level range of the *AS* path.

What range of the *AS* path the economy is in is important because that range determines how much real output can be expected to change in response to a shift in aggregate equilibrium demand. Committed Keynesians tend to see the economy in Range *A*—where the *AS* path is flat. Committed Classicals tend to see the economy in Range *C*—where the *AS* path is vertical and the price level is essentially considered perfectly flexible. Most economists today are somewhere in between committed Keynesians and committed Classicals; they see the economy in the intermediate range—Range *B*, where real output changes some, and the price level changes some as the *AED* curve shifts.

Where Is Potential Output?   How high a level of output an economy can achieve before it reaches its potential output (also called *potential income*) is an issue much in debate in economics. If the price level has remained constant but a small price level rise begins an accelerating inflation, the economy's true potential output is at the beginning of Range B. In that case, in the long run Range *B* collapses and the *AS* path becomes a right angle with only two ranges.

As Milton Friedman has said, given economists record on predicting where potential output is, much humility is in order.

If in Range *B* the price-level rise does not start an accelerating inflation, the economy can move up in Range *B*, depending on what type of rise in the price level the policy makers are willing to accept. (I discuss this issue in detail in a later chapter on growth, or inflation, and unemployment.) The economy's *target level* of output is that level of output where policy makers believe accelerating inflation will begin. This level of output is called *potential output*. It is the level of output that policy makers believe is achievable in the long run without generating accelerating inflation. It is the level of sustainable output that economists believe is achievable. That level grows by changes in inputs (capital and labor) and by increases in productivity—in output per unit input—brought about by improvements in technology. As we will see in our later discussion of policy, one of the key debates in macro policy is precisely where this level of potential output is.

A key debate in macro policy is: Precisely where is the economy's potential income?

The Macro Policy Model in an Economy with Ongoing Inflation   The above discussion of the macro policy model assumed that people believe the underlying price level would remain constant. When people believe that the underlying price level will not remain constant, it is helpful to interpret the vertical axis of the macro policy model slightly differently. To do so, start the analysis assuming an expected underlying level of inflation, and interpret the price level on the vertical axis as a deviation from that expected level of inflation.

Let's consider an example. Say you expect 2 percent inflation—the price level is expected to rise by 2 percent. Now say the price level unexpectedly increases by only 1 percent. In this interpretation, that price level rise of 1 percent would be considered a 1 percent *fall* in the price level relative to the expected price level. If the economy has an ongoing inflation, a movement down the *AS* path in Range *B* occurs when the price level relative to the expected price level falls. In Range *A* (the Keynesian Range), the rise in the price level (inflation) that accompanies economic expansion is expected.

Q–8:   What range is the economy in if bottlenecks are pervasive, the price level rises quickly, and the price rise accelerates in response to increases in aggregate equilibrium demand?

Interpreting the macro policy model in this fashion makes the model applicable to periods of **disinflation**—*a fall in the rate at which the price level is rising*—and makes movements down the *AS* path in Range *B* consistent with the observed reality that actual price levels seldom fall. When the macro policy model is interpreted as having the price level relative to expected inflation on the vertical axis, a movement down the *AS* path does not represent **deflation**—*a fall in the price level*—but instead represents disinflation. In our economy, we've seen significant decreases in inflation— that is, disinflation—which can occur even if there is an institutional limit on deflation—a fall in the price level.

Shifts of the Aggregate Supply Path   Now let's consider shifts in the *AS* path. As I stated above, the *AS* path traces the response of the price level to shifts in aggregate equilib-

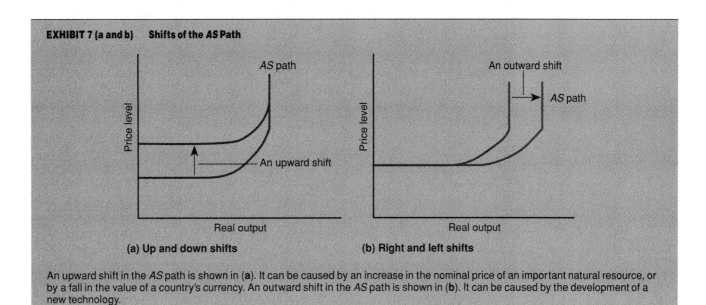

EXHIBIT 7 (a and b)   Shifts of the *AS* Path

(a) Up and down shifts

(b) Right and left shifts

An upward shift in the *AS* path is shown in (**a**). It can be caused by an increase in the nominal price of an important natural resource, or by a fall in the value of a country's currency. An outward shift in the *AS* path is shown in (**b**). It can be caused by the development of a new technology.

rium demand. If the price level shifts for some reason other than a shift in aggregate equilibrium demand, the *AS* path will shift up or down. For example, say that the nominal price of an important natural resource increases. That would cause the *AS* path to shift up as in Exhibit 7(a). It is also possible (but not likely) that the *AS* path can shift down. Say that, suddenly, institutions changed, and all firms lowered their nominal wages and prices by 20 percent. The result would be a fall in the *AS* path.

Since the *AS* path is flat at low levels of output relative to long-run potential income and becomes more vertical at long-run potential income, it is helpful to discuss two types of shifts: (1) those shift factors that move the horizontal part of the curve up and down, and (2) those shift factors that move the vertical portion of the curve to the right or left—that is, that shift long-run potential income. Let's first consider the up-and-down shifts.

Up and Down Shifts of the **AS** *Path*   Dramatic increases in nominal prices not due to a shift in aggregate equilibrium demand shift the *AS* path up. Nominal price shocks include changes in input prices and exchange rates. What happens if a country's exchange rate falls dramatically, as happened to Mexico in late 1994? Nominal import prices rose enormously—that is, the cost of U.S. goods in Mexico rose by more than 50 percent, and the Mexican price level rose, shifting up the horizontal portion of the *AS* path as in Exhibit 7(a). The increase in the nominal oil price did the same for the United States in the 1970s. Alternatively, say that suddenly, with no shift of the *AED* curve, workers demand, and get, a 25 percent wage increase. That would likewise shift up the horizontal portion of the *AS* curve, since it would significantly raise firms' costs.

Right and Left Shifts of the **AS** *Path*   The shifts of the vertical portion of the curve to the left or right are caused by changes in an economy's productive capacity. Productive capacity is difficult to measure, so what is often more important is perceived productive capacity. An increase in productive capacity will shift the *AS* path to the right. A decrease in productive capacity will shift it to the left.

Productive capacity is determined by technology, available resources (including labor and capital), institutions, and regulations. Technological advances, an increase in available resources, and improvements in institutional structure and regulations increase productive capacity. Decreases in available resources and negative changes in institutional structure and regulations decrease productive capacity. As you might

If the price level shifts for some reason other than a shift in aggregate equilibrium demand, the AS *path will shift up or down.*

4b The horizontal portion of the *AS* path can shift up or down due to nominal price level shocks. The vertical portion of the *AS* path can shift left or right due to changes in productive capacity.

Video Series, Economics USA: Economic Growth, Segments 25.1–25.3.

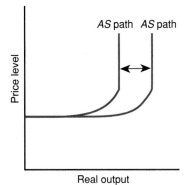

Price level (vertical axis)

AS path   AS path

Real output (horizontal axis)

The *AS* path shifts to the left (right) when actual or perceived productive capacity falls (rises).

imagine, there is debate about whether certain institutional and regulatory changes are positive or negative changes.

Let's first consider the effect of a technological change. Say that suddenly a new micro machine is developed that can change the molecular structure of atoms. This machine, called a replicater, allows one to change salt water into just about anything at a cost of almost zero. Want Earl Grey Tea? Simply put some salt water in the replicater and type in "tea, Earl Grey"—and out comes Earl Grey Tea. Ask yourself what effect this discovery would have on the *AS* path. If you answered that the economy's potential income, and hence the vertical portion of the *AS* path (which is determined by the economy's high level potential income), would shift out enormously, as in Exhibit 7(b), you've got it.

Next consider a decline in available resources—say a large decline in labor force participation. With fewer workers, firms initially would not be able to produce as much. Productive capacity would decline. Alternatively, say that the government suddenly decides that it wants lawyers to review every decision that firms make to ensure that the firms are making lawful decisions. Most economists agree that such a regulatory change would reduce the economy's productive capacity and shift the *AS* path to the left.

The *AS* path can also shift due to changes in perceived productive capacity. Perceived productive capacity can increase or decrease as a result of changing expectations. Thus, expectations can also shift the *AS* path, meaning that what people expect can play a role in what actually happens.

Say that for some reason all producers believe the economy's potential income is at current output, even though it technically could be higher. Given that expectation, whenever the economy exceeds the current level of output, producers expect inflation, and they raise their nominal prices to keep their relative prices in line with the other price rises they expect. As they do so, the expectations of low-level output become self-fulfilling: The price level rises because producers expect it to rise. What this means is that expectations for low-level output are acting as a self-fulfilling constraint on the economy. Given those expectations of low-level output, the economy's current equilibrium income becomes its long-run potential income—what it is technically capable of producing.

Now say expectations change, and that people believe the economy is capable of producing much more than is being currently produced. After expectations change, people no longer need believe they need to raise their nominal prices if demand increases. So they don't. Expectations of inflation are no longer a constraint and the vertical portion of the *AS* path shifts to the right until the actual technical constraints of the economy are reached. What is possible depends on what people believe is possible, and people's beliefs become causal determinants of economic reality.

Q–9: How can people's beliefs become causal determinants of economic reality?

Equilibrium in the Macro Policy Model

In Exhibit 8(a) I put the two curves together and discuss the complete macro policy model. Equilibrium is determined where the *AED* curve intersects the *AS* path. If either of the two curves shifts, the equilibrium will change. To see this let's begin with AED_0 and the *AS* path in Exhibit 8(b). The equilibrium price level will be P_e and equilibrium aggregate output will be Q_e. Now say the *AED* curve shifts in, to AED_1. Since the *AS* path is flat in this range, the price level will remain constant at P_e and output will fall to Q_1. Alternatively, say that the *AED* curve shifts out to AED_2. Since the *AS* path is upward sloping in this range, the price level rises to P_2 and output rises to Q_2.

Now let's consider a shift that is a little harder. Say instead of shifting out from AED_0 to AED_2, the shift had been the reverse—from AED_2 to AED_0. If there is no inflation, so this is a *de*flationary shift, the price level asymmetry comes into play. Instead of output shifting to Q_e, the price level remains constant and output falls all the way to Q_3 since the downward *AS* path is flat at P_2.

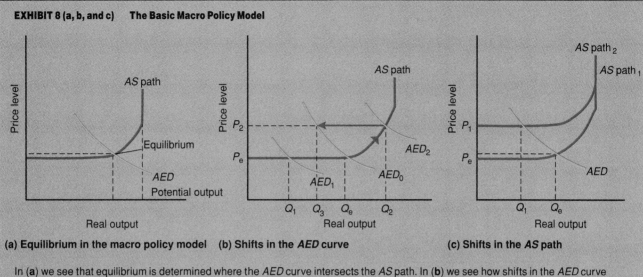

EXHIBIT 8 (a, b, and c)   The Basic Macro Policy Model

(a) Equilibrium in the macro policy model   (b) Shifts in the *AED* curve   (c) Shifts in the *AS* path

In (**a**) we see that equilibrium is determined where the *AED* curve intersects the *AS* path. In (**b**) we see how shifts in the *AED* curve change equilibrium price and output. A rightward shift (from AED_0 to AED_2) in the intermediate range increases the price level from P_e to P_2 and output from Q_e to Q_2. A leftward shift (from AED_0 to AED_1) causes output to fall to Q_1 while the price level remains at P_e. Similarly, if the *AED* curve had shifted from AED_2 to AED_0, and there was no underlying inflation, output would have fallen to Q_3. (If there had been inflation so that the shift from AED_2 to AED_0 caused *dis*inflation, not *de*flation, then output would have fallen only to Q_e.) In (**c**) we see how a shift in the *AS* path changes equilibrium. A shift upward of the *AS* path from *AS* path$_1$ to *AS* path$_2$ causes output to fall from Q_e to Q_1, and price level to rise from P_e to P_1. This basic policy model will be used throughout our study of macroeconomics to examine unemployment, growth, and inflation.

If, however, there had been inflation, so that this is a *dis*inflationary shift, not a *de*flationary shift, then the downward shift from AED_2 to AED_0 would have meant that the downward shift would have followed the reverse of the upward shift, and output would have fallen only to Q_e.

Now to make the example a little harder assume that, other things equal, an initial shift factor of the *AED* curve increases by 20. How much does the *AED* curve shift out? If you answered 20, that may be right, but it may not be. Remember the *AED* curve considers not only the initial shift, but also the multiplier effects that are caused by that initial shift. Thus the *AED* curve could shift out by a multiple of that amount—say two or three times that much. In the next chapter we will look at a model that tells us the relationship between an initial shift and a shift in the *AED* curve under specific assumptions. For now, just remember that the *AED* curve will likely shift out by more than the initial shift.

In Exhibit 8(c) I show the effect of a shift up in the *AS* path. How might such a shift occur? One way is for the nominal price of a basic commodity, such as oil, to increase and for no other nominal price to decrease. That occurred in the 1970s. When that happens, other things constant, output decreases from Q_e to Q_1 and the price level rises from P_e to P_1.

The *AS* path can also shift down. In the first half of the 1990s, for example, the effect of oil prices was in the opposite direction; they fell (shifting the *AS* path down), and, as they did, they had a tendency to make world output higher than it otherwise would have been.

Economists' penchant for creating models has drawn some light-hearted, friendly criticism from a variety of sources, including this author.

Let us now discuss some policy initiatives and other events that often occur in the economy and show why the shape of the aggregate supply path is central to policy debates. We do so in Exhibit 9(a), (b), and (c).

Alternative Shifts   In Exhibit 9(a), the initial equilibrium of the economy is in Range *A* of the *AS* path where the price level remains relatively constant. The economy is way below its potential income. In this range, a policy of increasing aggregate equilibrium

Macro Policy in the Macro Policy Model

EXHIBIT 9 (a, b, and c)   Adjustment in the Three Ranges of the AS Path

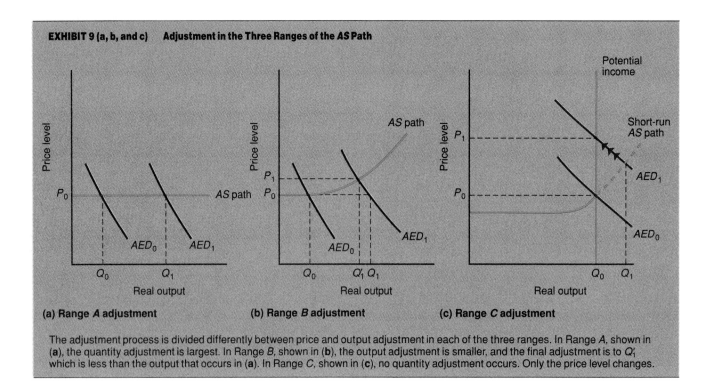

(a) Range *A* adjustment

(b) Range *B* adjustment

(c) Range *C* adjustment

The adjustment process is divided differently between price and output adjustment in each of the three ranges. In Range *A*, shown in (a), the quantity adjustment is largest. In Range *B*, shown in (b), the output adjustment is smaller, and the final adjustment is to Q_1' which is less than the output that occurs in (a). In Range *C*, shown in (c), no quantity adjustment occurs. Only the price level changes.

The macro policy model lets us interpret events that often occur in the economy.

demand from AED_0 to AED_1 will expand output and create jobs, and the price level will not change.

In Exhibit 9(b), the equilibrium of the economy is in Range *B* in which an increase in aggregate equilibrium demand will cause both the price level and real output to rise. The rise in the price level would mean that, for an equal increase in AED to that assumed in 8(a) (from AED_0 to AED_1), real output would increase by less, and the price level would rise. Economies are often thought to be in this in-between range and that is one of the reasons conducting macro policy is so difficult. To achieve one desired goal—higher output—you have to move further away from another—price-level stability.

In Exhibit 9(c), the equilibrium of the economy is at its potential income, and the *AS* path is vertical. This means that in the long run the increase in aggregate equilibrium demand will not bring about any increase in real output or any additional jobs at all; it will simply cause the price level to rise.

Because of pricing conventions, the fact that the economy has exceeded its potential output will not be immediatly apparent.

As I discussed above, however, the fact that the economy has exceeded its potential output will not be immediately apparent. Firms will supply greater than potential output (Q_1) by dipping into inventories, and labor markets will be tight. But initially, because of contractual obligations and inertia, wages will not rise. Soon, however, the inflation threshold will be broken; firms will change their pricing strategies—raising prices, and pushing up wages to keep their workers. As that happens, the price level will start rising faster than previously, and as that happens, real output will fall. The price level will rise to P_1.

Some Additional Examples   Just to be sure that you have the analysis down, let's make you an adviser to the president and give you a policy question. The economy initially has 12 percent unemployment and no inflation. Based on past history you believe that the economy is in the fixed price-level range. Now a demand shock hits the economy,

EXHIBIT 10 (a and b)   The Macro Policy Model in Action

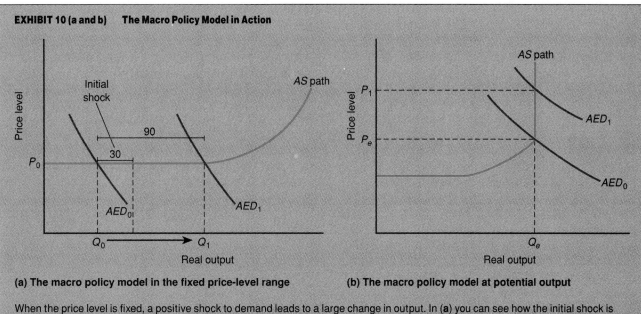

(a) The macro policy model in the fixed price-level range

(b) The macro policy model at potential output

When the price level is fixed, a positive shock to demand leads to a large change in output. In (a) you can see how the initial shock is multiplied by induced spending. In (b) I show how the same demand shock affects the economy when output is at its highest-level potential output. Output remains fixed and the price level rises to P_1.

which initially increases aggregate demand by 30. What do you predict will happen to the economy? Demonstrate your analysis graphically.

The answer is that aggregate equilibrium demand will increase by some multiple of 30 (because we must take into account multiplier effects), and the price level may initially stay constant, but may begin to rise depending on how close to the intermediate range (partial price-level flexibility) the economy was. Exhibit 10(a) demonstrates this prediction. Notice the *AED* curve shifts out by more than 30 (I have arbitrarily chosen 90), equilibrium output increases. If the *AED* curve had shifted out further, the price level might have risen slightly.

Alternatively, say that politicians suddenly cut the government budget deficit to zero, and even achieve a large surplus. What effect will you expect that action to have on the economy in the short run? The answer is that, assuming we aren't in the perfectly flexible price range, the *AED* curve shifts back by a multiple of the cut, and the economy goes into a recession.

Now let's try a different prediction. The economy initially has 5 percent unemployment and it is believed that 5 percent is the target rate of unemployment—the rate consistent with potential income. Now that same expansionary demand shock hits the economy. What do you predict will be the result? Demonstrate your analysis graphically.

The answer is that the *AED* curve will shift to the right by a multiple of the initial shift as before, but, because the economy is at its potential income, the effect of that shift will be a rise in the price level, not an increase in real output. That prediction is demonstrated in Exhibit 10(b). The initial price was P_e and the initial output was Q_e. After the shock, the price level rises to P_1 and the real output remains at Q_e.

As a final check on your understanding, let's say that you are asked to recommend policy. What policy would you suggest the government should follow in the previous example? If you answered, "Try to cut government spending or raise taxes so that the *AED* curve shifts in and the economy avoids the rise in prices," you've got the analysis down pat.

6 Shifts in aggregate equilibrium demand and the aggregate supply path can affect the price level and real output. How it does so depends upon the shift as well as where the economy is before the shift.

Q–10: Show the short-run and long-run effects on the economy of an increase in aggregate demand of 10, assuming it is currently at its potential output.

WHY MACRO POLICY IS MORE COMPLICATED THAN THIS MODEL MAKES IT LOOK

7 Knowing where potential output is and dealing with structural change are just two reasons why macro policy is more complicated than the model makes it look.

Structural readjustment   Phenomenon of an economy trying to change from what it had been doing to doing something new instead of repeating what it had done in the past.

Some Examples

I am generally very honest with my class about economists' poor record in predicting when potential income will be exceeded. Almost all economists missed the mark in the mid- and late 1990s.

The above macro policy model makes the analysis of the aggregate economy look easy. All you have to do is determine which part of the *AS* path the economy is in, and, based on that, choose the appropriate policy to shift *AED*. The problem is that we have no way of precisely determining for sure what range the economy is in, or precisely where the correct target level of potential output is.

One way of estimating the target level of potential output is to consider the normal unemployment rate that has caused accelerating inflation in the past, and calculate what output would be at that normal unemployment rate. But the normal rate of unemployment fluctuates and is difficult to predict.

The problem can be made clearer by relating it to an earlier chapter's discussion of cyclical and structural unemployment. There I stated that cyclical unemployment occurs when output is below potential output. Workers have been laid off, and it is relatively easy to call them back to work and increase production. Structural unemployment occurs when the economy is at its potential output. The problem isn't layoffs; it's appropriate jobs for the existing skills. But how does one determine which is which?

One way to determine potential income is to take the economy's previous income level and add the normal growth factor of 3 percent (the trend growth rate). This gives us a very rough estimate that needs to be adjusted for shift factors of the *AS* path. Regulations, technology, institutions, available resources, and expectations are always changing. This method can be problematic if these shift factors are changing quickly or dramatically.

In some cases, the economy can be undergoing significant **structural readjustment** in which *an economy is trying to change from what it has been doing to something new, not to repeat what it did in the past.* If that is true, the economy can find itself in the Classical range at less than the previously attained output. Unemployment may look like cyclical unemployment, but may actually be structural unemployment.

To see the problem of applying the model, let's consider some real-world examples, and see how they fit into the macro policy model.

The United States in the Mid-1990s   The mid-1990s U.S. economy expanded slowly, but that expansion was accompanied by major structural changes. This meant that firms expanded and increased output, but they often laid off workers simultaneously. Before these workers could be reemployed, they had to structurally change their professions rather than simply be hired back by their former companies. That takes a lot longer—first to realize that one must redefine one's profession, and then to actually do it.

So there was debate about what level of unemployment the United States could achieve. Initially, the majority of economists seemed united that anything below 6 percent unemployment would generate inflation. Then in 1996 unemployment fell to 5 percent, without generating inflation. Economists changed their estimates (and lost some credibility about being able to estimate the U.S. economy's potential income). Some argued the U.S. economy could expand still further without generating inflation. Others argued that the inflation had already started; it was simply taking time to show itself.

Canada   In Canada in the mid-1990s, unemployment was 9 percent—high by normal standards; inflation was 2 percent. But most economists felt that Canada had significant structural unemployment, and that a significant shift out of the *AED* curve would generate inflation. Thus, they saw the aggregate supply path as close to vertical, meaning that if the economy expanded, the result would be inflation, not strong growth. This was the majority view, and for Canada that fit the Classical laissez-faire view. Activist economists argued that the Canadian economy's potential income was much higher, and that shifting out the *AED* curve would cause significant real growth.

Japan   In the late 1990s Japan had the lowest unemployment rate of all major industrial countries—3 percent—and inflation was below 1 percent. It would seem that with such a low unemployment rate, most economists would believe that the Japanese economy was in the vertical range of the *AS* path. But that was not the case; the majority of economists felt that the Japanese economy had room for expansion and was in a flatter range than were the economies of the other major industrial countries.

The EU   Another example is Europe in the mid-1990s. Unemployment was over 10 percent, so it would seem the economy was in the *A* range. It didn't have to worry about inflation. But wait—there was major economic restructuring going on in Europe, and social welfare programs significantly reduced people's incentive to work. Thus some economists felt that Europe in the mid-1990s was at the outer edge of the intermediate range, and the "no expansionary demand" policy was called for. Others disagreed, and called for significant tax cuts to stimulate the economy. What range was Europe actually in? Economic theory doesn't tell us.

The Formerly Socialist Countries   The problem of structural change is even more real for the formerly socialist economies. Even though their output has fallen by 40 to 50 percent, many of them still find themselves in the Classical range—they don't want to produce what, or how, they did before. They are trying to develop whole new institutional structures, which means that neither their previous income nor their unemployment rates are especially relevant in determining their potential income. When there is major structural change, normal is no longer normal.

Making all these adjustments is complicated, and the resulting estimates of the target level of potential income leave much room for debate. There's usually a composite estimate, but actual potential income could be higher, or lower, than that composite, leaving room for disagreement about what the appropriate macro policy is.

The problems of estimating the target level of potential income have led some economists to argue that the best estimate of potential income that we have is the actual income in the economy. These economists believe the fluctuations in the economy are not caused primarily by fluctuations in aggregate demand, but are instead caused primarily by fluctuations in potential income. In terms of our macro policy model, they see Range *C* as fluctuating in and out as technological changes occur and desires to work change. Their Classical supply-side explanation is called a **real business cycle** theory, which *sees all changes in the economy as real shifts—shifts in potential income—that reflect real causes such as technological changes or shifting tastes.* Expressed in terms of our macro policy model, a real business cycle is a fluctuation that is caused by supply-side shifting of Range *C* on the *AS* path. For a real business cycle economist, the economy is always in the perfectly flexible price-level range, and the result of macro policy that shifts the *AED* curve out would be a rise in the price level, with no effect on real output. Thus it should not be a surprise when we tell you that real business cycle economists are Classical economists.

Let's conclude the chapter with a brief summary.

First, there is a difference between Classical and Keynesian economists; Classicals tend to favor laissez-faire policy. Keynesians tend to favor activist policy. These policy issues are often discussed in terms of the macro policy model, and the distinction between Keynesians and Classicals can be shown in that model. Essentially, Classicals see the *AS* path as vertical—they believe there is significant price-level flexibility in the economy. Keynesians see the *AS* path as flat as long as the economy is below its long-run potential income. Because it is flat, shifts in aggregate equilibrium demand will cause fluctuations in real output.

The Keynesian and Classical positions on the *AS* path give us the extremes. Most economists today are neither purely Classical nor purely Keynesian. They are a combination of the two; they see the economy in the intermediate range in which the *AS* path is upward sloping. Thus, the macro policy model provides us with a model that most economists today can accept. Understanding its foundations lets us understand the modern positions of activist and laissez-faire economists.

Debates about Potential Income

Real business cycle theory   Real business cycle theories see economic cycles that result from real shifts in the economy. Shocks to technology and tastes affect the supply side, leading to business cycles.

CONCLUSION AND A LOOK AHEAD

The appendix goes into the technical issues behind the macro policy model and the distinction between Classical and Keyesian analysis. It is far too technical for policy-related courses, but the intellectual issues it addresses have had a curious, almost addictive, hold on the profession and have been the center of key debates in macro theory.

CHAPTER SUMMARY

· The evolution of macroeconomic thinking has involved an evolving debate between Keynesian and Classical economists.
· The macro policy model consists of two curves—the *AED* curve and the *AS* path.
· The *AED* curve is downward sloping. The *AS* path has three segments: a fixed price-level range, a partially flexible price-level range, and an unsustainable, perfectly flexible price-level range.
· The *AED* curve is a curve that shows a variety of possible goods market equilibria.
· The *AS* path is institutionally determined. It shows

the path that adjustment follows when aggregate demand changes.
· The macro policy model can be used to explain how policy measures and other events will affect the price level and real output in the economy. Keynesians tend to see the economy in Range *A*—the fixed price-level range. Classicals tend to see the economy in Range *C*—the perfectly flexible price-level range.
· Macro policy is much more complicated than the macro policy model presents because we have no definitive way of deciding what range the economy is in.

KEY TERMS

activist economists *(246)*
aggregate equilibrium demand
  curve *(253)*
aggregate supply path *(258)*
deflation *(262)*
disinflation *(262)*
equilibrium income *(251)*
historical model *(253)*

international effect *(254)*
laissez-faire *(247)*
laissez-faire economists *(246)*
macro policy model *(246)*
multiplier effect *(256)*
potential income (output) *(251)*
price level *(252)*
quantity-adjusting markets *(259)*

quantity theory of money *(249)*
real business cycle *(269)*
real wage *(247)*
relative price *(253)*
Say's law *(248)*
structural readjustment *(268)*
supply/demand models *(252)*
wealth effect *(254)*

QUESTIONS FOR THOUGHT AND REVIEW

The number after each question represents the estimated degree of critical thinking required (1 = almost none; 10 = deep thought.)

1. Distinguish between a laissez-faire and an activist economist. *(3)*
2. Classicals saw the Depression as a political problem, not an economic problem. Why? *(6)*
3. What is the difference between a price level and a relative price? *(2)*
4. Explain how lowering the wage level will decrease unemployment if the price level doesn't change when the wage is lowered. *(5)*
5. Explain how lowering the wage level will decrease unemployment if the price level is flexible and hence changes when the nominal wage is lowered. *(7)*
6. A popular proposal to end the depression in the 1930s was to create a new money with coupons on it. If the money wasn't used within a specific period of time, the coupons would be worthless. Would that proposal help eliminate unemployment, given the Classical analysis? How? *(8)*
7. What are five factors that cause the *AED* curve to shift? *(4)*
8. What are two factors that cause the *AS* path to shift? *(4)*
9. What range of the *AS* path do you think the U.S. economy is in now? How does your answer to that determine what policy you would suggest the government should follow? *(8)*

10. How might "positive thinking" cause an economy to expand? *(5)*
11. In 1996 the U.S. Energy Department and Intel announced the invention of a supercomputer that could make 1 trillion calculations per second. A calculation that took the supercomputer 15 seconds to complete took the average desktop computer 2 days and took a hand calculator an estimated 250,000 years to complete. Show the likely effect of this innovation on the economy using the macro policy model. *(4)*
12. If the economy were at the end of Range *B* of the *AS* path, would policy makers present their policy prescriptions to increase real output any differently than if the economy were at the beginning of Range *B*? Explain. *(6)*
13. In a recent article, Paul Krugman argued that an economy needs inflation to operate smoothly. Show what he meant in reference to the distinction between deflation and disinflation in the macro policy model. *(8)*
14. In the late 1990s a growing number of economists argued that world policy makers were focusing too much on fighting inflation. According to the economists, the policy makers' actions were lowering potential output. The economists also argued that the technical level of potential output had risen. Show their argument using the macro policy model. *(8)*

PROBLEMS AND EXERCISES

1. The opening quotation of the chapter refers to Keynes's view of theory.
   a. What do you think he meant by it?
   b. How does it relate to the emphasis on the "other things constant" assumption?
   c. Do you think Keynes's interest was mainly in positive economics, the art of economics, or normative economics? Why?
2. In the library:
   a. Find the U.S. price level and the level of output (GDP) over the last 10 years.
   b. Graph the data with price level on the vertical axis and the level of GDP on the horizontal axis.
   c. Is the curve you have drawn a supply curve, a demand curve, or neither? Why?
3. Explain what will likely happen to the shape or position of the *AED* curve in the following circumstances:
   a. The exchange rate changes from fixed to flexible.
   b. A fall in the price level doesn't make people feel richer.
   c. A fall in the price level creates expectations of a further-falling price level.
   d. Income is redistributed from rich to poor people.
   e. Autonomous exports increase by 20.

   f. Government spending decreases by 10.
4. Explain what will happen to the slope or position of the *AS* path in the following circumstances:
   a. Available inputs increase.
   b. A civil war occurs.
   c. The relative price of oil quadruples.
   d. Wages that were fixed become flexible.
   e. The exchange rate changes from fixed to flexible.
5. Congratulations! You have been appointed an economic policy adviser to Textland. You are told that the economy is significantly below its potential income, and that the following shocks will hit the economy next year: World income will fall significantly; and the price of oil will rise significantly. (Your country is an oil importer.)
   a. Demonstrate graphically, using the macro policy model, your predictions.
   b. What policy might you suggest to the government?
   c. How would a real business cycle economist likely criticize the policy you suggest?
6. Write a short essay explaining why macro policy is more difficult than the simple model suggests. Choose a recent macroeconomic event to illustrate your point.

ANSWERS TO MARGIN QUESTIONS

1. False. The terms Keynesian and Classical are two boundaries to the spectrum of approaches to economic policy. Most economists fall in between those boundaries. *(246)*
2. False. According to Say and Ricardo, savings are not lost to the economy. The financial sector translates all savings into investment so that supply and demand are equal. Say's law will still be true. *(249)*
3. Expectations for Keynes are self-fulfilling as fear were self-fulfilling for President Roosevelt. Expectations of a downturn can lead to a downturn if producers lower supply in expectation of lower aggregate demand. This reduction in production lowers income, which will lower aggregate demand. Producers lower output still more. *(252)*
4. Calling the *AED* curve an *AD* curve would be misleading because in the aggregate when quantity demanded changes, aggregate supply also changes. The equilibrium part of *AED* tells you that the *AED* curve takes into account these interactions between supply and demand. *(253)*

5. A rise in the price level will make people poorer since the money and financial assets they hold will be worth less. As people get poorer, their expenditures decline—the quantity of aggregate demand falls. A rise in the price level relative to foreign prices also makes foreign goods relatively cheaper and domestic goods relatively more expensive. Exports will decline and imports will rise, thus further decreasing aggregate quantity demanded. *(254)*
6. The quantity of aggregate equilibrium demanded will increase by a multiple of 10 because of the multiplier effects. *(256)*
7. If expectations of inflation fall, the *AED* curve will shift to the left as people shift expenditures from the present to the future. *(257)*
8. The economy is in Range *C* if the price level is rising quickly and accelerating. Increases in aggregate equilibrium demand will result only in rises in the price level, not in real output only. *(262)*
9. People's beliefs can determine economic reality in many ways. Here is one example: If producers believe that the economy is at potential income, to keep their relative

prices constant they will respond to a rise in aggregate equilibrium demand by increasing their prices instead of increasing production. They will have, in effect, lowered potential output from its technical level of potential output. *(264)*

10. An increase in aggregate demand of 10 will lead to a shift in aggregate equilibrium demand of more than 10. In the short run, output can rise above potential, but significant bottlenecks will develop and input prices will rise sufficiently so that output falls to its potential level of output at a higher price level, as shown in the accompanying graph. *(267)*

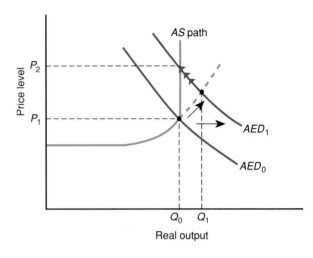

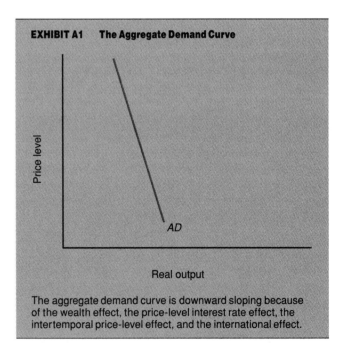

APPENDIX A

The Foundations of the Macro Policy Model

In the chapter I introduced you to the macro policy model. In this appendix I consider that model more carefully and relate it to a logically defined *AS/AD* model.

The **aggregate supply curve** is *a curve that relates the amount individuals as a whole want to supply and the price level, other things constant.* The **aggregate demand curve** is *a curve that relates the amount individuals as a whole want to consume and the price level, other things constant.*[1] These curves are derived analytically in the same way as micro supply and demand curves—through logical deduction from basic initial premises. Now that we've defined the *AS* and *AD* curves, let us briefly consider their derivation.

The Aggregate Demand Curve

Let's start with the *AD* curve. First let's ask: What will happen to the quantity of aggregate demand as the price level falls—assuming other things equal? The brief answer to that question was given in the main part of the chapter. The *AD* curve slopes downward, as in Exhibit A1, for the same reasons that the *AED* curve slopes downward, *except for the multiplier effects.*

EXHIBIT A1   The Aggregate Demand Curve

The aggregate demand curve is downward sloping because of the wealth effect, the price-level interest rate effect, the intertemporal price-level effect, and the international effect.

So the wealth effect and the international effect are two reasons the *AD* curve slopes downward. Let's consider these, and some of the other similar effects, more carefully.

Determinants of the Slope of the Aggregate Demand Curve

There are four effects that have been put forward as explanations of why a fall in the price level will increase quantity demanded, causing the aggregate demand curve to be

---

[1]This definition of the *AD* curve, while standard in most introductory books, is different from the aggregate equilibrium demand (*AED*) curve presented in the chapter. Some books even mix up the two curves; they define an *AD* curve, but then use an *AED* curve. The *AED* curve includes multiplier effects—induced spending resulting from the initial change in price. That *AED* curve derived from the Keynesian model is a locus of points tracing a shifting *AD* curve; it does not distinguish *shifts in* and *movements along* the *AD* curve. For further development of the problem, see David Colander, "The Stories We Tell: A Reconsideration of *AS/AD* Analysis," *Journal of Economic Perspectives,* Summer 1995.

downward sloping. These four effects are the *wealth effect, the price-level interest rate effect, the intertemporal price-level effect, and the international effect.* Each of these effects makes the aggregate demand curve downward sloping and thereby provides a mechanism through which the price level affects the total quantity demanded.

The Wealth Effect

The **wealth effect** explanation of why the aggregate demand curve slopes downward is that *if the price level falls, people feel wealthier because each of their dollars will buy more than those dollars did before, so people will increase their spending.* (The wealth effect is sometimes called the Pigou effect, for A.C. Pigou, one of the first economists to point it out.) If the price level falls and is perceived to have increased the value of money, you could say that the real money supply (the money supply divided by the price level) has increased. As the real money supply rises, the quantity of aggregate goods demanded increases until it has increased enough to equal aggregate supply.

To see how this occurs, let's consider an example. Assume the economy experiences a recession—there is an excess supply of workers and goods. The wage and price levels begin to fall. That fall in the price level increases the value of dollars in people's pockets, making them richer. Because they're richer, they spend more—the quantity demanded increases. With this adjustment mechanism, the Classicals had an answer to the question of how an aggregate disequilibrium could, in theory, be eliminated through a fall in the price level.

The Price-Level Interest Rate Effect

Another explanation of why the aggregate demand curve slopes downward (quantity of aggregate demand increases as price level falls) is called the price-level interest rate effect. According to the price-level interest rate effect, a decrease in the price level will increase the real money supply, as in the wealth effect. But the path of the interest rate does not depend on making holders of cash balances richer. Instead, the **price-level interest rate effect** *focuses on the effect of the increase in real money supply on interest rates: It will lower interest rates, which in turn will increase investment.* Why? Because at lower interest rates, businesses will find it cheaper to borrow and hence will undertake more investment projects.[2] Since investment is one component of aggregate demand, the quantity of aggregate demand will increase when the price level falls. Instead of relying on the effect that a lower price level has on cash balances (wealth effect), it concentrates on its effect on interest rates. The price-level interest rate effect is another reason why the aggregate demand curve slopes downward to the right.

The Intertemporal Price-Level Effect

A third effect is the **intertemporal price-level effect:** *If the price level falls, and is expected to rise in the next period, people will decide to purchase some goods now that they would have purchased in the future.* As they rearrange their intertemporal demand, they will increase their quantity demanded now and decrease their quantity demanded in the future. Thus, as long as the change in the current price level doesn't affect expectations of the future price level, this intertemporal shift in quantity demanded provides another explanation of why the aggregate demand curve slopes downward.

The International Effect

The price-level interest rate effect, the wealth effect, and the intertemporal price-level effect hold for a closed economy—an economy without international trade. As soon as we allow for international trade, there's another reason why the aggregate demand curve slopes downward: the **international effect.** *Given a fixed exchange rate, when the price level in a country goes down, the price of its exports decreases relative to the price of foreign goods.* You should note that most developed countries did have a fixed exchange rate in the early 1900s, since they were on the gold standard, which uses fixed exchange rates. The international effect works similarly for imports: When the price level in a country falls, the relative price of its imports rises, so a country's imports decrease.

For example, say the price level (including wages) in the United States falls by 50 percent. That means that a hamburger that previously cost $2 now will cost $1. Of course, people's incomes also fall, so a person who before had earned $400 per week now earns only $200 per week. However, a fall in the U.S. price level does not affect the price of imports. That means French perfume that previously cost $80 an ounce will still cost $80 an ounce. Since you're now earning only $200 a week, the relative price of French perfume to you will have doubled, and by the law of demand you'll consume less French perfume. You'll substitute U.S. perfume. As the U.S. price level falls, U.S. residents substitute U.S. goods for foreign goods, increasing the quantity of U.S. goods demanded.

The effect is the opposite with exports. Consider a reduction in the U.S. price of wheat. Foreigners' income won't have fallen, but the price of U.S. wheat will have declined. So, by the law of demand, foreigners will buy more U.S. wheat than before. As the U.S. price level falls, foreign residents substitute U.S. goods for their own goods, increasing the quantity of U.S. goods demanded. Both of these effects increase aggregate quantity demanded for U.S. goods. Thus, the international effect of a price change is a fourth reason why the aggregate demand curve slopes downward.

The importance of the international effect depends on the importance of international trade to a country. If the country trades very little, the international effect will

---

[2]The price-level interest rate effect can't be fully developed here because it depends on issues that themselves won't be fully developed until later chapters. I present it here for completeness, because it is one of the explanations of the downward-sloping aggregate demand curve.

be small. If, like the United States, the country trades a large amount, the international effect will be large.

If you reflect upon the international effect, you'll see a relationship between it and the reasoning underlying the partial-equilibrium downward-sloping demand curve. Internationally, a country's price level is a relative price. If economists open the analysis to include goods from other countries, a country's overall price level can be equated to the price for a single good—just the opposite of the case of a country's economy examined by itself. In an international context, the aggregate demand curve of a country is the equivalent of a partial-equilibrium demand curve for a single good within a country. So it isn't surprising that the international effect contributes to a downward-sloping aggregate demand curve.

The importance of the international effect depends on there being fixed exchange rates. If there are flexible exchange rates, a change in a country's price level will likely be accompanied by an offsetting change in the country's exchange rate. For example, say the price level in the United States rises by 10 percent but the value of the country's currency falls by 10 percent. For foreigners, the two effects will be offsetting, and the price they face for U.S. goods will be unchanged. Thus, with flexible exchange rates, the international effect may be inoperative.

These four effects—the wealth effect, the price-level interest rate effect, the intertemporal price-level effect, and the international effect—explain why the *AD* curve is downward sloping.

Difference between the *AED* Curve and the *AD* Curve   If the same effects are responsible for the *AD* and *AED* curves sloping downward, what is the difference between the *AD* curve and the *AED* curve? The difference is that the *AD* curve holds other things constant—specifically it holds supply decisions constant—while the *AED* curve does not. This means that the slope of the *AED* curve is also determined by any multiplier effects that the initial effect of the fall in the price level causes. To see the difference let's consider the definition of the aggregate equilibrium demand curve and compare it to the *AD* curve.

The Aggregate Equilibrium Demand Curve   The **aggregate equilibrium demand curve** is *a schedule, graphically represented by a curve, that shows, given a supply path, how a change in the price level will change equilibrium output after all interactive effects between aggregate supply and aggregate demand caused by that change are taken into account.* It is called an aggregate equilibrium demand curve because it tells us where the new equilibrium will be after aggregate production response to aggregate demand shifts is taken into account. It differs from the aggregate demand curve because it takes into account any assumed interaction between aggregate supply and demand.

If there is no interdependence, the *AD* curve is equivalent to the *AED* curve. If there is an interdependence, the

aggregate demand and the aggregate equilibrium demand curves are still related, but they are not equivalent. In fact they have the same general shape; they are both generally considered downward sloping. To see this, let's review the reason why the *AD* curve was downward sloping. The reason is that, as the price level fell, all other things equal, individuals are richer, so they increase their spending, increasing quantity demanded. This gave us the downward-sloping AD curve presented in Exhibit A1.

Now let's consider likely interactive effects such as those discussed above. When people increase their spending and the price level does not rise immediately, if there are workers to be hired, firms will likely increase output (moving along their supply path) which will increase income and cause individuals to buy even more, causing the *AD* curve to shift out again. The *AED* curve includes these induced effects on aggregate supply in its slope. Thus, it is a line which connects a set of points along a shifting *AD* curve. So the induced effects (often called multiplier effects), if there are any, reinforce the initial effect of a falling price level, making the aggregate equilibrium demand curve (*AED*) less downward sloping (flatter) than the *AD* curve. I draw the *AED* curve and show its relation to the *AD* curve in Exhibit A2.

As you can see, the dynamic interdependencies of aggregate supply and aggregate demand multiply any effect that the fall in the price level has on the aggregate quantity demanded and make the *AED* curve flatter than

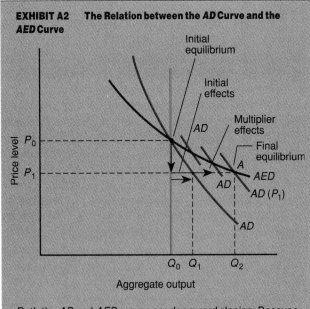

EXHIBIT A2   The Relation between the *AD* Curve and the *AED* Curve

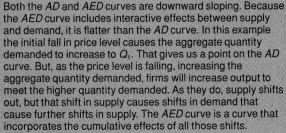

Both the *AD* and *AED* curves are downward sloping. Because the *AED* curve includes interactive effects between supply and demand, it is flatter than the *AD* curve. In this example the initial fall in price level causes the aggregate quantity demanded to increase to Q_1. That gives us a point on the *AD* curve. But, as the price level is falling, increasing the aggregate quantity demanded, firms will increase output to meet the higher quantity demanded. As they do, supply shifts out, but that shift in supply causes shifts in demand that cause further shifts in supply. The *AED* curve is a curve that incorporates the cumulative effects of all those shifts.

the *AD* curve. So, as the price-level decrease causes aggregate supply to increase, the *AD* curve shifts out. The *AED* curve combines these induced shifts with the initial change captured by the *AD* curve. In this example, the initial price-level fall caused quantity demanded to increase from Q_0 to Q_1, and the induced effects caused both aggregate supply and aggregate demand to increase from Q_1 to Q_2. So point $A(Q_2, P_1,)$ is a point on the *AED* curve. It includes both the initial and the induced quantity effects of a fall in the price level. If there are no secondary induced effects of a fall in the price level, the *AED* curve and the *AD* curve are identical.

Shifts in the *AD* Curve and Shifts in the *AED* Curve   Having considered its slope, let's consider shifts in the *AD* curve. The *AD* curve shifts for the same reason that the *AED* curve shifts, excluding the multiplier effects. Thus the discussion in the text is just as relevant for the *AD* curve as it is for the *AED* curve. The difference between the two is the amount of shifting that will take place in response to an autonomous shift. *The* AD *curve shifts only by the amount of the initial shift; the* AED *curve shifts by the amount of the initial shift plus an amount that reflects the dynamic interaction that the initial shift causes.* For example, say aggregate demand shifted out by 10. The *AD* curve would shift out by 10. But that shift might cause a supply response which would feed back on demand, etc. The *AED* curve would shift out by an amount that includes all the dynamic interactions. Thus it will not shift out by only 10. To say how much it will shift out one must specify what dynamic interactions one believes will occur in response to that autonomous shift. We consider that issue in the next chapter.

The Aggregate Supply Curve, the Effective Aggregate Supply Curve, and the *AS* Path

In the chapter I pointed out that many principles textbooks call the *AS* path an *AS* curve. They then go on to justify the shape of this terminology on institutional grounds involving real-world institutional limitations on changing nominal prices. Doing so presents logical problems since, technically, the *AS* curve exists only if the goods market is perfectly competitive—which means that the price level will always adjust to keep the goods market in equilibrium. In such markets there would be no multiplier effects, and no need to distinguish an *AD* curve from the *AED* curve.

In intermediate macro textbooks, the assumption of perfect competition in the goods market is made and students are led through a variety of formal specifications of aggregate supply curves based on the technical specifications of the production function, the supply curve of labor, and whether the labor market has fixed or flexible wages. The result is some wonderful mental gymnastics for students, but a formal model that does not nicely fit the institutional structure of the U.S. economy.

No principles textbook (that sells) goes through any of these mental gymnastics—principles students wouldn't put up with them—but other principles textbooks seldom make it clear that the institutional explanations of fixed and semi-fixed prices in the goods market that they are giving are inconsistent with their use of the *AS* curve. My discomfort with teaching the mislabeled *AS/AD* curves as the curves relevant to the macro policy model is a key reason why I decided to write my own principles textbook. In intermediate macro textbooks, however, you will be given the model based on perfectly flexible prices and, therefore, it is helpful for you to understand the relationship between the *AS* curve and the *AS* path. Let me first briefly discuss the *AS* curve.

Slope of the Aggregate Supply Curve   In the standard definition, the *AS* curve is essentially a factor market equilibrium curve. It tells us the amount of factors that will be supplied, given the institutional structure of the factor market. Economists usually distinguish two *AS* curves—a short-run *AS* curve and a long-run vertical *AS* curve. These two curves are drawn in Exhibit A3. The reasoning for the difference between the shapes of the two curves is that, in the short run, input prices, mainly wages, are assumed constant, so as output prices rise relative to input prices, profits increase and firms have an incentive to increase output. This leads to the short-run upward-sloping curve. As long as workers are willing to supply more labor even though their real wage has decreased, this reasoning makes sense.

In the long run, input prices and output prices are assumed to move in tandem. Thus, the prior reasoning for

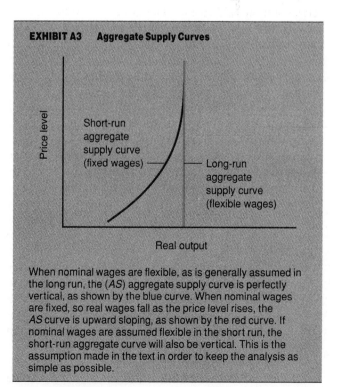

EXHIBIT A3   Aggregate Supply Curves

Price level / Real output

Short-run aggregate supply curve (fixed wages)

Long-run aggregate supply curve (flexible wages)

When nominal wages are flexible, as is generally assumed in the long run, the (*AS*) aggregate supply curve is perfectly vertical, as shown by the blue curve. When nominal wages are fixed, so real wages fall as the price level rises, the *AS* curve is upward sloping, as shown by the red curve. If nominal wages are assumed flexible in the short run, the short-run aggregate curve will also be vertical. This is the assumption made in the text in order to keep the analysis as simple as possible.

an upward-sloping *AS* curve does not apply—firms will not increase profits by increasing output. In the long run (or in the short run if input prices adjust as fast as output prices), the *AS* curve is perfectly vertical. A vertical curve means that a change in the price level, other things equal, will not cause the quantity of aggregate supply to change.

Foundation of the *AS* Path   The *AS* path does not come from the intermediate macro models; instead it comes from the macro econometric models that real-world policy makers use. These include the DRI model (the Data Resources Incorporated model), the CBO model (the Congressional Budget Office model), the Federal Reserve Bank model, the Macroeconomic Adviser's model (formerly Laurence H. Meyer and Associates model), and every other serious macroeconometric model that I know. They base their estimate of the price/real output trade-off on empirical evidence and *that empirical evidence is inconsistent with assuming perfect competition in the goods market.* You still get market clearing in these models, but the market clearing comes primarily from firms' inventory adjustments and production changes given their long-run pricing strategy, which generally involves some variation of cost-plus-markup pricing. There are, of course, exceptions, and in sectoral markets of these models the agricultural market is generally a price-adjustment rather than a quantity-adjustment market. But overall, quantity-adjusting markets prevail in these models, and the macro policy model is based on these models.

Making the jump between the model presented in intermediate macro textbooks and the model used by real-world policy makers has created much confusion in macro, and the current state of macro theorizing involves much debate. Perhaps the most serious confusion occurs in deciding whether fluctuations in output are caused by fluctuations in the real wage (the wage rate relative to the price level) or fluctuations in aggregate demand. In the intermediate macro model, it is the real-wage fluctuations that cause fluctuations in real output. Perfect price-level flexibility eliminates all fluctuations in real aggregate demand.

In the macroeconometric models, and hence in the macro policy model, it is fluctuations in aggregate demand that drive the economy in the short run since retail prices are, in large part, set by a cost-plus markup over raw material costs and labor costs. In these models, aggregate supply considerations enter into the model through their effect on potential income, as they do in the chapter's macro policy model. The intermediate and long-run connections to price-level changes are added separately, and are determined by how close the economy is to its potential income, as is the case with the macro policy model.

The Effective Aggregate Supply Curve   For pedagogical purposes I have found it helpful to relate the aggregate supply path to the aggregate supply curve by defining a new curve, which I call the effective aggregate supply curve.

The effective aggregate supply curve tells how, given an expectation of aggregate demand, the quantity of aggregate supply would change with a fall in the price level, other things constant. Thus, an **effective aggregate supply curve** is *a curve that tells us the quantity that firms choose to supply, given their expectations of demand, at different price levels.*

What the effective aggregate supply curve does is to capture the influence of real-wage changes on output in an economy with an institutional structure like ours. The slope of the effective aggregate supply curve is determined by the real wage—the wage/price level—so if wages and prices change equally, the effective aggregate supply curve is vertical. If the nominal wage is fixed, so that a rise in the price level decreases the real wage, the effective aggregate supply curve is upward sloping. Thus, the shape of the effective aggregate supply curve is governed by the same forces as govern the shape of the aggregate supply curve. The only difference between the two is that effective aggregate supply will shift when expectations of demand change.

Alternative Views of Aggregate Supply/Aggregate Demand Adjustment to Shifts in Aggregate Demand

Let's consider how the adjustment process works in practice where expectations of demand influence price/supply decisions—that is, when we have an effective aggregate supply curve and seller-determined prices.

Say suppliers expect aggregate demand to be low, and hence expect that demand for the product they produce will be low. They will likely decide to reduce supply, shifting the effective aggregate supply curve left. Alternatively, say expectations of aggregate demand are high, so that suppliers think that demand for their product will be high. Effective aggregate supply will increase. So, our general conclusion is that *expectations of an increase in aggregate demand will cause the effective* AS *curve to shift right, and expectations of a decrease in aggregate demand will cause the effective* AS *curve to shift left.* These shifts in expectations play a central role in leading an economy with seller-set prices to an aggregate equilibrium.

Just how important expectations of aggregate demand are can be seen by the amount of time and effort firms spend trying to measure what future demand will be. Firms use a large number of consumer sentiment surveys, polls, and market research surveys to decide how much to produce—what their supply will be. Recognizing the importance of expectations of demand to supply decisions is easy for businesspeople who are trying to predict demand, and for students trying to understand the economy.

It was somewhat more difficult for Classical economists who were trained to think about the economy as one in which firms had no short-run price-setting role, one in which firms produce and sell whatever they can at whatever price they can receive. In a perfectly flexible price-level world, the quantity demanded would always equal the quantity supplied, so expectations of aggregate demand should not play a role. In any other world—with less than perfectly flexible prices, such as the world we live in—expectations of aggregate demand are a central shift factor.

In Exhibit A4(a) we can see the Classical dynamic adjustment to a shift in aggregate demand.

For reasons discussed above, the *AD* curve is downward sloping and the *AS* curve is vertical at long-run potential output. A demand shock hits, shifting the *AD* curve to the left, to AD_1. Because the supply curve is upward sloping and fixed in the short run at its initial output, in the Classical case aggregate output never decreases by assumption—either because there is instantaneous price-level adjustment or because suppliers do not change output even though there is a shortfall of demand. Only one adjustment mechanism is possible. In the Classical adjustment, the price level (including the wage level) falls to P_1, keeping the aggregate economy in equilibrium. This assumption means that not only is the aggregate supply curve vertical, so too is the *AS* path. You are always in Range *C* of the *AS* path.

Keynes's Model   Keynes thought this Classical model of aggregate disequilibrium was too simple (as did many Classical economists such as Dennis Robertson). To see why, let's consider his argument against it. As before, let's say that the economy finds itself in aggregate disequilibrium at the existing price level, so the quantity of aggregate supply is greater than the quantity of aggregate demand. This disequilibrium may create a tendency for wages and prices to fall, but Keynes argued that a fall in the price level will not be instantaneous. Thus, the market is not perfectly competitive. He argued that, in the interim, a second adjustment force—expectations of demand—enters the picture.[3]

Specifically, in the short run, firms' expectations about demand cannot be assumed constant. When firms can't sell all their goods, they will cut production—decrease their effective aggregate supply. So unlike the Classical case where aggregate supply was fixed, in Keynes's view the effective aggregate supply would shift in response to a shortage in aggregate demand. The aggregate supply curve might be perfectly vertical, but the aggregate supply path was not. I show this Keynesian adjustment in Exhibit A4(b). In response to a shift in *AD*, the effective aggregate supply shifts back to point *C*. To understand aggregate equilibrium, Keynes argued, you had to understand the nature of these interdependent shift

[3]Keynes did not explore what would happen if nominal prices and wages did not move in tandem. He ruled that possibility out by a wage unit assumption that assumed wages and prices move in tandem. He argued, however, that (1) his conclusions were not based on this assumption, and (2) for the large movement in price level necessary for the Classical price-level adjustment mechanism to work, wages and prices would move roughly equally.

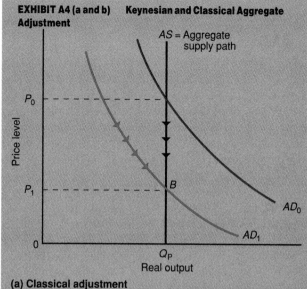

EXHIBIT A4 (a and b)   Keynesian and Classical Aggregate Adjustment

(a) Classical adjustment

If aggregate supply decisions and aggregate demand decisions are independent of each other and nominal wages and the price level are flexible, a decrease in aggregate demand from AD_0 to AD_1 will lead to an adjustment process in which output remains constant and the price level falls instantaneously to point *B*, in **(a)**.

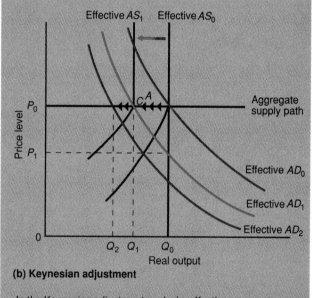

(b) Keynesian adjustment

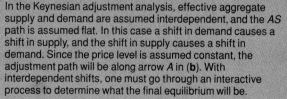

In the Keynesian adjustment analysis, effective aggregate supply and demand are assumed interdependent, and the *AS* path is assumed flat. In this case a shift in demand causes a shift in supply, and the shift in supply causes a shift in demand. Since the price level is assumed constant, the adjustment path will be along arrow *A* in **(b)**. With interdependent shifts, one must go through an interactive process to determine what the final equilibrium will be.

factors. *The interactions of these shift factors determined the income level at which the economy would equilibrate.*

So in Keynes's model, *effective aggregate supply depends on expected aggregate demand.* If demand isn't there to buy all that is supplied, the effective supply will shift back to meet the demand. But, Keynes argued, that shift back in effective aggregate supply would not bring about equilibrium. As effective aggregate supply shifts back, society's income will fall. Therefore the shift back in effective aggregate supply will cause the aggregate demand curve to shift back again. What Keynes called effective demand would fall because, in Keynes's model, not only is effective aggregate supply dependent on expected aggregate demand, aggregate demand is also dependent on effective aggregate supply. **Effective aggregate demand** is *the aggregate demand that exists after suppliers cut production in response to aggregate supply exceeding aggregate demand.* Comparing the two shifts in Exhibit A4(b), we see that the initial difference $(Q_0 - Q_1)$ between the AS_0 and AD_1 curves is more than the difference $(Q_1 - Q_2)$ between the AS_1 and AD_2 curves. So as I have drawn it, the effective AD curve shifts back by less than the effective AS curve shifts, which means with each shift the two curves move closer together; the shifting is an equilibrating force.

Where will the new equilibrium be in the Keynesian case? If the price level remains constant, short-run effective aggregate supply could shift back from AS_0 to AS_1 before the price level falls. Thus it might seem to you that the new equilibrium will be at the same price level P_0 and a lower output level Q_1 (point C). It won't be there. Why? Because of the interdependency between shifting effective aggregate supply and demand. Specifically, say effective aggregate supply shifts back to AS_1. As output falls, income falls, and income is a shift factor of demand. So as the effective AS curve shifts back, that very shift can cause a shift in effective aggregate demand from AD_1 to AD_2. But it's even more complicated—expected demand is a shift factor of supply, so the mere explanation of the shift in demand can bring about a further shift in supply. In this case the aggregate supply path is horizontal. The exact shape of the AS path depends upon these complicated interactions.

Keynes's conclusion from the above reasoning was that one cannot understand aggregate equilibrium without understanding the interrelation between effective aggregate supply and demand, and the effect that adjustment process has on the short-run equilibrium at which the economy arrives. For Keynes, this interrelationship between effective aggregate supply and demand is a fundamentally important insight because it undermines the logical underpinnings of a belief that, in the short run, a market economy will automatically gravitate toward its potential income. The interdependency of effective aggregate supply and demand can prevent the economy from arriving at its long-run potential income.

At this point in the analysis, we are not interested in determining where the aggregate equilibrium will be. The models in the next chapter will consider that in both the Classical and the Keynesian case. What I want to accomplish in this appendix is to impress upon you the complicated nature of aggregate disequilibrium adjustment analysis when all other things are not—as they cannot be

in the real world—assumed constant. There are many, many logical possibilities, and the process is mind-boggling. Such mind-boggling processes make theoretical economists' mouths water, and students' eyes gloss over. I won't be discussing them here.

The problem many economists have with what has become known as Keynesian theory and policy is not that it is too complicated; it is that it is too simple. It may well focus on only one of 100 interrelationships and in doing so make it look as if we understand something we do not. When one really looks into the interdependent shifting of the effective AS and AD curves, the analysis of aggregate equilibrium quickly becomes very complicated and it is not clear that formal AS/AD models are going to shed much light on the process. In making that adjustment, the U.S. economy has developed a variety of private institutions that adjust. Even though the U.S. economy is not perfectly competitive, these private institutions can help prevent the instability described by the model. So the policy implications of the model are unclear.

Justifying the Classical View of Aggregate Demand   On the surface, the above Keynesian discussion makes more intuitive sense to many students than does the Classical assumption that the AS curve is vertical and price-level adjustment brings the economy into equilibrium. In the short run most nominal prices are set, and adjusting them would have substantial costs.

Surface intuition can, however, be deceiving. For example, firms often meet a decrease in demand by increasing their inventory, not by decreasing production or price. If that decrease in demand continues, firms work out a strategy to maintain their market share—often by running a sale or by decreasing their costs and price. So the tendency toward price-level reduction is there. (On the up side, it's even easier—firms faced with an increase in demand for their good are often only too happy to increase prices and, if they do, they are often also forced to give their workers wage increases.) Moreover, there is a portion of the economy that has market-determined, rather than seller-determined, prices. These market-determined prices quickly adjust.

Even when the decrease in demand is met by laying off workers, it is possible for there to be little secondary effect if workers don't significantly decrease their expenditures. Why wouldn't laid-off workers decrease their expenditures? Perhaps they expect they are going to be hired again soon, or they may have a significant other who has a steady job. They dip into savings, and keep expenditures where they were before they were laid off. If people do so, the induced effect of the initial demand shift is eliminated.

So intuitively both views are possible, and the choice of which view must be based on empirical evidence. Alas, the empirical evidence is ambiguous, and it yields no definitive decision about which side is right. We'll deal with these issues in later chapters.

KEY TERMS

aggregate demand curve   *(272)*
aggregate equilibrium demand
  curve   *(274)*
aggregate supply curve   *(272)*

effective aggregate demand   *(278)*
effective aggregate supply curve   *(276)*
international effect   *(273)*
intertemporal price-level effect   *(273)*

price-level interest rate effect   *(273)*
wealth effect   *(273)*

QUESTIONS FOR THOUGHT AND REVIEW

1. Distinguish between an aggregate demand curve and an aggregate equilibrium demand curve.
2. Draw an aggregate equilibrium demand curve and explain the effect of shift factors on it.
3. Distinguish an aggregate supply path from an aggregate supply curve.

4. Why, in the Keynesian model, must one talk about shifts in the *AS* and *AD* curves as well as their slopes when discussing movement toward equilibrium?
5. Underlying the Classical and Keynesian *AS/AD* analyses are two differing views regarding the workings of the market. Characterize those views.

Eleven

The Macro Debate in Reference to the Aggregate Production/ Aggregate Expenditures Model

Keynes stirred the stale economic frog pond to its depth.

~ Gottfried Haberler

After reading this chapter, you should be able to:

1 Explain the difference between induced and autonomous expenditures.

2 Show how the level of income is graphically determined in the Keynesian aggregate production/ aggregate expenditures model.

3 Use the Keynesian equation to determine equilibrium income.

4 Explain the multiplier process.

5 Distinguish between mechanistic and interpretive use of Keynesian and Classical models.

6 Relate the *AP/AE* model to the macro policy model.

One of my kids' favorite books is *The Magic Schoolbus*. The kids in that book can go just about anywhere with their teacher, Ms. Frizzle, in their schoolbus—inside the human body, through ant hills, to outer space. Let's borrow that bus and go to a pretend policy meeting of the Japanese government. Some background: The Japanese economy has just fallen into recession, and the Japanese government is trying to determine why, and what to do about it. As we arrive, a man by the name of Tashi stands up. He tells the prime minister that the decrease in exports that resulted from the rise in the yen, combined with the effects of the enormous fall in the Japanese stock market, cut consumer expenditures, causing unemployment, and that unemployment caused further cuts, and those further cuts caused further cuts, and a downward spiral was in process. He suggests that to stimulate the economy the government should significantly increase its expenditures without raising taxes and that that policy will start a cumulative spiral going in the opposite direction. The prime minister agrees and, based upon that reasoning, the Japanese government increases its expenditures significantly.

I often tell relevant personal stories about my kids or life to my students to make me seem more real to them.

The schoolbus transports us back into the text. Let's consider what we have learned from the trip. We learned that some people think that increasing expenditures can expand the economy and that those expenditures can start the economy on a cumulative expansion path.

This little excursion was important because the same argument that Tashi made is often made in current policy debates. In this chapter we explore the recent history of the argument, and the model it is most often associated with—the Keynesian aggregate production/aggregate expenditure (*AP/AE*) model.

In the last chapter I developed the macro policy model. In that model I carefully differentiated between an initial shift in aggregate expenditures (other things equal) and a subsequent shift in aggregate equilibrium demand, after all multiplier effects of an initial shift are taken into account. I stated that the *AED* curve might shift by a multiple of the initial shift in aggregate expenditures but I did not say by how much of a multiple.

Such ambiguity was unacceptable to early Keynesians who wanted to have input into policy. They wanted their model to have direct policy relevance. To have direct policy relevance they needed to be able to discuss not only the *qualitative* direction of a shift in the *AED* curve, as we did in the last chapter, but also the *quantitative* amount of change. To do that they needed to know the exact induced or multiplier effects that would occur when there was an autonomous (outside the model) shock to aggregate equilibrium demand. Once they specified what the multiplier effects would be, they could give quantitative recommendations about policy—for example, they could say if government wanted to increase income by $20, it must increase autonomous government spending by, say, $8. Since the terms *autonomous* and *induced* used above are important, before proceeding let's consider them a bit more carefully. An **autonomous shift** is *a shift that occurs because of some change that the model does not consider.* A change in the weather increasing income, a change in government expenditures, or a change in exports due to a change in foreign income would all be autonomous changes. Induced changes are the multiplier effects that those initial autonomous changes bring about.

The Keynesian model the early Keynesians developed gives us a method for determining a quantitative estimate of the induced effects on income of an autonomous shift in expenditures. That model is called the **aggregate production/aggregate expenditures *(AP/AE)* model**. It is called that to separate it from the model presented in the last chapter. This Keynesian *AP/AE* model assumes the aggregate supply (*AS*) path is flat—that the price level remains constant—and then explores the question: When aggregate expenditures expand by, say, 20, by how much will aggregate equilibrium income expand? In terms of the macro policy model, the question it explores is shown by Exhibit 1: When a shift factor of aggregate expenditures increases by, say, 20, how much will the *AED* curve shift out if we are in the flat range of the aggregate supply path? The Keynesian *AP/AE* model is designed to fill in the question mark in Exhibit 1.

Whereas the macro policy model gives us insight into the general qualitative effects of shifts, hiding the induced effects, the Keynesian *AP/AE* model focuses on the induced effects. It looks specifically at the relationship between aggregate production and aggregate expenditures, and concentrates on the **income adjustment mechanism**—*the process by which initial changes in aggregate expenditures create a cumulative change in aggregate equilibrium income.* This process exists because of interdependencies between aggregate expenditures and aggregate production. That income adjustment mechanism contributes to the shape of the Keynesian *AED* curve, and is the reason why it shifts by a multiple of the initial shift in aggregate expenditures. That mechanism will be set in motion any time there is aggregate disequilibrium—any time that individuals' planned expenditures differ from firms' planned production. Thus, the Keynesian *AP/AE* model fills in a gap in the macro policy model by determining the size of the multiplier effects. It is, however, important to remember that this Keynesian *AP/AE* model is not a different model; it is totally consistent with the macro policy model and if you truly understand both of them you can move from one to the other, as long as you keep the assumptions of each model straight.

In this chapter we will consider the bare-bones *AP/AE* model and the Classical response to it. The Keynesian *AP/AE* model has the same horizontal axis—real

THE TEXTBOOK KEYNESIAN MODEL

Video Series, Economics U$A: John Maynard Keynes, Segments 5.1-5.3

An autonomous change is one that is not induced by variables considered within the model.

Aggregate production/aggregate expenditures **(AP/AE)** *model Keynesian model giving* aggregate supply *the name* aggregate production *and focusing on total production changes, not on changes in output caused by price-level changes. Emphasizes the difference between the Keynesian focus and the Classical focus on quantity of aggregate supply and demand changes resulting from changes in the price level.*

Income adjustment mechanism Process by which initial changes in aggregate expenditures create a cumulative change in aggregate equilibrium income.

The Keynesian AP/AE *model fills the gap in the macro policy model by determining the size of the multiplier effects.*

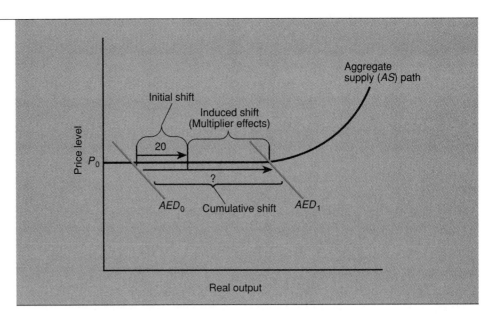

income—which is identical to real output—as does our macro policy model developed in the last chapter, but it does not put price level on the vertical axis. Instead, it measures real output (which equals real income) on the vertical axis. So the axes both measure the same thing.

To see Keynes's exposition of the model, we'll start, as Keynes did, by looking separately at production decisions and expenditure decisions.

Aggregate Production in the Keynesian *AP/AE* Model

Aggregate production is the total amount of actual production of all goods and services in every industry in an economy. It is at the center of the Keynesian model. Production creates an equal amount of income, so actual income and actual production are always equal; the terms can be used interchangeably.

While aggregate production creates an amount of income equal to that production, it does not necessarily create expenditures equal to that production. Expenditures can be higher or lower than planned production. If expenditures do not equal production, something has to change; plans must be adjusted. Given the institutional structure of our economy, that adjustment doesn't occur through price-level changes; firms' pricing strategy, especially when production exceeds expenditures, does not involve significant price changes. Instead, it initially involves inventory buildup, and then involves decreases in production. These changes occur until actual production equals expenditures.

In this view of the economy, expectations play a central role. Planned aggregate production depends on expectations of expenditures. If businesspeople expect high expenditures, they plan to produce a lot; if they expect low expenditures, they plan to produce a little. Keynes's model showed that these expectations of businesspeople can become partially self-fulfilling. Thus, while expectations of demand play no role in production decisions in the Classical model, expectations play a central role in the Keynesian model: Planned production will be driven by expected expenditures.

Graphically, aggregate production in the Keynesian model is represented by a 45° line through the origin.

Q–1: What is true about the relationship between income and production on the aggregate production curve?

Graphically, aggregate production in the Keynesian model is represented by a 45° line on a graph, with real income in dollars measured on the horizontal axis and real production measured in dollars on the vertical axis, as in Exhibit 2. Given the definition of the axes, connecting all the points at which real production equals real income produces a 45° line through the origin. Since, by definition, production creates an amount of income equal to the amount of production or output, this 45° line is the **aggregate production curve,** or alternatively the *aggregate income curve.* At all points on the aggregate production curve, income equals production. For example, consider point *A* in Exhibit 2, where real income (measured on the horizontal axis) is

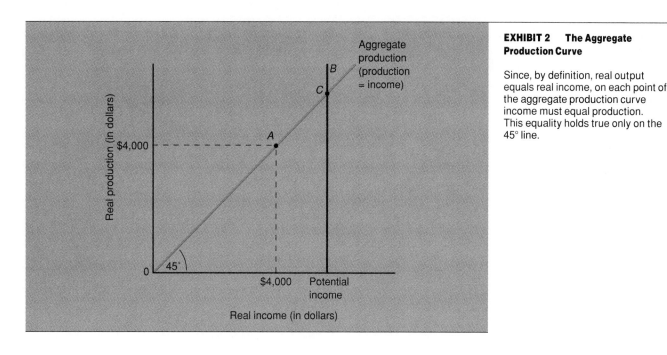

EXHIBIT 2   The Aggregate Production Curve

Since, by definition, real output equals real income, on each point of the aggregate production curve income must equal production. This equality holds true only on the 45° line.

$4,000 and real production (measured on the vertical axis) is also $4,000. That identity between real production and real income is true only on the 45° line. Output and income, however, cannot expand without limit. The model is relevant only when output is below its potential. Once production expands to the capacity constraint of the existing institutional structure—to potential income (line *B*)—no more output expansion is possible. At that point we are no longer in the Keynesian range of the economy.

In Classical analysis, the intersection of the potential income line with the aggregate production line at point *C* in Exhibit 2 would determine expenditures and output. The economy would produce the potential level of output, and the income in the economy would be just sufficient to buy the output; in the Classical model, income equals aggregate expenditures. If actual and potential output differed, changes in the price level would shift aggregate expenditures until the economy arrived at point *C*.

Keynes's analysis differs from the Classical analysis because Keynes said that planned aggregate expenditures, while they were related to income, need not be precisely equal to income (planned production). So there could be a difference between planned production and planned expenditures, and the aggregate economy would be in disequilibrium. That difference would require some adjustment mechanism to make planned expenditures and planned production equal if the economy is to move back to equilibrium. In the short run, that adjustment mechanism involved inventories—firms would accommodate or run down inventories to bring actual production and expenditures into equilibrium. But if inventories were changing, firms would change their planned production, which would have induced effects on people's planned expenditures. Keynes's model concerned how, ultimately, those adjustments would work.

Aggregate expenditures in the Keynesian model consist of *consumption (spending by consumers), investment (spending by business), spending by government, and net foreign spending on U.S. goods (the difference between U.S. exports and U.S. imports)*. These four components were presented in our earlier discussion of national income accounting, which isn't surprising since the national income accounts were designed around the Keynesian model. In that earlier discussion you saw that consumption was the largest component of expenditures. In the traditional approach to this model, aggregate expenditures are developed by specific consideration of each of

Classical and Keynesian Views of Production Compared

In the Keynesian model, planned expenditures need not equal production.

Aggregate Expenditures in the Keynesian Model

Aggregate expenditures   Total level of expenditures in an economy equals $C + I + G + (X - M)$.

olicy fights in economics occur on many levels. Keynes fought on most of them. But it wasn't Keynes who convinced U.S. policy makers to accept his ideas. (Indeed, then-President Roosevelt only met Keynes once and thought he was a pompous academic.) Instead, it was Alvin Hansen, a textbook writer and policy adviser to government who was hired away from the University of Wisconsin by Harvard in the mid-1930s, who played the key role in getting Keynesian economic policies introduced into the United States.

The story of how Hansen converted to Keynes's ideas is somewhat mysterious. At the time, almost all economists were Classicals, and Hansen was no exception. (Otherwise it's doubtful Harvard would have recruited him.) But, somehow, on the train trip from Wisconsin to Massachusetts, Hansen metamorphosed from a Classical to a Keynesian. His graduate seminar at Harvard in the late 1930s and the 1940s became the U.S. breeding ground for Keynesian economics.

What made Hansen and other economists switch from Classical to Keynesian economics? It was the Depression; the Keynesian story explained it much better than did the Classical real-wage story.

Hansen quickly realized that talking about interdependencies of supply and demand decisions didn't work for policy makers and businesspeople. They wanted numbers—specifics—and Keynes's work had no specifics. So Alvin Hansen and his students, especially Paul Samuelson, set about to develop specifics. They developed what is now called the textbook model of Keynesian economics. That textbook model gave the Keynesian ideas a structure embodied in the specific models that policy makers demanded. In the late 1940s, Hansen wrote a book, *A Guide to Keynes,* that was the bible for students studying macro in the 1950s and early 1960s. He also made weekly trips to Washington where he "sold" Keynesian ideas to policy makers.

Hansen's student, Paul Samuelson, wrote a textbook that changed the structure of the economics principles course. Samuelson's text provided an introduction to Keynesian ideas for millions of students throughout the world. At the same time, Dutch and Norwegian economists, including Jan Tinburgen and Ragnar Frisch, developed an empirically-determined macro model that policy makers could use. For their contributions, many in this group won Nobel prizes.

the components. To save time, in this chapter I concentrate on aggregate expenditures. (An algebraic model with the components is presented in the appendix.)

> Expenditures that are due to any factor other than income are considered autonomous expenditures. I prefer this to the algebraic interpretation of autonomous expenditures as the level of expenditures that takes place when income is zero.

Autonomous and Induced Expenditures   While expenditures are determined by many things, one of the most important is income. When income in society rises, expenditures rise. The Keynesian model is based upon this relationship being relatively stable and taking a specific nature: Specifically, as income changes, expenditures change, but not by as much as income.

Exhibit 3 shows a hypothesized relationship between possible income and expenditure levels for an economy. Notice that when income is zero, we still assume there is spending. How does that happen? By the economy borrowing or dipping into previous savings. Expenditures that would exist at a zero level of income are called **autonomous expenditures**—*expenditures that are independent of income*. They may change because something other than income changes. For example, if bad weather stops people from buying, *autonomous* expenditures would fall.

> *Autonomous expenditures   Expenditures that change because something other than income changes.*

Notice that as income rises, expenditures also rise, but not by as much as the rise in income. The relationship between changes in income and changes in expenditures is shown in columns 2 and 4. The numbers in these columns can be derived from columns 1 and 3. Each entry in column 2 represents the difference between the corresponding entry in column 1 and the entry in the previous row of column 1. Similarly, each entry in column 4 is the difference between the corresponding entry in column 3 and the entry in the previous row of column 3. For example, as income rises from $10,000 to $11,000 (column 1, row K to L), the change in income is $1,000 (column 2, row L). Similarly, as expenditures rise from $9,000 to $9,800 (column 3, row K to L), the change in expenditures is $800 (column 4, row L).

> **1** Autonomous expenditures are unrelated to income; induced expenditures are directly related to income.

Since much of Keynes's analysis focuses on changes in expenditures that occur in response to changes in income, it is important to distinguish that portion of expenditures that changes in response to changes in income from that portion that does not. As previously stated, that portion of expenditures that does not change when income

(1) Income (Y)	(2) Change in Income (ΔY)	(3) Expenditures (E)	(4) Change in Expenditures (ΔE)	Row
$ 0	—	$ 1,000	—	A
1,000	$1,000	1,800	$800	B
2,000	1,000	2,600	800	C
3,000	1,000	3,400	800	D
4,000	1,000	4,200	800	E
5,000	1,000	5,000	800	F
6,000	1,000	5,800	800	G
7,000	1,000	6,600	800	H
8,000	1,000	7,400	800	I
9,000	1,000	8,200	800	J
10,000	1,000	9,000	800	K
11,000	1,000	9,800	800	L
12,000	1,000	10,600	800	M
13,000	1,000	11,400	800	N
14,000	1,000	12,200	800	O
15,000	1,000	13,000	800	P

EXHIBIT 3   Expenditures Related to Income

Many professsors will be used to their relationship being presented as a relationship between income and consumption. By eliminating the divisions of expenditures, the math is made much easier and the essense of the Keynesian model is maintained.

changes is called *autonomous expenditures*. **Induced expenditures** are *expenditures that change as income changes.*

The relationship between expenditures and income—as in the table in our example—can be expressed more concisely as an **expenditures function** *a representation of the relationship between expenditures and income as a mathematical function*:

$$E = E_0 + mpeY$$

where:

E = expenditures
E_0 = autonomous expenditures
mpe = marginal propensity to expend
Y = income

why not AE??

The expenditures function corresponding to the table in Exhibit 3 is

$$E = \$1,000 + .8Y$$

I draw this expenditures function in Exhibit 4.

Notice that if you substitute the data from any row in the table in Exhibit 3, both sides of the expenditures function are equal. For example, in row C of Exhibit 3, we see that expenditures (E) = $2,600. So $2,600 = $1,000 + .8Y$. Since income (Y) = $2,000, we can calculate (.8)($2,000) = $1,600 and add it to $1,000, giving us $2,600. So the two sides are equal.

The Marginal Propensity to Expend   There is one part of the expenditures function we haven't talked about yet: the letters *mpe* (.8 in the numerical example). The letters *mpe* represent the marginal propensity to expend. Keynes was interested in what would happen to expenditures spending as income changed. He argued that when income fell by, say, $1,000, expenditures would fall by somewhat less than that amount ($800 in the example). He defined **marginal propensity to expend (*mpe*)** as *the ratio of a change in expenditures, ΔE, to a change in income, ΔY.* (The Greek letter Δ, or delta, which corresponds to the letter D in our alphabet, is commonly used to designate *change in*.) The *mpe* is the fraction spent from an additional dollar of income.

$$mpe = \frac{\text{Change in expenditures}}{\text{Change in income}} = \frac{\Delta E}{\Delta Y}$$

Induced expenditures (**mpeY**)
Expenditures that change as income changes.

Expenditures function   *A functional representation of the relation between expenditures and income* (E = E_0 + mpeY).

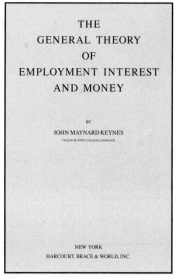

THE
GENERAL THEORY
OF
EMPLOYMENT INTEREST
AND MONEY

BY

JOHN MAYNARD KEYNES

FELLOW OF KING'S COLLEGE, CAMBRIDGE

NEW YORK
HARCOURT, BRACE & WORLD, INC.

The General Theory—the book that created macroeconomics as a separate subject.

Marginal propensity to expend (**mpe**)
The fraction spent from an additional dollar of income.

EXHIBIT 4   Graph of Expenditures Function

The expenditures function graphed here represents the function derived from the information in Exhibit 3. It has a slope of .8, the *mpe,* and an intercept of $1,000, the level of autonomous expenditures. The shaded area is the difference between production and expenditures. Thus, when real income is $14,000 expenditures are $12,200.

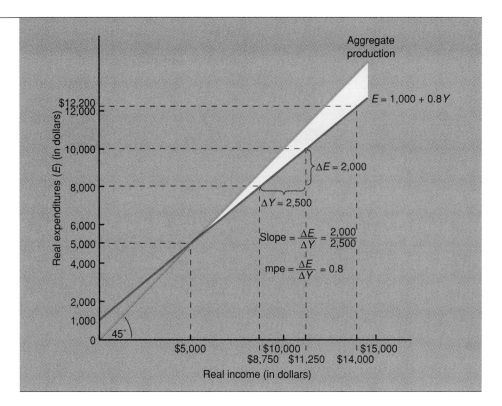

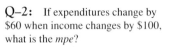

Q–2: If expenditures change by $60 when income changes by $100, what is the *mpe*?

Using the data in Exhibit 3, let's determine the *mpe* by dividing a change in expenditures by a corresponding change in income:

$$mpe = \frac{\Delta E}{\Delta Y} = \frac{\$800}{\$1,000} = .8$$

In thinking about the relationship, it is helpful to remember that the largest component of expenditures is consumption, and that the marginal propensity of individuals to consume out of their income is a key determinant of the marginal propensity to expend.

Graphing the Expenditures Function   Now that we're familiar with the terminology used with the expenditures function, let's see how to graph it. Exhibit 4 graphs the expenditures function represented by

$$E = \$1,000 + .8Y.$$

Notice that at zero income, expenditures are $1,000. This is the autonomous portion of expenditures.

     The expenditures function's slope tells us how much expenditures change with a particular change in income. In other words, the slope of an expenditures function graphically represents the marginal propensity to expend for an expenditures function.

The *AP/AE* Model Is an Historical Model in Time   While I will discuss the *AP/AE* model as if it relates to income levels over broad ranges, I must point out that, like the macro policy model, the *AP/AE* model is an historical model. It is useful to analyze shifts in aggregate expenditures from an historically given income level, not to determine income independent of the economy's historical position. Thus while we speak of what expenditures would be at zero income, or while we say the *mpe* is constant over all ranges of income, that is done simply to make the geometric portrayal of the model easier. What is actually assumed is that within the relevant range around existing

Here is a good place to make a mistake on the blackboard when you're graphing the expenditures function, just to see if students are awake.

     In beginning MBA courses and in schools where students have sufficient technical background to deal easily with algebra, I would suggest assigning Appendix A at this point and working the entire Keynesian model out algebraically. It provides a coherent structure of the model. For instructors who follow that route, it is important to remember that the model is far more than just the algebra. It also includes the stories and interpretations that go behind it. Thus, after the presentation of the algebra, students still need a week or two of discussion of the points in Chapters 10 and 11 in order for the model to become real to them.

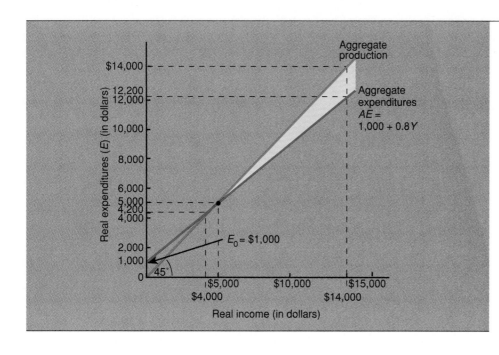

EXHIBIT 5   Comparing *AE* to *AP* and Solving for Equilibrium Graphically

Equilibrium in the *AP/AE* model is determined where the *AE* and *AP* curves intersect. That equilibrium is at $5,000. At income levels higher or lower than that, planned production will not equal planned expenditures.

income—say a 5 percent increase or decrease—the *mpe* remains constant, and the autonomous portion of the expenditures is the intercept that would occur if we extended the expenditures function.

Now that we've developed the graphical framework (the aggregate production/aggregate expenditure, or *AP/AE,* framework), we can put the aggregate production and aggregate expenditures together and see how the level of aggregate income is determined in the Keynesian model. Initially I assume the economy is in Range *A* of the aggregate supply path. In Range *A* the price level is constant, so all terms can be real terms. We begin by considering the relationship between the aggregate expenditures curve and the aggregate production curve more carefully. We do so in Exhibit 5.

The aggregate production curve is the 45° line up until the economy reaches potential income. It tells you the level of aggregate production and also the level of aggregate income since, by definition, income equals production when the price level does not change. Expenditures are shown by the *AE* line. Planned expenditures do not necessarily equal planned production or income. In equilibrium, however, expenditures must equal planned production. Let's see that that is the case.

Let's first say that planned production, and hence income, is $14,000. As you can see, at income of $14,000, expenditures are $12,200. Planned aggregate production exceeds aggregate expenditures. This is true for any income level above $5,000. Similarly, at all income levels below $5,000, planned aggregate production is less than aggregate expenditures. For example, at a production level of $4,000, aggregate expenditures are $4,200.

The only income level at which planned aggregate production equals aggregate expenditures is $5,000. Since we know that, in equilibrium, aggregate expenditures must equal planned aggregate production, $5,000 is the equilibrium level of income in the economy. It is the level of income at which neither producers nor consumers have any reason to change what they are doing. At any other level of income, since there is either a shortage or a surplus of goods, or firms' inventory is greater than or less than desired, there will be incentive to change. Thus, you can use the aggregate production curve and the aggregate expenditures curve to determine the level of income at which the economy will be in equilibrium.

I like to solve for equilibrium graphically and algebraically on two sides of the same blackboard. Then I move between the sides and show how they are two ways of achieving the same end.

DETERMINING THE LEVEL OF AGGREGATE INCOME

2 To determine income graphically in the Keynesian *AP/AE* model, you find the income level at which aggregate expenditures equals planned aggregate production.

For computer exercises using the AP/AE model, use module "Aggregate Production/Aggregate Expenditures" in *Macro Interactive.*

ADDED DIMENSION   SOLVING FOR EQUILIBRIUM INCOME ALGEBRAICALLY

For those of you who are mathematically inclined, the Keynesian equation can be derived by combining the equations presented in the text algebraically to arrive at the equation for income. Rewriting the expenditures relationship, we have:

$$E = E_0 + mpeY.$$

Aggregate production, by definition, equals aggregate income (Y) and, in equilibrium, aggregate income must equal the four components of aggregate expenditures. Beginning with the national income accounting identity, we have

$$Y = E.$$

Substituting the terms from the first equation, we have

$$Y = E_0 + mpeY.$$

Subtracting $mpeY$ from both sides,

$$Y - mpeY = E_0.$$

To arrive at the Keynesian equation we factor out Y:

$$Y(1 - mpe) = E_0.$$

Now solve for Y by dividing both sides by $(1 - mpe)$:

$$Y = \underbrace{\left[\frac{1}{(1 - mpe)} \right]}_{multiplier} \times \underbrace{[E_0]}_{autonomous\ expenditures}$$

This is the Keynesian equation.

Determining the Level of Aggregate Income with the Keynesian Equation

Keynesian equation   Equation showing the relationship between autonomous expenditures and the equilibrium level of income. Y = (multiplier)(autonomous expenditures).

Another useful way to determine the level of income in the Keynesian model is through the **Keynesian equation,** *an equation that tells us that income equals the multiplier times autonomous expenditures.*

$$Y = (multiplier)(autonomous\ expenditures)$$

The Keynesian equation does not come out of thin air. It comes from combining the set of equations underlying the graphical presentation of the Keynesian model into the two brackets. The Keynesian equation is derived in the accompanying box.

The Multiplier

Multiplier   A number that tells us how much income will change in response to a change in autonomous expenditures. [1/(1 − mpe)].

Q–3: If the *mpe* = .5, what is the multiplier?

"The Multiplier," by Henry Hazlitt, in *Classic Readings in Economics.*

The multiplier captures the key aspect of the Keynesian model that differentiates it from the Classical model. Specifically, the **multiplier** is *a number that tells us how much income will change in response to a change in autonomous expenditures.*

To calculate the multiplier, you divide 1 by (1 minus the marginal propensity to expend). Thus:

$$\text{Multiplier} = 1/(1 - mpe)$$

Once you know the value of the marginal propensity to expend, you can calculate the multiplier by reducing $[1/(1 - mpe)]$ to a simple number. For example, if *mpe* = .8, the multiplier is

$$1/(1 - .8) = 1/.2 = 5$$

The multiplier provided precisely the relationship policy makers needed. It gave them something specific. It gave them an intuitive story of why the Depression occurred and, as we will see in the next chapter, it gave them a story of how certain policies can change it. The story went as follows: When the stock market crashed, businesspeople and consumers got scared and cut their investment and consumption (both are components of expenditures). Aggregate expenditures decreased. That decrease sent the multiplier into action. It induced businesses to further decrease production (shift supply back), which lowered income and induced a further decrease in aggregate expenditures. This cumulative downward spiral of expenditures was the multiplier process. The multiplier story made sense to policy makers and, hence, played a big role in the acceptance of Keynesian economics into policy.

Since the multiplier tells you the relationship between autonomous expenditures and income, once you know the multiplier, calculating the equilibrium level of income is easy. All you do is multiply autonomous expenditures by the multiplier. For example, if autonomous expenditures are $4,000 and the multiplier is 5, equilibrium income in the economy will be $20,000.

Let's see how the equation works by considering another example. Say the *mpe* is .75. Subtracting .75 from 1 gives .25. Dividing 1 by .25 gives 4. (Remember, dividing 1 by 0.25 is asking how many 1/4ths there are in 1.) So our first term is 4. Say, also, that autonomous expenditures (E_0) are $750. The Keynesian equation tells us to multiply autonomous expenditures, $750, by 4. Doing so gives $4 \times \$750 = \$3,000$.

The Keynesian equation gives you a simple way to determine equilibrium income in the Keynesian model. You determine the multiplier $[1/(1 - mpe)]$ and multiply it by autonomous expenditures. Five different marginal propensities to expend and the multiplier associated with each are shown in the table below.

Marginal Propensities to Expend and Multipliers

mpe	multiplier = 1/(1 − mpe)
.5	2
.75	4
.8	5
.9	10
.95	20

Notice as *mpe* increases, the multiplier increases. The reason is that the larger the *mpe*, the more repercussions there are and the larger the induced effects of any initial shift in income are. Knowing the multiplier associated with each marginal propensity to expend gives you an easy way to determine equilibrium income in the economy.

Let's look at one more example of the multiplier. Say that the *mpe* is .75 but that autonomous expenditures are $1,000 instead of $750. What is the level of income? Multiplying autonomous expenditures, $1,000, by 4 tells us that income is $4,000. With a multiplier of 4, income rises by $1,000 because of the $250 increase in autonomous expenditures.

The preceding discussion provides a technical method of determining equilibrium income in the Keynesian model. But it doesn't help us understand what the model means for the economy and what forces are operating to ensure that the income level we determined is the equilibrium income level. For it to be the equilibrium level of income, there must be adjustment forces that push the economy toward that equilibrium whenever the economy is not in equilibrium. Let's now discuss those forces. Let's ask what happens when the macroeconomy is in disequilibrium—when aggregate production does not equal aggregate expenditures. Exhibit 6 shows us.

Let's first consider the economy at income level A where planned aggregate production equals $15,000 and planned aggregate expenditures equals $14,000. Since planned production exceeds expenditures by $1,000 at income level A, firms can't sell all they produce; inventories pile up. In response, firms make an adjustment. They decrease aggregate production and hence income. As businesses slow production, the economy moves inward along the aggregate production curve as shown by arrow A_1. As income falls, people's expenditures fall, and the gap between aggregate production and aggregate expenditures decreases. For example, say businesses decrease aggregate production to $14,000. Aggregate income also falls to $14,000, which causes aggregate expenditures to fall, as indicated by arrow A_2, to $13,200. There's still a gap, but it's been reduced by $200, from $1,000 to $800.

Since a gap still remains, production and income keep falling. A good exercise is to go through two more steps. With each step, the economy moves closer to equilibrium.

3 To determine equilibrium income using the Keynesian equation, you determine the multiplier and multiply it by the level of autonomous expenditures.

In the dynamic disequilibrium interpretation of Keynes presented in this chapter, the multiplier reflects a path dependency which is seen in the interconnection of aggregate supply and demand. This interconnection means that the disequilibrium adjustment affects the final equilibrium. The debate about the existence and importance of this path dependency is a key debate between New Keynesians and Classicals. The modern Classical position is the real business cycle theory; the modern Keynesian position is sunspot theories in which expectations are self-fulfilling. The multiplier captures one way in which expectations can be self-fulfilling.

Q–4: If autonomous expenditures are $2,000 and the *mpe* = .75, what is the level of income in the economy?

A Closer Look at the Income Adjustment Mechanism

4 The multiplier process works because when expenditures don't equal production, businesspeople change planned production, which changes income, which changes expenditures, which . . . .

Be sure to have your students work through some examples in which they find equilibrium income and the multiplier, either as in-class exercises or assignments that they hand in. I find it very useful to check my students' grasp of these concepts early on.

EXHIBIT 6   The Income Adjustment Mechanism

At income levels *A* and *B*, the economy is in disequilibrium. Depending on which direction the disequilibrium goes, it generates increases or decreases in planned production and expenditures until the economy reaches income level *C*, where aggregate expenditures equal planned aggregate production.

I usually go through this disequilibrium discussion two or three different times. Students seem to get it the first time as I say it, and then when I ask them about it, they've forgotten it. Usually, however, by the third time it has gone somewhat deeper into their brains and they remember it.

I like to make up a series of exercises that my students work through in class. I have them solve for equilibrium income and then I change one of the autonomous spending components. After the students finish the exercises, I work through them graphically for the class.

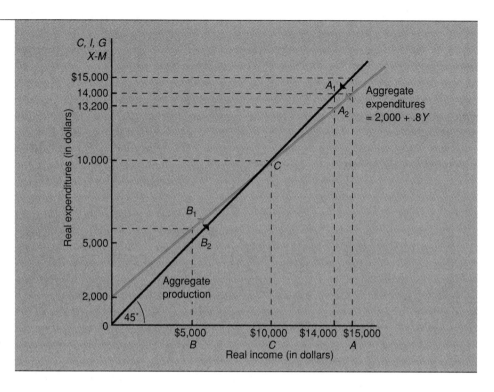

Q–5: When inventories fall below planned inventories, what is likely happening to the economy?

Now let's consider the economy at income level *B* ($5,000). Here planned production is less than expenditures. Firms find their inventory is running down. (Their investment in inventory is far less than they'd planned.) In response, they increase aggregate production and hence income. The economy starts to expand as aggregate production moves along arrow B_2 and aggregate expenditures move along arrow B_1. As individuals' income increases, their expenditures also increase, but by less than the increase in income, so the gap between aggregate expenditures and aggregate production decreases. But as long as expenditures and income exceed production, production and hence income keep rising.

Finally, let's consider the economy at income level *C*, $10,000. At point *C*, planned production and hence income is $10,000 and expenditures are $10,000. Firms are selling all they produce, so they have no reason to change their production levels. The aggregate economy is in equilibrium. This discussion should give you insight into what's behind the arithmetic of those earlier models.

The Multiplier and the Circular Flow Injections and Withdrawals

Another way to see intuitively what is going on with the multiplier is to think of the *AP/AE* model in terms of the circular flow. Expenditures are injections into the circular flow. The *mpe* measures the percentage of expenditures that get injected back into the economy each round of the circular flow. Thus if the *mpe* = .8, 80 percent of the expenditure flow is reinjected. This means that 20 percent is withdrawn from the circular flow each round. To focus on that withdrawal, some economists find it helpful

Q–6: If the marginal propensity to withdraw equals .4, what is the size of the multiplier?

It is useful to note that the income individuals receive can either be consumed (expended) or saved (withdrawn). If students recognize this, it is easier for them to understand the relationship between the *mpe* and the *mpw*.

to define a term that represents the withdrawals each round. Let us call that term the **marginal propensity to withdraw (*mpw*)**—*the percentage of income flow that leaks out of the economy each round of the circular flow.* By definition:

$$mpe + mpw = 1.$$

Alternatively expressed:

$$mpw = 1 - mpe$$

This means that the mutiplier can also be written as

$$\text{multiplier} = 1/mpw.$$

With leakages occurring each round of the circular flow, that circular flow would get smaller and smaller if that were all that were happening. But it isn't. Autonomous expenditures are being pumped into the circular flow, expanding the circular flow. Equilibrium occurs when the leakages equal the autonomous expenditures.

When thinking about this process, I often picture a group of economists under a leaking bathtub. They scurry around scooping up the leaking water, and, at intervals, dump it back into the tub. When they do so, there's an autonomous injection back into the bathtub.

Equilibrium occurs when the level of water in the tub remains constant—the injections equal the leakages.

Determining the equilibrium level of income using the multiplier is an important first step in understanding Keynes's analysis. The second step is to modify that analysis to answer a question that interested Keynes more: How much would a change in autonomous expenditures change the equilibrium level of income? This second step is important since it was precisely those sudden changes in autonomous expenditures Keynes said caused the aggregate disequilibrium, and it was these sudden changes he said the Classical model couldn't handle.

Because Keynes felt autonomous expenditures are subject to sudden shifts, I was careful to point out *autonomous* meant "determined outside the model and not affected by income." Autonomous expenditures can, and do, shift for a variety of reasons. When they do, the adjustment process is continually being called into play.

Anything outside the model that affects the level of any of the components of aggregate expenditures will shift aggregate expenditures. Some of the reasons autonomous expenditures shift include natural disasters, changes in consumption caused by changes in consumer choice, changes in investment caused by technological developments, shifts in government expenditures, changes in the exchange rate, and shifts in imports and exports. To focus on these shift factors, the expenditures function is often broken up into its component parts—consumption (C), investment (I), government spending (G), and net exports ($X - M$) (the difference between exports and imports). Thus:

$$\text{Expenditures } (E) = C + I + G + X - M$$

Changes in consumer sentiment affect C; changes in exchange rates affect X; major technological breakthroughs affect I, and changes in government's taxing and spending decisions affect G. For example, say a breakthrough in computer chip technology increases profit opportunities. National investment will likely increase. Alternatively, consider late 1996 when consumer confidence rose substantially. Autonomous consumption expenditures increased. Let's consider this last one to give you a sense of the reasoning behind these shifts.

Even if expenditures within a country are stable, outside expenditures often are not. A war or a shift in political alignments can totally change flows of exports and imports. For example, World Wars I and II brought U.S. trade with Germany to a halt, but significantly increased U.S. exports to other countries. The U.S. economy boomed. The depression in Europe in the middle and late 1920s cut back on European imports from the United States, significantly decreasing U.S. exports and further pushing the U.S. economy into a recession. In the 1990s, the events in the former Soviet Union lowered U.S. exports and lowered Eastern European countries' exports even more. We already know from history that exchange rates and tariff policies impact both imports and exports. All these changes show up as shifts in autonomous expenditures.

I chose this example because it relates back to the discussion with which I opened the chapter—the Japanese experience in 1995. The Japanese exchange rate rose dramatically, making Japanese goods much more expensive for Americans, and American goods much less expensive for Japanese. The result was a significant drop in expenditures on Japanese goods, leading to a recession in Japan.

SHIFTS IN AUTONOMOUS EXPENDITURES

For a real-world example of how autonomous expenditures can affect an economy and what policies can be used to affect these fluctuations see Chapter 11 in *Case Studies in Macroeconomics.*

Q–7:   Your study partner, Jean, has just said that autonomous means unchanging. How do you respond?

"The American Economy on the March," by Alvin H. Hansen, in *Classic Readings in Economics.*

✓ A REMINDER   DETERMINANTS OF THE *AE* CURVE

The *AE* curve is an upward-sloping curve whose slope is equal to the *mpe* and whose *Y*-intercept is equal to the level of autonomous expenditures.

Shifts of the *AE* curve

Anything that affects the level of autonomous expenditures will shift the *AE* curve. That is, anything that *lowers* (raises) autonomous

consumption
investment
government spending
net exports

will shift the *AE* curve *down* (up) by the amount of the change in autonomous expenditures.

Shifts in Autonomous Expenditures and Keynes's Model

Let's consider the Japanese case and the Keynesian explanation for what happens. The dramatic rise in the Japanese exchange rate cuts Japanese exports, decreasing aggregate expenditures so that aggregate production is greater than aggregate expenditures. Suppliers can't sell all they produce. Their reaction, Keynes would argue, would be to lay off workers and decrease output. That response would solve the problem if only one firm was in disequilibrium, but wouldn't solve the problem if all firms were in disequilibrium. When *all* producers respond in this fashion, aggregate income, and hence aggregate expenditures, will also fall. The suppliers' cutback will simply start a vicious cycle, which is multiplied. As the laid-off workers cut their consumption, total expenditures decrease; producers will cut back production, laying off more workers. The economy will enter into a downward spiral with aggregate production and expenditures chasing each other. The result will be an economic depression.

Will the downward spiral ever end? Keynes argued that eventually it would; fired individuals will dip into savings and not cut their expenditures by the full amount of their decrease in income. Because they do, as income falls, aggregate production and aggregate expenditures will get closer and closer together, and at some level of income aggregate production will equal aggregate expenditures. The models we considered in this chapter tell us how much income must fall to bring the economy to aggregate equilibrium.

The Income Adjustment Process: An Example

The income adjustment process is directly related to the multiplier. The reason is that any initial shock (a change in autonomous aggregate expenditures) is *multiplied* in the adjustment process. Let's see how this works in Exhibit 7's example, which will also serve as a review of the Keynesian model. In this example, let's say trade negotiations between the United States and other countries have fallen apart and U.S. exports decrease by $20. This is shown in the *AE* curve's downward shift from AE_0 to AE_1.

Q–8: If exports fall by $30 and the *mpe* = .9, what happens to equilibrium income?

How far must income fall until equilibrium is reached? To answer that question, we need to know the initial shock, $\Delta E = -\$20$, and the size of the multiplier, $[1/(1 - mpe)]$. In this example, $mpe = .8$, so the multiplier is 5. That means the final decrease in income that brings about equilibrium is $100 (five times as large as the initial shock of $20).

Be sure to draw your students' attention to Exhibit 7 (a and b). This figure should help them visualize the income adjustment process and see the role of the multiplier.

Exhibit 7(b), a blowup of the circled area in Exhibit 7(a), shows the detailed steps of the adjustment process so you can see how it works. Initially, autonomous expenditures fall by $20 (shift *A*), causing firms to decrease production by $20 (shift *B*). But that decrease in income causes expenditures to decrease by another $16 (0.8 × $20) (shift *C*). Again firms respond by cutting production, this time by $16 (shift *D*). Again income falls (shift *E*) causing production to fall (shift *F*). The process continues again and again (the remaining steps) until equilibrium income falls by $100, five times the amount of the initial shock. The *mpe* tells how much closer at each step aggregate expenditures will be to aggregate production. You can see this adjustment process in Exhibit 8, which shows the first steps with multipliers of various sizes.

EXHIBIT 7 (a and b)   Shifts in the Aggregate Expenditures Curve

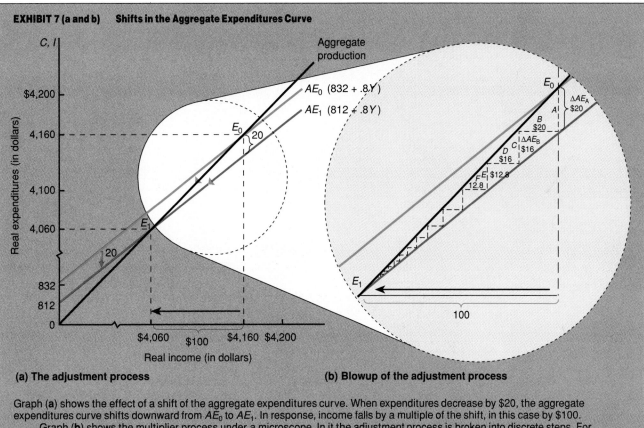

(a) The adjustment process

(b) Blowup of the adjustment process

Graph (**a**) shows the effect of a shift of the aggregate expenditures curve. When expenditures decrease by $20, the aggregate expenditures curve shifts downward from AE_0 to AE_1. In response, income falls by a multiple of the shift, in this case by $100.

Graph (**b**) shows the multiplier process under a microscope. In it the adjustment process is broken into discrete steps. For example, when income falls by $20 (shift B), expenditure falls by $16 (shift C). In response to that fall of expenditures, producers reduce output by $16, which decreases income by $16 (shift D). The lower income causes expenditures to fall further (shift E) and the process continues.

EXHIBIT 8   The First Five Steps of Four Multipliers

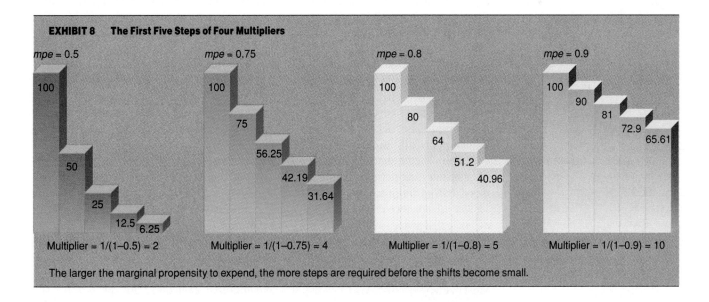

The larger the marginal propensity to expend, the more steps are required before the shifts become small.

Learning to work with the Keynesian model requires practice, so in Exhibit 9(a) and (b) I present two different expenditures functions and two different shifts in autonomous expenditures. Below each model is the equation representing how much aggregate income changes in terms of the multiplier and autonomous expenditures. As you see, this equation calculates the shift, while the graph determines it in a visual way.

FURTHER EXAMPLES OF THE KEYNESIAN MODEL

EXHIBIT 9 (a and b)   Two Different Expenditure Functions and Two Different Shifts in Autonomous Expenditures

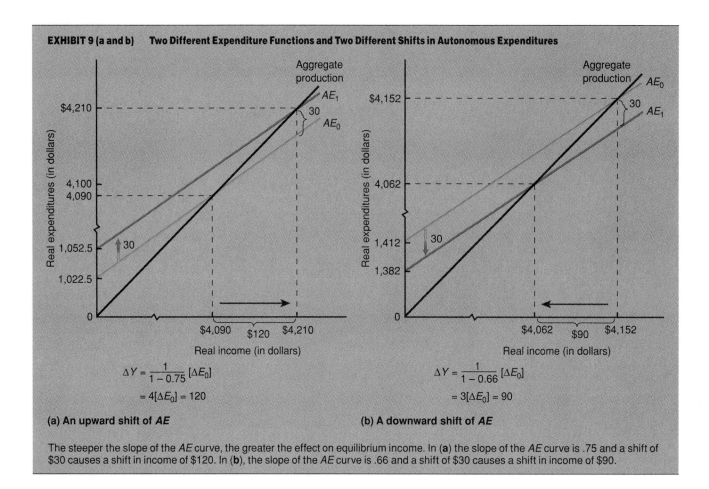

$$\Delta Y = \frac{1}{1 - 0.75}[\Delta E_0]$$
$$= 4[\Delta E_0] = 120$$

(a) An upward shift of AE

$$\Delta Y = \frac{1}{1 - 0.66}[\Delta E_0]$$
$$= 3[\Delta E_0] = 90$$

(b) A downward shift of AE

The steeper the slope of the *AE* curve, the greater the effect on equilibrium income. In (**a**) the slope of the *AE* curve is .75 and a shift of $30 causes a shift in income of $120. In (**b**), the slope of the *AE* curve is .66 and a shift of $30 causes a shift in income of $90.

Keynes's Explanation of the 1930s Depression

As a final example, let's see how Keynes used his model to explain the 1930s Depression. He argued the following: In 1929 there was a financial crash that continued into the 1930s. Financial markets were a mess. Businesspeople became scared, so they decreased investment; consumers became scared, so they decreased autonomous consumption and increased savings, thereby increasing withdrawals from the system. The result was a sudden large shift downward in the aggregate expenditures curve.

Businesspeople responded by decreasing output, which decreased income and started a downward spiral. This downward spiral confirmed business's fears. The decreased output further decreased income and expenditures. The process continued until eventually the economy settled at a low-income equilibrium, far below the potential, or full-employment, level of income.

Paradox of thrift   Individuals attempting to save more cause income to decrease; thereby they end up saving no more, or even less.

The process that Keynes argued played an important role in bringing about the Depression is sometimes called the **paradox of thrift.** *Individuals attempted to save more, but in doing so spent less and caused income to decrease, and they ended up saving no more, or even less.*

The Keynesian Model When the Price Level Is Not Fixed

The formal Keynesian *AP/AE* model depends on the economy being in Range *A* of the aggregate supply path, where the price level is fixed. This allows us to treat all changes in output and income as real changes. When the price level is not constant, the changes are divided between real and nominal changes, with the relative split determined by the degree of price-level flexibility determined by the supply path. How a change in the price level affects the *AE* curve can be explained by the wealth and international effects. A rise in the price level will cause the aggregate expenditures curve to shift down. Similarly a fall in the price level will cause the aggregate expenditures curve to shift up. (A much more detailed discussion of the relationship between the price level and expenditures can be found in the discussion of the slope of the *AED* curve in the previous chapter.)

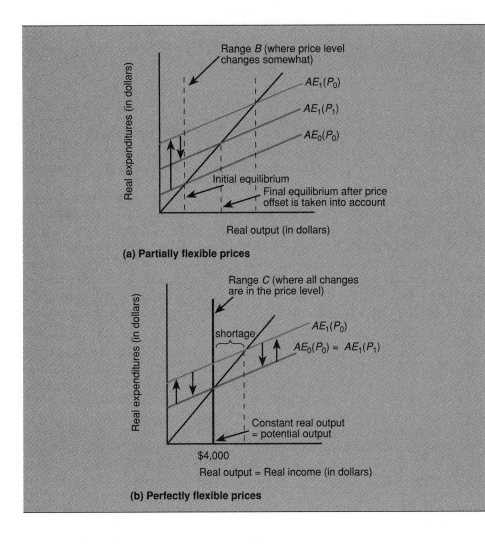

EXHIBIT 10 (a and b)   The Keynesian *AP/AE* Model When the Price Level Is Not Fixed

When the price level is not fixed, there is an offset to shifts in the *AE* curve because of the wealth and international effects discussed in the last chapter. Thus, in (**a**) if an autonomous shock shifts the *AE* curve up from AE_0 to AE_1, part of that upward shift would be offset by a rise in the price level that will shift the *AE* curve to $AE_1(P_1)$. In (**b**), the economy has reached Range *C*. All effects of changes in aggregate expenditures are on the price level. Any further shift up in the *AE* curve, such as the shift shown here from AE_0 to AE_1, will either cause a shortage if the price level is fixed, or will be countered by a rise in the price level which will shift the *AE* curve back to the original real income equilibrium of $4,000.

The Keynesian Model When the *AS* Path Is Upward Sloping   If we were doing the Keynesian model for Range *B*—where the supply path is upward sloping—part of the shift of the *AE* curve caused by a shift of autonomous expenditures would be offset by the change in the price level. The greater the slope of the *AS* path, the greater the shift back of the *AE* curves. For example, if the *AE* curve were to shift from AE_0 to AE_1 in Exhibit 10(a) with a constant price level P_0, it shifts only to $AE_1(P_1)$ when the price level rises to P_1. The rise in price from P_0 to P_1 shifts the *AE* curve down from $AE_1(P_0)$ to $AE_1(P_1)$, offsetting the initial increase in aggregate expenditures. Real income increases by a smaller amount when prices are flexible than when they are fixed.

The Keynesian Model Once Potential Income Is Reached   Once the *AS* path becomes vertical (the economy is in Range *C*), the price level offset is complete. In Range *C* it is clear what happens to real income at that point—it is constant, regardless of what aggregate expenditures are. In Range *C*, where the long-run aggregate supply path is vertical, all changes must be nominal, not real changes. Exhibit 10(b) shows what happens when aggregate expenditures increase but the economy is in Range *C*.

Initially the economy was in equilibrium with real income equal to $4,000. Now suddenly the *AE* curve shifts from AE_0 to AE_1. If the price level remains constant at P_0, there will be a shortage of goods since real output is fixed at $4,000 and the price level is fixed. If the price level rises, nominal income rises while real income remains constant. As the price level rises, the *AE* curve is pushed down until it is back to an equilibrium real expenditures of $4,000. This occurs at $AE_1(P_1)$.

Q–9: What happens to the size of the multiplier effects as the aggregate supply path becomes vertical?

THE CLASSICAL RESPONSE TO KEYNES

On the surface the Keynesian model makes a lot of intuitive sense to students. However, surface sense can often be misleading. Let's consider some of the ways in which it might be misleading, and in doing so highlight some important aspects of the Classical response to Keynes.

The Keynesian Model Is Not a Complete Model of the Economy

At best, what we can estimate are directions and rough sizes of autonomous demand or supply shocks.

The discussion of the Keynesian model presented in this chapter provides a technical method of determining equilibrium income. But in reality the model doesn't do what it purports to do—determine equilibrium income from scratch. Why? Because it doesn't tell us where those autonomous expenditures come from, or how we would go about measuring them.

At best, what we can measure, or at least estimate, are directions and rough sizes of autonomous demand or supply shocks, and we can determine the direction and possible over-adjustment the economy might make in response to those shocks. If you think back to our initial discussion of the Keynesian model, this is how I introduced it—as an explanation of forces affecting the adjustment process, not as a determinant of the final equilibrium independent of where the economy started. It was an historical, not an analytical, model. So, at best, the Keynesian model is not an alternative model, but is simply a representation of a more complicated unspecified model that explains where the autonomous expenditures came from. Without some additional information about where the economy started from, or what is the desired level of output, the Keynesian theory is not a complete theory.

Shifts Are Not as Great as One's Intuition Suggests

A second criticism that Classicals have of the Keynesian model is that it leads people to overemphasize the shifts that would occur in aggregate expenditures in response to a shift in autonomous expenditures. To show why, let's consider an example: Say people decide to save some more. You might think that that would lead to a fall in expenditures. But wait, that saving will go into the financial sector, and be translated back into the expenditures sector as loans to other consumers or as loans to businesses funding investment. So if you take a broad view of aggregate expenditures, many of the shifts in expenditures are simply rearrangements from one group of expenditures to another.

These differing views about the effectiveness of the financial sector in translating outflows from expenditures into other expenditures constitute an important difference between the Keynesian and Classical views, and one's intuition does not resolve which is right. That's why a study of the financial sector is an important aspect of macroeconomics. To the degree that outflows from expenditures are actually being channeled back into what the Keynesian model considers expenditures, there will be no shift in total expenditures, simply movements from one component to another. Thus, Classicals argue, the shifts will be much less than might be intuitively expected upon first glance.

The Price Level Will Often Change in Response to Shifts in Demand

One of the assumptions of the Keynesian model was that the price level was fixed—that made aggregate production a 45° line. But in reality the price level varies in response to increases in demand. That was the *B* range of the aggregate supply path that we assumed away for ease of exposition. But Classicals point out that the economy is often in that *B* range, and in that range, the price level can change, and that change in the price level will bring about an adjustment toward equilibrium.

People's Forward-Looking Expectations Make the Adjustment Process Much More Complicated

People's forward-looking expectations make the adjustment process much more complicated. The Keynesian model presented here assumes that people respond to current changes in income. Most people, however, act on the basis of expectations of the future. Consider the assumed Keynesian response of businesses to changes in expenditures. They lay off workers and cut production at the slightest fall in demand. In reality, their response is far more complicated. They may well see the fall as a temporary blip. They will allow their inventory to rise in the expectation that the next month another temporary blip will offset the previous fall. Business decisions about production are forward looking, and do not respond simply to current changes. As a contrast to the simple Keynesian model, some modern Classicals have put forward a **rational expectations model** of the macro economy in which *all decisions are based upon the expected equilibrium in the economy.* They argue that since people rationally expect the economy to achieve its potential income, it will do so.

There is an implicit assumption in the Keynesian model that shifts in demand are not simply reflections of shifts in desired production or supply. Reality is much more complicated. Shifts can occur for many reasons, and many shifts can reflect desired shifts in aggregate production, and they are accompanied by shifts in aggregate expenditures. Say, for example, that technology changes. There will be a shift out of one type of supply and into another type of supply, and there could be significant dislocation, and even decreases in expenditures as people try to adjust their lives to the new technology. These shifts may be simultaneous shifts in supply and demand and need not reflect suppliers' responding to changes in demand. Suppliers operate in the future—shifting supply, not to existing demand, but to expected demand, making the relationship between aggregate production and current demand far more complicated than it seems in the Keynesian model. Expansion of this line of thought has led to the **real business cycle theory** of the economy—*the theory that fluctuations in the economy reflect real phenomena—simultaneous shifts in supply and demand, not simply supply responses to demand shifts.* Let's consider an example—the expansion of the U.S. economy in 1995. The macro policy model would attribute that to a shift out of the *AED* curve, combined with a relatively flat *AS* path. The real business cycle theory would attribute that shift out to businesses' decision to increase supply due to technological developments, and a subsequent increase in demand via Say's law.

Shifts in Expenditures Might Reflect Desired Shifts in Supply and Demand

Let's say your income goes down 10 percent. The Keynesian model says that your expenditures will go down by some specific percentage of that. But will they? If you are rational, it seems reasonable to base your consumption on more than one year's income—say, instead, on your permanent or lifetime income. What happens to your income in a particular year has little effect on your lifetime income. If it is true that people base their spending primarily on lifetime income, not yearly income, the marginal propensity to expend out of changes in current income could be very low, approaching zero. In that case, the expenditures function would essentially be a flat line, and the multiplier would be one. There would be no secondary effects of an initial shift. This set of arguments is called the **permanent income hypothesis**—*the hypothesis that expenditures are determined by permanent or lifetime income.* It undermines the reasoning of much of the specific results of the simple Keynesian model.

Expenditures Depend on Much More than Current Income

Q–10: What effect would expenditures being dependent on permanent income have on the size of the multiplier?

The above arguments, and others like them, led to a demise in the use of the simple Keynesian model, and the movement back toward the Classical model and the macro policy model that better captured both contrasting views.

Keynesians agree in varying degrees with each of the Classical criticisms, and different groups of Classicals emphasize different criticisms. That's why the terms Classical and Keynesian have lost favor. There are so many alternative views and overlaps that few economists fit into one or the other. Still, I find the distinction useful pedagogically. So let me summarize the two alternative views.

SUMMARY OF THE DIFFERING VIEWS OF THE KEYNESIAN MODEL

The central Keynesian idea is that the economy will overreact to shocks—shifts in aggregate production and expenditure decisions—leading the income in the economy to fluctuate more than individuals desire. Without some additional information about where the economy started from, or what is the desired level of output, the Keynesian theory is not a complete theory. Put another way, *the Keynesian model is an historical model in time.* Each equilibrium that the economy arrives at is dependent on the past—the equilibrium that the economy arrives at is a **path-dependent equilibrium**—*an equilibrium that is influenced by the adjustment process to that*

The Keynesian model is an historical model in time.

In the interpretation of Keynesian economics presented here, it is important to emphasize that the disequilibrium adjustment process, captured by the multiplier is far too simple than is necessary to deal with the economy except in special circumstances. The interdependencies are enormous, and each of those interdependencies is adjusted for by certain institutional changes in the economy. Modern Classicals agree that these interdependencies exist, but argue that they are so complex that there are no specific policy implications forthcoming. Thus, the modern Classical work is returning to the early pre-Keynesian Classical work which recognized the short run complexities but saw them as too complicated to yield results. Thus, they focused on the long run and did not discuss short-run phenomena.

In the Keynesian model, the aggregate economy should be pictured as a pulsating spiral, expanding and contracting in response to unexpected shocks.

equilibrium. All history determines current reality and all models must reflect that historical connection. In any model that involves histories, you can't understand the current situation separately from the entire past. The future is unfolding in ways that can be understood only as part of historical time.

The last paragraph has a number of heavy philosophical points that have wild mathematical counterpart formulations. Path-dependent equilibria and hysteresis are all the rage in graduate economics schools today. Luckily, we don't have to get into any of that—the basic ideas are simple for introductory students to understand.

All that introductory students need understand is the different visions of the circular flow of income that follow from the Keynesian and Classical models. Those different visions can be seen by remembering the circular flow analysis.

The circular flow diagram expresses the national income identity: Aggregate income equals aggregate output. The Classical school saw forces outside of economics determining the size of the circular flow. It was indeed a circular flow. Keynes did not see outside forces determining the size of the circular flow; he saw the adjustment process to equilibrium changing the size of the income flow and hence changing the equilibrium. Any real shock to the economy would tend to be exaggerated, causing larger-than-desired fluctuations in income. Thus in a Keynesian model the aggregate economy should be seen as a pulsating spiral, expanding and contracting in response to unexpected shocks.

Understanding the pulsating income (business cycles) could not be accomplished by considering equilibrium separately from disequilibrium adjustment. Keynes's model offered one simple way of considering both simultaneously and arriving at a specific solution. Keynes asked: (1) does aggregate expenditure always equal aggregate production? and (2) if not, what will happen in the economy to bring them into equilibrium?

Mechanistic and Interpretative Keynesians

The "historical model in time" interpretation was not always the interpretation of Keynesian economics that students were taught. In the 1960s, the interpretation of the Keynesian model that was taught was mechanistic. A **mechanistic model** is *a model that pictures the economy as representable by a mechanically determined, timeless model with a determinant equilibrium*. It involved little or no discussion of the fleetingness of that equilibrium, or of the limitations of that equilibrium with respect to the starting position.

At that time, the Keynesian model was presented as definitive; all economists had to do was to go out and collect the measurements they needed and they could control the level of income in the economy, independent of where the level had been or of what people wanted. Reality proved that interpretation wrong; mechanistic Keynesian economics doesn't work, any more than mechanistic Classical economics does. Modern economists have come to the conclusion that *there is no simple way to understand the aggregate economy*. You can't separate dynamics from the equilibrium analysis; you can't study the economy in an historical vacuum, and any mechanistic interpretation of an aggregate model is doomed to failure.

The model I presented in this chapter was the mechanistic Keynesian model. However, the intepretation I give to it makes it what I call an **interpretive Keynesian model**—*a Keynesian model that views models as an aid in understanding complicated disequilibrium dynamics*. The specific results of the Keynesian model are a guide to one's common sense, letting one emphasize a particular important dynamic interdependency while keeping others in the back of one's head. With that addendum—that the Keynesian model is not meant to be taken literally, but only as an aid to our intuition—the simple Keynesian model of the 1950s and 1960s is extraordinarily modern and up to date, dealing with the issues with which the highest-level macro theorists of the 1990s are struggling.

5a A mechanistic Keynesian sees the model as a direct guide for policy; it tells you what policy to follow. An interpretative Keynesian sees the model as a guide to one's common sense, highlighting important dynamic interdependencies. Before applying the model, one must consider other interdependencies.

Mechanistic and Interpretive Classicals

The same distinction that holds for Keynesians holds for Classicals; there is both a mechanistic and an interpretive view of Classicals' ideas. The Classical criticisms of the Keynesian model listed above have all been extended into complicated models in their own right. I concentrate on the Keynesian model in this chapter because it was a good introduction into the complexities of the aggregate adjustment process, not because I necessarily believe it is the most descriptive of the actual adjustment process.

But I should not leave this discussion without mentioning that just as the mechanistic Keynesian model should not be seen as the model modern Keynesians believe, so too is it the case that the mechanistic Classical model should not be seen as the model modern Classicals believe. Most modern Classicals (and indeed most early Classicals) are quite willing to accept that there are induced effects of autonomous shifts. Most modern Classicals agree that the Classical flexible price assumption is far too simplistic, and most agree that the price level is fixed in the short run and that fluctuations occur in real output that exceed what people desire.

What they are not willing to accept is that the induced effects follow the simple pattern that the simple Keynesian model ascribes to them. They argue that the economy is so complicated that any formal model of it inevitably misses interconnections in the economy, and any intervention into the economy undermines subtle methods by which markets adjust to meet ever-changing problems. They are interpretive Classicals. They see the Classical model as an aid in understanding complicated disequilibrium dynamics. The specific results of the Classical model are a guide to one's common sense, letting one emphasize a particular important dynamic interdependency while keeping others in the back of one's head. With that addendum—that the Classical model is not meant to be taken literally, but only as an aid to our intuition—the Classical model presented in this book is extraordinarily modern and up to date, dealing with the issues with which the highest-level macro theorists of the 1990s are struggling.

5b A mechanistic Classical sees the Classical model as a direct guide for policy; an interpretive Classical sees the Classical model as an aid in understanding complicated disequilibrium dynamics with interdependencies.

As a summary and conclusion to the chapter, let's return to a consideration of the macro policy model, and see its relation to the Keynesian AP/AE model. Let's start with a consideration of the AED curve and the Keynesian model.

In the last chapter I emphasized that the AED curve was not a demand curve; it was an equilibrium curve—a curve that told us the relationship between different price levels and different equilibria in the goods market. It has traditionally been derived from the Keynesian model, and thus it has implicitly accepted the dynamics of that Keynesian model. To see how it is derived from the Keynesian model we must first recall how the AE curve shifts as the price level rises and falls.

In Exhibit 11(a) I draw three curves—one for each of the price levels P_0, P_1, and P_2, where $P_0 > P_1 > P_2$. The initial equilibrium is at point A. Notice that as the price level falls, aggregate expenditures rise, as I stated above. These initial increases cause induced expenditures; production shifts because of the induced effects, increasing output further than the initial shift in aggregate expenditures and the initial fall in output to Q_1'. The new equilibrium output at P_1 is Q_1 (point B), and at P_2 the new equilibrium output is Q_2 (point C).

In Exhibit 11(b) I show the equilibrium price levels and outputs on a graph, with price level on the vertical axis and real output on the horizontal axis. That gives us points A, B, and C, which correspond to points A, B, and C in Exhibit 11(a). Drawing a line through these points gives us the aggregate equilibrium demand curve: a curve that shows how a change in the price level will affect aggregate equilibrium demand. Notice that the AED curve includes both the effect of the initial shift in aggregate expenditures from a change in the price level and the multiplier effects as production and expenditures move to equilibrium. The initial shift in aggregate expenditures is shown by point B'. If there were were no multiplier effects, the AED curve would go through points A and B'.

The first thing to note when considering the two models is that the AP/AE model assumes the price level constant, so it assumes that the aggregate supply path is flat. This means that the AP/AE model tells us precisely how much the AED curve will shift when the autonomous expenditures shift by a specified amount. The difference

CONCLUSION: THE AP/AE MODEL AND THE MACRO POLICY MODEL

6 The macro policy model dynamics and the AE/AP model dynamics are equivalent when the price level is fixed. The AED curve can be derived from the AE/AP model.

EXHIBIT 11   Deriving the AED Curve

The AED curve is derived from the AP/AE model by asking what effect a fall in the price level has on equilibrium output. As we discussed in the last chapter, that fall in the price level increases equilibrium output, as shown in (a). In (b) we combine the price level with the equilibrium output it is associated with (points A, B, and C). Those points give us the AED curve.

Notice that the AED curve includes both the initial effect of a price-level change and the multiplier effect (the induced effects). If it did not include those effects, the AED curve would be steeper. For example, the initial effect of a fall in the price level from P_0 to P_1 is to increase output from Q_0 to Q_1'. Thus, if there were no multiplier effects, the AED curve would go through B'. The multiplier effects cause output to rise to Q_1, which means the AED curve goes through point B.

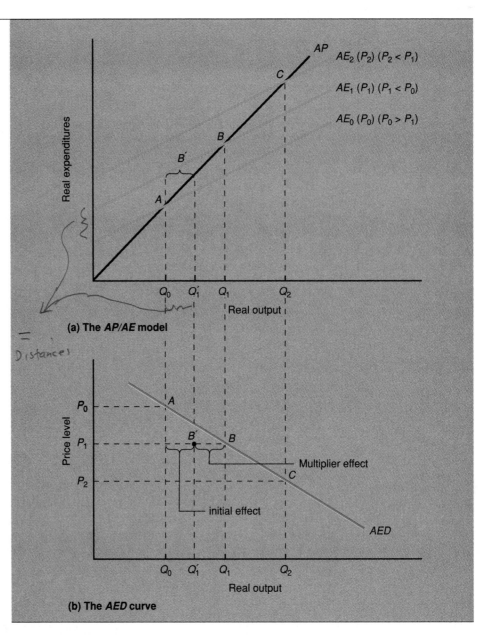

(a) The AP/AE model

(b) The AED curve

between the shift in autonomous expenditures and the AED curve shift is due to the multiplier.

The relationship between a shift in autonomous expenditures in the macro policy model and the AP/AE model can be seen in Exhibit 12. It considers a fall in autonomous expenditures of $20 when the multiplier is 2. In Exhibit 12(a) you can see that, in the AP/AE model, a fall in expenditures of $20 will cause income to fall by $40, from $4,052, to $4,012.

Exhibit 12(b) shows that same adjustment in the macro policy model. Expenditures fall by $20, but the AED curve shifts back not by $20, but by $40—the initial shift multiplied by the multiplier. That's because the AED curves take into account the interdependent shifts between supply and demand decisions that are set in motion by the initial shift. Thus we need the Keynesian model, or some alternative model of induced effects, before we can draw an AED curve. (I make the qualification "or some other model" to emphasize that the interdependent shifts assumed in the Keynesian model are not the only interdependent shifts that could occur. Had we assumed a different dynamic adjustment process, we would have had a different AED curve.)

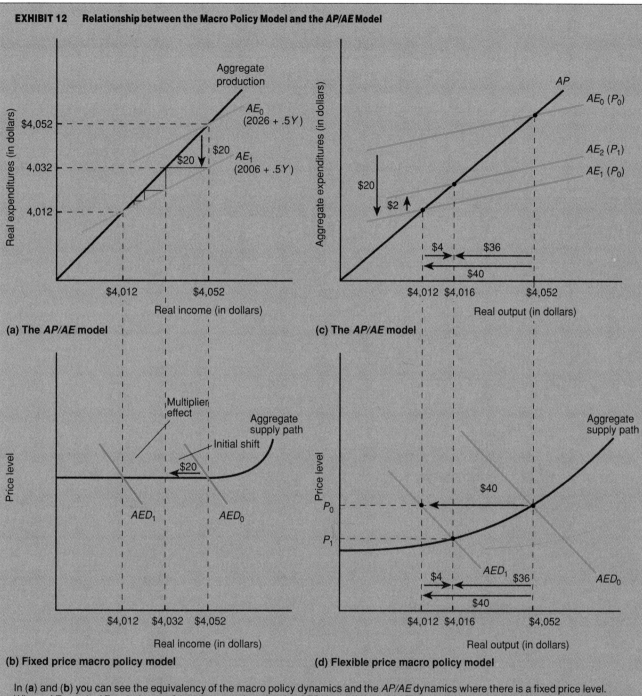

EXHIBIT 12   Relationship between the Macro Policy Model and the *AP/AE* Model

(a) The *AP/AE* model

(b) Fixed price macro policy model

(c) The *AP/AE* model

(d) Flexible price macro policy model

In (a) and (b) you can see the equivalency of the macro policy dynamics and the *AP/AE* dynamics where there is a fixed price level. Where *AE* equals *AP*, as it does at $4,012, we see how far the *AED* curve shifts back. Thus the initial shift in aggregate demand is $20, the same as the downward shift in the *AE* curve. The *AED* curve shifts back by $40, because its shift includes the induced effects. When the price level is flexible, as in (d), a reduction in aggregate demand reduces prices, leading to less of a change in output relative to the fixed-price model. The fall of the price level (from P_0 to P_1 in (d)) causes the *AE* curve to partially shift back up (from AE_1 to AE_2 in (c)), leading to a new equilibrium shift of only $36 rather than $40.

Exhibits 12(c) and (d) show what happens when the economy is in the partially flexible price-level range. Here the *AE* curve shifts down by $20, and the *AED* curve shifts in by $40. But the reduction in the *AED* curve causes the price level to fall, which causes income to rise somewhat so that the *AE* curve shifts up (from $AE_1(P_0)$ to $AE_2(P_1)$). The final decrease in income is now not $40, but is instead $36 in this example.

The points made in these last two pages are critical. Keynesian economics is very intuitive. In my experience, once the basic ideas of Keynesian economics are presented, students catch on easily. It is only after the formal model is presented that many of them become confused. I emphasize that they need to understand the formal model to provide some structure for their intuition.

A good test of your understanding here is to ask yourself what happens if the aggregate supply path is vertical. (In that case, the rise in aggregate equilibrium demand is fully offset by a rise in the price level, and the *AE* curve shifts right back where it started.)

Much of the modern debate in macro concerns the dynamic adjustment process that the Keynesian model is meant to describe. We won't go into that debate here since it quickly becomes very complicated, but I do want to point out to you that the Keynesian adjustment model is not the end of the analysis; it is simply the beginning—one of the simplest cases of dynamic adjustment. The real-world dynamic adjustment is more complicated, which is why there is so much debate about macroeconomic issues.

CHAPTER SUMMARY

- The Keynesian model focuses on the induced effects that a change in production has on expenditures, which affects production, and so on.
- The Keynesian model is made up of the aggregate production and aggregate expenditures curves. In equilibrium, planned aggregate production must equal planned aggregate expenditures.
- Aggregate expenditures (*AE*) is made up of consumption, investment, government spending, and net exports:

$$AE = C + I + G + (X - M)$$

- Expenditure depends upon the level of income; the *mpe* tells us the change in expenditure that occurs with a change in income.
- Withdrawals are the mirror image of expenditures.
- Shifts in autonomous expenditures can be the initial shock that begins the multiplier process.
- Keynes believed a business cycle is caused by (1) a shock creating a small disequilibrium, and (2) the multiplier, which expands that initial shock to a much

larger decrease or increase in production and income. The multiplier $(1/(1 - mpe))$ is the income adjustment mechanism.

- The Keynesian equation is

$$Y = \left[\frac{1}{(1 - mpe)} \right] \left[E_0 \right].$$

The multiplier tells us how much a change in autonomous expenditures will change income.

- Keynesians see aggregate equilibrium occurring in shifts of the aggregate production and aggregate expenditure decisions. Classicals see aggregate equilibrium occurring by changes in price bringing expenditures equal to potential output.
- The Keynesian model, like the Classical model, cannot be applied mechanistically; it is only a guide to common sense.
- The *AP/AE* model provides the reasoning behind the multiplier effects needed to derive an *AED* curve.

KEY TERMS

aggregate expenditures *(283)*
aggregate production curve *(282)*
aggregate production/aggregate
  expenditures (*AP/AE*) model *(281)*
autonomous expenditures *(284)*
autonomous shift *(281)*
expenditures function *(285)*
income adjustment mechanism *(281)*

induced expenditures *(285)*
interpretative Keynesian model *(298)*
Keynesian equation *(288)*
marginal propensity to expend
  (*mpe*) *(285)*
marginal propensity to withdraw
  (*mpw*) *(290)*
mechanistic model *(298)*

multiplier *(288)*
paradox of thrift *(294)*
path-dependent equilibrium *(297)*
permanent income hypothesis *(297)*
rational expectations model *(297)*
real business cycle theory *(297)*

QUESTIONS FOR THOUGHT AND REVIEW

The number after each question represents the estimated degree of critical thinking required. (1 = almost none; 10 = deep thought.)

1. If nominal income, rather than real income, were measured on the vertical axis, what would the *AP* curve look like in each of the three ranges of the aggregate supply path? *(9)*
2. If savings were instantaneously translated into investment, what would be the multiplier's size? What would be the level of autonomous expenditures? *(7)*
3. Name some forces that might cause shocks to aggregate expenditures. *(2)*
4. Mr. Whammo has just invented a magic pill. Take it and it transports you anywhere. Explain his invention's effects on the economy. *(10)*
5. The marginal propensity to expend is .8. Autonomous expenditures are $4,200. What is the level of income in the economy? Demonstrate graphically. *(3)*
6. The marginal propensity to expend is 0.66 and autonomous expenditures have just fallen by $20. What will likely happen to income? *(5)*
7. The marginal propensity to expend is .5 and autonomous expenditures have just risen $200. The economy is at its potential level of income. What will likely happen to income? Why? *(6)*
8. Demonstrate graphically the effect of an increase in autonomous expenditures of $20 in the Keynesian model if the *mpe* = .66. *(3)*
9. Why is the circular flow diagram of the economy an only partially correct conception of Keynesian economics? *(7)*
10. How does a mechanistic Keynesian differ from an interpretative Keynesian? *(3)*
11. Charlie Black, a GOP strategist, was quoted in a 1996 *Wall Street Journal* article as stating, "I can't tell you why this happens, but there's a lag time (before people tune into good economic news)." What is the effect of this delay in adjustment of expectations by consumers on the dynamics of the *AE/AP* model? *(9)*

PROBLEMS AND EXERCISES

1. Congratulations. You've been appointed economic adviser to Happyland. Your research assistant says the country's *mpe* is .8 and autonomous expenditures have just risen by $20.
   a. What will happen to income?
   b. Your research assistant comes in and says he's sorry but the *mpe* wasn't .8; it was .5. How does your answer change?
   c. He runs in again and says exports have fallen by $10 and investment has risen by $10. How does your answer change?
   d. You now have to present your analysis to the president, who wants to see it all graphically. Naturally you oblige.
2. Congratulations again. You've just been appointed economic adviser to Examland. The *mpe* is .6; investment is $1,000; government spending is $8,000; consumption is $10,000; and net exports are $1,000.
   a. What is the level of income in the country?
   b. Net exports increase by $2,000. What will happen to income?
   c. What will happen to unemployment? (Remember Okun's rule of thumb.)
   d. You've just learned the *mpe* changed from 0.6 to 0.5. How will this information change your answers in *a, b,* and *c*?
3. In 1992, as President Bush was running (unsuccessfully) for reelection, the economy slowed down; then in late 1993, after President Clinton's election, the economy picked up steam.
   a. Demonstrate graphically with the *AP/AE* model a shift in the *AE* curve that would have caused the slowdown. Which component of aggregate expenditures was the likely culprit?
   b. Demonstrate graphically with the *AP/AE* model a shift in the *AE* curve that would have caused the improvement. Which component of aggregate expenditures was likely responsible?
   c. What policies do you think President Bush could have used to stop the slowdown?
   d. What policies do you think President Clinton used to try to speed up the economy?
4. Demonstrate graphically the effect of an increase in autonomous expenditures when the *mpe* = .5 and the price level is fixed:
   a. In the *AP/AE* model.
   b. In the macro policy model.
   c. Do the same thing as in *a* and *b*, only this time assume prices are somewhat flexible.
5. State how the following information changes the slope of the *AED* curve discussed in the previous chapter.
   a. The effect of price level changes on autonomous expenditures is reduced.
   b. The size of the multiplier increases.
   c. Autonomous expenditures increase by $20.
   d. Falls in the price level disrupt financial markets, which offset the normally assumed effects of a change in the price level.

ANSWERS TO MARGIN QUESTIONS

1. Income equals production on the aggregate production curve. *(282)*
2. The *mpe* is .6. *(286)*
3. The multiplier is 2 when the *mpe* = .5. *(288)*
4. The level of income is $8,000. *(289)*
5. When inventories fall below planned inventories the economy is probably expanding; firms will likely increase production, which will cause expenditures to increase, which will further draw down inventories. *(290)*
6. If the *mpw* equals .4, the *mpe* equals .6, which means that the multiplier equals 2.5. *(290)*
7. I respond by saying that autonomous means "determined outside the model." That is, autonomous expenditures do not change in a predetermined way with income. Autonomous expenditures can, and do, change, and as they change, equilibrium income in the economy changes. *(291)*
8. Equilibrium income falls by $300. *(292)*
9. As the aggregate supply path becomes more vertical, price level changes absorb a larger percentage of shocks and the multiplier effects become smaller. *(295)*
10. If expenditures are dependent on permanent income, not current income, expenditures would not change as much with a change in current income and the multiplier would get smaller. *(297)*

APPENDIX A

An Algebraic Presentation of the Expanded Keynesian Model

In the chapter I developed the basic Keynesian model in reference to expenditures and withdrawals. Expenditures were injections into the circular flow; withdrawals were leakages. In equilibrium, injections had to equal withdrawals. This kept the math to a minimum, but obscured some of the ways in which the components of expenditures affected income, and in turn how those components of income are affected by income. This was a departure from the traditional approach, which is to assume initially all injections and withdrawals come from one subcomponent of expenditures, consumption, and then to expand the model to include the possibility of injections and withdrawals coming from other subcomponents of expenditures—generally taxes and imports. I made this departure to allow time for discussion of other issues, and to eliminate some of the mathematical complications that result in the disaggregated approach.

In this appendix I briefly outline a fuller presentation and show the relationship between the marginal propensity to expend (*mpe*), and the marginal propensity to consume (*mpc*), specified as *b* in the equations, and the marginal propensity to import (*mpm*), specified as *m* in the equations, and the marginal tax rate, specified as *t* in the equations.

The basic Keynesian model consists of the following equations:

$$(1)\ C = C_0 + bY_d$$
$$(2)\ Y_d = Y - T + R$$
$$(3)\ I = I_0$$
$$(4)\ G = G_0$$
$$(5)\ R = R_0$$
$$(6)\ T = T_0 + tY$$
$$(7)\ X = X_0$$
$$(8)\ M = M_0 + mY$$
$$(9)\ C + I + G + (X - M) = Y$$

Equation (1) is the consumption function. C_0 is autonomous consumption; bY_d is the *mpc* multiplied by disposable income.

Equation (2) defines disposable income as a function of real income minus taxes plus government transfers.

Equation (3) is the investment function. I_0 is autonomous investment.

Equation (4) is the government expenditures function. G_0 is autonomous spending.

Equation (5) is the government transfer function. R_0 is autonomous transfer payments.

Equation (6) is the tax function. Taxes are composed of two parts. The autonomous component, T_0, is unaffected by income. The induced portion of taxes is tY. The tax rate is represented by t.

Equation (7) is the exogenous export function.

Equation (8) is the import function. Imports are composed of two parts. M_0 is the autonomous portion.

The induced portion is mY. The marginal propensity to import is represented by m.

Equation (9) is the national income accounting identity: Total expenditures = income.

To use this model meaningfully, we must combine all these equations into a single equation, called a *reduced-form equation*, which will neatly show the effect of various shifts on the equilibrium level of income. To do so we first substitute Equation (2) into Equation (1) giving us:

$$(1a)\ C = C_0 + b(Y - T + R)$$

We then substitute (1a), (3), (4), (5), (6), (7), and (8) into Equation (9), giving:

$$C_0 + b[Y - (T_0 + tY) + R_0] + I_0 +$$
$$G_0 + (X_0 - (M_0 + mY)) = Y$$

Removing the parentheses:

$$C_0 + bY - bT_0 - btY + bR_0 + I_0 +$$
$$G_0 + X_0 - M_0 - mY = Y$$

Moving all of the Y terms to the right side:

$$C_0 - bT_0 + bR_0 + I_0 + G_0 + X_0 - M_0 =$$
$$Y - bY + btY + mY$$

Factoring out Y on the right side:

$$C_0 - bT_0 + bR_0 + I_0 + G_0 + X_0 - M_0 =$$
$$Y(1 - b + bt + m)$$

Dividing by $(1 - b + bt + m)$ gives:

$$(C_0 - bT_0 + bR_0 + I_0 + G_0 + X_0 -$$
$$M_0)[1/(1 - b + bt + m)] = Y$$

$1/(1 - b + bt + m)$ is the multiplier for a simple Keynesian model with endogenous taxes and endogenous imports.

The marginal propensity to expend, *mpe*, discussed in the text would equal $b - bt - m$. The additional terms adjust b, the *mpc*, for the other induced expenditures that the simple model did not consider. Notice that they both make the multiplier smaller. For example, if the *mpc* is .8, $t = .25$, and $m = .1$, the multiplier using only the *mpc* would be $1/(1 - .8) = 5$. Taking into account other induced expenditures we can calculate the *mpe*. It equals $.8 - .8(.25) - .1 = .5$. Substituting .5 into our generalized multiplier formula, $1/(1 - .5)$ we see that the multiplier becomes $(1/(.5)) = 2$.

Thus, the general structure of the reduced-form equation is:

$$Y = (\text{multiplier})(\text{autonomous expenditures})$$

When we discuss changes in autonomous expenditures, the general form is:

$$\Delta Y = (\text{multiplier})(\Delta \text{ autonomous expenditures})$$

To see whether you follow the argument, let's try another numerical example. Say you want to increase income (Y) by 100. Assume $b = .8$, $t = .2$, and $m = .04$. Substituting in these numbers you find that $mpe = .8 - .8(.2) - .04 = .6$. Thus, in this example we get a multiplier of 2.5. (The approximate multiplier for the United States is usually considered to be somewhere between 2 and 2.5; the additional terms play an important role in making it this small.)

Having calculated the multiplier we can now determine how much to change autonomous expenditures to affect income. For example, to increase income by 100, we must increase autonomous expenditures by $(100/2.5) = 40$.

QUESTIONS FOR THOUGHT AND REVIEW

1. You have just been made adviser to Keynesland. The president wants output to increase by 400 by decreasing taxes. Your research assistant tells you that the *mpc* is .8, and all other components of aggregate expenditures are determined outside the model. What policy would you suggest?

2. The president returns to you and tells you that instead of changing taxes, he wants to achieve the same result by increasing government expenditures. What policy would you recommend?

3. Your research assistant has a worried look on her face. "What's the problem?" you ask. "I goofed," she confesses. "I thought taxes were exogenous when actually there's a marginal tax rate of .1." Before she can utter another word, you say, "No problem. I'll simply recalculate my answers to Questions 1 and 2 and change them before I send them in." What are your corrected answers?

4. She still has a pained expression. "What's wrong?" you ask. "You didn't let me finish," she says. "Not only was there a marginal tax rate of .1; there's also a marginal propensity to import of .2." Again you interrupt to make sure she doesn't feel guilty. Again you say, "No problem. I'll simply recalculate my answers to Questions 1 and 2 to account for the new information." What are your new answers?

5. Explain, using the words "expenditures" and "leakages," why making taxes and imports endogenous reduces the multiplier.

6. Suppose imports were a function of disposable income instead of income. What would be the new *mpe*? How does it compare with the *mpe* when imports were a function of income?

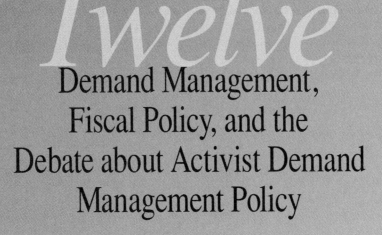

CHAPTER

Twelve

Demand Management, Fiscal Policy, and the Debate about Activist Demand Management Policy

An economist's lag may be a politician's catastrophe.
~ George Schultz

After reading this chapter, you should be able to:

1 Explain expansionary and contractionary fiscal policies.

2 Demonstrate fiscal policy using words and graphs.

3 List three alternatives to fiscal policy.

4 Distinguish a structural deficit from a passive deficit.

5 List six problems with fiscal policy and explain how those problems limit its use.

6 Define crowding out and explain how it can undermine the Keynesian view of fiscal policy.

7 Describe how automatic stabilizers work.

The previous two chapters highlighted the Classical and Keynesian views of how income was determined. Those chapters also introduced you to the Classical laissez-faire view of how macro policy worked and the Keynesian story of how small shifts in aggregate expenditure could be multiplied into larger fluctuations in aggregate production and aggregate income. That story underpins the Keynesian explanation of why there can be equilibrium at an income level below the full-employment income level and why income in the economy fluctuates.

The Keynesian model was not designed only to understand why fluctuations (booms and busts) occur in the economy; it was also designed to suggest *policies* to deal with the depression, policies that would get the economy out of its under-full-employment equilibrium. Keynes offered an alternative to the Classical laissez-faire policy.

Keynes's initial policy proposals were for public works (for the government to spend more without collecting more taxes to pay for the spending or, in other words, to run a deficit by spending more). Keynesians soon broadened that policy to include: (1) another way to stimulate the economy—by reducing taxes, (2) a way to slow down the economy when it was called for—by decreasing government spending or increasing taxes, (3) policies to change the money supply as a way of controlling the economy, and (4) general policies to influence components of aggregate expenditures.

We'll see Keynesian policy affecting the money supply in the next chapter. In this chapter, we consider government policies that change the level of government spending and taxes as a way of affecting the economy. First we consider the policies' effect in the Keynesian portion of the aggregate supply path. Then we consider the policies' effect in the Classical portion of the aggregate supply path. Finally we consider general problems of implementing such policies.

Government policies that change the level of government spending and taxes are termed **aggregate demand (expenditure) management policies.** One of the most well known of these aggregate demand management policies is **fiscal policy**—*the deliberate change in either government spending or taxes to stimulate or slow down the economy.* If aggregate income is too low (actual income is below target income), the appropriate fiscal policy is *expansionary fiscal policy:* decrease taxes or increase government spending. If aggregate income is too high (actual income is above target income), the appropriate fiscal policy is *contractionary fiscal policy:* increase taxes or decrease government spending.

Keynesians considered fiscal policy the steering wheel for the aggregate economy. They said Classical economists with their laissez-faire policy were trying to drive an economy without any steering wheel. If that were the case, is it any wonder the economy crashed?

In the Depression of the 1930s everyone agreed that income was too low and that, if fiscal policy worked, the appropriate fiscal policy was expansionary. Keynesians advocated that governments run deficits—spend more than the revenue they received. That advocacy made Keynesian economics the center of political debate at the time. Keynesians were accused of being communists, of looking for a way to destroy the U.S. economy, because they advocated running a deficit. In the late 1940s and early 1950s, textbooks that included the Keynesian model were subject to vehement attack; university presidents and trustees were pressured to fire any professor who used a "Keynesian" text. Much has changed since then. By the 1960s and 1970s, fiscal policy was a well-established tool of most governments, and Keynesian economics had become mainstream economics. Such was the influence of the Keynesian model.

Let's start this discussion with the story of fiscal policy for an economy in a depression. What caused that depression? As we saw in a previous chapter, when people got scared and cut back their spending, the multiplier took over and expanded that small negative shock into a full-blown depression. In a depression, the economy is at a level of income and production far below the potential level of income—below full employment of all productive resources.

Seeing this low level of income, and understanding the Keynesian model of the previous chapter, you should be led to the following insight: If somehow you can generate a countershock (a jolt in the opposite direction of the shift in aggregate demand that started the depression), you can get the multiplier working in reverse, expanding the economy in the same way the initial shock and multiplier effect had contracted it. You need a countershock to motivate people to spend, and as they increase their spending, society will be better off. But each individual, acting in her own interest, has no incentive to spend more. Each individual would reason: If I spend more, I'll be worse off. Theoretically, my additional spending might help society, but the positive effect would be so diluted that, in terms of my own situation, I don't see how my increased spending is going to benefit me.

For example, if a grocery store clerk increased her shopping expenditures by $100, only about $25 of that expenditure would go into food, so if her store is one of five stores selling various articles in the area where she shops, only $5 would go to her store. If she were one of 20 employees, her $5 represents only an additional 25¢ spending per employee at the store. If she were about to lose her job, her $100

Video Series, Economics USA: Fiscal Policy, Segments 6.1-6.2

FISCAL POLICY AND AGGREGATE DEMAND

1 Expansionary fiscal policy involves decreasing taxes or increasing government spending. Contractionary fiscal policy involves increasing taxes or decreasing government spending.

Keynesians argued that laissez-faire policy was the equivalent to driving a car without a steering wheel.

To give your students an introduction to how fiscal policy works, ask them to think of equilibrium income as the level of water in a bathtub. Full employment equilibrium occurs when the water is at the rim. If there is too much spending (water coming in from the tap) when the tub is full, there is an overflow, or inflation. If there is too little spending (water flowing out the drain), the water level falls and there is a recession. Fiscal policy is the act of draining more water out (reducing spending) when there is inflation, and adding more water to the tub (increasing spending) when there is a recession.

The Story of Keynesian Fiscal Policy

One individual spending more would not shift out the *AED* curve. All individuals spending more would, however, shift it out.

⊞ ADDED DIMENSION   THE ECONOMIC STEERING WHEEL

Our economic system is frequently put to shame by being displayed before an imaginary visitor from a strange planet. It is time to reverse the procedure.

Imagine yourself instead in a Buck Rogers interplanetary adventure, looking at a highway in a City of Tomorrow. The highway is wide and straight, and its edges are turned up so that it is almost impossible for a car to run off the road. What appears to be a runaway car is speeding along the road and veering off to one side. As it approaches the rising edge of the highway, its front wheels are turned so that it gets back onto the road and goes off at an angle, making for the other side, where the wheels are turned again. This happens many times, the car zigzagging but keeping on the highway until it is out of sight. You are wondering how long it will take for it to crash, when another car appears which behaves in the same fashion. When it comes near you it stops with a jerk. A door is opened, and an occupant asks whether you would like a lift. You look into the car and before you can control yourself you cry out, "Why, there's no steering wheel."

"Of course we have no steering wheel," says one of the occupants rather crossly. "Just think how it would cramp the front seat. It's worse than an old-fashioned gear-shift lever and it's dangerous. Suppose we have a steering wheel and somebody held on to it when we reached a curb. He would prevent the automatic turning of the wheel, and the car would surely be overturned. And besides, we believe in democracy and cannot give anyone the extreme authority of life and death over all the occupants of the car. That would be dictatorship."

"Down with dictatorship," chorus the other occupants of the car.

"If you are worried about the way the car goes from side to side," continues the first speaker, "forget it. We have wonderful brakes so that collisions are prevented nine times out of ten. On our better roads the curb is so effective that one can travel hundreds of miles without going off the road once. We have a very efficient system of carrying survivors of wrecks to nearby hospitals and for rapidly sweeping the remnants from the road to deposit them on nearby fields as a reminder to man of the inevitability of death."

You look around to see the piles of wrecks and burned-out automobiles as the man in the car continues. "Impressive, isn't it? But things are going to improve. See those men marking and photographing the tracks of the car that preceded us? They are going to take those pictures into their laboratories and pictures of our tracks, too, to analyze the cyclical characteristics of the curves, their degree of regularity, the average distance from turn to turn, the amplitude of the swings, and so on. When they have come to an agreement on their true nature we may know whether something can be done about it. At present they are disputing whether this cyclical movement is due to the type of road surface or to its shape or whether it is due to the length of the car or the kind of rubber in the tires or to the weather. Some of them think that it will be impossible to avoid having cycles unless we go back to the horse and buggy, but we can't do that because we believe in Progress. Well, want a ride?"

The dilemma between saving your skin and humoring the lunatics is resolved by your awakening from the nightmare, and you feel glad that the inhabitants of your own planet are a little more reasonable. But are they as reasonable about other things as they are about the desirability of steering their automobiles? Do they not behave exactly like the men in the nightmare when it comes to operating their economic system? Do they not allow their economic automobile to bounce from depression to inflation in wide and uncontrolled arcs? Through their failure to steer away from unemployment and idle factories, are they not just as guilty of public injury and insecurity as the mad motorists of Mars?

Source: Abba Lerner, "The Economic Steering Wheel," first published in *The University Review* (now *NEW LETTERS*), vol. 7, no. 4 (June 1941), pp. 257–65. Used by permission.

I ask my students whether anti-recession or anti-inflation policies can be thought of as public goods. After I pose the question I review the idea of the public good, and we work through how fiscal policy can be thought of as an application of this concept.

spending wouldn't save it. However, if *all* individuals, or a large proportion of all individuals, increased their spending by $100 each, spending at her store would rise considerably and her job would likely be saved.

How do you simultaneously get all or most individuals to spend more than they want to? In the 1930s, government found it wasn't easy. President Franklin Roosevelt went on radio to calm people's fears ("We have nothing to fear but fear itself") and to encourage people to spend to create more jobs.

According to the Keynesian model, these admonitions could have worked if they had generated sufficient initial spending; that initial increase would have generated some more spending which, in turn, would have generated even more spending. But

KEYNES AND KEYNESIAN POLICY

One of the subthemes of this book is that economic thought and policy are more complicated than an introductory book must necessarily make them seem. "Keynesian policy" is a good case in point. In the early 1930s, before Keynes wrote *The General Theory,* he was advocating public works programs and deficits as a way to get the British economy out of the Depression. He came upon what we now call the *Keynesian theory* as he tried to explain to Classical economists why he supported deficits. After arriving at his new theory, however, he spent little time advocating fiscal policy and, in fact, never mentions fiscal policy in *The General Theory,* the book that presents his theory. The book's primary policy recommendation is the need to socialize investments—for the government to take over the investment decisions from private individuals. When one of his followers, Abba Lerner, advocated expansionary fiscal policy at a seminar Keynes attended, Keynes strongly objected, leading Evsey Domar, another Keynesian follower, to whisper to a friend, "Keynes should read *The General Theory.*"

What's going on here? There are many interpretations, but the one I find most convincing is the one presented by historian Peter Clarke. He argues that, while working on *The General Theory,* Keynes turned his interest from a policy revolution to a theoretical revolution. He believed he had found a serious flaw in Classical economic theory. The Classicals assumed full employment, but did not show how the economy could move to that equilibrium from a disequilibrium. That's when Keynes's interest changed from a policy to a theoretical revolution.

His followers, such as Lerner, carried out the policy implications of his theory. Why did Keynes sometimes oppose these policy implications? Because he was also a student of politics and he recognized that economic theory can often lead to politically unacceptable policies. In a letter to a friend he later said Lerner was right in his logic, but he hoped the opposition didn't discover what Lerner was saying. Keynes was more than an economist; he was a politician as well.

---

these admonitions didn't work. The Keynesian model offered expansionary fiscal policy as an alternative.

With fiscal policy, government could provide the needed increased spending by decreasing taxes, increasing government spending, or both. Fiscal policy would provide the initial expansionary spending, increasing individuals' incomes. As individuals' incomes increased, they would spend more. As they spent more, the multiplier process would take over and expand the effect of the initial spending.

Keynesians argued that fiscal policy—the policy of government changing its spending and taxing to influence production and income levels in the economy—was the missing steering wheel of the economy.

Thus, both cutting taxes and increasing government expenditures are expansionary fiscal policy. The government provides the initial expansionary shock, and then the multiplier takes hold and expands the economy.

There is nothing special about government's ability to stimulate the economy with additional spending. If a group of individuals wanted to—and had spending power large enough to make a difference—they could do so, but private individuals don't have the incentive to do so. Their spending helps mainly other people and has only a small feedback on themselves. Unless they're altruistic, they don't take into account the effect of their spending on the aggregate spending stream and hence on aggregate income.

The significantly different effects when everyone does something rather than when only one person does it play an important role in economics. This difference has a number of names: the public goods problem, the tragedy of the commons, the fallacy of composition, and the multiperson dilemma.

The problem is neatly seen by considering an analogy to a football game. If everyone is standing, and you sit down, you can't see. Everyone is better off standing. No one has an incentive to sit down. However, if somehow all individuals could be enticed to sit down, all individuals would be even better off. Sitting down is a public good—a good that benefits others—but one that nobody on his or her own will do. Keynes argued that, in times of depression, spending is a public good because it benefits everyone, so government should spend or find ways of inducing private individuals to spend. This difference between individual and economy-wide reactions to spending decisions creates a possibility for government to exercise control over

2a Expansionary fiscal policy stimulates autonomous expenditures, which increases people's income, which increases people's spending even more.

Keynesians argue that fiscal policy was the missing steering wheel of the economy.

"The Economic Steering Wheel: The Story of the People's New Clothes," by Abba Lerner, in *Classic Readings in Economics.*

Aggregate Demand Management

Q-1: If spending in the economy is too low, why don't individuals simply increase their spending?

Note that this interpretation of Keynesian economics is quite consistent with individual rational expectations. Each individual has rational expectations, but because of macro externalities, the net effect of the collective decisions of individuals is not necessarily collectively rational. Thus there is an important distinction between individual rationality and collective rationality. The central policy issue of macroeconomics concerns this difference.

Keynes argued that, in times of depression, spending is a public good that benefits everyone.

EXHIBIT 1 (a and b)   Differing Views of Expansionary Fiscal Policy

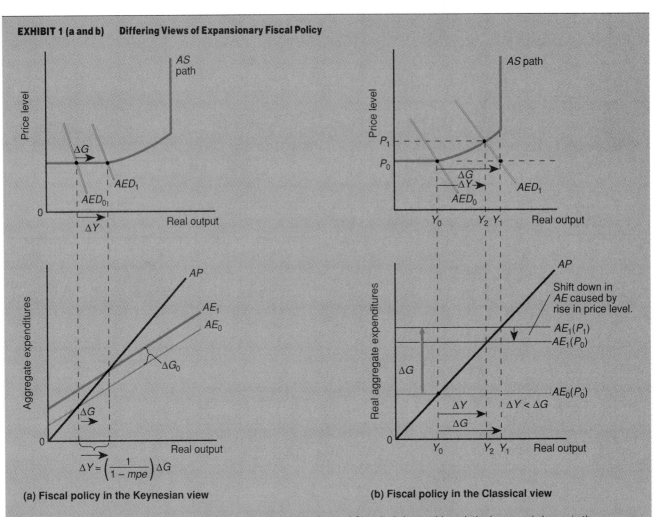

(a) Fiscal policy in the Keynesian view

(b) Fiscal policy in the Classical view

Expansionary fiscal policy expands real output in both the Keynesian and Classical views, although the increase is larger in the Keynesian view. The Keynesian view is shown in (**a**). The AS path is flat. Expansionary fiscal policy shifts the AED curve out by a multiple of the change in government spending, (ΔG), from AED_0 to AED_1. This is shown in the top part of (**a**). In the bottom part of (**a**) that same increase can be seen in the AE/AP model. There you can see the reason for the multiplier effect more explicitly; it is determined by the slope of the AE curve.

    The Classical view is shown in (**b**). The Classical view is different from the Keynesian view in two ways. The first difference is that the AED curve shifts out less, as you can see in the top graph in (**b**). The reason why can be seen in the bottom graph. The AE curve is flatter (in this case, horizontal), making the multiplier smaller or nonexistent. The second difference is that the AS path is upward sloping, or even vertical. Classicals believe it is far more likely that the equilibrium of the economy will be operating at its limit and that any further expansion of government spending will cause the price level to rise, perhaps even rise in an accelerating inflation. The rise in the price level causes the AE curve to shift down (to $AE_1(P_1)$), further reducing the expansionary effect of fiscal policy.

aggregate expenditures and thereby over aggregate output and income. As I stated above, government's attempt to control the aggregate level of spending in the economy is called aggregate demand management. It involves the government's influence of a shift factor of aggregate expenditures, and then relying on the multiplier effect to multiply that initial effect into a larger effect on aggregate equilibrium demand and thus on income.

Keynesian and Classical Views of Fiscal Policy

2b Expansionary fiscal policy shifts the AED curve out. The effect on prices and output depends upon where the economy is on the aggregate supply path.

Exhibit 1 shows the Keynesian and Classical views of fiscal policy in both the macro policy model and the AE/AP model.

    The Keynesian view of how fiscal policy works is presented in Exhibit 1(a). Expansionary fiscal policy initially shifts the AED curve out from AED_0 to AED_1 (in the top graph) and shifts the AE curve up from AE_0 to AE_1 (in the bottom graph). Aggregate equilibrium demand shifts through multiplier effects to AED_1 and income increases by a multiple of the initial increase in government spending, from Y_0 to Y_1.

The top graph in Exhibit 1(b) shows the Classical view of the effect of fiscal policy in the macro policy model. There are two major differences to note. The first difference is that, while, in the Classical case, fiscal policy shifts the *AED* curve out only by the initial increase in spending to AED_1, there are no multiplier effects; it does not shift it out as far as in the Keynesian case. The reason is that in the Classical case, it is generally assumed that there is significant offsetting effects, so the net expansionary effect of the spending is small; and there is no, or only a very small, amount of induced spending. (The multiplier is close to one.) The second difference to note is that the aggregate supply path is no longer assumed flat. It is upward sloping or close to vertical. This means that the increase in aggregate equilibrium demand is divided between a rise in the price level and a rise in real income. Real income will increase only to Y_2, not to Y_1, which it would have had the aggregate supply path been flat and the price level constant. So although fiscal policy still has an expansionary effect given the Classical assumptions, its effect on real income is much smaller than it is with the Keynesian assumptions.

The same differences are shown in the AE/AP model in the bottom graph of Exhibit 1(b). The initial shift in the AE curve is the same as in the Keynesian case. But, because the Classical expenditure function is flatter than the Keynesian expenditure function, the multiplier effect is smaller so there is less induced spending. (The reason is that Classical economists see expenditures depending upon permanent income, not current income—so the multiplier is much smaller, or even nonexistent.) Thus, the expansion in income that would occur even if the price level would remain constant is less than in the Keynesian case.

The second difference involves the price level. In the Classical model, the aggregate supply path is upward sloping, which means that the effect of fiscal policy will be to raise the price level from P_0 to P_1. That rise in price level in Exhibit 1(b) shifts the AE curve down from $AE_1(P_0)$ to $AE_1(P_1)$. In the absence of that price-level rise, real income would have increased to Y_1. But with the increase in the price level, real income rises only to Y_2. Notice that the net increase in income resulting from the increase in government spending in the Classical model is less than the initial increase in government spending. That's because most of the effects on income are eliminated by the rise in the price level. So you can see fiscal policy and demand management policy, in general, do not make much sense from a Classical view.

We'll return to a discussion of the Classical view below. For the moment, let's stay within the Keynesian view where the multiplier exists and the economy is far below its potential income so the *AS* path is flat. We'll consider how, given these assumptions, fiscal policy can be used to control the economy.

Fighting Recession: Expansionary Fiscal Policy   Let's now consider a numerical case where the economy is in a recession and is in the fixed-price-level range of the *AS* path. I consider this case in Exhibit 2.

For simplicity of exposition I assume that accelerating inflation occurs as soon as the price level rises slightly. This assumption eliminates Range *B* (the upward-sloping portion of the *AS* path), leaving only the Keynesian and Classical portions of the *AS* path.

The top panel shows the macro policy model; the bottom part shows the *AE/AP* model. Initially the economy is at equilibrium at income level $1,000, which is below the target potential income ($1,180). When equilibrium income is below potential income, this difference is called a **recessionary gap.** If everything goes as it should in the Keynesian story, this is what happens: The government recognizes this recessionary gap in aggregate income of, say, $180, and responds using expansionary fiscal policy (the policy of changing spending or taxes to affect the equilibrium income of the economy) by increasing government expenditures by $60. This shifts the *AED* curve out by three times that amount, or by $180. The initial shock shifts the *AED* curve out by $60; the $120 shift is due to the multiplier effects that the initial shift brings about.

"Fiscal Policy," by Milton Friedman, in *Classic Readings in Economics.*

The Classical view of fiscal policy is that it is far less effective than Keynesians believe it is.

For computer exercises on the effect of fiscal policy on the economy, use module "fiscal policy" in *Macro Interactive.*

Recessionary gap   *The difference between equilibrium income and potential income when potential income exceeds equilibrium income.*

If the economy is below its potential income level, the government can increase its expenditures to stimulate the economy. Doing so shifts the *AED* curve to the right. In the Keynesian view, the shift in the *AED* curve is greater than the initial shift in expenditures because the multiplier process takes over and expands the initial shock of the additional spending. If the government has chosen the right fiscal policy, income increases until actual income equals potential income.

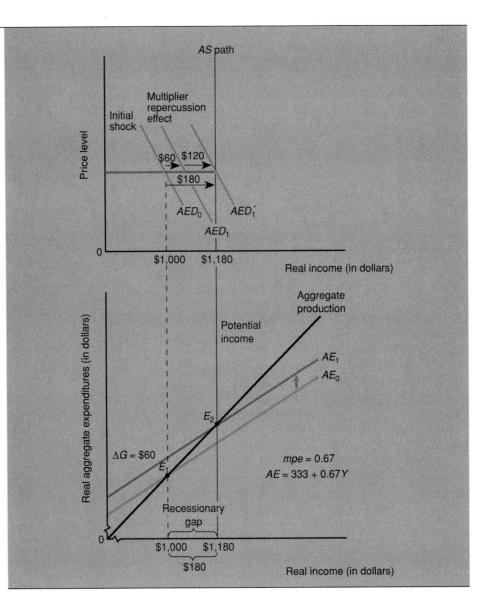

The same effects are shown in the *AE/AP* model in the bottom part of Exhibit 2. There the increased government spending shifts the *AE* curve from AE_0 upward to AE_1. Businesses that receive government contracts hire the workers who have been laid off by other firms and open new plants; output increases by the initial expenditure of $60. But the process doesn't stop there. At this point, the multiplier process sets in. As the newly employed workers spend more, other businesses find that their demand increases. They hire more workers, who spend an additional $40 (since their mpe = .67). This increases income further. The same process occurs again and again. By the time the process has ended, income has risen by $180 and is back at $1,180, the potential level of income.

How did the government economists know to increase spending by $60? It knew by backward induction. It empirically estimated that the mpe—the slope of the aggregate expenditures curve—was .67, which meant that the multiplier was $1/(1 - .67) = 1/.33 = 3$. It divided the multiplier, 3, into the recessionary gap, $180, and determined that if it increased spending by $60, income would increase by $180.

Q–2: Demonstrate graphically the effect of contractionary fiscal policy.

Fighting Inflation: Contractionary Fiscal Policy   Fiscal policy can also work in reverse, decreasing expenditures that are too high. Expenditures are "too high" when the economy temporarily exceeds its potential output. Doing so will generate accelerating

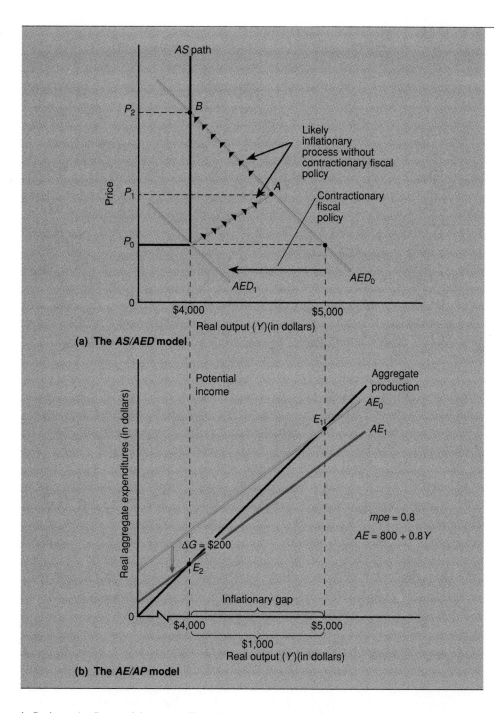

EXHIBIT 3 (a and b)   Demand-Pull Inflation and Fighting AS Path Inflation

Once the economy reaches its potential output, any further increase will lead to accelerating inflation. If the quantity of aggregate equilibrium demand exceeds potential income at that price level, there will be excess demand and pressures for demand-pull inflation. Temporarily, output may exceed potential output as firms and workers are slow to raise their prices and wages. But soon, shortages and accelerating inflation will drive the economy back to its potential income (at a point like B). To prevent this the government must use contractionary fiscal policy shifting the AED curve back from AED_0 to AED_1. This case is shown in (**a**). In (**b**), the same situation is shown in the AE/AP model. Again, contractionary fiscal policy, shifting the AE curve downward, from AE_0 to AE_1 is called for.

inflation. As I stated in an earlier chapter, there is debate about where accelerating inflation will begin: where the AS path starts to slope up or whether some price level rise will not generate accelerating inflation. For purposes of this chapter I will assume that accelerating inflation begins where the AS path begins to slope upward. This makes the AS path a right angle. It is important to remember, however, that in the short run, because of slowly adjusting prices, and firms selling off inventory, the economy can exceed its potential income. For practical purposes, however, the relevant AS path is considered a right angle, since exceeding potential income is not a viable long run policy. When the economy is above its potential output, additional expenditures cause accelerating inflationary pressure. People on average want to raise their prices, which either causes shortages if wages and prices are fixed (can't be raised) or inflation if wages and prices are not fixed.

The top graph in Exhibit 3 shows the situation in the macro policy model; the bottom graph shows it in the AE/AP model. Notice that at the existing price level, equilibrium income is at $5,000, while the economy's potential income is $4,000. Given this assumption there is no equilibrium in either model unless the price level increases, bringing real income back to $4,000.

What would likely happen in reality is that initially the expansion in aggregate equilibrium demand to AED_0 will be met by an increase in output above potential output and some increase in price level (from P_0 to P_1). But, at that output level, output exceeds potential output; workers and firms will adjust their pricing strategies, causing the price level rise to accelerate. This continuing increase in the price level would cause a movement along the AED curve from point A to point B. Thus, to prevent that inflation from occurring, the government must reduce aggregate equilibrium demand by $1,000, from $5,000 to $4,000 before the price level rises from P_0. Contractionary fiscal policy can be used to shift the AED curve back from AED_0 to AED_1 where there is no upward pressure on the price level.

To bring about that shift in the AED curve the government did not decrease its expenditures by $1,000. It decreased them by an amount less than that. How much less? To determine that, it had to calculate the multiplier. In this example the marginal propensity to expend was assumed to be .8, which means that the multiplier would be 5. So a cut in expenditures of $200 would cause the AED curve to shift back by $1,000.

The bottom part of Exhibit 3 shows contractionary fiscal policy in the AE/AP model. Potential income is $4,000, but the equilibrium level of income is $5,000. The difference between the two, $1,000, is an **inflationary gap**—*a difference between equilibrium income and potential income when equilibrium income exceeds potential income*. This inflationary gap causes upward pressure on wages and prices with no additional lasting output increase resulting. As the price level rises, the AE curve will shift down. If the government wants to avoid inflation, it can use contractionary fiscal policy. For example, a decrease in government spending of $200 shifts the AE curve down by $200 and decreases the equilibrium income by $1,000.

Q–3: The marginal propensity to expend is .33 and there is an inflationary gap of $100. What fiscal policy would you recommend?

Inflationary gap *The difference between equilibrium income and potential income when equilibrium income exceeds potential income.*

Applying the Models and the Questionable Effectiveness of Fiscal Policy

A high marginal propensity to expend means a large multiplier; a low marginal propensity to expend means a low multiplier.

When I discuss the effectiveness of fiscal policy, I like to ask my students to think about the consequences of fiscal policy tools that are powerful in their impact on the economy, but unpredictable in terms of their timing. This is a good way to lead into a discussion of the limitations of fiscal policy.
A countercyclical fiscal policy designed to keep the economy always at its target or potential level of income is called fine tuning.

Almost all economists, whether Keynesian or Classical, agree the government is not up to fine tuning the economy.

There are two ways to think about the effectiveness of fiscal policy—in the model, and in reality.

Effectiveness of Fiscal Policy in Reality   Models are great, and simple models, like the one I've presented in this book, that you can understand intuitively are even greater. You put in the numbers, and out comes the answer. Questions based on such models make great exam questions. But don't think that policies that work in a model will work in the real world.

The effectiveness of fiscal policy in reality depends on the government's ability to perceive a problem, and to react appropriately to it. The essence of fiscal policy is government changing its taxes and its spending to offset any deviation that would occur in other autonomous expenditures, thereby keeping the economy at its potential level of income. If the model is a correct description of the economy, and if the government can act fast enough and change its taxes and spending in a *countercyclical* way, depressions can be prevented. This type of management of the economy is called **countercyclical fiscal policy**—*fiscal policy in which the government offsets any shock that would create a business cycle*. The term **fine tuning** is used to describe such *fiscal policy designed to keep the economy always at its target or potential level of income*.

As I will discuss below, almost all economists, whether Keynesian or Classical, agree the government is not up to fine tuning the economy. The debate in the 1990s is whether it is up to any tuning of the economy at all.

At one time, some Keynesians thought the economy followed a simple adjustment process such as described by this model, and that it could be modeled simply and controlled. No more. Why? Because this, or any, simple model captures only one aspect of the dynamic adjustment process.

All economists now recognize that the dynamic adjustment in the economy is extraordinarily complicated and that, once you take into account reasonable expecta-

USING TAXES RATHER THAN EXPENDITURES AS THE TOOL OF FISCAL POLICY   **ADDED DIMENSION**

As a brain teaser you might try to figure out what you would have advised the government to do if it had wanted to increase taxes rather than decrease expenditures. By how much should it increase taxes? If you said by $200 since the multiplier is 5, you're on the right wave length, but not quite right. True, the multiplier, $[1/(1 - mpe)]$, is 5, but taxes affect expenditures in a slightly different way than do expenditures. Specifically, expenditures will not decrease by the full amount of the tax increase. The reason why is that people will likely reduce their savings in order to hold up their expenditures. Expenditures will initially fall by the mpe multiplied by the increased taxes, or $(.8 \times \$200) = \$160$, rather than by $200. To get the initial shift of $200 from increasing taxes, the government must increase taxes by $250. Then when people reduce spending by .8 of that, their expenditures will fall by $200.

tions of future policy, the formal model becomes hopelessly complex. Graduate students in economics get Ph.D.s for worrying about such hopeless complexities. At the introductory level, all we require is that you (1) know this simple Keynesian model, and (2) remember that, in the real world, it cannot be used in a mechanistic manner; it must be used with judgment.

As questions about the effectiveness of fiscal policy have developed, policy discussions have moved toward alternatives to fiscal policy. To understand how these alternatives work, you must simply remember that any change in autonomous expenditures, ΔE, not just changes in the government taxes and expenditures, will affect the level of income. You can see the alternatives to fiscal policy by breaking down autonomous expenditures into its components:

ALTERNATIVES TO FISCAL POLICY

$$\Delta Y = \text{multiplier} \times \begin{pmatrix} \Delta \text{ autonomous consumption} \\ + \\ \Delta \text{ autonomous investment} \\ + \\ \Delta \text{ autonomous government spending} \\ + \\ \Delta \text{ autonomous net exports} \end{pmatrix}$$

Any policy that affects any of these four components of autonomous expenditures — autonomous consumption, autonomous investment, autonomous government spending, and autonomous net exports—can achieve the same results as fiscal policy. So three alternatives to fiscal policy are directed investment policies, trade policies, and autonomous consumption policies. The above requires one addendum: any policy that can influence *autonomous* expenditures *without having offsetting effects on other expenditures* can be used to influence the direction and movement of aggregate income. That addendum in italics is important because, in the Classical view, no expenditure is autonomous. If you push on one type of expenditure, you simply pull on another, and the net effect will be a wash. But in the Keynesian view there is an autonomous component of each of those expenditures that in principle can be affected by policy. We have already considered government spending policy when we talked about fiscal policy. Let us briefly consider some of the other policies that could be used to influence income. I discuss investment first, then net exports, and, finally, consumption.

3 Three alternatives to fiscal policy are directed investment policies, trade policies, and autonomous consumption policies.

Let's first consider investment. Remember, Keynes thought that the Depression was caused by some type of collective psychological fear on the part of investors who, because they predicted that the economy was going into a recession, decided not to invest. As a result, the economy went into a recession, and then eventually a depression, as the fear built upon itself. If somehow government could have supported investment, it could have avoided the Depression.

Directed Investment Policies: Policy Affecting Expectations

A Numerical Example   To give you some practice with the model, let's consider a numerical example. Say that income is $400 less than desired and that the marginal propensity to expend is .5. How much will government policy have to increase autonomous investment in order to achieve the desired level of income? Working backwards, we see that the multiplier is 2, so autonomous investment must be increased by $200.

Rosy Scenario: Talking the Economy Well   Numerical examples like the one above are a bit far-fetched since it is difficult to relate a specific policy to a specific numerical result or investment. But the relationship is there, and you can see examples of government trying to exploit it every day. For example, listen to government officials on the radio or television. Almost inevitably you will hear rosy scenarios from them—the **Rosy Scenario policy**—*government policy of making optimistic predictions and never making gloomy predictions.* You almost never hear a policy-level government economist telling the newspapers how bad the economy is going to be. Why? Because a gloomy prediction could affect expectations and decrease investment and consumption spending. If you're a high-level government policy economist and you have a gloomy forecast, you're told to keep quiet or quit. In the Great Depression, President Roosevelt, in a famous radio address, told the nation not to fear—that the only thing it had to fear was fear itself. Bill Clinton's upbeat talk about the economy is another example: if he can get people to think the economy in the late 1990s will be in good shape, it will be in good shape because people expect it to be.

Of course, the upbeat talk must not only be rosy; it must also be credible—believable as a realistic policy. During the U.S. presidential campaign in 1996 when Bob Dole argued that he would cut taxes by 15 percent and eliminate the deficit (because, he said, the economy would grow by 5 or 6 percent a year), for a majority of voters he crossed the credibility line, and he lost the election. Bill Clinton in 1996 was in a better position; his rosy predictions of 1992—predictions of growth, low inflation, and declining unemployment—had come true. Business investment, consumer demand, and export demand had grown, while international competition had kept the inflation rate low. This helped establish his credibility and helped him win the 1996 election. Whether his good luck can continue through the end of the century remains to be seen.

Another way to influence investment is to protect the financial system by government guarantees or promises of guarantees. Nothing can decrease business confidence quite like a large number of bank and financial institution failures. Precisely that type of financial institution failure changed a recession in the 1930s to the Great Depression. As you saw in an earlier chapter, to prevent such failures in the future the government instituted a number of guarantee-type policies after the Depression.

Let's consider how such investment-expectations policies work in practice. Say the economy is in a slight recession, and because of that, banks are in financial trouble. The government recognizes that if the public decides that banks are in trouble, they will try to get their money out of the banks, in which case banks will have to close. As banks close, loans will dry up, investment will decrease, and the economy will fall into a deep recession. To prevent that, the government comes along and tells everyone that it will bail out the banks so that people's money is safe. If the government is believed, everything stays fine and the recession doesn't happen (and, hopefully, the banks get themselves out of their financial trouble).

Japan used such a "save the financial institutions" policy in the 1990s. When the Japanese stock and real estate markets collapsed in the early 1990s, the Japanese government loosened bank accounting rules in order to prevent banks from failing. Similarly, in the early 1990s, when the U.S. banking system was seriously in trouble due to loan losses, the U.S. government modified institutional rules to increase banking profitability. It worked, and by the mid-1990s the U.S. banking system had recovered.

Q-4: How is it possible to "talk" the economy into a boom?

If policy economists and government officials constantly try to "talk the economy well," the policy will gradually lose its effectiveness because they will lose credibility. The need to maintain credibility requires the judicious application of this policy approach.

Notice how in this interpretation, expectations play the central role and expectations are almost beyond policy formulation. The effect that policy has on expectations, and on expectations of expectations, is very much part of policy discussions in Washington today.

After the 1990s real estate collapse, Japan loosened bank accounting rules.

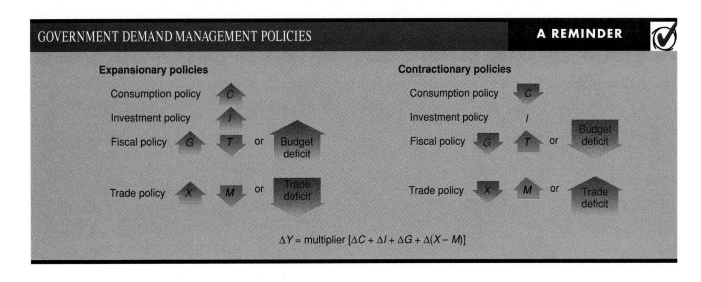

Another way in which the government can influence investment is through influencing the interest rate. I will discuss this policy in detail in the next chapter when we discuss monetary policy.

The answer to the question, "When do such policies affecting investment (through changing expectations or interest rates) make sense?" doesn't follow from the models; it is a matter of judgment. In the 1930s, Keynes didn't see any of these policies affecting investment as being sufficient; in his book, *The General Theory*, he advocated the government taking over the investment decisions—nationalizing investment. That policy didn't receive high marks in the United States.[1] Instead, Keynesian policy quickly came to mean fiscal policy. Why? Because politically, Keynesians quickly saw that fiscal policy could be sold to the public, whereas the more radical Keynesian nationalizing investment policies couldn't be.

Any policy that increases autonomous exports or decreases autonomous imports (and thereby increases autonomous expenditures) will also have multiplied effects on income. Examples of such policies abound. The U.S. Commerce Department has entire sub-departments assisting firms to develop their export markets. Similarly, U.S. trade delegations frequent other nations, pushing to get the other nations' trade restrictions on U.S. goods lowered. Those policies are called **export-led growth policies**—*policies designed to stimulate U.S. exports and increase aggregate expenditures on U.S. goods, and hence to have a multiplied effect on U.S. income.*

Notice that it is the trade balance (exports minus imports) that affects aggregate expenditures, so any policy that will reduce imports, such as tariffs, will have the same expansionary effect on income. That's why you hear so much about trade restrictions from Washington. They're a way of protecting U.S. jobs and of stimulating the U.S. economy in the short run. (In the long run most economists believe that tariff policies have serious problems.)

A Numerical Example   Let's start with a numerical example of a small country with a large percentage of imports. Say the country's income is $300 million too low and its marginal propensity to expend is .33. How must it affect net exports to achieve its desired income? Since the *mpe* is low, the multiplier is small (1.5), which means that net exports must be increased by approximately $200 million (either by decreasing imports or increasing exports by that amount).

In *The General Theory* there is no discussion of fiscal policy, or, for that matter, monetary policy. It is for political reasons that Keynesian economists started to focus on fiscal policy. Both Keynes and Classical economists such as A. C. Pigou were advocating fiscal policy long before Keynes developed the ideas that came out in *The General Theory*.

Trade Policy and Export-Led Growth

Export-led growth policies   Policies designed to stimulate exports and hence have a multiplied effect on U.S. income.

At this point I like to pose the following question to my class: If a country can expand its income by restricting imports, why can't all countries achieve the same end through such policies?

In 1994 there were negotiations among Japan, the United States, and Germany about the international relationship of these three economies. Pressure was brought on Japan and Germany to lower their interest rates and to expand their economics, and on the United States to raise its interest rates and keep its expansion lower than it otherwise would have been, and their policies since then reflected those negotiations.

---

[1]In some ways, the enormous defense expenditure made by the government after the 1940s was a version of such a policy, and it led to many complaints that the U.S. economy was a war-based economy.

For mathematical presentation of the interdependencies of the global economy, see Chapter 5, "The International Locomotive Effect" in *Economics: An Honors Companion*.

Q-5: In the 1990s, the value of the U.S. dollar has fallen. What effect would you expect that to have on income in the United States?

An important determinant of the price to U.S. consumers of Japanese cars is the exchange rate.

Autonomous Consumption Policy

Structural versus Passive Government Budget and Trade Deficits

Video Series, Economics U$A: Fiscal Policy, Segment 6-3

Higher tax rates and higher marginal propensities to import decrease the size of the multiplier.

Interdependencies in the Global Economy   I'll discuss these trade policies in much more detail in later chapters, but for now, let me remind you that one country's exports are another country's imports, so that every time the United States is out pushing its exports in an attempt to follow an export-led growth policy, it is the equivalent to getting another country to follow an *import-led decline* for its economy. Similarly, every trade restriction on foreign goods has an offsetting effect on another country's economy, an effect that will often lead to retaliation. So a policy of trying to restrict imports can often end up simultaneously restricting exports as other countries retaliate. Expectations of such retaliation is one of the reasons many economists support free trade agreements, such as the North American Free Trade Agreement (NAFTA), in which member countries agree not to engage in restrictive trade policies on imports.

A final way in which the trade balance can be affected is through **exchange rate policy**—*a policy of deliberately affecting a country's exchange rate in order to affect its trade balance*. In the long run, a low value of a country's currency relative to currencies of other countries encourages exports and discourages imports; a high value of a country's currency relative to other countries' currency discourages exports and encourages imports.

The effect of such exchange rates can be seen in the automobile industry. In the 1970s and 1980s, Japanese exports of cars were increasing enormously. An important reason for that was the relative value of the Japanese yen (somewhere around 300 to the dollar). In the 1990s, the value of the dollar fell relative to the yen, so that in the mid-1990s it was about one-third the value (around 100 to the dollar) of what it was in the 1970s. With this change, Japanese cars no longer seemed the good buy that they had been, and the U.S. automobile industry made a comeback. Again, we'll discuss such policies in more detail in a later chapter.

A third alternative to fiscal policy is consumption policies. Any policy designed to encourage autonomous consumption can hold autonomous expenditures up and have the same effect as fiscal policy. Increasing consumer credit availability to individuals by making the institutional environment conducive to credit is one way of achieving this.

The growth of the U.S. economy from the 1950s through the 1980s was marked by significant institutional changes that made credit available to a larger and larger group of people. This increase in consumer credit allowed significant expansion in income of the U.S. economy. In the 1990s, some consumers cut back as they tried to consolidate their financial obligations, and that has played a major role in the slow growth of the U.S. economy in the early 1990s. Similarly, the resolution of those problems played a major role in the rise in growth in the mid-1990s.

As a final review, to be sure you have the model down pat, calculate how much autonomous expenditures should change to decrease income by $60 if the *mpe* = ⅔.[2]

The above discussion of autonomous expenditure policy made it look as if there were a one-way flow from autonomous expenditure to income. Thus one could talk about fiscal policy, and the size of the deficit, or trade policy, and the size of the trade balance, as policies to control the level of income. But when one is thinking about such policies, it is important to remember that not all of these expenditures are autonomous. Changes in one component often induce changes in other components that can either augment or detract from the initial change. Consider a policy to increase consumption. That policy will lead to higher income, but when income goes up, so do taxes. The increase in taxes will partially offset the effect of the rise in consumption. Each of the components of aggregate expenditures has these induced effects that affect the analysis. Specifically, each of these induced elements affects the marginal propensity to expend, and thereby affects the size of the multiplier. (How these effects are mathematically related to the size of the multiplier is shown in Appendix A of Chap-

---

[2]If you came up with any answer but "Decrease autonomous expenditures by $20," a review is in order.

ADDED DIMENSION

REGIONAL MULTIPLIERS

ADDED DIMENSION

The macro policies discussed in the book are national policies. A parallel policy discussion goes on in just about every community when regional planning units consider the effect of the pullout of a military base, or the relocation of a new company into a community. All such policies to affect such decisions are based on the assumption that regional multipliers exist—that the impact of an expenditure will have a multiplied effect on the income of the community.

We can fit such policies into our Keynesian model by thinking of a community as having imports and exports. While exports and imports into and out of a community are not measured, they exist. For example, colleges are an export of a regional area (why?), and the maintenance of a college in an area can be seen as a regional export-led growth policy. Building expensive stadiums for professional sports teams is usually similarly justified by such multiplier-effect reasoning.

Looking in your local paper, you will most likely see evidence of such policies; most regional areas give tax benefits and other concessions to firms that locate there. (Ironically, many of these initiatives are supported by businesspeople who, on a national level, reject Keynesian policies.)

When thinking about these regional policies, it is important to remember that all the same problems that exist with Keynesian policy on the national level also exist on the local level: retaliation, inability to decide what to affect, and inability to decide what is the "appropriate" potential level of income. In the Classical view, in the aggregate, all these regional policies simply offset each other, and the net effect of such policies on the aggregate economy is more waste in government. But even if one is persuaded by this Classical argument, one might still support regional policies based on multiplier analysis. The reason is that unless such regional incentives are prohibited for all communities, once one area introduces them, the others must follow or lose out.

ter 11.) Higher tax rates and higher marginal propensities to import decrease the size of the multiplier; lower tax rates and lower marginal propensities to import increase the size of the multiplier.

The induced elements of taxes and imports mean that when we are discussing export-led growth policies or fiscal policy, we must remember that while *the budget deficit and the trade balance will affect aggregate income, simultaneously aggregate income will affect the budget deficit and trade balance.* So if we're using the size of the deficit or the size of the trade balance as a measure of our policy tools, they themselves will change as income changes, and the ending trade balance and ending budget deficit might be quite different than the initial trade balance or initial budget deficit.

The budget deficit and the trade balance will affect aggregate income, but they will also be affected by it.

For example, say the multiplier is 2 and the government is running expansionary policy. It increases government spending by $100 (increasing the budget deficit by $100), which causes income to rise by $200. If the tax rate is 20 percent, tax revenues will increase by $40 and the net effect will be to increase the budget deficit by $60, not $100. Alternatively, consider a successful export-led growth policy. Say the multiplier is again 2 and the government wants to eliminate a $40 billion trade deficit, but for every dollar of additional income people import 30¢ worth of goods. The government introduces policies that expand exports by $40 billion and income by $80 billion. That $80 billion increase in income causes imports to increase by $24 billion, so the $40 billion trade deficit will not be eliminated. It will instead be reduced by $16 billion.

This material is often a bit tricky for students, so explain it carefully.

To differentiate between a budget deficit being used as a policy instrument to affect the economy, and a budget deficit that is the result of income being below its potential, economists use a reference income level at which to judge fiscal policy. That reference income level is their estimate of the economy's potential level of income. They then ask: Would the economy have a budget deficit if it were at its potential level of income? If it would, that portion of the budget deficit is said to be a **structural deficit**—*the part of a budget deficit that would exist even if the economy were at its potential level of income.* On the other hand, if an economy is operating below its potential, the actual deficit will be larger than the structural deficit. In such an economy, that part of the total budget deficit is a **passive deficit**—*the part of the deficit that exists because the economy is operating below its potential level of output.* Economists believe that an economy can eliminate a passive budget deficit through growth in income, whereas it can't grow out of a structural deficit. Because the economy can't

4 A structural deficit is a deficit that would exist at potential income. A passive deficit is the deficit that exists because income is below potential income.

EXHIBIT 4   Structural and Passive Deficits

This exhibit graphs the actual and structural deficits from 1956 to 1996. The passive deficit is represented by the (dark blue) shaded area—the difference between the two. The passive deficit rises when output falls below potential, is zero when the economy is at its potential, and becomes a passive surplus represented by the (light blue) shaded area when the economy is above its potential output.

Source: CBO; The Economic and Budget Outlook (1996)

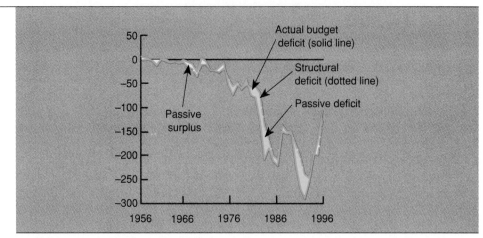

Q–6: An economy's actual income is $1 trillion; its potential income is also $1 trillion. Its actual deficit is $100 billion. What is its passive deficit?

grow out of structural budget deficits, they are of more concern to policy makers than are passive budget deficits.

Let me give an example. Say potential income is $7 trillion and actual income is $6.8 trillion, a shortfall of $200 billion. The actual budget deficit is $250 billion and the marginal tax rate is 25 percent. If the economy were at its potential income, tax revenue would be $50 billion higher and the deficit would be $200 billion. That $200 billion is the structural deficit. The $50 billion (25 percent multiplied by the $200 million shortfall) is the passive portion of the deficit.

In reality there is significant debate about what an economy's potential income level is, and hence there is disagreement about what percentage of a deficit is structural and what part is passive. Nonetheless, the distinction is often used and is important to remember. Exhibit 4 shows government estimates of the structural and passive deficits since 1956. As you consider it, ask yourself how those estimates would change if they were made by someone who felt a higher-level potential income was achievable. If you answered that the structural deficit would be lower, you've got the terms down.

So much for our discussion of the theoretical issues surrounding Keynesian economics and policies. Let's now turn to how they work in practice. To give you an idea of how fiscal and other expenditures policies work in the real world, we'll look at a couple of examples. Let's first consider what happened in World War II.

Fiscal Policy in World War II   The Depression in the United States continued through the 1930s. However, by the beginning of the 1940s it was no longer the focus of U.S. policy as the war in Europe (which had started in 1939) and in the Pacific (where it had started somewhat earlier) became more and more the central issue, especially after December 7, 1941, when Japan attacked the United States by bombing Pearl Harbor in Hawaii. At that point the United States entered the war against Japan and soon thereafter entered the war against Germany.

Fighting a war costs money, so economists' attention turned to how to raise that money. Taxes went up enormously, but government expenditures rose far more. The result can be seen in Exhibit 5(a), which tabulates GDP, the deficit, and unemployment data for the wartime time span 1937–46. As you can see, the deficit increased greatly and real income rose by more than the increase in the deficit. Exhibit 5(b) shows the effect in the macro policy model. The *AED* curve shifts out by more than the increase in the deficit. As predicted, the U.S. economy expanded enormously in response to the expansionary fiscal policy that accompanied the war. One thing should bother you about this episode. Where is the price-level increase that we would expect from the normal shape of the aggregate supply path? During this time aggregate equilibrium demand significantly exceeded the economy's previously estimated potential income, so we should have seen significant inflation. We didn't see that because the wartime expansion was accompanied by wage and price controls, which prevented price-level increases. The controls and rationing that accompanied them changed the shape of the *AS* path from the standard upward sloping path to the more L-shaped right angled

SHIFTING TERMS OF THE KEYNESIAN/CLASSICAL TRUCE

ADDED DIMENSION

Until the 1980s, most Keynesian economists were primarily interested in policy, and theoretical revolution in Keynes's work was not expanded upon. A truce was arrived at between Keynesians and Classicals. The truce stated that (1) Classical theory was theoretically correct, but the assumptions it made were inapplicable to many real-world situations, and (2) Keynesian theory was, theoretically, a special case of Classical theory, but it was a special case that just happened to be relevant to the real world. This gave Keynesians the policy applicability they were interested in, and Classicals the theoretical laurels.

In the 1980s, Keynesian policy came under fire and the truce broke down on the real-world policy side. More and more economists came to believe that Keynesian policy wasn't so relevant after all. As that happened, modern Keynesians returned to Keynes's work and argued against the other part of the truce that gave the theoretical laurels to the Classicals. These modern Keynesians argued that Keynes's theory was the more general theory since it allowed for the aggregate economy to have multiple equilibria, which modern theoretical work concluded it would likely have unless one assumed them away with ad hoc assumptions.

Thus in the 1990s, a new truce is developing. While modern macro theorists agree that the mechanistic multiplier

models of Keynesian economics are far too simple, they are more and more accepting that, in its general approach, Keynesian economics (the interpretive, not the mechanistic brand) is the more general theory because it includes the effects of dynamic disequilibrium feedback on the equilibrium—what in mathematics is called path dependency. Almost all modern theoretical work—both Keynesian and Classical—is being directed at such dynamic issues, making the Keynesian/Classical distinction almost irrelevant when talking about theoretical work. What this development means is that in theory, what in this book I call Keynesian economics has been accepted as more general than what in this book I call Classical economics (although many modern Classical economists would argue that it is they, not the Keynesians, who led the modern theoretical charge into path dependency).

In the real world, however, many Keynesian economists now also agree that the dynamic interactions are so complicated that, in most circumstances—except for serious recession—Classical economics, with its focus on establishing a system of rules within an institutional environment, is the most relevant. So the new truce is precisely the reverse of the old truce. In the new truce, Keynesians have the theoretical laurels and Classicals have the policy relevance.

EXHIBIT 5 (a and b)   War Finance: Expansionary Fiscal Policy

During wars, government budget deficits have risen significantly. As they have, unemployment has fallen and GNP has risen enormously. You can see the effect in the table in (a), which presents the U.S. government budget deficit and unemployment rate during World War II. The graph in (b) shows that this is what would be predicted in the Keynesian model.

Year	GDP (billions of 1958 dollars)	Deficit (billions of dollars)	Unemployment Rate
1937	$ 90	$ −2.8	14.3%
1938	84	−1.0	19.0
1939	90	−2.9	17.2
1940	99	−2.7	14.6
1941	124	−4.8	9.9
1942	157	−19.4	4.7
1943	191	−53.8	1.9
1944	210	−46.1	1.2
1945	211	−45.0	1.9
1946	208	−18.2	3.9

(a)

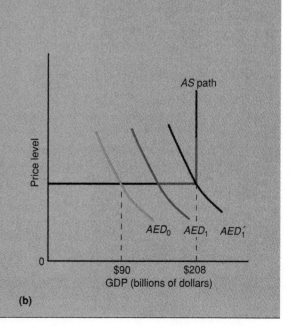

(b)

Source: *Historical Statistics of the United States; Colonial Times to 1970.*

path shown in red. During this period, the economy's potential output portion of the *AS* path was shifted out as far as anyone dared hope it could be. The economy responded by an enormous expansion. This expansion was also accompanied by a large increase in the money supply, so we must be careful about drawing too strong an inference about the effect of fiscal policy from the episode. (The importance of money will be discussed in the next chapter.)

A war can reduce unemployment, but it's not a good way to do so.

It is important to emphasize that in the 1990s the discussion of policy must go beyond fiscal policy. Politically, increasing the deficit is not an acceptable option.

Applying this simple Keynesian model is not going to give you an understanding of policy discussions today.

During World War II unemployment fell enormously, and the government issued many posters to get women to work. After the war. the government issued many posters to get women to give up their jobs for "their men." *Shaffer Archives.*

It might seem from the example of World War II, when the U.S. economy expanded sharply, that wars are good for the economy. They certainly do bring about expansionary policy, increase GDP, and decrease unemployment. But remember, GDP is *not* welfare and a decrease in unemployment is not necessarily good. In World War II people went without many goods; production of guns and bombs increased but production of butter decreased. Many people were killed or permanently disabled, which decreases unemployment but can hardly be called a good way to expand the economy and lower unemployment.

Fiscal Policy in the 1990s   As a second example of how economists think about fiscal policy, let's look into the beginning of the second millennium when the revenue that the U.S. government gets from social security taxes is predicted to be much higher than expenditures on benefits paid out to people in the form of Social Security (not including Medicare and Medicaid). Economists have pointed out that, because of this revenue in the absence of any change in policy, U.S. fiscal policy will likely turn highly contractionary. Using the simple Keynesian model, they have predicted that that surplus will slow down the economy and push it into a period of slow growth and possibly recession.

Now let's talk about a more recent example: 1993 and President Bill Clinton's policy proposal to keep the economy going—to increase income. Clinton, a Democrat, had generally Keynesian advisers. So what kind of policy do you think he advocated? If you said, "Increase the budget deficit to stimulate the economy," you've learned the model we discussed above, but you haven't been following what's been happening in the economy. Instead, from reading the newspaper you should know that he proposed a policy of *decreasing the deficit* to stimulate the economy! (The path by which a decrease in the deficit was to stimulate the economy was through the deficit's effect on the long-term interest rate and investment. A smaller deficit means less government borrowing which, as we will discuss later, means lower interest rates, which means higher investment.)

Actually, his policy was more complicated than that; he did propose to initially increase the budget deficit slightly to stimulate the economy, but Congress didn't go along. Moreover, like much in politics, a lot of his deficit reduction discussion was political rhetoric. But the lesson of this 1993 case is clear: applying the simple

Keynesian model we have been talking about in this chapter is not going to give you an understanding of policy discussions today.

But that does not mean you don't have to know the above models. It means you must know them better than did earlier students. As I've emphasized continually—to understand a model you must understand the limitations of the model and the assumptions that make it work, and determine whether those assumptions fit the reality. In the 1990s, it's clear that the assumptions of the simple model discussed above don't fit the facts of the 1990s. In the following pages I consider some reasons why.

PROBLEMS WITH FISCAL AND OTHER ACTIVIST KEYNESIAN POLICY

Keynesian fiscal policy, and activist government policy in general, sounds so easy— and in the model it is. If there's a contraction in the economy, the government runs an expansionary fiscal policy; if there's inflation, the government runs a contractionary fiscal policy, keeping the economy at the desired level of income.

In reality, that's not the way it is. A number of important problems arise, which makes the actual practice of fiscal policy difficult. These problems don't mean that the model is wrong; they simply mean that for fiscal policy to work, the policy conclusions drawn from the model must be modified to reflect the real-world problems. Let's consider how the reality might not fit the model. The model assumes:

1. Financing the deficit doesn't have any offsetting effect. In reality, it often does.
2. The government knows what the situation is (for instance, the size of the *mpe,* and other exogenous variables). In reality, the government must estimate them.
3. The government knows the economy's potential income level (the highest level of income that doesn't cause inflation). In reality, the government may not know what this level is.
4. The government has flexibility in changing spending and taxes. In reality, government cannot change them quickly.
5. The size of the government debt doesn't matter. In reality, the size of the government debt often does matter.
6. Fiscal policy doesn't negatively affect other government goals. In reality, it often does.

Let's consider each a bit further.

5 Six assumptions of the model that could lead to problems with fiscal policy are:
1. Financing the deficit doesn't have any offsetting effects.
2. The government knows what the situation is.
3. The government knows the economy's potential income level.
4. The government has flexibility in changing spending and taxes.
5. The size of the government debt doesn't matter.
6. Fiscal policy doesn't negatively affect other government goals.

Financing the Deficit Doesn't Have Offsetting Effects

One of the most important limitations of the Keynesian model is that it assumes that financing the deficit has no offsetting effects on income. Classicals argue that that is not the case. They argue that the government financing of deficit spending will offset the deficit's expansionary effect.

Classical economists say that the Keynesian model assumes savings and investment are unequal, and that the government can increase its expenditures without at the same time causing a decrease in private expenditures. Classical economists object to that assumption. They believe the interest rate equilibrates savings and investment. They argue that when the government borrows to finance the deficit, that borrowing will increase interest rates and crowd out private investment.

Interest rate **crowding out**—*the offsetting of a change in government expenditures by a change in private expenditures in the opposite direction*—occurs as follows: When the government runs a deficit, it must sell bonds (that is, it must borrow) to finance that deficit. To get people to buy and hold the bonds, the government must make them attractive. That means the interest rate the bonds pay must be higher than it otherwise would have been. This tends to push up the interest rate in the economy, which makes it more expensive for private businesses to borrow, so they reduce their

For a real-world example of the difficulties of implementing fiscal policy see Chapter 11 of *Case Studies in Macroeconomics.*

Interest rate crowding out reduces the effect of increases in government expenditures.

EXHIBIT 6 (a, b, and c)   A Schematic Representation of Crowding Out and Partial Crowding Out

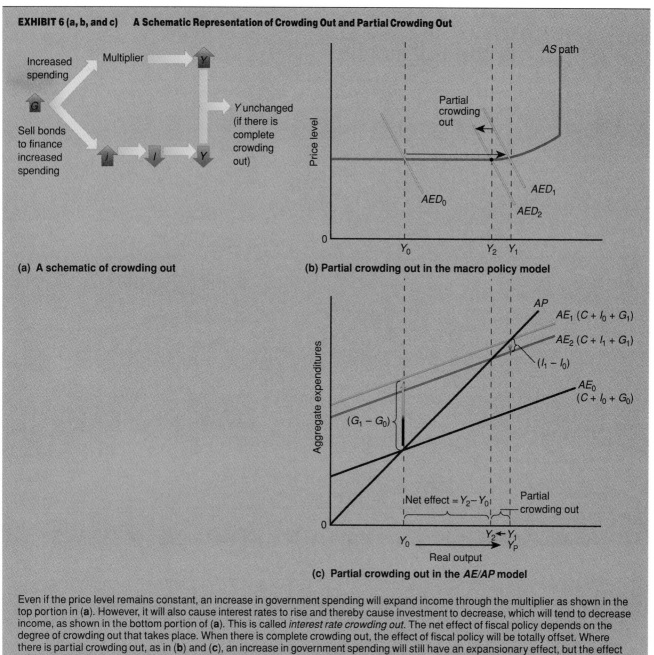

(a) A schematic of crowding out

(b) Partial crowding out in the macro policy model

(c) Partial crowding out in the AE/AP model

Even if the price level remains constant, an increase in government spending will expand income through the multiplier as shown in the top portion in (**a**). However, it will also cause interest rates to rise and thereby cause investment to decrease, which will tend to decrease income, as shown in the bottom portion of (**a**). This is called *interest rate crowding out*. The net effect of fiscal policy depends on the degree of crowding out that takes place. When there is complete crowding out, the effect of fiscal policy will be totally offset. Where there is partial crowding out, as in (**b**) and (**c**), an increase in government spending will still have an expansionary effect, but the effect will be smaller than it otherwise would have been.

borrowing and their investment. That private investment is crowded out by expansionary fiscal policy. Hence the name "crowding out." Increased government spending crowds out private spending.

Exhibit 6(a) shows the interconnection. The top arrows represent the direct effect of increased spending. The bottom arrows represent the effects of financing that increased spending. Each set of arrows works in the opposite direction from the other set. Crowding out is shown graphically in the macro policy model in Exhibit 6(b) and in the *AE/AP* model in Exhibit 6(c). Income in the economy is Y_0 and government has decided to expand that income to Y_1 by increasing its spending by ΔG (from G_0 to G_1).

If financing were not an issue, expansionary fiscal policy would shift up the *AED* curve by a multiple of the increase in government spending, increasing income from Y_0 to Y_1. Financing the deficit, however, increases interest rates and decreases investment by ΔI, which shifts the *AED* curve back to AED_2. Income falls back to Y_2.

Because of crowding out, the net expansionary effect of fiscal policy is much smaller than it otherwise would have been. Some Classicals argue that crowding out could totally offset the expansionary effect of fiscal policy, so the net effect is zero, or even negative, since they consider private spending more productive than government spending.

The crowding out effect also works in reverse on contractionary fiscal policy. Say the government runs a surplus. That surplus will slow the economy via the multiplier effect. But it also means the Treasury can buy back some of its outstanding bonds, which will have a tendency to push bond prices up and interest rates down. Lower interest rates will stimulate investment which, in turn, will have an offsetting expansionary effect on the economy. So when we include financing the deficit in our consideration of fiscal policy, the net multiplier effect is reduced.

How large this financing offset to fiscal policy will be is a matter of debate. Classicals see the crowding out effect as relatively large, in many cases almost completely negating the effect of expansionary fiscal policy. Keynesians see it as relatively small, as long as the economy is in a recession or operating below its potential income level. Some Keynesians even argue that often the crowding out will be offset by **crowding in**—*positive effects of government spending on other components of spending.* Where there is crowding in, the increased government spending will cause investment to increase as businesses prepare to meet the government's demand for goods.

The empirical evidence is mixed and has not resolved the debate. Both sides see some crowding out occurring as the debt is financed by selling bonds. The closer to the potential income level the economy is, the more crowding out is likely to occur.

6 Crowding out is the offsetting effect on private expenditures caused by the government's sale of bonds to finance expansionary fiscal policy.

Q–7: Demonstrate graphically what would happen if government expenditures policy stimulated private investment.

All our examples' numbers were chosen arbitrarily. In reality, the numbers used in the model must be estimated since data upon which estimates can be made aren't always available. Most economic data are published quarterly, and it usually takes six to nine months of data to indicate, with any degree of confidence, the state of the economy and which way it is heading. Thus, we could be halfway into a recession before we even knew it was happening. (Data are already three months old when published; then we need two or three quarters of such data before they compose a useful body of information to work with.)

In an attempt to deal with this problem, the government relies on large macroeconomic models and leading indicators to predict what the economy will be like six months or a year from now. As part of the input to these complex models, the government must predict economic factors that determine the size of the multiplier. These predictions are imprecise so the forecasts are imprecise. Economic forecasting is still an art, not a science.

Economists' data problems limit the use of fiscal policy for fine tuning. There's little sense in recommending expansionary or contractionary policy until you know what policy is called for.

Knowing What the Situation Is

I like to draw a graph of a business cycle downturn, and on the horizontal axis, show the lags involved as the government tries to react with fiscal policy. The recognition lag, the policy design and implementation lags, and the policy effect lag can be shown along the horizontal axis. This tool helps students to visualize an important problem with fiscal policy tools.

This problem of not knowing the level of potential income is related to the problem we just discussed. The target level of employment and the potential level of income are not easy concepts to define. At one time it was thought 3 percent unemployment meant full employment. Some time later it was generally thought 6 percent unemployment meant full employment. About that time economists stopped calling the potential level of income the *full-employment* level of income.

Any variation in potential income can make an enormous difference in the policy prescription that could be recommended. To see how big a difference, let's translate a 1 percent change in unemployment into a change in income. According to **Okun's law** *(the general rule of thumb economists use to translate changes in the unemployment rate into changes in income),* a 1 percentage point fall in the unemployment rate is associated with a 2.5 percent increase in income. Thus, in 1997 with income at about $7 trillion, a 1 percent fall in the unemployment rate would have increased income $175 billion.

Knowing the Level of Potential Income

Okun's law   A general rule of thumb economists use to translate the unemployment rate into changes in income. A 1 percentage point fall in the unemployment rate is associated with a 2.5 percent increase in income.

The CBO Report—The Economic and Budget Outlook is one of the many government publications that discusses macroeconomic policy options.

Differences in estimates of potential income often lead to different policy recommendations.

In most cases the U.S. economy is in an ambiguous state where some economists are calling for expansionary policy and others are calling for contractionary policy.

Q–8: Why don't economists have an accurate measure of potential income?

Expenditures on war-related products have been a major source of government expenditures in the past 60 years. Despite the end of the Cold War in the early 1990s these expenditures are proving hard to cut. *UPI/Bettmann.*

Now let's say one economist believes 6 percent is the long-run achievable target unemployment level, while another believes it's 4.5 percent. That's a 1.5 percentage point difference. Since a 1 percent decrease in the unemployment rate means an increase of about $175 billion in national income, their views of the income level we should target differ by over $263 billion (1.5 × $175 = $263). Yet both views are reasonable. Looking at the same economy (the same data), one economist may call for expansionary fiscal policy while the other may call for contractionary fiscal policy.

In practice, differences in estimates of potential income often lead to different policy recommendations. Empirical estimates suggest that the size of the multiplier is somewhere between 1.5 and 2.5. Let's say it's 2.5. That means autonomous expenditures must be predicted to shift either up or down by more than $105 billion before an economist who believes the target unemployment rate is 4.5 percent would agree in policy recommendation with an economist who believes the rate is 6 percent. Since almost all fluctuations in autonomous investment and autonomous consumption are less than this amount, there's no generally agreed-upon policy prescription for most fluctuations. Some economists will call for expansionary policy; some will call for contractionary policy; and the government decision makers won't have any clear-cut policy to follow.

You might wonder why the range of potential income estimates is so large. Why not simply see whether the economy has inflation at the existing unemployment and income levels? Would that it were so easy. Inflation is a complicated process. Seeds of inflation are often sown years before inflation results. The main problem is that establishing a close link between the level of economic activity and inflation is a complicated statistical challenge to economists, one that has not yet been satisfactorily met. That leads to enormous debate as to what the causes are.

Almost all economists believe that outside some range (perhaps 3.5 percent unemployment on the low side and 10 percent on the high side), too much spending causes inflation and too little spending causes a recession. That 3.5 to 10 percent range is so large that in most cases the U.S. economy is in an ambiguous state where some economists are calling for expansionary policy and others are calling for contractionary policy.

Once the economy reaches the edge of the range or falls outside it, the economists' policy prescription becomes clearer. For example, in the Depression, when this Keynesian model was developed, unemployment was 25 percent—well outside the range. Should the economy ever go into such a depression again, economists' policy prescriptions will be clear. The call will be for expansionary fiscal policy. Most times

the economy is within the ambiguous range so there are disagreements among economists.

For argument's sake, let's say economists agree that contractionary policy is needed and that's what they advise the government. Will the government implement it? And, if so, will it implement contractionary fiscal policy at the right time? The answer to both questions is: probably not. There are also problems with implementing economists' calls for expansionary fiscal policy. Even if economists are unanimous in calling for expansionary fiscal policy, putting fiscal policy in place takes time and has serious implementation problems.

Numerous political and institutional realities in the United States today make it a difficult task to implement fiscal policy. Government spending and taxes cannot be changed instantaneously. New taxes and new spending must be legislated. It takes time for the government to pass a bill. Politicians face intense political pressures; their other goals may conflict with the goals of fiscal policy. For example, few members of Congress who hope to be reelected would vote to raise taxes in an election year. Similarly, few members would vote to slash defense spending when military contractors are a major source of employment in their districts, even when there's little to defend against. Squabbles between Congress and the president may delay initiating appropriate fiscal policy for months, even years. By the time the fiscal policy is implemented, what may have once been the right fiscal policy may have ceased to be right, and some other policy may have become right.

Imagine trying to steer a car at 60 miles an hour when there's a five-second delay between the time you turn the steering wheel and the time the car's wheels turn. Imagining that situation will give you a good sense of how fiscal policy works in the real world.

There is no inherent reason why the adoption of Keynesian policies should have caused the government to run deficits year after year and hence to incur ever-increasing debt—accumulated deficits less accumulated surpluses. Keynesian policy is consistent with running deficits some years and surpluses other years. In practice, the introduction of Keynesian policy has been accompanied by many deficits and few surpluses, and by a large increase in government debt. If that increase in government debt hurts the economy, one can oppose Keynesian policy, even if one believes that policy might otherwise be beneficial.

There are two reasons why Keynesian policy has led to an increase in government debt. First, early Keynesian economists favored large increases in government spending as well as favoring the government's using fiscal policy. These early Keynesians employed the Keynesian economic model to justify increasing spending without increasing taxes. A second reason is political. Politically it's much easier for government to increase spending and decrease taxes than to decrease spending and increase taxes. Due to political pressure, expansionary fiscal policy has predominated over contractionary fiscal policy.

Whether debt is a problem is an important and complicated issue as we'll see in a later chapter devoted entirely to the question. For now, all you need remember is that if one believes that the debt is harmful, then there might be a reason not to conduct expansionary fiscal policy, even when the model calls for it.

An economy has many goals; achieving potential income is only one of those goals. So it's not surprising that those goals often conflict. In an earlier example in this chapter, we saw those conflicts. When the government ran expansionary fiscal policy, the balance of trade deficit grew. As the economy expands and income rises, exports remain constant but imports rise. If a nation's international considerations do not allow a balance of trade deficit to become larger, as is true in many countries, those governments cannot run expansionary fiscal policies—unless they can somehow prevent this balance of trade deficit from becoming larger.

The Government's Flexibility in Changing Taxes and Spending

The fiscal policy steering wheel can be insufficient to prevent the economy from crashing.

Draw a pie chart showing the broad categories of federal government spending, and then cross out those that represent long-term spending projects, contractual commitments, or entitlements.

Size of the Government Debt Doesn't Matter

Some professors like to assign the chapter on deficits and debt immediately following this chapter. Doing so allows them to expand on these issues enormously.

Fiscal Policy Doesn't Negatively Affect Other Government Goals

One time economists were united in their views on appropriate fiscal policy was during the Vietnam War, from the early 1960s until 1975, when the economy was pushed to its limits. About 1965, President Lyndon B. Johnson's economic advisers started to argue strongly that a tax increase was needed to slow the economy and decrease inflationary pressures. President Johnson wouldn't hear of it. He felt a tax increase would be political suicide. Finally in mid-1968, after Johnson had decided not to run for reelection, a temporary income tax increase was passed. By then, however, many economists felt that the seeds of the 1970s inflation had already been sown.

Fiscal Policy in Practice: Summary of the Problems

Fiscal policy is a sledgehammer, not an instrument for fine tuning.

Building Keynesian Policies into Institutions

7 An automatic stabilizer is any government program or policy that will counteract the business cycle without any new government action.

Automatic stabilizers do not reverse the direction of economic activity. That is, they do not turn recessions into recovery or expansions into recessions. Instead, they reduce the amplitude of the underlying cycle.

Q–9: What effect do automatic stabilizers have on the size of the multiplier?

So where do these six problems leave fiscal policy? While they don't eliminate its usefulness, they severely restrict it. Fiscal policy is a sledgehammer, not an instrument for fine tuning. When the economy goes into a depression, the appropriate fiscal policy is clear. Similarly when the economy has a hyperinflation, the appropriate policy is clear. But in less extreme cases, there will be debate on what the appropriate fiscal policy is—a debate economic theory can't answer conclusively.

Economists quickly recognized the political problems with instituting direct counter-cyclical fiscal policy. To avoid these problems they suggested policies that built fiscal policy into U.S. institutions so that it would be put into effect without any political decisions being necessary. They called a built-in fiscal policy an **automatic stabilizer,** which is *any government program or policy that will counteract the business cycle without any new government action.* Automatic stabilizers include welfare payments, unemployment insurance, and the income tax system.

To see how automatic stabilizers work, consider the unemployment insurance system. When the economy is slowing down or is in a recession, the unemployment rate will rise. When people lose their jobs, they will reduce their consumption, starting the multiplier process, which decreases income. Unemployment insurance immediately helps offset the decrease in individuals' incomes as the government pays benefits to the unemployed. Thus, the budget deficit increases, and part of the fall in income is stopped without any explicit act by the government. Automatic stabilizers also work in reverse. When income increases, they decrease the size of the deficit.

Another automatic stabilizer is our income tax system. Earlier in this chapter I said that tax revenue fluctuates as income fluctuates and that this makes the deficit hard to predict. When the economy expands unexpectedly, the budget deficit is lower than originally expected; when the economy contracts unexpectedly, the budget deficit is higher than expected. Let's go through the reasoning why. When the economy is strong, people have more income and thus pay higher taxes. This increase in tax revenue reduces consumption expenditures from what they would have been, and moderates the economy's growth. When the economy goes into a recession, the opposite occurs.

Automatic stabilizers may seem like the solution to the economic woes we have discussed, but they, too, have their shortcomings. One problem is that when the economy is first starting to climb out of a recession, automatic stabilizers will slow the process, rather than help it along, for the same reason they slow the contractionary process. As income increases, automatic stabilizers increase government taxes and decrease government spending, and as they do, the discretionary policy's expansionary effects are decreased.

Despite these problems, most Keynesians believe automatic stabilizers have played an important role in reducing fluctuations in our economy. They point to the kind of data we see in Exhibit 7, which they say show a significant decrease in fluctuations in the economy. Other economists aren't so sure; they argue the apparent decrease in fluctuations is an optical illusion. As usual, economic data are sufficiently ambiguous to give both sides strong arguments. The jury is still out.

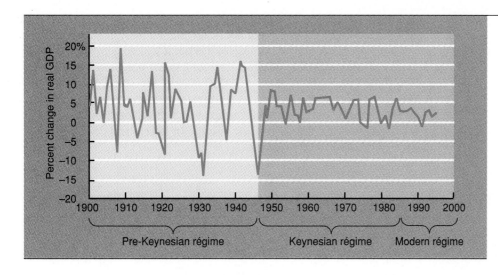

EXHIBIT 7   Decrease in Fluctuations in the Economy

One of the arguments in favor of Keynesian economics is that since it was introduced into the U.S. economy, fluctuations in the economy have decreased.

Source: Federal Reserve Historical Charts and Economic Report of the President. (http://www.doc.gov)

By now you should be able to think in terms of the Keynesian model and see how disequilibria between aggregate production and aggregate expenditures can be resolved by adjustments in aggregate income. But beware. The Keynesian model is only a model. It's a tool, a crutch, to help you see certain relationships. It does so by obscuring others, including interest rate adjustment, price level adjustment, and supply incentive effects.

Consideration of these aspects led to significant changes in macroeconomic thinking over the years. In the 1970s Classical economics rose like a phoenix from the ashes and reemerged. Modern Classical economists challenged the way Keynesian economists thought about expansionary effects of fiscal policy. They won many converts and modified the presentation of Keynesian economics so that it focuses on dynamic adjustment and is no longer presented mechanistically. The modern Classical economists argue that expectations of policy can change the dynamic adjustment process, and that any simple dynamic adjustment models are unlikely to describe the aggregate economy.

This chapter should have given you a good sense of how aggregate demand management is viewed by both Keynesians and Classicals. It should also have given you a good sense of the limitations of demand management policy—the foundation of traditional macro policy. Those limitations should not be downplayed, nor should they lead one to believe that traditional macro policy is dead. There are ongoing debates.

Most economists agree that demand management policies are useful for keeping the economy out of a serious recession and hyperinflationary boom (range A and range C of the aggregate supply path). Traditional macro policies are used and garner significant support when these ranges are reached. But that means that the economy is almost always in the intermediate range (range B) where there is significant debate about where within that range the target level of potential output is.

The problem is that there are no signposts on the economy saying, "This is the economy's potential income, and this is the appropriate target unemployment." Thus at the 1994 American Economic Association meeting you could have seen two former presidents of the American Economic Association, William Vickrey and Robert Eisner, arguing that the economy was in the Keynesian range, and the U.S. target unemployment rate should have been 3.5 percent, not the 6 percent it was thought to be by most other economists. That's the old-time Keynesian position. It places the target level of potential income closer to high-level potential output. The rise in the price level that might occur is a minor irritant, but not a serious problem.

Looking at the same reality, you could have some modern Classical economists, such as Robert Barro, arguing that even if the unemployment rate is 10 percent, if there is any inflation at all, it is likely to be a portent of accelerating inflation to come.

Fiscal Policy in Perspective

Fiscal policy in the 1990s is a good opportunity for class discussion. Perhaps you can have your students clip some articles about the Balanced Budget Amendment from 1996 and 1997.

THE PRACTICE OF FISCAL POLICY IN THE 1990s

Q–10: In what range is the economy operating most of the time?

William Vickrey won the Nobel prize in Economics in 1996; he argued that any unemployment rate above 3.5 percent is immoral.

The economy is generally in an ambiguous range; in this range macro policy is an art, not a science.

It sees a rise in the price level as a signal that the economy is in the "calm before the storm" range. Accelerating inflation might not occur immediately, but that accelerating inflation is simply lagging behind because of inertia; it will come.

The majority of the profession places the target level of potential income somewhere between these two extreme ranges. Unfortunately, the science of economics does not present a policy guide. In trying to estimate the correct potential level of output to aim for we enter the art of economics, which involves choosing between conflicting goals when one is not sure of the results. In later chapters I will discuss the dilemma posed by these conflicting goals.

CHAPTER SUMMARY

- Aggregate demand management policy attempts to influence the level of output in the economy by influencing aggregate demand and relying on the multiplier to expand any policy-induced change in aggregate demand.
- Fiscal policy—the change in government spending or taxes—works by providing a deliberate countershock to offset unexpected shocks to the economy.
- Expansionary fiscal policy is represented graphically as an upward shift of the aggregate expenditures curve.
- Contractionary fiscal policy is represented graphically as a downward shift of the aggregate expenditures curve.
- The effect of fiscal policy can be determined by using the Keynesian model.
- The size of the government deficit or surplus influences the level of income in the economy, but is also influenced by it.

- The size of the trade balance (net exports) influences the level of income in the economy but is also influenced by it.
- Fiscal policy is affected by the following problems, among others:
    1. Lack of knowledge of what policy is called for.
    2. Government's inability to respond quickly enough.
    3. Government debt.
    4. Interest rate crowding out.
- Keynesian fiscal policy is now built into U.S. economic institutions through automatic stabilizers.
- Aggregate demand management policies are most effective in the Keynesian range of the economy—when the economy is significantly below its potential income.

KEY TERMS

aggregate demand (expenditure) management policy *(307)*
automatic stabilizer *(328)*
countercyclical fiscal policy *(314)*
crowding in *(325)*
crowding out *(323)*

exchange rate policy *(318)*
export-led growth policies *(317)*
fine tuning *(314)*
fiscal policy *(307)*
inflationary gap *(314)*
Okun's law *(325)*

passive deficit *(319)*
recessionary gap *(311)*
Rosy Scenario policy *(316)*
structural deficit *(319)*

QUESTIONS FOR THOUGHT AND REVIEW

The number after each question represents the estimated degree of critical thinking required. (1 = almost none; 10 = deep thought.)

1. Explain how Franklin D. Roosevelt's statement, "We have nothing to fear but fear itself," pertains to macroeconomic policy. *(4)*

2. Congratulations! You've just been appointed chairman of the Council of Economic Advisers in Textland. The *mpe* is .8. There is a recessionary gap of $400, which the government wants to eliminate by changing expenditures. What policy would you suggest? *(4)*

3. Your research assistant comes running in and tells you that instead of changing expenditures, the government wants to achieve the same result by decreasing taxes. What policy would you recommend now? (Requires reading and using the math in Appendix A of Chapter 11.) *(4)*

4. Your research assistant has a worried look on her face. "What's the problem?" you ask. "I goofed," she confesses. "I thought taxes were exogenous when actually there's a marginal tax rate of .1." Before she can utter another word, you say, "No problem. I'll simply recalculate my answers to Questions 2 and 3 and change them before I send them in." What are your corrected answers? (Requires reading Appendix A of Chapter 11.) *(5)*

5. She still has a pained expression. "What's wrong?" you ask. "You didn't let me finish," she says. "Not only was there a marginal tax rate of .1; there's also a marginal propensity to import of .2." Again you interrupt to make sure she doesn't feel guilty. Again you say, "No problem," and recalculate your answers to Questions 2 and 3 to account for the new information. What are your new answers? (Requires reading Appendix A of Chapter 11.) *(5)*

6. That pained look is still there, but this time you don't interrupt. You let her finish. She says, "And they want to see the answers graphically." You do the right thing. *(4)*

7. Two economists are debating whether the normal rate of unemployment is 4 or 6 percent. Mr. A believes it's 4 percent; Ms. B believes it's 6 percent. One says the structural deficit is $40 billion; the other says it is $20 billion. Which one says which? Why? *(5)*

8. What is the current state of U.S. fiscal policy? Would you advise the United States to change its fiscal policy? Why? *(7)*

9. If interest rates have no effect on investment, what percentage of crowding out will there be? *(5)*

10. A country has a balance of trade deficit and a recessionary gap. Advise it how to eliminate both. *(9)*

11. When Professor Robert Gordon lowered his estimate of the target unemployment rate from 6 percent to 5.5 percent in early 1995, he quipped, "I've just created 600,000 jobs."

    a. What events in the 1990s most likely motivated his revision of the target unemployment rate?

    b. Show the effect this revision would have on the macro policy model.

    c. The unemployment rate at the time of the revision was 5.5 percent. Income was $7.3 trillion. Within 18 months the unemployment rate had fallen to 5 percent without signs of accelerating inflation. How much higher would the level of potential income have been in 1995 if the target unemployment rate were 5 percent rather than 5.5 percent?

PROBLEMS AND EXERCISES

1. Congratulations! You've just been appointed economic adviser to Easyland. You go to your first board meeting and are asked the following questions. What are the answers you would give?

   a. Why does cutting taxes by $100 have a smaller effect on GDP than increasing expenditures by $100?

   b. If they cut taxes and want a neutral fiscal policy, what should they do with their trade policy?

   c. Why does the trade deficit generally increase as the economy improves?

   d. How does your answer to c change if all world economies are moving together?

2. Congratulations! You've just been appointed economic adviser to Dreamland. The president wants your advice on how to reduce unemployment from 8 to 6 percent. Income is $40,000, and the *mpe* is .4.

   a. Advise her.

   b. She wants to know what would happen to her formerly balanced budget if she follows your advice. You naturally tell her.

   c. Now she wants to know what will happen to her formerly zero trade deficit. You tell her.

   d. Hearing your answers, she tells you that your policy is unacceptable. She wants to reduce unemployment and keep both the trade and the government budget in balance. How do you respond?

3. Condolences. You've been fired from your job in Dreamland, but you found another job in neighboring Fantasyland. Its economy is almost the same as Dreamland's but you must rely on your research assistant for the specific numbers. He says income is $50,000, *mpe* is .75, and the president wants to lower unemployment from 8 to 6 percent.

   a. Advise him.

   b. Your research assistant comes in and says "Sorry, I meant that the *mpe* is .66." You redo your calculations.

   c. You're just about to see the president when your research assistant comes running, saying "Sorry, sorry, I meant that the *mpe* is .5." Redo your calculations.

4. President Clinton's policy in 1993 was designed to reduce the deficit but increase employment.

   a. Why would such a policy not fit well in the Keynesian model presented in this chapter?

   b. Explain in words how such a policy might achieve the desired effect.

   c. Graphically demonstrate your answer in b.

   d. What data would you look at to see if your explanations in b and c are appropriate?

5. Explain the following observations in terms of the Keynesian model.

   a. In the late 1990s, the United States was pushing Japan to increase its budget deficit.

   b. In the late 1990s, the United States was pushing Japan to decrease its trade surplus.

   c. In the late 1990s, unemployment in Europe exceeded 10 percent but few economists were pushing for an increase in European governments' budget deficits.

   d. When running for reelection most presidents increase government spending programs.

   e. A maxim in politics is that if you are going to increase taxes, the time to do it is right after your election, when reelection is far off.

ANSWERS TO MARGIN QUESTIONS

1. Each individual's spending primarily affects others' income, not their own. The feedback effects on their own income are so small that they do not take them into account. Only coordinated effort, in which many people increase their spending simultaneously, will create a significant multiplier effect. Thus people's spending decision is a type of externality. *(309)*

2. As you can see, contractionary fiscal policy shifts aggregate expenditures to the left. The multiplier then takes over to shift the *AED* curve back by a multiple of the initial shift in aggregate expenditures. Income falls by a multiple of the initial shift. *(312)*

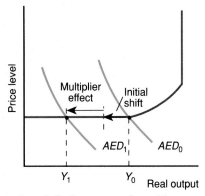

3. Since there is an inflationary gap, I would recommend contractionary fiscal policy. Since the multiplier is 1.5 (given the marginal propensity to expend of .33), I would recommend decreasing government spending by $66. *(314)*

4. Expectations play a central role in both spending and production decisions. If positive talk about the economy can influence expectations, it may be possible to "talk" an economy into a boom by increasing expenditures, or productivity, or both. *(316)*

5. According to the Keynesian model, a fall in the value of the dollar should increase exports, which would have a multiplied positive effect on income. *(318)*

6. Since the economy is at its potential income, its passive deficit is zero. All of its budget deficit is a structural deficit. *(320)*

7. If government spending stimulated private spending, the phenomenon of what might be called "crowding in" might occur. The increase in government spending would shift the *AE* curve up from AE_0 to AE_1 as in the diagram below. The resulting shift in income would cause a further shift up in investment, shifting the aggregate expenditure curve up further to AE_2. Income would increase from Y_0 to Y_2—by more than what the simple Keynesian model would predict. *(325)*

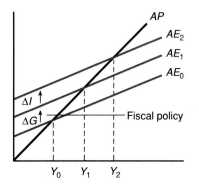

8. Potential income is not a measurable number. It is a conceptual number that must be estimated based upon observable information about such phenomena as inflation, productivity, and unemployment. Estimating potential income is a challenge. *(326)*

9. Automatic stabilizers tend to decrease the size of the multiplier, decreasing the fluctuations in the economy. *(328)*

10. Most of the time the economy is operating in the intermediate range where expansions in aggregate expenditures cause both an increase in real output and an increase in the price level. *(329)*

Thirteen

Monetary Policy and the Debate about Macro Policy

There have been three great inventions since the beginning of time: fire, the wheel and central banking.

~ Will Rogers

After reading this chapter, you should be able to:

1 Define monetary policy.

2 Summarize the structure and duties of the Fed.

3 List the three tools of monetary policy and explain how they work.

4 Define the Federal funds rate and discuss how the Fed uses it as an intermediate target.

5 Explain how monetary policy works in the Keynesian model.

6 Explain how monetary policy works in the Classical model.

7 List five problems often encountered in conducting monetary policy.

Monetary policy is *a policy of influencing the economy through changes in the banking system's reserves that influences the money supply and credit availability in the economy.* Monetary policy is one of the two main traditional macroeconomic tools (the other is fiscal policy) by which government attempts to control the aggregate economy. Unlike fiscal policy, which is controlled by the government directly, monetary policy is controlled by the central bank in the United States, the Fed. We'll discuss the Fed in more detail later in this chapter when we discuss the specific tools through which monetary policy is conducted. For now let me give you a sense of monetary policy and how it fits into our macro model.

Our familiar macro policy model is shown in Exhibit 1, and I have divided the aggregate supply path into three separate sections—range A, range B, and range C. What is the effect of monetary policy in the macro policy model? Expansionary monetary policy shifts the *AED* curve out; contractionary monetary policy shifts it in. As you can see, what effect contractionary or expansionary monetary policy will have on equilibrium income and the price level depends on the shape of the *AS* path. In range A, where the *AS* path is flat, real income will rise with expansionary monetary policy and decline with contractionary monetary policy. The price level is unaffected. In range C, where the *AS* path is vertical, real income does not change; the effect is on the price level and inflation. In range B, the intermediate range, the effects of monetary policy are divided between real income and the price level. Thus, the shape

1 Monetary policy is a policy that influences the economy through changes in the money supply and available credit.

In the United States, the Central Bank is the Fed, and much of this chapter is about its structure. But the Fed is only one of many Central Banks. Let's briefly introduce you to some of the others.

Bundesbank In Germany, the Central Bank is called the *Bundesbank*. It has a reputation as a fierce inflation fighter, in large part because of the historical legacy of the German hyperinflation of the late 1920s and early 1930s. To fight inflation in the mid-1990s, it maintained high interest rates relative to the rest of the world, causing international monetary disruption, which will be discussed in a later chapter. It has a much higher reserve requirement than does the Fed.

The Bank of England The Bank of England is sometimes called the Old Lady of Threadneedle Street (because it's located on that street, and the British like such quaint characterizations). It does not use a required reserve mechanism. Instead, individual banks determine their own needed reserves, so any reserves they have would, in a sense, be excess reserves. Needless to say, bank reserves are much lower in England than they are in Germany.

How does the Old Lady control the money supply? With the equivalent of open market operations and with what might

be called "tea control." Since there are only a few large banks in England, the Old Lady simply passes on the word at tea as to which direction she thinks the money supply should be going. Alas for sentimentalists, "tea control" is fading in England, as are many of the quaint English ways.

The Bank of Japan Of the three banks I discuss here, the Bank of Japan is most similar to the Fed. It uses primarily open market operations to control the money supply. Reserve requirements are similar to the Fed's, but because it allows banks a longer period in which to do their averaging, and Japan does not have the many small banks that the United States does—banks which often hold excess reserves—excess reserves are much lower in Japan than in the United States. Until the early 1990s the Bank of Japan held the Japanese interest rate far below the world rate, which caused an international outflow of savings and a corresponding trade surplus. In 1990 the Japanese interest rate has increased substantially, in part due to the actions of the Bank of Japan, but by the mid-1990s the Japanese interest rate was once again very low.

Clearly, there's more to be said about each of these central banks, but this brief introduction should give you a sense of both the similarities and the diversities among the central banks of the world.

EXHIBIT 1   Monetary Policy and the Macro Policy Model

The effect of monetary policy on the economy can be shown with the macro policy model. Expansionary monetary policy shifts the *AED* curve to the right. Contractionary monetary policy shifts the *AED* curve to the left. The effect on the price level depends upon the shape of the *AS* path. If there is underlying inflation and the price level is interpreted relative to expected inflation, contractionary monetary policy will lead to disinflation.

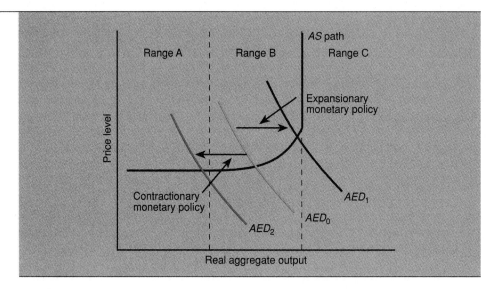

The effect of monetary policy depends on what range of the AS path the economy is in.

of the *AS* path is central to the effect one believes monetary policy will have on the economy.

As a review of previous chapters, see if you can answer the following: According to Classicals and Keynesians, what is the shape of the *AS* path and what effect on the economy does that shape tell you monetary policy will have on the price level and real income? If you said Classicals believe that the *AS* path is close to vertical and monetary policy mainly affects the price level, and Keynesians tend to believe that the *AS* curve is flat and that monetary policy has significant effects on real income, you've been doing your reading. If you didn't say that, you're in trouble, and you should think about spending more time studying.

You should also know that the Classical/Keynesian distinction is too sharp, and that a majority of economists are somewhere between the two—they see the economy as generally in the middle range, which means the effects of monetary policy are on both real output and price level. Let's now proceed to some specifics of how monetary policy shifts the *AED* curve.

We start by considering central banks—the institutions that conduct monetary policy.

A **central bank** is *a type of bankers' bank*. It conducts monetary policy and acts as a financial adviser for the government. If banks need to borrow money, they go to the central bank, just as when you need to borrow money, you go to a neighborhood bank. If there's a financial panic and a run on banks, the central bank is there to make loans to the banks until the panic goes away. Since its IOUs are cash, simply by issuing an IOU it can create money. It is this ability to create money that gives the central bank the power to control monetary policy. A central bank's duties also include advising government with its financial affairs. A central bank serves as a financial adviser to government. As is often the case with financial advisers, the government sometimes doesn't like the advice and doesn't follow it.

In many countries, such as Great Britain, the central bank is a part of their government, just as this country's Department of the Treasury and the Department of Commerce are part of the U.S. government. In the United States the central bank is not part of the government in the same way it is in some European countries.

Because of political infighting about how much autonomy the central bank should have in controlling the economy, the Federal Reserve Bank was created as a semiautonomous organization. The bank is privately owned by the member banks. However, member banks have few privileges of ownership. For example, the Board of Governors of the Federal Reserve is appointed by the U.S. president, not by the owners. Also, almost all the profits of the Fed go to the government, not to the owners. In short, the Fed is owned by the member banks in form only. In practice the Fed is an agency of the U.S. federal government.

Although it is an agency of the federal government, the Fed has much more independence than most agencies. One reason is that creating money is profitable, and while it returns its income after expenses to Congress, it is not dependent on Congress for appropriations. A second reason is that once appointed for a term of 14 years, Fed governors cannot be removed from office, nor can they be reappointed. Because they cannot be removed and because they have little incentive to try to get reappointed, they feel little political pressure. If the president doesn't like what they do, tough luck, until their appointments expire or one of them decides to resign or retire.

There are seven Governors of the Federal Reserve Bank. In practice, since pay at the Federal Reserve is much lower than at private banks and consulting firms, many appointees stay less than 14 years. When your job resumé includes "Governor of the Federal Reserve," private organizations are eager to hire you and pay you five or six times as much as you earned at the Fed. This means that none of the Federal Reserve Governors is hard up for a job. So while they are at the Federal Reserve, they can pretty much follow the policies they believe are best without being concerned about political retaliation, even if their terms aren't for life.

The president appoints one of the seven members to be chairman of the Board of Governors for a four-year term. The chairman has enormous influence and power, and is often called the second-most-powerful person in the United States. This is a bit of an exaggeration, but the chairman's statements are more widely reported in the financial press than any other government official's.

The Fed's general structure reflects its political history. Exhibit 2 demonstrates that structure. Notice in Exhibit 2(a) that most component banks are in the East and Midwest. The South and West have only three banks: Atlanta, Dallas, and San

---

While I make a sharp distinction between Keynesian and Classical views, you should recognize that most economists are somewhere between the two.

Video Series, Economics U$A: The Federal Reserve System, Segment 9.1

DUTIES AND STRUCTURE OF THE FED

It is the bank's ability to create money that gives the central bank the power to control monetary policy.

Historical Influences in the Federal Reserve Bank's Structure

Structure of the Fed

2a The Fed is a semiautonomous organization composed of 12 regional banks. It is run by the Board of Governors.

The Fed is a semiautonomous organization.

I like to talk about the Second Bank of the United States and the conflict between Andrew Jackson and Nicholas Biddle that led to its demise. I argue that this conflict was at the root of the decision to structure the Fed as a decentralized central banking system.

Q–1: Who appoints the chairman of the Board of Governors of the Federal Reserve System?

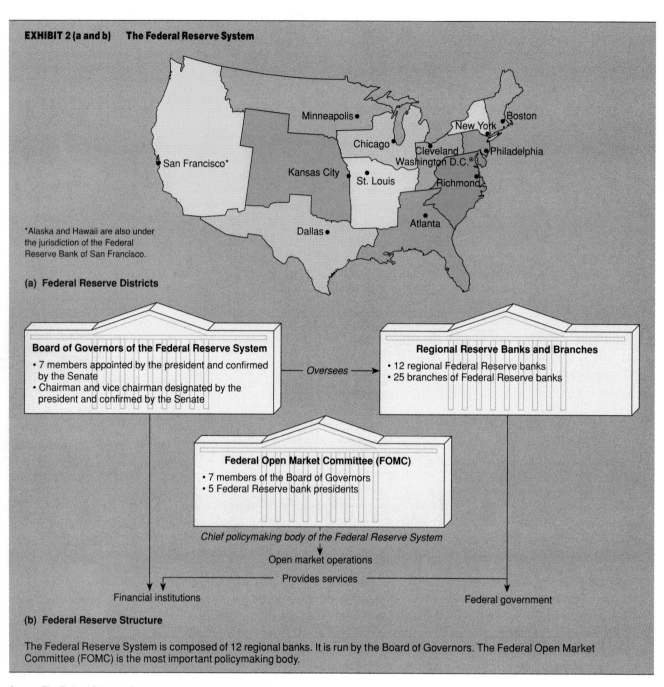

EXHIBIT 2 (a and b) The Federal Reserve System

*Alaska and Hawaii are also under the jurisdiction of the Federal Reserve Bank of San Francisco.

(a) Federal Reserve Districts

Board of Governors of the Federal Reserve System
• 7 members appointed by the president and confirmed by the Senate
• Chairman and vice chairman designated by the president and confirmed by the Senate

Oversees →

Regional Reserve Banks and Branches
• 12 regional Federal Reserve banks
• 25 branches of Federal Reserve banks

Federal Open Market Committee (FOMC)
• 7 members of the Board of Governors
• 5 Federal Reserve bank presidents

Chief policymaking body of the Federal Reserve System

Open market operations

Provides services

Financial institutions

Federal government

(b) Federal Reserve Structure

The Federal Reserve System is composed of 12 regional banks. It is run by the Board of Governors. The Federal Open Market Committee (FOMC) is the most important policymaking body.

Source: The Federal Reserve System. (http://www.bog.frb.fed.us)

Francisco. The reason is that in 1913, when the Fed was established, the West and South were less populated and less important economically than the rest of the country, so fewer banks were established there.

As these regions grew, the original structure remained because no one wanted to go through the political wrangling restructuring would bring about. Instead, the southern and western regional Feds established a number of branches to handle their banking needs.

Duties of the Fed

2b Congress gave the Fed six explicit duties. The most important is conducting monetary policy.

In legislation establishing the Fed, Congress gave it six explicit functions:

1. Conducting monetary policy (influencing the supply of money and credit in the economy).

In Chapter 9, which introduced you to financial institutions, there was a discussion of financial panics that can occur when people lose faith in one financial asset and want to shift to another. Financial panics are no stranger to banking. In the 1800s the United States suffered a financial panic every 20 years or so. Initially, a few people would suddenly fear they wouldn't be able to get their money out of their bank. They'd run down to the bank to get it. Others would see them getting their money and would do likewise. This was referred to as *a run on the bank*. As a result, their bank would have to close. If a bank closed, people would worry about other banks closing, and they'd run to *their* banks. That process could spread uncontrollably; banks would close and there would be a general financial panic. These panics led to considerable debate about what government should do to regulate and control the banking system.

Much of the initial debate about the U.S. banking industry concerned whether there should be a central bank (a bank that could make loans to other banks in times of crisis and could limit those banks' expansionary loans at other times). Supporters of a central bank argued that a central bank would create financial stability. Opponents argued that it would cause recessions and favor industrial interests over farming interests, and increase centralized power in the economy.

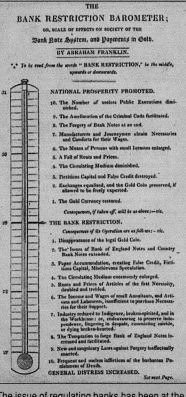

The issue of regulating banks has been at the forefront of economic policy discussions for centuries, as can be seen in this 19th-century English print of unknown origin, "The Bank Restriction Barometer." *Bleichroeder Print Collection, Baker Library, Harvard Business School.*

Initially central bank supporters predominated, and it wasn't long before the Bank of the United States, the first central U.S. bank chartered by the U.S. government, was established. Debates about the bank were rancorous and in 1811 its charter was not renewed. It went out of existence.

Five years later, in 1816, the political forces changed and the Second Bank of the United States was chartered. Its attempt to stop the inflationary spiral of 1817 and 1818 caused a depression. The bank was blamed. Political forces once again changed, and in 1832 the Second Bank was dismantled.

The next hundred years were marked by periodic financial crises and recessions—every 10 or 20 years. These crises led to arguments that the country needed a central bank to help prevent future crises, but when a particular crisis ended, the argument would fade away. In 1907, however, there was a major financial panic. In response the government established the Federal Reserve Bank (the Fed) in 1913. It empowered it to supply reserve assets to eliminate the incentive for depositors to panic and start a run on banks. The Fed failed to use these powers effectively during the 1929–33 period and thus bears some of the responsibility for the depth of the Great Depression. Despite this failure, the Federal Reserve Bank has remained in existence ever since and is now the United States central bank.

---

2. Supervising and regulating financial institutions.
3. Serving as a lender of last resort to financial institutions.
4. Providing banking services to the U.S. government.
5. Issuing coin and currency.
6. Providing financial services (such as check clearing) to commercial banks, savings and loan associations, savings banks, and credit unions.

Of these functions, the most important policy is conducting monetary policy, which is why I presented that first and will spend most of the chapter discussing it.

Not only is monetary policy the most important policy of the Fed, it is probably the most-used policy in macroeconomics. The Fed conducts and controls it, whereas fiscal policy is conducted directly by the government. Both policies are directed toward the same end: influencing the level of aggregate economic activity, hopefully in a beneficial manner. (In many other countries institutional arrangements are different; the central bank is a part of government, so both monetary and fiscal policy are directly conducted by the government, albeit by different branches of government.)

As of 1997, Alan Greenspan was the chairman of the Federal Reserve. A useful reference on how monetary policy actually works is the set of essays by real world practitioners in *The Art of Monetary Policy,* edited by Dewey Daane, a former Governor of the Federal Reserve, and myself (Armonk, NY: Sharpe Publishing, 1994).

THE IMPORTANCE OF MONETARY POLICY

Q–2: What is the difference between monetary policy and fiscal policy?

Actual decisions about monetary policy are made by the **Federal Open Market Committee (FOMC),** *the Fed's chief policymaking body.* All seven members of the Board of Governors, together with the president of the New York Fed and a rotating group of four of the presidents of the other regional banks, vote on the FOMC. The financial press and business community follow their discussions closely. There are even Fed watchers whose sole occupation is to follow what the Fed is doing and to tell people what it will likely do.

The Conduct of Monetary Policy

The monetary base consists of allowable reserves for banks. These allowable reserves are either vault cash or deposits at the Fed.

You've already seen that monetary policy shifts the *AED* curve. Let's now consider how it does so. We need to look more specifically at the institutional structure of the banking system and the role of the Fed in that institutional structure.

Think back to our discussion of the banking system. Banks take in deposits, make loans, and buy other financial assets, keeping a certain percentage of reserves for those transactions. Those reserves are IOUs of the Fed—*either vault cash or deposits at the Fed*—called the **monetary base.** The monetary base serves as legal reserves of the banking system. By controlling the monetary base, the Fed can influence the amount of money in the economy and the activities of banks.

The actual tools of monetary policy will affect the amount of reserves in the system. In turn, the amount of reserves in the system will affect the interest rate. Other things equal, as reserves decline, the interest rate will rise; and as reserves increase, the interest rate will decline. So monetary policy will also be associated with interest rates.

Let's now turn to the three tools of monetary policy and see precisely how they influence the amount of reserves in the system.

TOOLS OF MONETARY POLICY

3 The three tools of monetary policy are:
1. Changing the reserve requirement;
2. Changing the discount rate; and
3. Executing open market operations.

The three tools of monetary policy are:

1. Changing the reserve requirement.
2. Changing the discount rate.
3. Executing open market operations (buying and selling bonds).

Let's discuss each in turn.

Changing the Reserve Requirement   The total amount of money created from a given amount of cash depends on the percentage of deposits that a bank keeps in reserves (the bank's reserve ratio). Those reserves make up the monetary base of the economy. By law, the Fed controls the minimum percentage of deposits banks keep in reserve by controlling the reserve requirement of all U.S. banks. That minimum is called the **reserve requirement**—*the percentage the Federal Reserve System sets as the minimum amount of reserves a bank must have.*

Reserve requirement   Minimum ratio of reserves to deposits that a bank must have.

Required Reserves and Excess Reserves   For checking accounts (also called *demand deposits*), the amount banks keep in reserves depends partly on Federal Reserve requirements and partly on how much banks feel they need for safety (the cash they need to keep on hand at any time to give to depositors who claim some of their deposits in the form of cash). The amount most banks need for safety is much smaller than what the Fed requires. For them, it's the Fed's reserve requirement that determines the amount they hold as reserves.

Banks hold as little in reserves as possible. Why? Because reserves earn no interest for a bank. And we all know that banks are in business to earn profits. How much is as little as possible? That depends on the type of liabilities the bank has. In the late 1990s, required reserves for large banks for their checking accounts were about 10 percent. The reserve requirement for all other accounts was zero, making the reserve requirement for total liabilities somewhat under 2 percent.

In the late 1990s, total reserves were about $50 billion and required reserves were about $49 billion. This means excess reserves (reserves in excess of requirements) were about $1 billion. Thus, the reserve requirement generally plays a central role in how much money banks have to lend out. However, excess reserves can increase

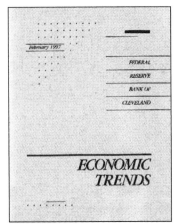

Economic Trends, a publication of the Federal Reserve Bank of Cleveland, is an excellent source for graphs and current information about monetary and fiscal policy.

substantially for short periods, as they did in the spring of 1992. Banks had reserves available, but did not lend them out.

The Reserve Requirement and the Money Supply   By changing the reserve requirements, the Fed can increase or decrease the money supply. If the Fed increases the reserve requirement, it contracts the money supply; banks have to keep more reserves so they have less money to lend out; the decreased money multiplier (the multiple contraction of deposits occurring in response to a change in reserves) further contracts the money supply. If the Fed decreases the reserve requirement, it expands the money supply; banks have more money to lend out; the money multiplier further expands the money supply.

The total effect on the money supply of changing the reserve requirement can be determined by thinking back to the approximate real-world money multiplier, which, as you saw in the earlier chapter on money, equals $1/(r + c)$ [1 divided by the sum of r (the percentage of each dollar that banks hold in reserves) plus c (the ratio of people's cash to deposits)]. When banks hold no excess reserves and face a reserve requirement of 15 percent, and people's cash-to-deposit ratio is 25 percent, the approximate money multiplier will be $1/.4 = 2.5$, so $1,000,000 in reserves will support a total $2,500,000 money supply. In reality the cash-to-deposit ratio is about 0.4 ($c = .4$), the average reserve requirement for demand deposits is about .1 ($r = .1$), and banks hold little in the way of excess reserves. So the realistic approximate money multiplier for demand deposits (M_1) is

$$1/(0.1 + 0.4) = 1/0.5 = 2$$

A $100 increase of reserves will support a $200 increase in demand deposits.[1] For other deposits the reserve requirement is much lower, so the money multiplier is larger for those.

What do you do if you're a bank and you come up short of reserves? In what's called the Federal funds market, the bank can borrow from another bank that has excess reserves. But if the entire banking system is short of reserves, that option won't work since there's no one to borrow from. Another option is to stop making new loans and to keep as reserves the proceeds of loans that are paid off. Still another option is to sell Treasury bonds to get the needed reserves. (Banks often hold some of their assets in Treasury bonds so that they can get additional reserves relatively easily if they need them.) These Treasury bonds are sometimes called *secondary reserves.* They do not count as bank reserves—only IOUs of the Fed count as reserves. But Treasury bonds can be easily sold and transferred into cash which does count as reserves. Banks use all these options.

Video Series, Economics USA: The Federal Reserve System, Segment 9.2
Show the potency of the reserve requirement as a tool of monetary policy by changing its value in a simple money multiplier by a small amount and view the impact on the size of the multiplier and the size of the money supply.

The approximate real-world money multiplier is $1/(r + c)$.

If one has time, a useful exercise is going through the balance sheet of a local bank.

---

[1]As c, the cash-to-deposit ratio, increases, the approximation becomes less exact. The actual multiplier is $(1 + c)/(r + c) = 1.4/.5 = 2.8$. Since the marginal amount held varies rather substantially, and various measures of money are used, this difference between our approximation and the actual cash multiplier is not of operational significance. In estimating the effect of policy on the different measures of the money supply, banks use only very rough estimates of the money supply.

Changing the Discount Rate   A second tool of monetary policy concerns another alternative banks have if they are short of reserves. A bank can also go to its bank (the Federal Reserve, the banker's bank) and take out a loan.

Discount rate   Rate of interest the Fed charges on loans it makes to banks.

The **discount rate** is *the rate of interest the Fed charges for those loans it makes to banks.* An increase in the discount rate makes it more expensive for banks to borrow from the Fed. A discount rate decrease makes it less expensive for banks to borrow. Therefore changing the discount rate is a second way the Fed can expand or contract the money supply.

On the surface, the reasoning seems straightforward. A discount rate decrease lowers the bank's cost and allows it to borrow more from the Fed. More reserves (IOUs of the Fed) are in the system so the money supply increases and the interest rates banks charge customers fall. An increase in the discount rate works in the opposite way.

Q–3: The discount rate works primarily through market channels. True or false? Why?

In practice, however, the way the discount rate works is more complicated. The discount rate that the Fed charges is usually slightly lower than competing interest rates that the banks would pay if they didn't borrow from the Fed. Thus, based on pure economic costs, banks should borrow lots of money from the Fed. But the invisible handshake is at work here, and the Fed discourages banks from using this option. It's a bit like having your parents lend you money. They'll lend you money, probably at a zero interest rate, but they may frown upon it and lecture you if you borrow from them. As a result, you use them only as a last resort. Similarly most banks borrow from the Fed only as a last resort.

I like to ask my students why banks should receive a subsidy in the form of a discount rate that is lower than the market rate.

Banks generally are very responsive to the Fed's desires. They know that the Fed controls the auditors of the banks, and if a bank borrows too often, the Fed may well suggest the auditors make a special visit to the bank to see why it needs to borrow. With such "moral suasion," the actual discount rate is not the determinant of how much a bank will borrow; the Fed's reproach is.

Nonetheless, the changes in the discount rate affect the money supply as we'd expect them to. The reason is that the Fed uses the discount rate as a signal to banks and to the general public: An increase in the discount rate signals that the Fed wants money tightened; a decrease signals that the Fed wants the money supply expanded. Banks usually respond appropriately.

Open market operations are the most often used tool of monetary policy because they can be easily undertaken, adjusted, timed, and reversed if necessary.

The Fed's use of this signal could be seen in 1993 when it cut the discount rate substantially (from 3.5 percent to 3 percent) as a signal that it believed more aggressive bank lending policy was warranted, or in mid-1994 when it raised it back to 3.5 percent.

The Federal Reserve banks process millions of checks every day through automated machines, such as this one. *Federal Reserve Bank of Boston.*

Open Market Operations   Changes in the discount rate and the reserve requirement are not used in day-to-day Fed operations. They're used mainly for major changes. For day-to-day operations, the Fed uses a third tool: **open market operations**—*the Fed's buying and selling of government securities* (the only type of asset the Fed is allowed by law to hold in any appreciable quantity). These open market operations are the primary tool of monetary policy.

When the Fed buys a Treasury bill or bond, it pays for it with its IOUs which serve as reserve assets for banks. This IOU doesn't have to be a written piece of paper. It may be simply a computer entry credited to the bank's account, say $1 billion. An IOU of the Fed is money.

Because the IOU the Fed uses to buy a government security serves as reserves to the banking system, with the simple act of buying a Treasury bond and paying for it with its IOU the Fed can increase the money supply (since this creates reserves for the bank). To increase the money supply, the Fed goes to the bond market, buys a bond, and pays for it with its IOU. The individual or firm who sold the bond now has an IOU of the Fed. When the individual or firm deposits the IOU in a bank, presto! The reserves of the banking system are increased. If the Fed buys $1,000,000 worth of bonds, it increases reserves by $1,000,000 and the total money supply by $1,000,000 times the money multiplier.

When the Fed sells Treasury bonds, it collects back some of its IOUs, reducing banking system reserves and decreasing the money supply. Thus,

> *To expand the money supply, the Fed buys bonds.*
> *To contract the money supply, the Fed sells bonds.*

Open market operations are the Fed's most-used tool in controlling the money supply. Periodically the Open Market Committee looks at trading in the financial markets and decides what its open market operations will be and whether it wants to expand or contract the money supply.

Examples of Open Market Operations   Understanding open market operations is essential to understanding monetary policy as it is actually practiced in the United States. So let us go through some examples.[2]

Open market operations involve the purchase or sale of federal government securities. When the Fed buys bonds, it deposits the funds in federal government accounts at a bank. Recall that banks can create money by lending out their excess reserves. When the Fed pays the government for its bonds, bank cash reserves rise. Banks don't like to hold excess reserves, so they lend out the excess, thereby expanding the deposit base of the economy. The money supply rises. Thus, an open market

Open market operations   The Fed's buying and selling of government securities.

Q–4: Besides open market operations, what are two tools of monetary policy?

Be sure to work through the transmission of an open market operation to a change in the money supply. This seems to be the point where many students lose their grip on the ideas behind monetary policy.

To expand the money supply, the Fed buys bonds. To contract the money supply, the Fed sells bonds.

---

[2]A discussion of the effects of open market operations using T–accounts is presented in Appendix A.

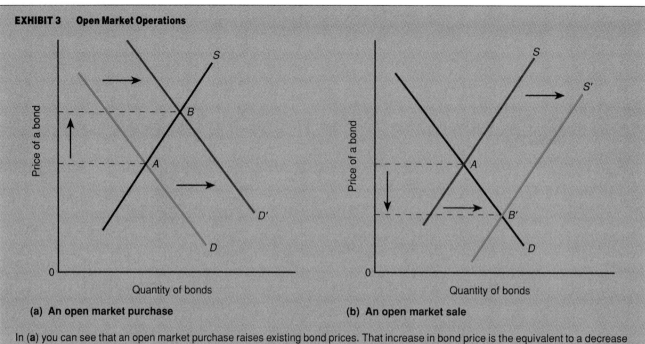

EXHIBIT 3   Open Market Operations

(a) An open market purchase

(b) An open market sale

In **(a)** you can see that an open market purchase raises existing bond prices. That increase in bond price is the equivalent to a decrease in the interest rate. In **(b)** you can see that an open market sale reduces existing bond prices. That reduction means that the interest rate rises.

Expansionary monetary policy
Monetary policy aimed at increasing the money supply and raising the level of aggregate demand.

Contractionary monetary policy
Monetary policy aimed at reducing the money supply and thereby restraining aggregate demand.

The Federal funds rate is the interest rate banks charge one another for overnight reserve loans.

purchase is an example of **expansionary monetary policy** (*usually defined to be monetary policy that tends to reduce interest rates and raise income*), since it raises the money supply (as long as the banks strive to minimize their excess reserves).

An open market sale has the opposite effect. Here, the Fed sells bonds. In return for the bond, the Fed receives a check drawn against a bank. The bank's reserve assets are reduced (since the Fed "cashes" the check and takes the money away from the bank), and the money supply falls. That's an example of **contractionary monetary policy** (*monetary policy that tends to raise interest rates and lower income*).

What happens to bond prices and interest rates during this process? Exhibit 3(a) illustrates the effects of an open market purchase in which the Fed buys bonds, thereby raising the demand for bonds. Bond prices rise, and since we know that bond prices and interest rates are inversely related (when one goes up the other goes down), interest rates fall. That's what we'd expect of an expansionary monetary policy.

Exhibit 3 (b) shows us what happens to bond prices in an open market sale. From that you can figure out the change in interest rates. As the Fed sells bonds, the supply of bonds shifts right, leading to lower bond prices. What happens to interest rates? If you said they go up, you're on track.

The Fed Funds Market   To get an even better sense of the way monetary policy works, let's look at it from the perspective of a bank. The bank will review its books, determine how much reserves it needs to meet its reserve requirement, and see if it has excess reserves or a shortage of reserves.

Say your bank didn't make as many loans as it expected to so that it has a surplus of reserves (excess reserves). Say also that another bank has made a few loans it didn't expect to make so it has a shortage of reserves. The bank with surplus reserves can lend money to the bank with a shortage—and it can lend it overnight as **Fed funds**—*loans of their reserves banks make to one another*. At the end of a day, a bank will look at its balances and see whether it has a shortage or surplus of reserves. If it has a surplus, it will call a Federal funds ("Fed funds") dealer to learn the **Federal funds rate**—*the interest rate banks charge one another for Fed funds*. Say the rate is 6 percent. The bank will then agree to lend its excess reserves overnight to the other bank for the daily equivalent of 6 percent per year. It's all simply done electronically, so there's no need actually to transfer funds. In the morning the money (plus overnight interest) is returned. The one-day interest rate is low, but when you're dealing with millions or billions, it adds up.

The **Federal funds market,** *the market in which banks lend and borrow reserves,* is highly efficient. When money is tight (most banks have shortages of reserves), the Fed funds rate is high; when money is loose (most banks have excess reserves), the rate is low. Generally, large city banks are borrowers of Fed funds; small country banks are lenders of Fed funds.

Offensive and Defensive Actions   Economists keep a close eye on the Federal funds rate in determining the state of monetary policy. I mention the Federal funds rate because it is an important intermediate target of the Fed in determining what monetary policy to conduct. Remember, the Fed sets minimum reserve requirements, but the actual amount of reserves available to banks is influenced by the amount of cash people hold and excess reserves that banks may choose to hold. That changes daily. For example, say there's a storm, and businesses don't make it to the bank with their cash. Bank reserves will fall even though the Fed didn't do anything. The Fed can, and does, offset such changes—by buying and selling bonds. Such actions are called *defensive actions*. They are designed to maintain the current monetary policy. These defensive actions are to be contrasted with offensive actions, which are actions meant to make monetary policy have expansionary or contractionary effects on the economy.

The Fed Funds Rate as an Intermediate Target   How does the Fed decide whether its buying and selling of bonds is having the desired effect? It has to look at intermediate targets—and in recent years the Federal funds rate has been the intermediate target of the Fed. Thus, the Fed determines whether monetary policy is tight or loose depending upon what is happening to the Federal funds rate. In practice it targets a range for that rate, and it buys and sells bonds to keep the Federal funds rate within that range. If the Federal funds rate goes above the Fed's target range, it buys bonds, which increases reserves and lowers the Federal funds rate. If the Federal funds rate goes below the Fed's target range, it sells bonds, which decreases reserves and raises the Federal funds rate.

There's another aspect of monetary policy that is extremely important in practice: the international aspect. In Chapter 4, I introduced you briefly to exchange rates and the importance of interest rates in their determination. A quick review: A rise in the domestic interest rate tends to increase the demand for a country's currency, and push up that country's exchange rate. That currency will cost more in terms of the currencies of other countries. Similarly, a fall in a country's interest rate works in the opposite direction.

To see how this international connection influences domestic monetary policy, let's say that a country has decided to run expansionary monetary policy, pushing its interest rate down. The fall in the interest rate will lead investors to invest elsewhere, lowering the value of that country's currency and causing an outflow of financial resources. That outflow will tend to push interest rates back up. If the country had international agreements to keep its exchange rate at a certain level—as do member countries of the European Union—this outflow must be offset in some way. Alternatively, if a country runs contractionary monetary policy and raises its interest rate, it will attract an inflow of funds, raising the value of the country's currency and causing an inflow of financial resources, which will tend to push the interest rate back down.

These international issues quickly get complicated and I will discuss them in more detail in later chapters. But, given the importance of these international considerations to the actual conduct of many countries' monetary policy, I wanted to alert you to the issues here.

4 The Federal funds rate is the interest rate banks charge one another for overnight reserve loans. The Fed determines whether monetary policy is loose or tight depending upon what's happening to the Fed funds rate. The Fed funds rate is an important intermediate target.

Q–5: There's been a big storm and cash held by individuals has increased. Should the Fed buy or sell bonds? Why?

Monetary policy affects interest rates such as the Federal funds rate. The Fed looks at the Federal funds rate to determine whether monetary policy is tight or loose.

Q–6: If the Federal funds rate is above the Fed's target range, is monetary policy too tight or too loose? Will the Fed buy bonds or sell bonds?

International Considerations in the Conduct of Monetary Policy

The interest rate plays an important role in exchange rate determination.

Contrasting Views of the Channels of Monetary Policy

Both Keynesians and Classicals agree that monetary policy is important, but they differ in how they see monetary policy affecting the economy, and in their recommendations to the Fed about how to conduct monetary policy. These differences will become more apparent when we discuss macro policy in later chapters, but to provide a good foundation for those later discussions, let's now briefly consider these differences. (The Keynesian and Classical theories of interest and their implications for monetary policy are discussed in Appendix B.)

MONETARY POLICY IN THE KEYNESIAN MODEL

5 In the Keynesian model, monetary policy works as follows:

$$M\downarrow \rightarrow i\uparrow \rightarrow I\downarrow \rightarrow Y\downarrow$$
$$M\uparrow \rightarrow i\downarrow \rightarrow I\uparrow \rightarrow Y\uparrow$$

Video Series, Economics U$A: The Federal Reserve System, Segment 13.1 and 13.2

In Keynesian terms, monetary policy is seen working primarily through its effect on interest rates. Let's see how. In Exhibit 4(a) we see that when the Fed decreases the money supply (uses contractionary monetary policy), it increases the interest rate. Exhibit 4(b) shows the effect of that increased interest rate on investment. As you can see, because the demand for investment is downward sloping, the rise in interest rate decreases the quantity of investment. (Lower interest rates lead businesses to borrow more, and to expand investment.)

A decrease in investment reduces aggregate demand. Through repercussion effects, aggregate equilibrium demand and income decrease by a multiple of the amount that investment decreased. Exhibit 4(c) shows the effect of a fall in investment on income. It has shifted the *AED* curve to the left by a multiple of the shift in investment. Thus, *contractionary* monetary policy tends to *decrease* the money supply, *increase* the interest rate, *decrease* investment, and *decrease* income and output:

contractionary monetary policy

$$M\downarrow \rightarrow i\uparrow \rightarrow I\downarrow \rightarrow Y\downarrow$$

Expansionary monetary policy works in the opposite manner, as Exhibit 4(d) shows. *Expansionary* monetary policy tends to *increase* the money supply, *decrease* the interest rate, *increase* investment, and *increase* income and output:

expansionary monetary policy

$$M\uparrow \rightarrow i\downarrow \rightarrow I\uparrow \rightarrow Y\uparrow$$

The preceding discussion of how monetary policy works in theory is helpful, but it probably isn't very intuitive. Let's go through the reasoning again, only this time focusing on trying to provide an intuitive feel for what is happening. Say the Fed uses open market operations. As the Fed either injects or pulls out reserves, it influences the amount of money banks have to lend and the interest rate at which they can lend it. When banks have more reserves than required, they want to lend. (That's how they make their profit.) To get people to borrow more from them, banks will decrease the interest rate they charge on loans. So expansionary monetary policy tends to decrease the interest rate banks charge their customers; contractionary policy tends to increase the interest rate banks charge customers. Expansionary monetary policy increases the amount of money banks have to lend, which tends to increase investment and leads to an increase in income. Contractionary monetary policy decreases the amount of money banks have to lend, which tends to decrease investment and leads to a decrease in income.

One of the best-known economists who developed the Keynesian analysis of monetary policy is James Tobin. He won a Nobel prize in 1981 for his contribution.

Keynesian Monetary Policy in the Circular Flow   Exhibit 5's familiar circular flow diagram shows how monetary policy works in the Keynesian model. In the Keynesian view monetary policy works inside the financial sector to help equate the flow of savings with investment. When the economy is operating at too low a level of income and when savings exceeds investment, in the absence of monetary policy, income will fall. Expansionary monetary policy tries to channel more savings into investment so the fall in income is stopped. It does so by increasing the available credit, lowering the interest rate, and increasing investment and hence income.

Contractionary monetary policy is called for when savings is smaller than investment and the economy is operating at too high a level of income, causing inflationary pressures. In this case, monetary policy tries to restrict the demand for investment

EXHIBIT 4 (a, b, c, and d)   Expansionary and Contractionary Monetary Policy and the Macro Policy Model

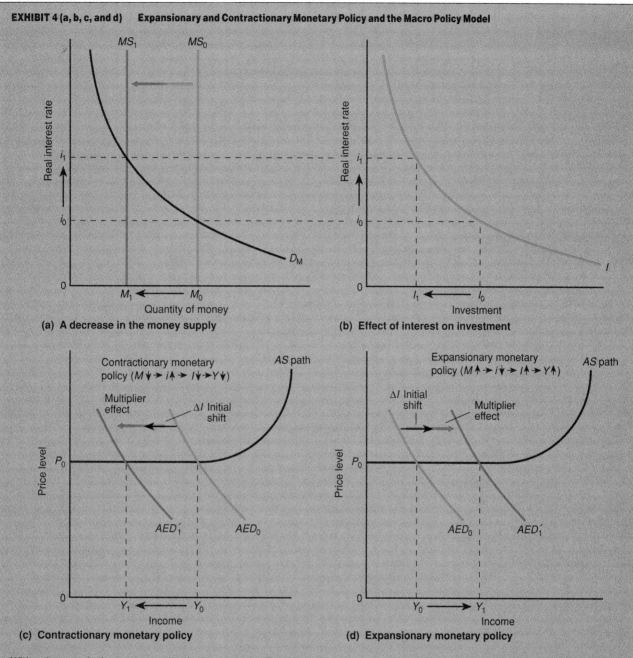

(a) A decrease in the money supply

(b) Effect of interest on investment

(c) Contractionary monetary policy

(d) Expansionary monetary policy

With a decrease in the money supply, the interest rate will rise from i_0 to i_1, as shown in (a). The rise in the interest rate results in a decrease in investment from I_0 to I_1, as shown in (b). The fall in investment shifts the aggregate equilibrium demand curve from AED_0 to AED_1'. Income decreases from Y_0 to Y_1, as shown in (c), which decreases savings sufficiently so that savings equal investment. In (d), expansionary monetary policy is shown working the opposite way. It shifts the AED curve to the right, from AED_0 to AED_1'. Income increases from Y_0 to Y_1.

and consumer loans. Thus, to control the economy, Keynesians tend to favor an activist monetary policy, with the Fed taking an active role in controlling the interest rate.

The Keynesian Emphasis on the Interest Rate   Because Keynesians see monetary policy working through the effect of interest rates on investment, they focus on the interest rate in judging monetary policy. They interpret a rising interest rate as a tightening of monetary policy. They interpret a falling interest rate as a loosening of monetary policy.

For a computer simulation of monetary policy in the macro model see the module, "Monetary Policy" in *Macro Interactive*.

EXHIBIT 5   Keynesian Monetary Policy in the Circular Flow

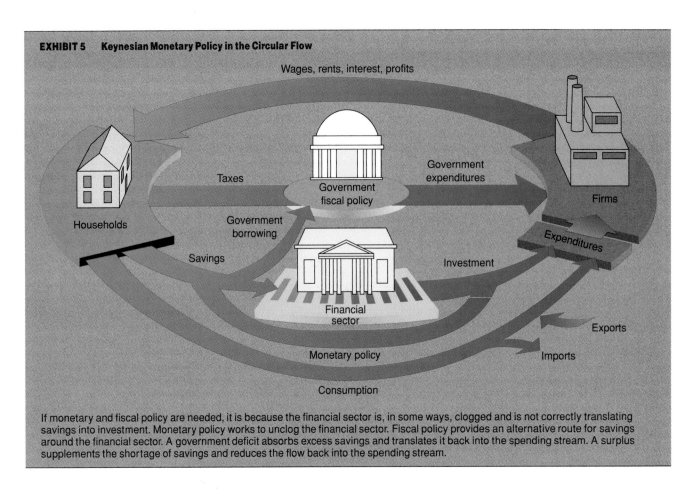

If monetary and fiscal policy are needed, it is because the financial sector is, in some ways, clogged and is not correctly translating savings into investment. Monetary policy works to unclog the financial sector. Fiscal policy provides an alternative route for savings around the financial sector. A government deficit absorbs excess savings and translates it back into the spending stream. A surplus supplements the shortage of savings and reduces the flow back into the spending stream.

Keynesians focus on interest rates as an indicator of monetary policy.

Keynesians believe the Fed should target interest rates in setting monetary policy. For example, if the interest rate is currently 6 percent and the Fed wants to loosen monetary policy, it should buy bonds until the interest rate falls to 5.5 percent. If it wants to tighten monetary policy, it should sell bonds to make the interest rate go up to, say, 6.5 percent.

In the 1950s, the early Keynesians advocated keeping the interest rate low. More recently, Keynesians have advocated keeping the interest rate low enough to foster growth, but high enough to prevent inflationary pressures. As you can imagine, it's a fine line between the two, so whatever policy the Fed chooses usually has critics.

Discussions of whether interest rates are too high or too low and the effect of monetary policy on interest rates fill our newspapers' financial pages. These articles reflect the Keynesian approach to monetary policy.

MONETARY POLICY IN THE CLASSICAL MODEL

Quantity theory of money *The quantity theory of money asserts that the price level varies in response to changes in the quantity of money.*

6 In the Classical model, monetary policy works through the quantity theory:

$$MV = PQ$$

It has short-run effects on real output, Q, but in the long run it affects only the price level, P.

In the Classical model, monetary policy is best seen in the **quantity theory of money**—*the theory that the price level varies in response to changes in the quantity of money.* The Classical quantity theory of money centers around the **equation of exchange,** *an equation for "quantity of money times velocity of money equals the price level times the quantity of real goods sold."* This equation is:

$$MV = PQ$$

where:

M = Quantity of money

V = Velocity

P = Price level

Q = Quantity of real goods sold.

Q is the real output of the economy (real GDP). P is the price level, so PQ is the economy's nominal output (nominal GDP—the quantity of goods valued at whatever price level exists at the time). Remember, real GDP equals nominal GDP divided by (deflated by) the price level, while nominal GDP equals nominal income.

V, the **velocity of money,** is *the number of times per year, on average, a dollar goes around to generate a dollar's worth of income.* Put another way, velocity is the amount of income per year generated by a dollar of money. MV also equals nominal output. Thus, if there's $100 of money in the economy and velocity is 20, nominal GDP is $2,000. We can calculate V by dividing nominal GDP by the money supply. Let's take Canada as an example. In Canada in 1996, nominal GDP was approximately $800 billion and M was approximately $60 billion (using M1), so velocity was about GDP/M = 13, meaning each dollar in the economy circulated enough to support approximately $13 in total income.

Velocity of money   *Number of times per year, on average, a dollar goes around to generate a dollar's worth of income; or amount of income per year generated by a dollar of money.*

Home page for Canadian statistics: http://www.statcan.ca.

The equation of exchange is a *tautology,* meaning it's true by definition. What changes it from a tautology to a theory are certain assumptions the Classicals make about the variables in the equation of exchange.

Q-7:   What's the difference between the equation of exchange and the quantity theory of money?

First, Classical economists assume velocity remains constant. They argue that money is spent only so fast; how fast is determined by the economy's institutional structure, such as how close to stores individuals live, how people are paid (weekly, biweekly, or monthly), and what sources of credit are available (can you go to the store and buy something on credit, that is, buying something without handing over cash?). This institutional structure changes slowly, they argue, so velocity won't fluctuate very much. Next year, velocity will be approximately the same as this year.

Velocity, of course, is not even close to constant in the short run, nor did Classicals consider it constant. Pointing this out sets up a discussion of how Classicals had a long-run, as opposed to a short-run, focus on their analysis.

If velocity remains constant, the quantity theory can be used to predict how much nominal GDP will grow if we know how much the money supply grows. For example, if the money supply goes up 6 percent, using the quantity theory a Classical economist would predict that nominal GDP will go up by 6 percent.

The second Classical assumption concerns Q, real output. Classical economists assume that Q is independent of the money supply. That is, the Classicals believe Q is **autonomous,** *meaning real output is determined by forces outside the quantity theory.* If Q grows, it is because of incentives in the real economy. Thus their policy analysis is on the real economy—the supply side of the economy, not the demand side.

Something that is determined outside the model is called autonomous.

This Classical assumption is sometimes called the **veil of money assumption,** which *holds that real output is not influenced by changes in the money supply.* Classical economists argue that in order to understand what is happening in the real economy, you must lift the veil of money.

The veil of money assumption says that real output isn't influenced by changes in the money supply.

This veil of money assumption makes analyzing the economy a lot easier than it would be if the financial and real sectors are interrelated and if real economic activity is influenced by financial changes. It allows Classical economists to separate two puzzles: how the real economy works, and how the price level and financial sector work. Instead of having two different jigsaw puzzles all mixed up, each puzzle can be worked separately. They can analyze what happens in the real economy (in the production of real goods and services) separately from what happens to the money supply and price level. Classical economists recognize that there are interconnections between the real and financial sectors, but they argue that most of these interconnections involve short-run considerations. Classical economists are primarily interested in the long run.

The veil of money assumption allows Classical economists to separate two puzzles—how the real economy works, and how the price level and financial sector works.

In the long run, there is a strong intuitive reason why the real and nominal economies are separate. Say one day you walk into work and your salary has doubled—but all prices also have doubled. What difference will these changes make in your behavior? Since no relative price has changed, it seems fair to say that your behavior won't be affected very much. That's what the Classical economists are saying with the veil of money assumption.

With both V (velocity) and Q (quantity or output) unaffected by changes in M (money supply), the only thing that can change is P (price level). Classical economists say that M and P will change by equivalent percentages.

Three assumptions of Quantity Theory:

1. Velocity constant

2. Real output independent of money supply

3. Causation goes from money to prices.

The final assumption of the Classical quantity theory is the *direction of causation*. Classical economists argue that changes in the money supply cause changes in the price level: In the quantity theory of money equation, the direction of causation goes from left to right,

$$MV \rightarrow PQ$$

not the other way around. Thus, when a Classical economist is asked to predict what would happen to inflation, he or she will ask what's happening to the money supply's growth rate. If the money supply is continually increasing at an 8 percent rate, the Classical economist's prediction would be that inflation would be 8 percent.

We've covered a lot of ground, so let me briefly summarize how we went from the equation of exchange to the quantity theory. We start with the equation of exchange:

$$MV = PQ$$

To that we add three assumptions:

1. Velocity is constant.
2. Real output is independent of the money supply.
3. Causation goes from money supply to prices.

The result is the quantity theory of money. It holds that real output is set at levels desired by individuals, and that real output is independent of the wage and price level. An increase in money will not increase real output; it will simply increase the wage and price level.

So, how do Classical economists view monetary policy? They see expansionary monetary policy as increasing the money supply (M), and in the long run they believe this will simply increase the price level (P):

$$\overset{\uparrow}{M}\overline{V} \Rightarrow \overset{\uparrow}{P}\overline{Q}$$

Thus, in the long run monetary policy has no effect on real economic variables such as income or employment. This view is consistent with the Classical proposition that there is a dichotomy between the real and nominal sectors. The Classical position on monetary policy is best seen in this theory.

The Classical Emphasis on Money Supply

Q–8: An economist emphasizes the interest rate in her discussion of monetary policy. Is she more likely to be a Keynesian or a Classical?

"Steady-as-You-Go" Policy

The quantity theory of money framework and the long-run relationship between money and prices that Classicals emphasize lead them to focus on the money supply as the key variable in judging whether monetary policy is tight or loose. A large increase in the money supply indicates expansionary monetary policy; a large decrease in the money supply indicates contractionary monetary policy.

Classicals oppose the Keynesian policy of an activist monetary policy.

Because of the Classicals' focus on the long run, they favor a "steady-as-you-go" monetary policy, increasing the money supply just enough each year to allow for the normal real growth in the economy. That increase is to be maintained regardless of the state of the economy. Following that rule, Classicals claim, is most likely to provide the stable financial setting necessary for a market economy to operate. Classicals believe discretionary monetary policy is as likely to destabilize as to stabilize the economy. Thus, Classicals oppose the Keynesian policy of an activist monetary policy. Because of ongoing changes in financial institutions that determine velocity and what is considered to be money, modern Classicals focus less on the money supply than earlier Classicals did. But modern Classicals still maintain that, after one adjusts for changing financial institutions, the general idea of the quantity theory is true.

The reason for their steady-as-you-go policy proposal is that, in the short run, Classical economists are much less certain about the workings of monetary policy. They argue that in the short run monetary policy operates in numerous ways that are too hard to analyze. How long monetary policy takes to work, by what channels it influences the real economy, and how, in the short run, it will influence prices versus

"Rules versus Authorities in Monetary Policy," by Henry C. Simons, in *Classic Readings in Economics.*

real income—all this is unknowable. But what is knowable is that expansionary monetary policy will have some unknown strong effect in the short run and will raise the price level in the long run.

Classicals don't believe that monetary policy can ease or hinder the link between savings and investment because they believe the financial markets are already coordinating the flow from savings into investment as well as possible. True, sometimes savings and investment might get screwed up a bit, but monetary policy, with its uncertain effect, will likely screw it up even more. Moreover, Classicals believe that since politicians focus on short-run effects, political pressures will generally be toward increasing the money supply. In the long run these increases in the money supply will lead to an increase in the price level, so a Keynesian activist monetary policy that does not follow a predetermined rule will have an undesirable effect on inflation.

Real and Nominal Interest Rates

In support of their argument that the money supply rather than the interest rate should be considered in judging the looseness or tightness of monetary policy, Classicals point out the distinction between real and nominal interest rates. **Nominal interest rates** are *the rates you actually see and pay*. When a bank pays 7 percent interest, that 7 percent is a nominal interest rate. **Real interest rates** are *rates adjusted for expected inflation*.

Nominal interest rates   Interest rates you actually see and pay.

Real interest rates   Nominal interest rates adjusted for expected inflation.

For example, say you get 7 percent interest from the bank, but the price level goes up 7 percent. At the end of the year you have $107 instead of $100, but you're no better off than before because the price level has risen—on average, things cost 7 percent more. What you would have paid $100 for last year now costs $107. (That's the definition of *inflation*.) Had the price level remained constant, and had you received 0 percent interest, you'd be in the equivalent position to receiving 7 percent interest on your $100 when the price level rises by 7 percent. That 0 percent is the *real interest rate*. It is the interest rate you would expect to receive if the price level remains constant.

Post-Keynesians, such as Paul Davidson, argue that it is primarily the nominal rate of interest that guides the economy and that the real rate is almost a meaningless concept. Their argument is that individuals think in money terms, and that either because of institutional constraints or illusions, individuals do not calculate the real rate. Most Keynesians do not go that far, but they do agree that the real interest rate can be hard for individuals to calculate, and that in the short run it is often the nominal interest rate that is the important rate.

The real interest rate cannot be observed because it depends on expected inflation, which cannot be directly observed. To calculate the real interest rate, you must subtract what you believe to be the expected rate of inflation from the nominal interest rate. For example, if the nominal interest rate is 7 percent and expected inflation is 4 percent, the real interest rate is 3 percent. The relationship between real and nominal interest rates is important both for your study of economics and for your own personal finances.

Nominal interest rate = Real interest rate + Expected inflation rate.

Nominal interest rate = Real interest rate + Expected inflation rate.

Real and Nominal Interest Rates and Monetary Policy

What does this distinction between nominal and real interest rates mean for monetary policy? It supports the Classical argument against using monetary policy to control the economy because it adds yet another uncertainty to the effect of monetary policy. Keynesians say that expansionary monetary policy lowers the interest rate and contractionary monetary policy increases the interest rate. However, if the expansionary monetary policy leads to expectations of increased inflation, Classicals point out that expansionary monetary policy can increase nominal interest rates (the ones you see). Why? Because of expectations of increasing inflation.

The distinction between nominal and real interest rates strengthens the Classical case that the best monetary policy is an unchanging policy. In the short run, monetary policy's effects are too uncertain; in the long run, they simply lead to changes in the price level.

Given the ambiguity of the short-run effect and the negative effect of the long run, monetary policy should not be used to influence the economy. Instead, according to Classical economists, the economy should be governed by a specific rule that sets the money supply at a predetermined level and either holds it there or increases it at a constant rate.

Q–9: Does Fed policy generally reflect Classical theory or Keynesian theory?

PROBLEMS IN THE CONDUCT OF MONETARY POLICY

7 Five problems of monetary policy:
1. Knowing what policy to use.
2. Understanding what policy you're using.
3. Lags in monetary policy.
4. Political pressure.
5. Conflicting international goals.

In spite of the problems associated with monetary policy, it is important to point out to students that it is the tool of choice for policy-makers in recent years.

Monetary Policy in the Fed Model of the 1990s   While it is important to know both the Keynesian and Classical models, it is also important to know that the Fed is eclectic, sometimes using a Keynesian model, sometimes a Classical model, but generally an eclectic model that combines both Keynesian and Classical models with a "feel of the markets." Thus, the Fed will use both interest rates and money supply measures, deciding on which to place more emphasis by using common sense and knowledge of institutional factors. The Fed is in constant communication with players in financial markets, and it has many economists whose jobs are to fit the theories into the institutions. This results in swings in focus. In the mid-1990s, the swing was toward emphasizing interest rates and away from emphasizing money supply measures, but if the past is any indication, this swing won't be permanent.

Earlier, after discussing fiscal policy's structure and mechanics, I presented the problems with using fiscal policy. Now that you've been through the structure and mechanics of monetary policy, let's consider the problems with using it, too.

Knowing What Policy to Use   To use monetary policy effectively, you must know the potential level of income. Otherwise you won't know whether to use expansionary or contractionary monetary policy. Let's consider an example: mid-1991. The economy seemed to be coming out of a recession. The Fed had to figure out whether to use expansionary monetary policy to speed up and guarantee the recovery, or use contractionary monetary policy and make sure inflation didn't start up again. Initially the Fed tried to fight inflation, only to discover that the economy wasn't coming out of the recession. In early 1992, the Fed switched from contractionary to expansionary monetary policy. It continued that policy through 1994 when fears of inflation caused it to start tightening the money supply slightly. Beginning in 1995 the Fed increased the money supply sufficiently to allow slow growth, as it tried to walk the tightrope between inflation and unemployment.

Understanding the Policy You're Using   To use monetary policy effectively, you must know whether the monetary policy you're using is expansionary or contractionary. You might think that's rather easy, but it isn't. In our consideration of monetary policy tools, you saw that the Fed doesn't directly control the money supply. It indirectly controls it, generally through open market operations. It controls what I earlier defined as the *monetary base* (the vault cash and reserves banks have at the Fed). Then the money multiplier determines the amounts of M_1, M_2, and other monetary measures in the economy.

That money multiplier is influenced by the amount of cash that people hold as well as the lending process at the bank. Neither of those is the stable number that we used in calculating the money multipliers. They change from day to day and week to week, so even if you control the monetary base, you can never be sure exactly what will happen to M_1 and M_2 in the short run. Moreover, the effects on M_1 and M_2 are sometimes different; one measure is telling you that you're expanding the money supply and the other measure is telling you you're contracting it.

And then, of course, there are changes in the interest rate—the measure of monetary policy that Keynesians focus on. If interest rates rise, is it because of expected inflation (which is adding an inflation premium to the nominal interest rate) or is it the real interest rate that is going up? There is frequent debate over which it is. Combined, these measurement problems make the Fed often wonder not only about what policy it should follow, but what policy it is following.

Lags in Monetary Policy   Monetary policy, like fiscal policy, takes time to work its way through the economic system. The Fed can change the money supply or interest rates; people don't have to borrow, however. An increased money supply may simply lead to excess reserves and have little or no influence on income. This is most likely when interest rates are very low. The belief that increases in the money supply would be ineffective in the 1930s led early Keynesians to focus on fiscal policy rather than monetary policy as a way of expanding the economy. They likened expansionary monetary policy to pushing on a string. The same problem exists with using contractionary monetary policy. Banks have been very good at figuring out ways to circumvent cuts in the money supply, making the intended results of contractionary monetary policy difficult to achieve.

Political Pressure   While the Fed is partially insulated from political pressure by its structure, it's not totally insulated. Presidents place enormous pressure on the Fed to use expansionary monetary policy (especially during an election year) and blame the Fed for any recession. When interest rates rise, the Fed takes the pressure, and if any members of the Board of Governors are politically aligned with the president, they find it difficult to persist in contractionary policy when the economy is in a recession.

For how Fed Chairman Greenspan deals with the political difficulties of monetary policy, see Chapter 14 in Case Studies in Macroeconomics.

Conflicting International Goals   Monetary policy is not conducted in a vacuum. It is conducted in an international arena and must be coordinated with other governments' monetary policy. Similarly, as we'll see a little later, monetary policy affects the exchange rate and trade balance. Often the desired monetary policy for its international effects is the opposite of the desired monetary policy for its domestic effects.

Q–10:   What are five problems in the conduct of monetary policy?

I could continue with a discussion of the problems of using monetary policy, but the above should give you a good sense that conducting monetary policy is not a piece of cake. It takes not only a sense of the theory; it also takes a feel for the economy. In short, the conduct of monetary policy is not a science. It does not allow the Fed to steer the economy as it might steer a car. It does work well enough to allow the Fed to *influence* the economy—much as an expert rodeo rider rides a bronco bull.

This chapter is not the end of our discussion of monetary policy. We'll see more of monetary policy when we discuss how to conduct macroeconomic policy in the next section. There you'll learn how monetary policy works in practice, the central role it plays in understanding inflation, and how it is integrated with fiscal policy. Before we turn to those issues, however, it is helpful to specifically consider the issue of inflation, and the role it plays in the policy debates about macroeconomic policy. That is what we do in the next chapter.

CONCLUSION AND A LOOK AHEAD

CHAPTER SUMMARY

- The Fed is a central bank; it conducts monetary policy for the United States and regulates financial institutions.
- Monetary policy influences the economy through changes in the money supply and credit availability.
- The three tools of monetary policy are:
    1. Changing the reserve requirement.
    2. Changing the discount rate.
    3. Open market operations.
- A change in reserves changes the money supply by the change in reserves times the money multiplier.
- Open market operations are the Fed's most important tool:
    To expand the money supply, the Fed buys bonds.
    To contract the money supply, the Fed sells bonds.

- In the Keynesian model, contractionary monetary policy works as follows:

$$M \downarrow \rightarrow i \uparrow \rightarrow I \downarrow \rightarrow Y \downarrow$$

Expansionary monetary policy works as follows:

$$M \uparrow \rightarrow i \downarrow \rightarrow I \uparrow \rightarrow Y \uparrow$$

- As an indicator of monetary policy, Keynesians focus on interest rates; Classicals focus on money supply.
- Classical economists see the short-run effects of monetary policy as ambiguous. They favor a long-run monetary rule.
- The Fed uses an eclectic model that combines both Keynesian and Classical insights.
- Problems of monetary policy include knowing what policy to use, knowing what policy you are using, lags, political pressure, and conflicting international goals.

KEY TERMS

autonomous *(347)*
central bank *(335)*
contractionary monetary policy *(342)*
discount rate *(340)*
equation of exchange *(346)*
expansionary monetary policy *(342)*
Fed funds *(342)*

Federal Open Market Committee
  (FOMC) *(338)*
Federal funds market *(343)*
Federal funds rate *(342)*
monetary base *(338)*
monetary policy *(333)*
nominal interest rates *(349)*

open market operations *(341)*
quantity theory of money *(346)*
real interest rates *(349)*
reserve requirement *(338)*
veil of money assumption *(347)*
velocity of money *(347)*

QUESTIONS FOR THOUGHT AND REVIEW

The number after each question represents the estimated degree of critical thinking required. (1 = almost none; 10 = deep thought.)

1. Is the Fed a private or a public agency? *(5)*
2. Why are there few regional Fed banks in the western part of the United States? *(2)*
3. The Fed wants to change the reserve requirement in order to increase the money supply (which is currently 4,000) by 200. The money multiplier is 3. What's the current reserve requirement and how should the Fed change it? *(6)*
4. The Fed wants to increase the money supply (which is currently 4,000) by 200. Assume that for each 1 percent the discount rate falls, banks borrow an additional 20. If instead of changing the reserve requirement, the Fed decides to change the discount rate, how much should the Fed change the rate to increase the money supply by 200? *(6)*
5. The Fed wants to increase the money supply (which is currently 4,000) by 200 as in (4). Only now, it decides to use open market operations. What should it do to achieve the desired change? *(6)*
6. You can lead a horse to water, but you can't make it drink. How might this adage be relevant to expansionary (as opposed to contractionary) monetary policy? *(7)*
7. The interest rate has just fallen. How might Classical and Keynesian economists draw different implications from that event? *(7)*
8. Investment increases by 20 for each interest rate drop of 1 percent. The income multiplier is 3. If the money multiplier is 4, and each change of 5 in the money supply changes the interest rate by 1 percent, what open market policy would you recommend to increase income by 240? *(6)*

9. What three assumptions turn the equation of exchange into the quantity theory of money? *(3)*
10. Assuming the quantity theory of money held true, what would happen if a country on a gold standard ran a balance of payments surplus? *(5)*
11. If the nominal interest rate is 6 percent and inflation is 5 percent, what's the real interest rate? *(3)*
12. "The effects of open market operations are somewhat like a stone cast in a pond." After the splash, discuss the first three ripples. *(4)*
13. Why would a bank hold Treasury bills as secondary reserves when it could simply hold primary reserves—cash? *(3)*
14. In 1968 Milton Friedman introduced the concept of the natural rate of unemployment. He said it was the "level of unemployment which has the property that it is consistent with equilibrium in the structure of real wage rates. At that level of employment, real wages are tending in the average to rise at a 'normal' secular rate, i.e., at a rate that can be indefinitely maintained so long as capital formation, technological improvements, etc. remain on their long-term trends." From this quotation, do you think Milton Friedman believes the Fed should adopt a target rate of unemployment? Why? *(7)*
15. The table below gives the Federal funds rate target at the end of each year shown.

Year	Federal Funds Target Rate
1993	3.00%
1994	4.75
1995	5.25
1996	5.00

Using these figures, describe how the monetary policy directions changed from 1993 through 1996. *(6)*

PROBLEMS AND EXERCISES

1. Suppose the Fed decides it needs to pursue an expansionary policy. Assume people hold no cash, the reserve requirement is 20 percent, and there are no excess reserves.

  a. Show how the Fed would increase the money supply by $2 million by changing the reserve requirement.
  b. Show how the Fed would increase the money supply by $2 million through open market operations.

2. Suppose the Fed decides that it needs to pursue a contractionary policy. It wants to decrease the money supply by $2 million. Assume people hold 20 percent of their money in the form of cash balances, the reserve requirement is 20 percent, and there are no excess reserves.
   a. Show how the Fed would decrease the money supply by $2 million by changing the reserve requirement.
   b. Show how the Fed would decrease the money supply by $2 million through open market operations.
   c. Go to your local bank and find out how much excess reserves they hold. Recalculate a and b assuming all banks held that percentage in excess reserves.

3. Some individuals have suggested raising the required reserve ratio for banks to 100 percent.
   a. What would the money multiplier be if this change were made?
   b. What effect would such a change have on the money supply?
   c. How could that effect be offset?
   d. Would banks likely favor or oppose this proposal? Why?

4. One of the proposals to reform monetary policy has been to have the central bank pay interest on reserves held at the bank.

   a. What effect would that proposal have on excess reserves?
   b. Would banks generally favor or oppose this proposal? Why?
   c. Would central banks generally favor or oppose this proposal? Why?
   d. What effect would this proposal probably have on interest rates paid by banks?

5. Assume the money supply is $500, the velocity of money is 8, and the price level is $2. Using the quantity theory of money:
   a. Determine the level of real output.
   b. Determine the level of nominal output.
   c. Assuming velocity remains constant, what will happen if the money supply rises 20 percent?
   d. If the government established price controls and also raised the money supply 20 percent, what would happen?
   e. How would you judge whether the assumption of fixed velocity is reasonable?

ANSWERS TO MARGIN QUESTIONS

1. The President of the United States appoints the Chairman of the Board of Governors of the Federal Reserve System.   *(335)*

2. Monetary policy is conducted by the Fed and involves changing the money supply or interest rates. Fiscal policy is conducted by the U.S. Treasury, or government, and involves running a surplus or deficit.   *(337)*

3. False. The Fed limits access to the discount window. Banks do not make decisions about borrowing from the Fed based on the fact that they can get a low interest rate at the discount window, but see it, instead, as a last resort.   *(340)*

4. The other tools of monetary policy are changing the discount rate and changing the reserve requirement.   *(341)*

5. The Fed should buy bonds to offset the unintended decline in reserves.   *(343)*

6. Monetary policy is too tight and the Fed will buy bonds.   *(343)*

7. The equation of exchange, $MV = PQ$, is a tautology. What changes it to the quantity theory are assumptions about the variables, specifically that velocity remains constant, that real output is determined separately, and

that the causation flows from money to prices. With these assumptions added, the equation of exchange implies that changes in the money supply are reflected in changes in the price level—which is what the quantity theory of money says.   *(347)*

8. Keynesians are more likely to emphasize the interest rate in discussions of monetary policy. Classical economists are more likely to emphasize measures of the money supply.   *(348)*

9. It depends. The Fed is generally eclectic, sometimes using a Keynesian model and sometimes a Classical model, combining the use of both of those models with a feel for the market. In other words, the Fed does what it wants. In 1993, the Fed leaned toward emphasizing interest rates and away from money supply measures, but, if the past is any indication, the swing won't be permanent.   *(350)*

10. Five problems of monetary policy are:
    1. Knowing what policy to use;
    2. Understanding what policy you're using;
    3. The lags in monetary policy;
    4. Political pressure; and
    5. Conflicting international goals.   *(351)*

The Effect of Monetary Policy
Using T-Accounts

The Fed uses the discount rate, the reserve requirement, and open market operations to change the money supply. Each of these tools works initially by affecting the amount of reserves in the banking system. Here, I will show you exactly how the Fed changes the money supply using T-accounts. To simplify things, say there's only one bank, Textland Bank, with branches all over the country. Textland is fully loaned out at a 10 percent reserve requirement. For simplicity, assume people hold no cash. Textland's beginning balance sheet is presented below in Exhibit A1.

Now say the Fed sells $10,000 worth of Treasury bonds to individuals. The person who buys them pays with a check to the Fed for $10,000. The Fed, in turn, presents that check to the bank, getting $10,000 in cash from the bank. This step is shown in Exhibit A2.

As you can see, bank reserves are now $290,000, which is too low to meet requirements on demand deposits of $2,990,000. With a 10 percent reserve requirement,

$2,990,000 in deposits would require (1/10) × $2,990,000 = $299,000, so the bank is $9,000 short of reserves. It must figure out a way to meet its reserve requirement. Let's say that it calls in $9,000 of its loans. After doing so it has assets of $299,000 in cash and $2,990,000 in demand deposits, so it looks as if the bank has met its reserve requirement.

If the bank could meet its reserve requirement that way, its balance sheet would be as shown in Exhibit A3. Loans would decrease by $9,000 and cash would increase by the $9,000 necessary to meet the reserve requirement.

Unfortunately for the bank, meeting its reserve requirement isn't that easy. That $9,000 in cash had to come from somewhere. Most likely, the person who paid off the loans in cash did it partly by running down her checking account, borrowing all the cash she could from others, and using whatever other options she had. Since by assumption in this example, people don't hold cash, the banking system was initially fully loaned out, and

---

EXHIBIT A1   Textland Bank Balance Sheet   Beginning Balance

Assets		Liabilities and Net Worth	
Cash (reserves)	$ 300,000	Demand deposits	$3,000,000
Loans	2,000,000	Net worth	1,000,000
Treasury bonds	400,000		
Property	1,300,000		
Total assets	$4,000,000	Total liabilities and net worth	$4,000,000

EXHIBIT A2   Transaction 1

Assets			Liabilities and Net Worth		
Cash (reserves)	$ 300,000		Demand deposits	$3,000,000	
Payment to Fed (person's Treasury purchase)	(10,000)		Deposit for cash (person's check)	(10,000)	
Total cash		$ 290,000	Total deposits		$2,990,000
Loans		2,000,000	Net worth		1,000,000
Treasury bonds		400,000			
Property		1,300,000			
Total assets		$3,990,000	Total liabilities and net worth		$3,990,000

EXHIBIT A3   Transaction 2

Assets			Liabilities and Net Worth	
Cash (reserves)	$ 290,000		Demand deposits	$2,990,000
Loans (repaid)	9,000		Net worth	1,000,000
Total cash		$ 299,000		
Loans	2,000,000			
Loans called in	(9,000)			
Total loans		1,991,000		
Treasury bonds		400,000		
Property		1,300,000		
Total assets		$3,990,000	Total liabilities and net worth	$3,990,000

Textland Bank was the only bank, the only cash in the economy was in Textland Bank's vaults! So that $9,000 in cash had to come from its vaults. Calling in the loans cannot directly solve its reserve problem. It still has reserves of only $290,000.

But calling in its loans did *indirectly* help solve the problem. Calling in loans decreased investment which, because it decreased aggregate demand, decreased the income in the economy. (If you're not sure why this is the case, think back to the macro policy model.) That decrease in income decreases the amount of demand deposits people want to hold. As demand deposits decrease, the bank's need for reserves decreases.

Contraction of the money supply in this example works in the opposite way to an expansion of the money supply. Banks keep trying to meet their reserve requirement by getting cash, only to find that for the banking system as a whole the total cash is limited. Thus, the banking system as a whole must continue to call in loans until that decline in loans causes income to fall sufficiently to cause demand deposits to fall to a level that can be supported by the smaller reserves. In this example, with a money multiplier of 10, when demand deposits have fallen by $100,000 to $2,900,000, total reserves available to the system ($290,000) will be sufficient to meet the reserve requirement.

QUESTIONS FOR THOUGHT AND REVIEW

1. Demonstrate, using T-accounts, the effect of the Fed selling $1 million of Treasury bonds.

APPENDIX B

Keynesian and Classical Theories of Interest and Their Implications for Monetary Policy

To understand the theoretical differences between Keynesian and Classical economists' theories of monetary policy, we must understand their alternative theories of interest. Unfortunately, these theories are complicated, confusing, and quite possibly confused—all at the same time.

The way these theories try to treat money is as simply another good—a good that has a supply and demand curve that can be analyzed separately from the other supply and demands. Having specified the analysis of the money market, both Keynesian and Classical theories

then try to integrate it back into the aggregate analysis. There have been many articles written trying to do this on both the Keynesian and Classical sides, but the formal attempts to do so lead to one of two conclusions: (1) that money doesn't matter; or (2) that money matters but only as a third- or fourth-order effect on the economy.

If one believes money matters in a more substantive way, one is forced to make some ad hoc assumptions that money *does* matter (it is desired for its own sake). That approach doesn't come close to making money matter as much as it seems to in the real world. Economists Robert

Clower, Peter Howitt, Xiaokai Yang and Siang Ng, in their recent work on the role of money, have, in my view, provided a reasonable discussion of how it might be integrated.

In the Clower view, money matters so much to the economy that its deep theoretical analysis must go beyond supply and demand analysis. Money is part of the institutional structure of our economy, and its effects are so substantial and interrelated with that institutional structure that it doesn't make a lot of sense to separate out the analysis of money independent of that institutional structure. Money is part of the macrofoundation of the economy. What this means is that output is not a function of money, i.e., $Q = F(M)$, but that the production function, F, itself is dependent on money and that the aggregate production function cannot be specified independently of the existence of money. At the introductory level, we needn't worry about such high-level theoretical issues. We simply need to recognize that money does matter, and it matters a lot.

An analogy might make this argument clear. Money's role in the economy is similar to the role of oil in a gas engine. As inputs into running an engine go, oil plays a supplemental role. Gas, together with electrical sparks, would be seen as the primary input. Oil would likely be seen as a tangential input. Moreover, any formal analysis of how oil reduces friction and heat would be extraordinarily complicated. But try running an engine without oil, and you will see oil's importance, just as you will also see the importance of money if you try to run an economy without money.

That said, let me now review very briefly the Keynesian and the Classical theories of money. Keynesians believe the interest rate is primarily a monetary phenomenon, so they have a monetary theory of the rate of interest. For Keynesians, the interest rate is determined by the supply and demand for money. Classicals believe the interest rate is a real phenomenon, so they have a real theory of the rate of interest. In an earlier chapter you were introduced to the Keynesian and Classical theories of the interest rate. This appendix further develops their theories and discusses their implications for conducting monetary policy.

The Keynesian Supply and Demand for Money Theory of the Interest Rate

As we saw in a previous chapter, money is a financial asset people want to hold. But how much do they want to hold? It shouldn't surprise you that economists' answer is that it depends upon the supply and demand for money.

The Supply of Money
The Fed determines the money supply by setting the amount of reserves in the system. Then the total amount of money in the economy is determined by the reserve requirement and the money multiplier. Here we'll assume that the Fed can perfectly determine the amount of money supplied to the economy and that that amount of money supplied isn't influenced by the interest rate. That makes the supply of money perfectly vertical, as in Exhibit B1.

The Demand for Money
As we saw in a previous chapter, people want to hold money because it's useful to them as a medium of exchange and as a store of wealth. But holding money isn't costless. *Money pays lower interest than other financial assets.* So how much money people want to hold depends on the interest rate on those other financial assets. The higher the interest rate on other financial assets, the greater the opportunity cost of holding money and the lower the quantity of money demanded. At lower interest rates, quantity of money demanded is larger because the opportunity cost of holding money is lower. Demand for money as a function of the interest rate is shown by the curve D_M in Exhibit B1.

The Keynesian theory of interest comes from combining the supply of money with the demand for money as in Exhibit B1. The interest rate is determined where the quantity of money supplied equals the quantity of money demanded (i_e). If the supply of money increases, say from S_0 to S_1 as in Exhibit B1(b), the interest rate will fall from i_0. If the demand for money increases, the interest rate will rise. Keynes argued that, in the short run, the money market determines the interest rate.

The Classical Savings Investment Theory of the Interest Rate

The supply and demand for money isn't the only market that plays a role in determining the interest rate. The Classical view is that the interest rate is determined by the supply of savings and the demand for those savings for investment purposes. Money doesn't affect the interest rate, so it doesn't affect the real economy. It only affects the price level. So the best monetary policy is a policy that provides stability of the price level. It's a long-run policy that emphasizes a constant predetermined growth rate of the money supply.

Implications of Keynesian and Classical Theories for Monetary Policy

In the Classical model, interest rate fluctuations keep savings equal to investment at the full-employment level of income. Changes in the interest rate equilibrate the savings/investment market.

That's not the way it works in Keynes's model. Income fluctuations, not interest rate fluctuations, bring the savings/investment market into equilibrium. As discussed in the text, this happens in the following way: Income

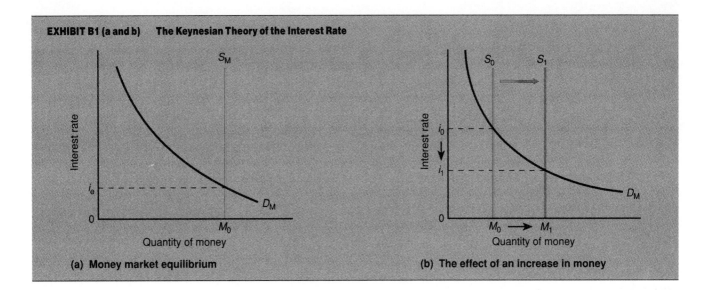

EXHIBIT B1 (a and b)   The Keynesian Theory of the Interest Rate

(a) **Money market equilibrium**

(b) **The effect of an increase in money**

fluctuates, which causes savings to fluctuate. That fluctuation in savings brings the savings/investment market into equilibrium.

So in Keynes's model, the real economy is affected by money. In the Classical model, money only affects the price level.

The implication of the Keynesian theory of interest for monetary policy is that it's necessary to maintain an active discretionary monetary policy to keep the interest rate at a level that will maintain a savings/investment equilibrium at the target level of income. Classicals believe in a monetary rule.

QUESTIONS FOR THOUGHT AND REVIEW

1. What does it mean to say that money is part of the macrofoundation of the economy?
2. If an economist said that the interest rate is determined primarily by the supply and demand for money, would that economist most likely be a Keynesian or Classical? Explain.

Fourteen

Inflation and Its Relationship to Unemployment and Growth

The first few months or year of inflation, like the first few drinks, seem just fine. Everyone has more money to spend and prices aren't rising quite as fast as the money that's available. The hangover comes when prices start to catch up.

~ Milton Friedman

After reading this chapter, you should be able to:

1 Explain why sustained high inflation is inevitably accompanied by a roughly equal increase in the money supply and expectations of inflation.

2 Differentiate between long-run and short-run Phillips curves.

3 Outline the Classical theory of inflation in reference to the quantity theory of money.

4 Explain why Classical economists favor a monetary rule.

5 Outline the Keynesian theory of inflation.

6 Distinguish the Keynesian and Classical views of the Phillips curve trade-off.

The last two chapters surveyed traditional macro policy—the use of monetary and fiscal policy as stabilization tools. In those chapters you saw that *if* (and it was a big if) the government can determine where potential income is, and *if* the government can significantly influence aggregate demand to offset undesirable shifts in autonomous aggregate demand before the autonomous expenditures shift in another direction (another big if), then there is a role for demand management as a stabilization tool to smooth out business cycles; the government could be in the economy's driving seat, with economists at the steering wheel.

You also were told about the reality that politicians, not economists, are at the steering wheel, and that politicians have a strong bias toward expansionary policy. Political pressures are to lower unemployment and stimulate growth. What prevents politicians from doing so is *inflation,* or at least the fear of generating an accelerating inflation. Real-world considerations of both fiscal and monetary policy involve discussions of what effect expansion might have on inflationary forces in the economy.

It is for that reason that inflation, and its relation to unemployment and growth, comes to center stage in any discussion of macro policy. Hence this chapter. It extends our earlier consideration of inflation, and considers different views on the existence and nature of a trade-off between inflation, unemployment, and growth.

Inflation is *a continuous rise in the price level*. All economists agree on that. They also agree (1) that high inflation rates are inevitably accompanied by a roughly proportional increase in the money supply, and (2) that high inflation rates are associated with expectations of inflation of approximately those rates. Thus, most economists accept that when inflation is really high, say 40 percent, the money supply will be increasing by about 40 percent, and people will be expecting approximately 40 percent inflation.[1] Why do these rough equalities hold? Let's consider the money supply and inflation first.

Say, for example, that the U.S. money supply growth rate is 40 percent. What will likely happen? From the equation of exchange discussed in the previous chapter ($MV = PY$), you can deduce that something else must also change. Assuming velocity, V, isn't decreasing enormously and real output, Y, isn't increasing enormously, that 40 percent increase in the money supply, M, must be accompanied by a rise in the price level, P, of about 40 percent. Otherwise there will be a shortage of goods. Alternatively, say prices are rising at a 40 percent rate but the money supply isn't growing at all. Unless velocity is increasing by 40 percent a year, firms will be unable to sell their goods at the higher prices because the amount of money people are spending won't buy the goods that firms are offering to sell at those higher prices. Given the shortage of aggregate demand, firms will be forced to stop increasing their prices.

Notice that so far we've said nothing about what's causing what to increase, which clearly is something policymakers would like to know. Determining the cause of inflation is important in determining how to fight it.

To distinguish cases in which price increases cause the money supply increases from cases in which money supply increases cause the price increases, inflation is divided into **cost-push inflation** (*inflation where price increases cause money supply increases*) and **demand-pull inflation** (*inflation where money supply increases cause price increases*).

In an ongoing inflation, it's often impossible to distinguish whether it's cost-push or demand-pull. The reason is expectations of inflation. Say money supply is expected to increase. Firms will expect demand for their goods to increase and will raise prices on the basis of that expectation. Then, even though price increases may come before money supply increases, it's the expected increase in the money supply that causes prices to rise. However, regardless of whether prices are being pulled by the money supply or are pushing the money supply, all economists agree that, for substantial inflation to continue, the money supply must rise.

The second relationship that most economists agree exists is between inflation and expectations of inflation. The relationship is based on common sense. For example, if inflation is currently 20 percent, assuming no major change in policy, it is reasonable to expect that it will remain about 20 percent. So people's natural tendency, often, is to base their expectations on conditions that already exist or have recently existed. That is, they use **adaptive expectations**—*expectations based, in some way, on what has been in the past.*

Adaptive expectations aren't the only reasonable type. People likely will also base their expectations of inflation on their understanding of the economy, economists' predictions of inflation, and their own past experience. For example, if the money supply is increasing substantially, many economists will predict high inflation. To the degree that people believe economists, people will expect high inflation, even though it's not yet high. So the relationship between current inflation and expectations of future inflation is not perfect.

INFLATION

Inflation   A continuous rise in the price level.

The Money Supply and Inflation

1 High inflation rates are inevitably accompanied by high money growth and high inflationary expectations. The reason is that the velocity of money generally cannot increase enormously and people's expectations of the future are determined in large part by what is occurring now.

Determining the cause of inflation is important to determining how to fight it.

When discussing this point I write the equation of exchange on the blackboard, review the elements of the equation, and use them to show the relationship between money and inflation.

Regardless of whether prices are being pulled by the money supply or are pushing the money supply, all economists agree that, for substantial inflation to continue, the money supply must rise.

Inflation and Expectations of Inflation

Q–1: If inflation exists when there are fairly large amounts of unemployment, is it more likely to be a cost-push inflation or a demand-pull inflation?

---

[1]Where economists disagree is on what causes what to increase. Is inflation causing the money supply to increase, or are increases in the money supply causing inflation? We'll address these issues shortly.

But, on average, most economists agree that expectations of inflation approximately equal the amount of inflation in the economy.

Inflation and Unemployment: Does a Phillips Curve Trade-Off Exist?

Video Series, Economics USA: Stagflation, Segments 10.1-10.2

Perhaps the most vexing dilemma policymakers face in dealing with inflation is the inflation/unemployment policy dilemma: Often when they try to fight inflation, unemployment seems to increase, and often when they try to fight unemployment, inflation seems to increase. The dilemma is captured graphically in a curve, shown in Exhibit 1(a), called the short-run Phillips curve.

In it, unemployment is measured on the horizontal axis; inflation is on the vertical axis. The **Phillips curve**—*a representation of the relation between inflation and unemployment*—shows us what combinations of those two phenomena are possible. It tells us that when unemployment is low, say 4 percent, inflation tends to be high, say 4 percent (point *A* on the short-run Phillips curve). It also tells us that if we want to lower inflation, say to 1 percent, we must be willing to accept high unemployment, say 7 percent (point *B* in Exhibit 1(a)).

Explanation of Why a Trade-Off Might Exist

Phillips curve   A representation of the relation between inflation and unemployment.

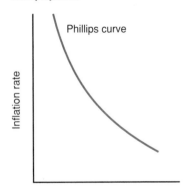

Why should there be such an inverse relationship between inflation and unemployment? One answer is that the Phillips curve is simply an aggregate representation of the dynamic laws of supply and demand. Unemployment represents excess supply of labor, and the greater the excess supply the greater the downward pressure on wages, and hence on prices. But there are two reasons that answer doesn't fully explain the slope of the Phillips curve. First, the laws of supply and demand refer to relative prices; inflation is about the price level. If the Phillips curve were an aggregate representation of the laws of supply and demand, everyone's expectation of the price level would have to remain constant, even as that price level was changing; that doesn't fit economists' view of people as rational. Second, the Phillips curve relationship shows a relationship between *inflation* and *unemployment,* whereas the laws of supply and demand suggest that, with enough unemployment, there should be a *fall* in the price level—deflation. We don't observe much deflation in our economy; in fact we haven't seen the U.S. price level fall in over 50 years. So the Phillips curve relationship represents something other than the laws of supply and demand.

A more satisfactory explanation for the short-run Phillips curve involves institutional factors inherent in the wage- and price-setting institutions and/or slowly adjusting expectations. These institutional factors, such as contracts and implicit agreements (the invisible handshake at work), prevent wages and prices from rising immediately when there is an increase in aggregate equilibrium demand, and create costs of changing wages and prices. These institutional factors result from institutions involving seller-set prices and negotiated wages.

Another explanation for the short-run Phillips curve involves individuals' expectation-forming process. Once people believe that a noninflationary environment has been achieved, they are slow to change their expectations of inflation. They are either fooled by the inflation, or they initially see inflation as a blip which does not

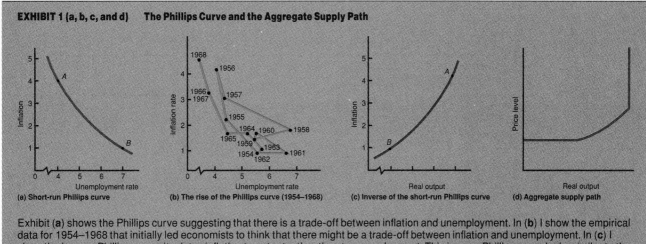

EXHIBIT 1 (a, b, c, and d)   The Phillips Curve and the Aggregate Supply Path

(a) Short-run Phillips curve

(b) The rise of the Phillips curve (1954–1968)

(c) Inverse of the short-run Phillips curve

(d) Aggregate supply path

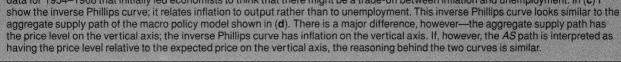

Exhibit (**a**) shows the Phillips curve suggesting that there is a trade-off between inflation and unemployment. In (**b**) I show the empirical data for 1954–1968 that initially led economists to think that there might be a trade-off between inflation and unemployment. In (**c**) I show the inverse Phillips curve; it relates inflation to output rather than to unemployment. This inverse Phillips curve looks similar to the aggregate supply path of the macro policy model shown in (**d**). There is a major difference, however—the aggregate supply path has the price level on the vertical axis; the inverse Phillips curve has inflation on the vertical axis. If, however, the *AS* path is interpreted as having the price level relative to the expected price on the vertical axis, the reasoning behind the two curves is similar.

change the expectations of future inflation. Since there are costs of changing nominal prices, they are initially slow to react to that inflation by increasing their own prices to keep their relative price constant.

A third explanation of why there is a trade-off involves the cost of processing information about inflation and the price level. Individuals aren't super-computers, and, were the CPI not reported in the newspapers, would only have a very rough idea of what is happening to the overall price level. (As we saw in our earlier discussion of inflation, even economists have a hard time determining precisely what the rate of inflation is.) Moreover, some rises in prices are necessary and, at times, the price level needs to rise relative to one's wage or price. People know this. Given the ambiguity about what the price level is, and what one's relative price ideally is, combined with the costs of changing nominal prices, a strong argument can be made that, often, rational individuals will not respond significantly to small increases in the price level. This tendency to not respond to price level changes has been called *money illusion*, but this line of reasoning does not see it as an illusion at all. It is individuals' rational reaction to the complexity of price levels and price determination. Given the costs and uncertainty surrounding the price-setting process, often small changes in the price level (i.e., 2–3%) do not warrant being taken into account. Only if inflation breaks what might be called an *inflationary psychological threshold* will workers and firms build a rise in the price level into their expectations and price-setting strategies.

Explanations for the shape of the short run Phillips curve include institutional factors, individuals' expectations formation process, and the cost of processing information.

These theoretical explanations are still being debated by economists and were not part of the initial Phillips curve presentation. The initial Phillips curve was an empirically based curve; it was based simply on the observed relationship between unemployment and inflation.

As I stated above, as economists looked at unemployment and inflation data over time, they noticed that there seemed to be a trade-off between inflation and unemployment. When unemployment was high, inflation was low; when unemployment was low, inflation was high. That empirical relationship seemed rather stable in the 1950s and 1960s. Exhibit 1(b) shows this empirical relationship for the United States for the years 1954–68, when it became built into the way economists looked at the economy.

Before we consider the Phillips curve in more detail, let's see how it relates to the macro policy model's aggregate supply path shown in Exhibit 1(d). In relating the two, it is helpful to create what might be called an inverse Phillips curve—a curve that

The Phillips Curve and the Aggregate Supply Path

While the aggregate supply path and the Phillips curve have somewhat the same shape, the aggregate supply path relates *price level* to output while the Phillips curve relates *inflation*—the change in the price level—to unemployment. While unemployment and output are probably inversely related most of the time, there is no general relationship between changes in the price level and changes in inflation. Just as the relationship between a variable and its derivative can be quite different, so, too, can the relationship between output and the price level and the change in the price level.

shows the relationship between inflation and output levels, rather than between inflation and unemployment. To create such a curve, you must remember that unemployment and output are inversely related—as unemployment falls, output increases. This inverse relationship between unemployment and output reverses the slope of the Phillips curve. Specifically, it makes the shape of the inverse Phillips curve upward sloping: As output increases, inflation also increases. In Exhibit 1(c) I show an inverse Phillips curve that relates inflation to output. It shows that as output increases, inflation has a tendency to increase.

This inverse Phillips curve shown in Exhibit 1(c) and the aggregate supply path shown in Exhibit 1(d) have the same upward-sloping shape, which leads some people to use them interchangeably. But there is a big difference between the two. The inverse Phillips curve has *inflation* on the vertical axis; it relates output to the change in the price level. The aggregate supply path has the *price level* on the vertical axis; it relates output to the price level. What's the difference? Think back to the definition of inflation as a *continuous* rise in the price level. A one-time rise in the price level is not necessarily inflation. It only becomes inflation when that is built into an inflationary process. So the curves correspond with quite different relationships. Still, there is a potential relationship between the two curves: If you flip through a large number of aggregate supply paths quickly, the continual one-time rises will become inflation.

History of the Phillips Curve

Because it seemed to represent a relatively stable trade-off, in the 1960s the short-run Phillips curve began to play a central role in discussions of macroeconomic policy. Republicans (often advised by Classical economists) generally favored contractionary monetary and fiscal policy, which maintained high unemployment and low inflation (a point like *B* in Exhibit 1(a and c)). Democrats (often advised by Keynesian economists) generally favored expansionary monetary and fiscal policies, which brought about low unemployment but high inflation (a point like *A* in Exhibit 1(a and c)). Keynesians believed the potential income was higher than what Classicals believed.

"Policy Implications of the Phillips Curve," by Paul Samuelson and Robert Solow in *Classic Readings in Economics* is the original Solow-Samuelson discussion of the Phillips. It is a useful reading because it shows how tentative they were in drawing policy conclusions about inflation.

The Breakdown of the Short-Run Phillips Curve In the early 1970s, the empirical short-run Phillips curve relationship seemed to break down. When one looked at the data, there no longer seemed to be a trade-off between unemployment and inflation. Instead, when unemployment was high, inflation was also high. This phenomenon is termed **stagflation**—*the combination of high and accelerating inflation and high unemployment.* Exhibit 2(a) shows the empirical relationship between inflation and unemployment from 1969 to 1981. Notice that the relatively stable relationship up until 1969 breaks down in the 1970s. In the 1970s, there doesn't seem to be any trade-off between inflation and unemployment at all. Something clearly changed in the 1970s. In the 1980s, inflation fell substantially, and beginning in 1986, a Phillips-curve-type relationship began to reappear, as can be seen in Exhibit 2(b). But then in the mid-1990s both inflation and unemployment remained low and the trade-off once again disappeared.

To discover what changed in the 1970s, economists devoted much thought to explaining the theory underlying the Phillips curve. What caused inflation? How would inflation interact with unemployment if people acted in certain reasonable ways? As economists thought about these problems, they developed and refined their understanding of inflation, unemployment, and growth.

Expectations of inflation The rise in the price level that the average person expects.

Short-run Phillips curve A curve showing the trade-off between inflation and unemployment when expectations of inflation are constant.

Long-run Phillips curve A curve showing the trade-off (or complete lack thereof) when expectations of inflation equal actual inflation.

The Distinction between the Short-Run and Long-Run Phillips Curves As views of the Phillips curve changed, economists began distinguishing between a short-run Phillips curve and a long-run Phillips curve. The key element of that distinction is based on **expectations of inflation** (*the rise in the price level that the average person expects*). The **short-run Phillips curve** is *a curve showing the trade-off between inflation and unemployment when expectations of inflation are constant.* On each point on the short-run Phillips curve, expectations of inflation do not change, and hence will not, generally, equal actual inflation. The **long-run Phillips curve** is *a curve showing the trade-off (or complete lack thereof) when expectations of inflation equal actual*

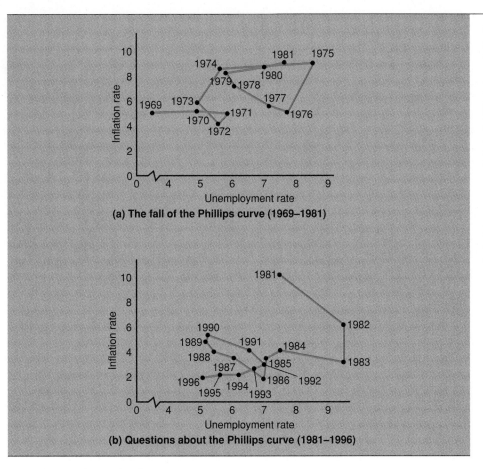

(a) The fall of the Phillips curve (1969–1981)

(b) Questions about the Phillips curve (1981–1996)

Source: Economic Report of the President.

EXHIBIT 2 (a and b)   The Empirical Data Underlying and Undermining the Phillips Curve Trade-Off

As you see in (**a**), in the 1970s the empirical Phillips curve relationship between inflation and unemployment broke down, leading many economists to question the existence of any Phillips curve relationship that allowed policy makers to choose between inflation and unemployment. In (**b**) you can see how in the 1980s and 1990s the evidence is mixed. Specifically, from 1985 to 1992, a Phillips curve relationship seemed to exist. This allows some economists to say a Phillips curve–type relationship exists and others to say it doesn't.

inflation. At each point on the long-run Phillips curve, expectations of inflation change so that they equal actual inflation. Economists used this distinction to explain why the short-run Phillips curve relationship broke down in the 1970s.

The reason expectations are so central to the Phillips curve is seen by considering an individual's decision about what wage or price to set. Say you expect 0 percent inflation and you want a 2 percent wage or price increase. You'll raise your wage or price by 2 percent. Now say you expect 20 percent inflation and you want a 2 percent real wage increase. To get it, you must increase your wage by 22 percent. If everyone expects 20 percent inflation, everyone will raise their wage or price by 20 percent just to keep up.

This was a recognition of the central role that expectations of inflation play in inflation. When expectations of inflation are higher, the same level of unemployment will be associated with a higher rate of inflation. To capture this relationship, it makes sense to assume that the short-run Phillips curve moves up or down as expectations of inflation change.

The Shape and Stability of the Long-Run Phillips Curve   To determine what the long-run Phillips curve would look like, economists asked themselves: What difference should expectations of inflation make to the target level of unemployment? Their answer was none. If people expect 20 percent inflation and are raising their wages and prices 20 percent on average, the situation is just the same as if they expect 4 percent inflation and are raising their wages and prices 4 percent on average. Since their real incomes will be the same in both situations, their real decisions—how much labor to supply and demand—will be the same, so employment will not change. People aren't fooled by expected inflation. Thus, economists theorized that the long-run Phillips curve

Q–2: Draw the long-run Phillips curve. Why does it have that shape?

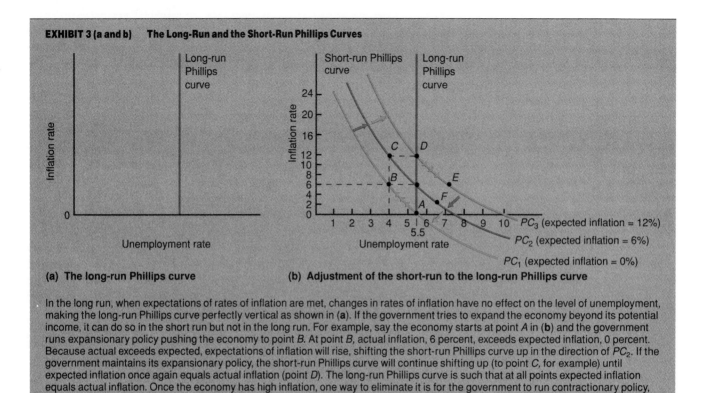

EXHIBIT 3 (a and b)   The Long-Run and the Short-Run Phillips Curves

(a) The long-run Phillips curve

(b) Adjustment of the short-run to the long-run Phillips curve

In the long run, when expectations of rates of inflation are met, changes in rates of inflation have no effect on the level of unemployment, making the long-run Phillips curve perfectly vertical as shown in (a). If the government tries to expand the economy beyond its potential income, it can do so in the short run but not in the long run. For example, say the economy starts at point A in (b) and the government runs expansionary policy pushing the economy to point B. At point B, actual inflation, 6 percent, exceeds expected inflation, 0 percent. Because actual exceeds expected, expectations of inflation will rise, shifting the short-run Phillips curve up in the direction of PC_2. If the government maintains its expansionary policy, the short-run Phillips curve will continue shifting up (to point C, for example) until expected inflation once again equals actual inflation (point D). The long-run Phillips curve is such that at all points expected inflation equals actual inflation. Once the economy has high inflation, one way to eliminate it is for the government to run contractionary policy, pushing the economy to point E where expected inflation exceeds actual inflation. As expectations of inflation fall, the short-run Phillips curve will shift back down to PC_2 and PC_1.

Be careful to discuss clearly why the long-run Phillips curve is positioned at the target rate of unemployment and why actual inflation always equals expected inflation along the long-run Phillips curve.

Q–3: If people's expectations of inflation didn't change, would the economy move from a short-run to a long-run Phillips curve?

For a computer simulation of policies that affect the Phillips curve see the module, "Phillips curve" in *Macro Interactive.*

2 The long-run Phillips curve is vertical; it takes into account the feedback of inflation on expectations of inflation. The short-run Phillips curve does not take this feedback into account.

would be a vertical line, as in Exhibit 3(a). As you can see, in the long run, when expectations of inflation are fully built into people's wage- and price-setting decisions, there's no trade-off between inflation and unemployment.

This vertical long-run Phillips curve fits the empirical data for the 1970s and provides an explanation for why the short-run trade-off broke down. To see this, let's consider the years 1964 and 1970. Unemployment in both years was approximately 5 percent, but inflation in 1970 was over 5 percent while inflation in 1964 was less than 2 percent. Why the difference? Consider what happened in the interim: Inflation was consistently rising, so it's reasonable to assume that expectations of inflation were higher in 1970 than in 1964. Expectations of inflation explain the difference. When expectations are higher, actual inflation at each level of unemployment will be higher.

Moving from a Short-Run to a Long-Run Phillips Curve   We can see how and why an economy moves from a short-run to a long-run Phillips curve by examining Exhibit 3(b). Say, for example, that initially the economy is at point *A*. Expected inflation is zero, and unemployment is 5.5 percent, a level consistent with potential income. Since expected inflation is zero, the relative short-run Phillips curve is PC_1, which assumes zero expected inflation. (Each short-run Phillips curve is consistent with one level of expected inflation.)

Now, say that the government expands aggregate demand with expansionary monetary policy. Initially, expectations of inflation remain constant, so the economy moves along the initial short-run Phillips curve, PC_1. Unemployment falls from 5.5 percent to 4 percent and inflation rises from 0 percent to 6 percent (point *B*).

If the rise of inflation to 6 percent caused no change in individuals' expectations, the economy could remain at point *B*. But generally people change their expectations to match the actual inflation. As they do, the short-run Phillips curve shifts, since each short-run Phillips curve represents the trade-off for a given level of inflationary expectation. Since inflation expectations have risen, the short-run Phillips curve shifts to PC_2. This means that people who wanted a 2 percent raise are now asking for a 2 + 6, or 8, percent raise. If the government wanted to maintain the 4 percent unem-

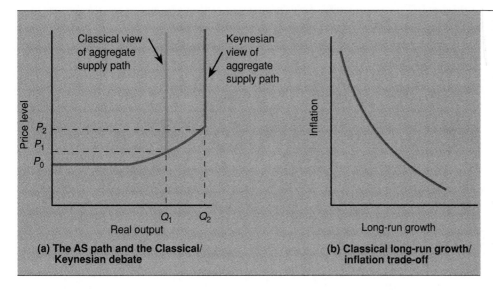

EXHIBIT 4 (a and b)   The Trade-Off between Inflation, High-Level Output, and Growth

Classicals are much more likely to err on the side of preventing inflation, estimating potential output at a low level (such as Q_1 in (**a**)). They see the inflation threshold at P_1 whereas Keynesians see it at P_2. Classicals justify erring on the side of preventing inflation by arguing that there is a high cost of allowing inflation—inflation undermines the economy's long-run growth and hence its future potential income. Thus, they emphasize a trade-off between inflation and growth as shown in (**b**).

Presenting the long-run Phillips curve as vertical gives students the sense that the government cannot affect the long-run rate of unemployment. Thus, it is appropriate to point out to students that there is enormous debate about estimates of the target rate of unemployment and that the target unemployment rate can shift around.

This ambiguity about the target rate is especially important in the 1990s in the United States, as significant restructuring is taking place. To bring home this issue, it is helpful to point out to students that there are jobs, and then there are *jobs*. If everyone desires high-level jobs, the target unemployment rate will be significantly higher than if everyone is willing to accept very low-paying jobs. The difference between the movements in the continental European unemployment rate and the U.S. and British unemployment rates in the late-1990s is an example of this. In Germany and other continental European countries, policy has been focused on guaranteeing high-level jobs for people, creating a much higher target rate of unemployment.

The Relationship between Inflation and Growth

ployment rate, it would have to use far more expansionary policies and accept 12 percent inflation (point C). But if the government did so, the short-run Phillips curve would shift up to PC_3, and the same expectation adjustment would occur. The short-run Phillips curve will continue to shift up as long as actual inflation exceeds expected inflation.

Now, the economy is on PC_3 where inflationary expectations are 12 percent. The only way for the government to stop this upward spiral is to back off on its unemployment goal, and to accept the level of unemployment consistent with potential income—5.5 percent unemployment. If it does so, the economy will arrive at point D—with expected inflation of 12 percent equaling actual inflation of 12 percent and with the unemployment rate at 5.5 percent. If you connect points A and D you will see that they are on a vertical line—the long-run Phillips curve—in which expectations of inflation equal actual inflation.

By the 1980s, most economists accepted the view that there was a short-run trade-off but no long-run trade-off. Once again, however, economists' beliefs were challenged by empirical observation. As unemployment decreased from 7 percent in 1986 to about 5 percent in 1989, inflation increased, but there were no signs of accelerating inflation, even though expectations had had time to adjust. Then in 1990 and 1991 as unemployment rose, inflation fell, and it remained low through the 1990s even as unemployment fell. This brought out another aspect of the debate concerning inflation—the relationship between inflation and growth.

We can see this debate by thinking back to the macro policy model and the aggregate supply path (see Exhibit 4(a)). As the economy expands and output increases, *at some point* the price level begins to rise. The problem is that no one knows precisely where that point is. The government wants to choose as high an output level as possible that is consistent with inflation remaining low and not accelerating. Where that point is is in debate. Keynesians argue that it is best to err on the high side, say at Q_2 in Exhibit 4(a). Classicals argue that it is best to err on the low side, say at Q_1. The reason for the difference is a difference of where the accelerating inflation threshold is. Classicals see that threshold at a low level of output.

Many people believe that a rise in price level is acceptable if it means higher output, lower unemployment, and more growth. If that were the entire trade-off, such a reaction is probably right. But Classical economists point out a problem with that reasoning, which might be called the "little bit pregnant problem." At the beginning of a pregnancy, it's true you are only a little bit pregnant, but that "little bit" has set in motion a set of cellular changes that will fundamentally alter your life. Classical economists say it is the same with a small rise in the price level: You can't have a

"The Stages of the Phillips Curve," by Milton Friedman, in *Classic Readings in Economics.*

Classicals see a long run tradeoff between inflation and growth.

"little bit of inflation." That little bit is setting in motion a series of events that will make the inflation grow and grow, unless the government gives up its attempt to achieve a high rate of output. The Classical solution is abstinence—just say no to any rise in the price level.

Classicals point out that erring on the low side pays off—it stops any chance of inflation. That inflation undermines the long-run growth prospects of the economy, and hence causes future levels of potential income to be lower than they otherwise would be. Put another way—*inflation undermines long-run growth;* abstinence creates the environment for long-run growth. Thus, for Classicals, while there is no long-run trade-off between inflation and unemployment, there is a long-run trade-off between inflation and growth: Higher inflation leads to low growth. This hypothesized relationship is shown in Exhibit 4(b). Thus, for Classicals, even if there is a short-run relationship between inflation and unemployment, it is precarious for government to try to take advantage of it, because doing so can undermine the long-run growth potential of the economy. For Classicals, government policy creating an environment of price level stability is the best policy—the policy most likely to lead to high levels of growth.

For Classicals, government policy creating an environment of price level stability is the best policy.

Keynesians waffle a bit more, and to be truthful, I've always found it hard to pin them down as to what precisely they do believe. (And I'm generally considered a Keynesian!) They agree that price level rises have the potential of generating inflation, and that high accelerating inflation undermines growth. But they argue that not all price level increases start an inflationary process. They often argue that a little bit of a rise in the price level is so nice, and if the government is really careful—I mean really really careful—it can avoid reaching the point where the little bit of rise in price level starts the monster of inflation growing within the economy. And besides, Keynesians reason, if inflation gets started, the government has some medicine to give the economy that will get rid of the inflation relatively easily.

In terms of policy differences, the different views come down to the following. The archetypical Classical economist would shoot for a potential income goal at a point close to where prices are starting to rise. They believe that the aggregate supply path quickly becomes vertical. This point is labeled Q_1 in Exhibit 4(a). He or she would argue that while, yes, in the short run one could lower the unemployment rate with more expansionary policy, such a policy would be inflationary, and would undermine the stability for long-run growth.

The archetypical Keynesian would be more likely to shoot for a potential output goal, such as Q_2 in Exhibit 4(a). This Keynesian view is that the aggregate supply path becomes vertical only after there are significant price level rises above those that were expected and that the gains in lower unemployment are worth the risk that the price level rise gets built into expectations.

The real-world difference can be seen in the debate about what to do about monetary policy in the late 1990s when the unemployment rate fell close to 5 percent. Until then, potential income had been estimated at an unemployment rate of 5.5 to 6 percent. So it seemed as if the economy were operating significantly beyond low-level potential output. But inflation remained low at about 2–3%. Classical economists argued that it was just a lag, and that unless the government instituted contractionary aggregate demand policy, the seeds of inflation would be sown. Keynesian economists argued that institutional changes in the labor market had reduced the inflation threat; some even argued that 4.5 percent unemployment was achievable. Only time will tell which group was right.

Now, let's look more carefully at the Classical and Keynesian underlying models of inflation.

THEORIES OF INFLATION AND THE PHILLIPS CURVE TRADE-OFF

Most economists accept the rough equality between expectations of inflation, increases in the money supply, and the actual rate of inflation. In a theory, however, one must blur out a number of aspects of reality to focus on those aspects one believes are most important. That's what Keynesians and Classicals do with their theories of inflation.

Keynesians blur the relationship between inflation and money in order to focus on the institutional process of setting prices and on cost-push pressures as the underlying causes of the inflationary process. According to Keynesians, the money supply increases with inflation, but these increases aren't the cause of inflation; the money supply increases occur because government tries to see that inflation (the rise in the price level) doesn't lead to unemployment and cost-push pressures. When government increases aggregate demand to see that the price increases don't lead to unemployment, it ratifies the inflation. According to Keynesians, money supply increases are a necessary, but not a causal, link in the inflation process.

Classicals blur the price-setting process and the cost-push pressures in order to focus on demand-pull pressure and the relationship between increases in the money supply and inflation. When Classicals see inflation they see the government increasing the money supply. Both theories shed light on inflation. Let's now consider them a bit more carefully.

As we saw in Chapter 13, Classical theory emphasized the money supply. Thus it isn't surprising that the Classical theory of inflation can be summed up in one sentence: *Inflation is everywhere and always a monetary phenomenon.* If the money supply doesn't rise, the price level won't rise. Forget all the other stuff. It obscures the connection between money and inflation. (This focus on money is why Classicals were called *monetarists* in the 1960s and 1970s.)

The Quantity Theory of Money and Inflation   That connection between money and inflation is relatively simple and can be seen in the Classical quantity theory of money: When the money supply rises, prices go up; if the money supply doesn't continue to rise, inflation won't continue. Reconsider the equation of exchange presented in the previous chapter:

$$MV = PQ$$

Classicals assume velocity, V, and real output, Q, are relatively constant. They also consider the price level, P, relatively flexible. These assumptions change the equation of exchange, which is true by definition, into the Classical quantity theory of money. According to the Classical quantity theory of money, any inflation is caused by

MIDAS, Transmuting all into GOLD PAPER.

Keynesians blur the relationship between inflation and money in order to focus on the institutional process of setting prices and on cost-push pressures as the underlying causes of the inflationary process.

Q–4: If an inflation theory focuses on the money supply and competitive markets, is it more likely to be a Keynesian theory or a Classical theory?

Classicals blur the price-setting process and the cost-push pressures in order to focus on demand-pull pressure and the relationship between increases in the money supply and inflation.

The Classical Theory of Inflation

3 The Classical theory of inflation is summarized by the sentence: Inflation is everywhere and always a monetary phenomenon.

Q–5: What is another name for Classical macroeconomists?

To illustrate the relationship between money and inflation, I give each of my students five pennies and auction off a candy bar. The first student to bid five cents gets the bar. Then I give them each ten pennies and auction another candy bar. The first student to bid ten cents gets the bar. Soon the students recognize that the price of the bar is directly related to the quantity of money that they have to bid. (With a big class this can get expensive, but you can play the game with fictional bank deposits.)

The Classical view that printing money causes inflation is seen in the 18th-century satirical drawing by James Gilray showing William Pitt spewing paper money out of his mouth while gold coins are locked up in his stomach.
Bleichroeder Print Collection, Baker Library, Harvard Business School.

Q–6: What one sentence best summarizes the Classical theory of inflation?

The policy response to the inflation of the late 1970s, tight monetary policy and a very deep recession, is a good example of the Classical approach to fighting inflation. Ask your students if they think the costs were justified.

Milton Friedman—Nobel prize, 1976, for work on macro-economist who most strongly argued the monetarist view. © *The Nobel Foundation.*

demand-pull pressures—which are generated by increases in the money supply. Therefore,

$$\Delta M \rightarrow \Delta P$$

Classical Modifications of the Quantity Theory   The quantity theory of money embodies the central element of the Classical theory of inflation. There are many modifications which explain why the connection between money and inflation in the short run isn't perfectly tight. One important modification is that Classicals believe that people are often fooled into thinking an increase in nominal demand caused by an increase in the money supply is actually an increase in real demand. The result will be a short-run expansionary effect on the real economy, as suggested in this chapter's opening quotation from Milton Friedman.

Examples of Money's Role in Inflation   Let's consider an example. In 1971 the Fed increased the money supply significantly; as a result, income rose and unemployment fell. In 1972 inflation fell slightly; however, in 1974 and 1975 both inflation and unemployment rose substantially. Here's an example of expansionary monetary policy increasing real output as prices are slow to respond to increases in aggregate demand. But in the long run the expansionary monetary policy caused inflation. Classical economists also believe that people can be fooled in the opposite direction—thinking that a decrease in nominal demand is actually a decrease in real demand. This makes it difficult to stop an ongoing inflation because the initial short-run effect is on real output. The effect on inflation occurs in the long run.

Let's consider another example, again from the 1970s, when significant inflation—10 percent—had become built into the economy. In late 1979 and the early 1980s, the Fed decreased the money supply growth significantly. This led to a leap in unemployment from 7 to 10 percent, but initially no decrease in inflation. By 1984, however, inflation had fallen to about 4 percent, and it remained low throughout the 1980s and 1990s.

Now let's consider a couple of more recent examples. In the early 1990s, the German central bank felt Germany's inflation rate was too high. It cut the money supply growth considerably. Initially, the impact was on output, and the tight money pushed the German economy into a recession. It remained in recession through early 1996, but the forecasts for the late 1990s were for growth, albeit slow.

Another example is Russia in the early 1990s. The Russian government was short of revenue and was forced to print money to finance its debt. As a result, inflation blew up into hyperinflation, and the Russian economy continued in a serious slump.

Despite these and many other examples, the simple view connecting inflation with money supply growth lost favor in the late 1980s and early 1990s as formerly stable relationships between certain measurements of money and inflation broke down. Part of the reason for this was the enormous changes in financial institutions that were occurring because of technological changes and changing regulations. Another part was the increased global interdependence of financial markets, which increased the flow of money among countries. In the 1990s it seemed that, for low inflation, the random elements (called *noise*) in the relationship between money and inflation overwhelmed the connection. For large inflation of the type experienced by many developing and transitional economies, the connection was still evident.

The Classical View of the Phillips Curve Trade-Off   The Classical view of the trade-off centers around the **natural rate of unemployment** (*the rate of unemployment to which the economy naturally gravitates*).[2] This natural rate of unemployment is independent of the inflation rate and expectations of inflation. It is the unemployment rate that will exist in long-run equilibrium when expectations of inflation equal the actual

---

[2]The natural rate concept is the Classical equivalent of what this book calls the *target rate of unemployment*. The Keynesian equivalent for the target rate is the *nonaccelerating inflation rate of unemployment* (NAIRU).

ADDED DIMENSION

By most accounts, Milton Friedman was a headstrong student. He didn't simply accept the truths his teachers laid out. If he didn't agree, he argued strongly for his own belief. He was very bright and his ideas were generally logical and convincing. He needed to be both persistent and intelligent to maintain and promote his views in spite of strong opposition.

Throughout the Keynesian years of the 1950s and 1960s, Friedman stood up and argued the Classical viewpoint of economics. He kept Classical economics alive. He was such a strong advocate of the quantity theory of money that, during this period, Classical economics was called monetarism. Friedman was the leader of the monetarists.

Friedman argued that fiscal policy simply didn't work. It led to expansions in government's size. He also opposed an activist monetary policy. The effects of monetary policy, he said, were too variable for it to be useful in guiding the economy. He called for a steady growth in the money supply, and argued consistently for a laissez-faire policy by government.

He has made his mark in both microeconomics and macroeconomics. In the 1970s, his ideas caught hold and helped spawn a renewal of the Classical school of economics. He was awarded the Nobel prize in economics in 1976.

---

level of inflation. The long-run Phillips curve is vertical at this natural rate of unemployment.

The basic argument why there is a natural rate is that people base their decisions on *relative* prices. Inflation involves a rise in the price level, so once inflation is fully expected, and adjusted for, it should have no effect on the real economy. So, if the normal level of unemployment were 5 percent when there is no inflation, unemployment should be 5 percent at a 10 percent fully expected inflation.

At unemployment rates to the left of the long-run Phillips curve (unemployment rates below the natural rate), actual inflation is above expectations of inflation. As people's expectations of inflation adjust up, the short-run Phillips curve will shift upward (shown by the upward arrows in Exhibit 5). To the right of the long-run Phillips curve (at unemployment rates higher than the natural rate), actual inflation is below expectations of inflation. As people's expectations of inflation adjust down, the short-run Phillips curve will shift downward (shown by the downward arrows in Exhibit 5).

Maintaining an unemployment rate below the natural rate would cause an ever-increasing acceleration of inflation. Classical economists see stagflation as either an ever-rightward-shifting short-run Phillips curve or a Phillips curve stuck in a high position resulting from too expansionary aggregate demand policies. Such an accelerating inflation is unsustainable because it destroys the benefits of money. It would cause hyperinflation and a breakdown of the economy. Eventually the government must give up its attempt to lower the unemployment rate below the natural rate. But even after giving up its attempt to achieve an unemployment rate below the natural rate, the government will have left a legacy of high inflation.

Classical Policy to Fight Inflation   In terms of policy, monetary policy is powerful, but unpredictable in the short run. Because of this unpredictability monetary policy cannot, and should not, be used to control the level of output in the economy. Thus, paradoxically, monetarists oppose an activist monetary policy.

Classicals, or monetarists as they are sometimes called because of their focus on money, believe that in the long run money affects only the price level. Since the short-run effects are unpredictable and in the long run only the price level is affected, Classicals say that monetary policy should follow a **monetary rule** (*a prescribed monetary policy that's to be followed regardless of what's happening in the economy*). They argue that:

1. The money supply should be increased by a determined percentage, say 3 percent per year, to allow for changes in productivity and real growth.

Natural rate of unemployment
Classical term for the unemployment rate in long-run equilibrium when expectations of inflation equal the actual level of inflation.

4 Classical economists favor a monetary rule because they believe the short-run effects of monetary policy are unpredictable and the long-run effects of monetary policy are on the price level, not on real output.

I think it is important to point out that there is much debate about the natural rate of unemployment and the lowest achievable level of unemployment that we should be shooting for.

Q–7: If the economy is at point *A* on the Phillips curve below, what prediction would you make for unemployment and inflation?

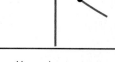

Monetary rule   *A prescribed monetary policy to be followed regardless of what is happening in the economy.*

EXHIBIT 5   The Classical View of the Phillips Curve Trade-Off

In the Classical view, the long-run Phillips curve is vertical at the natural rate of unemployment. Because expectations of inflation lag behind actual inflation, there exists a temporary trade-off between inflation and unemployment. But the trade-off is an illusion, and as soon as expectations catch up with actual inflation, the economy will return to the natural rate of unemployment.

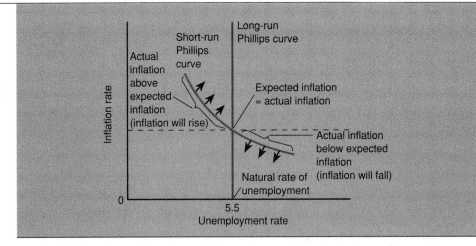

For a recent discussion of the debate over the natural rate of unemployment see Chapter 15 in *Case Studies in Macroeconomics*.

6a Classicals view the long run Phillips curve as vertical; the short run tradeoff is only a temporary illusion.

The Keynesian Theories of Inflation

5 The Keynesian theory of inflation holds that institutional and structural aspects of inflation, as well as increases in the money supply, are important causes of inflation.

Keynesian theories of inflation emphasize institutional and social causes of inflation.

It is at this point in Keynesian theory that the macrofoundations of microeconomics become important. Some Keynesians argue that the use of monetary institutions imposes an upward push on the nominal price level. That upward push must be offset or it will generate accelerating inflation. If it is not offset directly, then it must be offset indirectly through the maintenance of higher unemployment rates and excess supply markets than otherwise would be the case. It is this difference that accounts for the Keynesian NAIRU terminology, or the nonaccelerating inflation rate of unemployment, versus the Classical natural rate terminology.

2. Monetary policy should not be used in the short run to try to steer the economy.

Classicals believe that monetary policy should be used only to achieve long-run objectives, the most important of which is price stability.

There are many alternative ways in which short-run Classical theory of inflation makes adjustments for changes in velocity, real output, and inflationary expectations, but the core of that theory is inevitably that *inflation is everywhere and always a monetary phenomenon*. That core connection between money and inflation is pleasant for students because it makes it possible to present succinctly the Classical view.

Keynesians would agree with much of what the Classicals have to say but believe that they aren't focusing on the important institutional and structural aspects of inflation. Keynesians argue that when firms and individuals set prices, they do not take into account the effect of their pricing decisions on the price level. Since generally firms, rather than consumers, set prices, those prices quickly adjust upward in response to an increase in demand, but are much slower to adjust downward in response to a decrease in demand.

The revenue that firms receive is divided among profits, wages, and rent. All this income is ultimately paid to individual owners of the factors of production. Firms are simply intermediaries between individuals as owners of the factors of production and individuals as consumers. Keynesians argue that, given the institutional structure of our economy, it's often easier for firms to increase wages, profits, and rents to keep the peace with their employees and other factors of production than it is to try to hold those costs down. Firms then pay for that increase by raising the prices they charge consumers. That works as long as, in response to the rising price level, the government increases the money supply so that the demand is there to buy the goods at the higher prices.

Let's consider an example: A zuka firm is happy with its competitive position in the zuka market. It expects 0 percent inflation. Productivity (output of zukas per unit input) is increasing 2 percent, the same as the increase in productivity in the economy as a whole, so the firm can hold its nominal price of zukas constant even if it increases wages by 2 percent. Since the price level isn't expected to change, holding the price of zukas constant should maintain the firm's share of the zuka market. The firm offers workers a 2 percent pay increase.

The firm meets its workers to discuss the 2 percent offer. At that meeting it becomes clear to the firm that its workers will push for a 4 percent pay increase. What should the firm do? In a highly competitive market in which supply and demand forces alone determine wages and prices, there's no question what it would do; it would increase wages only 2 percent and hold its price constant. Real-world firms,

█f inflation is a distributional fight, who wins and who loses? The winners are people who can raise their wages or prices and still keep their jobs and sell their labor or goods. The losers are people who can't.

The composition of these groups changes over time. For example, at one time people on social security and pensions lost out during inflations since social security and pensions were, on the whole, set at fixed rates. Inflation lowered recipients' real income. But social security payments and many pensions are now indexed (automatically adjusted to compensate for inflation), so their recipients are no longer losers. Their real income became independent of inflation.

Similarly, it's sometimes said that bond holders are hurt by inflation, since the value of the money with which the bonds are redeemed falls during inflation. That's true, but whether bond holders lose depends on how the interest rate on bonds adjusts to the expected inflation rate. In recent years, the nominal interest rate has adjusted quickly to expectations

of inflation. When that happens, it is unclear how much bond holders have lost. If nominal interest rates adjust quickly to expectations of inflation, the real interest rate may remain as high as it otherwise would have been.

For example, in the 1950s bond holders received 2 percent interest; inflation was low, so 2 percent interest was close to a 2 percent real interest rate. In the early 1970s, interest rates on bonds were 8 percent, in large part because people expected 6 percent inflation. Six percent compensated bond holders for inflation, leaving them the same 2 percent real return they had received in the 1950s. So we must be careful in generalizing about distributional effects of inflation.

What we can say about the distributional consequences of inflation is that people who don't expect inflation and who are tied in to fixed contracts denominated in unindexed monetary values will likely lose in an inflation. However, these people are rational and probably won't let it happen again. They'll be prepared for a subsequent inflation.

however, often meet workers' demands under the expectation that other firms will do so too. Meeting these demands helps maintain morale and prevents turnover of key workers. This occurs whether or not there are unions. The result is an upward push on nominal wages and prices.

This upward push on nominal wages and prices can exist only if the labor and product markets are not highly competitive. In a highly competitive market, even small amounts of unemployment and excess supply would cause wages and prices to fall. Keynesians believe that most real-world markets are not highly competitive in this fashion. While they agree that some competition exists, they argue that in most sectors of the economy, competition works slowly. The invisible handshake, as well as the invisible hand, influences wages and prices. The result is that even when there is substantial unemployment and considerable excess supply of goods, existing workers can still put an upward push on nominal wages, and existing firms can put an upward push on nominal prices.

The Keynesian theory of inflation depends upon the view that markets are not highly competitive. Price will not fall in response to an excess supply.

The Insider/Outsider Model and Inflation   To get a better picture of how existing workers can push up wages despite substantial unemployment, let's consider a Keynesian model that divides the economy into insiders and outsiders. Insiders are workers who have good jobs with excellent long-run prospects, and current business owners. Both receive above-equilibrium wages, profits, and rents. If the world were competitive, their wages, profits, and rents would be pushed down to the equilibrium level. To prevent this from happening, Keynesians argue, insiders develop sociological and institutional barriers that prevent outsiders from competing away those above-equilibrium wages, profits, and rents. Because of those barriers, outsiders (often minorities) must take dead-end, low-paying jobs or attempt to undertake marginal businesses that pay little return for many hours worked. Even when outsiders do find better jobs or business opportunities, they are first to be fired and their businesses are the first to suffer in a recession. Thus, outsiders have much higher unemployment rates than insiders. For example, in the United States blacks tend to be outsiders; black unemployment rates are generally twice as high as white unemployment rates for the same age groups.

In short, Keynesians see an economic system that's only partially competitive. In their view, the invisible hand is often thwarted by other invisible forces. Such partially competitive economies are often characterized by insiders' monopolies. Insiders

Q–8: How would a Classical economist likely respond to an insider-outsider model of inflation?

get the jobs and are paid monopoly wage levels. Outsiders are unemployed at those higher wages. Imperfect competition allows workers (and firms) to raise nominal wages (and prices) even as unemployment (and excess supply of goods) exists. Then, as other insiders do likewise, the price level rises. This increase in the price level lowers workers' real wage. In response, workers further raise their nominal wages to protect their real wages. The result is an ongoing chase in which the insiders protect their real wage, while outsiders (the unemployed) suffer. (If the ideas of *nominal* and *real* are unclear to you, a review of earlier chapters may be in order.)

Within this imperfectly competitive system, both wages and prices develop their own inertia that causes inflation to take on a life of its own. Keynesians believe that to understand inflation you must understand the psychology of the individuals with wage- and price-setting power, including both firms and organizations of workers.

Keynesians see the nominal wage- and price-setting process as generating inflation.

Thus, Keynesians see the nominal wage- and price-setting process as generating inflation. As one group pushes up its nominal wage or price, another group responds by doing the same. More groups follow until finally the first group finds its relative wage or price hasn't increased. Then the entire process starts again. Once the nominal wage and price levels have risen, government has two options: It can either ratify the increase by increasing the money supply, thereby accepting the inflation; or it can refuse to ratify it, causing unemployment.

The Role of Unemployment in Keynesian Theories of Inflation

For Keynesians, what role does unemployment play in the inflation process? They see the fear of unemployment as a way of "disciplining" workers to accept lower pay. The reality that there are a number of unemployed people out there waiting to take the jobs of employed workers who ask for too high a wage increase helps prevent existing workers from raising their wage. Thus, unemployment helps fight inflation. But unemployment is not a complete retardant of inflation because many workers and firms have insulated themselves from unemployment through implicit or explicit contracts providing them with job and market security regardless of the level of unemployment. This means that the unemployment costs of fighting inflation are borne heavily by minorities and other outsiders. Insiders are more protected and have less to fear from unemployment. The resulting unemployment is not "natural" in the sense that it reflects people's choices; it is simply the amount of unemployment that is necessary to create competitive pressure on insiders and thereby limit their attempts at further monopolization.

Keynesians believe that, under current conditions, the costs of unemployment are borne heavily by minorities and other outsiders.

Another difference between Keynesians and Classicals is that Keynesians are far less likely to see a specific level of unemployment as the "natural rate" of unemployment. Because they believe that production and expenditure decisions are interrelated, they are far more cautious about specifying a single rate of unemployment toward which the aggregate economy gravitates. For them the target rate of unemployment can shift around; it is to be empirically determined, not theoretically deduced.

The Keynesian View of the Phillips Curve Trade-Off

As I've stated, Keynesians see an economy of imperfectly competitive markets. Keynesians believe that, in the short run, social forces (the invisible handshake, which creates a type of implicit contract between buyers and sellers) and explicit contracts play a large role in price determination. Because of these social forces, there is no reason that, in the short run, expected inflation must precisely equal actual inflation. Keynesians argue that if the economy is kept close to the existing level of inflation (say within 2 or 3 percent), these social forces can hold inflationary expectations in check at their existing level and prevent them from being built into higher inflationary demands, and thereby shifting up the short-run Phillips curve. Thus, within a limited range of inflation rates around the actual inflation rate, many Keynesians believe that the short-run Phillips curve can be relatively stable, and not shift up even though actual inflation exceeds expected inflation. They argue that the trade-off existing up to 1969 was not an illusion and that that relationship did exist in the late 1980s. There can be a long-run trade-off, between inflation and unemployment, as there was up until 1969. In a sense, Keynesians are saying that the Classical long run never comes.

6b Keynesians believe that institutional factors play a major role in determining inflation, and that expected inflation need not precisely equal actual inflation. Within a range of output levels, a trade-off is possible.

It is helpful here to discuss the costs of rationality and the imperfections in the inflation measure. Most individuals don't care about the rate of inflation; what they care about are those sets of prices that directly affect them. Each individual has their own personal inflation rate that directly affects their well-being.

The debate on what to do about inflation has an analogy to dieting. Fasting will cause you to lose about a pound a day. Want to lose 30 pounds? A Classical dietitian would say, "Fast. Thirty pounds equals 105,000 calories. When you've managed to complete a period in which you've eaten 105,000 fewer calories than are necessary to maintain your present weight, you'll have lost 30 pounds." A Keynesian dietitian would offer a variety of diets or would explore your soul to discover why you want to overeat, and would perhaps suggest a liquid protein plan. The Keynesian diet would also involve your taking in 105,000 fewer calories than if you'd continued to overeat. But, Keynesians argue, you can't stick with a diet unless you've discovered what makes you want to overeat.

The reason many Keynesians believe there can be a long-run trade-off between inflation and unemployment is not that they believe people are irrational; it is that they believe people are reasonable. Keynesians argue that, given the cost of rationality, it would be unreasonable for most people to make explicit calculations about inflation's effect on their incomes. People have a general feeling, but that is all they have. Consequently people's calculations about their relative wage and prices based on the price level are inexact. Three or four percent inflation per year is about .008 percent per day, meaning that $1,000 will lose about 8¢ in value each day. That 8¢ is hardly noticeable. Price indices are more inexact than that. Therefore, say many Keynesians, low inflation levels (2 or 3 percent) will be accepted by individuals without leading to immediate increases in their nominal wages or prices.

Keynesians argue that people will rationally respond quite differently to a 2 percent decrease in their real wage caused by a 2 percent decrease in their nominal wage than they would to a 2 percent decrease in their real wage caused by a 2 percent increase in the price level. They notice nominal wage changes. They are far less likely to notice and respond to real wage changes caused by a change in the price level. This argument accounts for the Keynesian explanation of the reasonably stable trade-off that existed before 1969.

How then do these Keynesians explain the stagflation of the 1970s? The answer is that the economy experienced a combination of unfortunate events, including oil price shocks and overly expansionary government policies. These events caused inflation to exceed what psychologists called the *just-noticeable difference*.

The **just-noticeable difference** is *the threshold where our senses realize that something has changed.* For example, say it gets 3°F warmer; most people won't notice. But if it gets 10°F warmer, most people will notice. Thus, the just-noticeable difference is a change of somewhere between 3°F and 10°F. Keynesians argue that, in the 1970s, inflation exceeded that threshold. As it did, inflation became built into people's expectations and everyone who previously had wanted a 4 percent wage hike now asked for a 9 percent hike, while firms that wanted a 3 percent price increase raised their prices by 8 percent to account for the expected higher price level due to inflation. The entire short-run Phillips curve shifted up, as suggested by the Classicals. But that happened only because the economy was pushed too far; it doesn't negate the existence of a continuing trade-off between inflation and unemployment within certain limits.

Thus, there is a central difference between the Keynesian and Classical views of the Phillips curve. The Keynesian view allows that, within a limited range, there is a long-run trade-off between inflation and unemployment. Moreover, in the Keynesian view equilibrium output and achievable unemployment rate can fluctuate around a lot more than Classicals believe it can. One year the achievable unemployment rate might be 6 percent; the next year it might be 5 percent. Those fluctuations, combined with institutional pressures pushing the price level up, make it difficult, if not impossible, to base one's macro policy decision about whether or not to use expansionary demand management policy on a one–time rise in the price level, or on some historically determined estimate of the natural rate of unemployment. The issues are simply too

Since rationality has a cost, it is rational not to take inflation into account in every decision.

It is not only expectations of inflation that are a necessary condition for people incorporating those expectations into their wage- and price setting process; they must also have the power of doing so. When contracts exist and institutions prevent passing on of price increases, at least for some time, the inflationary process can be a long drawn-out affair with underlying conditions changing by the time individuals have a chance to react. For example, wages in a three-year contract will not adjust for three years. At that point, when adjustment takes place, the past experience of catching up and adjusting for previous inflation plays a role. In such cases the wage and price-setting process can be both forward and backward looking.

Just-noticeable difference   A threshold below which our senses don't recognize that something has changed.

Q–9: How do Keynesians explain a relatively stable trade-off between inflation and unemployment that persists year after year?

This section is important because it not only compares and contrasts the Keynesian and Classical theories, but it also provides a chance to review the theories once again.

Keynesians tend to favor discretion; Classicals tend to favor rules over discretion.

complicated to do that. Discretionary judgments must be made about each case because each case is different.

Classical economists are concerned about government's ability to make these discretionary judgments in a responsible manner. They base this concern on past events. They point out that generally in making those judgments, decision makers have leaned more toward expansionary policy than toward contractionary policy, and have continually given in to political needs for a quick boost in the economy in order to strengthen the economy for the next election. They tend to forget the longer-run inflationary costs of their expansionary policy. Classical economists argue that the only way to stop such political pushes for expanding the economy is to give policy makers rules limiting their discretion. Their positions on what government will do if given discretion is why it is often said that Classicals favor rules and Keynesians favor discretion. In the Keynesian view, government macroeconomic policy can do good; in the Classical view, it cannot.

Keynesians see institutional and social forces determining the level of inflation and unemployment, and hence see a role for an incomes policy.

Keynesian Policies to Fight Inflation   As we saw above, Classicals say to stop inflation one must reduce the rate of growth of the money supply. Control the money supply and you will control inflation. Keynesians claim that governments can institute policies that either prevent inflation or abort it in its tracks.

Keynesians agree that the Classical solution to inflation—contractionary monetary policy until inflation stops—will ultimately control inflation, but they argue that it will do so in an inefficient and unfair manner. Keynesians argue that tight monetary policy usually causes unemployment among those least able to handle it. Keynesians ask, "Why should this group bear the cost of fighting inflation?" Their argument is that putting a brick wall in front of a speeding car will stop the car, but that doesn't mean that's how you should stop a car. Instead, Keynesians are more likely to favor the use of contractionary monetary policies in combination with additional policies that directly slow down inflation. One such additional policy is an **incomes policy,** *a policy that places direct pressure on individuals to hold down their nominal wages and prices.* Keynesians argue that because it holds down inflation directly, an incomes policy can help to eliminate expectations of inflation, thereby reducing the cost in unemployment necessary to fight inflation.

Incomes policy   *A policy placing direct pressure on individuals to hold down their nominal wages and prices.*

I like to ask my students if they think incomes policies are consistent with the values and ideology of American society.

Exhibit 6 shows how Keynesians think an incomes policy can reduce the amount of unemployment necessary to eliminate an ongoing inflation. It is a picture of two disinflationary paths along shifting short-run Phillips curves. (Remember, the short-run Phillips curve shifts down as inflationary expectations fall.) Path A, Keynesians claim, is the Classical path out of an initial high inflation. It involves running highly contractionary monetary policy, thereby inducing a recession with unemployment reaching, say, 10 percent, moving the economy along a path like A. Point A would be the trough of the recession. That recession would squeeze inflationary expectations out of the economy, shifting the short-run Phillips curve down, further decreasing inflation, even as unemployment fell.

An incomes policy can lead to a swifter adjustment to lower inflation.

Path B, Keynesians argue, is the disinflation path an economy would follow if it used an incomes policy in conjunction with contractionary monetary policy. Because the incomes policy puts direct downward pressure on inflation, expectations fall faster and the short-run Phillips curve shifts down faster. Thus the initial shift is to $SRPC_2$ at point *B,* the low point of the recession. Less unemployment would be needed.

An example of an incomes policy is a program of temporary wage and price controls which directly prohibit inflation. Keynesians argue that when people see that inflation is at a lower level, they'll expect less inflation, the Phillips curve will shift down, and the controls can be repealed. With wage and price controls, expectations of inflation are eliminated without a recession.

You may wish to point out, using the supply and demand model with a fixed price, how incomes policies can distort the price from its equilibrium level. If, however, one has a monopoly pricing model, incomes policies can lower price and increase ouput.

A program of temporary wage and price controls seems a highly desirable alternative to contractionary monetary policy and resulting unemployment. In 1971 President Nixon, a Republican, instituted wage and price controls to stem rising inflation. The initial results were encouraging—inflation fell substantially in 1972. But in 1973,

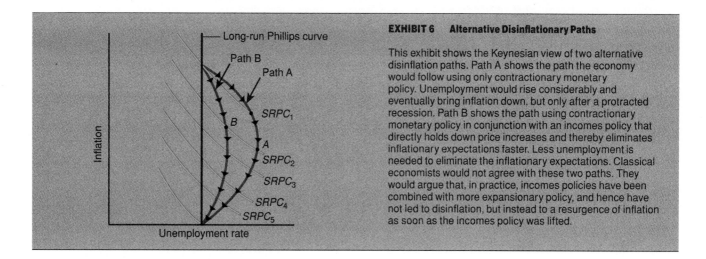

EXHIBIT 6   Alternative Disinflationary Paths

This exhibit shows the Keynesian view of two alternative disinflation paths. Path A shows the path the economy would follow using only contractionary monetary policy. Unemployment would rise considerably and eventually bring inflation down, but only after a protracted recession. Path B shows the path using contractionary monetary policy in conjunction with an incomes policy that directly holds down price increases and thereby eliminates inflationary expectations faster. Less unemployment is needed to eliminate the inflationary expectations. Classical economists would not agree with these two paths. They would argue that, in practice, incomes policies have been combined with more expansionary policy, and hence have not led to disinflation, but instead to a resurgence of inflation as soon as the incomes policy was lifted.

as controls were being lifted, inflation jumped. By 1974, unemployment was almost back to its 1972 level and inflation was over 8 percent.

What went wrong? One problem was bad timing. About the time controls were removed, an oil price shock generated more inflation. A second problem was that the fall in the inflation rate allowed aggregate policy to be more expansionary than it otherwise would have been. In 1972 and 1973, unemployment decreased. This suggests expansionary monetary and fiscal policies. Temporary wage and price controls can only temporarily hold down inflation. If controls are expected to have a long-run effect, they must be long-run controls—but no one expected the 1971–74 wage and price controls to be long-run. Thus, temporary controls change nothing in the underlying reality. Using controls often tempts government to be too expansionary. Classical economists argue that individuals know that governments will succumb to those temptations, and that knowledge will undermine the Keynesian story of how incomes policies would work.

The evidence on which policy is right is unclear since it is unknown what the inflation rate in the absence of these controls would have been. Supporters of temporary wage and price controls argue that the controls stopped a bad situation from getting worse. Opponents of temporary price controls as a way to reduce expectations of inflation argue that, inevitably, such price controls will be used to camouflage expansionary policy and thus should be avoided.

Similarities and Differences between Keynesian and Classical Theories

The preceding discussion highlighted differences between Keynesian and Classical theories of inflation. Keynesians see inflation as an institutional phenomenon; Classicals see it as a monetary phenomenon.

Classicals and Keynesians on Supply Shocks   The distinction between the Keynesian and Classical theories of inflation comes out most clearly when we consider the effects of a supply-price shock, such as a sudden increase in the price of oil. Keynesians see such a supply-price shock as a cost-push pressure, likely to lead to significant inflationary pressures as people try to maintain their relative income at their previous level.

Classical economists see a supply-price shock as simply a relative price change. They argue that as long as the government does not increase the money supply, other relative prices will fall and there will be little inflationary pressure from a supply-price shock. So they advocate maintaining a monetary rule and not increasing the money supply to accommodate higher prices.

The difference between the two views can be seen in reference to the aggregate supply path. Keynesians see a supply shock as causing a one-time increase in the price level, so it is a rise in the price level that will not lead to accelerating inflation.

Q–10: A price supply shock has just hit the economy. Who is likely to predict higher inflation, a Keynesian or a Classical? Why?

EXHIBIT 7   Inflation, Money Supply Growth, and Unemployment

| Year | Inflation (Measured by Implicit Price Deflator of GDP) | Rate of Money Supply Growth | | | Civilian Unemployment |
		M_1	M_2	M_3	
1990	4.4%	4.0%	3.7%	1.4%	5.6%
1991	3.9	8.6	3.1	1.3	6.8
1992	2.9	14.2	1.6	0.2	7.5
1993	2.6	10.2	1.6	1.5	6.9
1994	2.2	1.8	0.4	1.6	6.1
1995	2.5	−2.1	4.2	5.9	5.6
1996	2.0	−4.3	4.6	7.0	5.4

Therefore, Keynesians argue, people's expectations of inflation can remain low even in the face of continual upward shocks to the price level. They argue that accepting inflation of 2 or 3 percent can allow the economy to achieve a higher level of output than it otherwise could achieve. Classical economists see supply shock price–level rises as seeds for further accelerating inflation. For a Classical economist even 2 to 3 percent inflation would be an indication of the need to slow down money supply growth.

Classicals and Keynesians on Recent Inflation   To see these differences, let's compare how Classicals and Keynesians explain the inflation that's been occurring in the early 1990s.

First, the facts, which I present in Exhibit 7. As you can see, in the 1990s, inflation has remained low, while unemployment fluctuated. Different measures of the money supply were changing at different rates. There were no major price shocks during this time, but there were significant changes in financial institutions. The monetarists argued that, once one accounted for financial institutional changes, the core relationship between changes in the money supply and inflation could be seen.

Thus, the period, while not perfectly consistent with the Classical view, was not a refutation of it. Classicals claimed that if the Fed held constant an appropriate measure of the money supply, inflation could be totally stopped.

Keynesians would say that the inflation was relatively low because the unemployment rate was being kept higher than the economy could handle, and that the remaining inflation was a combination of supply shock inflation and inflation caused by existing institutions. They would claim that holding down the appropriate measure of the money supply was impossible (since one couldn't decide what the appropriate measure was), but that even if one could hold it down, holding it down further would only cause more unemployment since the inflation was inherent in the institutions.

Similarities in the Keynesian and Classical Views   These differences between the theories shouldn't obscure the similarities. Once the economy reaches its potential output, both Keynesians and Classicals see inflation as an excess demand phenomenon: too much money chasing too few goods. The differences in views occur when the economy is below its potential output. Keynesians believe inflation can still occur; Classicals believe it will not.

CONCLUSION

The Classical and Keynesian views of inflation and the Phillips curve trade-off reflect two consistent, but different, worldviews. Keynesians see a world in which sociological and institutional factors interact with market forces, keeping the economy in a perpetual disequilibrium when considered in an economic framework. Classicals see a world in which market forces predominate. They consider institutional and sociological factors insignificant, and view the overall economy as one in continual equilibrium. These two worldviews carry over to their analyses of the central policy issue facing most governments as they decide on their monetary and fiscal policies: the trade-off between inflation and unemployment.

These different worldviews are why there are major disagreements about policy. Classicals believe the best policy is laissez-faire; Keynesians believe an activist policy is needed. Given their contrasting worldviews, the debate will likely continue for a long time.

CHAPTER SUMMARY

- High inflation is inevitably accompanied by roughly proportional increases in the money supply and expectations of inflation.
- The short-run Phillips curve differs from the long-run Phillips curve because on the long-run Phillips curve expected inflation must equal actual inflation.
- The Classical theory of inflation blurs out the institutional process of setting prices and focuses on the relation between money and inflation.
- Classical economists favor a monetary rule that is to be followed regardless of economic conditions.
- Classicals argue that inflation undermines growth and that the relevant trade-off is between inflation and growth.

- The Keynesian theory of inflation blurs out the relationship between inflation and money and focuses on the institutional process of setting prices.
- In the Classical theory of inflation, the only equilibrium is on the long-run Phillips curve.
- In the Keynesian theory of inflation, a short-run Phillips curve trade-off can persist into the long run as long as inflation doesn't exceed a certain range.
- Classicals argue that the only way to stop inflation is to stop increasing the money supply. Keynesians argue that supplemental policies (such as an incomes policy) are needed.

KEY TERMS

adaptive expectations *(359)*
cost-push inflation *(359)*
demand-pull inflation *(359)*
expectations of inflation *(362)*
incomes policy *(374)*

inflation *(359)*
just-noticeable difference *(373)*
long-run Phillips curve *(362)*
monetary rule *(369)*
natural rate of unemployment *(368)*

Phillips curve *(360)*
short-run Phillips curve *(362)*
stagflation *(362)*

QUESTIONS FOR THOUGHT AND REVIEW

The number after each question represents the estimated degree of critical thinking required. (1 = almost none; 10 = deep thought.)

1. Distinguish cost-push from demand-pull inflation. *(2)*
2. Draw a short-run and a long-run Phillips curve. *(2)*
3. How would a Keynesian explain the relatively stable inflation/unemployment trade-off existing before 1969? *(5)*
4. How would a Classical economist explain the relatively stable inflation/unemployment trade-off existing before 1969? *(9)*
5. What policy implications would a Classical draw from the quotation at the beginning of the chapter? *(4)*
6. What policy implications would a Keynesian draw from the quotation at the beginning of the chapter? *(6)*
7. What implication does the insider/outsider view of the economy have for macroeconomic policy? *(6)*
8. What arguments would a Classical economist give in opposing an incomes policy? *(3)*

9. The Phillips curve is nothing but a figment of economists' imagination. True or false? *(9)*
10. A new approach to monetary policy in the mid-1990s, called "opportunistic disinflation," proposes that policy makers wait for a recession to lower inflation once it has fallen to a relatively low level—2 to 3%. Explain how this policy would work using the macro policy model and the Phillips curve framework. *(7)*
11. Wayne Angell stated in a *Wall Street Journal* editorial, "The Federal Reserve should get back on track getting inflation rates so low that inflation would no longer be a determining factor in household and business investment decisions." He views inflation as lowering long-term growth. Is he a Keynesian or a Classical? How does inflation affect household decisions and, consequently, growth? *(7)*

PROBLEMS AND EXERCISES

1. People's perception of inflation often differs from actual inflation.
   a. List five goods that you buy relatively frequently.
   b. Looking in old newspapers (found in the library on microfiche), locate sale prices for these goods since 1950, finding one price every five years or so. Determine the average price rise of each of these five goods from 1950 until today.
   c. Compare that price rise with the rise in the Consumer Price Index.

2. Congratulations. You've just been appointed finance minister of Inflationland. Inflation has been ongoing for the past five years at 5 percent. The target rate of unemployment, 5 percent, is also the actual rate.
   a. Demonstrate the economy's likely position on both short-run and long-run Phillips curves.
   b. The president tells you she wants to be reelected. Devise a monetary policy strategy for her that might help her accomplish her goal.
   c. Demonstrate that strategy graphically, including the likely long-run consequences.

3. In the early 1990s, Argentina stopped increasing the money supply and fixed the exchange rate of the Argentine austral at 10,000 to the dollar. It then renamed the Argentine currency the "peso" and cut off four zeros so that one peso equaled one dollar. Inflation slowed substantially. After this was done, the following observations were made. Explain why these observations did not surprise economists.
   a. The golf courses were far less crowded.

   b. The price of goods in dollar-equivalent pesos in Buenos Aires, the capital of the country, was significantly above that in New York City.
   c. Consumer prices—primarily of services—rose relative to other goods.
   d. Luxury auto dealers were shutting down.

4. Grade inflation is widespread. In 1990, 81 percent of the students who took the SATs had an A or B average, but 40 percent of them scored less than 390 on the verbal SAT. Students' grades are increasing but what they are learning is decreasing. Some economists argue that grade inflation should be dealt with in the same way that price inflation should be dealt with—by creating a fixed standard and requiring all grades to be specified relative to that standard. One way to accomplish this is to index the grades professors give: specify on the grade report both the student's grade and the class average, and deflate (or inflate) the professor's grade to some common standard.
   a. Discuss the advantages and disadvantages of such a proposal.
   b. What relationship does it have to economists' proposals for fixed exchange rates?

5. In the mid–1990s, Japan's annual money supply growth rate fell to 1–2 percent from an average annual rate of 10–11 percent in the late 1980s. What effect would you expect this decline to have had on:
   a. Japanese real output?
   b. Japanese unemployment?
   c. Japanese inflation?

ANSWERS TO MARGIN QUESTIONS

1. The more unemployment there is, the more inflation is likely to be cost-push, since unemployment relates to excess supply. One should keep in mind, however, that the cost-push/demand-pull distinction is more useful for describing the *initial causes* of inflation than it is for describing an ongoing inflation.   *(359)*

2. As you can see in the graph, the long-run Phillips curve is perfectly vertical. Its shape is dependent on the assumption that people's expectation of inflation completely adjusts to inflation in the long run, and that that adjustment is not institutionally constrained.   *(363)*

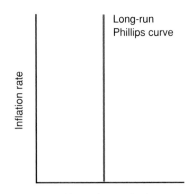

3. If people's expectations of inflation didn't change, the economy would stay on a short-run Phillips curve rather than move to the long-run Phillips curve. *(364)*

4. Classical theories of inflation are more likely to focus on money supply and competitive markets. Keynesian theories of inflation focus on institutional and structural problems in the market. *(367)*

5. Another name for Classical macroeconomists is "monetarists." *(367)*

6. "Inflation is everywhere and always a monetary phenomenon" is the sentence that best summarizes the Classical theory of inflation. *(368)*

7. If the economy is at point *A* on the Phillips curve below, inflation is below expected inflation and unemployment is higher than the target rate of unemployment. If this were the only information I had about the economy, I would expect both unemployment and inflation to fall. *(369)*

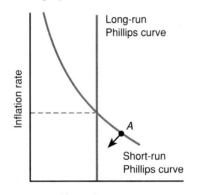

8. A Classical economist would likely say that the insider-outsider model of inflation tended to obscure the central cause of inflation: increases in the money supply. *(371)*

9. Keynesians would use the "just noticeable difference" concept to explain a relatively stable trade-off between inflation and employment that persists year after year. They see small changes in inflation as being too costly for people to adjust to, so they accept such changes without making adjustments. Most Keynesians see some flexibility between nominal and real rates. *(373)*

10. A Keynesian would be most likely to predict higher inflation. Classicals, who focus on the money supply, would say the price shock would be temporary and would essentially be a relative price change. *(375)*

Fifteen
International Dimensions of Monetary and Fiscal Policies

*The actual rate of exchange is largely governed by the expected
behavior of the country's monetary authority.*

~ Dennis Robertson

After reading this chapter, you should be able to:

1 Explain why there is significant debate about what
U.S. international goals should be.

2 State why domestic goals generally dominate
international goals.

3 Explain the paths through which monetary policy
affects exchange rates and the trade balance.

4 Explain the paths through which fiscal policy affects
exchange rates and the trade balance.

5 Summarize the reasons why governments try to
coordinate their monetary and fiscal policies.

6 State the potential problem of internationalizing a
country's debt.

In the 1990s, it's impossible to talk about macroeconomic policy without talking about
international issues. That's what I do in this chapter: I discuss the effect that monetary
and fiscal policies have on international macroeconomic goals, plus the effect that
certain international phenomena have on domestic macroeconomic goals of low inflation, low unemployment, and high growth.

The discussion in this chapter is not totally new to you. Earlier chapters introduced you to many international concepts and touched upon the international dimensions of fiscal and monetary policies. But now it's time to put those discussions
together and consider the issues more carefully. This discussion will provide you with
the necessary international base for understanding the macroeconomic policy you'll
be reading about in the newspapers.

THE AMBIGUOUS INTERNATIONAL GOALS OF MACROECONOMIC POLICY

Macroeconomics' international goals are less straightforward than its domestic goals.
There is general agreement about the domestic goals of macroeconomic policy: We
want low inflation, low unemployment, and high growth. There's far less agreement
on what a country's international goals should be.

Most economists agree that the international goal of U.S. macroeconomic policy
is to maintain the U.S. position in the world economy. But there's enormous debate
about what achieving that goal means. Do we want a high or a low exchange rate? Do
we want a balance of trade surplus? Or would it be better to have a balance of trade
deficit? Or should we not even pay attention to the balance of trade? Let's consider
the exchange rate goal first.

An **exchange rate** is *the rate at which one country's currency can be traded for another country's currency.* We discuss exchange rates at length in the next chapter; for now, let's briefly review the three types of exchange rates that exist.

Fixed and Flexible Exchange Rates   Countries can have a fixed exchange rate, a flexible exchange rate, or a partially flexible exchange rate. With a **fixed exchange rate,** *the exchange rate is set and government is committed to buying and selling its currency at a fixed rate.* With a **flexible exchange rate,** *the exchange rate is set by market forces (supply and demand for a country's currency). With a **partially flexible exchange rate,** the government sometimes buys and sells currencies to influence the price directly, and at other times the government simply accepts the exchange rate determined by supply and demand forces.* In the 1990s, the United States uses a partially flexible exchange rate.

In this chapter, to keep the analysis at a manageable level, I assume that the country in question has a flexible exchange rate. Thus, it accepts that its exchange rate will be determined by the forces of supply and demand. But that doesn't mean that the country can't indirectly influence the exchange rate through monetary and fiscal policies' effects on the economy and on the supply and demand for dollars. It is that indirect effect that we focus on in this chapter.

Do Countries Want a High or a Low Exchange Rate?   There is a debate over whether a country should have a high or a low exchange rate. A high exchange rate for the dollar makes foreign currencies cheaper, lowering the price of imports. Lowering import prices places competitive pressure on U.S. firms and helps to hold down inflation. All of this benefits U.S. residents' living standard. But a high exchange rate encourages imports and discourages exports. In doing so, it can cause a balance of trade deficit which can exert a contractionary effect on the economy by decreasing aggregate demand for U.S. output. So a high exchange rate also has a cost to U.S. residents.

A low exchange rate has the opposite effect. It makes imports more expensive and exports cheaper, and it can contribute to inflationary pressure. But, by encouraging exports and discouraging imports, it can cause a balance of trade surplus and exert an expansionary effect on the economy.

Thus, depending on the state of the economy, there are arguments both for high and low exchange rates. Hence there's often a divergence of views about what the exchange rate goal should be. Because of that divergence of views, many economists argue that a country should have no exchange rate policy because exchange rates are market-determined prices that are best left to the market. These economists question whether the government should even worry about the effect of monetary policy and fiscal policy on exchange rates. According to them, government should simply accept whatever exchange rate exists and not consider it in its conduct of monetary and fiscal policies.

A deficit in the **trade balance** (*the difference between imports and exports*) means that, as a country, we're consuming more than we're producing. Imports exceed exports, so we're consuming more than we could if we didn't run a deficit. A surplus in the trade balance means that exports exceed imports—we're producing more than we're consuming. Since consuming more than we otherwise could is kind of nice, it might seem that a trade deficit is preferred to a trade surplus.

But wait. A trade deficit isn't without costs, and a trade surplus isn't without benefits. We pay for a trade deficit by selling off U.S. assets to foreigners—by selling U.S. companies, factories, land, and buildings to foreigners, or selling them financial assets such as U.S. dollars, stocks, and bonds. All the future interest and profits on these assets will go to foreigners, not U.S. citizens. That means eventually, some time in the future, we will have to produce more than we consume so we can pay them *their* profit and interest on *their* assets. Thus, while in the short run a trade deficit allows more current consumption, in the long run it presents problems.

The Exchange Rate Goal

Exchange rate   The rate at which one country's currency can be traded for another country's currency.

Point out that an exchange rate is the price of one country's currency in terms of the currency of another country.

Q–1: If a country has flexible exchange rates, how can it influence those exchange rates?

Point out in the course of your lecture that when a country focuses its monetary policy on fixing the exchange rate it cannot use monetary policy to affect domestic goals.

Q–2: What effect does a low exchange rate have on a country's exports and imports?

1a Exchange rates have conflicting effects and, depending on the state of the economy, there are arguments both for high and low exchange rates.

Most major industrial economies rely on a system of partially flexible exchange rates.

The Trade Balance Goal

Trade balance   The difference between a country's exports and its imports.

Video Series, Economics USA: Exchange Rates, Segments 28.1-28.3 and Irwin Economic Video Series: "Foreign Exchange Markets."

Video Series, Economics U$A: International Trade, Segments 27.1-27.3.

1b Running a trade deficit is good in the short run but presents problems in the long run; thus there is debate about whether we should worry about a trade deficit or not.

Q–3: Why do some people argue that we should not worry about a trade deficit?

As long as a country can borrow, or sell assets, a country can have a trade deficit. But if a country runs a trade deficit year after year, eventually the long run will arrive and the country will run out of assets to sell and run out of other countries from whom to borrow. When that happens, the trade deficit problem must be faced.

The debate about whether a trade deficit should be of concern to policy makers involves whether these long-run effects should be anticipated and faced before they happen.

Opinions differ greatly. Some say not to worry—just accept what's happening. These "not-to-worry" economists argue that the trade deficit will end when U.S. citizens don't want to borrow from foreigners anymore and foreigners don't want to buy any more of our assets. They argue that the inflow of financial capital (money coming into the United States to buy our assets) from foreigners is financing new investment which will make the U.S. economy strong enough in the long run to reverse the trade deficit without serious disruption to the U.S. economy. So why deal with the trade deficit now when it will take care of itself in the future?

Others argue that, yes, the trade deficit will eventually take care of itself, but the economic distress accompanying the trade deficit taking care of itself will be great. By dealing with the problem now, the United States can avoid a highly unpleasant solution in the future.

Both views are reasonable, which is why there's no consensus on what a country's trade balance goal should be.

International versus Domestic Goals

2 Domestic goals generally dominate international goals because (1) international goals are ambiguous, and (2) international goals affect a country's population indirectly and, in politics, indirect effects take a back seat.

Be careful to work through the policy effects that are outlined in this section. My students tend to memorize at this point. Make certain that, instead, they know why the effects occur.

In the real world, when there's debate about a goal, that goal generally gets far less weight than goals about which there's general agreement. Since there's general agreement about our country's domestic goals (low inflation, low unemployment, and high growth), domestic goals generally dominate the U.S. political agenda.

Even if there weren't uncertainty about a country's international goals, domestic goals would likely dominate the political agenda. The reason is that inflation, unemployment, and growth affect a country's citizens directly. Trade deficits and exchange rates affect them indirectly—and in politics, indirect effects take a back seat.

Often a country responds to an international goal only when the international community forces it to do so. For example, in the 1980s when Brazil couldn't borrow any more money from other countries, it reluctantly made resolving its trade deficit a key goal. Similarly, when other countries threatened to limit Japanese imports, Japan took steps to increase the value of the yen and decrease its trade surplus. When a country is forced to face certain economic facts, international goals can become its primary goals. As countries become more economically integrated, these pressures from other countries become more important.

THE EFFECTS OF MONETARY AND FISCAL POLICIES ON INTERNATIONAL GOALS

For a computer simulation of the effects of monetary and fiscal policy effects on international goals, see Module, "International Monetary and Fiscal Policy" in *Macro Interactive* software.

To say that achieving international goals is not the determining factor in the choice of macroeconomic policies isn't to say that economists don't consider the effects of monetary and fiscal policies on international goals. They watch these carefully.

For example, the United States ran trade deficits through much of the 1980s and 1990s. In the late 1980s other countries were placing heavy pressure on the United States to do something. You can understand U.S. macroeconomic policy during that period only if you understand the international pressure. To follow the debates about macroeconomic policy, you must be familiar with how monetary and fiscal policies affect the exchange rate and the trade balance. Those effects often can significantly influence the choice of policies. We begin by considering the effect of monetary policy.

Monetary Policy's Effect on Exchange Rates

Monetary policy affects exchange rates in three ways: (1) through its effect on the interest rate, (2) through its effect on income, and (3) through its effect on price levels and inflation.

The Effect on Exchange Rates via Interest Rates   Expansionary monetary policy pushes down the U.S. interest rate, which decreases the financial capital inflow into the United States, decreasing the demand for dollars, pushing down the value of the dollar, and decreasing the U.S. exchange rate via the interest rate path. Contractionary monetary policy does the opposite. It raises the U.S. interest rate, which tends to bring in financial capital flows from abroad, increasing the demand for dollars, increasing the value of the dollar, and increasing the U.S. exchange rate.

To see why these effects take place, consider a person in Japan in the late 1980s, when the Japanese interest rate was about 2 or 3 percent. He or she reasoned, "Why should I earn only 2 or 3 percent return in Japan? I'll save (buy some financial assets) in the United States where I'll earn 8 percent." If the U.S. interest rate goes up due to contraction in the money supply, other things equal, the advantage of holding one's financial assets in the United States will become even greater and more people will want to save here. People in Japan hold yen, not dollars, so in order to save in the United States they must buy dollars. Thus, a rise in U.S. interest rates increases demand for dollars and, in terms of yen, pushes the U.S. exchange rate up.

It's important to recognize that it's the relative interest rates that govern the flow of financial capital. In the first part of the 1990s, Japan tightened its money supply, raising interest rates there to 6 percent. This relative increase in the Japanese interest rate decreased demand for dollars and thus lowered the U.S. exchange rate. In the second part of the 1990s, Japan reversed its policy and lowered its interest rate, thereby raising the U.S. exchange rate relative to the yen.

Another example of how important relative international interest rates are involves Germany and the European Union (EU). In 1992, the EU was heading toward a monetary union in which all member countries would use a common currency. As a stepping stone, the EU countries had exchange rates set within a narrow band. Because of fiscal problems caused by German reunification, the German central bank, the Bundesbank, felt it had to raise its interest rates. That rise put upward pressure on the mark, and destroyed the fixed exchange rate system and the upcoming monetary union. Many economists are willing to say that relative interest rates, because of their importance in the short run, are the *primary* short-run determinant of exchange rates.

The Effect on Exchange Rates via Income   Monetary policy also affects income in a country. As money supply rises, income expands; when money supply falls, income contracts.[1] This effect on income provides another way the money supply affects the exchange rate. As we saw earlier, when income rises, imports rise while exports are unaffected. To buy foreign products, U.S. citizens need foreign currency, which they must buy with dollars. So when U.S. imports rise, the supply of dollars to the foreign exchange market increases as U.S. citizens sell dollars to buy foreign currencies to pay for those imports. This decreases the dollar exchange rate. This effect through income and imports provides a second path through which monetary policy affects the exchange rate: Expansionary monetary policy causes U.S. income to rise, imports to rise, and the U.S. exchange rate to fall via the income path. Contractionary monetary policy causes U.S. income to fall, imports to fall, and the U.S. exchange rate to rise via the income path.

The Effect on Exchange Rates via Price Levels   A third way in which monetary policy can affect exchange rates is through its effect on prices in a country. Expansionary monetary policy pushes the U.S. price level up. As the U.S. price level rises relative to foreign prices, U.S. exports become more expensive, and goods the United States

Q–4:   What effect does the lowering of a country's interest rates have on exchange rates?

The keys to an extended European Monetary Union slipped away when Germany raised its interest rate.

In the real world, the issues become quite complicated. For example, in mid-1994, the Bundesbank was lowering its interest rates and the United States was raising its interest rates. Still, the U.S. dollar fell. The reason expressed in the market for this contra-expected phenomenon was that the United States had not raised its interest rates as much as expected. This is an example of why real-world policy must be interpreted in relation to the expectations of that policy.

Q–5:   What effect would contractionary monetary policy have on a country's exchange rates via the income and price routes?

---

[1]When there's inflation, it's the rate of money supply growth relative to the rate of inflation that's important. If inflation is 10 percent and money supply growth is 10 percent, the rate of increase in the real money supply is zero. If money supply growth falls to, say, 5 percent while inflation stays at 10 percent, there will be a contractionary effect on the real economy.

For international trade to take place, currencies must be convertible into other currencies. Here we see a Japanese currency trader taking bids on buying and selling currencies. *Fujifotos/ The Image Works.*

imports become cheaper, decreasing U.S. competitiveness. This increases demand for foreign currencies and decreases demand for dollars. Thus, via the price path, expansionary monetary policy pushes down the dollar's value for the same reason that an expansion in income pushes it down.

Contractionary monetary policy puts downward pressure on the U.S. price level and slows down any existing inflation. As the U.S. price level falls relative to foreign prices, U.S. exports become more competitive and the goods the United States imports more expensive. Thus, contractionary monetary policy pushes the value of the dollar up via the price path.

Expansionary monetary policy leads to a depreciation of a country's currency, while contractionary monetary policy causes the currency to appreciate.

The Net Effect of Monetary Policy on Exchange Rates   Notice that all these effects of monetary policy on exchange rates are in the same direction. Expansionary monetary policy pushes a country's exchange rate down; contractionary monetary policy pushes a country's exchange rate up. Summarizing these effects, we have the following relationships for expansionary and contractionary monetary policy:

3a Monetary policy affects exchange rates through the interest rate path, the income path, and the price level path, as shown in the accompanying diagram.

Expansionary monetary policy

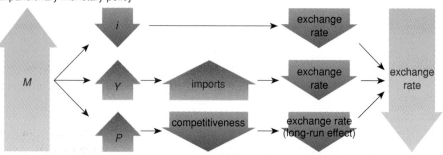

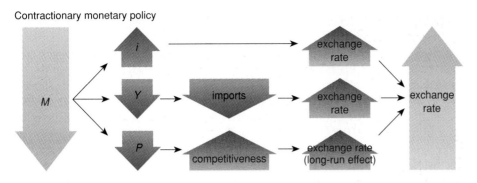

Contractionary monetary policy

There are, of course, many provisos to the relationship between monetary policy and the exchange rate. For example, as the price of imports goes up, there is some inflationary pressure from that rise in price and hence some pressure for the price level to rise as well as fall. Monetary policy affects exchange rates in subtle ways, but if an economist had to give a quick answer to what effect monetary policy would have on exchange rates it would be:

> *Expansionary monetary policy lowers exchange rates. It decreases the relative value of a country's currency.*
> *Contractionary monetary policy increases exchange rates. It increases the relative value of a country's currency.*

Expansionary monetary policy lowers exchange rates. It decreases the relative value of a country's currency.

Contractionary monetary policy increases exchange rates. It increases the relative value of a country's currency.

When a country's international trade balance is negative (in deficit), the country is importing more than it is exporting. When a country's international trade balance is positive, the country is exporting more than it is importing.

Monetary policy affects the trade balance in three ways: through income, through the price level, and through the exchange rate.

Monetary Policy's Effect on the Trade Balance

The Effect on the Trade Balance via Income   Expansionary monetary policy increases income. When income rises, imports rise, while exports are unaffected. As imports rise, the trade balance shifts in the direction of deficit. So, via the income path, expansionary monetary policy shifts the trade balance toward a deficit.

Contractionary policy works in the opposite direction. It decreases income. When income falls, imports fall, while exports are unaffected, so the trade balance shifts in the direction of surplus. Thus, via the income path, expansionary monetary policy increases the trade deficit; contractionary monetary policy decreases the trade deficit.

Expansionary monetary policy tends to increase the trade deficit while contractionary monetary policy tends to decrease the trade deficit.

The Effect on the Trade Balance via Price Levels   A second way monetary policy affects the trade balance is through its effect on a country's price level. Expansionary monetary policy pushes a country's price level up. This decreases its competitiveness and increases a trade deficit. So, via the price path, expansionary monetary policy increases a trade deficit.

Contractionary monetary policy works in the opposite direction. It tends to push a country's price level down; this fall makes exports more competitive and imports less competitive. Both these effects tend to decrease a trade deficit. So, via the price path, contractionary monetary policy decreases a trade deficit.

Monetary policy's effect on the price level is a long-run, not a short-run, effect. It often takes a year for changes in the money supply to affect prices, and another year or two for changes in prices to affect imports and exports. Thus, the price path is a long-run effect. Price level changes don't significantly affect the trade balance in the short run.

The Effect on the Trade Balance via Exchange Rates   A third path through which monetary policy influences the trade balance is the exchange rate. Expansionary U.S. monetary

Trade is central to the prosperity of modern economies.

policy decreases the interest rate which tends to push the dollar exchange rate down, increasing U.S. competitiveness. This decreases a trade deficit and hence works in a direction opposite to the effects of income changes and price level changes on the trade balance. Like the price level effect, the effect of the exchange rate on the trade balance is a long-run effect. This path doesn't have a significant effect in the short run.

Q–6: What effect will contractionary monetary policy have on the trade balance through the price level and income paths?

Contractionary monetary policy works in the opposite direction. It raises the exchange rate, increasing the relative price of U.S. exports and lowering the relative price of imports into the United States. Both effects tend to increase a trade deficit.

The Net Effect of Monetary Policy on the Trade Balance   Since the effects are not all in the same direction, talking about the net effect of monetary policy on the trade balance is a bit more ambiguous than talking about its net effect on a country's exchange rate. However, only one of these paths—the income path—is a short-run effect. Thus, in the short run the net effect of monetary policy is relatively clear: Expansionary monetary policy tends to increase a trade deficit; contractionary monetary policy tends to decrease it. Since, in the long run, the price path effect and the exchange rate effect tend to offset each other, the short-run effects of monetary policy through the income path often carry over to the long-run effect.

Q–7: What will be the net effect of contractionary monetary policy on the trade balance?

Summarizing these three relationships, we have the following relationships for expansionary and contractionary monetary policy:

3b Monetary policy affects the trade deficit through the income path, the price level path, and the exchange rate path, as shown in the accompanying diagram.

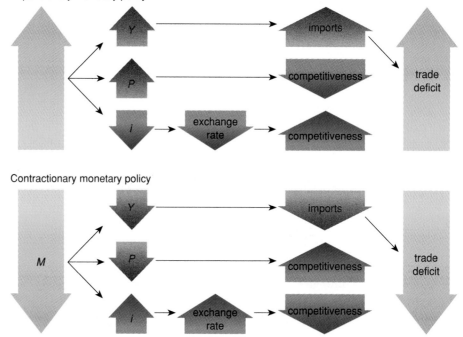

Expansionary monetary policy makes a trade deficit larger.

Contractionary monetary policy makes a trade deficit smaller.

While many complications can enter the trade balance picture, most economists would summarize monetary policy's short-run effect on the trade balance as follows:

Expansionary monetary policy makes a trade deficit larger.
Contractionary monetary policy makes a trade deficit smaller.

Fiscal Policy's Effect on Exchange Rates

Now we'll consider fiscal policy's effect on exchange rates. Fiscal policy, like monetary policy, affects exchange rates via three paths: via income, via price, and via interest rates. Let's begin with its effect through income.

The Effect on Exchange Rates via Income   Expansionary fiscal policy expands income and therefore increases imports, increasing the trade deficit and lowering the exchange rate. Contractionary fiscal policy contracts income, thereby decreasing imports and increasing the exchange rate. These effects of expansionary and contractionary fiscal policies via the income path are similar to the effects of monetary policy, so if it's not intuitively clear to you why the effect is what it is, it may be worthwhile to review the slightly more complete discussion of monetary policy's effect presented previously.

The Effect on Exchange Rates via Price Levels   Let's turn to the effect of fiscal policy on exchange rates through prices. Expansionary fiscal policy increases aggregate demand and increases prices of a country's exports; hence it decreases the competitiveness of a country's exports, which pushes down the exchange rate. Contractionary fiscal policy works in the opposite direction. These are the same effects that monetary policy had. And, as was the case with monetary policy, the price path is a long-run effect.

> The net effect of fiscal policy on the exchange rate is ambiguous because the income effect and the interest rate effect work in opposite directions.

The Effect on Exchange Rates via Interest Rates   Fiscal policy's effect on the exchange rate via the interest rate path is different from monetary policy's effect. Let's first consider the effect of expansionary fiscal policy. Whereas expansionary monetary policy lowers the interest rate, expansionary fiscal policy raises interest rates because the government sells bonds to finance that deficit. The higher U.S. interest rate causes foreign capital to flow into the United States, which pushes up the U.S. exchange rate. Therefore expansionary fiscal policy's effect on exchange rates via the interest rate effect is to push up a country's exchange rate.

Contractionary fiscal policy decreases interest rates since it reduces the bond financing of that deficit. Lower U.S. interest rates cause capital to flow out of the United States, which pushes down the U.S. exchange rate.

The Net Effect of Fiscal Policy on Exchange Rates   Of these three effects, the interest rate effect and the income effect are both short-run effects. These two work in opposite directions, so the net effect of fiscal policy on the exchange rate is ambiguous. Let's summarize these three effects.

> **Q–8:** What is the net effect of expansionary fiscal policy on the exchange rate?

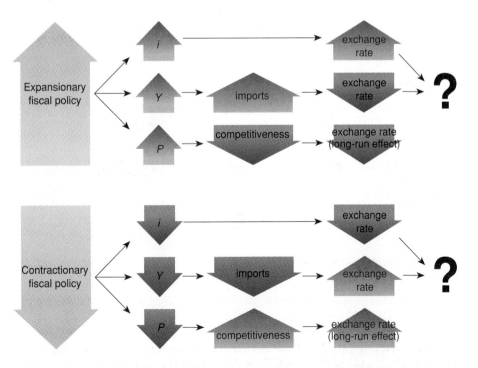

> **4a** Fiscal policy affects exchange rates through the income path, the interest rate path, and the price level path, as shown in the accompanying diagram.

It's unclear what the effect of expansionary or contractionary fiscal policy will be on exchange rates.

Fiscal policy works on the trade deficit primarily through its effects on income and prices. (Since fiscal policy's effect on the exchange rate is unclear, there is no need to consider its effect through exchange rates.)

Fiscal Policy's Effect on the Trade Deficit

The Effect on the Trade Deficit via Income   Let's begin by looking at the income path. As with expansionary monetary policy, expansionary fiscal policy increases income. This higher income increases imports, which increases the size of the trade deficit.

Contractionary fiscal policy decreases income and decreases imports. Hence it decreases the size of a trade deficit. These are the same effects as those of monetary policy.

The Effect on the Trade Deficit via Prices   The effect via the price level route is also similar to the effects of monetary policy. Expansionary fiscal policy pushes up the price level, increasing the price of a country's exports and decreasing its competitiveness. Hence it increases the trade deficit.

Contractionary fiscal policy pushes down the price level, decreasing the price of a country's exports, increasing its competitiveness, and decreasing the trade deficit. This effect via price is a long-run effect, as it is with monetary policy.

The Net Effect of Fiscal Policy on the Trade Deficit   Since these two effects work in the same direction, fiscal policy's net effect on the trade balance is clear:

Expansionary fiscal policy increases a trade deficit.

Contractionary fiscal policy decreases a trade deficit.

Expansionary fiscal policy increases a trade deficit.
Contractionary fiscal policy decreases a trade deficit.

Summarizing these two effects schematically, we have:

4b Fiscal policy affects the trade balance through the income path and the price level path, as shown in the accompanying diagram.

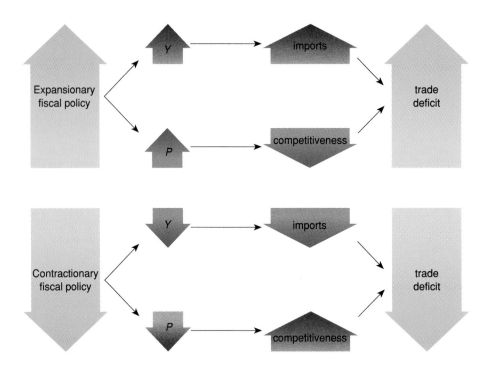

Q–9:   What is the net effect of expansionary fiscal policy on the trade deficit?

Exhibit 1 summarizes the primary net short-run effects of both expansionary monetary and fiscal policies on international goals. (The effects of contractionary policy work in the opposite direction.)

INTERNATIONAL PHENOMENA AND DOMESTIC GOALS

So far, we've focused on the effect of monetary and fiscal policies on international goals. But often the effect is the other way around: International phenomena change and have significant influences on the domestic economy and on the ability to achieve domestic goals.

For example, say that Japan ran contractionary monetary policy. That would increase the Japanese exchange rate and increase Japan's trade surplus, which means

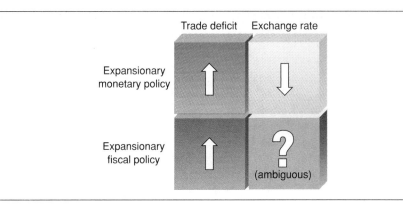

EXHIBIT 1   The Effect of Expansionary Monetary and Fiscal Policy on International Goals

In the short run, expansionary monetary policy tends to increase a trade deficit and decrease the exchange rate. Expansionary fiscal policy tends to increase the trade deficit. Its effect on the exchange rate is ambiguous.

it would decrease the U.S. exchange rate and increase the U.S. trade deficit, both of which would affect U.S. domestic goals. So the monetary and fiscal policies of other countries can have significant effects on the U.S. domestic economy. This has led to significant pressure for countries to coordinate their economic policies.

Unless forced to do so because of international pressures, most countries don't let international goals guide their macroeconomic policy. But for every effect that monetary and fiscal policies have on a country's exchange rates and trade balance, there's an equal and opposite effect on the combination of other countries' exchange rates and trade balances. When one country's exchange rate goes up, by definition another country's exchange rate must go down. Similarly, when one country's balance of trade is in surplus, another's must be in deficit. This interconnection means that other countries' fiscal and monetary policies affect the United States, while U.S. fiscal and monetary policies affect other countries, so pressure to coordinate policies is considerable.

Because of this interdependence, many economists argue that all countries must work together to coordinate their monetary and fiscal policies. For example, if Japan has a trade surplus and the United States has a trade deficit, the United States can run contractionary monetary policy or Japan can use expansionary monetary policy to help expand U.S. exports to Japan and thereby reduce the U.S. trade deficit. Why would Japan do something like that? Because, if it doesn't, the United States might threaten to directly limit Japanese exports to the United States through trade sanctions. So Japan must take U.S. desires into account in conducting its monetary and fiscal policies.

Coordination, of course, works both ways. If other countries are to take the U.S. economy's needs into account, the United States must take other countries' needs into account in determining its goals. Say, for example, the U.S. economy is going into a recession. This domestic problem calls for expansionary monetary policy. But expansionary monetary policy will increase U.S. income and U.S. imports and lower the value of the dollar. Say that, internationally, the United States has agreed that it must work toward eliminating the U.S. trade deficit in the short run. Does it forsake its domestic goals? Or does it forsake its international commitment?

There's no one right answer to those questions. It depends on political judgments (how long until the next election?), judgments about what foreign countries can do if the United States doesn't meet its international commitments, and similar judgments by foreign countries about the United States. The result is lots of international economic parleys (generally in rather pleasant surroundings) to discuss these issues. Nicely worded communiques are issued which say, in effect, that each country will do what's best for the world economy as long as it's also best for itself.

If you are teaching a technically oriented class, in the *Honors Companion* the Keynesian model with an international feedback is presented in Chapter 5. This provides a useful extra credit exercise to assign to students.

International Monetary and Fiscal Coordination

5 Governments try to coordinate their monetary and fiscal policies because their economies are interdependent.

Policy coordination may not work in practice because different countries have different preferences with respect to inflation and unemployment. They also have different economic structures so that policies that work for one may have adverse effects on another.

Coordination Is a Two-Way Street

Q–10: If domestic problems call for expansionary monetary policy and international problems call for contractionary monetary policy, what policy will a country likely adopt?

Each country will likely do what's best for the world economy as long as it's also best for itself.

The world has become much more interdependent in recent years. In this picture you can see cars made in Germany being unloaded for sale in the United States.   © *David Wells/The Image Works.*

Crowding Out and International Considerations

6 While internationalizing a country's debt may help in the short run, in the long run it presents potential problems since foreign ownership of a country's debts means the country must pay interest to those foreign countries and that debt may come due.

This is another opportunity to make the point that a country must often choose between domestic and international goals.

For a real-world example of a country subordinating its own domestic goals for an international goal, see Chapter 16 in *Case Studies in Macroeconomics.*

Initially, the European common currency was to be called the ECU. Later, for political reasons, it was decided to call it the Euro.

As a final topic in this chapter, let's reconsider the issue of crowding out that we considered in an earlier chapter, only this time we'll take into account international considerations. Say a government is running a budget deficit, and that the central bank has decided it won't increase the money supply to help finance the deficit. (This happened in the 1980s with the Fed and the U.S. government.) What will be the result?

The basic idea of crowding out is that the budget deficit will cause the interest rate to go up. But wait. There's another way to avoid the crowding out that results from financing the deficit: Foreigners could buy the debt at the existing interest rate. This is called *internationalizing the debt,* and is what happened to the U.S. economy in the late 1980s.

In the 1980s, there were massive inflows to the United States of financial capital from abroad. These inflows held down the U.S. interest rate even as the federal government ran large budget deficits. Thus, those large deficits didn't push up interest rates because foreigners, not U.S. citizens, were buying U.S. debt.

But, as we discussed, internationalization of the U.S. debt is not costless. While it helps in the short run, it presents problems in the long run. Foreign ownership of U.S. debt means that the United States must pay foreigners interest each year on that debt. To do so, the United States must export more than it imports, which means that the United States must consume less than it produces at some time in the future to pay for the trade deficits it's running now.

As you can see, the issues become complicated quickly.

Despite the complications, the above discussion gives you an understanding of many events that may have previously seemed incomprehensible. To show you the relevance of what I have said above about crowding out and international considerations, let's look at two situations that occurred in the early 1990s.

The first concerned Germany and the EU (discussed earlier in this chapter). For political reasons, Germany was running loose fiscal policy. Fearing inflation from this loose fiscal policy, the Bundesbank ran tight monetary policy, forcing both the German interest rate and the German exchange rate up. This disrupted the movement toward a European Monetary System and a common European currency—the Euro—as other European countries refused to go along. In the late 1990s those problems continued. Here we see domestic goals superseding international goals.

The second concerns Japan in 1993 and early 1994. Japan was experiencing a recession, in part because its tight monetary policy had pushed up interest rates and hence pushed up the exchange rate for the yen. Other countries, especially the United States and European countries, put enormous pressure on Japan to run expansionary

International Goal	Policy Alternatives
Lower exchange rate	Contractionary foreign monetary policy Expansionary domestic monetary policy
Lower trade deficit	Contractionary domestic fiscal policy Expansionary foreign fiscal policy Contractionary domestic monetary policy Expansionary foreign monetary policy

EXHIBIT 2   Selecting Policies to Achieve Goals

This table shows how alternative monetary and fiscal policies can be used to achieve the goal of a lower exchange rate and the goal of a lower trade deficit.

fiscal policy, which would keep the relative value of the yen high but simultaneously increase Japanese income, and hence Japanese demand for imports. In response, the Japanese ran expansionary fiscal policy and this helped to keep the value of the yen higher than it otherwise would have been. Soon thereafter, Japan simultaneously ran expansionary monetary policy, thereby offsetting the fiscal effect on the exchange rate.

There are many more examples, but these two should give you a good sense of the relevance of the issues.

CONCLUSION: SELECTING POLICIES TO ACHIEVE GOALS

Throughout this chapter I have organized the discussion around the effects of policies. Another way to organize the discussion would have been around goals, and to show how alternative policies will achieve those international goals.

The table in Exhibit 2 does this, and will serve as a useful review of the chapter. It shows alternative policies that will achieve specified goals.

You can see in the table why coordination of monetary and fiscal policies is much in the news, since a foreign country's policy can eliminate, or reduce the need for, domestic policies to be undertaken.

This brief chapter in no way exhausted the international topics. Countries use many policies to effect their international goals. But this chapter has, I hope, made you very aware of the international dimensions of our economic goals, and of how monetary and fiscal policies affect those goals. That awareness is absolutely necessary to discuss real-world macroeconomic policies.

CHAPTER SUMMARY

- The international goals of a country are often in dispute.
- Domestic goals generally dominate international goals, but countries often respond to an international goal when forced to do so by other countries.
- Expansionary monetary policy tends to lower a country's exchange rate and increase its trade deficit.
- Contractionary fiscal policy has an ambiguous effect on a country's exchange rate but tends to decrease its trade deficit.

- For every effect that monetary and fiscal policies have on a country's exchange rate and trade balance, there is an equal and opposite effect on the combination of foreign countries' exchange rates and trade balances.
- International capital inflows can reduce crowding out.
- Internationalizing a country's debt means that at some time in the future the country must consume less than it produces.

KEY TERMS

exchange rate   *(381)*

fixed exchange rate   *(381)*

flexible exchange rate   *(381)*

partially flexible exchange rate   *(381)*

trade balance   *(381)*

QUESTIONS FOR THOUGHT AND REVIEW

The number after each question represents the estimated degree of critical thinking required. (1 = almost none; 10 = deep thought.)

1. Look up the current U.S. exchange rate relative to the yen. Would you suggest raising it or lowering it? Why? *(7)*

2. Look up the current U.S. trade balance. Would you suggest raising it or lowering it? Why? *(7)*

3. What effect on the U.S. trade deficit and exchange rate would result if Japan ran an expansionary monetary policy? *(4)*

4. What would be the effect on the U.S. trade deficit and the U.S. exchange rate if Japan ran a contractionary fiscal policy? *(4)*

5. If modern Classicals are correct and expansionary monetary policy immediately increases inflationary expectations and the price level, how might the effect of monetary policy on the exchange rate be different than that presented in this chapter? *(9)*

6. What effect will a combination of expansionary fiscal policy and contractionary monetary policy have on the exchange rate? *(5)*

7. How would a Classical economist differ from a Keynesian economist in their policies for dealing with an oil price shock? Why? *(8)*

8. Is the United States justified in complaining of Japan's use of an export-led growth policy? Why? *(8)*

9. What effect would you expect a fall in the price of oil to have on the U.S. economy? Why? *(6)*

10. How is the Bundesbank's running a tight monetary policy in the early 1990s an example of domestic goals superseding international goals? *(2)*

11. In the mid-1990s, Japan's economic recession was much in the news. What would you suspect was happening to its trade balance during this time? What policies would you guess other countries (such as those in the Group of Seven) were pressuring Japan to implement? *(7)*

PROBLEMS AND EXERCISES

1. Draw the schematics to show the effect of contractionary fiscal policy on exchange rates.

2. Draw the schematics to show the effect of expansionary monetary policy on the trade deficit.

3. You observe that over the past decade a country's competitiveness has been continually eroded and its trade deficit has risen.
   a. What monetary or fiscal policies might have led to such results? Why?
   b. You also observe that interest rates have steadily risen along with a rise in the exchange rate. What policies would lead to this result?
   c. What policy might you suggest to improve the country's competitiveness? Explain how that policy might work.

4. Congratulations! You have been appointed an adviser to the IMF. A country that has run trade deficits for many years now has difficulty servicing its accumulated international debt and wants to borrow from the IMF to meet its obligations. The IMF requires that the country set

a target trade surplus.
   a. What monetary and fiscal policies would you suggest the IMF require of that country?
   b. What would be the likely effect of that plan on the country's domestic inflation and growth?
   c. How do you think the country's government will respond to your proposals? Why?

5. Congratulations! You've been hired as an economic adviser to Textland, a country that has perfectly flexible exchange rates. State what monetary and fiscal policy you might suggest in each of the following situations, and explain why you would suggest those policies.
   a. You want to lower the interest rate, decrease inflationary pressures, and lower the trade deficit.
   b. You want to lower the interest rate, decrease inflationary pressures, and lower a trade surplus.
   c. You want to lower the interest rate, decrease unemployment, and lower the trade deficit.
   d. You want to raise the interest rate, decrease unemployment, and lower the trade deficit.

ANSWERS TO MARGIN QUESTIONS

1. A country can influence its exchange rates indirectly through its monetary and fiscal policies. Contractionary monetary policy pushes up the exchange rate; contractionary fiscal policy pushes down the exchange rate. *(381)*

2. A low exchange rate of a country's currency will tend to stimulate exports and curtail imports. *(381)*

3. A trade deficit means a country is consuming more than it is producing. Consuming more than you produce is

pleasant. It also means that capital is flowing into the country, which can be used for investment. So why worry? *(382)*

4. A fall in a country's interest rate will push down its exchange rate. *(383)*

5. Contractionary monetary policy pushes up the interest rate, decreases income and hence imports, and has a tendency to decrease inflation. Therefore, through these paths, contractionary monetary policy will tend to

increase the exchange rate. *(383)*

6. Contractionary monetary policy will tend to decrease income and the price level, decreasing imports and increasing competitiveness. Since the income and price level paths work in the same direction, contractionary monetary policy is likely to decrease the trade deficit. The exchange rate path can, however, work in the opposite direction. *(386)*

7. In the short run, the net effect of contractionary monetary policy on the trade balance is to decrease the trade deficit, or increase the trade surplus. *(386)*

8. The net effect of expansionary fiscal policy on exchange rates is uncertain. Through the interest rate effect it pushes up the exchange rate, but through the income and price level effects it pushes down the exchange rate. *(387)*

9. The net effect of expansionary fiscal policy on the trade deficit is to increase the trade deficit. *(388)*

10. Generally, when domestic policies and international policies conflict, a country will choose to deal with its domestic problems. Thus, it will likely use expansionary monetary policy if domestic problems call for that. *(389)*

Sixteen

Open Economy Macro: Exchange Rate and Trade Policy

A foreign exchange dealer's office during a busy spell is the nearest thing to Bedlam I have struck.

~ Harold Wincott

After reading this chapter, you should be able to:

1 Describe the balance of payments and the balance on goods and services, and relate them to the supply and demand for currencies.

2 List three important fundamental determinants of exchange rates.

3 Explain how a country fixes an exchange rate.

4 Define purchasing power parity and explain its relevance to the debate about whether to have a fixed or flexible exchange rate.

5 Differentiate fixed, flexible, and partially flexible exchange rates, and discuss the advantages and disadvantages of each.

6 List some of the most important international trade restrictions.

7 Explain why economists generally support free trade.

The last chapter's consideration of the international dimensions of traditional macro policy assumed a flexible exchange rate. I discussed the effect of monetary and fiscal policy on exchange rates. As you saw in earlier chapters, flexible exchange rates are only one option that governments have. Other options are fixed exchange rates or an exchange rate system somewhere between flexible and fixed—partially flexible exchange rates. A consideration of macro issues from the perspective of such exchange régimes is called open economy macro.

The primary topics of open economy macro that have not been covered in the previous chapter are exchange rate policy and trade policy. In this chapter I consider these issues. I start with an in-depth consideration of the balance of payments, discussing how that balance of payments relates to exchange rates and tying that discussion into the consideration of the supply of and demand for currencies. Next I briefly consider some reasons why exchange rate determination is more complicated than it seems in supply/demand analysis. I then discuss exchange rate policy in some depth and present the arguments for and against various exchange rate régimes.

	1987		1996	
1. Current account				
2. Merchandise				
3. Exports	+250		+611	
4. Imports	−410		−799	
5. Balance of trade		−160		−188
6. Services				
7. Exports	+ 98		+224	
8. Imports	− 90		−150	
9. Balance on services		+ 8		+ 74
10. Balance on goods and services		−152		−114
11. Net Investment income	+ 8		− 8	
12. Net transfers	− 23		− 43	
13. Invest. trans. balance		− 15		− 51
14. Balance on current account		−167		−165
15. Capital account				
16. Capital inflows	+230		+525	
17. Capital outflows	− 71		−315	
18. Balance on capital account		+159		+210
19. Current and capital balance		− 8		+ 45
20. Statistical discrepancy		− 1		− 53
21. Official transactions account		+ 9		+ 8
22. Totals		0		0

EXHIBIT 1   The Balance of Payments Account, 1987 and 1996

Source: *Survey of Current Business* 1997. (http://www.census.gov)

The best door into an in-depth discussion of exchange rates and open economy macro is a discussion of **balance of payments** *(a country's record of all transactions between its residents and the residents of all foreign nations).*[1] These include a country's buying and selling of goods and services (imports and exports) and interest and profit payments from previous investments, together with all the capital inflows and outflows. Exhibit 1 presents the 1987 and 1996 balance of payments accounts for the United States. It records all payments made by foreigners to U.S. citizens and all payments made by U.S. citizens to foreigners in those years.

In the balance of payments accounts, flows of payments into the United States have a plus sign. Goods the U.S. exports must be paid for in dollars; they involve a flow of payments into the United States, so they have a plus sign. Similarly, U.S. imports must be paid for in foreign currency; they involve a flow of dollars out of the United States, and thus they have a minus sign. Notice that the bottom line of the balance of payments is $0. By definition, the bottom line (which includes all supplies and demands for currencies, including those of the government) must add up to zero.

As you can see in Exhibit 1, the balance of payments account is broken down into the current account, the capital account, and the official transactions account. The **current account** (lines 1–14) is *the part of the balance of payments account in which all short-term flows of payments are listed.* It includes exports and imports, which are what one normally means when one talks about the trade balance. The **capital account** (lines 15–18) is *the part of the balance of payments account in which all long-term flows of payments are listed.* If a U.S. citizen buys a German stock, or if a Japanese company buys a U.S. company, the transaction shows up on the capital account.

The government can influence the exchange rate by buying and selling **official reserves**—*government holdings of foreign currencies*—or by buying and selling other international reserves, such as gold. Such buying and selling is recorded in the **official transactions account** (line 21)—*the part of the balance of payments account that records the amount of its own currency or foreign currencies that a nation buys or sells.*

THE BALANCE OF PAYMENTS

1a The balance of payments is a country's record of all transactions between its residents and the residents of all foreign countries.

Current account The part of the balance of payments account that lists all short-term flows of payments.

Capital account The part of the balance of payments account that lists all long-term flows of payments.

[1]These records are not very good. Because of measurement difficulties, many transactions go unrecorded and many numbers must be estimated, leaving a potential for large errors.

To get a better idea of what's included in the three accounts, let's consider each of them more carefully.

The Current Account

At the top of Exhibit 1, the current account is composed of the merchandise (or goods) account (lines 2–5), the services account (lines 6–9), the net investment income account (line 11), and the net transfers account (lines 12 and 13).

You may wish to spend some extra time reviewing the historical trends and fluctuations in the trade balance that are outlined in Chapter 6.

Starting with the merchandise account, notice that in 1987 the United States imported $410 billion worth of goods and exported $250 billion worth of goods. *The difference between the value of goods exported and imported* is sometimes called the **balance of trade.** Looking at line 5, you can see that the United States had a balance of trade deficit of $160 billion in 1987 and $188 billion in 1996.

The trade balance is often discussed in the press as a summary of how the United States is doing in the international markets. It's not a good summary. Trade in services is just as important as trade in merchandise, so economists pay more attention to the combined balance on goods and services.

1b The balance on goods and services is the difference between the value of goods and services a nation exports and the value of goods and services it imports.

Thus, the **balance on goods and services**—*the difference between the value of goods and services exported and imported*—(line 10) becomes a key statistic for economists. Notice that in both 1987 and 1996 most of the U.S. trade deficit resulted from an imbalance in the merchandise or trade account. The service account worked in the opposite direction. It was slightly positive in 1987; in 1996 the services account reduced the trade deficit by $74 billion. Such services include tourist expenditures and insurance payments by foreigners to U.S. firms. For instance, when you travel in Japan, you spend yen, which you must buy with dollars; this is an outflow of payments, which is a negative contribution to the services account.

Recent changes in accounting procedures proposed by the National Academy of Sciences would treat production of goods by U.S. companies abroad as U.S. production. If accepted, this change would have major effects on the trade portion of the balance of payments accounts. Specifically, much of the trade deficit of the United States would be eliminated. Whether such a change makes sense is a complicated question, but it is helpful to point out to students that understanding the technical aspects of accounting is important to have an in-depth understanding of the international situation of an economy.

There is no reason that the goods and services sent into a country must equal the goods and services sent out in a particular year, even if the current account is in equilibrium, because the current account also includes payments from past investments and net transfers. When you invest, you expect to make a return on that investment. The payments to foreign owners of U.S. capital assets is a negative contribution to the U.S. balance of payments. The payment to U.S. owners of foreign capital assets is a positive contribution to the U.S. balance of payments. These payments on investment income are a type of holdover from past trade and services imbalances. So even though they relate to investments, they show up on the current account.

Q–1: If you, a U.S. citizen, are traveling abroad, where will your expenditures show up in the balance of payments accounts?

The final component of the current account is net transfers, which include foreign aid, gifts, and other payments to individuals not exchanged for goods or services. If you send $100 to your aunt in Mexico, it shows up with a minus sign here.

Adding up the pluses and minuses on the current account, we arrive at line 14, the current account balance. Notice that in 1987 the United States ran a $167 billion deficit on the current account, and in 1996 the United States had a deficit of $165 billion (line 14). That means that, in the current account, the supply of dollars greatly exceeded the demand for dollars. If the current account represented the total supply of and demand for dollars, the value of the dollar would have fallen. But it doesn't. There are also the capital account, statistical discrepancies, and the official transactions account.

The Capital Account

The capital account measures the flow of payments between countries for assets such as stocks, bonds, and real estate. As you can see in Exhibit 1, in 1987 there was a significant inflow of capital into the United States in excess of outflows of capital from the United States. Capital inflows (payments by foreigners for U.S. real and financial assets) were $159 billion more than capital outflows (payments by U.S. citizens for foreign assets). In 1996, there was an inflow of $525 billion (line 18), but there was also an outflow of $315 billion, so the net balance on the capital account was $210 billion as compared to $159 billion in 1987.

To buy these U.S. assets foreigners needed dollars, so these net capital inflows represent a demand for dollars. In 1987 the demand for dollars to buy real and financial assets went a long way toward balancing the excess supply of dollars on the current account. In 1996 it totally offset it.

Thus it would seem that the government would have had to buy dollars in 1987 and sell dollars in 1996. That wasn't the case, however. The reason is statistical discrepancies, as we see in line 20. In 1987 there was a small −$1 billion discrepancy, but in 1996 there was a much larger −$53 billion discrepancy. These discrepancies arise because many international transactions, especially on the capital account, go unrecorded and hence must be estimated. With these discrepancies taken into account, in the absence of government policy there would have been downward pressure on the value of the dollar both in 1987 and in 1996. Because of the importance of capital flows, when you think about what's likely to happen to a currency's value, it's important to remember both the demand for dollars to buy goods and services and the demand for dollars to buy assets.

In thinking about what determines a currency's value, it's important to remember both the demand for dollars to buy goods and services and the demand for dollars to buy assets.

There is, of course, a difference between demand for dollars to buy currently produced goods and services and demand for dollars to buy assets. Assets earn profits or interest, so when foreigners buy U.S. assets, they earn income from those assets just for owning those assets. The net investment income from foreigners' previous asset purchases shows up on line 10 of the current account. It's the difference between the income U.S. citizens receive from their foreign assets and the income foreigners receive from their U.S. assets. If assets earned equal returns, one would expect that when foreigners own more U.S. capital assets than U.S. citizens own foreign capital assets, net investment income should be negative. And when U.S. citizens own more foreign capital assets than foreigners own U.S. capital assets, net investment income should be positive. Why is this? Because net investment income is simply the difference between the returns on U.S. citizens' assets held abroad and foreign citizens' assets held in the United States.

1c Since the balance of payments consists of both the capital account and the current account, if the capital account is in surplus and the current account is in deficit, there can still be a balance of payments surplus.

In the 1980s, the inflow of capital into the United States greatly exceeded the outflow of capital from the United States, and this trend has continued into the late 1990s. As a result, the United States became a net debtor nation; the amount foreigners own in the United States now exceeds the amount U.S. citizens own abroad by well over $900 billion. So one would expect that U.S. investment income would be highly negative. But looking at Exhibit 1 we see that was not the case. The reason? Foreigners' returns have been low, and much of the U.S. investment abroad is undervalued. For example, the Japanese bought a lot of U.S. real estate at very high prices and have been losing money on those investments. But one cannot expect this trend to continue. In the late 1990s, net investment income became negative.

Q–2: How can net investment income be positive if a country is a net debtor nation?

The current account and the capital account measure the private and non-U.S. government supply of and demand for dollars. The net amount of these two accounts is called the balance of payments surplus (if quantity demanded of a currency exceeds quantity supplied), or deficit (if quantity supplied of a currency exceeds quantity demanded). In both 1987 and 1996 the private quantity of dollars supplied exceeded the private quantity demanded (taking statistical discrepancies into account), which means that the United States had a small balance of payments deficit in both years.

The Official Transactions Account

A balance of payments deficit will put downward pressure on the value of a country's currency. If a country wants to prevent that from happening, it can buy its own currency. The third component of the balance of payments account, the official transactions account, records the amount of dollars that the United States bought. As you can see on line 21 of Exhibit 1, in 1987 the government entered into the foreign exchange market and bought $9 billion worth of U.S. dollars, using $9 billion of foreign reserves that it had. In 1996, it bought $8 billion. When a government buys its own currency to hold up the currency's price, we say that the government has

A balance of payments deficit will put downward pressure on the value of a country's currency.

EXHIBIT 2   The Supply of and Demand for Francs

As long as one keeps "quantities and prices of what" straight, the standard, or fundamental, analysis of the determination of exchange rates is easy. Exchange rates are determined by the supply of and demand for a country's currency. Just remember that if you're talking about the supply of and demand for francs, the price will be measured in dollars and the quantity will be in francs, as in this exhibit.

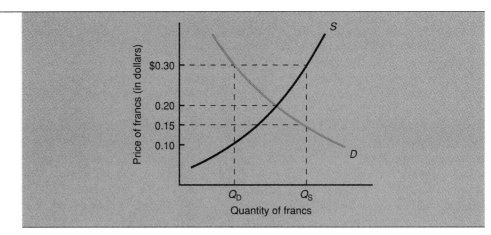

In mid-1994 the United States, in conjunction with Germany and Japan, made a concerted effort to hold up the value of the dollar and prevent the continued appreciation of the yen. They entered into the international markets buying dollars. They simultaneously changed their interest rates—the United States raising its interest rates; Japan and Germany lowering their interest rates. Most economists believe this accompanying domestic monetary policy is absolutely necessary to make foreign exchange intervention effective. The private international flows of money are simply too large for governments to affect them without changing their domestic monetary policy.

EXCHANGE RATES

Q–3: Show graphically the effect of an increase in demand for francs on the exchange rate for francs.

Ask your students to research the conversion of the East German mark to the West German mark after reunification. There were numerous accounts in the press in 1989 and 1990 of the problems associated with this conversion. In the late 1990s students will be able to find numerous articles about the European Monetary Union and the problems associated with converting to a common European currency.

supported its currency. It's holding the exchange rate higher than that rate otherwise would have been. If it sells its currency, it's attempting to depress the value of the currency.[2]

Now let's return to the point made at the beginning of the chapter: By definition the three accounts (current, capital, and official transactions) must sum to zero. Why is this? Because they are an accounting identity. The identity becomes something more than an identity if the currencies are freely exchangeable. In that case whenever anybody wants, they can take their currency and trade it for another. The quantity of currency supplied, including government's, must equal the quantity demanded, including government's.

The concepts *balance of payments* and *surplus* or *deficit* refer to the balance of payments not counting a country's official reserve transactions. Thus, any deficit in the balance of payments must be offset by an equal surplus in the official reserve transactions, and any surplus must be offset by an equal deficit. This means that the quantity of dollars supplied and the quantity of dollars demanded must be equal by definition.

We've already discussed exchange rate determination via supply and demand in an earlier chapter, but it is probably helpful to review our analysis.

In Exhibit 2, I present the supply of and demand for French francs in terms of dollars. Notice that the quantity of francs goes on the horizontal axis and the dollar price of francs goes on the vertical axis.

Let's first review where the supply of and demand for francs come from. The French who want to buy U.S. goods or assets supply francs to buy dollars. Let's consider an example. Say a French person wants to buy an IBM computer made in the United States. She has francs, but IBM wants dollars. So, in order to buy the computer, she or IBM must somehow exchange francs for dollars. She is *supplying* francs in order to *demand* dollars.

The supply curve of francs is upward sloping because the more dollars French citizens get for their francs, the cheaper U.S. goods and assets are for them and the greater the quantity of francs they want to supply for those goods. Say, for example, that the dollar price of one franc rises from 15¢ to 20¢. That means that the price of a dollar to a French person has fallen from 6.67 francs to 5 francs. For a French person, a good that cost $100 now falls in price from 667 francs to 500 francs. U.S. goods are cheaper, so the French buy more U.S. goods and more dollars, which means they supply more francs.

---

[2]Support for the dollar can also come from foreign central banks. In 1987, foreign central banks bought $45 billion worth of dollar-denominated assets, thereby playing a big role in holding the value of the dollar higher than it otherwise would have been.

The demand for francs comes from Americans who want to buy French goods or assets. The demand curve is downward sloping because the lower the dollar price of francs, the more francs U.S. citizens want to buy, for the same reasons I just described.

Equilibrium is where the quantity supplied equals the quantity demanded. In my example, equilibrium occurs at a dollar price of 20¢ for one franc. If the price of francs is above or below 20¢, quantity supplied won't equal the quantity demanded and there will be pressure for the exchange rate to move to equilibrium. Say, for example, that the price is 30¢. The quantity of francs supplied will be greater than the quantity demanded. People who want to sell francs won't be able to sell them. To find buyers, they will offer to sell their francs for less. As they do, the price of francs falls.

The supply/demand framework directly relates to the balance of payments. When quantity supplied equals private quantity demanded, the balance of payments is in equilibrium. If the exchange rate (the price of a country's currency in other currencies) is too high, there will be a deficit in the balance of payments; if the exchange rate is too low, there will be a surplus in the balance of payments. Thus, in Exhibit 2 when the price of francs is 30¢, the quantity of francs supplied exceeds the quantity demanded, so France is running a balance of payments deficit. When the price of francs is 15¢, the quantity of francs demanded exceeds the quantity supplied, so France is running a balance of payments surplus.

Exchange rate analysis is usually broken down into fundamental analysis and short-run analysis. In this next section I consider **fundamental analysis**—*a consideration of the fundamental forces that determine the supply of and demand for currencies,* and hence cause them to shift. These fundamental forces include a country's income, a country's prices, and the interest rate in a country. That means that changes in a country's income, changes in a country's prices, and changes in interest rates can cause the supply of and demand for a currency to shift. Let's consider how they do so.

Changes in a Country's Income   The demand for imports depends on the income in a country. When a country's income falls, demand for imports falls. Hence demand for foreign currency to buy those imports falls, which means that the supply of the country's currency to buy the foreign currency falls. That's why, in my presentation of the Keynesian model, I said that imports depend on income.

How important is this relationship? Very important. For example, in the mid-1990s the German economy went into recession and, as it did, its demand for imports fell and hence its supply of marks fell. This decrease in the supply of marks tended to push up the price of the mark relative to foreign currencies.

Changes in a Country's Prices   The United States's demand for imports and foreign countries' demand for U.S. exports depend on prices of U.S. goods compared to prices of foreign competing goods. If the United States has more inflation than other countries, foreign goods will become cheaper, U.S. demand for foreign currencies will tend to increase, and foreign demand for dollars will tend to decrease. This rise in U.S. inflation will shift the dollar supply outward and the dollar demand inward.

Changes in Interest Rates   People like to invest their savings in assets that will yield the highest return. Other things equal, a rise in U.S. interest rates relative to those abroad will increase demand for U.S. assets. As a result, demand for dollars will increase, while simultaneously the supply of dollars will decrease as fewer Americans sell their dollars to buy foreign assets. A fall in the U.S. interest rate or a rise in foreign interest rates will have the opposite effect.

Some Examples   To see that you have the analysis down pat, let's consider some examples. First, the U.S. economy goes into recession—what will likely happen to

---

In the *Honors Companion*, the backward-bending supply curve is presented as it relates to the J-curve. Going through that is a useful exercise for technically oriented students.

Q–4: Show graphically the effect of an increase in the demand for dollars by French people on the price of francs.

Exchange Rates and the Balance of Payments

1d A deficit in the balance of payments means that the private quantity supplied of a currency exceeds the private quantity demanded. A surplus in the balance of payments means the opposite.

Fundamental Forces Determining Exchange Rates

Exchange rate analysis is usually broken down into fundamental analysis and short-run analysis.

Q–5: In the early 1980s, the U.S. economy fell into a recession (the government faced the problem of both a high federal deficit and a high trade deficit, called the twin deficits), and the dollar was very strong. Can you provide an explanation for this sequence of events?

2 Three important fundamental determinants of exchange rates are prices, interest rates, and income.

For a computer simulation of the fundamental analysis of exchange rates, see module, "Foreign Exchange Markets" in *Macro Interactive* software.

Three shift factors relevant to the fundamental analysis of the supply and demand for currencies are:

   1. Changes in a country's income;

   2. Changes in a country's prices; and

   3. Changes in interest rates.

For a real-world example of a wildly fluctuating exchange rate in response to economic conditions, see Chapter 17 in *Case Studies in Macroeconomics*.

exchange rates? Second, the Mexican economy has runaway inflation—what will likely happen to exchange rates? And third, the interest rate on yen-denominated assets increases—what will likely happen to the exchange rate? If you answered: The value of the dollar will fall, the value of the peso will fall, and the value of the yen will rise, you're following the argument. If those weren't your answers, a review is in order.

Why Exchange Rate Determination Is More Complicated than Supply/ Demand Analysis Makes It Seem

Q–6: Why don't most governments leave determination of the exchange rate to the market?

When presenting the relationship between fundamental analysis and short-run analysis, I often draw the neat curves of fundamental analysis on the board. I then show a shift in demand due to expectations. I show how this shift can cause a shift in supply, which can cause a shift in demand, which can cause a shift in supply, etc. The result is an absolute mess on the board, which, I inform students, is about the state of the short-run analysis. These interdependencies are why traders rely on their gut instinct as opposed to fundamental analysis when trying to make money in the foreign exchange markets.

If real-world exchange rates are simply a matter of letting quantity supplied equal quantity demanded, why would any economist support the fixing of exchange rates? The answer is that the supply and demand curves for currencies can shift around rapidly in response to rumors, expectations, and expectations of expectations. As they shift, they bring about large fluctuations in exchange rates that make trading difficult and have significant real effects on economic activity.

Let me outline just one potential problem. Say you expect the price of the currency to fall one half of one percent tomorrow. What should you do? The correct answer is: Sell that currency quickly. Why? One half of one percent may not sound like much, but, annualized, it is equivalent to a rate of interest per year of 617 percent. Based on that expectation, if you're into making money (and you're really sure about the fall) you will sell all of that currency that you hold, and borrow all you can so you can sell some more. The reality is you can make big money if you guess small changes in exchange rates correctly. (Of course if you're wrong you can lose big money.) This means that if the market generally believes the exchange rates will move, those expectations will tend to be self-fulfilling. Self-fulfilling expectations undermine the argument in favor of letting markets determine exchange rates: When expectations rule, the exchange rate may not reflect actual demands and supplies of goods. Instead, the exchange rate can reflect expectations and rumors. The resulting fluctuations serve no real purpose, and cause problems for international trade and the country's economy.

International Trade Problems from Shifting Values of Currencies

Let's consider an example. Say, for instance, that a firm decides to build a plant in the United States because costs in the United States are low. But say the value of the dollar then rises significantly; the firm's costs rise significantly too, making it uncompetitive.

Or let's take a real-world example: South Korean companies decided to make a major drive to sell South Korean VCRs in the United States. They decided on a low-price strategy, which was justified by their cost advantage. Their export drive was a success, but the value of the South Korean won relative to the dollar rose significantly. The result was that in 1989 South Korean VCR companies were losing money on each VCR they sold in the United States. They kept the price low, hoping that the won would fall in value.

In summary, large fluctuations make real trade difficult, and cause serious real consequences. It is these consequences that have led to calls for government to fix or stabilize their exchange rates. (In Appendix B I give a more detailed discussion of other potential problems with exchange rate determination in the short run.)

How a Fixed Exchange Rate System Works

A fixed exchange rate policy is policy in which the government commits to holding the exchange rate at a specified rate.

Video Series, Economics USA: Exchange Rates, Segment 28.1 and 28.2 and Irwin Economic Video Series: "Foreign Exchange Markets" describes the history of the gold standard and the Bretton Woods system after World War II.

One way the government can set the exchange rate is by law: making its currency non-convertible. Major Western economies have agreed not to use this approach, so in what I discuss here I assume that this is not an option. (See the box for a discussion of how nonconvertible currencies work.) Another way is for the government to adopt a fixed exchange rate policy—*a policy in which the government commits to holding the exchange rate at a specified rate, either through direct or indirect intervention*.

Fixing the Exchange Rate The government has a number of methods of fixing its exchange rate. In the last chapter, you learned how monetary and fiscal policies can affect the value of a currency. These are indirect policies. It can also fix its exchange rates by a direct policy of **exchange rate intervention**—*buying or selling a currency to affect its price*. Let's consider an example of direct exchange rate intervention.

EXCHANGE RATES SET BY LAW: NONCONVERTIBLE CURRENCY AND CAPITAL CONTROLS   **ADDED DIMENSION**

A government can simply pass a law outlawing international currency trading and prohibiting the buying and selling of foreign currencies except at a rate determined by the government. Many developing countries set their exchange rates in this manner. When governments do so, they make international trade difficult because their currencies can't be freely exchanged with other currencies—that is, their currencies are nonconvertible.

Nonconvertible currencies' exchange rates don't fluctuate in response to shifts in supply and demand. Often the only legal way to deal in such currency is to buy it from the government and sell it to the government. It is illegal to trade nonconvertible currencies privately or even to carry large amounts of nonconvertible currency out of the country. Such prohibitions against currency flowing freely into and out of a country are called capital controls. If one country's currency can't be exchanged for another's at anything reflecting a market price, it's very difficult for them to buy each other's goods.

If nonconvertible currencies make trade so difficult, why do countries use them? The answer is: To avoid making the economic adjustments that international considerations would otherwise force upon them. Say that a country is running a large balance of payments deficit and the value of its currency is falling. This fall is pushing up the price of imports, causing inflation, and making the country's assets cheaper for foreigners. Foreigners can come in and buy up the country's assets at low prices.

The country can avoid this political problem simply by passing a law that fixes the exchange rate at a certain level. This action indirectly limits imports, since most foreign firms won't sell their goods at the official exchange rate. They don't want the country's currency at the official exchange rate. It also limits exports since the price of a country's exports is held high. The government can and often does give favored firms special dispensation to import or export. Thus, having a nonconvertible currency enables the government to control what can and can't be imported and exported. Generally when there's a nonconvertible currency, there is a large incentive for people to trade currencies illegally in a black market.

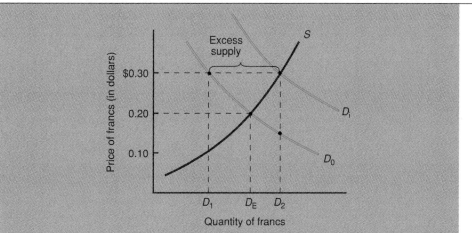

EXHIBIT 3   A Demonstration of Direct Exchange Policy

If the government chooses to hold the exchange rate at 30¢, when the equilibrium is 20¢, there is an excess supply given by $D_2 - D_1$. The government purchases this excess (using official reserves) and closes the difference, thus maintaining equilibrium.

Direct Exchange Rate Intervention—An Example   Suppose that, given the interaction of private supply and demand forces, the equilibrium value of the French franc is 20¢ a franc, but the French government wants to maintain a value of 30¢ a franc. This is shown in Exhibit 3. At 30¢ a franc, quantity supplied exceeds quantity demanded. The French government must buy the surplus, $D_2 - D_1$, using official reserves (foreign currency holdings). It thus shifts the total demand for francs to D_1, making the equilibrium market exchange rate (including the French government's demand for francs) equal to 30¢. This is called **currency support**—the *buying of a currency by a government to maintain its value at above its long-run equilibrium value*. It is a direct exchange rate policy. If a government has sufficient official reserves, or if it can convince other governments to lend it reserves, it can fix the exchange rate at the rate it wants, no matter what the private level of supply and demand is. In reality governments have no such power since their reserves are limited. Thus, in reality only temporary currency support is possible.

A country can maintain a fixed exchange rate only as long it has the reserves to maintain this constant rate. Once it runs out of reserves, it will be unable to intervene, and must then either borrow or devalue its currency.

3 A country fixes the exchange rate by standing ready to buy and sell its currency anytime the exchange rate is not at the fixed exchange rate.

ADDED DIMENSION   DETERMINING THE CAUSES OF FLUCTUATIONS IN THE DOLLAR'S VALUE

As you can see on the graph, the dollar's value has fluctuated considerably since 1973. A good exercise to see if you understand movements in the value of the dollar is to try to choose which factors caused the fluctuation.

Let's start with the relatively small fluctuations in 1973 and 1974. These probably reflected expectational bubbles—in which speculators were more concerned with short-run than long-run fundamentals—while the dollar's low value in 1979 and 1980 reflected high inflation, relatively low real interest rates, and the booming U.S. economy during this period.

The rise of the dollar in the early 1980s reflected higher real U.S. interest rates and the falling U.S. inflation rate, although the rise was much more than expected and probably reflected speculation, as did the sudden fall in the dollar's value in 1985. Similarly, the fluctuations in the late 1980s and early 1990s reflected both changing interest rates in the United States and changing foreign interest rates, as well as changing relative inflation rates.

In late 1996 and early 1997 the value of the dollar rose substantially. Part of the explanation for this lies in the weakness of the Japanese economy which led the Japanese central bank to increase the Japanese money supply, thereby lowering the Japanese interest rate. That weakness also was reflected in the fall in the prices of Japanese stocks. That fall led investors to shift out of Japanese stocks and into U.S. stocks, thereby

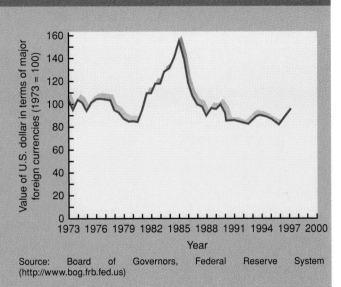

Source: Board of Governors, Federal Reserve System (http://www.bog.frb.fed.us)

increasing the demand for the dollar, and pushing up the U.S. effective exchange rate.

As you can see, after the fact we economists are pretty good at explaining the movements in the exchange rates. Alas, before the fact we aren't so good because often speculative activities make the timing of the movements unpredictable.

A more viable long-run exchange rate policy is **currency stabilization**—the *buying and selling of a currency by the government to offset temporary fluctuations in supply and demand for currencies*. In currency stabilization, the government is not trying to change the long-run equilibrium; it is simply trying to keep the exchange rate at that long-run equilibrium. Sometimes the government buys, and sometimes sells, currency, so the government is far less likely to run out of reserves.

Successful currency stabilization requires the government to choose the correct long-run equilibrium exchange rate. A policy of stabilization can become a policy of support if the government chooses too high a long-run equilibrium. Unfortunately, government has no way of knowing for sure what the long-run equilibrium exchange rate is, so how much stabilizing it can do depends on its access to reserves. If it has sufficient reserves, the government buys up sufficient quantities of its currency to make up the difference.

Once the government has dried up the sources of borrowing foreign currencies, if it wants to hold its exchange rate above the private equilibrium exchange rate it must move to indirect methods affecting its economy in order to affect private supplies and demands for its currency. In short, if a country wants to maintain a fixed exchange rate, it must adjust its economy to the fixed exchange rate.

Q-7: In general, would it be easier for the United States to push the value of the dollar down or up? Why?

The same argument about running out of reserves cannot be made for a country that wants to maintain a below-market exchange rate. Since a government can create all the domestic currency it wants, it's easier for the French government to push the value of its currency down by selling francs than it is for the government to hold it up by buying francs. By the same token, it's easier for another country (say, Japan) to push the value of the franc up (by pushing the value of the yen down). Thus, if the two countries can decide which way they want their exchange rates to move, they have a large incentive to cooperate. Of course, cooperation requires an agreement on the goals, and often countries' goals conflict. One role of the various international economic organizations discussed in Chapter 6 is to provide a forum for reaching agreement on exchange rate goals and a vehicle through which cooperation can take place.

Notice that, in principle, any trader could establish a fixed exchange rate by guaranteeing to buy or sell a currency at a given rate. Any "fix," however, is only as good as the guarantee, and to fix an exchange rate the trader would require many more resources than she has; only governments have sufficient resources to fix an exchange rate, and often even governments run out of resources.

In reality given the small level of official reserves compared to the enormous level of private trading, significant amounts of stabilization are impossible. Instead **strategic currency stabilization**—*buying and selling at strategic moments to affect expectations of traders, and hence to affect their supply and demand*—is used. Such issues are discussed in depth in International Finance courses.

Strategic currency stabilization
The process of buying and selling at strategic moments to affect the expectations of traders, and hence affect their supply and demand.

Stabilizing Fluctuations versus Deviating from Long-Run Equilibrium   The key to whether exchange rate intervention is a viable option or not involves the long-run equilibrium exchange rate. Direct exchange rate policy can succeed if the problem is one of stabilization. If, however, the problem is long run in nature, or if the government estimates the wrong equilibrium, eventually the government will run out of official reserves. Here's the rub: While, in theory, it is important to make the distinction, in practice it is difficult to do so. The long-run equilibrium rate can only be guessed at since no definitive empirical measure of this rate exists. The long-run equilibrium must be estimated. If that estimation is wrong, a sustainable stabilization policy becomes an unsustainable deviation from long-run equilibrium policy. Thus, a central issue in exchange rate intervention policy is estimating the long-run equilibrium exchange rate.

Estimating Long-Run Equilibrium Exchange Rates: Purchasing Power Parity   Purchasing power parity is one way economists have of estimating the long-run equilibrium rate. **Purchasing power parity (PPP)** *is a method of calculating exchange rates that attempts to value currencies at rates such that each currency will buy an equal basket of goods*. It is based on the idea that the exchange of currencies reflects the exchange of real goods. If you are able to exchange a basket of goods from country X for an equivalent basket of goods from country Z, you should also be able to exchange the amount of currency from country X that is needed to purchase country X's basket of goods for the amount of currency from country Z that is needed to purchase country Z's basket of goods. For example, say that the yen is valued at 100 yen to $1. Say also that you can buy the same basket of goods for 1,000 yen that you can buy for $7. In that case the purchasing power parity exchange rate would be 142 yen to $1 (1,000/7 = 142), compared to an actual exchange rate of 100 yen to $1. An economist would say that at 100 to the dollar the yen is overvalued—with 100 yen you could not purchase a basket of goods equivalent to the basket of goods you could purchase with $1.

Exhibit 4 shows various calculations for purchasing power parity for a variety of countries. The left-hand column shows the 1994 actual exchange rates. The second column shows purchasing power parity exchange rates. The third column shows the difference between the two, or the current distortion in the exchange rates (if you believe the PPP exchange rates are the correct ones).

Q–8: Ms. Economist always tries to travel to a country where the purchasing power parity exchange rate is lower than the market exchange rate. Why?

❹ Purchasing power parity is a method of calculating exchange rates such that various currencies will each buy an equal basket of goods and services. Those exchange rates may or may not be appropriate long-run exchange rates.

Criticisms of the Purchasing Power Parity Method   For many economists, estimating exchange rates using PPP has serious problems. If the currency is overvalued and will eventually fall, why don't traders use that information and sell that currency now, making it fall now? After all, they are out after a profit. So if there is open trading in a currency, any expected change in the exchange rate will affect exchange rates now. If traders don't sell now when there are expectations that a currency's undervaluation will eventually make its value fall, they must believe there is some reason that its value won't, in fact, fall.

Critics of the PPP method argue that the difficulty with purchasing power parity exchange rates is the complex nature of trade and consumption. They point out that

EXHIBIT 4   Actual and Purchasing Power Parity Exchange Rates for 1994

Country	Actual Exchange Rate (Currency per Dollar)	PPP Exchange Rate (Currency per Dollar)	Distortion
Japan	102.18	62.33	64%
Switzerland	1.3667	0.90	51
Germany	1.6216	1.23	32
U.K.	1.5319	1.50	2
U.S.	1	1	0
Russia	2191	3812	−43
Brazil	.000846	.001455	−42
India	31.374	125.50	−75
China	8.4462	40.03	−79
Uganda	979.4	7267	−87
Mozambique	6038.6	57125	−89

Source: *World Development Report*, 1996, *International Financial Statistics*, 1996, and author estimates.

the PPP will change as the basket of goods changes. This means that there is no one PPP measure. They also point out that, since all PPP measures leave out asset demand for a currency, the measures are missing an important element of the demand. Critics ask: Is there any reason to assume that in the long run the asset demand for a currency is less important than the goods demand for a currency? Because the asset demand for a currency is important, critics of PPP argue that there is little reason to assume that the short-run actual exchange rate will ever adjust to the PPP exchange rate. And if that rate doesn't adjust, then PPP does not provide a good estimate of the equilibrium rate. These critics further contend that the current exchange rate is the best estimate of the long-run equilibrium exchange rate.

Advantages and Disadvantages of Alternative Exchange Rate Systems

5a Three exchange rate régimes are:
1. Fixed exchange rate: The government chooses an exchange rate and offers to buy and sell currencies at that rate
2. Flexible exchange rate: Determination of exchange rates is left totally up to the market.
3. Partially flexible exchange rate: The government sometimes affects the exchange rate and sometimes leaves it to the market.

The problems of stabilizing exchange rates have led to an ongoing debate about whether a fixed exchange rate, a flexible exchange rate, or a combination of the two is best. This debate nicely captures the macro issues relevant to exchange rate stabilization, so in this section I consider that debate. First, a brief review of the three alternative régimes:

Fixed exchange rates: If the government chooses a particular exchange rate and offers to buy and sell currencies at that price, it is imposing a fixed exchange rate. For example, suppose the U.S. government says it will buy francs at 20¢ per franc and sell dollars at 5 francs per dollar. In that case, we say that the United States has a fixed exchange rate of 5 francs to the dollar.

Flexible exchange rates: When governments do not enter into foreign exchange markets at all, but leave the determination of exchange rates totally up to currency traders, the country is said to have a flexible exchange rate. The price of its currency is allowed to rise and fall as market forces dictate.

Partially flexible exchange rates: When governments sometimes buy or sell currencies to influence the exchange rate, while at other times letting private market forces operate, the country is said to have a partially flexible exchange rate. A partially flexible exchange rate is sometimes called a dirty float because it isn't purely market-determined or government-determined.

Fixed Exchange Rates   The advantages of a fixed exchange rate system are:
1. Fixed exchange rates provide international monetary stability.
2. Fixed exchange rates force governments to make adjustments to meet their international problems.

The disadvantages of a fixed exchange rate system are:
1. Fixed exchange rates can become unfixed. When they're expected to become unfixed, they create enormous monetary instability.

2. Fixed exchange rates force governments to make adjustments to meet their international problems. (Yes, this is a disadvantage as well as an advantage.)

Let's consider each in turn.

Fixed Exchange Rates and Monetary Stability   To maintain fixed exchange rates, the government must choose an exchange rate and have sufficient official reserves to support that rate. If the rate it chooses is too high, its exports lag and the country continually loses official reserves. If the rate it chooses is too low, it is paying more for its imports than it needs to and is building up official reserves, which means that some other country is losing official reserves. A country that is continually gaining or losing official reserves must eventually change its fixed exchange rate.

The difficulty is that as soon as the country gets close to its official reserves limit, foreign exchange traders begin to expect a drop in the value of the currency, and they try to get out of that currency because anyone holding that currency when it falls will lose money. False rumors of an expected depreciation or decrease in a country's fixed exchange rate can become true by causing a "run on a currency," as all traders sell that currency. Thus, at times fixed exchange rates can become highly unstable because expectation of a change in the exchange rate can force the change to occur. As opposed to small movements in currency values, under a fixed rate régime these movements occur in large, sudden jumps.

Fixed Exchange Rates and Policy Independence   Maintaining a fixed exchange rate places limitations on a central bank's actions. In a country with fixed exchange rates, the central bank must ensure that the international quantities of its currency supplied and demanded are equal at the existing exchange rate.

Say, for example, that the United States and the Bahamas have fixed exchange rates: \$1 B = \$1 U.S. The Bahamian central bank decides to run an expansionary monetary policy, lowering the interest rate and stimulating the Bahamian economy. The lower interest rates will cause financial capital to flow out of the country, and the higher income will increase imports. Demand for Bahamian dollars will fall. To prop up its dollar and to maintain the fixed exchange rate, the Bahamas will have to buy its own currency. They can do so only as long as they have sufficient official reserves of other countries' currencies.

Because most countries' official reserves are limited, a country with fixed exchange rates is limited in its ability to conduct expansionary monetary and fiscal policies. It loses its freedom to stimulate the economy in response to a recession. That's why, when a serious recession hits, many countries are forced to abandon fixed exchange rates. They run out of official reserves, and choose expansionary monetary policy to achieve their domestic goals over contractionary monetary policy to achieve their international goals.

Flexible Exchange Rates   The advantages and disadvantages of a flexible exchange rate (exchange rates totally determined by private market forces) are the reverse of those of fixed exchange rates. The advantages are:

1. Flexible exchange rates provide for orderly incremental adjustment of exchange rates, rather than large, sudden jumps.
2. Flexible exchange rates allow government to be flexible in conducting domestic monetary and fiscal policies.

The disadvantages are:

1. Flexible exchange rates allow speculation to cause large jumps in exchange rates, which do not reflect market fundamentals.

You may wish to discuss the breakdown of the European Exchange Rate Mechanism in late 1992 and its implication for the European Monetary Union. This breakdown in 1992 occurred largely because of a fundamental disequilibrium between Germany and Great Britain (and between Germany and some other European countries).

5b Fixed exchange rates provide international monetary stability and force governments to make adjustments to meet their international problems. (This is *also* a disadvantage.) If they become unfixed, they create monetary instability.

An important point to make in discussing exchange rate mechanisms is that when a country chooses to manipulate the value of its currency, it loses control of its money supply for domestic policy purposes. This fact has been at the root of the demise of many fixed exchange rate systems.

2. Flexible exchange rates allow government to be flexible in conducting domestic monetary and fiscal policies. (This is a disadvantage as well as an advantage.)

Let's consider each in turn.

Flexible Exchange Rates and Monetary Stability   Advocates of flexible exchange rates argue as follows: Why not treat currency markets like any other market and let private market forces determine a currency's value? There is no fixed price for TVs; why should there be a fixed price for currencies? The opponents' answer is based on the central role that international financial considerations play in an economy and the strange shapes and large shifts that occur in the short-run supply and demand curves for currencies. (These issues are discussed in Appendixes A and B.)

When expectations shift supply and demand curves around all the time, there's no guarantee that the exchange rate will be determined by long-run fundamental forces. The economy will go through real gyrations because of speculators' expectations about other speculators. Thus, the argument against flexible exchange rates is that they allow far too much fluctuation in exchange rates, making trade difficult.

5c Flexible exchange rate régimes provide for orderly incremental adjustment of exchange rates rather than large sudden jumps, and allow governments to be flexible in conducting domestic monetary and fiscal policy. (This is *also* a disadvantage.) They are, however, susceptible to private speculation.

Flexible Exchange Rates and Policy Independence   The policy independence arguments for and against flexible exchange rates are the reverse of those given for fixed exchange rates. Individuals who believe that national governments should not have flexibility in setting monetary policy argue that flexible exchange rates don't impose the discipline on policy that fixed exchange rates do. Say, for example, that a country's goods are uncompetitive. Under a fixed exchange rate system, the country would have to contract its money supply and deal with the underlying uncompetitiveness of its goods. Under a flexible exchange rate system, the country can maintain an expansionary monetary policy, allowing inflation simply by permitting the value of its currency to fall.

Advocates of policy flexibility argue that it's stupid for a country to go through a recession when it doesn't have to; flexible exchange rates allow countries more flexibility in dealing with their problems. True, policy flexibility may lead to inflation, but inflation is better than a recession.

In mid-1994, at about the time of the 50th anniversary of Bretton Woods, there was discussion of introducing a new system which would formalize the partially flexible exchange rate and try to add some stability to the international exchange rate system. Such proposals will likely be much in the news in the late 1990s.

Partially Flexible Exchange Rates   Faced with the dilemma of choosing between these two unpleasant policies, most countries have opted for a policy in between the two: partially flexible exchange rates. With such a policy they try to get the advantages of both a fixed and a flexible exchange rate.

When policy makers believe there is a fundamental misalignment in a country's exchange rate, they will allow private forces to determine it—they allow the exchange rate to be flexible. When they believe that the currency's value is falling because of speculation, or that too large an adjustment in the currency is taking place, and that that adjustment won't achieve their balance of payments goals, they step in and fix the exchange rate, either supporting or pushing down their currency's value. Countries that follow a currency stabilization policy have partially flexible exchange rates.

5d Partially flexible exchange rate régimes combine the advantages and disadvantages of fixed and flexible exchange rates.

If policy makers are correct, this system of partial flexibility would work smoothly and would have the advantages of both fixed and flexible exchange rates. If policy makers are incorrect, however, a partially flexible system has the disadvantages of both fixed and flexible systems.

Q–9: Does government intervention stabilize exchange rates?

Which View Is Right?   Which view is correct is much in debate. Most foreign-exchange traders that I know tell me that the possibility of government intervention increases the amount of private speculation in the system. In the private investors' view, their own assessments of what exchange rates should be are better than those of policy makers. If private investors knew the government would not enter in, private specu-

In the 1980s, it all looked so easy. After economic union in 1992 would come monetary union. A single European central bank would take over for individual banks, and a single currency—the ECU (European Currency Unit)—would replace the domestic currencies of Europe and would challenge the dollar as the reserve currency of the world economy.

But, as often happens with grand plans, there's a big jump between the plan and the reality. Let's consider the history of that case, and the case itself, now that we've discussed exchange rates.

The problems began when Germany, the dominant EU economy, changed its focus from EU unity to German reunification. Its fiscal policy turned expansionary in order to finance that reunification. The German government ran large deficits, which forced the German interest rate up as the Bundesbank refused to monetize the deficit. The high relative German interest rate increased demand for the German mark, putting pressure on other EU countries to keep their exchange rates within the agreed-upon band. After using all their reserves to defend their currencies, the only remaining tool available to them to keep within the range was contractionary monetary policy. (They had already agreed that goods could flow freely among member countries, and that no capital controls were allowed.)

But many of these countries were already in a recession; contractionary monetary policy would worsen the recession. Sensing a contradiction between EU commitments and domestic policy concerns, speculators entered the market, increasing the upward pressure on the mark. The result was inevitable. First Britain, Spain, and Italy, and finally France, broke their EU commitment to a fixed exchange rate, and let their currencies float to a lower level relative to the mark. Speculators made billions, and support for the EU having a single monetary policy and a single currency eroded, although many countries hoped that a single currency (now to be called the Euro) would be established before the end of the 20th century.

Eventually, in the autumn of 1993, the countries agreed to a wide 15 percent band within which EU countries would confine their currencies, but, given the experience of the early 1990s when domestic concerns overwhelmed EU concerns, this band was seen as a fixed exchange rate limit that would probably be broken as it imposed constraints on countries' domestic monetary policies.

lators would focus on fundamentals and would stabilize short-run exchange rates. When private speculators know government might enter into the market, they don't focus on fundamentals; instead they continually try to outguess government policy makers. When that happens, private speculation doesn't stabilize; it destabilizes exchange rates as private traders try to guess what the government thinks.

Many of my economics colleagues who work for the Fed aren't convinced by private investors' arguments. They maintain that some government intervention helps stabilize currency markets. I don't know which group is right—private foreign exchange traders or economists at the Fed. But to decide, it is necessary to go beyond the arguments and consider how the various exchange rate régimes have worked in practice. Appendix C gives you an introduction into the history of exchange rate régimes.

Let's now consider the problem of a government that decides that it will follow a fixed exchange rate, or even a partially fixed exchange rate, and the market rate differs from the rate it believes is appropriate, but it does not have sufficient official reserves to move the market exchange rate to the appropriate rate. In that case the only way it can achieve the exchange rate it believes proper is to *adjust the economy to the exchange rate*. Specifically, it must undertake policies that will either increase the private supply of its currency or decrease the private demand for its currency. Doing so either involves using the traditional macro policy—monetary and fiscal policy—to influence the economy, or using trade policy to affect the level of exports and imports.

To see the issues involved, let us return to the case of France that we considered initially in the chapter. That case is shown in Exhibit 5.

France's problem here is that it wants the exchange rate for the franc to be 30¢, not the 20¢ that it currently is. The French government has two options for raising the value of the franc: decrease the private supply of francs—shifting the supply curve in

ADJUSTING THE ECONOMY TO THE EXCHANGE RATE: TRADITIONAL MACRO POLICY AND TRADE POLICY

EXHIBIT 5   Adjusting the Economy to the Exchange Rate

If the French government wants to maintain an exchange rate for the franc at 30¢, and not 20¢, it can either (1) decrease the supply of francs, which causes a shift in the supply curve from S_0 to S_1 and results in an equilibrium at Q'_E, or (2) increase the private demand for francs, which shifts the demand curve out to D_1 and results in an equilibrium at Q''_E.

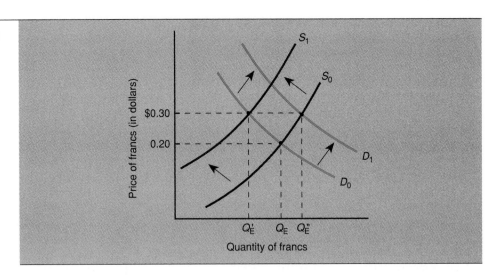

from S_0 to S_1, or increase the private demand for francs—shifting the demand curve out from D_0 to D_1. Let's see how it could accomplish its goal with trade policy or traditional macro policy.

Increase the Private Demand for Francs

To increase the demand for francs, the French government must create policies that increase the private demand for French assets, or for French goods and services. The primary way a government can do this in the short run is to increase the interest rate by running contractionary monetary policy. A higher interest rate increases the demand for the country's assets. The problem with this approach is that to maintain an exchange rate at a certain level, a country it must give up any attempt to target the domestic interest rate. Put another way: A country can achieve an interest rate target or an exchange rate target, but generally it cannot achieve both at the same time. The Added Dimension box on the preceding page gives such an example.

An interest rate policy can be combined with other longer-range policies. These include **export drives** *(in which the government assists exporters in the technicalities of exporting)*, **export subsidies** *(in which the government subsidizes exports)*, and making domestic financial assets more attractive to foreigners by, say, not reporting interest payments on them to the investor's government. (I'll leave it to you to figure out why not reporting interest payments might work.)

Decrease the Private Supply of Francs

To decrease the private supply of francs, the government can use direct trade policy, imposing tariffs on foreign goods in order to decrease demand for imports directly, or it can run contractionary monetary and fiscal policy, slowing down the domestic economy by inducing a recession. This recession decreases the demand for imports, and thereby decreases the private supply of francs. As I discussed in the last chapter, governments are usually loath to use contractionary policy because, politically, induced recessions are not popular. Therefore, trade policy is the politically popular option. So let us now turn to a consideration of trade policy.

TRADE POLICY

Trade policy involves government creating trade restrictions on imports in order to meet the balance of payments constraint without using traditional macro policy or exchange rate policy. Economists generally oppose such trade restrictions because (1) they prevent competition, (2) they lower world welfare, and (3) they lead other countries to retaliate. Despite economists' opposition, the world has many trade restrictions, and there is continual political pressure to institute more.

EXHIBIT 6 (a and b)   The Impact of Tariffs on Imported Goods, and Selected Tariff Rates

Industry	United States	European Union	Japan
Agriculture, forestry, and fisheries	1.8%	4.9%	18.4%
Food, beverages, and tobacco products	4.7	10.1	25.4
Textiles	9.2	7.2	3.3
Wearing apparel	22.7	13.4	13.8
Leather products.	4.2	2.0	3.0
Footwear	8.8	11.6	15.7
Furniture and fixtures.	4.1	5.6	5.1
Printing and publishing.	.7	2.1	.1
Chemicals	2.4	8.0	4.8
Petroleum and related products.	1.4	1.2	2.2
Glass and glass products	6.2	7.7	5.1
Iron and steel	3.6	4.7	2.8
Electrical machinery	4.4	7.9	4.3
Transportation equipment.	2.5	8.0	1.5
Miscellaneous manufacturers	4.2	4.7	4.6

(a) The impact of tariffs on imports   **(b) Selected tariff rates in the early 1990s.**

In **(a)** you see how tariffs affect the price and quantity of imports. A tariff raises the price of foreign goods because the foreign supplier cuts down his supply (shown by the shift in the supply curve from S_0 to S_1). The price to domestic consumers rises to P_1. As the price rises, demand shifts toward domestic goods. In **(b)** you see tariff rates for the United States, the EU, and Japan in the early 1990s. These rates will be continually changing as the changes negotiated in the last GATT negotiations and ongoing WTO negotiations are implemented.

Source: General Agreement on Tariffs and Trade *(GATT)* (http://www.unicc.org).

The most common trade restrictions are tariffs and quotas. Others are voluntary restraint agreements, embargoes, regulatory trade restrictions, and nationalistic appeals. Each of these restrictions will tend to reduce the private supply of a currency. I'll consider each in turn.

Tariffs   Tariffs, also called customs duties, are *taxes governments place on internationally traded goods—generally imports.* Tariffs are the most-used and most-familiar type of trade restriction. Tariffs operate in the same way a tax does: They make imported goods relatively more expensive than they otherwise would have been, and thereby encourage the consumption of domestically produced goods. How tariffs affect prices and quantity was presented in Chapter 4; Exhibit 6(a) provides you with a brief review.

As you can see, a tariff paid by the supplier shifts the foreign supply curve back from S_0 to S_1. This raises price from P_0 to P_1 and reduces the quantity of imports from Q_0 to Q_1. On average, U.S. tariffs raise the price of imported goods by 5 percent. Exhibit 6(b) presents tariff rates on various goods imposed by the United States, the European Union, and Japan. There is a wide variation of the level of tariff, depending on the industry.

Probably the most infamous tariff in U.S. history is the Smoot-Hawley Tariff of 1930, which raised tariffs on imported goods an average of 60 percent. It was passed in response to the Great Depression in the United States and to protect American jobs. It didn't work. Other countries responded with similar tariffs. As a result of these trade wars, international trade plummeted from $60 billion in 1928 to $25 billion in 1938, unemployment worsened, and the international depression deepened. These effects of the tariff convinced many, if not most, economists that free trade is preferable to trade restrictions. The dismal failure of the Smoot-Hawley Tariff was the main reason the **General Agreement on Tariffs and Trade (GATT),** the *regular international conference to reduce trade barriers,* was established immediately following World War II. Since then, rounds of negotiations have resulted in a decline in

Varieties of Trade Restrictions

Three types of trade restrictions are: (1) tariffs, (2) quotas, and (3) trade embargoes.

6 Some important international trade restrictions include tariffs, quotas, voluntary restraint agreements, and regulatory trade restrictions.

This discussion about trade restrictions duplicates the discussion of trade restrictions in the micro portion of the combined book. The reason for this is that different professors like to teach trade restrictions in different parts of the course. Having the same material in both facilitates flexibility.

worldwide tariffs and the establishment of GATT's successor, the **World Trade Organization (WTO)**—*an organization committed to getting countries to agree not to impose new tariffs or other trade restrictions.*

Quotas **Quotas** are *quantity limits placed on imports.* Their effect in limiting trade is similar to a tariff's effect. One big difference is in who gets the revenue. With a tariff, the government gets the revenue as tariff payments; with a quota, revenues accrue as additional profits to producers of the protected good. For example, if the United States places quotas on foreign textiles, producers of textiles will receive the proceeds of the resulting higher price. If the United States places a tariff on textile imports, the prices will also rise, but the U.S. government will receive the revenue.

A second big difference is that under a quota, any increase in domestic demand will be met by the less-efficient domestic producers (who would otherwise lose in the competition) since a quota places strict numerical limitations on what can be imported. Under a tariff, part of any increase in domestic demand will be met by more-efficient foreign producers since a tariff places a tax on imports but does not restrict their quantity. Needless to say, foreign producers prefer quotas to tariffs. A good exercise to make sure you understand the reason why foreign producers prefer quotas is to graphically show the relationship between a tariff and quota. (If you're not sure of the relationship you might review Chapter 4's discussion of tariffs and quotas.)

Voluntary Restraint Agreements Imposing new tariffs and quotas is specifically ruled out by the WTO, but foreign countries know that following WTO rules is voluntary and that if a domestic industry brought sufficient political pressure on its government, the WTO rules would be forgotten. To avoid the imposition of new tariffs on their goods, countries often enter into **voluntary restraint agreements**—*agreements in which countries voluntarily restrict their exports.* That's why Japan has agreed informally to limit the number of cars it exports to the United States.

The effect of such voluntary restraint agreements is identical to the effect of quotas: They directly limit the quantity of imports, increasing the price of the good and helping domestic producers. For example, when the United States encouraged Japan to impose "voluntary" quotas on exports of its cars to the United States, Toyota benefited from the quotas because it could price its limited supply of cars higher than it could if it sent in a large number of cars, so profit per car would be high. Since they faced less competition, U.S. car companies also benefited. They could increase their prices because Toyota had done so. Consumers lost because they paid higher prices both for domestic and imported cars.

Embargoes An **embargo** is *an all-out restriction on the import or export of a good.* Embargoes are usually established for international political reasons rather than for primarily economic reasons.

An example is the U.S. embargo of trade with Iraq. The U.S. government hoped that the embargo would so severely affect Iraq's economy that Saddam Hussein would lose political power. It did make life difficult for Iraqis, but it has not brought about the downfall of the Hussein government.

Regulatory Trade Restrictions Tariffs, quotas, and embargoes are the primary direct methods to restrict international trade. There are also indirect methods that restrict trade in not-so-obvious ways; these are called **regulatory trade restrictions**—*government-imposed procedural rules that limit imports.* One type of regulatory trade restriction has to do with protecting the health and safety of a country's residents. For example, a country might restrict import of all vegetables grown where certain pesticides are used, knowing full well that all other countries use those pesticides. The effect of such a regulation would be to halt the import of vegetables.

A second type of regulatory restriction involves making import and customs procedures so intricate and time-consuming that importers simply give up. For exam-

Trade restrictions, in practice, are often much more complicated than they seem in textbooks. Seldom does a country say, "We're limiting imports to protect our home producers." Instead the country explains the restrictions in a more politically acceptable way. Consider the fight between the European Union and the United States over U.S. meat exports. In 1988 the EU, in line with Union-wide internal requirements, banned all imports of any meat from animals treated with growth-inducing hormones, which U.S. meat producers use extensively. The result: the EU banned the meat exported from the United States.

The EU claimed that it had imposed the ban only because of public health concerns. The United States claimed that the ban was actually a trade restriction, pointing out that its own residents ate this kind of meat with confidence because a U.S. government agency had certified that the levels of hormones in the meat were far below any danger level.

The United States retaliated against the EU by imposing 100 percent tariffs on Danish and West German hams, Italian tomatoes, and certain other foods produced by EU member nations. The EU threatened to respond by placing 100 percent tariffs on $100 million worth of U.S. walnuts and dried fruits, but instead entered into bilateral meetings with the United States. Those meetings allowed untreated meats into the EU for human consumption and treated meats that would be used as dog food. In response, the United States removed its retaliatory tariff on hams and tomato sauce, but retained its tariffs on many other goods. In the 1990s, Europe's dog population seemed to be growing exponentially as Europe's imports of "dog food" increased by leaps and bounds. In 1996 the United States asked the WTO to review the EU ban. It did so in 1997, finding in favor of the US. An EU appeal was expected, so in 1997 the issue was still unresolved.

Which side is right in this dispute? The answer is far from obvious. Both the U.S. and the EU have potentially justifiable positions. As I said, trade restrictions are more complicated in reality than in textbooks.

ple, France requires all imported VCRs to be individually inspected in Toulouse. Since Toulouse is a provincial city, far from any port and outside the normal route for imports after they enter France, this inspection process can take months.

Some regulatory restrictions are imposed for legitimate reasons; others are designed simply to make importing more difficult and hence protect domestic producers from international competition. It's often hard to tell the difference. A good example of this difficulty occurred in 1988 when the EU disallowed all imports of meat from animals that had been fed growth-inducing hormones, as the accompanying box details.

Nationalistic Appeals   Finally, nationalistic appeals can help to restrict international trade. "Buy American" campaigns and Japanese xenophobia[3] are examples. Many Americans, given two products of equal appeal except that one is made in the United States and one is made in a foreign country, would buy the U.S. product. To get around this tendency, foreign and U.S. companies often go to great lengths to get a MADE IN U.S.A. classification on goods they sell in the United States. For example, components for many autos are made in Japan but shipped to the United States and assembled in Ohio or Tennessee so that the finished car can be called an American product.

Americans aren't the only nationalistic people on the international trade scene. Preference for Japanese goods is deeply ingrained in Japanese culture. Faced with U.S. demands that Japan reduce its trade surplus and with threats of retaliation if it doesn't, the Japanese government has attempted to change its people's cultural bias and to encourage consumption of U.S. goods.

When successful, these trade restriction policies decrease the demand for imports and decrease the private supply of domestic currency, thereby reducing its value relative to foreign currencies. The effect of trade restrictions on imports and a country's exchange rate is easy for politicans to explain, which is one reason why trade restrictions are so politically popular.

Despite the political popularity of trade restrictions, most economists support **free trade**—*a policy of allowing unrestricted trade among countries.* The reason is

Economists' Dislike of Trade Restriction Policies

[3]*Xenophobia* is a Greek word meaning "fear of foreigners." Pronounce the "x" like "z."

7 Economists generally support free trade because trade restrictions lower aggregate output, reduce international competition, and often result in harmful trade wars that hurt everyone.

Q–10: Why do many economists advocate free trade?

You may find it useful to role-play over the issue of trade restrictions. Divide your class into economists, consumers, workers impacted by trade, and elected policy-makers. Then ask them to discuss trade restrictions in the auto industry, steel industry, or some other high profile industry.

Strategic trade policies Threats to implement tariffs to bring about a reduction in tariffs or some other concession from the other country.

that, in their considered judgment, the harm done by trade restrictions outweighs the benefits.

Economists' first argument for free trade is that, viewed from a global perspective, free trade increases total output. From a national perspective, economists agree that particular instances of trade restriction may actually help one nation, even as most other nations are hurt. But they argue that the country imposing trade restrictions can benefit only if the other country doesn't retaliate with trade restrictions of its own. Retaliation is the rule, not the exception, however, and when there is retaliation, trade restrictions cause both countries to lose.

A second reason most economists support free trade is that trade restrictions reduce international competition. International competition is desirable because it forces domestic companies to stay on their toes. If trade restrictions on imports are imposed, domestic companies don't work as hard, and they become less efficient. For example, in the 1950s and 1960s the United States imposed restrictions on imported steel. U.S. steel industries responded to this protection by raising their prices and channeling profits from their steel production into other activities. By the 1970s the U.S. steel industry was a mess, internationally uncompetitive, and using outdated equipment to produce overpriced steel. Instead of making the steel industry stronger, restrictions made it a flabby, uncompetitive industry.

Economists' final argument against trade restrictions is: Yes, some restrictions might benefit a country, but almost no country can limit its restrictions to the beneficial ones. Trade restrictions are addictive—the more you have, the more you want. Thus, a majority of economists take the position that the best response to such addictive policies is "just say no."

Strategic Trade Policies While most economists favor free trade, there are times when trade restrictions can be used to promote free trade. For example, in the mid-1990s China was allowing significant illegal copying of U.S. software without paying royalties on the work. The United States exerted pressure to stop such copying but felt that China was not responding effectively. To force compliance, the United States made a list of Chinese goods that it threatened with 100 percent tariffs unless China complied.

The United States did not want to put on these restrictions, but felt that it would have more strategic bargaining power if it threatened to do so. Hence the name **strategic trade policies**—*threatening to implement tariffs to bring about a reduction in tariffs or some other concession from the other country.*

The potential problem with strategic trade policies is that they can backfire. One rule of strategic bargaining is that the other side must believe that you'll go through with your threat. Thus, strategic trade policy can lead a country that actually supports free trade to impose trade restrictions, just to show how strongly it believes in free trade.

Even though most economists support free trade, they admit that in bargaining it may be necessary to adopt a strategic position. A country may threaten to impose trade restrictions if the other country does so. When such strategic trade policies are successful, they end up eliminating or reducing trade restrictions. When they are unsuccessful, they can lead to a trade war. Thus, in response to the United States' threat, China made a threat of its own—to put prohibitive tariffs on U.S. goods. Just before the deadline the two countries had set, they agreed to avoid a trade war. China agreed to increase copyright enforcement and the United States agreed that China's proposed increased enforcement met U.S. objections.

When should trade restrictions be used for strategic purposes—and, just as important, when should they not be used for strategic purposes? Economic theory does not tell us. That question is part of the practice of the art of economics. (It should be pointed out that economic game theorists are adding insights into the issue and that the area of strategic trade policies is a hot one for research.)

As I hope has been apparent from reading the chapter, the issues in open-economy macro are extraordinarily interesting, but they are even more complicated, and even more politically charged, than the issues in domestic macro. Whatever the correct answers to the questions are, we can expect that the problems will become more and more important for the United States. With international transportation and communication becoming easier and faster, and with other countries' economies growing, the U.S. economy will inevitably become more interdependent with the other economies of the world, making the macroeconomics focus more and more on issues within an open economy framework.

CONCLUSION

CHAPTER SUMMARY

- The balance of payments is made up of the current account, the capital account, and the official transactions account.
- In the late 1980s the United States became a net debtor nation. In the 1990s it is the largest debtor nation in the world.
- Exchange rates in a perfectly flexible exchange rate system are determined by the supply of and demand for a currency.
- It is easier technically for a country to bring the value of its currency down than it is to support its currency.
- It is extraordinarily difficult to correctly estimate the long-run equilibrium exchange rate; one method of doing so is the purchasing power parity approach.

- Flexible, partially flexible, and fixed exchange rates each have advantages and disadvantages.
- Some important international trade restrictions include tariffs, quotas, voluntary restraint agreements, and regulatory trade restrictions.
- Economists generally support free trade because trade restrictions lower total world output, reduce international competition, and often result in harmful trade wars that hurt everyone.

KEY TERMS

balance of payments   *(395)*
balance of trade   *(396)*
balance on goods and services   *(396)*
capital account   *(395)*
currency stabilization   *(402)*
currency support   *(401)*
current account   *(395)*
embargo   *(410)*
exchange rate intervention   *(400)*
export drives   *(408)*

export subsidies   *(408)*
fixed exchange rate   *(404)*
flexible exchange rate   *(404)*
free trade   *(411)*
fundamental analysis   *(399)*
General Agreement on Tariffs and
  Trade (GATT)   *(409)*
official reserves   *(395)*
official transactions account   *(395)*
partially flexible exchange rate   *(404)*

purchasing power parity (PPP)   *(403)*
quota   *(410)*
regulatory trade restrictions   *(410)*
strategic currency stabilization   *(403)*
strategic trade policies   *(412)*
tariff   *(409)*
voluntary restraint agreements   *(410)*
World Trade Organization
  (WTO)   *(410)*

QUESTIONS FOR THOUGHT AND REVIEW

The number after each question represents the estimated degree of critical thinking required. (1 = almost none; 10 = deep thought.)

1. If a country is running a balance of trade deficit, will its current account be in deficit? Why?   *(3)*
2. When someone sends 100 British pounds to a friend in the United States, will this transaction show up on the

capital or current account? Why?   *(3)*
3. Support the statement: "It is best to offset a capital account surplus with a current account deficit."   *(7)*
4. Support the statement: "It is best to offset a capital account deficit with a current account surplus."   *(5)*
5. What are the advantages and disadvantages of a nonconvertible currency?   *(5)*

6. In Exhibit 3, a foreign government chooses to maintain an equilibrium market exchange rate of U.S. 30 cents per unit of its own currency. Discuss the implications of the government trying to maintain a higher fixed rate—say at 40 cents.   *(5)*

7. If you were the finance minister of Never-Never Land, how would you estimate the long-run exchange rate of your currency, the 'Neverback'? Defend your choice as well as discuss its possible failings.   *(8)*

8. Distinguish between the three types of regulatory restrictions and discuss their pros and cons.   *(6)*

9. Which is preferable: a fixed or a flexible exchange rate? Why?   *(7)*

10. Explain how high interest rates in Germany placed downward pressure on other EU countries' currencies and ended the European fixed exchange rate system.   *(5)*

11. Dr. Dollar Bill believes price stability is the main goal of central bank policy. Is the doctor more likely to prefer fixed or flexible exchange rates? Why?   *(3)*

12. If currency traders expect the government to devalue a currency, what will they likely do? Why?   *(4)*

13. What is the difference between a tariff and a quota?   *(4)*

14. How might a country benefit from having an inefficient customs agency?   *(5)*

15. Demonstrate graphically how the effects of a tariff differ from the effects of a quota.   *(6)*

16. If you were an economic adviser to a country that was following your advice about trade restrictions and that country fell into a recession, would you change your advice? Why or why not?   *(6)*

17. During the 1995–96 Republican presidential primaries, Patrick Buchanan wrote an editorial in *The Wall Street Journal* beginning, "Since the Nixon era the dollar has fallen 75 percent against the yen, 60 percent against the mark." What trade policies do you suppose he was promoting? He went on to outline a series of tariffs. Agree or disagree with his policies.   *(7)*

18. In an op-ed article, Paul Volcker, former chairman of the Board of Governors of the Federal Reserve, asked the question: "Is it really worth spending money in the exchange markets, modifying monetary policy, and taking care to balance the budget just to save another percentage or two [of value of exchange rates]?" What's your answer to this question?   *(8)*

19. In mid-1994 the value of the dollar fell sufficiently to warrant coordinated intervention among 17 countries. Still, the dollar went on falling. One economist stated, "[The intervention] was clearly a failure. . . . It's a good indication something else has to be done." Why would the United States and foreign countries want to keep up the value of the dollar?   *(6)*

PROBLEMS AND EXERCISES

1. Draw the fundamental analysis of the supply and demand for British pound sterling in terms of dollars. Show what will happen to the exchange rate with those curves in response to each of the following events:
   a. The U.K. price level rises.
   b. The U.S. price level rises.
   c. The U.K. economy experiences a boom.
   d. The U.K. interest rates rise.

2. The government of Never-Never Land, after much deliberation, finally decides to switch to a fixed exchange rate policy. It does this because the value of its currency, the 'Neverback,' is so high that the trade deficit is enormous. The finance minister fixes the rate at $10 a Neverback, which is lower than the equilibrium rate of $20 a Neverback.
   a. Discuss the trade or traditional macro policy options that could accomplish this lower exchange rate.
   b. Using the laws of supply and demand, show graphically how possible equilibriums are reached.

3. Will the following be suppliers or demanders of U.S. dollars in foreign exchange markets?
   a. A U.S. tourist in Latin America.
   b. A German foreign exchange trader who believes that the dollar exchange rate will fall.
   c. A U.S. foreign exchange trader who believes that the dollar exchange rate will fall.
   d. A Costa Rican tourist in the United States.
   e. A Russian capitalist who wants to protect his wealth from expropriation.
   f. A British investor in the United States.

4. You've been hired as an economic adviser to Yamaichi Foreign Exchange Traders. What buy or sell recommendations for U.S. dollars would you make in response to the following news?
   a. Faster economic growth in the EU.
   b. Expectations of higher interest rates in the United States.
   c. U.S. interest rate rises, but less than expected.
   d. Expected loosening of U.S. monetary policy.
   e. Higher inflationary predictions for the United States.

5. State whether the following will show up on the current account or the capital account:
   a. IBM's exports of computers to Japan.
   b. IBM's hiring of a British merchant bank as a consultant.
   c. A foreign national living in the United States repatriates money.
   d. Ford Motor Company's profit in Hungary.
   e. Ford Motor Company uses that Hungarian profit to build a new plant in Hungary.

6. One of the basic laws of economics is the law of one price. It says that given certain assumptions one would expect that if free trade is allowed, the prices of goods in multiple

countries should converge. This law underlies purchasing power parity.

a. Can you list what three of those assumptions likely are?

b. Should the law of one price hold for labor also? Why or why not?

c. Should it hold for capital more so or less so than for labor? Why or why not?

ANSWERS TO MARGIN QUESTIONS

1. The expenditures of a U.S. citizen traveling abroad will show up as a debit on the services account. As tourism or traveling, it is a service. *(396)*

2. Net investment income is the return a country gets on its foreign investment minus the return foreigners get on their investment within a country. A country is a net debtor nation if the value of foreign investment within a country exceeds the value of its investment abroad. A country can be a net debtor nation and still have its net investment income positive if its foreign investment is undervalued at market values (valuation is generally done at book value), or if its foreign investment earns a higher rate of return than foreigners' investment within that country. *(397)*

3. As in the following diagram, an increase in the demand for francs pushes up the exchange rate of francs in terms of dollars. *(398)*

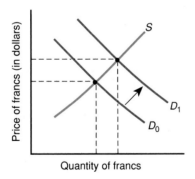

4. An increase in the demand for dollars is the equivalent of an increase in the supply of francs, so an increase in the demand for dollars pushes down the price of francs in terms of dollars, as in the following diagram. *(399)*

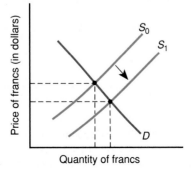

5. In the early 1980s the U.S. government was pursuing tight monetary policy and expansionary fiscal policy. The high exchange rate resulted in a strong dollar. Expansionary fiscal policy failed to stimulate domestic demand as export demand fell sharply due to the high dollar. This, accompanied by the high interest rate that had cut investment, drove the economy into a recession with twin deficits, but a strong dollar. *(399)*

6. In the short run, normal market forces have a limited, and possibly even perverse, effect on exchange rates, which is why most governments don't leave determination of exchange rates to the market. *(400)*

7. In general, it would be easier for the United States to push the value of the dollar down because doing so involves the United States buying up foreign currencies, which it can pay for simply by printing more dollars. To push the dollar up requires foreign reserves. *(402)*

8. When a foreign country's purchasing power parity exchange rate is less than the market exchange rate, the price of goods in that country tends to be relatively cheaper than at home. This tends to make traveling there less expensive. *(403)*

9. There is much debate about whether government intervention stabilizes exchange rates—private traders tend to believe it does not; government economists tend to believe that it does. *(406)*

10. Economists generally support free trade because trade restrictions lower aggregate output, reduce international competition, and often result in harmful trade wars that hurt everyone. *(412)*

The *J*–Curve

In the chapter I discussed the relationship between the demand/supply framework of exchange rates and the balance of payments account. In this appendix I consider some of the short-run problems that can develop in foreign exchange markets.

A decrease in a country's exchange rate—that is, a decline in its currency's value relative to that of another country's currency—pushes the price of imports up and the price of exports down. Thus, it tends to decrease the *quantity* of imports coming into a country and to increase the *quantity* of exports going out of a country. These changes in quantity *eventually* improve the balance of trade and hence the balance of payments.

I emphasize the words *eventually* and *quantity* to highlight a paradox that often occurs when exchange rates change. Often, initially, a fall in the exchange rate doesn't decrease the balance of trade deficit and the balance of payments deficit; it increases them. This phenomenon has occurred so often that it has acquired a name, the ***J*–curve**—*a curve describing the rise and fall in the balance of trade deficit following a fall in the exchange rate.* In a moment I'll explain why it's called that.

Why do trade deficit increases initially occur when a country's exchange rate falls? To answer that question, remember that a country's imports and exports are determined by two variables: price multiplied by quantity. When a country's exchange rate falls, the quantity of imports tends to decrease and the quantity of exports tends to rise, but the price of imports tends to rise and the price of exports tends to fall. In the short run these price effects tend to predominate over the quantity effects, so the balance of payments deficit and the balance of trade deficit become larger. Eventually, however, the quantity effects tend to predominate over the price effects, so the balance of trade and balance of payments deficits get smaller.

If one were graphing what happens to the balance of trade and balance of payments after an exchange rate falls, the graph would look something like Exhibit A1. The fall in the exchange rate occurs at time T_0, and initially the balance of trade and hence the balance of payments worsens. The balance of trade keeps worsening until time T_1, whereupon it starts to improve. At time T_2, it's back where it was at the start, and thereafter it substantially improves. The curve looks like a "J"—hence the name the *J*-curve.

Let's go through a numerical example to place the *J*-curve concept into your deep memory. Say that at an exchange rate of 2.5/1 (2.5 German marks to \$1.00), the United States is importing 40 Mercedes at \$50,000 (125,000 German marks) each, and is exporting to Germany 200,000 videos at \$9 (22.5 German marks) each. Imports are \$2,000,000 (40 × \$50,000) and exports are \$1,800,000 (\$9 × 200,000). The United States thus has a \$200,000 trade deficit with Germany.

Now say that the value of the dollar falls to 2.27/1 and the price of a Mercedes to U.S. citizens goes to \$55,000. In response, the quantity imported falls to 39. The price of videos falls to \$8.20, and the quantity exported rises to 210,000. Let's now calculate the trade deficit:

$$\text{Imports (\$55,000} \times \text{39)} = \$2,145,000$$
$$\text{Exports (\$8.20} \times \text{210,000)} = \$1,722,000$$
$$\text{Trade deficit} = \$423,000$$

In response to a fall in the relative value of the dollar, the trade deficit has increased from \$200,000 to \$423,000.

This result was dependent on the numbers I chose. Experience suggests that eventually, the quantity effect is much larger than this example indicates, and a fall in the value of a currency improves a country's trade balance.

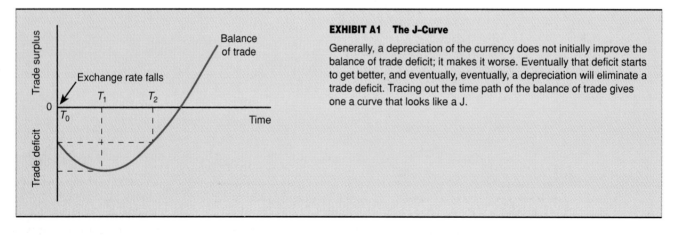

EXHIBIT A1   The J–Curve

Generally, a depreciation of the currency does not initially improve the balance of trade deficit; it makes it worse. Eventually that deficit starts to get better, and eventually, eventually, a depreciation will eliminate a trade deficit. Tracing out the time path of the balance of trade gives one a curve that looks like a J.

But that "eventually" can be as long as five to seven years. This possibility presents policy makers with a serious long-run/short-run dilemma in using exchange rate policy to achieve government's balance of trade and payments goals. Escaping that dilemma is one reason that many developing countries use nonconvertible currencies. Politically, often they can't afford to make their balance of payments deficit larger in the short run in order to achieve a long-run improvement.

The *J*-curve phenomenon—which suggests that normal market forces don't operate to keep the exchange rate in short-run equilibrium—is the reason that in our earlier discussion we separated the short-run determination of the exchange rate from the long-run determination of exchange rates. Fundamental analysis only works in the long run. In the short run, normal market forces don't determine exchange rates.

Understanding the limited, and possibly even perverse, short-run effect of normal market forces on achieving equilibrium is important to understanding why most governments don't leave determination of the exchange rate to the market, but instead play varying roles in its determination.

KEY TERMS

J–curve   *(416)*

QUESTIONS FOR THOUGHT AND REVIEW

1. What would happen to a country's balance of trade surplus if the country's exchange rate rose? In the short run? In the long run?
2. From 1980 to 1985 the value of the U.S. dollar relative to foreign currencies fell by more than 30 percent. What do you suppose was happening to the U.S. trade deficit? Confirm your answer with data.
3. From 1985 to 1990 the value of the U.S. dollar relative to foreign currencies rose by nearly 60 percent, more than reversing the previous 5-year decline. What do you suspect was happening to the U.S. trade deficit? Explain your answer with data.
4. What do your answers to questions 3 and 4 suggest about the long-run predictions of the *J*–curve phenomenon?

5. At an exchange rate of Rs20 to $1 (Rs is the sign for rupee), Pakistan is exporting 100,000 bales of cotton to the United States at $5 (or Rs100) each. It's importing 60 cars from the United States at $10,000 (Rs200,000) each. Now say that the value of the rupee falls to Rs22 to $1. Pakistan's exports rise to 103,000 bales of cotton while car imports fall to 58.
   a. What has happened to the trade balance?
   b. What will likely happen in the long run?
   c. What would happen if Pakistani exports raised their price for cotton so that they were getting the same revenue as before the rupee's fall in value?
   d. How would that response affect what would happen in the long run?

Why Exchange Rate Determination Is More Complicated than the Supply/Demand Model Would Suggest

It would appear from the supply/demand discussion in the chapter that the determination of exchange rates is a relatively simple process: All one need do is determine the supply and demand curves and decide where equilibrium occurs. And in some ways, it is relatively easy. But in other ways it isn't; if it were as simple as determining supply and demand curves and equilibrium, the quotation at the beginning of the chapter about the bedlam in a foreign exchange dealer's office wouldn't have been appropriate, and governments would not agonize over exchange rates as they do. There's more to the story of exchange rates than is told in those two curves. I hinted at the problem in the chapter, when I gave an example of how expectations of a change in exchange rates could influence demand for a currency. In this appendix I expand upon that argument.

The supply and demand curves presented in the text reflect long-run considerations; they reflect the effect of normal market forces on the supply and demand for currency. That's why I called it fundamental analysis. It was normal market forces that we used to justify the shapes of the curves. An analysis of curves based on normal market forces is often called fundamental analysis because the forces described are the forces one arrives at by applying normal or fundamental economic analysis. The normal market forces are the forces that will determine exchange rates in the long run—say in two, three, or four years.

Most movements in exchange rates that are discussed in the newspapers are influenced by these normal market forces, but are not determined by them. Thus, the short-run analysis of exchange rates (what will happen to the exchange rate in the next minute, week, month, or year) is not directly based on fundamental analysis but upon a variety of effects that influence traders' decisions whether to buy, sell, or hold a currency. In these decisions expectations play a central role. Let's see why.

The Important Role of Expectations

If the value of a currency falls, the holders of that currency and of assets denominated in that currency lose; if the value of a currency rises, the holders of that currency and of assets denominated in that currency gain. So everyone tries to hold currencies whose values will rise and get rid of currencies whose values will fall. Thus, expectations of whether a currency will rise or fall can cause large shifts in the supply and demand. Expectations can even be self-fulfilling. For example, the expectation of a rise in the dollar's value will increase the demand for dollars and decrease the supply, which will cause a rise in the value of the dollar. The dollar rises because it is expected to rise.

Stability and Instability in Foreign Exchange Markets

Given that these large shifts in the supply and demand for currencies based on expectations are constantly occurring, one might expect that there would be enormous shifts in exchange rates. But that doesn't often happen. Usually exchange rates are rather stable for two reasons. First, government sometimes enters into exchange markets to maintain stability. When people buy, the government sells; when people sell, the government buys. Government action counters the shifts.

A second reason is that foreign exchange traders and speculators stabilize the rates. Traders know that eventually market forces will be strong and will lead to fundamental forces that will control the exchange rates, and they base their expectations on those fundamentals. Which of these two reasons is more important is debatable. Since

that debate centers on whether private traders or government are better at stabilizing exchange rates, we need to look behind the supply and demand curves for currencies—at the traders who make the markets work.

Exchange Rate Markets, Traders, and the Spread   International currency traders are interested in making money. They buy and sell currencies. If they buy low and sell high, they make a profit. If they buy high and sell low, they lose money. The currency trader is constantly on the phone offering to buy a currency at one rate and to sell it at another rate.

The **spread** is *the difference between the price at which international currency traders buy a currency and the price at which they sell it.* To see how the spread works, let's consider a trader of francs and dollars. She might post the following rates:

Today's Rates
Sell: $1 . . . . 4.5 francs
Buy: $1 . . . . 4.4 francs
Sell: 1 franc . . . . 23¢
Buy: 1 franc . . . . 22¢

The spread is 1¢ for every franc traded, and 10 centimes (100 centimes equals one franc) for every dollar traded. The greater the spread, the greater the profit per transaction but the smaller the number of transactions that are likely to go through that trader. Traders become known as aggressive or nonaggressive. Aggressive traders have the smallest spread. They buy high and sell cheap, relying on volume for their profit.

How does an international currency trader choose what rates she will set? The answer is that she must choose a rate that brings her about the same amount of dollars that other people want to buy. That is, she must choose a rate for which the quantity of dollars supplied roughly equals the quantity of dollars demanded.

Thus, after a trader sets her rates, she will see how many dollars her advertised rates are bringing in, and how many dollars are going out. If fewer dollars are coming in than going out, she'll raise the price of dollars in terms of French francs. Instead of 4.5 francs to the dollar, she'll make it 4.6 francs to the dollar. Dollars become more expensive in terms of francs; francs become cheaper in terms of dollars. International traders hope that if everything goes right, that change will bring the two currencies into equilibrium. Traders set exchange rates to equate supply and demand for dollars.

The Short-Run Determination of Exchange Rates   Most currency traders will have taken an introductory economics course, so they'll look at the factors that cause shifts in supply and demand and think about the general long-run direction of exchange rates. As stated earlier, the analysis

ARBITRAGE

International currency traders often deal in a variety of currencies, and when they do they must be continually on the lookout for discrepancies among the exchange rates for various countries. For example, let's say a trader opens an office with several windows and sets up the following exchange rates:

Window 1: $1 = 4.5 francs or 1 franc = 22.2¢

Window 2: $1 = 707.9 won or 1 won = 0.14¢

Window 3: 1 won = 0.005 francs or 1 franc = 200 won.

Enter Mr. Arbitrage, who's always keeping his eye on international currency traders. Mr. Arbitrage goes up to window 1 and says, "I'll buy $1,000 worth of French francs." He receives 4,500 francs. He then goes to window 3 and says, "I'd like to buy Korean won for these 4,500 French francs, please." Handing over 4,500 francs, he receives 900,000 won. He then goes to window 2 and says, "I'd like to exchange these 900,000 won for dollars, please." He hands over 900,000 won, for which he receives $1,271. Next he takes the $1,271 back to window 1 and says, "I'd like to buy French francs, please." At this point the currency trader should know that she's goofed: In setting the exchange rates she has forgotten the principle of arbitrage.

Arbitrage is the buying of a good in one market at a low price and selling that good in another market at a higher price. It limits the exchange rates a currency trader can set in various markets and still make a profit. Specifically, the roundabout exchange rates must be identical to the direct exchange rates. Recognizing this, she changes the exchange rate between won and francs so that 1 won = 0.0063 francs and no arbitrage profits are to be made.

Our little story and example make it look as if arbitrage is simple. But remember, there are hundreds of currencies, and with even as few as 50 currencies there are many thousands of possible roundabout exchange rates. The table shows some of them.

Real-world arbitrageurs have computers that constantly monitor these exchange rates. If they find a difference, they buy and sell quickly, keeping the people who set exchange rates on their toes to set all exchange rates so that arbitrageurs can't make money by arbitraging markets.

Foreign exchange markets have become sophisticated and the spread is small. Computers, programmed to spot any potential for arbitrage, monitor exchange rates and keep exchange rates among currencies in line so that roundabout trading does not bring about long-term profits for arbitrageurs. Arbitrageurs, like others in a competitive market, cover their costs (which include normal profits) but don't make so much profit that they attract others into the business.

Currency traders are active in markets for most of the major currencies. The spreads are extremely narrow. The traders are constantly buying or selling—listening for trade figures, rumors on the street, and interest rate policy changes by governments. They don't limit themselves to buying and selling for customers. They can buy for their own accounts, speculating on whether a currency is about to go up or down. Often a trader has millions of dollars riding on whether a currency will go up or down a single percentage point.

Traders see only a small part of a currency's supply and demand—the part that flows through their offices as they buy and sell. Given their very limited observations, they have to guess what's going on. They're making judgments not about shifts in demand, but about their belief about other traders' beliefs about . . . Rumors can, and do, drive international currency markets wild.

Predicting how much of a foreign currency all the people in a country will want in the short run is a complicated task. If a currency trader predicts wrong, she gets stuck with some currencies that nobody wants. When the spread is wide, she can afford a few losses, but when the bid/ask spread is narrow, she must predict very carefully and must try to make sure that she chooses a rate for which the supply of and demand for various currencies flowing through her office are equal.

Key Currency Cross Rates

	Dollar	Pound	SFranc	Guilder	Peso	Yen	Lira	D-Mark	FFranc	CdnDlr
Canada	1.3516	2.2815	.99127	.76426	.17279	.01168	.00088	.85849	.25396	....
France	5.3220	8.9835	3.9032	3.0093	.68039	.04598	.00345	3.3803	....	3.9376
Germany	1.5744	2.6576	1.1547	.89025	.20128	.01360	.00102	....	.29583	1.1648
Italy	1542.5	2603.7	1131.3	872.21	197.2	13.326	....	979.74	289.83	1141.2
Japan	115.75	195.39	84.892	65.451	14.798	....	.07504	73.52	21.749	85.639
Mexico	7.8220	13.204	5.7367	4.4230	....	.06758	.00507	4.9682	1.4697	5.7872
Netherlands	1.7685	2.9852	1.2970	....	.22609	.01528	.00115	1.1233	.33230	1.3084
Switzerland	1.3635	2.3016	....	.77099	.17432	.01178	.00088	.86604	.25620	1.0088
U.K.	.59242	....	.43448	.33498	.07574	.00512	.00038	.37628	.11131	.43831
U.S.	....	1.6880	.73341	.56545	.12784	.00864	.00065	.63516	.18790	.73986

Source: Dow Jones Telerate Inc. January 8, 1997.

of the long-run determinants of exchange rates is called fundamental analysis. But traders recognize that in the very short run the quantities of currencies supplied and

demanded aren't significantly influenced by exchange rates, but are significantly influenced by expectations. They expect that supply and demand for currencies will

ADDED DIMENSION   LIMITS ON TRADERS' SPECULATION

When many U.S. banks first got seriously involved in international currency markets in the 1970s, traders had relatively loose limits on the speculative positions they could take. A speculative position is the net amount of a currency a trader holds from buying or selling currency for his or her own account in the hope that its value will rise or fall.

Speculative positions can be either long or short. Holding a currency in the hope that its price will rise is a long position; selling a currency you don't have but will buy when you must supply it, in the hope that its price will have fallen, is a short position.

Some traders lost millions of dollars for their banks in a short time. In the famous case of Franklin National Bank, the losses in trading currencies brought the bank under—that is, it went bankrupt and had to be bailed out by the Federal Deposit Insurance Corporation.

In response to such problems, most banks instituted stringent controls over the positions that traders could take. Most traders weren't allowed to have unauthorized positions at the end of each trading day.

Who are these foreign exchange traders? Usually they're not Ph.D. economists or even MBAs; such people often don't have the guts or personality to be traders. Instead traders are often people who are directly out of high school or college, people who have been discovered to have an ability to make split-second correct decisions (to buy or sell); who have few regrets ("If only I'd. . ."); and who want to earn about $60,000 a year to start. They're a bungee-type group. (Bungee is a sport in which you tie one end of an elastic rope to a rock or a tree and the other end to your feet and dive off a cliff, hoping the rope will stop you right before you hit the ground. If you're successful, you yo-yo up and down for two or three minutes.) Bungee is a trader's hobby. I prefer gardening.

shift enormously, which means the equilibrium price will fluctuate widely. Traders' time horizon is the very short run (minutes, hours, or days). Thus, you'll seldom hear currency traders talking about fundamentals of exchange rate determination. They're far more concerned with the short-run factors that shift demand, especially expectations.

Conclusion

Even if you've stayed with me through the discussion in this appendix, you still won't be able to predict exchange rates. Nobody can do that. But at least I hope you know why you can't. The most honest prediction that one can make is that exchange rates are likely to be highly volatile—unpredictable in the short run and even unpredictable in the long run as new short-run phenomena develop. To make even a reasonable guess about what will happen

in such markets, you will likely need a psychologist (who can tell you what other people are thinking, what other people think you're thinking, what other people think you think you're thinking, and so on), and perhaps also a psychiatrist to handle the mental marshmallow you might become if you get into international currency markets.

Being an international currency trader isn't for most people; when my students suggest that they'd like to become international currency traders, I suggest they go into a more pleasant, less stressful field—like, say, air traffic control.

Our story has a moral, however. The moral is that in many so-called economic phenomena, noneconomic criteria play a significant role in what happens; in the short run they swamp the long-run economic forces. Economists can predict which types of markets will have these fluctuations (foreign exchange markets are definitely one type), but they can't predict exactly how prices will fluctuate in these markets.

KEY TERMS

spread   *(418)*

QUESTIONS FOR THOUGHT AND REVIEW

1. Explain what will likely happen to the U.S. exchange rate based on fundamental analysis and on short-run analysis when:
   a. The United States goes into recession.
   b. The U.S. interest rate rises.
   c. The EU interest rate rises.
   d. The U.S. trade deficit increases.
2. The interest rate in the United States is 10 percent; the

Japanese interest rate is 3 percent. Over the next year you expect the Japanese yen to appreciate against the dollar by 5 percent. Where should you invest, and why?
3. How would your answer to question 2 differ if the yen were expected to appreciate by 5 percent in the next month?
4. Do currency traders make larger profits with a small spread or a large spread?

History of Exchange Rate Systems

A good way to give you an idea of how the various exchange rate systems work is to present a brief history of international exchange rate systems.

The Gold Standard: A Fixed Exchange Rate System

Governments played a major role in determining exchange rates until the 1930s. Beginning with the Paris Conference of 1867 and lasting until 1933 (except for the period around World War I), most of the world economies had a system of relatively fixed exchange rates under what was called a **gold standard**—*a system of fixed exchange rates in which the value of currencies was fixed relative to the value of gold and gold was used as the primary reserve asset.*

Under a gold standard, the amount of money a country issued had to be directly tied to gold, either because gold coin served as the currency in a country (as it did in the United States before 1914) or because countries were required by law to have a certain percentage of gold backing their currencies. Gold served as currency or backed all currencies. Each country participating in a gold standard agreed to fix the price of its currency relative to gold. That meant a country would agree to pay a specified amount of gold upon demand to anyone who wanted to exchange that country's currency for gold. To do so, each country had to maintain a stockpile of gold. When a country fixed the price of its currency relative to gold, it fixed its currency's price in relation to other currencies as a result of the process of arbitrage.

Under the gold standard, a country made up a difference between the quantity supplied and the quantity demanded of its currency by buying or selling gold to hold the price of its currency fixed in terms of gold. How much a country would need to buy and sell depended upon its balance of payments deficit or surplus. If the country ran a surplus in the balance of payments, it was required to sell its currency—that is, buy gold—to stop the value of its currency from rising. If a country ran a deficit in the balance of payments, it was required to buy its currency—that is, sell gold—to stop the value of its currency from falling.

The gold standard enabled governments to prevent short-run instability of the exchange rate. If there was a speculative run on its currency, the government would buy its currency with gold, thereby preventing the exchange rate from falling.

But for the gold standard to work, there had to be a method of long-run adjustment; otherwise countries would have run out of gold and would no longer have been able to fulfill their obligations under the gold standard. The **gold specie flow mechanism** was *the long-run adjustment mechanism that maintained the gold standard.* Here's how it worked: Since gold served as official reserves to a country's currency, a balance of payments deficit (and hence a downward pressure on the exchange rate) would result in a flow of gold out of the country and hence a decrease in the country's money supply. That decrease in the money supply would contract the economy, decreasing imports, lowering the country's price level, and increasing the interest rate, all of which would work toward eliminating the balance of payments deficit.

Similarly a country with a balance of payments surplus would experience an inflow of gold. That flow would increase the country's money supply, increasing income (and hence imports), increasing the price level (making imports cheaper and exports more expensive), and lowering the interest rate (increasing capital outflows). These would work toward eliminating the balance of payments surplus.

Thus, the gold standard determined a country's monetary policy and forced it to adjust any international balance of payments disequilibrium. Adjustments to a balance of payments deficit were often politically unpopular; they led to recessions, which, because the money supply was directly tied to gold, the government couldn't try to offset with expansionary monetary policy.

The gold specie flow mechanism was called into play in the United States in late 1931 when the Federal Reserve, in response to a shrinking U.S. gold supply, decreased the amount of money in the U.S. economy, deepening the depression that had begun in 1929. The government's domestic goals and responsibilities conflicted with its international goals and responsibilities.

That conflict led to partial abandonment of the gold standard in 1933. At that time the United States made it illegal for individual U.S. citizens to own gold. Except for gold used for ornamental and certain medical and industrial purposes, all privately owned gold had to be sold to the government. Dollar bills were no longer backed by gold in the sense that U.S. citizens could exchange dollars for a prespecified amount of gold. Instead dollar bills were backed by silver, which meant that any U.S. citizen could change dollars for a prespecified amount of silver. In the late 1960s that changed also. Since that time, for U.S.

residents, dollars have been backed only by trust in the soundness of the U.S. economy.

Gold continued to serve, at least partially, as international backing for U.S. currency. That is, other countries could still exchange dollars for gold. However in 1971, in response to another conflict between international and domestic goals, the United States totally cut off the relationship between dollars and gold. After that a dollar could be redeemed only for another dollar, whether it was a U.S. citizen or a foreign government who wanted to redeem the dollar.

The Bretton Woods System: A Fixed Exchange Rate System

As World War II was coming to an end, the United States and its allies met to establish a new international economic order. After much wrangling they agreed upon a system called the **Bretton Woods system,** *an agreement about fixed exchange rates that governed international financial relationships from the period after the end of World War II until 1971.* It was named after the resort in New Hampshire where the meeting that set up the system was held.

The Bretton Woods system established the International Monetary Fund (IMF) to oversee the international economic order. The IMF was empowered to arrange short-term loans between countries. The Bretton Woods system also established the World Bank, which was empowered to make longer-term loans to developing countries. Today the World Bank and IMF continue their central roles in international financial affairs.

The Bretton Woods system was based upon mutual agreements about what countries would do when experiencing balance of payments surpluses or deficits. It was essentially a fixed exchange rate system. For example, under the Bretton Woods system, the exchange rate of the dollar for the British pound was set at slightly over $4 to the pound.

The Bretton Woods system was not based on a gold standard. When countries experienced a balance of payments surplus or deficit, they did not necessarily buy or sell gold to stabilize the price of their currency. Instead they bought and sold other currencies. To ensure that participating countries would have sufficient reserves, they established a stabilization fund from which a country could obtain a short-term loan. It was hoped that this stabilization fund would be sufficient to handle all short-run adjustments that did not reflect fundamental imbalances.

In those cases where a misalignment of exchange rates was determined to be fundamental, the countries involved agreed that they would adjust their exchange rates. The IMF was empowered to oversee an orderly adjustment. It could authorize a country to make a one-time adjustment of up to 10 percent without obtaining formal approval from the IMF Board of Directors. After a country had used its one-time adjustment, formal approval was necessary for any change greater than 1 percent.

The Bretton Woods system reflected the underlying political and economic realities of the post-World War II period in which it was set up. European economies were devastated; the U.S. economy was strong. To rebuild, Europe was going to have to import U.S. equipment and borrow large amounts from the United States. There was serious concern over how high the value of the dollar would rise and how low the value of European currencies would fall in a free market exchange. The establishment of fixed exchange rates set limits on currencies' relative movements; the exchange rates that were chosen helped provide for the rebuilding of Europe.

In addition, the Bretton Woods system provided mechanisms for long-term loans from the United States to Europe that could help sustain those fixed exchange rates. The loans also eliminated the possibility of competitive depreciation of currencies, in which each country tries to stimulate its exports by lowering the relative value of its currency.

One difficulty with the Bretton Woods system was a shortage of official reserves and international liquidity. To offset that shortage, the IMF was empowered to create a type of international money called **Special Drawing Rights (SDRs).** But SDRs never became established as an international currency and the U.S. dollar kept serving as official reserves for individuals and countries. To get the dollars to foreigners, the United States had to run a deficit in its current account. Since countries could exchange the dollar for gold at a fixed price, the use of dollars as a reserve currency meant that, under the Bretton Woods system, the world was on a gold standard once removed.

The number of dollars held by foreigners grew enormously in the 1960s. By the early 1970s, those dollars far exceeded in value the amount of gold the United States had. Most countries accepted this situation; even though they could legally demand gold for their dollars, they did not. But Charles de Gaulle, the nationalistic president of France, wasn't pleased with the U.S. domination of international affairs at that time. He believed France deserved a much more prominent position. He demanded gold for the dollars held by the French central bank, knowing that the United States didn't have enough gold to meet his demand. As a result of his and other countries' demands, on August 15, 1971, the United States ended its policy of exchanging gold for dollars at $35 per ounce. With that change, the Bretton Woods system was dead.

The Present U.S. System: A Partially Flexible Exchange Rate System

International monetary affairs were much in the news in the early 1970s as countries groped for a new exchange rate system. The makeshift system finally agreed upon involved partially flexible exchange rates. Most Western countries' exchange rates are allowed to fluctuate, although at various times governments buy or sell their own currencies to affect the exchange rate.

Under the present partially flexible exchange rate system, countries must continually decide when a balance of payments surplus or deficit is a temporary phenomenon and when it is a signal of a fundamental imbalance. If they believe the situation is temporary, they enter into the foreign exchange market to hold their exchange rate at what they believe is an appropriate level. If, however, they believe that the balance of payments imbalance is a fundamental one, they let the exchange rate rise or fall.

While most Western countries' exchange rates are partially flexible, certain countries have agreed to fixed exchange rates of their currencies in relation to rates of a group of certain other currencies. For example, European Union countries maintained almost fixed exchange rates among their currencies until 1992, although this group of EU currencies could float relative to other currencies. Other currencies are fixed relative to the dollar.

Deciding what is, and what is not, a fundamental imbalance is complicated, and such decisions are considered at numerous international conferences held under the auspices of the IMF or governments. A number of organizations such as G-7 (Group of Seven), which were introduced in Chapter 6, focus much of their discussion on this issue. Often the various countries meet and agree, formally or informally, on acceptable ranges of exchange rates. Thus, while the present system is one of partially flexible exchange rates, the range of flexibility is limited.

KEY TERMS

Bretton Woods system *(422)*
gold specie flow mechanism *(421)*

gold standard *(421)*

Special Drawing Rights (SDRs) *(422)*

QUESTIONS FOR THOUGHT AND REVIEW

1. Explain why the gold standard broke down.
2. Explain why the Bretton Woods system broke down.
3. Describe the current exchange rate régime adopted by the United States.
4. What characteristics are desirable for an asset that serves as an official reserve?
5. The role of the dollar as an unofficial reserve currency has eroded in the past 10–15 years. What reason can you give for this?

Seventeen

The Art of Traditional Macro Policy

The worst episodes of recent monetary history—the great inflations—have been marked by the subjection of central bankers to overriding political pressures.

~ R. S. Sayers

After reading this chapter, you should be able to:

1 Summarize the conflicting goals of traditional macro policy.

2 Explain why macroeconomic policy is an art, not a science.

3 Distinguish a policy model from a theoretical model.

4 Explain why modern macro policy focuses on credibility.

5 State the main points of agreement on traditional macro policy between Keynesians and Classicals.

In earlier chapters I introduced you to the terminology, the institutions, and the theory of the macroeconomy. It's now time to put it all together.

- What should government do if the economy seems to be falling into a recession?
- What should government do if inflation seems to be increasing?
- What should government do if the economy seems to be falling into a recession but, simultaneously, inflation seems to be increasing?
- What should government do if there's a large trade deficit at the same time that it's worried about a recession?
- What should government do if its currency's value is falling and there's concern about inflation?

Policy makers face these and similar questions every day. In this chapter, using the terminology, knowledge of institutions, theory, and insights we developed in previous chapters, we'll try to come to grips with these difficult real-world issues.

In doing so I summarize and review similarities and differences between Keynesians and Classicals described in earlier chapters. First I update some recent theoretical developments relevant for policy and discuss the interaction between theory and policy. Then I consider the similarities and differences between Keynesians and Classicals on macro policy.[1]

---

[1] As I have emphasized throughout the book, the Keynesian/Classical classification is not a perfect one. That division both overestimates and underestimates the disagreements among economists. In Appendix A I consider some alternative classifications and briefly introduce you to some of the delightful diversity one finds in macroeconomics.

The last part of the chapter reviews important episodes in the recent history of macroeconomic policy, showing you how things worked out in real-world cases.

One reason why macroeconomic policy is so complicated is that it involves conflicting goals. As we saw in the chapter on inflation, the low inflation goal often conflicts with the low unemployment/high growth goal. And as we saw in a previous chapter, international trade balance and exchange rate goals often conflict with one another and with domestic goals. Thus, the government finds itself and the economy on a tightrope. Too expansionary a policy will accelerate inflation and expand trade deficits. But the government also knows that if it's too contractionary, it will cause a recession.

To maintain the economy on this tightrope, governments use monetary and fiscal policies as a balance bar. If the economy seems to be falling into inflation, governments can use contractionary monetary and fiscal policies; if it seems to be falling into recession, they can use expansionary monetary and fiscal policies. If they face both problems simultaneously, they must choose between the two strategies and hope for the best.

In thinking about these goals, we must recognize that there are limits to what can be achieved with macroeconomic policy. Economists often tell governments that they're asking for too much. These governments are like a patient who asks his doctor for a health program that will enable him to forget about a training program, eat anything he wants, and run a four-minute mile. Some things just can't be done, and it's important for governments to recognize the inevitable limitations and trade-offs, at least with the monetary and fiscal policy tools currently available. Good economists are continually pointing out those limits.

But, like the patient who doesn't like to hear there are limits, governments often go to other advisers who offer more upbeat advice. Economists are often put in the position of the stick-in-the-mud who sees only problems, not potentials.

This stick-in-the-mud image isn't appropriate. We economists are often dynamic, innovative, positive sorts of people (would you believe?) who've just been cast in a difficult role of pointing out that there are no free lunches. What makes economists' stick-in-the-mud role so difficult is that the trade-offs are often uncertain, meaning that once in a while the "promise-them-everything" advisers turn out to be right. Here's an example:

In 1984 and 1985, most economists were convinced that there was serious concern about inflationary pressures. Based on this concern, they warned against monetary and fiscal policies that were too expansionary. They kept predicting higher inflation. But due in part to some unexpected falls in the prices of oil and raw materials, that inflation didn't occur, even though government listened instead to a set of "full-speed-ahead" advisers. Because the inflation didn't occur, the advisers who said "full speed ahead" could point to this period and correctly say that they were right.

With policy effects so uncertain, most economists are hesitant to make unambiguous predictions about policy. But they do have a sense of the effects of certain policies and the trade-offs each involves. Exhibit 1 summarizes those trade-offs.

When advising governments about real-world macro policy, economists are very aware that they practice the **art of macro policy**—*macroeconomic policy based on rough estimates and judgments, rather than on precise relationships*—not the science of macroeconomics. In practicing the art of macro policy, Keynesians and Classicals have different styles, and before we talk about some real-world episodes, it's helpful to contrast those styles. We begin by reviewing some recent policy-relevant theoretical developments in macroeconomics.

In the 1980s and 1990s, there have been a lot of theoretical developments in thinking about macroeconomic problems, but most of those developments have had only tangential effects on macro policy makers. The reason is that those new developments lead to the conclusion that the aggregate economy is enormously complicated. Once

THE LIMITS OF TRADITIONAL MACROECONOMIC THEORY AND POLICY

1 Too contractionary a policy will cause unemployment and recession. Too expansionary a policy will accelerate inflation and expand trade deficits.

The Limits of Traditional Macroeconomic Policy

It is critical for students to understand the limitations of macroeconomic policy. Economists make policy prescriptions in light of those limitations.

Q–1: The President comes to you and says she wants very low unemployment, zero inflation, and very high growth. How do you respond?

When economists say that economic policy making is an art rather than a science, we are not claiming that the relationships that exist in the economy are completely open for discussion. They are, instead, uncertain and must be approached with a trained eye and interpreted with care. Policy making in this context requires very careful judgment about a range of possible policy effects and consequences.

With policy effects so uncertain, most economists are hesitant to make unambiguous predictions about policy.

2 Economic relationships are not certain, which makes macroeconomic policy an art rather than a science.

The Difference between Theoretical Models and Policy Models

EXHIBIT 1   Macroeconomic Policy Dilemmas

	Option	Advantages	Disadvantages
Monetary policy	Expansionary	1. Interest rates may fall. 2. Economy may grow. 3. Decreases unemployment.	1. Inflation may worsen. 2. Capital outflow. 3. Trade deficit may increase.
	Contractionary	1. Helps fight inflation. 2. Trade deficit may decrease. 3. Capital inflow.	1. Risks recession. 2. Increases unemployment. 3. Slows growth. 4. May help cause short-run political problems. 5. Interest rates may rise.
Fiscal policy	Expansionary	1. Maybe growth will continue. 2. May help solve short-run political problems. 3. Decreases unemployment.	1. Budget deficit worsens. 2. Hurts country's ability to borrow in the future. 3. Trade deficit may increase. 4. Upward pressure on interest rate.
	Contractionary	1. May help fight inflation. 2. May allow a better monetary/fiscal mix. 3. Trade deficit may decrease. 4. Interest rates may fall.	1. Risks recession. 2. Increases unemployment. 3. Slows growth. 4. May help cause short-run political problems.

one takes full account of that complexity, it's unclear, theoretically, what policies, if any, should be followed.

Recent theoretical work that often goes under the name rational expectations has focused on building dynamic feedback effects into macro models. **Rational expectations** are *expectations about the future based on the best current information available*. Such expectations are important because if people expect a policy, and make adjustments in anticipation of it, the policy will have a different effect than if they didn't expect it. Affecting the expectations becomes the channel through which policy actions affect the economy.

The influence of the rational expectations work is woven into much of the discussion in this book. It is why, for example, when I discuss monetary policy, I talk about Fed posturing—*seeming to be* absolutely resolute about fighting inflation—in addition to *being* resolute. If the Fed convinces the public that their sole goal is to fight inflation, people will react differently than if they do not believe that. One Fed economist nicely summarized the distinction between making people believe the Fed's goal, and the policy of actually pursuing that goal when he differentiated "bark policy" from "bite policy." If the Fed barks loudly and convincingly enough, it doesn't have to bite.

In this book Keynesian economics is interpreted as a theory where, because of interdependencies of individuals' expectations, what is individually rational is not

Q-2: What are rational expectations?

This is a good place at which to change one of the habitual actions as suggested in the *Experimental Economics* supplement, "A Rational Expectations Quiz Experiment."

necessarily collectively rational. This interpretation is influenced by the work on rational expectations. It is a modern interpretation of Keynesian economics that makes it theoretically sound, even if all individuals have rational expectations. In modern macroeconomic theory, a key Keynesian insight is that the aggregate economy involves enormous interdependencies and these interdependencies can cause the collective result to only poorly represent individuals' desires.

What is undermined by rational expectations is what has sometimes been called **mechanistic Keynesianism**—*the belief that the simple multiplier models (or even complex variations) actually describe the aggregate adjustment process, and lead to a deterministic solution that policy makers can exploit in a mechanistic way.*

Modern macroeconomists do not believe the economy works this way, and even the most complicated models leave out most interdependencies to make those models tractable. When one adds back these interdependencies, the solutions to the models are indeterminate. Once one takes into account these many interdependencies, one recognizes that Keynesian models, at best, describe tendencies toward an exaggeration of external real shocks to the economy. This more limited interpretation of Keynes's insight is the modern interpretation of Keynesian theory.

The last three paragraphs summarize about 5,000 articles and lots of fancy math over the past 10 years. This chapter is policy-oriented, so I can summarize that work briefly because, while recent theoretical developments have been influential in the interpretation given to macro models, they have not had a significant effect on macro policy. These developments have simply brought home the fact that if you build dynamic feedback effects into an aggregate model, you can come up with just about any result. Slightly different assumptions in models lead to substantially different results and policy recommendations. These models describing that complexity are grist for tenure for academic economists but are of little use to policy makers. Policy makers don't want complexity. They want models that come to definite conclusions, because policy makers don't have the luxury of waffling on issues.

Most theoretical work of macroeconomists involves abstract models that omit institutional context to try to capture those aspects of economic behavior that transcend institutions. However, most actions by individuals do not transcend institutions. So it should not be surprising that those theoretical models don't come to policy conclusions until the institutional context is added back. And adding back institutional context involves judgment—judgment about which reasonable people may differ.

This differing institutional judgment explains why no conclusion can be reached regarding whether the Keynesian model or the Classical model is the best guide for policy. Once one adds the institutional context back, both Classical and Keynesian macro models become reasonable guides, depending on the situation, and that's how policy makers use them—as guides, not as directives.

The introductory Keynesian and Classical models presented in the text are the ones in the back of policy makers' minds. They use them not as mechanical guides, but, with judgment, as working models—as descriptions of empirical regularities that they assume will be maintained—unless something else comes up. Policy makers do not care whether these models can be deductively derived from micro principles, or even whether they involve logical inconsistencies; what they care about is that these models fit with their intuition, describe observed reality, and predict reasonably well.

Let me give an example. Some farmers use the following rule of thumb: When the cows lie down, it is going to rain. The larger the percentage of their cows that lie down, the higher the probability of rain. If this rule of thumb usually works, it is a good rule of thumb. People who use this rule to predict don't care about the cows' decision-making process. They care about observable empirical regularity on which they can base policy decisions (such as whether to harvest the hay immediately, or wait a day).

Academic cowonomists would have a different focus. They would look into the cows' decision-making process and would try to explain the cow's lying-down decision in cost/benefit terms consistent with a cow's utility function.

Q–3: What is the problem with mechanistic Keynesianism?

Modern maco work on game theory and coordination problems in macro, which I sometimes called the macro-foundations of micro, comes to the conclusion, not surprisingly, that the macro economy is extraordinarily complicated and that the solutions are indeterminate, without limiting institutions. Students can understand this relatively easily. It is somewhat more difficult for theoretical economists, trained in models having unique equilibria, to accept.

Policy makers don't want complexity. They want models that come to definite conclusions.

The Interface between Theoretical and Policy Models

The introductory Keynesian and Classical models presented in the text are the ones in the back of policy makers' minds. They are used not as mechanical guides, but, with judgment, as working models.

What I am saying is that there are two fundamentally different types of models used in economics: policy models and theoretical models. A **policy model** is *a working tool that captures empirical regularities* that may be caused by features of the current institutional framework or by inherent economic tendencies; for short-run policy, policy makers don't care which, as long as the model leads to the best prediction. The macro policy model presented in Chapter 10 is such a model.

An academic theoretical model has a different purpose. Academic economists care passionately about whether an empirical regularity reflects inherent economic tendencies or the current institutional framework. Which of these is the cause of an empirical regularity has significant long-run policy relevance, and that is an academic economist's focus. By separating out institutionally-determined effects from institution-transcendent economic tendencies, their models can be used to predict whether a policy can be used indefinitely, or whether it only works temporarily—until institutions change. The recent Classical and Keynesian theoretical work on microfoundations is an attempt to make that separation for macroeconomics.

When teaching this subject, the instructor must discuss both types of models. That presents a problem, because on the one hand, the theoretical models are highly abstract and mathematically too complicated to present to anyone but specialists. On the other hand, the policy-oriented observational models are not really models at all. They are simply empirical generalizations, and they often fail to bring out the differences between those empirical regularities based on institutional constraints that will likely change and those that transcend existing institutions.

Let's now briefly consider the influence of some of this modern theoretical work on macro policy and some of the ideas underlying it.

3 Theoretical models are abstract; they try to capture certain aspects of economic behavior that transcend institutions. Policy models combine individuals' actions that transcend institutions and individual actions that depend on institutions; they try to capture empirical regularities.

Here one can mention the aggregate supply path that was used in the theoretical section. This curve reflects an empirical regularity; it is not a theoretically defined curve. Hence, for a theoretical model it is not helpful. For a policy model, it is very helpful.

People Aren't Stupid

Modern Classical economics is centered around rational expectations and the assumption that collective results will reflect individuals' desires.

Q–4: How does the fact that people aren't stupid tend to undermine activist policy?

In the 1990s, when one takes into account expectations of policies, the traditional discussion of policy changes to discussions of policy regimes. In terms of policy regimes, all the same issues and arguments exist as existed when the discussion centered around policy, except that they exist at a higher level, one taking into account the dynamic feedbacks of expected policy on the existing policy.

As I stated before, modern Classical economics is centered around rational expectations and the assumption that collective results will reflect individuals' desires. The essence of the modern Classical policy argument based on rational expectations is the following: Say the government uses an activist monetary and fiscal policy. People aren't stupid; they'll soon come to expect that activist monetary and fiscal policy will be used and, in anticipation, will change their behavior. But if they change their behavior, the government's estimates of what is going to be the effect of policy, based on past experience, will be wrong.

Let's consider an example. Say everyone knows government will run expansionary fiscal policy if the economy is in a recession. In the absence of any expected policy response by government, people would have lowered their prices when they saw a recession coming. Expecting government expansionary policy, however, they won't lower their prices. Thus, an activist policy creates its own problems, which can be avoided by establishing a set of rules that limit government's policy responses. Modern Classical economics has formalized that insight.

As we can see from this discussion, the key element of modern Classical ideas about policy is that you must consider the effects of policy on people's behavior, and that those effects place limits on policy options. Specifically, the fact that the economy is falling into a recession is not a sufficient reason for the government to run expansionary monetary and fiscal policies. Some modern Classicals go further than that, arguing that if all people have rational expectations and the economy is competitive, there's no room for any activist monetary policy.

Modern Keynesians generally agree with this modern Classical argument about expectations. But they argue that it doesn't rule out activist monetary and fiscal policies in all instances. As I discussed above, they argue that many fluctuations in the economy are due to a collective irrationality, which leaves room for government to correct that irrationality.

A good way to see how modern Classical and Keynesian ideas have affected macroeconomic policy, or at least the thinking about that policy, is the discussion in the 1990 *Economic Report of the President*. There's little or no mention of an activist fiscal policy and sizes of multipliers. Instead, the central theme is, "Fiscal policy should move toward *credible, systematic* policies that would promote strong noninflationary growth" (p. 77). By **credible systematic policies,** the report means *policies that people believe will be implemented regardless of the consequences.*

Similarly with the report's discussion of monetary policy. A key statement of principle for monetary policy is:

> Monetary policy needs to maintain credibility, because credibility helps ensure that the goals of policy will be attained during a period of dynamic economic and financial developments. Policy credibility is enhanced by building a record of achievement of the stated goals of policy and by consistently following stated policy principles.

I suspect the redundancy in those descriptions is by design. The economists who wrote the report wanted to emphasize that one cannot think of macroeconomic policy without thinking about what effect expectations of macroeconomic policy will have. The policy must be credible, systematic, and consistent. All these statements emphasize that you cannot think of policy choices in one time period as not affecting individuals' behavior in another time period.

An analogy to raising a child might make the point clear. Say that your child is crying in a restaurant. Do you hand out a piece of candy to stop the crying or do you maintain your "no candy" rule? Looking only at the one situation, it might make sense to give the candy, but doing so will undermine your credibility and consistency, and therefore has an additional cost. This emphasis on credibility is the primary effect modern theoretical work has had on macroeconomic policy. In conducting macro policy, one must consider the effect that expectations of that policy will have on the economy generally, and not only in a particular case.

The quotations from the 1990 *Economic Report of the President* reflect the Classical (or at least Republican) view of traditional macro policy. The same focus on credibilty shows up in the 1996 *Economic Report of the President,* which reflects the Keynesian (or at least Democratic) view of traditional macro policy. In a section entitled "The Importance of Forward-Looking Expectations" we find:

> Deficit reduction that is viewed as credible and likely to be accompanied by future monetary accommodation leads investors to expect a future decline in short-term rates.

In the 1990s credibility is a key element of all policy discussions.

Classicals and Keynesians also agree that, in practice, credibility is hard to achieve. The 1990 *Economic Report of the President* summarizes the problem nicely:

> Policy credibility is clearly useful to have, but achieving it may not be easy. Simply announcing a change in policy does not make it believable. Credibility depends in part on the plausibility and consistency of the announced policy in the context of the overall economic environment and other policies. Credibility probably depends most importantly on a track record of following the stated principles of policy.

Most economists can agree with this statement. Keynesians' and Classicals' disagreement concerns what policy is plausible and hence what policy can be credible.

Credibility and Macro Policy

When I introduce the ideas of credibility and macroeconomic policy, I change things a bit and discuss "credibility and class examination policy." I ask my class what would happen if I announced an exam, telling them that it would be very challenging, and then when the day came for the test, I announced that there would be no exam after all. They typically respond that I would achieve my desired goal of getting them to study the material, with the added benefit of not having to correct the exams. They also respond that they would be less likely to prepare as completely next time because they couldn't be sure that I would come through with the exam. I then point out that when I do not follow through with announced exams I lose credibility, much as the government suffers a loss of credibility when it does not follow through with its announced policies.

Emphasis on credibility is the primary effect modern theoretical work has had on macroeconomic policy.

The Classical view of government as a tool that individuals use to enrich themselves has been around for a long time, as can be seen in this 19th-century lithograph. *Bleichroeder Print Collection, Baker Library, Harvard Business School.*

4 Modern economists focus on credibility because they see macro policy operating through expectations as much as through the real channels emphasized in the traditional models.

THE KEYNESIAN/ CLASSICAL POLICY DEBATE

Debates about economic theory often mask debates about economic policy. Economists use theories to guide their reasoning, but before they can translate the results of a theory into a policy prescription, they must add a sense of institutions and history, adjusting the model to fit reality. Keynesians and Classicals differ not only in the theoretical models they prefer, but also, and probably more importantly, in their sense of institutions and history.

The Classical View of Government Policy

Classicals have a profound distrust of government and the political process.

Ask your students to discuss their own views of the role the government should play in making economic policy, and whether they see their own views as being closer to a Keynesian or Classical point of view.

In the Classical view, politicians often are guided by politics, not by society's best interest.

As you saw in earlier chapters, Classicals have a profound distrust of government and the political process. They tend to believe that, even if theoretically the government might be able to help solve a recession, there's a serious question whether, given the political process, it will do so. Politics will often guide government to do something quite different than "further the general good." In the Classical view, real-world government intervention is more likely to do harm than good.

Classicals see democratic government as being significantly controlled by special interest groups. While, in theory, government might be an expression of the will of the people, in practice it's not. Thus, government is not a legitimate method of correcting problems in the economy. True, government sometimes does good, but this is the exception. Overall the costs of government action outweigh the benefits.

In the Classical view, politicians often are guided by politics, not by society's best interest. Therefore any policy that increases the government's role is highly suspect and should be avoided. Modern Classical models reflect this view and focus on a model that highlights a laissez-faire policy for government.

The Keynesian View of Government Policy

Q–5: Distinguish between Keynesian and Classical views of government policy.

Keynesians tend to see government as an expression of the will of the people.

Keynesians tend to have more faith in government not only being able to recognize what's wrong, but also being willing to work to correct it. Thus, for a Keynesian it's worthwhile to talk about a model that highlights an activist role for government.

Keynesians tend to see government as an expression of the will of the people. Thus, they see it as a legitimate method of correcting problems in the economy. True, government is sometimes misled by interest groups who direct government to do their own bidding rather than follow the general interest, but this is simply a cost of government. In the Keynesian view, the benefits of government generally outweigh the costs.

Who's Right on Policy?

Notice that these differences between Keynesians and Classicals are based on judgment calls requiring a knowledge of the workings of the market and the social institutions that tie our country together. They're judgments upon which reasonable individuals may differ; between the two extremes are innumerable shades of Keynesians and Classicals. There's no objective way of deciding which group is right or wrong.

Similarities and Differences between Keynesians and Classicals on Traditional Macro Policy

For a discussion of the political realities of using Keynesian fiscal policy, see "The Consequences of Mr. Keynes," by James M. Buchanan and Richard E. Wagner, in *Classical Readings in Economics*.

With that update on modern theoretical developments and their relevance for policy, let's consider the three central problems of macroeconomics—inflation, unemployment, and growth—and see where Keynesians and Classicals tend to come out in their judgments about what to do about each of these. Exhibit 2 provides a summary comparison.

As you can see in Exhibit 2, there are some differences, but those differences reflect differences in emphasis, interpretation, and judgment as much as they reflect differences in theory.

Similarities and Differences between Keynesians and Classicals on Fiscal Policy   Classicals tend to worry slightly more about inflation than do Keynesians. Thus, Classicals tend to be more willing to believe that a higher unemployment rate is consistent with potential income than is a Keynesian. Moreover, Classicals see expansionary monetary and fiscal policy as having far less effect on real income and unemployment. It was this difference that was captured in the macro policy model in the shape of the aggregate supply path. I review that difference in Exhibit 3.

EXHIBIT 2   A Comparison of Classical and Keynesian Policies

Problem	Keynesian Policy	Classical Policy
Inflation	• *Cause: Inflation is a combination institutional and monetary problem.* • Use contractionary monetary and fiscal policy. • Supplement above policy with policies to change wage- and price-setting institutions—possibly consider a temporary incomes policy. • Some small amount of inflation may be good for economy, and it is not worth trying to push inflation to zero if doing so involves significant unemployment.	• *Cause: Inflation is a monetary problem.* • Avoid inflation by relying on strict monetary rule—use contractionary monetary policy. • Be careful about expanding output too high and causing inflation. • Push inflation to zero by following strict monetary rule.
Slow Growth	• *Cause: Slow growth is a combination institutional and aggregate demand problem.* • Use expansionary monetary and fiscal policy. • Supplement above policy with policies to establish incentives for growth.	• *Cause: Growth rate reflects people's desires; probable cause of slow growth is too much regulation, too-high tax rates, and too few incentives for growth.* • Remove government impediments to growth; go back to laissez-faire policy.
Recessionary Unemployment	• *Cause: Recessionary unemployment is a combination institutional and aggregate demand problem.* • Use expansionary monetary and fiscal policy.	• *Cause: Recessionary unemployment was probably caused by earlier government policies that were too expansionary, causing inflation.* • If unemployment is very high, use expansionary monetary and fiscal policy. Generally, however, government policies should focus on the long run.

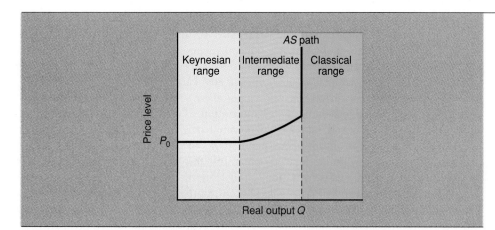

EXHIBIT 3   The *AS* Path in the Macro Policy Model

The differences between Keynesians and Classicals can be seen in the slope of the *AS* path. Classicals see the *AS* path as close to vertical; Keynesians see it as close to horizontal.

Video Series, Economics U$A: Fiscal Policy, Segments 6.1-6.3.

At this point, I often ask students whether they have considered the future taxes that they'll have to pay. Most haven't. This question generates significant discussion and brings home some of the problems with the assumptions of super-rationality in the future.

Ricardian Equivalence theorem *The argument that deficit spending will have no net effect on the economy's level of income.*

The theoretical differences between Keynesians and Classicals and among different subgroups of Classical economists on the expansionary effect of fiscal policy aren't too important in practice.

Q–6: Does a country's fiscal policy reflect political considerations more than it reflects stabilization policy considerations? Why?

At this point, I like to bring up the politics involved in contractionary fiscal policy, and I emphasize the asymmetry of fiscal policy; that is, it is easier to find political support for expansionary fiscal policy than for contractionary fiscal policy.

Q–7: Do Keynesians and Classicals agree or disagree more about the long-run or the short-run effects of monetary policy on inflation?

For a classical view, see "Rules versus Authorities in Monetary Policy," by Henry C. Simons, in *Classical Readings in Economics.*

There, you can see that when the economy is close to the Classical range, expansionary aggregate demand policy increases real output by a small amount. Much of the increase in aggregate demand leads to an increase in the price level. When the economy is close to the Keynesian range, expansionary aggregate demand policy has a much larger effect on real output, and a smaller effect on the price level.

The difference can be explained somewhat more precisely. All Classicals see expansionary monetary policy as inflationary. However, they are divided on their view of expansionary fiscal policy's effect on inflation. The monetarist school of Classical thought says expansionary fiscal policy financed by bonds isn't important with respect to inflation because the bonds crowd out an offsetting amount of private spending. Some modern Classicals say that deficit spending will have no effect on the economy. They argue that people with rational expectations will reduce their consumption and investment expenditures in order to be able to pay the future taxes necessary to finance the interest payments on the deficit. Since David Ricardo was the first to develop the argument that *deficit spending will have no effect on the economy's level of income,* it is often called the **Ricardian Equivalence theorem.** But the majority Classical position is that expansionary fiscal policy can contribute to inflationary pressures because it increases aggregate equilibruim demand, while the aggregate supply path doesn't shift out. The result is inflation.

These theoretical differences between Keynesians and Classicals and among different subgroups of Classical economists on the expansionary effect of fiscal policy aren't too important in practice, since, in the real world, fiscal policy is a difficult tool to use. A country's fiscal policy generally reflects political considerations as much as, or more than, economic stabilization considerations. Due to these political considerations, economists of all persuasions tend to believe that governments usually lean toward expansionary fiscal policy, regardless of economists' advice.

If expansionary aggregate policy is needed, fiscal policy generally turns expansionary. Tax cuts or spending increases are politically popular, and if the need for them is recognized in time, usually we can count on expansionary fiscal policy.

Turning the other way—contractionary fiscal policy—isn't so easy. When the U.S. president says, "Read my lips: No new taxes," and the U.S. Congress says, "No cuts in government programs," it's rather difficult to have contractionary fiscal policy. The fiscal policy steering wheel is consistently being pulled toward being inflationary.

Keynesians and Classicals both agree about the political difficulties of using fiscal policy to slow inflation. Thus, much of the debate about what types of macroeconomic policy to use generally focuses on monetary policy.

Similarities and Differences between Keynesians and Classicals on Monetary Policy The majority Keynesian and Classical views on monetary policy agree that expansionary monetary policy can stimulate the economy in the short run (although some modern Classicals argue that people with rational expectations will immediately push up prices, so expansionary monetary policy can only cause inflation, even in the short run). But Keynesians and Classicals disagree about the long run, and hence they disagree on the effectiveness of expansionary monetary policy. Classicals tend to see the long-run effect of monetary policy as exclusively on inflation; Keynesians believe that the inflationary effect of monetary policy is dependent on how close the economy is to its potential income. Because of this difference, Keynesians tend to advocate more activist policies, while Classicals tend to advocate more laissez-faire policies.

Theoretically these differences show up in their views on what determines aggregate output. Keynesians see the aggregate output as dependent upon expected aggregate demand. Thus, an increase in nominal demand can increase real output. Classicals see aggregate output as independent of expected aggregate demand. Unless expansionary monetary policy fools suppliers into thinking there's been an increase in real demand, it can only cause inflation.

Most Keynesians and Classicals agree that, in the short run, expansionary monetary policy can stimulate growth and keep the economy out of a recession. But it can do so only at the cost of creating inflationary pressure. That inflationary pressure leads to increased rates of inflation in the long run, as it breaks down institutional constraints on firms raising wages and prices and as it becomes built into expectations. Therefore, the initial inflationary side effects of expansionary monetary policy are often hidden. This hiding of costs creates enormous political pressure for expansionary monetary policy. With politicians' short-run time horizon, a push for expansionary monetary policy is almost inevitable, especially around election time. Given the Fed's quasi-independence, there is debate about whether the Fed responds to that pressure as well.

The debate about whether or not to use expansionary monetary policy arises because of disagreement about whether moderate expansionary pressures will always lead to inflation in the long run. This difference in views means that there's a range of inflation and unemployment where it's not clear whether expansionary or contractionary monetary policy should be used. The economy is often in this range. On the one hand, to use expansionary policy in that range is to take a chance that inflationary expectations will get built into expectations and institutions. On the other hand, to use contractionary policy can lead to a slow-growth, high-unemployment economy.

Amid these debates between Keynesians and Classicals we shouldn't lose sight of the convergence of views. There's more agreement about policy than disagreement. Both Keynesians and Classicals generally agree that:

1. *Expansionary monetary and fiscal policies have short-run stimulative effects on income.*
2. *Expansionary monetary and fiscal policies have potential long-run inflation effects.*
3. *Monetary policy is politically easier to use than fiscal policy.*
4. *Expansionary monetary and fiscal policies tend to increase a trade deficit.*
5. *Expansionary monetary policy places downward pressure on the exchange rate.*
6. *Expansionary fiscal policy has an ambiguous effect on the exchange rate.*

In the actual conduct of policy, these agreements often mean that various economists' advice is similar, whether they're Keynesian or Classical.

Another way to see the consistency of policy advice is to consider the macro policy model once again. I present that model again in Exhibit 4. In range *A* of the AS path, where unemployment is very high and the economy is a long way from potential output, both Classicals and Keynesians agree that expansionary macro policy is called for. In range *C*, where aggregate equilibrium demand exceeds potential income, both Keynesians and Classicals agree that contractionary macro policy is called for. The debate concerns range *B*, where unemployment may be too high but, simultaneously, there are inflationary pressures that could lead to an accelerating inflation. Because there is agreement about policy action in ranges *A* and *C*, the

For a discussion of the role of fiscal and monetary policy in the art of macro policy, see "Central Bankers Say: Look Elsewhere for Jobs," in *Case Studies in Macroeconomics*.

Video Series, Economics USA: Monetary Policy, Segments 13.1-13.3.

Agreement about Macroeconomic Policy

5 Both Keynesians and Classicals generally agree that:
1. Expansionary monetary and fiscal policies have short-run stimulative effects on income.
2. Expansionary monetary and fiscal policies have potential long-run inflation effects.
3. Monetary policy is politically easier to implement than fiscal policy.
4. Expansionary monetary and fiscal policies tend to increase a trade deficit.
5. Expansionary monetary policy places downward pressure on the exchange rate.
6. Expansionary fiscal policy has an ambiguous effect on the exchange rate.

It is very important that, even though economists differ over many issues, students recognize that there is substantial agreement over many policy effects. This will help you present macroeconomics as a more coherent area of economics.

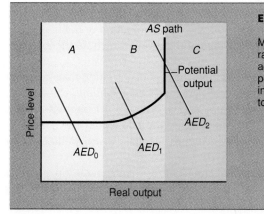

EXHIBIT 4   The Three Ranges of the Aggregate Supply Path

Most economists see the economy as having three ranges of price-level flexibility. In range *A*, when the economy is significantly below potential income, most economists agree that expansionary policy is useful. In range *C*, when the economy is above its potential income, most economists favor contractionary policy. In range *B*, the intermediate range, there is debate about policy. The economy is generally thought to be in range *B* so there is generally debate about what is the appropriate policy.

For a discussion of agreement among economists, see "The Monetarist Controversy, or Should We Forsake Stabilization Policies?" by Franco Modigliani, in *Classic Readings in Economics.*

RECENT HISTORY OF MACROECONOMIC POLICY

The 1990 Recession

Q–8: Describe monetary and fiscal policies just before the 1990 U.S. recession.

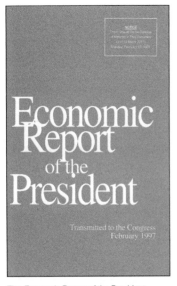

The *Economic Report of the President* provides a summary of the past year's economic events as well as a variety of data such as that found on the endpapers.

Depending on your point of view you can argue for or against Fed independence using evidence from the 1990 recession. One can claim that the Fed was too hasty in putting on the macroeconomic brakes, and could have been persuaded to ease up if its independence was more constrained. On the other hand, one can claim that the events of the 1990 recession prove the importance of Fed independence because the Fed was able to stand firm against the pleas for more expansionary monetary policy.

economy is generally pushed into range *B*, making it look as if there is more disagreement than there actually is.

Let's now turn to a consideration of recent macroeconomic policy. (Appendix B considers the history of macroeconomic policy over the past 50 years.)

The stage for the recent history of macro policy was set in the period 1983–90. This was a period of substantial growth in the economy. Ronald Reagan was president during most of this time. His successor, George Bush, was elected in 1988 on an economic platform similar to Reagan's: keep tax rates low, rely on growth and cutting government expenditures to cut the deficit, and enjoy the prosperity.

In the first half of Bush's term the economy kept on its path of growth, but in the fall of 1990 the string of good luck ended. Due to a Middle East military conflict, oil prices rose substantially, leading many to fear that inflationary pressures would result in an inflationary spurt like that of the mid- and late 1970s. Those fears of policy makers and businesspeople led to contractionary monetary policy and a fall in investment, and that led to the 1990 recession.

Going into the 1990s, the consensus view was that fiscal policy was expansionary, not for macroeconomic reasons, but for political reasons. This was unlikely to change significantly, so if inflationary pressures were going to be nipped in the bud, monetary policy had to provide the contractionary effect.

In 1990, regardless of how one measured monetary policy—by interest rates or by money supply—the Fed policy was contractionary, and there was significant debate about whether it should have loosened up policy to avoid a recession. The tight monetary policy had stronger-than-desired effects as banks limited loans to meet regulatory requirements, which had been tightened in response to the Savings and Loan problem of the 1980s. The arguments for loosening were countered by the fear that, if the Fed did loosen up, or even showed weakness in its resolve to fight inflation, inflation would take off. Whether that would have happened is unclear; what is clear is that there were problems with the anti-inflationary policy the Fed followed.

The Fed's resolve to fight inflation was strengthened by international pressures. In September 1990, as concern about the Middle East political situation grew, the G-7 countries met and decided to coordinate their monetary policies. All would maintain relatively contractionary policies, so that the 1974 and 1979 experiences, in which an oil price rise led to serious worldwide inflation, wouldn't be repeated—they would come down on the side of fighting inflation. Many economists felt that this would be the path to a serious recession, which would lead the Fed and other countries' central banks to change their policies from contractionary to expansionary, as they had in the past.

The United States had an even stronger reason to maintain contractionary monetary policy. The country already had a significant trade deficit which was expected to worsen due to rising prices of oil imports.

The policy most economists advocated for the United States was to reduce the trade deficit by tightening up somewhat on fiscal policy, but not too much—for fear of furthering recessionary pressures. This contractionary fiscal policy was meant to be counteracted by expansionary monetary policy. The combination of policies would lower the interest rate some, decreasing the value of the dollar, which, in the long run, would stimulate U.S. exports.

The Fed worked behind the scenes to achieve these goals, arguing that the economy could go a lot more smoothly if fiscal policy would become slightly more contractionary. It offered to loosen up on monetary policy, but only if Congress and the president made some movements toward tightening up the budget deficit (the difference between government spending and tax revenues) to make fiscal policies more contractionary.

By the end of summer 1990, the president and Congress hadn't made any progress in eliminating the budget deficit, which had actually increased because the government tax revenue was less than expected, thanks to a slowdown in the U.S. economy.

In October the budget deficit was reduced somewhat. In response, the Fed eased monetary policy slightly but, for fear of inflation, didn't ease up significantly. Once again the Fed and other central banks had to decide whether to accommodate and possibly trigger accelerating inflation, or to hold the line and possibly cause a recession. They tried to find a middle road: running expansionary, but not too expansionary, policy. It didn't work. In fall 1990 the economy went into recession. Unemployment increased from 5.1 to 7 percent and real GDP fell. The Fed's response was to fight the recession, although initially that response was muted because the Fed didn't want to rekindle inflation.

The recession lingered through early 1991. When it was clear that the recovery was slow in coming and that inflation was remaining low, the Fed forgot about inflation and its desire for tighter fiscal policy before it would institute a looser monetary policy. Despite the government's increasing budget deficit, the Fed loosened monetary policy significantly. Interest rates fell to their lowest level in 30 years. Their fall pushed down the U.S. exchange rate and that decrease, combined with the recession, temporarily lowered the U.S. foreign trade deficit. Simultaneously, recessions in the EU and Japan refocused international concern away from inflation.

Q–9: Describe monetary and fiscal policies shortly after the end of the 1990 U.S. recession.

The Sort-of Recovery, 1992—and the Debate about Structural Macro Policies

The pickup in the economy did not occur fast enough for George Bush. Entering the presidential election of 1992 with the economy in the doldrums, he lost the election to the Democratic nominee, Bill Clinton, who ran on a platform of getting the economy going again.

Precisely how Clinton planned to do this was unclear, not because he lacked an understanding of the economic problems facing the country, but because the situation the economy was in made traditional policies contradictory. The goal he set was to reduce the budget deficit while at the same time creating 8 million new jobs. Achieving this goal was beyond the normal macroeconomic tools of monetary and fiscal policy. His problems were compounded by recession in Europe and Japan that reduced U.S. exports and caused the U.S. trade deficit to expand.

Pointing out the limitations of normal macro policies would not have gotten him elected, so instead, he promised to achieve a self-contradictory goal. After he was elected, he had to figure out how to achieve the contradictory ends of that goal, or at least how to appear to be doing so.

A recent book by Bob Woodward, *The Agenda*, gives one a good sense of the confusion in the Clinton White House.

Q–10: Why could President Clinton use neither Keynesian nor Classical traditional macro policy?

Slow, Continued Growth from 1992 to 1997

By objective standards, the economy did well in President Clinton's first term. Growth continued at 2.5 percent per year and unemployment fell from 7.4 to 5.2 percent. Inflation remained relatively low at about 3 percent. Total employment in the U.S. rose from about 118 to about 127 million workers. The budget deficit fell from $290 billion to $107 billion. Despite this solid record of growth and expansion without accelerating inflation, there remained concern about downsizing of large U.S. firms, job and income insecurity, and the relatively unattractive nature of the jobs that the U.S. economy was creating. Still, the economic goals that Clinton had set for his first term were met, and he easily won reelection in 1996.

The dilemma Clinton faced provides a good statement of the modern confusion about macroeconomic policy. The difficulty was the following: To expand the economy and create jobs, both Keynesian and Classical economics tell us to run deficits and increase the money supply (although Classical economics says this will only work temporarily). But the political imperatives of the 1990s were to *decrease the size of the deficit* and to prevent inflation by not increasing the money supply.

Within this new situation, the difference between the traditional Classical and Keynesian theories becomes of minor importance, since both theories say that to stimulate the economy you must do what is politically infeasible. It is at this point that structural policies enter in. These policies will be the focus of the next chapter.

CONCLUSION

As you can see, real-world monetary and fiscal policies are not cut and dried. Working with these policies is an art, not a science, and involves politics and psychology as well as economics. But the messiness of real-world policy doesn't mean that one can forget the simplified theories and relationships of economic models. Far from it. Real-world policy problems require a much deeper understanding of the models so that one can see through the messiness and design a policy consistent with the general principles embodied in those models.

CHAPTER SUMMARY

The goals of macro policy often conflict with one another.

A policy model has a different focus than a theoretical model.

Modern macroeconomists emphasize the need for policy to be credible.

Keynesians tend to favor activist policy; Classicals tend to favor laissez-faire policy.

Keynesian and Classical economists agree about many aspects of macroeconomic policy.

Macro policy is chosen through a combination of economic and political considerations.

Macroeconomic policy is an art, not a science.

KEY TERMS

art of macro policy *(425)*
credible systematic policies *(429)*

mechanistic Keynesianism *(427)*
policy model *(428)*

rational expectations *(426)*
Ricardian Equivalence theorem *(432)*

QUESTIONS FOR THOUGHT AND REVIEW

The number after each question represents the estimated degree of critical thinking required. (1 = almost none; 10 = deep thought.)

1. What is the difference between a mechanistic Keynesian view and a modern Keynesian view? *(3)*
2. How do policy models and theoretical models differ? *(3)*
3. What is the relationship between rational expectations and the modern macro emphasis on credibility? *(4)*
4. Keynesians and Classicals are in direct opposition on macroeconomic policy. True or false? Why? *(5)*
5. Federal Reserve Board Chairman Greenspan has been known to "practice intentional ambiguity" when speaking about the future direction of the economy. What reasons might he have for this? When might he not want to be ambiguous? *(6)*

6. During the 1996 presidential campaign, Clinton praised recent economic growth as healthy while Dole criticized it as anemic. Dole promised a 15 percent across-the-board tax cut to "grow the economy." What range of the *AS* path did each candidate believe the economy was in? Explain why. *(7)*
7. How would Keynesian and Classical policy prescriptions likely differ as to what policy is needed if the economy is growing slowly and inflation is low? *(5)*
8. Name one advantage and one disadvantage of expansionary monetary policy. *(3)*
9. Name one advantage and one disadvantage of contractionary fiscal policy. *(3)*
10. What are the differences between the Keynesian and Classical policies to fight inflation? *(4)*

PROBLEMS AND EXERCISES

1. In the library, research one of the Fed's responses to a recession discussed in this chapter.
   a. Would you have done anything differently?
   b. If you did something differently, what would be the possible negative effects of your actions?
   c. Who was president, Fed chairman, and chairman of the Council of Economic Advisers during the recession you looked at? Give their political affiliations.

   d. If individuals from the opposite party were in office during that recession, how might the responses have been different?
2. Find the current unemployment, inflation, and growth rates.
   a. What fiscal policy is government using to deal with the problems?
   b. What monetary policy is government using?

c. Who is currently president, Fed chairman, and chairman of the Council of Economic Advisers? What are their political affiliations?

d. How might the policies be different if individuals from another party were in power?

3. In a recent article, two economists proposed that the United States implement a plan of mandatory forced savings of 4 percent of a person's income per year.

    a. Explain the likely effect of this plan on interest rates and savings.

    b. Discuss the macroeconomic implications of the plan.

    c. Discuss the administrative problems of the plan.

4. As Europe's unemployment rates rose to over 10 percent in the early 1990s, a number of proposals were put forward for work-sharing, in which individuals work one day less per week and have their pay reduced by from 10 to 20

percent. Do you think such proposals could play a significant role in reducing unemployment in Europe? Why or why not?

5. The U.S. unemployment insurance system spends about $26 billion a year. President Clinton's former Labor Secretary Robert Reich proposed that:

    a. Cash rewards be given to workers who find jobs quickly;

    b. Individuals be allowed to take their total unemployment benefits out in a lump sum, rather than over the normal 26-week period, if they are starting a small business; and

    c. Individuals who want to retool their skills be given the benefits as "training subsidies."

Discuss the advantages and disadvantages of each of these three proposals.

ANSWERS TO MARGIN QUESTIONS

1. I would respond that it is important for governments to recognize the inevitable limitations and trade-offs of goals, at least with the monetary and fiscal tools currently available. *(425)*

2. Rational expectations are expectations about the future based on the best information currently available. *(426)*

3. The simple multiplier model (or even complex variations of that model) does not include sufficient dynamic interdependencies. At best, the modern Keynesian model describes tendencies toward an exaggeration of autonomous real shocks to the economy. *(427)*

4. The fact that people aren't stupid tends to undermine activist monetary and fiscal policy because, in the expectation of policies, people will change their behavior. *(428)*

5. Classicals see democratic government as being significantly controlled by special interests, and believe that the costs of government action tend to outweigh the benefits. Keynesians tend to have more faith in government. *(430)*

6. A country's fiscal policy generally reflects political considerations. The reason why is that special interest groups and the political will of the people generally determine who gets reelected, and thus determine

government spending policies. Stabilization involves general, not special, interests. *(432)*

7. Keynesians and Classicals disagree more about the long-run effects of monetary policy on inflation. Both agree that monetary policy can have short-run real effects. Classicals tend to believe, however, that in the long run, the real effects will disappear, and only the inflationary effects will remain. Keynesians believe monetary policy can have long-run real effects. *(432)*

8. Going into the 1990 recession, fiscal policy was expansionary while monetary policy was contractionary. *(434)*

9. Shortly after the 1990 recession, once the expansion was viewed as slow and noninflationary, the Federal Reserve followed an expansionary monetary policy. Fiscal policy remained expansionary. *(435)*

10. President Clinton could use neither Keynesian nor Classical policy because both policies told him that to create jobs he had to run deficits and increase the money supply, but, in the early 1990s, the political imperatives were to decrease the size of the deficit and prevent inflation by refraining from increasing the money supply. *(435)*

A P P E N D I X   A

Nonmainstream Approaches to Macro

The Keynesian and Classical views presented in the main body of the chapter and carried through in remaining chapters differ in policy emphasis, but the policy im-plications of the differences are limited to slight varia-tions. Keynesians favor somewhat more-activist policies; Classicals favor somewhat less-activist policies—but both operate within the current institutional structure. I focus on these two groups for pedagogical reasons: there's only so much you can absorb in one semester. But that focus should not lull you into thinking that those are the only two views that economists hold. Not only are there many subdivisions of Classicals and Keynesians, but many economists don't fit into either group. They're called nonmainstream or heterodox economists.

A characteristic of nonmainstream, or heterodox, economists is that they are far more open to discuss major institutional changes than are mainstream economists. More specifically, a **heterodox economist,** or nonmainstream economist, is *one who doesn't accept the basic underlying model used by a majority of economists as the most useful model for analyzing the economy. Economists who do accept that model* are called **mainstream economists.**

In this section I will briefly introduce four heterodox macroeconomists' approaches to give you a sense of how their analyses differ from the mainstream analysis presented in this book. The four heterodox approaches are Austrian, Post-Keynesian, Institutionalist, and Radical.

Austrians

Austrian economists are *economists who believe in the liberty of all individuals first and social goals second.* They oppose state intrusion into private property and private activities. They are not all economists from Austria; rather, they are economists from anywhere who follow the ideas of Ludwig von Mises and Friedrich von Hayek, two economists who were from Austria. Austrian economists are sometimes classified as conservative, but they are more appropriately classified as **libertarians,** who *believe in liberty of individuals first and in other social goals second.* Consistent with their views, they are often willing to support what are sometimes considered radical ideas, such as legalizing addictive drugs or eliminating our current monetary system—ideas that conservative economists would oppose.

In macroeconomics, Austrian economists emphasize the uncertainty in the economy and the inability of a government controlled by self-interested politicians to undertake socially beneficial policy. Well-known Austrian macroeconomists include Murray Rothbard, Peter Boethke, and Mario Rizzo.

One proposal of Austrian economists will give you a flavor of their approach. That proposal is to eliminate the Federal Reserve System and to establish a **free market in money**—*a policy that would leave people free to use any money they want, and would significantly reduce banking regulation.* In a sense, their proposal carries the Classical argument in favor of laissez-faire to its logical conclusions. Why should the government have a monopoly of the money supply? Why shouldn't people be free to use whatever money they desire, denominated in whatever

unit they want? Why don't we rely upon competition to prevent inflation? Why don't we have a free market in money?

A sub-group of Austrian economists is *public choice* economists. They use the mainstream supply and demand approach, but apply it much more broadly than do mainstream economists. Specifically, they see government decisions as reflecting economic forces rather than attempts by government to do good. Well-known public choice economists include Gordon Tullock, James Buchanan, and Robert Tollison.

Post-Keynesians

Post-Keynesian macroeconomists are *economists who believe that uncertainty is a central issue in macroeconomics.* They follow Keynes's approach more so than do mainstream economists. They agree with Austrians about the importance of uncertainty in understanding the macro economy, but their policy response to that uncertainty is not to have government get out of the macro economy; it is for the government to take a larger role in guiding the economy.

One of their policy proposals that gives you a flavor of their approach is **tax-based incomes policies**—*policies in which the government tries to directly affect the nominal wage- and price-setting institutions.* Under a tax-based incomes policy, any firm raising its wage or price would be subject to a tax, and any firm lowering its wage or price would get a subsidy. Such a plan, they argue, would reduce the upward pressure on the nominal price level, and reduce the rate of unemployment necessary to hold down inflation. Well-known Post-Keynesian economists include Paul Davidson, Hyman Minsky, and John Cornwall.

Institutionalists

Institutionalist economists are *economists who argue that any economic analysis must involve specific considerations of institutions.* Institutionalists have a long history in economics; their lineage goes back to the early 1930s and the writings of Thorstein Veblen, J. M. Clarke, and John R. Commons. Institutionalists were early supporters of welfare capitalism, and they helped set up many of the institutions of welfare capitalism, such as Social Security, which we now take for granted. Institutionalists are very close to Post-Keynesians in their approach to macroeconomics, but they give stronger emphasis to the role of institutions, and to the role of government in establishing new institutions, than do Post-Keynesians.

You can get a sense of their policy approach from one of the policies many Institutionalists support: **indicative planning**—*a macroeconomic policy in which the government sets up an overall plan for various industries* *and selectively directs credit to certain industries.* Thus for Institutionalists the invisible foot directs the invisible hand. Well-known Institutionalists include Marc Tool, Warren Samuels, and John Adams.

Radicals

Radical economists are *economists who believe substantial equality-preferring institutional changes should be implemented to our economic system.* Radical economists evolved out of Marxian economics. Compared to mainstream economists, Radicals are far more willing to consider major institutional changes in our macro economy. They focus on the lack of equity in our current economic system, and their political discussions focus on institutional changes that might bring about a more equitable system. Specifically, they see the current economic system as one in which a few people—capitalists and high-level managers—benefit enormously, while others— minority groups such as African-Americans and Hispanics—are left out, without a job. To incorporate such issues, Radical economists often use a class-oriented analysis and are much more willing to talk about social conflict and tensions in our society than are mainstream economists.

Compared to mainstream economists, Radical economists' analysis focuses much more on distributional fights between capitalists and workers and their different savings propensities. According to one important branch of radical theory, when profits are high, because capitalists save a large portion of their income, aggregate demand will be too low, and the economy goes into a recession; then government must run a deficit to bail out the economy. Mainstream economists agree that such distributional effects exist, but they consider them too small to worry about. Mainstream economists focus on fluctuations in business investment and consumers' spending decisions, not on differences in people's consumption.

Policy proposals some Radicals favor and that give you a sense of their approach are policies to establish worker cooperatives to replace the corporation. Radicals argue that such worker cooperatives would see that the income of the firm was more equitably located. Well-known radical economists include Samuel Bowles, Herbert Gintis, and Howard Sherman.

Consistency of the Various Approaches

A characteristic of almost all heterodox economists of all types is that their analyses tend to be less formal than mainstream analysis. *Less formal* doesn't mean better or worse. There are advantages and disadvantages to formality, but *less formal* does mean that there's more potential for ambiguity in interpretation. It's easy to say whether the logic in a formal model is right or wrong. It's much harder to say whether the logic in an informal model is right or wrong because it's often hard to see precisely what the logic is. The advantage of an informal model is that it can include many more variables and can be made more realistic, so you can discuss real-world problems more easily with that model. Nonmainstream economists often want to talk about the real world, which is why they use informal models.

Often, after I discuss the mainstream and nonmainstream approaches, some student asks which is right. I respond with a story told by a former colleague of mine, Abba Lerner; the story goes as follows:

> "But look," the rabbi's wife remonstrated, "when one party to the dispute presented their case to you, you said, 'You are quite right,' and then when the other party presented their case you again said, 'You are quite right.' Surely they cannot both be right?" To which the Rabbi answered, "My dear, you are quite right!"

The moral of the story is that there's nothing necessarily inconsistent among mainstream and heterodox economists' approaches. They are simply different ways of looking at the same event. Which approach is most useful depends on what issues and events one is analyzing. The class analysis used by radicals is often more appropriate to developing countries than it is to the United States, and, in analyzing developing countries, many mainstream economists also include class fights in their approach. Similarly, Austrian analysis provides more insight into the role of the entrepreneur and individual in the economy than does mainstream analysis, while Post-Keynesian and Institutionalist analyses are useful when considering major institutional changes.

The distinctions between nonmainstream and mainstream economists can be overdone. One economist may well fall into two or three different groupings and use a combination of various analyses.

KEY TERMS

Austrian economists *(438)*	Institutionalist economists *(438)*	Post-Keynesian
free market in money *(438)*	libertarian *(438)*	macroeconomists *(438)*
heterodox economist *(438)*	mainstream economist *(438)*	radical economists *(439)*
indicative planning *(438)*		tax-based incomes policy *(438)*

QUESTIONS FOR THOUGHT AND REVIEW

1. Distinguish a heterodox from a mainstream economist.
2. Which heterodox group of economists would most likely support the following proposals?
   a. An incomes policy.
   b. A free market in monies.
   c. Indicative planning.
   d. Worker cooperatives.
3. Why are nonmainstream approaches to macroeconomics often less formal than mainstream approaches?
4. Explain what the author meant by the story of the rabbi.

APPENDIX B

Earlier History of Macroeconomic Policy

In the chapter I went through the recent history of macroeconomic policy. In this appendix I take a brief look back at the earlier history of macroeconomic policy to see how we got to where we are. That earlier history has been a history of the eclectic use of monetary and fiscal policy to attempt to stay within the boundary between too-high inflation and too-high unemployment.

The New Deal and the Rise of Keynesian Economics

Keynesian economics developed in the 1930s during the Depression. In the United States this early work was primarily theoretical, and Keynesian economists didn't have significant input into policy. President Franklin Roosevelt opposed deficits (and hence the use of expansionary fiscal policy). Moreover, he didn't like Keynes, whom he met during one of Keynes's visits to the United States. The Fed had a number of Keynesian advisers but, at the time, monetary policy wasn't the focus of Keynesian economics.

Nonetheless the U.S. government was running deficits and starting public works programs as part of the **New Deal**—*President Franklin Roosevelt's name for his practical "do-something" approach to economic policy.* These programs, however, reflected Roosevelt's approach to policy rather than the influence of Keynesian (or Classical) economics.

Post-War Macro Policy

The first half of the 1940s brought World War II. U.S. government spending increased enormously; U.S. taxes increased significantly (income tax rates were over 90 percent on high incomes). But the increase in spending was so large that the U.S. government started running wartime deficits significantly larger than anything it had run

in the Depression. The Fed agreed to hold interest rates on government bonds constant to help the government finance wartime spending. This agreement meant the Fed could not conduct an independent monetary policy, but was forced to accommodate a highly expansionary fiscal policy. In response, the U.S. economy boomed. Economic activity expanded enormously. Much of the production, however, was used for the war effort; consumer goods were in short supply. To keep the resulting inflationary pressures in check, wage and price controls were instituted.

Cycles of Inflation and Recession   During the war, the combination of price controls and high government expenditures led to low unemployment and low inflation. The U.S. economy came out of World War II operating at capacity output. The major economic questions of the immediate postwar period were: (1) how to convert the economy from wartime to peacetime production without falling back into a depression, and (2) how to eliminate price controls without generating a large inflation. Both questions were successfully answered.

The 1949 Recession   Soon after the war ended, price controls were lifted. The results were positive: While inflation picked up, it remained low, even as aggregate demand remained high.

The economy also avoided a recession or depression, at least initially, due in part to pent-up demand. Despite high tax rates, aggregate demand remained high as people spent some of their forced wartime savings. Their increased consumption offset much of the decrease in government spending. In spring 1948, the high wartime income tax rates were cut, giving the economy an additional expansionary push. But that push didn't offset the contractionary effect of the further decline in government spending, and the economy started to fall into a recession by the end of 1949.

That recession was short-lived because, in 1950, the Korean War started, the United States got involved, and government spending jumped due to rearmament. The economy quickly came out of the recession. Thus, in this first postwar recession we see fiscal policy working. But the fiscal policy (changes in government spending) was not implemented for stabilization purposes. Instead it reflected wartime and political needs.

The economy continued strong through the Korean War. Monetary policy during this period was still limited by the earlier agreement between the Fed and the Treasury that required the Fed to hold the interest rate on government bonds constant. In 1951, the Fed and the Treasury met to adjust this earlier agreement, and signed the **Treasury Accord**—*an agreement between the Fed and the U.S. Department of the Treasury in which the Fed was freed from holding the interest rate on government bonds constant.*

The 1953–54 Recession   In the summer of 1953, the Korean War ended and government expenditures decreased. Consumer confidence fell. To try to prevent a recession, the Fed loosened monetary policy. The expansionary monetary policy didn't work (or at least it wasn't enough), and industrial production fell almost 10 percent from July 1953 to May 1954. No specific expansionary fiscal policy was implemented, but automatic stabilizers, such as unemployment insurance, helped slow output's fall. By the end of 1954, consumer confidence was picking up and sales were increasing. By mid-1955, the economy was moving into a boom, and the concern turned from recession to inflation.

The 1955–56 Inflation   To fight this inflation, the Fed tightened the money supply, increasing the reserve requirement and raising the discount rate. It hoped that the tightened money supply would stop the inflation, but not stop real output from growing nor cause unemployment to increase. These hopes weren't met. The contractionary monetary policy did slow inflation, but it also decreased real output. By 1957, that decrease had become significant, and the concern changed back from inflation to unemployment and recession.

The 1957–58 Recession   The tight monetary policy of 1956 hit the capital goods industry especially hard; business investment dropped 16 percent, and consumers' expenditures for durable items fell almost as much. This decline was worsened by the end of a Middle East crisis (such crises have been almost continual since World War II), which caused U.S. exports to decrease. (During the crisis, U.S. exports had boomed as foreign countries bought food and goods from the United States to stockpile for a potential war.) During this period, the Fed was still concerned about inflation. This was the time when the inflation/

unemployment Phillips curve trade-off became part of economists' lexicon.

Faced with this dual problem, the Fed had to choose which problem to fight. Initially it chose to fight inflation; it didn't loosen monetary policy significantly. But in late 1958 and early 1959, the Fed reversed itself and moved toward a more expansionary monetary policy, causing interest rates to fall. Combined with a large increase in mortgages guaranteed by the Federal Housing Administration and the Veterans' Administration, this expansionary monetary policy worked. By mid-1959, the economy was in a boom. Once again the policy concern changed, and inflation, not unemployment, became the focus of policy makers' concern.

The 1960 Inflation and Recession   To fight the inflation, the Fed used contractionary monetary policy and decreased the money supply. The results were the same as they had been in the 1955–56 inflation. Contractionary monetary policy slowed the inflation, but it also brought the economy into recession.

Industrial production fell during the second half of 1960 and into the first part of 1961. Unemployment increased substantially. This was one of the few times that the economy had fallen into a recession during a presidential election. Many observers believe that the recession played a significant role in Richard Nixon's defeat by John F. Kennedy.

The Sustained Expansion of the 1960s   Partly because of the 1950s experience in fighting inflation and partly because of a change in policy advisers (from Classical economists advising Republicans to Keynesian economists advising Democrats), the focus of monetary and fiscal policies changed in the 1960s from fighting inflation to avoiding a recession. (John F. Kennedy's administration marked the first time that strong Keynesians were in key positions on the Council of Economic Advisers.[1]) The result was that generally, up until 1969, monetary policy was expansionary. The economy remained in a sustained expansion through much of the 1960s.

During the early 1960s, fiscal policy was also somewhat expansionary. Then, in 1966–67, it became highly expansionary as the government attempted to fight a large war in Vietnam while simultaneously maintaining domestic programs such as President Lyndon Johnson's War on Poverty. By 1966 most economists, Keynesian as well as Classical, had concluded that significant inflationary pressures were developing, and that monetary and fiscal policies both needed tightening. Politically, the government didn't want to hear such advice. It's true that monetary policy was tightened for about six months in 1966, but then it was loosened again until 1969, by which time infla-

---

[1]Actually, during Harry S Truman's presidency (1945–53), economists sympathetic to Keynes were on the council, but they were primarily Roosevelt New Dealers rather than Keynesian economists.

ADDED DIMENSION   POLITICS AND ECONOMICS

The discussion of economic policy history touched only briefly on the politics of the decisions, but as you read through it I hope you were thinking of who was in office. If you didn't, it might be helpful to reconsider that history, taking into account the following information about the presidents and their parties, the chairmen of the Council of Economic Advisers and their political classifications, and the chairmen of the Fed and their political affiliations.

Thinking about this information should convince you that while, in theory, the differences between Classicals and Keynesians are substantial, in practice they are often blurred by politics.

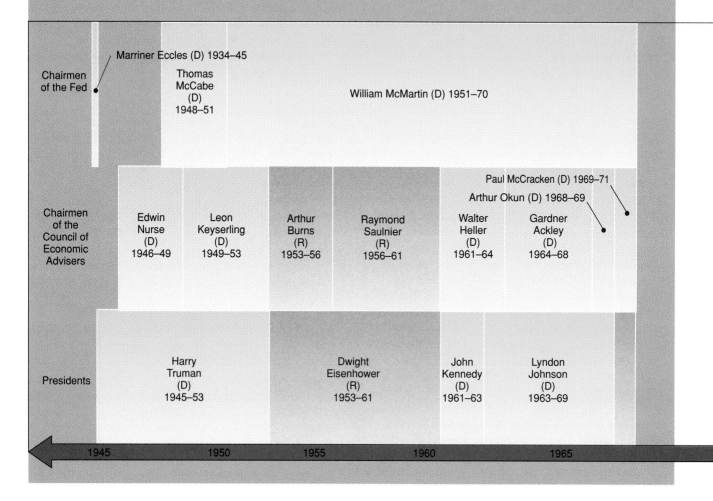

The 1968 tax increase and 1969 tight monetary policy both worked to slow down the economy. But about that same time, government war spending decreased. The result was a more contractionary fiscal policy than desired. Combined with a highly contractionary monetary policy, this policy led to a sudden braking of the economy which caused interest rates to rise to their highest levels in decades, leading to the 1969–70 recession. With this recession, the sustained expansion of the 1960s ended, as did economists' hopes of eliminating the business cycle with fine-tuning of monetary and fiscal policies.

tion had picked up significantly. Fiscal policy was even less responsive to economists' advice, and, for political reasons, fiscal policy remained highly stimulative until 1968, when the government instituted a 10 percent income tax surcharge.

The 1969 Recession and the 1970–73 Boom   Faced with a substantial economic downturn in 1969, the Fed acted relatively fast to reverse its policy to fight the recession. Since inflation hadn't yet responded to the tight monetary policy of 1969, fighting the recession required forgetting about using monetary policy to meet its inflation goals (which weren't being met anyway). Instead, the government instituted partial **wage and price controls** (*legal limits on prices and wages*).

Wage and price controls began in August 1971. The combination of price controls and expansionary monetary policy worked. In 1972, economic output increased significantly, and inflation stayed low. This significant monetary expansion right before a presidential election led some people to believe that Nixon and his economic advisers had learned a lesson from their 1960 election loss

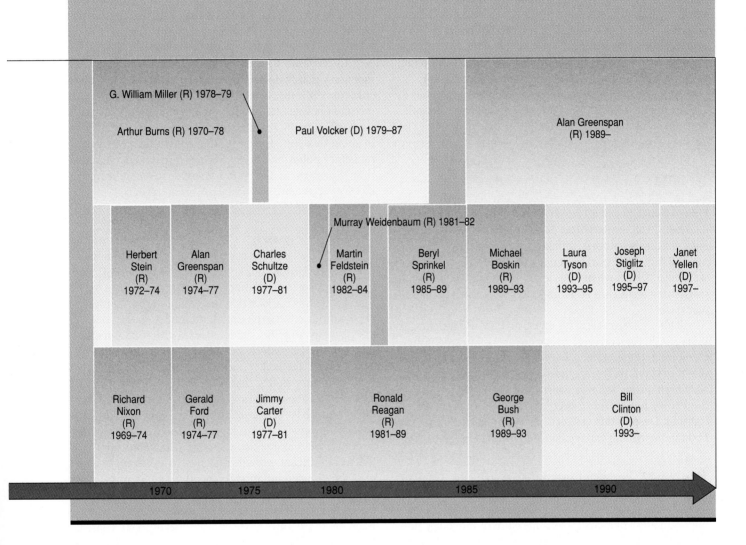

G. William Miller (R) 1978–79

Arthur Burns (R) 1970–78

Paul Volcker (D) 1979–87

Alan Greenspan (R) 1989–

Murray Weidenbaum (R) 1981–82

| Herbert Stein (R) 1972–74 | Alan Greenspan (R) 1974–77 | Charles Schultze (D) 1977–81 | Martin Feldstein (R) 1982–84 | Beryl Sprinkel (R) 1985–89 | Michael Boskin (R) 1989–93 | Laura Tyson (D) 1993–95 | Joseph Stiglitz (D) 1995–97 | Janet Yellen (D) 1997– |

| Richard Nixon (R) 1969–74 | Gerald Ford (R) 1974–77 | Jimmy Carter (D) 1977–81 | Ronald Reagan (R) 1981–89 | George Bush (R) 1989–93 | Bill Clinton (D) 1993– |

1970   1975   1980   1985   1990

when, as mentioned before, the economy went into a recession right before the election. You do not use contractionary monetary or fiscal policies right before a presidential election if you want to be reelected. In November 1972, President Nixon was reelected by a large majority.

Soon after the 1972 election, wage and price controls were loosened. Finally, in 1973, they were dismantled. The result was a significant increase in inflation which, by 1973, had reached 9 percent.

How much of this inflation was due to the removal of price controls and the expansionary monetary policy, and how much was due to exogenous supply price shocks, is a matter of debate between Keynesians and Classicals. Classicals argue that the inflation was primarily caused by the removal of price controls and the expansionary mone-

tary policy. Keynesians disagree, pointing out that three **supply price shocks**—*shocks that cause a rise in nominal wages and prices*—hit the economy during this period.

The first supply price shock concerned import prices. In 1972 and 1973, the U.S. economy had a fixed exchange rate with other major currencies, which meant that the U.S. government was committed to buying and selling currencies to maintain that fixed exchange rate whenever the quantity of dollars demanded didn't equal the quantity of dollars supplied. In 1971 the dollar was valued at a high relative exchange rate, imports significantly exceeded exports, and the United States had a significant balance of trade deficit. In response to that deficit, the United States and other countries agreed that the dollar would be devalued by 12 percent in December 1971. This raised import prices by 12 percent, causing a supply price shock.

The second supply price shock—the poor grain harvest of 1972—pushed up food prices. The third supply price shock—the Arab oil embargo—limited oil shipments to the United States and tripled the price of oil. Combined, these three supply price shocks caused significant inflationary pressure. They presented the Fed with a dilemma: either (1) expand the money supply, ratify the supply shock inflation, and allow other prices to rise in response, thereby avoiding a recession but building inflation into the economy, or (2) don't expand the money supply, trying to prevent the supply price shocks from being built into expectations of inflation, and risk recession.

Initially, the Fed expanded the money supply, but in 1973 it decided that it must do something about the inflation. It significantly tightened the money supply. The economy responded predictably and went into a recession.

The 1973–75 Recession The result of the tight monetary policy in 1973 was a severe recession, not only in the United States but in all major industrialized countries, as decreased U.S. imports had contractionary effects on foreign countries' exports. Inflation was reduced, but it remained high by historical standards. This recession lasted well into 1975, when the focus of policy once again shifted from concern about inflation to concern about the recession.

That concern led to an expansionary fiscal policy (a large 1975 tax cut) and expansionary monetary policy. Combined, these policies helped pull the economy out of the recession. Inflation, however, which had remained very high during the recession, grew even higher, causing the Fed serious concern over which problem it should be fighting. Despite this concern, through the late 1970s the Fed maintained an expansionary monetary policy.

The 1980–82 Recession-Expansion-Recession In October 1979, however, the Fed abruptly changed its focus from recession to inflation. At that point it also stopped focusing on interest rate targets as a measure of monetary policy, and announced that, henceforth, it would focus instead on the money supply.

The result was an enormous increase in short-term interest rates, which rose to more than 20 percent, and a sudden decrease in the money supply. In the short run, these policies had few effects upon inflation which, partly due to a second oil-price shock, had reached double digits in late 1979 and early 1980. But they significantly affected real output. In response to these measures the U.S. economy went into a large contraction. Industrial production fell by well over 10 percent.

In May 1980, the Fed moderated and backed off on its highly contractionary policy. In response, business activity picked up; by November 1980 the economy was in a major expansion. The expansion didn't take place soon enough for President Jimmy Carter. He was voted out of office partly because the public blamed him for the period's **stagflation** (*simultaneous high inflation and high unemployment*).

After the election, the concern changed from recession to inflation; the Fed tightened the money supply significantly. Again the interest rate rose to almost 20 percent, causing large decreases in spending on housing and consumer durables. By June 1981 the economy was deep into a recession. By November 1982, 12 million people were unemployed. The term *stagflation* was used with increasing frequency.

In response to this recession, both fiscal policy and monetary policy turned expansionary. On the fiscal policy side, in 1981 the United States enacted a major cut in income tax rates, although some of the effects of the cut were offset by increased Social Security taxes that kicked in about this same time. Simultaneously, the Fed loosened monetary policy and backed away from its strict monetary rule. Since then, the Fed has used an eclectic mix of money supply targets and interest rate targets.

The 1983–90 Expansion Combined, these expansionary policies helped pull the economy out of the recession. The 1981–82 recession, unlike the earlier one in 1980, had a major impact on inflationary expectations, and by the mid-1980s it was clear that the double-digit inflation and expectations of an exploding inflation rate had ended.

Exactly why this sudden decrease in inflation and inflationary expectations occurred is a matter of debate. Traditional Classical economists attributed it primarily to tight monetary policy that convinced people that the Fed was serious about fighting inflation. **Supply-side Classical economists**—*economists who strongly emphasize the short-run influence of economic incentives*—attributed it to cuts in the income tax rates that stimulated supply and led to significant growth. Keynesian economists attributed the reduced inflation to negative supply price shocks during this period: Oil prices fell, food and raw materials prices fell, and labor relations were relatively smooth. Each of these three explanations (traditional Classical, supply-side Classical, and Keynesian) probably captures part of the truth.

Whatever the cause, throughout this period employment was increasing substantially, inflation stayed low, and the U.S. economy seemed strong. But there were problems. The banking and financial system significantly overextended itself during this period, resulting in hundreds of billions of dollars of government-guaranteed loans which came due in 1989 and 1990. Additionally, both the U.S. trade deficit and government budget deficit remained high, creating serious potential long-term problems.

So the debate remains about this period: Was it a time of sustained positive growth, or was it merely a time in which a group of yuppies and rich people became richer while creating serious long-term problems for the United States?

Assessment of Policy   The history of macroeconomic policy since the 1930s should have given you a sense of the changing focus, the political difficulties of using the fiscal policy tool, and the shifting back and forth over concern about inflation and recession. A natural reaction to that history is that, in hindsight, the handling of monetary and fiscal policy leaves much to be desired.

Fiscal policy has often had the wrong effects at the right time, or the right effects at the wrong time, but it has seldom had the right effect at the right time. There wasn't much discussion of fiscal policy in this history because it hasn't been used much to try to direct the economy. That's why most of this history concerned monetary policy.

In its conduct of monetary policy, the Fed has seemed to switch goals from one moment to the next and to continually go too far in both directions. The result has been a stop-go set of policies, causing the economy to alternate between inflationary booms and recessions. This leads modern Classical economists to argue that the Fed's policies have lacked credibility. Keynesians emphasize, however, that such an assessment can only be made with hindsight. Given the knowledge available to policy makers and the political and institutional constraints under which they operate, many Keynesians believe that the past 50 years, while not pretty, are representative of about as good a macroeconomic policy as can be expected. In short, macroeconomics is an art, and art isn't always pretty or neat.

KEY TERMS

New Deal   *(440*
stagflation   *(444)*

supply price shock   *(443)*
supply-side Classical
   economists   *(444)*

Treasury Accord   *(441)*
wage and price controls   *(442)*

QUESTIONS FOR THOUGHT AND REVIEW

1. The experience with price controls during World War II demonstrates that price controls work. True or false? Why?
2. The experience of the New Deal suggests that economists' theoretical debates have little effect on government's real-world policies. True or false? Why?
3. Give three possible explanations for the increase in inflation in the 1970s.
4. What well-known policy change did the Fed implement in October 1979?
5. Give three possible explanations for the 1983–90 decrease in inflation.
6. How does a Classical supply-side economist differ from a traditional Classical economist?

CHAPTER

Eighteen

Structural Supply-Side Macro Policies

The ideas of economists and political philosophers, both when they are right and when they are wrong, are more powerful than is commonly understood. Indeed, the world is ruled by little else.

~ J. M. Keynes

After reading this chapter, you should be able to:

1 Distinguish a structural supply-side macro policy from a traditional macro policy.

2 List three general Classical laissez-faire structural supply-side policies.

3 Explain the debate about the Laffer curve.

4 Explain how reducing government spending can increase potential output and how increasing government spending can increase potential output.

5 Differentiate a Keynesian and a Classical view of the excess burden of taxes.

6 List three Keynesian activist structural supply-side policies.

7 Define activist industrial policy and discuss its advantages and disadvantages.

8 Explain how an incomes policy is supposed to work and how it often works in practice.

1 Structural supply-side macro policies are policies that increase the potential output the economy can achieve, thereby allowing a reduction in unemployment, by changing the structure of the economy and the incentives inherent in that structure.

Q-1: True or false: An increase in the structural deficit is an example of a structural supply-side policy.

If the majority of economists are correct in their belief that much of the unemployment Western economies are now facing is immune to expansionary monetary and fiscal policy, does that mean that macro policy has no place in modern economic policy? The answer is: No, not necessarily. A variety of alternative policies have been suggested to reduce unemployment and increase potential income beyond the level achievable with monetary and fiscal policy. Economists call these alternative policies *structural supply-side macro policies.* **Structural supply-side macro policies** are *policies that increase the potential output the economy can achieve.* They work by changing the structure of the economy and the incentives inherent in that structure.

A key characteristic of structural supply-side macro policies is that they can affect unemployment and equilibrium output of the economy, even if they have a fiscally neutral effect. That is, they work not through their effect on government spending, on the interest rate, or on the money supply, but through changing supply incentives directly. Because structural supply-side policies expand potential output, they allow the economy to grow; that growth decreases the budget deficit and creates jobs. Thus, structural supply-side policies offer the hope of having it all—growth,

EXHIBIT 2   The Laffer Curve

(a) The Laffer curve shows a proposed relationship between tax revenue and tax rates used to argue that lowering tax rates would increase tax revenue. At zero tax rate, revenue is zero. At 100 percent tax rate no one would supply labor or capital, so revenue would also be zero. Somewhere in between is a maximum revenue. The traditional Laffer curve shown in (a) implicitly assumed the point of maximum revenue would be at 50 percent. But that assumption was arbitrary. The point of maximum revenue could as well be that shown in (b), at 80 percent, or it could be at a lower tax rate—perhaps 25 percent.

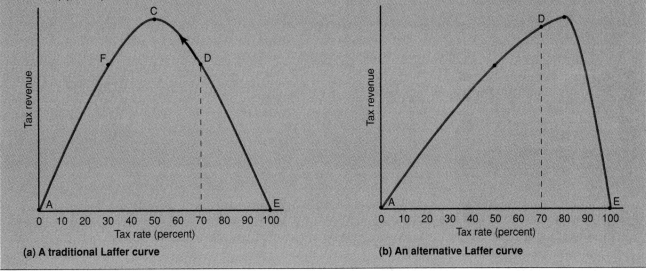

(a) A traditional Laffer curve   **(b) An alternative Laffer curve**

Now let's say that the economy is at point D with the tax rate at 70 percent. What happens if the government decreases the tax rate from 70 percent to 50 percent? The answer is: Tax revenues increase. So if the economy were at a point such as D, as supply-side advocates in the 1980s argued it was, cutting tax rates would increase tax revenues.

Do Tax Cuts Increase or Decrease the Budget Deficit?   In the 1980s the Laffer curve was a strong political prop which helped bring about tax reductions. Most economists, however, did not accept the conclusion that tax cuts would decrease the budget deficit, as the above example suggests they would. Why? The answer is that while there is nothing wrong with the logic, most economists questioned the specific shape that early advocates gave to the curve. They asked why the Laffer curve had the shape shown in Exhibit 2(a). Why wouldn't it have the shape shown in Exhibit 2(b)? The difference between the shapes of the two curves is the tax rate at which tax revenue starts falling. In Exhibit 2(a) tax revenue starts falling at a tax rate above 50 percent, which makes any tax rate above 50 percent have a cost in lost revenue. In Exhibit 2(b) tax revenue starts falling at a tax rate of 80 percent, which means that tax revenues increase up until tax rates hit 80 percent.

The point at which the Laffer curve peaks is important because it determines whether or not tax cuts from their current rates will increase the budget deficit. If the economy is at a 70 percent tax rate (point D) in the traditional Laffer curve (Exhibit 2(a)), it is beyond the point of maximum revenue; tax cuts will stimulate the economy and increase revenue. In the alternative Laffer curve point D is below the point of maximum revenue, and a decrease in tax rates decreases tax revenue, and hence increases the budget deficit.

So where is the U.S. economy on the Laffer curve? That is impossible to answer because the discussion of these issues quickly becomes time and tax specific. The reason is that economic incentives take time to work, and the long-run incentive effects of a tax cut are generally much stronger than are the short-run incentive effects. But the Laffer curve has no time dimension and thus does not distinguish between short-run and long-run effects.

Moreover, one cannot just talk about some ambiguous tax cut. One must talk about specific tax cuts: Each tax has its own incentive effect and its own point of

The Laffer curve is an empirical curve. Its shape and where the economy is on the curve are matters of debate.

I sometimes ask students to explain how they think tax rates affect their behavior.

maximum revenue. For example, a cut in a state business income tax could have enormous effects in attracting business from other states. The same business income tax cut on the national level would have much smaller effects.

The above complications made much of the discussion about the Laffer curve unfruitful. Laffer curve supporters and opponents had in the backs of their minds different taxes and different time periods. If, however, the reference was to the federal income tax and the time period was the immediate short run (i.e., the year following the tax cut), then most economists felt that the economy would be on the upward-sloping part of the Laffer curve and lower income tax rates would decrease tax revenue and increase the deficit. And that is what happened in the 1980s—tax revenues fell and the budget deficit increased when tax rates were lowered from a maximum rate of about 70 percent to a maximum rate of about 36 percent.

3 Much of the discussion of the Laffer curve has been unfruitful because that discussion has not made clear what time dimension or specific tax one is talking about.

THE BROADER QUESTION ABOUT TAX CUTS

None of the above arguments tells us whether lowering income tax rates was a good or bad idea—there are many different views on that issue. Even if a cut in tax rates increases deficits in the short run, in the long run most economists agree that a tax cut can stimulate growth, and thereby increase tax revenue higher than it otherwise would have been. Moreover, simply because a tax reduction will increase the budget deficit in the short run does not mean that tax reduction isn't a good policy. Whether it is good policy depends on the entire set of effects that the tax cuts bring about.

To make a judgment about whether a tax cut makes sense or not requires a much broader range of judgments than simply what happens to tax revenue. For example, many Classical economists see tax rate cuts as a way of forcing the government to face decisions that it otherwise would not face. They believe that, in the absence of tax cuts, government programs are not closely scrutinized. Thus, most Classical economists support this tax rate cut policy as the best way to increase potential output and allow the economy to grow, if it is used in combination with a reduction in government spending, much of which they think is wasteful and some of which has negative incentive effects of its own.

Q–3:   Tax cuts increase budget deficits and therefore should be avoided. True or false? Why?

Reduce Government Social Welfare Spending

In a pure capitalist economy, to get anything you must work—no work, no eat. As I discussed in earlier chapters, the United States is far from a pure capitalist economy; it has been modified by numerous social programs that allow people to eat when they have not worked. Classical economists argue that these social welfare programs have reduced people's incentive to work, and have thereby reduced our economy's potential income. By reducing these social welfare programs we can increase people's incentive to work, and thereby increase the economy's potential income.

The general argument of how a reduction in **need-based social welfare programs**—*social welfare programs in which eligibility is determined by need*—will increase potential income goes as follows: much of government social welfare spending is need-based: the greater one's need, the more one gets. This tie-in between need and how much one gets from social welfare programs creates perverse incentives: people have an incentive to appear needy so that they receive the benefits of the social welfare programs.

To see this, let's look at the incentives of individuals to work in relation to these need-based programs. Say you get a need-based payment of $700 a month if you have no income, but you receive a need-based payment of only $100 a month if you already have an income of $700 a month. You are trying to decide whether or not to take a job that pays $7 per hour for 25 hours per week (100 hours per month). Your income at that rate of pay would be $700 a month. But your incremental income (the net after you take into account the $600 reduction in your need-based payment) is only $100 per month, or $1 per hour! This gives you little incentive to take the job, and a large incentive to work "off the books," taking a job where you are paid cash, or where you get "in kind" pay. The implicit tax rate on your wage is almost 86 percent.

4a Social welfare programs can reduce people's incentive to work, thereby decreasing potential output.

Need-based social welfare programs *Social welfare programs in which eligibility is determined by need.*

Q–4   In what way do need-based social welfare programs create perverse incentives?

This is a good place to discuss the recent reform in U.S. welfare laws.

TRADITIONAL KEYNESIAN AND CLASSICAL EXPLANATIONS OF THE EFFECTS OF A TAX CUT   **ADDED DIMENSION**

We can see the theoretical difference between the Keynesian traditional explanations and Classical supply-side explanations of how a tax cut affects the economy by considering the following thought experiment: Assume the government replaced the income tax (a tax in which the total amount a person pays changes with the amount of income she earns) with a poll tax (a tax in which the total amount an individual pays is constant regardless of his income). Also assume that the poll tax generated as much revenue as the income tax, and that the proportion of money spent on consumption was equal for all income groups. What would be the effect on the aggregate economy?

Classical supply-siders would say that the aggregate output would increase enormously since the reward for additional work would be increased significantly. For Classical supply-siders, a cut in tax rates, not a cut in tax revenues, is what stimulates the economy.

A traditional Keynesian would say that a shift from an income tax to a poll tax would have no effect on the economy. Why? Because tax revenues wouldn't change; only the method of assessing the taxes would change. In the traditional Keynesian model, it is the amount of tax collected, not the tax rate, that affects the economy. A change in the tax rates, tax revenue remaining constant, would have no effect.

In reality, tax revenues are almost invariably changed by changing tax rates, so the effect of a tax cut is difficult to discover, which is why there is so much debate about which side is right.

Your net increase in income is only an additional $1 an hour out of each $7 an hour, which means you lose 86 cents out of each additional dollar earned. This is the basic irony of all need-based programs—they discourage work effort, and create incentives for people to become needy.

Many need-based programs are structured in this way, and hence they embody a strong incentive not to work, or at least to work "off the books." By eliminating these programs or, at least, by significantly restructuring such programs, government can ensure that more people will choose to work more. Potential output can be increased by cutting government spending. The downside is that if many of these programs were eliminated, individuals who were genuinely and unavoidably in need would get less help.

Many need-based programs involve an incentive to appear needy and to avoid accepting a job.

Reduce Government Regulation

The third general laissez-faire policy to increase potential output is to reduce regulation. For example, to start a business in the United States, one must go through an enormous amount of bureaucracy and red tape. Often one must get an environmental impact study and follow rigid regulations. The complicated regulatory system discourages new businesses and the jobs they create. Streamlining, modifying, or eliminating many of these regulations will encourage the starting of more businesses; there will be more competition, and potential output will increase.

You were introduced to one example of the impact of regulations on business in the appendix to Chapter 5 when we considered the starting of the Vermont Country Kitchen. There we saw how the owners had to plow through enormous regulations simply to start a small business, and how they reduced its size to meet the regulations. And that was a small business—as businesses get bigger the regulations become more complex, and to avoid dealing with these regulations the incentive not to expand becomes greater.

Let's consider some other examples. Say you want to start a business in an old building. Before you can do so, you had better check whether the old building is registered as a historic landmark. If it is, you cannot renovate the building unless you get permission from government authorities. You also better check whether any endangered species are living in the building or on its grounds. If they are, regulations prevent you from endangering their habitat by starting a business there.

EXHIBIT 3   The Regulated Hamburger

These kinds of U.S. regulations have been applied to restaurant hamburgers in the past. Today although the regulations have been modified they have not necessarily been simplified or reduced.

Source: *US. News & World Report*

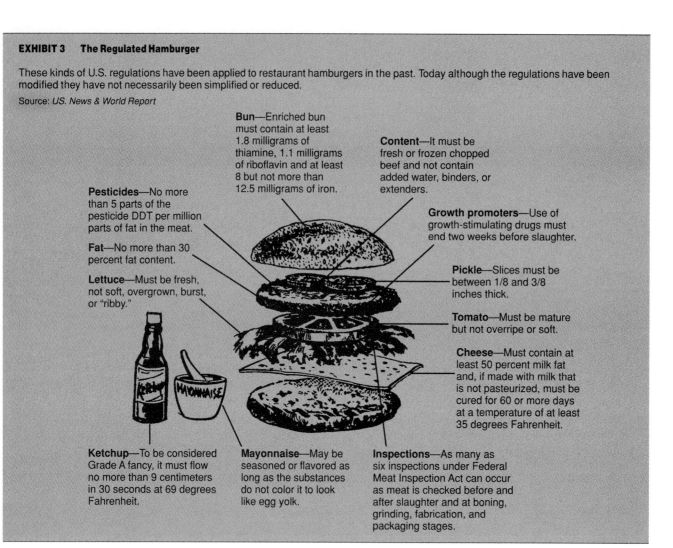

Bun—Enriched bun must contain at least 1.8 milligrams of thiamine, 1.1 milligrams of riboflavin and at least 8 but not more than 12.5 milligrams of iron.

Content—It must be fresh or frozen chopped beef and not contain added water, binders, or extenders.

Pesticides—No more than 5 parts of the pesticide DDT per million parts of fat in the meat.

Fat—No more than 30 percent fat content.

Lettuce—Must be fresh, not soft, overgrown, burst, or "ribby."

Growth promoters—Use of growth-stimulating drugs must end two weeks before slaughter.

Pickle—Slices must be between 1/8 and 3/8 inches thick.

Tomato—Must be mature but not overripe or soft.

Cheese—Must contain at least 50 percent milk fat and, if made with milk that is not pasteurized, must be cured for 60 or more days at a temperature of at least 35 degrees Fahrenheit.

Ketchup—To be considered Grade A fancy, it must flow no more than 9 centimeters in 30 seconds at 69 degrees Fahrenheit.

Mayonnaise—May be seasoned or flavored as long as the substances do not color it to look like egg yolk.

Inspections—As many as six inspections under Federal Meat Inspection Act can occur as meat is checked before and after slaughter and at boning, grinding, fabrication, and packaging stages.

Classical economists believe our economy is over-regulated and that reducing regulation would cause potential output to increase.

You also better check whether that particular building is zoned for your new use. For example a restaurant in my town closed, and a young couple bought it, wanting to reopen it. Unfortunately, the restaurant had been closed for more than one year, which meant the preexisting use zoning that the original restaurant had was voided, and having a restaurant there would no longer be allowed. Luckily for the couple, the Board of Zoning Adjustment (of which I'm a member) found a loophole which allowed them to open, but otherwise they would have been out of luck.

Exhibit 3 gives a visual sense of how pervasive regulations are in our economy. It provides a listing of some of the more than 41,000 regulations that governed the process of transforming the raw materials into a hamburger in the 1980s.

There are many more examples of the ways in which regulations decrease output, but these should give you a good idea of the Classical view of how regulations decrease potential output. Now, no Classical economist is saying that all these regulations should be eliminated—many serve useful functions—but what Classical economists are saying is that many of the existing regulations can be modified and streamlined, and doing so will cause potential output to increase.

Specific Classical Laissez-Faire Structural Policies

Let's now consider some specific examples of Classical structural policies that have been proposed either in the United States or in other countries.

Reduce Payroll Tax   Reducing payroll taxes has been advocated in Europe where, because the incentives embodied in taxes and social programs are so substantial, the

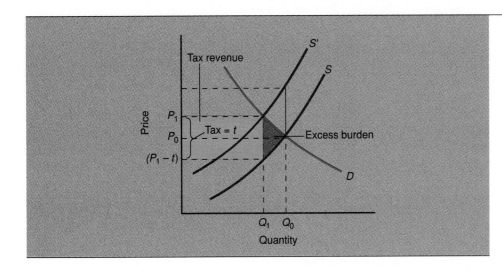

EXHIBIT 4   Keynesian and Classical Views of the Excess Burden of a Tax

A tax decreases output from Q_0 to Q_1; it increases the price consumers pay from P_0 to P_1 and it decreases the price suppliers receive from P_0 to $P_1 - t$. All economists agree that a tax creates an excess burden equal to the red triangle. Classicals see the tax revenue of the government (the blue rectangle) as additional excess burden. Keynesians see it as a transfer and, thus, not an excess burden.

economy's potential income seems to be consistent with a 10 percent unemployment rate. To see why, consider the case of Germany. Germany's payroll tax approaches 50 percent of the wage. That means that when a firm hires a person for, say, 10 marks per hour, that worker costs the firm 15 marks per hour. The higher price that the firm must pay for labor makes it far more likely that the firm will decide to produce elsewhere—say in Mexico where not only is the wage lower, but so, too, are the taxes. If Germany reduces its payroll tax, it will reduce the incentive for firms to move jobs from Germany to Mexico. Thus, reducing the level of payroll taxes is an example of a specific structural macro policy that will reduce unemployment.

Of course, in distinguishing the supply-side effect from the demand-side effect, it is necessary to keep the tax cut revenue-neutral. One can do this by offsetting a tax cut with a tax increase in some other sector of the economy, or by cutting government spending. Both might have offsetting effects that must be considered when determining the net effect of a specific tax cut.

Most Classical economists would agree that increasing other taxes will have significant negative offsetting effects that will make the net effect of the policy weak. But Classical economists do not argue that other taxes should be increased in order to keep a tax cut revenue-neutral. Instead, they argue that cutting government spending is the appropriate choice. For a Classical economist a cut in government spending will have little offsetting effect on production.

Exhibit 4 shows the standard supply and demand curves with taxes, and contrasts the two different views of Classical laissez-faire economists on the effects of taxes.

All economists agree that taxes raise equilibrium price and reduce equilibrium quantity, and that these taxes involve what is called an **excess burden**—*a loss to consumers and producers that is not gained by anyone else.* All economists also agree that that excess burden includes the red triangle in Exhibit 4. The disagreement concerns the tax revenue resulting from the tax, shown by the blue rectangle. In the Keynesian activist view, this government tax revenue is used to support government programs and therefore this tax revenue is more valuable to the people who benefit from the programs than it was to the people who paid the tax. Thus, the blue rectangle represents a transfer of resources and is not a burden to society. A Classical laissez-faire economist would disagree. In the laissez-faire view, this tax revenue is, to a large degree, wasted. Thus, the blue rectangle should be counted as a burden to society, as well as the red triangle.

In fact, for Classical economists some of the tax revenue is used for purposes that are worse than wasting it—it is used to support spending programs that reduce individuals' desire to work. To the degree that a cut in taxes eliminates social welfare programs, it will increase individuals' desire to work, and to the degree that it transfers workers from the unproductive government sector to the productive private sector, it

Classical economists favor cutting taxes and simultaneously cutting government spending.

5 Classicals see a much bigger excess burden of taxation than Keynesians do, because they see the revenue from taxation as being wasted; Keynesians see it as being transferred to more productive uses.

Excess burden *A loss to consumers and producers that is not gained by anyone else.*

Q–5: What is the difference between the Keynesian and Classical views of government spending?

will increase the economy's productivity—real output per worker will increase. So, by cutting the payroll tax, and accompanying that cut with cuts in social welfare spending, government can cause the economy to win two ways: (1) in cutting taxes, it will increase private employment, and (2) in cutting government spending, further increases in employment will be gained.

Some Classical supply-side structural policies are: (1) cutting taxes; (2) reducing unemployment benefits; and (3) eliminating the minimum wage.

Reduce Benefits to the Unemployed   A second specific policy that has been advocated by some Classical laissez-faire economists is to reduce the benefits of unemployment insurance. To see the effect of unemployment insurance benefit payments on unemployment, put yourself in the place of the worker who has been laid off. That worker must decide whether to look, or how hard to look, for another job. Should she move to find another job or take a job in a different industry or area? If the worker had no income after becoming unemployed, the worker would probably be rather flexible in the type job she would accept, and quite active in searching for another job. The worker would likely take another job relatively quickly, even if it meant moving and accepting a substantial cut in pay.

Unemployment benefits reduce an unemployed worker's incentive to find another job.

With the government providing an unemployment insurance check for 50 to 60 percent of the previous wage each month—up to about $1,500 per month, as is the case in Germany—the worker will probably be far less flexible in the type of job she will accept. She will be tempted to follow another strategy—collecting the unemployment benefits for as long as she can, reducing her consumption expenditures by, say, 20 percent, and making up the difference by borrowing and dipping into savings. Thus, she could keep almost the same lifestyle, at least for as long as the benefits and borrowing power hold out. Classicals claim that it is precisely such liberal social benefit policies that have led to the high unemployment rate in Europe, and point out that in the United States, where policies are much less liberal, unemployment rates, and duration of unemployment, are lower.

For a discussion of the distinction between voluntary and involuntary unemployment (is there one?), see "Unemployment Policy," by Robert Lucas in Classic Readings in Economics.

If the government cut those benefits, it would increase the likelihood that the worker would find another job quickly. Thus, cutting and modifying benefits given to unemployed workers is another type of macro structural policy. By cutting payroll taxes, and by cutting benefits given to unemployed workers, the government can have a fiscally neutral policy that will reduce unemployment on both the tax and the expenditure sides.

Eliminating the minimum wage would increase the quantity of labor demanded and reduce the quantity of labor supplied. It would reduce unemployment.

Eliminate Minimum Wage   A third specific structural macro policy that is often discussed as a way of reducing unemployment is lowering, or eliminating, the minimum wage. The way in which the minimum wage will reduce unemployment can be seen in Exhibit 5.

In it you can see how the minimum wage, W_{min}, set above the equilibrium wage, W_e, increases the gap between the quantity of labor supplied and the quantity demanded, and thereby creates unemployment equal to $Q_s - Q_d$.

There is enormous debate about the degree to which the elimination of the minimum wage would reduce unemployment, but all agree that eliminating it would increase employment.

The Political Problem of Laissez-Faire Policies

Many social programs were instituted for reasons of fairness. Eliminating them might increase output but also eliminate the positive contributions those programs were making to fairness or other social goals.

Most economists would agree that to varying degrees each of the Classical proposals put forward would increase potential output and allow the economy to grow and expand. But most people also recognize that there are social costs of doing so. Government social spending and regulation came about because of problems in society. There were people in need whom society wanted to help and there were abuses and externalities in private relations that government wanted to prevent. By giving the programs up, one is eliminating not only the negative effects, but also the positive effects of these policies.

Consider the minimum wage. The Classical argument focused on the employment loss caused by the minimum wage. It did not take into account the potential benefits from establishing a minimum wage. The simple argument for the minimum

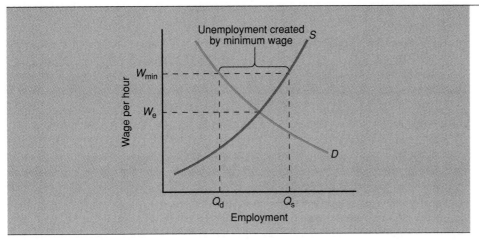

EXHIBIT 5   The Minimum Wage

Classicals argue that eliminating the minimum wage would reduce unemployment and increase the economy's potential output. At the market wage W_e, firms would hire more workers and the unemployment created by the minimum wage $Q_s - Q_d$ would be eliminated.

wage is that it transfers income to those who need it. It can be supported for that reason even if it raises unemployment. That is why in 1996 the U.S. raised the minimum wage with broad support from both Democrats and Republicans.

In short, in making the decision whether any of the above are desirable policies, one must weigh the good and the bad, judging each policy separately on its specific characteristics. But that individual judging is often subject to enormous political pressure and, in today's economy, many economists are skeptical that the political structure arrives at reasonable decisions. So while, theoretically, laissez-faire policies offer significant advantages, politically, the policies that get through often are not the policies that Classical laissez-faire economists advocate.

KEYNESIAN ACTIVIST STRUCTURAL POLICIES

Compared to Classical policies, Keynesian proposals for supply-side structural policies are more varied, and the reasoning behind them more complicated. Much of the difference comes from their alternative underlying visions of how competition works in an economy. Classicals tend to see a unidimensional ranking of economies as more or less competitive, depending on the level of government involvement—less government involvement means a more competitive economy. Keynesians see a much more complicated relationship between competitiveness and government involvement.

Keynesians see regulation as a necessary part of a functioning economy.

Specifically, Keynesians see regulation as a necessary part of a functioning economy. In their view removing regulations can cause the economy to function worse—removing regulation can reduce potential output. Similarly with tax decreases. Keynesians tend to see taxes as achieving important equity goals and as a necessary part of a functioning economy. Taxes determine who bears the burden of the costs of government, and any cuts in taxes, unless they are structured to benefit primarily the poor, reduce that role. Keynesians argue that an economy with zero taxes would have a very low potential income because it would have no government structure holding it all together.

Consistent with this view, one general set of Keynesian supply-side structural proposals—which might be called *productivity-enhancing social spending* and *productivity-enhancing regulatory programs*—focuses, not on cutting social programs and regulations, as do the Classical proposals, but on modifying them, improving the positive aspects of the programs while eliminating the negative aspects.

6 Three Keynesian structural supply-side policies are: (1) productivity-enhancing regulatory reforms; (2) activist industrial policies; and (3) incomes policies.

The other two general sets of proposals are variations of active cooperation among government, businesses, and households. These proposals increase government's role in the economy. They involve government, business, and labor working together to achieve better results and higher productivity. One of these new sets of proposals, called *activist industrial policies,* focuses on establishing a positive relationship between government and business to further their mutual benefit.

A third set of proposals are *incomes policies*—polices which hold down wages and prices directly, and thereby lessen the need to have unemployment to hold them down. Let's consider each briefly.

Productivity-Enhancing Social Spending and Regulatory Programs

Let's first consider the arguments Keynesians put forward to support their contention that the correct social programs and regulations can increase the economy's potential income. Consider, for example, welfare programs. Keynesians argue that, appropriately designed, welfare programs help maintain social order and cohesion. They prevent people from starving, and from being too weak to work. They reduce crime. All these effects increase productivity and the economy's potential income. Welfare programs that accomplish these ends are called **productivity-enhancing social welfare programs**—*social welfare programs designed to increase potential output.*

Say that the government cut expenditures on welfare programs. Those welfare cuts could leave some of those on welfare with no alternative but to resort to crime, increasing costs for legitimate businesses. The cuts could also lead to significant social and political unrest, and possibly rioting, making economic activity impossible. So even if one does not support social programs for their equity aspects, one can support them on selfish grounds for their ability to increase potential output.

To Keynesians many of the social welfare programs that Classicals see as waste are actually investments in the future. For example, consider the food stamp program, which provides vouchers for food for individuals whose income falls below a certain level. Without that food their nutrition falls, their performance in school or at work falls, and their health suffers. As a result, they are less productive students or workers now and in the future.

Thus, ironically, Keynesians see as supply-enhancing some of the same social spending programs that Classicals see as supply-decreasing government programs. Keynesians do not deny that the taxes to pay for these programs have some negative incentive effects, but their view is that the supply-enhancing effects of social spending programs often outweigh the negative incentive effects.

The same argument can be used for regulatory policies that were so maligned by many Classicals, as I discussed above. In the absence of these regulatory policies some firms would produce goods that are unsafe and will kill or injure consumers. For example, before it became regulated the pesticide DDT was widely used, creating health problems for many people. Similarly with lead-based paint, which can cause serious brain damage to young children. In the absence of regulation it is likely that such long-run damages would be taken less into account than they are now.

The above justification for certain social spending programs and regulations makes appropriate government supply-side structural policy far less certain than it is in the Classical view. One cannot simply cut social and regulatory programs and expect that the economy's productivity will increase. One must cut the negative aspects of the programs, and keep the positive aspects. Unfortunately, often, the supply-enhancing and supply-reducing aspects of the programs are intertwined and highly political, making the practical application of this reasonable approach impossible.

4b Social welfare programs can increase peoples' nutrition, and increase society's social cohesion, thereby increasing potential output.

Q-6: Explain how increasing spending on social welfare programs can increase potential income.

The very same programs Classical economists see as reducing potential output are seen by Keynesians as supply-enhancing.

Activist Industrial Policy

7 An activist industrial policy is a policy under which the government works directly with businesses, providing funds, background research, and encouragement to specific industries. It has serious potential political problems.

The second general type of activist structural policy that has been proposed is an industrial policy. An **industrial policy** is *the formal policy that government takes toward business.* In actual fact, the United States has always had, and always will have, an industrial policy—it is embodied in the laws and antitrust policy of the government. An **activist industrial policy** is *a policy under which the government works directly with businesses,* providing funds, background research, and encouragement to specific industries in order to keep a country internationally competitive. Keynesian advocates claim that if the United States introduced such a policy there would be large gains from cooperation and increased international competitiveness as funds are channeled to high-growth industries, increasing the United States's potential output.

Export-Encouraging Partnerships of Government and Business   One of the aspects of an industrial policy that has received much attention in the United States is a government partnership with business to encourage exports. A laissez-faire position is that exports take care of themselves. The activist position is that other invisible forces play a major role in determining exports. Thus, active government involvement is necessary to encourage and expand exports. This includes **strategic trade policy,** by which *one country threatens to retaliate unless other countries reduce their explicit and implicit trade barriers.* Let me give two examples.

Strategic trade policy Where one country threatens to retaliate unless other countries reduce their explicit and implicit trade barriers.

In 1996 China allowed Chinese businesses to copy or "pirate" U.S. software and CDs. Since the pirating firms did not have to pay any development cost, they could sell the software and CDs at a much lower cost than U.S. firms could, hurting production and employment in the United States. (For example, Windows 95 software sold in China for $4 while in the U.S. it sold for over $100.) In response the United States threatened China with $2 billion of tariffs on Chinese goods. These tariffs were to go into effect if China did not stop the illegal production of the CDs and software. At the last minute the U.S. and China came to an agreement and avoided the fight.

Q-7: Explain how strategic trade policy might go wrong.

Government-led economic missions are another example. Top government officials frequently travel abroad with CEOs from business to meet with their foreign counterparts, in an effort to establish opportunities to export U.S. goods. It was on such an economic mission that former U.S. Commerce Secretary Ronald Brown and a number of U.S. CEOs were killed in a plane crash in 1996.

The Example of Japan's MITI   Advocates of an activist U.S. industrial policy point to **MITI**—*Japan's Ministry of International Trade and Industry, which guides Japan's activist industrial policy*—as an example of how an activist industrial policy can work. MITI is credited by these advocates with engineering Japan's economic growth over the past 40 years (although how successful MITI was is debatable). MITI worked closely with Japanese companies to improve their competitiveness. The ministry provided money and research, and saw to it that companies focused on international, rather than domestic, competition. It smoothed the flow of capital to certain industries it wanted to promote, such as the electronics industry. It did this by taking such measures as consulting with banks and encouraging loans. MITI would say, "So-and-So is a good company," and that statement was a code to banks that they should approve So-and-So's loan application.

MITI Japan's Ministry of International Trade and Industry, which guides Japan's activist industry policy.

Q-8: What is MITI, and what is its relevance to structural supply-side policies?

Questions about an Activist Industrial Policy   Japan's activist industrial policy success did not come without problems. Its activism involved government in business decisions. This opened up significant possibilities for graft. In the late 1980s and 1990s, a number of major scandals erupted in Japan when it was revealed that Japanese corporations had given many politicians in the ruling Liberal Democratic Party options to buy stock in the companies at low prices.

Such problems are likely to arise under any activist industrial policy. Because government decisions can mean a difference of hundreds of millions of dollars to firms, companies will inevitably spend money to influence those decisions, either legally through lobbying or illegally through bribery and graft. The exposure of the scandals in Japan has already changed the composition of its elected ruling party. Whether the scandals will change Japan's industrial policy remains to be seen.

Critics of an activist industrial policy also argue that Japan's success came not as a result of MITI and its activist industrial policy, but in spite of it. They point out that MITI's strategy was to develop a number of industries that, as it turned out, did not succeed in the international competitive market. These critics argue that it was only skillful decision making on the part of private firms that finessed MITI's inappropriate directives and allowed those firms to follow other paths, and that it was these firms' actions that ultimately led to MITI's success. The available information is contradictory, and the debate is likely to continue through the next decade.

Critics argue that Japan's success came, not as a result of MITI, but in spite of it.

While the United States has never had an activist industrial policy like Japan's, it has developed a **military-industrial complex**—*a close connection among the armed forces, the industries that manufacture weapons, and members of Congress from states and districts that depend heavily on the defense industry.* This relationship of mutual benefit is an activist relationship in that it involves government in the decisions of privately owned defense manufacturers.

This involvement often prevents government from making tough economic choices. For example, in 1989 Congress seemed about to cut production of the B-2 Stealth bomber. Northrup, the plane's manufacturer, took out full-page newspaper ads, pointing out that parts of the B-2 were produced in 48 states and that thousands of jobs would be lost if the government canceled the contract. Congress gave in, as it has done on many other defense items that are widely regarded as nonessential to national security.

With the ending of the Cold War in the early 1990s, many have felt that defense spending could be cut substantially. But whenever specific cuts have been suggested, the military-industrial complex has fought hard against them.

Targeted Employment Subsidy Policies

Targeted Employment Subsidy Policies   An example of the type of specific government supply-side structural policy that the Keynesian activist view leads to is a policy that enjoys a fair amount of political support, especially from Keynesians, in Europe. This policy is a targeted employment subsidy for low-wage workers. A **targeted employment subsidy policy** is *a policy in which government pays business to hire specific groups of workers.* The reasoning in support of this policy is the same as the reasoning used by Classicals to support the payroll tax reduction. An employment subsidy encourages firms to hire targeted workers rather than to transfer their production activities abroad.

A typical employment subsidy plan that has been proposed would be that all firms that hire a worker at, say, below a wage of 16 marks an hour will receive a subsidy of, say, 10 marks, so the actual cost of the worker is the 6 marks in direct costs and 8 marks in indirect payroll tax cost, or 14 marks. Thus the unemployment subsidy is essentially the equivalent of a targeted payroll tax reduction.

What has not received much political support in Europe is a fiscally neutral payroll subsidy—that is, a payroll subsidy financed by a tax increase. The problem is that any tax that finances it has efficiency costs of its own, and creates a political group strongly against it—the group that will have to pay the tax.

Should the United States Adopt an Activist Industrial Policy?

Should the United States Adopt an Activist Industrial Policy?   Any time economic decisions are made on a political basis, waste is inevitable. It's the cost of an activist industrial policy in a democratic government. But there are also benefits. Competition can be wasteful, especially in research. That's why scientific conventions (rules limiting scientists' behavior) exist that support openness and sharing of scientific knowledge. Cooperation by firms with government and universities can lead to more productive research.

Even with the problem of wasteful defense spending, the United States has maintained a technological lead in aerospace in large part because of the government's support for that industry. Some economists have argued that the United States wouldn't have remained highly competitive without the defense industry's close connection with, and subsidies by, the government. As with every decision in economics, there are both costs and benefits.

In weighing these costs and benefits, a majority of economists come out on the side of opposing an activist industrial policy for the United States. This includes most conservative economists who generally oppose activist government policies plus a number of liberal economists who are concerned about the politics of an industrial policy. They believe that a formal activist industrial policy would probably lead to

Nineteen
Deficits and Debt

Any government, like any family, can for a year spend a little more than it earns. But you and I know that a continuance of that habit means the poorhouse.

~ Franklin D. Roosevelt

After reading this chapter, you should be able to:

1 Define the terms *deficit* and *debt*.

2 State why economists focus on financial health rather than on deficits.

3 Explain why, in an expanding economy, a government can run a limited, but continual, deficit without serious concern about the consequences.

4 Differentiate between a real deficit and a nominal deficit.

5 Explain why, even though the real budget deficit of the United States is much lower than the nominal deficit, there is still reason for concern about the deficit.

6 Explain why there are alternative reasonable views about the deficit.

In our discussion of macroeconomic policies and problems, two concepts come up continually: deficits and debt. Is the U.S. budget deficit something we have to worry about? Is the $5 trillion U.S. government debt going to be an unbearable burden on our grandchildren? These and similar questions are sufficiently important to warrant a separate chapter that explores the government budget deficit and debt.

Before we begin the exploration, let's briefly consider the definitions. A **deficit** is *a shortfall of revenues under payments;* it is a flow concept. If your income (revenues) is $20,000 per year and your expenditures (payments) are $30,000 per year, you are running a deficit. If revenues exceed payments, you are running a surplus. This means that a *government budget deficit* occurs when government expenditures exceed government revenues.

Debt is *accumulated deficits minus accumulated surpluses;* it is a stock concept. For example, say you've spent $30,000 a year for 10 years and have had annual income of $20,000 for 10 years. So you've had a deficit of $10,000 per year. At the end of 10 years, you will have accumulated a debt of $100,000:

$$10 \times \$10,000 = \$100,000.$$

(Spending more than you have in income means that you need to borrow the extra $10,000 per year from someone, so in later years much of your expenditure will be on interest on your previous debt.)

1 A deficit is a shortfall of incoming revenue under outgoing payments. A debt is accumulated deficits minus accumulated surpluses.

There are various measures of U.S. government debt, depending on how one includes U.S. government trust funds and Federal Reserve holdings. These measures of the U.S. debt can vary.

Deficit is a flow concept; debt is a stock concept.

Remember that large deficits have become so routine during the lifetimes of most students that the numbers on the deficit and the debt have lost some of their meaning. I like to spend some extra time covering the historical data to demonstrate that large deficits and rapidly growing federal debts are a relatively recent phenomenon.

U.S. GOVERNMENT DEFICITS AND DEBT: THE HISTORICAL RECORD

Video Series, Economics USA: Federal Deficit, Segments 12.1-12.3.

Policy Régimes, the Deficit, and the Debt

For a real-world example of the political-budget nexus and its effect on policy regimes in Japan, see "In Japan, It Takes a Lot of Sashimi to Build a Budget," in *Case Studies in Macroeconomics.*

The adoption of Keynesian policies—using deficits to stimulate the economy—in the late 1940s has led to nearly continual budget deficits ever since the end of World War II.

Q–1: In the 1980s, when the United States changed to a modern Classical supply-side policy régime, what happened to the size of the deficit?

Let's begin with a consideration of the historical record of deficits in the United States. Exhibit 1(a) graphs the U.S. budget deficits since 1945. As you can see, for many years the U.S. budget has been significantly in deficit. But that hasn't always been the case. Before the 1940s, the U.S. government ran a budget surplus sometimes (mainly in peacetime) and a budget deficit at other times (mainly during wartime). After World War II—that is, after 1945—that changed, and since that time the United States has run consistent deficits.

Because debt is accumulated deficits, and the United States has a deficit almost every year, you would expect United States debt to have increased substantially since World War II. Exhibit 1(b) shows that is indeed the case.

Why was there a change after World War II? A reason many economists suggest is the change in macroeconomic **policy régimes**—*the general set of rules that governs the monetary and fiscal policies that a country follows*—that occurred after World War II.

The big difference in policy régimes before and after World War II was the introduction of Keynesian economics and its use of discretionary fiscal policy. Before World War II, Classical economics dictated that government budget deficits were bad and that, except in wartime, they should be avoided. And that was the policy the U.S. government followed. That was changed by Keynesian economics that prescribed deficits to stimulate the economy and achieve a higher level of output. According to Keynesian economics, deficits were not necessarily bad. You had to look at the state of the economy to decide whether a deficit was good or bad.

Because Keynesian economics removed the stigma connected with deficits, some economists argue that government budget deficits are the result of Keynesian policies. Others argue that view is too simplistic. They point out that Keynesian economics never said that all deficits are good—it only said that deficits aren't necessarily bad, and when the economy is in a recession deficits might actually be good.

The argument that Keynesian economics accounts for the deficit is weakened by the fact that, in the 1980s, when there was a second change in policy régimes—Keynesian economics was discarded and replaced with a modern Classical supply-side economic policy régime—the deficit did not disappear. In fact, the deficit grew. The modern Classical supply-side policy régime has led to an even larger deficit than existed in the Keynesian policy régime.

The modern Classical supply-side régime focuses on the need for tax cuts whenever they can possibly be implemented. This supply-side Classical focus on tax cuts

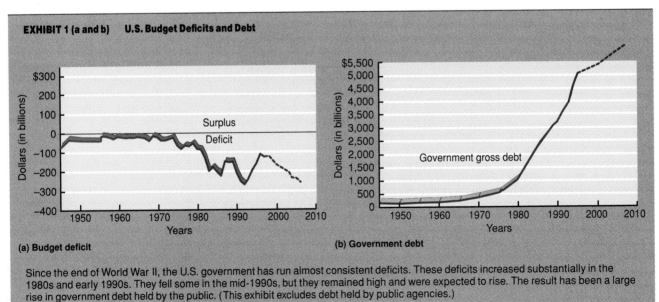

EXHIBIT 1 (a and b)   U.S. Budget Deficits and Debt

(a) Budget deficit

(b) Government debt

Since the end of World War II, the U.S. government has run almost consistent deficits. These deficits increased substantially in the 1980s and early 1990s. They fell some in the mid-1990s, but they remained high and were expected to rise. The result has been a large rise in government debt held by the public. (This exhibit excludes debt held by public agencies.)

Source: *The Economic and Budget Outlook,* 1997. (Congressional Budget Office.)

as the key to economic prosperity with little concern about the deficit is why you are now likely to see role reversals—Keynesians arguing against a deficit and Classicals arguing in favor of government running a deficit!

Differing groups of economists' changing views of deficits have had little impact on the lay public's view about deficits and debt. The lay public doesn't like either. In response, politicians say that they too don't like deficits and debt and that they're greatly concerned about the deficit problems.

In the 1980s political concern about the deficit grew so large that Congress passed the **Gramm-Rudman-Hollings Act** in 1985, *a law establishing mandatory deficit targets for the United States.* This act was designed to eliminate deficits by 1991. When it became clear that it would not achieve its goals, it was supplemented by the **Budget Enforcement Act of 1990,** *a law that put caps on certain aspects of federal spending, and established a "pay-as-you-go" test for new spending or tax cuts so that, through 1996, any new legislation, except for emergencies, had to be accompanied by offsetting tax increases or spending cuts.*

In 1993, as deficits continued high, the Clinton administration pushed through a deficit reduction law, the Omnibus Budget Reconciliation Act of 1993, that consisted of a combination of tax measures, spending cuts, and some new spending programs. Even with these laws, most observers projected that deficits would continue in the future, as government spending increased due to already-passed health and income maintenance entitlement programs. The reality of the budget process is that most federal spending programs are not voted upon by Congress. Only about 34 percent of total outlays are discretionary in any one year. Mandatory spending, which includes Social Security, Medicare and Medicaid, and interest payments on the debt, accounts for the remaining 66 percent. This percentage of spending that is mandatory is increasing. By 2007, the Congressional Budget Office projects that mandatory spending plus net interest payments will account for 75 percent of total outlays.

For some politicians, the laws discussed above were not strong enough. They suggested a balanced budget amendment to the U.S. Constitution that would make it unconstitutional for the government to run a deficit. Support for such an amendment grew in the early 1990s as budget deficits approached $300 billion. Even economists who support that balanced budget amendment agree that the reason for not running a budget deficit is not the immediate economic consequences of a deficit. The reason is political. They believe that a balanced budget requirement would work like a lock on

Politics and the Deficit

This is a useful point in the course to emphasize the role of politics in the chronic deficits our country ran in the 1980s, which have continued into the 1990s.

Since 1985 public and political concerns about the size of the deficit have led to the passage of three acts of Congress in an effort to reduce that size.

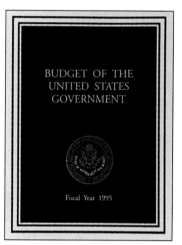

Each year the federal government publishes its budget, which details its spending programs.

This lithograph, entitled "Legislative assault (on the budget)," appeared in a French newspaper in 1835. *Bleichroeder Print Collection, Baker Library, Harvard Business School.*

the refrigerator and that the political structure of the United States lacks self-control in spending and hence needs that lock. If you unlock a refrigerator, people without self-control will grow fat. Similarly, without the discipline of a mandatory balanced budget, government and politicians without self-control won't make the hard choices. Instead they'll say, "We can have both guns and butter. We'll pay for them by running a deficit."

Judging by events since the 1940s, there's substance to the political argument that most democracies lack self-control in spending and taxing decisions. Most political observers agree that democracy tends to put off difficult decisions. People want lots of goods and services from government, but nobody wants to pay for them with taxes. Running a deficit (buy now, pay later) allows democracies to buy current goods and services but delay paying for them, and hence to avoid the hard choices for the present.[1]

Most political observers agree that democracy tends to put off difficult decisions.

ECONOMISTS' WAY OF LOOKING AT DEFICITS AND DEBT

Where do economists come out in the debate about the deficit? On most sides of the issue. But the reasons for their differences are quite unlike the reasons lay people and politicians differ. Why? Because there are a number of technical aspects behind the deficits and debt that most economists understand, and most lay people (and politicians) don't. Thus, to understand economists' views on deficits and debt, you've got to understand these technical aspects behind applying those definitions. We'll now examine these technical aspects and see how understanding them changes our ideas about some problems that deficits and debt pose for society.

Arbitrariness in Defining Deficits

Q–2: Distinguish between deficit and debt.

The definitions of *deficits* and *debt* are simple, but their simplicity hides important aspects that will help you understand current debates about deficits and debt. Thus, it's necessary to look carefully at some ambiguities in the definitions. Let's start with deficits.

Deficits are a shortfall of revenues compared to expenditures. So whether you have a deficit depends on what you include as a revenue and what you include as an expenditure. How you make these decisions can make an enormous difference in whether you have a deficit.

For example, consider the problem of a firm with revenues of $8,000 but no expenses except a $10,000 machine expected to last five years. Should the firm charge the $10,000 to this year's expenditures? Should it split the $10,000 evenly among the five years? Or should the firm use some other approach? Which method the firm chooses makes a big difference in whether its current budget will be in surplus or deficit.

This accounting issue is central to the debate about whether we should be concerned about the U.S. budget deficit. Say, for example, that government promises to pay an individual $1,000 ten years from now. How should government treat that promise? Since the obligation is incurred now, should government count as an expense now an amount that, if saved, would allow government to pay that $1,000 later? Or should government not count it as an expenditure until it actually pays out the money?

The same ambiguity surrounds revenues. For example, say you're holding government bonds valued at $100,000, which pay $10,000 interest per year, while you're spending $10,000 per year. You might think your budget is balanced. But what if the market value of the bonds (the amount you can sell them for) rises from $100,000 to $120,000? Should you count that $20,000 rise in value of the bonds as a revenue? Using an opportunity cost approach that economists use, a person holding bonds should count the rise in the bond's market value as revenue, which means that your income for the year is $30,000, not $10,000. Similarly the government that issued the

---

[1]The fact that democracy has problems doesn't mean that some other form of government is preferable to democracy. As Winston Churchill said, democracy is the worst form of government, except for all the other forms.

bond should count the rise in the market value of the bond it issued as an expenditure and count any fall in the market value of a bond it issued as income.[2]

Many such questions must be answered before we can determine whether a budget is in deficit or surplus. Some questions have no right or wrong answer. For others there are right or wrong answers that vary with the question being asked. For still others, an economist's "right way" is an accountant's "wrong way." In short, there are many ways to measure expenditures and receipts so there are many ways to measure deficits.

To say that there are many ways to measure deficits is not to say that all ways are correct. Pretending to have income that you don't have is wrong by all standards. Similarly, inconsistent accounting practices—sometimes to measure an income flow one way and sometimes another—are wrong. Standard accounting practices rule out a number of "creative," but improper, approaches to measuring deficits. But even eliminating these, there remain numerous reasonable ways of defining deficits, which accounts for much of the debate.

There are many ways to measure expenditures and receipts, so there are many ways to measure deficits.

Deficits as a Summary Measure

The point of the previous discussion is that deficits are simply a summary measure of a budget. As a summary, a deficit figure reduces a complicated set of accounting relationships down to one figure. To understand whether that one summary measure is something to worry about, you've got to understand the accounting procedures used to calculate it. Only then can you make an informed judgment about whether a deficit is something to worry about.

2 The deficit is simply a summary measure of the financial health of the economy. To understand that summary you must understand the methods that were used to calculate it.

The Need to Judge Debt Relative to Assets

Debt is accumulated deficits. If you spend $1,000 more than you earn for each of three years, you'll end up with a $3,000 debt. (To make things simple, we assume that spending includes paying interest on the debt.)

Debt is also a summary measure of a country's financial situation. As a summary measure, debt has even more problems than deficit. Unlike a deficit (which is the difference between outflows and inflows and hence provides at least a full summary measure), debt by itself is only half of a picture. The other half of the debt picture is assets. For a country, assets include its skilled work force, its natural resources, its factories, its housing stock, and its holdings of foreign assets. For a government, assets include the buildings and land it owns but, more importantly, it includes a portion of the assets of the people in the country, since government gets a portion of all earnings of those assets in tax revenue.

Q-3: Why is debt only half the picture of a country's financial situation?

Ask your students whether they think it is appropriate to judge the government's debt against the value of the country's assets.

To get an idea why the addition of assets is necessary to complete the debt picture, consider two governments: one has debt of $3 trillion and assets of $500 trillion; the other has $1 trillion in debt but only $1 trillion in assets. Which is in a better position? The government with more debt is, because its debt is significantly exceeded by its assets. The example's point is simple: To judge a country's debt, you must view its debt in relation to its assets.

To judge a country's debt, you must view its debt in relation to its assets.

Arbitrariness in Defining Debt

Like income and revenues, assets and debt are subject to varying definitions. Say, for example, that an 18-year-old is due to inherit $1 million at age 21. Should that expected future asset be counted as an asset now? Or say that the government buys an aircraft for $1 billion and discovers that it doesn't fly. What value should the government place on that aircraft? Or say that a country owes $1 billion, due to be paid 10 years from now, but inflation is ongoing at 100 percent per year. The inflation will reduce the value of the debt when it comes due by so much that its current real value will be $1 million—the approximate present value of $1 billion in 10 years with

---

[2]Since a fixed-rate bond's price varies inversely with the interest rate in the economy, a rise in the interest rate creates an income for bond issuers and an expense for bond holders. Reviewing the reasons why in relation to the present value formula is a good exercise.

100 percent inflation. It will be like paying $1 million today. Should the country list the debt as a $1 billion debt or a $1 million debt?

As was the case with income, revenues, and deficits, there's no unique answer to how assets and debts should be valued. So even after you take assets into account, you still have to be careful when deciding whether or not to be concerned about debt.

Difference between Individual and Government Debt

Three reasons government debt is different than individual debts are:

1. The government lives forever; people don't.

2. The government can print money to pay its debt; people can't.

3. Much of government debt is owed to itself—to its own citizens.

Another important fact about debt is that all debt is not the same. In particular, government debt is different than an individual's debt. There are three reasons for this.

First, government is ongoing. There's no real need for government ever to pay back its debt. An individual's lifespan is limited; when a person dies, there's inevitably an accounting of assets and debt to determine whether anything is left to go to heirs. Before any part of a person's estate is passed on, all debts must be paid. The government, however, doesn't ever have to settle its accounts.

Second, government has an option that individuals don't have for paying off a debt. Specifically, it can pay off a debt by creating money. As long as people will accept a country's currency, a country can always exchange its interest-bearing debt for money (noninterest-bearing debt). By doing so, it pays off its debt.

Third, much of a government debt is **internal government debt** (*government debt owed to its own citizens*). Paying interest on the debt involves a redistribution among citizens of the country, but it does not involve a net reduction in income of the average citizen. For example, say that a country has a $3 trillion debt, all of which is internal debt. Say also that the government pays $300 billion interest on its debt each year. That means the government must collect $300 billion in taxes so people are $300 billion poorer; but it pays out $300 billion in interest to them, so on average, people in the country are neither richer nor poorer because of the debt.[3]

External government debt (*government debt owed to individuals in foreign countries*) is different, being more like an individual's debt. Paying interest on it involves a net reduction in domestic income. U.S. taxpayers will be poorer; foreign holders of U.S. bonds will be richer.

These three differences between government debt and individual debt must be continually kept in mind when considering governments' debt problems.

Deficits, Debt, and Debt Service Relative to GDP

Deficits and debt relative to GDP provide a measure of a country's ability to pay off a deficit and service its debt.

Let's now apply some of these insights. In Exhibits 1(a) and (b), we saw that U.S. government debt and deficits have been increasing since World War II. Let's now consider the question from a slightly different perspective, taking into account government's ability to handle debt and deficits. That different perspective is to look at deficits and debt relative to GDP, as in Exhibits 2(a) and (b). As you can see, relative to GDP, recent deficits look much smaller. As a percentage of GDP, deficits haven't shown the same alarming trend as when they're considered in absolute terms. And it's the same with debt. Relative to GDP, debt has not been continually increasing. Instead, from after World War II to the 1970s and in the period from 1988 to 1990, the debt/GDP ratio actually decreased. In the mid-1990s it stabilized at somewhat under 70 percent of GDP.

Why measure deficits and debt relative to GDP? Because the ability to pay off a deficit depends upon a nation's productive capacity. Government's ability to bring in revenue depends upon GDP. So GDP serves the same function for government as income does for an individual. It provides a measure of how much debt, and how large a deficit, government can handle.

Q-4: Why is it reasonable to measure debt relative to GDP?

Considering deficits and debt relative to GDP should ease our concern about the large U.S. deficit and growing U.S. debt. Although the absolute size of the deficits is much larger today than earlier, their relative importance compared to GDP is not. Similarly for debt. Though the debt has been increasing continuously, the problem it presents hasn't necessarily increased.

---

[3]There are, of course, distributional effects. The people who pay the taxes are not necessarily the same people who receive the interest.

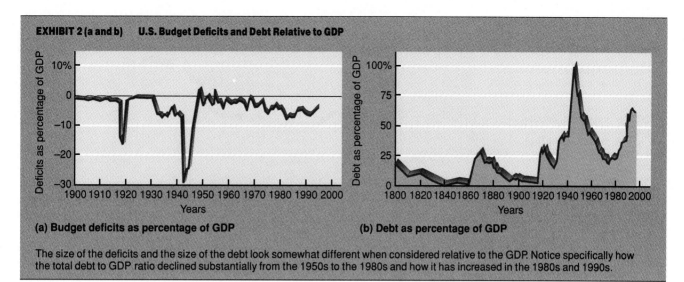

EXHIBIT 2 (a and b)   U.S. Budget Deficits and Debt Relative to GDP

(a) Budget deficits as percentage of GDP

(b) Debt as percentage of GDP

The size of the deficits and the size of the debt look somewhat different when considered relative to the GDP. Notice specifically how the total debt to GDP ratio declined substantially from the 1950s to the 1980s and how it has increased in the 1980s and 1990s.

Source: *The Economic and Budget Outlook*, 1997 (Congressional Budget Office), and *Historical Statistics* (U.S. Bureau of the Census).

Considering debt relative to GDP is still not quite sufficient. Economists are also concerned about the interest rate paid on the debt. How much of a burden a given amount of debt imposes depends on the interest rate that must be paid on that debt. It determines annual **debt service**—*the interest rate on debt times the total debt.*

In 1996, the U.S. government paid out approximately $240 billion in interest. A larger debt would require even higher interest payments. The $240 billion in interest payment is government revenue that can't be spent on defense or welfare; it's a payment for past expenditures. Ultimately the interest payments are the burden of the debt. That's what people mean when they say a deficit is burdening future generations. That burden is the interest payments future generations will have to make to the holders of U.S. debt.[4]

Over the past 50 years, the interest rate has fluctuated considerably; when it has risen, the debt service has increased; when it has fallen, debt service has decreased. Exhibit 3 shows the federal interest rate payments relative to GDP. This ratio increased substantially in World War II and then again in the 1970s and early 1980s. In the early 1990s it rose, but in the mid-1990s it has fallen to slightly over 3 percent of GDP. Thus, this measure suggests that the debt is more of a problem than the debt/GDP measure, but less of a problem than when we simply looked at debt as an isolated figure.

The United States can afford its current debt in the sense that it can afford to pay the interest on that debt. In fact, it could afford a much higher debt/GDP ratio since U.S. government bonds are still considered one of the safest assets in the world. No one is worried about the U.S. government defaulting. So technically the current debt can be handled, and can probably be increased by trillions of dollars without problem.

Let's now turn to a consideration of how growth in GDP reduces problems posed by deficits and debt service.

GDP can grow either because there's *real* growth or because there's *inflationary* growth. Both types of growth play major roles in economists' assessment of deficits. So we must consider how both types of GDP growth affect deficits and debt.

Debt service   The interest rate on debt times the total debt.

Two Ways GDP Growth Reduces Problems Posed by Deficits

[4]This statement about the burden of the debt doesn't contradict my earlier statement that government's internal debt doesn't directly decrease income in a country. With internal debt, those interest payments are paid to someone in the country. Thus, the burden of the debt isn't the loss of income to society. The burden is the prior commitment of government revenue to paying interest on government bonds. If collecting those tax revenues necessary to pay off bond holders has negative incentive effects and reduces income, then the debt indirectly lowers income in the economy.

EXHIBIT 3   Federal Interest Payments Relative to GDP

Interest payments as a percentage of GDP remained relatively constant until the 1970s, after which they rose significantly due to high interest rates and large increases in debt. In the late 1980s, they fell as GDP increased, but with the recession in the early 1990s they rose substantially again, even as interest rates fell.

Source: *The Economic and Budget Outlook,* 1997 (Congressional Budget Office).

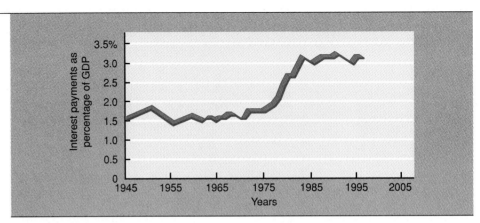

As the economy grows, the deficit relative to GDP is reduced. Thus, expansionary policies can actually lead to a smaller deficit problem.

Structural deficit *The deficit that would remain when the cyclical elements have been netted out.*

When a society experiences real growth, it becomes richer, and, being richer, it can handle more debt.

3 Since in a growing economy a continual deficit is consistent with a constant ratio of debt to GDP, and GDP serves as a measure of the government's ability to pay off the debt, a country can run a continual deficit.

Q–5: Explain how inflation can wipe out debt.

Structural Deficits, Cycles, and Growth   In my earlier discussion of fiscal policy, I pointed out that the level of income in the economy affected the deficit. As income increases, tax revenue increases and the deficit declines. This means that in a cyclical downturn, the deficit increases, and in a cyclical upturn, the deficit decreases. In talking about the problem of total debt, economists generally focus on the **structural deficit**—*the deficit that would remain when the cyclical elements have been netted out (when the economy is at its potential income)*. In theory, determining the structural deficit is easy to do; in practice, it is difficult since there is significant debate about where potential income is and how much it is increasing from one year to the next. Despite this, in discussing the deficit problem, economists focus on the structural deficit; the cyclical component of the deficit will solve itself.

Real Growth and the Deficit   When a society experiences real growth, it becomes richer, and, being richer, it can handle more debt. Real growth in the United States has averaged about 2.5 percent per year, which means that U.S. debt can grow at a rate of 2.5 percent without increasing the debt/GDP ratio. But for debt to grow, government must run a deficit, so a constant debt/GDP ratio in a growing economy is consistent with a continual deficit.

How much of a deficit are we talking about? U.S. federal government debt in 1996 was about $5.0 trillion and GDP was about $7.5 trillion, so the government debt/GDP ratio was about 67 percent. A real growth rate of 2.5 percent means that real GDP is growing at about $190 billion per year. That means that government can run a deficit of $127 billion a year without increasing the debt/GDP ratio:

$$67\% \times \$190 \text{ billion} = \$127 \text{ billion.}$$

Of course, for those who believe that total U.S. government debt is already too large relative to GDP, this argument (that the debt/GDP ratio is remaining constant) is unsatisfying. They'd prefer the debt/GDP ratio to fall.

Summarizing: Real growth makes it possible for a country to run a deficit without increasing the debt/GDP ratio. Since that ratio is a key ratio for judging economists' concern about debt, real growth lessens concern about the deficit.

We now turn to inflation's effect on deficits and debt.

Inflation, Debt, and the Real Deficit   Inflation's subtle effect on deficits and debt requires careful consideration. The first key point is that *inflation wipes out debt*. How much does it wipe out? Consider an example. Say a country has a $2 trillion debt and inflation is 4 percent per year. That means that the real value of all assets denominated in dollars is declining by 4 percent each year. If you had $100 and there's 4 percent inflation in a year, that $100 will be worth 4 percent less at the end of the year—the equivalent of $96 had there been no inflation. By the same reasoning, when there's inflation the value of the debt is declining 4 percent each year. Four percent of $2 trillion is $80 billion, so with an outstanding debt of $2 trillion, 4 percent inflation will eliminate $80 billion of the debt each year.

The larger the debt and the larger the inflation, the more debt will be eliminated with inflation. For example, with 10 percent inflation and a $2 trillion debt, $200 billion of the debt will be eliminated by inflation each year. With 4 percent inflation and a $4 trillion debt, $160 billion of the debt will be eliminated.

If inflation is wiping out debt, and the deficit is equal to the increases in debt from one year to the next, inflation also affects the deficit. Economists take this into account by defining two types of deficits: a nominal deficit and a real deficit.

A **nominal deficit** is *the deficit determined by looking at the difference between expenditures and receipts.* It's what most people think of when they think of the budget deficit; it's the value that is generally reported.

A **real deficit** is *the nominal deficit adjusted for inflation's effect on the debt.* It is the nominal deficit *minus* the decrease in the value of the government's total outstanding debts due to inflation. Thus, to calculate the *real* deficit one must know the nominal deficit, the rate of inflation, and the total outstanding government debt. Let's consider some examples.

Inflation reduces the value of the debt. That reduction is taken into account when the real deficit is calculated.

In our first example, assume:

Nominal deficit = $100 billion
Inflation = 4%
Total debt = $2 trillion.

The definition of *real deficit* states:

Real deficit = Nominal deficit − (Inflation × Total debt).

4 Real deficit = Nominal deficit − (Inflation × Total debt).

Substituting in the numbers gives us:

Real deficit = $100 billion − (4% × $2 trillion)
= $100 billion − $80 billion
= $20 billion

Though the nominal deficit is $100 billion, the real deficit is only $20 billion.

In our second example, assume:

Nominal deficit = $100 billion
Inflation = 10%
Total debt = $2 trillion.

The only change from the first example is the inflation rate. But look what happens to the real deficit.

Real deficit = $100 billion − (10% × $2 trillion)
= $100 billion − $200 billion
= −$100 billion

In this case, the country is not running a real deficit. After adjusting for inflation, the $100 billion nominal deficit becomes a −$100 billion deficit (a $100 billion real surplus)!

Let's consider 1996 as our third example.

Q–6: The nominal deficit = $40 billion; inflation = 2 percent, and the total debt = $4 trillion. What is the real deficit?

Nominal deficit = $107 billion
Inflation = 3%
Total debt = $5 trillion.

Now see what happens:

Real deficit = $107 billion − (3% × $5 trillion) = −$43 billion.

The nominal $107 billion deficit became a real $43 billion surplus. As you can see, the real deficit can differ significantly from the nominal deficit.

Inflation, Debt, and Nominal Deficits   This distinction between the nominal deficit and the real deficit is not an illusion. Inflation wipes out debt, and that fact must be considered when evaluating the effect of a deficit. Inflation is an important reason why the U.S. debt/GDP ratio declined in the postwar period. When inflation increases, the debt/GDP ratio can decrease even when the nominal deficit is large.

Inflation wipes out debt, and that fact must be considered when evaluating the effect of a deficit.

You may be somewhat hesitant to accept the preceding argument about how inflation eliminates debt and can change a nominal deficit into a real surplus. The first time I was presented with the argument, I was dubious. Somehow, inflation as a way of reducing debt's burden sounds too good to be true. If you are hesitant, it's with good reason. While the argument that inflation wipes out debt is correct, your fears are not groundless. Inflation is not a costless answer to eliminating debt.

To see that it isn't, let's carefully consider how inflation eliminates the debt. Say you bought U.S. bonds in denominations of $100 each and with a 4 percent annual interest rate, with the expectation that the price level would remain constant. That's not a bad return; in each year you expect $4 for each $100 you loaned the government, and as each bond matures you also expect to get your $100 back. Now let's say that inflation is 6 percent per year. For each year of the loan, the dollars with which the government pays you back are worth 6 percent less than the dollars you loaned the government, so instead of gaining 4 percent, you're losing 2 percent—the 4 percent interest you get minus the 6 percent inflation.

The cost of eliminating the debt through inflation is paid by creditors who do not anticipate the inflation.

For you (the holder of debt), inflation isn't a costless way to eliminate a debt. It's very costly to creditors, who lose what the government gains. The government's gain from an inflation is the bond holder's loss from inflation. So the effect of inflation on debt is no illusion; it is simply a transfer of money from bond holders to the government.

Nominal and Real Interest Rates and Deficits   Such transfers of income do not make bond holders (creditors) very happy. Yes, the government's real debt is being reduced by inflation, but it's being reduced by bond holders' losses. And bond holders aren't helpless people. What can they do about it? For the fixed interest rate bonds they already hold, they can do nothing. When they bought the bonds, the contract was set. But they can do something about future bonds. The next time a bond salesman suggests buying government bonds, purchasers will likely take any expected inflation into account. Instead of buying a bond with a 4 percent interest rate, they will require an additional 6 percent to compensate them for the 6 percent expected inflation, for a total of 10 percent.

Expectations of inflation push up the nominal interest rate and cause bond holders to demand an inflation premium on their bonds. Expected future inflation causes the real interest rate to be different from the nominal interest rate. Thus, in the absence of inflation the nominal interest rate might be 4 percent. With 6 percent inflation, the nominal interest rate might be 10 percent: 4 percent real interest rate plus 6 percent expected inflation.

When I deal with this issue, I work through a couple of bond transactions, with and without full expectations adjustment. Through the examples students can see that if expectations adjust completely, debtors are protected from inflation.

If the nominal interest rate is 6 percent higher than the real interest rate, bond holders have fully adjusted their 6 percent expectations of inflation into their bond purchases. In this case they won't lose if there's 6 percent inflation. Bond holders do not lose when they correctly expect inflation and build that expectation into their financial dealings. But if bond holders don't lose when they make a full adjustment for expected inflation, government can't win.

With Full Adjustment in Expectations, Creditors Don't Lose

To see that with full interest rate adjustment for inflation, creditors don't lose, it is helpful to divide the government's deficit into two components: a spending-on-current-needs component and a debt service component.

Let's say the government has a total debt of $2 trillion, total expenditures of $500 billion, and a nominal deficit of $100 billion. Let's also assume that initially there's no expected inflation. Because there's no expected inflation, the 4 percent nominal interest rate will also be the real interest rate, and the nominal deficit will equal the real deficit. This means that the government is paying $80 billion a year in interest ($2 trillion debt × 4 percent interest). The debt service component of the deficit is $80 billion, leaving $420 billion to finance spending on current needs.

Now assume that there's a 6 percent inflation but the interest rate remains 4 percent. That 6 percent inflation decreases real debt by $120 billion (6 percent $\times$ $2 trillion). Using the real deficit formula, you can calculate that the government is actually running a real surplus of $20 billion:

$$\text{Real deficit} = \$100 \text{ billion} - (6\% \times \$2 \text{ trillion})$$

$$= \$100 \text{ billion} - \$120 \text{ billion}$$

$$= -\$20 \text{ billion}$$

Q–7: Explain why, when there is full adjustment for expectations, creditors don't lose in an inflation.

But what happens if the 6 percent inflation were fully expected? In that case, the nominal interest rate on the debt, assuming it's all short term, will rise from 4 to 10 percent to account for the expected inflation. Debt service will be $200 billion (10 percent $\times$ $2 trillion), $120 billion more than government would have had to pay had there been no inflation adjustment to the interest rate. That $120 billion increase in the debt service expenditures just equals the $120 billion that the inflation wiped out.

This $120 billion increase in the debt service component of the deficit decreases the $420 billion current-spending component of the budget to $300 billion. So when nominal interest rates go up, simply in order to maintain the nominal deficit at its current level government must either reduce spending on current needs or it must raise taxes and collect more in revenues. It's paying extra interest to bond holders to compensate them for their loss due to inflation.

This distinction between nominal and real is necessary to make a judgment about a given nominal deficit. When there's high expected inflation and a large debt, much of the nominal deficit is a debt service component that is simply offsetting the decrease in the debt due to inflation.

This insight into debt is directly relevant to the budget situation in the United States. For example, back in 1990 the nominal U.S. deficit was about $280 billion, while the real deficit was about half of that—$140 billion. But that low real deficit was not costless to the government. When inflationary expectations were much lower, as they were in the 1950s, government paid 3 or 4 percent on its bonds. In 1990 it paid 8 or 9 percent, which is about 5 percent more than it paid in the 1950s. With its $2.75 trillion debt, the United States was paying about $140 billion more in interest than it would have had to pay if no inflation had been expected and the nominal interest rate had been 3 rather than 8 percent. That reduced the amount it could spend on current services by $140 billion. This means that much of the 1990 nominal U.S. deficit existed because of the rise in debt service necessary to compensate bond holders for the expected inflation.

Expected inflation adds a cost to government in higher interest payments to holders of government debt. In the 1990s this was a sizable portion of federal expenditures.

As inflationary expectations and nominal interest rates fell in the 1990s, the difference between the real and nominal deficit decreased. Still, a 2 percent gap between nominal and real interest rates and a $5 trillion debt would mean that $100 billion of any deficit is due to the inflation premium raising the nominal interest rate.

We've covered a lot of material, so before we move on let's review four important points:

Summary to This Point

1. Deficits are summary measures of the state of the economy. They are dependent on the accounting procedures used.

2. It is the financial health of the economy, not the deficit, with which we should be concerned.

3. Deficits and debt should be viewed relative to GDP to determine their importance.

4. The real deficit is the nominal deficit adjusted for the inflation reduction in the real debt:

$$\text{Real deficit} = \text{Nominal deficit} - (\text{Inflation} \times \text{Debt})$$

Deficits are a summary measure of the state of the economy.

It is the financial health of the economy, not the deficit, that we should be concerned with.

Here's a proposal that some economists have suggested could significantly reduce the nominal U.S. deficit. Currently most bonds are fixed-interest bonds. They pay back a stated number of dollars in a given period. For example, at 10 percent interest a $1,000 five-year bond pays $100 interest each year for five years, and pays back another $1,000 at the end of five years.

Some economists have proposed the following: make the amount that is to be paid back, the $1,000, indexed to inflation. Thus, if the price level rises 40 percent, the amount paid back would be $1,400 rather than $1,000. Bonds that pay back an amount dependent on inflation are called *indexed bonds*.

Let's now ask: What would happen if the United States were to issue only indexed bonds? Since bond holders are compensated for inflation, the interest on bonds would fall. If 5 percent inflation were the expected rate and the nominal interest rate were 7 percent, the real interest rate would be 2 percent—so the interest rate on bonds would be 2 instead of 7 percent, U.S. debt service would fall from about $200 billion to between $50 billion and $60 billion, and the measured U.S. deficit would decrease significantly. (In January 1997 the Treasury Department introduced inflation-indexed bonds for the first time. Such issues are expected to increase.)

Many economists oppose having the government issue indexed bonds. Yes, they agree, it would lower the measured deficit, but it would not change real U.S. debt. At the same time, indexing would introduce new complexities of government finance as the inflation index comes under even more scrutiny because so much money would be riding on it.

Whether or not you favor the proposal, it is a superb proposal from an academic perspective. It helps us recognize the difference between real and nominal deficits.

Some Reasons for Concern about the U.S. Government Budget Deficit

Considering real deficits rather than nominal deficits and viewing the deficit and debt relative to GDP should have lessened your concern about the size of the U.S. deficit. Given inflation, the real deficit is lower than the nominal deficit, and given real economic growth we can stand an increase in total debt without the burden becoming intolerable.

But, as with most issues in economics, we must think about "on the other hand." The most important "on the other hand" concerns how future commitments are calculated in the U.S. budget, and the accounting gimmicks used to make the nominal deficit seem low. To see how these work, let's consider the accounting system used by the U.S. government budget.

The U.S. Budget Does Not Include Many Government Obligations   The U.S. government uses a **cash flow accounting system**—*an accounting system entering expenses and revenues only when cash is received or paid out.* When it spends or collects money, these outflows or inflows show up on the budget. When the government doesn't have a cash inflow or outflow, nothing shows up on the budget. This cash flow accounting system leads to a number of important aspects of the budget and the deficit.

First, a number of obligations government incurs do not show up as part of the deficit. One such obligation is federal loan guarantees, such as guarantees on student loans, pensions, and deposits in banks. Since no cash is spent when these guarantees are made, they don't show up as expenditures.

Just how important these can be became apparent in 1989 when numerous savings and loan associations went bankrupt and the Federal Savings and Loan Insurance Corporation (FSLIC), the organization that guaranteed S&L deposits, was called upon to meet its obligation. The cost to government was over $200 billion—all from off-budget obligations that never showed up in the government budget when they were incurred! So here we have a case of government incurring a huge obligation that never showed up as an expense at the time it was incurred.

In the 1990s the FSLIC was merged into the **Federal Deposit Insurance Corporation (FDIC)**—*a government organization that guarantees bank deposits.* The FDIC is an agency whose outstanding obligations don't appear in the budget, and it isn't the only agency with such an accounting practice. There are many others, such as Penny Benny (Pension Benefit Guarantee Corporation), a government organization that guarantees pension payments by firms through pension benefits insurance. Through these programs, the U.S. government has guaranteed trillions of

Cash flow accounting system   An accounting system entering expenses and revenues only when cash is received or paid out.

Q–8:   How can a government that isn't running a deficit still get itself into financial trouble?

dollars of obligations out there, meaning that even if it had a real deficit of zero, its overall financial health might still be questionable.

The Government Uses Accounting Tricks to Make the Deficit Look Smaller   Of even more concern is the way in which the U.S. government met its obligation to bail out the savings and loan corporations. What it did not do is admit to the obligation and enter it into the books as an expense. Entering the S&L bailout on the books would have increased the nominal deficit and made it look as if the government weren't reducing the deficit—but the government was committed to reducing the deficit.

Instead, the government increased insurance fees on savings and loans institutions slightly and counted those fees as additional current revenue. Those fees were no way near enough to cover the cost of the S&L bailout. To cover most of the costs, the government sold special bonds. But these expenditures were *not* counted as expenditures so they didn't increase the deficit in 1989 or 1990. Instead, they were called **off-budget expenditures** (*expenditures of money that are not to be counted as expenditures in the budget*).

So here's what happened with the S&L bailout. The fees increased current revenues; the expenditures weren't entered on the books. As it worked out, incurring a multibillion dollar obligation in 1989 *lowered* the measured budget deficit for 1989!

Were this FSLIC action an isolated incident, it could be shaken off. It's much like failing a quiz: It might be no problem if the reason you failed the quiz was that your child or your father was sick that day: not to worry, because it was an isolated incident. But if you failed a quiz because you did no studying, failing is much more important. It suggests that, unless you start studying, you will likely fail all your other quizzes. The FSLIC fiasco was the government equivalent to not studying.

The U.S. government has often dealt with its budgetary problems with gimmicks to make the deficit look smaller than it is. Thus, many economists argue that the government has serious financial health problems that are hidden by the accounting procedures it uses. And it has those problems even if its real deficit is zero or in surplus.

5 Even though the real deficit is lower than the nominal deficit, there is still cause for concern because the U.S. budget fails to include many obligations and the government uses many accounting tricks.

Let's consider the old-age retirement portion of the social security system as another example of how the government's financial health may be questionable even when its budget is not in deficit. According to some observers, that system has a built-in financial problem that will likely explode some time about the year 2020.

The Social Security Retirement System

Funded and Unfunded Retirement Systems   Pension systems can be either funded or unfunded. A **funded pension system** is *a pension system in which money is collected and invested in a special fund from which pension payments are made*. An **unfunded pension system** is *a pension system in which pensions are paid from current revenues*.

The social security system, which provides pensions for a large majority of the U.S. population, is largely an *unfunded* pension system. Until recently, most of the social security taxes that the government collected as part of that pension system were not invested in a special fund to be used to pay out benefits when the person retires or otherwise becomes eligible to receive benefits. Instead, to a large degree, the government paid social security benefits from current tax revenue.

An unfunded pension system is not necessarily unsound. In an ongoing system, there will always be revenue coming in and payments going out. There are always current workers to support a system that pays the aged. The benefit of the unfunded system is that it allows initial payments to individuals to exceed what they paid in. The problem with an unfunded system is that there's no trust fund of assets earning interest to cover future payments.

A Potential Problem with Unfunded Systems   As long as the population's age distribution, the annual death rate, and the number of people working do not change much, an

Funded pension system   One in which money is collected and invested in a special fund from which payments are made.

Unfunded pension system   One in which pensions are paid from current revenues.

It is important for students to understand the true nature of Social Security system. Too often people believe that Social Security is a funded system, when actually the opposite is the case.

One way to get a handle on whether the U.S. government debt is "too high" is to compare it to the debt of some other countries, as is done in the bar chart. Since debt is defined slightly differently in different countries, and since fluctuation in GDP can change ratios, these percentages should be interpreted as measures of magnitude only.

In the chart you can see that the United States comes out in the middle of these eight countries. Of course, there is no economic law stating that the other countries are right, or that the economic situation might not change, making these current ratios unsustainable. Still, it's nice to know that the United States is not alone in its deficit and debt problems.

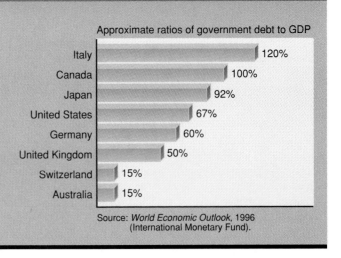

Approximate ratios of government debt to GDP

Italy	120%
Canada	100%
Japan	92%
United States	67%
Germany	60%
United Kingdom	50%
Switzerland	15%
Australia	15%

Source: *World Economic Outlook*, 1996 (International Monetary Fund).

unfunded system presents no problem. But an unfunded system does present a potential problem if the amount paid in and the amount paid out differ.

To see this, say we have only three groups of people: workers, the retired elderly, and the very young (who aren't yet working). Now suddenly we start a pension program. We use the money that we collect from the workers to pay pensions to the elderly retired people. These elderly people have paid nothing in, because they retired before the system started up. In short, this group gets benefits without having paid anything into the system. In the next generation, the elderly die, the workers become elderly, and the young become workers. The new group of elderly get paid by the new workers. As long as the three groups remain at equivalent relative sizes, the process works neatly—each generation will get paid when its time comes.

But let's consider what happens when there's a "baby boom" and one group suddenly has a large number of children in a short period of time. In this case, the sizes of the generations are no longer equal. Initially things work out well. The baby boom young become workers, and there are lots of them relative to the elderly. There's plenty of money coming in and comparatively little going out. This allows for an increase in payments to the elderly, or a decrease in the taxes paid by the working group, or both.

But what happens in the next generation when the baby boom workers become elderly? Then, assuming the baby boomers have a "normal" number of children, rather than the larger numbers of children their own parents had, the number of people collecting benefits becomes larger but the number of workers contributing to the system becomes smaller. In this case, payments per person must decrease, contributions coming in per worker must increase, or some combination of the two must occur. None of these alternatives is particularly pleasant.

This example doesn't come out of nowhere. It represents the current situation in the U.S. social security system. From 1946 through the late 1960s there was a baby boom, and these baby boomers are currently in the labor force. They'll start retiring in large numbers in the early 2000s and, when they do, the number of workers per retiree will decrease dramatically, so that in 2020 there will be about 2.5 workers per retiree instead of more than 15 workers per retiree as in the 1950s and 1960s. Exhibit 4 shows these unpleasant projections.

There are a number of ways to avoid these unpleasant alternatives. One way is to partially fund the system. With a partially funded pension system, some of the money paid in by the baby boom generation is put in a trust fund (when the proportion of workers to elderly is high). That trust fund and the interest it earns are used to pay part of the benefits of the elderly when the proportion of workers to elderly is low.

Q–9: How can a baby boom cause problems for an unfunded pension system?

Social Security also encompasses Medicare. While the old age retirement portion has a surplus, the Medicare portion has a deficit and will be exhausted early in the next century. At that time, there will be pressure to use the surplus in the Old Age benefit trust fund to balance some of the shortfall of the Medicare trust fund.

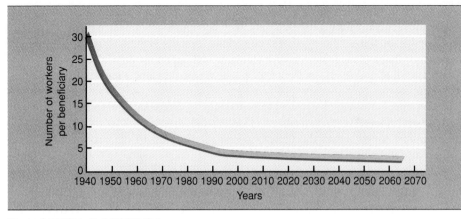

Source: Social Security Administration.

EXHIBIT 4   Projection of Workers Compared with Social Security Retirees

The number of workers per retiree declined considerably from 1940 to 1997, and it will continue to decline until about 2020. The following decade will be the crunch period for Social Security.

A second way is to vary the retirement age so that a large group of workers retires later and a small group of workers retires earlier. After age 65, people in each age group die off faster than people in younger age groups. This means that if the retirement age were raised, there would be fewer people to collect benefits than there are when the retirement age is 65. This higher retirement age would help keep the ratio of workers to elderly roughly equal, again eliminating the mismatch of revenue coming in with payments going out.

Social Security and the Budget Deficit   In the 1970s and 1980s, economists pointed out that this problem would be occurring. In response, the government made a number of changes. The retirement age was moved up slightly and, most important, there was a large increase in the rate of social security or FICA (Federal Insurance Contribution Act) contributions. This tax increase was to create a large trust fund that would provide significant budget surpluses in the 1980s and 1990s. These surpluses could be used to make the payments coming due in the 2000s without requiring huge tax increases or massive borrowing at that future time. Thus, in 1996, about $65 billion more in social security taxes was collected than was paid out. Therefore it seems as if the supplemental trust fund solution is the one the government is following.

Unfortunately, that tax increase is not resulting in government surpluses. Instead, the government is running large current deficits, so it is financing the trust fund with government bonds (promises to pay). (The only asset the trust fund is allowed to hold is government bonds.) But the social security system has already promised to pay anyway. So the only difference the trust fund makes is that, with the "trust fund," the government has issued pieces of paper (bonds) as backing for that promise.

An Alternative   Let's look at another possible solution to the social security problem. Say that the retirement age at which people become eligible to receive social security payments were raised in increments so that, in 2010, the retirement age at which they could get full benefits would be 70. (It's now about 65.)[5] Then say that the current social security tax rates were lowered 10 percent. This combination of policies would increase the current budget deficit, but would significantly improve the U.S. financial picture because future commitments would have been so significantly lowered that there would be no need to collect as much current social security tax revenue. So here's a case in which the deficit would increase, but the United States would be in better financial shape.

Charles Schultze—Chairman of the Council of Economic Advisers under President Carter. *UPI/Bettmann.*

Q–10: How could raising the retirement age at which people become eligible to receive social security payments help the economy without affecting the deficit?

---

[5]Government pension systems were started by the 19th-century German leader Otto von Bismarck. He reportedly chose 65 as the retirement age because his advisers told him that vital statistics for the country showed most people died before age 65.

THE DEFICIT DEBATE: WOLVES, PUSSYCATS, OR TERMITES

6 Because the deficit has many dimensions and each is widely debated, there are many alternative reasonable views about the deficit.

The accounting used in the social security system is only one of the U.S. government's many problem accounting areas. That's why economists emphasize that it's the financial health of the economy that's important, not the deficit. But economists also recognize that the measured deficit will be at the center of the debate about government spending and taxes, so they take positions on the deficit and its meaning to the economy.

Charles Schultze, chairman of the Council of Economic Advisers in the Carter administration and currently an economist at the Brookings Institution, has divided economists' views about the deficit and its relationship to the economy's financial health into three groups:

1. The wolf-at-the-door group, who believe the deficit will bring about imminent doom.
2. The domesticated-pussycat group, who believe the deficit doesn't matter.
3. The termites-in-the-basement group, who believe the deficit will cause serious problems in the long run.

Few economists belong to the wolf-at-the-door group. A small but vocal group of economists comprise the domesticated pussycats. They include both liberal Keynesian economists who feel the economy needs more expansion, and conservative Classical economists who believe deficits don't influence behavior and hence make no difference to the real economy. The largest group of economists belong to the termites-in-the-basement group.

Three Alternative Views of the Deficit

Three alternative views about the deficit are demonstrated in an exchange between William Proxmire, Robert Eisner, Robert Solow, and Franco Modigliani. Proxmire is a retired politician. Eisner, Solow, and Modigliani are well-known economists.

'WIZARDS' SAY FORGET THE DEFICIT—DON'T LISTEN

William Proxmire
U.S. Senator
Washington, D.C.

Now some eminent economists are telling Congress and the administration to forget the deficit and the $2.6 trillion national debt. These objects of our deepest concern don't matter, they say. When people of the stature of Robert Eisner, a former president of the American Economic Association, whisper these seductive words, it's going to be hard for members of Congress to resist. And when the view is echoed by such Wall Street wizards as John Gutfreund and Peter Bernstein, it's like a teen-ager being told by her revered family doctor that smoking doesn't really threaten her health—it might even relax her and ease tensions.

After more than 30 years in the Senate, I cannot think of a more alluring or dangerous philosophy for a member of Congress than the economic gospel according to Mr. Eisner. How irresistible it would be if a congressman could justify voting for increased spending and cutting taxes because it's good, hard economic sense.

The two most painful actions a member of Congress can take are first, a vote to cut popular spending programs, and second—and even more painful—a vote to increase taxes. But if these economic and Wall Street gurus are right, every day of a congressman's service in this debt-ridden government can be Christmas. A few years ago the so-called supply-side economists promised that a cut in taxes, even without a corresponding reduction in spending, would permit the country to grow its way out of deficits and debt. A trillion and a half dollars of additional national debt has made the supply siders a laugh.

Now we're told by Mr. Eisner that the $155 billion deficit for 1988 is a mirage. In the Eisner view, expenditures on roads, aircraft carriers and fighter planes are not really spending. They're investments. Mr. Eisner claims that when we include state and local surpluses, and then allow for inflation, the government at all levels is running an Eisner surplus. Mr. Eisner computes that surplus at $42 billion for 1988. Right now, in his view, Congress isn't spending enough—it's taxing too much. According to him, this surplus is a serious drag on the economy. So come on Congress, spend more. Tax less. The deficit is not big enough. It's not even a deficit.

What's wrong with this Eisner analysis? Plenty. First, buying a highway or a warship is indeed an investment. It's also something else. It's a cost. When this kind of investment is made with borrowed money, it can be an exacting and painful cost.

Here's "an investment" that rarely pays a tangible cash return to the government. Take the federal government's biggest spender, the military: 85% of its expenditure is for military

(continued)

personnel, including retired pay, operations and maintenance, and procurement. None of these expenditures yield a penny of return to the government. In fact, military procurement, far from being an investment representing a source of future income, creates an "asset"—an aircraft carrier, for example, that will, once constructed, cost tens of billions of dollars to operate throughout its useful life in addition to its original cost. Some investment.

Overwhelmingly, government "investment" is of the same "wasting-asset" kind. Yes indeed, government expenditures may constitute useful services, often services to be consumed for years to come. During those years the government that borrows to "buy" the investment—the building or highway—must pay interest on its borrowing. It must maintain and operate its public asset.

As time goes on, the government must rehabilitate or replace the public asset or terminate the service it provides. Certainly the present govern-

ment accounting system of counting all expenditures as outlay without offsetting credit for their future value is crude. But it is also roughly accurate and fair. This follows because every year Americans live off past government "investments" as well as buy "investments" that provide government services for the future. One could argue that, by failing to maintain the pace of highway building and other capital construction, recent congresses have been accumulating bigger deficits than reported. On this basis, I could as easily contend that the true federal deficit is $300 billion for 1988 as Mr. Eisner can argue that it is not a deficit at all, but a surplus.

The simplest, most obvious evidence that the federal government is living beyond its means is the colossal new burden of an immensely expanded national debt that now commands $155 billion a year in interest. That interest is both the fastest growing cost of government and the one cost that must be paid on time, in full. Interest and inter-

est alone cannot be cut, stretched out, or reduced. It is a grim, unavoidable reminder of debt that all the sophistries of the brightest on Wall Street and academia cannot diminish.

The Eisner argument should be very appealing to your 19-year-old son who wants you to buy him a $30,000 Porsche. His pitch to you goes like this: "We're not really and truly going into debt when we spring for this Porsche. This isn't debt. This is an investment. Look, we can finance it over five years. You'll pay only about $45,000 total. I know you think I'm nuts, Dad, but this is the way the former president of the American Economic Association and the brightest guys on Wall Street see it. So how about it, Daddio? Let's get with it."

DEFICIT ISN'T TOO TAXING

Robert Eisner
Professor of Economics
Northwestern University
Evanston, Ill.

Re William Proxmire's Feb. 3 editorial-page article " 'Wizards' Say Forget the Deficit—Don't Listen": Despite his alarm, deficits—at least as they are conventionally measured—may not be bad for the economy. Mr. Proxmire taxes me—forgive the expression—for pointing out that by meaningful measure the official 1988 budget deficit of $155 billion was actually a real surplus of $42 billion. The calculations, though, are simple and illuminating.

Apply standard business accounting practices to the federal budget and include as expenses or costs only the depreciation of capital, not capital

expenditures. Substituting a reasonable estimate of depreciation for the more than $200 billion of federal investment spending (Office of Management and Budget estimate) would knock some $70 billion off the deficit, reducing it to $85 billion.

Recognize that deficits are significant because they add to debt but what matters then is the real debt, adjusted for inflation. With inflation running at 3.6 percent, there was an "inflation tax" of some $72 billion on the $2 trillion of Treasury debt held by the public. Counting this inflation tax reduces the deficit to $13 billion.

In terms of impact on the economy, we are interested in all of government, not just Washington. State and local governments over the past fiscal year ran a surplus of some $55 billion—not unrelated to $108 billion of federal

grants in aid that amounted to more than two-thirds of the official federal deficit. If we add the plus $55 billion to the minus $13 billion we reach that real government budget surplus of $42 billion.

The critical issue—however we measure the budget—is what it does to the economy. Republicans since the days of Franklin D. Roosevelt have been denouncing Democratic budget deficits. Democrats have tried to have a field day denouncing the Reagan deficits that began in 1982. (They are in fact now much less, running some 3 percent of gross national product while they were more than 6 percent of GNP a few years ago.) Few politicians have been inspired to face the facts.

Despite recent record deficits, the sky has not fallen. Rather, the economy

(continued)

moved from deep recession and 10.7 percent unemployment to more than six years of sustained recovery. Unemployment fell by half. Corporate profits and the stock market soared. Business investment grew smartly.

All this indeed occurred not in spite of the budget deficits but in large part because of them. Government spending in excess of what it took from the public in taxes fueled aggregate demand, private and public, so that we were able to purchase more and more of what our productive economy could offer.

This is not to argue, contrary to Mr. Proxmire's charge, that there should be no limit to deficits. They can be too large if they bring us to the point where we are trying to buy more than can possibly be produced, a point that, despite our relative prosperity, we have hardly yet reached. And this is not to argue for wasteful government spending—or any other kind of wasteful spending. It makes a difference whether a person borrows to finance a gambling binge in Las Vegas or to buy a house or pay for his child's education. It makes a difference whether

a firm borrows to finance productive capital expenditures or frivolous extravagance.

It is vitally important that in addition to maintaining current prosperity—it hardly makes sense to slow down the economy now because it might slow down later—we invest adequately in the future. I see no reason to second-guess household and business decisions on how much to save and invest as long as the economy is prosperous. But by far the greatest portion of investment in the future is by its nature public. Private productivity and our future well-being depend critically on public investment in human capital—in education, training, and health, in basic research, in our vast tangible infrastructure of roads, bridges, and airports, and in the protection of natural resources of land, water, and air.

This is where Mr. Proxmire's counsel and all the near-hysteria about our mismeasured budget deficits can lead us seriously astray. Our 13-year-olds score last in international comparisons on tests of math and science ability. Much of a generation grows up semiliterate or illiterate and crazed by

drugs. Workers spend hours on choked highways and business travelers spend hours waiting for clearance to land at or fly to our congested airports.

Yet our "education president" is told that there is little or no more money to be invested in education, that the war to end the scourge of drugs will have to be fought on a shoestring, that there is virtually no room for new expenditures of any kind because "the deficit" must be brought down to some arbitrary target.

I am not telling "Daddio" to borrow to buy his 19-year-old son a $30,000 Porsche—although something that will give service for five years is properly considered an investment. But worthwhile public investment does have a payoff to the economy in higher productivity and national income. And indeed out of this higher income flows increased government revenues, even if Mr. Bush keeps that famous pledge to lip readers.

Who's Right?

William Proxmire—Former senator from Wisconsin who chaired the Senate Budget Committee. *UPI/Bettmann.*

The three perspectives presented here provide tremendous fuel for debate.

The Proxmire letter is typical of many intelligent lay people's view of the deficit. Proxmire attacks the adjustments that almost all economists believe should be made to the deficit. He represents the wolf-at-the-door view, which few economists endorse.

Eisner's response represents the domesticated-pussycat view held primarily by liberal Keynesian economists (of whom Eisner is one) and some Classical economists, although their reasons for holding that view are quite different from those of liberal Keynesians. Liberal Keynesians believe that it is important to stimulate the economy by running a deficit. As long as the economy needs stimulation, deficits don't matter. Classical economists who fall into this group of domesticated pussycats believe that deficits don't influence the economy, period: Since people are rational and fully discount expected future tax payments that the deficit would entail, deficits make no difference to the economy.

The termites-in-the-basement view in the Solow/Modigliani letter below represents the ideas of the majority of economists. They see the deficit gnawing away at the structure of the economy. They agree that the deficit per se doesn't matter, but they believe that the economy's underlying health isn't good and that it needs to be treated. Superficial cover-up work that makes the deficit look smaller, but doesn't deal with the underlying health problems, won't treat the disease.

CUTTING DEFICIT IS OUR ONLY ACCEPTABLE COURSE

Franco Modigliani
Robert Solow
*Professors of Economics
M.I.T., Cambridge, Mass.*

To the Editor:

It is unfortunate that Prof. Robert Eisner, whose contributions have made him a leading member of the economics profession, has now chosen to devote much of his attention to a contrary campaign in favor of more government expenditure and bigger deficits. Does he have a point?

Many of the arguments in "Let's Stop Worrying About the Budget Deficit" (letter, Feb. 19) are perfectly acceptable; for example, his assertion that any expenditure that primarily benefits future generations might be paid out of deficits without damaging them. The same goes for his assertion that the deficit, as measured in the budget, has numerous shortcomings. He calls attention to some that go in the direction of exaggerating the deficit (though one could argue with his specific corrections).

But he fails to mention others going in the opposite direction. Of these the most conspicuous is the treatment of Social Security; as a pension system it should not be included in the budget. It is running a surplus of some $50 billion (which should be devoted to capital formation to meet the coming bulge in the population of old relative to young). Hence, if Social Security were properly taken out of the budget, the deficit would be $50 billion larger.

But his argument is faulty on other grounds. The first is his concern that reducing the deficit at this time is likely "to slow the economy and hence bring less investment." This preoccupation must be regarded as entirely misplaced under conditions of high demand pressure and high interest rates.

Even more serious is Mr. Eisner's failure to come to grips with the fact that, since the beginning of the huge fiscal deficits in 1982, national savings (inclusive of durable goods accumulation) have plummeted from a comparatively low level of around 10 percent in the 1960's and 70's to a distressingly low one of around 5 percent in recent years. Though net national saving may not be exactly measured, there is no ground to doubt the trend. Only the large increase in capital imports (the trade deficit) has made it possible nearly to maintain the level of investment.

Professor Eisner seems to agree about some proper concern over our presumed growing debt to the rest of the world. But what he fails to realize is that none of his proposed solutions will reduce the trade deficit, unless we free resources to be used for more net exports. This requires that we either cut the deficit or cut investment. Failure to do so under conditions of full, if not overfull, employment would threaten to overload the economy, courting the risk of serious inflation.

Most thoughtful people agree that cutting investment is the last thing we should consider, and no one in his right mind thinks we should push output at the risk of inflation. This leaves cutting the deficit as the only acceptable option.

Reprinted by courtesy of Franco Modigliani and Robert Solow from a letter in the *New York Times* of March 12, 1989.

CHAPTER SUMMARY

A deficit is a shortfall of incoming revenues over outgoing payments; debt is accumulated deficits minus accumulated surpluses.

A budget deficit should be judged in light of economic and political conditions.

The deficit is a summary measure of a budget.

Whether a deficit is a problem depends on the budgeting procedures that measure it.

A country's debt must be judged in relation to its assets.

To judge the importance of deficits and debt, economists look at them relative to GDP.

A real deficit is a nominal deficit adjusted for the effect of inflation.

When expectations of inflation have fully adjusted, inflation involves no transfer from creditors to debtors.

The U.S. government often deals with its deficit problem by using gimmicks.

There are various reasonable views about the U.S. budget deficit.

KEY TERMS

Budget Enforcement Act of
 1990 *(465)*
cash flow accounting system *(474)*
debt *(463)*
debt service *(469)*
deficit *(463)*

external government debt *(468)*
Federal Deposit Insurance Corporation
 (FDIC) *(474)*
funded pension system *(475)*
Gramm-Rudman-Hollings Act *(465)*
internal government debt *(468)*

nominal deficit *(471)*
off-budget expenditure *(475)*
policy régime *(464)*
real deficit *(471)*
structural deficit *(470)*
unfunded pension system *(475)*

QUESTIONS FOR THOUGHT AND REVIEW

*The number after each question represents the estimated
degree of critical thinking required. (1 = almost none;
10 = deep thought.)*

1. Your income is $40,000 per year; your expenditures are
   $45,000. Ten thousand dollars of your $45,000
   expenditure is for tuition. Is your budget in deficit or
   surplus? Why? *(6)*
2. "The deficit should be of concern." What additional
   information do you need to undertake a reasonable
   discussion of that statement? *(5)*
3. "The debt should be of concern." What additional
   information do you need to undertake a reasonable
   discussion of that statement? *(5)*
4. Inflation is 20 percent. Debt is $2 trillion. The nominal
   deficit is $300 billion. What is the real deficit? *(2)*
5. How would your answer to Question 4 differ if you knew
   that expected inflation was 15 percent? *(5)*

6. The government began to issue inflation-adjusted bonds
   in 1997. Will the deficit fall as a result? Why or why
   not? What benefits do such bonds provide to bond
   holders? *(9)*
7. State the arguments of the pussycat view of the deficit.
   (6)
8. State the arguments of the wolf-at-the-door view of the
   deficit. *(6)*
9. State the arguments of the termites-in-the-basement view
   of the deficit. *(6)*
10. In what sense is the social security trust fund an
    accounting gimmick? *(7)*
11. In an op-ed article in *The Wall Street Journal*, Paul W.
    McCracken said: "A decision to go with budgets that
    involve deficits is a decision to have a future economy
    delivering lower incomes." Do you agree or disagree?
    Why? *(9)*

PROBLEMS AND EXERCISES

1. Calculate the real deficit in the following cases.
   a. Inflation is 10 percent. Debt is $3 trillion. Nominal
    deficit is $220 billion.
   b. Inflation is 2 percent. Debt is $1 trillion. Nominal
    deficit is $50 billion.
   c. Inflation is −4 percent. (Price level is falling.) Debt is
    $500 billion. Nominal deficit is $30 billion.
2. Using the latest figures available from your library, or the
   World Wide Web, calculate the real budget deficits for the
   United States, Britain, France, Brazil, and Nigeria.
3. Assume a country's nominal GDP is $600 billion,
   government expenditures less debt service are $145 billion,
   and revenue is $160 billion. The nominal debt is $360
   billion. Inflation is 3 percent while real interest rates are
   3 percent. Expected inflation is fully adjusted.
   a. Calculate debt service payments.
   b. Calculate the nominal deficit.
   c. Calculate the real deficit.

   d. What would you expect to happen if expectations of
    inflation fall? Why?
4. Assume a country's real growth is 2 percent per year,
   while its real deficit is rising by 5 percent per year. Can a
   country continue to afford such deficits ad infinitum? What
   problems might this country face in the future?
5. You've been hired by Creative Accountants, consultants to
   Textland. Your assignment is to make suggestions about
   how to structure its accounts so that the current deficit
   looks as small as possible. Specifically, they want to know
   how to treat the following:
   a. Government pensions.
   b. Sale of land.
   c. Social security taxes.
   d. Proceeds of a program to allow people to prepay taxes
    for a 10 percent discount.
   e. Expenditures on F-52 bombers.

ANSWERS TO MARGIN QUESTIONS

1. When the United States changed to a modern Classical supply-side policy régime, the size of the deficit increased, suggesting that it was politics as much as Keynesian economics that led to deficits. *(464)*
2. The deficit is a flow concept, the difference between income and expenditures. A debt—accumulated deficits minus accumulated surpluses—is a stock concept. *(466)*
3. To get a full picture of a country's financial situation, you have to look at assets as well as debt, since a large debt for a country with large assets poses no problem. *(467)*
4. GDP provides a measure of an economy's ability to service the debt and hence it is reasonable to measure the debt relative to GDP. *(468)*
5. Inflation reduces the value of the dollars with which the debt will be repaid and hence, in real terms, wipes out a portion of the debt. *(470)*
6. The real deficit equals the nominal deficit minus inflation times the total debt. Inflation times the total debt in this case equals $80 billion (.02 × $4 trillion). Since the nominal deficit is $40 billion, the real deficit is actually a surplus of $40 billion. ($40 billion − $80 billion = −$40 billion). *(471)*
7. When there is full adjustment for expectations, nominal interest rates rise to fully compensate creditors for any loss due to inflation. *(473)*
8. Deficits are simply a summary measure of an economy's health. By undertaking obligations in the future that don't show up as a deficit, a country can still get itself into financial trouble. *(474)*
9. An unfunded pension system is a pay-as-you-go system. It collects taxes from current workers and uses the proceeds to pay out benefits to current retirees. A baby boom changes the ratio between workers and retirees. Initially, it increases the number of workers to retirees, lowering the tax rate that must be paid to meet a given per-person retirement goal. However, when the baby boomers retire, it increases the necessary tax rate because there are so many more retirees for whom a per-person retirement goal must be met, and there are fewer working taxpayers from whom the necessary amount of taxes must be collected. *(476)*
10. Raising the social security retirement age does not reduce the deficit, but it does significantly reduce the future obligations of the country and hence can help the country's fiscal health. *(477)*

Twenty

Growth and the Macroeconomics of Developing and Transitional Economies

*Rise up, study the economic forces which oppress you. . . . They
have emerged from the hand of man just as the gods emerged from
his brain. You can control them.*

~ Paul LaFargue

After reading this chapter, you should be able to:

1 Distinguish between growth and development.

2 Explain why there might be a difference in normative goals between developing and developed countries.

3 Explain why economies at different stages in development have different institutional needs.

4 Explain what is meant by "the dual economy."

5 Distinguish between a régime change and a policy change.

6 Explain why the statement that inflation is a problem of the central bank issuing too much money is not sufficient for developing and transitional countries.

7 Distinguish between convertibility on the current account and full convertibility.

8 Explain the "borrowing circle" concept and why it was successful.

In this edition I have spread the international chapters throughout the book, instead of leaving them as a separate section. I have divided growth and development into a micro section and a macro section to better fit development into both courses. I have found that the issues involved in macro development are exciting to students, and it's too bad that they often are not covered.

Throughout this book I have emphasized that macro policy is an art in which one takes the abstract principles learned in *positive economics*—the abstract analysis and models that tell us how economic forces direct the economy—and examines how those principles work out in a particular institutional structure to achieve goals determined in *normative economics*—the branch of economics that considers what goals we should be aiming for. In this chapter we see another aspect of that art.

Most of this book has emphasized the macroeconomics of Western industrialized economies, the United States in particular. That means I have focused on their goals and their institutions. In this chapter I shift focus and discuss the macroeconomic problems of *developing economies* and *transitional economies*. As discussed in Chapter 6, a **developing economy** is *an economy that has a low level of GDP per capita and a relatively undeveloped market structure, and has not recently had an alternative, developed economic system.* A **transitional economy** is *an economy that has had an alternative, developed, socialist economic system, but is in the process of changing from that system to a market system.*

Economists use the terms developing and transitional, rather than growing, to emphasize that the goals of these countries involve more than simply an increase in output; these countries are changing their underlying institutions. Put another way, these economies are changing their production function; they are not increasing inputs given a production function. Thus *development* refers to an increase in productive capacity and output brought about by a change in the underlying institutions, and *growth* refers to an increase in output brought about by an increase in inputs.

The distinction can be overdone. Institutions, and hence production functions, in developed as well as in developing countries are continually changing, and output changes are essentially a combination of both changes in production functions and increases in inputs. For example, in the 1990s the major Western economies have been **restructuring** their economies—*changing the underlying economic institutions*—as they work to compete better in the world economy. As they restructure, they change their methods of production, their laws, and their social support programs. Thus, in some ways, they are doing precisely what developing and transitional countries are doing—developing rather than just growing. Despite the ambiguity, the distinction between growth and development can be a useful one if you remember that the two blend into each other.

The reason economists separate out developing and transitional economies is that these economies have (1) different institutional structures and (2) a different weighting of goals than do Western developed economies. These two differences—in institutional structure, and in goals—change the way in which the lessons of abstract theory are applied and discussed.

The chapter begins with a consideration of how the goals of developing countries differ from the goals of developed countries. Then I turn my attention to how the institutions differ. In the process of that discussion, I consider the general conduct of macro policy in developing countries, and present some case studies that bring to life important aspects of the macroeconomic problems they face.

When discussing macro policy within Western developed economies, I did not dwell on questions of normative goals of macroeconomics. Instead, I used generally accepted goals in the United States as the goals of macro policy—achieving low inflation, low unemployment, and an acceptable growth rate—with a few caveats. You may have noticed that the discussion focused more on what might be called stability goals—achieving low unemployment and low inflation—than it did on the acceptable growth rate goal. I chose that focus because growth in Western developed countries is desired because it holds unemployment down, and because it avoids difficult distributional questions, as much as it is desired for its own sake. Our economy has sufficient productive capacity to provide its citizens, on average, with a relatively high standard of living. The problem facing Western societies is as much seeing that all members of those societies share in that high standard of living as it is raising the standard.

In the developing countries, the weighting of goals is different. Growth—an increase in the economies' output—and development—a transition of the economies' institutions so that the economies can achieve higher levels of output—are primary goals. When people are starving and the economy isn't fulfilling people's **basic needs**—*adequate food, clothing, and shelter*—a main focus of macro policy will be on how to increase the economy's growth rate through development so that the economy can fulfill those basic needs.

When Classical economics developed, its focus was almost totally on economic growth. Early developers of that Classical economics—Adam Smith, Thomas Malthus, and David Ricardo—took growth as economics' central area of concern. As Western market economies grew, the focus of macroeconomics changed from issues of long-run growth to issues of short-run stability. The macroeconomic models

1 Growth occurs because of an increase in inputs, given a production function; development occurs through a change in the production function.

Q-1: Why does restructuring in developed countries suggest that the distinction between growth and development can be overdone?

When discussing development, I like to point out that in some ways the United States economy is a developing economy. We talk about some of the institutional changes that are a part of that development process. In the last two years the discussion has focused on changes in trading institutions such as NAFTA and the GATT.

While the lessons of abstract theory do not change when we shift our attention to developing and transitional economies, the institutions and goals change enormously.

DIFFERING GOALS OF DEVELOPED AND DEVELOPING COUNTRIES

Growth and Basic Needs

2 There are differences in normative goals between developing and developed countries because their wealth differs. Developing countries face true economic needs whereas developed countries' economic needs are considered by most people to be normatively less pressing.

Economic Growth as an Appropriate Goal for Developing Countries

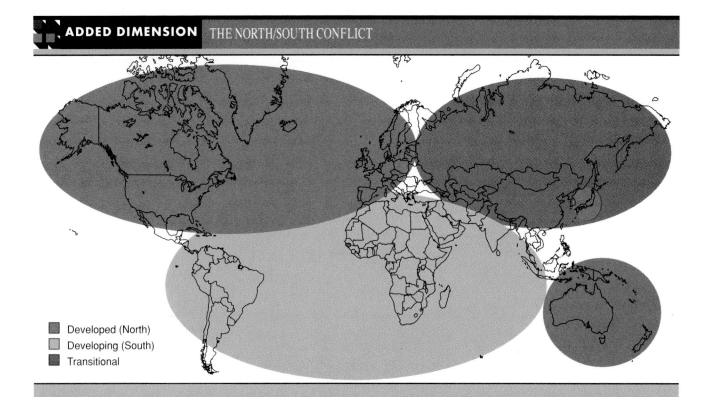

Developed (North)
Developing (South)
Transitional

Consider the map of the world and you will see that most of the developed nations are in the Northern hemisphere and most of the developing nations are in the Southern hemisphere. This has led to a characterization of the normative questions about growth as the "North/South conflict." Roughly, "North" refers to North America and Western Europe (together with Japan and Australia). "South" refers to Latin America and Africa.

The South's Position

In this conflict, the "South" takes the following position:

Economic growth uses natural resources or, more precisely, modifies the forms certain resources take. Much of the modification of resources that occurs due to current Northern production processes is, in the South's view, undesirable. For example, in many production processes we start with beautiful raw materials—forests, mountains, and pristine rivers—and we end up with trash heaps—dumps and polluted cesspools. In short, current production processes create too many of what society considers waste products in order to create goods that people don't really need, but which, instead, reflect needs created for them by society. The South asks: "Do Northern industrialized economies really need closets filled with this year's fashions—to be thrown out and replaced with next year's fashions? Or would something simpler—less resource-intensive—suffice?" Alternatively, think of automobiles. Do Western consumers really need air-conditioned automobiles at the cost of the depletion of the ozone layer?

The normative value judgments that must be made to answer these questions posed by the South are enormous, and I do not intend to deal with them here. But that does not mean that such judgments are not important. It is, in my view, legitimate to question whether further growth along the lines that Western economies are currently following is a goal to which the majority of people in Western society would subscribe, if they thought seriously about the issue.

The South points out that even if Northern societies have chosen the growth path, that path may still be suspect when one considers the normative issue of growth from an international perspective. Western economic growth imposes costs on the rest of the world. The world has a population of about 5.5 billion. The population of the industrialized countries is less than 1 billion, or 17 percent of the world's population, yet they use 60 percent of the world's resources and create many of the waste products that influence the entire atmosphere of the world. The South argues that, if we had a worldwide democratic government and a vote were taken on whether the majority of all people felt that physical growth in Western economies was a worthwhile goal, that growth would not be supported.

The North's Response

The Northern response to this philosophical question is varied. One response is to feel somewhat guilty about the North's success and use of the world's resources, and to establish aid programs to try to assuage that guilt. A number of international development programs have been started to try to offset the costs of the North's economic growth, but these programs are not large.

A second response is that the world isn't a democracy, and so in reality the question is moot. It doesn't matter what is right in some abstract philosophical sense. What matters simply is "what is."

A third response is that the South has the argument backwards. True, the North uses resources, but it is also creating new technologies. Technological changes are occurring faster than resource depletion, and with modern technological improvements in waste disposal, wastes are decreasing, not increasing. These pro-economic-growth economists argue that economic growth of Northern industrial countries is good not only for people in Northern countries; it is good for the entire world.

CLASSICAL ECONOMISTS AND LONG-RUN GROWTH

ADDED DIMENSION

How did Classical economists advise countries to grow? They advised: (1) keep the government out of the economy; (2) channel income to entrepreneurs and capitalists who consume little and who have a fetish for investing; (3) channel income away from landowners, who use it on servants and good living, not on growth-creating activities; and (4) channel income away from government that spends it on who-knows-what (but certainly not on growth-creating activities).

They also generally opposed programs to raise wages of workers because (1) workers would use the raises to have more children (the Malthusian doctrine), and (2) high wages would make the economy internationally uncompetitive in a fixed exchange rate system as then existed.

Early Classical economists—Adam Smith, Thomas Malthus, and David Ricardo—were strongest in their support of these propositions. Later Classical economists—John Stewart Mill and Alfred Marshall—were less adamant in their

support and often advocated contrary policies. Likely reasons for the change include changing institutions and increased wealth in the economy.

Democracy developed together with capitalism, and as the democratic nature of government became part of the institutional structure, the Classical arguments against government intervention were modified. Similarly, as industrialists lost their investment fetish and started to enjoy life (i.e., as they (or their children) started to consume some of their profits, not invest), it made less sense to channel income to industrialists to bring about investment and growth. Also, with the development of financial markets, savings from others, such as landowners or workers, could be channeled into investment and hence into growth. And finally, as society got richer, other goals besides growth became more important. In short, as Western institutions changed and Western wealth grew, so, too, did Classical economists' proposed policies.

---

developed in this book reflect that change in focus. Keynesian economics, specifically, has a short-run focus, and has little relevance to long-term growth. That part of Classical economics that we concentrated on in earlier chapters was a response to Keynes, which means that the Classical economics I presented earlier concerned more short-run than long-run issues. I left out a discussion of Classical long-run economics, which did focus on growth. (See the accompanying box for a brief discussion of Classical long-run economics.)

In summary, the goals of developed and developing countries differ; for developing countries, growth in economic output is a more generally agreed-upon goal than it is for developed countries. The central policy question facing these developing countries is: What set of macro policies will lead to growth?

Developing and transitional countries differ from developed countries not only in their goals, but also in their macroeconomic institutions. These macroeconomic institutions are qualitatively different from institutions in developed countries. Their governments are different; their financial institutions—the institutions that translate savings into investment—are different; their fiscal institutions—the institutions through which government collects taxes and spends its money—are different; and their social and cultural institutions are different. Because of these differences, the way in which we discuss macroeconomic policy is different.

One of the differences concerns very basic market institutions—such as Western-style property rights and contract law. In certain groups of developing countries, most notably sub-Saharan Africa, these basic market institutions don't exist; instead, communal property rights and tradition structure economic relationships. In the transitional economies, where the government previously owned large portions of the economy, ownership is often unclear. Decades ago, before the government owned large portions of the economy, there was private ownership, and claims based on those old conditions are surfacing, often placing clouds on current "ownership" and control. How can one talk about market forces in such economies?[1] On a more mundane level, consider the issue of monetary policy. Talking about monetary policy via open market operations (the buying and selling of bonds by the central bank) is not all that helpful

INSTITUTIONAL DIFFERENCES

Q–2: What are two ways in which developed countries differ from developing countries?

■ Economies at different stages of development have different institutional needs because the problems they face are different. Institutions that can be assumed in developed countries cannot necessarily be assumed to exist in developing countries.

---

[1]One can, of course, talk about economic forces. But, as discussed in Chapter 1, economic forces only become market forces in a market institutional setting.

when there are no open market operations, as there are not in many developing countries.

Let's now consider some specific institutional differences more carefully.

Political Differences and Laissez-Faire

In many developing countries, institutional checks and balances on government leaders often do not exist.

For a real-world example of the political difficulties facing a transitional economy, see "East-West Divide Lives On in Germany," in *Case Studies in Macroeconomics.*

Q–3: Why might an economist favor activist policies in developed countries and laissez-faire policies in developing countries?

Views of how activist macroeconomic policy should be are necessarily contingent on the political system an economy has. One of the scarcest commodities in developing countries is socially-minded leaders. Not that developed countries have any overabundance of them, but at least in most developed countries there is a tradition of politicians seeming to be fair and open-minded, and a set of institutionalized checks and balances that limits leaders using government for their personal benefit. In many developing countries, those institutionalized checks and balances on governmental leaders often do not exist.

Let's consider a few examples. First, consider Saudi Arabia, which, while economically rich, maintains many of the institutions of a developing country. It is an absolute monarchy in which the royal family is the ultimate power. Say a member of that family comes to the bank and wants a loan that, on economic grounds, doesn't make sense. What do you think the bank loan officer will do? Grant the loan, if the banker is smart. Thus, despite the wealth of the country, it isn't surprising that many economists believe the Saudi banking system reflects that political structure, and may soon find itself in serious trouble.

A second example is the new transitional countries of the former Soviet Union. They face enormous political instability problems, and in the 1990s the largest growth industry there was the private protection agency business. In such an institutional setting, government policy often has little to do with economics or what's good for the economy, and any proposed macroeconomic policy must take that into account.

A final example is Nigeria, which had enormous possibilities for economic growth in the 1980s because of its oil riches. It didn't develop. Instead, politicians fought over the spoils, and bribes became a major source of their income. Corruption was rampant, and the Nigerian economy went nowhere. I will stop there, but, unfortunately, there are many other examples.

Because of the structure of government in many developing countries, many economists who, in Western developed economies, favor activist government policies may well favor Classical laissez-faire policies for the same reasons that early Classical economists did—because they have a profound distrust of the governments. That distrust, however, must have limits. As I discussed in Chapter 5, even a laissez-faire policy requires some government role in setting the rules. So there is no escaping the need for socially-minded leaders.

The Dual Economy

4 "The dual economy" refers to the existence of the two sectors in most developing countries: a traditional sector and an internationally-oriented modern market sector.

Q–4: What is meant by the term "dual economy"?

A second institutional difference between developed and developing countries is the dual nature of developing countries' economies. Whereas it often makes sense to talk about a Western economy as a single economy, it does not for most developing countries. A developing country's economy is generally characterized by a **dual economy**—*the existence of two sectors: a traditional sector and an internationally-oriented modern market sector.*[2]

Often, the largest percentage of the population participates in the traditional economy. It is a local currency, or no currency, sector in which traditional ways of doing things take precedence. The second sector—the internationally-oriented modern market sector—is often indistinguishable from a Western economy. Activities in the modern sector are often conducted in foreign currencies, rather than domestic currencies, and contracts are often governed by international law. This dual economy aspect of developing countries creates a number of policy dilemmas for them and affects the way they think about macroeconomic problems.

---

[2]I discuss these two economies as if they were separate, but in reality, they are interrelated. Portions of the economy devoted to the tourist trade span both sectors, as do some manufacturing industries. Still, there is sufficient independence of the two economies that it is reasonable to treat them as separate.

For example, take the problem of unemployment. Many developing countries have a large, subsistence farming economy. Subsistence farmers aren't technically unemployed, but often there are so many people on the land that, in economic terms, their marginal product is minimal or even negative, so for policy purposes one can consider the quantity of labor that will be supplied at the going wage unlimited. But to call these people unemployed is problematic. These subsistence farmers are simply outside the market economy. In such cases one would hardly want, or be able, to talk of an unemployment problem in the same way we talk in the United States.

A third institutional difference concerns developing and transitional countries' fiscal systems. To undertake discretionary fiscal policy—running a deficit or surplus to affect the aggregate economy—the government must be able to determine expenditures and tax rates, with a particular eye toward the difference between the two. As discussed above, discretionary fiscal policy is difficult for Western developed countries to undertake; it is almost impossible for developing and transitional economies. Often, the governments in these economies don't have the institutional structures with which to collect taxes (or, when they have the institutional structure, it is undermined by fraud and evasion), so their taxing options are limited; that's why they often use tariffs as a primary source of revenue.

In the traditional sector of many developing and transitional countries, barter or cash transactions predominate, and such transactions are especially difficult to tax. For example, consider Bulgaria, which at the beginning of the 1990s was attempting to transform itself from a centrally-planned economy to a market economy. Initially it had no agency for tax collection since all previous economic activity was under the control of the state. Under its old institutional structure, revenues automatically flowed into the state. As the country shifted to a market economy, that changed dramatically. With no experience in tax collection, and with no tradition of paying taxes, initially all the fiscal policy discussion concerned how to collect enough to finance the basic core of government in order to keep it functioning.

Similar problems exist with government expenditures. Many expenditures of developing countries are mandated by political considerations—if the government doesn't make them, it will likely be voted out of office. Within such a setting, to talk about Keynesian fiscal policy—choosing a deficit for its macroeconomic implications—even if it might otherwise be relevant, is not much help since the budget deficit is not a choice variable, but instead is a result of other political decisions.

The political constraints facing developing and transitional countries can, of course, be overstated. The reality is that developing countries do institute new fiscal régimes. Take, for example, Mexico. In the early 1980s, Mexico's fiscal problems seemed impossible to solve, but in the late 1980s and early 1990s, Carlos de Salinas, a U.S.-trained economist, introduced a fiscal austerity program and an economic liberalization program that lowered Mexico's deficit and significantly reduced its inflation. But such changes are better called a **régime change**—*a change in the entire atmosphere within which the government and the economy interrelate*—rather than a **policy change**—*a change in one aspect of government's actions, such as monetary policy or fiscal policy*. Régimes can change suddenly. For example, in Mexico soon after President Salinas left office, his brother was implicated in a murder and drug scandal. Foreign investors became worried and pulled money out of Mexico. The peso fell, inflation and interest rates rose, and the Mexican economy fell into a serious recession. In one day the régime of confidence had changed to a régime of uncertainty and confusion, full of questions about what policy actions the Mexican government would take.

I spent two chapters discussing the complex financial systems of developed countries because you had to understand those financial systems in order to understand macro policy. While some parts of that discussion carry over to developing countries, other parts don't, since financial systems in developing countries are often quite different than those in developed countries.

You may need to remind your students that the marginal product of a worker is the additional amount of output that the worker can produce.

Fiscal Structure of Developing and Transitional Economies

Often developing countries do not have the institutional structures with which to collect taxes.

Many government expenditures in developing countries are mandated by political considerations.

The assassination of Carlos de Salinas's chosen successor in Mexico, Luis Colosio, demonstrates some of the political problems that remain in countries that have almost escaped the "developing" name.

5 A régime change is a change in the entire atmosphere within which the government and the economy interrelate; a policy change is a change in one aspect of government's actions.

Financial Institutions of Developing and Transitional Economies

The primary difference between financial institutions in developing countries and developed countries arises from the dual nature of developing countries' economies.

The primary difference arises from the dual nature of developing countries' economies. In the traditional part of developing economies, the financial sector is embryonic; trades are made by barter, or with direct payment of money; trades requiring more sophisticated financial markets, such as mortgages to finance houses, just don't exist.

In the modern international part of developing economies, that isn't the case. Developing countries' international financial sectors are sometimes as sophisticated as Western financial institutions. When one walks into a currency trading room in Bulgaria or Nigeria, one will see a room similar to a room that one would see in New York, London, or Frankfurt. That modern financial sector is integrated into the international economy (with pay rates that often approach or match those of the West). This dual nature of developing countries' financial sectors imposes constraints on the practice of monetary policy and changes the regulatory and control functions of central banks.

An Example of the Different Roles of Financial Institutions in Transitional Economies

Let's consider an example of a transitional economy—Bulgaria, where I spent some time trying to understand the banking system and teaching Bulgarian professors about Western banking. Before going over there, I had expected to teach about money and banking the same way I had done in the West, explaining how the quantity of high-powered money serves as a basis for loans, and how the money multiplier works. Then, I had expected to explain how the banks made decisions on long-term loans, and how those decisions were related to central bank policy.

I soon discovered that much of this was not directly relevant for Bulgaria. While Bulgarian private banks had many long-term loans on the books, when I was there they were making almost no new long-term loans, and those that already existed were, in large part, worthless. The reason was that the Bulgarian private banks had been created out of the former Bulgarian National Bank. In the transition, that single bank was broken up into the Central Bank and a number of private banks, with the private banks carrying on their books some portion of the loans of the central bank from which they were created. These loans had little value; as part of the planned economy, the bank had systematically extended whatever credit was needed to the companies it served. These firms simultaneously extended **interfirm credit** (*loans from one firm to another*) to other firms so that monetary payment for whatever they wanted was easy to obtain. This is what Harvard economist James Kornai called the **soft budget constraint**—*loose financial constraints on firms' decisions in centrally planned economies.* By this term he meant that, since firms could get loans without difficulty, financial constraints—the need to pay for inputs—placed little constraint on firms' decisions in centrally planned economies. With the end of the central planning and an attempt to switch their economies from centrally planned to market economies, the soft budget constraint came to a hard end.

Soft budget constraint   Loose financial constraints on firms' decisions in centrally planned economies.

The private banks that evolved from the government bank inherited the loans of their predecessor bank, and it was these long-term loans that they carried on their books. The loans were uncollectable. Even if the firms to whom the loans were made were still viable, those viable firms had so many trade credits extended to other, unviable firms that the viable firms couldn't pay off the loans. Most firms couldn't even afford to pay the interest, and the only reason they didn't default was that the banks kept lending them the money to pay the interest. Luckily or unluckily, depending on where you stood, the real interest rate was negative, and inflation was wiping out many of these loans, making the debtor firms better off. (For whom was this unlucky? Remember: inflation makes the society neither richer nor poorer, so someone was losing. Who? Holders of cash whose wealth was being wiped out.)

Inflation makes society neither richer nor poorer. It transfers money from creditors to debtors.

There were three reasons that new long-term loans weren't being made. The first was that the central bank was attempting to restrict credit in order to restrain the inflationary pressures. Thus, private banks had a hard time getting loans from the central bank. An important reason why the central bank was concerned about making too much credit available was, in turn, a second reason why new long-term loans weren't being made. Since the private banks had never made loans based on sound lending principles (remember the soft budget constraint), they had no loan officers or procedures to determine who should get loans.

Third, even if they had had such a system, there was little demand for what I'd call sound long-term loans. These were two reasons for their low demand. First, the Bulgarian economy was in a serious downward spiral. With expectations of a downward economic spiral, sound long-term investment doesn't make much sense. Second, the interest rate charged by the Bulgarian banks was about 50 percent. Such high nominal interest rates have a tendency to discourage loans. But, you must remember, the inflation was around 60 percent, making the real interest rate minus 10 percent. A negative real interest rate should, according to simple economic theory, encourage firms to take out loans. That wasn't taking place. Why? It seems that once inflation and nominal interest rates get that high, they are accompanied by enormous uncertainty about future inflation and, in particular, about relative prices of products. To make a business plan work with a 60 percent rate of inflation and a 50 percent nominal interest rate, you must build a 50 or 60 percent price rise into your business plan, making your profitability analysis on the basis of an expected rise in prices.

When I asked businesspeople why they didn't do that, I discovered that the business texts that they were using to guide them didn't include such an inflation adjustment—their texts did break-even analysis (an analysis of whether an investment makes sense or not) at fixed prices. (Remember, these were people new to business, and they were looking to the Western textbooks to guide them.) Even those who understood that the break-even analysis could be adjusted for expected inflation didn't want their success or failure to be dependent on an inflation rate over which they had no control. Entrepreneurial types generally like control, and the inflation made them feel controlled rather than in control. In short, they felt the financial situation was too uncertain to take a chance, and so they didn't want to invest.

To say that there was no demand for solid productive investment loans is not to say there was no demand for loans. There was a large demand for long-term loans, but most of that demand was connected to high-risk investments in which the borrower received most of the return in the unlikely event that the project turned out to be successful and the bank bore all the loss in the likely event the project was unsuccessful. The end result was that the banks were making almost no long-term loans.

Despite the fact that the banking system was not making long-term loans, it provided **trade credits**—*significant short-term loans (one to two weeks) to facilitate interfirm trade.* In Western economies this necessary function for a working economy is provided primarily by firms. When a firm orders a product from another firm, the bill is sent payable in about 30 days—weeks after the product is sent. Accounts payable and accounts receivable, representing short-term loans from one firm to another, are parts of every Western firm's balance sheet. The Bulgarian firms were unwilling to extend such trade credits to other Bulgarian firms; they wanted payment guaranties before they would sell to another firm. (In the United States, firms want such guaranties when the firms they are dealing with are close to bankruptcy.) The Bulgarian banking system was providing this guarantee function. It extended large amounts of trade credits, making interfirm trade possible.

This trade credit role of banking is hardly mentioned in modern Western money and banking books, and is not even discussed in the financial and monetary institutions chapters of this book. It is, however, an absolutely necessary function for an economy to work. In developed countries, one takes the fulfillment of that function for granted; in Bulgaria one couldn't. (This function of banking was not always taken for granted in the United States; academic discussion of banking in the early 1800s often included discussion of this vital role and how to maintain sufficient "elasticity" in the money supply to meet the trade credit needs. Western institutions simply became so good at fulfilling this function that we don't discuss it.)

It is important to have specific knowledge of a country's institutions before one can understand its economy and meaningfully talk about policy.

The above is one of many institutional examples of differences that exist and that change the nature of the macro problem. What's important is not so much the specifics of the example but, rather, the general point it brings home. Economies at different stages of development have different institutional, and policy, needs. Institutions with the same names in different countries can have quite different roles. Such institutions can differ in subtle ways, making it important to have specific knowledge of a country's institutions before one can understand its economy and meaningfully talk about policy.

Monetary Policy in Developing and Transitional Countries

Now that I've discussed some of the ways in which financial institutions differ in developing and transitional countries, let's consider some issues of central banking and monetary policy for those economies.

The first thing to note about central banking in developing and transitional countries is that its primary goal is often different than a central bank's primary goal in developed countries. The reason is that, while all central banks have a number of goals, at the top of them all is the goal of keeping the economy running. In the 1990s, Western central banks have the luxury of assuming away the problem of keeping the economy running—inertia, institutions, and history hold Western industrial economies together, and keep them running. Central banks in developing and transitional countries can't make that assumption.

Central banks in developing and transitional countries have far less independence than do central banks in developed countries.

What this means in practice is that central banks in developing and transitional countries have far less independence than do central banks in developed countries. With a political and fiscal system that generates large deficits and cannot exist without those deficits, the thought of an independent monetary policy goes out the window.

You may find it useful to refresh your students' memories concerning how the central bank can monetize the government's debts.

A second difference concerns the institutional implementation of monetary policy. In a developing or a transitional country, a broad-based domestic government bond market often does not exist. So if the government runs a deficit and is financing it domestically, the central bank usually must buy the bonds, which means that it must increase the money supply.

Monetary Policy and Inflation   The above institutional background gives us some insight into the significant inflation problem many developing and transitional countries face. The extent of that inflation can be seen in Exhibit 1.

It shows recent inflation rates for various regions. Notice that for a number of developing countries, the U.S. inflation rate wouldn't be seen as inflation at all, but only as background noise in the price level. For example, in the early 1990s inflation in some Latin American countries has exceeded 10,000 percent per year. Thus, talking about inflation as a macroeconomic problem of developing countries would seem to make sense. But it cannot be talked about as a simple economic problem; it must be talked about as a macro-political problem.

Q–6: If everyone knows that the cause of inflation in developing countries is the creation of too much money, why don't these countries stop inflation?

Let me explain. In the United States, there's significant debate about the cause and nature of inflation. The cause and nature of developing and transitional countries' inflation is clear. Economists of all persuasions agree that large inflations can continue only if the central bank issues large amounts of money. So the cause of developing countries' inflation is that the central banks are issuing too much money. But, as discussed above, the central banks know that. The real policy debate is not about the economic cause but is about the political cause—whether the central bank has a choice about issuing so much money. That debate concerns issues related to the political consequences of not issuing too much money.

6 Central banks recognize that printing too much money causes inflation, but often feel compelled to do so for political reasons. Debate about inflation in developing and transitional countries generally concerns those political reasons, not the relationship between money and inflation.

As I discussed above, often, in developing countries, the government's sources of tax revenue are limited, and the low level of income in the economy makes the tax base small. A government attempting to collect significantly more taxes might risk being overthrown. Similarly its ability to cut expenditures is limited. If it cuts expenditures, it will almost certainly be overthrown. With new tax sources unavailable and with no ability to cut expenditures, the government uses its only other option to meet its obligations—it issues debt. And, if the central bank agrees with the conclusion that

Inflation Rate			
	1993	1994	1995
Latin America	209.5%	223.9%	37.9%
Africa	27.4	33.8	25.8
Asia	9.5	13.5	10.9
U.S.	2.6	2.3	2.5
E.U.	3.6	2.6	3.0
Eastern Europe	364.5	152.9	75.3

EXHIBIT 1   Inflation Rates of Selected Areas

Inflation is a problem of many developing countries, especially in Latin and South America. Notice the generally lower rates of inflation in the developed as compared to the developing regions.

Source: *World Economic Outlook, 1996* (International Monetary Fund).

the government is correct in its assessment that it has no choice, then if the central bank doesn't want the government to be overthrown, it has no choice but to monetize that debt (print money to pay that debt). Sometimes the central bank's choices are even more limited; dictatorships simply tell the central bank to provide the needed money, or be eliminated.

The problem for transitional economies is slightly different. As socialist countries, they had their taxes built into their pricing structure. Their government received the difference between the revenue received for the goods they sold and the cost to them to produce those goods. Their "tax" was that difference. As they moved toward a market economy, this source of revenue was eliminated and they had no taxing institutions—such as the U.S. Internal Revenue Service—in place to implement new taxes and supply that revenue. Moreover, people had no tradition of paying taxes and, hence, avoided and evaded taxes whenever they could. With the legal system in transition, the government could do little to force individuals to pay taxes.

The Inflation Tax   Issuing money to finance budget deficits may be a short-term solution but it is not a long-term solution. It is an accounting identity that real resources consumed by the economy must equal the real resources produced or imported. If the government deficit doesn't increase output, the real resources the government is getting because the central bank is monetizing its debt must come from somewhere. Where do those real resources come from? From the **inflation tax**: *an implicit tax on the holders of cash and the holders of any obligations specified in nominal terms.* Inflation works as a type of tax on these individuals.

Let's consider that inflation tax in relation to the transitional economies. With the end of central planning, there was an enormous monetary overhang—large stores of currency in excess of real goods in the economy at market prices. This monetary overhang existed because most individuals had stored their financial wealth in the currency of their country. This currency represented the enormous past obligations of the former socialist governments—obligations that far exceeded the governments', or the economies', ability to meet them.

As they moved to a market economy without an acceptable tax base, there was no way for these governments to meet their current obligations, let alone their past obligations. Something had to give; accounting identities are unforgiving. Either the government must default, or prices must rise enormously.

The central banks generally chose to keep the governments operating (which isn't surprising, since they were often branches of the government). To do that they increased the money supply enormously, causing hyperinflation in many of these countries. These hyperinflations soon took on a life of their own. The expectation of accelerating inflation created even more inflationary pressure as individuals tried to spend any money they had quickly, before the prices went up. This increased velocity, nominal demand for goods, and inflationary pressures. These hyperinflations wiped out (taxed away) the monetary overhang, allowing most of those transitional countries to rein in their inflation, getting it down to double digits (less than 100 percent per

If there are international students in your class, it is helpful to ask them to describe some of their fiscal and taxpaying institutions at home. Such questions usually generate signifiant interest among U.S. students and start good discussions.

Inflation works as a tax on holders of obligations specified in nominal terms.

I like to spend some extra time to make sure my students understand how the inflation tax works. It is a different kind of tax than they are used to thinking about.

year). This was possible because, with the overhang wiped out, the inflation tax only had to make up for the government budget deficit; it no longer had to be used to eliminate past obligations.

Q-7: In an inflation, who else, besides government, gets revenue from an inflation tax?

One problem with the use of an inflation tax is that in an inflation, the government is not the only recipient of revenue; any issuer of fixed-interest-rate debt denominated in domestic currency also gains. And the holder of any fixed-interest-rate debt denominated in domestic currency loses. This income redistribution caused by an inflation can temporarily stimulate real output, but it can also undermine the country's financial institutions.

The point of the above discussion is that the central banks know that issuing large quantities of money will cause inflation. What they don't know, and what the policy discussions are about, is which is worse: the inflation or the unpleasant alternatives. Should the central bank bail out the government? There are legitimate questions about whether countries' budget deficits are absolutely necessary or not. It is those assessments in which the debate about developing countries' inflation exists; the debate is not about whether the inflation is caused by the issuance of too much money.

The fact that inflation is only a temporary solution doesn't stop developing and transitional countries' leaders from using it.

Opponents of any type of bailout point out that any "inflation solution" is only a temporary solution that, if used, will require ever-increasing amounts of inflation to remain effective. Proponents of bailouts agree with this argument, but argue that inflation buys a bit more time, and the alternative is the breakdown of the government and the economy. Because of the unpleasant alternative, the fact that inflation is only a temporary solution doesn't stop developing and transitional countries' leaders from using it. They don't have time for the luxury of long-run solutions, and are often simply looking for policies that will hold their governments together for a month at a time.

Focus on the International Sector and the Exchange Rate Constraint

Another difference between the monetary policies of developed and developing countries concerns the policy options they consider for dealing with foreign exchange markets. Developed countries are generally committed to full exchange rate convertibility on both the current and capital accounts. With full exchange rate convertibility, individuals can exchange their currency for any other country's currency without significant government restrictions.

Transitional and developing countries often do not have fully convertible currencies. Individuals and firms in these countries face restrictions on their ability to exchange currencies—sometimes general restrictions and sometimes restrictions depending on the purpose for which they wish to use the foreign exchange.

Various Types of Convertibility   Since convertibility plays such a central role in developing countries' macro policies, let's review the various types of convertibility. The United States has **full convertibility**—*individuals may change dollars into any currency they want for whatever legal purpose they want.* (There are, however, reporting laws about movements of currency.) Most Western developed countries have full convertibility.

Q-8: Distinguish between convertibility on the current account and full convertibility.

A second type of convertibility is **convertibility on the current account**—*a system that allows people to exchange currencies freely to buy goods and services, but not to buy assets in other countries.*

The third type of convertibility is **limited capital account convertibility**—*a system that allows full current account convertibility and partial capital account convertibility.* There are various levels of restrictions on what types of assets one can exchange, so there are many types of limited capital account convertibility.

7 Full convertibility means one can exchange one's currency for whatever legal purpose one wants. Convertibility on the current account limits those exchanges to buying goods and services.

Almost no developing country has full convertibility.

Almost no developing country allows full convertibility. Why? One reason is that they want to force their residents to keep their savings, and to do their investing, in their home country, not abroad. Why don't their citizens want to do that? Because when there is a chance of a change in governments—and government seizure of assets—as there often is in developing countries, rich individuals generally prefer to have a significant portion of their assets abroad, away from the hands of their government.

These limits on exchange rate convertibility explain a general phenomenon found in most developing countries—the fact that much of the international part of the dual economy in developing countries is "dollarized"—contracts are framed in, and accounting is handled in, dollars, not in the home country's currency. Dollarization exists almost completely in the international sectors of countries that have nonconvertible currencies, and largely in the international sectors of countries where the currency is convertible on the current account but not on the capital account. This dollarization exists because of nonconvertibility, or the fear of nonconvertibility. Thus, ironically, nonconvertibility increases the focus on dollarized contracts in the international sector, and puts that sector beyond effective control by the central bank.

Nonconvertibility does not halt international trade—it merely complicates it, since it adds another layer of uncertainty and bureaucracy to the trading process. Each firm that is conducting international trade must see that it will have sufficient foreign exchange to carry on its business. Developing and transitional governments will often want to encourage this international trade, while preventing outflows of their currencies for other purposes.

Nonconvertibility does not halt international trade; it merely makes it more difficult.

When developing countries have partially convertible exchange rates, **exchange rate policy**—*buying and selling foreign currencies in order to help stabilize the exchange rate*—often is an important central bank function. This is such an important function because trade in most of these countries' currencies is *thin*—there is not a large number of traders or trades. When trading is thin, large fluctuations in exchange rates are possible in response to a change in a few traders' needs. Even the uncertainties of the weather can affect traders. Say an expected oil tanker is kept from landing in port because of bad weather. The financial exchange—paying for that oil—that would have taken place upon landing does not take place, and the supply/demand conditions for a country's currency could change substantially. In response, the value of the country's currency could rise or fall dramatically unless it were stabilized. The central bank often helps provide exchange rate stabilization.

Since the collapse of the communist empire, the Russian ruble has become convertible. For a discussion of the difficulties of a market determined exchange rate in a transitional economy, see "Ruble Stages 21.5% Decline Against the Dollar," in *Case Studies in Macroeconomics.*

Conditionality and the Balance of Payments Constraint   In designing their policies, transitional and developing countries often rely on advice from the International Monetary Fund (IMF). One reason is that the IMF has economists who have much experience with these issues. A second reason is that, for these countries, the IMF is a major source of temporary loans that they need to stabilize their currencies.

These loans usually come with conditions that the country meet certain domestic monetary and fiscal stabilization goals. Specifically, these goals are that government deficits be lowered and money supply growth be limited. Because of these requirements, IMF's loan policy is often called **conditionality**—*the making of loans that are subject to specific conditions.*

The basis for most IMF loans is conditionality.

Even a partially flexible exchange rate régime presents the country with the **balance of payments constraint**—*limitations on expansionary domestic macroeconomic policy due to a shortage of international reserves.* Attempts to expand the domestic economy with expansionary monetary policy continually push the economy to its balance of payments constraint. To meet both its domestic goals and international balance of payments constraints, many developing countries turn to loans from the IMF, not only for the exchange rate stabilization reasons discussed above, but also for a more expansionary macro policy than otherwise would be possible. Because of the IMF's control of these loans, macro policy in developing countries is often conducted with one eye toward the IMF, and sometimes with a complete bow.

Balance of payments constraint
Limitation on expansionary domestic macro policy due to a shortage of international reserves.

The above discussion may have made it seem as if conducting domestic macro policy in developing countries is almost hopelessly dominated by domestic political concerns and international constraints. If, by macro policy, one means using traditional monetary and fiscal policy tools as they are used in standard ways, that's true. But macro policy, interpreted broadly, is much more than using those tools. It is the development of new institutions that expand the possibilities for growth. It is creating a new production function, not operating within an existing one. Macro policy, writ large to

MACRO INSTITUTIONAL POLICY IN DEVELOPING COUNTRIES

include the development of new institutions, can have enormous effects. To undertake such policies requires an understanding of the role of institutions, the specific nature of the problem in one's country, and creativity.

Let's consider a recent World Bank report on the developmental success of "The Asian Tigers" to see how economists view what might be called **macro institutional policies**—*policies to change the underlying macro institutions and thereby increase output.* The report asked what were the causes of these countries' high growth rates, and whether their success provides lessons for other developing countries.

The report concluded that the most important reason for these countries' success was that they "got the economic fundamentals right, with low inflation, sound fiscal policies, high levels of domestic savings, heavy investment in education; and they kept their economies more open to foreign technology than most other developing countries." In a sense, what the World Bank concluded was that these high growth rates were not a miracle at all, but simply the result of sound economic policies.

While economists will disagree with particulars of many of these fundamentals, almost all would agree with the general argument: macro policy in developing countries involves getting the infrastructure right—creating a climate within which individual initiative is directed toward production.

Generating Savings and Investment and the Lingering Shadow of the Debt Crisis

Let's now consider some of these fundamentals more carefully.

Growth depends on investment, and investment depends on savings. This savings can come from domestic sources, or it can come from international sources, either in the form of foreign private investment or foreign aid.

Because it is difficult to generate domestic savings, developing countries often look abroad for savings to finance investment. But many of the firms in these countries are unable to borrow abroad because they lack creditworthiness. This leads the governments of many of these developing countries to guarantee loans by private firms, thereby creating large government debt overhangs, all denominated in dollars, leaving the monetary policy with a serious external debt problem.

Had the loans that led to this debt gone for productive investments that paid a return greater than the principal and interest on the loans, these investments would have been helpful. But in reality, as a result of political corruption and economic mismanagement, the investments were often unproductive. Returns on the investments didn't even cover the interest payments, let alone the principal. The situation was worsened by tight U.S. monetary policy that simultaneously raised interest rates, increasing the interest burden of these floating-rate loans, and raised the value of the dollar, increasing the developing countries' indebtedness far beyond their expectations. In short, the governments that had guaranteed the loans found themselves responsible for repaying the loans without the wherewithal to do so. They found themselves in a debt crisis.

In the mid-1990s, the total debt of Latin American countries was about $600 billion, much of it owned by U.S. banks, while all the developing countries combined had about $1.9 trillion in outstanding debt. That meant that they had to have a large annual trade surplus simply to pay the interest of about $100 billion a year on their debt. Some countries' annual interest was more than they could afford to pay from their export earnings. But if they paid only the interest on the debt and did not make payments on the principal, the debt would remain as large as ever. And as long as that debt remained unpaid, there would be no new incoming foreign investment to devote to development. The developing countries found themselves trapped by debt, and that trap became known as the debt crisis.

How the Debt Crisis Was Managed   There's a saying in banking, "If you owe the bank a million, you're in trouble; if you owe the bank a billion, your trouble is the bank's trouble." When a lender will go broke if a borrower defaults, the lender will try as

---

Macro institutional policies Policies to change the underlying macro institutions and thereby increase output.

Macro policy in developing countries involves getting the infrastructure right—creating a climate within which individual initiative is directed toward production.

Growth depends on investment, and investment depends on savings.

Q-9: How can loans to developing countries cause problems?

If you owe a bank a million, you are in trouble; if you owe a bank a billion, your trouble is the bank's trouble.

hard as it can to work something out. Accordingly, the 1980s were years of intense negotiation designed to prevent developing countries from defaulting on their loans. The U.S. government, other Western governments, and the International Monetary Fund were active in these negotiations.

In the late 1980s, default was prevented by (1) restructuring the debt, (2) lending developing countries even more money to pay the interest on the debts, (3) writing off some of the old loans (essentially forgiving them), and (4) lowering the interest rate on the remaining loans.

The Debt Restructuring Strategy   Since the process by which these debts were reduced shows the role of the IMF in developing countries' economies, let's consider portions of it a bit more carefully.

The fall in the value of developing countries' debt led to a debt restructuring strategy. The basic plan of debt restructuring was called The Brady Plan. It involved banks accepting a reduction in indebtedness of the developing country (at, say, 40¢ on the dollar) in trade for either a U.S. government or IMF guarantee of the "restructured" debt. These restructuring plans were instituted in the early 1990s and, by the mid-1990s, the developing countries were once again in a reasonably strong debt position and banks were making new, unguaranteed loans to them.

Because of the problems of international debt, generating domestic saving is, in many ways, preferable to borrowing from abroad. But it is a difficult strategy—poor people don't have much discretionary income, and hence can't save much, and rich people are concerned about confiscation of their wealth, and hence save abroad, either legally or illegally. Moreover, for the small middle class that does exist, there are few financial instruments that effectively channel savings into investment. Macro monetary policy in such countries involves setting up such institutions. Let's now consider a case study that gives some insight into these issues.

Generating Domestic Savings

Our case study considers the development of an institution in one of the poorest countries of the world—Bangladesh. There, Mohammed Yunus, a U.S.-trained economist, created a bank—the Grameen Bank—that made market-rate-interest loans to poor village women. According to reports, the loans had a 97 percent payback rate, and Yunus made a profit.

A Case Study: The Borrowing Circle

How did he do it? As I discussed above, most banks in developing countries are internationally oriented. They use the same structure that Western banks use. This leaves the traditional part of many developing countries' economies without an effective way to translate savings into investment, stranding many entrepreneurial individuals without ways to develop their ideas.

Yunus recognized that Western financial institutional structures were not well suited to the traditional sectors of developing countries. He further recognized that the purpose of financial institutions is to direct resources to those with good ideas who can back up their promises to pay back their loans in the future with increased output.

What Yunus did was to reconsider the fundamental role of banking in an economy—to make it possible for people with good ideas to develop those ideas by providing them with funds to develop their ideas—and to devise a structure that allowed such lending to take place.

He saw that Western banking institutions did not provide the answer for Bangladesh. By basing their lending decisions on the amount of collateral a borrower had, they essentially made it impossible for most people in Bangladesh to get loans. But Yunus also recognized that the collateral function served a useful purpose: it forced people to make the difficult decision about whether they really needed the loans, and to work hard to see that they could pay the loans back, even if the going got tough. If you eliminate the role of collateral, something else must replace it.

ADDED DIMENSION   THE SIXTEEN DECISIONS

Making productive loans in developing countries involves more than simply lending money. It involves changing cultural norms and creating a market economy. Thus, when the Grameen Bank makes a loan, it has the borrower promise to abide by the following 16 decisions, in an effort to change the culture and ways of life of the borrower.

The 16 Decisions

1. The four principles of Grameen Bank—discipline, unity, courage, and hard work—we shall follow and advance in all walks of our lives.
2. We shall bring prosperity to our families.
3. We shall not live in dilapidated houses. We shall repair our houses and work towards constructing new houses as soon as possible.
4. We shall grow vegetables all the year round. We shall eat plenty of them and sell the surplus.
5. During the planting seasons, we shall plant as many seedlings as possible.
6. We shall plan to keep our families small. We shall minimize our expenditures. We shall look after our health.
7. We shall educate our children and ensure that they can earn enough to pay for their education.
8. We shall always keep our children and the environment clean.
9. We shall build and use pit latrines.
10. We shall drink tube-well water. If it is not available, we shall boil water or use alum.
11. We shall not take any dowry in our sons' weddings, neither shall we give any dowry in our daughters' weddings. We shall keep the center free from the curse of dowry. We shall not practice child marriage.

In developing countries, public health is a major concern. Rivers that serve as sources of drinking water also serve as sewers.

12. We shall not inflict any injustice on anyone, neither shall we allow anyone to do so.
13. For higher income we shall collectively undertake bigger investments.
14. We shall always be ready to help each other. If anyone is in difficulty, we shall all help.
15. If we come to know of any breach of discipline in any center, we shall all go there and help restore discipline.
16. We shall introduce physical exercise in our centers. We shall take part in all social activities collectively.

---

8 The "borrowing circle" concept replaced traditional collateral with guarantees by friends of the borrower. It was successful because the invisible handshake in Bangladesh, where the borrowing circle originated, was very strong.

Q–10: What made the borrowing circle a success in Bangladesh?

Discussing the sixteen decisions listed in the accompanying box is a useful way of bringing home to students the fundamental difference of economic problems in developing countries and in developed countries.

The ingenious solution he came up with was the **borrowing circle** concept—*a credit system that replaces traditional collateral with guarantees by friends of the borrower.* Recognizing that the invisible handshake was extremely strong in Bangladesh, he made use of that handshake in his bank's lending practices. He offered to make loans to any woman who could find four friends who would agree that they would, if necessary, help her pay the loan back. If the borrower defaulted, the others could not borrow until the loan was repaid. The invisible handshake replaced the traditional collateral.

Notice several things about the concept:

- It used economic insights creatively, and it recognized the essence of the problem, not the superficial aspects.
- It relied on an individual rather than governmental initiative. Yunus made a profit, and the individuals getting the loans made profits. Thus it encouraged development without a government plan.
- It created a new institution that fit the social structure, rather than importing outside institutions.
- It was directed at the traditional economy, rather than the international economy, and the successful loans improved the lot of millions.

This simple concept worked. In ten years it developed into a large bank that has made more than 1,600,000 loans. The loans have been taken out to buy such things as a cow or material to make a fishing net—not large items, but items to use in precisely the types of activity that generate bottom-up development.

Mr. Yunus' work has received enormous accolades (President Clinton said he should get a Nobel prize), and even developed countries are looking into the borrowing circle concept as a way of getting credit to the poor. While the concept was extraordinarily simple, his borrowing circle concept made use of economic insights but simultaneously reflected an understanding of and concern about the cultural and social dimensions of the economy. It is the type of macro policy most needed in developing countries.

To undertake beneficial macro institutional policy requires an understanding of the role of institutions, the specific nature of the problems in one's country, and creativity.

CONCLUSION

Examples of macro policy in developing countries like the above exist, but not as often as I would like to report. Asian and Latin American countries have a number of bright spots; Africa remains a problem. These examples show that creative macro institutional policies play an important role in development, and that the future of developing countries can be brighter than the present is.

Whether their futures will be brighter depends on the imagination, drive, and creativity of their policy makers. It doesn't surprise me that the originator of this Bangladeshi plan (whom, in case you haven't guessed, I greatly admire) studied economics, because economic thinking directs one to solutions that combine economic insight with existing institutions. It doesn't promise easy answers, but it does allow one to see the types of institutions that are sustainable. The economic way of thinking can lead to institutional change and economic takeoff.

CHAPTER SUMMARY

- Economists separate out developing and transitional economies because these economies have different institutional structures and different weighting of goals than do Western economies.
- Many developing economies have serious political problems that make it impossible for government to take an active, positive role in the economy.
- Many developing countries have dual economies—one a traditional, nonmarket economy, and the other an internationalized market economy.
- Inflation in developing countries is usually related to the printing of too much money; the debate is about the political reasons why this occurs, and the viability of the alternatives.

- Most monetary policies in developing countries focus on the international sector and are continually dealing with the balance of payments constraint.
- Most developing countries have some type of limited convertibility.
- Macro policies in developing and transitional countries are more concerned with institutional policies and régime changes than are macro policies in developed countries.
- The debt crisis of the 1980s was resolved by a combination of write-downs and restructuring.
- The borrowing circle is an example of an innovative macro institutional policy designed to better translate savings into investment.

KEY TERMS

balance of payments constraint   *(495)*
basic needs   *(485)*
borrowing circle   *(498)*
conditionality   *(495)*
convertibility on the current
   account   *(494)*
developing economy   *(484)*

dual economy   *(488)*
exchange rate policy   *(495)*
full convertibility   *(494)*
inflation tax   *(493)*
interfirm credit   *(490)*
limited capital account
   convertibility   *(494)*

macro institutional policies   *(496)*
policy change   *(489)*
régime change   *(489)*
restructuring   *(485)*
soft budget constraint   *(490)*
trade credits   *(491)*
transitional economy   *(484)*

QUESTIONS FOR THOUGHT AND REVIEW

The number after the questions represents the estimated degree of critical thinking required. (1 = almost none; 10 = deep thought)

1. Do different economic theories apply to developing countries than apply to developed countries? *(2)*
2. What is the difference between development and growth? *(2)*
3. What are three ways in which the institutions of developing countries differ from those in developed countries? *(2)*
4. Why do governments in developing countries often seem more arbitrary and oppressive than governments in developed countries? *(3)*
5. What is meant by "the dual economy"? *(2)*
6. How does a régime change differ from a policy change? *(2)*

7. What was the soft budget constraint? *(2)*
8. What is the inflation tax? *(2)*
9. Why doesn't the fact that the "inflation solution" is only a temporary solution stop many developing countries from using it? *(4)*
10. What is conditionality, and how does it relate to the balance of payments constraint? *(4)*
11. In 1996 Serbia faced a debt of $10 million and an inflation of 500 percent. Serbia did not adopt an austerity program to stabilize its currency. Furthermore, Serbia shunned foreign investment that might have provided needed capital. What are the pressures that typically confront such transitional economies and lead them to reject programs that, according to standards of industrialized nations, would appear to work? *(8)*

PROBLEMS AND EXERCISES

1. Could the borrowing circle concept be adopted for use in the United States?
   a. Why or why not?
   b. What modifications would you suggest if it were to be adopted?
   c. Minorities in the United States often do not use banks. In what ways are U.S. minorities' problems similar to those of people in developing countries?
2. Choose any developing country and answer the following questions about it:
   a. What is its level of per capita income?
   b. What is its growth potential?
   c. What is the exchange rate of its currency in relation to the U.S. dollar?
   d. What policy suggestions might you make to the country?
3. Bulgarian private banks rarely made long-term loans, but made substantial short-term loans in the early 1990s.

   a. List three reasons why long-term loans were not made and two reasons why short-term loans were extended.
   b. Contrast this with banking practices in the United States.
4. It has been argued that development economics has no general theory; it is instead the application of common sense to real-world problems.
   a. Do you agree or disagree with that statement? Why?
   b. Why do you think this argument about the lack of generality of theories is made for developing countries more than it is made for developed countries?
5. In 1993 and 1994 President Fujimori of Peru instituted a set of policies that turned the Peruvian economy around. Research the following questions:
   a. How did he engineer this turnaround?
   b. Why has the U.S. government limited aid to Peru?
   c. What monetary and fiscal policy did he use?
   d. How would you judge his policies?

ANSWERS TO MARGIN QUESTIONS

1. Restructuring in developed countries suggests that the distinction between growth and development can be overdone since it is an example of developed countries' growth occurring through changing institutions—development—rather than through increasing inputs—growth. *(485)*
2. Two ways in which a developed country differs from a developing country are: (1) its institutions are qualitatively different; and (2) its goals are different. *(487)*
3. An economist might favor activist policies in developed countries and laissez-faire policies in developing countries because the policies one favors depend upon

the desire and ability of government to work for and achieve the goals of its policies. Different views of government can lead to different views of policy. Since many economists have a serious concern about the political structure in developing counties, but less such concern about it in developed countries, they can favor one set of policies for developing countries and another set for developed countries. *(488)*
4. The "dual economy" refers to a developing country's tendency to have two economies that have little interaction—one a traditional nonmarket economy, and one an internationally-oriented modern market economy. *(488)*

5. The trade credit function of banks in Western market economies is barely mentioned because the institutional structure almost eliminates it as a function.   *(491)*

6. While everyone agrees that inflation in developing countries is caused by the central bank issuing too much money, the real policy question concerns what the political consequences of not issuing too much money may be. Sometimes the cure for inflation can be worse than the problem.   *(491)*

7. In an inflation, any issuers of fixed-interest-rate debt denominated in the domestic currency gain from the holders of these debts.   *(494)*

8. Full convertibility includes convertibility on the capital account as well as on the current account. It means that people are allowed to buy foreign financial assets—to save abroad. Convertibility on the current account means that people are allowed to buy foreign currencies in order to buy foreign goods, but not necessarily in order to buy foreign financial assets.   *(494)*

9. Loans to developing countries can be helpful if they are used for productive purposes, but they can cause problems if they are used for unproductive purposes. When governments guarantee loans, the lenders do not have an incentive to see that the loans are used for productive purposes.   *(496)*

10. A strong invisible handshake made the borrowing circle a success. In particular, to avoid social punishment, a borrower would work hard to repay a loan.   *(498)*

Economic and the Internet Web Sites

In previous editions I have included data at the end of this section. In this edition, I do not include data; instead I include a variety of internet sources of data in the hope that this information will lead some of you to explore these sources of data. Updating the data in the text, and checking out various web sites relevant to economics, is a useful exercise.

For those who do not have easy access to the Internet, often you can get access through your college library. If not, don't despair. Data are still available in a variety of print sources, and will likely remain available for years to come.

Selected U.S. Research and Policy Organization Sites

National Bureau for Economic Research: http://www.nber.org/RAND: http://www.rand.org/
The Brookings Institutions: http://www.brook.edu/
Resources for the Future: http://www.rff.org/
Institute for International Economics: http://www.iie.com/

Selected U.S. Government Sites

Fed Stats: http://www.Fedstats.gov/
The White House, Economic Statistics Briefing Room: http://www.whitehouse.gov/fsbr/esbr.html
The White House, Council of Economic Advisers: http://www.whitehouse.gov/WH/EOP/CEA/html/CEA.html
Bureau of Economic Analysis: http://www.bea.doc.gov/
CIA World Factbook: http://www.odci.gov/cia/publications/nsolo/factbook/global.htm
U.S. Census, International Trade Statistics: http://www.census.gov/foreign-trade/www/
Department of Justice: http://www.ojp.usdoj.gov/bjs/
Bureau of Labor Statistics: http://www.bls.gov/
Bureau of Transportation Statistics: http://www.bts.gov/
Economic Research Service (U.S. Department of Agriculture): http://www.econ.ag.gov/
Energy Information Administration: http://www.eia.doe.gov/
Federal Trade Commission: http://www.ftc.gov/
Internal Revenue Service, Statistics of Income: http://www.irs.ustreas.gov/prod/tax_stats
National Agricultural Statistics Service: http://www.usda.gov/nass
National Center for Health Statistics: http://www.cdc.gov/nchswww/nchshome.htm
Social Security Administration: http://www.ssa.gov/
U.S. Census Bureau: http://www.census.gov/
U.S. Department of Commerce: http://www.doc.gov/
U.S. Department of Transportations: http://www.bts.gov/
U.S. Department of the Treasury: http://www.ustreas.gov/

Antitrust Policy: http://www.antitrust.org/

Thomas (Legislative information): http://thomas.loc.gov/

Selected State Statistical Agency Sites

Alabama: http://www.cba.ua.edu/~cber/

Arkansas: http://www.aiea.ualr.edu/depts/csdc/about.html

California: California Department of Finance, http://www.dof.ca.gov/html/Demograp/druhpar.htm

Delaware: http://www.state.de.us/govern/agencies/dedo/dsdc/dsdc.htm

Hawaii, Hawaii State Data Center: http://www.hawaii.gov/dbedt/sdcrpt.html

Illinois, Regional Research and Development Services: http://www.rrds.siue.edu/

Indiana, Indiana Business Research Center: http://www.iupui.edu/it/ibrc

Kansas: http://kufacts.cc.ukans.edu/cwis/units/IPPBR/IPPBR_main.html

Kentucky, State Data Center: http://www.louisville.edu/cbpa/sdc

Louisiana, Louisiana State Data Center: http://www.state.la.us/state/census/census.htm

Maryland: http://www.inform.umd.edu:8080/UMS+State/MD_Resources/MSDC/

Massachusetts: http://www-unix.oit.umass.edu/~miser

Michigan, Michigan Information Center: http://www.michigan.state.mi.us/michome/mic.htm

Minnesota: http://www.mnplan.state.mn.us/demography/demog_01.html

Missouri, University of Missouri-Columbia Office of Social & Economic Data Analysis: http://www.oseda.missouri.edu/

Montana, Research & Analysis Bureau: http://jsd.dli.mt.gov/lmi/lmi.htm

Nevada: http://www.clan.lib.nv.us/docs/sdc.htm

New Jersey: http://www.state.nj.us/labor/lra/njsdc.html

New Mexico, Bureau of Business and Economic Research: http://www.unm.edu/~bber

North Carolina: http://www.ospl.state.nc.us/OSPL/

North Dakota: http://www.sdc.ag.ndsu.nodak.edu/

New York, New York State Department of Labor: http://www.labor.state.ny.us/

Ohio, Southwest Ohio Regional Data Center: http://www.ipr.uc.edu/sordc/welcome.htm

Ohio, Northern Ohio Data And Information Service: http://cua6.csuohio.edu/~ucweb/nodis/nodis.htm

Oklahoma, Oklahoma State Data Center: http://www.odoc.state.ok.us/osdc.htm

Oregon: http://www.upa.pdx.edu/CPRC/

Pennsylvania: http://www.hbg.psu.edu/

Rhode Island, Economic Development Corporation: http://www.riedc.com/

Texas: http://www-txsdc.tamu.edu/

Utah:http://www.governor.state.ut.us/dea/sdc.htm

Vermont: http://www.uvm.edu/~cdae/crs

Wisconsin, Department of Administration: http://www.doa.state.wi.us/deir/boi.htm

Federal Reserve System and Related Sites

Board of Governors: http://www.bog.frb.fed.us/

Regional Banks

Boston: http://www.bos.frb.org/

New York: http://www.ny.frb.org/

Philadelphia: http://www.libertynet.org/~fedresrv/fedpage.html

Cleveland: http://www.clev.frb.org/

Richmond: http://www.rich.frb.org/

Atlanta: http://www.frbatlanta.org/

Chicago: http://www.frbchi.org/

St. Louis: http://www.stls.frb.org/

Minneapolis: http://woodrow.mpls.frb.fed.us/

Kansas City: http://www.kc.frb.org/

Dallas: http://www.dallasfed.org/

San Francisco: http://www.frbsf.org/

Federal Reserve System's National Information Center: http://www.ffiec.gov/nic/

Federal Deposit Insurance Corporation: http://www.fdic.gov/

U.S. Department of Treasury: http://www.ustreas.gov/

Selected Foreign Statistics Sites

Algeria, Office National de Statistiques: http://ist.cerist.dz/sie/ons/ons.htm

Argentina, National Institute of Statistics and Censuses: http://www.indec.mecon.ar/default.htm

Australia, Australian Bureau of Statistics: http:///www.abs.gov.au/

Brazil, Brazilian Institute of Geography and Statistics (IBGE): http://www.ibge.gov.br/english/e-home.htm
Bulgaria, National Statistical Institute: http://www.acad.bg/BulRTD/nsi/index.htm
Canada, Statistics Canada: http://www.statcan.ca/
Colombia, National Administrative Department of Statistics (DANE): http://www.sin.com.co/Clientes/DANE
Croatia, Central Bureau of Statistics: http://www.dzs.hr/
Czech Republic, Czech Statistical Office: http://infox.eunet.cz/csu/
Denmark, Statistics Denmark: http://www.dst.dk/internet/startuk.htm
Finland, Statistics Finland: http://www.stat.fi/sf/home.html
France, National Institute of Statistics and Economic Studies (INSEE): http://www.insee.fr/
Germany, Federal Statistical Office: http://www.statistik-bund.de/e_home.htm
Hong Kong, Census and Statistics Department: http://www.info.gov.hk/censtatd
Hungary, Hungarian Central Statistical Office: http://www.ksh.hu/eng/homeng.html
Iceland, Statistics Iceland: ttp://eldur.stjr.is/en/stjren01.htm
Indonesia, Central Bureau of Statistics: http://www.bps.go.id/
Ireland, Bank of Ireland: http://www.treasury.boi.ie/
Israel, Central Bureau of Statistics: http://www.cbs.gov.il/engindex.htm
Italy, National Institute of Statistics: http://www.istat.it/Inglese.html
Japan, Japanese Statistics Bureau: http://www.stat.go.jp/
Korea, National Statistical Office: http://www.nso.go.kr/
Latvia, Central Statistical Bureau of Latvia: http://www.latnet.lv/ligumi/CSBL
Lithuania, Department of Statistics: http://www.std.lt/
Luxembourg, National Institute of Statistics and Economic Studies: http://statec.gouvernement.lu/
Morocco, Ministry of Population: http://194.204.215.1/
Mexico, National Institute of Statistics, Geography, and Informatics: http://www.inegi.gob.mx/paginamenu.html
Netherlands, Central Bureau of Statistics (CBS): http://www.cbs.nl/
New Zealand, Statistics New Zealand: http://www.govt.nz/ps/min/stats
Norway, Statistics Norway: http://www.ssb.no/www-open/english/
Peru, National Institute of Statistics and Informatics: http://www.inei.gob.pe/
Poland, Central Statistical Office: http://di3.gus4.stsp.gov.pl/
Portugal, National Institute of Statistics: http://www.ine.pt/ine/
Russia, Russian State Committee for Statistics: http://feast.fe.msk.ru/koi/infomarket/emn/rating/gstat.html
Singapore, Department of Statistics: http://www.singstat.gov.sg/
Slovenia, Statistical Office of the Republic of Slovenia: http://www.sigov.si/zrs/index_e.html
South Africa, Central Statistical Service: http://www.css.gov.za/
Spain, National Institute of Statistics: http://www.ine.es/
Sweden, Statistics Sweden: http://www.scb.se/indexeng.htm
Switzerland, Swiss Federal Statistical Office: http://www.admin.ch/bfs/eindex.htm
Taiwan, Directorate General of Budget, Accounting and Statistics: http://www.dgbasey.gov.tw/
Turkey, State Institute of Statistics: http://www.die.gov.tr/ENGLISH/index.html
United Kingdom, Office for National Statistics: http://www.emap.co.uk/cso
Venezuela, Central Office of Statistics and Informatics (OCEI)

Selected Foreign Central Bank Sites
Bank of Canada: http://www.bank-banque-canada.ca/english/intro-e.htm
Deutsche Bundesbank: http://www.bundesbank.de/index_e.html
Bank of Japan: http://www.boj.go.jp/en/index.htm
Bank of England: http://www.bankofengland.co.uk/
Central Bank of Kenya: http://www.arcc.or.ke/cbk.htm
Reserve Bank of India: http://www.reservebank.com/
Central Bank of Thailand: http://www.bot.or.th/
Central Bank of Jordan: http://www.cbj.gov.jo/
Bank of Ireland: http://www.treasury.boi.ie/

Selected Sites of International Organizations
European Community, EUROSTAT: http://europa.eu.int/en/comm/eurostat/eurostat.html
European Union: http://europa.eu.int
Organization for Economic Cooperation and Development (OECD): http://www.oecd.org/
International Labour Organization (ILO): http://www.ilo.org/
International Monetary Fund (IMF): http://www.imf.org/external/
International Statistical Institute (ISI): http://www.cbs.nl/isi/

The Statistical Office of the European Communities (EUROSTAT)
The World Bank: http://www.worldbank.org/
United Nations: http://www.un.org/
UN Economic Commission for Europe (UN/ECE) Statistical Division: http://www.unicc.org/unece/
UN Statistics Division: http://www.un.org/Depts/unsd/
United Nations Food and Agriculture Organization (FAO): http://www.fao.org/waicent/waicent.htm
United Nations Economic Commission for Latin America and the Caribbean (UN/ECLAC): http://www.eclac.cl/
United Nations Educational, Scientific and Cultural Organization (UNESCO): http://www.unesco.org/
United Nations Population Information Network (POPIN): http://www.undp.org/popin/
World Health Organization (WHO): http://www.who.ch/
World Trade Organization (WTO): http://www.wto.org/Welcome.html

Selected Sites of Economic Periodicals
Forbes: http://www.forbes.com
The Wall Street Journal: http://wsj.com
The New York Times: http://www.nytimes.com/
The Financial Times: http://www.nytimes.com/
The Economist: http://www.ECONOMIST.com/

Selected Investing Sites
Invest-o-rama: http://www.investorama.com/
Morningstar: http://www.morningstar.net
Wall Street Directory: http://www.wsdinc.com/

Fun Sites
Economist jokes: http://www.etla.fi/pkm/jtxt.html
The Humor House: http://www.challenger.net/local/jokes/
The Prisoner's Dilemma: http://serendip.brynmawr.edu/~ann/pd.html
Tom and Ray Magliozzi's CarTalk: http://www.cartalk.com/
Fun, games and entertainment: http://escher.cs.ucdavis.edu:1024/fundandgames.html

Large-scale macro models
The Fair Model: http://fairmodel.econ.yale.edu/
Macroadvisers: http://www.macroadvisers.com/
The WEFA Group: http://www.wefa.com/
DRI McGraw-Hill: http://www.dri.mcgraw-hill.com/

Links to other pages
Statistical links: http://www.cbs.nl/eng/link/index.htm
Statistical Resources on the Web (University of Michigan):
   http://www.lib.umich.edu/libhome/Documents.center/stcomp.html
Fedworld Information Network: http://www.fedworld.gov/
Resources for Economists on the Internet: http://econwpa.wustl.edu/EconFAQ/EconFAQ.html
GPO Gate: http://www.gpo.ucop.edu/
Louisiana State University: http://www.lib.lsu.edu/bus/economic.html
Dr. Ed Yardeni: http://www.webcom.com/~yardeni/economic.html
Resources for Economists on The Internet: http://coba.shsu.edu/EconFAQ/EconFAQ.html
Colander Home Page: http://www.mhhe.com/economics/colander

Glossary

A

Activist economists. Economists who believe that the government can create and implement policy proposals that can positively impact the economy.

Activist industrial policy. Policy under which the government works directly with businesses.

Activist structural policy. Policy that involves more government activity than currently exists.

Adaptive expectations. Expectations based, in some way, on what has been in the past.

Aggregate demand curve. Curve that relates the amount individuals as a whole want to consume and the price level, other things constant.

Aggregate demand (expenditure) management policy. Policy aimed at changing the level of income in the economy by a combination of a change in autonomous expenditures and the multiplied induced expenditures resulting from that change.

Aggregate equilibrium demand (AED) curve. Curve that shows how a change in the price level will change aggregate equilibrium demand after all the dynamic interactive effects between production and expenditures are taken into account.

Aggregate expenditures. Consumption (spending by consumers), investment (spending by business), spending by government, and net foreign spending on U. S. goods (the difference between U.S. exports and U.S. imports).

Aggregate production curve. Forty-five-degree line representing aggregate production, with real income in dollars measured on the horizontal axis and real production measured in dollars on the vertical axis.

Aggregate production/aggregate expenditures (AP/AE) model. Keynesian model giving aggregate supply the name aggregate production and focusing on total production changes, not on changes in output caused by price-level changes. Emphasizes the difference between the Keynesian focus and the Classical focus on quantity of aggregate supply and demand changes resulting from changes in the price level.

Aggregate supply curve. Curve that relates the amount individuals as a whole want to supply and the price level, other things constant.

Aggregate supply path. A curve that tells us how changes in aggregate equilibrium demand will be split between real output changes and price level changes.

Appreciation. An increase in value.

Approximate real-world money multiplier. One divided by the sum of the percentage of deposits banks hold in reserve and the ratio of money people hold in currency to the money they hold as deposits. $(1 / (r + c)$.

Art of economics. The relating of positive economics to normative economics.

Art of macro policy. Macroeconomic policy based on rough estimates and judgments, rather than on precise relationships.

Asset management. How a bank handles its loans and other assets.

Austrian economist. Economist who believes in the liberty of all individuals first and social goals second.

Automatic stabilizer. Any government program or policy that will counteract the business cycle without any new government action.

Autonomous expenditures. Expenditures that are independent of income.

Autonomous shift. A shift that occurs because of some change that the model does not consider.

B

Balance of payments. A country's record of all transactions between its residents and the residents of all foreign nations.

Balance of payments accounts. Accounts that record all transactions between the residents of a country and residents of all foreign nations.

Balance of payments constraint. Limitations on expansionary domestic macroeconomic policy due to a shortage of international reserves.

Balance of trade. The difference between the value of the goods a country imports and the value of the goods it exports.

Bank. A financial institution whose primary function is holding money for, and lending money to, individuals and firms.

Bar graph.   Graph where the area under each point is filled to look like a bar.

Basic needs.   Adequate food, clothing, and shelter.

Bond.   A promise to pay a certain amount of money plus interest in the future.

Boom.   In the business cycle, a very high peak, representing a big jump in output.

Borrowing circle.   A credit system that replaces traditional collateral with guarantees by friends of the borrower.

Bretton Woods system.   An agreement about fixed exchange rates that governed international financial relationships from the period after the end of World War II until 1971.

Budget Enforcement Act of 1990.   A law that puts caps on certain aspects of federal spending, and established a ''pay-as-you-go'' context for new spending or tax cuts so that, through 1996, any new legislation, except for emergencies, had to be accompanied by offsetting tax increases or spending cuts.

Business.   Private producing units in our society.

Business cycle.   The upward or downward movement of economic activity, or real GDP, that occurs around the growth trend.

C

Capacity utilization rate.   Rate at which factories and machines are operating compared to the maximum sustainable rate at which they could be used.

Capital account.   The part of the balance of payments account in which all long-term flows of payments are listed.

Capital markets.   Markets in which financial assets having a maturity of more than one year are bought and sold.

Capitalism.   An economic system based upon private property and the market in which, in principle, individuals decide how, what, and for whom to produce.

Cash flow accounting system.   An accounting system entering expenses and revenues only when cash is received or paid out.

Central bank.   A type of bankers' bank.

Certificate of deposit (CD).   A piece of paper certifying that you have a sum of money in a savings account in the bank for a specified period of time.

Classicals.   Macroeconomists who generally favor laissez-faire or non-activist policies.

Commercial paper.   Short-term promissory note that a certain amount of money plus interest will be paid back on demand.

Comparative advantage.   The ability to be better suited to the production of one good than to the production of another good.

Competition.   Ability of individuals or firms to freely enter into business activities.

Competitiveness.   The ability to produce goods and services more cheaply than other countries can.

Conditionality.   The making of loans that are subject to specific conditions.

Consumer Price Index (CPI).   Measure of prices of a fixed ''basket'' of consumer goods, weighted according to each component's share of an average consumer's expenditures.

Consumer sovereignty.   Principle that the consumer's wishes rule what's produced.

Contractionary monetary policy.   Monetary policy that tends to raise interest rates and lower income.

Contractual intermediary.   Financial institution that holds and stores individuals' financial assets.

Convertibility on the current account.   A system that allows people to exchange currencies freely to buy goods and services, but not to buy assets in other countries.

Coordinate system.   Two-dimensional space in which one point represents two numbers.

Corporation.   Business that is treated as a person, legally owned by its stockholders. Its stockholders are not liable for the actions of the corporate ''person.''

Cost-push inflation.   Inflation that occurs when the economy is below full employment, with prices rising even though there are no shortages of goods or workers.

Countercyclical fiscal policy.   Fiscal policy in which the government offsets any shock that would create a business cycle.

Credible systematic policies.   Policies that people believe will be implemented regardless of the consequences.

Crowding in.   Positive effects of government spending on other components of spending.

Crowding out.   The offsetting of a change in government expenditures by a change in private expenditures in the opposite direction.

Cultural norms.   Standards people use when they determine whether a particular activity or behavior is acceptable.

Currency stabilization.   Buying and selling of a currency by the government to offset temporary fluctuations in supply and demand for currencies.

Currency support.   Buying of a currency by a government to maintain its value at above its long-run equilibrium value.

Current account.   The part of the balance of payments account in which all short-term flows of payments are listed.

Cyclical unemployment.   Unemployment resulting from fluctuations in economic activity.

D

Debt.   Accumulated deficits minus accumulated surpluses.

Debt service.   The interest rate on debt times the total debt.

Decision tree.   A visual description of sequential choices.

Deficit.   A shortfall of revenues under payments.

Deflation.   A fall in the price level.

Demand.   Schedule of quantities of a good that will be bought per unit of time at various prices, other things constant.

Demand curve.   Graphic representation of the law of demand.

Demand-pull inflation.   Inflation that occurs when the economy is at or above full employment.

Demerit goods or activities.   Goods or activities the government deems bad for you even though you choose to use the goods or engage in the activities.

Depository institution. A financial institution whose primary financial liability is deposits in checking or savings accounts.

Depreciation. A decrease in the value of a currency. Also the decrease in an asset's value.

Depression. A large recession.

Developing economy. An economy that has a low level of GDP per capita and a relatively undeveloped market structure, and has not recently had an alternative, developed economic system.

Direct relationship. Relationship in which when one variable goes up, the other goes up too.

Discount rate. The rate of interest the Fed charges for loans it makes to banks.

Discouraged workers. People who do not look for a job because they feel they don't have a chance of finding one.

Disinflation. A fall in the rate at which the price level is rising.

Disintermediation. The process of lending directly and not going through a financial intermediary.

Disposable personal income. Income that is roughly equal to national income less taxes paid by individuals plus transfer payments made to individuals.

Diversification. Spreading the risks by holding many different types of financial assets.

Domestic income (DI). The total income earned by residents and businesses in a country.

Downturn. Segment of the business cycle characterized by the economy starting to fall from a peak.

Dual economy. The existence of two sectors: a traditional sector and an internationally-oriented modern market sector.

Durable goods. Goods expected to last more than one year.

E

Economic decision rule. If the relevant benefits of doing something exceed the relevant costs, do it. If the relevant costs of doing something exceed the relevant benefits, don't do it.

Economic forces. The necessary reactions to scarcity.

Economic institution. Physical or mental structure that significantly influences economic decisions.

Economic model. Framework that places the generalized insights of the theory in a more specific contextual setting.

Economic policy. An action (or inaction) taken, usually by government, to influence economic events.

Economic principle. Commonly held economic insight stated as a law or general assumption.

Economic reasoning. Thinking like an economist, making decisions on the basis of costs and benefits.

Economic system. System (set of economic institutions) by which an economy is organized.

Economic theory. Generalizations about the working of an abstract economy.

Economics. The study of economies.

Economy. The institutional structure through which individuals in a society coordinate their diverse wants or desires.

Effective aggregate demand. Aggregate demand that exists after suppliers cut production in response to aggregate supply exceeding aggregate demand.

Effective aggregate supply curve. A curve that tells us the quantity that firms choose to supply, given their expectations of demand, at different price levels.

Efficiency. Achieving a goal using as few inputs as possible.

Embargo. An all-out restriction on the import or export of a good.

Employee compensation. Wages and salaries paid to individuals, along with fringe benefits and government taxes for social security and unemployment insurance.

Entrepreneurship. The ability to organize and get something done.

Equation of exchange. An equation for "quantity of money times velocity of money equals the price level times the quantity of real goods sold": $MV = PQ$.

Equilibrium. A concept in which the opposing dynamic forces cancel each other out.

Equilibrium income. The level of income toward which the economy gravitates in the short run.

Equilibrium price. The price toward which the invisible hand drives the market.

European Union (EU). An economic and political union of European countries that is both an economic free trade area and a loose political organization.

Excess burden. A loss to consumers and producers that is not gained by anyone else.

Excess demand. Quantity demanded is greater than quantity supplied.

Excess reserve ratio. The additional percentage of deposits that banks choose to hold over their amount of required reserves.

Excess reserves. Reserves held by banks in excess of what banks are required to hold.

Excess supply. Quantity supplied is greater than quantity demanded.

Exchange rate. The rate at which one country's currency can be traded for another country's currency.

Exchange rate intervention. Buying or selling a currency to affect its price.

Exchange rate policy. Buying and selling foreign currencies in order to help stabilize the exchange rate.

Excise tax. A tax that is levied on a specific good.

Expansion. Upturn that lasts for at least two consecutive quarters of a year.

Expansionary monetary policy. Monetary policy involving increase in the money supply that tends to reduce interest rates and raise income.

Expected inflation. Inflation people expect to occur.

Expenditures function. A representation of the relationship between expenditures and income as a mathematical function.

Export drive. Government promotion of exports through assisting exporters in the technicalities of exporting.

Export subsidy. Government promotion of exports through the subsidy of exports.

Export-led growth policies. Policies designed to stimulate a country's exports and increase aggregate expenditures on its goods.

Exports. Goods produced in the home country but sold in foreign countries.

External government debt. Government debt owed to individuals in foreign countries.

Externality. The effect that an action may have on a third party that the person who undertook that action did not take into account

F

Factors of production. Inputs, or resources, necessary to produce goods.

Fallacy of composition. The false assumption that what is true for a part will also be true for the whole.

Fed funds. Loans of their reserves banks make to one another.

Federal Deposit Insurance Corporation (FDIC). A government organization that guarantees bank deposits.

Federal funds market. The market in which banks lend and borrow reserves.

Federal funds rate. The interest rate banks charge one another for Fed funds.

Federal Open Market Committee (FOMC). The Fed's chief policymaking body.

Federal Reserve Bank (the Fed). The U.S. central bank whose liabilities (Federal Reserve Notes) serve as cash in the United States.

Feudalism. Economic system in which traditions (the invisible handshake) rule.

Financial assets. Assets, such as stocks or bonds, whose benefit to the owner depends on the issuer of the asset meeting certain obligations.

Financial institution. A business whose primary activity is buying, selling, or holding financial assets.

Financial liabilities. Liabilities incurred by the issuer of a financial asset to stand behind the issued asset.

Financial market. An institution that brings buyers and sellers of financial assets together.

Fine tuning. Fiscal policy designed to keep the economy always at its target or potential level of income.

Firms. Organizations of individuals that transform factors of production into usable goods.

First dynamic law of supply and demand. When quantity demanded is greater than quantity supplied, prices tend to rise; when quantity supplied is greater than quantity demanded, prices tend to fall.

Fiscal policy. The deliberate change in either government spending or taxes to stimulate or slow down the economy.

Fixed exchange rate. The exchange rate is set and government is committed to buying and selling its currency at a fixed rate.

Fixed exchange rates. Rates, set by government, at which a currency can be freely exchanged among individuals.

Flexible exchange rate. The exchange rate is set by market forces (supply and demand for a country's currency).

Foreign exchange market. Market in which one country's currency can be exchanged for another country's.

Free market in money. Policy that would leave people free to use any money they want, and would significantly reduce banking regulation.

Free rider. Person who participates in something for free because others have paid for it.

Free trade. A policy of allowing unrestricted trade among countries.

Free trade associations. Groups of countries that have reduced or eliminated trade barriers among themselves.

Frictional unemployment. Unemployment caused by new entrants into the job market and people quitting a job just long enough to look for and find another one.

Full convertibility. An exchange rate system under which individuals may change dollars into any currency they want for whatever legal purpose they want.

Full employment. An economic climate in which just about everyone who wants a job at the going wage rate can have one.

Fundamental analysis. A consideration of the fundamental forces that determine the supply of and demand for currencies.

Funded pension system. Pension system in which money is collected and invested in a special fund from which pension payments are made.

G

GDP deflator. Index of the price level of aggregate output or the average price of the components in total output (or GDP) relative to a base year.

General Agreement on Tariffs and Trade (GATT). An agreement among many subscribing countries on certain conditions of international trade; it has been replaced by the World Trade Organization.

Global corporations. Corporations with substantial operations on both the production and sales sides in more than one country.

Gold specie flow mechanism. The long-run adjustment mechanism that maintained the gold standard.

Gold standard. System of fixed exchange rates in which the value of currencies was fixed relative to the value of gold and gold was used as the primary reserve asset.

Government failures. Situations where the government intervenes and makes things worse.

Government purchases. Government payments for goods and services and investment in equipment and structures.

Gramm-Rudman-Hollings Act. A law establishing mandatory deficit targets for the United States.

Graph. Picture of points in a coordinate system in which points denote relationships between numbers.

Gross domestic product (GDP). The total market value of all final goods and services produced in an economy in a one-year period.

Gross national product (GNP). Aggregate final output of citizens and businesses of an economy in a one-year period.

Gross private domestic investment. Expenditures by firms or households on goods, often called capital goods, that are used over and over to make products or provide services.

Group of Five.   Group that meets to promote negotiations and coordinate economic relations among countries. The Five are Japan, Germany, Britain, France, and the United States.

Group of Seven.   Group that meets to promote negotiations and coordinate economic relations among countries. The Seven are Japan, Germany, Britain, France, Canada, Italy, and the United States.

Growth-compatible institutions.   Institutions that foster growth.

H

Heterodox economist.   Economist who doesn't accept the basic underlying model used by a majority of economists as the most useful model for analyzing the economy.

Historical model.   Model that starts at a point in time, and tells one what will likely happen when shocks hit the economy.

Households.   Groups of individuals living together and making joint decisions.

Human capital.   People's knowledge.

Hyperinflation.   Inflation that hits triple digits—100 percent or more.

I

Ideology.   Set of values held so deeply that they are not questioned by the majority of the population.

Imports.   Goods produced in foreign countries but sold in the home country.

Income adjustment mechanism.   Process by which initial changes in aggregate expenditures create a cumulative change in aggregate equilibrium income.

Incomes policy.   A policy that places direct pressure on individuals to hold down their nominal wages and prices.

Indicative planning.   Macroeconomic policy in which the government sets up an overall plan for various industries and selectively directs credit to certain industries.

Induced expenditures.   Expenditures that change as income changes.

Industrial policy.   Formal policy that government takes toward business.

Industrial Revolution.   A period (about 1750-1900) during which technology and machines rapidly modernized industrial production and mass-produced goods replaced handmade goods.

Inflation.   A continual rise in the price level.

Inflation tax.   An implicit tax on the holders of cash and the holders of any obligations specified in nominal terms.

Inflationary gap.   A difference between equilibrium income and potential income when equilibrium income exceeds potential income.

Input.   What you put into a production process to achieve an output.

Institutionalist economist.   Economist who argues that any economic analysis must involve specific considerations of institutions.

Interest.   The income private businesses pay to households that have lent the businesses money.

Interfirm credit.   Loans from one firm to another.

Intermediate products.   Products used as input in the production of some other product.

Internal government debt.   Government debt owed to its own citizens.

International effect.   As the price level in the United States falls (assuming the exchange rate does not change), the quantity of U.S. goods demanded will increase.

International Monetary Fund (IMF).   A multinational, international financial institution concerned primarily with monetary issues.

Interpolation assumption.   Assumption that the relationship between variables is the same between points as it is at the points.

Interpretive Keynesian model.   A Keynesian model that views models as an aid in understanding complicated disequilibrium dynamics.

Intertemporal price-level effect.   If the price level falls, and is expected to rise in the next period, people will decide to purchase some goods now that they would have purchased in the future.

Inverse relationship.   A relationship between two variables in which when one goes up the other goes down.

Invisible foot.   Political and legal forces.

Invisible hand.   The price mechanism, the rise and fall of prices that guides our actions in a market.

Invisible hand theory.   A market, through the price mechanism, will allocate resources efficiently.

Invisible handshake.   Social and historical forces.

J

J-curve.   A curve describing the rise and fall in the balance of trade deficit following a fall in the exchange rate.

Just-noticeable difference.   The threshold where our senses realize that something has changed.

K

Keynesian equation.   An equation that tells us that income equals the multiplier times autonomous expenditures.

Keynesians.   Macroeconomists who generally favor activist government policy.

L

Labor force.   Those people in an economy who are willing and able to work.

Laffer curve.   A curve that shows the relationship between tax rates and tax revenues.

Laissez-faire.   Leave the market alone. The philosophy that government should intervene in the economy as little as possible.

Laissez-faire economists.   Economists who believe that most government policies would probably make things worse, so the best policy is (relatively) little government involvement with the economy.

Law of demand.   More of a good will be demanded the lower its price, other things constant. Also can be stated as: Less of a good will be demanded the higher its price, other things constant.

Law of supply. More of a good will be supplied the higher its price, other things constant. Also can be stated as: Less of a good will be supplied the lower its price, other things constant.

Leading indicators. Indicators that tell us what's likely to happen 12 to 15 months from now.

Liability management. How a bank attracts deposits and what it pays for them.

Libertarian. Economist who believes in liberty of individuals first and in other social goals second.

Limited capital account convertibility. A system that allows full current account convertibility and partial capital account convertibility.

Limited liability. The liability of a stockholder (owner) in a corporation; it is limited to the amount the stockholder has invested in the company.

Line graph. Graph where the data are connected by a continuous line.

Linear curve. A curve that is drawn as a straight line.

Liquidity. Ability to turn an asset into cash quickly.

Long-run Phillips curve. A curve showing the trade-off (or complete lack thereof) when expectations of inflation equal actual inflation.

M

M1. Currency in the hands of the public, checking account balances, and travelers' checks.

M2. M1 plus savings deposits, small-denomination time deposits, and money market mutual fund shares, along with some esoteric financial instruments.

Macro institutional policies. Policies to change the underlying macro institutions and thereby increase output.

Macro policy model. Model that demonstrates the effects of macro policy on output and prices.

Macroeconomic externality. Externality that affects the levels of unemployment, inflation, or growth in the economy as a whole.

Macroeconomics. The study of inflation, unemployment, business cycles, and growth primarily from the whole to the parts.

Mainstream economist. Economist who accepts the basic underlying model used by a majority of economists as the most useful model for analyzing the economy.

Marginal benefit. Additional benefit above what you've already derived.

Marginal cost. Additional cost to you over and above the costs you have already incurred.

Marginal propensity to expend (mpe). The ratio of a change in expenditures to a change in income.

Marginal propensity to withdraw (mpw). The percentage of income flow that leaks out of the economy each round of the circular flow.

Market demand curve. The horizontal sum of all individual demand curves.

Market failures. Situations where the market does not lead to a desired result.

Market force. Economic force that is given relatively free rein by society to work through the market.

Marshallian economics. Economic analysis that sees economics as a way of thinking and integrates insights from other disciplines.

Mechanistic Keynesianism. The belief that the simple multiplier models (or even complex variations) actually describe the aggregate adjustment process, and lead to a deterministic solution that policy makers can exploit in a mechanistic way.

Mechanistic model. A model that pictures the economy as representable by a mechanically determined, timeless model with a determinant equilibrium.

Mercantilism. Economic system in which government (the invisible foot) determines the what, how, and for whom decision by doling out the rights to undertake certain economic decisions.

Merit goods or activities. Goods and activities that government believes are good for you, even though you may not choose to consume the goods or engage in the activities.

Microeconomics. The study of individual choice, and how that choice is influenced by economic forces.

Military-industrial complex. A combination of defense industry firms and the U.S. armed forces, which have vested interests in keeping defense spending flowing, regardless of whether that spending is good for society.

MITI. Japan's Ministry of International Trade and Industry, which guides Japan's activist industrial policy.

Monetary base. Banks' allowable reserves, consisting of vault cash or deposits at the Fed.

Monetary policy. Influencing the economy through changes in the banking system's reserves.

Monetary rule. A prescribed monetary policy that's to be followed regardless of what's happening in the economy.

Money. A highly liquid financial asset that's generally accepted in exchange for other goods. It is used as a reference in valuing other goods, and can be stored as wealth.

Money markets. Markets in which financial assets having a maturity of less than one year are bought and sold.

Money price. Actual price you pay for the goods you buy.

Monopoly power. Ability of individuals or firms currently in business to prevent other individuals or firms from entering the same kind of business.

Mortgage. A special name for a secured loan on real estate.

Movement along the demand curve. The graphic representation of the effect of a change in price on the quantity demanded.

Movement along the supply curve. The graphic representation of the effect of a change in price on the quantity supplied.

Multiplier. A number that tells us how much income will change in response to a change in autonomous expenditures.

Multiplier effect. The multiplication of the initial effects of the price–level change on aggregate expenditures as the economy adjusts to equilibrium.

N

National income (NI). The total income earned by citizens and businesses of a country.

National income accounting. A set of rules and definitions for measuring economic activity in the aggregate economy—that is, in the economy as a whole.

National income accounting identity. The accounting equality of output and income.

Natural rate of unemployment. The rate of unemployment to which the economy naturally gravitates.

Need-based social welfare program. Social welfare program in which eligibility is determined by need.

Neomercantilism. A market economy guided by government.

Net domestic product (NDP). The sum of consumption expenditures, government expenditures, net foreign expenditures, and investment less depreciation.

Net exports. Exports minus imports.

Net foreign factor income. Income from foreign domestic factor sources minus foreign factor income earned domestically.

Net national product. GNP adjusted for depreciation.

Net private investment. Gross private domestic investment minus depreciation.

New Deal. President Franklin Roosevelt's name for his practical "do-something" approach to economic policy.

NIMBY. Not In My Back Yard. Phrase used by people who may approve of a project, but don't want it to be near them.

Nominal concepts. Concepts specified in monetary terms.

Nominal deficit. The deficit determined by looking at the difference between expenditures and receipts.

Nominal GDP. GDP calculated at existing prices.

Nominal interest rates. The rates you actually see and pay.

Nominal output. Output as measured at current prices.

Nonconvertible currency. A currency that cannot be freely exchanged except at the government set rate.

Nondurable goods. Goods that last less than one year.

Nonlinear curve. A curve that is drawn as a curved line.

Nonprofit businesses. Businesses that try only to make enough money to cover their expenses with their revenues.

Nontariff barriers. Indirect regulatory restrictions on exports and imports.

Normative economics. The study of what the goals of the economy should be.

North American Free Trade Agreement (NAFTA). A U.S.-Canada-Mexico free trade zone that is phasing in reductions in tariffs.

O

Objective analysis. Analysis that keeps the analyst's value judgments separate from the analysis.

Off-budget expenditures. Expenditures of money that are not to be counted as expenditures in the budget.

Official reserves. Government holdings of foreign currencies.

Official transactions account. The part of the balance of payments account that records the amount of its own currency or foreign currencies that a national buys or sells.

Okun's rule of thumb. (Sometimes called Okun's Law.) A one-percentage-point change in the unemployment rate will cause income to change in the opposite direction by 2.5 percent.

Open market operations. The Fed's buying and selling of government securities.

Opportunity cost. The benefit forgone by undertaking a particular activity.

Other things constant. All other factors that could affect the analysis are assumed to remain constant (whether they actually remain constant or not).

Output. A result of a productive activity.

P

Paradox of thrift. Individuals attempted to save more, but in doing so spent less and caused income to decrease, and they ended up saving no more, or even less.

Partial equilibrium analysis. Analysis in which other things can reasonably be assumed to remain constant.

Partially flexible exchange rate. The government sometimes buys and sells currencies to influence the price directly, and at other times the government simply accepts the exchange rate determined by supply and demand forces.

Partnership. Business with two or more owners.

Passive deficit. The part of the deficit that exists because the economy is operating below its potential level of output.

Path-dependent equilibrium. An equilibrium that is influenced by the adjustment process to that equilibrium.

Permanent income hypothesis. Expenditures are determined by permanent or lifetime income.

Personal income (PI). National income plus net transfer payments from government minus amounts attributed but not received.

Phillips curve. A representation of the relation between inflation and unemployment.

Pie chart. A circle divided into "pie pieces," where the individual pie represents the total amount and the pie pieces reflect the percentage of the whole pie that the various components make up.

Policy change. A change in one aspect of government's actions, such as monetary policy or fiscal policy.

Policy régime. The general set of rules that governs the monetary and fiscal policies that a country follows.

Positive economics. The study of what is, and how the economy works.

Post-Keynesian macroeconomist. Economist who believes that uncertainty is a central issue in macroeconomics.

Potential income. The level of income that the economy technically is capable of producing without generating accelerating inflation.

Potential output. The highest achievable output level without accelerating inflation.

Present value.   The value now of income payments in the future.

Price ceiling.   A government-imposed limit on how high a price can be charged.

Price floor.   A government-imposed limit on how low a price can be charged.

Price index.   A composite of prices—a series of numbers that summarizes what happens to prices of a selection of goods (often called a market basket of goods) over time.

Price level.   The price of a composite of all goods.

Price-level interest rate effect.   Focuses on the effect of the increase in real money supply on interest rates: It will lower interest rates, which in turn will increase investment.

Primary financial market.   Market in which newly issued financial assets are sold.

Principle of increasing marginal opportunity cost.   In order to get more of something, one must give up ever-increasing quantities of something else.

Private good.   A good that, when consumed by one individual, cannot be consumed by other individuals.

Private property rights.   Control a private individual or a firm has over an asset or a right.

Producer Price Index (PPI).   An index or ratio of a composite of prices of a number of important raw materials, such as steel, relative to a composite of the prices of those raw materials in a base year.

Production possibility curve.   A curve measuring the maximum combination of outputs that can be obtained from a given number of inputs.

Production possibility table.   Table that lists a choice's opportunity costs by summarizing what alternative outputs you can achieve with your inputs.

Productive efficiency.   Achieving as much output as possible from a given amount of inputs or resources.

Productivity-enhancing social welfare program.   Social welfare program designed to increase potential output.

Profit.   What's left over from total revenues after all the appropriate costs have been subtracted. Alternatively, what's left over from total revenues after all the appropriate costs have been subtracted.

Progressive tax.   Tax whose rates increase as a person's income increases.

Proletariat.   The working class.

Proportional tax.   Tax whose rates are constant at all income levels, no matter what your total annual income is.

Public good.   A good whose consumption by one individual does not prevent its consumption by other individuals.

Purchasing power parity (PPP).   A method of calculating exchange rates that attempts to value currencies at rates such that each currency will buy an equal basket of goods.

Q

Quantity demanded.   A specific amount that will be demanded per unit of time at a specific price, other things constant.

Quantity supplied.   A specific amount that will be supplied at a specific price.

Quantity theory of money.   The price level varies in response to changes in the quantity of money.

Quantity-adjusting markets.   Markets in which firms bring about equilibrium by modifying their supply instead of changing prices.

Quota.   A quantitative restriction on the amount that one country can export to another.

R

Radical economist.   Economist who believes substantial equality-preferring institutional changes should be implemented to our economic system.

Rational expectations.   Expectations about the future based on the best current information available.

Rationing.   Structural mechanism for determining who gets what.

Real business cycle theory.   A theory that views fluctuations in the economy as reflecting real phenomena—simultaneous shifts in supply and demand, not simply supply responses to demand shifts.

Real concepts.   Concepts adjusted for inflation.

Real deficit.   The nominal deficit adjusted for inflation's effect on the debt.

Real GDP.   Nominal GDP adjusted for inflation.

Real gross domestic product (real GDP).   The market value of goods and services produced in an economy stated in the prices of a given year.

Real interest rates.   Interest rates adjusted for expected inflation.

Real output.   The total amount of goods and services produced, adjusted for price level changes.

Real wage.   The wage level relative to the price level.

Recession.   A decline in real output that persists for more than two consecutive quarters of a year.

Recessionary gap.   The difference between equilibrium income and potential income when potential income exceeds equilibrium income.

Régime change.   A change in the entire atmosphere within which the government and the economy interrelate.

Regressive tax.   Tax whose rates decrease as income rises.

Regulatory trade restrictions.   Government-imposed procedural rules that limit imports.

Relative price.   Nominal price of the good relative to the price level. Also, the price of a good compared to the price of another good or combination of goods.

Rent control.   A price ceiling on rents, set by government.

Rents.   The income from property received by households.

Reserve ratio.   The ratio of reserves to total deposits.

Reserve requirement.   The percentage the Federal Reserve System sets as the minimum amount of reserves a bank must have.

Reserves.   Currency and deposits a bank keeps on hand or at the Fed or central bank, enough to manage the normal cash inflows and outflows.

Restructuring.   Changing the underlying economic institutions.

Ricardian equivalence theorem. Deficit spending will have no effect on the economy's level of income.

Rosy Scenario policy. Government policy of making optimistic predictions and never making gloomy predictions.

S

Say's law. Supply creates its own demand.

Scarcity. The goods available are too few to satisfy individuals' desires.

Second dynamic law of supply and demand. In a market, the larger the difference between quantity supplied and quantity demanded, the greater the pressure on prices to rise (if there is excess demand) or fall (if there is excess supply).

Secondary financial market. Market in which previously issued financial assets can be bought and sold.

Shift factors of demand. Factors that cause shifts in the demand curve.

Shift in demand. The effect of anything other than price on demand.

Shift in supply. The graphic representation of the effect of a change in price on the quantity supplied.

Short-run Phillips curve. A curve showing the trade-off between inflation and unemployment when expectations of inflation are constant.

Simple money multiplier. The measure of the amount of money ultimately created per dollar deposited in the banking system, when people hold no currency.

Slope. The change in the value on the vertical axis divided by the change in the value on the horizontal axis.

Social capital. The habitual way of doing things that guides people in how they approach production.

Socialism. Economic system based on individuals' good will toward others, not on their own self-interest.

Soft budget constraint. Loose financial constraints on firms' decisions in centrally planned economies.

Sole proprietorship. Business that has only one owner.

Soviet-style socialism. Economic system that uses administrative control or central planning to solve the coordination problems: what, how, and for whom.

Special Drawing Rights (SDRs). International reserves created by the IMF.

Spread. The difference between banks' costs and the interest they pay out, and the interest they take in minus bad loans, or, in international currency markets, the difference between the price at which international currency traders buy a currency and the price at which they sell it.

Stages of production. The various levels, such as manufacturing, wholesaling, or retailing, that U.S. businesses adopt.

Stagflation. Combination of high and accelerating inflation and high unemployment.

State socialism. Economic system in which government sees to it that people work for the common good until they can be relied upon to do that on their own.

Stock. Financial asset that conveys ownership rights in a corporation.

Strategic currency stabilization. Buying and selling at strategic moments to affect expectations of traders, and hence to affect their supply and demand.

Strategic trade policy. Policy by which one country threatens to retaliate unless other countries reduce their explicit and implicit trade barriers.

Structural deficit. The part of a budget deficit that would exist even if the economy were at its potential level of income.

Structural readjustment. An economy is trying to change from what it has been doing to something new, not to repeat what it did in the past.

Structural supply-side macro policies. Policies that increase the potential output the economy can achieve.

Structural unemployment. Unemployment caused by economic restructuring making some skills obsolete.

Subjective analysis. Analysis that reflects the analyst's views of how things should be.

Sunk costs. Costs that have already been incurred and cannot be recovered.

Supply. A schedule of quantities a seller is willing to sell per unit of time at various prices, other things constant. Put another way, a schedule of quantities of goods that will be offered to the market at various prices, other things constant.

Supply curve. Graphic representation of the law of supply.

Supply price shock. Shock that causes a rise in nominal wages and prices.

Supply-side Classical economist. Economist who strongly emphasizes the short-run influence of economic incentives.

Supply/demand models. Microeconomic models in which the shapes of supply and demand curves are based on the principle of substitution and opportunity costs.

T

Target rate of unemployment. Lowest sustainable rate of unemployment that policymakers believe is achievable under existing conditions.

Targeted employment subsidy policy. A policy in which government pays business to hire specific groups of workers.

Tariff. A tax on an imported good.

Tax-based income policies. Policies in which the government tries to directly affect the nominal wage- and price-setting institutions.

Third dynamic law of supply and demand. When quantity supplied equals quantity demanded, prices have no tendency to change.

Trade balance. The difference between imports and exports.

Trade credits. Significant short-term loans (one to two weeks) to facilitate interfirm trade.

Trade deficit. The result of a country's imports exceeding its imports.

Trade surplus. The result of a country's exports exceeding its imports.

Transfer payments. Payments made to individuals that aren't payment for a good or service.

Transitional economy. An economy that has had an alternative, developed, socialist economic system, but is in the process of changing from that system to a market system.

Treasury Accord. An agreement between the Fed and the U.S. Department of the Treasury in which the Fed was freed from holding the interest rate on government bonds constant.

U

Underemployed. Part-time workers who would prefer full-time work.

Unemployment. Description of situation that occurs when people are looking for a job and cannot find one.

Unemployment rate. The number of people who cannot find a job as a percent of those people in the economy who are willing and able to work.

Unexpected inflation. Inflation that surprises people.

Unfunded pension system. Pension system in which pensions are paid from current revenues.

V

Value added. The increase in value that a firm contributes to a product or service.

Veil of money assumption. Real output is not influenced by changes in the money supply.

Velocity of money. The number of times per year, on average, a dollar goes around to generate a dollar's worth of income.

Voluntary restraint agreements. Government-imposed procedural rules that limit imports.

W

Wage and price controls. Legal limits on prices and wages.

Walrasian economics. Economic analysis that sees economics as a logical science.

Wealth Accounts. A balance sheet of an economy's stock of assets and liabilities.

Wealth effect. As the price level falls, people are richer, so they buy more.

Welfare capitalism. An economic system in which the market is allowed to operate but in which government plays dual roles in determining distribution and making the what, how, and for whom decisions.

World Bank. A multinational, international financial institution that works with developing countries to secure low-interest loans.

World Trade Organization (WTO). An organization committed to getting countries to agree not to impose new tariffs or other trade restrictions.

Colloquial Glossary

A

Ad infinitum. (adjective). Latin for "forever" (literally, it means "unto infinity").

Ain't. (verb). An ungrammatical form of "isn't," sometimes used to emphasize a point even when the speaker knows that "isn't" is the correct form.

Airtight. (adjective). Completely secure; impregnable.

All the rage. (descriptive phrase). Extremely popular, but the popularity is likely to be transitory.

Allied forces. (descriptive phrase). In World War II the Allied forces were made up of military from more than 20 countries, some of whom were the United States, Canada, Great Britain, France, Poland, the Netherlands, the USSR, and China. They were allied against a group of opponents comprised of Germany and the countries it had occupied plus Italy and Japan.

Apple pie. (descriptive phrase). A dessert that is considered distinctively and traditionally American, symbolizing warm family values.

B

Baby boom. (noun). Any period when more than the statistically predicted number of babies is born.

Baby boomers. (descriptive phrase). People born in the years 1945 through 1964. This is an enormous and influential group of people whose large number is attributed to the "boom" in babies that occurred when military personnel, many of whom had been away from home for four or five years, were discharged from service after the end of World War II.

Back off. (verb). To retreat from.

Back to the drawing board. (descriptive phrase). To start all over again after having your plan or project turn out to be useless.

Bads. (noun). Bad things; the opposite of good things.

Bailed out. (descriptive phrase). To be rescued. It has other colloquial meanings as well, but they do not appear in this book.

Bedlam. (noun). Chaotic and apparently disorganized activity. Today the word is not capitalized. A few hundred years ago in England the noun meant the Hospital of St. Mary's of Bethlehem, an insane asylum. The hospital was not in Bethlehem; it was in London. "Bedlam" was the way "Bethlehem" was pronounced by the English.

Best possible light. (descriptive phrase). To present an issue in the most favorable way.

Better off. (descriptive phrase). In a more advantageous situation, whether financial, emotional, physical, or in some other way.

Big Mac. (proper noun). Brand name of a kind of hamburger sold at McDonald's restaurants.

Binge. (noun). Irrational and undisciplined pursuit of a single activity, usually in the context of drinking alcoholic beverages but applicable to any obsession.

Bit the dust. (descriptive phrase). To bite the dust is to die. (Comes from movies about old times in the United States, in which victims would be shot and fall to the ground—i.e., fall in the dust.)

Blip. (noun). A sharp, momentary eruption. It may derive from the sound a bubble makes when it bursts.

Broke. (adjective). Effectively bankrupt; sometimes even actually bankrupt.

Buck Rogers. (proper name). 1930s comic book figure famous for exploring other planets. His inventor apparently had a phenomenal ability to look into the future.

C

Calvin Coolidge. (proper name). President of the United States from 1923–1928.

Central Park West. (proper name). A fashionable and expensive street in New York City.

Choosier. (adjective). More choosy than someone else. ("Choosy" means to be very particular in deciding which of two or more alternatives to accept.)

Coined. (verb). Used to mean "invented" or "originated."

Cornrows. (noun). Hair style in which hair is braided in shallow, narrow rows over the entire head.

Corvette. (noun). A type of expensive sports car.

Couch potato. (descriptive phrase). Person who shuns exercise. Comes from a person who spends the entire day on the couch in front of the TV set, possibly with a big bag of potato chips.

Crunch period.   (noun). Period when a crisis that has been approaching arrives and must be dealt with.

Cut and dried.   (descriptive phrase). Simple, obvious, and settled.

D

Daddio.   (form of address). Slang for "Daddy," "Father," or a male figure who would ordinarily command some respect but who is being addressed irreverently. Spelled "Daddy-O" by people who use the expression habitually and "Daddio" by people who have heard others use it and adopt it once in a while to show that they are up-to-date.

Dead end.   (noun). A road that ends without reaching an intersection. There is no way out of such a road, unless you turn around and go back. The term is metaphorically applied to any situation in which you come to an abrupt halt with no way to advance.

Deadbeat.   (noun). Lazy person who has no ambition, no money, and no prospects.

Decent.   (adjective). Of high quality.

Designer.   (adjective). A product from a designer who is well-known, a celebrity. Example: "Elizabeth Taylor perfume."

Do the right thing.   (verb). Phrase that can be used in many situations. Usually means to resign yourself to doing whatever the situation calls for even if you'd rather not. Sometimes has a nobler meaning: heroically resolving to carry out an almost impossible and probably dangerous and/or repugnant task.

Dry up.   (verb). To eliminate.

E

Expertise.   (noun). Quality of being an expert.

F

Fact of life.   (descriptive phrase). Designation of a phenomenon as a simple reality. You may not like it, but there's nothing you can do about it.

Far cry.   (descriptive phrase). A long distance; very different from (something else).

Field day.   (noun). Exciting, noisy, and exuberant occasion. Comes from the custom of holding fairs out-of-doors, i.e., in a field.

Fix.   (verb). To prepare, as in "fixing a meal." This is only one of the multiplicity of meanings of this verb.

Foundations.   (noun). Nonprofit organizations that foster charitable, educational, artistic, religious, and other philanthropic enterprises.

Free lunch.   (descriptive phrase). Something you get without paying for it in any way. Usually applied negatively to mean that there is no "free lunch."

Fries.   (noun). French fried potatoes.

Full-speed-ahead.   (adjective). Adventurous, energetic, sometimes accompanied by a tendency to be thoughtless.

Fun.   (adjective). When used as an adjective, as in "fun chapter," it means something that is fun. (In formal English, "fun" is a noun, not an adjective.)

Funky.   (adjective). Eccentric in style or manner.

Funny.   (adverb). Peculiar.

G

Gay.   (adjective). Same-gender sexual preference.

Gee.   (expletive). Emphatic expression signaling surprise or enthusiasm.

Get with it.   (admonition). Wake up; recognize reality; join the majority opinion.

Gimmick.   (noun). Contrivance or trick.

Go-cart.   (noun). A small engine vehicle that is used for racing and recreation.

Going.   (adjective). Prevailing.

Going.   (noun). Conduct or course of an activity.

Good cop/bad cop.   (noun). Alternating mood shifts. It comes from the alleged practice of having two police officers interview a suspect—one officer is kind and coaxing while the other is mean and nasty. This is supposed to make the suspect feel that the nice cop is a good person to confide in.

Good offices.   (descriptive phrase). An expression common in 18th century England, meaning "services."

Gooey.   (adjective). Sticky or slimy.

Goofed.   (verb). Past tense of the verb "to goof," meaning to make a careless mistake.

Grade school.   (descriptive phrase). School in the first few years of formal education (sometimes called "elementary school").

Graft.   (noun). Bribery and financial corruption, often in connection with government officials.

Grocery store coupons.   (descriptive phrase). Coupons appearing in print publications or displayed in a store. They offer you a discount redeemable from the cashier when you buy a particular item.

Groucho Marx.   (proper name). A famous U.S. comedian (1885–1977).

Guns and butter.   (descriptive phrase). Metaphor describing the dilemma whether to devote resources to war or to peace.

Guts.   (noun). Courage.

H

H. G. Wells.   (proper name). English author (1866–1946).

Handout.   (noun). Unearned offering (as distinct from a gift); charity.

Handy.   (adjective). Convenient.

High-end.   (adjective). A good that is at the high end of the price range for various qualities of that good.

Hot air.   (descriptive phrase). An empty promise.

I

In line.   (descriptive phrase). To be "kept in line" is to be encouraged or forced to act the way your colleagues want you to act.

IOU. (noun). A nickname applied to a formal acknowledgment of a debt, such as a U.S. Treasury bond. Also an informal but written acknowledgment of a debt. Pronounce the letters and you will hear "I owe you."

J

Jazz Jackrabbit CD. (noun). A computer game that young children like.

K

Keeping track. (descriptive phrase). Following the course of something and recording your observations.

Kick in. (verb). to start or begin

Killer. (noun). An extremely daunting task.

Klutz. (noun). Awkward, incompetent person.

Knights of the Round Table. Fictional group of aristocrats at the court of semi-fictional King Arthur. Their story is set in Britain in the 8th century A.D.

L

Laurels. (noun). Symbol of honor and victory. In ancient Greece winners of physical or intellectual contests were awarded wreaths made of laurel leaves (as in "poet laureate").

Lead banker. (descriptive phrase). Primary or principal bank or banker in an enterprise.

Leads. (noun). Persons or institutions that you think will be interested in whatever you have to sell. Also the information you have that makes you think someone or something is worth pursuing.

Left the nest. (descriptive phrase). To have left one's parental home, usually because one has grown up and become self-sufficient.

Legal fiction. (descriptive phrase). Concept that has a definition in the law but the definition is invented solely for purposes of the law in which it appears.

Levis. (noun). Popular brand of jeans.

Like Greek to you. (descriptive phrase). Incomprehensible (because in the United States, classical Greek is considered to be a language that almost no one learns).

Little bit. (descriptive phrase). A small quantity.

Lord Tennyson. (proper name). Alfred Tennyson, 19th century English poet who wrote a poem, Ulysses, about the nobility of effort ("To strive, to seek, to find and not to yield").

Lousy. (adjective). Incompetent.

M

Mall. (noun). Short for "shopping mall." A variety of stores grouped on one piece of land, with ample parking for all the mall's shoppers and often with many amenities such as covered walkways, playgrounds for children, fountains, etc.

MasterCard. (proper noun). Brand name of a widely-issued credit card.

McDonald's. (proper name). Large chain of restaurants featuring convenience and inexpensive food.

Mind boggling. (descriptive phrase). Overwhelming.

Motherhood. (noun). Symbol used to designate any concept that is immune from criticism.

N

Nature of the beast. (descriptive phrase). Character of whatever you are describing (need not have anything to do with a "beast").

Nicholas Apert. (proper name). Nineteenth-century French experimenter who discovered how to preserve food by canning or bottling it.

Nip in the bud. (verb). To cut off a process soon after it has begun in order to prevent it from coming to a result toward which it seems to be progressing.

No way. (exclamation). Emphatic expression denoting refusal, denial, or extreme disapproval.

Nuts. (adjective). Crazy.

O

Off the books. (descriptive phrase). Not officially recorded (and hence it's an untaxed transaction).

Off-the-cuff. (adjective). A quick, unthinking answer for which the speaker has no valid authority (comes from the alleged practice of writing an abbreviated answer on the cuff of a shirt, to be glanced at during an exam).

Oliver Wendell Holmes. (proper name). A justice of the U.S. Supreme Court, famous for his wit, his wisdom, his literary ability, his advocacy of civil rights, and his very long life (1841-1935).

On their toes. (descriptive phrase). Alert; ready for any eventuality.

Op-ed. (adjective). Describes an article that appears on the "op-ed" page of a newspaper, which is a page devoted to opinion and editorials.

Overfull. (adjective). More than full, whatever that is.

P

Paid cash. (descriptive phrase). "Paid in cash" can convey the implication that neither the employer nor the employee treated the payment as taxable.

Partying. (verb). Attending parties, relaxing; sometimes refers to use of drugs.

Peer pressure. (descriptive phrase). Push to do what everyone else in your particular group is doing.

Phoenix from the ashes. (descriptive phrase). Metaphor for coming to life after having been thought to be dead. In ancient Greek mythology the phoenix was a bird said to (really) rise from the ashes after a fire.

Pick up. (verb). To start to increase.

Pickle. (noun). Dilemma.

Picky. (adjective). Indulging in fine distinctions when making a decision.

Pitch. (noun). An impassioned argument designed to convince a currently neutral audience.

Pitcher. (noun). In the U.S. game of baseball, the pitcher is the player who throws the ball to the batter, hoping to throw it so skillfully that the batter cannot hit it.

Poorhouse. (noun). Public institution where impoverished individuals were housed. These institutions were purposely dreary and unpleasant. They no longer officially exist, but they have a modern manifestation: shelters for the homeless.

Preseason. (noun). Short period before the season for a sport or the run of a film or play starts.

Press. (noun). Media, such as newspapers, magazines, and TV; also, anyone employed in such media.

Pretend. (adjective). Used as an adjective, as in "pretend policy meeting," it means "imaginary." (In formal English, "pretend" is a verb, not an adjective.)

Pub. (noun). Short for "public house," an expression used in England to mean a commercial establishment where alcoholic drinks are served, usually with refreshments and occasionally with light meals.

Q

Quite a bit. (descriptive phrase). A rather large quantity.

Quote. (noun). Seller's statement of what he or she will charge for a good or service.

R

Raised eyebrows. (descriptive phrase). Reaction of disapproval to an objectionable expression or action.

Read my lips. (admonition). Pay close attention because what I am saying is what I really mean.

Red flag. (descriptive phrase). To raise a red flag means to become very alert to a danger or perceived danger. (Ships in port that are loading fuel or ammunition raise a red flag to signal danger.)

Red tape. (noun). Frustrating, petty requirements that must be fulfilled before the goal you have in mind is accomplished. Before the existence of file cabinets and computer directories, it was the practice in many offices to tie up bundles of paperwork with red tape.

Red-lined. (adjective). On a motor vehicle's tachometer, a red line that warns at what speed an engine's capacity is being strained.

Retool. (verb). To refresh and improve.

Ride on. (verb). To depend on; to be inextricably connected to.

Ritzy. (adjective). Very expensive, fashionable, and ostentatious. Comes from the entrepreneur César Ritz, a Swiss developer of expensive hotels, active in the first quarter of the 20th century.

Robin Hood. (proper name). Semi-fictional English adventurer of the 12th or 13th century. He "stole from the rich and gave to the poor."

Rolling Stones. (proper name). One of the origninal rock band of musicians.

Rub. (noun). Dilemma.

Rule of thumb. (descriptive phrase). An estimate that is quick and easy to make and is reliable enough for rough calculations. Comes from using the space from the tip of your thumb to the first joint as being about an inch.

S

Saks. (proper name). A mid-size department store that sells expensive, fashionable items. There are very few stores in the Saks chain, and Saks stores are considered exclusive.

Scab. (noun). Person who takes a job, or continues in a job, even though the workers at that firm are on strike.

Screw it up. (verb). To meddle with a situation to the extent that you get it into a worse position than it was before you started to repair or improve it.

Second-guess. (verb). To contend that your opinion of a decision or situation is more accurate and useful than that of the person or institution whose business it was to assess a decision or situation.

Sell out. (verb). A good or service that sells out is a good or service that you cannot buy because all have been sold to previous buyers.

Shake. (noun). Milkshake, a type of cool drink.

Shell out. (verb). To pay money, often somewhat more than you want to pay for the item in question.

Shivering in their sandals. (descriptive phrase). Standard English idiom is "shivering in their shoes." Here it has been adapted to the circumstances (i.e., that the persons referred to are wearing sandals, not shoes). Means being afraid.

Shoestring. (noun). Used in relation to money, "on a shoestring" means to have a stingy and insufficient amount.

Shopping mall. (descriptive phrase). A variety of stores grouped on one piece of land, with ample parking for all the mall's shoppers and often with many amenities such as covered walkways, playgrounds for children, fountains, etc.

Show up. (verb). To put in an appearance, to arrive.

Sky has not fallen. (descriptive phrase). Disaster has not struck. Comes from the fable of Chicken Little, who was constantly crying, "The sky is falling! The sky is falling!" when she believed there was a disaster, but she was mistaken.

Slow as molasses. (descriptive phrase). Very slow physically. Molasses is a thick, sweet syrup made from sugar cane (known as "treacle" in the United Kingdom) that pours with agonizing slowness from its container.

Smartly. (adverb). In a spirited or exuberant way.

Spell. (noun). Period or amount of time.

Spending a penny. (descriptive phrase). Spending any money at all. Do not confuse with usage in England, where the phrase means to go to the bathroom.

Spoils. (noun). Valuable items that probably belong to someone else but are being carried away and fought over by unscrupulous or desperate contestants.

Spring for. (verb). To pay for something that the payer would not ordinarily buy at all, or would buy only at a lower price. Frequently the purchase is made because of social pressure, in order not to appear stingy.

Star Trek. (proper name). Famous U.S. TV series about life in outer space.

Steady. (noun). A person to whom you are romantically committed and with whom you spend a lot of time, especially in social activities.

Steady as you go. (admonition). Just keep going calmly along the way you have been going. It's a nautical term, derived from keeping a ship on an even, or steady, course.

Stick-in-the-mud. (noun). A conservative person, not open to new ideas.

Stiff upper lip. (noun). Stoicism and determination.

String. (noun). Uninterrupted succession of identical occurrences.

Stuck with. (descriptive phrase). To be unable to sell or otherwise get rid of something that you don't want and, apparently, no one else wants either.

Swell. (adjective). Excellent, wonderful, astonishingly good.

T

Tacky. (adjective). In very poor taste.

Taco. (noun). Type of food, somewhat like a pancake, used in Mexican cuisine to wrap around a filling such as ground meat.

Tad. (noun). A very small quantity.

Take a back seat. (descriptive phrase). To be accorded scant attention or respect, or to be relegated to a secondary position.

Temp. (noun). Worker whose job is temporary and who accepts the job with that understanding.

The likes of. (descriptive phrase). Things or people that are like other things or other people.

Tickle Me Elmo. (proper name). Name of an extravagantly popular toy, especially in the 1996 Christmas season. Basically it is a stuffed figure, but whether the name represents a command to tickle the figure, or whether the figure has a first name, "Tickle Me," and a last name, Elmo, is a matter for speculation.

Ton. (noun). A large quantity.

Tough. (adjective). Very difficult.

Track record. (noun). Record of accomplishment with respect to a particular type of endeavor; for instance, a horse's record of having consistently lost races on a particular racetrack.

Trendy. (adjective). A phenomenon that is slightly ahead of traditional ways and indicates a trend. Something trendy may turn into something traditional, or it may fade away without ever becoming mainstream.

Truck. (verb). To exchange one thing for another. This was Adam Smith's definition in 1776 and it is still one of the meanings of the verb.

True to form. (descriptive phrase). Performed in the way the action is almost always performed; consistent over time.

Twinkies. (noun). Brand name of an inexpensive small cake.

U

Under the table. (descriptive phrase). To accept money surreptitiously in order to avoid paying taxes on it or to conceal the income for other reasons. Also, to proffer such money to avoid having it known that you are making a particular deal.

Under-the-counter. (adjective). Secret or concealed by an unscrupulous person.

V

Vanity license plate. (descriptive phrase). One-of-a-kind motor vehicle license plate issued to your individual specification. It might have your name, your profession, or any individual set of letters and numbers that will fit on the plate.

Village watchman. (descriptive phrase). Before modern communication technology, in small communities local news was gathered and reported by an official, the village watchman or town crier, who walked around collecting facts and gossip.

W

Waffling. (adjective). Vacillating or evasive. Derives from a Scottish word, "waff," meaning to wave or flap.

Wal-Mart. (proper name). A very large store that sells thousands of inexpensive items. There are hundreds of Wal-Marts in the United States.

Whiz. (noun). An expert.

Wild about. (descriptive phrase). Extremely enthusiastic about undertaking a particular action or admiring a particular object or person.

Wind up. (descriptive phrase). To discover that you have reached a particular conclusion or destination.

Wipe out. (verb). To eliminate.

With it. (descriptive phrase). Up-to-date, knowledgeable about current issues.

Wolf-at-the-door. (descriptive phrase). Describes imminent danger. Comes from the fable of the Three Little Pigs, the door to whose cottage was besieged by a wolf who cried, "I'll huff and I'll puff and I'll blow your house down!"

Writ large. (metaphorical phrase). Emphasized; put in emphatic terms. Note that "writ" is an archaic form of "written."

Z

Zebot. (proper noun). A children's action figure.

Zuka. (noun). Word invented by the author to represent a product—any product—manufactured by a firm.

Photo Credits

Index

Economic Report of the President
Supplementary Table
Selected Historical Series on Gross Domestic Product and Related Series, 1929–58
(billions of dollars; except as noted)

Year	Gross Domestic Product — Current Dollars	Gross Domestic Product — 1987 Dollars	Gross Domestic Product — Implicit Price Deflator (1987 = 100)	Percent Change from Preceding Period — Current Dollars	Percent Change from Preceding Period — 1987 Dollars	Percent Change from Preceding Period — Implicit Price Deflator	Constant (1987) Dollars — Personal Consumption Expenditures	Constant (1987) Dollars — Gross Private Domestic Investment	Constant (1987) Dollars — Net Exports	Constant (1987) Dollars — Government Purchases	Disposable Personal Income — Total	Disposable Personal Income — Per Capita (Dollars)	Saving as Percent of Disposable Personal Income[1]	Population (thousands)[2]
1929	103.1	821.8	12.5				554.5	152.8	1.9	112.6	558.8	4,807	3.0	121,878
1930	90.4	748.9	12.1	−12.4	−8.9	−3.2	520.0	107.2	−.3	122.0	542.2	4,402	2.5	123,188
1931	75.8	691.3	11.0	−16.2	−7.7	−9.1	501.0	67.2	−2.3	125.5	519.7	4,186	2.1	124,149
1932	58.0	599.7	9.7	−23.5	−13.3	−11.8	456.6	25.0	−2.4	120.5	449.8	3,600	−3.1	124,949
1933	55.6	587.1	9.5	−4.1	−2.1	−2.1	447.4	26.6	−3.0	116.1	437.0	3,477	−3.9	125,690
1934	65.1	632.6	10.3	17.1	7.7	8.4	461.1	41.1	−1.0	131.4	462.0	3,652	−1.1	126,485
1935	72.3	681.3	10.6	11.1	7.7	2.9	487.6	65.2	−7.2	135.7	505.2	3,967	2.3	127,362
1936	82.7	777.9	10.6	14.4	14.2	.0	534.4	89.9	−5.1	158.6	565.9	4,415	4.4	128,181
1937	90.8	811.4	11.2	9.8	4.3	5.7	554.6	106.4	−1.9	152.2	585.5	4,540	4.0	128,961
1938	84.9	778.9	10.9	−6.5	−4.0	−2.7	542.2	69.9	4.2	162.5	547.6	4,213	−.3	129,969
1939	90.8	840.7	10.8	7.0	7.9	−.9	568.7	93.4	4.6	174.0	590.3	4,505	2.4	131,028
1940	100.0	906.0	11.0	10.2	7.8	1.9	595.2	121.8	8.2	180.7	627.2	4,747	3.8	132,122
1941	125.0	1,070.6	11.7	25.0	18.2	6.4	629.3	149.4	2.8	289.1	713.9	5,352	10.7	133,402
1942	158.5	1,284.9	12.3	26.8	20.0	5.1	628.7	81.4	−11.1	586.0	824.7	6,115	23.1	134,860
1943	192.4	1,540.5	12.5	21.3	19.9	1.6	647.3	53.5	−28.1	867.7	863.8	6,317	24.5	136,739
1944	211.0	1,670.0	12.6	9.7	8.4	.8	671.2	59.8	−29.0	968.0	901.8	6,516	25.0	138,397
1945	213.1	1,602.6	13.3	1.0	−4.0	5.6	714.6	82.6	−23.9	829.4	890.9	6,367	19.2	139,928
1946	211.9	1,272.1	16.7	−.6	−20.6	25.6	779.1	195.5	26.5	271.0	860.0	6,083	8.5	141,389
1947	234.3	1,252.8	18.7	10.6	−1.5	12.0	793.3	198.8	41.9	218.8	826.1	5,732	3.0	144,126
1948	260.3	1,300.0	20.0	11.1	3.8	7.0	813.0	229.8	16.6	240.6	872.9	5,953	5.8	146,631
1949	259.3	1,305.5	19.9	−.4	.4	−.5	831.4	187.4	17.3	269.3	874.5	5,862	3.7	149,188
1950	287.0	1,418.5	20.2	10.7	8.7	1.5	874.3	256.4	3.2	284.5	942.5	6,214	5.9	151,684
1951	331.6	1,558.4	21.3	15.5	9.9	5.4	894.7	255.6	11.1	397.0	978.2	6,340	7.3	154,287
1952	349.7	1,624.9	21.5	5.4	4.3	.9	923.4	231.6	2.3	467.6	1,009.7	6,433	7.2	156,954
1953	370.0	1,685.5	22.0	5.8	3.7	2.3	962.5	240.3	−7.1	489.8	1,053.5	6,603	7.0	159,565
1954	370.9	1,673.8	22.2	.2	−.7	.9	987.3	234.1	−2.3	454.7	1,071.5	6,598	6.2	162,391
1955	404.3	1,768.3	22.9	9.0	5.6	3.2	1,047.0	284.8	−5.2	441.7	1,130.8	6,842	5.7	165,275
1956	426.2	1,803.6	23.6	5.4	2.0	3.1	1,078.7	282.2	−1.2	444.0	1,185.2	7,046	7.1	168,221
1957	448.6	1,838.2	24.4	5.2	1.9	3.4	1,104.4	266.9	1.6	465.3	1,214.6	7,091	7.2	171,274
1958	454.7	1,829.1	24.9	1.4	−.5	2.0	1,122.2	245.7	−14.9	476.0	1,236.0	7,098	7.4	174,141

[1] Percents based on data in millions of dollars.
[2] Population of the United States including Armed Forces overseas; does not include data for Alaska and Hawaii.

Source: Department of Commerce, Bureau of Economic Analysis.